INTERNATIONAL
ENCYCLOPEDIA
OF THE
STOCK MARKET

INTERNATIONAL ENCYCLOPEDIA OF THE STOCK MARKET

VOLUME TWO
M through Z

Editor
MICHAEL SHEIMO

Associate Editor
ANDREAS LOIZOU

Executive Editor
ALISON AVES

Picture Editor
ANTONIA BOSTRÖM

FITZROY DEARBORN PUBLISHERS
CHICAGO • LONDON

© Copyright 1999 by
FITZROY DEARBORN PUBLISHERS

FITZROY DEARBORN PUBLISHERS
919 North Michigan Avenue
Chicago, Illinois 60611
U.S.A.

or

FITZROY DEARBORN PUBLISHERS
310 Regent Street
London W1R 5AJ
England

British Library and Library of Congress Cataloging-in-Publication Data Is Available

ISBN 1-884964-35-4

First published in the USA and UK 1998

Typeset by Andrea Rosenberg
Printed by Edwards Brothers, Ann Arbor, Michigan

Cover designs by Peter Aristedes

LIST OF ENTRIES

Volume 2

INTERNATIONAL
ENCYCLOPEDIA
OF THE
STOCK MARKET

M

MACROECONOMICS

Macroeconomics is the branch of economics that studies economic aggregates and grand totals.

Macroeconomics studies the determination of national output and its growth over time. It also studies the problems of stagnation, unemployment, and inflation; the balance of international payments and cyclical instability; and the policies adopted by governments to deal with these problems.

Macroeconomic problems are closely related to the balance between aggregate demand and aggregate supply, and the conflict of objectives that governments face. Because resources are scarce, societies are concerned that their resources should be used as fully as possible, and that over time national output should grow. The achievement of growth and the full use of resources is not easy, and in the 1930s, 1980s, and 1990s, economies throughout the world experienced stagnation and unemployment. Attempts by governments to stimulate growth and employment have often resulted in inflation and balance of payments crises. Even when economies do achieve growth it is often short-lived and alternated with periods of stagnation.

In the 1980s many governments implemented demand management policies to control the economy and implemented supply-side policies to improve the supply potential of the economy, and to create conditions for sustainable, non-inflationary growth. Many of these policies focused on the economy on a microeconomic level.

See also BALANCE OF PAYMENTS; INFLATION; KEYNES, JOHN MAYNARD; MICROECONOMICS.

MACROECONOMIST

A *Macroeconomist* studies the concept of economics as a complete interactive unit, with consideration of the international balance of payments, exchange rates, foreign trade, capital flow, and aggregated data on both a domestic and international scale.

At the opposite end of the economic study spectrum is the microeconomist, who researches economic issues at the company and consumer level.

See also ECONOMIC INDICATORS; ECONOMICS; MICROECONOMICS.

MAINTENANCE CALL

A *Maintenance Call* is a notice of funds or marginable securities due on a margin account.

Sent from a broker to an investor, the maintenance call informs the investor that a deposit of funds in his margin account is required to restore the equity value of the account to the minimum maintenance margin requirement. A maintenance call must be paid promptly either by a cash deposit or by the deposit of marginable securities.

If a maintenance call is not promptly satisfied, the terms of the margin agreement allow the broker to sell a portion of the securities in the account to raise the required equity. Most brokerage firms usually attempt to contact the investor before liquidating securities in the account; however, they are not required to do so.

Multiple maintenance calls will be made if the market or individual securities are dropping rapidly in price.

See also MAINTENANCE REQUIREMENT; MARGIN ACCOUNT; REGULATION G–X/REGULATION T.

MAINTENANCE REQUIREMENT

When an investor opens a margin account, a minimum deposit of cash or marginable securities must be deposited with a broker; this amount is referred to as the *Maintenance Requirement.*

If the equity value (the cash value less any debits) in the margin account drops below the maintenance requirement, a broker can call for a deposit of cash or securities to bring the equity up to the minimum. The broker is also able to liquidate the account if the equity in the account falls below the maintenance requirement.

See also MAINTENANCE CALL; MARGIN ACCOUNT; REGULATION G–X/REGULATION T.

MAJORITY CONTROL

An investor or a group of investors owning a controlling interest in the voting shares of a publicly traded company are said to have *Majority Control.* In most cases, a shareholder owning more than 50% of a company's shares will have undeniable control over the company. However, majority control can exist with a smaller percentage of shares, especially in situations in which there are a large number of shareholders.

Majority control allows a wide range of powers to the controlling shareholder(s), including the ability to obtain a position on the board of directors and the ability to restructure the company to conform to their business practices.

It is common for a group to take majority control of a company, realign the business to make it more efficient and effective, then sell the group's stake for a substantial profit.

See also BOARD OF DIRECTORS; MERGER; TAKEOVER/ TAKEOVER BID.

MAKING A MARKET

When a market maker (broker/dealer) quotes a buying and selling price for a security, they are said to be *Making a Market* in that stock. The market maker is then obliged to trade the stock at the quoted buy and sell prices, and therefore maintains an inventory of the relevant stock to satisfy orders. In some situations the market maker acts as a principal, buying what an investor is selling and selling to the investor who is buying.

Many stock exchanges have instigated rules of fair practice that disallow a market maker to back away from a firm quote once it is made. There are also regulations limiting the amount of money a market maker is allowed to earn on mark ups or mark downs, and prohibiting the dealer from creating a situation in which they only accept those deals that are financially favorable to them.

See also BACKING AWAY; BROKER/DEALER; MARKET MAKER.

MAKLER (Germany)

Makler is a general term for a dealer on the German Stock Exchanges. They may be official dealers such as the borsenmakler or kursmakler, or independents such as the freie makler. All are market makers on the floor of the exchanges.

See also FREIE MAKLER; GERMANY; KURSMAKLER; MARKET MAKER.

MALAYSIA, FEDERATION OF

Malaysia is a country of southeast Asia. It is bordered on the north by Thailand, on the south by Singapore, on the west by the Strait of Malacca.

Area: 127,584 square miles (330,442 square km)

Population: 19,948,000 (54.0% urban; 46.0% rural)

Form of Government: Federal constitutional monarchy, with two legislative houses: Senate—69 members; House of Representatives—192 members. Chief of state: Paramount Ruler. Head of government: Prime Minister.

Official Language: Malay

Capital: Kuala Lumpur

Largest Cities: Kuala Lumpur, 1,145,075; Ipoh, 382,633; Johor Baharu, 328,646; Melaka, 295,999; Petaling Jaya, 254,849

Economy:

Currency: Malaysia Ringgit (M$)

National Budget: Revenue—M$44.7 billion; expenditures—M$33.3 billion (social services: 33.9%; security: 15.2%; administration: 10.5%; economic services: 8.4%)

Public Debt: US$13.9 billion

Gross National Product: US$60.1 billion

Principal Products: Palm oil, rice, rubber, bananas, livestock; machinery; fuels; basic manufactures

Foreign Trade (Imports): M$117.4 billion (machinery and transport equipment: 55.6%; basic manufactured goods: 15.1%; chemicals: 7.6%; food: 5.0%; mineral fuels: 3.6%; inedible crude materials: 2.7%; from Japan: 27.4%; United States: 16.9%; Singapore: 15.2%; Taiwan: 5.4%; Germany: 3.8%; United Kingdom: 3.1%; South Korea: 3.0%; Australia: 2.8%)

Foreign Trade (Exports): M$121.2 billion (machinery and transport equipment: 48.5%; mineral fuels: 10.3%; basic manufactures: 9.6%; inedible crude materials: 9.1%; animal and vegetable oils: 6.0%; food, beverages, and tobacco: 3.4%; to Singapore: 21.7%; United States: 20.3%; Japan: 13.0%; United Kingdom: 4.2%; Hong Kong: 4.1%; Germany: 3.7%; Thailand: 3.6%)

Stock Exchanges: 2
Kuala Lumpur Stock Exchange (KLSE)
3rd, 4th, & 5th Floors, Exchange Square
Off Jalan Semantan
Damansara Heights
50490 Kuala Lumpur
Malaysia
Phone: (60-3) 254 6433, 254 6513
Fax: (60-3) 255 7463, 256 1291

Internet Address: www.klse.com.my

Trading Hours: Monday–Friday, 9:30 to 12:30 and 2:30 to 5:00

Office Hours: Monday–Friday, 9:00 to 5:30

Exchange Holidays:

2, 30, 31 January	1 June
1, 2 February	9, 31 August
2, 3 March	23 October
1, 10, 15, 31 May	25 December

Listed Companies: 529

526 domestic

  3 foreign

Total Market Capitalization:

At 31 December 1997

Local Currency (Millions)	US Dollars (Millions)
250,083	64,250

Major Sectors: Industrial, finance, palm oils, properties, rubber plantations

Share Price Performance:

(% Change)

1992	54
1993	134
1994	-24
1995	9
1996	32
1997	-47

History: Malayan securities trading began in the latter part of the 19th century as a result of the British corporate presence in the rubber and tin industries, and became formally established with the formation of the Singapore Stockbrokers Association on 23 June 1930. Trading grew and expanded, but was soon interrupted by World War II. It recommenced in 1946. The Malayan Sharebrokers' Association existed until 21 March 1960, when the Malayan Stock Exchange was formed. Public trading of shares began on 9 May 1960, when four stockbrokers gathered together in the clearing house of the Central Bank to mark prices. At that time clerical assistance and telephone facilities were provided by the Central Bank.

Facilities for share trading improved in 1961 with the addition of a board system. In 1962 trading rooms in Singapore and Kuala Lumpur were linked by telephone lines to provide investors with the latest available prices. The link eliminated arbitraging by integrating the two trading rooms into a single market with the same stocks and shares listed at a single set of prices on both boards.

On 16 September 1963, the Federation of Malaysia was formed. Malayan Stock Exchange operations were strengthened during the following year by the adoption of new rules and by-laws, the creation of a fidelity fund, and implementation of more stringent listing requirements. On 8 May 1973, the stock exchanges of Malaysia and Singapore split into two separate entities. This action was taken in order for Malaysia to develop a strong and healthy national capital market, closely tied to the country's objectives and developmental priorities.

The Kuala Lumpur Stock Exchange Berhad (KLSEB) was established 2 July 1973 and operates in accordance with provisional rules, by-laws, listing requirements, and a corporate disclosure policy. When the Securities Industry Act (SIA) of 1973 was brought into force in 1976, a new company called the Kuala Lumpur Stock Exchange took over from the KLSEB. The Foreign Investment Committee was formed in 1974.

To provide greater orderly conduct of the securities business, a new Securities Industry Act came into force in July 1983, replacing the old SIA. It provides for greater supervision and control of the industry by regulating the operations of dealers, prohibiting artificial trading and market rigging, and empowers the Minister of Finance to amend the rules of the stock exchange. The new act formalized the status of the Capital Issues Committee.

On 15 May 1989 the exchange entered the technological age with the introduction of a semiautomated trading system—the System on Computerized Order Routing and Execution (SCORE). The conversion from open-outcry to the electronic system improved the speed of transactions and their volume. More importantly, through SCORE, the investor can verify the time at which an order is given and executed.

In February of 1990 the exchange implemented the Fixed Delivery and Settlement System, adding further efficiency to the trading system. On 26 April 1994 the exchange became officially known as Kuala Lumpur Stock Exchange.

Although the KLSE is the only official market for trading in securities, there is an exchange called Pasaran Saham Bumiputera (Bumiputera Stock Exchange or BSE) set up for the Bumiputera companies. The latter was established in 1969, under the Majlis Amanah Rakyat Act 20, 1966, and began operations in 1971.

Classes of Securities: Ordinary shares/stocks, preference shares, bonds, loan stocks, loan notes, property trust units, warrants, transferable subscriptions rights, call warrants.

Indices:

Name	Number of Shares
EMAS	335
KLSE Composite (KLSE)	86
KSLE Industrial	30
KLSE Consumer Products	50

Name	Number of Shares
KLSE Industrial Products	70
KLSE Construction	16
KLSE Trading/Services	56
KLSE Finance	43
KLSE Property	43
KLSE Mining	11
KLSE Plantation	38
KLSE Second Board	106
The New Straits Times Industrial Index	30

The indices are calculated by the weighted average method. The weight used is the number of ordinary shares outstanding.

The KLSE indices are calculated by the exchange every 15 minutes. The Second Board Index was launched on 2 January 1991, and the Exchange Main Board All-Share Index (EMAS) on 16 October 1991. Another four new indices—Consumer Products, Industrial Products, Construction, and Trading/Services—were introduced on 1 September 1993.

Supervisory Organizations:

The Securities Commission

Registrar of Companies

Licensing Officer, (Securities/Futures Trading) Ministry of Finance

Kuala Lumpur Stock Exchange

Foreign Investment Committee

Depository: The Malaysian Central Depository (CDS)

Settlement Details:

Shares:

Ready Basis:

Trade date + 4 (to the selling broker), + 5 (to Scans clearinghouse), +6 (to the buying broker), +7 (to the buyer)

Physical

Receive versus payment, but not delivery versus payment

Turnaround trades on the same day are not allowed.

Immediate Basis:

Next day settlement

Trading: The KLSE's open-outcry system was replaced by the System on Computerized Order Routing and Execution (SCORE) in 1989. SCORE began as a semiautomated trading system by which computer terminals located in the exchange member companies offices could be used to enter orders. Orders were routed to the exchange's matching room to be handled by the KLSE staff. As of 19 October 1992 the

KLSE established the automatic matching of orders. Implementation continued in stages and by 30 November 1992 matching became completely automatic. Both cash and margin transactions can be entered. Under the margin requirements, an investor must place certain acceptable forms of collateral when purchasing securities and the sum of these must not be less than 15% of the outstanding balance.

Trading Lots:

Market Price	Board Lot
M$10.00 or less	1,000 shares or units
More than M$10.00	100 shares or units
	500 shares or units
	1,000 shares or units

Price Fluctuation Regulations:

1. As a matter of policy, the exchange will query a company if the price or volume of its securities moves by a certain percentage in a day or given week.
2. For SCORE trading, there is a limit set on the highest and lowest price that a stock can be traded for each trading session of the day. The limit is presently a 30% from the previous day's closing price.

Listing Requirements:

Main Board Listing

Prerequisites for Admission (Ordinary Shares)

1. Minimum paid-up of M$20 million
2. At least 25% of the issued and paid-up capital is in the hands of the public and a minimum percentage is in the hands of 500 shareholders holding between 500 to 10,000 shares as follows:

Issued and Paid-Up	Minimum %
Not exceeding M$50m	15.0%
Not exceeding M$100m	12.5% or M$8m, whichever is greater
M$100m and above	10.0% or M$15m, whichever is greater

3. Issue of a prospectus regardless of the method of flotation and the advertisement of the full prospectus
4. A three- to five-year track record

Corporate Disclosure Policy

1. A listed company is required to make immediate public disclosure of all material information concerning its affairs, except in exceptional circumstances.
2. A listed company is required to release material information to the public in a manner designed

to achieve the fullest possible public dissemination.

3. Whenever a listed company becomes aware of a rumor or report that contains information likely to either have an effect on the trading of the company's securities or have a bearing on investment decisions, the company is required to publicly clarify the rumor or reports as promptly as possible.

4. Whenever unusual market action takes place in a listed company's securities, the company is expected to make inquiry to determine whether rumors or other conditions requiring corrective action exist, and if so, to take whatever action is appropriate. If, after the company's review, the unusual market action remains unexplained, it may be appropriate for the company to announce that there has been no material development in its business and affairs not previously disclosed nor, to its knowledge, any other reason to account for the unusual market action.

5. A listed company should refrain from promotional disclosure activity that exceeds that which is necessary to enable the public to make informed investment decisions. Such activity includes inappropriately worded news releases, public announcements not justified by actual developments in a company's affairs, exaggerated reports or predictions, flamboyant wording, and other forms of overstated or overzealous disclosure activity that may mislead investors and cause unwarranted price movements and activity in a company's securities.

6. Insiders should not trade on the basis of material information that is not known to the investing public. Moreover, insiders should refrain from trading, even after material information has been released to the press and other media, for a period sufficient to permit thorough public dissemination and evaluation of the information.

Second Board Listing

The Second Board Listing Requirements are essentially the same as for the Main Board. Second Board companies are subject to the same Corporate Disclosure Policy. There are, however, some different requirements for Second Board Listing:

1. The company must be incorporated in Malaysia.
2. The company must have a 2–3 year track record.
3. Minimum capital of M$5 million and a maximum of up to M$20 million.

4. At least 25%, but not more than 50%, of the issued and paid-up capital is in the hands of the public, provided that at least 15% of the issued and paid-up capital is in the hands of 500 shareholders holding not more than 10,000 shares each and not less than 500 shares each.
5. Only a summary of the prospectus is to be advertised.
6. The exchange may impose a moratorium on the sale of major shareholdings for one year from the date of admission of the company to the Second Board. Thereafter, the major shareholders are allowed to divest a maximum of 15% per annum of their respective shareholdings.

Procedures for Initial Listing Applications:

1. An application is submitted by the company to the Securities Commission.
2. The company submits a Memorandum and Articles of Association of the company to the exchange for approval.
3. The company files an Initial Listing Application and supporting papers with the exchange.
4. The Securities Commission reviews and approves the listing.
5. The company files a final copy of the prospectus with the Registrar of Companies and the exchange.
6. The company advertises and issues the prospectus to the public and offer period opens.
7. The company announces the basis for allotment.
8. The company issues shares pursuant to the allotment.
9. Shares are admitted to the Official List.
10. Shares trade on the exchange three market days after certificates have been dispatched.

Investor Taxation: Taxes withheld on dividends is 35% deducted at source.

Dividend Income: There is a deduction of 30% corporate tax at source for all dividends other than for tax exempt dividends. The tax deducted is treated as a tax credit when a resident files his tax returns. A non-resident will receive the full amount of the dividend less corporate tax, but will not be entitled to any refunds. However, under tax treaties with some countries, double tax relief may be available.

Interest Income: Interest earned by individuals from investment in Malaysian government securities or bonds issued by the Malaysian government are exempt from tax. Interest earned by individuals from investment in bonds issued by public companies listed on the KLSE are tax exempt provided that these bonds are not convertible into equity shares. Tax exemption is also extended to interest earned by individuals from investment in bonds issued by any company not listed on the KLSE but rated by Rating Agency Malaysia Berhad provided these bonds are not convertible into equity shares.

Interest earned by the individual resident on all other fixed interest bearing securities is subject to tax. For non-residents, a withholding tax of 20% is deducted at source for countries which do not have tax treaties with Malaysia.

Capital gains are not taxed.

There is a clearing fee of 0.05% of transacted value (paid by buyer and seller).

Stamp Duty:
   a. Contract Notes: M$1.50 for M$1,000 or fractional part of value of securities paid by buyer and seller. With effect from 13 May 1988, all contract notes made in connection with any transaction between a local broker and a foreign broker in stocks and marketable securities are exempted from stamp duty.
   b. Transfer: M$3.00 for M$1,000 or fractional part of value of shares (paid by buyer if registration is desired).
   c. Share Certificate: As of 1 January 1994, no stamp duty shall be paid on a share certificate.

M$3.00 is paid to the company registrar for issuance of share certificate.

Limitations: Foreign ownership of companies is generally restricted to 30%. The following are subject to Foreign Investment Committee approval:

• Any proposed acquisition of 15% or more of the voting power by any foreign interest or associated group or by foreign interests in the aggregate of 30% or more of the voting power of a Malaysian company or business

• Any proposed acquisition of interest exceeding M$5 million

• Any proposed acquisition of substantial assets

These guidelines, however, do not apply to specific projects approved by the government.

Securities Lending: None

Brokerage Firms:
1 Arab-Malaysian Securities SDN BHD
15th Floor, Bangunan Arab-Malaysian
55, Jalan Raja Chulan
50200 Kuala Lumpur
Malaysia
Phone: (60-3) 238 2788/99
Fax: (60-3) 238 3162

BIMB Securities SDN BHD
1st & 2nd Floor, Podium Block
Bangunan AMDB, No. 1, Jalan Lumut
50350 Kuala Lumpur
Malaysia
Phone: (60-3) 443 3533
Fax: (60-3)441 3433/2622

Capitalcorp Securities SDN BHD
Level 1& 2, Block G Central
Pusat Bandar Damansara
50490 Kuala Lumpur
Malaysia
Phone: (60-3) 254 9966
Fax: (60-3) 254 8595

CIMB Securities SDN BHD
9th Floor, Commerce Square
Jalan Semantan, Damansara Heights
PO Box 10126
50704 Kuala Lumpur
Malaysia
Phone: (60-3) 253 2288
Fax: (60-3) 253 5533

Pengkalen Securities SDN BHD
(formerly EN-J Securities SDN BHD)
Box 100, Lot One 4th Floor
KL Plaza, 170 Jalan Bukit Bintang
55100 Kuala Lumpur
Malaysia
Phone: (60-3) 244 8044
Fax: (60-3) 244 8082
Telex: MA 31186

Inter-Pacific Securities SDN BHD
Level 7, Shahzan-Prudential Tower
30 Jalan Sultan Ismail
50250 Kuala Lumpur
Malaysia
Phone: (60-3) 244 1888
Fax: (60-3) 244 1686
Telex: MA 34469 IPSEC

Kuala Lumpur City Securities SDN BHD
3.07 Level 3, Bangunan Angkasaraya
Jalan Ampang
50450 Kuala Lumpur
Malaysia
Phone: (60-3) 244 9322
Fax: (60-3) 244 8099

Mayban Securities SDN BHD
30th Floor, Menara Maybank
100 Jalan Tun Perak
50050 Kuala Lumpur
Malaysia
Phone: (60-3) 232 3822/33
Fax: (60-3) 232 3807
Telex: MAYSEC MA 20294

PB Securities SDN BHD
20th and 21st Floor
Menara Sabre
No. 8 Lorong P Ramlee
50250 Kuala Lumpur
Malaysia
Phone: (60-3) 201 3011
Fax: (60-3) 201 2533

Seagroatt and Campbell SDN BHD
Wisma Hamzah-Kwong Hing
7th Floor, No. 1, Leboh Ampang
50100 Kuala Lumpur
Malaysia
Phone: (60-3) 232 7122/03/8
Fax: (60-3) 232 7420
Telex: MA 32816 SEAGRO

UMBC Securities SDN BHD
21st Floor, Bahgunan UMBC
Jalan Sultan Sulaiman
50000 Kuala Lumpur
Malaysia
Phone: (60-3) 274 9288/778/779
Fax: (60-3) 274 9907

Apex Securities SDN BHD
3rd Floor, Wisma Apex
145 A-C, Jalan Bukit PO Box 16
43007 Kajang
Malaysia
Phone: (60-3) 836 1118/32135
Fax: (60-3) 837 4532
Telex: MA 31617 CHLICK

Halim Securities SDN BHD
4th Floor Menara MPPJ
Jalan Tehgah
46770 Petaling Jaya
PO Box 561
Malaysia
Phone: (60-3) 755 5777/008/025
Fax: (60-3) 755 4612
Telex: MA 36007

SJ Securities SDN BHD
Level 3, Holiday Villa
No. 9, Jalan SS 12/1, Subang Jaya
47500 Petaling Jaya
Malaysia
Phone: (60-3) 734 0202
Fax: (60-3) 734 8342, 733 0649

South Johore Securities SDN BHD
(formerly Koh & Lee Securities)
3rd Floor, Penggaram Comples
1 Jalan Abdul Rahman
83000 Batu Pahat
Kuala Lumpur
Malaysia
Phone: (60-7) 434 2282
Fax: (60-7) 431 6766
Cables: SAHAM BATU PAHAT

ENG Securities SDN BHD
Suites 1001, 1003, and 1005
10th Floor, Merlin Inn Tower, Jalan Meldrum
8000 Johore Bahru, Johore
Malaysia
Phone: (60-7) 231 211,212
Fax: (60-7) 246 266
Cables: ENGSEC JOHOR BARU

JB Securities SDN BHD
Suite 8.1, Level 8 Menara Pelangi
2 Jalan Kuning, Taman Pelangi
80400 Johore Bahru
Malaysia
Phone: (60-7) 332 800/000/798
Fax: (60-3) 332 798
Telex: JBSEC MA 060166

Botly Securities SDN BHD
1st Floor, Plaza Teh Teng Seng
No. 227, Jalan Kampar
30250 Ipoh, Perak
Malaysia
Phone: (60-5) 531 313
Fax: (60-5) 253 6785
Cables: TRANSFER, Ipoh

YK Fung Securities SDN BHD
65, Clarke Street
30300 Ipoh, Perak
Malaysia
Phone: (60-5) 241 5100/200/249
Fax: (60-5) 253 1778
Cable: FUNGSEC, Ipoh

Labuan Securities SDN BHD
Level 2, Wisma Oceanic
Jalan Okk Awang Besar
87008 Wilayah Persekutuan Labuan
Kuala Lumpur
Malaysia
Phone: (60-87) 410 621
Fax: (60-87) 410 620

Company Information:

The Best Performing Shares in the Country

Company Name	Share Price Change 1 January 1997 to 31 December 1997 (%)
Omega Holdings	179
Leisure Management	101
Kuala Lumpur Kepong	31

The Largest Companies in the Country by Market Capitalization as of 31 December 1997

Company Name	Market Capitalization Local Currency (Millions)	Market Capitalization US Dollars (Millions)
Telekom Malaysia	34,502	8,864
Tenaga Nasional	25,730	6,610
Petronas Gas	15,959	4,100
Malayan Banking	12,921	3,319
Sime Darby	8,699	2,235
Rothmans Of Pall Mall	8,637	2,219
Resorts World	7,152	1,837
Genting	6,846	1,759
Ytl Corp.	6,223	1,599
Kuala Lumpur Kepong	5,960	1,531
Ytl Power	5,703	1,465
Berjaya Sports Toto	5,692	1,462
Malaysia Intl.Shipping	4,980	1,279
Golden Hope Pltn.	4,519	1,161
Nestle (Malaysia)	4,221	1,084
Renong	3,998	1,027
Magnum Corporation	3,512	902
Rhb Capital	3,136	806
Public Bank	2,801	719
United Engineers (Mal.)	2,585	664
Kumpulan Guthrie	2,500	642
Tanjong Plc	2,425	623
Highlands & Lowlands	2,405	618

Company Name	Market Capitalization Local Currency (Millions)	Market Capitalization US Dollars (Millions)
Malaysian Airline Sy.	2,402	617
Hicom Holdings	2,330	598
Oriental Holdings	2,115	543
Omega Holdings	2,077	534
Proton (Perusahaan Otomobil)	2,063	530
Uniphoenix Corp.	2,058	529
Perlis Plantations	2,024	520
Mutiara Swisscom	1,970	506
Malaysian Pacific Inds.	1,960	504
Sarawak Enter.Corp.	1,913	491
Carlsberg Brewery Malaysia	1,913	491
Leisure Management	1,840	473
Shell Refining	1,830	470
Malakoff	1,826	469
Jaya Tiasa Holdings	1,814	466
Edaran Otomobil Nasional	1,803	463
Technology Resources Industries	1,736	446
Rj Reynolds	1,661	427
Berjaya Land	1,637	420
Hong Leong Credit	1,565	402
Hap Seng Consolidated	1,494	384
Commerce Asset-Hdg.	1,478	380
Hong Leong Bank	1,478	380
Guinness Anchor	1,450	373
Mni Holdings	1,449	372
Ekran	1,414	363
Pacific Bank	1,357	349
Petronas Dagangan	1,320	339
Ramatex	1,282	329
Southern Bank	1,281	329
Malaysia Mining	1,279	329
Ppb Oil Palms	1,255	322
Batu Kawan	1,253	322
Malayan United Inds.	1,235	317
Oyl Industries	1,231	316
Malaysian Oxygen	1,204	309
Ban Hin Lee Bank	1,198	308
Kfc Holdings (Malaysia)	1,177	302

Company Name	Market Capitalization Local Currency (Millions)	Market Capitalization US Dollars (Millions)
Esso Malaysia	1,172	301
Rashid Hussain	1,166	300
Tan Chong Motor Holdings	1,142	294
Bimb Holdings	1,139	293
Pan Malaysia Cement	1,109	285
Malayan Cement	1,095	281
Ioi Corporation	1,064	273
Ammb Holdings	1,017	261
United Malayan Land	1,014	260
Hume Industries Mal.	1,011	260
New Straits Times Press	956	246
Powertek	920	236
Island & Peninsular	916	235
Pelangi	896	230
Hong Leong Industries	889	228
Boustead Holdings	878	226
Malaysian Resources	867	223
Amsteel Corp.	856	220
Farlim Group (M)	846	217
Sime Uep Properties	841	216
Metroplex	841	216
Country Heights Hdg.	818	210
Lingui Development	814	209
Sungei Way Hdg.	785	202
Chemical Co.Malaysia	784	201
Umw Holdings	784	201
Multi-Purpose Holdings	781	201
Cahya Mata Sarawak	764	196
Mal.Nat.Reinsurance	759	195

Regional Stock Exchanges: None

Other Stock Exchange:

The Bumiputera Stock Exchange
4th Floor, Medan MARA
21 Jalan Raja Laut
50350 Kuala Lumpur
Malaysia
Phone: (60-3) 261 9682

Other Investment Information:

Malaysian Industrial Development Authority (MIDA)
3rd-6th Floor
Wisma Damansara, Jalan Semantan
PO Box 10618
Kuala Lumpur
Malaysia
Phone: (60-3) 254 3633
Telex: MIDA MA 30752

Chamber of Commerce and Industry of Malaysia
Bangunan Angkass Raya, 13th Floor
Jalan Ampang
Kuala Lumpur
Malaysia
Phone: (60-3) 433 090

MALONEY ACT (United States)

The *Maloney Act* refers to section 15A of the Securities Exchange Act of 1934. This amendment, so named for its sponsor, Senator Maloney, permits the registration of self-policing associations of securities dealers.

Due to the vast amount of unique technical knowledge necessary to formulate meaningful and effective regulations, self-regulation is essential to the securities industry. It is the keystone to establishing a free market for the trading of securities under a system that is fair and orderly. The National Association of Securities Dealers (NASD) is registered with the Securities and Exchange Commission in accordance with the Maloney Act.

While the Maloney Act is unique to the United States, similar self-regulatory securities organizations are established in most countries.

See also NATIONAL ASSOCIATION OF SECURITIES DEALERS (NASD); SECURITIES AND EXCHANGE COMMISSION (SEC); SELF-REGULATING ORGANIZATION (SRO).

MALTA, REPUBLIC OF

Malta is an archipelago in the central Mediterranean Sea 58 miles south of Sicily.

Population: 369,609

Form of Government: Parliamentary democracy (unicameral). Chief of state: President.

Official Languages: Maltese; English

Capital: Valletta

Largest Cities: Valletta and Marsaxlokk.

Economy:

Currency: Maltese Lira (LM)

National Budget: Revenues—$1.4 billion; expenditures—$1.4 billion

Public Debt: US$603 million

Gross National Product: US$3.9 billion

Principal Products: Machinery; transport equipment; agricultural products

Foreign Trade (Imports): US$2.1 billion (commodities: food, petroleum, machinery and semimanufactured goods; from Italy: 27%; Germany: 14%; United Kingdom: 13%; United States: 9%)

Foreign Trade (Exports): US$1.3 billion (commodities: machinery and transport equipment, clothing and footware, printed matter; to Italy: 32% Germany: 16%; United Kingdom: 8%)

Stock Exchanges: 1

Malta Stock Exchange
Pope Pius V Street
Valletta
Malta CMR 01
Phone: (356) 244-051
Fax: (356) 244-071

Trading Hours: Wednesday 9:00 to 12:00

Office Hours: Monday–Friday 7:45 to 5:15

Exchange Holidays:

1, 2, 17, 31 January	30 August
27 February	23 October
3, 12 March	1 November
1 April	25 December
1 May	

Other Investment Information:

Malta Development Corporation
PO Box 571
House of Catalunya
Marsamxewtto Road
Valletta
Malta
Phone: (356) 221-431/222-691
Fax: (356) 606-407

Central Bank of Malta
Castille Place
Valletta
Malta
Phone: (356) 247-480
Fax: (356) 243-051
Telex: 1262

Ministry of the Environment
Floriana
Valletta
Malta
Phone: (356) 222-378
Fax: (356) 231-293
Telex: 1861

MALTHUS, THOMAS ROBERT

Thomas Robert Malthus (1766–1834) was an English classical economist, educated in mathematics at Cambridge. Malthus was appointed Professor of Political Economy of the East India College in 1804. He wrote works on economic methodology and principles and, most famously, on population.

In his essay titled "Principles of Population as It Affects the Future Improvement of Society" (1798), Malthus argued that population growth would outstrip food supplies. Malthus proposed that population had a natural growth rate described by a geometric progression, whereas the natural resources necessary to support the population grew at a rate similar to an arithmetic progression and featured diminishing returns. Without restraints on population there would be a continued pressure on living standards, both in terms of room and output, and a downward pressure on subsistence wages. Malthus's gloomy prognosis, however, underestimated the pace and impact of technological progress and the benefits of overseas trade.

Malthus and David Ricardo were involved in a debate with the French classical economist J.B. Say regarding Say's law of markets. Say argued that there could be no general overproduction or underproduction of commodities in an economy, since whatever was bought must have been sold by someone else and any disequilibrium was therefore temporary. Malthus's observation of the post-Napoleonic economy and the persistence of gluts led him to argue that overproduction was not a temporary phenomenon resolved by the market, but could be general and chronic. In the case of nonessential goods, market clearance depended upon the tastes of those with incomes to purchase them.

Malthus's solution to the problem of gluts was the provision of public works, and this has been described as an anticipation of later Keynesian arguments on the importance of aggregate demand in the economy. His arguments, however, remained in the classical school: underconsumption was the result of an increase in planned savings, which increased funds for investment and led to an increase in the output of consumer goods. Since the labor supply was inelastic, wages rose with costs.

Thomas Malthus, 1830, engraving by John Linnell. *(Corbis-Bettmann)*

Malthus was interested in the codification of technical terminology and sought to place political economy on solid empirical foundations, although his work is often criticized for its generalizations. His public debate with Ricardo and Say led to important developments in classical economic theory and his willingness to support the Corn Laws further reinforced his qualified support for the efficacy of the market in certain situations. Malthus, and other classical economists, argued against the prevailing Poor Laws, a system of charitable works for the extremely poor in parish workhouses. He argued that the system had the effect of swelling claims on the nation's food supplies while making no contribution to their enlargement. Classical criticism pointed to the impact of the Poor Laws on incentives to work and their interference with labor mobility, but Malthus added that the system enabled recipients to reproduce at higher rates than otherwise possible and further exacerbate the problem.

See also CLASSICAL SCHOOL OF ECONOMICS; KEYNES, JOHN MAYNARD; RICARDO, DAVID; SAY, JEAN-BAPTISTE.

MANAGED FUND

A *Managed Fund* is an open-ended mutual fund in which securities are actively bought and sold on behalf of small investors.

Managed funds follow a set strategy in order to achieve a defined objective, while remaining within stated risk parameters. New money is constantly entering the fund and must be invested within a specified amount of time. Money will leave the fund as investors cash out or subscribe to automatic withdrawal programs. The success of any fund is largely dependent on the quality and continuity of its managers.

Closed-end mutual funds, which only make available a limited amount of shares, are referred to as *nonmanaged* or *unmanaged funds*.

See also MUTUAL FUND; UNIT INVESTMENT TRUST/ UNIT TRUST.

MANAGEMENT BUY-OUT (MBO)

A *Management Buy-Out (MBO)* is the acquisition of the share capital of a company by its directors and top-level managers.

MBOs became popular during the 1980s when many large conglomerates sought to dispose of non-core subsidiaries and peripheral operating units. MBOs have often taken place as an alternative to closure or forced trade sales and are normally achieved with the help of loans from supportive banks and ven-

ture capital funds. Financial backers are generally supportive of management who are sufficiently knowledgeable about their own business to achieve a return to full profitability.

When large sums of money are borrowed the MBO may be referred to as a leveraged buy-out (LBO).

See also CONTROLLING INTEREST; LEVERAGED BUY-OUT (LBO); TAKEOVER/TAKEOVER BID.

MANAGEMENT COMPANY

A *Management Company* manages mutual funds (either open-end or closed-end funds), and serves in an administrative capacity for the trading of shares and the reinvestment of dividends. Each management company has an investment manager to buy and sell securities in the portfolio, reinvesting the proceeds according to a set of investment objectives.

Investment strategies are set by the company and the investment manager, often with the input of an investment adviser who is well acquainted with investment objectives of the individual funds and the management company as a whole. Management companies may be linked with insurance companies, pension funds, or families of mutual funds.

See also INVESTMENT ADVISER; MANAGEMENT GROUP; OPEN END FUND; UNIT INVESTMENT TRUST/ UNIT TRUST.

MANAGEMENT FEE

A *Management Fee* is any fee charged that is not a commission based on securities transactions. Examples of management fees include:
- Annual fee charged by a brokerage firm for the maintenance of an account
- Investment adviser fee based on assets under management
- Administrative fee charged by a closed-end fund
- Administrative fee charged by an open-end fund
- Administrative fee charged by a limited partnership
- Administrative fee for an annuity containing a mutual fund

See also ASSET MANAGEMENT ACCOUNT; OPEN END FUND; UNIT INVESTMENT TRUST/UNIT TRUST.

MANAGEMENT GROUP

A *Management Group* serves as an investment adviser to an investment company. Well acquainted with the objectives of managed funds, management groups offer investment analysis and advice on how to implement effective strategies.

Many investment adviser groups also provide legal, clerical, public relations, and trade execution services. They often work with several clients (usually at an institutional level) and many also manage assets for larger net worth individuals.

Fees are based on a percentage of the assets under management for each client or fund. Some management groups will charge an additional fee for certain investments that they themselves offer to clients.

See also INVESTMENT ADVISER; MANAGEMENT FEE; STOCKBROKER.

MANAGING UNDERWRITER

The *Managing Underwriter* is the investment banker representing a company issuing securities. The managing underwriter organizes the syndicate, keeps the books, establishes the selling group, and stabilizes a securities price during the distribution.

The managing underwriter is compensated by profits received from the other underwriters.

See also INVESTMENT BANKER; SELLING GROUP; SYNDICATE.

MANDATAIRE (France)

See PROXY.

MANI (Italy)

Mani is an Italian term referring to any group of unknown investors behind large movements in the stock market.

As a general rule institutional investors accumulate positions slowly, not wanting to attract attention that will drive up the price of securities. Large movements either up or down can be caused by a number of things. For example, if a company's share price jumps, it could signal the beginning of a corporate takeover or the issue of a favorable report. It could also be a sign that an institutional investor is trying to see how much interest exists in the company.

Conversely, if there is a marked fall in a company's share price, it could be the result of a large group of investors liquidating their position in the company and selling off all their shares in one tranche because the present share price performance has not been in line with an institution's objectives.

There are exceptions, however, particularly during a corporate takeover.

See also INSTITUTIONAL INVESTOR; LIQUIDATE; TAKEOVER/TAKEOVER BID.

MANIPULATION

Manipulation is the intentional influencing of the price of a security in order to profit from the change.

Manipulation can occur in many ways. It might involve starting a rumor about a company's prospects, or buying up large quantities of a security to create the impression of increased popularity. These techniques are designed to attract new investors, whose interest will push the price even higher.

Price manipulation runs contrary to the idea of a free market and is therefore an illegal activity. Most countries have adopted laws prohibiting manipulation.

Buying shares to stabilize a falling price is also a form of manipulation; however, it may be allowed if the action is considered to be in the public's best interest. Companies are permitted to make stabilization purchases when the overall market is declining or the company's share price is in a serious decline.

See also INSIDER DEALING/INSIDER TRADING; NATIONAL ASSOCIATION OF SECURITIES DEALERS (NASD); SECURITIES AND EXCHANGE COMMISSION (SEC).

MANIPULATOR

A *manipulator* is a person or group of persons engaged in price manipulation.

See MANIPULATION.

MANUFACTURERS HANOVER CORPORATION

Before its 1991 merger with Chemical Banking Corporation, *Manufacturers Hanover Corporation*, the holding company of Manufacturers Hanover Trust, was one of the world's leading banking and financial institutions. The company relied on a long series of mergers and acquisitions to boost its influence nationally and worldwide. The headquarters of "Manny Hanny," as the bank was nicknamed, were in New York City—directly across the street from those of Chemical Bank—where it was founded. The company's history paralleled New York City's transformation from a post-colonial port into the world's most important financial center.

Manufacturers Hanover Trust's earliest predecessor could be traced to 1812, when the New York Manufacturing Company was founded. Although it was ostensibly a textile company, the New York Manufacturing Company's charter included the authorization to conduct banking activities. In 1817 its banking business was acquired by the Phenix Bank. With the passing of the Banking Act of 1865, the Phenix Bank became a national bank. The legendary J. P. Morgan was among the bank's original incorporators. In 1851 the Chatham Bank, named after William Pitt, Earl of Chatham, was established by another group of prosperous merchants. One of these merchants, Earl G. Drake, served as the bank's first president.

In 1911 the Phenix and Chatham banks merged to form the Chatham and Phenix National Bank of New York. In 1915 Chatham and Phenix merged with the Century Bank. Century brought 11 branches to the partnership, and special arrangements had to be made to retain these, since only state banks were allowed to have branches. In the end Chatham and Phenix was the only national bank in New York City allowed to own branches.

The word *Manufacturers* in the name of the bank came not from the New York Manufacturing Company of 1812 but from the Manufacturers National Bank of Brooklyn, which was established in 1853. In 1914 this bank merged with the Citizens Trust Company, a bank that opened its doors in 1905. After the merger of the Manufacturers National Bank and the Citizens Trust Company, the bank became Manufacturers Trust.

By 1921 Manufacturers Trust had $40 million in deposits; by 1929 the bank had absorbed 11 other banks and had a total of 47 offices. This expansion continued, and in 1931 Manufacturers Trust obtained more deposits and offices in the liquidation of five banks. This activity culminated in 1932 with the merger of Manufacturers Trust and the Chatham and Phenix National Bank.

The bank continued to expand through more mergers and outright purchases, solidifying its position in the New York banking industry. In 1950 Manufacturers Trust made one of its largest mergers ever when the Brooklyn Trust Company became part of the organization. Chartered in 1866 by contractors William C. Kingly and Judge Alexander McGee, and given solid support by an influential state senator, Henry C. Murphy, Brooklyn Trust undertook the expensive and politically divisive task of physically linking Manhattan and Brooklyn. The total cost of the Brooklyn Bridge—$15 million—was an enormous amount at the time, and could not have been financed had it not been for Brooklyn Trust's determination. The merger of the two banks in 1950 increased the number of Manufacturers Trust's branch offices to 100, the most in New York City at the time.

The corporation's other constituent bank, Hanover Bank, also traced its history to the early 19th century. The National Bank of the City of New York was chartered in 1829, funded largely by John Jacob Astor. Its first president, Albert Gallatin, had served

as Secretary of the Treasury under presidents Thomas Jefferson and James Madison, and had helped negotiate the Louisiana Purchase of 1803. During Gallatin's tenure as the bank's president, the nation experienced a serious economic downswing, culminating in the Panic of 1837. Gallatin is credited with guiding the banking system through this crisis and with establishing New York City as the financial hub of the country. In his honor, National Bank was renamed Gallatin Bank. This bank merged with the Hanover Bank in 1912.

By 1875 Hanover Bank, now a member of the national banking system, held a deposit line of $6 million. Under James T. Woodward, a noted city merchant who became president of the bank in 1876, Hanover Bank took the lead in the redevelopment of the post-Civil War South and provided financial support and banking services to entrepreneurs and companies engaged in the industrial expansion of the American West. By the time of Woodward's death in 1910, Hanover Bank had built up a deposit line of more than $100 million and had total resources of $117 million.

The constant pursuit of new markets, a trademark of both Hanover and Manufacturers, and intense competition among banking institutions for new accounts (pension funds in particular) led to the merger of these two banks in 1961. With $6 billion in assets and $7.5 billion in the trust and investment-management business, the new Manufacturers Hanover Trust Company (MHT) ranked at the top of the business. Its pension-plan clients included Union Carbide, Chrysler, Texaco, and American Motors.

However, the combination of Manufacturers Trust's strength in retail banking and Hanover Bank's strength in wholesale banking created fears of overconcentration in the industry. The Justice Department claimed the consolidation violated antitrust laws and moved to break up the company. The merger, however, survived.

Under President Gabriel Hauge, MHT expanded into the international market, much as Hanover Bank had once expanded into the reconstructing South and developing West. In 1968 Manufacturers Hanover, like the other New York money center banks, created a holding company, Manufacturers Hanover Corporation, and MHT became this company's subsidiary.

Despite problems, the corporation continued to grow. Its subsidiaries' assets alone totaled $2.8 billion, and by 1973 the corporation was worth $20 billion. Manufacturers Hanover continued to expand during the 1970s by acquiring several subsidiary banks and opening more branch offices, and in 1974, it opened a branch in Bucharest. This was the first such Western banking office in the Soviet bloc.

As loans on more than $30 billion in long-term debt at fixed rates began to mature, earnings rose to $211 million in 1979, up from $85 million in 1970. Manny Hanny by then had 436 offices in 20 states and 78 facilities in 37 countries with a wide range of financing alternatives and noncredit services.

John F. McGillicuddy became president of Manufacturers Hanover in 1973, when Hauge became chairman. By 1979, despite high earnings, it was ominously apparent that Manny Hanny had, like so many other banks, become overdependent on international loans. Loan-loss reserves were bolstered 25%, as debt repayments from Third World borrowers became increasingly uncertain.

In late 1983 Manny Hanny bought CIT Financial Corporation from RCA for $1.5 billion, at the time the largest sum a bank had ever spent for an acquisition. The following year McGillicuddy announced a major shift in the company's strategic thinking. Corporate streamlining and decentralization became the new order.

The bank was divided into five sections to place direct responsibility for performance on managers, and 5,000 employees were let go between 1986 and 1988 alone. Unprofitable services were discontinued, and less-profitable operations such as the Belgian subsidiary and the British consumer units were sold off to reduce overhead. Manny Hanny used the $1.6 billion earned through these sales to help raise reserves of $2.3 billion.

Despite strong earnings of $200 million in 1986, troubles continued as the bank's large Third World, energy, and real-estate loans continued to plague it. Continuing to sell off smaller, less-profitable operations, the bank earned $966 million in 1988.

On 31 December 1991 Manufacturers Hanover Corporation merged with Chemical Banking Corporation—another banking giant of similar size in assets, number of employees, and number of offices—under the latter's name. This formed the fifth largest bank holding company in the United States, with assets of almost $183 billion and major franchises in key regional, national, and international markets. In 1996 Chemical Banking Corporation merged with Chase Manhattan Corporation to form the largest bank in the United States, and effecting what was at that time the largest merger in world banking history. As of 31 March 1997, their combined assets totaled $336.1 billion.

See also GALLATIN, ALBERT-ABRAHAM.

MARCHÉ (France)

Marché is the French term for market.

See also STOCK MARKET.

MARCHÉ À OPTIONS (France)

Marché à Options are similar to the conventional options market in the United Kingdom.

MARCHÉ À PRIMES (France)

Marché à Primes gives an investor the right to buy shares at a set price at any time during a one- to three-month period. The investor can cancel the option before the settlement date for a fee.

MARCHÉ À TERME (France)

Marché à Terme refers to the forward delivery market. Trades are firm, but settlement is delayed to the next settlement period. Margin collateral must be supplied by the investor and will be adjusted according to market changes.

MARCHÉ À TERME D'INSTRUMENTS FINANCIERS (MATIF; France)

Marché à Terme d'Instruments Financiers (MATIF) is the financial futures market.

MARCHÉ APRÈS BOURSE (France)

Marché après Bourse refers to after-hours trading.

MARCHÉ AU COMPTANT (France)

Marché au Comptant refers to the spot or cash market, in which securities can be bought or sold for immediate settlement.

MARCHÉ DE L'ARGENT (France)

Marché de l'Argent refers to money market short-term funds.

MARCHÉ DES CAPITAUX (France)

Marché des Capitaux refers to long-term funds.

MARCHÉ DES REPORTS (France)

Marché des Reports refers to the contango market, operated once a month, in which investors can sell securities at a fixed price and buy them back for the same price on the settlement day in the following month. A contango rate is paid by the investors. If the selling position exceeds the buying position, a special deportation or backwardation rate is paid.

See also BACKWARDATION; CONTANGO.

MARCHÉ DES VALEURS (France)

Marché des Valeurs refers to the securities market.

MARCHÉ HORS COTE (France)

Marché Hors Cote is the over-the-counter unofficial market of the bourses. In this market, agents de change are responsible for maintaining prices, although they are not responsible for the quality of the securities. Securities are separated into two categories: the special section and the other section.

Special section securities are those belonging to companies that have an agreement with the Commission des Operations de Bourse to publish the same information as listed companies. These companies must make an application for listing within three years.

All remaining companies on the over the counter market appear on the other section.

See also LISTED SECURITIES; OVER THE COUNTER (OTC).

MARGE (Germany)

See SPREAD.

MARGIN

Margin is the amount paid by an investor for a security.

Margin is a fractional amount of the price of a security. Since the balance of the price is paid by the broker, margin usually involves a loan from a brokerage firm or a bank against the value of the securities. The amount borrowed is limited by regulation, but can be further limited by the lending institution.

Not all securities are allowed to be used as collateral for margin. In the United States, for instance, shares with a value of less than $3 are often restricted. This is due to the additional risk inherent in lower priced securities, which are subject to more extreme price fluctuations than listed stocks. If the price falls below minimum requirements, many positions in smaller securities will be liquidated, thereby causing the price to drop further. To avoid such problems, some firms will not lend money on shares with a value of less than $5.

Margin is a form of market leverage, allowing the investor to make full use of investment funds. It does, however, present a greater risk than dealing in cash, as the investor must deposit cash (margin maintenance) if the price of the securities used as collateral is dropping. Maintenance calls are often made when the owner's equity drops to 25%, but this limit is often set at higher levels by brokerage firms.

An example helps to explain how margin buying can benefit the investor:

Investor buys 200 shares of ABE, Inc. at $50 per share for a total of $10,000.

Investor borrows $5,000 and buys another 100 shares at $50.

Investor sells all 300 shares of ABE, Inc. for $55 for a total of $16,500.

The profit of $1,500 would have only been $1,000 without the margin purchase. The investor will, however, pay commissions and margin interest on the loan.

Margin loans are computerized to show an investor's available cash and borrowing power. An investor should be able to get the information at any time the office is open. Margin clerks regularly monitor the accounts for possible discrepancies or extraordinary changes.

See also CASH ACCOUNT; EQUITY.

MARGIN ACCOUNT

A *Margin Account* is a form of investment account in which sales and purchases of listed stocks are made with the aid of credit provided by the investor's broker. A margin account requires a signature or signatures on a margin agreement, and a deposit of cash or securities to meet the minimum equity requirement.

When buying on margin, the investor provides only a percentage of the total cost of the securities, while the broker provides the balance. The broker then charges the investor interest on the outstanding amount.

In the United States, a margin account cannot be used as an Individual Retirement Account (IRA) because the funds allowed to be contributed annually to these accounts are a set amount. A situation could arise in which additional funds are required for a margin maintenance call, but the investor has already contributed the maximum annual amount.

Important to note: The majority of brokerage firms require all options trading to be done in a margin account (with a special options agreement form), even when no money has been borrowed.

See also CASH ACCOUNT; EQUITY; MARGIN.

MARGIN AGREEMENT

See MARGIN ACCOUNT.

MARGIN CALL

A *Margin Call* is a request for additional securities or payments to offset a loss in the market value of securities pledged as collateral.

In the United States, Federal Reserve Board Regulation T covers credit extension to customers by securities brokers, dealers, and members of the national securities exchanges; sets the initial margin requirement; and strictly defines registered (eligible), unregistered (ineligible), and exempt securities.

Although the requirements are subject to change, the initial equity in a margin account is a minimum of $2,000. Up to 50% of eligible marginable securities can qualify for a margin loan. For example, if an investor paid $10,000 to buy 200 shares of XYZ Corporation at $50 per share, the investor could then borrow $5,000 to buy another 100 shares at $50 per share. This transaction is referred to as a *Reg-T.*

If the market value of the shares drops from $50 to $45 per share, the bank or brokerage firm that loaned the $5,000 can issue a margin call requesting that the investor submit funds ($500) to cover the $5 drop per share in the market value of the 100 shares purchased with borrowed money.

The maintenance requirement in a margin account is a minimum of 25% of marginable equity securities. Many firms increase that amount to 30% and will issue a maintenance call if the account equity falls below the 30% level. So, although the investor would also incur a loss of $1,000 on the 200 shares purchased with his own funds, because the present market value of $45 per share maintains the account at $9,000 ($45 a share x 200 shares), the investor would not be required to replenish any amount, as $9,000 is well above the minimum maintenance requirement of $2,000.

If an investor makes a margin account purchase but doesn't have the funds in the account to meet the minimum Regulation T requirements, the firm issues a Reg-T Call. This is simply a request for additional funds.

See also MARGIN; REGULATION G–X/REGULATION T; SETTLE.

MARGIN LOANS
See MARGIN.

MARGIN MAINTENANCE
See MAINTENANCE REQUIREMENT; MARGIN.

MARGIN OF PROFIT
See PROFIT MARGIN.

MARK DOWN (United States)
The lowering of a price of a security or proceeds is referred to as a *Mark Down.* Mark downs appear in the following three forms:

1. A cash amount to be subtracted from the selling price of an over-the-counter security when sold to a broker/dealer. In the United States, the National Association of Securities Dealers limits the amount to no more than 5% for mark downs and mark ups on the buy side (with some exceptions involving low-priced securities). In this case the mark down is, effectively, a commission.
2. A price reduction on a bond offer to meet the current market demands.
3. The revaluation of securities by banks and investment firms, based on market moves.

See also COMMISSION; MARK TO THE MARKET; MARK-UP.

MARK TO THE MARKET
Mark to the Market is the process of re-evaluating a security, or portfolio of securities, to more closely reflect current market prices, resulting in one of the following situations:

1. A margin call if the price of shares sold short rises to a high enough level
2. A margin call if a short option goes against the option writer
3. A margin call if a margined portfolio drops low enough in price
4. A change in the net asset value of a mutual fund when it is calculated at the end of the day
5. A change in a when-issued security if it declines in value before settlement date

See also MARGIN; REGULATION G–X/REGULATION T, SELLING SHORT.

MARK UP
Effectively, *Mark Up* is the commission charged for buying an over-the-counter security.

In the United States, the National Association of Securities Dealers, under the Rules of Fair Practice, limits broker/dealers to a mark up of not more than 5%, except in situations in which there is an unusually low price or an unusually small amount of securities involved.

Some broker/dealers list the mark up as a commission charge to avoid any possible confusion about the charges associated with over-the-counter trading. A mark down will be charged when selling an over-the-counter security.

See also COMMISSION; MARK DOWN; OVER THE COUNTER (OTC).

MARKET AVERAGE

See DOW JONES AVERAGES; DOW THEORY.

MARKET BOTTOM

Market Bottom refers to the lowest point of a stock during its decline on the market. This is the level at which everyone would like to buy shares, but never seems to do so. Technical analysts call this point a level of support, during which buyers enter the market and cause it to rise. Market bottom is the exact opposite of resistance, a market high point at which the market will struggle to break through.

Studies of technical analysis can give investors an explanation for the market bottom, but this form of analysis is rarely reliable when forecasting the state of the market.

See also DOW THEORY; MARKET TOP; TECHNICAL ANALYSIS.

MARKET CAPITALIZATION

Market Capitalization is calculated by multiplying the number of outstanding ordinary shares by the current market price of each ordinary share, and is synonymous with the total value of the company. Many institutional investors consider market capitalization when selecting companies in which to buy shares. It is regularly used to screen out companies below a certain size.

Calculating the market capitalization of each company trading on the stock exchange and adding them all together produces the market capitalization for the total stock exchange.

See also INSTITUTIONAL INVESTOR; MARKET PRICE; OUTSTANDING SHARES.

MARKET CORRECTION/MARKET CRASH

A *Market Correction* is a temporary sell-off of securities during which the market drops for a day or a few days, then begins to climb higher again. Most corrections are between 2% and 5% and tend to last for less than a week.

A *Market Crash* is a sudden and potentially ruinous drop afflicting all shares listed on a stock exchange. The worst one-day market crash was on 19 October 1987, when the Dow Jones Industrial Average dropped more than 500 points in one single day. This decline, of more than 20%, was an example of a bear market.

See also BLACK MONDAY; DOW THEORY; TECHNICAL ANALYSIS; TREND.

MARKET IF TOUCHED (MIT)

Market If Touched (MIT) is a qualifier placed on an order that stipulates that the order be executed only in the event that the market price reaches or passes a stated price. Only some exchanges allow MIT order designation.

Buy orders designated MIT are entered below the current trading price, and sell orders are entered above the current trading price. Their relationship to current prices is the opposite of that of a stop order, but the same as a limit order.

MIT orders occur most often with futures trading in commodities.

See also LIMIT ORDER; MARKET ORDER; STOP ORDER.

MARKET INDEX

Market Index is a term used to describe both indices and averages.

The first widely publicized market average was the Dow Jones Industrial Average, which became official on 26 May 1896, although it started several years earlier as a combination of industrial and railroad shares.

The Dow Jones Industrial Average is a true average, but with the individual share prices added together and divided by a total number called a divisor. The divisor is not the total number of companies, but a figure that is adjusted to reflect changes such as share splits and bonus issues.

Other market indices, such as the Standard and Poor's 500 Index, take into account the number of shares, and are based more on value changes.

Market indices are indicators of market trends, and offer investors a benchmark by which to measure performance.

See also DOW JONES AVERAGES; DOW THEORY; STANDARD AND POOR'S 500 INDEX (S&P 500).

MARKET LETTER

Published by a brokerage or investment firm and sold by subscription to interested investors, a *Market Letter* contains articles regarding various economic situations impacting on investing. These publications also contain investment analysis of the stock market and chart the progress of individual companies or business sectors.

Subscription newsletters are frequently narrow in their subject focus. They might only address growth shares, high-tech companies, technical analysis, the Dow Theory, or utility shares.

In addition to a market letter, many companies (in the interest of timeliness) provide a phone service for current market analysis updates.

See also DOW THEORY; TECHNICAL ANALYSIS.

MARKET MAKER

A *Market Maker* (broker/dealer) trades securities for both the firm's account and for the accounts of investors. The market maker does not trade from the floor of the stock exchange, but rather from the trading desk in the brokerage firm's home office.

The market maker is obliged to quote firm two-way prices for securities on a continuous basis in order to facilitate public trading. Market makers will often keep an inventory of the stocks in which they make a market, and will consequently have to accept the risks and rewards inherent in proprietary trading.

If a brokerage receives an order for a security for which it does not make a market (quote a buying and selling price), the firm usually acts as agent and has the trade executed through a market maker. However, when securities are thinly traded, it can be difficult to find a market maker to conduct a buy or sell transaction.

See also PROPRIETARY TRADING; SPECIALIST; STOCK EXCHANGE; THINLY TRADED; TRADING DESK.

MARKET MANIA

Prices on stock markets throughout most of the world shot up in the mid-1990s, setting off a controversy among investors and analysts. Was the bull market based on a firm foundation of profitability, increased productivity, low interest rates, and low inflation? Or was it a result of the reckless investments of a growing number of shareholders who, afflicted with *Market Mania*, had bid share prices up to a point beyond all reason?

In 1996 stocks rose 35.5% in Finland and 34.2% in Taiwan. During the first seven months of 1997, they rose 53% in the Netherlands, 50% in Germany, 35% in Italy, 28% in the United States, and 22% in Great Britain. In Britain and France, they had doubled since 1991; in the United States and Germany, they had more than tripled. Worldwide, the capitalization of stock markets tripled between 1986 and 1996. Among the developed countries, the sole exception to this trend of heady growth was Japan.

The U.S. bull market had continued virtually without interruption since 1982, with the Dow Jones Industrial Average increasing from 2,000 to 4,000 points between 8 January 1987 and 23 February 1995, then doubling again to 8,000 by 16 July 1997—a period of two years and five months, the shortest doubling time in the Dow's history. Other indexes of the gains in the U.S. market, including the Standard and Poor's 500 (S&P 500) Index, the National Association of Securities Dealers Automated Quotation System (NASDAQ), and the Russell 2000 index of small-capitalization stocks, all registered very significant increases. Even initial public offerings—new stocks—showed unprecedented gains. Yet for all these bullish indicators, some discerned deep problems.

One concern was that the price to earnings ratio (p/e) of stocks had reached a level significantly higher than its historic average. For example, the p/e ratio for companies on the S&P 500 had averaged 14 for 1926–97, but by July 1997 it had reached 23. This ratio was not so far out of line by comparison to previous periods of very low inflation. However, it did mean that the rate of return on stock investments, which is the inverse of the p/e, stood at around 5%, or about one-fifth lower than the rate of return on 30-year U.S. Treasury bonds. Thus, stocks were said to be overvalued by about 20% in comparison to bonds. The last time they had been at least that overvalued—32% in October 1987—a major crash in the stock market followed shortly.

Another view held that share prices had been bid up because of several new sources of cash that were entering the stock market. Individuals' mutual funds were being invested at the rate of $20–$30 billion per month in 1996, and there was potentially much more. Corporations increasingly engaged in stock-repurchase programs. And foreign investors began to enter the U.S. market in unprecedented numbers.

The heightened volatility of the U.S. market in 1997 was seen by some as a sign of investor confusion and a precursor of a major correction. Nine of the ten largest daily increases in the history of the Dow were recorded that year, along with five of the ten biggest losses. Major gyrations within one session had become common.

Others feared that inflationary pressures would force the Federal Reserve to raise interest rates, or that foreign investors might pull out for various reasons, either of which could cause a downturn. Some saw the growth of indexing (investing in a representative mix of all the stocks on the market), increasingly relied upon by mutual funds, as proof that investing was characterized by blind speculation more than by any serious attempt to evaluate particular stock prices in relation to their real values. Other analysts noted a tendency for the big increases to become more concentrated in narrower sectors of the market.

Assessing the market meant figuring out to what extent the market accurately reflected the state of the economy and also figuring out what the state of the economy was. The U.S. economy had made the transition from an emphasis on manufacturing to an emphasis on information and services in an increasingly globalized economic environment, and there were many new phenomena to understand. By mid-1997 the U.S. gross domestic product had grown for 78 consecutive months, whereas wholesale prices had fallen for 7 consecutive months (the first time that had happened in the 50 years they had been computed). How could there be such low inflation in the U.S. economy—even some deflation at the wholesale level—during a period of sustained expansion?

Real wages were one reason. Depending on how one evaluated consumer prices, real wages had either decreased slightly, held steady, or increased slightly over the previous 25 years. Even though the official unemployment rate fell below 5% in 1997, there was little upward pressure on wages. The spread of low-paying service jobs, the decline of unions, the increased use of temporary and part-time workers, and increased competition from lower-paid labor in the Third World tended to keep wages down.

Another reason was productivity. According to the standard statistical measures, productivity was increasing at only about 1% per year in the United States—not enough to explain the coexistence of high growth, low inflation, and relatively low unemployment. However, some argued that the old measures missed the effects of widespread computerization—greater production, reduced delivery time, better inventory management, and heightened synchronization of local supply and demand.

Some theorize that in the new conditions of the 1990s, business cycles in the worldwide capitalist economy will be dampened, opening the prospects of more prolonged periods of fairly steady growth. If these views are correct, and barring external shocks, the stock market's rise might continue for some time. However, the possibility of major economic or political disruptions, especially with increased economic polarization in society, remain.

See also PSYCHOLOGY OF SPECULATION.

MARKET MULTIPLE
See PRICE/EARNINGS RATIO.

MARKET ON CLOSE
Market on Close is a qualifier placed on an order to buy or sell securities stipulating that the order is executed during the last 30 seconds of exchange trading. There is no guarantee that a market on close order will be executed, since unqualified market orders always have precedence. The order might be executed at the final price of the day or remain unfulfilled.

A market on close order can be used by an investor to buy or sell securities when prices are moving in a favorable direction during the trading session. The investor believes the closing price will be the most acceptable for the day and will place a market on close order.

See also LIMIT ORDER; MARKET ORDER, ON THE OPENING.

MARKET ORDER
Any order of securities designated to be bought or sold at the best available price is referred to as a *Market Order*. The "best available price" will be either the highest possible bid or the lowest possible offer.

Because they involve less risk than limit orders or sell limits, the vast majority of orders placed are market orders. Many institutional traders place market orders only, rather than chase the price of a share by constantly changing a limit order. In addition, market orders always take precedence in being filled.

Limit orders can sometimes be frustrating for investors. Often, the price seems to hover around the limit and then move up. The buying investor then raises the limit, only to see the price advance further. Invariably, it proves better to buy the shares for a three-to-five-year growth rate at the market price.

Sell limits can be even more frustrating and costly. As the investor chases the elusive price, the market can unexpectedly correct and be down for the next few months. Many investment gurus recommend selling at the market and moving on to other investment selections.

Although the price quotation doesn't guarantee the execution price, most orders are filled reasonably close to the information given in a quote.

See also ALL OR NONE (AON); AT THE MARKET; LIMIT ORDER; STOP ORDER.

MARKET OVERSIGHT AND SURVEILLANCE SYSTEM (MOSS; United States)
The *Market Oversight and Surveillance System (MOSS)* is a Securities and Exchange Commission (SEC) system for overseeing market activity.

MOSS specifically monitors the trading activities of stock exchange specialists, with particular attention to the liquidity of each company's shares, price differentials, and trading patterns. If the SEC believes the public will be better served, MOSS has complete authority to assign new listings to specialists or to reassign listed issues to other specialists.

Although self-regulation is an important concept to securities trading, some direct regulation is also necessary and the SEC takes an active role in maintaining compliance with the concept of a "fair and orderly market."

See also FAIR AND ORDERLY MARKET; SECURITIES AND EXCHANGE COMMISSION (SEC); SPECIALIST.

MARKET PRICE

In regard to exchange traded securities, *Market Price* is the price of the last trade reported.

For example, if a price quotation shows XYZ Corporation to have a bid $50, an ask $50 1/8, and a last trade of $50 1/8, the market price is $50 1/8.

Historically, prices most often use daily closing prices, although sometimes a price half way between a specific session's high and low for the day can be used. Sometimes a market price of a poorly traded security has to be estimated based on the opinion of analysts and traders who deal with similar securities.

Within certain limitations, a time and sales report can be obtained if an investor believes a trade was executed at an inaccurate price. However, a time and sales report might not be available from some stock exchanges.

See also LIMIT ORDER; MARKET ORDER; STOP ORDER.

MARKET STABILIZATION

Market Stabilization is an attempt to control the price of a share by interfering with the free working of market forces. Stabilization, pegging, and fixing are normally prohibited by stock exchange regulators, and if found guilty, the underwriter or investment bank responsible will be heavily fined and censured.

On rare occasions, a stock exchange will accept limited market stabilization to guarantee effective trading of a new issue or, still more rarely, a rights issue. A firm that has permission to perform market stabilization must state the fact on all issue documents and prospectuses.

MARKET TOP

A *Market Top* is the highest level ever reached by a stock market or stock market index. The phrase is also commonly used to refer to the most recent high point in a stock market average or index.

From a technical perspective, the market top represents the level at which there appear more sellers than buyers and can become a point of resistance. It is the opposite of support, where more buyers than sellers appear. Resistance is the market or share price level that continually attracts sellers. It is a point where a trend line turns downward, usually resulting in more than one fall. Technical analysts believe a strong rally

will follow if resistance is strongly penetrated and a breakout occurs.

See also DOW THEORY; MARKET BOTTOM; TECHNICAL ANALYSIS.

MARKET VALUE

See CURRENT MARKET VALUE; MARKET PRICE.

MARKETABLE LIMIT ORDER

A *Marketable Limit Order* is a limit order placed at or close enough to the current market price so as to allow for an immediate execution.

Investors want orders to be filled as quickly as possible, but wish to avoid losing money or paying extra costs if there is a sudden surge or fall in the market price. Placing a limit on the order provides a form of insurance. Such an order is often placed at or near the open, or to be filled on the re-open after trading has been halted for a time.

For example, XYZ Corporation began trading at $50 per share and trading was halted for an announcement. An investor believes the announcement will be positive news and places a buy order for 100 shares at $50 1/4 or better (OB). The "or better" is added to let the trader know that this order is intentionally being placed above the current market price (limit buy orders are usually placed below the current market price). When XYZ Corporation resumes trading, the investor's order will be filled if it can be filled at a price of $50 1/4 or less. If trading reopens above $50 1/4, the investor's order missed the market and is unlikely to be filled.

See also DAY ORDER; LIMIT ORDER; MARKET ORDER.

MARKETABLE PARCEL (Australia)

A *Marketable Parcel* is the minimum number of shares necessary for a normal transaction. The market price of the shares determines the number of shares in a parcel. Shares can also be traded in multiples of a marketable parcel.

Grouping shares in marketable parcels, also known as round lots, enhances speed and accuracy in any stock market. This was especially true when all trades were accomplished by individuals rather than by computer.

Shares not in marketable parcels can be traded, but are handled through an odd-lot broker and usually attract an extra fee.

See also ODD-LOT; ODD-LOT DIFFERENTIAL; ROUND LOT.

MARKT (Germany)

See MARKET.

MARKT BEHERRSCHEN (Germany)

See CORNERING THE MARKET.

MARKTHEWERTUNG (Germany)

See MARKET CAPITALIZATION.

MARKTPREIS (Germany)

See MARKET PRICE.

MARRIED PUT

A *Married Put* is an investor's immediate purchase of a put option on newly acquired securities in order to protect, or hedge, their price. The purchase of the put option limits the selling price of the shares until the option expires. The amount of risk is limited to the amount of money paid for the put, which is absorbed into the cost of the shares.

If the share price drops, the put can be exercised before expiration and the shares are sold at the put strike price. Alternatively, the put option can be sold for a profit.

For example: An investor buys 100 shares of XYZ Corporation at $55 and buys an October 55 put for $4 for a total effective cost of $59.

If the share price drops to $50, the investor can either exercise the put and sell at the strike price of $55 or sell the put for a profit ($5 plus any remaining time value).

If the price of the shares rises, the put can be held until expiration or sold for a loss on the premium. Any loss is married to the put and is netted for tax purposes in the United States and many other countries.

See also OPTION; PREMIUM; PUT; PUT PREMIUM; STRIKE PRICE.

MARTILLO SYSTEM (Colombia)

The auction system for transferring securities registered on the Bogota Stock Exchange is known as the *Martillo System*. Shares not registered on the Bogota Exchange can also be transferred if they are listed in the National Securities Register. When prior authorization is obtained by the board of directors, other types of assets can also be traded. Auctions are chaired by a legal representative of the BSE or a person so delegated.

See also COLOMBIA; TRANSFER.

MARX, KARL

Karl Marx was a German philosopher, historian, sociologist, political theorist, and economist. Exiled from Germany in 1849, Marx lived in London and was supported financially by the industrialist Friedrich Engels, coauthor with Marx of *The Communist Manifesto* (1848). In 1859 Marx published *The Critique of Political Economy*, followed by the first volume of *Das Kapital* in 1867. Volumes two and three were edited by Engels and published posthumously in 1885 and 1894.

Marx's education in philosophy at the universities of Bonn, Berlin, and Jena provided a strong influence of Hegelian political philosophy in his thinking. In Marx's analysis, economic circumstances were the determinants of all social relationships and even of human consciousness itself. To Marx, the mode of production of the material means of existence conditioned the whole process of social, political, and intellectual life. This economic determinism allowed Marx to develop comprehensive ideas about society and to challenge the classical economic tradition. Within a historical framework, policies intended to remedy economic evils, Marx argued, were useless. The function of economic analysis was restricted to exposing the laws of historical change and the inevitable destruction of capitalism.

Marx's economics were essentially those of the classical school, especially the work of David Ricardo. For Marx, capitalism was a stage in the process of evolution removed from the primitive agricultural economy and moving toward the inevitable elimination of private property and the class structure. Continuous change in the methods of production and exchange cause social relations and political structures to become outmoded. Marx identified four evolutionary stages through which the relations of production and society had passed: primitive communism, slavery, feudalism, and capitalism.

In *Das Kapital*, his major work, Marx attempted to discover the economic law of motion of capitalism. He argued that capitalism is characterized by two antagonistic classes, the capital-owning bourgeois class and the propertyless proletariat. The proletariat is required to offer itself as wage labor in order to survive. Marx developed from Adam Smith and Ricardo their labor theory of value, which also provided him with a system of prices. The quantity of labor used up in the manufacture of a product determined value, and this value was fundamental and immutable. Labor consumption determined exchange value, which Marx critically distinguished from use value. The exchange value is paid by capitalists as wages determined by the

Karl Marx, 1878. *(AP/Wide World Photos)*

socially necessary labor time to "produce" the worker. The labor inputs required to rear, feed, clothe, and educate the worker (the subsistence level in order to keep the population constant) determined the exchange value. The value of the laborer to the capitalist (the use value) is greater than the exchange value the capitalist pays for labor, and "surplus value" accrues to the capitalist.

Marx argued that labor was the sole source of surplus value and that other factors of production, such as plant and machinery, only reproduced themselves in the productive process. Marx termed these constant capital in contrast to the variable returns from labor. The desire for further wealth, combined with competition and technological change, induced capitalists to invest from their surplus. The ratio of constant capital to labor variable capital, Marx argued, would rise as accumulation proceeds so that the rate of surplus value, and presumably the rate of profit, would eventually fall.

Marx believed that diminishing profits and stronger competition would lead to monopoly and the concentration of wealth in a few hands, while also imposing a downward pressure on wages. The emergence of a large "reserve army of unemployed" arising from mechanization would add to the polarization of the system into a few rich capitalists and a mass of discontented workers. As a result, the class conflict would increase until the economic structure would evolve again through the overthrow of capitalism, giving way to socialism and finally to communism.

Marx's ingenious extension and modification of the classical school and his focus on the social process have had a dramatic impact upon economic and political thinking. Marx's greatest challenge was to 19th-century society's self-confidence in economic progress, and he alerted many to the unequal realities of capitalism. His work provided the impetus for the neoclassical emergence that challenged Marx's belief that labor was the sole source of surplus income.

Marx is criticized for predicting the decline of capitalism as a result of falling wages and profits, both of which have stubbornly resisted his theoretical claims. Later economists within the Marxist tradition have attempted to explain this by the ability of capitalists to invest in colonies. In adapting Marxist analysis to the problems of economic planning and administration in a postcapitalist society, 20th-century economists and politicians have extended Marxist analysis beyond its originator's brief. Marx offered no systematic analysis of the economic system that would replace capitalism following its inevitable decline.

Marx's influence is unparalleled and his ideas and tradition provided the rationale and rhetoric for some of the greatest social and political changes of the 20th century.

See also CLASSICAL SCHOOL OF ECONOMICS; NEO-CLASSICAL SCHOOL OF ECONOMICS; RICARDO, DAVID.

MASTER OF BUSINESS ADMINISTRATION (MBA)

Master of Business Administration (MBA) is an advanced degree granted for study beyond the bachelor's degree. Approximately 750 colleges and universities offer MBA programs in the United States. Of these, only about one-third have received accreditation from the prestigious American Assembly of Collegiate Schools of Business. In Britain over 100 schools provide MBA programs, and the Association of Business Schools is the largest academic grouping in British higher education. Several universities in Europe offer the MBA, including France's INSEAD (European Institute of Business Administration), generally regarded as Europe's best business school. In Asia there has recently been a proliferation of MBA programs, even though most Japanese companies feel the MBA is not helpful unless the business is export oriented.

Annually, various organizations and publications, such as *Business Week* and *U.S. News & World Report*, publish rankings of U.S. business schools based on surveys of the businesses that hire the schools' graduates and the graduates themselves. The following are perennially ranked among the top 25:

• Northwestern University (Kellogg School of Business)

• University of Pennsylvania (Wharton School of Business)

• Harvard University

• University of Virginia (Darden School of Business)

• Stanford University

• University of Chicago

• Massachusetts Institute of Technology (Sloan School of Business)

• Columbia University

• University of Michigan

• Dartmouth University (Amos Tuck School of Business)

In Europe a list of top business schools would usually include the following:

• INSEAD

• London School of Business

- International Institute for Management Development (IMD) in Lausanne, Switzerland
  - Manchester (England)
  - Warwick (England)
  - Erasmus-Rotterdam (in the Netherlands)

Asia's top-rated business schools are as follows:

- International University of Japan
- Chinese University of Hong Kong
- Indian Institute of Management

The top-ranked U.S. business schools are very selective regarding admissions, most accepting only 7% to 45% of their applicants. An almost universal admission requirement is the Graduate Management Admission Test (GMAT). Significant work experience in a managerial position normally enhances an applicant's chances of admission.

The course of study for the MBA includes courses in accounting and finance, economics, marketing, human resource and conflict management, production management, organizational and consumer behavior, business law, business ethics, international business, statistics and quantitative methods, and management information systems. Many students choose an area of concentration such as accounting/finance or management/marketing.

Many MBA programs extend over a two-year period to accommodate students who continue to work and those whose backgrounds require that they make up prerequisite courses. Also, various part-time MBA programs are available—from two years of alternate weekends to a few years of evening classes, and from on-line study to a year's worth of Saturdays plus study abroad.

The 1960s and 1970s were a period of business growth and expansion, and large companies needed many intelligent, well-educated managers to control their operations and to staff their corporate headquarters. This fueled a boom in businesses recruiting and hiring MBAs, usually at premium salaries. In the 1980s the bull market spurred a surge in investment banking, and Wall Street joined in the boom of hiring MBAs. For example, 30% of Harvard's 1987 MBA graduates accepted positions in investment banking. Many of these MBAs joined the investment banks' merger-and-acquisitions teams that were reshaping corporate America.

After the October 1987 stock market crash known as Black Monday, many newly graduated MBAs and MBA candidates saw their future dim considerably. The Dow Jones had dropped 508 points and many brokerage firms began laying off employees. However, not all MBAs lost out as a result of Black Mon-

day. Many investment banks began laying off middle managers and hiring entry-level MBAs to take their place.

There are now more than one million MBAs in the United States, and 75,000 new MBAs graduate each year. One-third of the graduates are women. This abundance of MBAs comes at a time when many business executives are wary of hiring them. These executives criticize MBAs as being too steeped in theory with too little practical business sense and being prone to expect advancement at an unrealistically fast pace. Competition among MBAs for the better jobs is intense. Nevertheless, in a recent survey of 600 business leaders 78% responded yes when asked if they would recommend an MBA to a son or daughter interested in a business career.

MBAs work in a variety of industries, including automotive, banking, consulting, consumer products, data processing, financial services, food and beverage, and insurance. In these industries the majority of MBAs work in the areas of marketing and finance. They also work in the areas of administration and general management, information management, production, and operations.

See also HARVARD BUSINESS SCHOOL.

MATCHED ORDERS

Matched Orders are two orders—one to buy securities with a brokerage firm, and an identical one to sell securities with another firm—placed simultaneously for the purpose of creating the impression of trading activity.

For example:

Buy 1,000 shares of XYZ Corporation at brokerage firm A.

Sell 1,000 shares of XYZ Corporation at brokerage firm B.

This will appear as 2,000 shares of activity when, in reality, there is no real trading activity. Such trades were made illegal in the United States under the terms of the Securities Exchange Act of 1934.

See also BUY; FREE RIDING; SELL; SETTLE.

MAURITIUS, REPUBLIC OF

The *Republic of Mauritius* is an island country. It is the central independent island state of the Mascarene group, lying about 500 miles east of Madagascar in the Indian Ocean.

Area: 788 square miles (2,040 square km)

Population: 1,128,000 (40.7% urban; 59.3% rural)

Form of Government: Republic, with one legislative house: Legislative Assembly—70 members. Chief of state: President. Head of government: Prime Minister.

Official Language: English

Capital: Port Louis

Largest Cities: Port Louis, 142,850; Beau Bassin-Rose Hill, 94,299; Vacoas-Phoenix, 92,072; Curepipe, 74,738; Quatre Bornes, 71,534

Economy:

Currency: Mauritian rupee (Rs)

National Budget: Revenue—Rs 12.9 billion; expenditures—Rs 12.7 billion (social services: 35.6%, of which education, art, and culture: 14.6%; social security: 10.9%; health: 8.2%; public-debt service: 27.7%)

Public Debt: US$884.0 million

Gross National Product: US$3.3 billion

Principal Products: Sugarcane; green tea; potatoes and other vegetables; livestock; clothing and textiles

Foreign Trade (Imports): Rs 30.3 billion (manufactured goods classified chiefly by material: 36.4%; machinery and transport equipment: 22.4%; food: 12.3%; mineral fuels and lubricants: 6.4%; chemicals: 6.3%; inedible crude materials excluding fuels: 3.1%; animal and vegetable oils and fats: 1.0%; from South Africa: 14.2%; France: 12.6%; Japan: 7.2%; United Kingdom: 5.8%; Hong Kong: 4.6%; India: 4.4%; Taiwan: 4.2%; Germany: 4.1%)

Foreign Trade (Exports): Rs 23.0 billion (clothing and textiles: 55.3%; sugar: 25.1%; yarn: 2.5%; pearls and precious stones: 1.8%; to United Kingdom: 32.4%; France: 20.5%; United States: 17.9%; Germany: 7.1%; Italy: 4.0%)

Stock Exchanges: 1
Stock Exchange of Mauritius (SEM)
6th Floor, Cascades Bldg.
33 bis, Edith Cavell St.
Port Louis
Mauritius
Phone: (230) 212 9541, 42, 43
Fax: (230) 208 8409

Internet Address: www.zlynx.com/semdex/home

Trading Hours:

Monday, Wednesday, Friday	11:00 to 12:00	Official Market
Tuesday, Thursday	11:00 to 12:00	OTC Market

Office Hours: Monday–Friday, 8:45 to 4:00

Exchange Holidays:

1, 2, 17, 31 January	30 August
27 February	23 October
3, 12 March	1 November
1 April	25 December
1 May	

Listed Companies: 41

Total Market Capitalization:

At 31 December 1997

Local Currency (Millions)	US Dollars (Millions)
37,021,056	1,667,289

Major Sectors: Banking and insurance, industry, investment, sugar, commerce, leisure and hotels, transportation

Share Price Performance:

(% Change)

1994	91
1995	-3
1996	20
1997	11

History: Mauritius has a background of brokerage activities that dates back to the 18th century, when it existed as a colony of France. A Chambre des Courtiers was established in 1804, followed by the Mauritian Chamber of Commerce in 1827. With the establishment of commercial banks in the mid-19th century, securities trading became regular. Docks, insurance companies, and sugar factories were among the first traded securities.

After World War II, the Brokers Ordinance (1945) and the Transfer of Shares and Debentures Ordinance (1953) updated the procedures of the existing stock market.

The present-day Stock Exchange of Mauritius (SEM) falls under the authority of the Stock Exchange Act of 1988, and the Companies Act. Eleven brokerage firms are shareholders of the Exchange. The SEM is supervised by the Stock Exchange Commission, which assumes the role of regulating authority.

The Stock Exchange of Mauritius is a member of both the Fédération International des Bourses de Valeurs, an international association of stock exchanges, and the African Stock Exchanges Association, a regional organization.

The current market started trading the securities of five companies in July 1989 and has a current listed market of 30 companies and an over-the-counter market of 74 companies.

Classes of Securities: Ordinary shares, preference shares, corporate debentures, government bonds

Indices: SEMDEX Index (5 July 1989 = 100)

Formula:

$$\text{SEMDEX} = \frac{\text{Current market value of all listed shares}}{\text{Base market value of all listed shares}} \times 100$$

The market value of any class of shares is equal to the number of shares outstanding multiplied by its market price.

Supervisory Organizations:

Minister of Finance

Stock Exchange Commission (SEC)

Controller of Securities

Depository: None (being developed)

The Stock Exchange of Mauritius is developing a Central Depository System that will eventually eliminate certificates and operate solely with a book-entry system.

Settlement Details:

Shares: Friday of the following week

Trading: The two operating markets on the Securities Exchange of Mauritius are the Official Market, which trades the securities of all listed companies, and the over-the-counter (OTC) Market for the trading of unlisted companies.

Until December 1993 there were two trading mechanisms: the open-outcry method for listed securities and the *casier*, or box, method for the OTC. As of January 1994, trading on both markets converted to open-outcry (*à la criée*). Depending on market activity, prices are allowed to vary between sessions. The maximum variation is 6% for the Official Market and 10% for the OTC Market. Daily sessions last between 30 minutes and one hour. At the end of the trading session, all transactions are netted.

Effectively, the system is an order-driven, single-price auction. The casier method is used in situations of unusual market disequilibrium, when a price cannot be reached by the outcry method. Buy and sell orders are matched by a computer to determine a quoted price. If a quotation exercise cannot be accomplished, a market sheet with details of existing orders is provided for the brokers, who can then solicit new orders for 30 minutes.

An investor can place market orders, limit orders, and stop orders. All trading is for spot transactions and current delivery.

Brokerage rates are fixed at 1% of the value of every trade. Of that 1%, 25% goes to the SEM in the form of a fee.

Listing Requirements: Companies wishing to list on the Mauritius Securities Exchange must have an adequate trading record with published or filed accounts for three years prior to the listing request. The market capitalization must be at least Rs 20 million. A minimum of 25% of the shares must be publicly held and spread among at least 200 shareholders, although this rule does not apply to the holdings of company directors and substantial shareholders with more than 5% of the issued capital.

Documentation providing detailed information on the company, conformation with the rules and regulations of the stock exchange, and an information sheet must be issued to the public just prior to listing. The information sheet must also detail the company's present business and future prospects. A number of post-listing obligations must also be met, including the public release of any information that is expected to affect the company's share prices.

Provisional financial statements must be made public within three months of the financial year end, and intermediate financial reports must be distributed every six months.

Application for listing is filed with the Stock Exchange of Mauritius Listing Committee, which is constituted by the Minister of Finance. Following the report and recommendations of the listing committee, the SEM Executive Committee may grant or reject the listing application pending approval of the Stock Exchange Commission.

Further details on listing can be obtained by contacting the Mauritius Securities Exchange.

Investor Taxation: None; foreign investors have the same tax treatment as residents for dividends and capital gains.

Limitations: Non-citizens can subscribe to new issues and invest in unit trusts.

Securities Lending: None

Brokerage Firms:

Asma Securities & Investment Ltd.

43, Sir William Newton Street

Port Louis

Mauritius

Phone: (230) 212 1269, 211 0697

Fax: (230) 208 8508

Associated Brokers Ltd.
10, Sir William Newton Street
Port Louis
Mauritius
Phone: (230) 212 3038
Fax: (230) 212 6690

Capital Markets Brokers Ltd.
3rd Floor, Moorgate House
29, Sir William Newton Street
Port Louis
Mauritius
Phone: (230) 211 1934, 212 1336
Fax: (230) 212 3557/2

Compagnie des Agents de Change Ltee
9th Floor, Stratton Court
Pondrière Street
Port Louis
Mauritius
Phone: (230) 212 2578, 212 0454
Fax: (230) 208 3455

First Brokers Ltd.
4th Floor, R. Li Wan Po Building
12, Remy Ollier Street
Port Louis
Mauritius
Phone: (230) 211 0582/83, 228 0458
Fax: (230) 211 0584

General Brokerage Ltd.
8th Floor, Les Cascades Building
33 bis, Edith Cavell Street
Port Louis
Mauritius
Phone: (230) 212 9863/4/5
Fax: (230) 212 9867

MCB Stockbrokers Ltd.
Aux Galeries Reunies Building
5, Bourbon Street
Port Louis
Mauritius
Phone: (230) 208 2801
Fax: (230) 211 0239

Ramet & Associés Ltée
16, Queen Street
Port Louis
Mauritius
Phone: (230) 212 3535, 212 2661
Fax: (230) 208 6294

State Stockbrokering Co. Ltd.
2nd Floor, Fon Sing Building
12, Edith Cavell Street
Port Louis
Mauritius
Phone: (230) 208 8055/ 8096, 212 2978
Fax: (230) 208 8948

Newton Securities Ltd.
3rd Floor, Nirmal House
22, Sir William Newton Street
Port Louis
Mauritius
Phone: (230) 208 8626, 212 6768, 208 2597
Fax: (230) 208 8749

Cavell Securities Ltd.
Harel Mallac Building
18, Edith Cavell Street
Port Louis
Mauritius
Phone: (230) 208 0808/09
Fax: (230) 208 8798

Company Information:

10 Major Companies

Name of Company	Market Capitalization (US$ in millions)
Mauritius Commercial Bank	243.95
State Bank of Mauritius	161.23
Rogers & Company	160.76
Sun Resorts	157.09
Air Mauritius	150.93
Ireland Blyth	72.51
Mon Tresor & Mon Desert	59.91
Grand Baie Hotel	41.45
National Investment Trust	38.60
Fincorp Investment	36.43

Regional Exchanges: None

Other Investment Information:
Mauritius Export Development and Investment
   Agency
PAI Building, 2nd Floor
Pope Hennessy Floor
Port Louis
Mauritius
Phone: (230) 208 7750
Fax: (230) 208 5965

Mauritius Offshore Business Activities Authority
Government House
Port Louis
Mauritius
Phone: (230) 201 2557 or (230) 201 1840 or (230)
   201 1146
Fax: (230) 208 8622
Telex: 4249 EXTERN IW

Ministry of the Environment and Quality of Life
Barracks Street
Port Louis
Mauritius
Phone: (230) 208 2831
Fax: (230) 208 6579

Bank of Mauritius
Sir William Newton Street
Port Louis
Mauritius
Phone: (230) 208 4164
Fax: (230) 208 9204

Mauritius Chamber of Commerce and Industry
Royal Road
Port Louis
Mauritius
Phone: (230) 208 3301
Fax: (230) 208 0076

MAXIMUM PRICE FLUCTUATION

Maximum Price Fluctuation is the percentage amount by which a share price is allowed to vary. Several exchanges, especially those operating by computer, establish maximum price fluctuations. Some exchanges allow a maximum fluctuation of between 5% and 10% of the share price at the previous session's close. If an individual share price moves past the maximum fluctuation, trading is halted and the situation is examined. Depending on the results, trading may either resume or continue to hold for a forthcoming corporate announcement.

Since many of the fully computerized systems have virtually eliminated the specialist and the market maker functions of buying when there are no buyers and selling when there are no sellers, the maximum fluctuation is a way to prevent or at least moderate unusually severe market swings.

See also MARKET MAKER; SPECIALIST; SUSPENDED TRADING.

MAXWELL, ROBERT

The sudden death of *Robert Maxwell* in 1991 brought to an end one of the most extraordinary business careers the world has ever seen. His financial dealings on the stock exchange and his greedy acquisitions of hundreds of companies left over 30,000 people facing a massive drop in the value of their pensions and led to shame and embarrassment for some of the best established names in the City of London. The total indebtedness of the Maxwell empire was at least £2.4 billion, of which only a fraction will ever be recovered.

Maxwell died on 5 November 1991 after falling from his 60 meter yacht, *The Lady Ghislaine*. The skipper of the yacht reported that Maxwell was missing off the Canary Islands. Like most aspects of Maxwell's life, his death was shrouded in controversy.

Maxwell's early childhood was in a region of Czechoslovakia that was annexed by the Soviet Union during World War II. He lost many members of his immediate family in the Nazi concentration camps and joined the Allied forces to fight against the Axis powers. His facility with languages led to assignments with the British Secret Service, and he was awarded several medals for his bravery.

He settled in England and soon began his controversial career in publishing. His early success was achieved at the price of a number of lawsuits from disgruntled partners. An official inquiry into his business affairs ruled in 1971 that Maxwell was unfit to run a public company. Undaunted, Maxwell returned to the business world after a brief interlude as an elected politician. Maxwell was fascinated by politics and held a seat in the House of Commons as a Labour Member of Parliament between 1964 and 1970. His largely unsuccessful political career was characterized by scandal; in 1968 he was accused of stealing from the House of Commons's wine cellar and of making false entries in the accounts of the Commons' Catering Committee.

Maxwell worked hard to establish a business empire that encompassed newspapers, academic publishing, sport and leisure interests, and stock market speculation. His two best-known vehicles were Mirror Group Newspapers (MGN) and the Maxwell Communication Corporation (MCC), but Maxwell owned at least 800 different companies during a lifetime of wheeling and dealing. Maxwell installed two of his sons, Kevin and Ian, as key executives in his business empire. Kevin, who was made chief executive of MCC, took on the burden for financial planning and

Robert Maxwell, chairman and CEO of Maxwell Communication Corporation, announces the creation of *The European*, a pan-European weekend newspaper. (Reuters/Corbis-Bettmann)

the treasury department for many companies within the group. Ian was promoted to deputy chairman of MGN.

Many commercial banks were prepared to lend to Maxwell, often preferring to accept his word rather than asking for proof of his financial stability. Maxwell recognized early that the City's lack of external regulation and tendency to accept a man's word as his bond could be used to his advantage. MCC's purchase of Macmillan in 1989 was largely funded by the banks that had advanced MCC a total of £1.3 billion by the end of the year. The private companies, which had grown into an inordinately complicated web of more than 400 entities, were lent an additional £970 million.

Goldman Sachs was the main market maker in MCC shares and earned considerable fees from buying and selling the quoted shares. It held approximately 25% of the available shares in MCC and accounted for nearly 50% of trading in the shares. Maxwell used the bank's corporate finance arm to buy and sell companies, and Goldman lent money to

Maxwell, taking MCC and MGN shares as collateral. For several years, the bank's busy trading floor was even located in Maxwell House, the headquarters of MCC.

As Maxwell's debts increased and the value of his companies fell, Goldman attempted to call in its loans. On three occasions Goldman requested Maxwell to repay $75 million but met with a negative response. On the day that Maxwell took his last, fateful boat trip, traders at Goldman were instructed to sell off their MCC shares. On 5 November 1991 dealing screens in the City displayed the message that shares in MGM and MCC were suspended. Ten minutes later, a second message reported that Maxwell was missing at sea, presumed dead.

Those people charged with securing the continued existence of the Maxwell companies were soon to find out that Maxwell had spent huge amounts of money during the last months of his life. Senior management at MCC filed for Chapter 11 bankruptcy protection in the United States and for administration in the United Kingdom in December 1991.

A large group of angry pensioners gathered in front of the Houses of Parliament on 8 June 1992 to complain about their shoddy treatment by Maxwell. They angrily demanded cash compensation, citing the government bailout of Barlow Clowes as a precedent for state aid. Their anger had been increased by disclosures that the company pension schemes were excluded from stricter levels of regulatory control by Investment Management Regulatory Organisation (IMRO), the City regulator. Kevin Maxwell, who worked tirelessly with his brother to save the group of companies, became Britain's largest ever bankruptcy case when the High Court announced that he had debts of over £400 million.

Subsequent investigations revealed that, although IMRO had authorized the two investment companies Maxwell used to run the pension funds, there were doubts as to the thoroughness of their investigation. One company was not visited for nearly two years, and even when irregularities had been found, IMRO failed to check that problems had been rectified.

On 16 June 1993 the Securities and Futures Authority (SFA) fined Goldman Sachs £160,000 plus £125,000 in costs. Goldman Sachs was censured for failing to report three breaches of City law when it paid for shares from Maxwell before receiving them. Staff at the bank were, however, cleared of any knowledge of or involvement in "illicit conduct."

An Israeli printing company, Scitex, was at the center of Maxwell's suspicious share dealings. Bishopsgate Investment Management (BIM), which controlled the pension funds for approximately 30,000 people, officially owned the Scitex shares. However, the shares were signed over to the Robert Maxwell Group, a Maxwell company that had its ultimate holding company in an offshore tax haven. The Robert Maxwell Group was supposed to sell the Scitex shares in the open market and return the funds to the pensions account at BIM. What actually happened was that the large profits made on the sale of the Scitex shares were given by the Robert Maxwell Group to its banks to reduce its debts.

In December 1993 the High Court ruled that Maxwell had misappropriated pension fund assets and fraudulently dealt in shares of Berlitz, a language teaching company, in a desperate attempt to fortify his crumbling business empire. The judge ruled that Maxwell had misled three banks—Lehman Brothers, Swiss Volksbank, and Credit Suisse—who had acquired the Berlitz shares in good faith only to find out later that Maxwell had used them as collateral against other loans. The prosecution showed how Maxwell had transferred the ownership of the shares from a publishing company, Macmillan, to Bishopsgate Investment Trust in November 1990. The shares were subsequently pledged as security against loans for one of Maxwell's private companies.

Maxwell had a talent for self-mythology, and it is occasionally difficult to separate fact from fiction when stories about his life are recounted. Maxwell's wooing of foreign ministers and statesmen led some people to suggest he was a spy. Indeed, Maxwell spent so much money and time flying around the world in his Gulfstream aircraft, carrying its cargo of champagne and caviar to the governments of the world, that he was often distracted from the day-to-day running of his press empire.

In May 1983 the general secretaries of the Central Committee met in Moscow's Kremlin in the Soviet Union to grant an honorary doctorate from Moscow State University to Maxwell. Maxwell was cited as a "well-known specialist in the field of economics who actively campaigns for the strengthening of friendship and mutual understanding between the Soviet and English peoples." Declassified documents indicate that Maxwell was close to Yuri Andropov, who became Soviet leader in 1982, and who Maxwell kept informed about events in Europe and the United States. There is strong evidence to suggest that Maxwell also briefed Israeli and Bulgarian ministers on similar matters.

Maxwell's involvement in Bulgaria is a perfect example of how he used his financial power and political contacts to his own advantage. He courted communist party officials with donations for charitable funds in the names of their relatives and gave Bulgaria's top football club $100,000 to buy a new strip emblazoned with one word, *Maxwell*. More useful schemes, such as setting up a new Bulgarian bank or solving the country's chronic toothpaste shortage, were forgotten as Maxwell diverted his energies into self-aggrandizing projects. A farfetched plan to establish a Hollywood-style film industry in Bulgaria came to nothing. More important, though, was the hard currency that Maxwell supplied to Bulgaria once the near-bankrupt country defaulted on its foreign debt repayments.

Maxwell's relationship with Israel was more complex. He enjoyed considerable financial and political success in the country and frequently announced his intention to retire to Israel. He invested $6.5 million in 1988 to buy a stake in the Hebrew-language newspaper *Ma'ariv,* and followed this purchase with so many other investments that bumper stickers on Tel Aviv cars appeared with the slogan "Robert Maxwell - Buy Me!" One of Maxwell's closest friends, Tommy

Lapid, who worked on *Ma'ariv*, summed up the symbiotic relationship between Maxwell and Israel: "Either we knew, and so we were crooks, or we didn't know, and we were fools."

With a mouthpiece for his views guaranteed by his *Ma'ariv* stake, Maxwell began to assiduously court political leaders in Israel. He simultaneously developed relationships with the liberal Shimon Peres, the right wing health minister Ehud Olmert, and the right wing extremist Arik Sharon, who was the minister of industry and trade. Prime Minister Yitzhak Shamir was not won over by Maxwell's mixture of charm and bullying and forever remained skeptical of his motives.

Maxwell's desire to be at the center of political power occasionally stretched to unbelievable lengths. When the black South African leader Nelson Mandela arrived in the United Kingdom following his release from prison he was invited to a formal dinner at the Commonwealth Institute in London. When Maxwell found out that he had not been invited to the dinner he frantically phoned the organizers and begged for an invitation. When his request was politely refused Maxwell forced his way into the dinner and sat down next to a perplexed Mandela.

Maxwell's 47-year marriage to his wife, Betty, and their seven children became the subject of immense media speculation after his death. Betty's oft-proclaimed protestations of love suggested that theirs was a marriage of true equals. In a magazine article in 1987 she stated that, "Our love for each other is not in doubt, it is the rock and rudder of my life." As with many aspects of Robert Maxwell's life, the reality was very different from the public appearance.

In Betty Maxwell's autobiography, *A Mind of My Own*, she revealed that Maxwell frequently threatened her with divorce and that they spent the last years of his life living apart. Far from being a loving husband, Maxwell treated his wife in exactly the same way that he treated his colleagues. In her words, he was "harsh, cruel, uncompromising, dictatorial, exceedingly selfish and inconsiderate." Many books have been published about Robert Maxwell and, since most of them display a personal bias about the subject, it is hard to recommend one particular book as a source for further enlightenment. Nevertheless, Tom Bower's unauthorized book, *Maxwell the Outsider*, gives interesting accounts of some of Maxwell's worst excesses.

Even Maxwell's dealings in football, long the preserve of monied tycoons in Europe, were colored by financial skullduggery and arrogance. Maxwell bought into his local club, Oxford United, and took part in the team's lap of honor when it won promo-

tion. Maxwell misunderstood the strong feelings that football engendered among its supporters and was roundly booed when he appeared in the stadium of the next football club he bought, Derby County. He also tried to take over a third club, the prestigious Tottenham Hotspur, but was defeated after a bitter struggle with the consumer electronics millionaire, Alan Sugar.

Maxwell's death is surrounded by mystery. Two autopsies were performed with inconclusive results. The first suggested death by accident or natural causes, but the second raised the possibility of suicide or even murder. Some accounts of Maxwell's last days indicate the actions of a man who was preoccupied with his failing business empire and who seemed to lack the will to continue the fight any longer. Other commentators, particularly those who knew Maxwell closely, are adamant that a strong character like Maxwell could never consider suicide. There are others who point to Maxwell's antagonistic links with political figures and secret services throughout the world and raise the probability of assassination.

If a Hollywood scriptwriter had submitted Maxwell's life as the basis for a film, it would have been rejected for implausibility. Maxwell was a larger-than-life character, a physically domineering individual whose corpulence became a cipher for the worst excesses of capitalism. His life story, from penniless refugee to one of the largest fraudsters in the history of finance, was packed with international leaders, powerful business brokers, fervent enemies, and loyal supporters. His behavior often showed signs of megalomania and paranoia, yet his opinions were sought by many of the high and mighty in several countries. For a man who courted publicity and craved adoration, he died a lonely death and left behind a terrible legacy.

The truth about Robert Maxwell is unlikely to ever surface. The complex financial structures, shady deals, and political intrigues have all conspired to make his motives and methods impossible to divine. The sheer number of his personal contacts and the vast size of his business deals multiplies the intrigue and deception. Above all else, it is likely that even Robert Maxwell lost track of the lies and conspiracies to which he was a party.

MEGLIO (Italy)

See AT BEST.

MEMBER

A corporation, firm, person, or other entity that has joined a stock exchange organization, pays dues as required, and has access to the benefits thereof is called a *Member*.

Some stock exchanges require memberships—often called seats—to be owned by individual persons rather than by companies. Other exchanges allow memberships to be owned by either individuals or companies. Some exchanges also offer limited, partial, or representative memberships.

Stock exchange members are responsible for running the stock exchanges and are directly involved with making transactions.

See also BROKER/DEALER; FLOOR BROKER; SPECIALIST; TRADE.

MEMBER CORPORATION
See MEMBER.

MEMBER FIRM
See MEMBER.

MEMBER ORGANIZATION
See MEMBER.

MERCATO (Italy)
See MARKET.

MERCATO AZIONARIO (Italy)
See STOCK MARKET.

MERCATO DEBOLE/MERCATO PESANTE (Italy)
See BEAR MARKET.

MERCATO (IN) DENARO (Italy)
See BULL MARKET.

MERCHANT BANKER
See INVESTMENT BANKER.

MERCOSUR
MERCOSUR, also known as *MERCOSUL*, is a customs union of six South American countries: Argentina, Bolivia, Brazil, Chile, Paraguay, and Uruguay. Formed in 1991, by the mid-1990s it had established a number of tariff reductions and had removed other trade barriers among its member states, whose collective gross domestic product was nearly $1 trillion. MERCOSUR is a Spanish acronym for "Mercado Común del Sur" (Common Market of the South). It aspires to establish free movement among member states, not only of goods and services but also of capital and labor, by 2001.

MERCOSUR is the product of an off-and-on process of regional economic integration that began in the late 1950s. The 1960 Treaty of Montevideo created the Latin American Free Trade Association (ALALC). In addition to the seven initial signatories of the treaty, there were four other countries that joined ALALC by the mid-1960s. While some steps were taken toward economic integration, they encountered numerous obstacles from certain national business interests and military dictatorships with hegemonic ambitions. Another obstacle was the prevailing development philosophy of the time, which favored import substitution (the development of local industry and greater national self-sufficiency) over development of trade, including intraregional trade.

Some of the forces opposing the development of ALALC were strengthened by the oil crises of the 1970s and the huge pileup of debt in some of the Latin American countries, which reached extreme crisis proportions by the start of the 1980s. A second Treaty of Montevideo in 1980 attempted to revive ALALC by restructuring it into a Latin American Integration Association (ALADI). ALADI attempted to develop a system of preferential tariffs and a more flexible structure of intraregional trade agreements, but it made little progress.

Acting bilaterally, the heads of state of Argentina and Brazil signed a "Program for Integration and Economic Cooperation" in 1986. This agreement, which emphasized the development of trade between the two countries, especially in capital goods and steel, was the precursor of MERCOSUR. In December 1990 the two countries signed an "Economic Complementation Accord," calling for a gradual reduction of bilateral tariffs until they would disappear at the end of 1994. As Paraguay and Uruguay wished to be included in this agreement, the Treaty of Asunción was signed a few months later. This treaty created MERCOSUR, which the four countries agreed would be a customs union by the end of 1994 and ultimately a common market.

Tariffs were reduced to zero between 1991 and 1994 for 90% of intraregional trade, which increased in volume from $3.5 billion in 1990 to $12.5 billion in 1995. The vast majority of this increase resulted from trade between Argentina and Brazil, particularly in the automotive, agricultural, and energy sectors. (Much of this increase could not be attributed to tariff reductions, since both countries had also vastly increased trade with countries outside the region in the early 1990s.) Every member country was able, taking into account its own plans for development, to specify products that were exempted from these tariff reductions for a certain number of years; for example, Brazil's list included chemicals and petrochemicals, milk products, and raw materials for textiles.

Chile, Latin America's most developed country, joined MERCOSUR in 1996 as an associate member, maintaining a number of reciprocal preferential tariff agreements with other countries, mainly in Latin America. Bolivia became an associate member in 1997. The addition of these two countries to the customs union facilitated various infrastructural and mining projects.

Additional protocols that were adopted by MERCOSUR stipulated that every member would agree to promote and facilitate the entry of foreign investment from other members. By mid-1996 approximately 100 companies in the region had plans to invest in other member states. Financial institutions within the region signed agreements calling for various forms of cooperation, and the four official banks of the MERCOSUR states called for their own integration into one bank and the increase of their participation in international trade.

In 1995 MERCOSUR and the European Union set forth plans for development of a free trade area comprising both regions, as well as for economic cooperation. By contrast, the United States was slow to develop relations with MERCOSUR.

A certain stabilization of the economic and political situation in MERCOSUR's member states in the 1990s, as well as their increased integration into the global economy, allowed MERCOSUR to grow in a way that previous economic integration attempts in Latin America had not been able to achieve. MERCOSUR itself had made a substantial contribution to improving the investment climate in the member states, and had also enhanced Latin America's exports to countries outside the region. MERCOSUR expected to sign free trade pacts in 1997 with Venezuela, Colombia, Peru, and Ecuador. Its goal was to become a common market of all the Latin American countries by 2005, before linking up with the North American Free Trade Agreement (NAFTA).

See also CUSTOMS UNIONS.

MERCURY ASSET MANAGEMENT LIMITED (MAM)

Mercury Asset Management Limited (MAM) was formed in 1969 as Warburg Investment Management Limited. In 1986 it changed its name to Mercury Warburg Investment Management Limited and then to Mercury Asset Management Holdings Limited. In March 1987 Mercury Asset Management (MAM) became known by its present name and became nominally independent from SG Warburg (which still owned 75% of it) as part of a move to protect Warburg against hostile takeovers. In 1995 MAM became fully independent when the Swiss Bank Corporation acquired the rest of Warburg.

In 1997 MAM, which is based in London, was Britain's largest independent investment bank, engaging in advisory services and investment management for investment trusts, pension funds, charities, other institutions, private clients, and unit trusts. It had more than $147 billion in client assets under management, an increase of roughly 500% in the previous ten years. Its pretax profit for the fiscal year ending 30 March 1997 was $277.5 million, or 22% more than for the previous year.

MAM manages pension fund investments for more than 50 of Britain's 100 largest companies and their subsidiaries. It also manages approximately $19 billion in funds through its private investors' division. MAM has more than 1,000 employees, of whom more than 200 are investment professionals. It has offices in 17 countries and a capitalization of $3.78 billion on the London Stock Exchange. MAM was named Fund Management Group of the Year 1997 from *Investment Week*, one of Britain's leading financial newspapers.

For its private clients, MAM provides a range of investment options, from balanced portfolios to investments concentrating in a particular country, region, or industry. MAM's unit trusts provide international diversification, risk reduction, and enhanced returns, in addition to offering many clients a tax-efficient investment. MAM managed investment trusts for more than 50,000 shareholders and portfolios for more than 2,500 private clients in 1997. It managed approximately $35 billion worldwide in fixed interest markets, seeking to add value to portfolios by making use of changes in global currency and capital markets. It also managed or advised approximately 140 different insurance companies worldwide.

MAM's fund managers continually visit the leading central banks in the world to evaluate different countries' economies, in addition to calling on approximately 3,000 companies each year to assess their prospects. Their investment decisions are based on asset allocation; weighting according to country, currency, and sector; and stock selection. They develop their investment strategies based on four principles:
1. Active management adds value.
2. Active fund management should be based on research.
3. Focused portfolios bring discipline.

4. House views should be balanced with the skill of the individual.

Whereas many British pension fund managers give individual managers quite a lot of leeway from which to choose stocks, MAM takes a more controlled approach. For global funds, a strategy committee of four decides how much to allocate to each market. Subcommittees decide how to distribute investments between the sectors in each market. Then fund managers pick the particular stocks. MAM feels this centralized setup allows it to act quickly, despite its relatively large size.

In 1997 MAM was purchased by Merrill Lynch and Company for approximately $5.2 billion. Through the deal, MAM hoped to increase its access to markets in the United States. The combined entity, Merrill Lynch Mercury Asset Management, with assets of $450 billion under management, is one of the largest asset management groups in the world.

See also WARBURG DYNASTY.

MERGER

A *Merger* is the joining of two or more companies. A merger differs from a takeover in that the arrangement is usually amicable and agreed to by all concerned parties.

Mergers can be accomplished in one of three ways: through the pooling of interests by combining accounts; through the acquisition of a company, in which the amount paid over the company's book value remains on the books of the purchaser as "goodwill"; or through the formation of a new company in order to acquire the net assets of the combining companies (consolidation).

Companies will merge for several reasons, including the following:

• To achieve additional capacity located in new markets

• To expand markets (horizontal)

• To diversify product line (conglomerate)

• For backward (vertical) integration (manufacturers that acquire raw material suppliers)

• For forward (vertical) integration (manufacturers acquiring sales outlets)

• To reduce competitors in a saturated market

Although mergers and acquisitions will often cause a company's share price to rise, there is considerable debate as to whether or not this is an advantage to the shareholders over the long-term.

See also ACQUISITION; GOODWILL; TAKEOVER/TAKEOVER BID; VALUE.

MERRILL LYNCH

Merrill Lynch is a unique Wall Street firm: while its peers have chosen to develop business with institutional clients, Merrill Lynch has remained focused on the private investor. Affectionately known as the "thundering herd" because of its size and financial clout, Merrill Lynch has consistently headed the league tables that measure the performance of investment banks and stockbrokers.

Charles E. Merrill's background was unconventional. He was born in Jacksonville, Florida, in 1885 and was educated at Worcester Academy, Massachusetts, and Amherst College in Massachusetts. He dropped his studies at the University of Michigan Law School in favor of a season in minor league baseball. When he realized that he wouldn't make the grade as a pitcher, Merrill tried a number of jobs before finding a post as a salesman at an investment house called George H. Burr and Company. Merrill's interest in the equity market resulted in his famous article, "Mr. Average Investor," which appeared in *Leslie's Illustrated Weekly*. Merrill presented his views on the smaller, private investor and voiced concern about the occasionally shabby service that they received. He proposed an ethical approach to investment sales, one that would treat all customers equally no matter the size of their portfolio.

In 1913 Merrill left George H. Burr for a short-lived stint as the sales manager for Eastman Dillon. In January 1914 he set up Charles E. Merrill and Company and was soon joined in business by his long-time friend, Edmund C. Lynch. Merrill Lynch and Company was now open for trading. Both Merrill and Lynch were called up for military service during World War I and they were forced to leave their business in the hands of associates. The entrepreneurial Merrill moved the firm into the underwriting business and developed a reputation as a specialist in the retail sector. The fast-growing list of clients at this time included J.C. Penney, McCrory Stores, and Western Auto Supply. Merrill, a natural dealmaker, also undertook a series of direct investments that were to prove immensely profitable. A stake in the film company Pathe was sold to Joseph Kennedy. Safeway Stores, a food retail chain based in California and largely founded by Merrill, eventually became a major presence in towns and cities throughout the United States.

Merrill was one of the first investment managers to realize that Wall Street was overheating in the last years of the 1920s. He advised clients to sell both equities and debt securities and to hold their wealth in cash. Merrill reduced his involvement in the firm after the 1929 crash and Lynch took over the running of the firm until his death in 1938.

In 1930 the firm sold its retail business to E.A. Pierce and Company, which had its roots in a partnership called Burrill and Housman, founded in 1885. The managing partner of the firm, Edward Allen Pierce, increased the firm's presence across the United States by establishing a network of branches linked together by telegraph connections. In 1939, Pierce, suffering from the long-term depression that had taken hold of the U.S. economy, convinced Merrill to return to the broking world. The firms merged their interests. Two years later a New Orleans investment firm, Fenner and Beane, was added to the partnership's interests.

Fenner and Beane was the second largest retail "wire house" brokerage in the United States. Merrill Lynch became known as the "king of the wire houses" because of its extensive use of telegrams, teleprinters, and telephones. As the firm spread across the United States investment in new telecommunications technology became a paramount concern. A network of 9,000 salesmen and 430 offices, servicing the needs of close to 5 million clients, was built up over the next 40 years. The management of the firm was content to leave its rivals to fight for prestigious institutional investors, safe in the knowledge that no firm could rival their distribution channels.

Merrill's philosophy was to accept small investors and the relatively tiny commissions they provided in the first years of the relationship. If the client was satisfied with the service that was offered and was happy with the advice provided by the broker, then the size of the portfolio would grow; the firm benefited from the long-term relationship with the client. Merrill Lynch was one of the most vociferous campaigners for the abolition of fixed rates of commission and made a point of charging less than its peers for client services. Brokers were actively discouraged from dubious practices such as "churning" clients' accounts, and the firm developed a reputation for fairness and financial probity. Unusual for the high-pressure world of Wall Street, Merrill Lynch's brokers were paid salaries and were, therefore, less reliant on forcing commissions from their clients.

Merrill Lynch displayed a genius for marketing and self-promotion that advanced the firm after the end of World War II. An Investment Information Center was built in New York's Grand Central Station, showing the latest prices and giving investment advice to commuters. Full-page newspaper advertisements and special investment seminars for women successfully attracted new clients. In 1955 Merrill Lynch was responsible for 10% of all transactions on the New York Stock Exchange. Charles Merrill died in 1956, apparently content to have founded one of Wall Street's most popular firms. In 1959 the partners decided to change the firm's corporate structure and Merrill Lynch led the trend on Wall Street toward incorporation.

The 1960s saw many positive developments for Merrill Lynch. In 1964 the company bought C J Devine, a specialist in government-issued securities. The first steps in Merrill Lynch's property program were taken when a real estate financing division was set up. Four years later the real estate firm and mortgage experts Hubbard, Westervelt and Motteley was taken over. Twenty offices were established abroad, and in 1964 Merrill Lynch became the first Wall Street brokerage to open an office in Tokyo. The firm was the lead underwriter for the public offering of shares in Comsat, the innovative company that manufactured the first commercially viable telecommunications satellite. Howard Hughes paid for Merrill Lynch's services in 1965 when he sold off his stake in TWA. In 1968 Donald Regan became president of Merrill Lynch, and two years later he was made chairman and chief executive officer.

The next decade also saw periods of rapid growth. In 1970 the New York Stock Exchange asked Merrill Lynch to help out the fifth largest U.S. broker, Goodbody and Company, which was in danger of collapse. Goodbody, which had expertise in unit trusts and options dealing, had become swamped by increased volumes of trading and found that the back office was not able to cope with the paperwork. Clients left Goodbody as the firm lost control over its administration. Merrill Lynch stepped in to rescue Goodbody and acquired the firm relatively cheaply. In the following year, shares in Merrill Lynch were traded for the first time on the New York Stock Exchange.

During the 1970s Merrill Lynch introduced many innovative products that encouraged savings and investment. The Cash Management Account was first marketed in 1977, much to the consternation of retail banks, which launched a legal campaign against it. This account allowed investors to write checks and borrow money against the securities held by the account holder. Merrill Lynch was also heavily involved in the Ginnie Mae market, which dealt in government-backed mortgages.

The mutual fund division, an area neglected by the original founders of the firm, grew steadily during the 1970s and 1980s. By 1993 the fund was second only to Fidelity Investments in terms of the value of assets under management.

Donald Regan left the firm in 1981 to join the U.S. Treasury and later became chief of staff at the White House. Roger Birk became the new chairman in 1981; he was eventually superseded by William Schreyer in 1984. The firm recovered from the Black Monday crash of 1987 to overtake Salomon Brothers as the largest underwriter in the United States.

Regan had been a firm believer in long-term, relationship-based marketing. He instinctively understood that satisfied customers would use Merrill Lynch for a wide variety of financial services. His personal and business ethics were eventually codified into the set of principles that still guide employees at Merrill Lynch:

- Client focus
- Respect for the individual
- Teamwork
- Responsible citizenship
- Integrity

The sheer size of Merrill Lynch has brought problems for the firm. The retail and institutional equity sales divisions were separated during the 1980s and management was forced to install new operating controls. In 1987 the firm lost $377 million in the mortgage-backed securities market and in 1990 the firm took a $470 million charge against profits to cover the cost of restructuring operations. Remuneration schemes that stressed teamwork and long-term planning, rather than individual performance, were implemented. Loyalty was encouraged by bonus shares, and approximately one-quarter of the firm's shares are currently owned by members of staff. Risk management was recognized as a vital discipline, and the company has largely avoided the trading scandals, both deliberate and accidental, that have marred several other firms.

Charles Merrill has left behind a potent legacy to the North American stockbroking industry. His methods and ethical approach led to a wide ownership of shares across the country, and by 1970 it was estimated that one in six people in the United States directly owned equities. His insistence on client service and repeat business changed the public perception of brokers from dishonest hustlers to college-educated professionals. In 1994, when many competitors suffered from a stagnant equity market and the fall-off in bond prices, Merrill Lynch made a larger profit than any other firm on Wall Street. In July 1995 Merrill Lynch increased its presence in the European stock markets when it bought the City of London broker Smith New Court. The deal gave greater exposure to the primary equity market in London and across continental Europe, but integrating the slightly stuffy English firm into the "thundering herd" has caused occasional difficulty.

Smith New Court was founded in 1924 and grew into one of the largest market makers and institutional brokers in the UK equities sector. The firm specializes in the research, origination, distribution, and trading of equity shares and their derivatives. Smith New Court has a significant corporate brokering business. Headquartered in London, the company also has principal offices in New York, Tokyo, Hong Kong, and Singapore, as well as an associated company in Malaysia.

The merger between Merrill Lynch and Smith New Court formed the largest brokerage in the world. Particularly impressive was the combined equity research department, which had 370 equity analysts and a significant number of strategists and economists. The acquisition of Smith New Court was part of Merrill Lynch's globalization strategy. The merger put considerable pressure on competing firms to merge to remain competitive with this colossus of the financial world.

The firm currently employs more than 44,000 people. The success of the international expansion plan has clearly succeeded: the firm has operations in 31 countries and more than 20% of revenues are earned outside of the United States. Merrill Lynch has consistently led the way in cross-border financing and has an apparently insurmountable position as the dominant underwriter in the United States.

See also HUGHES, HOWARD.

MEXICAN COLLAPSE OF 1994

The *Mexican Collapse of 1994* refers to Mexico's near default on foreign loans at the end of that year, the Mexican government's devaluation of the peso, and the resulting effects on Mexico's economy as well as the international investment climate. Mexico's persistent trade deficit over a number of years had been compounded by the large debt service payments flowing out of the country. As the end of 1994 approached, the Mexican government needed $50 billion in foreign exchange to meet its obligations, but had only $6 billion available. President Ernesto Zedillo and his advisers saw the devaluation of the peso as necessary to improve the country's trade balance and to help offset the debt service payments. However, the 13.5% devaluation, in the context of Mexico's international financial instability and investors' lack of confidence in Mexico's economy and political stability, had numerous complex economic effects. Mexico's inflation soared to 52% by the end of 1995 and still stood at more than 31.4% six months later. The peso's exchange rate against the dollar fell nearly 50% in one month. Internationally, capital flowed out of countries in which the investment picture was considered similar to Mexico's.

The Mexican government had looked forward to a measured devaluation for some time. However, a series of unexpected political events during 1994 had caused repeated postponement of this move. These events included the uprising of peasants in Chiapas on 1 January, several political kidnappings and assassinations, and widespread exposures of official corruption. The government's postponement of any intervention caused what could have been a more contained financial adjustment to develop into a liquidity crisis that had international ramifications.

Despite some of the negative indicators, Mexico's economy was by no means the weakest among those developing countries that had taken on large debts. In fact, relative to its gross domestic product, Mexico's debts were only one-third as high as those of Italy, Belgium, and Greece. Mexico had eliminated the largest budget deficits of the 1980s and had achieved a balanced budget. Its inflation rate in 1994 was only 7%, and its 16% savings rate was higher than that of the United States. In many ways, Mexico, with its large-scale moves toward privatization of the economy and its entry into both the North American Free Trade Agreement (NAFTA) and the Organization for Economic Cooperation and Development (OECD), was considered a model of economic reform. Nevertheless, Mexico's announced inability to pay its loans in December 1994 struck a nerve in the international financial community, given that a similar Mexican announcement in 1982 had marked the beginning of the debt crisis of many developing countries.

The devaluation of the peso did lead to the disappearance of Mexico's trade deficit within two months. This did not, however, give Mexico the ability to meet its immediate debts. Foreign investors removed large amounts of capital from the country following the devaluation, since they feared even greater additional devaluations. Their worries were compounded by reports that the Zapatista National Liberation Army planned a resumption of its armed offensive in Chiapas. For similar reasons, capital was removed precipitously from developing countries around the world. The possibility that Mexico might default on its loans caused great concern internationally, especially since this could set off a chain reaction of defaults among other poor, overindebted countries.

In an attempt to forestall this, the United States moved in late December to allow Mexico to exchange 6 billion pesos for US$6 billion, and Canada offered a similar exchange for C$1 billion. Yet these sums were not enough to cover Mexico's short-term loan obligations. So the United States, the International Monetary Fund (IMF), other industrialized nations, and even some developing countries put together a rescue package consisting of more than $52 billion and constituting the largest loan ever made. The IMF could not lend sufficient funds to Mexico under NAFTA's rules. The United States had much at stake in stabilizing Mexico's economy, including hundreds of billions in pension funds. Subsequently the peso was stabilized and Mexico was able to avoid defaulting on its loans.

However, as a result of the stipulations of the loan, Mexico lost a good deal of control over its economy. The IMF and the United States required 60% interest for 28-day peso loans to the Mexican government, as well as 100% interest for loans to consumers in the winter of 1995. Although Mexico's budget had been balanced before the peso devaluation, sharp cutbacks in government spending were required. Revenues from Mexico's substantial oil sales were to go directly into an account at the Federal Reserve Bank in New York and be controlled by the United States to guarantee repayment to non-Mexican bondholders. The Mexican government's decision to allow the substitution of almost all the stock of peso-dominated short-term government securities held by foreigners with instruments indexed to the dollar meant that the investors were protected against devaluation, but this arrangement carried the risk for Mexico that the investors might withdraw their investments after they had matured. Among Mexico's industries, the banks were most sharply affected, with defaults on about 14% of the loans they had outstanding. The rescue of these banks was to prove costly for Mexico's federal Treasury.

The average Mexican's standard of living had been reduced during the previous 13 years because of free market reforms. As a result of the terms of the $52 billion loan package, it was expected that the average Mexican family's income would fall another 33%. Within four months, Mexico had lost 500,000 jobs, and another 4 million workers had been reduced to 15 hours per week; within nine months, official unemployment had doubled and retail sales were down 40%. Gross domestic product fell 6.2% in 1995. Plans were accelerated to allow foreign investment in areas from which it had previously been barred, including petrochemicals, real estate, airports and harbors, railroads, and communications.

It should be noted that the actions of U.S. investors played an important role in precipitating the Mexican financial crisis. During the 1990–91 recession, U.S. banks lowered their interest rates. As a result, hundreds of billions of dollars were moved from American savings accounts into mutual funds, which offered a higher return. Mutual fund managers, in turn, moved some of their funds into Mexico, where they could earn higher amounts. Later, when interest rates in the United States went back up, these fund managers started to move their investments back into the United States. With this money flowing out of the country, Mexico, which was already running a current account deficit (the sum of its trade imbalance and debt service, minus new loans coming into the country), quickly ran out of foreign exchange reserves.

One result of the 1994 Mexican collapse is that investors are more carefully scrutinizing opportunities in the developing countries, taking into account the need to monitor the macroeconomic conditions in those markets. Various plans are under discussion regarding this monitoring as well as the establishment of an internationally funded facility that would provide quick and sufficient assistance to countries facing a liquidity crisis. One form this might take would be a North American Exchange Facility that could facilitate a minimum degree of macroeconomic coordination and monetary cooperation among trade partners.

See also DEVELOPING COUNTRIES; MEXICAN DEBT CRISIS OF 1982; MEXICO.

MEXICAN DEBT CRISIS OF 1982

The *Mexican Debt Crisis of 1982* was brought about by Mexico's inability to pay interest on many of the $80 billion in loans that it had received from various governments and private banks and agencies. The nine largest U.S. banks were particularly affected, having committed 44% of their capital to these loans. Overall, Mexican debts amounted to 17.1% of total U.S. bank loans to developing countries and the Soviet bloc. Factors contributing to the crisis included Mexico's program of oil-based growth (1976–82), which was paid for by taking out huge loans and relied on massive imports of machinery, technology, and technical expertise from developed countries. In addition, the 1981–82 drop in oil prices caused a steep decline in Mexico's export income.

The high point of the crisis was reached at the end of August, when Mexican president José López Portillo nationalized the banks and imposed exchange controls. Both of these moves were strongly opposed by the International Monetary Fund (IMF). López Portillo blamed the crisis on the large foreign powers, with their high-interest loans and unfair treatment of the

developing countries, as well as on Mexico's private bankers. But in the following weeks, with Mexico running out of money and López Portillo scheduled in any case to turn over the presidency to Miguel de la Madrid, Mexico had to come around to the terms that the IMF insisted on as part of its rescue package. In addition to these conditions, Mexico had to devalue the peso by 53%.

In mid-November, the IMF's acting director, Jacques de Larosière, announced that Mexico would need, within one month, an additional $8.3 billion in new loans to pay the scheduled amounts on its old loans. He proposed that the IMF contribute $1.3 billion, various governments $2 billion, and the banks $5 billion. Through a series of negotiations, the bankers' advisory committee decided that every bank that had previously made loans to Mexico would be charged 7% of the amount it was still owed. The banks recovered much of this money by charging higher interest rates and various fees. In this way, Mexico's creditors weathered the immediate crisis.

Many people in Mexico did not fare as well as a result of the debt crisis and the measures taken in its wake. In the 1980s, as the Mexican government cut subsidies for basic foods and services in order to reduce deficits, consumer prices for these items shot up. The purchasing power of salaries declined 50% during the 1980s. By 1988 more than half of all Mexicans lived below minimum international nutritional levels.

Beginning with the 1982 crisis Mexico's capital account became negative, as its debt service payments far exceeded new loans that it received. Trade surpluses had to be generated to cover the difference. While there was a moderate increase in exports, Mexico mainly tried to achieve a trade surplus by reducing its imports.

While Mexico was the first developing country unable to service its debts, several others followed. The way in which the Mexican debt crisis was dealt with was used as a model when similar situations arose with countries such as Venezuela, Brazil, and Argentina. Mexico itself received many financial injections designed to prevent it from defaulting. From 1980 to 1991 Mexico received more structural and sectoral adjustment loans from the World Bank than any other country—13 in all. For example, a $12 billion loan package was put together in 1987 and early 1988. It was also pressured to liberalize its trade and investment policies—that is, to become more open to free trade and foreign investment—by virtue of signing six agreements with the IMF. And after Mexico joined the General Agreement on Tariffs and

Trade (GATT) in 1986, it received a huge loan from the World Bank. During this period, the World Bank offered Mexico relatively low interest rates and easy payment terms. The pace of economic liberalization increased further after Carlos Salinas de Gortari became president in 1988.

The United States instituted its own program for dealing with the Mexican debt crisis. It mobilized emergency credits to stave off possible defaults; it increased imports from Mexico to provide Mexico with needed foreign exchange; it allowed enough Mexican immigrants into the United States to keep Mexico's unemployment rate from soaring too high; and it gave more direct attention to the development of the border region.

By late 1983, although the peso continued to devalue, inflation was approximately 100%, and Mexico's economic output was down 3% for the year. The Mexico City stock exchange, Bolsa Mexicana de Valores, was doing quite well. The Bolsa's index of leading stocks had more than doubled in the previous seven months.

See also DEVELOPING COUNTRIES; INTERNATIONAL MONETARY FUND (IMF); MEXICAN COLLAPSE OF 1994; MEXICO; THIRD WORLD DEBT.

MEXICO

Mexico (Estados Unidos Mexicanos) is the third largest country of Latin America. It is bordered by the United States on the north, and Belize and Guatemala on the southeast.

Area: 756,066 square miles (1,958,201 square km)

Population: 91,145,000 (71.3% urban; 28.7% rural)

Form of Government: Federal republic, with two legislative houses: Senate—128 members; Chamber of Deputies—500 members. Chief of state and head of government: President.

Official Language: Spanish

Capital: Mexico City

Largest Cities: Mexico City, 9,815,795; Guadalajara, 1,650,042; Ciudad Netzahualcoyotl, 1,255,456; Monterrey, 1,068,996; Puebla, 1,007,170; Juarez, 789,522; Leon, 758,279; Tijuana, 698,752; Merida, 523,422; Chihuahua, 516,153

Economy:

Currency: New Mexico Peso (Mex$)

National Budget: Revenue—Mex$192.8 billion; expenditures—Mex$185.2 billion (transfers: 30.4%;

interest on public debt: 15.3%; wages and salaries: 13.1%).

Public Debt: US$86.0 billion

Gross National Product: US$325.0 billion

Principal Products: Fruits and vegetables; petroleum; machinery

Foreign Trade (Imports): US$65.4 billion (manufactured products: 94.2%; food and food products: 4.2%; minerals and mineral products: 0.6%; from United States: 68.9%; Japan: 5.0%; Germany: 4.2%; Brazil: 1.8%; Canada: 1.7%; Spain: 1.7%; France: 1.6%; Italy: 1.2%)

Foreign Trade (Exports): US$60.9 billion (metallic products, machinery, and equipment: 58.0%; crude petroleum: 12.2%; metal and metal products: 6.3%; processed food, beverages, and tobacco: 3.3%; to United States: 83.1%; Canada: 3.0%; Spain: 1.7%; Japan: 1.3%; France: 0.8%; Germany: 0.8%; Brazil: 0.6%; Belgium-Luxembourg: 0.5%; Argentina: 0.5%)

Stock Exchanges: 1

Mexican Stock Exchange (MSE; Bolsa Mexicana de Valores, S.A. de C.V.; BMV)

Paseo de la Reforma, 255

Col. Cuauhtemoc

Mexico D.F. 06500

Phone: (52-5) 726-66-00

Fax: (52-5) 726-68-05

Internet Address: www.bmv.com

Trading Hours:

Monday–Friday, 8:30 to 3:00 (Fall/Winter)

Monday–Friday, 7:30 to 2:00 (Spring/Summer)

Office Hours: Monday–Friday, 8:30 to 2:30/3:30 to 5:30

Exchange Holidays:

1 January	1, 5 May
5 February	1, 16 September
21 March	2, 20 November
13, 14 April	12, 25 December

Listed Companies: 186

Total Market Capitalization:

At 31 December 1997

Local Currency (Millions)	US Dollars (Millions)
1,029,912	127,752

Major Sectors: Services, communications, transportation, industrials, commerce, construction

Share Price Performance:

(% Change)

1992	56
1993	66
1994	-6
1995	14
1996	34
1997	52

History: The Mexico Stock Exchange (MSE) was established in 1894 in Mexico City. It began as a private institution and, until the mid 1970s, was much overlooked as a means for raising capital. Early listings were comprised mainly of banks and industrial and mining companies.

In 1975 securities legislation strengthened the Mexican Securities Commission, and regulations came into effect requiring banks to invest 8% of their savings deposits in shares or mortgage bonds, while also allowing them to make loans to brokerage firms. Reforms were also enacted to increase investment opportunities through a wider self-regulatory plan and the quotation of foreign securities.

The MSE, owned by 30 brokerage firms, or *casas de bolsa* (two of which are foreign), handles the monitoring and registration of all new issues of shares, bonds, and commercial paper, establishes the disclosure and reporting standards, and regulates the stock exchange and broker activities.

In accordance with Mexican Securities Market Law, standards are set for the registration of brokers in the National Registry of Securities and Brokers.

Classes of Securities: Shares are classified as either B, C, or L. Shares for foreign investors are classified as A shares. Although they are held in a "Neutral Trust," A shares can be purchased directly by residents. Other classes of securities include: development bonds, petro bonds, adjustment bonds, Treasury bonds, bankers acceptances, commercial paper, promissory notes, Treasury bills and repurchase agreements. Options and derivatives are expected to be traded in the near future.

Indices:

IPC Index, 35 most representative issues traded

INMEX Index, 20 issues, designed for derivative products

Supervisory Organizations:

The Treasury and Public Credit Board

Commision Nacional de Valores (CNV)

Depository:

INDEVAL S.A de C.V. (1978), for shares, bankers' acceptances, and commercial paper

Banco de Mexico (Central Bank) serves as auction and clearinghouse as well as book entry depository for government fixed-income securities.

Settlement Details:

Shares:

Trade date + 2 (T + 2)

Most are book-entry

Receive and delivery versus payment is allowed.

Turnaround trades for the same day are possible.

Trading: Auction open-outcry is the method used on the trading floor. Orders can also be entered in writing. Written orders will bypass the system if the details of a buy and sell can be matched.

An automated system—Automated Transaction Operating System (SATO)—handles the majority of company shares and all the money market instruments. Trading can be temporarily suspended if a price change exceeds 5% (1% for debentures), and can be indefinitely suspended if important company information is not filed. Company shares that also have an ADR program and are traded on a foreign exchange are not subject to the 5% rule.

A second tier market started trading in July 1993. It is a parallel market attracting medium-sized companies to the stock market.

Plans are being implemented to launch an options and futures market in late 1998. It will have an automated trading system with the securities depositary (SD Indeval) performing the function of a central clearing organization.

Listing Requirements: To list on the Mexico Stock Exchange a company must meet specific requirements regarding operating history and management. Securities must be approved by the Commission.

Companies are required to publish audited financial statements on an annual basis together with unaudited quarterly financial statements and other financial and operations information.

Investor Taxation:

No reciprocal tax treaties

Withheld by issuers

Petrobonds, corporate bonds, commercial paper, and bankers acceptances have a 15% tax on interest

No capital gains tax on equity shares, corporate bonds, or government bonds

No registration or exchange fees

No stamp duty

Although there are no tax exemptions, a reduction on commercial paper tax is available to some foreign pension funds registered with the Mexican Ministry of Finance and Public Credit.

Limitations: Non-citizens of Mexico can hold as much as 49% of any company's "B" shares. They may also purchase "C" and "L" shares, although these shares allow them no voting rights. Only "A" shares registered with the Neutral Trust can be purchased by non-residents.

Shareholders owning 10% or more of a company's shares are required to report all purchases or sales of shares representing 10% or more of that company's share capital to the MSC within ten days of the transaction.

Securities Lending: None

Brokerage Firms:
Acciones Bursatiles
Hamburgo No. 190
Col. Juarez
06600 Mexico, D.F.
Phone: (52-5) 533-06-25
Fax: (52-5) 207-39-44

Acciones y Valores de Mexico
Paseo de la Reforma 398
Col. Juarez
06600 Mexico, D.F.
Phone: (52-5) 584-29-77
Fax: (52-5) 208-50-48 and 584-29-77

Afin
Perferico Sur 4355
Col. Jardines de la Montana
01900 Mexico, D.F.
Phone: (52-5) 652-92-44 and 652-94-88
Fax: (52-5) 652-63-98

Arka
Emilio Castelar No. 75
Chapultepec Polanco
11560 Mexico, D.F.
Phone: (52-5) 255-21-55 and 203-40-34
Fax: (52-5) 203-52-87

Bursamex
Fuente de Piramides 1 pisos 6 y 7
Lomas de Tecamachalco
53950 Naucalpan,
Mexico

Phone: (52-5) 294-63-44 and 61-58
Fax: (52-5) 294-76-13

C.B.I.
Insurgentes Sur 1886
Col. Florida
01030 Mexico, D.F.
Phone: (52-5) 575-31-33
Fax: (52-5) 534-96-67 and 534-88-46

Cremi
Paseo de la Reforma No. 144, piso 1
Col. Juarez
06600 Mexico, D.F.
Phone: (52-5) 566-62-11
Fax: (52-5) 566-62-11 ext. 1525

Estrategia Bursatil
Camino al Desierto de los Leones 19
Col. Guadalupe Inn
01020 Mexico, D.F.
Phone: (52-5) 550-71-00
Fax: (52-5) 550-71-00 ext. 4018

Fimsa
Jaime Balmes 11
Edificio B, Piso 6
Col. Polanco
11510 Mexico, D.F.
Phone: (52-5) 207-02-02
Fax: (52-5) 208-49-11

Interacciones
Paseo de la Reforma 383
Planta Baja
Col. Cuauhtemoc
06500 Mexico, D.F.
Phone: (52-5) 264-18-00 and 208-00-66
Fax: (52-5) 525-39-42

Inverlat
Bosques de Ciruelos 120
Col. Bosques de las Lomas
11700 Mexico, D.F.
Phone: (52-5) 596-62-22
Fax: (52-5) 596-25-55

Invermexico
Blvd. Manuel Avila Camacho 170
Col. Lomas San Isidro
11620 Mexico, D.F.
Phone: (52-5) 570-70-00 and 570-50-22
Fax: (52-5) 202-10-70

Inversora Bursatil
Paseo de las Palmas 736
Planta Baja
11000 Mexico, D.F.
Phone: (52-5) 259-15-42 and 202-11-22
Fax: (52-5) 540-74-92

Mexival
Paseo de la Reforma 359 piso 1
Col. Cuauhtemoc
06560 Mexico, D.F.
Phone: (52-5) 208-20-44
Fax: (52-5) 208-52-15 and 202-21-07

MultiValores
Blas Pascal 105
Col. Morales Polanco
11510 Mexico, D.F.
Phone: (52-5) 557-62-55 and 28-33
Fax: (52-5) 557-62-55 ext. 3720

Operadora de Bolsa
Rio Amazonas 62
Col Cuauhtemoc
06500 Mexico, D.F.
Phone: (52-5) 592-69-88
Fax: (52-5) 592-69-88 ext. 2821

Prime
Paseo de la Reforma 243
Torre B, piso 3
Col. Cuauhtemoc
06500 Mexico, D.F.
Phone: (52-5) 533-59-70
Fax: (52-5) 207-01-81

Probursa
Blvd. Adolfo Lopez Mateos 2448
Col. Altavista
01060 Mexico, D.F.
Phone: (52-5) 660-11-11 and 13-35
Fax: (52-5) 660-11-11 ext. 2235

Valores Bursatiles de Mexico
Insurgentes Sur 670, Piso 6
Col. de Valle
03100 Mexico, D.F.
Phone: (52-5) 536-30-60 and 687-90-11
Fax: (52-5) 510-89-80

Valores Finamex
Rio Amazonas 91
Col. Cuauhtemoc

06500 Mexico, D.F.
Phone: (52-5) 525-90-20 and 208-00-33
Fax: (52-5) 208-17-56

Value
Liverpool 54
Col. Juarez
06600 Mexico, D.F.
Phone: (52-5) 207-27-26 and 525-46-00
Fax: (52-5) 207-27-26 ext. 3323

Vector
Av. Roble 565 Oriente
Col. Valle del Campestre
Garza Garcia
66265 Monterrey, Nuevo Leon
Phone: (52-8) 35-67-77 and 35-77-77
Fax: (52-8) 35-78-97

Company Information:

The Best Performing Shares in the Country

Company Name	Share Price Change 1 January 1997 to 31 December 1997 (%)
Elektra 'L'	1,672
Herdez 'B'	542
Argos 'B'	241
Cifra 'V'	233
Hilasal 'A'	223
Cifra 'A'	221
Iusacell 'D'	215
Cie 'B'	197
Elektra Cpo (Cpo = 1 Sr.L + 2 Sr. B)	191
Dina	178
Gserfin 'L'	155
Vitro	149
Iusacell 'L'	146
Femsa 'B'	139
Visa	137
Soriana 'B'	135
Ara	118
Kof 'L'	106
Promex 'B'	101
Empaq 'B'	100
Gfnorte 'B'	99
Ich 'B'	99
Livepol 1	96
Livepol C-1	92
Cifra 'C'	89
Gph 1	87
Contal	83
Desc 'B'	79

Company Name	Share Price Change 1 January 1997 to 31 December 1997 (%)
Desc 'C'	79
Telecom 'A1'	76
Tribasa	76
Desc 'A'	75
Sigma 'B'	74
Pepsigx 'Cpo'	67
Segcoam 'A'	67
Segcoam 'B'	67
Comerci Ubc	66
Bimbo 'A'	66
Gfb 'B'	65
Bbvpro 'B'	59
Bevides 'B'	58
Cydsasa 'A'	57
Hylsamx 'B'	57
Gfb 'A'	56
Televisa 'Cpo'	56
Telmex 'L'	55
Celanes 'B1'	52
Cintra 'A'	50
Alfa 'A'	49
Gmodelo 'C'	48
Banacci 'B'	45
Cemex Cpo	45
Banacci 'A'	43
Tamsa	41
Ttolmex 'B2'	40
Cemex 'B'	39
Durango 'A'	39
Telmex 'A'	37
Comerci 'Ub'	36
Gissa B	36
Banacci 'L'	34
Sanluis Cpo	33
Gigante 'B'	33
Tmm 'A'	31

The Largest Companies in the Country by Market Capitalization as of 31 December 1997

Company Name	Market Capitalization Local Currency (Millions)	Market Capitalization US Dollars (Millions)
Telmex 'L'	131,468	16,308
Gcarso 'A1'	49,351	6,122
Cifra 'A'	39,338	4,880
Cifra 'V'	37,795	4,688
Televisa 'Cpo'	35,680	4,426
Femsa 'B'	34,919	4,331
Alfa 'A'	32,820	4,071
Telecom 'A1'	31,097	3,857
Kimber 'A'	28,035	3,477
Bimbo 'A'	26,130	3,241
Soriana 'B'	21,300	2,642
Cemex 'A'	20,865	2,588
Moderna 'A'	20,204	2,506
Tvaztca Cpo	19,788	2,455
Cemex 'B'	18,793	2,331
Banacci 'B'	17,478	2,168
Gfinbur 'B'	16,897	2,096
Banacci 'A'	16,685	2,070
Visa	16,148	2,003
Livepol 1	15,798	1,960
Apasco	15,590	1,934
Gmexico 'B'	15,318	1,900
Cemex Cpo	14,927	1,852
Gfinbur 'A'	14,922	1,851
Penoles	14,764	1,831
Cifra 'C'	14,480	1,796
Ica	13,749	1,705
Gfb 'B'	13,500	1,675
Vitro	12,798	1,587
Tamsa	12,127	1,504
Hylsamx 'B'	11,579	1,436
Celanes 'B1'	11,507	1,427
Elektra 'L'	11,482	1,424
Gruma 'B'	11,159	1,384
Gmodelo 'C'	11,023	1,367
Contal	10,763	1,335
Gissa B	9,462	1,174
Desc 'A'	8,946	1,110
Desc 'B'	8,732	1,083
Cremi B	8,642	1,072
Ahmsa	7,767	963
Comerci 'Ub'	7,684	953
Cintra 'A'	7,453	925
Gfb 'A'	7,399	918
Hilasal 'A'	6,857	851
Ttolmex 'B2'	6,777	841
Pepsigx 'Cpo'	6,493	805
Segcoam 'A'	6,227	772
Segcoam 'B'	5,983	742
Imsa Ubc	5,505	683
Gsanbor 'B'	5,415	672
Telmex 'A'	5,413	671
Elektra Cpo	5,360	665
Sigma 'B'	5,121	635
Gigante 'B'	4,896	607
Tribasa	4,840	600
Aty	4,801	596
Desc 'C'	4,662	578

Company Name	Market Capitalization Local Currency (Millions)	Market Capitalization US Dollars (Millions)
Ara	4,289	532
Kof 'L'	4,242	526
Banacci 'L'	4,165	517
Geo 'B'	4,044	502
Bachoco Ubl	3,968	492
Gfb 'L'	3,688	458
Nadro 'B'	3,627	450
Ich 'B'	3,585	445
Maseca 'B'	3,455	429
Empaq 'B'	3,444	427
Comerci Ubc	3,341	414
Cie 'B'	3,333	413
Durango 'A'	3,274	406
Argos 'B'	3,274	406
Gfnorte 'B'	3,224	400
Gph 1	3,212	398
Iusacell 'D'	3,212	398
Sanluis Cpo	2,891	359
Cydsasa 'A'	2,700	335
Livepol C-1	2,666	331
Iusacell 'L'	2,459	305
Bbvpro 'B'	2,369	294
Confra 'A'	2,321	288
Acerla	2,302	286
Gserfin 'L'	2,266	281
Dina	2,262	281
Almaco 1	2,203	273
Herdez 'B'	2,197	273
Promex 'B'	2,136	265
Tmm 'A'	2,136	265
Bevides 'B'	2,118	263
Gserfin 'A'	2,101	261

Regional Exchanges: None

Other Investment Information:
Mexican Investment Board (MIB)
Paseo de la Reforma 915
Lomas de Chapultepec
11000 Mexico, D.F.
Phone: (52-5) 202-78-04
Fax: (52-5) 202-79-25

National Commission on Foreign Investment
Office of the President
Los Pinos
Mexico, D.F.
Phone: (52-5) 515-33-53
Telex: 1760010

Secretariat of State for Commerce and Industrial Development
Alfonso Reyes 30
Mexico, D.F.
Phone: (52-5) 286-18-23
Telex: 1775718

Secretary of State for Foreign Affairs
Ricardo Flores Magon 1
Tiateloco 06995
Mexico, D.F.
Phone: (52-5) 277-54-70
Telex: 1763478

MICROECONOMICS

Microeconomics is the study of individual economic units, such as households, firms, and industries. It studies the interrelationship between these units in determining the pattern of production and distribution of goods and services. Microeconomics is concerned with the demand and supply of a particular good, service, or resource.

Economists attempt to explain the behavior of individuals and firms faced with a multitude of options. They are often portrayed as making rational choices that involve weighing up the benefits of any activity and its opportunity cost (the next best alternative foregone as a result of the decision). Both firms and individuals are assumed to be maximizers of either profit or satisfaction.

Because resources are scarce, people have to make choices. Microeconomics studies the choices of what goods and services to produce, how to produce them, and for whom to produce them.

The use of supply side policies by governments in recent years has been an attempt to alter the supply decisions of individuals and firms and to facilitate the operation of market forces.

See also MACROECONOMICS.

MIDDLE AGES, BANKING IN THE

Banking in the Middle Ages had its origins as money-lending in Italy. Money changing had been conducted for centuries in the Orient, but it came to Europe only gradually, through the influence of the Arab peoples and the Crusades. Indeed, it was Italian bankers who financed the Crusades in 1191.

The development of banking in medieval Europe necessitated the lending of money at interest. Traditionally, however, the Catholic Church had forbade this practice, considering any interest equivalent to usury. If a Christian lent money, it should be as an act of charity, and only the amount that had been lent should be repaid.

By the 11th century, however, the developing economy of Europe required moneylending. For this reason the first large-scale moneylenders in Europe were the Jews, who were not bound by the Church's views on usury. The Jews justified the rather high interest rates they charged by the fact that many of the loans they extended were not paid back. For more than 200 years they remained Europe's primary lenders.

By the 13th century some merchants were finding ways to circumvent the usury laws. For example, an Italian merchant might lend money to an English nobleman, and this loan would be repaid in a larger quantity of wool than the market price would indicate, effectively paying the merchant interest. Under the pressure of the financial needs of commerce and the Church itself, Christian doctrine began to adjust. St. Thomas Aquinas (1225–74), for example, held that a good's just price was determined not by greed, but by the seller's needs, which were thereby recognized as legitimate. By the 15th century it had become acceptable for Christians to lend money for interest, whether the loans were for consumption goods, manufacturing, agriculture, or trade.

The justification for this was that since there were great risks of losing money when lending, interest had to be charged as a way of repaying the lenders for bad debts, much as a merchant was entitled to mark up his price to guard against shipwreck or piracy. More decisive, however, was the Church's need for the Vatican to collect papal revenues throughout Europe, a task that the incipient bankers needed to carry out in context of the difficulty of transporting money and the variety of European currencies.

The first Christian bankers were probably goldsmiths who held in their vaults surplus money for merchants over long periods and lent some of it for interest. With the spread of lending by Christians, the Jews were repeatedly expelled from England and France in the 13th century.

One of the services provided by the first medieval bankers was currency exchange. A great many kinds of coins existed in medieval Europe—whereas the pound sterling was uniform throughout England in the 12th and 13th centuries. In France, by contrast, different coins were issued by Paris, Tours, Anjou, and Provins. Bankers, by establishing offices in different European cities, could facilitate exchanges by issuing notes of credit and bills of exchange, thus obviating the need for their customers to transport bulky quantities of coins.

The most powerful medieval bankers came from the ranks of merchants in Italy, based in cities such as Florence, Venice, Siena, and Genoa. These merchants had accumulated more capital than they could use in the purchase of land or government bonds. They therefore went into banking, which was initially conducted outdoors, using *banca* (tables or benches).

The most well known and successful were the Medici family in Florence, who had made much of their money in the textiles trade. The Medicis established houses throughout Europe. They profited handsomely from foreign exchange. They also extended loans to various monarchs, whether for royal consumption or for war, although, as the disastrous experience of other bankers of that period illustrated, these were decidedly high-risk ventures. Kings and princes might be defeated or deposed, or they could simply decide not to repay a loan—or even find some excuse to get rid of the lender.

Other influential bankers in medieval Europe were the Knights Templar and the Knights of the Hospital (Hospitallers). The Templars, especially, made huge sums of money by financing the Crusades up until the late 13th century, by which time their vast land holdings throughout Europe, their exemptions from tolls and taxes, and other privileges they enjoyed allowed them to rival the Italians and Jews as the biggest financiers. They lent money to nobles, bishops, abbeys, merchants, and kings.

By the 15th century a number of European banks had gone bankrupt as a result of bad loans and the fiscal chaos resulting from multiple currencies. Others, which had functioned primarily as deposit banks, suffered losses on direct investments in businesses. Some European cities, such as Barcelona and Genoa, established their own central currencies to control inflation. The surviving banks were to be in great demand during the next period of civic growth and industrial development.

See also ANCIENT EGYPT, BANKING IN; ANCIENT GREECE, BANKING IN; ANCIENT ROME, BANKING IN; BABYLON, BANKING IN; ISLAMIC BANKING.

MIDLAND BANK PLC

Midland Bank PLC is one of the four largest deposit banks in the United Kingdom. In the first half of the

20th century, the Midland Bank PLC was the largest bank in the world.

The Birmingham and Midland Bank was founded in 1836. The leading figure among its founders was Charles Geach, a 28-year-old Bank of England clerk who quit his job to become the new institution's general manager (he remained in this position until his death in 1854).

It prospered quietly until 1851, when it acquired Bates and Robins, a Stourbridge private bank. In 1862 it added Baker and Crane, another private bank. These two acquisitions marked the beginning of a long series of amalgamations that would turn Midland into a banking powerhouse by the early years of the next century.

By the 1880s the bank began to expand again when it acquired the Union Bank of Birmingham, and amalgamated with Coventry Union Banking Company, the Leamington Priors and Warwickshire Banking Company, the Derby Commercial Bank, the Leeds and County Bank, and the Exchange and Discount Bank.

In 1891 Edward Holden became Midland's general manager. Also that year, Midland acquired the Central Bank of London. This acquisition changed Midland from a provincial institution to one with nationwide ambitions. Midland's expansion continued into the early years of the 20th century, and in 1918 the bank made its largest acquisition in its history to date, the London Joint-Stock Bank.

In 1919 Sir Edward Holden died. Reginald McKenna became the new general manager; he was known for his outspokenness on economic matters and for being a noted ally of John Maynard Keynes. McKenna's term saw the end of expansion through acquisition due to the Treasury regulations of the 1920s. Midland's last acquisition was the purchase of the North of Scotland Bank in 1924. By 1934, however, it had become the largest deposit bank in the world, with more than £457 million in assets, and by 1939 the bank had more than 2,100 branch offices. Reginald McKenna died in 1943.

In 1963 the Midland International Bank was formed by the combination of the Commercial Bank of Australia, Canada's Standard Bank, and the Toronto-Dominion Bank. In 1967, Midland achieved another first by purchasing 33% interest in the merchant bank Samuel Montagu. This was the first merger in Britain between a merchant bank and a deposit bank. Then in 1974 Midland increased its stake in Montagu to 100%, only to sell 40% of it to Aetna Life and Casualty and then buy it back again in 1985.

The decade of the 1980s was indeed a challenge for Midland. In 1980 Midland purchased 60% of Trinkaus und Burkhardt, West Germany's biggest privately owned bank, from Citicorp. In 1982 it acquired 69% of Handesfinanz Bank of Geneva from Italy's Banca Commerciale Italiana. These acquisitions gave Midland a substantial expertise in the international market.

Ultimately this strategy became an unqualified failure. In 1981 Midland had acquired a 57% stake in Crocker National Bank, the 12th largest bank in the United States (the fourth largest bank in California). This was the largest takeover of an American bank to date and cost Midland $820 million. When the deal was consummated, Midland became the tenth largest banking organization in the world. Almost from the moment that Midland took over, however, Crocker's financial performance faltered; in 1983 it collapsed, posting a $62 million loss for the fourth quarter.

Irrespective of the calamity, Midland stuck by its subsidiary, even buying out the rest of its stock in 1985 for $16.25 per share. In 1986 Midland sold Crocker to Wells Fargo and Company for $1.1 billion, roughly the amount that Midland had sunk into it.

By the late 1980s, Midland was on the defensive, with several parties purchasing part interests in the bank. Hanson Trust acquired 6.5%, Robert Maxwell acquired 2.5%, Prudential Insurance Company bought 2%, and in 1988 the Kuwaiti Investment Office disclosed that it owned 5.1% of the bank. Reacting to rumors that it might become a target for takeover, Midland agreed to allow the Hongkong and Shanghai Banking Corporation to acquire 14.9% of its stock in a "friendly" transaction.

Despite all of Midland Bank PLC's trials and tribulations, it remains one of Britain's Big Four deposit banks and one of the largest banks in the world. The Midland has in fact gone from strength to strength following the deal with the Hong Kong and Shanghai Banking Corporation in 1992. In August 1998 the Midland announced record pre-tax profits of £1.63 billion. The Midland's groundbreaking telephone bank, First Direct, has more than 800,000 customers, with about 150,000 of them recruited in 1997. The Midland has launched PC banking and is considering television banking and opening branches in supermarkets.

See also WELLS FARGO AND COMPANY.

MILKEN, MICHAEL

Michael Milken's mastery of the junk bond revolution made him one of the central figures of the 1980s boom. Unphotogenic and unglamorous, Milken nevertheless made it onto the front covers of most business magazines. From his elevated status as one of the most prolific salesmen of all time, Milken ended the most productive decade of his career in prison.

Stories about Milken's journey to fortune have reached near-mythic status. His colleagues would rush to work at 4:30 in the morning, only to find that Milken had already started work on the first deal of the day. He used to wear a miner's metal hat during his train journey to work so that he could read annual reports and analyst reports by the light of its torch. His immense salary, $550 million in 1986, earned him a place in the *Guinness Book of Records* as the highest paid person in the history of the world. His arrogance and his oft-proclaimed assertion that money meant nothing to him made Milken a convenient hate figure for the popular press.

Milken had begun as a lowly salesman in the bond department of Drexel Burnham Lambert. He focused on the unfashionable world of "fallen angels," bonds that had been downgraded to below investment grade by the rating authorities. The persuasive Milken was able to convince his clients that the bonds, which were shunned by the majority of investors, would make excellent, high-yielding additions to their portfolios. Milken revitalized the market in so-called junk bonds, and soon Drexel began to issue bonds for grateful corporate clients. By 1980, ten years of nonstop work by Milken had made Drexel the preeminent bond house in the United States, and the firm claimed to have more than 1,000 clients.

Frederick Joseph, a colleague of Milken's in the bond department, became Drexel's chief executive officer in 1985 and quickly saw the potential of junk bonds in the financing of corporate takeovers. Drexel began to earn fees comparable to those paid to the established players on Wall Street and was associated with the great entrepreneurial spirits that revitalized corporate America. Drexel put together financing packages for T. Boone Pickens's hostile bid for Gulf Oil and Carl Icahn's attempted takeover of Phillips Petroleum, together with numerous other buyouts, hostile takeovers, and corporate restructurings. For each transaction, Milken received an advisory fee worth half a million dollars plus up to 5% of the value of the deal. It is a tribute to Milken's analytical skills that less than 2% of the high-risk deals put together by Drexel during this boom defaulted on payment.

The good days came to an end in 1986. One of Milken's investment banking colleagues, Dennis Levine, was arrested on insider dealing charges. It later surfaced that the regulators in the United States had acted after receiving a tip-off from a branch of Merrill Lynch in Caracas, Venezuela. Levine struck a bargain with the authorities to exchange names and details of insider trading at Drexel for a lighter sentence. Ivan Boesky, the notorious arbitrageur, was among those named by Levine. The aggressive New York attorney Rudolph Giuliani began a concerted campaign against the junk bond masters. Drexel was heavily fined and forced into bankruptcy, while Boesky was sentenced to three years in prison. Giuliani's attention now focused on Milken, who was widely perceived to be the major villain in the affair.

Milken was indicted on 98 criminal charges. If found guilty on all charges, he would have faced a maximum of 520 years in jail and fines totaling $18 billion. Milken quickly agreed to plead guilty to six charges of security fraud. He was sentenced to ten years in prison for violating U.S. rules on securities, but the term was reduced to five years on appeal.

It is important to keep in mind that none of Milken's bond issues or takeover deals were judged to be against either the spirit or the letter of the law. He was found guilty of largely technical offenses and, instead of the lengthy show trial that many had expected, Milken was convicted at a fairly low-key trial that lasted only a week. He was sentenced to ten years in prison and 1,800 hours of community service, and was fined $600 million. Milken had his sentence reduced again to 33 months in August 1992 and was released in January 1993 having served 22 months for his part in the scandal.

Shortly after leaving prison in 1993 Milken was diagnosed as having prostate cancer, and despite a course of hormone therapy, he was given only a limited chance of long-term survival. He has personally contributed $17.5 million to the Association for the Cure of Cancer of the Prostate (CaP CURE), his cancer research charity, and has raised a further $23 million from an impressive list of sponsors. The interpreters of myth who seek to use Milken's life story as a parable have interpreted Milken's illness as a punishment for his past sins. Milken himself has also seen a connection: "I rightly or wrongly believe that all the aggravation I had contributed to my cancer."

Milken has underwritten a number of expensive research projects to help find a cure for cancer. With his prostate cancer apparently in remission, Milken has adroitly used his contacts to ensure the success of CaP CURE. Top businessmen, famous academics, and respected scientists have all been cajoled into helping the charity.

The Milken story has been endlessly retold in the main protagonists' autobiographies, in newspapers, in film, and in court. Perhaps the most bizarre version of

Michael Milken addressing the Mexican and American Foundation's California Forum, 9 June 1989. *(UPI/Cor-bis-Bettmann)*

the junk bond bonanza appeared in 1996 when the Brooklyn Academy of Music produced a musical satire, *The Predators' Ball*, based on his life and set to a hip-hop and rap score. At a particularly dramatic moment in the musical, Milken's notorious X-shaped desk rises above the stage.

James B. Stewart's account of Milken's career, *Den of Thieves*, certainly paints a portrait of Milken as an amoral and avaricious trader who put personal wealth above all other objectives. He is shown as ruthless and obsessive, a bitter man who displays little humanity toward others. In one episode, which becomes painfully ironic in the light of Milken's subsequent ill health, he displays little sympathy for a colleague whose mother has been diagnosed as having cancer. His only concern is when his worker can return to making money for Drexel. Stewart also has little doubt as to Milken's guilt on the insider dealing charges. In Stewart's opinion, Milken was the originator of "the greatest criminal conspiracy the financial world has ever known."

Apologists for Milken believe that the passage of time will radically alter these negative perceptions. Junk bonds, largely Milken's invention, revolutionized the way in which corporate America was financed. Milken enabled hungry entrepreneurs who lacked capital to attack corporations that had become bloated and lethargic. It was almost as if a form of financial Darwinism, where the strong superseded the weak, was in force. Milken's legacy resides in entrepreneurs such as Ted Turner, who have set up companies from scratch and seen them grow to global status in less than a decade.

The pro-Milken camp is also strongly critical of the manner in which Milken was tried and convicted. While the other main players in the scandal were allowed to plea bargain their way to a shorter sentence and benefited from publicly blaming their former colleagues, Milken was made a scapegoat and forced to accept the blame for others' transgressions. He was found guilty by the press many months before he took the witness stand.

A further twist to the Milken tale came with the publication of *Highly Confident*, written by the *Vanity Fair* journalist Jesse Kornbluth. The main argument of the book is that Milken was a borderline schizophrenic who became unable to distinguish between ethically good and bad as the stress of junk bond trading increased. Kornbluth, who interviewed Milken in prison and had access to his psychologist, also believes that the prosecuting authorities deliberately placed extreme psychological pressure on Milken to

coerce a conviction from him. Not surprisingly, the book was not well received in the Milken camp and was dismissively labeled as "psycho-babble" by Alan Dershowitz, Milken's high-profile attorney.

Dangerous Dreamers by Robert Sobel presents an interesting account of the details of how the junk bond market operated. Sobel explains how businessmen such as T. Boone Pickens and Carl Icahn were able to make fortunes with Milken's help.

Although Milken's recent profile in the business community has, of necessity, been far lower than in the 1980s, he has made a number of investments. He worked with Larry Ellison, the founder of Oracle, to set up a multimedia company, Education Technology, and has also used the Milken Family Trust to fund ventures in real estate and cable communications. Despite the continuing legal restrictions on his ability to give investment advice, he has been paid several large consultancy fees for helping with mergers.

See also BOESKY, IVAN; *DEN OF THIEVES*; DREXEL BURNHAM LAMBERT; JUNK BOND.

MILL, JOHN STUART

John Stuart Mill was an English radical, philosopher, moralist, political economist, and Member of Parliament. His major economic work, *Principles of Political Economy with Their Application to Social Philosophy* (1848), dominated British economic thinking in the mid-19th century and synthesized Mill's political philosophy with economic doctrines.

Mill's professed objective was to consolidate classical economic analysis as it had evolved since Adam Smith, and he also recognized the considerable economic changes that had occurred since David Ricardo and Thomas Malthus. The result was to move political economy toward neoclassical marginal analysis. In his exposition of the theory of value, Mill showed how price is determined by the equality of demand and supply. He combined with this an embryonic notion of elasticity, and thus provided the foundations of later neoclassical theory of value. Mill used the concept of demand and supply in the case of commodities with joint costs and demonstrated how the reciprocal demand for each others' products affected countries' terms of trade.

Arguably Mill's most significant modification in the orthodox classical tradition was his reinterpretation of the laws of production and distribution. Mill argued that production was immutable—fixed by nature and technology—but that distribution of the outcome was socially determined. By accepting a far more optimis-

John Stuart Mill, 1873, by George Frederic Watts. *(Courtesy of National Portrait Gallery, London)*

tic view of population growth than earlier classical economists, Mill challenged the view that the net product of society should be identified with the profit and rent shares of income.

Mill also challenged the view that uninterrupted expansion was a goal that required no justification. In his description of the "stationary" state, Mill criticized the social manifestations of affluence and of the tendency toward increasingly risky behavior by entrepreneurs faced with a declining rate of profit. Mill looked forward to the coming of a society in which the struggle for survival ended and people were able to enjoy the fruits of past abstinence.

Mill's frame of reference contained the outlines of a more active intervention in economic life than the classical school called for. The stationary state had a role as "civilizer," to educate the working classes and reduce population growth, and also in performing a stabilizing function. In the stationary state, taxation would reduce the volatility in rates of return on investment and the channeling of domestic savings into more lucrative foreign markets. Results would be even more beneficial if foreign investment were directed into the development of low-cost sources of food and raw materials required in the lending country.

In his most famous work of political philosophy, *On Liberty* (1859), Mill pioneered the principle of noninterference with individual liberty. In matters of practical action he saw a role for the state. The spirit of compromise and eclecticism in Mill's writings are perhaps their strongest feature and greatest influence on subsequent thinkers. Pure economics to Mill was only a part of the whole discipline of moral and social philosophy.

See also CLASSICAL SCHOOL OF ECONOMICS; MALTHUS, THOMAS ROBERT; RICARDO, DAVID; SMITH, ADAM.

MINIMUM MAINTENANCE REQUIREMENTS
See MARGIN; REGULATION G–X/REGULATION T.

MINNEAPOLIS GRAIN EXCHANGE (MGE)
130 Grain Exchange Building
400 South 4th Street
Minneapolis, MN 55415
Phone: (612) 321-7101
Internet Address: www.mgex.com

The origin of the *Minneapolis Grain Exchange (MGE)* can be traced to the 19th century, when farmers had no way of knowing if they were getting the best price for their grain. Processors and millers did not know if they were buying economically. Since farmers were harvesting and selling their crops at the same time, subsequent floods and gluts of grain on the market set the supply and demand curve askew; obviously supply was highest at harvest time. Many farmers had to sell their grain for prices far below a break even point.

In 1881, 21 businessmen formed the Minneapolis Chamber of Commerce, an organization designed to encourage and promote trade in corn, oats, and wheat, as well as prevent abuses. The objectives of the original chamber of commerce were "To facilitate the buying and selling of all products, to inculcate principles of justice and equity in trade, to facilitate speedy adjustments to business disputes, to acquire and disseminate valuable commercial information, and generally to secure to its members the benefits of cooperation in the furtherance of their legitimate business pursuits, and to advance the general prosperity and business of Minneapolis." The Minneapolis Chamber of Commerce became a centralized grain market for farmers, processors, elevator operators, and others needing to buy and sell grain. By providing a location in which grain buyers and sellers could conduct business, farmers gained easy access to buyers and current market prices, elevator operators could locate farmers and merchants, and investors had a market in which to speculate.

By 1946 the term *chamber of commerce* became associated with organizations devoted mainly to civic and social issues. So, in 1947, the Minneapolis Chamber of Commerce officially became the civic organization and the grain business became the Minneapolis Grain Exchange.

After more than 100 years, the Minneapolis Grain Exchange still provides an auction site, as well as many services for buyers and sellers of grains grown in the Upper Midwest and Pacific Northwest. The Minneapolis Grain Exchange continues today as a time-honored, nationally respected institution. It has built a worldwide reputation for honesty and integrity. The grain exchange boasts the only authorized market for Hard Red Spring Wheat and White Wheat Futures and Options, trading an average of ten million bushels daily. It is also the largest cash exchange market in the world, trading a daily average of one million bushels of grain including wheat, barley, oats, durum, rye, sunflower seeds, flax, corn, soybeans, millet, and milo. In addition, the Minneapolis Grain Exchange is the world's only seafood complex. In July 1993 the exchange introduced and began trading the White Shrimp futures and options contract, and added the Black Tiger shrimp contract in November 1994.

The Minneapolis Grain Exchange's favorable reputation is due in part to its commitment to excellence through self-governing departments and outstanding services.

Compliance Department: This is the internal affairs division or policing arm of the Minneapolis Grain Exchange. This department investigates potential members and analyzes the financial statements of member organizations to determine whether they will be able to meet their financial obligations. The Compliance Department oversees futures trading, investigates rule violations, and works closely with the Commodity Futures Trading Commission (CFTC) to ensure that federal regulations are met.

Weighing Department: This department supervises grain weighing at terminal elevators, monitors the condition of rail cars, investigates weight disputes, and is certified by the Association of American Railroads to issue weight certificates on grain that is shipped or received from terminal elevators. These certificates are used to resolve weight disputes and provide a basis for cash settlement. Because of the care that is taken in weighing and the daily enforcement of industry regulations, certificates issued by the MGE have an excellent national reputation for honest reputable weights.

Sampling Department: Here, grain samples are collected from inspection agencies in the Midwest. These samples, which represent grain for sale on the cash market, are taken from rail cars and serve to give buyers a tangible idea of what they are purchasing. Samples are also used to settle any grain quality disputes. The sampling department compiles and posts the Daily Market Report, which lists the number of rail cars for sale or application. It is also licensed by the State Department of Agriculture to use fumigants in rail cars.

Clearing House: The Clearing House functions as a financial intermediary, or bank, between buyers and sellers. It is the buyer of every futures contract and the seller of every purchase. It keeps accounts for members, making sure that they have enough "margin" deposit money to cover their trades. By monitoring members' trades and accounts, the Clearing House guarantees that all futures trades will be honored with prompt payment or delivery.

From 9:30 A.M. to 1:30 P.M. each day the traders and members of the exchange buy and sell futures and options through a type of free form auction called open-outcry. As bids and offers are shouted or signaled through a series of hand signals, trades are made and prices are set and reported to the trading world.

The futures market allows farmers, processors, and merchants to buy and sell grain that, in some cases, has not even been planted yet. This is not as risky as it may seem. Futures contracts eliminate risk by enabling buyers and sellers to lock in a price today for some time in the future. For example, a farmer can sell a futures contract guaranteeing a certain market price. If the price indeed goes down, he or she can purchase that futures contract for a profit and then sell that grain for the cash market price—the grain in futures offsets any loss in cash. Farmers can avoid losing money on their investments by using futures and options. Futures contracts are simply insurance policies against rapid price fluctuations. The practice is called hedging.

Hedgers leave all the guesswork and the risk-taking to those who invest in commodity futures the way others invest in stocks, bonds, and real estate. Investors, in essence, seek to profit by taking advantage of price fluctuations. By assuming the risk that hedgers (primarily farmers, processors, and grain elevator operators) wish to avoid, investors keep the market from becoming stagnant.

See also COMMODITIES; COMMODITY FUTURES TRADING COMMISSION (CFTC); FUTURES TRADING.

MINOR (United States)

A *Minor* is someone who is under 18, the age of majority.

See also UNIFORM GIFT TO MINORS ACT (UGMA).

MINORITY INTEREST

An individual or group that owns less than 50% of the voting shares of a company is called a *Minority Interest*. This includes another corporation that might hold less than 50% of another corporation, often as an investment.

On the consolidated balance sheets of companies that have subsidiaries that are not wholly owned, the minority interest is shown as either a separate equity account or a liability with an indefinite term. The minority interest's share of income is subtracted from profits in the income statement of the holding company to arrive at the figure for consolidated net income.

See also AFFILIATED PERSON; BALANCE SHEET; CONSOLIDATED REPORT.

MINORITY SHAREHOLDER

See MINORITY INTEREST.

MINUS TICK

See DOWNTICK.

MISSING THE MARKET

The execution—due to broker negligence—of an investor's order at an unfavorable price is called *Missing the Market*.

Missing the market might be caused by a broker either forgetting to place an order, or placing an order incorrectly without making the proper adjustments prior to execution.

An investor's first recourse is to discuss the problem with the brokerage firm's branch office manager. Most situations can be adjusted or corrected at this level. If this proves unsatisfactory, an investor may wish to contact the firm's compliance officer or, if necessary, contact the National Association of Securities Dealers.

Ultimately, the investor can demand that the brokerage firm make good any loss, or appeal to the Securities and Exchange Commission for an arbitration hearing to have an adjustment made.

See also ARBITRATION; NATIONAL ASSOCIATION OF SECURITIES DEALERS (NASD); SECURITIES AND EXCHANGE COMMISSION (SEC).

MISSISSIPPI BUBBLE

The roots of the *Mississippi Bubble* lie in the characters of two men from very different backgrounds. King Louis XIV was a ruler of extravagant tastes whose excesses drained the resources of the French government. John Law, by contrast, was a goldsmith from Edinburgh, Scotland, whose financial acumen led him to develop a plan to shore up France's finances. The combined efforts of King Louis XIV and Law almost bankrupted 18th-century France.

John Law was born in Edinburgh in 1671. His father, a prosperous goldsmith, taught the young John the intricacies of deposit taking and loan making in the firm's counting house. His charge showed a talent for mathematics far beyond his age and an amazing aptitude for finance. At the age of 17, Law left Edinburgh, determined to seek his fortune in London.

Accounts of his sojourn in London read like a true-life version of the *Rake's Progress*. Fascinated by the high life, Law became a ladies' man, dressing in high-fashion clothes and making contacts in court circles. His math skills and sharp mind led him to London's casinos, where he enjoyed considerable success for many years until his luck spectacularly ran out. The Law family estate, Lauriston, was mortgaged to cover his huge gambling losses.

Worse still were indiscretions in Law's personal life. Rumors of shady business dealings and affairs with married women began to circulate about the dashing Scotsman. Eventually Law was challenged to a duel, something of an occupational hazard in 18th century polite society. Law's opponent, Edward "Beau" Wilson, received a fatal stomach wound from Law's first sword stroke, and Law was charged with murder. He pleaded for clemency and the charge was reduced to manslaughter. Wilson's relatives appealed against this decision and, fearing the worst, Law's associates sprung him from Newgate jail.

Law fled to the continent, spending time in Holland, Italy, and Austria before arriving in France in 1715. He published two anonymous pamphlets that proposed the widespread introduction of paper money in place of bullion for business transactions. Law's gambling skills did not desert him, and he was rumored to have earned a fortune worth $4 million (£2.5 million) in today's money. France at this time was a country in turmoil, thrown into confusion by the death of King Louis XIV after a reign of 72 years. The five-year-old Louis XV held nominal power, but the country was run by his uncle, Philippe, who became the regent.

King Louis had left his successors a terrible legacy. A long series of wars, designed to prove France as the strongest military power in Europe, had cost millions of livres. Decades of profligate spending on palaces, parties, mistresses, and illegitimate children took their toll on the French taxpayers. Corruption and bribes to court favorites exacerbated the problem. The French people found that the interest payments on the national debt swallowed the major part of the national income. The regent, who had seen Law's financial ability at the gaming table, had also been impressed by Law's ideas for economic reform. Although the French Council of Finance repeatedly rejected Law's proposals, the regent, sensing a chance to solve a desperate problem, allowed Law to set up a private bank.

Law was given French nationality and opened the Banque Générale in May 1716. The initial capital structure provided an omen of the financial complications that were to come: the equity was 6 million livres, one-quarter paid fully in cash with the remainder paid in promissory notes that were sold at a heavy discount. The bank was assured of a steady flow of money—essential in any weakly constructed company—when the French laws were changed to make regional taxes only payable in Banque Générale notes.

Law was able to put his theories on the advantages of paper money to the test. First, the bank issued notes that could be redeemed against silver coinage. After

John Law, engraving by R. Grave. *(Mary Evans Picture Library)*

many years of fluctuating currency, the French people were pleased to put their money in an instrument backed by a precious metal. The notes held their value, paid interest, and were easily transportable. Within a short time they traded at a premium to their issue price. As the circulation of the notes increased, usurers were forced out of business and interest rates fell. For a time the French economy boomed. Law, finally realizing his dream, opened branches of the bank throughout France.

With success came ambition. The compliant regent granted Law a license in August 1717 to commercially exploit France's Louisiana territory. This massive swath of land, which had originally been claimed for France by the explorers Marquette and La Salle, stretched from the Mississippi River to the Rocky Mountains and the Great Lakes. Law formed a company, the Compagnie de la Louisiane ou d'Occident, and prepared to benefit from the abundant wealth of the New World. By 1719 Law's company had taken control of the Senegal Company, the China Company, the Africa Company, and the French East Indies Company. Law, who renamed his enterprise the Compagnie des Indes, now dominated over the whole of France's trading beyond the boundaries of Europe.

Almost incredibly to modern readers, by 1719 the Compagnie des Indes acquired the Royal Mint. In August of the same year the Compagnie des Indes received the right to function as the collector of national tax in France for nine years. With a near monopoly over France's finances and the exciting prospect of the boom in the New World, shares in Compagnie des Indes zoomed. When it became public knowledge that the very bullish Law had bought a large number of futures contracts in the stock, the share price reached 8,000 livres, against an issue price of 500 livres only two years earlier.

France became gripped by Mississippi fever. People flocked from the outlying regions to Paris intent on making their fortunes. Informal markets sprang up in shops and on sidewalks to trade the shares. Some unfortunates, aware of the booming South Sea Company on the other side of the channel in England, even mortgaged their homes to buy shares. The announcement of a 40% dividend in 1720 drove the price up to 20,000 livres.

The collapse, inevitable once the shares had reached such a peak, was prompted by rumors of difficult conditions in the Louisiana Territory. Swamps and mountains, rather than gold and silver deposits, were the order of the day, and many of the first group of colonizers returned to France. Suddenly, the idea of a 40% dividend every year became unlikely. The first

selling orders could not be funded by the bank's silver resources, and confidence plummeted.

Law used his power over the French currency system to print more livres, but his theories on money proved to be incorrect. The extra supply of paper money devalued the currency, causing inflation to soar in France. People now wanted to be paid in gold or silver and rightly regarded the new bank notes, still wet from the presses, as worthless.

Shares in Compagnie des Indes became untradeable and Law was now regarded as a villain. The regent disowned him and an angry mob ransacked his offices. He was forced to flee, first to Latin America and then to Venice, where he died in abject poverty.

See also SOUTH SEA BUBBLE; TULIPMANIA.

MITARBEITERAKTIEN (Germany)
See SHARES.

MITSUBISHI TRUST AND BANKING CORPORATION

Mitsubishi Trust and Banking Corporation is the leading trust bank in Japan. The Mitsubishi group, originally a shipping and warehousing conglomerate, first created a bank in 1919.

In 1927 various members of the Mitsubishi conglomerate, led by the Mitsubishi Bank, capitalized and incorporated the Mitsubishi Trust and Banking Corporation. Although it was an entirely separate company, Mitsubishi Trust was controlled by other Mitsubishi companies through cross-ownership of stock and broad representation.

Mitsubishi Trust spent much of its early existence busily building market share. In 1929 the company opened a branch office in Osaka. Mitsubishi Trust opened its third branch in Nagoya in 1940 and additional branches in Fukuoka and Yokohama in 1941.

Mitsubishi Trust served as a capital resource for the Mitsubishi group, which had become intimately involved with government as a military and public projects contractor. In 1942, with the war well under way, Mitsubishi Trust opened two additional branches in Kyoto and Kobe. After World War II, however, Mitsubishi Trust was effectively closed, only to reopen its doors again in 1948. It was authorized to deal in foreign exchange the following year.

While the Mitsubishi group never regained the power it held before the war, Mitsubishi Trust had become more important to the organization than ever before. As it entered the 1970s, it became increasingly involved in a financial combine within the group. This miniature conglomerate, consisting of the Trust, Mitsubishi Bank, Tokio Marine and Fire Insurance, and Meiji Mutual Life Insurance, acted as a major multi-service financial institution.

When by the mid-1980s it was clear that deregulation would come, Mitsubishi Trust finally adopted a more aggressive attitude. Eager to exploit new opportunities in the United States, Mitsubishi Trust opened a branch office in New York in 1988.

After a banking law that had forbidden mergers between banks was amended in 1995, Mitsubishi Bank acquired the Bank of Tokyo in April 1996, creating the largest bank in the world, the Bank of Tokyo-Mitsubishi, Ltd.

See also BANK OF TOKYO-MITSUBISHI; JAPAN; JAPANESE FINANCIAL MARKETS; MITSUI KOBE BANK.

MITSUI KOBE BANK
See SAKURA BANK LTD.

MONETARY POLICY

Any decision made concerning a country's money supply is regarded as *Monetary Policy.*

In the United States, the Federal Reserve Board controls all monetary policy. For example, if the country's economy needs stimulation, the Federal Reserve Board can supply additional credit to the banking system through its open-market operators, lower the member bank reserve requirements, or lower the Federal Discount Rate.

Likewise, if the economy is growing too fast and threatening to overheat, the Federal Reserve can withdraw money from circulation, raise the reserve requirements, or raise the Federal Discount Rate.

Important to note: Monetary policy should not be confused with fiscal policy. Although each of these policies attempts to control the level of economic activity (including industrial production, employment, and prices), fiscal policy is carried out through government spending and taxation.

See also FEDERAL DISCOUNT RATE/FED FUNDS; FISCAL POLICY; INTEREST/INTEREST RATES.

MONEY LAUNDERING

Money Laundering is the process of turning money obtained from illegal sources into funds that appear to be legitimate.

A successful money laundering operation will hide the true source of the money, whether it is from organized crime, drug smuggling, or illegal stock market speculation. The ultimate owner of the money should also be obscured. Any money in paper and coin form must be fed into the banking system; once in an account, the money can easily be transferred around the world. Once the money is in the banking systems, any trails that can link the cash to its source and to the launderers must be obliterated.

Law enforcement specialists have identified three distinct stages that money passes through in the money laundering cycle.

Immersion Immersion turns physical cash into banked deposits. A common way to accomplish this task is to deposit criminal proceeds at the same time as legitimate earnings. For example, the owner of a cash-based business, such as a take-out restaurant or video rental store, could bank the profits from crime with the daily receipts. The criminal may, of course, be liable for paying tax on this income if it enters the banking system, but the additional tax would be a small price to pay for legitimizing the income.

Layering Layering hides the original source of the money. Layering involves moving the funds through as many accounts as possible, using bogus companies and offshore banks to create a complex network of obscure connections. The aim of layering is to destroy any trail that might connect the original "dirty" money with the "clean" money that appears at the end of the operation. The criminal may have to pay a percentage as a fee to each person who handles the money and will incur bank charges and legal expenses. Again, he or she might decide that these are worthwhile costs if they help to legitimize the money.

Integration Integration is the return of the money to the criminal in a clean, untraceable form. There are many ways to integrate the money. For example, a Cayman-based company may buy an office block in London, then sell the same property and remit the cash to a New York company. The owner of the New York company can then pay a large dividend to the firm's largest shareholder—himself.

Many countries have developed antilaundering laws that are designed to catch people depositing large sums of cash in banks. In the United States, all deposits over $10,000 must be recorded on special forms. Germany (DM 20,000), the UK (£10,000), and Italy (L 10 million) have all imposed specific limits on the amount of cash that can be deposited without filling out a form, while obliging bank staff to report any suspicions to the police. Some launderers have responded to these maximum deposits by recruiting teams of people whose sole task is to make small deposits at a number of different banks. These workers, known as "smurfs" in the criminal fraternity, will open multiple accounts in many branches to avoid detection.

Money laundering operations often cross national boundaries in an attempt to hinder investigators. New technology has made it easy to wire funds electronically across the globe, and some commentators believe that as much as $1,000 billion is transferred between the world's banks on a daily basis. The first attempt to counter global laundering began in Paris in 1989, when the heads of the G-7 industrialized countries met to discuss the problem. The countries invited customs staff, banking supervisors, and drug enforcement agents to be members of the Financial Action Task Force (FATF). Member countries of the Organization for Economic Cooperation and Development (OECD) were also invited to join.

The International Monetary Fund (IMF) estimated in 1996 that the business of crime is worth approximately $500 billion per year, equivalent to 2% of the world's economy.

See also RACKETEER INFLUENCED AND CORRUPT ORGANIZATIONS (RICO) ACT; WHITE COLLAR CRIME.

MONEY MARKET

The *Money Market* exists, primarily, for the trading of short-term debt securities. These securities include banker's acceptances (BAs), negotiable certificates of deposit, Eurodollar certificates of deposit, commercial paper, Treasury bills (T-bills), Federal Home Loan Bank discount notes, and discount notes from both the Federal National Mortgage Association and the Federal Farm Credit System.

Also considered a part of the money market are Fed Funds, and inter-bank and bank borrowing from the Federal Reserve Bank Window.

Repurchase agreements (repos) and reverse repurchase agreements are also considered to be part of the money market, but technically are agreements rather than securities.

The world's leading money market is in New York City, with London and Tokyo second and third, respectively. Maintaining constant contact among themselves allows money market traders to, whenever possible, take advantage of arbitrage situations. Arbitrage (the simultaneous buying and selling of a specific item or its equivalent in the same or separate market) helps worldwide money market prices remain uniform.

See also FEDERAL DISCOUNT RATE/FED FUNDS; MONEY MARKET FUND.

MONEY MARKET ACCOUNT

A *Money Market Account*, operating much like a no-load, open-end, mutual fund, invests in government securities, certificates of deposit, commercial paper, banker's acceptances, repurchase agreements, and other low-risk investments that benefit from high liquidity.

The value of money market funds remains constant at $1 per share and the interest paid fluctuates on a daily basis. Many money market funds also have check-writing privileges. Although they are not federally insured (by the Federal Deposit Insurance Corporation or the Federal Savings and Loan Insurance Corporation), some are insured privately.

Many brokerage firms offer money market funds attached to an account through which open cash balances are swept into the money market on a regular basis.

See also ASSET ACCOUNT; CASH ACCOUNT; MARGIN ACCOUNT.

MONEY SUPPLY

Primarily composed of the sum of circulating currency and savings and checking account deposits, the *Money Supply* is the total amount of money in an economy.

Since the early 1970s, controlling the money supply has been a favored method employed by many central governments in an attempt to control price increases. However, the quantity theory of money proposes that an increase in the money supply will be followed by a corresponding increase in inflation.

The money supply in the United States is divided into four basic categories. Each new category is inclusive of its predecessor. They are as follows:

M-1 circulating currency
       commercial bank demand deposits
       NOW and ATS (automatic transfer from
          savings accounts)
       credit union share drafts
       mutual savings bank demand deposits
       nonbank travelers checks

M-2 M-1
       overnight repurchase agreements issued by
          commercial banks
       overnight Eurodollars
       savings accounts
       time deposits under $100,000
       money market mutual fund shares

M-3 M-2
       time deposits over $100,000
       term repurchase agreements

L   M-3 plus other liquid assets such as:
    Treasury bills
    savings bonds
    commercial paper
    bankers' acceptances
    Eurodollar holdings of United States
        residents (nonbank)

See also FEDERAL DISCOUNT RATE/FED FUNDS; MONETARY POLICY; MONEY MARKET.

MONOPOLY

A *Monopoly* is the control of a market structure by one or a limited number of suppliers in order to prevent the entry of competitors to the market.

Monopolies enjoy the absence of competition, but as a result, have little motivation to meet the needs of consumers. The majority of monopolies have their origins in those services or products that are an essential part of a consumer's life. Food, electricity, heating fuel, telephone, and postal systems have all been or continue to be monopolies in some areas of the world.

Many countries have adopted strong antitrust laws to prevent the formation of new monopolies, while controlling others such as electricity, natural gas, and railroads, which are already in existence. In some cases, governments force monopolies to break apart into different companies and create a competitive situation. In theory, competition will force companies to improve products and supply services at reasonable prices, thereby benefiting the consumer and stimulating economic growth.

See also CAPITALISM; ECONOMICS; MONEY SUPPLY.

MOODY'S INVESTOR'S SERVICES (United States)

Formed by John Moody in 1903, *Moody's Investor's Services* provides analytical services. Merging with Dun & Bradstreet in 1961—but continuing to trade as a separate entity—Moody's originated the practice of rating investments with Moody's Bond Ratings, which are used by financial institutions and corporations for analysis.

Moody's provides several investment services including specialized research or economic advisory work for banks, brokers, financial institutions, companies, estates, pension funds, and individual investors.

The current list of periodicals published by Moody's includes:

Municipals and Governments
Banks and Finance
Industrials
OTC Industrials
Public Utilities
Transportation
International
Stock Survey
Bond Survey
Dividend Record
Bond Record
Advisory Reports
Handbook of Widely Held Common Stocks

Together with Standard & Poor's and Fitch, Moody's is one of the three prominent bond rating services of the United States. In fact, it is possibly more renowned for its bond and commercial paper rating than for the many other services it provides.

See also ANALYST; FITCH INVESTOR'S SERVICE INC.; FUNDAMENTAL ANALYSIS; RATING; STANDARD & POOR'S RATINGS; VALUE LINE INVESTMENT SURVEY.

MORGAN, J.P., AND COMPANY, INC.

J.P. Morgan and Company, Inc. is a holding company formed in 1969 whose subsidiaries engage in corporate financial advising, securities, trusts, and other financial services. At the end of 1996, J.P. Morgan and Company had $222 billion in assets and 15,527 employees.

Junius Spencer Morgan (J.P. Morgan's father) became an American officer in the influential London banking firm of George Peabody and Company in 1854. In 1864 Peabody retired and Morgan changed the name of the company to J.S. Morgan and Company. This bank became an important link between London and bankers in America.

In 1854, when J.P. Morgan was 17, he joined his father's banking house. In 1857 he was sent to New York to work for the firm Duncan, Sherman and Company. Duncan, Sherman was the correspondent of his father's firm. By 1860 J.P. Morgan had left Duncan, Sherman and founded J.P. Morgan and Company to act as agent for J.S. Morgan and Company. In 1864 Morgan asked Charles H. Dabney to become a senior partner in a new firm, which became Dabney, Morgan and Company.

In 1869 Morgan successfully took on Jay Gould and James Fisk (two of America's most notorious financial buccaneers) for control of the Albany and Susquehanna Railroad. This was the first of many battles, buyouts, and reorganizations—some done at government behest—stretching over the following 30 years, by the end of which J.P. Morgan had achieved control over the vast majority of U.S. railway systems. In 1879 Morgan arranged for the sale of $25 million worth of Vanderbilt interest in the New York Central railroad through his father's firm in England. This

J. P. Morgan, American banker and financier. *(Corbis)*

action gained Morgan a seat on the board of directors of the New York Central and the praise of Vanderbilt.

In 1886 Morgan implemented plans to reorganize both the Reading and Philadelphia railroads. He also implemented plans to reorganize the Chesapeake and Ohio railroads and later played an important role in reorganizing the Baltimore and Ohio Railroad.

After the Interstate Commerce Act was passed in 1887, Morgan helped to persuade the country's railroad executives to abide by the law and cooperate with the Interstate Commerce Commission. After the Panic of 1893, Morgan was called on by the government to reorganize a number of the leading railway systems in the nation, including the Southern, the Erie, the Philadelphia and Reading, and the Northern Pacific. By the end of the century only two American railroad systems were outside of J.P. Morgan's control.

When Junius Morgan died in 1890, J.P. Morgan became head of the London house. Three years later, Anthony Drexel also died, and in 1895 Morgan reorganized the Morgan and Drexel firms. New York-based Drexel Morgan became J.P. Morgan and Company, in which the Philadelphia-based Drexel and Company was partially merged.

Morgan was now an impressive figure in international finance as head of the houses in New York, Philadelphia, London, and Paris. In 1895 President Grover Cleveland turned to international bankers for help in controlling the flow of the U.S. Treasury's gold reserves. Morgan, with his connections to the European banking community, was able to help supply the government with $56 million in gold. Morgan's later refusal to answer questions at a congressional hearing regarding his profits was said to have contributed to Cleveland's fall from power in 1896.

Despite extremely high regard in which Morgan was already held by the American people, his power was further enhanced by publicity. Morgan had already organized the railroads and guided the Edison Electric Company through its infant stages. Ultimately, Morgan saw to the merger of the Edison Electric Company with the Thomson-Houston Electric Company to create the General Electric Company. Having accomplished all of this, Morgan turned to the steel industry.

In the late 1890s, Morgan helped to create the Federal Steel Company, the National Tube Company, and the American Bridge Company. Morgan also assisted in arranging the takeover of the giant Carnegie Steel Company to form the U.S. Steel Corporation in 1901. In 1902, Morgan financed the consolidation of five harvesting companies to form International Harvester Company.

As Morgan grew older he began to focus on banking and insurance (although his influence continued in a number of fields). Morgan owned a controlling interest in the First National Bank of New York and his bank's future partner, Guaranty Trust Company of New York. In 1909, he acquired controlling interest in the Equitable Assurance Society and already held a significant voice in the New York Life Insurance Company. Because of this the New York banking and insurance community feared Morgan's power, and a congressional investigation was instigated by the Pujo Committee in 1912. Although the committee attempted to measure the extent of Morgan and his associates' huge empire in banking, insurance, transportation, public utilities, and trade, it did not recommend that any action be taken.

J.P. Morgan died in 1913. His son J.P. Morgan Jr. (known as Jack) became the head of the family business. Morgan became the commercial agent for the French and British governments in the United States during World War I, accommodating orders for more than $3 billion in war supplies for France and Britain and organizing more than 2,000 banks to underwrite bonds for those two countries even before America entered the war. After the war the bank floated approximately $12 billion in bonds for these and other countries, thus helping finance reconstruction. In the postwar era, Morgan was the leading banker, as the United States became a creditor nation and the most important financial market in the world.

When the stock market crashed on 22 October 1929, J.P. Morgan and Company initiated a major attempt to avert financial disaster. A meeting was held in Morgan's office on 24 October with five major bankers to formulate a plan to stave off disaster by creating a pool to preserve order in the stock market. After the crash, J.P. Morgan and Company and the other companies involved were kept under close observation as the government tried to determine whether or not they had actually contributed to the stock market crash.

During the 1930s the bank underwent drastic changes. The Banking Act of 1933 (also known as the Glass-Steagall Act) required a separation of deposit and investment banking. As a result of this, in 1934 J.P. Morgan and Company left the investment banking business and became a private commercial bank. Some of its partners left to form Morgan Stanley and Company, which took over the investment banking.

Although Jack Morgan continued as head of the commercial bank, by the mid-1930s he had become chiefly a figurehead, with the actual management being handled by other partners. In 1940, J.P. Morgan and Company was incorporated as a state bank under the laws of New York and it began the sale of common stock on the New York Stock Exchange.

As a publicly owned, state-chartered bank, Morgan could now open a trust department (something private partnerships were not allowed to do). Morgan's new chairman, Thomas Lamont, formed the new entity, which soon became the new center of Morgan's power.

Jack Morgan died on 13 March 1943. His eldest son, Junius S. Morgan II, took over as director of the firm. During the late 1940s and 1950s, Morgan concentrated on its trust and wholesale banking; in 1959 Morgan shocked the world financial community by announcing the merger between J.P. Morgan and Company and Guaranty Trust Company of New York (GTC).

GTC itself had two predecessors: the New York Guaranty Trust and Indemnity Company, founded in 1864 and renamed the Guaranty Trust Company of New York in 1896, and the National Bank of Commerce, a subsidiary of the Bank of Commerce, founded in 1839. Initially, New York Guaranty Trust lent money against warehouse receipts. The National Bank of Commerce, also a commercial bank, mainly lent to manufacturers and traders. Both New York Guaranty Trust and National Commerce had close ties to J.P. Morgan and Company. J.P. Morgan was director of the National Bank of Commerce from 1875 to 1910. The merger in 1929 between New York Guaranty Trust and National Commerce worked to increase their strength and position in order to broaden the range of wholesale services they could offer. After the merger with J.P. Morgan and Company, Inc., the new bank, Morgan Guaranty Trust, was one of the largest and most prominent trust banks in New York.

In 1960 Morgan Guaranty Trust established the Morgan Guaranty International Banking Corporation and Morgan Guaranty International Finance Corporation to further its expansion in international markets. In 1961 Morgan Guaranty Trust made an attempt to enter retail banking. The Federal Reserve rejected the plan in 1962, however, fearing that the move would create too great a power concentration. The plan involved a proposed affiliation with six upstate New York banks. In 1968 it set up the Euroclear System, based in Brussels, which went on to facilitate the distribution, clearance, and settlement of Eurobonds on behalf of hundreds of banks, brokers, and investment institutions. In 1969 the J.P. Morgan and Company

holding company was created and Morgan Guaranty Trust became one of its wholly owned subsidiaries.

The 3 foreign branches that J.P. Morgan and Company had at the time of its merger jumped to 26 branches and representative offices by 1978. By the late 1970s Morgan's total assets equaled $43.5 billion dollars. The firm by now had become the largest stockholder in America, with more than $15 billion invested in the stock market in companies such as IBM, Sears, and Citicorp.

The 1980s saw tremendous change in the banking industry as major companies more often than not chose to raise their own capital in the securities markets rather than to aquire it from the banks. Through its subsidiaries, J.P. Morgan and Company put renewed emphasis on investment and merchant banking and achieved notable success in international corporate finance and mergers and acquisitions advisory, and was involved in some of the largest cross-border and U.S. transactions of the year. Also, in the late 1980s Morgan's London-based securities subsidiary, J.P. Morgan Securities Ltd., was given greater leeway to invest and underwrite both corporate debt and equity. By the mid-1990s, J.P. Morgan and Company had offices in seven U.S. cities and 35 other countries.

Morgan Guaranty Trust, as before, continued to emphasize low-risk, high-quality, high-return ventures, focusing on work with corporations, governments, and wealthy individuals. Compared to other banks, its rate of profit was very high, particularly in Europe, where it was active in international bonds, futures, gold, energy financing, ship mortgage lending, and commodities trading.

J.P. Morgan and Company continues to be the "blue blood" of American banks. Its capital strength and long-established reputation for high ethical standards have been valuable advantages as the markets of the world become more competitive. J.P. Morgan and Company, Inc. has emerged as a front-runner in the world's most active capital markets as an adviser to governments and international corporations, and the provider of innovative services.

See also MORGAN GRENFELL GROUP PLC; MORGAN STANLEY, DEAN WITTER, DISCOVER & COMPANY (MWD).

MORGAN GRENFELL GROUP PLC

Morgan Grenfell Group PLC has been one of the most prestigious names in the City of London for 150 years. Its history was shaped by some of the great personalities of banking lore, and its fortunes were dependent on wars, international trade, banking booms, and economic recessions. It lost its indepen-

Line engraving of George Peabody, founder of Morgan Grenfell Group PLC. *(Courtesy of Peabody Trust)*

dence because of greed and an apparent disregard for business ethics and company law.

The roots of Morgan Grenfell can be traced to the famous American trader George Peabody, who operated a successful import and export business with branches in Baltimore, New York, and Philadelphia. In 1838 Peabody, the son of a leather worker from Massachusetts, opened a London branch to import cotton, textiles, and tobacco into the United Kingdom. The demand for his services led the entrepreneurial Peabody to open a counting house and a currency exchange. Like his contemporaries in the trading world, Rothschilds and Barings, Peabody soon discovered that there was more profit in money brokering than in transporting corn to Ireland and spices from Asia. In 1851 the house of George Peabody and Company was established to deal in securities rather than commodities.

In 1854 Peabody accepted his fellow American, Junius Spencer Morgan, into the partnership and took a less high-profile role. Peabody increasingly devoted his time and considerable fortune to charitable work, and many Peabody buildings designed for the working class still remain in central London. When Peabody formally retired in 1864 the firm was renamed J.S. Morgan and Company. The end of the U.S. Civil War caused a boom in railroad construction and domestic and civic rebuilding. Expansion into the lucrative field of lending to foreign governments began when J.S. Morgan arranged financing for Chile in 1867 and France in 1870.

Junius Morgan introduced his son, J. Pierpont Morgan, to the banking world, and the firm forged a number of important alliances. Pierpont Morgan was admitted into the partnership of Drexel and Company, based in New York, and the two partnerships began to refer significant amounts of work to each other. The industrialization of the United States and the Latin American boom provided opportunities for many bankers and merchants. The spread of the railways, the building of new factories, and improved standards of infrastructure all demanded equity capital and loan financing. With the passage of time, the U.S. operation became more important than the London office, and Pierpont Morgan became senior partner upon the death of his father in 1890.

The firm's success in North America and Latin America and the relatively lackluster performance of the London partnership led to a certain amount of frustration on the part of the aggressive Pierpont Morgan. A planned merger with Barings, which had seen most of its capital destroyed after a period of reckless lending in Argentina, was tentatively proposed but firmly rejected. E.C. Grenfell was admitted into the partnership in 1904, and a new partnership called Morgan Grenfell and Company was established in 1909. The American firm, called J.P. Morgan and Company since 1893, took a half stake in Morgan Grenfell in exchange for £1 million in equity capital.

During World War I Morgan Grenfell and J.P. Morgan worked closely together to finance the war effort and to organize supplies for those countries opposed to the German forces. J.P. Morgan was estimated to have lent more than $1.5 billion to the governments of Britain, France, and Russia during the war. When the war ended, Morgan Grenfell took a full part in the financial restructuring of the European economy and helped with the important task of currency stabilization. The period between the wars was a time of unprecedented turmoil in the financial markets, with hyperinflation in Germany, food shortages in Eastern Europe, and a damaging general strike in England. Morgan Grenfell became heavily involved with advising industrial companies, particularly those involved in steel manufacturing.

In common with many of their merchant banking colleagues, the partners of Morgan Grenfell encountered both problems and profits during World War II. The demand for financing increased dramatically as the Allies fought a long, drawn-out campaign on several fronts. In 1953 Morgan Grenfell took a major part in the postwar denationalization of UK industry and was especially involved in returning the steel industry to private hands. Morgan Grenfell, which was known as the "steel house" in some circles, had such a firm grip over the UK manufacturing sector that it accounted for more than half of the debt issues for industrial companies during the 1950s.

Edward Grenfell had died in 1941 and his replacement, Vivian Smith, traveled abroad extensively to build up the firm's overseas network. Smith was in turn replaced by Lord Catto in 1956. The 1960s saw a slight retrenchment in foreign business for the bank, largely as a result of the restrictions placed by successive governments on foreign exchange. Sir John Stevens, who was managing director from 1967 to 1973, counteracted the exchange controls by expanding the bank's operations in Europe, Africa, and Asia. Expansion into North and South America, however, was not without its problems, and the increasing competition between Morgan Grenfell and its U.S. correspondent, J.P. Morgan, led to an ending of the formal partnership between the two firms. In 1981 J.P. Morgan sold its stake in Morgan Grenfell to a number of institutional investors in the City of London.

The character of Morgan Grenfell changed during the 1980s as the "Big Bang" exploded in the City of London. The Big Bang promised an end to fixed commissions on stock market deals and encouraged competition among the different stockbroking houses. Large UK retail banks and foreign investment banks were actively encouraged to enter the City. New capital would increase profits, and firms would be free to act as both agent and principal in transactions. The years between the first announcement of the planned changes and the actual Big Bang on 27 October 1986 saw frantic deal-making between the established City firms and the new entrants, as corporations jockeyed for a position in the new market. In 1984 Morgan Grenfell bought the stock jobber Pinchin and Denny and the gilt-edged broker Pember and Boyle. External capital came from Deutsche Bank, which bought a 4% stake that same year. The importance of pleasing external owners became even more marked when the bank became a listed company, the Morgan Grenfell Group PLC, in February 1986.

The downfall of Morgan Grenfell was the takeover of the Scottish brewers Distillers by Arthur Guinness and Sons. Ernest Saunders, the chief executive of Guinness, had developed a close relationship with Roger Seelig, a senior banker at Morgan Grenfell who had a rising reputation as a dynamic and entrepreneurial corporate financier. The two worked frantically to seize Distillers from the clutches of a rival bidder, Argyll, and were prepared to put City rules and regulations to the test. In a move that ran contrary to the rather genteel spirit of the old City, a series of advertisements that disparaged Argyll were issued. Morgan Grenfell bought £70 million worth of shares in Distillers and received an indemnity against loss; the Bank of England responded to this purchase by announcing measures that prohibited a merchant bank from supporting the share price of a client.

Guinness proposed to pay for its acquisition of Distillers with an exchange of new Guinness shares. The market value of Guinness shares would be all-important, and Saunders and Seelig hatched a plan to ensure that the price of the shares stayed high. A number of insiders were recruited into a "fan club," a group of individuals who were indemnified against any fall in the share price if they continued to buy the shares. Mercury Asset Management offered a large tranche of shares in Distillers to the highest bidder. Seelig phoned Tom Ward, a nonexecutive director at Guinness, and asked him to arrange immediate payment for the shares. The chairman of Bank Leu in Switzerland, Dr. Arthur Furer, was contacted, and he sent £76 million to Guinness in exchange for a fee and an indemnity against loss. The actions of Furer, who was also a nonexecutive director on the Guinness board, guaranteed that Guinness would hold the majority of shares in Distillers.

The share support operation came to an end when members of the fan club tried to sell their shares. In November 1986 the Securities and Exchange Commission (SEC) in the United States announced that Ivan Boesky had admitted to insider dealing in a number of cases. Boesky provided the SEC with information on the Guinness affair and the SEC passed this information to the Department of Trade and Industry (DTI). On 1 December, DTI inspectors visited the head offices of Guinness, Morgan Grenfell, and Cazenove. The announcement of the raid on City dealing screens instantly cut 35 pence from the Guinness share price. The Morgan Grenfell press office hurriedly denied that insider dealing and illegal share supporting had been essential features of the Guinness bid.

On 30 December Seelig resigned, complaining that he was made into the scapegoat for the actions of others. The Bank of England threatened to suspend Morgan Grenfell's banking license and demanded the resignation of senior staff at the merchant bank. A lengthy series of legal cases followed the investigation, and Saunders and several members of the fan club were imprisoned and fined.

The Guinness affair destroyed Morgan Grenfell's long-held reputation. The diversification into international equities and gilts was generally held to be unsuccessful, and the bank withdrew from these activities to concentrate on corporate finance and banking. In 1989 Deutsche Bank took control of the bank, and now the once-proud firm lives on only in the name of the wholly owned subsidiary, Deutsche Morgan Grenfell.

There are two published versions of the Morgan Grenfell story that can be recommended. Kathleen Burk, a history professor at University College, London, relies heavily on the extensive archive kept by the bank for her book, *Morgan Grenfell 1838–1988: The Biography of a Merchant Bank*. An alternative history, which is especially detailed when describing the Guinness affair, is presented in Dominic Hobson's *The Pride of Lucifer, Morgan Grenfell 1838–1988: The Unauthorized Biography of a Merchant Bank*.

See also BIG BANG; DREXEL BURNHAM LAMBERT; GUINNESS TRIAL; MORGAN, J.P., & COMPANY.

MORGAN GUARANTY TRUST

See MORGAN, J.P., & COMPANY.

MORGAN STANLEY, DEAN WITTER, DISCOVER AND COMPANY (MWD)

In mid-1997 the Morgan Stanley Group, Inc., one of the world's top investment banking firms, merged with Dean Witter, Discover and Company, a leader in securities and credit services, to form *Morgan Stanley, Dean Witter, Discover and Company (MWD)*. The merger created the largest securities firm in the United States, with a market capitalization of $21 billion. MWD is a leader in three primary businesses—securities, asset management, and credit and transaction services—and has 409 offices in 22 countries.

MWD's securities business provides a wide range of products and services to both the institutional and individual investor. Such investment banking activities as equity and debt underwriting and mergers and acquisitions are carried out by Morgan Stanley, as are most institutional securities activities. Dean Witter caters primarily to individual investors through more than 9,000 account executives in approximately 370 branch offices. Dean Witter has more than 3 million securities clients and had record assets of $271 billion in June 1997.

MWD had approximately $303 billion in assets under management and administration in June 1997. Asset management is offered to individuals primarily through Dean Witter InterCapital and Van Campen American Capital. Asset management is provided to institutions primarily through Morgan Stanley. As of June 1997, assets under supervision were $410 billion, reflecting in part the April acquisition of Barclay's global custody business. MWD also participates in merchant banking through its holdings of Ford Howard Corporation, which announced in 1997 its merger with James River Corporation. MWD's credit and transaction services business is conducted through four business units: (1) NOVUS Services, which markets the Discover, the BRAVO, and the Private Issue credit cards, (2) Prime Option Services, which markets the cobranded Prime Option MasterCard, (3) SPS Transactional Services, and (4) NOVUS Financial Corporation. In number of accounts, MWD's credit services is the largest single issuer of general purpose credit cards in the United States, with over 38 million accounts in 1997 reaching about one-third of U.S. households. SPS Transaction Services is a publicly held subsidiary that is 74% owned by MWD. NOVUS Financial Corporation is a consumer finance company concentrated in real estate-secured lending.

Chronology of Significant Events

1920s Dean Witter, his brother Guy, and cousin Jean found a securities firm dealing in corporate and municipal bonds in San Francisco (1924). Dean Witter purchases its first seat on the San Francisco Stock Exchange, which later becomes part of the Pacific Stock Exchange (1928). Dean Witter and Company opens a New York office and purchases a seat on the New York Stock Exchange (1929).

1930s In response to the Banking Act of 1933, which prohibited commercial banks from engaging in investment banking activities, J.P. Morgan and Company divests itself of its investment banking operations, which are organized as Morgan Stanley (1935).

1940s Stock market and investment banking activity is dormant during World War II. Morgan Stanley restructures from a corporation to a partnership in order to join the New York Stock Exchange (1941). After the war, as the economy resurges and capital markets expand, Dean Witter and Company and Morgan Stanley resume their growth.

1950s Morgan Stanley participates in European reconstruction by co-managing an offering of triple-A rated bonds issued by the World Bank (1952). Dean Witter acquires its first international office in Geneva, Switzerland (1959).

1960s Morgan Stanley and Morgan Guaranty Trust form Morgan and Cie International in Paris (1967). Dean Witter and Company, a California partnership, becomes Dean Witter and Company, Inc., a Delaware corporation (1968).

1970s Dean Witter and Company goes public (1972). Morgan Stanley shifts its primary focus from underwriting to expanded market activities and develops a mergers and acquisitions division. In the largest merger in the U.S. securities industry at that time, Dean Witter joins with Reynolds Securities International to form Dean Witter Reynolds, Inc. (1978).

1980s Dean Witter Reynolds, Inc. joins Sears Roebuck and Company as the nucleus of its financial services network (1981). Dean Witter Financial Services launches Discover Card (1985). Dean Witter Financial Services Group restructures, forming three separate business units—Discover Card Services, Inc., Dean Witter Financial, and Dean Witter Capital (1989). Morgan Stanley goes public and accelerates its international expansion, opening offices in Sydney, Melbourne, Zurich, Frankfurt, Hong Kong, Milan, and Luxembourg, and expanding its operations in London and Tokyo.

1990s Dean Witter Financial Services Group changes its name to Dean Witter, Discover and Company and becomes an independent, publicly traded company (1992). Sears sells 20% of its equity in Dean Witter, Discover and Company to the public and plans to spin off the remaining 80% to Sears shareholders. Morgan Stanley continues its global expansion by opening offices in Singapore, Paris, Taipei, Madrid, Seoul, Shanghai, Johannesburg, Geneva, Bombay, Moscow, Beijing, São Paulo, and Mexico City. Morgan Stanley and Dean Witter, Discover and Company merge.

See also MORGAN GRENFELL GROUP PLC; MORGAN, J.P., & COMPANY; WARBURG DYNASTY.

MOROCCO, KINGDOM OF

Morocco (al-Mamlakah al-Maghribiyah) is a country located on the northwestern corner of Africa. It is bordered on the east and southeast by Algeria, and on the south by the Western Sahara.

Area: 177,117 square miles (458,730 square km)

Population: 26,980,000 (48.4% urban; 51.6% rural)

Form of Government: Constitutional monarchy, with one legislative house: House of Representatives— 333. Chief of state: King. Head of government: King assisted by Prime Minister.

Official Language: Arabic

Capital: Rabat

Largest Cities: Casablanca, 2,943,000; Rabat, 1,220,000; Fes, 564,000

Economy:

Currency: Dirham (DH)

National Budget: Revenue—DH 89.8 billion; expenditures—DH 93.4 billion (current expenditure: 50.4%; debt payments: 29.1%; investment expenditures: 20.4%)

Public Debt: US$20.3 billion

Gross National Product: US$27.6 billion

Principal Products: Barley, wheat, sugar beets; oranges, sugarcane, and other fruits and vegetables; livestock; consumer goods

Foreign Trade (Imports): DH 66.1 billion (capital goods: 27.6%; food, beverages, and tobacco: 14.5%, of which wheat: 5.3%; consumer goods: 10.9%; crude oil: 10.8%; from France: 23.0%; Spain: 10.5%; United States: 10.1%; Italy: 6.3%; Germany: 5.9%; United Kingdom: 2.7%; Iran: 2.5%)

Foreign Trade (Exports): DH 36.8 billion (consumer goods: 28.8%, of which clothing: 11.7%; food: 26.1%, of which fresh, canned, and frozen fish: 14.4%; minerals: 10.2%, of which phosphates: 7.0%; to France: 33.3%; Spain: 8.8%; Japan: 5.6%; Italy: 5.2%; Germany: 4.4%; India: 3.9%; United Kingdom: 3.6%)

Stock Exchanges: 1

Casablanca Stock Exchange (CSE; Bourse des Valeurs de Casablanca)
Avenue de l'Armée Royale
Casablanca
Morocco
Phone: (212-2) 45 26 26
Fax: (212-2) 45 26 25

Internet Address: www.mbendi.co.za/exmo

Trading Hours: Monday–Friday, 11:00 to 12:15

Office Hours: Monday–Friday, 8:30 to 12:00 and 2:30 to 6:30

Exchange Holidays:

1 January	7, 8, 9 July
3 March	14, 20 August
8, 9, 28 May	6, 18 November

Listed Companies: 49

Market Capitalization: US$6.0 billion

Major Sectors: Banking, leisure, finance, holding companies

History: The roots of the Casablanca Stock Exchange date back to the establishment of a private stock exchange in 1929. The Moroccan government assumed control of the Casablanca exchange in 1948. An open-outcry trading system was used through the 1950s and 1960s. Substantial reforms began in the early 1970s, and the government has recently passed laws to increase the level of regulation. The CSE was privatized in 1995.

Classes of Securities: Ordinary shares, government obligations, and other securities

Indices: CFG 25 Index

Trading: Open-outcry auction method of floor trading

Investor Taxation:
No capital gains tax
Dividends have a 10% withholding tax

Limitations: None

Regional Exchanges: None

Company Information:

10 Most Active Companies

Name of Company	Trading Value (US$ in millions)
Banque Commercials du Maroc	270.66
BMCE	241.97
SNI	198.34
ONA	115.83
Wafabank	103.62
Brasseries do Maroc	41.61
Lesieur	25.37
Credit Eqdom	25.01
Credit du Maroc	24.90
BMCI	24.19

10 Major Companies

Name of Company	Market Capitalization (US$ in millions)
Banque Commercials du Maroc	765.38
ONA	670.90
SNI	789.39
BMCE	462.36
Credit du Maroc	344.04
Cosumar	308.00
Brasseries do Marocq	276.47
Lesieur	275.16
BNDE	248.96
Wafabank	239.36

Other Investment Information:

Office of Industrial Development (ODI)
10 Rue Ghandi
PO Box 211
Rabat
Morocco
Phone: (212-7) 70 84 60
Fax: (212-7) 70 76 95
Telex: 36053

Moroccan Center for Export Promotion (CMPE)
23 Boulevard Giradot
Casablanca
Morocco
Phone: (212-7) 30 22 10
Fax: (212-7) 30 17 93
Telex: 27847

La Fédération des Chambres du Commerce et
    d'Industries du Maroc

56 Avenue de France
Rabat
Morocco
Phone: (212-7) 76 52 30
Telex: 31884

MOZER, PAUL

Paul Mozer was one of the most successful traders in government bonds at the U.S. brokers Salomon Inc. during the great boom years of the 1980s. His part in the wrongdoing that surrounded the auction of U.S. Treasury bonds in February 1991 cost Salomon heavy fines and severely damaged the bank's reputation. When Salomon publicly admitted that the auction had been rigged, its share price fell by 30% and several major institutional clients were lost.

The abuse of the Treasury bond market struck a particular resonance in the United States. Salomon was America's primary dealer of U.S. bonds, and, since the end of World War I, no firm had raised more money for successive U.S. governments. The public had almost become accustomed to scandals in the junk bond market, but allegations of market rigging and record falsification in the normally spotless world of government bond trading were a shocking revelation.

The 1980s started in difficult fashion for Salomon. The partners of the firm decided to follow Wall Street's trend and incorporate as a limited liability company. The new entity would protect partners from unlimited liability in the event of heavy losses, but also introduced a new class of external shareholders who were not part of the day-to-day running of the business. The senior partners at Salomon faced two vital challenges. First, employees who were denied the lure of a partnership would have to be appropriately rewarded to prevent their defection to competitors. Second, a division of profits between the workers who earned it and the shareholders who provided the capital had to be agreed upon.

Some commentators believe that the Mozer scandal could have been avoided if top management had paid more attention to these issues. Instead, their attempts to please all parties led to an atmosphere of suspicion, lack of cooperation, and mutual distrust.

The partners sold the partnership to Phibro, a large commodities trading company, for $550 million in 1981. A new company, called Phibro-Salomon, was set up and Salomon's partners were rewarded with cash payments, shares in Phibro-Salomon, and large salaries. (By 1986 the charismatic chairman of Salomon, John Gutfreund, and his former partners were so dominant in the new entity that its name was changed to Salomon Inc.) The external capital raised by Salomon ensured its position as a global player and provided the finance to make large profits on proprietary trading, but the end of the partnership structure also gave rise to some less tangible losses.

Partnerships bred loyalty and a strong team ethic, with the promise of riches acting as a powerful motivating force. Retiring partners relied on the capital they had invested in the firm for their pension and therefore had a vested interest in the continued success of the business. But those senior employees who were denied the chance to attain partnership were less pleased with their lot. Appeasement came in the form of a "phantom share" scheme. One hundred top executives were allotted a stake in a cash pool that would grow in line with the firm's share price. Any member of the scheme who left Salomon, Inc. within five years would lose his or her stake.

The mid-1980s were great years for Salomon. The large debts of the U.S. government and the flurry of debt-funded corporate takeovers occasioned heavy demand for bond trading and the underwriting of new issues. In the four years from 1982 to 1986 Salomon's annual revenues grew from $2 billion to $5 billion. The heady atmosphere of bond trading, and the excesses it led to, are entertainingly described in Michael Lewis's book *Liar's Poker*. Salaries and bonuses soared and the size of the phantom share pot grew from $30 million in 1981 to $100 million by the mid-1980s. Pool members, however, soon began to quarrel about how the cash should be divided.

The bond traders were disgruntled by the concept of equal shares in the pool for the rest of the firm. Their department consistently made more money than the equities division and the investment banking arm of Salomon and they felt they should take the lion's share of the fund. The global stock market crash of 1987 abruptly ended Salomon's boom years. Bonuses were cut for the first time since the firm went public and the arguments about the pool intensified.

John Meriwether, a former academic who had built up the spectacularly successful bond-arbitrage desk at Salomon Inc., felt particularly aggrieved. Unlike many senior executives at the company, Meriwether was a proponent of strict budgeting and genuinely performance-related pay. His department made more

Paul Mozer (center) leaves the federal courthouse in New York after being arraigned on charges stemming from the Salomon Brothers Inc. Treasury bond scandal, 7 January 1993. *(AP/Wide World Photos)*

money than the rest of the firm, and he demanded increased compensation. John Gutfreund was faced with the difficult task of keeping many aggressive and money-oriented people happy. His solution proved disastrous. In 1990 he secretly allowed the arbitrage desk to keep 15% of its own profits to fund a separate, and highly confidential, performance-related pay scheme. Many of the traders received bonuses of $10 million; Lawrence Hildebrand, who had taken over from Meriwether as head of arbitrage, was paid $23 million.

Of course, the supposedly secret bonus pool soon became common knowledge at Salomon, Inc. Paul Mozer was a highly-rated trader who had moved from the bond arbitrage desk to head up the government bonds trading desk. He was angry that he had missed out on the huge bonuses in his former department, and Mozer convinced Gutfreund that the profit share deal he had covertly offered the arbitrageurs should be extended to all traders. Mozer now saw the way to huge profits for himself and his department.

In 1991 Mozer was involved in a series of transactions that baffled the markets. In February Salomon submitted a fake bid in the name of Mercury Asset Management for an auction of bonds. Mozer's actions broke the Securities and Exchange Commission rules that prohibit a single bidder from dominating the auction market, and he was subsequently shown to have falsified records to cover up the transaction. No single firm was allowed to buy more than 35% of an issue of bonds. In December 1990, however, Salomon placed a bid for 35% of the issue and also put in a $1 billion bid in the name of a customer. It subsequently transpired that the customer had not authorized the bank to bid on its behalf and Salomon ended up with 48% of the issue. In February the ruse was repeated, and this time the bank walked away with 57% of the issue. Similar transactions occurred in April.

In May, Salomon Inc. put in a 35% bid for its own account and also acted as an agent for two large institutional clients. Mozer, in his capacity as both principal and agent, now owned 85% of the issue. Other firms who wanted to buy into the issue were caught out by the restricted supply, and the price of the bonds increased sharply. Salomon made a large, instant profit of which Mozer would be guaranteed a healthy slice.

Worse still, Gutfreund stayed silent on the matter and was widely believed to be attempting to cover up the deals. In August Salomon admitted that Gutfreund, Meriwether, and the firm's president, Thomas Strauss, had all known of Mozer's irregularities since April.

The well-known investor Warren Buffett had been Salomon's largest shareholder since 1987. He publicly expressed his displeasure at the remuneration squabble at the bank, acerbically pointing out that while Salomon employees were the most expensive of any company within the Standard and Poor's Index of the top 500 corporates in the United States, the return to shareholders was toward the bottom of the list.

Mozer was forced to resign, and Gutfreund and Meriwether soon followed suit. Buffet became emergency chairman and publicly stated his dissatisfaction with Gutfreund and his colleagues. Salomon, Inc. set up new management reporting structures and redrew its performance agreements. Senior staff were now offered shares in the company at a discounted price and the phantom share schemes were abandoned. Buffet, who had kept his dignity throughout the whole affair, was pleased to see his concepts on management and ownership achieve acceptance at the company. Staff were financially encouraged to remain loyal to the firm, but shareholders' interests were also considered.

See also GUTFREUND, JOHN; *LIAR'S POKER*; SALOMON INC.

MULTINATIONAL COMPANY (MNC)

A *Multinational Company (MNC)* is a company that has at least one production facility or other fixed asset in a foreign country, and makes corporate decisions in an international context. All decisions regarding marketing and production, as well as research and development and labor relations, are made with regard to the customs, laws, and traditions of the host country.

In addition to normal business risks, MNCs must be prepared to take on additional levels of financial risk (e.g., devaluation, inflation, exchange rate), economic risk, political instability risk, and legal risk, as well as the social risk of operating in an unfamiliar environment.

See also CONGLOMERATE; EXCHANGE RATE; INTEREST/ INTEREST RATES.

MULTIPLE

See PRICE/EARNINGS RATIO.

MULTIPLE LISTING

Listing shares on more than one stock exchange is referred to as *Multiple Listing*. Shares might be listed on several stock exchanges within a single country or listed on several stock exchanges in different countries.

Multiple listing not only offers the advantage of added liquidity to the shares of a company but also can benefit a company by creating a feeling of goodwill within the foreign country on whose exchange the shares are listed.

The company may list its securities as ordinary shares, international depository receipts, or global depository receipts in non-domestic countries.

See also AMERICAN DEPOSITORY RECEIPTS/SHARES (ADR); EUROPEAN DEPOSITORY RECEIPTS (EDR); GLOBAL DEPOSITORY RECEIPTS (GDR).

MUTILATED SECURITY

A *Mutilated Security* is a paper certificate so badly damaged that it cannot be considered good delivery. In such cases it becomes the obligation of the seller to obtain a guarantee of the rights of ownership from the transfer agent.

Damage to paper certificates is one of the disadvantages of a certificate-based system. If the certificates are old, it can take time to research the changes and find out which firm is currently acting as the transfer agent. Payment for the sale of such securities cannot be achieved until the shares are in good delivery form.

The increasing popularity of electronic computer book-entry systems alleviates this problem.

See also BOOK-ENTRY; CERTIFICATE; GOOD DELIVERY; SETTLE.

MUTUAL FUND

A *Mutual Fund* is an investment company that manages a portfolio of securities for individuals or institutional investors. Portfolios are assembled according to a variety of interests or investment objectives and are actively managed by a professional portfolio manager.

The main advantages of a mutual fund are:

Diversification: The money is spread among the shares of several companies, thereby protecting investors from the risk of any one company suffering a decline.

Ease: The money is easily invested, with additional amounts added in small quantities on a regular basis, therefore allowing investors to take advantage of dollar cost averaging.

Variety: The wide variety of funds allows the investor to select the fund of greatest interest, whether for income, growth, total return, or aggressive growth speculation.

Professional fund management: The performance of the fund is the responsibility of a professional investor who has an understanding of the stock market.

Easy access to funds: Money can be accessed at any time, but may be subject to regular-way settlement.

The greatest risk to mutual funds is the risk of a fall in the overall market. There can be no protection for investors from an overall decline in the stock market.

See also MARGIN; SHARES; UNIT INVESTMENT TRUST/ UNIT TRUST.

MUTUAL FUND CUSTODIAN

Mutual Fund Custodian refers to any commercial bank or trust company that holds money and securities owned by a mutual fund in safekeeping. The custodian can also act as a transfer agent, managing the details of investor buying and selling, as well as a disbursing agent for payments from the mutual fund. The custodian takes care of the basic maintenance services necessary for the operation of a mutual fund.

Custodians are required to qualify under the provisions of the U.S. Investment Company Act of 1940. They charge a fee to the mutual fund for the custodial services provided.

See also MUTUAL FUND; UNIT INVESTMENT TRUST/ UNIT TRUST.

N

N/A

The initials *N/A* (N.A., n.a.) refer to information that is not available or to statistics that are not applicable. Sometimes, earnings reports will include a note that states certain figures were not available.

The N/A notation can also denote an issue will not be available to the public. On occasions, entire issues of shares have only one buyer.

See also EARNINGS REPORT; INITIAL PUBLIC OFFERING (IPO).

NAAMLOZE VENNOOTSCHAP (NV; The Netherlands)

A *Naamloze Vennootschap (NV)* is a public limited company whose shares are listed on the Amsterdam Stock Exchange.

See also NETHERLANDS, THE.

NADIR, ASIL

The collapse of Polly Peck was one of the most spectacular corporate insolvencies of the 1980s. The company had grown from a tiny fruit exporter to a large conglomerate that was the darling of the UK stock market. Shares in Polly Peck, which were worth only five and half pence in 1979, reached £23 each by 1982. Its success, and subsequent failure, were largely dependent on one man, *Asil Nadir.*

Nadir was Turkish; his family had left the Mediterranean island of Cyprus in 1959 when it became clear that British forces would withdraw and the Greek population would gain greater control over the political affairs of the island. Nadir established a garment business in cramped premises in the East End of London. His years of struggling to make money in the cutthroat world of textiles ended when Turkish forces illegally invaded the north of Cyprus in 1974, and the land stolen from Greek-Cypriots ended up in Turkish hands. The opportunistic Nadir ended up controlling a packaging plant that processed the citrus fruits that grew in abundance in Cyprus.

Nadir's conspicuous success was noticed by the Turkish political leader, Turgut Ozal, who offered him a number of opportunities on the economically backward Turkish mainland. Fruit-growing farms were set up to export produce to the European Community and the Middle East. Nadir also diversified Polly Peck into low-priced consumer electronics and mass tourism.

Political success was guaranteed when Nadir bought two newspapers and a magazine that were pro-Ozal.

The company's share price jumped more than a thousand-fold in ten years, and it was soon a constituent of the Financial Times-Stock Exchange (FT-SE) Index. Among the operations owned by Polly Peck, the best performing stock of the 1980s, were Del Monte, a fresh fruit business, and Sansui, a Japanese electronics company.

On 17 August 1990 the stock exchange announced that it was requesting Nadir to explain the suspicious circumstances surrounding his attempt to turn the publicly quoted Polly Peck back into a private company. The surveillance unit of the exchange, which was commonly referred to as the insider dealing group, had spent much time investigating trading in Polly Peck shares and an illegal share support operation that appeared to have been in operation for several months.

The Serious Fraud squad raided Nadir's luxurious offices in September 1990 after it received information from both the stock exchange and the Inland Revenue. Shares in Polly Peck collapsed as the market digested the news that one of the great growth stocks of recent years had been an illusion. It was later publicized that for several years the stock exchange had been investigating manipulation of the Polly Peck share price by a group of Switzerland-based nominee companies that were linked to Nadir.

Many of the reasons for Polly Peck's failure can be attributed to Nadir's personal shortcomings. Like many businessmen who succeeded during the boom years of the 1980s, he became obsessed with his image to the detriment of his company. A number of interviews in prominent newspapers gave Nadir the opportunity to present himself as a sophisticate who wore expensive suits, bought fine art, and socialized with the European aristocracy. The truth was less impressive, and Nadir became distracted by the effort required to keep up his facade of urbanity. His refusal to delegate and an inability to accept that he needed help to run such a large business eventually cost him dearly.

Nadir's cavalier approach to accounting standards also planted the seeds of destruction for Polly Peck. A large portion of the company's profits appeared to arise from its fruit interests in Turkey and the illegally occupied Turkish enclave in Northern Cyprus. Because of rampant inflation in Turkey the Turkish

Asil Nadir. *(AP/Wide World Photos)*

lira was constantly devalued during the 1980s and early 1990s. The significant losses that Polly Peck incurred on these foreign exchange transactions were not revealed in its profit and loss statements but were hidden in the reserves section of the balance sheet. The net effect was to persuade investors that the company was profitable even though its earning power was largely an illusion.

Polly Peck, which had been one of the star performers on the London Stock Exchange in the early 1980s, was placed into administration in October 1990 with estimated debts of £1.15 billion. One of the companies in the Polly Peck groups, a fruit business called Meyna, was discovered to have a turnover equal to only one-fifth of the amount claimed for it in the group accounts. Auditors, accountants, and analysts were all taken in by Nadir's smooth charm and plausible explanations, even though some of his deceptions should have put them on alert.

A quick check of records at Sunzest, the fruit exporter based in northern Cyprus, would have shown that the company claimed to export more oranges than were grown on the whole of the island. Polly Peck's external auditors, Stoy Hayward, were widely criticized for overlooking the inconsistencies in the firm's accounts.

The collapse of Polly Peck gave rise to one of the most complicated liquidations ever seen. The Turkish Cypriot authorities refused to allow the liquidators to sell Nadir's assets to pay off investors who had been duped by the phenomenal price rise in Polly Peck shares. The company owned two hotels, eight apartment blocks, a citrus fruit packing unit, and a factory that made cardboard boxes. Two partners of Cork Gully, the insolvency arm of Coopers and Lybrand that led the investigation, were found guilty of professional misconduct by the Institute of Chartered Accountants in England and Wales. The partners had not revealed a potentially serious conflict of interest in their relationship with Nadir.

A team of liquidators from the accountants Touche Ross who worked with Cork Gully discovered secret payments made by companies controlled by Nadir to the Conservative party. The donations, with a minimum value of £130,000, showed that Nadir's simple methods of gaining political credibility were as effective in Whitehall as they had been in Istanbul.

The investigation and trial uncovered a number of amazing subplots. A liquidator working on the case was shot in Northern Cyprus by an unknown assailant. A little-known novelist forged a letter that implied a relationship between two Conservative ministers, David Mellor and Kenneth Baker, and Nadir. The let-

ter, which purported to thank Nadir for his donations to the Conservative party, was offered for sale to two tabloid newspapers in the United Kingdom.

A Tory Member of Parliament, Michael Mates, who had once been the Northern Ireland Security Minister, was forced to resign after his links with Nadir became public. Mates further clouded the legal proceedings when he alleged that the Serious Fraud Office had put unfair pressure on the judiciary to prosecute Nadir. Mates also bizarrely alleged that Nadir was the victim of a secret service plot to destabilize the unrecognized enclave of northern Cyprus.

An Inland Revenue investigator, Michael Allcock, who was later jailed for accepting cash from businessmen in exchange for favorable tax treatment, was suspended from his duties as head of the Inland Revenue's Special Office due to allegations of bribery. Allcock had been a successful investigator charged with investigating "rich and powerful people."

In May 1993 Nadir jumped bail and fled to Northern Cyprus. The occupied section of the island is not recognized by any country apart from Turkey and, as a consequence, no extradition treaties exist between it and any other country. Nadir was obviously aware of this loophole but declared his reasons for fleeing the United Kingdom with typical arrogance. "I do assure you it wasn't an easy decision to leave Great Britain, knowing as I do the consequences of jumping bail. But the chances of me receiving a fair trial were receding by the day. Ladies and gentlemen, nobody can live without hope. Sadly, the authorities had during the past two and a half years demolished my hope of receiving a fair trial. I had to have freedom to move, to think, to talk. They had killed that, and so I came here so that I could at long last obtain for myself the basic human right to defend myself."

Nadir used the *Hurriyet* newspaper in Turkey to provide a highly fictionalized version of his flight from England. He claimed to have organized the escape with military precision, boasting that he carried a gun to shoot any policemen that got in his way. Nadir's tale of a 162 miles-per-hour car chase conducted by a professional formula one driver was flatly contradicted by the pilot who flew him to Northern Cyprus. The ease with which Nadir fled the country amazed the UK public and led to calls for a tightening of the laws on bail. Ramadan Guney, a close friend of Nadir who posted £1 million of his bail, was excused from paying the bail after another lengthy court case.

The Istanbul police arrested a Polly Peck administrator, Michael Jordan of Coopers and Lybrand, and a legal adviser in November 1993. The police, who acted on a complaint from lawyers representing Nadir, claimed that Jordan was guilty of "illegality and irregular conduct" in his attempts to sell off Polly Peck assets for the benefit of creditors. When the two men were released, Nadir retaliated by threatening to sue the Home Secretary, the Serious Fraud Squad, and the director of Public Prosecutions over what he claimed was his "ill-treatment" while being investigated in the United Kingdom.

Elizabeth Forsyth, a grandmother with conservative tastes in politics, was arrested and tried for laundering money for Nadir, who had stolen the cash from his Polly Peck empire. Forsyth was jailed for five years for handling £400,000 of stolen money for Nadir. She had first met Nadir while working at Citibank in a department that set up schemes to reduce the tax liabilities of foreign nationals living in Britain. Nadir offered her a £70,000 per annum role to look after his personal tax affairs.

John Turner, Polly Peck's head accountant, was cleared of ten charges of false accounting by a judge at the Old Bailey. The Serious Fraud Office agreed that it would not press charges since it would be "unjust" to prosecute Turner while Nadir was hiding in Turkey and northern Cyprus.

Creditors in the company have received only a tiny fraction of the money owed to them when Polly Peck collapsed in 1990. Authorities in Turkey and Northern Cyprus have consistently frustrated liquidators in their attempts to recover money stolen by Nadir. Elizabeth Forsyth was freed from her prison sentence in 1997 after having served ten months in prison and was awarded damages by the High Court against the administrators appointed to deal with Polly Peck's collapse. Nadir, who orchestrated the astounding rise of Polly Peck, has thus far escaped justice.

See also SOUTH SEA BUBBLE; TULIPMANIA.

NAFTA

See NORTH AMERICAN FREE TRADE AGREEMENT (NAFTA).

NAKED OPTION/NAKED CALL

A *Naked Option*, also known as an uncovered option, is a position held by an option writer (seller) who does not have an offsetting position to limit risk.

The highest-risk strategy is the *Naked Call*, in which the writer sells calls and does not have an offsetting option position or ownership of the underlying security. If the call sold is exercised, the call writer will have to buy the securities at the current market price in order to fulfill the contract. There is no way to know ahead of time what the market price will be.

Although prices often move within certain limits, unusual situations (i.e., a takeover) can occur. Such a situation can cause a significant price increase in a short period of time.

A short put can be covered by selling short. If the put is exercised when the price of the underlying shares drops, the investor buys the shares at the strike price, but can deliver them to close out the short position. By employing this strategy, the level of maximum risk is known in advance. The premium on the sale of puts gives the investor some protection against a price increase of the underlying shares.

See also CALL; OPTION; PUT.

NAMIBIA, REPUBLIC OF

Namibia (Afrikaans Namibie, Suidwes-Afrika) is a country on the southwest coast of Africa. It is bordered by Angola and Zambia on the north, Botswana on the east, and South Africa on the south and southeast.

Area: 318,580 square miles (825,118 square km)

Population: 1,651,000 (35.2% urban; 64.8% rural)

Form of Government: Republic, with two legislative houses: National Assembly—72 members; National Council—26 members. Head of state and government: President.

Official Language: English

Capital: Windhoek

Largest Cities: Windhoek 125,000; Swakopmund 15,500; Rundu 15,000; Rehoboth 15,000; Keetmanshoop 14,000

Economy:

Currency: Namibia Dollar (N$)
   (Linked 1-1 with the South African Rand, which is also legal tender.)

National Budget: Revenue—N$3.4 billion; expenditures—N$3.9 billion (education: 23.5%; transportation: 18.4%; health and welfare: 13.1%; national defense: 5.3%; agriculture: 5.0%)

Public Debt: US$3.2 million

Gross National Product: US$2.6 billion

Principal Products: Fruits and vegetables; livestock; minerals

Foreign Trade (Imports): US$1.2 billion (chemical and petroleum products: 21.5%; food and agricultural products: 17.1%; machinery and transport equipment: 6.6%; other: 46.2%; from South Africa: 75-100%)

Foreign Trade (Exports): US$1.3 billion (minerals: 50.2%, of which diamonds: 31.4%; agricultural products: 36.1%, of which cattle: 11.0%; karakul pelts: 0.2%; to United States: 25%; South Africa: 19%; Japan: 15%)

Stock Exchanges: 1

Namibia Stock Exchange (NSE)

PO Box 2401

Kaiserkrone Centre Shop 11

Windhoek

Namibia

Phone: (264-61) 227 647

Fax: (264-61) 248 531

Internet Address: www.mbendi.co.za/exna

Trading Hours: Monday–Friday, 10:00 to 12:00 and 2:00 to 4:00

Office Hours: Monday–Friday, 8:00 to 4:30

Exchange Holidays:

1 January	1, 4, 16 May
21 March	26 August
5, 8 April	10, 25, 26 December

Listed Companies: 33

Market Capitalization: US$200 million

Major Sectors: Industrial, agricultural, mining, financial, fishing, retail

History: In 1992 Namibian businesses and individuals formed an association to raise the capital and start-up funds for a stock exchange; each member contributed N$10,000.

Amendments were made to the 1985 Stock Exchanges Control Act and on 30 September the Namibian Finance Minister launched the Namibian Stock Exchange. Trading began with the dual-listings of bigger Namibian companies that had previously listed on the Johannesburg Stock Exchange, and grew with further dual-listings of major financial institutions that possessed extensive operations in Namibia. The first Namibian-only listings and capital raising exercises appeared in 1994. By the end of December 1995, there were 23 companies listed on the Namibia Stock Exchange.

Classes of Securities: Shares, preferred shares, government bonds, corporate bonds, options

Fredis, a form of loan stock linked to the JSE All-Share index but paying interest, are a cross between a derivative and bond.

Indices:

The NSE Overall Index was recalculated July 1995 to a market capitalization weighted index. The base was recalculated to October 1992 = 100.

NSE Local Index (1 July 1995 = 100)

Namibian-owned companies with the majority of operations located in the country

Supervisory Organizations:

Ministry of Finance Permanent Secretary

Namibian Stock Exchange (37 associate members)

Executive Committee (9 members of the business community)

Subcommittees

Compliance is overseen by the Registrar of Stock Exchanges (the Permanent Secretary at the Ministry of Finance, assisted by the Department of Financial Institutions Supervision)

Depository: Central Depository (Pty) Ltd. (under development)

Settlement Details:

Shares: Trade date + 1 day (T + 1) for individual investors.

By arrangement, a value-for-value settlement, with agreement from NSE, for recognized institutions

Trading: Stockbrokers place orders on remote computer terminals. The orders are ranked by time and price priority. Deals are matched individually on agreement between brokers and the NSE computer handles contract notes.

The NSE and a Namibian computer firm have developed a computer system that they co-own. This system handles all trading, with settlement being through the NSE. The system incorporates a Transfer Secretaries service and a Central Depository, although the last is not yet in operation.

Investor Protection: The NSE has established a Guarantee Fund to protect investors in the event of default by a broker on the exchange. The NSE also has a fidelity insurance policy against fraud or misappropriation of investor's funds of up to N$100,000. However, it should be noted that the stockbroker involved bears full liability before responsibility shifts to the NSE.

Listing Requirements: There are no restrictions on foreign companies listing on the NSE, provided they meet the requirements of the Listing Committee and are approved by the Executive Committee.

Main Listing Requirements:

1. Must have share capital and reserves of at least N$1 million.
2. A minimum of one million shares must be in issue.
3. Must have acceptable and profitable trading record for at least three years with current audited pretax profit of N$500,000.
4. Must be no qualified auditors report for two years.
5. Minimum of 20% of issued shares must be held by the public.
6. At least 75 shareholders must represent the public.

   (There is a provision for newer companies that includes additional conditions.)

Investor Taxation:

- No capital gains tax (unless the investor is a very frequent trader)
- 10% non-resident tax on dividends
- General sales tax of 11% is added to the handling charge and commission.

Limitations: There are no restrictions on foreign investment (although foreigners need special permission if they wish to take control of a bank). Foreign exchange regulations are as they are in South Africa, and the Namibia dollar is linked 1-to-1 with the rand. Investors must apply through an authorized dealer, usually a commercial bank, to ensure the free remittance of dividends and the proceeds of sales.

When an investor makes a deal, it must be for lots of 100 shares. The investor must be able to pay if buying, or must produce the share certificates if selling, either on the day of the deal or the following morning to the NSE. The charges for dealing include a N$15.00 handling charge on every deal, plus a commission (minimum N$2.50) per transaction. The commission will consist of the following percentage of the deal value:

1.00% deals up to N$10,000
0.85% portion up to N$20,000
0.65% portion up to N$100,000
0.50% portion up to N$500,000
0.40% portion up to N$1,000,000
0.20% portion above N$1,000,000

(Lower rates apply to trading on bonds and debt instruments.)

Brokerage Firms:

Wikus Hanekom, Wilfried Moroff
PO Box 1272, Windhoek/ Shop 8
Kaiserkrone Centre

Windhoek
Namibia
Phone: (264-61) 239 708
Fax: (264-61) 232 513

Jean Simonis,
PO Box 196, Windhoek/ Nimrod Building
Casino Street
Windhoek
Namibia
Phone: (264-61) 237 477
Fax: (264-61) 227 321

Company Information:

10 Major Companies

Name of Company	Type of Business	Market Capitalization (N$ millions)
Standard Bank Inv Corp.	Banking	20,947.4
Southern Life Assc.	Life Insurance	7,706.3
Afrox	Health, Gas Prod., Welding	4,930.5
Genbel	Portfolio Management	4,845.6
Engen	Fuel Distributor/ Refinery	4,390.2
Mutua & Federal	Short-Term Insurance	4,071.8
Metropolitan Life	Life Insurance	3,801.6
Servgro	Tourism, Liesure	2,655.0
First Nat. Bank Hld.	Banking	583.7
Stocks and Stocks Ltd	Holding Company	563.2

Other Investment Information:

The Investment Centre
Ministry of Trade and Industry
Private Bag 13340
Windhoek
Namibia
Phone: (264) 289 911
Fax: (264) 220 148

Namibia National Chamber of Commerce and Industry
PO Box 9355
Windhoek
Namibia
Phone: (264) 228 809
Fax: (264) 228 009

NARROW MARKET

See THINLY TRADED.

NARROWING A SPREAD

Narrowing a Spread is an action by a broker/dealer or market specialist to achieve either a higher bid (investor selling price) or a lower offer (investor buying price).

In an order-driven auction market, however, narrowing a spread (closing a spread) usually reflects the actions of investors who cause the current market price to advance or decline.

See also ASK PRICE; BID PRICE; LAST TRADE.

NASDAQ

See NATIONAL ASSOCIATION OF SECURITIES DEALERS AUTOMATED QUOTATION SYSTEM (NASDAQ).

NATIONAL ASSOCIATION OF SECURITIES DEALERS (NASD; United States)

The *National Association of Securities Dealers (NASD)* came into existence through an authorization described in the Maloney Act of 1938, which was an amendment to the Securities Exchange Act. The authorization permits brokers and dealers to form a membership organization made up of members registered with the Securities and Exchange Commission (SEC).

The NASD regulates the over-the-counter market in the United States, including more than 5,200 firms having more than 460,000 employees. The regulation comes under the oversight of the SEC. NASD owns and operates the National Association of Securities Dealers Automated Quotation System (NASDAQ) (over the counter), an automated communication and quotation system. NASD financing comes from the securities industry and NASDAQ issuers.

The NASD is a self-regulatory organization meeting regulatory responsibilities by means of an integrated program of:

1. On-site inspections of member firms
2. Computerized surveillance of NASDAQ securities trading
3. Enforcement of rules covering special product areas such as municipal and government securities
4. Formal review of arrangements for underwriting regarding publicly issued securities
5. Testing procedure and activity for personnel
6. Cooperative actions with the exchanges, individual states, and the Securities and Exchange Commission

With regard to brokerage firm regulation, the NASD Rules of Fair Practice require a member to conduct business with high standards of commercial honor and just and equitable principals of trade. Strict standards of honesty, integrity, and fair dealing with customers, including the prompt delivery of funds and securities, as well as a faithful adherence to customers' instructions, are demanded from all members.

The Rules of Fair Practice list details actions that are clear violations. Violations include the following:

- Recommending low-priced, speculative securities to customers when the broker has no idea of the investor's financial status
- Excessive activity (churning), designed to generate commissions
- Fraudulent activity, establishment of fictitious accounts, or exceeding discretionary authority
- Recommending purchases beyond the investor's financial means

The NASD also acts as the enforcer for federal laws and SEC rules, such as:

- Net-capital rule governing financial requirements for securities firms
- Requirements for submission of monthly and quarterly statements of financial condition
- Enforcement of the customer-protection rule governing custody and segregation of customer funds and securities
- SEC anti-fraud rules, prohibiting the use of manipulative, deceptive, or other fraudulent devices in security transactions
- SEC cold-call rule addressing high pressure and other abusive sales tactics involving the trading of penny stocks.

See also NATIONAL ASSOCIATION OF SECURITIES DEALERS AUTOMATED QUOTATION SYSTEM (NASDAQ); SECURITIES AND EXCHANGE COMMISSION (SEC); SELF-REGULATING ORGANIZATION (SRO).

NATIONAL ASSOCIATION OF SECURITIES DEALERS AUTOMATED QUOTATION SYSTEM (NASDAQ)

The *National Association of Securities Dealers Automated Quotation System (NASDAQ)* provides three primary, basic services:

1. The NASDAQ Quotation System
2. The Small Order Execution System (SOES)
3. The Trade Acceptance and Reconciliation Service (TARS)

Quotation System: The NASDAQ Quotation System gathers, verifies, and distributes quotation information to system subscribers. The Level 1 service provides the best bid and ask prices in all securities to salespeople and dealers in the OTC market. It also broadcasts last-sale price and volume data on more than 3,000 issues of the NASDAQ National Market System.

Level 2 service is provided through NASDAQ-owned computer terminals. It is available to both member and non-member subscribers and is a composite display with current quotes submitted by the market makers in each issue. The quotes provide the best available bid and ask prices (referred to as "the inside market"), indexes, volume, and market summary information.

Small Order Execution System (SOES): SOES is a Tandem-Based system that enables all securities orders, up to 1,000 shares for the 3,000 NASDAQ National Market System issues and 500 shares for nearly 3,000 other NASDAQ issues, to be automatically executed by computer.

Trade Acceptance and Reconciliation Service (TARS): Also a Tandem-Based system, the TARS assists the back offices of member firms to resolve uncompared and advisory OTC transactions processed through participating clearing organizations.

NASDAQ is also linked electronically to London's International Stock Exchange.

See also LISTED SECURITIES; NATIONAL ASSOCIATION OF SECURITIES DEALERS (NASD); REGULATIONS; UNITED STATES/NASDAQ (OTC) STOCK MARKET.

NATIONAL DEBT

National Debt is a cumulative quantity that is a result of a nation's annual operating deficits exceeding revenues, and tends to increase because of the accumulation of interest. The debt consists of both an interest-bearing component and a non-interest-bearing component.

In the United States, national debt refers to the total outstanding obligations of the federal government, including bonds, notes, bills, and certificates of indebtedness. In Great Britain, by contrast, it is sometimes taken to include the debt of the entire public sector, including nationalized industries, local authorities, and so forth. These differences in definition must be borne in mind when comparing the national debts of different countries; generally speaking, a more useful figure is the ratio of national debt to national income.

Government borrowing is generally thought to have a stimulating effect on consumption, investment, and employment. Whether and to what extent this is so depends on the nature of the government expenditures that are underwritten by the borrowing as well as the nature of alternative private investments that it may displace. Also, in general, government borrowing con-

tributes to inflation. When the U.S. Federal Reserve has moved to lower the inflation rate, the stock market has responded very well.

Some of the major capitalist countries have dynamic histories of national debt. In France the national debt grew to sizable proportions in the 17th and 18th centuries, but about two-thirds of it was repudiated following the 1789 revolution. The Napoleonic wars in the early 1800s and the Franco-German War in 1870–71 raised the national debt to more than 21 billion francs. It was financed by government bonds, but increased again as a result of the two world wars. In 1960, following decades of inflation, a new franc valued at 100 old francs was issued, so the nominal value of the debt decreased 99%. But since then it has risen again, reaching 3.217 trillion francs in 1995.

In Great Britain, periods of rapid increase in national debt have also tended to be associated with wars. During World War II, British national debt reached £21.366 billion. After the war, when the British government nationalized various sectors of industry, the national debt rose further. By 1992 it was £168.613 billion.

In Germany most financial powers were retained by the individual states until the formation of the Weimar Republic following World War I. Germany's debt from the war led to hyperinflation and financial chaos. Following World War II the German national debt was more than DM 300 billion. A currency reform in 1948 wiped out most of this, but it resumed a steady increase in the following decades. By 1994 it stood at a little more than DM 1 trillion.

In Japan the government began issuing bonds in the 1870s following the Meiji Restoration. Financing the wars with Japan in 1894–95 and with Russia in 1904–95 cost a total of approximately 1.75 billion yen, which was mainly raised by foreign borrowing. Increases in taxation stabilized the national debt, even through the course of World War I; however, the debt doubled between 1918 and 1930. With rapid militarization and war in China, by 1940 the Japanese national debt was more than three times what it had been a decade earlier. It reached 150.795 billion yen during World War II and continued to increase sharply after the war, reaching 212.474 trillion yen by 1993.

In the United States, when the federal government was first formed it assumed the Revolutionary War debts of the various states. In 1790 the national debt stood at $75 million. For several decades the government avoided additional borrowing, except for during the War of 1812, and in 1835 the cumulative national debt was eliminated. It accumulated again during the

Civil War and World War I, but following several years of budgetary surpluses in the 1920s the national debt fell to a little more than $16 billion in 1930. However, during the Depression, government efforts to stimulate economic recovery caused an increase in the debt. During World War II it grew rapidly, reaching $269 billion by 1946. By 1970 it had reached $380 billion. During the 1980s huge increases in expenditures for national defense and a wide range of social welfare transfer payments greatly increased the national debt. By 1996 it had reached approximately $5.2 trillion. As a fraction of gross domestic product, it stood at approximately 71%, the highest proportion in four decades.

Analysts view the current trends in the U.S. national debt with varying degrees of alarm. They hold that the buildup of debt and associated inflationary pressures must weaken the dollar as an international unit of reserve currency. The level of U.S. foreign debt, it is feared, can undermine its power and influence in the world.

Others argue that the U.S. national debt is still a relatively small portion of gross domestic product, smaller than for other developed countries. Further, they say, contrary to the notion that it represents a burden bequeathed to future generations, it represents an intragenerational transfer, from those whose taxes pay the interest on the national debt to those who lend to the government by purchasing bonds and the like. For investors, government securities can provide convenient investments. Major holders include pension funds, savings and loan associations, and money market mutual funds.

See also WAR AND STOCK MARKETS.

NATIONAL MARKET SYSTEM (United States)

The National Association of Securities Dealers (NASD) in the United States sponsors an operation known as the *National Market System*. Shares trading in the system have to meet certain criteria for size, profitability, and trading activity.

Companies with shares in the National Market System provide more information than for other over-the-counter shares. Information such as the company name, dividend, high-low for 52 weeks, trading volume, high-low during the trading session, closing price, and price change for the most recent session are listed for these companies.

See also LISTED SECURITIES; NATIONAL ASSOCIATION OF SECURITIES DEALERS AUTOMATED QUOTATION SYSTEM (NASDAQ); UNITED STATES.

NATIONAL SECURITIES CLEARING CORPORATION (NSCC; United States)

The *National Securities Clearing Corporation (NSCC)* is a securities clearing organization formed in 1977 by a merger of the subsidiaries of the New York Stock Exchange, the American Stock Exchange, and the National Clearing Corporation. It reconciles brokerage firm transactions executed on the exchanges.

See also SETTLE; UNITED STATES.

NATIONSBANK

NationsBank, incorporated in 1991, has expanded across the United States with unprecedented speed and aggressiveness, in three decades becoming the largest and fastest growing banking supergiant in the country. NationsBank's history dates to the Commercial National Bank of Charlotte, founded in 1874 with $50,000 in capital. After only nine months in business the bank's first president, Major Clement Dowd, announced the first of what would become an unbroken string of dividend payments; Commercial National Bank survived the banking storms of 1893, 1907, and 1929–1933 with its assets relatively intact.

George Stephens and Word H. Wood formed the Southern States Trust Company in Charlotte in 1901; in 1907 they changed its name to American Trust Company. Security National Bank was formed in Greensboro, North Carolina nearly 30 years later at the height of the Depression, which it survived surprisingly well.

In November 1957 Commercial National and American Trust pooled their complementary portfolios and became American Commercial Bank, to which the First National Bank of Raleigh was soon added. Not long after, Security National merged with Depositers National Bank of Durham, and on 1 July 1960 the two giants, American Commercial and Security National, merged, forming the North Carolina National Bank (NCNB).

In 1974 NCNB suffered huge losses in its real estate investment trust—in response, the bank became still more aggressive in its acquisitions, finishing the 1970s with $100 million mergers with the Bank of Asheville and Carolina First National in Lincolnton. This brought its assets to $6 billion, and NCNB was finally forced to look outside the state of North Carolina for its next acquisition.

Looking for ways to end restrictions on interstate banking, in 1981 the bank took advantage of a loophole in Florida law which would allow it to purchase banks via a subsidiary it had owned in that state since

1972. It proceeded to buy First National Bank of Lake City, Gulfstream Banks of Boca Raton, Ellis Banks of Bradenton, and Pan American Banks; by the time its acquisitions slowed in 1987, NCNB National Bank of Florida had become Florida's fourth largest financial institution.

In 1985 the southeastern United States agreed to allow reciprocal interstate banking, after which NCNB acquired banks in Georgia, South Carolina, Virginia, and Maryland, making it the only bank to operate in six southern states. In 1988, with the purchase of the First Republic Bank of Texas, NCNB Chairman Hugh McColl Jr. quintupled his bank's assets in only five years and elevated it from a regional financial leader to a national powerhouse. Other financial institutions awaited NCNB's next attack with trepidation, some going to great lengths to avoid a takeover. Chairman McColl is an ex-Marine who, according to *Fortune*, once considered adopting this motto, "crush the sons-of-bitches and have a nice day."

On 31 December 1991 NCNB Corporation merged with C&S/Sovran of Atlanta, Georgia and changed its name to NationsBank. As the 1990s progressed, NationsBank sustained NCNB's voracious appetite, averaging approximately five acquisitions per year. On 13 April 1998 history was made when Nations-Bank announced a stock-for-stock merger with BankAmerica Corporation, another banking giant based in San Francisco, California. The merger created the first truly national U.S. banking franchise, with $570 billion in assets, $45 billion in shareholders' equity, and a market capitalization of $133 billion.

See also ACQUISITION; MERGER; TAKEOVER/TAKEOVER BID.

NATURAL SELLER
See LONG POSITION.

NATWEST GROUP
NatWest Group, formerly National Westminster Bank PLC, is the United Kingdom's second largest bank and operates in 33 countries. As of early 1997, NatWest's total assets were approximately £168 billion. The group's headquarters are in London, and its stock is traded on the London, New York, and Tokyo exchanges. NatWest divides its business operations into the following sectors and subsidiaries: NatWest UK, NatWest Markets, NatWest Wealth Management, Coutts and Company Group, Ulster Bank, and Lombard.

NatWest UK is the group's principal domestic services arm, offering retail and corporate banking services, insurance services, card services, and mortgage services. NatWest Markets is the group's worldwide corporate and investment banking division whose activities comprise a variety of wholesale financial services, such as debt and equity issuance, investment products, Treasury operations, financial advice, and risk management. NatWest Wealth Management brings together the group's businesses that focus on wealth creation and management, including pension and investment services and asset management. Coutts and Company Group is NatWest's private banking arm, operating both in the United Kingdom and internationally for trust and banking services. Ulster Bank provides a full range of retail, commercial, and investment banking services throughout Ireland.

Lombard is the United Kingdom's largest finance house. This sector of NatWest operates in the business, vehicle, and personal finance markets and, in early 1997, had customer balances of £10.6 billion, while advancing another £120 million to its customers every week. Lombard is structured into three divisions: Lombard Business, Lombard Motor, and Lombard Personal. Lombard Business includes a variety of funding facilities for business clients to lease or purchase all types of assets from agricultural implements to computerized industrial machinery. Lombard Business operates not only in the United Kingdom but also has leasing and agricultural finance facilities in France and Germany. The business division also provides businesses with working capital through specialized factoring and invoice discounting facilities for both the domestic and export markets.

Lombard Motor offers point-of-sale vehicle financing for both private customers and business users through motor car dealers. Largely because of links with major manufacturers of vehicles, Lombard finances approximately one out of every five new cars purchased on credit in the United Kingdom. Lombard motor also offers motor car dealers financing for stocking their operations.

Lombard Personal is one of the United Kingdom's largest providers of retail credit, offering point-of-sale financing through an array of retail outlets, as well as offering personal loan service via direct mail. In addition to its extensive credit operations in the United

Kingdom, Lombard Personal engages in point-of-sale retail credit activities in Holland, Belgium, and Germany. The personal division also provides sterling and dollar deposit facilities for nonresidents of the United Kingdom.

NatWest was created under the name National Westminster Bank in 1968 by combining three major banks established in the early 1800s: the National Provincial Bank, its subsidiary the District Bank, and the Westminster Bank. The transfer of the undertakings of the merged organizations did not take effect until 1 January 1970. NatWest started business with a "bang" by rapidly expanding and significantly improving the quality of its customer services. For example, only three months after its official start of business, the group acquired Lombard Banking Limited, a bank whose history dates back to 1861, and merged it with the successful subsidiary North Central Finance Company to form Lombard North Central PLC. After additional acquisitions and expansion, Lombard North Central became the present-day Lombard sector. This strategy of rapid, early expansion enabled NatWest to overtake Barclays and become, at that time, Britain's largest commercial bank.

In the late 1970s and early 1980s, after undertaking a tremendous restructuring, NatWest began a concerted effort to expand its international operations. In 1975 it expanded into Scotland, opening offices in Edinburgh, Glasgow, and later Aberdeen, in an effort to help support the bank's participation in North Sea fuel projects. In 1977 Robin Leigh-Pemberton became chairman and oversaw the company's purchase of the National Bank of North America in New York. By 1979 NatWest had extended its bases of operation in France, Belgium, and West Germany, and had established overseas representatives in Australia, Bahrain, Canada, Greece, Hong Kong, Japan, Mexico, Singapore, Spain, and what was then the Soviet Union.

In 1983 Thomas Boardman replaced Robin Leigh-Pemberton as chairman of NatWest. Leigh-Pemberton went on to be appointed governor of the Bank of England. Boardman and Tom Frost, NatWest's CEO since 1987, continued to transform NatWest from a domestic banking institution into an international financial organization. Part of the plan included forming NatWest's Investment Bank through the acquisition of a medium-sized stock exchange jobber and broker. By 1987 NatWest expanded its American subsidiary, NatWest USA, by acquiring First Jersey National Bank and Ultra Bancorp (another New Jersey-based bank) in 1989. These holdings became National Westminster Bancorp, which had 340 offices in New York and New Jersey.

NatWest lived up to its reputation for caution with its handling of the Third World debt crisis. In June 1987, it added £246 million to its reserves, becoming the first British bank to follow the lead of the American money-center banks by limiting its exposure to Third World loans.

In December 1988 NatWest's good name was tarnished. The Department of Trade and Industry (DTI) began to investigate the role played by the bank's investment-banking subsidiary, County NatWest, in an acquisition by the employment agency Blue Arrow. In 1987 County NatWest underwrote a stock offering for Blue Arrow to raise cash for the deal, but the results were disappointing. County NatWest was left with an interest in a 13.5% stake in Blue Arrow, having concealed a substantial interest by dividing the stake between itself, its own market-making arm, County NatWest Securities, and the Union Bank of Switzerland (UBS, to which it granted an indemnity against losses).

These actions were undertaken secretly, but after the October stock market crash, the Blue Arrow wound opened even further; its actions could no longer be concealed. In December 1987, County NatWest made a payment to UBS to release the indemnity, purchased County NatWest Securities' holding, and announced that it held a total stake of 9.5% in Blue Arrow.

The DTI released the results of its investigation in July 1989, sharply criticizing County NatWest actions in failing to report its stake in Blue Arrow. The report stated "County NatWest violated a law requiring any party holding a 5% or greater interest in a company to report that fact in a timely fashion. This served to deceive both regulators and the financial markets about the true value of Blue Arrow stock." Although the DTI report did not criticize Lord Boardman, he announced that he would retire from the bank in September, five months ahead of schedule. Three other NatWest executives also resigned. On 1 October 1989, Lord Alexander, the former head of the British government body overseeing corporate takeovers, became chairman.

NatWest's once-sterling reputation and its budding investment banking business had been tainted, but the bank's strength and reputation for caution continued nevertheless. It is because of this that the group was able to make a quick recovery with very little disruption of its successful operations.

In 1994 NatWest acquired a 20% interest in HDFC Bank, a new financial institution in India. In the same year the group, along with a Hong Kong merchant house, formed Wheelock NatWest to engage in corporate finance, investment management, and equities stockbroking in Southeast Asia. In 1995 National Westminster Bank PLC reorganized as NatWest Group. In that year the Lombard sector had pretax profits of £234.9 million—more than a 70-fold increase from pretax profits of £3.2 million recorded by Lombard just four years earlier. By 1996 NatWest decided it was no longer profitable to compete with the American banking conglomerates, so it sold NatWest Bancorp, its American subsidiary, for $3.5 billion principally in cash. Later in 1996 NatWest purchased Gartmore Investment Management from Banque Indosuez for $727 million. Gartmore was placed in the newly created NatWest Wealth Management sector, along with NatWest Life and Investment Services and NatWest Ventures.

See also COUTTS & COMPANY.

NAVNE-AKTIE (Denmark)

Navne-Aktie denotes a share as registered on the Copenhagen Stock Exchange. The majority of shares listed on the Copenhagen Stock Exchange are issued in bearer form, meaning they are not registered to a specific investor. For the shareholder to vote, the shares must be registered in the holder's name through the Danish Securities Centre, with the name being sent to the company's register of shareholders.

A company's Articles of Association may require the shares to be registered.

See also BEARER CERTIFICATE/SECURITY/SHARE; REGISTERED SECURITY; REGISTRAR.

NAZI GOLD

The scandal of *Nazi Gold* has become a very public issue in recent years. Neutral countries, with Switzerland foremost among them, have been accused of benefiting financially from World War II by accepting gold from the senior-ranking Nazi officials.

Secret papers released by the British secret service in 1997 showed that the Allied forces were monitoring the movement of Nazi gold even before the war started. Just before Germany invaded Poland, the Reichsbank in Germany received $97 million in gold bars from Austria, Czechoslovakia, and Danzig. As German reserves became depleted during the war and trade became impossible, the Nazis turned to the systematic theft of gold and other precious items to finance the war effort. Along with the many millions stolen from Jewish families, gold from Belgium ($223

million) and state treasures from Holland ($193 million) were used to keep Germany armed and fed.

The records of the Reichsbank were confiscated by the Allies once the war was over. They showed a systematic pattern of theft, laundering, and concealment. Under interrogation in 1945, Dr. Puhl of the Reichsbank admitted that all the plundered gold was melted down and that the majority was sent abroad in exchange for vital raw materials and foreign currency. The Allies knew that the majority of money flowed through Switzerland, but other neutral countries, such as Sweden, Spain, and Portugal, also received ingots.

The Allies tried to pressurize the Swiss into refusing to accept any more Nazi gold but were hamstrung by their own need for Swiss francs. The Bank of England warned all of the neutral countries that any money that was illegally obtained would be claimed by the Allies at the end of the war. The Swiss Embassy in London was informed that Switzerland would suffer "the maximum amount of trouble" if it continued to deal with the Nazis.

Once peace was achieved the Allies attempted to force the Swiss to hand over the gold, but soon realized that there was no legal way to ensure that they complied. Moral pressure, however, forced the Swiss to make a payment of 250 million Swiss francs in May 1946, which was soon followed by a second payment of 121.5 million Swiss francs. The Allies forewent any further claims on the gold, even though some experts believed that Switzerland had only parted with a small fraction of the money it banked from the Nazis.

One of the great problems facing investigators is that the provenance of the gold cannot be proven. The jewelry, coins, and even the tooth fillings that were stolen from their original Jewish owners were melted down in a central smithy and turned into gold bars. In many cases the original owners had either died or could not be traced. The long period between the loss of gold and the submission of claims further complicated the problem. Several hoards of Nazi gold were also uncovered in Germany, including a large amount in a disused gold mine in Merkers and a cache secreted away by the Nazi Foreign Minister, von Ribbentrop.

Many bureaucratic obstacles were placed in the way of the rightful heirs to the gold. Ironically, the growth of money laundering has been one of the major factors in motivating the Swiss bankers to resolve the problem of Nazi gold. Continued allegations that the Swiss were still laundering funds from modern-day dictators and drug barons has changed Swiss laws on banking secrecy and has made the bankers slightly more open when dealing with Jewish groups and representatives from American congress.

A highly secretive committee, the Tripartite Gold Commission, was set up in 1946 to track down the gold and return it to its rightful owners. Located in Brussels, the commission was manned by representatives from Britain, the United States, and France. In September 1996 the Swiss government published a decree ordering all bank records and accounts of financial dealings with the Nazis to be turned over to a special investigating committee. Anybody found guilty of destroying documents or preventing their publication would be liable for a fine and a spell in prison. Inspectors were given far-reaching powers to inspect bank records and other relevant archive materials.

Jewish action groups have also complained about the Swiss bankers' attitude toward sums deposited by Jewish people for safekeeping during the war. The bankers demanded written proof of death from relatives of depositors who had been killed in the concentration camps. The dormant funds could not be claimed, since no death certificates were issued by the Nazis. The action groups have also accused the bankers of planning with the Nazis to set up an international fund to finance Nazi leaders once the war ended.

NEAR MONEY

Near Money is a general term used to describe cash equivalents and liquid securities that are easily converted to cash.

Government securities, bank demand or time deposits, money market shares, and bonds close to maturity are all examples of near money.

See also CASH; CASH EQUIVALENTS; MONEY SUPPLY.

NEARBY FUTURES

Futures contracts trading close to the present time are known as *Nearby Futures*. In January, the "nearbys" would be considered to be February and March. Nearby futures contracts are more actively traded than later months.

See also FUTURES CONTRACT.

NEGATIVE YIELD CURVE

See INVERTED YIELD CURVE.

NEGOTIABLE

A type of security which has transferable ownership is known as *Negotiable*. The term *negotiable* is synonymous with *transferable* and *marketable*.

With securities, the transfer of ownership is commonly accomplished by the act of buying and selling for cash compensation. If a security cannot be resold, it is a non-negotiable security.

Negotiable also refers to a topic involved in the bargaining process in which two or more parties debate in order to reach mutual agreement. Discussions will be held until all parties arrive at a mutual agreement.

See also LIMIT ORDER; SETTLE; STOP ORDER; TRANSFER.

NEGOTIATED BID

An issuer of ordinary shares will negotiate a price, known as a *Negotiated Bid*, with a single underwriter, rather than have several underwriters bid on the issue. Working with a single underwriter creates a working business relationship in which the underwriter learns about the issuer's business and can effectively promote it. The majority of common stock underwritings are negotiated bids.

In the United States, municipal debt securities underwritings are commonly done on a competitive, rather than negotiated, bid basis. Municipalities often require that any dealings regarding financial matters have bids submitted.

See also HOT ISSUE; INITIAL PUBLIC OFFERING (IPO); UNDERWRITING.

NEGOTIATED COMMISSION

Negotiated Commission is the term used to describe the compensation a brokerage firm charges for providing the investment service of trading securities. Some countries have maximum commissions set by legislation, others have commissions set by common practice, and others have negotiated commissions.

Although the theory of negotiated commissions involves the concept of bargaining on the amount of charges paid, in most situations the commissions are firmly quoted by the brokerage firm involved. The negotiation is more a matter of price competition between firms to have the lowest commissions available.

See also BROKERAGE HOUSE; COMMISSION; SALES CHARGE.

NEOCLASSICAL SCHOOL OF ECONOMICS

The *Neoclassical School of Economics* is the system of economic thought in the tradition of classical economics, characterized by microeconomic theoretical systems constructed to explore conditions of static equilibrium. The term *neoclassical* derives from the view that the originators of the so-called marginalist revolution were extending and improving on the basic foundations of the classical economists, such as David Ricardo and J. S. Mill. The main contributors to the neoclassical system, John Bates Clark, F.Y. Edgeworth, Irving Fisher, Alfred Marshall, Vilfredo Pareto, Léon Walras, and K. Wicksell used the concepts of marginal utility and marginal productivity to analyze the pricing of goods, services, and factors of production in competitive markets.

Neoclassical economists focus on decision-making units (households, firms, and industries) and on the way choices made by their economic agents are converted into an orderly process. Neoclassical statements about macroeconomics derive from the aggregation of the micro units.

The operation of the market system under competitive conditions ensures the optimum allocation of resources—the maximum societal welfare. The neoclassical approach elevated the theory of market price to the center of economic analysis and involved the creation of abstract models of economic agents' behavior, isolating the economic process, and providing a theoretical benchmark against which to compare real economic performance.

Some of the most important contributions to microeconomic theory were made by Alfred Marshall (1842–1924). In *Principles of Economics* (1890) he focused on the study of man "in the ordinary business of life," and his theory of value brought together the diverse elements of previous theories. Rational consumers aim to maximize their satisfaction from consumption, and suppliers of productive services are expected to seek maximum rewards. Marshall formulated the concept of demand as a relationship between quantities demanded and prices. For each good, a range of price and quantity was conceivable and could be depicted diagrammatically. In neoclassical economics, price is determined by the interaction of the demand for a good or service and the supply curve, which depicts the willingness of suppliers to supply different quantities at differing prices to the market. Production involved costs and sacrifices that were expected to rise as quantity offered increased, hence supply was positively related to price.

Marshall's concept of "diminishing marginal utility," which states that with the addition of an extra unit of consumption the incremental increase in an individual's total satisfaction declines, led to a downward sloping demand curve and an inverse price-quality relationship. The degree to which quality varies with price was explained using the concept of elasticity—the responsiveness of a variable to a change in

another. The aggregation of all individual demand schedules provides the market demand curve. Marshall argued that consumers maximize utility obtainable from a given income by adjusting their expenditure patterns such that the marginal utility deriving from each good or service relative to price was equal.

The result of Marshall's procedure was to remove the classical distinction between value and market price. The neoclassical approach also assigns, in the laws of supply and demand, the rewards to suppliers of productive services—land, labor, and capital—while removing traditional concerns of surplus and value.

Neoclassical production theory addresses itself to two principal issues: the combination of factors of production and the adjustments made when market conditions are altered. In the perfectly competitive market assumed by neoclassicists, firms are unable to influence price and therefore they aim to minimize costs through the least costly combination of factors of production.

Léon Walras (1834–1910) approached the neoclassical problem with far more theoretical rigor, presenting the analysis of the competitive process in the form of simultaneous equations and emphasizing the interdependence of all prices within the economic system.

John Bates Clark (1847–1938) applied the tools of marginal analysis to income distribution, arguing that productive factors are optimally engaged if each are hired to the point at which the marginal unit of each factor is equal to its marginal product.

The achievement of neoclassical economists is their piecing together of a complex system into a coherent analysis, in which the economic order is viewed as an organic unit with interdependent components. The system was challenged by the events of the 1930s and by the work of John Maynard Keynes (1883–1946), who identified aggregate demand operating below full employment equilibrium, contradicting the neoclassical premise of full employment being the normal operating level of the economy. Clark's pupil Thorstein Veblen (1857–1929) provided the most vociferous contemporary refute of neoclassicism. Veblen argued that its methodology was too formal, deductive, and static to apply to economic problems; human action was more instinctive than reflective; and the behavior of individuals was governed by emulation and that of firms by workmanship. Later economists such as J.K. Galbraith (1908–) have echoed these criticisms of neoclassicism, but it has nevertheless retained a powerful force in modern economic thought and provided the rationale for the emergence of "supply side" policies in the 1980s.

See also CLASSICAL SCHOOL OF ECONOMICS; FISHER, IRVING; GALBRAITH, JOHN KENNETH; KEYNES, JOHN MAYNARD; MARX, KARL; PARETO, VILFREDO; RICARDO, DAVID; THEORY OF MARKETS.

NEPAL, KINGDOM OF

Nepal (Nepal Adhirajya) is a landlocked country of southern Asia. It is bordered on the north by Chinese Tibet and the Himalayas, and on the east, south, and west by India.

Area: 56,827 square miles (147,181 square km)

Population: 20,093,000 (9.6% urban; 90.4% rural)

Form of Government: Constitutional monarchy, with two legislative houses: National Council—60 members; House of Representatives—205 members. Chief of state: King. Head of government: Prime Minister.

Official Language: Nepali

Capital: Kathmandu

Largest Cities: Kathmandu, 419,073; Biratnagar, 130,129; Lalitpur, 117,203; Pokhara, 95,311; Birganj, 68,764

Economy:

Currency: Nepalese rupee (NR)

National Budget: Revenue—NR 22.4 billion; expenditures—NR 35.5 billion (development: 63.7%; regular: 36.3%)

Public Debt: US$1.9 billion

Gross National Product: US$3.2 billion

Principal Products: Rice, sugarcane, corn, wheat, and other vegetables; livestock

Foreign Trade (Imports): NR 37.0 billion (basic manufactured goods: 29.2%; machinery and transport equipment: 19.5%; chemicals: 12.3%; mineral fuels and lubricants: 10.5%; food and live animals, chiefly for food: 9.3%; crude materials except fuels: 8.5%; from India: 40.5%; Singapore: 31.8%; Japan: 15.6%; West Germany: 4.3%; China: 3.8%; South Korea: 3.7%)

Foreign Trade (Exports): NR 17.3 billion (basic manufactures: 59.3%; food and live animals, chiefly for food: 11.4%; crude materials except fuels: 2.8%; animal and vegetable oils: 0.9%; to Germany: 49.0%; United States: 25.9%; India: 22.1%; Belgium: 2.2%)

Stock Exchanges: 1

Nepal Stock Exchange
PO Box 1550
Kathmandu
Nepal
Phone: (977-1) 224 467/415 210
Fax: (977-1) 416 461

Exchange Holidays:

1, 2, 17, 31 January	30 August
27 February	23 October
3, 12 March	1 November
1 April	25 December
1 May	

NET

A *Net* figure is an amount attained after all deductions and additions have been made. It is sometimes referred to as a *bottom line* or *final figure*. Bottom line is derived from the customary physical location of the net profit figure on a company's financial statement.

A company's net sales figure might be the gross sales minus discounts, any returns, and allowances for bad debts. Net profits are gross profits less operating and other expenses. Net assets are the difference between total assets and total liabilities, a figure also known as equity or net worth.

An initial public offering (IPO) is frequently described in a price that is net to the investor, meaning no additional commission will be charged (as compensation for the broker) and calculated into the issue price. If this is the case, the IPO will be referred to as a net transaction.

With an investment in securities, net profits are the cash received in excess of the cash paid for buying the securities, less any expenses involved in making the transaction.

See also CAPITAL GAIN; RETURN ON INVESTMENT; YIELD.

NET ASSET VALUE (NAV)

A mutual fund *Net Asset Value (NAV)* consists of the total asset value of the fund, less any fees and expenses, expressed in terms of the value per share. It is the price an investor would have received if mutual fund shares had been sold (redeemed) during that day's trading session. Net asset values are calculated at the end of each trading session.

The public offering price (POP) is a term used to describe the price of mutual fund shares with the maximum sales charge applied. The POP is also called the maximum offering price. It is the price an investor would pay to buy shares in minimal quantities.

When a mutual fund quotation appears in the newspaper, it shows the NAV, the POP, and the net change on the NAV from the most recent trading session.

See also MUTUAL FUND; SALES CHARGE.

NET BALANCE SYSTEM

A *Net Balance System* is used by many stock exchanges to simplify the buying and selling of securities. Instead of delivering shares for each sell, all of the buys and sells for a specific security are netted by subtracting the sells from the buys.

For example, if the total trades for a session amounted to 100,000 shares of IBM sold and 70,000 shares purchased, it leaves the firm's net position on IBM at a negative 30,000 shares to be delivered to cover the sells. The clearing corporation notifies the firm and the contra parties of the net position.

The process eliminates needless repetition and the unnecessary delivery and redelivery of shares, thereby cutting cost and saving time.

See also BROKERAGE HOUSE; SETTLE.

NET CAPITAL REQUIREMENT (United States)

A rule for brokerage firms set by the Securities and Exchange Commission under Rule 15c3-1, the *Net Capital Requirement* requires a ratio of net capital to be maintained. This ratio measures the proportion of cash, and assets readily converted to cash, against the aggregated indebtedness of investors. The indebtedness cannot exceed the cash by more than 1500%.

Calculations must be made by the firm on a daily basis and are monitored by the SEC.

See also BROKERAGE HOUSE; CASH; SECURITIES AND EXCHANGE COMMISSION (SEC).

NET CHANGE

Usually, the *Net Change* for exchange traded shares is the difference between closing prices from one day to the next. However, for over-the-counter (OTC) shares the difference in bid prices is commonly used as the basis for calculating the net change. For mutual funds, net change is the change in the net asset value.

When price information appears in the newspapers for shares, bonds, and mutual funds, the net change per individual unit will also be listed.

See also ASK PRICE; BID PRICE; LAST TRADE; NET ASSET VALUE (NAV).

NET CURRENT ASSETS

Current assets minus current liabilities gives the figure for a company's *Net Current Assets*. This amount is also known as the company's working capital, or the money they need to conduct day-to-day operations.

Security analysts subtract preferred stock and divide the net current assets by the number of ordinary shares outstanding to calculate the working capital per share. The per share figure is believed to be a conservative figure for the company's liquidation value.

If the net current assets per share are higher than the market price, an analyst may conclude that the market price is undervalued and will rate the share as a possible buy. Other analysts disagree with this form of analysis, believing the theory ignores the efficiency of capital markets in general. Long-term items such as pension plan obligations do not appear on the balance sheet and may have some impact on the company.

Net quick assets (NQA) is a stricter measurement of liquidity, because it removes inventories from current assets. Net current assets minus inventories minus current liabilities reveals net quick assets. When the NQA is divided by current liabilities it provides investors with the acid test ratio.

See also ACID TEST RATIO; CURRENT ASSETS; CURRENT LIABILITIES; QUICK ASSET RATIO; QUICK ASSETS.

NET PRICE

A *Net Price* is a quotation with any commission, mark up, mark down, or fees included.

Initial Public Offerings are usually quoted at a net price, and no additional commission is added on to the price. All fees and commissions are paid by the issuer out of the proceeds from the issue offering.

See also COMMISSION; INITIAL PUBLIC OFFERING (IPO); SALES CHARGE.

NET PROCEEDS

Net Proceeds are the total amount of cash received when an investor sells a securities position. They have all commissions and any other fees deducted as noted on the trade confirmation. The net proceeds figure is important when calculating capital gains for tax purposes. Ordinarily, the total cost of the purchase has the net proceeds subtracted from it, and the remainder represents the capital gain or capital loss.

For example, if an investor buys 100 shares of XYZ Corporation for a price of $50 per share and a commission of $40, with an exchange fee of $1.25, the total cost to buy would be $5,041.25. If the shares are later sold for $55 per share, with a commission of $40 and an exchange fee of $1.25, the net proceeds would be $5,541.25. The capital gain on the transaction would be:

Net proceeds	$5,541.25
−Total buy cost	$5,041.25
Capital gain	$ 500.00

NET QUICK ASSETS (NQA)

See NET CURRENT ASSETS.

NET SALES

Net Sales (revenues) is the total amount of sales or revenues minus any adjustments for refunds or returns of product. It represents the inflow of cash to the company and can be an important analytical tool.

Earnings can be massaged by changing accounting methods, laying off staff, or repurchasing stock. However, sales revenue is used by many analysts as an important indicator of a company's progress.

See also EARNINGS; FUNDAMENTAL ANALYSIS; NET.

NET WORTH

Net Worth is the amount by which total assets exceed total liabilities. For a company, net worth is also known as *shareholder's equity* or *net assets*.

An individual's net worth is calculated by totaling the complete value of possessions (e.g., house, car, securities) minus all debts and liabilities (e.g., mortgage, credit balances, and other debts).

Individual net worth can become an important consideration for qualifying as a buyer for some of the more speculative investments. Brokerage firms will often require a minimum net worth to buy such investments.

See also ASSET; LIABILITIES; SUITABILITY/SUITABILITY RULE.

NETHERLANDS, KINGDOM OF THE

Netherlands (Nederland (Dutch), Koninkrijk der Nederlanden; Holland) is a country located in northwestern Europe. It is bordered on the east by Germany and on the south by Belgium.

Area: 16,163 square miles (41,863 square km)

Population: 15,487,000 (90.4% urban; 9.6% rural)

Form of Government: Constitutional monarchy, with a parliament comprised of two legislative houses: First Chamber—75 members; Second Chamber—150 members. Chief of state: Monarch. Head of government: Prime Minister.

Official Language: Dutch

Capital: Amsterdam (Seat of government: The Hague)

Largest Cities: Amsterdam, 724,096; Rotterdam, 598,521; The Hague, 445,279; Utrecht, 234,106; Eindhoven, 196,130

Economy:

Currency: Guilder (G)

National Budget: Revenue—G 180.4 billion; expenditures—G 197.2 billion (social security and public health: 38.0%; education and culture: 10.5%; debt service: 9.2%; defense: 4.2%; transportation: 2.9%).

Public Debt: US$195.9 billion

Gross National Product: US$316.4 billion

Principal Products: Vegetables; livestock; machinery; chemicals; fuels

Foreign Trade (Imports): G 235.0 billion (machinery and transport equipment: 28.5%, of which road vehicles: 6.5%; foodstuffs, beverages, and tobacco: 11.7%; chemicals and chemical products: 10.7%; mineral fuels: 8.8%, of which petroleum: 5.1%; clothing: 3.8%; from Germany: 23.5%; Belgium-Luxembourg: 11.7%; United Kingdom: 9.6%; United States: 8.0%; France: 7.5%)

Foreign Trade (Exports): G 258.2 billion (machinery and transport equipment: 23.6%, of which road vehicles: 2.9%; foodstuffs, beverages, and tobacco: 19.4%; chemicals and chemical products: 15.0%; mineral fuels: 8.5%, of which petroleum products: 5.5%; iron and steel: 2.0%; clothing: 1.7%; to Germany: 29.1%; Belgium-Luxembourg: 12.7%; France: 10.6%; United Kingdom: 9.4%; Italy: 5.7%)

Stock Exchanges: 1
Amsterdam Stock Exchange (AEX)
Beursplein 5
PO Box 19163
1000 GD Amsterdam
The Netherlands
Phone: (31-20) 550 4444
Fax: (31-20) 550 4950

Internet Address: www.aex.nl/aexhome

Trading Hours: Monday–Friday, 9:30 to 4:30

Listed Companies: 650

Total Market Capitalization:

At 31 December 1997

Local Currency (Millions)	US Dollars (Millions)
1,013,557	499,972

Major Sectors: Banking, energy, food/spirits, airlines, industrial

The trading floor of the Amsterdam Stock Exchange. *(Courtesy of Amsterdam Exchanges NV)*

Share Price Performance:

(% Change)

1992	6
1993	44
1994	8
1995	16
1996	39
1997	43

Indices: CBS All Share Index

Supervisory Organizations:

Ministry of Finance
Association of Dutch Stockbrokers

Depository:

Central Securities Depository (Necigef)
Securities Clearing Corporation (Effectenclearing)

Settlement Details:

Shares:
Trade date + 3 days (T + 3)
Delivery versus payment available

Trading: A new equity trading system called the Trading System Amsterdam (TSA) was launched in September 1994 for the trading of equities in Holland. The system is made up of both a wholesale and retail segment. The retail segment is a central market for transaction below the wholesale limit, and is managed by a single market maker (Hoekman). The Hoekman fixes quotes on bids and offers for banks and brokers.

The wholesale system allows banks and brokers to deal directly with one another on the computer through the Automatic Interprofessional Dealing System Amsterdam (AIDA). Bid and offer prices can be announced on an advertisement screen called ASSET.

A quotation officer supervises trading and monitors the observance of trading rules on the trading floor. The officer can suspend or halt trading if necessary.

Listing Requirements:

The Application for Listing:

According to the Association in the Securities Regulations, the following documents must be included with an application:

• A copy of the prospectus, certified by the signatories, and a copy of each type of prospectus on the security that has been published outside the Netherlands

• A statement, addressed to the Association from the auditor, together with the auditor's report will be included in the prospectus testifying approval

• A statement indicating the amount or number of securities that have been placed

• A specimen of a security in each denomination

With shares, the following documents must also be included:

• A notarial deed containing the articles of association of the issuing institution, or a copy of the articles certified by a notary public, together with a certificate proving the issuing institution was created in accordance with the laws of the country of incorporation (for a Dutch corporate body this is a "declaration of no objection")

• A copy of the annual accounts and annual reports for the past five financial years

• For shares issued by a non-EU institution, a declaration from a stock exchange in the company's home country, specifying the amount or number of shares of the issuing institution that have been included in the listing and the denominations and number of the securities. This statement must also state that the issuing institution was created in accordance with the laws of the country of incorporation.

With share certificates, the same information provided with shares must be supplied, together with the following additional items:

If the certificates are issued by a trust office:

• The advert announcing the commencement of the trust activities and the availability of the trusteeship conditions

• A declaration of the trust office in accordance with Appendix VI of the Securities Regulations

If the certificates have been issued by an anti-takeover committee or association, the following must be included:

• The notarial deed containing the articles of association of the anti-takeover committee or association, or a copy of these articles of association certified by or on behalf of the board of this committee or association

• The notarial deed containing the trusteeship conditions or a copy of the trusteeship conditions, certified by the trust office or notary public

• A declaration of the anti-takeover committee or of the association in accordance with Appendix VI of the Securities Regulations

In the case of "introduction by trading," a statement from the jobbers trading in the relevant securities must be submitted declaring their willingness to:

a. Provide, on a date set by the Stock Exchange Association, a statement of the turnover volumes since the beginning of trading on the stock exchange, itemized per day, as well as the total number of members who have participated in the trading.

b. Permit the Control Office of the Stock Exchange Association to conduct an audit in respect to the above statement, as intended in the Stock Exchange Association's articles of association.

Investor Taxation: Dividends have a 25% withholding tax for non-residents, which can be reduced if a tax treaty is in operation.

There is no capital gains tax and no withholding tax on income from bonds.

Limitations: In general, there are no control restrictions on repatriation of capital and earnings.

Brokerage Firms:
ABN AMRO Bank NV
Foppingadreef 22
1102 BS Amsterdam
Netherlands
Phone: (31-20) 628 9393

Bank Bangert Pontier NV
Keizersgracht 472
1017 EG Amsterdam
Netherlands
Phone: (31-20) 520 6520

Bank Mendes Gans NV
Herengracht 619
1017 CE Amsterdam
Netherlands
Phone: (31-20) 523 5311

Bond Center Amsterdam BV
Herengracht 493
1017 BT Amsterdam
Netherlands
Phone: (31-20) 626 5535

Cate and Cie NV Effectenbank Ten
Keizersgracht 215
1016 DT Amsterdam
Netherlands
Phone: (31-20) 626 4500

Citco Bank-Nederland-NV
Strawinskylaan 3053
1077 ZX Amsterdam

Netherlands
Phone: (31-20) 662 4181

Citicorp Investment Bank (The Netherlands) NV
Hoogoorddreef 548
1101 BE Amsterdam
Netherlands
Phone: (31-20) 691 7275

CS First Boston (Nederland)-NV
Johannes Vermeerstraat 9
1017 BS Amsterdam
Netherlands
Phone: (31-20) 575 4444

Deutsche Bank-De Bary NV
Herengracht 450
1017 CA Amsterdam
Netherlands
Phone: (31-20) 555 4911

Extra Clearing BV
Papenbroekssteg 2
1012 NW Amsterdam
Netherlands
Phone: (31-20) 626 5911

Geston NV
Minervalaan 103
1077 NV Amsterdam
Netherlands
Phone: (31-20) 676 9445

IMG Holland
Investment Management Group NV
Spuistraat 114b
1023 VA Amsterdam
Netherlands
Phone: (31-20) 638 3366

Institutional Brokerage Services NV
Herengracht 467-469
1017 BS Amsterdam
Netherlands
Phone: (31-20) 523 2650

KBW Effectenbank NV
De Ruyterkade 113
1011 AB Amsterdam
Netherlands
Phone: (31-20) 626 1811

Kollem and Broekman BV, Van
Keizersgracht 317
1016 EE Amsterdam
Netherlands
Phone: (31-20) 524 9444

Leemhuis and Van Loon BV
Rokin 92-96
1012 KZ Amsterdam
Netherlands
Phone: (31-20) 556 3131

Nomura Bank Nederland NV
De Boelelaan 7
1083 HJ Amsterdam
Netherlands
Phone: (31-20) 549 6969

Dudhof Effecten NV
Rokin 99
1012 KM Amsterdam
Netherlands
Phone: (31-20) 622 0982

Perk and Schmidt International BV
Dam 3-7
1012 JS Amsterdam
Netherlands
Phone: (31-20) 626 6686

Rocorp and Partners Effecten BV
Herengracht 199-201
1016 BE Amsterdam
Netherlands
Phone: (31-20) 627 1948

Company Information:

The Best Performing Shares in the Country

Company Name	Share Price Change 1 January 1997 to 31 December 1997 (%)
Unique International	315
Asm Lithography Hldg. Nv	208
Simac Techniek	202
Axa Actief Beheer Nl	182
Volker Wessels Stevin	150
Athlon Groep	145
Kempen & Co	139
Baan	139
Nbm-Amstelland	115
Fugro	109
Arnhemsche	94
Ordina Beheer	92

Company Name	Share Price Change 1 January 1997 to 31 December 1997 (%)
Uni-Invest (Verenig)	87
Heijmans	82
Asr Verzekeringsgroep	80
Aegon	79
Philips Eltn.	77
Moolen (Van Der)	74
Ing Groep Certs.	67
Unilever Certs.	63
Calve-Delft Cert.	60
Draka Hdg.	59
Kas-Associatie	59
Vnu	59
Randstad Hldg.	53
Ahold Kon.	53
Haltrust 'B'	52
Internatio Muller	51
Schuttersveld	50
Haltrust Unit	50
Abn Amro Holding	49
Akzo Nobel	49
Fortis Amev Certs	48
Nat.Investgbk.	48
Royal Dutch Ptl.	47
Nedap	46
Moeara Fndrs.	45
Vendex Intl.Certs.	45
Moeara Enim Ptl.	43
Moeara(Winstbew)	41
Atag Hldg.	41
Getronics	40
Nbm Amstelland Pref.	40
Norit	40
Dordtsche Ptl.Inds.	40
Cap Gemini Group	39
Aalberts Inds.	36
De Boer Unigro	35
Polynorm	34
Ahrend(Kon.) Gp.Certs.	33
Robeco	33
Hagemeyer	33
Samas Cert.	33
Hoogovens	32
Kpn	30

The Largest Companies in the Country by Market Capitalization as of 31 December 1997

Company Name	Market Capitalization Local Currency (Millions)	Market Capitalization US Dollars (Millions)
Royal Dutch Ptl.	238,660	117,727

Company Name	Market Capitalization Local Currency (Millions)	Market Capitalization US Dollars (Millions)	Company Name	Market Capitalization Local Currency (Millions)	Market Capitalization US Dollars (Millions)
Ing Groep Certs.	81,452	40,179	Wereldhave	2,101	1,037
Unilever Certs.	80,020	39,473	Vib	2,057	1,015
Abn Amro Holding	55,679	27,466	Gist-Brocades Cert.	2,056	1,014
Aegon	52,281	25,789	Volker Wessels Stevin	2,042	1,007
Philips Eltn.	43,046	21,234	Calve-Delft Cert.	2,025	999
Kpn	39,952	19,707	Telegraaf Hdg.	2,011	992
Ahold Kon.	27,521	13,576	Npm	1,901	938
Akzo Nobel	24,923	12,294	Kon.Pakhoed	1,879	927
Elsevier	23,157	11,423	Moeara(Winstbew)	1,778	877
Robeco	22,726	11,210	Moeara Enim Ptl.	1,718	848
Wolters Kluwer Cert	17,901	8,830	Internatio Muller	1,592	786
Heineken	17,711	8,737	Moeara Fndrs.	1,536	758
Polygram	17,460	8,613	Kon.Bijenkorf	1,511	745
Fortis Amev Certs	16,282	8,032	Draka Hdg.	1,447	714
Dordtsche Ptl.Inds.	16,133	7,958	Nbm-Amstelland	1,435	708
Baan	13,811	6,813	Belindo Certs.	1,424	703
Rorento	11,856	5,848	Kon.Van Leer	1,367	674
Rolinco	11,226	5,537	Endemol Entertainment	1,320	651
Vnu	10,838	5,346	Wegener Arcade Certs.	1,301	642
Rodamco	9,462	4,667	Haltrust Unit	1,298	640
Asm Lithography Hldg. Nv	9,177	4,527	Hollandsche Beton Groep	1,248	616
Vendex Intl.Certs.	8,587	4,236	Van Melle	1,238	611
Hagemeyer	8,314	4,101	Nutreco	1,153	569
Randstad Hldg.	8,240	4,065	Hoek's Machine	1,141	563
Heineken 'A'	7,697	3,797	Uni-Invest (Verenig)	1,132	558
Nutricia Vern.Bedr.	7,662	3,780	Van Ommeren	1,070	528
Getronics	5,655	2,789	Nedlloyd	1,051	518
Dsm	5,395	2,661	Ballast Nedam Ccp	1,050	518
Klm	5,162	2,546	Ahrend(Kon.) Gp.Certs.	998	492
Ispat International	4,890	2,412	Otra	989	488
Kon.Knp Bt	4,854	2,394	Boskalis Westminster	928	458
Gucci Group	4,774	2,355	Alpinvest Holding	919	454
Oce	4,446	2,193	Nbm Amstelland Pref.	894	441
Benckiser	4,398	2,169	Aalberts Inds.	859	424
Asr Verzekeringsgroep	3,871	1,909	Ing Pref	858	423
Csm Cert.	3,585	1,769	Schuitema	852	420
Hoogovens	3,077	1,518	Brunel Intl.	852	420
Cap Gemini Group	2,928	1,445	Opg Certs.	850	419
Ihc Caland	2,833	1,397	Axa Actief Beheer Nl	841	415
Bolswessanen	2,670	1,317	Grolsch (Kon.)	840	414
Arnhemsche	2,602	1,284	Vastned Retail	831	410
Hunter Douglas	2,553	1,259			
Nat.Investgbk.	2,325	1,147			
Abn Amro Hldg.Pref.	2,211	1,091			
Haltrust 'B'	2,153	1,062			
Stork	2,142	1,057			

Company Name	Market Capitalization Local Currency (Millions)	Market Capitalization US Dollars (Millions)
Rodamco Retail Ned.Fd.	823	406
Heijmans	814	401
Twentsche Kabel	782	386
Kempen & Co	778	384
Ceteco Holding	778	384
Unique International	748	369
Fugro	737	364
De Boer Unigro	731	361
Vedior	702	346
Gamma Holding	688	339
Ordina Beheer	684	337
Evc International	658	325
Moolen (Van Der)	559	276
Holland Chemical Intl.	551	272
Asm International	543	268
Vastned Offices Indl.	534	263
Besi	529	261
Kon.Knp Bt Pref.	510	252
Schuttersveld	464	229
Simac Techniek	448	221
Gti Holding	447	220
Sligro Beheer	443	219
Smit Intl.Certs.	432	213
Arcadis	429	212
Beers	423	209
Toolex-Alpha	422	208
Samas Cert.	418	206
Letterhaave	410	202
Chicago Bridge & Iron	394	195
Kas-Associatie	391	193
Athlon Groep	385	190
Cate(Kon.Ten)	378	187
Mendes Gans	374	185
Norit	372	183
Kon.Frans Maas Groep	366	180
Nedap	359	177
Nagron	350	173
Nkf Holding	333	164
Atag Hldg.	327	161
Macintosh	319	157
Polynorm	289	142
P.&C. Group	201	99

Regional Stock Exchanges: None

Other Investment Information:
Netherlands Foreign Investment Agency
Ministry of Development Corporation
PO Box 20061
Bezuidenhoutseweg 67
2500 EB The Hague
Netherlands
Phone: (31-70) 348 6486
Telex: 31326

Ministry of Housing Physical Planning and the Environment
Van Alkemadelaan 85
2597 AC The Hague
Netherlands
Phone: (31-70) 326 4201
Telex: 34429

Ministry of Social Affairs and Employment
PO Box 90801
Anna Van Hannoverstraat 4
2509 LV The Hague
Netherlands
Phone: (31-70) 333 4444
Fax: (31-70) 333 4023
Telex: 331250

De Netherlands Bank NV
PO Box 98
Westeinde 1
1000 AB Amsterdam
Netherlands
Phone: (31-20) 524 9111
Telex: 11355

NETTOHANDEL (Germany)
See NET PRICE.

NEUAUSGABE, NEUEMISSION (Germany)
See INITIAL PUBLIC OFFERING (IPO).

NEURAL NETWORK
A *Neural Network* or, more fully, an Artificial Neural Network, is a structure of electronic computer components designed to simulate a portion of the human nervous system, the main component of which is the brain. The nervous system is a complex of neurons (fundamental nerve cells) connected in an extensive network that can generate, codify, store, and use information. An impulse traveling in part of the nervous system can have the following effects:

• Induce a neuron to release another impulse into the network

• Inhibit a neuron from releasing another impulse

• Combine with other incoming impulses to reach a threshold needed for exciting a neuron

• Remain confined in a section of the network and travel in a closed loop, providing what is called "feedback"

Using an array of simple processors, each of which is called a processing element, or neuron, arranged in a specially designed pattern of interconnections, a neural network models the nervous system's capacity for processing information. The pattern of interconnections is the architecture of the neural network.

Electronic impulses in a neural network behave much as they do in the nervous system. Each processing element is programmed to perform the same basic function, using a small local memory area. A processing element receives more than one input but has only one output, which becomes an input to another processing element or an output of the network. An output may be fed back into the same processing element as input.

A feedforward network is one whose architecture contains no feedback connections. This is the most common architecture in neural networks applied to investment decision making. Various feedback configurations are also in common use. The processing that occurs in most networks is relatively simple: multiplying each input by a weighting factor, adding the resulting products, and computing an output value that is a function of that sum. Symbolically, the process is as follows:

$$x_j = T(\Sigma w_{ij}x_i)$$

where:

x_j is the output of processing element j

x_i is the input received from processing element i (or by direct input)

w_{ij} is the weighting factor, or weighting coefficient, of the link between processing elements i and j

Σ represents finding the sum of all the $w_{ij}x_i$

T represents applying a transfer, or activation, function to the sum

The most commonly used transfer functions are variations of the S-shaped sigmoid:

$$T(y) = (1 - e^{-y})^{-1}$$

where $y = \Sigma w_{ij}x_i$ and $e \approx 2.7183$.

The main distinguishing characteristic of neural networks is their architecture. Approximately 20 different architectures exist and approximately 12 of these are in common use. Most of these configurations employ layers of processing elements—normally an input layer, an output layer, and between them, one or more "hidden" layers. Most neural networks used in investment decisions have the multilayered (one or two hidden layers) feedforward architecture.

An essential feature of neural networks is that "learning" takes place. This is neural network parlance for saying the system has the capability of making adjustments to the weighting coefficients according to a built-in rule. For example, using the delta rule, the adjustment in the weighting coefficient w_{ij} is made proportional to the difference between the desired output and the actual output. About six such learning rules are in common use. A problem in the application of neural networks is the time needed by the system to learn, or to become "trained."

An experiment with applying a neural network to financial decision-making was conducted by the researchers Y. Yoon and G. Swales. To predict how the stock of a firm would perform, they used a four-layered architecture with an input layer, an output layer, and two hidden layers. See the figure below, in which each circle represents a processing element. The inputs include the following nine variables: confidence, economic factors outside the firm's control, growth, strategic plans, new products, anticipated loss, anticipated gain, long-term optimism, and short-term optimism. Values for these factors were selected from studies of the *Fortune 500* and *Business Week*'s top 1,000 firms. There were only two outputs: well-performing firm and poor-performing firm. The network correctly classified 77.5% of the test cases, compared to 65% correct using multiple discriminant analysis.

Four-Layered Network

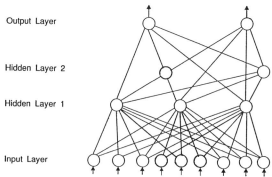

Output Layer

Hidden Layer 2

Hidden Layer 1

Input Layer

In another experiment with the application of neural networks to financial decision making, a group sponsored by Fujitsu Laboratories and Nikko Securities built a network to determine the best buy-and-sell time for the Tokyo Stock Exchange Price Index (TOPIX). The input variables were turnover, interest rate, foreign exchange rate, Dow Jones average, and several others. There was a single numerical output. An output greater than or equal to 0.5 meant "buy," while a value less than 0.5 signified "sell." The network was trained and tested during the period from January 1987 to September 1989. The network outperformed the TOPIX by 487 points—a significant difference.

Since the early 1990s, neural networks have been used extensively to assist in financial analyses. Financial areas in which neural networks are being applied include the following:
- Risk rating of fixed income investments
- Detecting irregularities in price movements of securities
- Selecting or diversifying a portfolio
- Making economic predictions
- Simulating market behavior
- Constructing security indexes
- Identifying explanatory economic factors
- "Mining" financial databases

The following are examples of some of these applications:
- A forecasting company in the United Kingdom, in association with a U.S. insurance company, used neural networks to predict returns on bonds. From November 1992 to October 1994 with $250 million under management, they achieved a 25.2% return compared to 13.6% for the Salomon index.
- LBS Capital management uses neural networks to select stocks in the management of more than $300 million in assets.
- Dai-ichi Kangyo Bank and Fujitsu developed a neural network to assist in predicting the interest rate on Treasury bonds. Since 1990, the system has been 75% accurate, compared to 60% accuracy by human experts.
- Swiss Bank Corporation uses neural networks for market-timing decisions.
- Siemens/Siemens-Nixdorf developed a neural network to predict day-to-day movements in the Deutsche Aktienindex (DAX), a capitalization-weighted index of 30 blue chip stocks. In an 11-month test the system achieved a 41% return. The system is now being used by a financial institution in Germany.
- Siemens/Siemens-Nixdorf also developed a neural network to predict the exchange rate between the German mark and the U.S. dollar. A one-year test of the network yielded a 50% return. This system is also now being used by a financial institution in Germany.

Neural networks differ significantly from so-called expert systems, the operation of which depends on programmer-supplied formulas and algorithms (rules of procedure) correlating input to output. Because of their learning feature, neural networks are particularly suited to making associations, classifying, and recognizing patterns, and thereby making their own correlation of input to output. In performing these tasks neural networks are many times faster than conventional computers. Today, there is a great deal of interest in integrating neural networks with rule-based systems.

Neural network financial software that will run on a personal computer is now available for as little as $200, but in evaluating this technology one should remember that the computer dictum "garbage in, garbage out" still applies. That is, neural networks do fall into the realm of artificial intelligence, and they are constructed with the view of simulating the brain. However, in the final analysis these devices still depend on the expertise of their programmers and the currency and suitability of the input data.

See also COMPUTER TRADING; DEALING ROOM TECHNOLOGY.

NEW ACCOUNT FORM

A *New Account Form* is a form used to set up a brokerage investing account.

See also CASH ACCOUNT; MARGIN ACCOUNT.

NEW ISSUE

See INITIAL PUBLIC OFFERING (IPO).

NEW YORK COMMODITY EXCHANGE (COMEX)

See NEW YORK MERCANTILE EXCHANGE (NYMEX).

NEW YORK COTTON EXCHANGE (NYCE)

Four World Trade Center
New York, NY 10048
Phone: (212) 938-2650
Fax: (212) 839-8061
New York E-mail: nyce.marketing@mcimail.com
Europe E-mail: 2031220@mcimail.com
Internet: www.nyce.com

The *New York Cotton Exchange (NYCE)* was founded in 1870 by a group of cotton brokers and merchants. It was incorporated by the New York State Legislature in 1871, and is the oldest futures exchange in New York. NYCE is organized under and governed by the New York Not-For-Profit Corporation Law, and it provides a facility for its members to trade commodity futures and futures options contracts. NYCE is owned by its members who represent either commercial users, commission houses, or themselves.

Cotton futures were launched in 1870, and cotton futures options were introduced in 1984, after a ban on agricultural options was lifted by the government. Today, the exchange is the premier marketplace for cotton futures and futures options trading. In the fall of 1996, NYCE introduced the Special Potato Underlying Division (SPUDs), a division that trades potato futures and futures options. Over the years, the exchange and its affiliates have expanded and enhanced services to meet the needs of the marketplace.

Affiliated Exchanges/Divisions

The Commodity Clearing Corporation (CCC) has been a wholly owned subsidiary of NYCE since December 1992. The CCC is incorporated under and governed by the New York Business Corporation Law. The CCC acts as the central clearing organization for contracts made on NYCE including its FINEX (financial instruments) division and the Citrus Associates of the New York Cotton Exchange, Inc. (Citrus Associates). The CCC is made up of its clearing members who must meet the requirements set forth in the CCC's by-laws and rules.

Citrus Associates is organized under and subject to the New York Not-For-Profit Corporation Law. Trading Frozen Concentrated Orange Juice (FCOJ) futures began in 1966, and options on FCOJ futures were introduced in 1985. It is a contract market designated by the Commodity Futures Trading Commission (CFTC) for trading in FCOJ futures and futures options contracts. Citrus Associates is made up of Class-A members (full NYCE members) and associate members.

New York Futures Exchange, Inc. (NYFE) is a wholly owned subsidiary of NYCE. NYFE was incorporated in New York in 1979, and acquired by NYCE on 31 December 1993. It consists of 361 members and currently has 434 seats. NYFE offers trading in futures and futures options in the NYSE Composite Index, KR-CRB Index, and PSE Technology 100 Indexes. NYFE has shared trading space with NYCE at the Commodities Exchange Center, Inc. since 1988. NYFE trades are cleared through Intermarket Clearing Corporation (ICC), a subsidiary of Options Clearing Corporation (OCC).

FINEX, established in 1985 as the financial division of NYCE, offers trading of futures and futures options in various financial products. FINEX first began listing futures and futures options on the U.S. Dollar Index (USDX) in 1985. FINEX continued to diversify its product base, and in 1994, FINEX Europe in Dublin, Ireland, was created as a complementary trading facility. FINEX Europe provides the European market with access to an open-outcry exchange. Coinciding with the opening of FINEX Europe, currency futures and futures options against the Deutschemark and U.S. dollar were introduced.

For more than 125 years, NYCE has been a leading force in the futures industry. Today, the exchange is meeting the needs of market participants by providing a diverse range of agricultural and financial products. The exchange and its affiliates have and will continue to introduce innovative products to meet global demands.

See also NEW YORK FUTURES EXCHANGE (NYFE).

NEW YORK FUTURES EXCHANGE (NYFE)
Four World Trade Center
8th Floor Boardroom
New York, NY 10048
Phone: (212) 938-4940
Fax: (212) 488-8135
Internet: www.nyfe.com

The *New York Futures Exchange (NYFE)* is a wholly owned subsidiary of the New York Cotton Exchange (NYCE), the oldest futures exchange in New York. NYFE trades financial products, including futures and futures options, on the New York Stock Exchange (NYSE) Composite Index, CRB, and the PSE Technology 100 Indexes. NYFE's products are traded alongside a variety of financial and agricultural products, making NYCE one of the first international exchanges to so broadly diversify its product line.

Trading was first approved for the NYFE as a contract market to trade futures contracts for certain foreign currencies and U.S. government instruments. Trading started 7 August 1980, with 20-year U.S. Treasury bond futures contracts. NYFE also received authorization to trade futures in five foreign currencies—the British pound, Canadian dollar, German mark, Japanese yen, and Swiss franc.

New York exchanges were late entering the financial futures market. The American Stock Exchange experimented with financial futures trading in August 1978. After two years the activity was merged into the New York Futures Exchange. The Commodity Exchange, Inc. expanded futures trading in 1979, and included U.S. Treasury bills and Government National Mortgage Association certificates of deposit, expanding further into Treasury notes in 1980. The New York Mercantile Exchange discontinued the trading of foreign currency futures including the British pound, Canadian dollar, German mark, Japanese yen, Belgian franc, and Swiss franc.

On 3 February 1997 the Commodity Futures Trading Commission (CFTC) approved expanded trading limits for the NYFE's NYSE Composite Index futures contract. These new limits will have the effect of keeping trading in the NYSE Index and other stock index futures contracts synchronized with one another and with the NYSE's expanded circuit breakers during times of market duress by coordinating the trading halt periods and price limits of the futures contracts.

In addition to the expanded opening period limit, which applies when the futures contract moves 4.00 points up or down from the prior day's close, further limits may trigger trading halts when the futures contract moves 9.00, 17.00, 25.00, 40.00, or 50.00 points down from the prior day's close.

According to Norman Eisler, Chairman of the NYFE, the expanded trading limits recognize the higher levels that the equities market has attained since the original limits were set, and also help ensure that the market continues to function effectively as a price discovery and hedging mechanism.

See also COMMODITY FUTURES TRADING COMMISSION (CFTC); FUTURES CONTRACT; FUTURES TRADING.

NEW YORK MERCANTILE EXCHANGE (NYMEX)

One North End Avenue
World Financial Center
New York, NY 10282
Phone: (212) 299-2000
Fax: (212) 301-4700
Internet: www.nymex.com

On 3 August 1994 the *New York Mercantile Exchange (NYMEX)* bought the New York Commodity Exchange (COMEX) for $62 million. The result of this merger between New York's two largest exchanges was the fifth largest futures exchange in the world, which by 1996 was trading approximately 400 million commodity contracts each year. Trading is conducted through two divisions. The NYMEX Division has 816 seats held by members who trade in energy and platinum group metals futures and options.The COMEX Division has 772 seats held by futures and options traders in gold, silver, copper, and the European Options Exchange.

Commodity exchanges in the United States date back to the mid-19th century. Businessmen began organizing market forums to make the buying and selling of commodities easier. These central market-places provided a place for buyers and sellers—essentially farmers and grain dealers—to meet, set quality and quantity standards, and establish rules of business. Over a period of 50 years—from the mid- to late 19th century—approximately 1,600 exchanges sprang up across the United States, mostly at major railheads, inland water ports, and seaports.

Agricultural commodities were the most commonly traded, but a market will flourish for almost any commodity as long as there is an active pool of buyers and sellers. There is no telling what will lubricate the wheels of commerce—cat pelts were once a hot item in St. Louis, and today dried cocoons are a major exchange-traded commodity in Japan.

In 1872 a group of Manhattan dairy merchants got together to bring some order to the chaotic conditions that were prevalent in the New York markets. The city had the nation's most poorly organized and least economical system for the storage, pricing, and transfer of agricultural products. The merchants hoped that the newly established Butter and Cheese Exchange of New York would improve the efficiency of the marketplace.

Within a few years, the egg trade became an important part of the business conducted on the exchange, and the name was modified to the Butter, Cheese and Egg Exchange. Efforts were also made to attract traders of groceries, dried fruits, canned goods, and poultry, and in 1882 the name was changed again to the New York Mercantile Exchange.

In the early 1900s the number of commodity exchanges in the United States declined sharply. The main reasons for this were the development of means of communication and transportation; the building of centralized warehouses in the main market centers; the creation of a national market that superseded the regional markets; and the consolidation of exchanges in the principal market centers. By the mid-1990s only nine of the more than 1,600 commodity exchanges of a century earlier still existed.

In 1933, during the Great Depression, the Commodity Exchange, Inc., was established in New York through the merger of four small exchanges—the National Metal Exchange, the Rubber Exchange of New York, the National Raw Silk Exchange, and the New York Hide Exchange. A variety of commodities were traded on the new exchange: copper, hides, rubber, silk, silver, and tin. Because of the national economic crisis at the time, the use of gold as money in the United States had been discontinued shortly before COMEX was founded. Private ownership of the metal was forbidden until 31 December 1974, when the restrictions were lifted, and gold finally opened for trading on COMEX.

In the 1970s and 1980s COMEX experienced a number of problems. The most important were the difficulties with the Hunt brothers and their near cornering of the futures market in silver in 1979–80; the massive outtrade problem of 1983; the 1985 default of one of the exchange's clearing firms, Volume Investors, which missed a $26 million margin call; and the silver crash of April 1987.

A gradually worsening problem during this period was the fact that COMEX did not deal in financial futures at all. As these futures assumed increasing importance, they tended to displace the two major contracts of COMEX, gold and silver, as a hedge against volatile interest or exchange rates. For the years 1988–93, options on gold, silver, and copper dropped 10%. For all these reasons as well as more positive ones, such as taking advantage of economies of scale, COMEX was ripe to be purchased by NYMEX in 1994.

In 1993 NYMEX opened its after-hours electronic trading system, NYMEX ACCESS. With the addition of slightly extended hours on the exchange floor, NYMEX ACCESS made it possible for commodities to be traded 22 hours per day. Buyers and sellers around the world could thus exchange futures and options contracts at virtually any time for crude oil, heating oil, gasoline, natural gas, and platinum, and futures contracts for gold, silver, copper, and propane. As a result, the exchange became more competitive internationally vis-à-vis such exchanges as the London Metals Exchange and the International Petroleum Exchange.

See also CHICAGO MERCANTILE EXCHANGE; HUNT BROTHERS.

NEW YORK STOCK EXCHANGE (NYSE)

See UNITED STATES/NEW YORK STOCK EXCHANGE (NYSE).

NEW ZEALAND, DOMINION OF

New Zealand (Aotearoa (Maori)) is an island nation in the South Pacific.

Area: 104,454 square miles (270,534 square km)

Population: 3,568,000 (68.6% urban; 31.4% rural)

Form of Government: Constitutional monarchy, with one legislative house: House of Representatives—99 members. Chief of state: British Monarch, represented by Governor-General. Head of government: Prime Minister.

Official Languages: English; Maori

Capital: Wellington

Largest Cities: Auckland, 336,500; Christchurch, 308,800; Manukau, 243,400; North Shore, 163,600; Wellington, 153,800

Economy:

Currency: New Zealand Dollar (NZ$)

National Budget: Revenue—NZ$29.6 billion; expenditures—NZ$29.2 billion (social services: 36.1%; education: 15.9%; health: 14.1%; administration: 10.2%)

Public Debt: NZ$29.6 billion

Gross National Product: US$44.7 billion

Principal Products: Food and livestock; minerals and metals; basic manufactures

Foreign Trade (Imports): NZ$18.5 million (machinery: 24.6%; minerals, chemicals, and plastics: 22.2%; transport equipment: 13.5%; basic manufactures: 7.6%; metals and metal products: 5.9%; textiles, clothing, and footwear: 5.7%; from Australia: 21.5%; United States: 18.1%; Japan: 15.8%; United Kingdom: 6.1%; Germany: 4.4%)

Foreign Trade (Exports): NZ$19.8 billion (food and live animals: 46.5%; basic manufactures: 25.4%; minerals, chemicals, and plastics: 11.5%; metals and metal products: 6.5%; to Australia: 21.0%; Japan: 14.6%; United States: 11.2%; United Kingdom: 6.0%; South Korea: 4.7%; Germany: 2.5%)

Stock Exchanges: 1
The New Zealand Stock Exchange (NZSE)
ASB Bank Tower
Level 9
2 Hunter Street
Wellington
New Zealand
Phone: (64-4) 472-7599
Fax: (64-4) 473-1470
Telex: NZ3424

Internet Address: www.nzse.co.nz

Trading Hours:
Monday–Friday   8:30 to 9:30   Pre-opening session
                 9:30 to 3:30

Exchange Holidays:
1, 2 January   1 June
6 February   26 October
25 April   24*, 25, 26, 31* December
(*Half-day, settlement remains unchanged.)

Listed Companies: 225 total

146 domestic
 79 foreign

Total Market Capitalization:

At 31 December 1997

Local Currency (Millions)	US Dollars (Millions)
50,814	29,505

Major Sectors: Agriculture and associated services, automotive, building, chemical and fertilizer, construction, electrical, energy and fuel, engineering, finance and banks, food, forestry and forest products, insurance, investments

Share Price Performance:

(% Change)

1992	16
1993	42
1994	-2
1995	13
1996	-1
1997	20

History: The first stock exchanges in New Zealand were formed in Auckland, Thames, Dunedin, and Reefton in the 1870s. These were the financial centers of the early goldfields. As gold fever waned, the Thames and Reefton exchanges fell by the wayside. Auckland and Dunedin developed commercially and industrially, along with Wellington and Christchurch, and exchanges were established. No attempt was made to provide a system that would directly facilitate the transfer of shares and the dissemination of market information. In 1872, however, 12 brokers formed the Auckland Sharebrokers' Association, with Joseph Newman as chairman. This move signaled the first stages in the development of a fair market in New Zealand.

In 1897 the Auckland Sharebrokers Association changed its name to the Auckland Stock Exchange. It was 1910 before a meeting could be convened with other exchanges to agree on common rules. In 1915 the Stock Exchange Association of New Zealand, a loose-knit body of regional exchanges and forerunner to the present New Zealand Stock Exchange, was formed.

The NZSE today operates under the Sharebrokers Act Amendment, which became effective in 1983.

Classes of Securities: Fully or partly paid ordinary, specified preference, redeemable specified preference, and cumulative preference shares, options, rights and equity warrants

Indices:

NZSE Top 40 Gross and Capital Indices (base = 1,000 1 July 1986):

Covers 40 of the largest and most liquid stocks listed and quoted on the NZSE, weighted by market capitalization. Membership is reviewed quarterly. Gross indices calculate dividends reinvested. Capital indices are without dividends reinvested.

NZSE 30 Selection Gross and Capital Indices (back calculated to January 1991):

Covers the 30 stocks in the NZSE-40 Index with the largest float capital. The float capital of each company is established by removing all known blocks of shares held, or more-or-less controlled, by one person or a group of related persons and amounting to 30% or more of the share capital. This reflects, as nearly as practical, the shares normally available to investors. The NZSE-30 Selection Index is weighted by float (available) capital and membership is reviewed quarterly.

Top 10 Gross and Capital Indices: (base = 1,000 July 1988)

The NZSE developed this index to reflect the movement of prices in the shares of major companies in which there is greater public interest and in which the majority of turnover on the exchange takes place. As such, the index is of interest to private investors as well as to institutions and companies who closely follow the performance of leading companies.

The Top 10 securities are defined as the top ten listed securities by capitalization among the top 20 trading. The Top 10 is calculated in the same way as the NZSE Gross and Capital Indices. Each security is weighted by its capitalization. Capitalization is the latest market price multiplied by the same number of shares issued in the security. This is not the same as a companies capitalization, in that it only counts head shares.

The Top 10 Capital Index is the basis for the TOP futures contract offered by the NZ Futures and Options Exchange, since 4 August 1995. The Top 10 has defined restricted membership. Members are not necessarily New Zealand shares or securities. Overseas securities are eligible for inclusion in the index if trading on the New Zealand market represents a major proportion of the total trading.

Capital Index Formula:

$$\frac{\text{Sum of (last sale price} \times \text{current number of shares)}}{\text{Sum of (adjusted opening price today not adjusted for dividends} \times \text{current number of shares)}} \times \text{End-of-Day index previous day}$$

Gross Index:

$$\frac{\text{Sum of (last sale price} \times}{\text{current number of shares)}} \times \frac{\text{End-of-Day index}}{\text{previous day}}$$

Sum of (opening price today adjusted for dividends × current number of shares)

The rules on processing Diary Adjustments for the NZSE Gross and Capital Indices are:

1. The market value of the security is taken to be the latest market price multiplied by the number of shares. When a Diary Adjustment is applied, an adjusted price is calculated which reflects the expected effect of the adjustment. The index calculations for the next day are based on the adjusted price.

2. The basic principle is that each Dairy Adjustment may change the total number of shares outstanding (e.g. the issue of bonus shares) and may change the market value of the security (e.g. payment of a dividend). The adjusted price of the shares is calculated so that the adjusted price, multiplied by the new number of shares, equals the new market value.

3. A Bonus Issue of shares increases the number of shares without any movement of money. The price is therefore reduced in the same proportion as the shares are diluted. A bonus of M new shares for every N old shares held means:

New Price = Old Price × N / (M+N)

In effect, the market value (old price × N) is divided among the new number of shares (M+N).

4. In the case of a Rights Issue, the number of shares is increased and money is brought into the company by the payment of money from subscribers. The adjusted price is calculated on the assumption that all rights are exercised. A rights issue of M new shares for each N old shares held means:

New Price =
(Old Price × N + Appl'n Money × M) / (M+N)

In effect, the old market value (old price × N) plus the additional value (appl'n money × M) is divided among the new number of shares (M+N).

5. Dividends in New Zealand are quoted net of imputation tax. The amount payable directly to the shareholder may then be reduced by deduction of resident withholding tax. For the purpose of calculating adjusted prices, the relevant figure is taken to be the total payment by the company (i.e., the raw dividend plus imputation tax).

Supervisory Organizations:
Securities Commission
New Zealand Stock Exchange

Depository: None

Settlement Details:

Shares:
Trade date + 5 days (T + 5)
Notification of buy-ins after T + 8 days

The first phase of Electronic Registration, implemented in August 1992, was a system called Fully Automated Screen Trading and Electronic Registration (FASTER). It allows for the electronic transfer of securities in settlement of market transactions between brokers.

Brokers maintain accounts (broker transfer account) at the share registry and electronically transfer shares in and out of their accounts at the share registry. Transfers are made directly on company share registers and not through a depository or through a subregister. At the same time, the NZSE processes the settlement between brokers in respect of broker to broker transfers. An electronic transfer is initiated by a selling broker's in-house system interfaced to the NZSE's computer system. The NZSE's computer system will then connect to the respective share registry's computer in order to transfer securities to the buying brokers transfer account. The NZSE's computer system effectively acts as a message switch between broker and the share registry systems operating in New Zealand.

Electronic registration also allows for the movement of shares between broker transfer accounts and their clients. These are referred to as client inward and outward transfers. The second stage of electronic registration is to remove the requirement for physical delivery of certificates for the sale.

Trading: Trading is done via a National Automated Screen Based trading system. The screen based trading system allows brokers to enter bids and offers into a terminal based in their individual offices. Bids and offers are captured on a time priority basis at each successive price level. The screen based trading system is interfaced to the Broker-to-Broker Accounting system of settlement. Brokers may communicate inter-office and inter-broker via the screen trading system. All quotations are captured electronically and disseminated by broadcast signal to brokers and other media. The computer system provides a matched sale advice to each party. Matched trades generate automated trade reports at the end of each trading day. Sales data is also disseminated via the broadcast signal.

Listing Requirements: The listing rules of the New Zealand Stock Exchange contain the terms of a contract under which issuers wishing to have their securities traded throughout the NZSE agree to abide by the rules imposed to facilitate the efficient operation of the market in the interests of securities issuers, buyers, sellers, and brokers.

The NZSE requires listed issuers to supply all relevant information promptly to them for immediate dissemination to inform both existing shareholders and prospective shareholders, who may wish to trade on the market. Preliminary company announcements for the full and half year are required by the NZSE within three months of balance date with the annual audited accounts required within four months of balance date.

In July 1989, the Securities (Substantial Security Holders) Regulations 1989 were introduced pursuant to the Securities Amendment Act of 1988. These regulations require holders of securities of listed companies to disclose their shareholding if they hold more than 5% of the listed issuer.

Investor Taxation: Non-resident withholding tax (NRWT) is currently imposed on New Zealand dividends paid to non-resident shareholders at the rate of 30% of the amount of the dividend. When the shareholder resides in a country with which New Zealand has a double tax treaty, a lesser rate, usually 15%, applies. Where a non-resident shareholder receives a dividend from a New Zealand resident company, the amount received will be the dividend reduced by NRWT. Interest payments are also subject to non-resident withholding tax at a current rate of 15%, or at 0% in cases in which an approved issuer levy has been paid. There is no formal capital gains tax.

Limitations: New Zealand has a policy of actively encouraging foreign investment. Although a range of proposals for investment in New Zealand require official consent (namely investments exceeding NZ$10 million and investments in commercial fishing and rural land), as a general policy such approval can be obtained without difficulty. Such areas as broadcasting and telecommunications are relatively open to foreign investment.

These matters are regulated by the Overseas Investment Commission (OIC) pursuant to the provisions of the Overseas Investment Act of 1973, and the Overseas Investment Regulations 1985.

Securities Lending: Allowed

Brokerage Firms:
Access Brokerage Ltd
SP 22010
Wellington Central
PO Box 1293
Wellington
New Zealand
Phone: (64-4) 473-4644
Fax: (64-4) 473-4681

ANZ McCaughan Securities (NZ) Ltd.
CP 25506
PO Box 6243
Auckland
New Zealand
Phone: (64-9) 308-9867
Fax: (64-9) 309-9410

Baldwin Smith & Co.
PO Box 140
Blenheim
New Zealand
Phone: (64-3) 578-9869
Fax: (64-3) 578-0832

Broad & Piper
YA 90049
PO Box 844
Invercargill
New Zealand
Phone: (64-3) 218-4167
Fax: (64-3) 218-2238

BZW New Zealand Ltd.
CP21009
PO Box 3464
Auckland
New Zealand
Phone: (64-9) 358-7500
Fax: (64-9) 377-9797

H.J. Chapman
SP20019
PO Box 749
Taupo
New Zealand
Phone: (64-7) 378-7150
Fax: (64-7) 378-0110

Clavell Equities
PO Box 1917

Auckland
New Zealand
Phone: (64-9) 309-1553
Fax: (64-9) 309-3048

CS First Boston NZ Securities Ltd.
SP20056
PO Box 3394
Wellington
New Zealand
Phone: (64-4) 474-4400
Fax: (64-4) 472-3764

County Natwest Securities New Zealand Ltd.
SX10047
PO Box 1821
Wellington
New Zealand
Phone: (64-4) 496-9100
Fax: (64-4) 499-9940

Direct Broking Ltd.
SP20049
PO Box 1790
Wellington
New Zealand
Phone: (64-4) 499-6655
Fax: (64-4) 499-5757

Egden Wignall & Co.
WP20153
PO Box 2335
Christchurch
New Zealand
Phone: (64-3) 379-2600
Fax: (64-3) 379-1196

Esam Cushing & Company
MA75092
PO Box 241
Hastings
New Zealand
Phone: (64-6) 876-8129
Fax: (64-6) 878-5059

Garlick & Co. Ltd.
SP20042
PO Box 2098
Wellington
New Zealand
Phone: (64-4) 473-4620
Fax: (64-4) 472-5712

Gould Steele & Co.
PO Box 1739
Wellington
New Zealand
Phone: (64-4) 472-8211
Fax: (64-4) 473-9991

Jordan Sandman Were Ltd.
CP22007
PO Box 887
Auckland
New Zealand
Phone: (64-9) 309-9800
Fax: (64-9) 309-9861

Ming Shan Sharebrokers Ltd.
CP27504
PO Box 5632
New Zealand
Phone: (64-9) 373-5888
Fax: (64-9) 373-3739

Noble & Co.
GA27001
PO Box 76
Matamata
New Zealand
Phone: (64-7) 888-7033
Fax: (64-7) 888-7554

SBC Warburg New Zealand Equities Ltd.
CP241129
PO Box 45
Auckland
New Zealand
Phone: (64-9) 307-4800
Fax: (64-9) 307-4888

R.M. Story
PO Box 979
Wanganui
New Zealand
Phone: (64-6) 345-7950
Fax: (64-6) 345-8310

Young & Co.
PP82001
PO Box 1144
Palmerston North
New Zealand
Phone: (64-6) 358-4029
Fax: (64-6) 356-4082

Company Information:

The Best Performing Shares in the Country

Company Name	Share Price Change 1 January 1997 to 31 December 1997 (%)
Colonial Motor	745
Nzse 10 Index Fund	241
Baycorp Holdings	67
Tr City Of London	61
Fletch.Chal.Energy Divn.	47
Progressive Enterprises	40
Corporate Invs.	38
Warehouse Group	35

The Largest Companies in the Country by Market Capitalization as of 31 December 1997

Company Name	Market Capitalization Local Currency (Millions)	Market Capitalization US Dollars (Millions)
Telecom Corp.Of Nz.	15,778	9,162
Carter Holt Harvey	4,599	2,670
Brierley Invs.	3,292	1,912
Fletch.Chal.Energy Divn.	2,324	1,350
Lion Nathan	2,114	1,228
Fletch.Chal.Paper Divn.	1,738	1,009
Tr City Of London	1,390	807
Templeton Emerg	1,286	747
Fletch.Chal.Forest Divn.	1,235	717
Fletch.Chal.Bldg.Divn.	1,182	686
Inde.Newspapers	1,108	643
Wilson & Horton	1,033	600
Air New Zealand 'B'	958	556
Colonial Motor	931	540
Power New Zealand	916	532
Ports Of Auckland	842	489
Tranz Rail Holdings	824	478
Sky Network Tv.	794	461
Kiwi Inc.Pr.Tst. Convertible Notes	727	422
Air New Zealand 'A'	676	393
Warehouse Group	658	382
Fernz	643	373
Fisher & Paykel Inds.	619	359
Gpg	600	349
Sky City	585	340
Enerco New Zealand	484	281
New Zealand Refining	480	279
Transalta New Zealand	468	272
Progressive Enterprises	446	259

Company Name	Market Capitalization Local Currency (Millions)	Market Capitalization US Dollars (Millions)
Corporate Invs.	391	227
Kiwi Inc.Pr.Tst.	330	192
Milburn New Zealand	286	166
Trustpower	281	163
Sanford	278	162
Db Group	277	161
Amp Nz Office	250	145
Baycorp Holdings	243	141
Port Of Tauranga	241	140
Waste Management Nz.	241	140
St.Lukes Group	231	134
Nzse 10 Index Fund	210	122
Shortland Properties	199	116
Trans Tasman Properties	195	113
Independent Press Preference Division	193	112
Lyttelton Port Company	192	111
Steel & Tube Holdings	189	110
Infrastructure & Utils.	186	108
Hellaby Hdg.	151	88
Nuplex Industries	149	86
Rest.Brands Of Nz.	145	84

Regional Stock Exchanges: None

Other Investment Information:

Overseas Investment Commission
PO Box 2498
Wellington
New Zealand
Phone: (64-4) 472-2029
Fax: (64-4) 472-3262

Ministry of Commerce
PO Box 1473
32 Bowen Street
Wellington
New Zealand
Phone: (64-4) 472-0030

Ministry of the Environment
PO Box 10362
Wellington
New Zealand
Phone: (64-4) 473-4090
Fax: (64-4) 471-0195

Immigration Service
Business Immigration Section
PO Box 4130
120 The Terrace
Wellington
New Zealand
Phone: (64-4) 473-9100
Fax: (64-4) 471-2118

Reserve Bank of New Zealand
PO Box 2498
2 The Terrace
Wellington
New Zealand
Phone: (64-4) 472-2029
Fax: (64-4) 473-8554
Telex: NZ3368

NICARAGUA

Nicaragua (Republica de Nicaragua) is the largest country in Central America. It is bordered by Honduras on the north and Costa Rica on the south.

Area: 50,464 square miles (130,700 square km)

Population: 4,340,000 (61.6% urban; 38.4% rural)

Form of Government: Unitary multiparty republic, with one legislative house: National Assembly—92 members. Head of state and government: President.

Official Language: Spanish

Capital: Managua

Largest Cities: Managua, 973,759; Leon, 172,042; Masaya, 101,878; Chinandega, 101,605; Matagalpa, 95,268; Granada, 91,929

Economy:

Currency: Gold cordoba (C$)

National Budget: Revenue—C$2.5 billion; expenditures—C$2.8 billion (current expenditure: 79.3%; development expenditure: 20.7%)

Public Debt: US$8.8 billion

Gross National Product: US$1.4 billion

Principal Products: Fruits and vegetables; coffee; livestock

Foreign Trade (Imports): US$727.7 million (nondurable consumer goods: 29.9%; raw materials for industry: 22.1%; capital goods for industry: 14.6%; petroleum products: 14.6%; from United States: 20.0%; Venezuela: 17.0%; Costa Rica: 13.0%; Guatemala: 10.0%; El Salvador: 7.0%)

Foreign Trade (Exports): US$266.9 million (fresh and frozen meat: 22.8%; nontraditional industrial exports: 21.2%; coffee: 12.0%; crustaceans: 10.0%: gold: 9.8%; sugar: 6.5%; to United States: 42.0%; Germany: 9.0%; Belgium-Luxembourg: 6.0%; El Salvador: 5.0%; Mexico: 5.0%)

Stock Exchanges: 1
National Stock Exchange
Edificio Oscar Perez Cassar
Centor Banic
KM 4 1/2 Carretera a Masaya
Managua
Nicaragua
Internet Address: www.bolsanic.com

NIESSBAUCHNUTZER (Germany)
See BENEFICIAL OWNER.

NIGERIA, FEDERAL REPUBLIC OF
The *Federal Republic of Nigeria* is a country situated on the southern coast of western Africa. It is bordered by Niger on the north, Cameroon on the east, and Benin on the west.

Area: 356,669 square miles (923,768 square km)

Population: 95,434,000 (37.7% urban; 62.3% rural)

Form of Government: Military regime. Head of state and government: President (assisted by Provisional Council).

Official Language: English

Capital: Abuja (Federal Capital Territory)

Largest Cities: Lagos 1,347,000; Ibadan 1,295,000; Kano 699,900; Ogbomosho 660,600; Oshogbo 441,600; Ilorin 430,600

Economy:

Currency: Naira (N)

National Budget: Revenue—N 350.7 billion; expenditures—N 351.2 billion (recurrent expenditure: 64.3%, of which debt service: 53.7%; defense: 2.9%; education: 2.8%; police: 2.5%; health: 1.4%; capital expenditure: 35.7%).

Public Debt: US$29.5 billion

Gross National Product: US$32.5 billion

Principal Products: Yams, cassava, sorghum, rice, and other vegetables; plantains and bananas, and other fruits; livestock

Foreign Trade (Imports): N 143.2 billion (machinery and transport equipment: 43.2%; manufactured goods, mostly iron and steel products, textiles, and paper products: 27.8%; chemicals: 16.0%; food: 8.8%; from Germany: 13.8%; United Kingdom: 13.6%; United States: 11.8%; France: 8.9%)

Foreign Trade (Exports): N 205.6 billion (crude petroleum: 97.9%; cocoa beans: 0.6%; rubber: 0.4%; fertilizer: 0.2%; to United States: 40.7%; Spain: 12.6%; Germany: 8.6%; the Netherlands: 5.0%; France: 5.0%; Italy: 4.0%)

Stock Exchanges: 1
The Nigerian Stock Exchange (NSE)
Stock Exchange House
8-9th Floors
2/4 Customs Street
PO Box 2457
Lagos
Nigeria
Phone: (234-1) 266-0287/266-0305/266-0335
Fax: (234-1) 266-8724
Telex: (961) 23567

Internet Address: www.nse.com.ng

Trading Hours: Monday–Friday, 11:00 to 1:00

Office Hours: Monday–Friday, 7:30 to 4:30

Exchange Holidays:

1 January	11 October
7 April	25 December
8 July	

Listed Companies: 181

Market Capitalization: US$775 million

Major Sectors: Manufacturing, wholesale, finance, insurance, real estate

History: The Nigerian Stock Exchange began in 1960 as the Lagos Stock Exchange, a limited liability private company. It was renamed the Nigerian Stock Exchange in 1977, following a reorganization that included a total of six trading floors.

A Securities and Exchange Commission was established to register all new securities issues and to determine the price, amount, and timing of the share issue. The Securities and Exchange Commission is responsible for ensuring a fair and orderly market. The Commission also supervises the actions of brokers, underwriters, and other stock market participants.

The NSE now has branches and trading floors in five cities in Nigeria.

Classes of Securities: Ordinary shares, preference shares (voting), bonds, and other securities

Indices: NSE General Index (1984 = 100)

Supervisory Organizations:
Securities and Exchange Commission
Nigerian Stock Exchange

Depository: Central Securities Clearing House

Settlement Details:

Shares: Trade date + 3 days to 5 days (T + 3 to T + 5)

Trading: Trading on the Nigerian Stock Exchange is by "call-over" and involves fixing prices at a specific time, when members gather around to bid and offer. Currently the exchange does not have enough trading volume to conduct a continuous auction approach. Trading of equities is conducted by stockbrokers acting as brokers and jobbers.

Delays can occur in the receiving of certificates due to the transfer and registration procedures. The NSE provides custodial services through the Central Securities Clearing House.

Although merchant banks are allowed to underwrite new issues of shares and bonds, brokers handle all the trading of securities.

Listing Requirements: Full listing requirements are outlined in the *Green Book*, published in 1992. Listed companies must notify the exchange in the event of any of the following events:

1. Distributions of dividends, changes in capital structure, or any moves that might affect the price of the shares
2. Proposed changes in the character or nature of business of the company or group, or a change in voting control or in beneficial ownership of voting securities
3. The date and time when the board of directors will meet to discuss dividends
4. Proposed alterations to the memorandum or articles of association of the company
5. Changes in company directorship
6. Takeover intentions, acquisition moves, and other related activities to provide information to members as required by the NSE

Immediately after a board meeting the NSE must be notified of the following:

1. Intentions for a redemption of securities, stating the date and time of striking the balance for the drawing
2. Security amount outstanding after a purchase
3. Preliminary profits for the year, half year, or quarter and comparative figures relating to pre-tax profits and after-tax profits (required even if the figures are subject to change or audit)

4. Dividends or other distributions to members recommended or declared to be paid, including approval for payment of dividends, interest rights, or scrip issues

The Second-Tier Securities Market (SSM) began in April 1985. It is regulated by the Nigerian Securities and Exchange Commission and was originally formed to encourage investment and support of the equities market by wholly-owned Nigerian companies. The qualifications for issue are less restricted, and a three-year trading record (compared with five years) is required.

Investor Taxation: Withholding tax on rents, dividends, interests, and directors' fees is 10%. It is levied on all shareholders. Deductions, computations, payments, and receipts of income tax and withholding tax must be in the currency in which the income was received. Assessments, payments, and giving of receipts are also required to be in the currency of transaction.

Capital gains tax is 20%.

Limitations: Ownership of 5% or more of a companies shares requires notification to the NSE. Acquisitions, mergers, or takeovers are required to put the matter before the shareholders of the companies involved and also require the approval of the court.

Brokerage Firms:
Icon Stockbrokers
63/71 Broad Street
Lagos
Nigeria
Phone: (234-1) 662-607

Nigeria Stockbrokers
Stock Exchange Building
2/3 Customs Street
PO Box 4591
Lagos
Nigeria
Phone: (234-1) 665-694

Company Information:

10 Major Companies

Name of Company	Market Capitalization (US$ millions)
Union Bank of Nigeria	29.0
PZ Industries	37.0
UAC Nigeria	24.1
W Africa Portland	28.4
Cadbury Nigeria	31.5
Lever Brothers Nigeria	73.8
Nigerian Bottling Company	43.7
Nigerian Tobacco Company	28.9
Guiness Nigeria	47.6
Nigerian Breweries	94.4

Regional Exchanges: (Trading Floors)
Ibadan
Kano
Kaduna
Onitsha
Port Harcourt

Other Investment Information:
Nigerian Association of Chambers of Commerce, Industries and Agriculture
Commerce House
Idowu Taylor Street
Victoria Island
Lagos
Nigeria
Phone: (234-1) 964-737
Telex: 21368

NIKKEI STOCK INDEX
See JAPAN.

NIKKO SECURITIES COMPANY LIMITED

The *Nikko Securities Company Limited,* based in Japan, is one of the largest securities companies in the world, with assets of more than ¥3 trillion. Nikko is represented in all the major capital and equities markets around the world, and has 116 branch offices in Japan as well as 15 subsidiaries and nine representative offices overseas.

Founded in 1944, Nikko is the youngest of Japan's Big Four securities houses. Nikko was formed as a merger between the Kawashimaya Securities Company and the Nikko Securities Company, which was at the time part of the Industrial Bank of Japan (IBJ). In 1918 Genichi Toyama founded the Kawashimaya Shoten to buy and sell stocks and bonds; two years later his company was incorporated as Kawashimaya Shoten Inc., Ltd.

The Nikko Securities Company grew out of the securities department of the Industrial Bank of Japan. Although Nikko separated from IBJ in 1920 and operated autonomously on a day-to-day basis, it remained under the ultimate control of IBJ. In 1943 Nikko strengthened its position in the markets when it acquired the Kyodo Securities Company, Ltd. A year later it merged with Kawashimaya, formally separating itself from IBJ and creating the present-day Nikko Securities Company.

In 1997 the Securities and Exchange Surveillance Committee raided Nikko's main office amid suspicions that the company had disguised illegal payoffs to a corporate extortionist, Ryuichi Koike. Nikko was accused of making the payoffs to Koike as compensation for his losses on Tokyo Electric shares that he'd purchased through the firm. The resulting fallout from the scandal included the resignation of Nikko's chairman, president, and six other executive board members, as well as the suicide of Shokei Arai, a Liberal Democratic Party legislator who'd been accused of receiving favors from Nikko. Fines levied against Nikko as a result of the illegal payoffs totaled more than $1.15 million.

See also INDUSTRIAL BANK OF JAPAN LTD. (IBJ).

NIL DISTRIBUTION BASIS
See PRICE/EARNINGS RATIO.

NIL PAID
Shares traded on a "when issued" basis, usually coming from a new issue or a rights issue, are known as *Nil Paid*.

In the United Kingdom, nil paid issues can be traded in the form of the provisional allotment letter form for up to 21 days, until the call on the issue is made. During this period, the value of the shares is a combination of theoretical and supply-demand factors. Payment is not required until the market value is determined.

See also ALLOTMENT LETTER; SUBSCRIPTION RIGHTS; SUBSCRIPTION WARRANT; WHEN ISSUED (WI).

NIPPON CREDIT BANK (NCB)
The *Nippon Credit Bank (NCB)* has been one of only three long-term credit banks in Japan for more than 40 years. Chartered by the government in 1957, and having survived some severe challenges following the collapse of Japan's real estate market in 1990, Nippon Credit Bank was facing a period of deregulation and increased competition in the late 1990s that would require further adjustments.

In the 1920s the Japanese government formed the Industrial Bank of Japan (IBJ) to manage and regulate long-term credit for industries. After World War II, IBJ was privatized, and two more long-term credit banks were formed: the Long-Term Credit Bank of Japan and the Bank of Chosen. The latter had been a colonial bank in Korea. In 1957 the Bank of Chosen became a public company called the Nippon Fudosan Bank (*Fudosan* means "real estate"). Nippon Fudosan was licensed to issue three- and five-year debentures. Its customers were companies that needed investment capital in such industries as steel, chemicals, and heavy manufacturing. It changed its name to Nippon Credit Bank (NCB) in 1977.

The oil price shocks in 1973–74 and 1978–79 destroyed many of the small and medium-sized companies that NCB served. Thus NCB began to do more lending to service industries and foreign companies. It entered the American and European bond markets, and carried out a variety of banking activities, the breadth of which would have been prohibited in Japan. As some of its old customers began issuing their own bonds to raise money, NCB moved further away from its original business.

In 1985 NCB began a process of putting even more emphasis on its foreign banking. It maintained offices in New York, Los Angeles, Singapore, Hong Kong, and London. As the 1980s came to a close, its primary business was divided among the manufacturing, real estate, and finance industries, and it also provided loans in construction, communication, transportation, and retailing. By itself and through its subsidiaries, it was involved in financial debentures, deposits, loans, securities, and trust services. The financing it provided was essential to the national housing system.

The collapse of the real estate and stock markets in Japan in 1990 had a powerful impact on NCB. In 1996 it showed a loss for the second year in a row, this time amounting to $3.35 billion, the third largest loss for any company in the *Fortune Global 500*. By early 1997 the bank admitted to carrying $11 billion in bad loans, although some analysts estimated the actual figure was twice as high. Its assets at the end of March 1997 stood at $122.8 billion, down from $155.9 billion two years earlier. It had 2,877 employees working in its network of 18 offices, five branches, and one agency in Japan, plus five branches and eight representative offices overseas. All in all, it was one of the two most overextended banks in Japan, and corrective action was urgent.

On 1 April 1997, acting in concert with the country's central bank, the Bank of Japan, NCB announced a major restructuring plan. The following were its major components:

• Writing off all anticipated losses related to problem loans and recording a loss for the fiscal year ending 31 March 1997

• Closing all overseas offices, which required (not only by the logic of NCB's consolidation but also by the Bank for International Settlements' requirement) that its capital-to-risk assets ratio be at least 8%, whereas NCB's had fallen to 6%

• Implementing a fundamental restructuring, including salary cuts, a 20% reduction of staff within one year, and sale of all business sites, including the Tokyo head office

• Terminating support for the affiliated three non-banks

• Enhancing NCB's capital

The plan for capital enhancement, amounting to $2.5 billion, involved getting assistance from insurance companies, other long-term credit banks, and city banks, as well as drawing on the Bank of Japan's New Financial Stabilization Fund.

NCB's president stated that these steps would reduce the bank's assets to $83 billion by the year 2000 but would restore profitability.

Despite this restructuring plan, NCB's stock continued to fall until 10 April, when NCB and Bankers Trust New York Corporation announced in a joint statement that they were forming an alliance. NCB stock shot up 20% in one day. In the agreement, NCB would market mortgage-backed securities and other asset-backed securities; Bankers Trust would provide overseas services to NCB clients and would take more than $18 million in NCB assets, thus absorbing some of NCB's loan risk. The agreement was seen as a potential model for greater future cooperation between banks in the two countries, especially following the "Big Bang" deregulation of banking in Japan.

For the future, NCB's management planned to focus on: the securitization of property holdings and of all types of credit and loans; risk management, using derivatives transactions such as interest rate and currency swaps; and asset management.

See also BANKERS TRUST COMPANY; INDUSTRIAL BANK OF JAPAN LTD (IBJ); JAPANESE BOOM AND BUST 1988–90; LONG-TERM CREDIT BANK OF JAPAN LTD. (LTCB).

NIPPON SHINPAN COMPANY, LIMITED (NSC)

The *Nippon Shinpan Company, Limited (NSC)*, the first consumer credit company in Japan, was begun in 1951 when the entrepreneur Mitsunari Yamada made a deal with several Japanese department stores to accept his coupons. By 1996 the company had grown into the parent company of a group engaged in credit card services, shopping loan contracts, guarantees of mortgages and personal loans, loan contracts, resort and leisure business, leasing, real estate sales, bill collection, insurance brokerage, automated teller machine operations, and real estate-related services. It is the largest source of consumer credit in the country, with 23.3 million cardholders, and one of the largest leasing firms. Its assets are approximately $69 billion. It has 13 consolidated subsidiaries in Japan, four in the United States, and one each in Great Britain, Hong Kong, and Australia.

NSC's predecessor, founded in 1951, was the Nippon Shinyo Hanbai Company. From its Tokyo office it gave consumers the chance to buy goods on installment. In 1956 the company became engaged in real estate activities, marketing Japan's first luxury condominium. From there it expanded to handling mortgages and selling homes and home sites.

In 1959 the Japanese Ministry of International Trade and Industry (MITI) set guidelines restricting the geographic area within which credit services could issue coupons. This severely truncated Nippon Shinyo's business. Accordingly, the company adjusted its focus and became the first provider of housing loans in Japan. It got more involved in housing and condominium development.

In 1963 the company found a way to get around the 1959 MITI guidelines. Instead of offering coupons, it came up with the idea of "shopping loans." Consumers could apply for credit at member stores. Once they were approved, Nippon Shinyo would pay the purchase price for the goods, and the consumers could repay the loan over time.

In 1966 the company assumed its present name. It made plans for an expanded network of offices, and started making loans backed by securities. Also that year, NSC issued its first credit cards, opening a door to greatly increased business in the coming decades. In 1969 NSC reached an agreement with Interbank Card Association (later known as MasterCard International) that made it possible for NSC credit cards to be accepted overseas. By 1973 NSC was issuing Master-Cards in other countries.

In the 1970s and 1980s NSC engaged in numerous new ventures. It established business with retailers and banks in Hong Kong and Hawaii; it developed its business with resorts and tourist attractions; it issued bonds in European currencies (Swiss francs in 1976 and German deutsche marks in 1978); and in 1989 it issued an additional $450 million in bonds and warrants in Europe and Asia. In 1981 NSC and the BankAmerica Group set up a joint venture, the International Factoring Corporation, to purchase the debt and service the accounts of small and medium-sized companies.

Throughout this period, however, the most dynamic aspect of NSC's business was its credit cards. From 1984 to 1988, card circulation grew from

10 million to almost 18 million. The number of Japanese stores participating in NSC's credit program grew to 334,000 in 1988. NSC also formed joint-card agreements with Japan's Postal Savings system and VisaInternational. The arrangement with Visa, established in 1987, put the Visa logo on NSC's 13 million cards in Japan. (At that time, Japanese banking regulations prevented banks from offering revolving credit, but did not prohibit finance companies such as NSC from doing so.) In 1988 NSC established the International Credit Card Business Association to promote MasterCard and Visa credit cards. By 1991 NSC's credit card network included 275 agencies and 560,000 shops.

In 1991 NSC purchased a 70% stake in the Equitable Life Assurance Society, becoming the first Japanese company to acquire a U.S.-owned life insurer. NSC assumed control over Equitable's six branches and its retail network in Japan. In 1993 NSC signed an agreement with R.R. Donnelley Japan to market Donnelley's American Showcase/Japan catalog. As part of this deal, NSC's entire list of nearly 25 million cardholders was made available to Donnelley. The two companies shared the costs of the marketing effort and split a share of merchandise sales with the companies whose catalogs were listed in Donnelley's master catalog.

In 1994 NSC issued $200–$300 million in asset-backed securities on the Euromarket. Such a securitization deal was illegal in Japan, but an exception was made in this case, perhaps as a step toward overall deregulation of this type of activity.

By 1996 NSC's business had become quite diversified. As a percentage of total company revenue, loan contract fees accounted for 35%, shopping loan contract fees 19%, credit card contract fees 14%, guarantee contract fees 13%, leasing revenue 11%, financial revenue 2%, real estate sales revenue 1%, and other business 5%. Overseas revenues accounted for less than 10% of the total.

See also JAPAN; JAPANESE FINANCIAL MARKETS.

NO LOAD (United States)

"No Load" is a popular description for several types of open-end mutual funds that do not have an up-front sales charge. Some of them have a sales charge if the fund shares are sold within the first three to five years (called a 12-B1 or back-end load), but others have no charge to enter or leave the fund. With a no-load fund, the net asset value and public offering price are identical every day.

No-load mutual funds do charge an annual management fee to cover the costs of administering the day-to-day activities of the fund.

See also MUTUAL FUND; NET ASSET VALUE (NAV); PUBLIC OFFERING PRICE (POP).

NOBEL PRIZE FOR ECONOMIC SCIENCES

The *Nobel Prize for Economic Sciences* is an international prize, worth more than $1,000,000, awarded annually for achievement in the field of economic science.

The Nobel prizes were founded in 1901 by the legacy of Alfred Nobel, the Swedish inventor of dynamite. Since 1969 a Nobel Prize financed by the Swedish National Bank has been awarded for outstanding work in economics.

The recipients of the Nobel Prize for Economic Sciences through 1996 are as follows:

1969 Ragnar Frisch (Norway) and Jan Tinbergen (Netherlands): Developed and applied dynamic models for the analysis of economic processes.

1970 Paul A. Samuelson (United States): Developed static and dynamic economic theory and actively contributed to raising the level of analysis in economic science.

1971 Simon Kuznets (Russia): Empirically interpreted economic growth, leading to new and deepened insight into economic and social structure and the process of development.

1972 Sir John R. Hicks (Great Britain) and Kenneth J. Arrow (United States): Made pioneering contributions to general economic equilibrium theory and welfare theory.

1973 Wassily Leontief (Russia): Developed the input-output method and applied it to important economic problems.

1974 Gunnar Myrdal (Sweden) and Friedrich August von Hayek (Austria): Pioneered work in the theory of money and economic fluctuations and analyzed the interdependence of economic, social, and institutional phenomena.

1975 Leonid Vitaliyevich Kantorovich (U.S.S.R.) and Tjalling C. Koopmans (Netherlands): Contributed to the theory of optimum allocation of resources.

1976 Milton Friedman (United States): Achieved in the fields of consumption analysis and monetary history and theory, and demonstrated the complexity of stabilization policy.

1977 Bertil Ohlin (Sweden) and James E. Meade (Great Britain): Made a pathbreaking contribution to the theory of international trade and international capital movements.

1978 Herbert A. Simon (United States): Was a pioneer in research into the decision-making process within economic organizations.

1979 Theodore W. Schultz (United States) and Sir Arthur Lewis (British West Indies): Were pioneers in research into economic development research with particular consideration for the problems of developing countries.

1980 Lawrence R. Klein (United States): Created econometric models and applied them to the analysis of economic fluctuations and economic policies.

1981 James Tobin (United States): Analyzed financial markets and their relations to expenditure decisions, employment, production, and prices.

1982 George J. Stigler (United States): Studied industrial structures, functioning of markets, and causes and effects of public regulation.

1983 Gerard Debreu (France): Incorporated new analytical methods into economic theory and reformulated the theory of general equilibrium.

1984 Sir Richard Stone (Great Britain): Made fundamental contributions to the development of systems of national accounts and hence greatly improved the basis for empirical economic analysis.

1985 Franco Modigliani (Italy): Was a pioneer in analyses of saving and of financial markets.

1986 James M. Buchanan, Jr. (United States): Developed the contractual and constitutional bases for the theory of economic and political decision making.

1987 Robert M. Solow (United States): Contributed to the theory of economic growth.

1988 Maurice Allais (France): Made pioneering contributions to the theory of markets and efficient utilization of resources.

1989 Trygve Haavelmo (Norway): Clarified the probability theory foundations of econometrics and analyzed simultaneous economic structures.

1990 Harry M. Markowitz, Merton M. Miller, and William F. Sharpe (United States): Were pioneers in the theory of financial economics.

1991 Ronald H. Coase (Great Britain): Discovered and clarified the significance of transaction costs and property rights for the institutional structure and functioning of the economy.

1992 Gary S. Becker (United States): Extended the domain of microeconomic analysis to a wide range of human behavior and interaction, including non-market behavior.

1993 Robert W. Fogel and Douglas C. North (United States): Renewed research into economic history by applying economic theory and quantitative methods in order to explain economic and institutional change.

1994 John C. Harsanyi (Hungary), John F. Nash (United States), and Reinhard Selten (Germany): Were pioneers in analysis of equilibria in the theory of non-cooperative games.

1995 Robert Lucas (United States): Developed and applied the hypothesis of rational expectations, thereby transforming macroeconomic analysis and deepening our understanding of economic policy.

1996 James A. Mirrlees (United Kingdom) and William Vickrey (Canada): Made fundamental contributions to the economic theory of incentives under asymmetric information.

See also ALLAIS, MAURICE; CHICAGO SCHOOL OF ECONOMICS.

NOMURA SECURITIES COMPANY, LIMITED

Nomura Securities Company, Limited is the largest securities brokerage in the world and one of the world's largest investment bankers. In Japan, it is the leader of the so-called big four brokerages, along with Daiwa Securities, Nikko Securities, and Yamaichi Securities. Nomura provides individual and institutional trading services, as well as securities underwriting, asset management, project finance, leveraged leasing, real estate, and mergers and acquisitions services. The firm's client base consists primarily of Japanese companies, but Nomura is increasing its presence in international markets in order to compete for foreign business, especially in Asia.

Nomura's headquarters are in Tokyo, and it has offices in almost 30 countries in the Americas, Europe, and Asia. As of March 1996, Nomura had shareholders' equity of $17 billion and total assets of $120 billion. The corporation's stock is traded on the Tokyo, Osaka, Nagoya, Amsterdam, and Luxembourg stock exchanges.

Chronology of Significant Events

1872 Tokushichi Nomura opens the Nomura Shoten in Osaka. (*Shoten* means "store" or "shop.") This is basically a money-changing business, but as the Japanese industrial revolution gains momentum, the business transforms rapidly to include other financial services, among them stock trading.

1890 Although the Japanese stock market is not well developed—with very few joint-stock companies, no government regulation of exchanges, and many corrupt brokers—the stock trading department of Nomura Shoten consistently makes a profit.

1906 Nomura Shoten establishes the first research department at a Japanese financial company and begins publishing a daily financial newsletter, the *Osaka Nomura Business News*.

1908 Nomura enters the bond trading and underwriting fields, regularly participating in underwriting syndicates.

1910–19 Nomura's bond business expands rapidly during World War I as Japanese heavy industry floats bond issues. Nomura Shoten reorganizes as Nomura Shoten Incorporated. Osaka Nomura Bank (now Daiwa Bank) opens and sets up a securities department to handle bond sales and underwriting.

1920s Nomura and Company is founded as a holding company for the entire Nomura group. Bond market activity increases continually, causing Nomura to split off the securities department of Osaka Nomura Bank and set it up as a separate company—the Nomura Securities Company. The new company concentrates on the bond market, ignoring stocks.

1930s The government begins to assume control of the economy. Nomura is one of eight houses allowed to underwrite and sell bonds for the government and corporations. Government control of the bond market pushes investors toward stocks, so Nomura Securities opens a stock department.

1940s Nomura manages to expand right up to the end of World War II. After the war, as part of the break-up of family-controlled business groups, the occupation forces dissolution and reorganization of Nomura Securities Company.

1950s Nomura's New York office, closed since 1936, is reestablished. Nomura is the first Japanese company to introduce a computer system—a Univac 120. Nomura Real Estate Development Company begins operations.

1960s Nomura Investment Trust Management Company and Nomura Investment Trust Sales Company begin operations. Nomura comanages the first Japanese stock and bond offerings in the United States. Nomura Research Institute begins serving the needs of Japan. Nomura International opens in Hong Kong. Nomura incorporates a subsidiary in the United States and becomes member of American (Boston) Stock Exchange.

1970s Despite two oil crises that cause stock prices to plunge, Nomura continues to prosper and expand. Activities in Europe increase.

1980s Nomura's American subsidiary is the first Japanese company to become a member of the New York Stock Exchange. Nomura has great success in Japan and the European markets but has trouble competing in the United States market against the large American securities houses. Nomura continues to incorporate the latest computer hardware and software both at home and abroad. By the end of the decade Nomura is the world's largest and wealthiest securities firm.

1990s At start of the decade Nomura suffers from the stagnation of the Japanese market and from the penalties imposed for illegal activities associated with compensating favored clients for losses. By the middle of the decade both the Japanese market and Nomura largely recover their former positions, only to be hit by another scandal in 1997. Nomura admits to making payoffs of protection money to the Japanese underworld. Nomura's president is arrested in connection with the scandal. The government imposes restrictions, shutting down some Nomura operations until the end of the year and prohibiting Nomura from underwriting government-backed bonds and from participating in government bond auctions. Nomura is fined $1.7 million, and a number of Nomura officials and employees receive salary cuts and reprimands. Private sector clients curtail business with Nomura, but then relent and resume business dealings because of the convenience afforded by Nomura's size and market dominance.

See also JAPAN; JAPANESE BOOM AND BUST 1988–90; JAPANESE FINANCIAL MARKETS; NIKKO SECURITIES COMPANY LIMITED; YAMAICHI SECURITIES COMPANY LIMITED.

NON-BUSINESS DAY

A *Non-Business Day* is a national holiday on which normal business operations do not occur. Financial dealings such as settlement or due payments are automatically delayed to the next business day. In many parts of the world, religious holidays, political holidays, and New Year's Day are non-business days.

Settlement terms are commonly stated in business days; any days of the weekend or holidays are not included in calculations of the date of settlement.

NON-CLEARING MEMBER (United States)

A *Non-Clearing Member* is a member of the National Association of Securities Dealers (NASD) or an exchange that does not have an operations function, but hires the services of another member to clear trades and arrange for settlement. Non-clearing members pay a fee for this service.

See also BROKER/DEALER; MEMBER; SETTLE.

NON-PRECIOUS METALS

The *Non-Precious Metals* include iron, steel, aluminum, copper, nickel, tin, lead, and zinc. These metals are relatively abundant and are critical to the world's industries. Growth of the markets for these metals tends to be slow and steady, with prices sensitive to changes in supply and demand. In turn, the supply and demand for non-precious metals are sensitive to international events. Demand for non-precious metals comes primarily from industry. It declines during periods of worldwide recession, when industries slow down, and increases at the ends of recessionary periods, during periods of economic recovery. In years of moderate economic growth, the peaks and valleys in the metals market tend to level out. Most non-precious metals are available in many parts of the world, so tumultuous events in any one country are unlikely to devastate the world supply of one metal. In addition, recycling has increased the availability of some non-precious metals, such as aluminum, from secondary sources. However, suppliers, particularly mining companies, may respond to decreases in world demand by gearing down their production.

Non-precious metals do not consistently outperform the stock market, but price spikes occasionally occur. Investors can follow the progress of these metals through various exchanges and indexes, but two of the most useful indicators in the metals industry are the London Metal Exchange (LME); and Metallgesellschaft Metal Index (MGMI), an index created by Metallgesellschaft (MG), a German metals, engineering, and chemicals firm. Metals industry analysts offering regular forecasts of the status of nonferrous metals markets include London-based Wolff and Company, Limited; Billiton Metal Limited; Brandeis (Brokers) UK Limited; and Wirtschaftsvereinigung Metalle, Germany's nonferrous metals industry trade association.

Investors who are interested in non-precious metals have several options. As with any commodity, one option is to buy the metal itself. A more common option is to invest in stock in mining companies or in mutual funds that specialize in metals. An investor who is willing to accept higher levels of risk might prefer options and futures contracts.

Specific Metals

Iron and steel are abundant, cheap, and always in demand. These metals are used in the manufacturing, construction, mining, transportation, agriculture, and defense industries. Iron deposits exist throughout the world. Iron and steel are constantly in demand in the developed countries, and there is an emerging demand in developing countries.

Aluminum is the world's most abundant metal and most demanded nonferrous metal. Much aluminum is used in packaging. However, aluminum and its alloys are also used to construct buildings and aircraft, and to manufacture large appliances, electrical conductors, and chemical and food-processing equipment. Most aluminum is mined from bauxite deposits. Recycled aluminum available from secondary sources in the developed countries tends to drive down the price. However, in recent years, participation in the metals market by mutual funds has driven up the price of aluminum.

Copper is used to make cables that carry high-voltage electricity underground, and most residential electric wires are made of copper. Copper is also used in radiators, plumbing, air conditioning, roofing, and the manufacture of industrial machines. As a result, the demand for copper usually increases during housing construction booms and during periods of rising manufacturing. Copper's price is probably more sensitive to changes in the world economy than that of any other metal. However, other factors sometimes play an important role in influencing the demand for copper. In 1997 copper prices improved in response to supply problems and participation by mutual funds in the metals market. Demand for copper is greatest in the developed countries. In recent years, China has become an important market for copper—its copper consumption rate rises 4–5% annually.

The prices of nickel, tin, and zinc are tied to the fortunes of the steel industry. Most nickel is used to produce stainless steel. The steel industry uses tin to plate steel cans that are used as food containers, but demand for this use of tin has decreased because many manufacturers have shifted to aluminum. Most zinc is used to galvanize iron and steel. Mutual funds participating in the metals market have helped to raise the price of zinc in recent years.

Lead is demanded more by battery manufacturers than by any other market. Most batteries are produced in the United States, which is the world's largest market for lead. Lead is also used to cover underground or underwater electric cables, to line water pipes, and as a roofing material. Lead is used in ammunition, sol-der, type metal, and pewter; in the walls and foundations of buildings to absorb sound and vibrations; and to prevent radioactive leakage from nuclear reactors, particle accelerators, X-ray equipment, and containers used to transport and store radioactive materials.

See also PRECIOUS METALS.

NON-QUALIFYING STOCK OPTION

An option often granted to a corporate executive to buy a certain number of shares at a specified price within a certain time period is called a *Non-Qualifying Stock Option*. Such options are usually part of a compensation package for executives.

It is referred to as non-qualifying because the difference between the option price and the fair market value is considered to be income and has a liability for withholding tax.

See also EMPLOYEE STOCK OWNERSHIP PLAN (ESOP); PENSION PLAN/FUND.

NON-RECURRING CHARGE

See EXTRAORDINARY ITEM.

NO-PAR VALUE (United States)

No-Par Value shares have no-par value specified in either the corporate charter or on the share certificate. Companies that issue no-par value shares may carry the money received as part of the capital stock account or a part of the capital surplus (paid-in capital) account. The amount carried as capital stock has an implicit value, stated as the number of shares outstanding divided into the dollar amount of the capital stock.

Corporations have avoided no-par value shares in the past because many states based taxes on the par value. However, some states, such as Delaware, encouraged companies to issue shares with no-par value. No-par value shares are not permitted in the United Kingdom.

See also CERTIFICATE; INITIAL PUBLIC OFFERING (IPO).

NO-REVIEW OFFERING (United States)

No-Review Offering is a fast-track offering made by a large and frequent issuer of securities. A no-review offering can be fast-tracked through the Securities and Exchange Commission (SEC) if the company is up-to-date in all reports filed with the SEC.

With a no-review offering, it is possible to file a registration statement and receive a no-review commen-

tary from the SEC. An underwritten offering can appear in as few as two to three days.

See also INITIAL PUBLIC OFFERING (IPO); SECURITIES AND EXCHANGE COMMISSION (SEC).

NORINCHUKIN BANK

Norinchukin Bank, a cooperative agricultural bank owned by farming, fishing, forestry, and other rural cooperatives, was set up by the Japanese government in 1923 to help modernize and stimulate growth in the country's agricultural sector. The name *Norinchukin*, which the bank adopted in 1943, derives from the Japanese words for agriculture (*no*), forestry (*rin*), cooperative (*chu*), and bank (*kin*). In 1995 Norinchukin had 41 branch offices throughout Japan. By early 1997 it had assets of $378.7 billion, making it one of the largest banks in the world.

As a cooperative, Norinchukin has been oriented first and foremost toward its long-established goal of supporting agriculture, and only secondarily toward making money through banking. It may seem highly unusual that one of the world's largest banks could have maintained such a philosophy, but the huge number of cooperatives at its base have made it possible. However, Norinchukin has had to diversify its business, including internationally, since the late 1980s, due to the changes affecting Japanese agriculture, the decline of the interest rate offered on Japanese government bonds (which had traditionally been a major investment for Norinchukin), the deregulation of Japanese banking, and heightened competition. Nevertheless, the bank still opposes agricultural imports and supports the development of self-sufficiency by Japanese agriculture.

Norinchukin almost went bankrupt during World War II as a result of the government's restrictions on banking. During the postwar agricultural reform, the bank played a major part in financing the revival of Japanese farming. Concerned that the government might cut its support for agriculture, through the farmers' cooperative organization Norinchukin formed a political lobby that won more support for import quotas, subsidy programs, and measures to strengthen agricultural institutions.

Tapping its large savings base, which consisted of thousands of cooperatives (more than 5,600 of them in 1989), Norinchukin could buy government bonds that yielded 6–7% and could enjoy a good spread even after offering better interest rates on deposits than commercial banks did. The bank collected deposits according to the following arrangement: The *nokyo*, or agricultural cooperatives, as well as fishing cooperatives deposited two-thirds of the funds they had collected (minus their investments in local government bonds or projects serving primary industries) with prefectural agricultural banks called *shinnoren*. The *shinnoren*, in turn, could also make investments, but they were required to deposit one-half of the remainder with Norinchukin.

Norinchukin's margins began to disappear in the 1980s, as the government issued bonds less frequently and at lower interest rates. At the same time, farmers' demand for loans declined. Norinchukin accumulated an enormous amount of funds that it was unable to invest profitably.

A major part of the bank's response was to expand internationally. In 1979 it had been given permission by the Japanese agricultural and finance ministries to buy foreign bonds, and it had set up an international department, which started by buying foreign government-backed bonds and some Japanese-backed Eurobonds. Norinchukin set up a working relationship with the Bank of Tokyo to learn more about bond markets and international finance. With the Bank of Tokyo's assistance, Norinchukin set up a representative office in New York in 1982 (upgraded to a branch in 1984). In turn, Norinchukin purchased Bank of Tokyo debentures, and the two banks shared clients, information, and computer systems. Norinchukin also established an office in London in 1985, a securities brokerage in London in 1986 (elevated to a branch in 1991), a subsidiary bank in Zurich in 1989, and a representative office in Singapore in 1990 (elevated to a branch in 1993). In April 1989 the bank became entitled to invest in foreign equity.

In 1986 the Norinchukin Law, which had made the bank a nonprofit institution and restricted its business activities, was revised. Norinchukin could then, in principle, offer the same services as Japan's national commercial banks, and it proceeded to move into the trustee business. In 1993 the Japanese Ministry of Finance approved three long-term credit banks, including Norinchukin, to open securities subsidiaries. The ruling meant that these banks could underwrite Japanese corporations' debts and could compete in international capital markets. Later that year Norinchukin established the Norinchukin Securities Company, Limited, and Norinchukin Investment Trust Management Company, Limited. The following year the Norinchukin Securities Company became a member of the Tokyo International Futures Exchange.

By the mid-1990s Norinchukin's slowly diversifying services included loans to the primary sector and public entities; financial services and derivative products; trade in open market certificates of deposits, commercial paper, futures, options, the Euroyen money market, over-the-counter public bonds, and government bonds; and the underwriting of Euroyen bonds.

See also CRÉDIT AGRICOLE; JAPAN.

NORMAL INVESTMENT PRACTICE (United States)

Under the rules of fair practice, the National Association of Securities Dealers (NASD) places restrictions on the marketing of securities expected to be a "hot issue." Such issues cannot be sold as hot issues and can only be sold to investors as part of their *Normal Investing Practice*. If an investor shows a pattern of buying 1,000 shares of new issues of a particular industry and a hot issue comes along, it would be fair for that investor to pick up 1,000 shares.

Solely buying hot issues would not be considered part of an investor's normal investing practice.

See also HOT ISSUE; INITIAL PUBLIC OFFERING (IPO); NATIONAL ASSOCIATION OF SECURITIES DEALERS (NASD).

NORMAL TRADING UNIT
See ROUND LOT.

NORTH AMERICAN FREE TRADE AGREEMENT (NAFTA)

The *North American Free Trade Agreement (NAFTA)*, joining Canada, the United States, and Mexico in a set of policies designed to reduce trade barriers, went into effect on 1 January 1994. The new arrangements represented an extension of those that had been reached in the U.S.-Canada Free Trade Agreement of 1988. At the time NAFTA was signed, the three countries had a total population of approximately 370 million, somewhat greater than that of the European Community.

Under NAFTA, tariffs on 99% of the goods traded between Mexico and the United States were to be phased out over a period of ten years. Certain agricultural products that were important to either country's economy would not be tariff-free until another five years after that. In addition to physical goods, NAFTA's terms affected telecommunications, patents, investments, and financial services.

Although many sections of the U.S. economy stood to gain from the opening of the Mexican market that NAFTA called for, there were those in the United States who opposed the treaty, expressing concerns about the loss of American jobs, the inability of certain American industries to compete with their Mexican counterparts because of the low cost of Mexican labor, and the looser environmental regulations in Mexico.

There was also substantial objection to the agreement in Mexico, where the economy was weakened by the collapse of the peso in 1994. The resulting austerity program that was demanded by the United States and the International Monetary Fund (IMF) in exchange for loans was expected to cost 750,000 jobs and to cut the average Mexican family's real purchasing power by one-third. Canada, too, was experiencing economic difficulties. Its budget deficit in proportion to its gross domestic product was three times that of the United States, and interest payments on its federal debt consumed 40% of its total spending.

In 1996 some of the stipulations of NAFTA came into conflict with the rewritten 1994 specifications of the General Agreement on Tariffs and Trade (GATT). Canada moved to replace its import quotas with tariffs on poultry, eggs, and other dairy products imported from the United States. This was permissible under GATT, according to which Canada had five years to reduce its tariffs by 15%. The U.S. dairy industry then charged that Canada's action was in violation of NAFTA. However, later in the year a World Trade Organization panel ruled in favor of Canada, holding that GATT superseded NAFTA.

As far as U.S.-Mexico trade, on the one hand, it was expected that the full effect of NAFTA on the agricultural balance of trade between the United States and Mexico would not be known until 2009, when all tariffs were to be eliminated. But barring a huge increase in Mexico's agricultural exports, it is likely that the effects of NAFTA will include a weakening of Mexican farming, growth in Mexico's agricultural trade deficit with the United States, and deepened dependence on U.S. investment and trade. The impact on Mexico's production of corn, beans, and dairy products will be particularly serious. This is a result not only of the overall advantages of U.S. agriculture (greater productivity, greater profitability, more technology, more available financing) but also of the fact that the more developed system of import standards in the United States, involving classification, grading, and marketing of domestic goods, makes it relatively harder for Mexican agricultural products to penetrate the U.S. market. For example, even after NAFTA, there are still U.S. federal marketing orders in effect for nearly 50 fruits, vegetables, nuts, and other specialty crops.

In 1993 the Mexican stock market rose 51%. However, on the day that NAFTA went into effect a group of Mayan Indians and peasants in the Mexican state of Chiapas launched a bloody rebellion against the Mexican government. The rebels chose to initiate their rebellion on the same day as NAFTA's implementation in order to draw attention to their belief that NAFTA would only benefit Mexico's rich. In the wake of the uprising and the weak peso, Mexican stocks recorded their largest one-day fall in more than 18 months on 3 January 1994. A few days later it rebounded, then climbed to an all-time high in February. The Mexican equity market surged throughout 1994, as investors, confident about Mexico's prospects with NAFTA in effect, moved funds from U.S. stocks and Asian markets. For the first eight months of 1994, foreign investment was up 29%, and about half the $9 billion in foreign investment was in the Mexican stock market.

In 1994, U.S. agricultural exports to Mexico increased 24%, with especially notable gains in grains, oilseeds, and animal products. By contrast, Mexican agricultural exports to the United States increased only 4%. The differential effect on the two countries' economies was increased by the fact that 24% of Mexico's population was engaged in agriculture, compared to only 2.4% in the United States. One effect of the inability of many Mexican farmers to compete in the global market is increased migration from the countryside to urban areas, especially Mexico City, as well as emigration to the United States. Estimates of the number of Mexican farmers that will leave agriculture and migrate from the rural areas by the year 2010 range from 500,000 to 15 million.

See also CUSTOMS UNIONS; EUROPEAN COMMUNITY (EC); EUROPEAN FREE TRADE ASSOCIATION (EFTA); GENERAL AGREEMENT ON TARIFFS AND TRADE (GATT).

NORWAY, KINGDOM OF

Norway (Kongeriket Norge) is Europe's fifth largest country. It is bordered by Skagerrak on the south, and Sweden, Finland, and Russia on the east.

Area: 125,050 square miles (323,878 square km)

Population: 4,360,000 (75.0% urban; 25.0% rural)

Form of Government: Constitutional monarchy, with one legislative house: Parliament—165 members. Chief of state: King. Head of government: Prime Minister.

Official Language: Norwegian

Capital: Oslo

Largest Cities: Oslo, 482,555; Bergen, 221,645; Trondheim, 142,792; Stavanger, 103,496; Baerum, 95,612

Economy:

Currency: Norwegian Krone (NKr)

National Budget: Revenue—NKr 339.2 billion; expenditures—NKr 339.1 billion (social security and welfare: 25.2%; health: 7.9%; debt service: 6.0%)

Public Debt: US$23.4 billion

Gross National Product: US$113.5 billion

Principal Products: Fish; agricultural produce; fuels; machinery and metals

Foreign Trade (Imports): NKr 193.0 billion (machinery and transport equipment: 34.0%; of which road vehicles: 7.7%; ships: 4.0%; metals and metal products: 11.0%; of which iron and steel: 4.3%; food products: 4.8%; of which fruits and vegetables: 1.6%; petroleum products: 2.2%; from Sweden: 14.9%; Germany: 13.9%; United Kingdom: 10.3%; Denmark: 7.4%)

Foreign Trade (Exports): NKr 244.5 billion (fuels and fuel products: 48.8%; of which crude petroleum: 37.7%; natural gas: 6.8%; machinery and transport equipment: 16.4%; metals and metal products: 11.4%; of which aluminum: 4.9%; food products: 8.3%; of which fish: 7.7%; to United Kingdom: 20.7%; Germany: 12.1%; Sweden: 9.5%; the Netherlands: 9.5%)

Stock Exchanges: 3

Oslo Bors (Oslo Stock Exchange; OSE)
P.O. Box 460 Sentrum
0152 Oslo
Norway
Phone: (47-2) 234 1700
Fax: (47-2) 241 6590

Internet Address: www.ose.no

Trading Hours:
| Monday–Friday | 10:00 to 4:00 | Shares and Options |
| | 9:00 to 3:00 | Bonds and Futures |

Exchange Holidays:
| 1 January | 24, 25, 26, 31 December |
| 4, 5, 8 April | |

Listed Companies: 217

Total Market Capitalization:

At 31 December 1997

Local Currency (Millions)	US Dollars (Millions)
389,632	52,852

Major Sectors: Industry, shipping, banks, insurance

Share Price Performance:

(% Change)

1991	-3
1992	-6
1993	62
1994	20
1995	12
1996	24
1997	35

History: The Oslo Stock Exchange (OSE), established in 1819, is the only organized marketplace where shares, bonds, and derivatives are traded in Norway. On 30 June 1995, the total market capitalization of listed Norwegian shares totaled NKr 263.7 billion. The nominal value of listed bonds totaled NKr 741.5 billion. Turnover is high and market liquidity compares with other major international exchanges.

The Oslo Stock Exchange underwent major revisions in 1994 as new regulations came into effect. The change was marked by instituting international standards, especially those standards applying to the European Union. Greater emphasis was placed on control and surveillance functions, as well as standards for companies' reports and accounting practices.

OSE now uses an electronic trade support and information system, facilitating control of the market and dissemination of information impacting prices.

Classes of Securities: Ordinary and preference shares, bonds, options, derivatives

Electronic ownership of securities through the Norwegian Registry of Securities (Verdipapirsentralen, VPS) began in 1986, and greatly improved the efficiency of securities trading. In addition to the Oslo Stock Exchange, the Norwegian Futures & Options Clearing House (NOS) represents an integral part of the Norwegian financial community. Established in 1990, NOS serves as a legal counterpart for the issuer and buyer of derivatives.

Classes of Securities: A and B shares, primary capital certificates, stock options, bonds, bills, certificates, index options, index futures, interest rate futures

Indices:

OSE Index of 50 issues (base = 100 1 January 1983)

Totalindeksen All-shares Index (base = 100 December/January 1983 shown), encompasses all the shares listed on the main list

Bank (sector index for listed banks, main list) (base = 100 December/January 1983)

Insurance (base = 100 December/January 1983)

Industry (base = 100 December/January 1983)

Shipping (base = 100 December/January 1983)

SMB-Index (base = 500 December/January 1995)
  Small and medium sized companies listed

Primary Capital Certificate Index (base = 500 December/January 1983)

OBX Index (base = 200 December/January 1987)

Supervisory Organizations:

Ministry of Finance

Banking, Insurance, and Securities Commission

The Stock Exchange Council

Depository: The Norwegian Registry of Securities (Verdipapirsentralen (VPS))

Settlement Details:

Shares: Trade date + 3 days (T + 3)

Trading: The trading system is an Automatic Trade Support and Information System. It allows decentralized trading in bonds and futures. Stocks and options trading is centralized.

A new generation trading system to enable decentralized trading in all three markets became available in 1996–97.

The Oslo Stock Exchange and the Swedish Derivatives Exchange (OM) had a common options market by the end of 1996. OM's automatic trading system is used for both Norwegian and Swedish products, and trading will be available in Oslo, Stockholm, and London.

Securities trading is regulated by the Securities Trading Act of 1985. The Oslo Stock Exchange regulations define rules for the following areas:

- Generally accepted trading practice
- Reportable securities trading
- Misuse of confidential and price-sensitive information in securities trading (insider trading)
- Issues of securities
- Listed companies' duties to provide information

Listing Requirements:

Main Listing Requirements:

- Share capital (market value based) NKr 10 million
- At least 500 shareholders
- 25% of share capital to be held by non-related parties
- Minimum three years of trading history

SMB Listing Requirements:

- Share capital of at least NKr 8 million
- At least 50 shareholders

- 25% of share capital to be held by non-related parties
- Minimum three years of trading history

The Observation List: Introduced 11 July 1994, any company's securities may be transferred to the observation list when trading and pricing require extra care and attention. It is considered a warning to investors that pricing is uncertain.

The most common reason to transfer securities to the observation list is when the company indicates the existence of negotiations that can strongly impact the organization of the company. Mergers, acquisitions, and financial restructuring can be reasons for a movement to the observation list.

When the complete information is relayed to the public and the market, the company is removed from the observation list and normal trade resumes.

Foreign companies must also file a listing agreement with the Oslo Stock Exchange.

Investor Taxation:

Non-residents:

- No capital gains tax
- No interest payments taxation
- No stamp duty

- 25% withholding tax on dividends unless the investor's country has a double taxation agreement with Norway. Under such an agreement the withholding tax is normally 15%.

Limitations: The laws limiting the right of foreigners to acquire more than one-third of Norwegian companies and institutions were abolished and now coincide with the non-discrimination principle of the European Economic Area Agreement (EEA).

Securities Lending: Currently not allowed, but expected to be changed

Brokerage Firms:

Alfred Berg Norge AS

PO Box 483

N-0105 Oslo

Norway

Phone: (47-2) 200 5000

Fax: (47-2) 241 7480

Bergen Fondsmegler-forretning AS

Jernbanetorget 4a

N-0154 Oslo

Norway

Phone: (47-2) 233 4910

Fax: (47-2) 233 6700

Bergen Fondsmegler-forretning AS
PO Box 933
N-5001 Bergen
Norway
Phone: (47-5) 531 6130
Fax: (47-5) 532 3493

Carnegi AS
PO Box 684, Sentrum
N-0106 Oslo
Norway
Phone: (47-2) 200 9300
Fax: (47-2) 242 5855

Chemical Bank Norge AS
PO Box 1224 Vika
N-0110 Oslo
Norway
Phone: (47-2) 294 1919
Fax: (47-2) 242 5861

Christiania Bank og Kreditkasse AS
PO Box 1166, Sentrum
N-0107 Oslo
Norway
Phone: (47-2) 248 5000
Fax: (47-2) 256 8650

Den norske Bank AS
DnB Fonds
PO Box 1171, Sentrum
N-0107 Oslo
Norway
Phone: (47-2) 294 8850
Fax: (47-2) 283 2523

Den norske Bank AS
DnB Fonds
N-5020 Bergen
Norway
Phone: (47-5) 521 1353
Fax: (47-5) 521 1586

Elcon Securities AS
PO Box 153, Sentrum
N-0102 Oslo
Norway
Phone: (47-2) 233 0240
Fax: (47-2) 241 8961

Fearnly Fonds AS
PO Box 1158, Sentrum
N-0107 Oslo

Norway
Phone: (47-2) 293 6000
Fax: (47-2) 293 6360, 293 6361

FIBA Nordic Securities AS
PO Box 1351 Vika
N-0113 Oslo
Norway
Phone: (47-2) 283 8870
Fax: (47-2) 283 8801, 283 8805

Fondsfinans AS
PO Box 1782, Vika
N-0113 Oslo
Norway
Phone: (47-2) 283 6690
Fax: (47-2) 283 1620

Handelsbanken
PO Box 332, Sentrum
N-0101 Oslo
Norway
Phone: (47-2) 294 0900
Fax: (47-2) 233 6915

Industri and Skipsbanken Fonds AS
PO Box 1692, Vika
N-0110 Oslo
Norway
Phone: (47-2) 242 2104
Fax: (47-2) 242 3732

Noka Securities AS
PO Box 1253, Vika
N-0111 Oslo
Norway
Phone: (47-2) 283 6300
Fax: (47-2) 283 6306

Norse Securities AS
PO Box 1474, Vika
N-0116 Oslo
Norway
Phone: (47-2) 283 1183
Fax: (47-2) 283 1242, 283 1243

R.S. Platou Securities AS
PO Box 10
N-1322 Hovik
Norway
Phone: (47-7) 759 2030
Fax: (47-7) 759 2675

Saga Securities AS
PO Box 1770 Vika
N-0122 Oslo
Norway
Phone: (47-2) 201 0000
Fax: (47-2) 283 0122

Sparebanken Nord-Norge Fondsadelingen
Sjogt. 39
N-9005 Tromso
Norway
Phone: (47-7) 762 2000
Fax: (47-7) 768 8684

Sundal Collier and Co AS
PO Box 1444, Vika
N-0115 Oslo
Norway
Phone: (47-2) 283 1460
Fax: (47-2) 283 0792, 283 0794

Company Information:

The Best Performing Shares in the Country

Company Name	Share Price Change 1 January 1997 to 31 December 1997 (%)
Det Sondenfjeld	295
Tandberg Data	223
Ask	195
Netcom	193
Ncl Holding	147
Merkantildata	117
Ptl. Geo-Services	87
Aker Maritime Asa	80
Wilhs.Wilhelmsen A	75
Tomra	66
Bonheur	59
Ganger Rolf	59
Transocean Offshore	59
Fokus Bank	56
Olav Thon	55
Christiania Bank	48
Orkla 'A'	43
Den Norske Bank	43
Orkla 'B'	42
Storebrand	41
Stolt Nielsen 'B'	40
Sparebanken Nor	32

The Largest Companies in the Country by Market Capitalization as of 31 December 1997

Company Name	Market Capitalization Local Currency (Millions)	Market Capitalization US Dollars (Millions)
Norsk Hydro	82,352	11,171
Transocean Offshore	33,490	4,543
Royal Crbn. Cruises Ltd.	29,905	4,056
Orkla 'A'	25,076	3,401
Den Norske Bank	22,289	3,023
Ptl. Geo-Services	16,703	2,266
Christiania Bank	16,424	2,228
Storebrand	14,403	1,954
Saga Petroleum 'A'	13,055	1,771
Kvaerner 'A'	12,749	1,729
Bergesen D.Y. 'A'	9,239	1,253
Aker Maritime Asa	8,905	1,208
Fred Olsen Energy	8,874	1,204
Schibsted	8,760	1,188
Netcom	8,441	1,145
Aker Rgi 'A'	7,391	1,002
Sparebanken Nor	6,823	926
Tomra	6,348	861
Norske Skog 'A'	6,162	836
Orkla 'B'	5,650	766
Ncl Holding	5,425	736
Stolt Nielsen 'B'	5,104	692
Det Sondenfjeld	4,889	663
Elkem	4,829	655
Bonheur	4,826	655
Leif Hoegh	4,500	610
Fokus Bank	4,500	610
Smedvig 'A'	4,255	577
Frontline Ltd	4,074	553
Merkantildata	4,021	545
Bergesen D.Y. 'B'	3,898	529
Ganger Rolf	3,843	521
Saga Petroleum 'B'	3,838	521
Dyno Industrier	3,633	493
Norex Industries	3,514	477
Kvaerner 'B'	3,310	449
Wilhs.Wilhelmsen A	3,079	418
Hafslund 'A'	3,073	417
Alcatel Stk	2,940	399
Rieber & Son 'A'	2,921	396
Olav Thon	2,832	384
Tandberg Data	2,801	380
Ocean Rig Asa	2,791	379
Steen & Strom Asa	2,788	378
Rieber & Son 'B'	2,729	370
Nera	2,653	360

Company Name	Market Capitalization Local Currency (Millions)	Market Capitalization US Dollars (Millions)
Aker Rgi 'B'	2,598	352
Tandberg Television	2,476	336
Ask	2,461	334

Regional Exchanges: None

Other Investment Information:
Ministry of Industry
Ploensgt 8
PO Box 8014
Department 0030
Oslo 1
Norway
Phone: (47-2) 34-9090
Fax: (47-2) 34-9525
Telex: 21428

Ministry of the Environment
Myntgt 2
PO Box 8013
Oslo 1
Norway
Phone: (47-2) 34-9090
Fax: (47-2) 34-9560

Norges Bank (Bank of Norway)
Bankplassen 2
PO Box 1179
Sentrum
N-0107 Oslo 1
Norway
Phone: (47-2) 31-6000
Fax: (47-2) 41-3105
Telex: 71369

NOTOWANIA JEDNOLITE (Poland)

Trades based on a single price quotation are known as a *Notowania Jednolite* (e.g., a situation where several trades can be executed at the price established during the beginning of a trading session). Executions are concluded on the basis of orders received.

See also ON THE OPENING, POLAND/TRADING.

OBJECTIVE

An *Objective* is a planned or desired end result. By forming a clear, precise, and well-defined objective, an investor can measurably increase the return on an investment.

In order to be successful an objective should be:

1. Specific, in order to be well understood
2. Based on observation and analysis
3. Reasonable in its expectations
4. Appropriate to the investor's level of risk
5. Limited by a reasonable time frame
6. Measurable, in order to be properly evaluated

Objectives for ordinary share investing can be divided into four general categories.

1. Income (dividends)
2. Growth (long-term price growth)
3. Total Return (dividends and price growth)
4. Speculation (short-term price growth)

See also EARNINGS; GROWTH; SPECULATION; TOTAL RETURN.

OBLIGATION CONVERTIBLE EN ACTION (France)

See CONVERTIBLE.

OBR' OT (Poland)

Obr' ot is a term meaning turnover of securities.

See also COMMISSION; MEMBER; TURNOVER.

ODD LOT

Odd Lot refers to any group of shares to be traded whose quantity is less than the standard unit of trading, known as a round lot. In most cases a round lot is 100 shares, although on occasion ten shares can be considered a round lot.

The terminology used for odd lots differs on the world stock exchanges. They can be referred to as board lots, trading lots, or trading units.

See also ODD LOT DIFFERENTIAL; ODD LOT THEORY; ROUND LOT; SETTLE.

ODD LOT DIFFERENTIAL

Odd Lot Differential is the fee charged for odd lot trading.

In investment trading, all orders are subject to standard fees and commissions. However, because odd lot orders must be routed through a broker specializing in odd lot trades, odd lot trading suffers an additonal fee in order to cover extra handling costs.

Strictly speaking, there is no odd lot differential charged for over-the-counter (OTC) transactions, since these transactions are negotiated. In reality, however, brokerage firms tend to charge more for trading quantities of shares not in round lots, and thus the odd lot differential is worked into the price.

See also ODD LOT.

ODD LOT THEORY

First hypothesized by Garfield Drew, the *Odd Lot Theory* suggests that odd lotters (small investors who cannot afford to invest in round lots) are naive and ignorant in regard to the market and tend to buy and sell securities at the wrong time. According to Drew, the time to buy, then, was when odd lotters were selling, and conversely, to sell when they were buying.

Drew's theory has been largely discredited. Recent research indicates that many odd lots are the result of dividend reinvestment programs, and as such, do not necessarily appear as buy transactions. In fact, many dividend payments are automatically reinvested. Therefore, purchase orders involving odd lot numbers have little or nothing to do with the market rising or falling.

At present, this theory exists more as an historical curiosity than an actively followed trading strategy.

See also FUNDAMENTAL ANALYSIS; ODD LOT; ROUND LOT; TECHNICAL ANALYSIS.

OECD

See ORGANIZATION FOR ECONOMIC COOPERATION AND DEVELOPMENT (OECD).

OEX (United States)

OEX is the trading, or "ticker," symbol for the Standard & Poor's 100 Index options traded on the Chicago Board of Options Exchange (CBOE). Put and call options are available and have five-point strike price intervals. The options have a three-month duration and are "American style" in that they may be exercised at any time during their lifetime. Settlement is in cash and is calculated on the deviation of the strike price from the index value multiplied by $100.

For example, if a call is exercised at 405, and the strike price of the OEX is 445, the writer would pay the holder $40 x 100, or $4,000. OEX options are used primarily to hedge systematic market risk.

See also DOW JONES INDUSTRIAL AVERAGE (DJIA); DOW THEORY; TECHNICAL ANALYSIS.

OFERTA (Poland)

Oferta is a term that refers to an order balancing phase that occasionally becomes necessary during a trading session on the Polish Stock Exchange.

If there is a preponderance of buy or sell orders during a period of time, a specialist will invite other brokers to place counterbalancing orders from the "lighter" side of the market to eliminate the existing imbalance.

Because a preponderance of orders on one side of the market tends to cause extraordinary price fluctuations, stock exchanges attempt to moderate these price changes by balancing. The purpose of such balancing is to maintain price stability for securities and therefore ensure that the stock market is fair and orderly.

Some fully computerized stock markets have effectively replaced the order balancing system by setting limits on price fluctuations. If the limit is reached, trading is suspended until the exchange can ascertain the reason for the fluctuation and notify the public of any significant changes affecting the company involved.

See also FAIR AND ORDERLY MARKET; MARKET MAKER; ORDER IMBALANCE; SPECIALIST.

OFF FLOOR

Off Floor refers to any method of trading—usually by telephone, fax, or other electronic means—that does not occur on the floor of the stock exchange.

Off floor securities are those securities that are traded off floor. Under exchange regulations, off floor orders receive priority over those orders originating on the exchange floor. These regulations are in keeping with the mandate of a fair and orderly market, since on floor orders are usually between traders trading for their own accounts.

See also MARKET MAKER; SPECIALIST; TRADE.

OFFER

Also known as offer price or ask price, an *Offer* represents the price at which a seller is willing to sell a security to an investor.

A price quotation on a broker's computer terminal would show the following information:

Bid	Ask (offer)	Size	Last Trade
60	60 1/8	100x200	60 1/8

Price quotations can change at any time, even when an order to buy or sell is being entered into the computer. Price quotations also follow a time priority, meaning they can change as the order is on its way to the exchange.

See also LIMIT ORDER; MARKET ORDER; STOP ORDER.

OFFER FOR SALE (United Kingdom)

An *Offer for Sale*, the most popular of four methods used for the distribution of new issues, is the method recommended by the stock exchange when a new issue is valued at more than £15 million on the listed market. This method is encouraged by the stock exchange because it allows a large number of investors to participate, thereby ensuring broad distribution and an active market for the security.

A typical offer for sale will see the issuing house buying shares from the issuing company and selling them to the investing public. A prospectus detailing the company's share capital and debt, along with information on directors, senior employees, professional advisers, bankers, auditors, attorneys, stockbrokers, and registrars is sent to each investor. A history of the company, a description of the company's main business activities, major customers, and most important suppliers, information on the planned use of proceeds, and a statement regarding the adequacy of working capital are included as well.

A section of the prospectus is devoted to accounting reports covering the past five years of trading, along with a recent consolidated balance sheet, and notes regarding fixed assets, investments, share capital, reserves, and debt. The prospectus is also required to include a history of the company's share capital structure, information about its subsidiaries, and the details of the Articles of Association that outline voting rights, the powers of directors, and borrowing powers. It must also include details of directors' share ownership, extraordinary contracts, and finally, a statement, signed by the financial advisers, consenting to the issuance of the prospectus.

Included with the prospectus is an application for an allotment of shares. Once the application has been completed, it is sent to the receiving banker who examines all applications and sends out allotments.

The offer for sale will be either a fixed price or a tender offer. The fixed-price offer for sale is the most common, leading to a scaling down of the shares received by each investor if the offer is over-subscribed. A tender offer involves the fixing of a minimum price, with investors submitting bids at the minimum price or higher.

According to stock exchange rules, the offer for sale must be advertised in at least two major newspapers.

See also INITIAL PUBLIC OFFERING (IPO); PROSPECTUS; REGISTRAR.

OFFER PERIOD (United Kingdom)

The *Offer Period* is the required time for a takeover offer to remain open.

Rules set by the City Code on Takeovers and Mergers require a minimum offer period of 21 days following the announcement of a takeover. In cases in which the offer is revised, a 14-day extension is allowed. The maximum period an offer is allowed to remain open is 60 days from the date of the original announcement, unless the panel on takeovers and mergers grants a special exception. Usually, such extensions are granted only if a competing offer is involved.

Shares are allowed to trade as normal during the offer period. All such trades are reported to stock exchange authorities and the press by noon on the day following trading.

See also MERGER; SHARK REPELLENT; TAKEOVER/TAKEOVER BID.

OFFER PRICE

See OFFER.

OFFER WANTED (United States)

Offer Wanted is the designation given to the form sent from one dealer to another requesting an offer on company shares listed on the pink sheets, published by the National Quotations Bureau, which contain low-priced, infrequently traded securities that are not listed in the daily newspapers.

Since many of these shares are thinly traded and are therefore considered to be highly speculative, obtaining a quote often takes time and can be delayed even further due to changing market makers. Therefore, brokerage firms subscribe to the pink sheets not so much for price quotations, but rather for the market makers listed for the securities.

See also PINK SHEETS; SPECULATION; THINLY TRADED.

OFFERING DATE

Offering Date is the date an initial public offering begins to trade and refers only to over-the-counter (OTC) trading. It does not include presold offerings.

The offering date also marks the beginning of a 90-day "quiet period," during which research reports are not available.

See also HOT ISSUE; INITIAL PUBLIC OFFERING (IPO); QUIET PERIOD.

OFFERTA (Italy)

See OFFER.

OFFERTA DI ACQUISTO (Italy)

See TAKEOVER/TAKEOVER BID.

OFFERTE (Germany)

See OFFER.

OFFICE OF FAIR TRADING (OFT; United Kingdom)

The *Office of Fair Trading (OFT),* a supervisory organization formed as part of the Fair Trading Act of 1973, attempts to control restrictive trading agreements that are not in the public interest. Its director general is empowered to take a company to court if necessary.

The OFT was responsible for many changes in stock exchange practices, including the decision to appoint lay members to its ruling council and the change in policy regarding minimum commission rules.

See also FAIR AND ORDERLY MARKET; NATIONAL ASSOCIATION OF SECURITIES DEALERS (NASD); SECURITIES AND EXCHANGE COMMISSION (SEC).

OFFICIAL ASSIGNEE

The *Official Assignee* is the person appointed by the stock exchange to supervise the concluding affairs of a member firm declared by the exchange to be in default. The official assignee administrates the collection of any debts and due payments on outstanding claims against the defaulting firm.

To help facilitate these matters, the official assignee is allowed to make use of funds in the stock exchange compensation fund.

See also COMMON STOCK; PREFERRED STOCK (PFD); SECURITIES INVESTOR PROTECTION CORPORATION (SIPC).

OFFRE PUBLIQUE D'ACHAT, OFFRE PUBLIQUE D'ÉCHANGE (France)

Offre Publique d'Achat / Offre Publique d'Échange are bids to take over a company. The former involves settlement in cash terms; the latter, settlement through an exchange of the shares in the target company for those of the bidder. Takeover offers are controlled by the government.

Takeover bids are submitted by application to a committee of the Chambre Syndicale de la Compagnie des Agents de Change for approval. The application lists the minimum and maximum number of shares in the bid and states the settlement terms: cash or shares. The offer to buy shares from investors is dependent upon a minimum number of acceptances being received. Bids are not usually approved unless they involve more than 10% of the company's shares. Approved offers have to post a notice in the Bulletin de la Cote Officielle, which spells out all of the relevant details.

All bids remain open for a month. Shareholders can back out of the deal up to ten days before the expiration of the takeover. The company attempting the takeover can only withdraw if a competitive bid is made. The Ministry of the Economy can stop a takeover at any time.

Regular share trading of a company involved in a takeover bid requires 100% margin on the forward market.

See also ACQUISITION; LEVERAGED BUYOUT (LBO); TAKEOVER/TAKEOVER BID.

OIL

Oil, the drilling of which was first undertaken systematically in the 1860s, surpassed coal as the leading energy source in industrialized countries in the mid-20th century. Since the 1860s approximately 40,000 oil fields have been discovered. However, approximately 300 world-class giant fields plus 37 supergiant fields contain approximately 80% of the world's known recoverable oil. Saudi Arabia has more than one-fourth of the world's proven reserves, followed by Kuwait, the former Soviet Union, Iran, the United Arab Emirates, and the United States. Counting both proven reserves and estimated undiscovered sources, the Middle East has approximately 39% of the world's total oil endowment. On a world scale, oil production stands at about 20 billion barrels per year. The United States leads all countries in cumulative oil production, even though it imports about half of its oil consumption, which greatly contributes to its trade deficit.

Oil drilling and refining is the world's biggest business. Of the top 20 companies in the *Fortune 500*, seven are oil companies. The business of oil is thoroughly interwoven with global power politics.

After World War II, Middle Eastern oil became increasingly important to Western Europe, Japan, and the United States as the automobile industry took off. It also became the principal export of several Middle Eastern countries. Between 1949 and 1972, total world energy consumption tripled. Consumption of oil tripled in the United States, increased by a factor of 15 in Western Europe, and shot up by a factor of 137 in Japan. As oil became more abundant, it became

much cheaper than coal. One industry after another converted to oil as its main energy source.

Since 1970, increased consciousness of the environment has led to an awareness that air pollution, acid rain, oil spills, destruction of the ozone layer, and global warming are among the by-products of an overreliance on oil.

The price and supply of oil experienced some sharp swings in the 1970s and 1980s. In 1973 the Organization of Petroleum Exporting Countries (OPEC) sought to gain more control over prices and output, which led to an oil shortage and a sharp increase in the price of oil. An even sharper 150% increase in the price of crude oil occurred in 1979–81, even though supply was only down by 4% or 5%. By this time, the development of large oil fields in Mexico, Alaska, and the North Sea had begun, lessening Western dependence on OPEC oil.

In 1985 a glut of oil production caused a sharp fall in its price. In the ensuing shakedown, 170 independent U.S. oil producers lost $3.5 billion in the first half of 1986, leading to a collapse of real estate values and the regional banking structure. Meanwhile, the Big Five U.S. oil companies had profits of $5.5 billion.

In the 1980s, oil had a greater impact on stock markets than ever before. In the previous decade, the world economy had become more volatile as a result of deregulation. Futures markets were set up for gold, interest rates, and currencies. Then, the first futures contract in crude oil was set up on the New York Mercantile Exchange on 30 March 1983. Completed two weeks after a major OPEC meeting, this move was designed to undermine OPEC's price-setting powers. The rights to a single barrel of oil could now be repeatedly bought and sold, with profits going to traders and speculators. During the restructuring of the oil industry in the mid-1980s, institutional and individual investors, pension funds, and arbitrageurs reaped more than $100 billion.

Historically, the price of oil was first set by the 19th-century monopoly Standard Oil. Later, it was determined by the Texas Railroad Commission in the United States and the major oil-producing companies around the world. By the early 1970s OPEC had emerged as a major force influencing the global price of crude oil, and by the mid-1980s, the price was being set through the activity of the futures market. A complex interplay developed involving world events, economic conditions, the oil industry, and the stock markets. For example, in anticipation of an OPEC meeting in February 1983, the British National Oil Corporation expected to lower prices by at least $2 a barrel to remain competitive. The British pound then fell to US$1.54, an all-time low. But the OPEC ministers could not agree on a price. The day following the announcement of OPEC's internal disagreements, the U.S. Dow Jones Industrial Average fell 23 points, with oil stocks showing an especially sharp fall. Another example occurred in the fall of 1990 during the Persian Gulf crisis, when the price of crude oil on the futures market doubled, leading to higher consumer prices.

See also ORGANIZATION OF PETROLEUM EXPORTING COUNTRIES (OPEC).

OKUN'S LAW
Okun's Law (named for the late Arthur Okun, a Yale University economist who investigated the relationship between output and employment) describes the statistical relationship between the increase or decrease in real output and the rate of unemployment. The theory states that any increase in real output of more than 4.0% will create new jobs, and any increase of less than 3.5% will raise unemployment. A 3.5% to 4.0% growth in real output will mean that the unemployment rate remains stable.

See also ECONOMICS; GROWTH.

OLD LADY OF THREADNEEDLE STREET, THE
The Old Lady of Threadneedle Street is an affectionate term used to refer to the Bank of England.

First bestowed upon the bank by dramatist R.B. Sheridan, it remains a compliment to the bank's long history of stability, as well as a reference to its location on Threadneedle Street at the heart of the City of London.

The Bank of England is similar to the Federal Reserve Bank in the United States. It acts as a central bank, issuing currency and regulating credit, and regulating the money supply in the United Kingdom as well. The Bank of England has a well-deserved reputation for using firm persuasion to exercise influence on credit.

See also BANK OF ENGLAND; LOMBARD STREET; WALL STREET.

The "Old Lady of Threadneedle Street"—the Bank of England. *(Mary Evans Picture Library)*

OMAN, THE SULTANATE OF

Oman (Saltanat 'Uman (Arabic)) is a country occupying the southeastern coast of the Arabian Peninsula. It is bordered on the southwest by Yemen, on the west by Saudi Arabia, and on the northwest by the United Arab Emirates.

Area: 118,150 square miles (306,000 square km)

Population: 2,163,000 (13.2% urban; 86.8% rural)

Form of Government: Monarchy. Head of state and government: Sultan and Prime Minister.

Official Language: Arabic

Capital: Muscat

Largest Cities: Muscat, 100,000; Nizwa, 62,880; Sama'il, 44,721; Salalah, 10,000

Economy:

Currency: Riyal-Omani (RO)

National Budget: Revenue—RO 1.8 billion; expenditures—RO 2.2 billion (recurrent budget: 78.9%; of which defense: 43.8%; education: 12.0%; general public services: 6.8%; fuel and energy: 6.8%; health: 5.4%; capital development projects and subsidies: 21.1%)

Public Debt: US$2.3 billion

Gross National Product: US$9.6 billion

Principal Products: Vegetables, melons, and dates; livestock; oil

Foreign Trade (Imports): US$4.7 billion (machinery and transport equipment: 42.7%; basic manufactured goods: 15.1%; food and live animals: 13.0%; miscellaneous manufactured articles: 9.9%; beverages and tobacco: 6.4%; chemicals: 5.5%; from United Arab Emirates: 29.1%; Japan: 19.9%; United Kingdom: 8.8%; United States: 6.7%; Germany: 4.9%; India: 3.1%)

Foreign Trade (Exports): US$4.8 billion (petroleum: 76.3%; metals and metal products: 1.6%; live animals and products: 1.4%; textiles: 1.2%; to United Arab Emirates: 41.9%; Hong Kong: 16.9%; Iran: 9.1%; Saudi Arabia: 4.2%; United States: 4.1%; Tanzania: 3.6%)

Stock Exchanges: 1
Muscat Securities Market (MSM)
Quaboos Mosque Street
MBD, RUWI, Muscat
PO Box 3262 Postal Code 112
Ruwi
Oman

Phone: (968) 702665
Fax: (968) 702691, 799266
Telex: 3220 MSM ON

Internet Information: www.msm-oman.com

Trading Hours:
Sunday–Wednesday, 10:00 to 12:30
Monday–Tuesday, 5:00 to 6:00

Office Hours:
Sunday–Wednesday, 7:30 to 2:30
Monday–Tuesday, 4:30 to 7:30

Exchange Holidays:

31 January	6 July
1 February	18 November
7, 8 April	

Listed Companies: 114

Market Capitalization: US$3.2 billion

Major Sectors: Banks and investment companies, industrial, services, insurance

Growth:
28.6% growth in MSM Index 1994
8.1% growth in MSM Index 1995

History: The Muscat Securities Market, established in 1989, celebrated its fifth year with the adoption of four Royal Decrees that are of importance to non-Omani investors:

Royal Decree No. 5/94 added two articles to the Muscat Securities Market Laws:

1. Joint stock investment and inter-mediation companies with capital of not less than RO 2 million are now allowed to open investment accounts on behalf of clients.
2. Non-Omanis may own units of such accounts provided they do not represent more than 49% of their total investments.

Royal Decree No. 53/94 formed the Muscat Securities Market's Board of Directors, increased and outlinded their powers, and enabled the Chief Executive to contact and coordinate with senior government staff in order to issue decisions on urgent matters.

Royal Decree No. 83/94 amended the provisions of the Commercial Companies Law, thereby facilitating procedures for establishing new commercial companies and for reducing government intervention in the affairs of joint stock companies. This amendment also contained a provision stating that authorized capital may be higher than the issued capital and allowed for the issue of convertible bonds.

Royal Decree No. 102/94 established laws on foreign capital and governs all matters relating to foreign investment. It allows foreign investment in companies with capital of at least RO 150,000 provided that the foreign ownership is limited to 49%. This percentage can be raised to 65% with approval of the Ministry of Commerce and Industry, and increased further to 100% with the approval of the Development Council if the project contributes to national economic development and is valued at not less than RO 500,000. The law offers protection and safeguards for investment projects and states that such projects cannot be confiscated or expropriated unless it is in the public interest.

Classes of Securities: Shares, bonds, bills, investment accounts

Indices: MSM Index (1 January 1992 = 100)

Index = Current Total Market Value/Base Total Market Value × Base Price Index (100)

Supervisory Organizations:

Ministry of Finance

MSM Board of Directors

Chief Executive

Depository: None

Trading: Trading occurs in several ways on the Muscat Securities Market. They are as follows:

Primary Market trading, during which securities are offered to the public and issued within the prevailing law, regulations, instructions, and conventions of the exchange.

Secondary Market trading, during which securities are bought or sold directly or through an intermediary, and exchange and transfer of ownership may take place on the floor, in the offices of intermediaries, or in the offices of the market.

Regular Market trading (part of the Secondary Market), in which dealing in shares is organized on the floor according to specific listing requirements specified by the board.

Parallel Market trading (part of the Secondary Market), in which dealing in companies shares is organized on the floor and governed by easy listing requirements. This market provides liquidity for securities prior to their listing in the regular market.

Third Market trading (part of the Secondary Market), in which off-floor trading takes place in an intermediary's offices or the market offices. The third market is also used for those companies whose shares do not meet the specific listing requirements on the floor.

Listing Requirements:

1. All listing companies must be Omani joint stock companies.

2. Subscribed capital must be a minimum RO 500,000.

3. The company must have been trading for a minimum of one year.

4. The company must have a net profit from business within one complete fiscal year, prior to listing.

5. The company must have a minimum of 50 shareholders, and a minimum of 20 small shareholders (1,000 to 2,000 shares). Small shareholders must own at least 5% of the total subscribed shares.

6. The company's shares must have been traded for a minimum of one year on the parallel market prior to application for listing on the regular market.

7. Comprehensive financial statements for the most recent period must be available. These statements must indicate fairly and clearly the company's financial position.

8. The company must publish its final accounts and balance sheet in two daily newspapers for at least one day if a period of six months has lapsed since the publication of a previous balance sheet and final accounts.

9. At the board's discretion, the MSM board of directors may exempt a company from the above terms if they decide doing so would be in the public's interest.

New companies can also list on the parallel market, which is governed by less strict rules.

1. A company must be newly established and have completed the requirements of incorporation as a legal entity.

2. A newly formed company must submit a listing application and the following supporting documents:

• Articles of incorporation and articles of association

• Certificate of registration from relevant authorities

• List of names of the directors

• Sample stock certificate

• List of persons authorized to sign for the company and samples of their signatures

A prospectus must be prepared and approved by the MSM. A general requirement states that all information that may assist an investor in making an investment decision must be included.

Investor Taxation: Overseas investors are taxed under the same rules as Omani nationals.

A number of double taxation treaties are under consideration.

Limitations: Non-Omanis are limited to holding up to 49% of some companies.

Securities Lending: None

Brokerage Firms:
Oman Security Portfolio Co.
PO Box 3591 Postal Code 112
Muscat
Oman
Phone: (968) 700842, 700298
Fax: (968) 703448

Financial Services Co.
PO Box 2777 Postal Code 112
Muscat
Oman
Phone: (968) 702729, 702355
Fax: (968) 702353

Al Ahlia Security Portfolio Co.
PO Box 2232 Postal Code 112
Muscat
Oman
Phone: (968) 709421, 706737
Fax: (968) 786020

Al Shalman Securities Co.
PO Box 577 Postal Code 114
Muscat
Oman
Phone: (968) 702713
Fax: (968) 797331

Al Baraka Financial Securities Co.
PO Box 1464 Postal Code 112
Muscat
Oman
Phone: (968) 796345, 702721
Fax: (968) 704381

International Financial Servicies
PO Box 1261 Postal Code 112
Muscat
Oman
Phone: (968) 702692, 703111
Fax: (968) 708200

Al Amin Securities Co.
PO Box 1853 Postal Code 112

Muscat
Oman
Phone: (968) 787475
Fax: (968) 787476

United Securities (Associated)
PO Box 2566 Postal Code 112
Muscat
Oman
Phone: (968) 787481, 796951
Fax: (968) 787479

Gulf Investments Services
PO Box 358 Postal Code 115
Muscat
Oman
Phone: (968) 787472
Fax: (968) 787469

Oman International Dev. & Inv. Co.
PO Box 3886 Postal Code 112
Muscat
Oman
Phone: (968) 707772
Fax: (968) 707519

Oman Investments Services
PO Box 3886 Postal Code 112
Muscat
Oman
Phone: (968) 707772
Fax: (968) 707519

Company Information:

10 Major Companies

Name of Company	Market Capitalization (US$ millions)
Oman Flour Mills	177.40
Oman Cement Co.	171.95
Bank Muscat Al Alhi Al Omani	137.92
National Bank of Oman	103.90
United Bank of Oman	98.44
Oman International Bank	89.35
Oman National Insurance	85.97
Raysut Cement Co.	77.66
Dhofar Cattlefeed	67.53
Oman Fisheries	60.52

Other Investment Information:
Committee on the Investment of Foreign Capital
Ministry of Commerce and Industry
PO Box 550
Muscat

Oman
Phone: (968) 79950
Fax: (968) 794238
Telex: 3665 WIZARA ON

Ministry of Environment and Water Resources
PO Box 323
Muscat
Oman
Phone: (968) 696444
Fax: (968) 602320
Telex: 54404 A/B MININVOY ON

Ministry of Finance and Economy
PO Box 506
Muscat
Oman
Phone: (968) 738201
Telex: 5333 MALIYA ON

Ministry of Social Affairs and Labor
PO Box 560
Muscat
Oman
Phone: (968) 602444
Telex: 5002 MOSAL ON

Central Bank of Oman
PO Box 4161
Ruwi
Oman
Phone: (968) 702222
Fax: (968) 707913
Telex: 3070 MARKAZI ON

Oman Development Bank
PO Box 309
Muscat
Oman
Phone: (968) 738021
Telex: 5179 OBEDE ON

Oman Chamber of Commerce and Industry
PO Box 4400
Ruwi
Oman
Phone: (968) 70764
Telex: 33889 AL-GURFA MB

ON BALANCE VOLUME

On Balance Volume refers to the net of buying and selling volume. It also refers to the technical analysis approach that attempts to specifically calculate the point at which a share, bond, or commodity is being distributed by sellers or the subject of accumulation of buyers. It is calculated in the following way:

On balance volume is plotted on a graph against a line showing share price. A signal is given at the point at which the lines cross, indicating either the time to buy (with regards to accumulation), or the time to sell (with regards to distribution). This technique can be used for the entire market, as well as individual company shares.

See also DOW THEORY; TECHNICAL ANALYSIS; VOLUME.

ON FLOOR ORDER (United States)

On Floor Order is the designation used for orders originating on the floor of the exchange. The purpose of the designation, in keeping with the the mandate of a fair and orderly market, is to prohibit any benefit to exchange members who might take advantage of buyers and sellers who are unaware of such information.

See also FAIR AND ORDERLY MARKET; MEMBER; STOCK EXCHANGE.

ON THE OPENING

On the Opening is an instruction given by the investor to buy or sell a defined amount of shares only if the order is part of the initial transaction of the security involved on that market day. If the instruction cannot be followed, the order is canceled.

This differs from the rule that all market orders received before the open must be included in the initial transaction.

See also LIMIT ORDER; MARKET ORDER.

ONGOING BUYER / ONGOING SELLER

Ongoing Buyer/Ongoing Seller describes an investor who buys or sells the same security on a continuous basis. For example, an investor wants to buy 1,000 shares of XYZ Corporation and does so by placing an order to buy 100 shares of the company every Monday for ten weeks. In doing so, the investor is taking advantage of the short-term cyclical nature of share prices and the stock market. As a result of this ongoing purchase, the average price per share is lower than it would be if the stocks were purchased all at once. Obviously, the current pattern of the market will affect the success of the strategy.

The same technique can be applied to a selling strategy, although selling will work best when it is "selling into strength" during a time of rising prices.

See also BLOCK TRADE; LIMIT ORDER; STOP ORDER.

ON-REGISTER DAY (United Kingdom)
See DATE OF RECORD; EX-DATE.

OPEC
See ORGANIZATION OF PETROLEUM EXPORTING COUNTRIES (OPEC).

OPEN
In stockbroking there are three main uses of the word *Open*. They are:

1. The time at which a trading session begins on a stock exchange. The open is usually at a set time; however, a variety of occurrences can cause delay. A price gap is the most common cause of delay, due to the amount of time necessary to match disparate buy and sell orders. Events such as fires, floods, electrical blackouts, computer problems, wars, and assassinations have all been known to delay the opening of stock markets around the world.

2. The establishment of an account with a stock broker for the purpose of buying or selling investments. Individuals can open an account by filling out a new account form. The information included on the form can help a broker to better understand the investor's goals and objectives. Each investor is then assigned an account number. This important number is used to access the investor's account status on a computer.

3. The designation on an order for securities. An open order is one that is placed at a limit price or as a stop order and remains open until it is either canceled or executed.

See also ACCOUNT; LIMIT ORDER; STOP ORDER.

OPEN CONTRACT
An *Open Contract* is a futures contract that grants the buyer the right—without obligation—to buy a designated number of securities at a specific price before the expiration date.

Once it has been purchased, however, the writer is obliged to sell the futures contract with the option to buy it back from the original buyer if the option is exercised prior to expiration.

See also CALL; OPTION; PUT.

OPEN INTEREST
In reference to commodity or options trading, *Open Interest* is the total number of contracts remaining open that have not been executed, closed out, or allowed to expire.

Open interest statistics are often employed as a means of indicating the prevailing sentiment of investors in commodities and options. Figures for open interest are reported in newspapers carrying commodity and options information.

See also EXPIRATION; OPTION; UNDERLYING SECURITY.

OPEN MARKET OPERATIONS
Open Market Operations are strategies employed to control interest rates and involve the buying and selling of bonds by a central government. If a government sells bonds, the price of bonds will fall. As a result, interest rates will rise. Conversely, if a government buys more bonds, the price of bonds will rise, and interest rates will come down.

Because the buying and selling of bonds can influence the level of money rates (through its quantitative effect upon bank excess reserves), open market operations are also used to contract or expand the volume of excess reserves of a country's member banks, thereby influencing their power to grant credit to businesses. Additionally, open market operations can cause a knock-on effect upon foreign exchange markets and international capital movements.

In America, the New York Federal Reserve Bank is authorized to carry out transactions for the system open market account as per the directives of the Federal Open Market Committee. These transactions include: the buying or selling of government securities in the open market and the exchange of such securities at maturity; the purchase and sale of bankers' acceptances in the open market for their own accounts; the purchase of securities and acceptances under Repurchase Agreements; the purchase and sale of foreign currencies in the form of cable transfers in the open market; and the direct purchase of government securities from the United States.

See also CENTRAL BANK; KEYNES, JOHN MAYNARD; MONETARY POLICY.

OPEN ORDER
An *Open Order* is an order to buy or sell that has not been executed.

In most cases the term refers to limit orders or stop orders designated good till canceled. These orders remain open until they are either executed by the brokerage, canceled by the investor, or expire.

If the investor wishes to make a change in an open order, it is necessary to place the same order as a change rather than to place a new order. If another open order were to be entered, both might be executed, leaving the investor in a position of liability for any loss.

See also DAY ORDER; GOOD TILL CANCELED (GTC); MARKET ORDER; STOP ORDER.

OPEN-END FUND

An *Open-End Fund,* also referred to as an open end management company, is a common type of mutual fund in which the money from all investors is pooled and invested in a portfolio of securities designed to meet a specific investment objective.

An open-end fund differs from unit trusts and other closed-end funds in that new investors can buy shares in the open-end fund on any business day. The funds are priced at the end of each day and funds of significant size will have their closing price quoted in the mutual fund section of the newspaper. Day end quotes show the net asset value (NAV), which represents the price per share if the fund had been sold that day; the public offering price (POP), which represents the maximum price an investor would have paid per share to buy the minimum quantity of the fund that day; and the net change in the value of the fund on the previous day.

Some open-end funds have their own exclusive sales forces. Others sell through designated brokers. *Important to note*: Some funds cannot be transferred from one brokerage firm to another. Before transferring an account between brokerage firms, the investor should confirm that the mutual funds in the account can be handled by the receiving firm. If a fund cannot be transferred, it might be possible to have the shares mailed to the individual or held by the manager of the mutual fund. In some cases, however, the funds will have to be liquidated unless the investor wants to have more than one investing account.

In the past 20 years, open-end funds have experienced tremendous growth in size and quantity. Such funds are used to invest for children's education, save for retirement, or for general wealth accumulation.

See also REDEMPTION; UNIT INVESTMENT TRUST/UNIT TRUST.

OPENING PURCHASE

Also called buying to open, an *Opening Purchase* is the buying of an option and payment of the premium.

For example, an investor purchases 5 calls on XYZ Corp. April 40s with a premium of $1. The total premium of $500 is paid along with any brokerage commission. The option stays in effect until the end of the third week of April and can be exercised at any time.

If the price of XYZ Corp. rises to $60 a share, the investor can exercise the option and buy XYZ Corp. shares for $40 a share, receiving a $20 profit before deducting the cost of the premium and commission charges included in the opening purchase.

The investor can also sell the call options and profit from a higher premium.

See also CALL; OPENING SALE; OPTION; PREMIUM; PUT; PUT PREMIUM.

OPENING SALE

Also called selling to open, an *Opening Sale* is the selling of an option for the purpose of receiving the premium. In the event that the investor's account does not meet the conditions for covering, such options are referred to as naked or uncovered.

A conservative opening sale would be to sell calls on stock held in an account. For example, 500 shares of XYZ Corp. are held in an account and are fully paid. The investor sells 5 calls on XYZ Corp. April 40s and receives a premium of $1 per share. Although the investor still has price risk on the stock, he or she has moderated that risk by receiving the $1 per share premium. In addition, the investor runs the risk that the share price will rise high enough above the strike price of $40 to be called away.

See also CALL; OPTION; PUT; STRIKE PRICE.

OPERATING RATIO

Operating Ratio, a test of operating efficiency, is the mathematical comparison of sales and revenues to the costs associated with their generation. The most common formula used is:

$$\frac{\text{direct cost of goods sold} + \text{selling, administrative and general costs}}{\text{sales, net of taxes}}$$

If a company receives $1,000,000 from sales and it costs $750,000 to produce those sales, the operating ratio is 75%. Subtract the operating ratio from 100% and it gives a margin of profit ratio of 25%.

A low operating ratio generally suggests higher efficiency and the ability to carry a larger debt.

See also PROFIT MARGIN.

OPERATIONS

Operations is the name given to the department of a brokerage firm that is responsible for the execution, clearance, and settlement of investor securities transactions and the care and maintenance of customer accounts. Clearing, delivery, and settlement are often referred to as the street side, while setting up new accounts, attracting assets, and generating trade is known as the customer side. All are handled by brokers.

See also DELIVERY NOTICE; MARGIN; SETTLE.

OPÉRATIONS D' INITIÉS (France)

See INSIDER.

OPERATOR

Operator is an old-fashioned term for a speculator.

Before laws mandating a fair and orderly market were enacted, wealthy individuals invested large sums of their own money (or money from the the formation of pools) in order to create a corner on gold, or on the securities of a specific company. Famous operators such as Cornelius Vanderbilt, James Hill, or Jamie Fisk would gain control of the price of a security or commodity, thereby making the market unfairly difficult for any short sellers.

The situations that allowed an operator to create a corner were often created by the relatively low number of shares issued for a specific company. The actions of these big investors were said to cause ripples on Wall Street because other investors would try to follow in their wake.

Today, corners are considered to be a form of manipulation. Outlawing price manipulation and mandating higher minimums for the submission of securities and commodities has helped the stock market to remain fair and orderly for the individual investor.

See also SECURITIES AND EXCHANGE COMMISSION (SEC); SELF-REGULATING ORGANIZATION (SRO); SPECULATION.

OPERAZIONE (A) CONTANTI (Italy)

See CASH TRANSACTION.

OPTION

An *Option* is a certificate that allows the bearer certain rights in regards to the buying or selling of securities. The two main types of options available are call options and put options.

See also CALL; EXPIRATION CYCLE; INTRINSIC VALUE; PUT; SELLING TO OPEN; TIME VALUE.

OPTION CONTRACT

An *Option Contract* is the unit of measure for the number of calls or puts an investor desires to buy or sell.

An equity option contract normally consists of 100 shares of the underlying security. Thus, 5 contracts represent 500 shares and 10 contracts represent 1,000 shares. The premium is multiplied by the total number of shares involved to calculate the cost of the option contracts. A quantity of five contracts with a premium of $3 would lead to a total cost of $1,500 plus commission.

5 contracts multiplied by 100 shares per contract =	500	Total shares
500 shares multiplied by a $3 premium =	$1,500	Contracts cost
Plus commission (estimated) for 5 contracts =	$ 30	Commission cost
	$1,530	Total option cost

Commissions are estimated in the preceding example to stress the importance of calculating their cost when trading options. Frequent option trades can have the profits eaten up by the commission charges.

Option contracts are designated by their owners as being in the money, at the money, or out of the money.

See also CALL; PUT.

OPTION CYCLE (United States)

An *Option Cycle* refers to the following cycles of American equity options:

Cycle 1: January, April, July, October

Cycle 2: February, May, August, November

Cycle 3: March, June, September, December

Although there are four months in each cycle, only three of the four months trade at one time. For example, during Cycle 1, January, April, and July options will trade until the January options expire. Once the January options are dropped, the October options begin to trade. Likewise, April, July, and October options trade until the April options expire. Once the April options are dropped, January begins to trade again. The expiration date is always the Saturday following the third Friday of the expiration month.

Treasury bond options and index options expire according to the following cycle: March, June, September, December.

As in the previous example, only three months trade at once, and the expiration date is always the Saturday following the third Friday of the expiration month.

OPTION D'ACHAT (France)

See CALL.

OPTION DE VENTE (France)

See PUT.

OPTION HOLDER

An *Option Holder* is an investor who buys an option contract to open a position until the option is either sold to close the position, is exercised, or expires.

The option holder has the right to exercise an American option contract or they can be sold to close the position at any time before expiration. An option holder's risk is limited to the premium paid for the option contracts.

See also EXPIRATION; PREMIUM.

OPTION PREMIUM

The *Option Premium* is the amount paid for the sale of an option. Option premiums are either call premiums or put premiums.

See also CALL PREMIUM; OPTION; PUT PREMIUM; STRIKE PRICE; TRIPLE WITCHING HOUR.

OPTION SERIES

Put or call options with the same underlying security, strike price, and expiration date are said to be part of the same *Option Series*.

All calls for the January 60 XYZ Corporation make a series. Similarly, all puts for the January 60 XYZ Corporation make a separate series.

Any difference in the four items (class, expiration, strike price, underlying security) produces a different option series.

See also CALL; EXPIRATION; OPTION; PUT; STRIKE PRICE; UNDERLYING SECURITY.

OPTION SPREAD

The *Option Spread* is the difference between the buy and sell premiums of options of the same class.

OPTION SPREADING

Option Spreading is the simultaneous buying and selling of options in the same class. The options may either have the same exercise price but different expiry dates, or may have different exercise prices but the same expiry date.

See also CALL; OPTION; OPTION SERIES; PUT; STRADDLE.

OPTION WRITER

The *Option Writer* is an investor who sells a put or call contract to open a position.

Options are written, or sold, to obtain premium income. For example, if an investor writes 5 November 60 calls on XYZ Corporation for $3, the investor will receive $1,500 for the calls (5 calls times 100 shares per contract equals 500, which is multiplied by the $3 premium for a total of $1,500). The call option writer believes the share price will decline and the option will expire worthless. Also, if the price declines, the option premium will drop and the writer can buy to close and take the profit reflected in the difference between the selling and buying prices. The writer might sell at $3 and buy back at $1, securing a $1,000 profit.

If the writer also owns 500 shares of XYZ Corporation, the 5 calls are covered, meaning the shares can be delivered if the share price rises above the strike price when the investor exercises the option. If the writer does not own the 500 shares of XYZ Corporation, he or she is said to be writing naked, or uncovered, calls. If these calls are exercised, the writer will have to buy the shares at the current market price in order to deliver them.

See also BUYING TO CLOSE; CALL; OPTION; PUT.

OPTIONS AGREEMENT

An agreement to trade options is known as an *Options Agreement.* This agreement contains three important segments:

1. Verification of the investor's financial status
2. Acknowledgment of the Option Clearing Corporation disclosure statement
3. Agreement to abide by exercise and position limits and other rules and regulations for options trading

Many U.S. brokerage firms will not allow an investor to trade options until the agreement is signed and approved by their compliance department.

See also COMPLIANCE; OPTIONS CLEARING CORPORATION (OCC); REGISTERED OPTIONS PRINCIPAL (ROP).

OPTIONS CLEARING CORPORATION (OCC; United States)

The *Options Clearing Corporation (OCC)* is an organization, owned by the exchanges, that issues contracts and guarantees the fulfillment of obligations by all parties involved.

An OCC prospectus outlining all the rules (and risks) of trading is given to the options investor. Accompanying the prospectus is an options agreement that must be signed by the investor before trading is allowed to commence.

The OCC also processes the exchange of option transaction funds, keeps a record of those trades, and is responsible for assigning exercised options to brokerage firms. It sets ethical standards for options traders, as well.

See also CALL; PUT.

OPZIONE DOPPIA (Italy)
See STRADDLE.

OR BETTER (OB)

Or Better, a designation that appears on the order ticket of a limit order, indicates that the broker should, if possible, perform the transaction at a price better than that stated by the limit order.

Limit buy orders are normally placed below the current trading price. For instance, if the current price of XYZ Corp. is $50, a limit order might be placed at $48 5/8. However, if the price is expected to suddenly increase, some investors will place a limit order above the current market price.

Although the designation "or better" is always assumed on a limit order, the occasion can arise in which the instruction verifies the order to be correct as entered.

See also LIMIT ORDER; MARKET ORDER; STOP ORDER.

ORANGE COUNTY

Orange County in southern California is an economic powerhouse in which output of goods and services would rank it among the top ten countries in the world, and in which per capita income is 60% higher than the average in the United States. With international trade in the billions of dollars, it ranks third among all regional areas in the United States for exports. It is home to thousands of businesses with international ties, including a number of *Fortune 500* companies.

Yet on 6 December 1994, Orange County declared bankruptcy. In the biggest municipal bankruptcy in U.S. history, county representatives filed petitions on behalf of the county itself as well as its investment pool, which had had $7.5 billion prior to the debacle and had received investments from nearly 200 cities, school districts, and agencies in Orange County and throughout the western United States. Two days later Orange County defaulted on a $110 million pension bond it had just issued, and later that month it could not muster the $169 million needed to pay bond holders. By mid-December, financial advisers had begun to sell what was left of Orange County's investment pool. Total losses were later determined to be $1.64 billion. The Orange County financial scandal attracted national attention as it focused concerns on the liquidity of public funds and sent a shock through financial markets.

Orange County Treasury officials had used the $7.5 billion investment pool to borrow another $12 to $14 billion. Combining all these funds, and rejecting the idea of a diversified portfolio, they invested in derivatives, which are contracts that link the value of one type of investment to that of others. Some of Orange County's derivatives depended on the relationship between U.S. and Swiss interest rates. When the U.S. Federal Reserve Board raised interest rates relative to Swiss rates, the spread between Orange County's borrowing rate and its investment returns disappeared. Some of Orange County's investments were derivatives known as "inverse floaters," which offer a higher rate of interest if interest rates go down. But when U.S. interest rates went up, the county's profits suffered.

The Securities and Exchange Commission (SEC) filed a civil suit against the county treasurer, Robert Citron, and his assistant treasurer, Matthew Raabe. In the suit, the SEC alleged that the county had committed fraud against people who bought its bonds but were not advised of the county's true financial condition, and that the county had misled investors about a risky strategy involving the $20 billion investment pool run by Citron. The suit raised serious questions about the propriety of the behavior of Orange County's principal broker, Merrill Lynch and Company. In fact, the county sued Merrill Lynch for $2.4 billion. However, in its own defense, Merrill Lynch said that it had given Citron and Raabe detailed advice, in October 1992 and again in January 1993, about how rising interest rates would decrease the value of their fund.

After the initial layoff of 500 county employees in early 1995, Orange County was able to put together a viable recovery plan, despite a defeat by county voters of a proposed 0.5% sales tax hike in June 1995. The county was the beneficiary of a $520 million bond recovery plan put together by Wall Street advisers, which allowed the county to mortgage landfills and county buildings. In addition, Orange County was able to shore up its finances by diverting transport and park taxes, raising dump fees, and importing trash. This made it possible for the county to sell $550 million in new bonds and thus pay current bondholders, vendors, and some other high-priority creditors.

Meanwhile, companies based in Orange County increased their sale of stock to the public from $377 million to $1.37 billion during the year following the bankruptcy. However, the county's annual general fund budget dropped 41% from 1995 to 1996.

Several lessons can be drawn from the Orange County fiscal crisis. In all likelihood such a crisis could occur somewhere else soon, because few public officials or people they serve have a thorough understanding of municipal finance. First, the Orange County investors put considerations of yield ahead of safety and liquidity, just the opposite of what is prudent for public officials who must regularly pay for teacher salaries, road repairs, and the like. Second, they did not build a diverse portfolio, instead banking everything on the erroneous prediction that U.S. interest rates would fall. Third, they used short-term loans to finance their investments in long-term assets; unable to realize profits from their assets quickly enough, they could not repay the loans. Fourth, they engaged in excessive leveraging, using a $7.5 billion fund to borrow nearly twice that amount. Finally, they did not agree on and implement a policy of stopping losses before they had grown too great.

See also DERIVATIVE INSTRUMENT; LEVERAGE.

ORDER BOOK OFFICIAL (OBO; United States)

Order Book Officials are Pacific Stock Exchange (PSE) options employees who take orders for options not able to be immediately executed. When the order can be filled, the OBO functions as agent, executing the order and sending notification to the member firm who placed it.

Their function is similar to board brokers on the Chicago Board Options Exchange (CBOE).

See also AGENCY; EXECUTION; OPTION.

ORDER IMBALANCE

An *Order Imbalance* is an overabundance of either buys or sells.

An order imbalance can make fair pricing very difficult. To correct it, trading is temporarily suspended in order to provide sufficient time to arrive at a new fair market price and allow the trading public access to any information that has given rise to the order imbalance.

Allowing information to be disseminated to the investing public is part of creating a fair and orderly market.

See also ASK PRICE; BID PRICE; LAST TRADE.

ORDER TICKET

An *Order Ticket* is the form (either paper or computer entry) that, when filled out by a broker, contains all the customer's instructions regarding a security. Included on the form are any special designations, such as all or none (AON), immediate or cancel (IOC), limit price and stop price, etc.

Once the order ticket is completed and the order is verified, it is sent to the exchange floor by computer or by wire. For an over-the-counter (OTC) transaction, the form is sent to the firm's trading desk, where it is executed as agent or principal.

Federal laws require the order ticket to be retained for a specific period of time to enable backtracking in the invent of lost investor records or other discrepancies.

See also ALL OR NONE (AON); IMMEDIATE OR CANCEL (IOC); LIMIT ORDER; STOCKBROKER; STOP ORDER.

ORDINARY INCOME

For tax purposes, *Ordinary Income* is any income that is not a result of investment or capital gain.

No matter what the source, ordinary income is aggregated and taxed at the same effective rate as the individual's non-investment income. If investment income is calculated as capital gains income, it can be taxed at differing rates depending on whether the gains are long-term or short-term.

Long-term gains receive preferential treatment in order to encourage individuals to invest money and hold the securities for extended periods of time. Investing money in companies supplies the capital necessary for corporate growth and development.

See also INDIVIDUAL COUNTRIES' STOCK EXCHANGE PROFILES/INVESTOR TAXATION.

ORDINARY SHARES
See COMMON STOCK.

ORGANIZATION FOR ECONOMIC COOPERATION AND DEVELOPMENT (OECD)

The *Organization for Economic Cooperation and Development (OECD)* was formed in September 1961. It was an outgrowth and extension of the Organization for European Economic Cooperation (OEEC), which had been formed in 1947 to coordinate Western Europe's economic recovery. OEEC had consisted of 16 countries: Austria, Belgium, Denmark, France, Greece, Iceland, the Republic of Ireland, Italy, Luxembourg, the Netherlands, Norway, Portugal, Sweden, Switzerland, Turkey, and the United Kingdom. When OECD was formed, the United States, Canada, and Spain joined. Since then 10 other countries have joined OECD: Germany, Japan, Finland, Australia, New Zealand, Mexico, the Czech Republic, Poland, Hungary, and South Korea.

The goals of OECD are to promote a high rate of sustainable economic growth, with high employment, a rising standard of living, and stable finances among all member countries; to contribute to the economic development of all member as well as non-member countries; and to facilitate the expansion of world trade on a multilateral, non-discriminatory basis.

Lacking enforcement powers, OECD is a consultative body that holds conferences and seminars, and publishes materials totaling more than 10,000 pages annually, covering subjects such as economic statistics of member countries, agriculture, scientific research, capital markets, tax structures, energy resources, environmental issues, education, and development assistance. Its chief publication is its bimonthly magazine, *The OECD Observer*.

OECD is headquartered in Paris and has a staff of more than 1,000 persons. Structurally, it consists of committees that are responsible for research and policy formation in specific areas, as well as a secretariat, consisting of 20 directorates and services whose professional and administrative staff support the work of those committees.

The structure of OECD's directorates reflects an interdisciplinary perspective based on an understanding of the increasing globalization of the economy, the greater interpenetration of different policy areas, and the heightened interdependence of member and non-member countries. Part of OECD's increased concern with some non-member countries relates to its efforts to get those countries to adopt market economies. In particular, OECD has taken on the task of assisting the former members of the Soviet bloc in their efforts to make the transition to private capitalist economies. Three of these countries—the Czech Republic, Poland, and Hungary—have recently joined OECD.

Among the Western European OECD countries, both Britain and France carried out privatization campaigns in the 1980s. These were intended to stimulate the economy and broaden the base of stockholders. French privatized companies, however, did not fare so well in the late 1980s, partly because of the weak French stock market.

Some of the main directorates of the OECD secretariat are as follows:

• The Trade Directorate analyzes the development of rules needed to deal with the expanding volume and diversity of trade. It addresses environmental issues, competition policy, industrial policy, and technology.

• The Directorate for Financial, Fiscal, and Enterprise Affairs seeks to promote a fair and predictable groundwork for investment. It monitors statistics and analyzes phenomena in banking, securities, and insurance. It also guides opposition to bribery in international commerce, fosters antitrust policies, promotes cooperation among different countries' law enforcement agencies, and provides information for consumers.

• The Directorate for Science, Technology, and Industry examines the interrelations among scientific advancement, technology, and economic growth. It conducts international comparisons and helps to develop scientific and industrial policies.

• The Directorate for Education, Employment, Labor, and Social Affairs investigates education and training systems in member countries. It carries out policy reviews in these areas as well as the areas of health care and social welfare programs and immigration.

• The Agriculture Directorate promotes the cutting of farm subsidies while planning assistance to farmers. It establishes international codes for maintaining the quality of fruits, vegetables, seeds, forest products, and tractors, and monitors the management of fisheries.

• The Environment Directorate addresses the interplay between environmental policy and competition, trade, investment, and employment. It monitors member countries' environmental policies and supports international cooperation on such issues as climate change, waste management, and biological diversity.

• The Development Cooperation Directorate monitors aid budgets and studies whether they are sustainable in terms of population growth and the environment.

• The Public Management Service deals with governments' public policy effectiveness, service quality, and responsiveness to citizens.

• The Statistics Directorate maintains macroeconomic data needed for economic forecasting. These data include information on national accounts, the labor force, foreign trade, prices, output, and money.

• The Territorial Development Service studies how urban, regional, and rural policies and local efforts can give rise to jobs and higher living standards, promote development, and protect the environment.

• The International Energy Agency oversees energy sharing in cases of emergency disruptions.

• The Nuclear Energy Agency seeks to facilitate safe, peaceful uses of nuclear energy.

• The International Futures Programme helps government and industry decision-makers to understand long-term economic forecasts and prepare for their implications.

See also EUROPEAN BANK FOR RECONSTRUCTION AND DEVELOPMENT (EBRD); INTERNATIONAL MONETARY FUND (IMF); UNITED NATIONS CONFERENCE ON TRADE AND DEVELOPMENT (UNCTAD).

ORGANIZATION OF PETROLEUM EXPORTING COUNTRIES (OPEC)

The *Organization of Petroleum Exporting Countries (OPEC)* is a group of 13 countries that are major producers and exporters of crude oil. The organization includes Iran, Iraq, Kuwait, Saudi Arabia, Venezuela, Qatar, Libya, Indonesia, United Arab Emirates (UAE), Algeria, Nigeria, Ecuador, and Gabon. OPEC opened offices in Vienna, Austria, in 1960.

OPEC was started as a reaction to British Petroleum's decision in 1959 to cut the posted price of petroleum. This action angered the oil-producing Arab countries, who decided to meet in Cairo, Egypt, to discuss the situation. The conference was also attended by delegates from non-Arab petroleum-exporting countries. The results of the meeting were little more than an expression of increasing frustrations. Not long afterward, however, another meeting was called, this one attended by Juan Pablo Perez Alfonzo (Venezuela's oil spokesman), Abdullah Tarki (Saudi Arabia), and representatives from Iran and Iraq (who had boycotted the first conference). Out of this meeting, held on 14 September 1960, OPEC was born.

OPEC's influence eventually grew, and by the end of 1973 the organization had become a major player on the international oil market. Its major impact came as a result of an oil embargo. In 1973 Saudi Arabia, the dominant member of OPEC by virtue of owning more than twice as many oil reserves as other OPEC members, ordered cuts in oil production to reduce the oil supply to the United States and other countries friendly to Israel. The embargo was designed to show support for Egypt's war with Israel. Panic from the embargo caused the spot price for oil to increase to several times the posted price that had been established by the major producers. In 1973 oil prices rose from $3 per barrel to $34 per barrel. OPEC seized its opportunity to become a powerful influence on the price of oil in the following decades by controlling the amount of oil produced.

OPEC's high prices eventually forced oil-dependent countries to seek alternative forms of energy and to expand the imports of oil from non-OPEC countries. As a result, by 1990 OPEC's share of world exports fell below 50%. In 1994 OPEC members attempted to promote an oil price of $21 per barrel, but the lack of solidarity among members and world market conditions would only support a maximum price of $16 per barrel.

ORIX CORPORATION

In the mid-1990s, Japan's *Orix Corporation* was in the process of evolving from one of the biggest leasing firms in the world to a more diversified financing company. Its business activities include residential lending, installment sales, consumer credit, venture capital financing, securities brokerage, futures fund management, life insurance, and property management. In addition, it leases a broad range of items, including computers, office machines, construction equipment, semiconductor manufacturing plant and machinery, cars, trucks, ships, and jumbo jets to businesses across Asia, Europe, and the United States. At the end of 1996 Orix had 78 offices in Japan and 2,705 employees. Leasing and installment loan sales comprised 76% of Orix's revenues in 1996. On 31 March 1997, Orix's assets were $41.8 billion.

Orix was formed as Orient Leasing Company, Limited (OLC) in 1964. OLC's business grew slowly throughout the 1960s, as Japanese businesses and consumers were not accustomed to leasing. In the 1970s OLC established itself throughout Asia. In 1974 it set up its first wholly owned subsidiary, Orient Leasing (Asia), in Hong Kong. The subsidiary handled mortgage loans, did financing in multiple currencies, and leased major items such as ships and planes.

In 1972 OLC established its first major subsidiary in Japan, Orient Leasing Interior Company, and also created the Korea Development Leasing Corporation and Orient Leasing Singapore, which leased vehicles, machinery, furniture, medical and dental equipment, and vessels. OLC proceeded to set up subsidiaries in several other Asian countries—Malaysia in 1973, Indonesia in 1975, the Philippines in 1977, and Thailand in 1978. OLC also set up subsidiaries in Brazil in 1973 and in Chile in 1977.

In the 1980s OLC expanded into the United States, Europe, and China. In 1981 OLC founded the China Orient Leasing Company, the first leasing company in that country, in partnership with two Chinese companies. Within three years, this new leasing firm was writing $40 million in contracts for plant machinery, film development equipment, printing presses, and other varied equipment. OLC opened a representative office in Greece in 1982, set up Orient Leasing (UK) in London in 1983, and established Lombard Orient Leasing Limited in England in 1986. In 1988 OLC formed a leasing company in Spain. In the United

States, OLC set up Orient Leasing USA Corporation in 1981 and Orient-U.S. Leasing Corporation in 1982.

In the late 1980s OLC began to diversify and engage in an increasing quantity and variety of non-leasing businesses. In the United States, it invested in a hotel chain and a real estate company. In Japan, it purchased a small brokerage firm in 1986. As part of its plan to diversify, OLC renamed itself Orix on its 25th anniversary in 1989. To help establish its corporate identity in the marketplace, Orix purchased a Japanese baseball team and named it the Orix Blue Wave.

In 1990 Orix Corporation founded Orix Commodities in a joint venture with Commodities Corporation of the USA. In 1997 Orix's subsidiary, Orix USA Corporation, in a joint venture with Banc One Capital Corporation, formed Banc One Mortgage Capital Markets (BOMCM). BOMCM's main activities were securitizing loans on commercial property, servicing loans, and investing in securitized loans. In 1995 Orix helped set up the first leasing company in Egypt. In China in 1997 Orix's subsidiary joined with another firm to offer credit sales of air conditioners—the first time they had been made available in China. Also in the 1990s, Orix invested in a resort in Hawaii, urban real estate and an airlines company in Japan, and personal computer sales over the Internet in Japan.

Orix continued to dominate the Japanese leasing market in the 1990s, and it was among the top five leasing companies in the world. Leasing continued to provide more than half its receivables and revenues in 1994. However, profit rates in leasing had declined because of the Japanese stock market crash and recession. The fall in real estate prices and equity markets in Japan had a significant effect on the company in the early 1990s. The proliferation of bad debt tended to affect leasing companies such as Orix even more than banks, since the leasing companies had typically financed more risky credits. Orix's write-offs on bad loans peaked at $221 million in the 1992 fiscal year. Japanese domestic leasing contracts declined for 27 consecutive months ending in June 1994.

Orix thus found it necessary to diversify, as did many other Japanese financing companies. Some changes in Japanese regulations aided this process. In 1993 the Ministry of Finance lifted the ban on issuance of commercial paper by nonbank financial companies. A new law recognized the sale of securities backed by lease receivables, and a revised commercial code removed issue limits for debentures. These changes made it simpler for Orix to raise funds and reduce costs.

See also JAPANESE BOOM AND BUST 1988–90; NIPPON SHINPAN COMPANY LTD.

ORPHAN STOCK (United States)

Orphan Stock is a slang expression referring to a company whose shares are not examined by a research analyst.

Because companies rely heavily on analysts to inform the public of profitable activities and growth developments, those not covered by independent research tend to have lower market values than similar companies that are covered.

See also ANALYST; DOW JONES INDUSTRIAL AVERAGES (DJIA); STANDARD & POOR'S.

OTC OPTION

An *OTC Option* is an option purchased over the counter.

See also CALL; PUT.

OTHER INCOME

A line item entry appearing on the balance sheet of a corporation, *Other Income* refers to any revenue other than that which is accrued through the normal course of business. Such sources include interest and dividends from investments, profits from asset liquidation, gains on foreign exchange, and rental income.

Items under this category are listed separately so as not to confuse main line business revenues with other sources. If combined, these figures could easily mislead investors.

See also EARNINGS; EXTRAORDINARY ITEM.

OUT OF THE MONEY

Out of the Money is one of three possible descriptions given to the relationship between the strike price of an option and the price of the underlying security. An option is said to be out of the money when its exercise would yield negative results for the holder.

For example, if the exercise price of a call on XYZ Corporation is $50, an investor would lose money when exercising the option if the current market price was $45 a share; the investor's option would be $5 out of the money.

If the market price of the shares and the strike price are identical, the option is said to be at the money. If the market price of the shares is higher than the strike price, the option is said to be in the money. An option that is five or more points out of the money is said to be deep out of the money.

See also AT THE MONEY; CALL OPTION; IN THE MONEY; STRIKE PRICE; UNDERLYING SECURITY.

OUTSTANDING SHARES

See ISSUED AND OUTSTANDING.

OVER THE COUNTER (OTC)

Over the Counter (OTC) refers to those securities not traded on organized stock exchanges but rather on telephones and computers from the trading desks in various brokerage firms.

In the United States, rules for OTC trading are set and implemented by the National Association of Securities Dealers (NASD). Price quotations are calculated and reported by the National Association of Securities Dealers Automated Quotations (NASDAQ). Other countries have similar self-regulating organizations.

See also NATIONAL ASSOCIATION OF SECURITIES DEALERS (NASD); NATIONAL ASSOCIATION OF SECURITIES DEALERS AUTOMATED QUOTATION SYSTEM (NASDAQ); SELF-REGULATING ORGANIZATION; UNITED STATES.

OVERBOUGHT

Overbought is a term used by technical analysts when describing a sharp increase in the price of shares or the level of the market. An overbought condition is believed to signify a future drop in prices because of the threat of profit taking. To the technical analyst, a common signal of overbuying is a price gap when the security or the market opens higher than it closed on the previous session.

Although a designation of "overbought" is considered to be a fairly reliable indicator of the current situation, it is not reliable in regard to the long-term approach. Technical investors tend to focus on short-term price swings, rather than growth from year to year.

See also INDICATOR; OVERSOLD; TECHNICAL ANALYSIS.

OVERHEATING

Overheating describes the growth of an economy in which expansion is thought to be too rapid. When an economy is overheating, the country's productive capacity is near the full limit. Economists fear inflation as a result of an overheating economy, as too much money begins to pursue too few goods.

In the United States, the usual remedy for an overheating economy is the restriction of the money supply by the Federal Reserve, and reduced spending by the government. While this action can be effective in slowing down the economy, it also runs the risk of creating a recession.

See also FEDERAL RESERVE SYSTEM; INTEREST/INTEREST RATES; RECESSION.

OVERREACHING

Overreaching is the unethical action of a broker/dealer who, when acting as market maker in the over-the-counter market, charges a higher price as a principal than he or she would charge as an agent.

Until recently, the amount of mark-up did not appear on a trade confirmation. In effect, this hid the charges from the investor. Securities and Exchange Commission (SEC) regulations now require the amount of mark up to be listed separately on the confirmation. By doing so, the SEC has been successful in reducing the occurrences of overreaching.

See also MARK DOWN; MARK UP; SECURITIES AND EXCHANGE COMMISSION (SEC).

OVERSOLD

Oversold is a term used by technical analysts when describing a sharp decrease in the price of shares or the level of the market. An oversold condition is believed to signal a drop in prices and market levels. A common signal of overselling is the existence of a price gap when the security or the market opens lower than it closed on the previous session.

Although overselling is considered to be a signal that a correction is overdue, like many indicators, it is not reliable in the long-term approach.

See also INDICATOR; OVERBOUGHT; TECHNICAL ANALYSIS.

OVERVALUED

When a technical analyst reviews a company's shares and reaches the conclusion that the shares are trading at significantly higher prices than are justified by the company's earnings and growth prospects, the shares are said to be *Overvalued.*

If well-regarded analysts determine that certain shares are overvalued, the share prices could fall. It is often difficult, however, to determine if a decline is caused by the actual overvalue of the shares, or is a result of the publication of an analyst's opinion.

See also FUNDAMENTAL ANALYSIS; OVERBOUGHT; UNDERVALUED.

P

PACHETTO (Italy)

See STOCK.

PACIFIC COMPUTERIZED ORDER ACCESS SYSTEM (P/COAST; United States)

The *Pacific Computerized Order Access System (P/Coast)* executes market orders for the Pacific Stock Exchange.

See also UNITED STATES/PACIFIC STOCK EXCHANGE (PSE).

PACIFIC STOCK EXCHANGE

See UNITED STATES/PACIFIC STOCK EXCHANGE (PSE).

PAC-MAN DEFENSE

Pac-Man is a popular computer game in which players are eaten up by their opponents if they are slow in responding to the opponents' threat. For investment bankers, the *Pac-Man Defense* signifies a strategy against a hostile takeover made by the proposed takeover target. The target, once aware of the threat to its independence, will attempt to take control of the unwanted raider before it can put its takeover plans into action. This may be achieved by buying stock in or launching a full bid for the raiding company, or by influencing the company's board members and investors that a friendly merger, rather than an aggressive takeover, will be better for their interests.

The term is associated with William Agee, who was chairman of the U.S. company Bendix. In 1982 Agee launched a hostile bid for the defense contractor Martin Marietta. Martin Marietta in turn made a hostile bid for Bendix. Agee was forced to hastily arrange a defensive merger in order to protect his company.

See also HOSTILE TAKEOVER; TAKEOVER/TAKEOVER BID.

PAID IN CAPITAL/PAID UP CAPITAL

Paid In Capital/Paid Up Capital is the money a company receives from its shareholders as a result of an initial sale of shares, or an initial public offering. The paid in capital is adjusted downward if a company repurchases some of its own shares. The figure for paid in capital appears on a company's balance sheet.

See also AUTHORIZED SHARES; CAPITAL; INITIAL PUBLIC OFFERING (IPO).

PAINEWEBBER

PaineWebber is one of the largest financial service companies in the world. Founded in 1879, it serves more than two million clients, including individuals, institutions, state and local governments, and public agencies. The services that PaineWebber provides include private client investment services, municipal securities, securities lending, asset management, investment banking, research, global fixed income, global equity sales and trading, and transaction services. At the end of 1996 the firm had approximately $52.5 billion in assets and employed approximately 16,000 people in more than 300 offices around the world.

Paine and Webber was founded in 1879 in Boston, and in 1880 it acquired a seat on the Boston Stock Exchange. The following year the firm changed its name to Paine, Webber and Company. It joined the New York Stock Exchange in 1890, the Chicago Board of Trade in 1909, and the Chicago Stock Exchange in 1916.

Paine Webber opened its first branch office in 1899 in Michigan. It opened up nine more branches during World War I, including one in New York City. In the 1920s it opened five more offices and moved six to larger quarters. By 1930 Paine Webber had 25 branch offices in 22 cities throughout the northeastern and upper midwestern portions of the United States, although it lost six of these offices during the Great Depression.

Recovering during World War II, in 1942 Paine Webber merged with Jackson and Curtis to form Paine, Webber, Jackson and Curtis. This privately owned brokerage house focused on the retail trade, buying and selling securities for private customers. It moved its headquarters to New York City in 1963.

In 1974 the Employee Retirement Income Security Act was passed. This increased the importance of institutional investors as a revenue source in the U.S. stock market. In May 1975 the fixed-rate commission structure for brokers ended. These legislative changes, combined with the lower trading volume that the U.S. stock market experienced for several years beginning in the late 1960s, led to lower profit margins and increased competition among U.S. brokerage houses. Expansion into new markets, as well as mergers, became the practice of the companies that were to survive. Paine Webber itself underwent a period of very rapid growth, going from fewer than 40 branch offices and annual revenues of $30 million in 1964, to 229 branches and revenues of $900 million in 1980.

Paine Webber's acquisitions during this period included the Kansas City brokerage house of Barret Fitch North in 1967; the securities firm of Abbott, Procter and Paine, based in Richmond, Virginia, in 1970; the Abacus Company, an investment firm, in 1972; and the securities research firm Mitchell Hutchins in 1977. Paine Webber merged with the investment bankers Blyth Eastman Dillon and Company in 1980. Meanwhile, Paine Webber had become a public corporation in 1970, enhancing its ability to find dependable capital sources.

In 1973 the firm opened its first offices overseas, in London and Tokyo.

In the 1980s Paine Webber continued to diversify through acquisitions and reorganizations. In 1983 it acquired Rotan Mosle Financial Corporation, as well as First Mid-America. In 1984 it acquired Becker Paribas Futures, a commodity futures trading firm, and purchased Rouse Real Estate Finance. Also in 1984 the firm reorganized to set up three subsidiaries under one name, PaineWebber Incorporated. In 1986–88, acting as investment banker, it participated in the buyouts of National Car Rental, Greyhound, and Braniff Airlines.

Following the October 1987 stock market crash, PaineWebber moved to consolidate, selling its commercial paper and venture capital operations. To acquire more capital, it sold an 18% equity interest to Yasuda Mutual Life Insurance. In turn, PaineWebber moved to acquire Manufacturers Hanover Investment Corporation in 1988. As of this time, PaineWebber's strategy was to focus on four core businesses: investment and merchant banking, capital trading, asset management, and retail and institutional sales.

But in the coming years further consolidation became necessary. In 1994 PaineWebber pulled out of the commodities business, even at a time when most investors were getting more involved in this area because of worries about inflation. PaineWebber's decision was influenced by its difficulties with the volatile mortgage derivatives in its Short-Term U.S. Government Income Fund, and by its desire to reduce the amount of risk in its investments.

In 1995 the firm scaled back its mortgage-backed securities and largely got out of the equity derivatives business. It also slowed its plans for international expansion. Then in 1996 it restructured its investment banking activities to cover five to seven industries, down from ten. Mainly a move to cut expenses, this restructuring was also a sign that PaineWebber's investment banking had not developed as it had hoped, despite its acquisition of Kidder Peabody in 1994 from General Electric. However, the Kidder Peabody deal had stimulated PaineWebber's groups in health care, real estate, and energy.

By 1997 PaineWebber had raised its return on equity to 20%, up from 13% in 1995. Rather than trying to dominate in all industries or reinvent itself as a niche brokerage, PaineWebber sought to expand itself into specific areas where it saw the most growth. PaineWebber combined its energy and utility divisions, and increased its number of analysts in the new department. Also in 1997 PaineWebber announced that it would hire approximately 1,200 new brokers in the hopes of securing a larger share of the retail investment market. As more private investor money entered the stock market, PaineWebber looked to improve its responsiveness to those clients, recasting stock brokers as "personal chief financial officers," and research analyses as "investment themes."

See also INVESTMENT BANKER; KIDDER PEABODY & COMPANY; MANUFACTURERS HANOVER CORPORATION.

PAINTING THE TAPE
See CROSS.

PAKISTAN, ISLAMIC REPUBLIC OF
Pakistan (Islam-i Jamhuriya-e Pakistan) is Asia's seventh largest country. It is bordered to the west by Iran, to the north by Afghanistan, to the northeast by China, and to the east and southeast by India.

Area: 307,374 square miles (796,095 square km)

Population: 140,497,000 (32% urban; 68.0% rural)

Form of Government: Multiparty federal Islamic republic, with two legislative houses: Senate—87 members; National Assembly—217 members. Chief of state: President. Chief of government: Prime Minister.

Official Language: Urdu

Capital: Islamabad

Largest Cities: Karachi, 5,208,132; Lahore, 2,952,689; Faisalabad, 1,104,209; Rawalpindi, 794,843; Islamabad, 204,364

Economy:

Currency: Pakistan rupee (Rs)

National Budget: Revenue—Rs 288.7 billion; expenditures—Rs 272.5 billion (public debt service: 48.1%; defense: 32.7%; subsidies: 1.8%; law and order: 1.7%).

Public Debt: US$20.3 billion

Gross National Product: US$54.0 billion

Principal Products: Sugarcane; wheat, rice, corn; livestock; textiles

Foreign Trade (Imports): Rs 258.3 billion (petroleum products: 16.3%; specialized machinery: 9.1%; road vehicles: 6.3%; vegetable oil and fats: 5.7%; organic chemicals: 4.1%; iron and steel manufactures: 3.8%; electrical machinery: 3.4%; general industrial machinery: 3.2%; from Japan: 11.8%; United States: 10.6%; Malaysia: 5.5%; Saudi Arabia: 5.4%; Kuwait: 5.3%; China: 5.1%; United Kingdom: 4.9%; France: 4.0%; Germany: 3.9%)

Foreign Trade (Exports): Rs 205.5 billion (textile fabrics: 53.6%; ready-made garments: 22.0%; rice: 3.6%; leather and leather goods: 3.5%; fresh fish: 2.3%; cotton: 2.1%; sugar and honey: 1.8%; to United States: 14.4%; Japan: 8.0%; Germany: 8.0%; United Kingdom: 7.8%; Dubayy: 6.3%; France: 4.1%; Saudi Arabia: 3.5%; the Netherlands: 3.1%)

Stock Exchanges: 3

Karachi Stock Exchange (KSE)
Stock Exchange Building
Stock Exchange Road
Karachi-74000
Pakistan
Phone: (92-21) 241-2425
Fax: (952) 241-0825
Telex: 20046 KASEX-PK

Internet Address: www.kse.org

Trading Hours: Sunday–Thursday, 11:00 to 2:00

Office Hours: Sunday–Thursday, 10:30 to 6:30

Exchange Holidays:

20, 26, January	15 October
8–10 April	9 November
6, 14 August	6, 25 December

Listed Companies 781

Market Capitalization: US$11.9 billion

Major Sectors: Mining, construction, manufacturing, transportation, communication, utility, finance, insurance, real estate

History: The Karachi Stock Exchange, registered under the Companies Act of 1913, began trading in September 1947. Initially, although there were 100 members, fewer than 6 were active traders. Today, membership has risen to 200 with nearly 70% of members being active brokers.

Trading activity has grown to more than 7.5 million shares a day, with much of the trading done by foreign investors. Only active exchange members are permitted to trade in the trading hall and appoint authorized agents to act on their behalf. Foreign brokers are not allowed to trade on the exchange.

Classes of Securities: Ordinary shares, modarabas (similar to mutual funds), Foreign Exchange Bearer Certificates (issued by the federal government in exchange for foreign currency deposits), bonds for the Water and Power Development Authority, and Bearer National Fund Bonds

Indices:

The KSE Index is an arithmetic average of 50 actively traded shares, based at 1000 on 1 November 1991.

The State Bank of Pakistan (SBP) produces both the General Index (all listed shares with a composite weighted average of ten sector indices) and the Sensitivity Index

The General Index (all ordinary shares listed on the KSE, weighted by paid-up capital)

IFC Total Return Index, which adjusts for cash dividends and implied stock dividend of rights issues

Supervisory Organizations: The Securities and Exchange Ordinance (SEO) is the main governing organization, and the Corporate Law Authority (CLA) is the agency that supervises the information requirements for the stock exchanges and the licensing of brokers. The Investment Promotion Bureau (IPB) is the foreign investment regulatory body.

Depository: Central Depository

Settlement Details:

Shares:

Ready basis: Trades on Saturday–Wednesday are settled on the Sunday of the following week (by 11:30 A.M.)

Spot basis: 24 hours between buyer and seller

Forward trading: Delivery and settlement at the end of each month

Fixed income: Spot basis; mostly owned by banks and institutions with very little trading

Trading: Trading on the exchange is done by open-outcry. A calling member is obliged to trade in at least one marketable lot (100 shares of Rs 10 each) if the call is accepted.

The market information system has been computerized and a computerized trading system is expected to follow in the near future.

Listing Requirements A formal application must be made to the exchange in compliance with the KSE or Lahore Stock Exchange (LSE) listing regulations. If the application complies with the requirements, a report is sent to the company affairs committee. A prospectus must be published in a newspaper with a circulation in the province in which the exchange is situated. Listing takes place about five weeks from the publication of a prospectus in the newspapers.

The Controller of Capital Issues must approve an issue and the publishing of a prospectus. Permission of the controller is not required for an issue of shares at par where the value does not exceed Rs 100 million, unless the issuer is involved in banking, insurance, leasing, investment, finance, or housing. Permission is required for a provident society or a company in which foreign capital is associated and which has operations relating to arms and ammunition, security printing, currency minting, high explosives, or radioactive substances.

The general exemption is subject to compliance with conditions set in the Schedule to the Order. The Exemption Order additionally permits the issuance of bonus shares by listed companies subject to defined conditions.

Investor Taxation: Dividend income is taxed at 15%, and there is an added surcharge of 10% if dividend income exceeds Rs 100,000 (effective tax 16.5%). Unlisted securities are taxed at a reduced rate of 27.5% when shares are held for longer than 12 months. Foreign companies pay tax at an effective rate of 55%.

Limitations: There are few restrictions on foreign investment in ordinary shares listed on the exchanges or for subscriptions to public offerings. Some approvals are only occasionally necessary from the IPB and the SBP.

The four restricted industries (arms, security and currency printing, explosives, and radioactive materials) are restricted only if the promoter of the project is a foreigner.

For exchange control, SBP approval is necessary for:

1. Corporate securities other than shares
2. Shares of unlisted companies
3. New share issues from unlisted companies.

Securities Lending: None

Brokerage Firms:
Jahandir Siddiqui & Co. Ltd.
90 KSE Bldg.
Karachi

Pakistan
Phone: (92-21) 241-9491 and 241-9001
Fax: (92-21) 241-5106

Khadim Ali Shah Bukhari & Co. Ltd.
95 KSE Bldg.
Karachi
Pakistan
Phone: (92-21) 241-9210 and 2914
Fax: (92-21) 241-5762

Amin Issa Tai
615 KSE Bldg.
Karachi
Pakistan
Phone: (92-21) 241-9381 and 241-1722
Fax: (92-21) 242-3469

Firozuddin A. Cassim
26 KSE Bldg.
Karachi
Pakistan
Phone: (92-21) 241-5459 and 4742
Fax: (92-21) 241-1933

Aziz Fida Hussein
4 KSE Bldg.
Karachi
Pakistan
Phone: (92-21) 241-5076 and 241-5042
Fax: (92-21) 241-6051

Sarmad Husseini
4 LSE Bldg.
Lahore
Pakistan
Phone: (92-0) 63768
Fax: (92-0) 56950

N.F. Dastur
LSE Bldg.
Lahore
Pakistan
Phone: (92-0) 57666 and 57777
Fax: (92-0) 56950

Company Information:

The Best Performing Shares in the Country

Company Name	Share Price Change 1 January 1997 to 31 December 1997 (%)
Schon Bank	155
Pakistan Burma Shell	131

Company Name	Share Price Change 1 January 1997 to 31 December 1997 (%)
Lever Brothers	99
Pakistan State Oil	68
Al-Faysal Inv. Bank	59
Nat. Dev. Leasing	58
Muslim Commercial Bank	55
Dawood Hercules	53
Picic	48
Bank Commerce Al Hab	39
Boc Pakistan	34
Khadim Ali Shah Bu	31
Pak Telecom (Ptcl)	30

The Largest Companies in the Country by Market Capitalization as of 31 December 1997

Company Name	Market Capitalization Local Currency (Millions)	Market Capitalization US Dollars (Millions)
Pak Telecom (Ptcl)	166,260	3,778
Pakistan State Oil	90,174	2,049
Fauji Fertilizer	22,487	511
Lever Brothers	13,090	297
Muslim Commercial Bank	8,559	195
Sui Southern Gas	8,530	194
Sui Northern Gas	7,706	175
Engro Chemical	6,731	153
Pakistan Burma Shell	4,897	111

Regional Exchanges:

Islamabad Stock Exchange
101-E Fazal-Ul-Haq Road
Blue Area
Islamabad
Pakistan
Phone: (92-51) 215-047
Fax: (92-51) 215-051
Telex: 54673 ISE GL PK

Lahore Stock Exchange
19 Khayaban-e-Aiwan-e-lqbal
PO Box 1315
Lahore 54000
Pakistan
Phone: (92-42) 636-8000
Fax: (92-42) 636-8484/636-8485
Telex: 44821 STOK PK/ 47887 STOK PK

Other Investment Information:
Investment Promotion Bureau
Kandawala Building
M.A. Jinnah Road
Karachi
Pakistan
Phone: (92-21) 714289
Fax: (92-21) 713572
Telex: 3137 SUPLS PK

Ministry of Industries
Block-A, Pak Secretariat
Islamabad
Pakistan
Phone: (92-51) 820235
Fax: (92-51) 825130
Telex: MIND PK 5774

Federation of Pakistan Chambers of Commerce and Industry
Federation House, Clifton
Karachi
Pakistan
Phone: (92-21) 532179
Fax: (92-21) 570277
Telex: 25370 FPCC&J

PANAMA, REPUBLIC OF

Panama (Republica de Panama) is a country of Central America. It is bordered on the east by Colombia and on the west by Costa Rica.

Area: 29,157 square miles (75,517 square km)

Population: 2,631,000 (53.3% urban; 46.7% rural)

Form of Government: Multiparty republic, with one legislative house: Legislative Assembly—72 members. Head of state and government: President.

Official Language: Spanish

Capital: Panama City

Largest Cities: Panama City 450,668; San Miguelito 293,564; David 65,763; Colon 54,654; Baru 46,093

Economy:

Currency: Balboa (B)

National Budget: Revenue—B 1.9 billion; expenditures—B 1.9 billion (current expenditure: 80.2%; of which public debt payments: 25.6%; current transfers: 14.0%; education: 11.1%; administration: 7.8%; health: 7.2%; development expenditure: 19.8%).

Public Debt: US$3.7 billion

Gross National Product: US$6.6 billion

Principal Products: Sugarcane, coffee, tobacco, rice, bananas, and other fruits and vegetables; livestock; fish

Foreign Trade (Imports): B 2.2 billion (machinery and apparatus: 17.7%; transport equipment: 13.2%; mineral fuels: 13.2%; chemicals and chemical products: 11.1%; from United States: 36.5%; Colón Free Zone: 16.6%; Japan: 7.8%; Ecuador: 3.8%; Netherlands Antilles: 3.1%; Costa Rica: 2.8%)

Foreign Trade (Exports): B 508.0 million (bananas: 39.6%; shrimp: 11.2%; raw sugar: 4.3%; clothing: 4.2%; fish products: 3.7%; to United States: 34.6%; Germany: 14.1%; Sweden: 9.5%; Costa Rica: 6.7%; Italy: 5.5%)

Stock Exchanges: 1

Panama Stock Exchange (PSE)
Calle Elvira Mendez y Calle 52
Edificio Vallarino/Planta Baja
PO Box 87-0878
Panama
Phone: (507) 269-1966
Fax: (507) 269-2457

Internet Address: www.urraca.com/bvp

Trading Hours: Monday–Friday, 11:00 to 12:00

Office Hours: Monday–Friday, 8:00 to 5:00

Exchange Holidays:

1, 12 January	1 May
28 February	3, 10, 28 November
14 April	25, 26 December

Listed Companies: 81 total
14 domestic
67 foreign

Market Capitalization: US$4.3 billion

Major Sectors: Banking, finance, insurance, industrial, construction materials

History: The Panama Stock Exchange was opened on 26 June 1990. Its stated goal is to create and maintain a continuous market for the trading of local and foreign securities, both public and private, as well as currencies, futures, and options.

The PSE is owned by more than 60 shareholders, including national banks, international banks, broker/dealers, insurance companies, industrial companies, commercial companies, professional, and private investors.

The value of equity trading increased by more than 950% to a level of US$70.2 million in 1994. Much of the increase was due to the privatization program of state-owned cement manufacturers. Domestic market capitalization showed an increase of 82% from US$419 million in 1993 to US$762 million in 1994.

Classes of Securities: Shares, preferred shares, government bonds, corporate bonds, and commercial paper

Indices: PSE General Index (December 1992, base = 100) weighted by capitalization of 10 listed securities on the Panama Stock Exchange

Supervisory Organizations:
Ministry of Commerce and Industry
Comision Nacional de Valores (CNV)

Settlement Details:
Shares:
Same day—(T) at 3:00
Regular—Trade date + 2 days (T + 2)
Period—Mutual agreement on a future date

Trading: Open-outcry auction is the method of floor trading. Trades are locked in and matching takes place on the trade date. Panama Stock Exchange members are the only people allowed to be a part of the matching and settlement system.

Listing Requirements: Authorization for listing is obtained from the CNV. A prospectus is required and must include information about the business (three years of audited financial statements), the industry, and the securities to be issued.

Investor Taxation:
All income is subject to domestic income tax liabilities.
Dividends are subject to a 10% withholding tax at the source.
Capital gains on CNV authorized shares are tax exempt.

Limitations: There are no restrictions on owning shares or on repatriation of capital and income from dividends or capital gains.

Brokerage Firms:
Cambios
PO Box 44341
Panama 5
Panama
Phone: (507) 64 6655
Fax: (507) 64 5204

Isthmian Financial Services
PO Box 55-2647
Paitilla
Panama
Phone: (507) 26 1769/63 9766
Fax: (507) 26 3967/63 9969

Inversiones Bursatiles de Panama
PO Box 6-497
Panama 6A
Panama
Phone: (507) 63 7150
Fax: (507) 663 7995

Citivalores
PO Box 11181
Panama 6
Panama
Phone: (507) 63 5544
Fax: (507) 69 0659

Bincap Brokers
PO Box 11181
Panama 6
Panama
Phone: (507) 64 6833
Fax: (507) 63 4096

Valores Commerciales de Panama
PO Box 5198
Panama 5
Panama
Phone: (507) 63 6800
Fax: (507) 63 8033

Company Information:

10 Most Active Companies

Name of Company	Trading Value (US$ millions)
Golden Forest	199.02
Cerveceria Nacionales	118.03
Empresa General de Inversiones	103.28
Financiera Automotriz	85.00
Geofino International	62.67
Capatales Nacionales	46.08
Coca Cola de Panama	45.59
Cerveceria Baru-Panama	39.10
Minamerica Corporation	35.94
Grupo Assa	34.00

10 Major Companies

Name of Company	Market Capitalization (US$ millions)
Empresa General de Inversiones	199.02
Grupo Assa	118.03
Cervecerial Nacionales	103.78
Primer Banco de Ahorros	85.00
Capatales Nacionales	62.67
Minamerica Corporation	46.08
Cerveria Baru-Panama	45.59
Coca Cola de Panama	39.10
Financiera Automotriz	35.94
Banco International de Panama	34.00

Other Investment Information:
Panama Trade Development Institute
Banco Exterior Building
PO Box 6-1897
El Dorado
Panama
Phone: (507) 257244
Fax: (507) 252193
Telex: 3499 Invest PG

Chamber of Commerce, Industry and Agriculture of
   Panama
Avda Samuel Lewis
Panama City
Panama
Phone: (507) 648498
Telex: 2434

PANTY RAID
Panty Raid is a slang term used to denote an attempt to buy a company's shares at a price below their fair value. A raider may make a low bid in an attempt to woo disgruntled institutional investors who hold a significant tranche of a stock but cannot find a buyer for such a large stake. If unsuccessful, a panty raid may be followed by another bid at a fairer level. The technique is occasionally used by some raiders to boost the value of their holding by making other investors aware of the true value of the company.

PAPER LOSS
See UNREALIZED PROFITS/LOSSES.

PAPIER WARTOS'CIOWY (Poland)
See SECURITY.

PAR

Derived from the Latin word for *equal, Par* describes a situation in which a security's price is equal to its face value.

Those securities that trade at par have neither premium nor discount. Bonds that trade at par would most commonly do so at $1,000—the same as the face value per bond.

As applied to ordinary shares, par is an identifier used to evaluate the shares on the balance sheet of the company and is synonymous with nominal value.

For preference shares or preferred stock, par can be the redemption value when the company decides to retire the issue, although such redemptions are often performed at a premium over par.

See also ASK PRICE; BID PRICE; BOOK VALUE; LAST TRADE; MARKET CAPITALIZATION.

PAR OPPOSITION (France)

One of three methods of quotation on the bourses, *Par Opposition* determines quotes on the cash market for securities that also trade in the forward market.

See also MARCHÉ À TERME.

PAR VALUE

See PAR.

PARAGUAY, REPUBLIC OF

Paraguay (Republica del Paraguay (Spanish); Teta Paraguaype (Guarani)) is a landlocked country of south-central South America. It is bordered on the east by Brazil, on the southeast, south and southwest by Argentina, and on the north and northwest by Bolivia.

Area: 157,048 square miles (406,752 square km)

Population: 4,828,000 (50.5% urban; 49.5% rural)

Form of Government: Multiparty republic, with two legislative houses: Senate—45 members; Chamber of Deputies—80 members. Head of state and government: President.

Official Languages: Spanish; Guarani

Capital: Asunción

Largest Cities: Asunción, 502,426; Ciudad del Este, 133,893; San Lorenzo, 133,311; Lambare, 99,681; Fernando de la Mora, 95,287

Economy:

Currency: Guarani (G)

National Budget: Revenue—G 4.3 trillion; expenditures—G 1.7 trillion (education: 19.3%; public works:

14.4%; defense: 10.5%; public health: 7.5%; interior: 7.0%; agriculture: 5.8%; housing: 5.4%)

Public Debt: US$1.3 billion

Gross National Product: US$7.0 billion

Principal Products: Sugarcane; seed cotton; cassava, soybeans, corn, oranges, and other fruits and vegetables; livestock

Foreign Trade (Imports): US$2.1 billion (machinery and transport equipment: 33.2%; of which transport equipment: 12.9%; fuels and lubricants: 7.4%; chemicals and pharmaceuticals: 6.8%; iron products: 5.5%; from Brazil: 31.3%; United States: 22.7%; Argentina: 11.7%; Hong Kong: 8.8%; Japan: 4.9%; United Kingdom: 2.2%; Chile: 1.6%; France: 1.3%; Italy: 1.3%)

Foreign Trade (Exports): US$816.8 million (soybean flour: 27.2%; cotton fibers: 20.9%; timber: 9.6%; vegetable oil: 7.7%; of which tung oil: 0.6%; hides and skins: 7.7%; processed meat: 6.9%; perfume oils: 1.2%; tobacco: 0.8%; oilseed cakes: 0.5%; to Brazil: 39.6%; the Netherlands: 19.6%; Argentina: 11.1%; United States: 7.0%; Italy: 3.0%; Germany: 1.6%; France: 1.5%)

Stock Exchanges:
Bolsa de Valores y Productos de Asunción
Calle Estrella 540
Asunción
Paraguay
Phone: (595-21) 422-445
Fax: (595-21) 442-446

Internet Address: www.pdv.com.py

Trading Hours: Monday–Friday, 8:00 to 2:30

Other Investment Information:
Investment Council Office
Ministry of Industry and Commerce
Avda Espana 323
Asunción
Paraguay
Phone: (595-21) 204-693
Fax: (595-21) 210-570
Telex: 259

Central Bank of Paraguay
Avda Pablo VI
Asunción
Paraguay
Phone: (595-21) 608-019 or (595-21) 608 020
Fax: (595-21) 608 150
Telex: 134

Chamber of Commerce of Paraguay
Estrella 540
Asunción
Paraguay
Phone: (595-21) 473-12

PARCEL
See BLOCK.

PARETO, VILFREDO

Vilfredo Pareto (1848–1923) was a French-born Italian engineer, economist, and sociologist. In his early works Pareto was a keen advocate of economic liberalism, but he is best remembered for his developments in welfare economics.

In *Cours d'economie politique* (1896), Pareto advanced the general equilibrium analysis of the neoclassical economist Léon Walras, setting out the mathematical conditions of a general equilibrium system based on the interdependence of all economic quantities. Pareto advocated positive economics, aspiring to give economics an ethically neutral, scientific status comparable to the physical sciences, and to distill its findings into the form of predictive mathematical propositions.

In *Manuale di Economica Politica* (1906), Pareto highlighted the shortcomings in any theory of value so far as it rested upon measurable or "cardinal" utility rather than ordinal utility. Pareto demonstrated that exchange would take place in a competitive market between individuals, such that the ratios of the marginal utilities of the goods traded equaled the ratio of their prices. An optimum point of exchange could be defined without the need to compare individual's total utility. Pareto referred to utility as "ophelimity." A Pareto optimum is a welfare maximum defined as a position from which it is impossible to improve anyone's welfare by altering production or exchange. Any change will necessarily impair someone else's welfare. The Pareto criterion was intended to represent a neutral standard of welfare, but nevertheless a standard against which the effects of economic change could be judged. Further developments of Pareto optimality by J.R. Hicks and N. Kaldor are the basis of cost-benefit analysis.

Pareto's study of the distribution of personal incomes led to Pareto's Law, a supposed intertemporal constancy of income distribution across countries that has not proved to be valid. Pareto argued that whatever the political or taxation conditions, income will be distributed in the same way. He noted that the distribution of a large number of incomes is heavily concentrated among the lower income groups and that the number of incomes was inversely proportional with the size of income.

Pareto is often seen as the founder of modern welfare economics, while his extension of the work of Walras at the University of Lausanne established a definite Lausanne School within neoclassical economics. The inherent contradiction between his positivism and welfare analysis contributed to Pareto's disillusion with economics as a discipline, and he focused upon sociology in his later works.

See also NEOCLASSICAL SCHOOL OF ECONOMICS.

PARI (France)
See PAR.

PARITY

Parity is a word with several meanings on the stock exchanges of the world.

Parity can refer to a situation in which the price of a share is equal to the market price of a convertible on that same share.

Parity can occur when equity shares are trading at the same price as a related option plus premium.

In reference to an auction market, parity is a situation in which a broker with priority has a fill and other brokers can compete for the remaining order. Sometimes the flip of a coin determines the contra broker for the transaction.

See also CONVERTIBLE; OPTION; PREMIUM.

PARKING

Parking is an illegal practice whereby a dealer sells a security to another dealer for the purpose of reducing its net capital requirement. Once the first dealer finds a buyer for the security, he buys it back and compensates the firm for the parking.

The word also refers to the illegal practice of one brokerage firm parking a brokerage registration with another firm during a temporary layoff situation. Transferring the registration back at a later time allows the firm to avoid incurring the expense of re-examination.

See also NATIONAL ASSOCIATION OF SECURITIES DEALERS (NASD); SECURITIES AND EXCHANGE COMMISSION (SEC).

PARQUET (France and Others)
See TRADING FLOOR.

PARTICIPATE BUT DO NOT INITIATE (PNI)

Placed by institutional investors on significant buy or sell orders, *Participate But Do Not Initiate (PNI)* is an instruction stipulating that the order be filled by market forces creating any new price, rather than this order causing any changes. It is likely to be used by an investor who wishes to either accumulate or sell off a position with the minimum effect on market prices. Some institutions are not allowed to create an uptick when buying nor a downtick if selling.

See also BLOCK TRADE; DOWNTICK; UPTICK.

PARTICIPATING PREFERENCE SHARES
(United Kingdom)

Preferred stock that pays a regular, set dividend and an additional dividend when the company is profitable is referred to as *Participating Preference Shares*. The preference shares are allowed to participate along with the ordinary shares in the extra dividend. The United States has similar preference shares (preferred stock), but the situation is rare.

See also COMMON STOCK; DIVIDEND; PREFERRED STOCK (PFD).

PARTICIPATION AUX BÉNÉFICES (France)

See PROFIT SHARING PLAN.

PARTNERSHIP

Partnership describes a business arrangement in which two or more persons pool capital and abilities in order to run a company. When individuals are responsible for liabilities they are known as general partners. If their risk is limited to the amount of money contributed, and they do not participate in the business operations, they are known as limited partners.

See also CORPORATION; PUBLIC LIMITED COMPANY (PLC).

PASSED DIVIDEND

The term *Passed Dividend* describes any unpaid dividends on preferred shares.

Under normal circumstances, a corporation annually pays preferred share dividends to its investors. Passed dividends are usually the result of insufficient earnings. If the dividends on cumulative preferred shares are missed, they must be paid before any further ordinary or preferred share dividends can be paid.

In addition, most preferred share dividends are cumulative. As a result, any passed dividends from previous years must be paid to investors before ordinary shareholders can receive a dividend in the current year.

Ordinary share dividends do not have to be paid and can be passed. Once a company begins paying dividends on ordinary shares, missing a dividend payment sends a negative signal to potential investors. Most companies try to avoid this situation.

See also COMMON STOCK; DIVIDEND; PREFERRED STOCK (PFD).

PASSIFS (France)

See LIABILITIES.

PAWNBROKING

Pawnbroking is the business of making loans to individuals who provide security for the loan in the form of personal belongings, such as jewelry, cameras, or other goods. The item pledged as security, called the pawn, is said to be pawned, or hocked. A pawnbroker's place of business is usually a storefront shop, called a pawnshop.

A pawnbroker provides clients with a chit, or claim check, for use when redeeming the pawned item. Clients redeem a pawn by repaying the loan, including interest and other charges. Pawnshop loans may be as small as $20 or as large as several thousand dollars, but most are for $70–$100. Loan periods are short; most are for 30 to 160 days, averaging 90 days. Interest rates are high, and vary with the amount of the loan, being higher for smaller loans. Additional charges that a pawnbroker might assess include a storage fee for large items and a flat fee for each transaction or for each item pawned.

As a means of providing further security for the loan, a pawnbroker limits the amount of a loan to a fraction (one-third to one-half) of the resale value of the item being pawned. If the owner does not redeem a pawned item within a stipulated grace period, generally 30 to 90 days after the loan repayment is due, ownership of the item is forfeited, and a pawnbroker may legally sell the item to recoup the investment. Pawned items that are available for sale are said to be "out of pawn." Most states require the pawnbroker to notify the owner by mail that an item will be out of pawn after the required grace period. Between 70% and 80% of all items pawned are redeemed.

Practically every state in the United States has enacted legislation regulating pawnbroking in various ways. State laws set limits on the loan periods and the interest rates and other permissible fees. Pawnbrokers must keep written records of every transaction, and make them readily available to police and other authorities who are attempting to trace stolen property. Pawnshops must refuse to do business with anyone who is underage or under the influence of alcohol or drugs.

Pawnbroking is one of mankind's oldest financial institutions, dating back at least 3,000 years to ancient China. Pawnbroking in Europe originated during the Middle Ages (A.D. 500–1500) and evolved into three forms: (1) private pawnbrokers, (2) public pawnshops, and (3) *montes pietatis*. The latter were charitable funds supported by gifts and bequests that initially gave interest-free loans to the poor, who had to secure the loans with pawns. Later, the *montes pietatis* began charging interest to preclude abrupt depletion of funds. Private pawnbrokers were individuals exempt from the usury laws that were common at that time. One of the reasons for such exemption was religion. For example, the usury laws did not allow Christians to charge interest but did not so restrict Jews.

Public pawnshops were enterprises established by towns, often in the form of a municipal bank that would accept pawns. In 1198 the Bavarian town of Freising set up one of the earliest public pawnshops. These public pawnshops were an early attempt to combat the exorbitant interest rates often charged by private pawnbrokers. The moderate interest rates charged by the public institutions made it difficult for them to succeed in such a high-risk business. Nevertheless, public pawnshops predominated in Europe during the 1700s and 1800s—in some countries to the exclusion of private pawnbrokers and in other countries alongside them. Public pawnshops never made an appearance in the United States.

Pawnshops conducted business in many cities in the United States as early as 1800. They were an early necessity because of the scarcity of banks. By the late 1800s states began to pass laws regulating pawnshops because abuses were prevalent. Today, there are between 12,000 and 14,000 pawnshops operating in the United States.

Several large pawnbroking companies are publicly held, and their stock is traded on the New York Stock Exchange. A few major banks have bought shares as an investment. Also, a few brokers have observed that in the future, banks may enter the pawnbroking business through separate subsidiaries.

Pawnbrokers are often called the bankers of the poor. They make loans readily available to people who have no credit history and, frequently, no means of support or gainful employment. In bad economic times, such as when the stock market is falling or stagnant, pawnshops must make adjustments in pricing and loans. For example, the value of a pawnshop's merchandise goes down because retail discounters sell for less to maintain or broaden their market share. Selling for less affects the amount pawnbrokers may loan, and because people have less access to discre-tionary income during poor economic times, borrowing continues with larger risk to the pawnbroker.

PAYMENT DATE (United Kingdom)

The date for sending dividends or interest payments to securities holders is called the *Payment Date*.

See also DIVIDEND.

PEABODY, GEORGE

George Peabody (1795–1869) was one of the best known international businessmen of the 1800s and the first great American philanthropist. His hometown of South Danvers, Massachusetts honored its most famous native son by changing its name to Peabody. George Peabody's family was poor, and his formal education ended at the age of 11 when his father apprenticed him to the owner of a general store. After four years Peabody completed his apprenticeship and moved on.

By the time he was 17 Peabody was managing his uncle's general store in the Georgetown section of Washington, D.C. At 19 he was junior partner of the firm of Riggs and Peabody, which sold dry goods. The company then moved from Washington, D.C. to Baltimore, and, besides wholesaling dry goods, established itself as a shipping agent. In 1822 the firm opened branches in Philadelphia and New York. When Elisha Riggs retired from the business in 1829, Peabody continued the business with Elisha's nephew and changed the name of the firm to Peabody, Riggs, and Company.

Peabody made his first trip to Great Britain in 1827 to sell cotton and to buy machinery for clients in Maryland and the South. Soon he was making annual voyages to Britain, and his business dealings there increasingly took on the functions of merchant banker and investment banker. His reputation as an honest, dependable businessman grew in the United States and in Britain. At a time when many state governments were having financial difficulties, Peabody was able to sell bonds for Maryland and other states to British bankers. When the states' financial fortunes improved and their bonds paid off, Peabody's reputation in Britain soared.

By 1830 Peabody, Riggs, and Company was a full-fledged investment banking house as well as a thriving dry goods wholesaler. In 1836 Peabody sensed that the dealings of land speculators in the United States would soon depress the economy. By the time Peabody's fears were fully realized a year later, Peabody, Riggs, and Company had collected their outstanding debts and thus weathered the economic

The Hall of the East India Marine Society, now the Peabody Museum, Salem, Massachusetts. *(Spectrum Photo)*

downturn. That same year Peabody moved the company to London, which remained his base of operations until his death.

In 1843 Peabody withdrew from Peabody, Riggs, and Company to devote his energy toward his investment banking operations, Peabody and Company. During this time, most British bankers had little confidence in the American market and distrusted practically all American businessmen. As a result, they charged 10% interest on loans to Americans and discounted U.S. notes at an even higher percentage. Peabody charged only 5% on these transactions, so Peabody and Company soon became the repository of most of the business between the United States and Britain. Eventually many of his contemporaries looked upon Peabody as the U.S. financial ambassador in Britain.

In 1854 Peabody took on Junius Spencer Morgan as a partner, who at the time was studying at the University of Goettingen. The partnership was a perfect match. Thus, from Peabody and Company, the foundation was laid for the great international banking house J.S. Morgan and Company and eventually J.P. Morgan and Company, Inc.

Junius Morgan assumed more and more of the business duties as Peabody began to occupy his time with philanthropic pursuits. In London, Peabody established the Peabody Donation Fund, which to this day provides subsidized housing for that city's working class. In the early 1860s the fund built several apartment settlements for London's working people. Peabody also established a number of charities in the United States. A list of some of Peabody's benefactions follows (in purchasing power, the dollar amounts would be considerably higher today):

1852 The Peabody Institute; Peabody, Massachusetts—$217,000

1856 The Peabody Institute; Danvers, Massachusetts—$100,000

1857 The Peabody Institute; Baltimore, Maryland—$1,400,000

1862 The Peabody Donation Fund; London—$2,500,000

1866 The Peabody Museum; Harvard—$150,000

1866 The Peabody Museum; Yale—$150,000

1867 The Peabody Museum; Salem, Massachusetts—$140,000

1867 The Peabody Education Fund—$3,500,000

When George Peabody died, he was temporarily interred in Westminster Abbey. Later, his body was carried back to the United States on the HMS *Monarch*, the newest and largest ship of Her Majesty's Navy. He was buried in Peabody, Massachusetts. George Peabody and General Dwight D. Eisenhower are the only Americans to receive the Freedom of the City of London. A statue of Peabody stands in London's financial district.

See also MORGAN, J.P., & COMPANY, INC.

PEGGING (United States)

Pegging refers to the stabilization of securities prices.

Pegging is a form of price manipulation and, in most cases, is illegal. There are circumstances, however, under which pegging is legal.

When offering a new issue of shares, a managing underwriter is permitted to peg the market price, then stabilize the market in the issuer's shares by buying some of the shares in the open market. Such an action is considered legal, as it is in the public interest and helps establish a fair and orderly market.

Pegging is also regularly used to stabilize currency exchange rates and is often employed by some governments to support agricultural product prices. Again, under these circumstances this activity is meant for the public interest and not for the purpose of creating a false impression of stability.

See also ASK PRICE; BID PRICE; LAST TRADE; MANIPULATION.

PENN SQUARE FAILURE

The *Penn Square Failure* refers to the 1982 bankruptcy of Penn Square Bank in Oklahoma City. The collapse of Penn Square, with its $400 million in assets—which grew out of the extension of an excessive quantity of loans to oil and gas exploration and drilling companies, along with a number of irregular banking practices—had a significant impact on a number of other U.S. banks.

Penn Square opened in 1960. It was still a relatively small, conservative bank with assets of only $30 million in 1975. By the time it failed on 5 July 1982, Penn Square's assets had increased by a factor of more than 13. Most of the $2 billion in loans it had made consisted of high-risk loans to independent oil producers in Oklahoma.

Penn Square extended these loans during a period when there was great interest in the United States in developing domestic energy sources, so that the country would be less dependent on foreign oil. In Oklahoma there was much enthusiasm about the possible reserves in the area's oil fields.

Most often Penn Square would extend a loan to an oil producer, requiring only minimal, if any, documentation at that stage. Then it would sell the greater part of the loan to one of several larger banks, a procedure made necessary because of legal limits on the size of loans that Penn Square could extend to any one customer—no more than 10% of its capital. But the procedure displaced the burden of carrying the loans onto the banks that bought the participations—Continental Bank, Seattle First ("Seafirst"), Chase Manhattan, Michigan National Bank of Detroit, and Northern Trust Company of Chicago.

Much of Penn Square's operating capital resulted from the sale of its certificates of deposit by money brokers. This gave the bank just enough money to maneuver between the time when it would extend a loan and when it would receive money from the larger bank that was purchasing the loan participation. In 1980 alone, Penn Square's assets doubled, and the volume of its loan participations increased by $300 million, or a factor of five. But by the end of the year, approximately three-quarters of Penn Square's loans were classified as dubious, substandard, or in some way noteworthy.

When oil prices began to decline in late 1981, Penn Square was in a very tenuous position. Loans that were written off as bad increased from $405,000 in 1980 to $4.2 million in 1981. When Penn Square was declared bankrupt in 1982, some of the larger banks that had lent it money nearly failed. In 1983 Seafirst, the 13th largest bank in the country, which had purchased $400 million in loans from Penn Square, was essentially rescued when it was purchased by Bank-America Corporation. Continental Bank of Illinois, whose loan participation purchases through Penn Square came to half of its net worth, was rescued from near failure by the federal government in 1984.

In terms of the state's economy, the impact was considerable. In 1983 employment in the oil and gas industry declined by one-third, and the unemployment rate in Oklahoma doubled. More than 150 companies that had banked with Penn Square went bankrupt.

In the aftermath of Penn Square's failure, investigators for the Federal Deposit Insurance Corporation (FDIC) found widespread evidence of possible criminal activity, including misapplication of funds, embezzlement, falsification of financial statements, and other instances of bank fraud. Within six months they had identified 451 possible criminal violations. But the initial round of prosecution against William

Patterson, the chief energy lender at Penn Square, did not result in any convictions.

There were some other interesting legal rulings. In one, a court ruled that a "constructive trust" judgment should be made against FDIC, the receiver for Penn Square, to reimburse uninsured depositors of the failed bank.

In addition, a number of changes were made in banking practices and banking regulation. The most important were these:

• Regulators tightened requirements for reporting loan participations sold to and purchased from other banks.

• Banks improved their credit analysis procedures and expanded and refined documentation policies.

• Examiners, auditors, and directors of banks improved their communications.

• The need for banking laws to allow interstate takeovers of troubled banks was more widely recognized.

Despite these changes, many U.S. banks failed in the competitive 1980s. In 1984 a total of 79 failed, more than in any year since the Great Depression. By 1985 more than 1,000 banks were classified as problem banks in the lists of the FDIC, the Comptroller of the Currency, and the Federal Reserve Board.

In 1988 William Patterson pleaded guilty to a charge of misapplication of bank funds and was sentenced to two years in prison. John R. Lytle, former Continental Illinois vice president, who pleaded guilty to the same charge, was sentenced to three and a half years in prison.

See also BANK OF NEW ENGLAND CORPORATION; CONTINENTAL BANK OF ILLINOIS; INSOLVENCY.

PENNY STOCK

Penny Stock refers to different prices of shares, all of which range from a few cents to about five dollars.

Different people and organizations have their own meanings and levels for penny stocks. These shares are considered by many to be highly speculative and extremely risky. They are often thinly traded due to a lack of market makers willing to conduct transactions. Many penny stocks in the United States are only quoted on the pink sheets.

Brokerage firms can place extra restrictions on such shares being held or traded in accounts, and they might make a requirement for the broker to accept unsolicited orders only. Many firms will not allow such shares in a margin account and many of them do not qualify for margin loans.

See also JUNK BOND; PINK SHEETS; THINLY TRADED.

PENSION PLAN/FUND

A *Pension Plan/Fund* is a sum of money laid aside or invested to provide an income for a person after he or she retires. The pension may also provide compensation for disablement. With private pension plans, pension contributions are placed in managed pension funds that receive favorable tax benefits. With occupational pension plans, a portion of an employee's earnings is put into a fund that is invested for all employees as a group. Employers sometimes contribute all of the money to the pension plan. When employers pay part of it, employees usually make up the difference.

See also MUTUAL FUND; PRUDENT MAN RULE; UNIT INVESTMENT TRUST/UNIT TRUST.

PENSION REVERSION (United States)

The cancellation of a pension fund in order to reorganize the plan from defined benefit to defined contribution is referred to as a *Pension Reversion*. This activity allows for the termination of over-funded plans and the purchase of annuities in order to cover existing employee benefits. Any excess becomes part of the company's assets.

Pension plans are redefined as defined contribution, in which the employee can select the investment strategy. The plan is usually based on company shares or a selection of mutual funds. The success of a defined contribution plan depends on the performance of the strategy selected.

See also DEFINED BENEFIT/DEFINED CONTRIBUTION; MUTUAL FUND; UNIT INVESTMENT TRUST/UNIT TRUST.

PENTAPHILIA

Pentaphilia is one of the increasing number of stock market theories that employ numerology. Supporters of pentaphilia believe that the market will always rise in years that are divisible by the number five.

Recent analysis of this theory shows the following changes in the value of market indices.

Year	Dow Jones Composite Index	FT-SE 100 Index
1980	+25.2	+27.1
1985	+25.9	+14.6
1990	−11.1	−11.5
1995	+32.9	+20.3

Source: Datastream.

Investors who plan to rely on this method of investment to decide their strategy for the year 2000 should be aware that no causal reason has been found for these results. As with many of the esoteric investment techniques put forward by numerologists, coincidence plays a very active part.

See also FIBONACCI SEQUENCE; SUPER BOWL THEORY.

PER KASSA (Germany)
See CASH TRANSACTION.

PERELLA, JOSEPH R.
An investment banker who specializes in mergers and acquisitions, *Joseph R. Perella* is by training and background a certified public accountant. Perella was born in Newark, New Jersey, in 1941. His parents, Dominic and Agnes, had immigrated from Italy. Perella graduated from Lehigh University in 1964 and received an MBA from Harvard in 1972. He was an accountant with the firm of Haskins and Sells in New York City from 1964 to 1970, and in 1971 he was a consultant for the International Bank for Reconstruction and Development in Washington, D.C.

In 1972 Perella joined The First Boston Corporation, an investment banking firm in New York. Merger and acquisition (M&A) activity was on the increase in the early 1970s (this trend would continue, resulting in the "merger mania" of the 1980s). First Boston, which had no M&A department, placed Perella in charge of M&A services with the intention he would establish that department. Development proceeded slowly for the first few years, during which time the firm represented Cargill, a private grain-trading company with assets of $1 billion, in a raid on Missouri Portland Cement, and advised International Paper Company on its acquisition of General Crude Oil.

Late in 1976 Combustion Engineering hired First Boston to represent it as a potential white knight in the takeover of Gray Tool. In these dealings Perella worked with a young lawyer named Bruce Wasserstein, an associate in the law firm of Cravath, Swaine and Moore, which had been retained by Perella. Wasserstein's ability to take charge of a meeting or situation so impressed Perella that a few months later he hired him as a member of First Boston's M&A department. For the next 15 years the pair was one of the most successful M&A teams in investment banking.

As a team, Perella and Wasserstein were in many ways an odd couple. Wasserstein was short, pudgy, and somewhat unkempt; Perella was tall, slender, and polished in appearance and manner. Wasserstein was the gruff expert of the facts and figures; Perella was the charming and attentive master of client relationships. Perella had the reputation of being an extraordinary team leader, a good teacher, and a patient mentor.

He was known to be even-tempered with peers and subordinates, but always ready and able to speak his mind, especially if he perceived a business deal to be poorly conceived or in danger of going awry.

Fearful that Wasserstein might be hired away from First Boston by a competing firm, Perella requested that his superiors appoint Wasserstein as a codirector of the M&A department. The two men shared the directorship until 1988, participating in some of the biggest mergers and acquisitions of the 1980s. The volume of M&A transactions at First Boston increased from four per year in the late 1970s to 200 per year in 1987, and the number of personnel in the M&A department increased from four to 160 during that period. By 1987 Perella's annual earnings had grown to $5 million. Some of the major deals that Perella took part in at First Boston were the acquisition of Conoco by Du Pont, Capital Cities' purchase of ABC, thwarting a takeover of Marathon by Mobil and arranging its sale to USX (then U.S. Steel), and the takeover of Allied Stores by the Canadian retailer, the Campeau Corporation.

In 1988 Perella and Wasserstein both left First Boston Corporation to start their own company, Wasserstein, Perella and Company, which soon became known on Wall Street as "Wasserella." Within a few months the giant Japanese securities brokerage Nomura bought a 20% share of the new company for $100 million. Three major deals that Perella participated in while at the new firm were the purchase by Beecham, the British pharmaceutical giant, of its American counterpart Smith-Kline Beckman; Philip Morris's acquisition of Kraft; and the takeover by Georgia Pacific of Great Northern Nekoosa. Perhaps Perella's greatest deal while with Wasserstein, Perella and Company was the $13 billion purchase of Warner Communications by Time, Inc. in the face of a very strong effort by Paramount Communications to scuttle the deal.

The 1990s brought a marked slowdown in the mergers advisory business, and in 1993 Perella left the company that still bears his name. The split with his longtime partner Wasserstein was not amicable, according to close associates of the two men. In fact, they describe the entire partnership with Wasserstein as difficult for Perella because Wasserstein always insisted on playing the dominant role. Perella was also unhappy with some of Wasserstein's recent business decisions, such as the firm's $350 million investment in Isosceles, the holding company for a struggling British supermarket chain.

The top investment banking firms on Wall Street— Merrill Lynch, Bear Stearns, Donaldson Lufkin and

Jenrette, and Morgan Stanley and Company—pursued Perella. He decided on Morgan Stanley, who wanted his services in mergers and acquisitions to replace another M&A expert, Robert Greenhill, who left four months earlier under acrimonious circumstances after a 31-year career at the firm.

The first year at Morgan Stanley was relatively quiet for Perella, but soon he was displaying his M&A talents and know-how, particularly his ability to bring in new clients. He found a buyer—Sandoz Corporation in Switzerland—for the Gerber Products Company, and advised Sandoz throughout the $3.7 billion deal. Perella was an adviser to American Cyanamid Company in its successful resistance of a hostile takeover bid by American Home Products Corporation—a two-week stint that earned Morgan Stanley a handsome $23.8 million in fees. He was instrumental in securing for Morgan Stanley the business of Conseco Inc. in that company's $3.25 billion bid to acquire Kemper Corporation.

Perella secured for Morgan Stanley another blue chip client, Time-Warner, winning that company away from his previous firm, Wasserstein, Perella and Company. Time-Warner had blacklisted Morgan Stanley for having earlier, during the tenure of Robert Greenhill, represented Paramount in its attempt to block the Time-Warner merger. On the other hand, Perella, then of Wasserstein, Perella and Company, was credited with helping save the merger. Now, Time-Warner needed Morgan Stanley's help to resist a potential takeover by Seagram Company, Limited.

In 1995 Perella was placed in charge of Morgan Stanley's corporate finance operation. This position required less involvement in structuring individual deals, with much more time spent overseeing overall client relations and the flow of the firm's M&A business. He is also a member of Morgan Stanley's operating committee.

Early in 1997, in a strange twist of fate, Wasserstein and Perella again found themselves involved in the same merger deal. Wasserstein through the Wasserstein, Perella Group was an adviser to Dean Witter, Discover and Company in its $10.2 billion merger with none other than Morgan Stanley—Perella's employer. The deal, consummated in mid-1997, formed the largest securities firm in the United States, with a market capitalization of $21 billion.

See also MORGAN STANLEY, DEAN WITTER, DISCOVER & COMPANY (MWD); WASSERSTEIN, BRUCE.

PERELMAN, RONALD
Owner, chairman, and CEO of a giant diversified holding company, *Ronald Perelman* acquired many of his holdings as an audacious corporate raider during the 1980s. At one time, he was the richest person in the United States, but his wealth has been surpassed by that of several others, particularly heads of computer software enterprises. Perelman was born in Greensboro, North Carolina, in 1943, but he was raised in Philadelphia, Pennsylvania. The son of Raymond Perelman, who was himself a corporate raider, he received a bachelor's degree in 1964 from the University of Pennsylvania and an MBA in 1966 from the University of Pennsylvania's Wharton School of Finance.

Perelman's father introduced him at an early age to the business of acquiring and managing companies. During his preteen years, Perelman accompanied his father on visits to companies that the elder Perelman was considering acquiring. Then the two would discuss the pros and cons of each potential transaction. By the time he was 11, Perelman was attending board meetings, and in his teens he was conversant with balance sheets and annual reports. After graduate school, Perelman worked with his father for 12 years building Belmont Industries, a conglomerate based in Philadelphia. The younger Perelman was eager to assume control of the company; his father would not relinquish it, and in 1978 Perelman set out on his own, to his father's great displeasure.

Perelman moved to New York and managed to obtain a $1.9 million bank loan. With it he purchased a controlling interest in Cohen-Hatfield, an unprofitable chain of New Jersey jewelry stores. By selling the chain's stores and liquidating its inventory, Perelman raised $15 million in cash. From this beginning he was to go on to acquire more than 40 companies during the next two decades. Perelman resold most of his acquisitions for handsome profits, but he kept a select few to build a diversified conglomerate in which his share is estimated to be anywhere from $5 billion to $9 billion.

In 1983 Perelman purchased Technicolor, the film processing company, for $125 million, and less than two years later he sold the company, reaping $625 million in profit. This transaction provided considerable funding for Perelman's future wheeling and dealing. It also led to a lawsuit. Cinerama, which held approximately 4% of the stock of Technicolor, alleged that Perelman was able to buy the company at a bargain price because its directors did not solicit competing bids. Cinerama further alleged that Perelman compensated the directors for their dereliction of duty. The case meandered through the Delaware courts for 13 years. In 1993 a lower court concluded that Perelman paid one director $150,000 for an introduction to Technicolor's CEO, and he then promised to increase the CEO's earnings in return for the CEO's support of Perelman's bid. Finally, in 1995 the Delaware Supreme Court concluded in Perelman's favor, finding that although Technicolor's directors were negligent, Perelman still paid a fair price for the company.

In the 1980s Perelman acquired the reputation of being a corporate raider who made flagrant use of Michael Milken's junk bonds and was always on the prowl for greenmail payoffs. For example, in a hostile takeover he acquired Revlon in 1986 with the backing of Milken, who was at Drexel, Burnham, Lambert. Perelman also attempted a hostile takeover of Gillette in 1986 and came away with $39 million in greenmail.

However, Perelman's reputation for being aggressive is matched by his reputation for being shrewd. His present holdings are structured into a few levels of holding companies. Overall, there is MAFCO Holdings, which is the holding company for MacAndrews and Forbes Holdings. The latter is the holding company for a level of principal holding companies, which in 1995 were Revlon Worldwide (cosmetics), Coleman Holdings (outdoor recreation equipment), C&F Holdings (cigars, flavorings, and aerospace), First Nationwide Holdings (banking), and Andrews (entertainment and publishing). Below each principal holding company may be other holding companies. For example, below Revlon Worldwide is Revlon, Inc., which is the holding company for Revlon Consumer Products, a privately held operating company owned outright by Perelman. Below Coleman Holdings is Coleman Worldwide, which is the holding company for Coleman Company, a public corporation in which Perelman has an 83% stake. This multilevel structure allows debt to be shared among different entities, limiting the liability of MacAndrews and Forbes, the umbrella holding company.

Although there are multiple holding companies interposed between MacAndrews and Forbes and the operating companies, MacAndrews and Forbes usually retains at least an 80% stake in each operating company. This makes possible the consolidation of income from the various companies, so that one company's profits can be offset by another company's losses, thereby effecting a tax saving. Perelman has been able to benefit from the tax laws in other ways. In 1988 he purchased First Gibraltar, a group of failing savings and loans located in Texas, from the Federal Savings and Loan Insurance Corporation. The sweetheart deal gave Perelman the right to deduct $3 billion in net operating losses during the succeeding

15 years. Because the Texas savings and loan market recovered in a short time, Perelman has since been able to sell First Gibraltar at a $1 billion profit. However, he still retains the tax write-off for use elsewhere in his conglomerate.

During the 1990s Perelman has been able to discard some of his raider image. He has acquired companies whose nationally known brand name products were faltering in sales, and he has stayed with them for years, rebuilding their operations and revamping their products to regain strong national sales. For example, at Revlon, after struggling for five years to bring about a turnaround, Perelman changed the CEO, and adopted a new market strategy, which he called "mass, not class." Revlon stopped selling its products in department stores and started selling exclusively through discount outlets, such as Kmart and Wal-Mart, and drugstore chains, such as Osco and Walgreens. The company also released two new products, Color Stay lipstick and Age Defying Makeup, that were huge successes. Revlon moved from third place to second in cosmetic sales.

Similarly, Perelman stayed with a stagnating level of sales at Coleman from its purchase in 1989 until 1993. Since then he has infused $150 million in Coleman, buying seven new companies, including a camping equipment firm in Italy, an aluminum furniture manufacturer, and a backpack company. Coleman sales increased dramatically—from $575 million in 1993 to $950 million in 1995.

In the late 1990s Perelman was pursuing a policy of expanding his vast holdings through constant small acquisitions, while continuing to leverage his companies heavily and building cash reserves for the next big deal. According to one estimate, Perelman's holding companies were $2.6 billion in debt, and his operating companies had a market value of $8.1 billion, suggesting a debt-to-equity ratio of 32%. Perelman disputed those figures, claiming the ratio is only 20%. He also points out that his companies grow 20% annually—double the 10% annual cost of the debt. At the same time, one of Perelman's top lieutenants estimated that the holding companies had $700 million of free cash ready to spend.

In 1997 one of Perelman's companies, Marvel Entertainment Group, the publishers of comic books, encountered severe cash flow problems and filed for Chapter 11 bankruptcy. Perelman's proposed reorganization plan included a provision that would reduce bondholders' claims from 80% of Marvel stock to 16%. The bondholders, led by Carl Icahn, another corporate raider, objected and put forth an alternate reorganization plan. After considerable maneuvering, the Icahn group wrested control of Marvel away from Perelman, but he emerged from the fray with a profit of $50 million.

Many in the financial community felt that Perelman had abandoned his fellow investors (the Marvel bondholders) to enrich himself. They insisted that the incident damaged Perelman's reputation and impaired his ability to borrow money in the future. Perelman replied that his reorganization proposal provided for a cash infusion of $365 million, which the bondholders rejected. He claimed further that the bondholders led by Icahn were opportunists who recently bought the distress bonds at a deep discount, and the original bondholders were knowledgeable investors who had long since sold the instruments. In less than a month after the Marvel affair, Perelman readily raised $500 million for another of his holdings.

See also GREENMAIL; HOSTILE TAKEOVER; ICAHN, CARL; MILKEN, MICHAEL.

PERFECT HEDGE
See SHORT AGAINST THE BOX.

PERFORMANCE FUND
A *Performance Fund* is a mutual fund with a stated objective of capital growth.

Performance funds invest in the shares of companies expected to grow rapidly in the next few years. Such companies do not normally pay dividends, as the earnings are used for growth, expansion, and new developments.

Performance funds accept higher than average risk in order to achieve higher returns on the funds invested.

See also DIVIDEND; MUTUAL FUND; OBJECTIVE.

PERFORMANCE STOCK
See PERFORMANCE FUND.

PERIOD OF RETENTION (United Kingdom)
As applied to an approved profit sharing scheme, the *Period of Retention* refers to the time limit before which employees are not allowed to sell shares. Currently, this period is two years from receipt.

See also EMPLOYEE STOCK OWNERSHIP PLAN (ESOP); PENSION PLAN/FUND.

PERIODIC PAYMENT PLAN
A *Periodic Payment Plan* is a mutual fund program whereby a certain amount of money is added to a mutual fund on a regular basis. Many funds are set up

to directly transfer a set amount from an investor's bank account to the mutual fund on a monthly basis.

The program carries the advantage of dollar cost averaging, which benefits the investor. It also carries the advantage of not requiring a decision to make an investment every month. The money invested can be easily accessed by selling shares as necessary.

Important to note: Above normal sales charges may occur in the event that a one-off payment is made.

See also CONSTANT DOLLAR PLAN; MUTUAL FUND; PUBLIC OFFERING PRICE (POP).

PEROT, H. ROSS
H. Ross Perot was born on 27 June 1930 in Texarkana, Texas. Perot was an average student but a first-rate Boy Scout; he once cited the *Boy Scout Handbook* as his favorite book. After attending Texarkana Junior College for two years, in 1949 Perot entered the United States Naval Academy at Annapolis, Maryland, graduating with an ensign's commission in 1953. He then served four years of active duty with the United States Navy. After leaving the Navy in 1957, Perot joined International Business Machines Corporation (IBM) as a computer sales representative. He left IBM in 1962 to start his own company, Electronic Data Systems Corporation (EDS), which designed, installed, and operated computer data-processing systems for clients on contract. Most of EDS's early clients were insurance companies, and business boomed in 1965 when, with the start of Medicare, the number of insurance claims processed increased dramatically.

In 1968 Perot took EDS public. The New York investment banking firm of R.W. Pressprich and Company was the underwriter. The initial stock price of $16.50 was 118 times EDS's earnings. (Usually an offering is set at 10 to 20 times earnings.)

Several factors made EDS's numbers acceptable. High-tech stocks were the darlings of Wall Street. Although EDS's 1965 pretax profits were $26,487 on revenues of $865,000, in 1968 these numbers had soared to pretax profits of $2.4 million on revenues of $7.5 million—an increase in profit margin from 3% to 31%. The EDS prospectus was written in such a way that even though the business was almost completely dependent on processing Medicare claims, it appeared to be highly diversified, serving clients in several fields including insurance, finance, and health care.

On 12 September 1968, only 650,000 of the 11.5 million outstanding shares were offered for sale. Investors snapped up the shares and drove the opening price up to almost $23 at the close of the trading day.

The offering was one of the year's most successful. As the majority shareholder, Perot held stock valued at $230 million, which appreciated to $1.5 billion in 18 months.

In the late 1970s and early 1980s EDS received several long-term contracts from the U.S. government, including one very lucrative contract to overhaul the computer systems at 47 army bases. In spite of his bright and secure future with EDS, in 1984 Perot sold the company to General Motors for $2.5 billion of GM stock. The transaction made Perot GM's largest shareholder, and the company offered him a seat on its board of directors. He also retained his chairmanship of EDS's board. Perot was an active director; he visited factories and lunched with assembly-line workers. He also was outspoken in his criticism of GM management. Company executives viewed him as a meddler who was trying to reform GM in the mold of EDS. By 1986 the company had its fill of Perot, and they paid him $700 million to relinquish both his seat on the GM board and his chairmanship of EDS. Perot soon established a new company, Perot Systems Corporation, which actively competed with EDS.

As a sought-after public speaker, Perot used his rousing speaking style to criticize government policies and practices. His supporters began urging him to run for president. In February 1992 Perot became an independent candidate for the U.S. presidency, which he largely financed from his own money. Then in July, just when a large number of voters began viewing him as a viable candidate, Perot withdrew from the race, first explaining that he felt he could not receive enough votes to win the election, and later citing "unimaginable" pressures on his family brought on by Republican dirty tricks. However, he continued to fund his support groups.

By October, his supporters succeeded in getting Perot's name on the ballot in all 50 states, and he reentered the race. Perot campaigned almost exclusively through the media, especially television. His frank talk and populist image generated so much excitement among voters that the Republican and Democratic parties felt it was more prudent to include him in televised debates than to ignore him. Perot later remarked that the 19% of the popular vote he received in the election was worth the $65 million he personally spent on his campaign.

After the election, Perot publicly opposed the North American Free Trade Agreement (NAFTA). He participated in 100 rallies in all 50 states, as well as infomercials and TV talk shows. He also appeared before Congress, wrote two books, and debated with Vice President Gore.

Perot resisted his followers' urgings to enter the 1996 presidential race until very near the election, when he decided to run as the Reform Party candidate. Perot never mounted a serious campaign, however, and accumulated only 9% of the popular vote.

PERPETUAL WARRANT

A *Perpetual Warrant* is enacted to purchase a set number of common shares at a predetermined price. It has no expiration date. The warrants can be exercised for the shares or can be traded as warrants.

See also OPTION; SUBSCRIPTION RIGHTS; SUBSCRIPTION WARRANT.

PERSONAL INVESTMENT AUTHORITY (PIA)

The *Personal Investment Authority (PIA)* is part of the self-regulatory structure established by the British financial industry since the passage of the 1986 Financial Services Act (FSA). As a result of the act, five self-regulatory organizations (SROs) were formed, as well as various recognized professional bodies and recognized investment exchanges. All of these organizations, bodies, and exchanges were supervised by the Securities and Investments Board (SIB), which was the ultimate regulator for 6,500 firms in 1997. The PIA itself was created in 1994 as part of a streamlining of the structure.

The British financial industry instituted a number of changes in the mid-1980s, collectively referred to as the Big Bang. One consequence of these changes was that they put an end to many investor protections that had existed within the old system. The FSA was intended to re-create the necessary regulations and regulatory bodies under the new conditions.

The five SROs that were formed in 1986 were The Securities Association (TSA), which regulated market makers (jobbers), brokers, and dealers in corporate and British government securities; the Association of Futures Brokers and Dealers (AFBD), which oversaw financial and commodities futures exchanges; the Investment Managers Regulatory Organisation (IMRO), which regulated the work of pension funds, trusts, and merchant banks; the Life Assurance and Unit Trust Regulatory Organisation (LAUTRO), which had responsibility for insurance companies, unit trusts, and friendly societies; and the Financial Intermediaries, Managers and Brokers Regulatory Association (FIMBRA), which monitored a broad range of securities firms and independent brokers of life assurance unit trusts.

In the early 1990s, TSA and AFBD joined, forming the Securities and Futures Authority (SFA). In addition, a retail self-regulatory organization, the PIA, was formed to oversee the entire retail sector. A plan was made for FIMBRA and LAUTRO gradually to be phased out by October 1997 and replaced by PIA. In addition, PIA would take responsibility for regulating other institutions in the retail sector, specifically the banks and building societies that are IMRO members (IMRO, however, would continue to exist and to regulate the other members of its sector). In addition, the PIA ombudsman would take over from several different ombudsmen as the main independent arbiter of investors' complaints.

The overall duty of PIA was to regulate nearly all types of investment business conducted by private investors. The specific services it provided were these:

• Ensuring that investors received appropriate investment advice from a firm regulated by PIA.

• Ensuring that members operated to the highest professional standards. This applied to many areas, covering life insurance (including endowment policies); pensions, unit trusts, and personal equity plans; guaranteed income bonds; investment trust savings schemes; offshore funds (for example, gilt funds or bond funds); advice on dealings in shares and traded options; portfolio investments and broker funds; and advice on Enterprise Investment Schemes.

• Providing advice to consumers through a help desk and a leaflet, "How to Complain."

• Providing a mechanism for redress (PIA ombudsman) if poor investment advice were provided by members.

In 1997 PIA regulated approximately 4,000 firms, including independent financial advisers who advised on or marketed retail investment products or acted for private investors in relation to such products. It also was the main regulator of firms advising on and arranging life assurance and personal pensions, friendly society investments, unit trusts, and investment trust savings schemes.

One of the principal regulatory issues for PIA, which it inherited from LAUTRO, concerned the proper training of sales representatives dealing in life assurance. Related to this was the question of whether firms were selling their customers the appropriate policies in a climate in which sales had typically become product-driven rather than customer-driven. PIA recommended programs for companies to retrain their staff.

There remained some well-defined political differences in Britain about how to regulate the financial industry. Controversy surrounded the selection of members of PIA's disciplinary committee, which had

power to levy fines on companies that violated the regulations. Some politicians, particularly in the Labor Party, were advocates of statutory regulation, in which a body of laws governing acceptable practices in the industry would be adjudicated by government authorities. The backers of self-regulation, however, continued to argue for some version of the existing regulatory structure.

In early 1997 the new Labor government proposed that, because of the ever-greater blurring of the boundaries between banking, insurance, and financial services, the three existing self-regulatory organizations—PIA, SFA, and IMRO—should be merged into the single overarching body, SIB. In turn, SIB would assume responsibility for banking regulation, which had been carried out by the Bank of England, and possibly also for Lloyd's of London, which had not been regulated.

See also BIG BANG; FINANCIAL SERVICES ACT 1986; SECURITIES AND INVESTMENTS BOARD (SIB); SELF-REGULATING ORGANIZATION (SRO).

PERU, REPUBLIC OF

Peru (Republica del Peru (Spanish)) is the third largest nation in South America. It is bordered on the northwest by Ecuador, on the northeast by Colombia, on the east by Brazil and Bolivia, and on the south by Chile.

Area: 1,325 square miles (2,132 square km)

Population: 23,489,000 (71.8% urban; 28.2% rural)

Form of Government: Unitary multiparty republic, with one legislative house: Congress—120 members. Head of state and government: President.

Official Languages: Spanish; Quechua; Aymara

Capital: Lima

Largest Cities: Lima (metropolitan), 5,706,127; Arequipa, 619,156; Callao, 615,046; Trujillo, 509,312; Chiclayo, 411,536

Economy:

Currency: Nuevo Sol (S)

National Budget: Revenue—S 9.2 billion; expenditures—S 12.5 billion (current expenditure: 64.1%, of which wages and salaries: 20.2%; transfer payments: 18.9%; capital expenditure: 19.4%; public debt amortization: 16.5%)

Public Debt: US$16.1 billion

Gross National Product: US$34.0 billion

Principal Products: Sugarcane; potatoes, rice, plantains, corn; coffee; livestock; minerals

Foreign Trade (Imports): US$3.6 billion (raw and intermediate materials: 48.2%; machinery and transport equipment: 31.4%; consumer goods: 20.4%; from United States: 27.6%; Japan: 7.6%; Argentina: 6.4%; Brazil: 6.2%; Colombia: 5.7%; Germany: 4.3%; Chile: 4.0%)

Foreign Trade (Exports): US$3.3 billion (copper: 17.4%; fish flour: 16.3%; zinc: 7.9%; gold: 6.2%; petroleum and derivatives: 4.3%; lead: 2.8%; silver: 2.2%; to United States: 20.9%; Japan: 9.2%; United Kingdom: 8.5%; Germany: 6.2%; Italy: 4.8%; China: 4.2%; Taiwan: 3.5%; the Netherlands: 3.5%)

Stock Exchanges: 2

Lima Stock Exchange (Bolsa de Valores de Lima)
Pasaje Acuna 191
Lima
Casilla Postal 1538
Peru
Phone: (51-14) 260 714, 327 939, 620 837, 260 961, 267 939, 302 082
Fax: (51-14) 267 650

Internet Address: www.bvl.com.pe

Trading Hours: Monday–Friday, 10:00 to 1:30

Office Hours: Monday–Friday, 9:00 to 5:15

Exchange Holidays:

1 January	28 July
9, 10 April	8 October
1 May	25 December

Listed Companies: 330

Market Capitalization: US$17.3 billion

Major Sectors: Mining, manufacturing, transportation, finance, insurance, real estate

History: The Lima Mercantile Exchange (Bolsa Mercantil de Lima) was established more than 140 years ago and was reorganized in 1898 as Bolsa Comercial de Lima. In 1949 it was reorganized again and renamed Bolsa de Comercio de Lima. In 1979 the National Supervisory Commission of Companies and Securities (CONASEV) was created, and a major reformation resulted in the current name Bolsa de Valores de Lima (Lima Stock Exchange).

Classes of Securities: Common shares, preferred shares, labor shares (non-voting), government bonds, corporate bonds, rights

Indices: Lima Stock Exchange Index (December 1991 = 100)

Supervisory Organizations:
Minister of Finance
National Supervisory Commission of Companies and Securities (CONASEV)
Lima Stock Exchange

Depository: Securities Depository and Settlement House - CAVAL

Settlement Details:

Shares: CAVAL Trade date + 3 days (T + 3).

Trading: Trades are accomplished through CAVAL, a system designed to settle securities transactions and register those securities that are represented by book-entry accounts. The CAVAL system was developed with a high-technology client server. Securities are no longer represented by certificates, but registered through book-entry accounts.

CAVAL settles the cash transactions performed at the stock exchange 72 hours after the trading date (T + 3) facilitating delivery versus payment (DVP). CAVAL has been accepted as a member of the Association of National Numbering Agencies (ANNA) and recognized as the sole National Numbering Agency for Peru. As such, it is responsible for allocating ISIN codes to securities in Peru.

Each investor, local or foreign, has an individual account in CAVAL, which contains all purchased securities. The brokerage houses and stock brokers have a main account made up of all the accounts of their clients' securities. An investor with several brokerage accounts will have a different account number for each. CAVAL registers the transfer of securities by automated book-entry accounts, by crediting securities to the buyer's account, and by debiting the seller's account.

A CAVALCARD is issued to the investor. This allows consultations regarding holdings, by means of terminals located in the brokerage firms' offices. Use of the card requires a four-digit access code that can be modified at any time by the investor.

CAVAL offers many advantages to the investor. It eliminates the risk of certificate loss or forgery. It eliminates the cost of certificate custody. It eliminates delivery (allowing for the purchase or sale of securities to occur within a shorter time period, thus preventing price distortions). Cash dividends can be sent to the investor's bank or designated address. Finally, the system provides information on security holdings on a monthly basis (by mail) or at any time through CAVALCARD. Investors must register at the Unique Holders Registry (RUT; Registro Unico de Titulares) through a brokerage house or broker. The registry implies the allocation of a CODE, which the investor uses for all transactions on the exchange.

CAVAL MAIL offers an electronic mailing service that provides information on the movement of securities. This reduces administrative costs related to certificate issues, transfer of registries, and delivery of rights.

CAVAL LINK is an "on line" computer service of investment information for investors to use from their office or home. It can be connected to Investment Mutual Fund Administrators, Pension Fund Administrators, Custodians, other institutional investors, and insurance companies.

CAVAL SWIFT provides information to foreign investors through its International Services Division. Foreign institutional investors have access to information about their holdings as well as the market, delivery of benefits, and corporate information through SWIFT or by fax.

Listing Requirements: Securities must be recorded in the public registry of securities and intermediaries administered by CONASEV. Contact the National Supervisory Commission of Companies and Securities for full listing details.

Issuers are required to inform CONASEV and the stock exchange of the listing of any transformation, merger, or dissolution of the company. Furthermore, modifications to corporate objectives, treatment of profits, distributions, an increase or reduction of capital, and labor strikes are cause for notifications being sent to the exchange and CONASEV.

Quarterly financial statements, as well as annual reports, are also required to be sent to CONASEV and the stock exchange.

Investor Taxation: Corporate dividends are not taxed.

Capital gains and readjustment of capital paid to bond holders are tax exempt until the year 2000.

Limitations: Capital, dividends, and profits can be freely repatriated.

There are no limits on share ownership for foreign investors.

Securities Lending: Available

Brokerage Firms:
ABACO SAB S.A.
Jr. Chinchon 910 San Isidro
Lima
Peru
Phone: (51-14) 401 533, 403 748, 408 112
Fax: (51-14) 415 723

Abila & Calpe SAB S.A.
Independencia 842
Miraflores
Peru
Phone: (51-14) 478 219, 478 349

Acciones Y Valores SAB S.A.
Pasaje Acuna 127 OF. 701
Lima
Peru
Phone: (51-14) 270 071, 275 151, 302 237
Fax: (51-14) 260 916

Cartisa Peru SAB
Jr. Miro Quesada 247 Of. 503-504
Lima
Peru
Phone: (51-14) 283 949, 278 742

Coril SAB S.A.
Republica de Panama N° 3420
San Isidro
Peru
Phone: (51-14) 421 888
Fax: (51-14) 417 745

Credibolsa SAB S.A.
Centenario 156,
La Molina
Peru
Phone: (51-14) 373 838, 378 133
Fax: (51-14) 378 877

Cruzblanca S.A. SAB
Francisco Masias 544, Piso 12
San Isidro
Peru
Phone: (51-14) 220 294, 220 400
Fax: (51-14) 220 360

Divisas & Valores S.A. SAB
Miro Quesada 221 Of. 6003-604-605
Lima
Peru
Phone: (51-14) 274 997, 284 970, 274 852
Fax: (51-14) 274 852

Financiera Peruana-Interfip
Av. Felipe Pardo y Aliaga 634
San Isidro
Lima
Peru
Phone: (51-14) 404 970, 407 198
Fax: (51-14) 215 296

Finanval SAB
Los Laureles 235
San Isidro
Peru
Miro Quesada 247 Of. 508
Lima
Peru
Phone: (51-14) 211 727, 211 737, 271 701
Fax: (51-14) 314 188

Finvest SAB
Av. San Felipe 370
Jesus Maria
Peru
Pasaje Acuna 127 Of. 801
Lima
Peru
Phone: (51-14) 635 010, 630 443
Fax: (51-14) 632 297

Fortuna S.A. SAB
Miro Quesada 221 Of. 402
Lima
Peru
Phone: (51-14) 282 535, 282 689, 282 749

Godoy & Barclay SAB S.A.
Miro Quesada 260 Of. 1002
Lima
Peru
Phone: (51-14) 287 006
Fax: (51-14) 269 434

Helvetia SAB
Dean Valdivia 241
San Isidro
Peru
Phone: (51-14) 425 330, 424 310, 411 068
Fax: (51-14) 410 426

La Moneda SAB S.A.
Av. Juan de Aliaga N° 426
Mag. del Mar
Peru
Phone: (51-14) 619 720, 618 082
Fax: (51-14) 619 971

Montabetti Valmont SAB S.A.
Miro Quesada 247 Of. 201
Lima
Peru
Phone: (51-14) 289 797, 270 592
Fax: (51-14) 262 304

Plusvalor SAB S.A.
Miro Quesada 251 of. 500
Lima
Peru
Phone: (51-14) 419 067, 418 700, 210 884
Fax: (51-14) 419 070, 286 476

Wiese SAB S.A.
Miro Quesada 260 2° piso
Lima
Peru
Phone: (51-14) 302 213, 277 831
Fax: (51-14) 277 831

Company Information:

The Best Performing Shares in the Country

Company Name	Share Price Change 1 January 1997 to 31 December 1997 (%)
San Juan Cap	154
Fam Trab	103
Atacocha Trab	101
Aceros Trab	98
Morococha Trab	96
Milpo Cap	84
Cementos Trab	72
Credisa Trab	41
Manufacturera Trab	37
Norte Pacasmayo Trab	37
Arcata Trab	36
Milpo Trab	31

The Largest Companies in the Country by Market Capitalization as of 31 December 1997

Company Name	Market Capitalization Local Currency (Millions)	Market Capitalization US Dollars (Millions)
Telefonos 'B' Cap	9,051	3,320
Cnc Trab	8,868	3,253
Credito Cap	2,536	930
Buenaventura Cap	2,506	919
Backusac1	1,076	395
Wiese Cap	914	335
Banco Continental Cap	900	330
Backus Trab	507	186
Milpo Cap	332	122
Buenaventura Trab	325	119

Regional Exchange:

Arequipa Stock Exchange (Bolsa de Valores de Arequipa)
Sucre 209
Arequipa

Peru
Phone: (51-54) 244 452
Fax: (51-54) 218 117

Other Investment Information:

National Commission on Foreign Investment and
    Technology (CONITE)
Ministry of Industry, Commerce, Tourism, and
    Integration
Calle 1 Oeste
Corpac, San Isidro
Lima
Peru
Phone: (51-14) 407 120
Telex: 21094

Confederation of Chambers of Commerce of Peru
Avda Gregorio Escobedo 398
Lima
Peru
Phone: (51-14) 633 434

PETERSON, PETER G.

Peter G. Peterson (b. 1926) is a prominent U.S. business leader. He held various governmental positions during the Nixon administrations, including Secretary of Commerce. Peterson was CEO of Bell and Howell Company from 1966 to 1971, and currently serves on the boards of several prestigious corporations and charitable organizations. His many friends are among the wealthiest and best-known personages in the nation. Peterson's achievements in the world of high finance include rescuing the distinguished investment banking house of Lehman Brothers from bankruptcy during the 1970s. In this endeavor and subsequent ten-year employment with Lehman, Peterson's fortunes became inextricably enmeshed with those of Lewis L. Glucksman, a notable Wall Street veteran.

Peterson was born and reared in Kearney, Nebraska, the son of Greek immigrant parents. His father, following the lead of an older brother, had changed the family name from Petropoulos, which means "son of Peter." After first attending Kearney State Teachers College for one year and the Massachusetts Institute of Technology for one and one-half years, Peterson graduated summa cum laude from Northwestern University in 1947. While working days at Market Facts, Inc., a market research company in Chicago, Peterson studied marketing at night at the University of Chicago, receiving an MBA after five quarters. He joined the faculty at the University of Chicago, teaching evening classes and continuing to work during the day for Market Facts. After a few years Peterson went to the firm of McCann-Erickson in Chicago as a market researcher. He secured such new accounts as Peter Pan Peanut Butter, Swift Meat Packing, and Rival Dog Food, and was soon managing the Chicago office.

In 1953 Peterson and his family moved to the fashionable Chicago suburb of Kenilworth and became the neighbors of Charles Percy, president of Bell and Howell. A former movie camera company, Bell and Howell has become an information-access and mail-processing company, and was a high-profile advertising account of Peterson's in the 1950s. Under Peterson's guidance Bell and Howell sponsored Edward R. Morrow's CBS Reports. Seeing qualities in Peterson that he valued, Percy hired him as executive vice president for marketing. In 1961 Peterson became president of Bell and Howell, and in 1966 he replaced Percy as CEO when the latter won a seat in Washington as a senator from Illinois.

Peterson spent 13 years at Bell and Howell. Then in 1971 he went to Washington when President Nixon appointed him Assistant to the President for International Economic Affairs. Peterson also served in the Nixon administrations as Executive Director of the Council on Economic Policy in 1971 and 1972, and as Secretary of Commerce in 1972 and 1973. Because of clashes with Nixon's Secretary of the Treasury, John Connally, and because Nixon was irritated by Peterson's largely liberal social circle in Washington, Peterson was asked to resign from the Commerce Department. Peterson decided to seek a position in investment banking, hoping to improve his net worth dramatically. His new interest coincided with a need at Lehman Brothers.

Lehman Brothers, founded in 1850, had long been one of the most prestigious investment banking houses in the United States. In 1969 Robert (Bobbie) Lehman, the extremely well-liked and highly respected chairman of the board, died. Beset with this loss and the collapse of the bond market, the always irascible and contentious partners were in a state of chaos. Many withdrew from the partnership, taking their capital with them. Lehman Brothers was losing $9 million annually. Frederick Ehrman, who by virtual default had become chairman of the board, was looking for help for his ailing firm. Ehrman offered Peterson a vice chairmanship. Peterson accepted, and two months later, in August 1973, he became chairman.

Peterson launched an attack on expenditures—for example, the workforce was cut from 955 to 663 within one year. He also launched a study of Lehman Brothers' competition, which was judged to be the following ten banking firms: A.G. Becker; Dillon, Read; First Boston Corporation; Goldman, Sachs and Company; Halsey, Stuart; Kidder, Peabody and Company; Lazard Frères; Merrill Lynch; Morgan Stanley; and Salomon Brothers Inc. A more important study was that of Lehman's internal weaknesses. Two partners, Kenneth Lipper and Joseph J. Gal, studied Lehman's internal weaknesses and submitted a 100-page confidential report to the board. The report pinpointed the following significant weaknesses:

• Lack of a carefully defined business strategy

• Fragmented and undisciplined approach to running its business

• Portion of the partnership whose ability, training, and/or work habits are inconsistent with the competitive demands of the marketplace and with Lehman's present business

• Too small a professional staff relative to the number of clients to be serviced and transactions to be processed

• Bond distribution system in chaos and an equity distribution system experiencing declining market share

• Recent management changes throughout the organization

• High overhead relative to current revenue levels

• Comparatively limited capital

Although some of the partners were concerned about his lack of experience in the finance field, Peterson was confident that his executive background had prepared him remarkably well for the tasks at hand. He was eager and, he felt, very well schooled to plan strategy, devise organization charts and marketing plans, and create and sell new products. He culled the partnership, replacing some of them with new blood, but he proceeded with caution. By mid-1976 he replaced seven board members and reduced the average age of the board from 56 to 47.

In 1974 Peterson approached the need for additional capital by selling 15% of Lehman's stock to Banca Commerciale Italiana (BCI) for $7 million. He developed an extensive cost-cutting plan that cut the payroll and included reductions in partners' salaries. Later, he induced BCI to invest more heavily in Lehman. Peterson also effected two mergers—one with Abraham and Company, a brokerage firm, and a second with Kuhn Loeb and Company, a prestigious investment banking firm with blue chip clients. By 1975 Lehman was again profitable, earning $24 million before taxes and bonuses. During Peterson's ten-year chairmanship, Lehman's capital increased tenfold.

While Peterson was championing Lehman's fortunes through his contacts with the outside world, he relied heavily on Lew Glucksman to keep the inside corporate mechanisms functioning smoothly and effectively. Early on, when some partners blamed Glucksman for large losses and called for his dismissal, Peterson became his backer, and literally saved Glucksman's job. Glucksman received regular promotions under Peterson, and by 1983 had advanced to the level of co-CEO alongside Peterson. Glucksman was not satisfied and decided to try to oust Peterson and take sole control of Lehmans. Peterson chose to voluntarily step aside rather than force a showdown, receiving a severance package that included immediate withdrawal of $7 million in equity, 1% of Lehman's profits over the next five and one-half years, $300,000 annual supplemental retirement benefits for five and one-half years, a $5 million investment by Lehmans in Peterson's new venture capital firm, and other considerations.

As chairman of Lehman, Lew Glucksman was not able to gain the full support of the other partners, who forced a sale of the firm to Shearson/American Express within a few months after Glucksman replaced Peterson. The sale caused some alterations in Peterson's severance package. Primarily, the payment of 1% of Lehman profits was replaced with a flat payment of $200,000 annually for five years. Additionally, Peterson received a premium of $6 million on the $7 million in equity he previously withdrew. In all, Peterson took leave of Lehman $18 million wealthier—not counting the $5 million investment in his new firm that Shearson honored.

Since 1985 Peterson has been chairman of the Blackstone Group, the venture capital firm he cofounded with his friend Eli Jacobs. He is also director of Rockefeller Center Properties, Inc.; Sony Corporation; and Transtar, Inc. He is chairman of the board of the Council on Foreign Relations and Institute for International Economics; president of the Concord Coalition; and a trustee for the Committee for Economic Development, the National Bureau of Economic Research, and the New York Museum of Modern Art.

See also GLUCKSMAN, LEWIS L.; LEHMAN BROTHERS HOLDINGS INC.

PETITE BOURSE (France)

Petite Bourse denotes late afternoon trading on the Paris Bourse, which coincides with the opening of the New York markets.

See also FRANCE/PARIS BOURSE.

PHANTOM INCOME (United States)

Phantom Income is taxable income that must be reported to the IRS even though there is not any cash flow involved.

Some limited partnerships and zero coupon bonds that are not held in a tax sheltered account (e.g., Keogh, IRA, or SEP) will give rise to phantom income. The price of zero coupon bonds is accreted upward each year. The increase is considered taxable, even though no cash is paid until the bonds are sold or reach maturity.

See also CASH FLOW; TAXABLE EVENT.

PHILADELPHIA STOCK EXCHANGE (PHLX)

See UNITED STATES/PHILADELPHIA STOCK EXCHANGE (PHLX).

PHILIPPINES, REPUBLIC OF

The *Philippines* (Republika ng Pilipinas (Pilipino)) is an archipelago of about 7,100 islands and islets lying about 500 miles off the southeastern coast of Asia.

Area: 115,800 square miles (300,000 square km)

Population: 70,011,000 (54.0% urban; 46.0% rural)

Form of Government: Unitary republic, with two legislative houses: Senate—24 members; House of Representatives—204 members. Chief of state and head of government: President.

Official Languages: Pilipino; English

Capital: Manila

Largest Cities: Manila, 1,894,667; Quezon City, 1,627,890; Davao, 867,779; Cebu, 641,042; Caloocan, 629,473; Zamboanga, 453,214

Economy:

Currency: Peso (PhP)

National Budget: Revenue—P 334.5 billion; expenditures—P 309.9 billion (debt service: 30.7%; education: 15.4%; transportation and communications: 11.0%; defense: 10.2%; general public services: 10.0%; agriculture: 8.4%; health: 4.2%)

Public Debt: US$27.5 billion

Gross National Product: US$54.6 billion

Principal Products: Fruits and vegetables; livestock; machinery; clothing

Foreign Trade (Imports): US$22.6 billion (machinery and transport equipment: 33.5%; basic manufactures: 13.9%; chemicals: 9.7%; mineral fuels and lubricants: 9.5%; food and live animals: 6.7%; inedible crude materials: 4.3%; from Japan: 24.1%; United States: 18.5%; Singapore: 6.6%; Taiwan: 5.7%; South Korea: 5.2%; Hong Kong: 5.1%; Saudi Arabia: 4.4%; Germany: 3.5%; Australia: 2.8%; Malaysia: 1.9%)

Foreign Trade (Exports): US$13.5 billion (machinery and transport equipment: 21.6%; food and live animals: 9.9%; clothing and accessories: 6.7%; basic manufactures: 6.5%; animal and vegetable oils and fats: 3.6%; inedible crude materials: 3.0%; to United States: 36.8%; Japan: 15.0%; Singapore: 5.3%; Germany: 4.9%; Hong Kong: 4.8%; United Kingdom: 4.7%; the Netherlands: 3.8%; Taiwan: 3.4%; Thailand: 2.7%)

Stock Exchanges: 2

Philippine Stock Exchange (PSE)
Philippine Stock Exchange Centre
Exchange Road
Ortigas Center
Pasig, Metro Manila 1605
Philippines
Phone: (63-2) 636-0122 to 41
Fax: (63-2) 634-5920

Internet Address: www.pse.com.ph

Trading Hours: Monday–Friday, 9:30 to 12:00

Office Hours: Monday–Friday, 8:00 to 5:00

Exchange Holidays:

1 January	30 August
9 April	1, 30 November
1 May	25, 30, 31 December
12 June	

Listed Companies: 221

Total Market Capitalization:

At 31 December 1997

Local Currency (Millions)	US Dollars (Millions)
1,005,916	25,212

Major Sectors: Commercial/industrial, property, mining, oil

Share Price Performance:

(% Change)

1991	53
1992	46
1993	182
1994	29
1995	-11
1996	59
1997	-36

History: The Philippine Stock Exchange began trading in 1927. In 1963 the Makati Stock Exchange was established. Although they were separate entities, the two exchanges traded the same issues. President Fidel V. Ramos envisioned the joining of the two exchanges, with management by a professional group. In 1992 this vision was realized through the formation of the present Philippine Stock Exchange (PSE).

The first election of the PSE Board of Governors, held on 20 March 1993, elected 14 member-brokers. A 15th position was reserved for the PSE President Atty. Eduardo de Los Angeles, a non-broker. On 4 March 1994, the Securities and Exchange Commission granted the Philippine Stock Exchange, Inc. a license to operate, simultaneously canceling the licenses of the former separate exchanges. In March of 1994, One Price-One Market became a reality through a computer link between the two trading floors, assuring the best bid and offer no matter where the orders originated.

Classes of Securities: Class A shares for Philippine citizens, Class B shares for foreigners

Indices: PSE Composite Index (30 September 1994 = 100) Calculated daily, based on market capitalization of constituent stocks, using the weighted market capitalization method. The index is computed by comparing the total market capitalization of constituent stocks with the total market capitalization on the previous date. Weightings for each stock vary daily as market capitalization changes. A recomposition was accomplished on 3 October 1994 to further reflect the general movement of the market, and Class B shares of each component company were added.

The PSE Composite Index is evaluated on a six-month basis and contains a basket of stocks selected on the basis of liquidity, market capitalization, and profitability.

Components of the PSE Composite Index:

Composite Index	30 companies
Commercial-Industrial	31 companies
Property	10 companies
Mining	7 companies
Oil	10 companies

The computation formula is:

$$\text{Current index} = \frac{\text{Yesterday's}}{\text{Closing Index}} \times \frac{\text{Today's Market Capitalization}}{\text{Yesterday's Market Capitalization}}$$

Market capitalization = Closing Price × Outstanding Shares

Allowances are made for capital changes in the constituent stocks or changes in the constituent stocks themselves. Consequently, the previous revised aggregate market value is the previous day's aggregate market value adjusted for any capital changes in the constituent stocks. Capital changes include changes in number of the total outstanding shares due to stock dividends and preemptive rights.

Supervisory Organizations:

Securities and Exchange Commission of the Philippines: A quasi-judicial government agency, it regulates the securities industry through powers granted by laws such as Presidential Decree No. 902-A and the Revised Securities act. It administers and implements other laws such as the Corporation Code, the Law on Partnership, the Investment Act, and the Investment Houses Law.

Securities Investors Protection Fund (SIPF): Manages a fund contributed to largely by member-brokers for the purpose of protecting investors against losses due to fraud, failure, or insolvency of a member-broker/dealer. The fund is available only to customers of securities firms which are forced to liquidate.

Philippine Association of Securities Brokers & Dealers, Inc. (PSBDI): An organization representing all licensed stockbrokers and independent securities brokers and dealers, as well as investment houses, in the Philippines. The organization serves as the voice of the securities industry vis-à-vis the public and the government in matters affecting the members. It promotes projects for the development of the securities industry and protects members whenever their interests are affected by certain factors, such as proposed government measures, which might be adverse to the securities industry.

Depository: Philippine Central Depository, Inc.

Settlement Details:

Shares: Trade date + 4 days (1:00 P.M.)

Trading: Fully automated continuous auction trading occurs on the Philippine Stock Exchange every business day, officially beginning at 9:30 and ending at 12:00. Pre-open trading actually begins at 9:00 and extends until 12:10 for executing orders at closing prices. The exchange is closed on Saturdays, Sundays, legal holidays, and days when the Central Bank Clearing Office is closed.

SEC rules require a trading halt whenever the price of a security of a company listed on the stock exchange moves 50% up or 40% down on a particular day, to be reckoned from the last closing price or the last posted bid price, whichever is higher. The price of the security is automatically frozen by the exchange upon reaching the limit, unless there is an official announcement from the company or the proper government agency.

Types of Orders Acceptable to the System:

Pre-Open A pre-open limit is an order placed in the half hour prior to the opening of the regular session, specifying the price at which the investor is willing to buy or sell. A pre-open limit order not matched during the pre-open time is automatically forwarded to the daily market trading.

Daily Market

1. Limit Order (good for the day): Specifies the price at which an investor is willing to buy or sell. If the order is not able to be executed during the trading session in which it is entered, the order is canceled.
2. Limit Order (good till canceled): A limit order that is automatically canceled after 15 calendar days if it cannot be executed.
3. Cross Transaction: An order whereby the same broker has identical buy and sell orders from clients.

Post-Close

1. Limit Order: An order valid during the ten minute extension at the end of the trading session. The price is limited to the closing price of the issue involved.
2. Limit Order (good till canceled): Same as a limit order, but if the order cannot be matched it is automatically forwarded to the following trading day. It expires after 15 calendar days and is canceled.

   Except for special block sales and odd lots, the system shall not execute any order at a price inferior to the best bid offer (BBO).

Listing Requirements: Over-the-counter shares, not listed on the exchange but registered and licensed by the SEC for sale to the public, may be traded by brokers outside the PSE trading hours. OTC transactions are conducted by direct inquiry and negotiation among dealers using mail, telephone, telegraph, teletype, or any other form of communication. OTC can act as principals or agents in conducting buys and sells.

Investor Taxation:

Brokerage Commissions—These are limited to a maximum rate of 1.5% of the total transaction cost.

Transfer Fee—A transfer fee of P 45 per share certificate is charged by the transfer agent for every transfer.

Documentary Stamp Tax—This amount is based on the par value of the stock. The tax is P 0.50 for every P 200.00 par value of or any fraction thereof.

Value Added Tax—A 10% value added tax is charged on the transfer fee.

Final Transfer Tax—Shares traded on the Exchange are subject to a final transfer tax of one-half of 1% of the value of transaction in lieu of capital gains tax.

On dividends:

A. Dividends received by non-resident alien individuals from domestic corporations are subject to a 30% tax.
B. Dividends received by a domestic corporation from another domestic corporation are not subject to tax.
C. Dividends received by non-resident foreign corporations from domestic corporations are subject to a 35% tax.
D. Dividends received by individuals, citizens, or resident aliens, from domestic corporations are not subject to tax.

Limitations: When a securities transaction involves a non-resident, whether affected in the domestic or foreign market, it is the responsibility of the securities dealer/broker to register the transaction, using the prescribed registration form, with the Central Bank within three business days from the transaction date. The Central Bank will issue a Certificate of Registration upon approval of the registration.

Non-residents are restricted to the purchase and sale of Class B shares. Class A shares are traded by Philippine residents. The purpose of this restriction is to monitor alien equity ownership, which is limited by the Philippines constitution to 40% maximum ownership in a Filipino company.

Foreign investors must register with the Central Bank for funds repatriation, which takes place through a local custodian.

Restrictions:

1. Under the new Constitution of the Republic of the Philippines
   A. Franchise, certificate or authorization for the operation of a public utility shall be granted only to citizens of the Philippines or to a corporation of which at least 60% of the capital is owned by such citizens. Participation of foreign investors in governing body shall be limited to their proportionate share in the capital and all executive and managing officers of such corporation must be Filipino citizens.
   B. Disposition, exploration, development, exploitation, or utilization of natural resources

shall be limited to citizens of the Philippines or to corporations or associations of which at least 60% of the capital is owned by such citizens. The word *capital* should be understood to mean "outstanding capital stock" in case of stock corporation.

C. Ownership and management of mass media shall be limited to citizens of the Philippines or to corporations or associations wholly owned and managed by such citizens.

D. Educational institutions other than those established by religious orders, mission boards, and charitable organizations, shall be owned solely by citizens of the Philippines, or corporations or associations 60% of the capital of which is owned by citizens of the Philippines.

2. *Atomic Energy:* Issuance of license to acquire, own, or operate atomic energy facility is limited to Philippine citizens or entities with at least 60% Philippine capital.

3. *Civil Aeronautics:* Granting of permit to engage in domestic air commerce and/or air transportation must be made to Filipino citizens or juridical persons with at least 60% Filipino capital.

4. *Coconut Industry:* Granting of loans to finance establishment of coconut centrals and mills must be made to a Filipino citizen or a corporation or association with majority Filipino capital.

5. *Property:* No condominium unit shall be conveyed or transferred to persons other than Filipino citizens, or corporations at least 60% of the capital stock of which belong to Filipino citizens, except in cases of hereditary succession.

6. *Cottage Industry:* All cottage industries shall be owned and operated by Philippine citizens or by juridical person with at least 75% Philippine capital. All members of its board of directors shall be Filipino citizens.

7. *Financing Companies:* At least 60% of the capital stock of financing companies should be owned by citizens of the Philippines; two-thirds of the members of the board of directors must be Filipino citizens. In the case of partnerships, all the managing partners must be citizens of the Philippines.

8. *Fishing and Other Aquatic Rights:* Limited to citizens of the Philippines or a juridical person with at least 61% Filipino capital.

9. *Investment Incentives:* Board of Investments registered enterprises limited to corporations at least 60% voting capital stock of which is owned and held by Philippine nationals, and at least 60% of the members of the board of directors of which are citizens of the Philippines. Tax incentives for investments in pioneer enterprises and preference in grant of government loans is limited to Philippine nationals.

10. *Minerals and Mineral Lands, Coal and Petroleum:* Lessee of unreserved and unappropriated coal-bearing lands must be a Filipino citizen or juridical person with at least 60% Filipino capital.

11. *Private Lands:* (a) Sale or lease of lands of the private domain of the government of the Philippines is limited to persons qualified to acquire public lands. (b) Mortgagee of private real property may be any person, but only Filipino citizens or corporations or associations with 60% Filipino capital can bid for such mortgaged property if foreclosed.

12. *Public Lands:* Applicants for homestead, free patents, and judicial confirmation of imperfect or incomplete title to public lands shall be Filipino citizens. Applicants for sale and lease shall be Philippine citizens or juridical person with at least 60% Filipino capital.

13. *Retail Trade:* Retail trade business is limited to Filipino citizens or juridical persons with 100% Filipino capital.

14. *Rice and Corn:* Only Filipino citizens or 100% Filipino-owned corporations may engage in the rice and/or corn industry; but foreign equity participation in alien or business organization that may be allowed by NGA to engage in the rice and corn industry shall be transferred to Filipino citizens within a period established by NGA.

15. *Shipping:* Issuance of certificate of Philippine register to vessels of domestic ownership for coastwide trade is limited to Filipino citizens or juridical persons with at least 60% Filipino capital. The president and managing director of corporations or associations that will engage in coastwide trade shall be citizens of the Philippines; also members of the crew shall be citizens of the Philippines.

16. *Tobacco:* Amending tobacco laws concerning the Virginia Tobacco Industry authorization given by the Philippine Virginia Tobacco Administration Board to import foreign leaf tobacco for blending purposes is limited to bona fide cigarette manufacturers owned or controlled by Filipino citizens.

17. *Employment:* The issuance of a license or authority to recruit or hire workers is limited to citizens of the Philippines or corporations, partnerships, or entities at least 60% of the authorized capital stock of which is owned and/or controlled by Filipino citizens.

18. *Banking:* (a) 70% of voting stock of the banking institutions shall be owned by Filipino citizens, except new banks established by consolidation of branches or agencies of foreign banks in the Philippines. Two-thirds of the members of the board of directors shall be Filipino citizens. (b) 70% of voting stock of the private development banks shall be owned by Filipino citizens, except new banks established by consolidation of branches or agencies of foreign banks in the Philippines. Two-thirds of the members of the board of directors shall be Filipino citizens. (c) Capital stock of rural banks shall be 100% owned and held (directly or indirectly) by Filipino citizens. All members of the board or directors shall be Filipino citizens. (d) 70% of the voting stock of savings and loan associations shall be owned by citizens of the Philippines. Two-thirds of the members of the board of directors shall be Philippine citizens.

Securities Lending: None

Brokerage Firms:
A&A Securities, Inc.
1906 Y. Ayala Ave. Condominium
6776 Ayala Avenue
Makati City
Philippines
Phone: (63-2) 891-1008 to 10
Fax: (63-2) 891-1179

AGJ Securities Corporation
9/F Royal Match Building
6780 Ayala Ave.
Makati City
Philippines
Phone: (63-2) 893-4170 to 71, 893-4176 to 79
Fax: (63-2) 810-5416

Alpha Securities Corporation
18/F The Pacific Star Building
Makati Ave., cor. Sen Gil Puyat Ave.
Makati City
Philippines
Phone: (63-2) 892-8561 to 63, 893-6457
Fax: (63-2) 894-5750

Amon Securities Corporation
5/F The Pacific Star Bldg.
Makati Ave., cor. Sen Gil Puyat Ave.
Makati City
Philippines
Phone: (63-2) 815-0811 to 21, 893-2450
Fax: (63-2) 894-5475

Baring Securities (PHILS), Inc.
18/F The Pacific Star Bldg.
Sen Gil Puyat Ave. cor. Makati Ave.
Makati City
Philippines
Phone: (63-2) 810-7701, 815-2240
Fax: (63-2) 819-1256

Bernad Securities, Inc.
1057 M.H. del Pilar St.
Ermita, Manila
Philippines
Phone: (63-2) 503-897, 505-388, 505-267
Fax: (63-2) 599-215

Campos, Lanuza & Company, Inc.
Unit 2003-B Tektite Tower I, Exchange Road
Ortigas Center
Pasig City
Philippines
Phone: (63-2) 634-6881 to 87
Fax: (63-2) 636-1167

Citibank Securities, Inc.
5/F Citibank Centre
8741 Paseo de Roxas
Makati City
Philippines
Phone: (63-2) 894-7677, 894-7692 & 94
Fax: (63-2) 894-7014

Connell Securities, Inc.
G/F Alsco Building
116 Herrera St., Legaspi Village
Makati City
Philippines
Phone: (63-2) 893-2001 to 05, 816-3108
Fax: (63-2) 818-3969

Diversified Securities, Inc.
Unit 2304-B Tektite Tower I.
Exchange Road, Ortigas Center
Pasig City
Philippines
Phone: (63-2) 635-2009 to 10, 635-2674
Fax: (63-2) 635-2009

Evergreen Stock Brokerage & Sec., Inc.
5/F Prudence Mansion, Fernandez cor.
Ongpin Sts. Sta. Cruz, Manila
Philippines
Phone: (63-2) 7337241 to 42
Fax: (63-2) 733-7240

Fidelity Securities, Inc.
21/F Philippine Stock Exchange Centre
Exchange Road, Ortigas Center
Pasig City
Philippines
Phone: (63-2) 634-7110
Fax: (63-2) 634-5043

Globalinks Securities & Stocks, Inc.
Mezzanine Floor, Belson House, 271 EDSA
Mandaluyong City
Philippines
Phone: (63-2) 709-329, 796-101
Fax: (63-2) 789-655

Investors Securities, Inc.
Unit M-VI-A Gallery Bldg.
Amorsolo St.
Makati City
Philippines
Phone: (63-2) 843-1877, 843-1210
Fax: (63-2) 817-9989

James Capel Securities (PHILS.), Inc.
13/F Royal Match Bldg.
6780 Ayala Ave.
Makati City
Philippines
Phone: (63-2) 810-5106
Fax: (63-2) 810-5108

Jardine Fleming Exchange Capital Securities, Inc.
2/F Corporate Business Center
151 Paseo de Roxas cor. Pasay Road
Makati City
Philippines
Phone: (63-2) 813-8519 to 26
Fax: (63-2) 817-5366, 816-0569

Kerry Securities (PHILS.), Inc.
9/F Dona Salustiana D. Ty Tower
104 Paseo de Roxas cor. Perea St., Legaspi Village
Makati City
Philippines
Phone: (63-2) 812-6661 to 68
Fax: (63-2) 812-4839

Kim Eng Securities (PHILS.), Inc.
Rm 1106 Pacific Bank Bldg.
6776 Ayala Ave.
Makati City
Philippines

Phone: (63-2) 891-1152 & 56, 891-1031 to 33
Fax: (63-2) 894-5308

Nomura International (H.K.) Ltd.
20/F-21/F, 3 Garden Road
Central, Honkong
Phone: (852) 536-1950
Fax: (852) 536-1959

Philippine Asia Equity Securities, Inc.
25/F Pacific Star Building
Sen Gil Puyat Ave. cor Makati Ave.
Makati City
Philippines
Phone: (63-2) 816-3471 to 76
Fax: (63-2) 819-2653 & 54

Company Information:

The Best Performing Shares in the Country

Company Name	Share Price Change 1 January 1997 to 31 December 1997 (%)
Centro Escolar Uvty.	547
Rfm	47
Manila Bulletin Pbl.	43
Music Corporation	23
Philp.Long Dsn.Tel.	22

The Largest Companies in the Country by Market Capitalization as of 31 December 1997

Company Name	Market Capitalization Local Currency (Millions)	Market Capitalization US Dollars (Millions)
Ayala Corp.	129,724	3,251
Ayala Land	115,928	2,906
Philp. Long Dsn. Tel.	95,681	2,398
San Miguel 'A'	63,613	1,594
Metropolitan Bk. & Tst.	61,318	1,537
Sm Prime Holdings	59,584	1,493
Bk. of the Philp.Isle.	50,014	1,254
Manila Electric 'B'	44,872	1,125
Manila Electric 'A'	41,440	1,039
San Miguel 'B'	32,358	811
Petron Corp.	31,406	787
Benpres Holdings	27,443	688
Far East Bk. & Trust	26,460	663
Filinvest Dev.	20,246	507
Equitable Banking Corp.	18,530	464
Pci Bank	17,508	439
Jollibee Foods	14,753	370

Company Name	Market Capitalization Local Currency (Millions)	Market Capitalization US Dollars (Millions)
Abs-Cbn Bcast.	14,032	352
Jg Summit Hdg.	13,914	349
Philippine Nat. Bk.	12,236	307
C&P Homes	9,827	246
Union Bk. of the Philps.	9,647	242
Digital Telecom.	9,281	233
Rfm	9,237	232
China Banking	8,390	210
Universal Robina	7,365	185
Philtrust Bank	7,227	181
Aboitiz Equity Vent.	7,175	180
Alsons Consolidated	7,172	180
Ionics Circuits	7,090	178
Filinvest Land	6,763	169
Intl. Ctnr. Term. Svs.	6,501	163
Rizal Coml. Bkg. 'A'	6,494	163
La Tondena Distillers	5,947	149
Cosmos Bottling	5,693	143
Centro Escolar Uvty.	5,588	140
Fortune Cement	5,539	139
Metro Pacific	5,100	128
Music Corporation	5,091	128
Belle	4,878	122
Anscor Soriano	4,795	120
Primetown Property Group	4,762	119
Solidbank	4,673	117
Pilipino Telephone	4,645	116
Security Bank	4,644	116
Manila Bulletin Pbl.	4,195	105

Regional Exchange:

Makati Stock Exchange
Ground Floor
Makati Stock Exchange Building
Ayala Avenue
Makati, Metro Manila
The Philippines
Phone: (63-2) 810-1145

Other Investment Information:
Department of Trade and Industry
385 Sen. Gil J. Puyat Avenue
1200 Makatu, Metro Manila,
Philippines
Phone: (63-2) 868-403, 867-895, 875-602
Fax: (63-2) 632-851166
Telex: 45555 BOI/PM OR 122661 BOI PH

Philippine Chamber of Commerce
ODC International Plaza Building
219 Salcedo Street
Makati, Metro Manila 2801
Philippines
Phone: (63-2) 8176981
Telex: 62042

PHILLIPS, ALBAN

Alban Phillips (1914–1975) was a British economist who defined the empirical relationship between the percentage change of money wages and the level of unemployment. His work has been in the middle of the debate between Keynesian and Monetarist economists in subsequent decades.

Phillips was primarily concerned with macroeconomics and explored the time-lagged relationships between the multiplier and accelerator in mathematical models of the economy. Phillips also applied the engineering technique of closed-loop control systems to the analysis of macroeconomic relationships.

It was for his work on the relationship between inflation and unemployment that Phillips's work created most discussion. In an article in *Economica* in 1958 Professor Phillips plotted a graph showing their relationship in the United Kingdom from 1861–1957. With wage inflation on the vertical axis and unemployment on the horizontal axis, a scale of points was obtained. The resulting curve showed an inverse relationship between inflation and unemployment. Given that wage increases during the period were approximately 2% above price increases, a similarly shaped curve could be plotted showing the relationship between price inflation and unemployment. The main implication of Phillips's analysis was that, since a particular level of employment in the economy will imply a particular rate of wage increase, the aims of low unemployment and a low rate of inflation may be inconsistent. The government must then choose between the feasible combinations of unemployment and inflation.

The inverse relationship between wage inflation and unemployment was explained by changes in aggregate demand and the existence of "money illusion." When aggregate demand rose relative to potential output, inflation rose and unemployment fell: there was an upward movement along the curve. If wages rose, the unemployed may have believed that the higher wages they were offered represented a real wage increase and accepted jobs more readily. The position of the Phillips curve depended upon non-demand factors causing inflation and unemployment, and in the century for which Phillips studied these factors conditions had changed little. From the mid-1960s onward, however, the Phillips curve relationship appeared to break down with the experience of stagflation, the phenomenon of unemployment and inflation rising simultaneously in Western economies.

Milton Friedman introduced the idea of adaptive expectations, and later work by Robert Lucas of the Chicago School of Economics applied the notion of rational expectations to explain the breakdown of the Phillips curve. In adaptive expectations the Phillips curve relationship works only in the short run, as workers temporarily suffer from money illusion before recognizing the real value of wages. Under rational expectations, money illusion is deemed non-existent. The long-run Phillips curve at the non-accelerating inflation rate of unemployment (NAIRU) is vertical at the national rate of unemployment, the level of unemployment where the labor market is in equilibrium. The adaptive expectations and rational expectations Phillips curve both argued against the viability of demand-side policies and advocated that supply-side policies were the only means of altering the levels of unemployment and inflation in an economy.

See also CHICAGO SCHOOL OF ECONOMICS; KEYNES, JOHN MAYNARD; MACROECONOMICS; SUPPLY-SIDERS.

PHILLIPS' LAW
See PHILLIPS, ALBAN.

PHYSICAL ACCESS MEMBER (United States)
Physical Access Member refers to an individual who purchases the right to use the trading facility of the New York Stock Exchange by paying an annual fee, but who has no voting nor ownership privileges on the exchange. The individual can buy and sell securities.

See also MEMBER; UNITED STATES/NEW YORK STOCK EXCHANGE (NYSE).

PHYSICALS
See ACTUALS.

PHYSIOCRATS
The *Physiocrats* are widely regarded as the first formal school of economists. Led by François Quesnay, the physiocrats first published works in France during the 1750s. Their work relied on theoretical models and analytical frameworks that provided the basis for deriving solutions.

Physiocrats, writing in the preindustrial age, concentrated on an analysis of surpluses and deficits produced by agriculture. The classical school of economics sustained interest in the origins and nature of an economic surplus and followed the physiocrats in arguing that it was the result of production. Classical analysis believed that manufacturing as well as agriculture could produce a surplus, reflecting the emerging industrialization in the economy.

See also CLASSICAL SCHOOL OF ECONOMICS.

PICKENS, T. BOONE
T. Boone Pickens was an extremely successful oil explorer for many years until he turned his attention to the far more lucrative task of corporate raiding. During the 1980s he made a string of hostile takeover bids for, among others, Gulf Oil, Philips, and Unocal via his own company, Mesa.

Pickens spent many years searching for companies that were rich in assets but were undervalued by the stock market. Financing was available via high-yielding junk bonds, which became an acceptable form of security during the 1980s. Each deal had to be completed swiftly; the stripped assets were sold off and the borrowings were paid down with the proceeds. The profits earned by Pickens, and contemporaries such as Carl Icahn and Ivan Boesky, were huge. It took several years for the U.S. public to appreciate that the age of the friendly merger had been replaced by the epoch of the corporate raid.

Pickens operated with a mixture of arrogance and cunning on the way to amassing his personal fortune. He displayed a willingness to aggressively employ a wide range of innovative tactics to gain control over companies. In 1985, for example, New York City and the State of California joined together to resist Pickens' demand for "greenmail" in a bid for Phillips Petroleum. Pickens attempted to get $53 per share, while forcing the other shareholders to accept only $42 per share, paid in a mixture of debt and equity. His offer failed when the pension funds called for and received equal treatment.

In 1995 Pickens experienced the threat of takeover from the less agreeable position of corporate target. A takeover bid for Mesa, financed by businessmen Dennis Washington and Marvin Davis, was masterminded by one of Pickens' former codirectors, David Batchelder. To add to the irony, the bidder criticized Pickens for many of the errors that he had attacked during the 1980s. Pickens was accused of unfocused management, poor control over spending, and running an unnecessary corporate jet. Mesa had built up a collection of natural gas-producing sites in the United States but had been squeezed by a steady fall in the market price of gas. Interest payments on the company's debt

T. Boone Pickens, February 1985. *(Walz; UWE/Corbis)*

mountain have turned any apparent trading profits into net losses. A plan to sell off the massive Hugoton gas field, which stretches from Kansas to the Texas panhandle, was abandoned when auction bids failed to reach the company's reserve price.

See also BOESKY, IVAN; GREENMAIL; ICAHN, CARL; JUNK BOND; RAIDER; TAKEOVER/TAKEOVER BID.

PIGGYBACK EXCEPTION (United States)

A *Piggyback Exception* is the name given to the 1984 amendment of Securities and Exchange Commission Rule 15c2-11. Although factual information must be reported to the SEC, the amendment presumes that regular and frequent quotations in an actively traded market are an acceptable substitute for such information.

See also ANNUAL REPORT; EARNINGS; SECURITIES AND EXCHANGE COMMISSION (SEC).

PIGGYBACK REGISTRATION (United States)

Piggyback Registration refers to the practice of making an initial public offering while allowing private shareholders to include their shares in the offering. The issue is called a primary/secondary distribution, and the full information disclosure will appear in the prospectus. It will include the major sellers of securities that were privately purchased before the public offering.

See also INITIAL PUBLIC OFFERING (IPO); PRIMARY DISTRIBUTION; PROSPECTUS.

PIGGYBACKING (United States)

Piggybacking is the unethical practice of a stockbroker making personal transactions based on information given by an investor who is also a customer.

Not only does the practice of piggybacking present a conflict of interest, it places other investors at a disadvantage. It would also be unethical for the broker to use the information as a way to convince other clients to invest, unless the information has been released to the public and is verified.

Such information could also be construed as insider information and would, therefore, be a direct violation of U.S. securities laws.

See also INSIDER INFORMATION; NATIONAL ASSOCIATION OF SECURITIES DEALERS (NASD); REGISTERED REPRESENTATIVE (RR).

PINK SHEETS (United States)

Pink Sheets refers to a tablet of pink-colored pages containing price quotations and market makers for thinly traded securities that do not trade on an exchange or are not quoted through NASDAQ. These shares, however, do trade over-the-counter. The sheets are mailed from their publisher, the National Quotation Bureau, to brokerage firms on a daily basis. Debt securities quotations are printed on yellow sheets.

In most cases the market maker must be contacted by telephone to obtain a current price quotation.

See also QUOTE; THINLY TRADED.

PIOVE (Italy)

See BEAR MARKET.

PIT TRADING/PIT BOSS (United States)

The term *Pit Trading* refers to the trading of futures and options and is derived from the description of the trading floor. Most are ring shaped, with many levels of steps that enable several traders to see and be seen easily as they make trades.

In options trading on the Chicago Board of Options Exchange, the *Pit Boss* is a member who is appointed by the CBOE to assist the floor officials. The pit boss resolves non–rule violation disputes and keeps track of quotation quality, accuracy, and the open and close prices.

The pit boss also functions as a liaison between the trading crowd and the CBOE regulatory staff members.

See also CALL; OPTION; PUT; PUT PREMIUM.

PLACEMENT (France)

See INVESTMENT.

PLACING

See INITIAL PUBLIC OFFERING (IPO).

PLAGE DE COURS (France)

See PRICE RANGE.

PLAIN VANILLA

Plain Vanilla has two meanings in the world of the stock market. In one instance, it refers to an easy solution to a problem. It is also used to describe a new issue of securities that offers no extra benefits to aid in its promotion.

Brokers tend to like plain vanilla securities. Because additional benefits require more explanation, thereby creating more questions and additional time delays, there exists a negative feeling about securities with extra benefits. The general feeling is that if the underlying security is sound, the extras are not necessary.

See also INITIAL PUBLIC OFFERING (IPO); SUBSCRIPTION RIGHTS; SUBSCRIPTION WARRANT.

PLAN COMPANY (United States)

An organization registered with the Securities and Exchange Commission, a *Plan Company* sells contractual funds for the fund's underwriter.

A contractual plan purchaser receives two prospectuses, one from the plan company and the second prospectus from the mutual fund involved.

See also MUTUAL FUND; SECURITIES AND EXCHANGE COMMISSION (SEC); UNIT INVESTMENT TRUST/UNIT TRUST.

PLAN D'INVESTISSEMENT (France)

A *Plan D'Investissement* is an investment plan involving monthly contributions to a unit investment trust.

See also UNIT INVESTMENT TRUST/UNIT TRUST.

PLAYER

In the world of securities trading, the term *Player* is used to describe two classes of individuals. The first type buys several shares of a company, the second buys the entire company.

The first group includes frequent, or day, traders, comprised of institutional and individual investors who regularly buy several shares of a company. Frequent trading of securities is considered a speculative activity, often involving technical market analysis. Trades are made on market forecasts for the short term.

The second group is comprised of individuals who are regularly involved with large-scale leveraged buyouts.

A leveraged buyout (LBO) can take many forms. Some are kept private, closely held by a small group of individuals. Other LBOs are broken up—each part being sold and the remainder being reissued to the public. Still other buyouts are reorganized to make a more productive company and are resold to the public at a profit.

Players such as T. Boone Pickens, Carl Icahn, Saul Steinberg, and Ted Turner tend to move swiftly in a leveraged buyout situation. Speculators often try to accompany the situation, buying shares of the target to ride it up and taking gains as the share price rises. However, this can be a risky strategy because takeovers can fall through. One of the most noteworthy was the management-led LBO of UAL Corporation in 1989. The financing fell through, the price of UAL collapsed, and the Dow Jones Industrial Average fell more than 180 points all in the same day.

See also ICAHN, CARL; LEVERAGED BUYOUT (LBO); PICKENS, T. BOONE; TAKEOVER/TAKEOVER BID; THEORY OF SPECULATION.

PLAYING THE MARKET

Playing the Market is securities jargon for share trading on the stock market.

Those who play the market have various approaches. Many just buy shares, wait for them to rise to an acceptable level, and then sell. If the increase does not occur in a certain period of time the shares are sold and reinvested. There are essentially no set objectives and no planned strategies other than to buy and sell at a profit. Others might use technical analysis, buying and selling based on forecasts taken from price trend charts.

See also FUNDAMENTAL ANALYSIS; OBJECTIVE; TECHNICAL ANALYSIS.

PLC

See PUBLIC LIMITED COMPANY (PLC).

PLUS TICK

See UPTICK; ZERO PLUS TICK.

PLUS VALORE DI CAPITALE (Italy)

See CAPITAL GAIN.

PNC BANK CORPORATION

PNC Bank Corporation had grown to be the 11th largest bank holding company in the United States by 1997, despite its relatively brief history. As of 30 June 1997, its assets stood at $72 billion, and it had a total of 850 branches in Pennsylvania, Kentucky, Delaware, Ohio, Indiana, Florida, Massachusetts, and New Jersey. Its nonbanking subsidiaries provide corporate, retail, investment management, trust, and investment banking services.

In 1983 Pittsburgh National Corporation merged with Provident National Corporation, forming PNC Financial Corporation. Pittsburgh National Bank had originated in 1852, when Pittsburgh Trust and Savings opened. Provident National Bank went back to the Tradesmens National Bank, which opened in Philadelphia in 1847, and the Provident Life and Trust Company, which was established in 1865 by Quakers as an insurance company. Both Pittsburgh National and Provident National went through various acquisitions and name changes until the state of Pennsylvania changed its banking laws in 1982 to permit statewide banking, paving the way for their merger the following year.

PNC distinguished itself in the 1980s for its unusual management style, known as "bottom-up management," in which senior executives were granted sufficient latitude by the chief executive to make their own decisions. In addition, PNC's attitude toward growth was somewhat unusual, especially in the highly competitive environment of the 1980s, in that it focused on the provision of high-quality products and services and viewed quantitative growth as rather secondary.

Ironically, PNC grew rapidly, both through the expansion of its own activities and through acquisitions. Beginning in 1983 with $16.4 billion in assets, by 1988 it had doubled in size to $36.5 billion, and within nine more years it had doubled once again. This extremely impressive growth rate was seen by many as a vindication of PNC's beliefs.

In the 1980s, bank mergers in the United States were facilitated by banking deregulation. PNC's acquisitions strategy emphasized purchasing healthy, well-run banks of medium size ($2–$6 billion in assets). PNC also looked for banks with an excellent return on equity and assets, and that had expertise in some area of financial services that would benefit the entire PNC group. Finally, PNC looked to merge with banks that had management philosophies similar to its own.

In 1984 PNC acquired the Marine Bank of Erie, Pennsylvania; in 1985, the Northeastern Bancorp of Scranton, Pennsylvania; in 1986, Hershey Bank of Hershey, Pennsylvania; in 1987, Citizen's Fidelity Corporation of Louisville, Kentucky; and in 1988, Central Bancorp of Cincinnati, Ohio, the First Bank and Trust of Mechanicsburg, Pennsylvania, and the Bank of Delaware. In 1987 PNC began work on a single corporation-wide infrastructure, developing common systems, a single data center, uniform financial reporting, and the like.

PNC's second stage of acquisitions commenced in 1991 with its purchase of First Federal Savings and Loan Association of Pittsburgh. This deal made PNC the largest bank in Pittsburgh. In the years 1991–96, PNC acquired nine financial institutions that improved its market share in all the places where it already existed. In addition, PNC moved into new markets, purchasing the CCNB Corporation in Harrisburg and United Federal Bancorp of State College, thus creating what is now the central Pennsylvania market of PNC Bank. In 1995 PNC acquired most of the New Jersey franchise of Chemical Bank. Later that year, PNC and Midlantic Corporation joined forces in a $3 billion merger.

During the early 1990s PNC's major nonbank acquisitions were Sears Mortgage Company, which operated in 30 states, and BlackRock Financial Management, a leading manager of fixed-income investments. In 1997 it acquired five retail mortgage origination offices from Fleet Mortgage.

Thus by the mid-1990s, PNC was strong in several areas: corporate banking (PNC Capital Markets, Inc. was a leading underwriter of health care and education credits), consumer banking (3.3 million households and 135,000 small businesses), mortgage banking (479,000 loans with an outstanding principal balance of approximately $41 billion), real estate banking (a portfolio of more than $4 billion), and asset management (PNC was the nation's fifth largest bank money manager, with discretionary authority over $114.9 billion and approximately $346.4 billion in assets under administration). In addition, PNC offered credit cards, institutional investment management (through Provident Capital Management), leasing, mutual funds and securities (through PNC Securities), and trust services. In the early 1990s, PNC's securities business grew 25–30% per year, its corporate services and cash management grew approximately 20% a year, and its mutual fund business grew more than 20% a year.

PNC had established itself as a "super-regional" bank. It aspired to develop its business within the entire northeast quadrant of the United States, and to develop its money management and corporate services sectors internationally.

POINT

Point is the term used to define the degree by which an index, average, or price moves.

When a share price changes by $1 it is said to have changed by a point. When a bond price changes by one point, it changes $10 per $1,000 face value. In reference to yields, a 100 basis-point move will cause a change of 1% (100 basis points = 1%). If the Dow Jones Industrial Average goes from 5,600 to 5,601 it has moved one point.

Indices are described in point or partial point moves. Partial point moves are indicated by the use of a decimal point.

See also ASK PRICE; BID PRICE; CURRENT MARKET PRICE.

POINT AND FIGURE CHART

A *Point and Figure Chart* is used by some technical analysts to forecast changes in trends. Daily highs and lows are also often used for this analysis in order to measure momentum with the time factor removed. If used, they will often have minimums established for marking reversals. For example, three points might be required before moving to each new column.

A price increase causes an *X* to be placed on the graph paper (price range by minimal tick, normally indicated on the left). As long as the price continues to be higher each day, an *X* is placed in the same column, corresponding to the price scale. The scale is determined by the person doing the analysis, but should be calibrated to a realistic price movement. For share price movements, the minimal tick of 1/8 might be too small a calibration, but $10 could be too large.

If a price is lower than the preceding day, an *O* is placed at the corresponding level in the immediate column to the right. If the price continues lower, the *O*s are marked in the same column. Each time a direction change occurs, the marking moves one column to the right. No record is kept of individual dates, although an investor might want to note the starting date on the chart. Here is a simple example:

Point and Figure Chart for XYZ Corporation:
Price Scale in $. Daily highs and lows with a minimum 3 point difference to show a reversal

```
65
64
63
62
61                          X      < Buy signal
60    X          X    O    X
59    X    O     X    O    X
58    X    O     X    O    X
57    X    O          O
56    X
55    X
54
53
52
51
50
```

For the simplified example, marks are added each time the closing is at least $1 away from the previous mark. The system measures momentum separated from time. The amount of movement necessary to indicate a reversal from advancing to declining or vice-versa can be adjusted by the person doing the analysis. Even though the chart shows price differences of $1, greater reversal moves can be required to show direction change if the analyst so chooses. It can be a one-point change, smaller to show more volatility, or a greater minimum change to moderate volatility.

It is considered a sell signal if the declining column drops below the preceding declining column and a buy signal if an ascending column rises above a preceding ascending column.

See also DOW THEORY; FUNDAMENTAL ANALYSIS; RESISTANCE; SUPPORT/SUPPORT LEVEL; TECHNICAL ANALYSIS.

POISON PILL

Poison Pill is the name given to a corporate strategy that seeks to prevent a takeover by making the acquisition too expensive.

Often poison pill strategies are set up with convertible preferred stock distributed to shareholders as a share dividend. The preferred stock is convertible into a quantity of common shares equal to or in excess of the total number of outstanding shares. The conversion would cause dilution, but would also make a target considerably more expensive.

The ideal poison pill is one that will make the company more expensive if taken over, but cause no harm to the company if the takeover falls through.

See also MERGER; PREFERRED STOCK (PFD); TAKEOVER/ TAKEOVER BID.

POLAND, REPUBLIC OF

Poland (Rzeczpospolita Polska) is one of the largest countries in Europe. It is bordered on the east and northeast by Ukraine and Belarus, on the northeast by Lithuania and Russia, on the south by the Czech Republic and Slovakia, and on the west by Germany.

Area: 120,727 square miles (312,683 square km)

Population: 38,641,000 (61.8% urban; 38.2% rural)

Form of Government: Unitary multiparty republic, with two legislative houses: Senate—100 members; Diet—460 members. Chief of state: President. Head of government: Prime Minister.

Official Language: Polish

Capital: Warsaw

Largest Cities: Warsaw, 1,642,700; Lodz, 833,700; Krakow, 745,100

Economy:

Currency: Polish Zloty (Zl)

National Budget: Zl 459.0 trillion; expenditures—Zl 502.4 trillion (social benefits: 20.7%; interest on debts: 18.1%)

Public Debt: US$47.2 billion

Gross National Product: US$87.3 billion

Principal Products: Potatoes, wheat, rye, sugar beets; livestock; machinery; industrial products

Foreign Trade (Imports): Zl 340.2 trillion (machinery and transport equipment: 34.4%; chemicals: 17.5%; fuel and power: 12.6%; light-industrial products: 10.0%; food: 7.6%; from Germany: 28.0%; Italy: 7.8%; Russia: 6.8%; United Kingdom: 5.8%; United States: 5.1%; the Netherlands: 4.7%)

Foreign Trade (Exports): Zl 257.6 trillion (machinery and transport equipment: 25.8%; light industrial products: 15.3%; steel products: 14.6%; chemicals: 9.8%; fuel and power: 9.5%; food: 9.1%; to Germany: 36.3%; the Netherlands: 5.9%; Italy: 5.2%; Russia: 4.6%; United Kingdom: 4.3%)

Stock Exchanges: 1

Warsaw Stock Exchange (WSE; Gielda Papierów Wartosciowych)
ul. Nowy Swiat 6/12
Warsaw 00-400
Poland
Phone: (48-22) 628 3232
Fax: (48-22) 628 1754

Internet Address: www.fuw.edu.pl/gielda.eng

Trading Hours: Monday–Friday, 11:00 to 1:00

Office Hours: Monday–Friday, 9:00 to 5:00

Exchange Holidays:

1, 2 January	15 June
3, 10 April	11 November
1 May	24, 25 December

Listed Companies: 99

Total Market Capitalization:

At 31 December 1997

Local Currency (Millions)	US Dollars (Millions)
24,690	7,004

Major Sectors: Construction, manufacturing, wholesale/retail trade, finance insurance, real estate

Share Price Performance:

(% Change)

1995	22
1996	104
1997	34

History: Originating in 1817, the Warsaw Stock Exchange (WSE) reopened in April 1991 after a 52-year closure. When the exchange closed in 1939, it was trading more than 150 securities and accounted for more than 90% of the total trading on the six Polish exchanges of that time.

Political changes and a non-communist government began creating a capital market structure in 1989. The Act on Public Trading in Securities and Trust Funds was adopted in March 1991, and the Warsaw Stock Exchange joint stock company was established by the State Treasury in April 1991. Simultaneously, the Polish Securities Commission, with a chairman appointed by the Prime Minister, was activated.

The structure and legal regulation of the modern Polish capital market were patterned after the most modern and efficient systems used elsewhere in the world. After a comprehensive review of the world markets, a system based on the French capital market was adopted and implemented with much help from Societe des Bourse Francaises and the French Depository SICOVAM.

The WSE is presently the only securities exchange in Poland. It is a self-regulated organization, although all rules and statutes must have the approval of the Polish Securities Commission.

Classes of Securities: Common shares, warrants, corporate bonds, government securities

Indices: Warszawski Indeks Gieldowy, Wig (April 1991 = 1,000) indicates the average price change of securities traded on the Warsaw Stock Exchange.

Supervisory Organizations: Polish Securities Commission (PSC) supervises a self-regulated securities industry as well as the National Depository of Securities, banks, and brokerage firms.

Depository: The National Depository of Securities (NDS), managed by the Warsaw Stock Exchange

Settlement Details:

Shares: Trade date + 3 days (T + 3)
Book-entry for exchange traded shares.
Physical delivery for OTC is also available.
Receive and delivery versus payment is allowed.
Turnaround same day trades cannot be performed.

Investor Taxation: Dividends and interest suffer 30% withholding tax, which can be reduced if a tax treaty exists.

Trading:
Structure of the Equity Trading Market
• Three segments of the market with different listing requirements
Main Market—The official, regulated market that has the most rigorous listing requirements.
Parallel Market—Offers advantages of an official, regulated market to smaller and newer companies.

Free Market—A trading mechanism for companies not able to meet the listing requirements of the main or parallel markets.

- Single-price auction system of trading (call market)

- Specialist brokers ensure liquidity

- Settlement between members is completed through the National Securities Depository on a T + 3 and delivery versus payment basis

Trading on the Warsaw Stock Exchange is order-driven, centralized, and paperless. The system of trading for shares is as a call market or single-price auction (in French: *par casier* or in German: *einheitskurs*). Its main feature is that a single price per share emerges at the end of each session based on the orders submitted. During trading sessions, a key role is played by brokerage firms acting as specialists.

In the single-price auction system the specialist broker balances the market and ensures liquidity. Appointed by the issuer of the securities, with the approval of the stock exchange management board, a specialist broker helps to balance the market during the trading session by buying or selling from inventory and organizing additional trading after the daily price has been fixed. The latter is known as "extra-time trading" and is defined as the period during which balancing orders can be executed. The specialist/broker will also scale orders back, should one side of the market predominate.

Listing Requirements: Listing on the Warsaw Stock Exchange requires approval by the Polish Securities Commission. When granted, the company must then apply to the WSE Supervisory Board for admission to trading on the exchange. The following are listing criteria for the Warsaw Stock Exchange markets:

Main Market

- The value of shares to be admitted must be at least Zl 5 million and not less than the equivalent of 1.6 million ECU.

- The book value of the company must be at least Zl 9 million and not less than the equivalent of 3 million ECU.

- The value of the share capital of the company must be at least Zl 4.5 million and not less than the equivalent of 1.5 million ECU.

- Shares of at least Zl 4 million, and not less than the equivalent of 1.5 million ECU, must be distributed among small shareholders, defined as those who individually own no more than 5% of total number of votes.

- At least 25% of shares to be listed must be distributed among small shareholders.

- At least 500 shareholders must hold the shares to be admitted.

- The company must have registered pretax combined profits for the past three financial years of at least Zl 3 million, and not less than the equivalent of 1 million ECU.

Parallel Market

- The value of shares to be admitted must be at least Zl 1.2 million and not less than the equivalent of 350 thousand ECU.

- The book value of the company must be at least Zl 3 million and not less than the equivalent of 1 million ECU.

- The value of the share capital of the company must be at least Zl 1.5 million and not less than 0.5 million ECU.

- Shares of at least Zl 1.5 million, and not less than the equivalent of 0.5 million ECU, must be distributed among small shareholders.

- At least 10% of shares to be listed must be distributed among small shareholders.

- At least 300 shareholders must hold the shares to be admitted.

- The company must have registered a pretax profit for the last financial year.

- A financial report for the last year must be presented.

Free Market

- A company that does not meet requirements for listing on either the main or parallel market may be admitted to trading on the free market if the shares are admitted to public trading and their transferability is not limited. Statements of recommendation are required from two stock exchange member firms. Companies still have to be admitted to public trading by the Securities Commission after they present a prospectus.

Continuous Disclosure Obligations

All the companies admitted to public trading are subject to a continuing obligation to submit quarterly reports. Short reports on sales and earnings must be submitted monthly. Also, the company must immediately report all price-sensitive information to the Polish Securities Commission, the Warsaw Stock Exchange, and the Polish Press Agency (PAP).

Limitations: All cash transactions must be processed by a licensed Polish bank.

Interest repatriation requires a permit from National Bank of Poland and the Ministry of Finance.

Special investment permission is required for seaport management, real estate dealings, companies involved with defense, and finance companies.

Securities Lending: None

Brokerage Firms:

Central Brokerage Office of PKO
Warsaw
Poland
Phone: (48-22) 640 2840
Fax: (48-22) 640 2800

Brokerage Office of Bank Zachodni we Wroclawiu
Warsaw
Poland
Phone: (48-22) 442 296
Fax: (48-22) 442 954

Bank Brokerage House of PKO
Warsaw
Poland
Phone: (48-22) 661 7886
Fax: (48-22) 661 7880

Brokerage House of Powszechny Bank Gospodarczy
Warsaw
Poland
Phone: (48-22) 367 395
Fax: (48-22) 368 795

Brokerage Office of Bank Gdanski S.A.
Warsaw
Poland
Phone: (48-22) 379 912
Fax: (48-22) 379 913

Centrum Operacju Kapitalowych of Bank Handlowy
Warsaw
Poland
Phone: (48-22) 661 7125
Fax: (48-22) 625 6949

Warszawski Dom Maklerski
Warsaw
Poland
Phone: (48-22) 625 5794
Fax: (48-22) 625 4744

Brokerage Office of Kredyt Bank
Warsaw
Poland

Phone: (48-22) 614 5572
Fax: (48-22) 614 5562

Brokerage Office of Bank Gospodarki Zywnosciowej
Warsaw
Poland
Phone: (48-22) 291 939
Fax: (48-22) 297 858

Brokerage Office of Bank Depozytowo-Kredytowy w Lublinie
Warsaw
Poland
Phone: (48-22) 201 71
Fax: (48-22) 253 32

Brokerage Office of Bank Inicjatyw Gospodarczych BIG
Warsaw
Poland
Phone: (48-22) 693 6710
Fax: (48-22) 693 6714

Brokerage Office of Bank Przemyslowo-Handlowy
Warsaw
Poland
Phone: (48-22) 231 471
Fax: (48-22) 223 586

Brokerage House Criditanstalt Securities
Warsaw
Poland
Phone: (48-22) 630 6272
Fax: (48-22) 630 6268

Dom Maklerski DML Sp.
Warsaw
Poland
Phone: (48-22) 621 0370
Fax: (48-22) 621 0275

Brokerage House of Bank Amerykanski w Polsce
Warsaw
Poland
Phone: (48-22) 672 4769
Fax: (48-22) 372 4830

Citibrokerage Sp.
Warsaw
Poland
Phone: (48-22) 657 7870
Fax: (48-22) 657 7880

CS First Boston Polska
Warsaw
Poland
Phone: (48-22) 630 5656
Fax: (48-22) 630 6212

Polski Dom Maklerski
Warsaw
Poland
Phone: (48-22) 290 716
Fax: (48-22) 297 873

Inwestycyjny Dom Maklerski PBI
Warsaw
Poland
Phone: (48-22) 297 009
Fax: (48-22) 628 1868

Dom Maklerski "Penetrator"
Warsaw
Poland
Phone: (48-22) 215 444
Fax: (48-22) 225 072

Company Information:

The Best Performing Shares in the Country

Company Name	Share Price Change 1 January 1997 to 31 December 1997 (%)
Zywiec	123
Optimus	95
Jelfa	71
Kabelbfk	65
Polifarbc	40
Kredyt 'B'	38
Debica	34
Elektrim	31
Mostalexp	31
Okocim	30

The Largest Companies in the Country by Market Capitalization as of 31 December 1997

Company Name	Market Capitalization Local Currency (Millions)	Market Capitalization US Dollars (Millions)
Bank Handlowy	2,925	830
Kghm	2,600	738
Elektrim	2,281	647
Bph	1,896	538
Bsk	1,806	512
Pbk	1,598	453
Bre	1,387	393
Wbk	1,218	346
Debica	1,187	337
Wedel	1,078	306
Zywiec	888	252
Celuloza	885	251
Agros Holding	803	228
Kabelbfk	756	214
Stomil Olsztyn	735	209
Polifarbc	689	195
Orbis Sa	668	189
Gorazdze	644	183
Optimus	603	171
B I G	564	160
Kety	540	153
Jelfa	530	150
Okocim	528	150
Amica	524	149
Grajewo	434	123
Mostalexp	409	116
Polifarbw Susp - 25/09/97	380	108
Kredyt 'B'	365	103

Regional Exchange:
 OTC Market

Other Investment Information:
Ministry of Privatization
ul. Krucza 36
00-525 Warsaw
Poland
Phone: (48-22) 628 0281
Fax: (48-22) 625 1114

Ministry of Industry and Trade
ul. Wspo'lna 4
00-921 Warsaw
Poland
Phone: (48-22) 210 351
Fax: (48-22) 212 550

Ministry of Environmental Protection, Natural
 Resources and Forestry
ul. Wawelska 52/54
00-922 Warsaw
Poland
Phone: (48-22) 250 001, 254 001
Fax: (48-22) 253 335, 253 972

National Bank of Poland
ul. Swietokrzyska 11/12
00-950 Warsaw
Poland
Phone: (48-22) 200 321
Fax: (48-22) 269 95

Polish Chamber of Commerce
Promotion Center
ul. Trebacka 4
00-074 Warsaw
Poland
Phone: (48-22) 260 221, 267 376
Fax: (48-22) 2274 673, 6355 137

PONZI SCHEME

Originating in the 1920s and named for its creator, a *Ponzi Scheme* refers to an illegal trading practice.

Charles Ponzi originated a currency trading scheme in order to make money based on arbitrage situations on foreign currency. Unfortunately, the money he collected from investors was never invested. Instead, Ponzi used the money from new investors to pay out large sums to earlier investors until the process became too large to manage.

Ponzi schemes are also known as pyramids, because of their tendency to build large sums of cash, based on new money coming into the scheme. Although early investors get some money in return, it usually encourages them to invest higher amounts, and eventually everyone sustains losses.

All such schemes are illegal in the United States, but they crop up in various formats from time to time. Sometimes the perpetrators escape with the funds before they can be prosecuted. A variation of the Ponzi scheme recently appeared in Albania.

See also NATIONAL ASSOCIATION OF SECURITIES DEALERS (NASD); SECURITIES AND EXCHANGE COMMISSION (SEC).

POOL

A *Pool* refers to any group of investors joining funds for purposes of buying shares of a company or group of companies.

A pool might be an investment group in which contributions are made on a regular basis to invest in shares, or it could be a group of large net-worth individuals pooling funds to accomplish a corporate takeover.

Pooling is legal as long as it does not involve the control of market competition or the manipulation of prices, and as long as securities laws are not violated.

See also INVESTMENT CLUB; LEVERAGED BUYOUT (LBO); TAKEOVER/TAKEOVER BID.

POOLING OF INTERESTS

Pooling of Interests is an accounting method that can be employed when two businesses join together.

The pooling of interests is accomplished through an exchange of common shares and accounted for on a book value basis. The concept recognizes the facts that common shareholders continue as holders of the combined company and that the transaction is a merger rather than an acquisition.

The book value of the assets and the equities of the combined enterprises are added together. The combining corporation makes a record of the assets and liabilities received.

The following criteria, designed to assure a continuity of ownership, are used when assessing whether the deal represents a pooling of interests:

Attributes of combining companies:

1. Each company is autonomous and has not been a subsidiary or division of another within two years prior to the plan of combination.

Manner of combining interests:

1. The combination is done with a single transaction and completed in accordance with a specific plan within one year after initiation.
2. The corporation issues only common shares, with rights identical to those of the majority of its outstanding voting common stock, in exchange for substantially all the voting common shares of another company at the date the plan of combination is consummated.
3. Neither of the combining companies changes the equity interest of the voting common shares either within two years before the plan of combination is initiated or between the dates the combination is initiated and consummated.
4. Each of the combining companies reacquires shares of voting common shares only for purposes other than business combinations.
5. The ratio of the interest of an individual common shareholder to those of other common shareholders in a combining company remains the same, as a result of the exchange of shares to effect the combination.

See also ACQUISITION; MERGER; TAKEOVER/TAKEOVER BID.

Charles Ponzi after receiving his sentence. *(UPI/Corbis-Bettmann)*

PORTAFOGLIO TITOLI (Italy)

See PORTFOLIO.

PORTARE (Italy)

See BEARER CERTIFICATE/SECURITY/SHARE.

PORTFEUILLE (France)

See PORTFOLIO.

PORTFOLIO

A *Portfolio* is a list of the total investment holdings of an individual or institution, including items such as shares of companies, bonds, commodities, real estate investments, cash equivalents, and other marketable assets. Most hard assets, such as metals, gems, and art works, are usually excluded.

See also ASSET; MONEY MARKET; MUTUAL FUND.

PORTFOLIO MANAGER

A professional investment manager for an institution, a *Portfolio Manager* administers the strategy of a securities portfolio. Portfolio managers work for investment companies, mutual funds, pension funds, insurance companies, corporations, investment advisers, or any other company directly involved with market investing.

Portfolio managers are also called money managers or investment counsels. Their strategies are set by the fund they manage, the company they work for, or their own objectives. As a group they tend to be aggressive investors and seldom, if ever, hold cash for more than a few days. Many are required to be totally invested, only keeping enough cash on hand for basic maintenance needs.

See also MUTUAL FUND; PORTFOLIO; UNIT INVESTMENT TRUST/UNIT TRUST.

PORTFOLIO THEORY

Portfolio Theory allows an investor to classify, project, and monitor the expected risk and return of investments. It is often referred to as modern portfolio theory (MPT), especially since the 1952 publication of Harry Markowitz's paper "Portfolio Selection." Markowitz shared the 1990 Nobel Prize for Economics with Merton Miller and William Sharpe, with whom he further developed the theory of portfolio selection and corporate finance.

The theory recognizes that different investors will have different utilities in regard to rates of return and different tolerances for risk. Its objective is to identify the most efficient group of securities at a given time that produces the maximum expected return for a given level of risk and the minimum level of risk for a given expected return. Risk refers to the chance that the actual rate of return on an asset will differ from the expected rate of return. Often, a reward-to-risk ratio is computed, and some market analysts track thousands of stocks according to this measure. To protect against excessive risk, an efficient portfolio is diversified.

Avoidance of risk must always be weighed against the rate of return, which will tend to be diluted as an increasing number of different assets are included in an investment portfolio. The methods of evaluation and control of risk may be altered depending on market conditions, as for example in Japan following the speculative bubble of the late 1980s when stocks were overpriced and sometimes manipulated by security houses. In addition, in analyzing the price movements of a particular asset, a further distinction is made between securities whose movements are largely independent of those of the market as a whole, and those whose movements tend to be in phase with those of the market.

While there are many detailed and highly quantifiable factors that may be considered in evaluating portfolios—some of which will be summarized here—it is important to note that in one study of a number of U.S. pension fund managers, more than 90% of the difference in performance was found to be the result of the mix of assets in stocks, bonds, or cash. This particular study stressed that the timing of investments was not such an important factor. Most analysts would disagree with this idea, pointing to periods such as 1980–82 when stocks in high technology, defense, oil, and oil service became highly overpriced, then later in that period became underpriced. In fact, some investors use formula plans, utilizing programs that provide an automatic device for timing buy-and-sell decisions.

However, placing emphasis on the kinds of holdings—stocks, bonds, or cash—serves as a verification of a major tenet of portfolio theory going back to at least the 1930s. Investment plans would be weighted partly toward common stocks and partly toward bonds and high-grade preferred stocks. The former were considered the aggressive part of the portfolio, whose price would move with the general movement of stock prices, thus providing profits when the market is on the rise. The latter were considered the defensive part of the portfolio, designed to protect the investor against a decline in stock prices. In a fixed ratio plan, the relative weight between these two types of investments was held constant; in a variable ratio plan, it might typically range from 35% to 65% for either type. The third element mentioned above, cash, would be held in reserve to allow the investor to take advantage of new investment opportunities.

In addition to this balancing of stocks, bonds, and cash in an investment plan, a number of other considerations enter into the design of a diversified portfolio. These include buying issues in a mix of industries and in a mix of companies, spreading investments over a wide geographic area (including internationally), investing in emerging and pre-emerging markets, buying issues of companies with diversified products, timing purchases over different periods of the stock cycle, and selecting bonds with different maturity dates.

More generally, in arriving at an ideal portfolio, each investment must be scrutinized from a number of standpoints. The following listing is adapted from *The Stock Market*, 6th edition, by Richard Teweles, Edward Bradley, and Ted Teweles:

1. Safe principal—the original investment is safe, including against inflation
2. Safe income
3. Stable income—a constant flow of income, with constant purchasing power
4. Maximum income
5. Acceptable maturity
6. Acceptable denomination
7. Potential appreciation—the potential for future growth
8. Freedom from management cares
9. Freedom from taxation
10. Marketability or liquidity
11. Noncallable—the issuer cannot deprive the investor of his or her ideal investment
12. Convertible—the investor can convert preferred stock or bond into common stock whenever that is profitable
13. Low commissions
14. Strong issuer—a growth company, long established, with good finances and management

MPT, which endeavors to make a precise mathematical assessment of the merits of different investment mixes, is based on a number of assumptions about the stock market and investor preferences. First, it is assumed that the market is efficient, that is, that everything is known or knowable about each stock. While this is akin to the classical economic theory of the market, it contrasts with traditional, or fundamental, stock market analysis, which assumes market inefficiency, meaning that an investor can achieve a rate of return superior to that of the general market return rate by purchasing undervalued securities and selling overvalued ones.

Second, issues that offer higher rates of return generally entail higher risks. Third, investors prefer higher returns (although with a declining marginal utility as the returns get higher), but they also prefer lower risks. The implication is that if there is to be successful portfolio management, analysts must be able to identify securities that are exceptions to the general rule stated in the second assumption and that have both a relatively high return rate and a relatively low risk (that is, a low standard deviation of their return rate). In addition, once a set of securities is selected, their relative weight—how much is invested in each—can be adjusted to optimize the mix of expected return and risk.

Fourth, risk is a function not only of the properties of each particular issue, but also of the degree of correlation of these issues' price movements. The rationale for diversification (by industry, by company, by location, by time of investment, according to the aggressive/defensive dimension, and so forth) flows directly from this concern to have a set of investments that will not all rise—or fall—together. Specifically, in MPT, the aim is to acquire a set of securities that are negatively correlated or have a low positive correlation, and to avoid a portfolio whose components' price movements have high positive correlations.

Interestingly, although MPT starts off with the assumption of an efficient market and some think this leads to the conclusion that the market "cannot be beaten," it is possible to achieve an above-market rate of return through the proper selection of securities. In one study of an application of Markowitz's principles, the investor achieved a rate of return 2% better than that of the market as a whole. Clearly, there are time lags, and not all investors are applying MPT or applying it equally well.

Of course, different investors' assessments of acceptable return and risk will vary. Technically, MPT speaks of an investor's "indifference curve" on a graph of return against risk; each point on the curve is equally acceptable to the investor, while constituting a different mix of return and risk. Typically, investors will differ in age, marital status and family responsibilities, health, personal habits, willingness to accept risks, and so forth. Given their different needs and preferences, investors may choose either an income portfolio, which offers more immediate, steady, and reliable income, or they may choose a growth portfolio, which offers a higher rate of return in the longer run but lower dividend payouts.

See also FUNDAMENTAL ANALYSIS; RISK/REWARD RATIO; STOCK MARKET EFFICIENCY THEORY.

PORTUGAL, REPUBLIC OF

Portugal (Republica Portuguesa) is a country lying along the Atlantic coast of the Iberian Peninsula in southwestern Europe. It is bordered on the east and the north by Spain.

Area: 35,672 square miles (92,389 square km)

Population: 9,906,000 (34.8% urban; 65.2% rural)

Form of Government: Parliamentary state, with one legislative house: Assembly of the Republic—230 members. Chief of state: President. Head of government: Prime Minister.

Official Language: Portuguese

Capital: Lisbon

Largest Cities: Lisbon, 681,063; Porto, 309,485; Vila Nova de Gaia, 247,499; Amadora, 176,137

Economy:

Currency: Portuguese Escudo (Esc)

National Budget: Revenue—Esc 5.6 trillion; expenditures—Esc 6.4 trillion (education: 12.4%; health: 9.8%; defense: 6.6%; administration: 5.3%; public works: 2.8%)

Public Debt: US$39.9 billion

Gross National Product: US$77.7 billion

Principal Products: Fruits and vegetables; livestock; textiles and clothes; machinery

Foreign Trade (Imports): Esc 3.9 billion (machinery and transport equipment: 35.7%, of which road vehicles and parts: 15.1%; food and live animals: 13.8%; mineral fuels: 8.8%; chemicals and chemical products: 7.9%; textiles: 7.1%; office machines: 2.4%; from Spain: 17.8%; Germany: 15.0%; France: 12.7%; Italy: 8.7%; United Kingdom: 7.4%; The Netherlands: 4.9%)

Foreign Trade (Exports): Esc 2.5 billion (textiles and wearing apparel: 28.4%; machinery and transport equipment: 21.3%, of which transport equipment: 6.5%; footwear: 9.6%; cork and wood products: 5.5%; chemicals and chemical products: 3.3%; to Germany: 19.6%; France: 15.2%; Spain: 14.4%; United Kingdom: 11.4%)

Stock Exchanges: 2

Stock Exchange of Lisboa (LSE; Bolsa de Valores de Lisboa; BVL)

Edificio da Bolsa
Rua Soeiro Pereira Gomes
1600 Lisbon
Portugal

Phone: (351-1) 790-99-04, 795-20-31

Fax: (351-1) 795-20-21, 795-20-24

Internet Address: www.bvl.pt

Trading Hours: Monday–Friday

Market With Official Quotations:
  Continuous: (TRADIS system) National Trading System

Automated System Pre-Opening	9:30 to 10:00
Open-Outcry + Automated System	10:00 to 1:00
Automated System	1:00 to 3:00

  Two Daily Fixing (Automated System / general rule)
  (Separate Trading Floor) (1) (2)

Automated System (1st Fixing)	9:30 to 10:30
Open-Outcry (2nd Fixing)	11:00 to 1:00 & 2:00 to 4:00

  Two Daily Fixing Open-Outcry (4)

1st Fixing	10:30 to 1:00
2nd Fixing	2:00 to 4:00

Second Market: (Separate Trading Floors) (2)
  Continuous:

Automated System Pre-Opening	9:30 to 1:30
Open Outcry	10:30 to 12:00

Market Without Quotations: (Separate Trading Floors) (Exception 3)
  Two Daily Fixing

Automated System (1st Fixing)	9:30 to 1:30
Open-Outcry (2nd Fixing)	11:00 to 1:00

(1) Securities not yet integrated in the National Trading System.

(2) One in Lisbon Stock Exchange and the other in Oporto Stock Exchange.

(3) Rights are traded through the system applied to the securities from which they are detached.

(4) According to the Lisbon Stock Exchange Association Circular no. 2/92, the 20 most liquid securities selected among bonds and participation bonds listed on the Market With Official Quotations and traded through the separate trading floors, are weekly selected to be traded through two open-outcry fixings.

Office Hours: Monday–Friday, 9:00 to 5:00

Exchange Holidays:

1 January	10, 11 June
24 February	5 October
10, 13 April	1, 24, 25 December
1 May	

Listed Companies: 78

Total Market Capitalization:

At 31 December 1997

Local Currency (Millions)	US Dollars (Millions)
9,156,685	49,807

Major Sectors: Banking and financial, metal products, machinery and equipment, insurance, foodstuffs, beverages and tobacco, retail trade

Share Price Performance:

(% Change)

1992	2
1993	68
1994	9
1995	30
1996	59
1997	121

Classes of Securities: Common shares (both bearer and registered) corporate fixed income securities, government fixed income securities, convertible securities, and warrants. Derivatives are traded on the Oporto Exchange.

Indices:

BVL Index—General (5 January 1988 = 1,000)

BVL 30 Index (4 January 1993 = 1,000)

BVL—INC National Continuous Index (16 September 1991 = 1,000)

BVL—Sector Indices (5 January 1988 = 1,000)
food, paper, chemicals, metal products, construction, banks, real estate Op.

BVL—ORF Index (fixed income)

BTA Index (1977 = 100)

Supervisory Organizations:

The Banco de Portugal (Central Bank) regulates currency movement.

The Commissao de Mercado de Valores Mobiliarios (C.M.V.M.) oversees the capital markets.

The Instituto do Comercio Externo de Portugal

Depository: The Central Depository (The Central de Valores Mobilarios)

Settlement Details:

Shares:

Trade date + 3 days

Physical and book-entry (fungible bearer shares only)

Receive or delivery versus payment is allowed.

Turnaround trades can be done on the continuous market or by using a combination of the exchange and OTC.

Trading: The 1991 reforms of the Portuguese securities market created three segments within the stock market: the Market with Official Quotations, the Second Market, and the Market without Quotations.

The Second Market is intended for securities issued by small- to medium-sized companies and has entry requirements that are easier to meet than the stipulations imposed by the Market with Official Quotations. The regulations for minimum capital, reserves, and dispersion of capital are less stringent than for the Official Market. These advantages can be important for new, small, and medium-sized companies or larger companies wishing to disperse a small part of their capital. A single full year of activity is adequate for a company's admission to the Second Market.

The Market without Quotations includes securities that have not fulfilled the listing requirements of the other two markets.

With the new Securities Act, a nationwide continuous trading system was implemented in September of 1991 and started trading with issues from three companies. By the end of 1994, nearly 50 securities were being traded. In the near future, all securities listed on the Market with Official Quotations will be traded in this continuous system.

Currently, securities listed on the Market with Official Quotations not traded on the continuous system, and all securities listed on the Market without Quotations, may have two daily prices—one on the computer system and another on the open-outcry system. The securities listed on the Second Market are traded on a continuous open-outcry system.

Listing Requirements: The following securities may be traded on the Lisbon Stock Exchange:

• National and foreign public funds and all similar securities

• Shares and bonds, including cash certificates, issued by domestic or foreign companies and other entities

• Participation bonds

• Closed-end investment fund units

• Other securities considered tradable on the stock exchange by legal provision, by ministerial order of the Finance Minister

• Rights attaching to the securities mentioned in the previous items or constituted on them and likely to be traded autonomously

The designation of public funds includes:

• Securities representing the domestic public debt

• Securities issued by public institutes and public funds

• Securities issued by the Portuguese Autonomous Regions and local municipalities

• Any other national securities legally classified as public funds

• Securities issued by foreign public bodies and other foreign entities, whenever similar to those mentioned in the previous items

Those securities issued by any companies or other entities with unconditional and joint guarantee of the Portuguese State or of a foreign state are considered similar to national or foreign public funds, respectively. Those bonds and other debt securities issued by international organizations of public status or international financial institutions included on a list to be established in a ministerial order of the Finance Minister, after consultation with the Bank of Portugal and the C.M.V.M., may also be admitted to listing under the same conditions as public and similar funds. The securities issued by those entities not included on the list contained in the ministerial order will be admitted to listing under the general conditions.

Any issuer to the Lisbon Stock Exchange must comply with the following rules:

• Appoint a representative to be directly responsible for the company's relations with the securities market, except in the case of securities representing the national public debt. The representative must be a member of the board of directors or a manager.

• The securities to be admitted to listing must comply with the conditions required for trading on the stock exchange, namely to be fully paid, free from any pledges or charges, or any limitations in relation to the rights attached to them or to their transferability.

• The characteristics and legal situation of the securities must be in accordance with the applicable legal, regular, or statutory provisions.

Admission to each of the three segments of the Lisbon Stock Exchange requires compliance with some specific requirements.

Market with Official Quotations

Admissions to this market are the responsibility of both stock exchanges and must be approved by the C.M.V.M. Securities issued by the Portuguese State or by other states have a special statute, being admitted by decision of the Finance Ministry.

Admission to Listing Requirements:

• The issuer must have at least two full years of activity.

• The issuer must have regularly published their annual reports and accounts, at least for the three financial years preceding the request for admission.

• It must be proved that the company has a sound economic and financial situation.

• The request for admission must encompass all the shares of the same class already admitted.

• At least 25% of the share capital or 500,000 shares must be in public hands, so as to guarantee sufficient liquidity for the shares to be admitted.

• The issuer must have capital and reserves of 500 million escudos or an estimated stock capitalization to that amount.

Securities issued by foreign entities, others than public or similar funds, can only be admitted to listing if they meet all the requirements applicable to the admission of domestic securities of the same nature.

Request for Listing Admission: The application for admission to the Market with Official Quotations must be submitted by the interested company to the Stock Exchange Associations. It can be presented either in Lisbon Stock Exchange or in the Oporto Stock Exchange and must contain the following:

• A summary description of the issuer, line of business, economic, financial situation, profits, and losses

• A certified copy of the minutes or decisions of the company's governing bodies approving the issue, in accordance with the applicable legal and statutory provisions

• An updated copy of the issuing company's statutes or of its internal rules and regulations

• The date of incorporation of the issuer

• The amount of share capital

• The identification of all the members of the governing bodies and authorized signatories

• Annual reports and accounts, reports of the supervisory board and of the financial auditors for the past three financial years or, in the case of companies existing for less than three years, for the last completed financial years

• Original specimen of the certificates representing the securities to be admitted

• Auditors' report on the company's economic and financial situation, not required whenever the reports of the official financial auditor certify that the company's activity, management, accounts, economic, and financial situation meet the required standards

• Prospectus for admission to listing, drawn up in accordance with the provisions of Regulation no. 91/7 of the C.M.V.M.

• All other data that may become necessary to verify that all legal conditions for admission to listing, namely public dispersion of capital, have been complied with

After submission of the request for admission to listing, the stock exchanges analyze the information and make a decision, which must be ratified by the C.M.V.M. within 30 days. After this ratification, the admission is subordinated to the publication of a prospectus and an advertisement in the official stock exchange journal of each one of the two stock exchanges. The admission is in full force and effective 8 working days after the date of the publication of the said advertisement.

Prospectus: The prospectus is an essential element in the admission procedure. It must be drawn up in accordance with the provisions of Regulation no. 91/7 of the C.M.V.M. and must contain the following chapters:

- Preliminary information
- Notices to investors
- Information concerning those responsible for listing particulars
- Information concerning the securities for the admission of which application is being made
- Identification and description of the issuer
- Information concerning the issuer's activity
- Information concerning the issuer's assets, liabilities, financial position, profits, and losses
- Information concerning issuer's estimates for the near future
- Report of the auditor
- Economic and financial viability study
- Liquidity contract

The competent authorities may waive the issuer from publishing the prospectus under the following circumstances:

- Shares allotted free of charge to holders of already listed shares of the same issue;
- Shares resulting from the conversion of convertible bonds, or from the exercise of the right to subscribe shares by the holders of bonds or any other securities conferring that right, if the previously issued shares are already listed on the same stock exchange;

Any prospectus published within a six-month period prior to a request for admission is acceptable, since the changes occurring in the meanwhile are introduced. The prospectus must be published as a brochure and made available to the public, free of charge, at the issuer's head offices, at the offices of the financial organizations selected to act as paying agents, and at the stock exchanges. In addition to this publication, an advertisement must be published in the official stock exchange journals announcing the publication of the prospectus and where it can be obtained.

Duties of Admission: Listed companies must:

- Assure all payments inherent in their securities;
- Provide the C.M.V.M. and the stock exchanges with general information, such as extracts from the minutes of general meetings, changes in the social contract, any other information considered relevant, and all publications made available to the public by the issuer or on behalf of the issuer;
- Publish annual and interim reports and accounts, accompanied by their legal certification, reports of the auditors, and extract from the minute of approval of the accounts concerning the profit allocation approved by the general meeting;
- Inform the public of any exceptional events affecting its activity, changes in managing bodies, acquisition or alienation of major capital holdings, and voting rights attributed to those capital holdings;
- Provide reasonable information to the holders of listed securities, by means of publications, within the legal periods, of all events concerning the issuer or the listed securities.

Second Market: Admission to the Second Market is the sole responsibility of the stock exchange to which the application is submitted. The exchange will report its decision to the C.M.V.M. The shares representing the share capital of a company may be admitted to listing on the Second Market provided they meet the following:

- The issuer must have at least one full year of activity.
- The issuer must have regularly published their annual reports and accounts for the two financial years preceding the request for admission.
- It must be proved that the company has an accurate economic and financial situation.
- The request for admission must encompass all the shares of the same class already admitted.
- At least 10% of the share capital must be in public hands.
- The issuer company must have capital and reserves of 125 million escudos or an estimated stock capitalization to that amount.

The new Securities Act also envisages a "conditional admission" to the Second Market. There are some companies that comply with all the conditions to be admitted to the Second Market except the required dispersion of capital. Companies in this situation are conditionally allowed to be listed on the Second Market provided they sign a contract for dispersion of capital with an authorized financial intermediary.

Three years after the definitive admission of the securities to the Second Market, the board of directors of the Stock Exchange Association where they are listed will analyze their market performance and consider a transfer to the Market with Official Quotations. The transfer may be applied for by the issuer or officially decided by the Stock Exchange Association after prior consultation with the issuer. The transfer to the Market with Official Quotations may take place sooner if the issuing company fulfills the requirements.

The admission of securities to listing on the Second Market is subject to an application to be submitted by the interested company to the stock exchange where it wishes to be listed. The said application must contain, with the necessary adaptations, the information requested for admission to the Market with Official Quotations.

Prospectus: The prospectus on admission to listing on the Second Market is simpler than the one required for the Market with Official Quotation, but must contain the information provided for by Regulation no. 91/7 of the C.M.V.M. with the necessary modifications.

In a "conditional admission" the prospectus must also:

• State the procedures to be adopted in the sale of shares for dispersion of the company's capital, identify the financial intermediary or intermediaries in charge of such sale, and transcribe the relevant conditions included in the contract established between the company and the financial intermediary;

• Indicate the fixed or minimum price at which the shares will be sold and the basis for that price;

• Emphasize that the admission is conditional and the requirements it must meet to become effective;

• Include all other information demanded by C.M.V.M.'s regulations or deemed necessary by the Stock Exchange Association to ensure the protection of investors' interests.

The prospectus for conditional admission must be published at least 15 days before the date on which the sale of the shares on the Market without Quotations is scheduled to begin.

As in the case of admission to the Market with Official Quotations, in the situation of a normal admission to the Second Market, the competent authorities may waive the issuer from publishing the prospectus. Whenever the issuer has published a complete prospectus in the six months preceding the request for admission, that prospectus may be used with the inclusion of any material changes that have occurred.

The prospectus must be published as a brochure made available to the public, free of charge, at the issuer's head offices, at the offices of the financial organizations chosen to act as paying agents, and at the stock exchange. In addition to this publication, an advertisement must be published in the Official Stock Exchange Journal giving information on how the prospectus was published and where it can be obtained. The admission will become effective within eight working days after the referred publication.

Duties of Admission:

• The issuers of securities listed on the Second Market have the same duties as the issuers of securities listed on the Market with Official Quotations, although some of the requirements to publish information are less onerous.

• The issuer of securities listed on the Second Market must publish, among other information, annual and semi-annual statements of accounts and the corresponding legal certification, so as to keep the market informed of the evolution of its activity.

Market without Quotations: Requirements for listing on this market are less rigorous than those imposed on the other two markets, with regard to admission, maintenance, and information. In fact, to be admitted to listing the issuer only needs to be incorporated and operating in accordance with the applicable legislation. There are no requirements concerning minimum capital dispersion nor economic and financial situation.

As regards the maintenance of listing on the Market without Quotations, issuers must apply for admission of securities for a limited period of time. In this case, they will not have to pay the admission fee. Furthermore, they may also require exclusion of their securities from trading, stating the reasons for such a request.

The requirements concerning information are much simpler than those imposed on the other two markets. However, a level of information is required from issuers sufficient to keep the market reasonably informed about issuers and relative securities.

The following securities may be traded on this market:

• Rights attaching to or constituted on securities listed on the Market with Official Quotations or on the Second Market or traded autonomously on the Market without Quotations;

- Securities excluded or suspended from listing on the Market with Official Quotations or on the Second Market;
- Any other securities, trading of which is specifically required.

Admission to Trading: Rights are automatically tradable on the Market without Quotations. Subscription rights are traded in a period commencing on the date from which they may be exercised and ending the fifth working day before the deadline for such exercise. In the case of incorporation rights, this deadline is the 30th day.

The securities suspended or excluded from the Market with Official Quotations or the Second Market may be traded on the Market without Quotations, respectively, of both or of only one of the stock exchanges for a period and in the conditions established by the board of directors of the corresponding Stock Exchange Associations. The issuers of securities admitted to listing for a limited period may request its conversion into a definitive listing before expiration of the initial deadline. If this request is not made before expiration of the trading period, the admission of the same securities to trading can only be applied for 180 days later.

The decision to admit securities to trading on the Market without Quotations of the Lisbon Stock Exchange is made by the board of directors of the Lisbon Stock Exchange Association, without need for approval by the C.M.V.M. The decision to admit securities to trading on Market without Quotations of the Lisbon Stock Exchange must be made public by a notice officially published in the Official Stock Exchange Journal. The admission to trading becomes effective only eight days after publication of the referred notice. The notice must state the date of the stock exchange session in which the securities will begin to be traded.

Duties of Admission: All companies with securities admitted to trading for an unlimited period of time on the Market without Quotations must publish annual reports and accounts. This must be accompanied by their legal certification, board of auditors' report, official auditors' report, and extract from the minutes of approval of the accounts concerning the profit allocation approved in the general meeting.

Issuers must also provide general information, in particular relating to the acquisition and alienation of major capital holdings. Companies with securities admitted to trading for a limited period of time are waived from these obligations, except in cases in which the deadline for compliance with these obliga-

tions falls within the period in which they are admitted to trading.

When the admission of securities to trading on the Market without Quotations results from their suspension from the Market with Official Quotations or the Second Market, the issuer must comply throughout the suspension period with all the provisions regarding information to which it was subject before the suspension.

Investor Taxation:
Dividends are taxed at 20%.
There is no capital gains tax for long-term share holdings.
OTC transactions carry a stamp duty charge.
Transaction fees of .40 to .50 per MIL are charged by the stock exchange for some securities.
A stock exchange tax of .05% is charged on all off exchange trades.
Double taxation treaties with Portugal can allow investors to reclaim taxes withheld at the source.

Limitations:
Foreign investors must have a local cash account for capital market transaction.
Overdrafts and cash loans are prohibited.
Approval from the Central Bank is required for primary market transactions.
Foreign ownership of utilities and communications is prohibited.
No foreign ownership restrictions are imposed by the government, but individual companies can set limits.

Securities Lending: Available

Brokerage Firms:
CFI
Rua Braancamp, 52 - 5° Esq.
1200 Lisbon
Portugal
Phone: (351-1) 315-57-70/1/2
Fax: (351-1) 352-90-47

Douro
Rua Rodrigo Sampaio, 170 - 2°
1100 Lisbon
Portugal
Phone: (351-1) 352-23-45/46
Fax: (351-1) 352-23-39

Finantia Corretora
Av. dos Combatentes, Torre 1, Lote H -1ª
1100 Lisbon
Portugal

Phone: (351-1) 726-75-40
Fax: (351-1) 726-53-10

Midas Corretora
Roa do Comercio, 14 r/c
1100 Lisbon
Portugal
Phone: (351-1) 888-44-54
Fax: (351-1) 863-69-6

Titulo
Avenida da Republica, 60 - 9°
1000 Lisbon
Portugal
Phone: (351-1) 793-74-24
Fax: (351-1) 793-72-67

Pars
Av. da Boavista, 3521, 3°, Sala 302
Porto
Portugal
Phone: (351-2) 610-41-67
Fax: (351-2) 610-41-64

Fincor
Rua Braamcamp, 9-7°
1200 Lisbon
Portugal
Phone: (351-1) 315-58-99
Fax: (351-1) 540-91-9

Ascor Dealer
Rua do Ouro, 95, - 1°e 2°
1100 Lisbon
Portugal
Phone: (351-1) 347-82-87
Fax: (351-1) 347-82-80

BSN Dealer
Av. Eng° Duarte Pacheco, Torre 1 - 6° - Sala 1
1000 Lisbon
Portugal
Phone: (351-1) 387-71-35
Fax: (351-1) 387-70-19

Comercial Dealer
Avenida Jose Malhoa, Lote 1686 - 3°
1000 Lisbon
Portugal
Phone: (351-1) 727-01-10, 727-02-78
Fax: (351-1) 727-09-76

Corretora Atlantico

Avenida Jose Malhoa, Lote 1686 -3°
1000 Lisbon
Portugal
Phone: (351-1) 793-28-62, 727-02-78
Fax: (351-1) 727-09-76

Eser
Rua de Sao Juliao, 30
1100 Lisbon
Portugal
Phone: (351-1) 888-53-33
Fax: (351-1) 863-27-8

NCO Dealer
Rua Barata Salgueiro, 33 - 2°
1200 Lisbon
Portugal
Phone: (351-1) 352-15-60
Fax: (351-1) 352-49-17

BFE Dealer
Av. General Firmino Miguel, 3 - 6°
1600 Lisbon
Portugal
Phone: (351-1) 727-21-63
Fax: (351-1) 727-20-58

Central de Investimentos
Rua Castilho, 233 - 4°
1070 Lisbon
Portugal

Sofin
Av. Eng° Duarte Pacheco, Torre 1,8°Salas 9, 10, 11
1000 Lisbon
Portugal
Phone: (351-1) 387-15-27
Fax: (351-1) 651-74-6

Tottadealer
Avenida da Republica, 64 - 1°
1000 Lisbon
Portugal
Phone: (351-1) 793-91-32, 793-90-66
Fax: (351-1) 796-48-71

M. Valores
Avenida 24 de Julho, 50
1200 Lisbon
Portugal
Phone: (351-1) 395-38-86
Fax: (351-1) 395-39-16

BBV Interactivos (Portugal)
Avenida da Liberdade, 222 - 6°
1200 Lisbon
Portugal
Phone: (351-1) 311-72-58, 311-74-92
Fax: (351-1) 311-75-84

Company Information:

The Best Performing Shares in the Country

Company Name	Share Price Change 1 January 1997 to 31 December 1997 (%)
Sonae Industria	165
Bnc.Pinto & Sotto Mayor	147
Bpi-Sgps	132
Mundial Confianca R	116
Bcp R	102
Bnc.Espr.Santo (Bescl)R	101
Telecel	98
Portugal Telecom 'B'	93
Cin	92
Inapa	89
Jeronimo Martins	83
Atlantis Cristais De Alcobaua	75
Semapa	61
Banco Essi	56
Modelo Continente	56
Somague Sgps	56
Banco Mello	55
Sonae Investimento	52
Atlantis Cristais De Alcobaua Pref.	45
Cimpor	45
Salvador Caetano	42
Credito Predial	39
Seguros Imperio	36
Tranquilidade	33

The Largest Companies in the Country by Market Capitalization as of 31 December 1997

Company Name	Market Capitalization Local Currency (Millions)	Market Capitalization US Dollars (Millions)
Electricidad De Portugal	2,090,999	11,374
Portugal Telecom 'B'	1,622,599	8,826
Bcp R	564,600	3,071
Bnc.Espr.Santo (Bescl)R	478,504	2,603
Telecel	421,615	2,293
Cimpor	405,216	2,204
Jeronimo Martins	399,766	2,174

Company Name	Market Capitalization Local Currency (Millions)	Market Capitalization US Dollars (Millions)
Brisa-Auto Estradas Priv	354,875	1,930
Bpi-Sgps	348,817	1,897
Modelo Continente	302,940	1,648
Sonae Investimento	297,760	1,620
Bnc.Prtg.Atlantico	279,400	1,520
Bnc.Pinto & Sotto Mayor	271,405	1,476
Bnc.Totta Acores R	216,840	1,179
Soporcel	169,395	921
Mundial Confianca R	162,810	886
Banco Mello	115,566	629
Semapa	106,142	577
Inparsa	99,742	543
Portucel Industrial	97,701	531
Tranquilidade	83,980	457
Sonae Imobilaria	83,662	455
Credito Predial	58,212	317
Seguros Imperio	56,647	308
Sonae Industria	53,734	292
Unicer R	50,700	276
Cin	40,565	221
Inapa	38,700	211
Banif R	31,950	174
Corticeira Amorim	31,460	171
Colep Portugal	30,155	164
Salvador Caetano	29,323	160
Somague Sgps	27,585	150
Engil Sgps	26,096	142
Banco Essi	22,660	123
Mundicenter	19,325	105
Mague	18,908	103
B A Barbosa & Almeida	17,880	97
Centralcer	17,585	96
Mota & Cia.	17,520	95
Madeirense Tabacos	16,425	89
Imperio Imobilario	16,200	88
Soares Da Costa	15,488	84
Efacec	14,377	78
Ibersol	13,730	75
Atlantis Cristais De Alcobaua	12,713	69
Ctl.Banco De Investiment	12,600	69
Atlantis Cristais De Alcobaua Pref.	12,450	68
Cr.Lyonn.Portl. R	11,868	65
Espart	11,604	63

Regional Stock Exchange:

Oporto Derivatives Exchange (Bolsa de Derivados do Porto; BDP)
Av. de Boavista 3433
4100 Porto
Portugal
Phone: (351-2) 618-58-58
Fax: (351-2) 618-56-66
Internet: www.bdp.pt

Other Investment Information:

Portugese Foreign Trade Institute
Avenue 5 de Outubro 101
Lisbon
Portugal
Phone: (351-1) 793-01-03
Fax: (351-1) 793-50-28
Telex: 16498

Ministry of Trade and Tourism
Avenue de República 79
Lisbon
Portugal
Phone: (351-1) 730412
Telex: 13455

Bank of Portugal
Rua do Comercio 148
Lisbon
Portugal
Phone: (351-1) 346-29-31
Fax: (351-1) 346-73-41
Telex: 16554

POSITION

A more specific description than portfolio, a *Position* can be either long (in which securities are purchased before being sold) or short (in which securities are sold before being purchased). An investor buying 100 shares of XYZ Corporation has a long position in the security.

Position can also refer to a broker/dealer's holding or short sale. These positions are also called inventory.

See also GROWTH; OBJECTIVE; PORTFOLIO; SELLING SHORT.

POSITION LIMIT (United States and Others)

The limit imposed on the number of option contracts an investor can have on the same side of the market is referred to as the *Position Limit.*

The Options Clearing Corporation and the exchanges limit the option contracts of each class an investor is allowed to control. The limits are determined by the underlying security price and daily trading volume.

If a position limit is set at 3,000 contracts, it means that an investor can only control that number of contracts on the same side of the market. The following are several examples;

    3,000 calls purchased long or sold short
    3,000 puts purchased long or sold short
    2,000 long puts and 1,000 short calls
    2,000 long calls and 1,000 short puts
Current lists of position limits can be obtained from the exchanges.

See also CALL; FUTURES CONTRACT; OPTION; PUT; PUT PREMIUM.

POSITION OFFER/BID

An offer or bid made by a broker/dealer to buy or sell a block of securities to accommodate an institutional customer is known as a *Position Offer/Bid.* The quote given is normally made far enough away from the current market to provide partial protection against market risk, while the broker/dealer looks for customers with which to close out their position.

Over-the-Counter trading desks seek to maximize order flow, not to build, buy and hold positions for profit. When they are holding a position in a security, their risk increases significantly. Keeping order flow constant reduces their risk and makes them profitable.

See also BROKER/DEALER; TRADING DESK.

POSITIVE CARRY

A *Positive Carry* is a leveraged investment in which the return on investment is higher than the interest, commissions, and fees paid. It can be a special concern when interest rates are high or rising. If an investor pays interest of 10% and is earning 7% on the leveraged investment, it is a negative carry and not profitable. If interest of 6% is paid on a leveraged portfolio returning 10%, the investor is getting a return of 4%, a positive carry.

See also INTEREST/INTEREST RATES; MARGIN.

POSITIVE YIELD CURVE

Interest yields on long-term debt instruments higher than those on short-term investments create a situation known as a *Positive Yield Curve.* For example, when 30-year Treasury bonds are paying 7% and the yield on three-month T-bills is less than 6%, it is a positive yield curve.

The positive curve is the most common shape for the yield curve. Those committing their investment funds for a longer time period want a higher yield, otherwise they would only invest short-term.

See also CURRENT YIELD; INTEREST/INTEREST RATES; INVERTED YIELD CURVE; YIELD.

POST

See TRADING POST.

POST EXECUTION REPORTING (PER; United States)

Post Execution Reporting (PER) is a system of the American Stock Exchange. It allows members to send market orders, limit orders, and odd lot orders to specialists at their respective posts. A report of the execution is returned to the member and does not require their presence at the post.

PER can also appear as an abbreviation for Price/Earnings Ratio (earnings multiple) in some countries, although the abbreviation p/e is more commonly used.

See also PRICE/EARNINGS RATIO; SPECIALIST; UNITED STATES/AMERICAN STOCK EXCHANGE (AMEX).

POUND

The *Pound* is the primary currency of the United Kingdom and some other countries. When referring specifically to the United Kingdom, pound sterling is the term often used.

See also CURRENCY; DOLLAR; UNITED KINGDOM.

POWER OF ATTORNEY

Power of Attorney is the name given to a legal document—witnessed or acknowledged—that gives authorization to a person designated to act for and in place of the signing party. The power of attorney can be general, specific, or limited to acts defined in the document.

In reference to securities trading, limited power of attorney can be used with some custodial accounts. It can also be used to transfer share certificates, or to authorize a separate party (such as an investment adviser) to make trades in a brokerage account.

See also CUSTODIAL ACCOUNT; DISCRETIONARY ACCOUNT.

PRAEFERENCE AKTIE (Denmark)

Benefits attached to *Praeference Aktie* (preference shares) will vary with different companies, but can include:

- Receiving dividends before other shareholders

- Cumulative basis if dividend payments are missed

- Preference on liquidation of company

See also AKTIE (DENMARK); COMMON STOCK; DIVIDEND; EX-DIVIDEND (XD); PREFERRED STOCK (PFD).

PRECIOUS METALS

Technically, the term *Precious Metals* refers to those elements that are sometimes called "noble metals" because they resist oxidation and corrosion. They are gold, silver, and the platinum-group metals: platinum, palladium, rhodium, iridium, osmium, and ruthenium. However, when investors and analysts refer to precious metals they generally mean gold, silver, and platinum.

The prices of precious metals are extremely volatile and tend to move independently of the stock market as a whole. Despite the industrial importance of these metals, an analysis of precious metals markets based purely on fundamentals of supply and demand may prove to be seriously inaccurate. Precious metals prices are particularly sensitive to world events such as wars, political and economic crises, and inflation. Because of their independence from the rest of the market, many analysts recommend investing in bullion or coins as tangible assets that can balance the "paper assets"—stocks and bonds—in a portfolio. Precious metals can help to control the risk in a portfolio because their prices tend to move in the opposite direction from that of the paper assets. Because their prices are volatile, investments in precious metals can result in dramatic gains—and equally dramatic losses. For this reason, many analysts recommend limiting the quantity of precious metals investments in a portfolio to approximately 10% of the total holdings, and diversifying one's investments by buying more than one metal. Investors in this area must be able to risk large amounts of capital and hold on to their investments for long periods of time, riding out the inevitable drops in price.

There are some drawbacks to investing in precious metals in addition to the risks an investor must take in a volatile market. Precious metals do not pay interest or dividends. Investors holding a metal and waiting for a price spike may have to pay 1% of the value of the metal per year in storage and insurance costs. Dealers charge fees for buying and selling metals. Investors can avoid the cost of holding metals by investing in mining company stocks, mutual funds, or metals futures. The prices of mining company stocks are typically more volatile than the price of the metal itself. Futures contracts are risky, but require a smaller capital investment.

Specific Metals

Gold has retained its importance to the international monetary system even after the end of the gold standard because it is still the only universally accepted currency. Gold is important to the jewelry, electronics, computer, defense, and commercial aerospace industries. Nevertheless, the price of gold is primarily influenced by investor demand. Many investors consider gold to be a conservative way to diversify their portfolios, because gold tends to maintain the same value over long periods of time. Investors typically buy gold in response to inflation, international economic uncertainty or crisis, a decline in the value of the dollar, or a bearish stock market. The price of gold declines when investors fear that central banks may sell their reserves. A prediction of future gold prices should refer, at a minimum, to the following indicators: the inflation rate, commodity indices, the value of the dollar (gold's price varies inversely with the value of the dollar), traders' commitments reported by futures markets such as COMEX, and the behavior of other precious metals prices.

The price of silver is much more volatile than that of gold, and sometimes provides an early signal of what may happen to gold prices. Because of silver's greater volatility, a smaller amount of silver in a portfolio can provide as much risk protection as a larger amount of gold. The jewelry, photographic, and electronics industries generate the greatest demand for silver. Only a few countries find it economical to mine silver, and the amount of silver that is mined annually is not enough to satisfy international demand. Therefore, much of the demand for silver must be met by secondary sources, such as scrap silver recovered by industries, and silver that is dishoarded. The secondary supply of silver varies with silver's price.

Platinum is used by the jewelry, automobile, petrochemical, and agricultural industries. It is especially important to Japan's jewelry industry. Platinum is used to make razor blades, explosives, high-octane gasoline, laser rubies, optical glass, fiberglass, and pacemakers. It is also used as a catalytic electrode coating in electromechanical fuel cells. Cancer researchers are experimenting with the use of platinum-based drugs to attack DNA in cancer cells. Like gold, platinum's price is sensitive to changes in the value of the dollar and to periods of international crisis. However, platinum's price changes more quickly and more often than the price of gold because the market for platinum is smaller and more liquid. Politi-

cal developments in South Africa, the major producer of platinum, have a pronounced effect on its price.

See also GOLD; NON-PRECIOUS METALS; SILVER.

PRECOMPTE MOBILIER (Belgium)
See WITHHOLDING TAX.

PRE-EMERGING MARKETS
Pre-Emerging Markets are those developing countries in which conditions have not yet been established for foreign investment to play more than a very limited role, but which investors think have the potential for rapid growth. As the end of the 20th century approached, the increasing globalization of the world economy and the development of dynamic industrial sectors in some developing countries, along with the end of the cold war and the breakup of the Soviet bloc, presented international investors with a new situation. Many more countries than previously, at least since the 1960s, opened to trade and foreign investment, and carried out the structural reforms required to attract foreign capital. A number of these countries created particularly hospitable conditions for foreign investors, and some of them began to show rapid economic growth. Such countries are referred to as *emerging growth markets*. For a variety of political and economic reasons, pre-emerging markets have not yet developed to this stage.

Because there is no hard-and-fast rule distinguishing an emerging market from a pre-emerging one, and some investors would say that some countries could probably fit into either category, it is helpful to review some of the differences between them. The world's pre-emerging markets are principally located in places such as Africa, the Middle East, southern and central Asia, and Central America and the Caribbean. There are many pre-emerging markets that have large populations and are endowed with great and largely untapped stores of natural resources. However, their markets are limited by the extreme poverty of the people, the minimal development of industry, and the lack of infrastructure. Their stock markets, in particular, tend to have limited volume, listings, liquidity, and hours of operation, as well as insufficient regulation. Their economies are frequently subject to hyperinflation.

Market activity is highly seasonal, given agriculture's share in the total economy. In some of these countries, roads, bridges, and ports have been destroyed in the course of many years of anticolonial and civil war. Indeed, ethnic rivalries remain a disruptive threat in some. Corrupt authoritarian regimes, such as the Mobutu government in the former Zaire, can do a great deal to block development by siphoning off a country's economic surplus into various bureaucratic and luxury expenditures. In Mobutu's 32 years of rule, which ended in 1997, there were no schools or hospitals built in the country, road construction was neglected, and the country's rich deposits of gold, diamonds, and strategic metals were little exploited. Countries with a very large state sector, such as the neighboring Congo-Brazzaville, have a long way to go to carry out the degree of privatization that will attract foreign investors. And sometimes there are large outstanding debts owed to the World Bank, the International Monetary Fund (IMF), and commercial creditors that must first be dealt with before a country will receive significant quantities of investments. Thus, there are many different factors that can stall or arrest development in pre-emerging markets.

Sub-Saharan Africa contains the greatest concentration of pre-emerging markets. Among these countries, Botswana, Ghana, Kenya, Côte d'Ivoire, Malawi, Mauritius, Mozambique, Namibia, Nigeria, Swaziland, Tanzania, Uganda, Zambia, and Zimbabwe had stock markets in 1997, with a total capitalization of $9.2 billion. Except for Côte de'Ivoire, Kenya, Nigeria, and Zimbabwe, all of these had been established since 1989. Despite their limitations and the sometimes uncertain environments in which they operated, values in some of these markets rose rapidly: 144% in Nigeria and more than 50% in Côte d'Ivoire, Namibia, and Zimbabwe in 1995, and 72% in Zimbabwe and 56% in Nigeria in 1996. A number of countries reduced their debts through trades, in which a foreign bank assumes the debt in exchange for gaining ownership of certain properties in the country. In light of these conditions, the Morgan Stanley Africa Investment Fund, which had 70% of its holdings in South Africa when it was established in 1994, had 56% of its holdings in other African countries by 1997. An additional benefit for investors was that these markets were barely synchronized with those in developed countries; further, they were largely independent of each other. Thus investments in them constituted diversification. Nevertheless, most investors considered it prudent to invest no more than 10% of their international portfolio in African countries.

Those African pre-emerging markets showing the most growth potential in the mid-1990s were Ghana, Zimbabwe, Namibia, Botswana, and Kenya. Ghana was of great interest because of the 1994 sale of government's 25% of the Ashanti Goldfields, one of the world's largest gold mines, one-fifth of it on Ghana's own stock exchange and the remainder on the London market. Zimbabwe's strengths in agriculture, mining, and tourism were considered a good basis for market development, especially since the government had broken with its commitment to expanding the state sector and had reduced formerly galloping inflation to a manageable 8% in 1995.

Other sub-Saharan African countries were still further from emerging, such as Angola, the second largest producer of petroleum in sub-Saharan Africa (after Nigeria). It is home to the largest fisheries in southern Africa. At one time Angola was the world's fourth largest coffee producer and an exporter of cacao, cotton, sisal, corn, tobacco, and timber. It has major deposits of diamonds, copper, and gold. But it was burdened by severe poverty, destruction of its infrastructure (the long war against Portugal, followed by many years of war against rebels), and the potential for further conflict. Under the direction of the IMF and the World Bank, it planned to privatize 80–90% of its state-controlled companies, but it owed at least $11 billion to foreign creditors.

During the 1990s the majority of emerging markets were located in Southeast Asia, Eastern Europe, and Latin America. In terms of the capitalization of their stock markets, 54% are in Southeast Asia, 41% in Latin America, and 5% in Eastern Europe. Investments in these countries grew rapidly and were generally very profitable. In 1995 approximately 14% of U.S. holdings of foreign stocks, or $50 billion, was invested in emerging markets (70% of this amount had been invested in the previous five years). It was expected that this figure could grow to more than $70 billion by 2000, constituting roughly 25% of total U.S. foreign investment. Of course, investments in emerging markets carried a bigger risk than in developed countries, owing to political instability, currency volatility, and other factors. Nevertheless, investors were drawn to these markets by a wide range of investment opportunities, including futures and options, options on individual stocks, over-the-counter index swaps, options on index-linked notes, and domestic equity derivatives, plus the prospects of long-term growth rates two or three times those in developed markets.

The biggest emerging markets (BEMs) were Argentina, Brazil, China, Indonesia, India, Mexico, Poland, Russia, South Africa, South Korea, and Turkey. The distinguishing characteristics of these countries were their large populations, the richness of their natural resources, their drives to have greater international roles, their rapidly expanding markets, and the relatively advanced state of their reforms (including balancing budgets and paying off external debts, privatizing formerly state-run enterprises, and carrying out political liberalization; the BEMs fulfilled these criteria to varying degrees). If one relaxes one or two of these requirements, a number of other countries qualified as emerging markets, including Thailand, Singapore, Hungary, the Czech Republic, Chile and Ecuador.

See also EMERGING GROWTH MARKETS.

PREEMPTIVE RIGHTS

The rights that allow shareholders to purchase additional shares of a new issue before they are offered to the general public are called *Preemptive Rights.* The original purpose of these rights was to protect shareholders from dilution if new shares were issued.

In the United States, 48 of the 50 states have preemptive rights, but subsequent changes have reduced much of the benefit. Most states allow preemptive rights to be waived if shareholders are paid by the company, and limit the validity of the preemptive rights only in the event that they are set down in the corporate charter.

In the United Kingdom the term *preemption rights* is employed.

See also SUBSCRIPTION RIGHTS; SUBSCRIPTION WARRANT.

PREFERENCE SHARES (United Kingdom)

See PREFERRED STOCK (PFD).

PREFERRED STOCK (PFD)

Also known as preference shares, *Preferred Stock (PFD)* is usually considered to be a debt instrument. Its price is interest rate sensitive and represents equity ownership of the company—with a claim on assets in liquidation—ahead of all ordinary shares, but after creditors and bonds.

Preferred stock can be in several forms, including convertible into ordinary shares, cumulative dividend payments, non-cumulative, fixed rate dividends, or adjustable rate dividends (usually based on another security such as Treasury bills or other money market rates).

Convertible preferred prices tend to follow the common share prices and at some point can be converted to equity common shares.

Most preferred stock is non-voting and cumulative, meaning any passed dividends must be paid up before any other dividends, including dividends for common shares, can be paid out.

Preferred stock can be participating or non-participating, with regards to the receiving of extra dividends declared by the company. Participating stock receives extra dividends; whole non-participating stock does not.

Companies have tried to make preferred stock more attractive to investors with additional provisions, including:

1. Preference to assets
2. Cumulative dividends
3. Limited issue
4. Provision for partial or total redemption of the issue at a future date, paid, usually with a premium, by a sinking fund
5. Provision for placing control in the hands of preferred stockholders if dividends fail

Preferred stock (in the United Kingdom, preference shares) represent a special kind of ownership with less risk, but there are limitations regarding control and capital gains.

See also COMMON STOCK; DIVIDEND; EX-DATE.

PREISVERDIENST-RELATION (Germany)

See PRICE/EARNINGS RATIO.

PRELIMINARY AGREEMENT

When an underwriter and a new issuer first come together, they form a *Preliminary Agreement* to assemble the details of a new issue of securities. The underwriter then draws up the necessary paperwork and estimates the success of the new issue. The two then look at the details of the proposed new issue and decide if they want to proceed.

If the decision is made to go ahead with the issue, the two sign a formal agreement to proceed.

See also INITIAL PUBLIC OFFERING (IPO); ISSUE; UNDERWRITING.

PRELIMINARY PROSPECTUS

A *Preliminary Prospectus,* also called a "red herring," is a document that offers a description of a new securities issue. The term has long held a meaning of something ingenuous since some of the information in a preliminary prospectus is subject to change before the final prospectus is published.

A cautionary statement printed on the cover of a preliminary prospectus informs the investor that the information is incomplete and subject to change. The red-colored print and the incomplete nature of the information gave rise to the phrase "red herring."

Even though it is incomplete and some of the information is subject to change, the preliminary prospectus does provide the prospective investor with considerable information regarding the new issue.

Brokers send out preliminary prospectus to prospective buyers to obtain an indication of interest.

See also INDICATION OF INTEREST; INITIAL PUBLIC OFFERING (IPO); OBJECTIVE; PROSPECTUS; RED HERRING.

PREMIER OU DERNIER COURS (France)

Premier ou Dernier Cours is an order for the opening or closing price on the Bourse. Closing price orders are accepted on the forward market (Marché à Terme) but not for the cash market (Marché au Comptant).

See also AT THE CLOSE; AT THE OPEN.

PREMIO A VENDRE (Italy)

See PUT; PUT PREMIUM.

PREMIO D'ACQUISTO (Italy)

See CALL.

PREMIUM (Option)

The *Premium*, the price an option buyer pays or an option writer receives for an option, is the price per single unit based on the underlying security.

Essentially, the premium is composed of two values: the intrinsic value, which is based on the current price of the underlying security, and the time value, which is based on the remaining time until expiration.

If XYZ Corporation shares are trading at $55 and an investor wants to buy the November 50 calls with the option premium at $8, the $5 difference between the strike price and the current market price represents the intrinsic value. The remaining $3 in the option premium represents the time value of the option.

See also CALL; OPTION; PUT; PUT PREMIUM; SELLING TO OPEN.

PRESENTAZIONE FOGLI (Italy)

See SETTLE.

PRESIDENT

The highest ranking officer of a company after the chairman of the board, a company *President* is appointed by the board of directors and answers directly to them.

In smaller companies, the president may also be the chief executive officer (CEO) and take responsibility for the management of the daily operations and the policy decisions of the company. With many larger companies, the chairman of the board is also chief executive officer (CEO), effectively making the president more of a chief operating officer.

See also AFFILIATED PERSON; BOARD OF DIRECTORS.

PRESUMPTIVE UNDERWRITER (United States)

The Securities and Exchange Commission calls any person or group buying 10% or more of a new issue and selling the position within two years a *Presumptive Underwriter*. Such transactions are allowed under SEC regulations.

See also INITIAL PUBLIC OFFERING (IPO); ISSUE; UNDERWRITING.

PREZZO (DI) EMISSIONE (Italy)

See ISSUE PRICE.

PREZZO LIMITATO (Italy)

See LIMIT ORDER.

PREZZO LORDO (Italy)

See MARKET PRICE.

PRICE GAP

See GAP.

PRICE LIMITS

See LIMIT ORDER.

PRICE RANGE

The *Price Range* is an indicator of the highest and lowest prices calculated over an extended time period.

See also RANGE.

PRICE SPREAD

See SPREAD.

PRICE/EARNINGS RATIO (P/E)

The *Price/Earnings Ratio (p/e)* is the ratio arrived at by dividing the current market price of a share by the current earnings per share.

If XYZ Corporation is currently at $50 per share and has annual earnings of $4 per share, the p/e ratio is 12.5.

Current price	$50	Equals a price/earnings
Current annual earnings	4	ratio of 12.5.

The p/e ratio of a company is an important item of analysis for investors. Companies that have a relatively low p/e ratio, when compared to similar companies in their sector or a stock market index, are considered conservative. Relatively high p/e ratios are often considered the sign of a more speculative stock.

Some analysts look at the current p/e ratio in relation to the historic ratio. Such analysis tends to bring up other questions for research. If a company has traded at a p/e ratio of 15 to 17 for the past five years and is now at a ratio of 12, is it undervalued and a good buy or has something happened to lower expectations? If the current p/e ratio is 20, has the change been caused by an increase in the overall stock market, or has something happened to attract buyers to the company?

A p/e ratio is also known as an earnings multiple.

See also DIVIDEND; EARNINGS; MARKET PRICE.

PRICEY

Anything more expensive than is believed to be fair is referred to as *Pricey*. The term might refer to the price of a group of shares experiencing a sudden increase, as in "the Dow Jones Industrials are getting pricey." It can also refer to a specific company whose shares have been increasing, as in "XYZ Corporation is getting pricey."

The term can also refer to the spread between the bid and ask as being too wide or too pricey. The term is not specific, although some analysts talk of shares as being pricey in relation to their earnings.

See also ASK PRICE; BID PRICE; EARNINGS; MARKET PRICE; PRICE/EARNINGS RATIO.

PRIMARY DEALER (United States)

A *Primary Dealer* is a bank or other investment dealer who is authorized to buy and sell government securities, and also deals directly with the Federal Reserve Bank of New York (the Fed) in the Fed Open Market Operations. Such dealers qualify for the position of primary dealer by reputation, capacity, and by having adequate facilities to trade large deals.

When the Fed wishes to tighten the money supply, it sells government securities to primary dealers, thus removing cash from circulation. The primary dealers pay for the government securities with cash. If the Fed wants to expand the money supply, it buys government securities from those dealers, thus putting cash into the system.

When new issues come from the government, the primary dealers make competitive bids for those securities.

List of the Primary Government Securities Dealers Reporting to the Market Reports Division of the Federal Reserve Bank of New York
Aubrey G. Lanston & Co., Inc.
BancAmerica Robertson Stephens
Bear, Stearns & Co., Inc.
BT Alex. Brown Incorporated
BZW Securities Inc.
Chase Securities Inc.
CIBC Oppenheimer Corp.
Citicorp Securities, Inc.
Credit Suisse First Boston Corporation
Daiwa Securities America Inc.
Dean Witter Reynolds Inc.
Deutsche Morgan Grenfell/C.J. Lawrence Inc.
Donaldson, Lufkin & Jenrette Securities Corporation
Dresdner Kleinwort Benson North America LLC.
Eastbridge Capital Inc.
First Chicago Capital Markets, Inc.
Fuji Securities Inc.
Goldman, Sachs & Co.
Greenwich Capital Markets, Inc.
HSBC Securities, Inc.
J. P. Morgan Securities, Inc.
Lehman Brothers Inc.
Merrill Lynch Government Securities Inc.
Morgan Stanley & Co. Incorporated
NationsBanc Montgomery Securities LLC.
Nesbitt Burns Securities Inc.
The Nikko Securities Co. International, Inc.
Nomura Securities International, Inc.
Paine Webber Incorporated
Paribas Corporation
Prudential Securities Incorporated
Salomon Brothers Inc.
Sanwa Securities (USA) Co., L.P.
SBC Warburg Dillon Read Inc.
Smith Barney Inc.
UBS Securities LLC.
Zions First National Bank

Note: This list has been compiled and made available for statistical purposes only and has no significance with respect to other relationships between dealers and the Federal Reserve Bank of New York. Qualification for the reporting list is based on the achievement and maintenance of the standards outlined in the Federal Reserve Bank of New York's memorandum of January 22, 1992. January 2, 1998 effective date (Source: Federal Reserve Bank of New York)

PRIMARY DISTRIBUTION

With bonds, every new issue is a *Primary Distribution*. With shares, only the sale of authorized but previously unissued shares are primaries. The sale of U.S. Treasury shares is a secondary offering.

See also INITIAL PUBLIC OFFERING (IPO); SECONDARY DISTRIBUTION; TREASURY STOCK.

PRIMARY EARNINGS

Primary Earnings are net post-tax earnings and after-preferred dividends stated on a per share basis. Primary earnings are not figured after dilution, which also takes into account warrants, rights, convertibles, and corporate share options.

See also CONVERTIBLE; SUBSCRIPTION RIGHTS; SUBSCRIPTION WARRANT.

PRIMARY MARKET

The *Primary Market* is the market for new issues of securities. In a primary market, the proceeds from the sale go directly to the issuer.

When securities publicly trade on an exchange or over-the-counter they trade in the secondary market.

See also SECONDARY MARKET.

PRIMARY MARKET PROTECTION (PMP; United States)

When a regional stock exchange specialist accepts an order "away from the market" they must provide *Primary Market Protection (PMP),* which guarantees the customer a fill of at least a partial execution if a trade occurs on the primary exchange (New York Stock Exchange).

See also LIMIT ORDER; SPECIALIST; UNITED STATES/ NEW YORK STOCK EXCHANGE (NYSE).

PRIME (France)

See MARCHÉ À PRIMES.

PRIME RATE

The *Prime Rate* is the rate of interest charged by commercial banks in the United States to their best customers on short-term maturities. Its level is influenced by the Federal discount rate and the Federal funds rate, and can be changed on a regular basis. Other lending rates, such as the rates for consumer debt and mortgages, are also based on the prime rate. It is the interest rate most closely representing the riskless rate of money offered to clients with the highest quality credit rating. The prime rate is an important guideline for the calculation of actual rates charged.

See also FEDERAL DISCOUNT RATE/FED FUNDS; INTEREST/INTEREST RATES.

PRINCIPAL

The *Principal* is the face amount or par value of a debt security. It is the amount exclusive of interest or premium that the holder receives at settlement. The principal also serves as the base for calculating the interest amount on the security.

Principal also refers to the original amount of money an investor uses to buy an investment, plus any additional amounts that might have been added later. It is the amount before any interest or capital gains or losses are incurred. It is basically the amount of money a person invests.

A principal can also be a person or organization who is the main party entering into an agreement or transaction and acting as a buyer or a seller.

See also CAPITAL GAIN; COMMISSION; INTEREST/INTEREST RATES.

PRINCIPAL SHAREHOLDER (United States)

According to the Securities and Exchange Commission (SEC), a *Principal Shareholder* is a person or group of persons acting in concert who own more than 10% of a registered company's voting shares.

Such shareholders are frequently on the board of directors and are considered insiders by the SEC. Any buys or sells of the company's shares by the principal shareholder must be reported to the SEC.

See also AFFILIATED PERSON; CONTROL STOCK; INSIDER.

PRIORITATSAKTIE (Germany)

See PREFERRED STOCK (PFD).

PRIORITY

In reference to share trading, *Priority* is the main factor considered when determining the order in which offers to buy or sell a security are accepted. There are two main priorities observed on stock exchanges: time and place of origin.

In an auction market procedure, the first bid or offer placed is executed before other bids and offers, even if subsequent orders are larger. Orders coming to the exchange from off-floor, that is orders originated by investors rather than traders, have priority over orders originating on the exchange floor.

The first order to arrive from an investor, rather than from an exchange member, is the order granted the highest priority. The integrity of these order priorities is essential for an exchange to maintain a fair and orderly market.

Priority is also an important concern in the winding-up of a company. In the event of corporate default, payment of liabilities generally follows a set order of priority. It is as follows:

1. Preferred creditors
2. Secured creditors

3. Unsecured or general creditors

4. Contingent liabilities

5. Shareholders or other owners

PRIS D'ÉMISSION (France)

See EXERCISE PRICE.

PRIVATE PLACEMENT (United States)

Private Placement is the sale of shares, bonds, private limited partnerships, or other investments. Usually these sales are made to an institutional investor. However, qualifying individuals can participate in some private placements.

Private placements do not require registration with the Securities and Exchange Commission (SEC), since they are not a public offering and are not being immediately resold.

At a later date, the private placement may result in an Initial Public Offering (IPO) for the investors to take gains. Normal underwriting and registration requirements will be used and attended to when the public offering is made.

Private Placement Memorandum (PPM): A document similar to a registered offering prospectus, the PPM discloses all pertinent information to the investor interested in a private placement. Even though the placement is private, the issuer is still required to supply information on which an investor can make an informed decision, including any future marketability of the issue and the intended use of the funds invested.

Usually the number of investors in any one private placement cannot be more than 35, although "accredited investors" are not included in this number.

Accredited investors are those in the United States who are allowed, under SEC rules and regulations, to participate in placing shares. The following are three examples:

1. An investor with a net worth of more than $1 million

2. An investor receiving $200,000 income currently and for the past two years

3. A senior official of the issuer

See also INITIAL PUBLIC OFFERING (IPO); INSTITUTIONAL INVESTOR; NET WORTH; SECURITIES AND EXCHANGE COMMISSION (SEC).

PRIVATIZATION

Privatization is the term used to describe programs to sell shares in government-owned companies. Various industries are involved in these programs. Airlines, manufacturing, telecommunications, transportation, hotel, banking, and insurance are among the most popular.

The greatest amount of privatization is occurring in countries changing from a communist system to a capitalist system of government. Additionally, noncommunist countries such as Japan, France, and the United Kingdom are converting some government-owned businesses into shares that can be privately owned and publicly traded. This process of denationalization has often proved to be controversial, with much criticism arising because of the size of stock market inducements added to the shares to guarantee investor interest.

See also CAPITAL; COMMON STOCK; PUBLICLY HELD AND TRADED COMPANY.

PROCEEDS

Proceeds are the funds received by a borrower after fees and interest are deducted. It is the net amount of money the borrower has to work with on the project for which the money was borrowed.

Proceeds are also the funds received when an investor sells securities. Net proceeds amount to the market price of the security multiplied by the number of shares sold, with any fees and commissions or markdowns deducted.

If the proceeds from a sale of securities are used to purchase other securities, it is called a proceeds sale, and the NASD Rules of Fair Practice Five Percent Rule comes into effect.

See also COMMISSION; FIVE PERCENT RULE; NATIONAL ASSOCIATION OF SECURITIES DEALERS (NASD).

PRODUCER PRICE INDEX (PPI; United States)

The *Producer Price Index (PPI)* is an index produced by the U.S. Department of Labor Bureau of Statistics that measures the average price change in producer goods.

Nearly 3,000 products, such as chemicals, feeds, textiles, fibers, and machinery, are examined. Some analysts consider the PPI a more accurate indicator of rising prices than the Consumer Price Index.

See also CONSUMER PRICE INDEX (CPI); INFLATION; INTEREST/INTEREST RATES.

PROFILE YOUR CUSTOMER RULE (United States)

Under Rule 405, the New York Stock Exchange requires stockbrokers to know information regarding the financial status and investment objectives of their customers. This is known as the *Profile Your Customer* rule.

Additionally, the rule expects the broker to know a customer's investment objectives and only make suitable recommendations within the scope of those objectives. Many brokerage firms have a customer profile form that the stockbroker must complete when opening a new account. Brokers are usually also required to profile existing customers on a periodic basis because their status and objectives can change.

The intent of the rule is to prohibit the broker or the firm from using "I didn't know" as an excuse for making an improper or unsuitable investment recommendation. The language of the rule is written to reflect this.

See also OBJECTIVE; REGISTERED REPRESENTATIVE (RR); RULE 405; SUITABILITY/SUITABILITY RULE.

PROFIT

Profit is the economic reward paid to the entrepreneur for taking risk and being a successful manager. It is a business's net gain, after taxes and expenses, from manufacturing, merchandising, and selling of products or services. It represents the increase in the firm's net worth. Profit is used as one measure of success with individuals and companies. It is their reward for making decisions and taking risk.

With investing, profit is the money returned for buying and selling securities or commodities.

See also EARNINGS; GAIN.

PROFIT AND LOSS

Profit and Loss is part of a company's bookkeeping procedure. Debits and credits are netted to observe whether a company, a product, or a special project has made or lost money. The statement is a useful tool in finding problems and making decisions on the continuation or cancellation of a company, product, or service.

An individual's performance is often measured by his or her impact on a company's profit and loss. A high level of profits can mean extra compensation in the form of a bonus, continuation of employment, stock options, or other benefits for an individual. Losses, especially if they are continual, can have the opposite impact on an individual.

See also BALANCE SHEET; EARNINGS; PROFIT.

PROFIT MARGIN

There are two important ratios employed by financial analysts when considering the *Profit Margin* of a firm: The gross profit margin, and the net profit margin.

The gross profit margin measures gross profit as a percentage of sales:

$$\frac{\text{Gross Profit}}{\text{Sales}} \times 100 = \text{GP\%}$$

This ratio measures the efficiency of a company in the vital area of buying and selling goods and services. The gross profit margin will be affected by many factors, including changes in selling price, fluctuations in the cost of raw materials, theft of goods, supplier discounts, and rebates offered to customers.

The net profit margin measures net profit as a percentage of sales:

$$\frac{\text{Net Profit}}{\text{Sales}} \times 100 = \text{NP\%}$$

Any changes in the net profit margin that are unexplained by changes in selling price or the cost of raw materials (and which, therefore, will become apparent in analysis of the gross profit margin) will be caused by changes in overhead expenses. These changes may be due to factors such as increased marketing costs, a reduction in the wage bill, technological advances in production, or greater electricity costs.

PROFIT SHARING PLAN

A *Profit Sharing Plan* is a plan established by a company and managed by an investment professional that allows employees to share in the profits of the company.

Upon the establishment of a profit sharing plan, a portion of the company profits are contributed to the employee plan on an annual basis. If there are no profits, no contribution is made. Contributions are made either in cash or to a deferred plan that can be used for a variety of investments. Funds accumulate on a tax-deferred basis until the employee retires or leaves the company.

Some plans allow the employee to borrow funds from the profit sharing plan for certain major expenses such as buying a house or paying for children's education.

See also INDIVIDUAL RETIREMENT ACCOUNT (IRA); INSTITUTIONAL INVESTOR; PENSION PLAN/FUND.

PROFIT TAKING

See REALIZED PROFIT/LOSS.

PROGRAM EXECUTION PROCESSING (PEP; United States)

Endorsed by the New York Stock Exchange (NYSE) and tied into the Super DOT system, *Program Execution Processing (PEP)* facilitates the execution of orders in multiple issues entered at the same time. It is used with the institutional investor's index-based port-folios.

In order for share portfolios to mirror or better the performance of indices, large trades involving several issues have to be made simultaneously. Any delays in the execution of orders could skew the figures. The Program Execution Processing program offers the institutional investor a tool to have the necessary trades executed.

See also INDEX NUMBERS; INSTITUTIONAL INVESTOR; PORTFOLIO.

PROGRAM TRADING

A term used to describe the strategy of many institutional investors, *Program Trading* involves a shift in positions between index options, futures, and the underlying shares of the indexes. It is essentially an arbitrage strategy and is called program trading because computer programs are used to give buy and sell signals, telling the money manager to change from securities to futures or options.

Professional investors might buy a stock index futures contract (e.g., on the Standard & Poor's 500 Index) when it is cheap compared to the underlying share prices. The futures are sold when they rise in value, but before expiration. By selling futures and buying the underlying shares, the trader creates a fully hedged position.

The strategy also captures the spread between the futures and the share prices. When the futures contract expires, the spread becomes zero, at the same price as the shares. Positions are then unwound by selling the shares and letting the futures expire. The captured spread becomes profit with minimal risk. At the end of each quarter—March, July, October, and December—program traders must unwind positions because all index futures, options, and index options expire. This gives rise to the phenomenon known as the triple-witching hour, the last trading hour of the last trading day.

Program trading was also part of the portfolio insurance designed to protect the portfolio of an institutional investor when the stock market experiences a decline. Much of the U.S. market volatility during the mid-1980s was blamed on program trading. Circuit breakers to limit volatility were added after the market crash on 19 October 1987, and curtailed many of the program trading strategies. Such limits are important for an exchange to maintain a fair and orderly market.

See also ARBITRAGE; FUTURES CONTRACT; INDEX OPTION; INSTITUTIONAL INVESTOR.

PROPERTY AS INVESTMENT

Property as Investment, also known as real estate (property in buildings and land), has assumed increasing importance in the economies of the developed countries in recent decades. By the mid-1990s it had become not only one of the more profitable forms of investment, but also one in which risks could be relatively well controlled.

In general, real estate investments offer four forms of income. First, there is the gross (pretax) disposable income, or cash flow, which is equal to the rents collected, minus the operating expenses and mortgage payments. The rental income from a property is affected by numerous factors—the strength of the economy, the supply of and demand for space, the market rate for space, the tenants, the type of property, and the type of contract. Second, there is equity income, also known as equity buildup or principal reduction, which results from the gradual increase in the portion of the total property's price that is owned by the investor as he or she pays off the mortgage. Third, there is income resulting from various tax shelters, which are not offered to any other common form of investment. Fourth, there is appreciation, that is, the inflation in the price of the real estate. (There are exceptions to this last form of income when the price of land depreciates, such as during the crisis in Japan in the late 1980s and early 1990s.)

The overall value of a real estate investment is estimated by investors using one of two methods, the capitalization rate model or the discounted cash flow model. The real estate market is not considered to be as efficient as the stock market for several reasons. The real estate market is mostly local, whereas the stock market is national and international. Information flows more easily in the stock market than in the real estate market. In addition, inside information, illegal in the stock market, is legal in the real estate market.

In the United States in the 1990s, new investment vehicles developed that made it possible for many more people to invest in real estate. Until that time, most real estate was owned by private, family-owned companies. However, the collapse of real estate values in California and elsewhere in 1989–90 largely put an end to private financing. Real estate firms turned to the public market for equity capital by making use of initial public offerings (IPOs), a time-tested device in the stock market.

The revival and increasing importance of real estate investment trusts (REITs) dates to this time, although they had existed some 30 years earlier. REITs are companies that pool many people's capital to purchase, manage, and develop groupings of properties, including apartments, office buildings, warehouses, shopping centers, and even prisons. Because of the diversification of their holdings, they provide a relatively low-risk method for more people to invest in real estate. They also are only moderately leveraged, with debts of approximately 30% of equity as opposed to the very high leverage figures of 70% or more that were common among real estate firms in the 1980s. The bulk of their investments, then, are in physical assets rather than mortgages.

In 1996 the U.S. commercial real estate market was in its fourth consecutive year of recovery. Overall economic growth, minimal new construction, and low interest rates combined to increase rents and decrease metropolitan vacancy rates. Total returns for REITs were approximately 30%, as compared to 27.8% for the Standard and Poor's 500 Index. For the years 1993–96, only 2% of REITs registered negative average returns, compared to 16% of stocks in the Russell 3000 Index. By 1997 the total value of U.S. commercial real estate was approximately $4 trillion. It should be noted that REITs accounted for only 4% of the market at this point, with the great majority of purchases done on the private markets, whether through purchases of equity (direct property investments, private placements, venture capital, or commingled funds) or assumptions of debt (mortgages or high-yield commercial mortgage-backed securities).

All of this success led some analysts to worry that a period of overbuilding, resulting in higher vacancy rates and lower values, would ensue. Others argued, however, that this was not likely, given the elimination of incentives for speculative construction under the Tax Reform Act of 1986, the enforcement of new restraints on banks' and insurance companies' real estate lending, and the inactivity of thrift institutions in real estate financing since the failures of 1990. The pessimists were in the majority, although they did not envision as big a collapse in real estate values as had occurred in 1989. Others, looking at longer-term trends, projected that increased computerization, telecommuting, electronic shopping, and just-in-time production would reduce the market for office buildings, shops, and warehouses.

See also DIVERSIFICATION; JAPANESE BOOM AND BUST 1988–90; PORTFOLIO THEORY; REAL ESTATE INVESTMENT TRUST (REIT).

PROPRIETARY

Strictly speaking, something is *Proprietary* if it is owned by a person or organization. It might be a line of products, information, or brand names.

Stock market quotations can be described as being proprietary if they are in real-time, meaning a fee is charged if someone wants to know the current information. Quotes with a time delay can often be obtained at no charge. Cable television and the Internet are two possible sources of delayed information.

See also ASK PRICE; BID PRICE; LAST TRADE; QUOTE.

PROPRIETARY TRADING

Proprietary Trading refers to investment activities undertaken by a bank for its own account. Banks will allocate a certain amount of their own capital for speculation in shares, bonds, currency, and derivatives such as futures and options. A clear distinction must be drawn between proprietary trading and trading undertaken on behalf of clients.

In the 1990s many banks have been forced to turn to proprietary trading operations to compensate for lower profits from traditional income sources such as loans. In years when stock markets are booming, investing a bank's capital in trading activities can be extremely profitable. However, in times of turbulence and decline—such as the Asian financial crisis of 1997–98—proprietary trading in stocks, derivatives, and options has led to significant losses. The British investment bank Barings was brought to its knees by the activities of one derivatives trader and there have been many other examples of the volatile nature of proprietary trading.

Institutional investors are often unsure of how to value banks with substantial proprietary trading operations. The volatility of the income stream from proprietary trading increases the risk of insolvency but offers greater scope for profit.

See also BARINGS; TRADING.

PROSPECTUS

A *Prospectus* is a document in the form of a circular, letter, notice, or advertisement offering a security for sale.

In the United States, a copy of a prospectus must be filed with the Securities and Exchange Commission (SEC) as part of the securities registration procedure. The requirement of a full disclosure prospectus is covered under the Securities Act of 1933 and states that all material facts must be disclosed and communicated to investors. It is an integral part of the Registration Statement, which is a matter of public record.

The SEC requires that "all information required to be included in a prospectus shall be clearly understandable without the necessity of referring to the particular form or the General Rules and Regulations. Financial statements included in a prospectus are to be set forth in comparative form if practicable and shall include the notes thereto and the accountants' certificate."

The prospectus is meant to be an objective statement describing the company, without puffing or slanting, and should be something on which intelligent investment decisions can be made. However, many prospectuses display many of the characteristics of sales documents.

See also INITIAL PUBLIC OFFERING (IPO); REGISTRATION; SECURITIES AND EXCHANGE COMMISSION (SEC).

PROSPEKT (Germany)

See PROSPECTUS.

PROSPEKTHAFTUNG (Germany)

See PROSPECTUS.

PROSPETTO (Italy)

See PROSPECTUS.

PROVVIGIONE (Italy)

See COMMISSION.

PROXY

A *Proxy* is the form sent to shareholders enabling them to vote on company matters. A proxy can also be used to transfer the voting power to someone who will vote in place of the shareholder.

The normal form sent out by companies is for voting purposes, but a shareholder can request a form to add specific voting instructions. The proxy enables the shareholder to make use of the voting power without attending a meeting.

See also VOTING SHARE.

PROXY STATEMENT (United States)

The information required by the Securities and Exchange Commission (SEC) to be provided to shareholders before they can vote by proxy on various company matters is called a *Proxy Statement*.

Such a statement might refer to the election of members of a board of directors. It would describe factual information on the proposed additions, including their bonus and option plans. It can also contain descriptions of any other resolutions to be voted on, such as the selection of a new accounting firm.

See also PREFERRED STOCK (PFD); PROXY; VOTING SHARE.

PRUDENT MAN RULE (United States)

A standard adopted by some states in the United States, the *Prudent Man Rule* is an imprecise guide for those investing for others.

Persons or organizations referred to as fiduciaries, such as will executors, trustees, banking trust departments, and estate administrators, are expected to manage the funds entrusted to them as a prudent man or woman would be expected to act. This involves acting with discretion and intelligence to seek a reasonable income, preserve capital, and generally avoid speculation.

States not using the Prudent Man Rule often fall back on the use of a legal list, allowing fiduciaries to invest in a specific list of securities. The major problem with a legal list is that it is not regularly updated to include or exclude new investment products (such as derivatives and futures) and might not make a ruling on such items until a serious problem involving capital loss occurs.

See also FIDUCIARY; MUTUAL FUND; OBJECTIVE.

PRUDENTIAL SECURITIES

Prudential Securities is the fifth largest full service brokerage firm in the United States. Its history dates back to 1879. In that year Leopold Cahn founded Leopold Cahn and Company, Brokers and Investment Bankers, in New York City. The following year his nephew, Jules Bache, joined the firm.

In 1890 Leopold Cahn and Company opened a second office in New York City and one in Albany. In 1892 it reorganized as J. S. Bache and Company, and in 1896 it opened eight more branches around the country. J. S. Bache and Company had seats on the New York Stock Exchange, New York Produce Exchange, New York Cotton Exchange, Chicago Board of Trade, and Philadelphia Stock Exchange. In addition, it had correspondents in London and Paris.

During World War I the firm was involved in large-scale purchasing of strategic materials and commodities for the United States and its allies. It also sold large quantities of Liberty Bonds to support the United States war effort.

In the 1920s J. S. Bache and Company became a leading financier of railroad, automobile, and mining companies. It was a major stockholder of the Chicago, Great Western Railway and the Ann Arbor Railroad. It helped finance the New York City subways, and was a leader in providing financing to the Chrysler Corporation during its early years.

J. S. Bache and Company suffered little from the stock market crash of 1929, since it had no money invested in the stock market. During the 1930s it was able to expand internationally, establishing correspondents in Tokyo, Hong Kong, Singapore, Berlin, and Amsterdam.

During World War II it had to close all its overseas branches except the one in London. In 1944 Jules Bache died and was succeeded by Harold Bache, and the company's name was changed to Bache and Company.

After the war, six new branches were opened in New York, as well as several others around the country. Most of the overseas branches were reopened, and new ones were set up in Geneva, Frankfurt, and Rome.

In 1971 Bache and Company became a public corporation. Its offering of shares raised $40 million in new capital. In 1973 it acquired Halsey, Stuart and Company, one of the country's leading corporate bond and municipal underwriting houses.

In 1975 the holding company Bache Group Inc. was formed. In 1977 Bache and Company acquired Shield Model Roland, an institutional brokerage and investment banking firm. The Bache Group also purchased Harrison and Company in Cincinnati, Ohio, and the Albert M. Bender Company, one of the largest private insurance brokers in the western United States.

In 1981 the Prudential Insurance Company of America, the world's largest insurance company, acquired Bache and Company. In 1982 Bache and Company. changed its name to Prudential-Bache Securities. The firm continued to expand, acquiring in 1989 Thompson McKinnon Securities Inc., the ninth largest brokerage house in the United States, which had 4,700 employees and 154 branches. This acquisition made Prudential-Bache the third largest brokerage in the country.

In the late 1980s Prudential-Bache changed its approach, deemphasizing merchant-bank capabilities and stressing retail brokerage, mutual funds, and selected capital markets business.

The firm was involved in the costliest financial scandal in the history of Wall Street in the 1980s and early 1990s. Prudential-Bache was charged with the fraudulent sale of billions of dollars of worthless investments to hundreds of thousands of investors, many of whom had low or fixed incomes. For years it had distributed literature that falsely portrayed the limited partnerships it was selling, such as in real estate and oil wells, as safe and tax-efficient investments. As part of the settlement, the firm had to pay more than $1.4 billion in fines to regulators and compensation to investors. Approximately one-quarter of Prudential-Bache's 340,000 investors were participants in a class-action suit against it.

Some analysts identified the causes of these abuses as twofold. The management of Prudential-Bache was very much caught up in the no-holds-barred, more-is-better greed that became especially prominent among a section of U.S. businesses in the 1980s. Also, the company's sales representatives were rewarded for making greater sales, with little regard for whether the products they were selling actually met the needs of their customers.

Prudential-Bache experienced a particularly bad year in 1990, when it lost more than $250 million. In 1991 The Prudential, whose long-standing and carefully cultivated reputation for reliability had been significantly damaged by the scandal, infused $200 million into its brokerage subsidiary and renamed it Prudential Securities Inc. By the mid-1990s Prudential Securities had more than 2.2 million accounts and was engaged in more than 60,000 trades per day.

PSYCHOLOGY OF SPECULATION

The *Psychology of Speculation* refers to the whole set of ideas, habits, passions, calculations, insights, ignorances, stratagems, and occasional impetuosities—in other words, all the rational and irrational mental processes—that are associated with the activities of speculation, whether one is dealing in currencies, bonds, stocks, or commodities.

Speculation itself is somewhat easier to define. In general, it is the process of buying and/or selling with an eye to holding things that can be bought and/or sold at a profit later on.

There is also the distinction between a bear, one who sells stocks or shares because of an expectation that they will fall in price, and a bull, one who buys them in anticipation that their price will rise. In either case, the speculator must have confidence in his or her predictions about market trends. However, since it is often very difficult to predict futures markets, the position of the speculator generally entails a good deal of risk, and the willingness to accept risks is a necessary part of the speculator's psychological makeup.

Historically, three kinds of speculators—scalpers, day traders, and position traders—have been distinguished, according to the different degrees or kinds of risk that they have assumed, as well as differences in their available resources. Scalpers are those who make a futures trade, for example, buying some goods, and then enter into the reverse trade, that is, selling those goods, within a matter of a few minutes. They are oriented toward making a profit after a minimal price movement. Day traders hold their positions for a number of hours, seeking to profit from price fluctuations that take place during a single trading day and always reversing their trade before the exchange's closing time. Position traders take a position in the futures market and may hold it for weeks or even months. Position traders potentially can reap the greatest profit on a given trade, but they also incur the largest risks, given the difficulty of forecasting market movements over longer periods of time.

In today's futures markets, with 18 exchanges around the world, a new dimension has been added to speculative possibilities through the linking of exchanges in different countries. Several of these links make 24-hour-a-day trading possible. For example, the New York Mercantile Exchange (NYMEX) and the Sydney Futures Exchange opened an electronic trading link in 1996. The Chicago Mercantile Exchange is linked with the Singapore International Monetary Exchange, and the London International Financial Futures and Options Exchange is linked with the Tokyo International Financial Futures Exchange. Similar links exist or are under discussion between other exchanges. In this context, unceasing restless activity has become a more pronounced part of the speculator's mental makeup.

Studies indicate that smaller speculators tend to lose in the markets rather than make any profits. Nevertheless, there is no shortage of such people. They are drawn to speculative activity for a number of reasons: they enjoy engaging in it; they believe that they can forecast accurately—a belief that is fostered by a selective memory of their previous record; and they discount a series of relatively small losses and feel they are immune to large losses, while holding out hope that they will make large profits.

On the one hand, speculators play a necessary role under capitalism by supplying capital, taking risks, holding goods, and the like, and there are many kinds of production that could not go forward today but for their activities. Yet they are often thought of in the public imagination as greedy, self-serving individuals. This view is fed by the perception that they are profiteers who do not actually produce, or organize or assist the production of, anything of substance. As an increasing share of the economic transactions in the developed countries have taken on a speculative cast in the 1980s and 1990s, and the distribution of wealth and income has become more polarized, this view has crystallized.

In addition, there are concerns about how speculation has triggered a number of frauds, financial panics, collapses, and crashes in the history of capitalism. In such situations, a "speculative bubble" has formed in which the price of an asset, or in more generalized cases, the prices of assets as a whole, have climbed to levels far in excess of their values.

In such bubbles, there is a tendency on the part of the chief speculators to forget about history and to think that their means of stimulating prices to ever greater heights is original and infallible (for example, buying on the margin, that is, having to put down only 10% of the value of a stock, a practice that has a very long history). As profits spiral ever higher, the speculators forget that they must inevitably come down; or they assume that they will be able to see the warning signs and sell off in time. Historically, the majority have not gotten out in time.

See also CHAOS THEORY; MARKET MANIA; SPECULATION.

PUBLIC LIMITED COMPANY (PLC; United Kingdom)

A *Public Limited Company (PLC)* is the legal form for a publicly traded company in the United Kingdom.

It is a company limited by shares or by guarantee and the words "Public Limited Company" or initials "PLC" follow the company name. PLCs can have an unlimited number of shareholders and are the only type of UK company that can offer shares for public subscription.

See also CORPORATION; PUBLICLY HELD AND TRADED COMPANY.

PUBLIC OFFERING

See INITIAL PUBLIC OFFERING (IPO).

PUBLIC OFFERING PRICE (POP; United States and Others)

Public Offering Price (POP) is a term used to describe the price of mutual fund shares with the maximum sales charge applied. It is also called the maximum offering price. It is the price an investor would pay to buy shares in minimal quantities.

When a mutual fund quotation appears in the newspaper it shows the net asset value (NAV), the public offering price (POP), and the net change on the NAV from the most recent trading session.

A mutual fund net asset value consists of the total asset value of the fund, less any fees and expenses, expressed in terms of the value per share. It is the price an investor would have received if mutual fund shares had been redeemed during that day's trading session. Net asset values are calculated at the end of each trading session.

See also MUTUAL FUND; UNIT INVESTMENT TRUST/ UNIT TRUST.

PUBLICLY HELD AND TRADED COMPANY

A *Publicly Held and Traded Company* is one whose shares are traded on a stock exchange or in an over-the-counter market. Publicly traded shares can be bought or sold among individual and institutional investors. Such companies are also referred to as joint stock companies and limited companies—referring to the limited liability of the shareholders. Their liability is limited to the price paid for the securities.

If a company is not publicly held, it will be privately held by one or more individuals. Private companies often have shares, but the purchase or sale of such shares is specifically restricted. If shares of privately held (also called "closely held") shares are distributed to employees, they are usually restricted to being sold back to the company.

See also INITIAL PUBLIC OFFERING (IPO); LISTED OPTION; OVER THE COUNTER (OTC).

PUNKT (Germany)

See POINT.

PURCHASING POWER

In general, *Purchasing Power* is the ability to buy as related to price levels.

For someone on a fixed income, the purchasing power varies inversely to the price level. As prices rise a person's purchasing power drops. If prices fall, the purchasing power of an individual rises.

An index of purchasing power is computed by reversing an index of commodity prices. The United States Bureau of Labor Statistics computes an index of purchasing power based on the reciprocal numbers from a commodity price index.

Increases in purchasing power can also be effected by wage increases or lower taxes. The increase generally provides the consuming public with additional disposable income with which to buy consumer goods. Purchases of consumer goods are generally perceived as beneficial to a country's economic growth.

See also INCOME; INFLATION; INTEREST/INTEREST RATES.

PURE PLAY

Pure Play describes the practice of investing in the securities of a company that has one primary business (e.g., a company that makes hard drives for computers or a fast-food company) as opposed to a company made up of several different types of businesses (conglomerate). The objective is to focus on what a company does best. Therefore, the best pure plays tend to be leaders in their type of business. It is the opposite of selecting the shares of a diversified company.

A pure play can also be a way to describe an initial public offering which does not have one or more "kickers" involved. Instead, the new issue offers only common shares or only corporate bonds, rather than shares or bonds with features or other securities attached.

See also DIVERSIFICATION; INITIAL PUBLIC OFFERING (IPO); KICKER.

PUT

A *Put* option gives the holder (owner) the right to sell a specific amount of the underlying security at a set price (strike price) in a defined period of time (prior to expiration). The option holder pays a price (premium) for this right. Options are either American or European. American options can be exercised (sold) at any time before the expiration date. European options may only be exercised at the expiry date.

For example: If XYZ Corporation has a market price of $55 per share and an investor currently owns 500 shares, but fears the price will temporarily drop, the investor can buy American puts to protect the price.

The investor buys 5 November puts at a strike price of $55 for a premium of $3 (total cost 500 shares times $3 = $1,500). No matter how low the price of XYZ Corporation declines, the put holder has the right to exercise and put (sell) the shares for $55 until the option expires in November.

The put was sold by an investor who believes the price of XYZ Corporation will either remain the same or rise between the time it was sold and the November expiration. For selling the put the investor received $3 per share or the $1,500 total premium.

If the price stays at or above the $55 level, the put will expire worthless.

See also CALL; EXPIRATION CYCLE; OPTION; PUT PREMIUM; SELLING TO OPEN.

PUT PREMIUM

In reference to options, the amount paid by the buyer and received by the seller of a put option is called the *Put Premium*. The put premium includes intrinsic value (the profitable difference between a strike price and the current market price) and time value (any amount more than the intrinsic value). Time value declines as the expiration date is approached.

For example, if the April 50 puts on XYZ Corporation have a premium of $5 and the current market price is $47, the put's intrinsic value is $3 and the time value is $2. Premium is stated on a per share basis. An investor buying 2 puts (100 shares per call) would pay a $1,000 put premium (200 x $5).

See also CALL PREMIUM; OPTION; STRIKE PRICE.

PYRAMIDING

In the modern business world the term *Pyramiding* has a number of meanings.

Pyramiding is sometimes used to describe a business expansion that makes use of leverage to build a larger production base. It is also a description for building on strength and becoming more efficient by eliminating waste or non-productive assets.

In reference to investing, pyramiding is making use of equity positions to leverage additions to an investor's portfolio of securities.

In fraudulent schemes, pyramiding has been used in the form of chain letters, where each recipient sends money to those on the list and adds new names. Pyramid fraud also occurs when incoming funds from new investors are used to pay out funds to current holders, giving the impression of high performance.

See also MARGIN; MUTUAL FUND; PONZI SCHEME.

QUALITATIVE ANALYSIS

Evaluating shares on the basis of non-financial data, *Qualitative Analysis* focuses on factors that are expected to affect revenues and earnings, but are not empirically measurable. These factors might include brand recognition, new products, labor relations, and quality of management. As a result of this kind of analysis, qualitative changes that have recently affected the share prices of many companies include environmental awareness and agreement with international trade rules. On the other hand, a company lacking in social responsibility may suffer negative sentiment if it is guilty of pollution and poor labor practices. These are negative attributes that can affect a company's bottom line but cannot be precisely measured.

Qualitative analysts are a vital complement to quantitative analysis when making buy or sell recommendations on shares.

See also BOTTOM LINE; EARNINGS; ETHICAL INVESTMENT; SOCIALLY RESPONSIBLE INVESTMENT (SRI); TECHNICAL ANALYSIS.

QUANTITATIVE ANALYSIS

Evaluating shares by examining financial data, *Quantitative Analysis* focuses on a company's financial information (typically the balance sheet and the income statement), while also considering economic trends within the relevant industry sector and the economy as a whole. Earnings growth trends, debt levels, and cash flow are among the areas of study for quantitative analysts who employ the data as a basis for projecting the company's growth.

Decisions to buy or sell shares of a company will be affected by qualitative analysis, but the main focus will be on the quantifiable numbers.

See also ANALYST; BUY; SELL.

QUANTITATIVO MINIMO DI NEGOZIAZIONE (Italy)

Quantitativo Minimo di Negoziazione refers to the minimum number of shares for a stock exchange trading in Italy. This number is set by the Commissione Nazionale per la Societa e la Borsa (CONSOB).

Many stock exchanges set minimum share availability requirements to provide the market with sufficient liquidity for trading. Poor liquidity adds to price volatility and can encourage inconsistent price quotations. These are problems that exchanges are eager to avoid, as shares that trade infrequently are difficult to buy and sell, thus creating an unfair and often unstable market.

Setting minimum quantity levels helps to ensure that enough shares are available for a broader base of investors, thereby creating an active market.

See also ITALY; THINLY TRADED.

QUARTERLY REPORT

A *Quarterly Report* is a three-month record of a corporation's financial condition.

In the United States the Securities and Exchange Commission requires annual reports to be distributed to stockholders. These reports contain balance sheet and income statements as well as other corporate information. In the United States, annual and quarterly reports can be requested from a company's investor relations department.

See also BALANCE SHEET; BOTTOM LINE; EARNINGS.

QUICK ASSET RATIO

Quick Asset Ratio is used by analysts to measure corporate liquidity. The ratio compares current assets (minus current inventory) to current liabilities. The most common version of the formula is as follows:

$$\frac{\text{Current Assets (including cash, accounts receivable net of bad debt provision, readily marketable securities but excluding stock and work in progress)}}{\text{Current Liabilities (including trade creditors, loan repayments within 12 months, tax payments due within 12 months)}}$$

A ratio in excess of 1 suggests a positive quick asset ratio, but a significant caveat must be mentioned. If the ratio is very high, it may indicate the presence of large amounts of cash, which can be attractive to companies looking for takeovers.

See also ACID TEST RATIO; NET CURRENT ASSETS; QUICK ASSETS.

QUICK ASSETS

Quick Assets are those assets that can be turned into cash in a short period of time without a significant sacrifice in value. A sample balance sheet serves as an example:

Current Assets	$6,000,000
Minus Current Inventory	$2,500,000
Equals Quick Assets	$3,500,000

Quick assets differ from net quick assets, which are current assets minus current liabilities.

See also ACID TEST RATIO; NET CURRENT ASSETS; QUICK ASSET RATIO.

QUIET PERIOD

Quiet Period refers to a 90-day span, after an issuer's initial public offering, during which underwriters are not permitted to distribute research about the company's business.

Designed to allow for the placement of securities into investment portfolios based solely upon the information provided in the prospectus, this Securities and Exchange Commission rule is intended to moderate the impact of positive research reports on new offerings by discouraging speculation and short-term trading.

The quiet period also allows the shares to receive a broad-based distribution that will help to prevent severe price volatility.

See also INITIAL PUBLIC OFFERING (IPO); SECURITIES AND EXCHANGE COMMISSION (SEC); VOLATILE.

QUOTARE (Italy)

Quotare means to quote prices for equity shares.

See also QUOTE.

QUOTATION

A *Quotation* is the inclusion by a stock exchange of the price of a particular security on its official list. Only public companies that meet specified requirements are granted quotations on the exchanges. Less stringent standards apply to unlisted securities markets.

Quotations include price information about particular stocks, bonds, commodity and financial futures, options, mutual funds, or money markets. They may also indicate the volume of trading and other information. Nonetheless, they by no means contain all the data relevant for investors. They do not indicate, for example, the overall financial condition of a firm whose stock is listed, nor the quality or location of delivery of a listed commodity future.

In Germany, the first list of market quotations for the Borse was published in 1625. In the United States, stock prices were first listed on a ticker tape by the New York Stock Exchange (NYSE) in 1867. Improvements were gradually made in the stock ticker so that it could list a greater number of prices more rapidly. By 1930 the printer used could print 500 characters per minute, and this level of performance remained standard for more than 30 years. Developments in computerization and teleprocessing in the 1960s and 1970s allowed much greater speeds. In 1966 the NYSE introduced the Market Data System, which provided nearly instantaneous collection and display of data, linking the exchange with member firms' offices around the world. By 1976 the NYSE had a system that could handle 36,000 characters per minute. The increase in the volume of trade on the exchange ran more or less in parallel, however, so that even the new technology was hard pressed to keep pace with the market's activity.

The development of one central reporting system, called the consolidated tape, made it possible to produce one list for all NYSE–listed securities transactions, regardless of where the transactions were carried out. Other exchanges participating in the consolidated tape are the American, Pacific, Midwest, Philadelphia, Boston, and Cincinnati, plus the National Association of Securities Dealers and the Instinet. Further advances have made it possible to dispense with trading floors and have fully computerized systems in the National Association of Securities Dealers Automated Quotation (NASDAQ) system. In 1990 NASDAQ introduced Portal, a trading and quotation system for unregistered securities. Later it created SelectNet, an on-line negotiating system that allows order entry firms to negotiate buy and sell orders directly with market dealers.

With the broad dissemination of computers, and the existence of services such as Free Internet equity news, it has become possible for brokers and other individuals to access updated stock price information continuously. Similar technical advances have been made in other countries. For example, in 1995 the German Borse's electronic bond quotation and trading system was launched. The London Stock Exchange Automated Quotation system (SEAQ), which replaced floor trading at the time of London's Big Bang in 1986, uses a screen display to provide information about securities.

Daily quotations for the NYSE are listed in the greatest detail in the *Wall Street Journal*. Quotations for securities that are mainly of local interest are found in most local newspapers. The Associated Press provides automated transmission of stock tables to newspapers around the world. The *Commercial and Financial Chronicle*, which is published weekly, contains very comprehensive securities quotations, and it is the only publication to carry complete NASDAQ quotations every week.

For a typical stock quotation from a major exchange, the information displayed includes the stock's high and low prices for the previous 52 weeks;

the amount of any dividends distributed; the yield (annual dividend returns divided by current purchase price); the p/e ratio (the price of one share of stock in proportion to how much that share represents in the company's total earnings); the volume of sales in the time period in question; the prices (high, low, and closing) of the stock during that period (session, week, etc., depending on what is covered in the publication where the quotation is listed); and the net change in closing value since the close of the previous period.

Quotations for over-the-counter stocks, such as those traded in NASDAQ, or for some tax-exempt municipal bonds, will include bid and ask prices, with the bid price being the highest bid offered during the period in question. Quotations for corporate bonds will include the coupon rate and the current percentage yield. Futures contracts, which are often grouped into agricultural and metallurgical commodities, interest rate futures, foreign exchange futures, and stock index futures, have quotations that include information such as the size of the contract unit (for example, 5,000 bushels of corn) and the open interest, which means the number of contracts currently obligated for delivery.

See also ASK PRICE; BID PRICE; COMPUTER TRADING; REAL TIME; TICKER/STOCK TICKER; TICKER TAPE; UNITED STATES/NEW YORK STOCK EXCHANGE (NYSE).

QUOTATION SPREAD

Quotation Spread refers to the money difference between a bid and ask in a price quote.

If shares of a company show a quote of 39 5/8 bid to 39 3/4 ask, the spread is 1/8 of a dollar on the exchanges denominated in dollars. A quote of 5 1/2 bid to 6 ask shows a spread of 1/2 dollar. The quotation on a computer screen will look something like the following:

(*spread*)

Bid	Ask	Size	Last Trade
39 5/8	39 3/4	100x200	39 5/8

See also ASK PRICE; BID PRICE; LAST TRADE.

QUOTE

Quote refers to the current market price information of a publicly traded security.

Sometimes called the full quote or quotation, a quote is a statement of the highest bid and lowest offer for a security. For example, if the shares of a company are trading at 50 1/4 to 50 3/8, a shareholder can currently sell 100 shares at $50.25 per share or an investor can buy 100 shares at a price of $50.375 per share. On exchanges, quotes will usually indicate the last trade price and the size, which represents the quantities available at the current quote.

Bid	Ask	Size	Last Trade
50 1/4	50 3/8	100x200	50 3/8

See also ASK PRICE; BID PRICE; QUOTATION; QUOTATION SPREAD.

QUOTIENT COURS BÉNÉFICE (France)
See PRICE/EARNINGS RATIO.

R

RACCATTORE (Italy)

Raccattore refers to the accumulation of shares in a slow manner, so as not to arouse suspicion or other interest in the particular company.

Even though the term is Italian, the concept is universal. Too much attention to an investor's accumulation in the shares of a company could attract the interest of other buyers, causing the price of the shares to rise more than normal.

Sellers of large stakes often take the opposite approach, disposing of their holdings in one transaction known as a block trade.

See also BLOCK; BLOCK TRADE; INSTITUTIONAL INVESTOR; POSITION.

RACHAT (France)

See REDEMPTION.

RACKETEER INFLUENCED AND CORRUPT ORGANIZATIONS ACT (United States)

The *Racketeer Influenced and Corrupt Organizations Act (RICO)* was passed by the U.S. Senate on 15 October 1970. The act's impact has been felt by Wall Street members as well as by the criminal mobs that were its original target.

The roots of the RICO Act lie in the Senate's many investigations into organized crime in the United States. In open and closed sessions in the 1950s, Senate members were told that organized crime gangs, particularly the Mafia, had infiltrated legitimate businesses. Organized crime was alleged to have influence over numerous industries, particularly shipping, trucking, construction, gambling, and waste disposal. Large profits were made from bribes, illegal cartels forced prices up, and crime bosses legitimized their funds by laundering them through a wide variety of front companies. Several years of prevarication were followed by a number of ineffective acts that did little to curtail the problem.

Attorney G. Robert Blakey was responsible for drafting the bill that eventually became the RICO Act in 1969. The act covered the following illegal activities:

- The establishment and operation of any illegal enterprise
- The collection of unlawful debts
- The counterfeiting of money and documents
- Embezzlement from pension funds
- Extortion

RICO also allowed prosecutions for gang-related murder, narcotics trading, illegal gambling, bribery, insurance fraud, arson, and robbery.

The act was careful not to offend the large and politically important Italian-American community. Interestingly, the phrase "organized crime" did not appear in the act: instead Blakey used the phrase "racketeering activities" to define RICO's scope. Some wits pointed out, however, that the title of the act provided a sardonic echo of a character in a famous gangster movie. In 1930 Edward G. Robinson had enthralled movie audiences with his portrayal of the mobster Rico Bendello in *Little Caesar.*

The regulations pertaining to the stock exchange were primarily designed to prosecute criminals who "washed" their money by buying stocks and bonds and then reinvested the proceeds in legitimate businesses. Provision was also made to prosecute any member of an organized group who was suspected of share price manipulation or stock market fraud. Brokers who provided false information to clients and those who churned accounts in order to generate extra commission could also be prosecuted. The RICO law threatened stiff penalties for those found guilty of such crimes. Any business purchased with illegal money could be confiscated, and treble damages could be levied in civil cases. Assets of suspected criminals could be frozen by the authorities even before a trial opened.

Wall Street legend is full of tales about the effects of organized crime on the "fair and orderly" world of the stock exchange. For example, Yiddy Bloom, a known associate of the Mafia's most respected financier, Meyer Lansky, was found guilty in 1978 of manipulating the share price of the Magic Marker Corporation with the aim of making profits from illegal stock dealing. Bloom organized a massive "concert party," opening hundreds of accounts in different names across the United States. The share price rose from $6.50 to $30, boosted by many small purchases from these accounts and a number of large bribes to salesmen. Bloom and his associates, who had effectively cornered the market in Magic Marker stock, sold at the peak and pocketed huge profits.

Another Mafia scam involved blackmailing or bribing back office staff to steal certificates for bearer securities. The certificates were pledged as collateral against loans with gullible or compliant banks; the money received in exchange was then shifted overseas or used to fund a business. By the time the banks discovered that the certificates were stolen, the cash was long gone.

The first years of RICO were inauspicious. Only a limited number of cases were brought to trial and relatively few convictions were achieved. The takeover boom of the 1980s, however, provided many occasions for RICO to come into play. In 1982 the feared corporate raider Carl Icahn made an audacious bid for the Marshall Field department store group. Attorneys for Marshall Field claimed that Icahn had partly funded his raid from racketeering. When Marshall Field merged with Batus, however, the charges were not pressed further.

RICO was shown to be a truly effective law during the legal investigations that followed allegations of illegal share dealing at the U.S. investment bank Drexel Burnham Lambert. Rudolph Giuliani, the high profile U.S. New York attorney, led a campaign against Wall Street crime that resulted in a successful prosecution and a $650 million fine. The case destroyed Drexel's reputation and crippled the bank's finances, and it came as no surprise when Drexel filed for bankruptcy in 1990.

The plethora of books dealing with the insider dealing scandal at Drexel Burnham Lambert provide a number of useful insights into the practical application of the RICO Act. Fenton Bailey's *Fall from Grace: The Untold Story of Michael Milken* is critical of the power of the act but, as the book is largely supportive of Milken, this is not entirely surprising. Connie Bruck is more in favor of RICO in her exposé of Milken in *The Predators' Ball*, as is James Stewart in his enjoyable *Den of Thieves*.

See also MONEY LAUNDERING; WHITE COLLAR CRIME.

RAIDER

A corporation or individual investor seeking to purchase a controlling interest in a firm is referred to as a *Raider*.

Often heading a company with significant liquid assets (known as a war chest), a corporate raider actively searches for companies in which he or she might buy either a controlling interest or all of the shares. The company may be added to a portfolio of companies, sold off in pieces, or resold to the public at a later time.

Greenmail—a situation in which a target company buys back the shares purchased by the raider at a premium if the raider agrees to cease the takeover attempt—is one means by which to avoid a takeover. Another is the poison pill defense, in which the management of the target company threatens to implement strategies designed to make the company much less attractive if the prospective purchaser continues with the takeover attempt.

In the United States, Carl Icahn, T. Boone Pickens, Ted Turner, and Saul Steinberg have all held the distinction of being referred to as corporate raiders. In the United Kingdom, Hanson Trust developed a reputation for aggressively taking over undervalued companies.

See also GREENMAIL; POISON PILL; TAKEOVER/TAKEOVER BID.

RALLY

Rally refers to a rise in the value of a market or an individual share after a decline in prices.

Any event perceived as improving the investment climate is capable of causing a stock market rally. One of the strongest of these events is the lowering of interest rates. Another strong influence is the announcement of increased corporate earnings.

A rally in the price of shares of an individual company can be caused by a variety of factors. Improved earnings, a takeover attempt, the settlement of a costly lawsuit, or the announcement of a new product can all have a positive impact on a company's share prices.

The opposite of a rally is often referred to as a correction, in which prices decline due to the presence of more sellers than buyers.

See also DOW THEORY; FUNDAMENTAL ANALYSIS; MARKET CORRECTION/MARKETCRASH; TECHNICAL ANALYSIS.

RANDOM WALK THEORY

The *Random Walk Theory* is a theory of stock price movements that posits that fluctuations in the market value of a security are unpredictable. Analysts and economists who follow the theory believe that price changes over a period of time will follow a random pattern.

The theory first appeared in the doctoral thesis of Louis Bachelier at the turn of the century. It became popular in the late 1950s and early 1960s, and has been a constant influence on stock market thinking ever since.

In its simplest form, the random walk theory states that the next price change of stock is based on the current market price adjusted for an unknown change, which may be either positive or negative. Random walk theory is closely related to the weak form of the "Efficient Market Hypothesis."

See also DART THROWERS; DOW THEORY; FIBONACCI SEQUENCE; FUNDAMENTAL ANALYSIS; STOCK MARKET EFFICIENCY THEORY; TECHNICAL ANALYSIS.

RANGE

Range refers to the price trading pattern of shares or the point movement of a stock market index between a high and low level.

A general range for both shares and indexes is the year high and year low. These figures will show both the growth and volatility for a 52-week period.

In reference to technical analysis, the range is between a selected area of support and resistance. The information contained in a range is used to forecast short-term trading patterns.

Fundamental analysts also make use of trading ranges to assist in trend observation and to forecast future ranges. For example, if XYZ Corporation is trading at a range of $35 to $50 per share, it might be forecast to trade at $50 to $60 per share with a specified increase in earnings.

See also FUNDAMENTAL ANALYSIS; TECHNICAL ANALYSIS; YEAR HIGH/YEAR LOW (HI-LO).

RAPPORT (France)

See ANNUAL REPORT.

RAPPORTE (DI) CONVERSIONE (Italy)

Rapporte (di) Conversione means exchanging convertible securities for shares.

See also CONVERTIBLE.

RAPPORTO PREZZO-UTILE (Italy)

See PRICE/EARNINGS RATIO.

RATE OF INTEREST

See INTEREST/INTEREST RATES.

RATE OF RETURN

When looking at a new investment and deciding whether or not to purchase a security, investors often calculate the *Rate of Return*, also referred to as current yield. It is essentially the money paid out to the investor divided by the price of the security.

For example: If an investor is interested in buying 500 shares of XYZ Corporation at $50 per share, with a current annual dividend of $3.67, the rate of return is calculated as follows:

Cost of 500 shares of XYZ Corporation:

$50 x 500 = $25,000

The annual dividend to the investor:

$3.67 x 500 = $1,835

$$\frac{\$1{,}835 \text{ total annual dividend}}{\$25{,}000 \text{ cost of the investment}} = 7.34\% \text{ rate of return}$$

If the amount of the annual dividend is increased, the rate of return will increase.

See also DIVIDEND; TOTAL RETURN; YIELD.

RATING

A *Rating* offers a guide to the quality of bonds and securities.

A credit rating uses a combination of letters and numbers, generally with "A" and "1" representing the lowest risk. As applied to bonds, ratings indicate the current opinion on whether principal and interest will be paid on a timely basis.

In the United States, three of the leading bond rating services are Fitch, Moody's, and Standard & Poor's. The following is a summary of their ratings for corporate and municipal bond ratings:

Description of Rating:	Fitch	Moody's	Standard & Poor's
Highest quality	AAA	Aaa	AAA
High quality	AA	Aa	AA
Upper medium grade	A	A	A
Medium grade	BBB	Baa	BBB
Speculative	BB	Ba	BB
Speculative low grade	B	B	B
Poor to default	CCC	Caa	CCC
Highest speculation	CC	Ca	CC
Lowest quality/ no interest	C	C	C

Ratings on company shares are more indicative of the stability of the dividend payments and are often stated as letters "A, B, or C," with a plus or minus added as a further modifier.

Some analysts also rate the debt on companies as to the ability of companies to service that debt, based on cash flows.

See also FITCH INVESTORS' SERVICE INC.; MOODY'S INVESTOR'S SERVICES; STANDARD AND POOR'S RATINGS; VALUE LINE INVESTMENT SURVEY.

RATIO WRITER

A *Ratio Writer* is an investor who participates in the risk-moderating strategy of writing (selling) call contracts, some of which are covered by the underlying security.

Using this strategy, if a person owning 500 shares of XYZ Corporation writes (sells) 10 call contracts, five of the contracts are covered by the 500 shares and five of the contracts are uncovered (naked). In this case the investor is a ratio writer of 2 for 1.

See also CALL; NAKED OPTION/NAKED CALL; OPTION; UNDERLYING SECURITY.

REACTION
See MARKET CORRECTION/CRASH.

READY MARKET
Ready Market is a description of the marketability of a security. This status is determined by the existence of legitimate bids and offers, a reasonable amount of regular trading to provide liquidity, and timely settlement of transactions. A security with a ready market is characterized by ongoing trading activity rather than occasional activity.

The U.S. Securities and Exchange Commission (SEC) uses the description in determining a securities firm's net capital compliance. The value of the securities that have a ready market must be reasonably related to the last sale price in bona fide competitive markets.

Brokerage firms must maintain certain net capital requirements as required by the SEC.

See also LIQUIDITY; NET CAPITAL REQUIREMENT; SECURITIES AND EXCHANGE COMMISSION (SEC).

REAL ESTATE INVESTMENT TRUST (REIT; United States)
A *Real Estate Investment Trust (REIT)* is a company trust in which to invest a portfolio of real estate ventures.

Publicly owned REITs must register with the Securities and Exchange Commission. Many REITs trade in the same way as ordinary shares, with a bid, ask, and last trade. The value of the security is directly linked to the value fluctuations and productivity of the underlying real estate and often include a variety of holdings in shopping centers, office buildings, apartment complexes, and hotels.

The marketing theory behind such trusts is that they offer considerable diversification in real estate, with the added bonus of the liquidity found in ordinary share investments.

Equity REITs take ownership positions in the properties, and the shareholders receive income from rents received. When properties are sold, shareholders can also receive capital gains. Mortgage REITs solely own mortgages on properties and pass interest income to shareholders.

To avoid corporate taxation, 75% or more of the REIT's income must be from real property and 95% of its taxable income must be distributed to shareholders.

See also CAPITAL GAIN; LIQUIDITY; PROPERTY AS INVESTMENT; PUBLICLY HELD AND TRADED COMPANY.

REAL TIME
Real Time refers to the simultaneous inputting and generation of data in a computer system.

The most common form of real time data is the share price information that appears on Reuters screens in broker's dealer rooms.

While surfing the Internet for stock market information, the term *real time quotes* will frequently be seen and usually carries an extra fee for the service. Real time means that quotations are as current as they can possibly be, whether during the time of trading sessions or at the end of the day. The provider of these quotations must pay a fee for the service and passes that fee along to the Internet end-user.

Another form of price quotation is available without any extra fees both on the Internet and on network television. Although these quotations are delayed 15 minutes, they enable the investor to get some feel for what the market and individual company shares are doing.

See also ASK PRICE; BID PRICE; QUOTE.

REAL TIME TRADE REPORTING (United States)
Real Time Trade Reporting is a requirement imposed on market makers (and in some instances, non-market makers) to report each trade immediately after completion of the transaction. Shares traded on the NASDAQ Stock Market are subject to real time trade reporting within 90 seconds of execution.

See also MARKET MAKER; STOCK MARKET; UNITED STATES/NASDAQ (OTC).

REALIZED PROFIT/LOSS
A *Realized Profit/Loss* results from the sale of an investment. It differs from a paper profit or loss, a situation in which the shares are not sold.

For example, if an investor owns 100 shares of XYZ Corporation for which he or she paid $50 per share and the current market price is $40 per share, there would be a $10 per share loss. The loss is referred to as realized only in the event that the shares are sold. If the shares are not sold, the loss is referred to as an unrealized or paper loss.

Brokerage firms and investment advisers often show realized and unrealized losses or gains in the periodic statements sent to investors.

See also CAPITAL GAIN; CAPITAL LOSS; COST BASIS; WASH SALE RULE.

RECEIVE VERSUS PAYMENT (RVP)

Receive Versus Payment (RVP) is a method whereby institutional investors receive cash settlement for the sale of a security. Only cash will be accepted by the investor in exchange for the delivery of the securities.

When buying securities, the institutional investor will use delivery versus payment (DVP), a situation in which the securities are sent to the institution's bank and payment is given on delivery.

See also CASH ACCOUNT; DELIVERY VERSUS PAYMENT (DVP); MARGIN ACCOUNT.

RECESSION

A *Recession* can be categorized by a pronounced downturn in the level of economic activity, often shown by two or more successive quarters of negative growth in GDP.

Recessions are a cyclical phenomenon of trade cycles, usually short in duration and characterized by increases in company liquidations, low levels of consumer confidence, and a drop in personal and business expenditure. A downturn in consumer demand can lead to a fall in levels of investment and a negative multiplier effect, causing a severe contraction in the capital goods industry. Destocking further reduces production, with high interest rates, often at the onset of recession, increasing the opportunity cost of holding inventory. Prior to recession, productivity often falls, with companies slow to respond to a fall in demand and reluctant to reduce their labor force.

Keynesian demand management of the economy attempts to stabilize fluctuations in the trade cycle by counter-cyclical fiscal policy, such as expanding aggregate demand and deficit financing. The fine-tuning of policy is often hampered by the effect of time lags, as individuals' expectations of recession have a cumulative negative effect on aggregate demand.

See also FISCAL POLICY; KEYNES, JOHN MAYNARD.

RECORD DATE

See DATE OF RECORD.

RED HERRING

Red Herring is securities industry jargon for the preliminary prospectus for a new securities issue. The term *red herring* has long held a meaning of something ingenuous, since some of the information in a preliminary prospectus might be changed for the final prospectus. A cautionary statement printed near the left side of the cover of a preliminary prospectus informs the investor that the information is incom-

plete and subject to change. The red-colored print and a disclaimer stating that the information is not final are all typical signs of a red herring prospectus.

Even though it is incomplete and some of the information is subject to change, the red herring does provide the prospective investor with considerable information regarding the new issue. Brokers send out red herrings to prospective buyers to obtain indications of interest.

See also INDICATION OF INTEREST; INITIAL PUBLIC OFFERING (IPO); OBJECTIVE; PRELIMINARY PROSPECTUS.

REDEMPTION

Redemption refers to a company's repurchase of callable debt securities (bonds or preferred shares) before their maturity date, commonly at a premium over their par value.

Companies employ redemptions as a means of restructuring or reducing their debt. This activity can be particularly advantageous when interest rates have dropped and the company can refinance at lower rates.

Redemption is also the term used to describe the selling of the shares of a mutual fund by an investor. Mutual fund open end shares are redeemed at the net asset value, which is normally calculated at the end of each trading session.

Closed end mutual fund shares, also known as unit investment trusts, are not usually redeemed by the investor; rather, they are resold to another investor.

See also MUTUAL FUND; NET ASSET VALUE (NAV); UNIT INVESTMENT TRUST/UNIT TRUST.

REGISTERED CERTIFICATE

A *Registered Certificate* is a paper certificate for a registered security.

See also REGISTERED SECURITY.

REGISTERED COMPANY (United States)

A *Registered Company* is a company that has filed a registration statement with the Securities and Exchange Commission (SEC) and has expressed its intent to conduct a public offering.

A registered company is required to meet SEC disclosure requirements. These requirements help to ensure that companies provide investors with enough information to decide whether or not to include the shares of a publicly traded company in their portfolios. The aim is for the company's statistics to be transparent, so there are no hidden secrets or problems. The same basic financial and other company information is available to all investors who might be interested.

See also ANNUAL REPORT; BALANCE SHEET; INTERIM REPORT; SECURITIES AND EXCHANGE COMMISSION (SEC).

REGISTERED COMPETITIVE MARKET MAKER (RCMM; United States)

A *Registered Competitive Market Maker (RCMM)* is a member of the New York Stock Exchange who is allowed to make trades for a personal account or for the account of a firm. These members are expected to provide bids and offers (on either a voluntary basis or on request), which help to contribute to the stability of the market when an imbalance exists in buy or sell orders.

Effectively, RCMMs help to enhance the dealer function of the exchange specialists.

See also BID PRICE; SPECIALIST; UNITED STATES/NEW YORK STOCK EXCHANGE (NYSE).

REGISTERED COMPETITIVE TRADER (RCT)

A *Registered Competitive Trader (RCT)* is a member of the New York Stock Exchange who can make trades for a personal account or an account for a firm, and who invests to make profits on short-term trades.

RCTs are required to abide by the same trading rules as the exchange specialist. Since it is required that 75% of their transactions be stabilizing trades, they cannot buy above the sale price of a previous trade nor sell below a previous trade. The bids and offers placed by an RCT cannot take precedence over a public customer of a member firm at the same price.

On the American Stock Exchange a registered equity market maker (REMM) performs essentially the same function as the RCT, but must adhere to stricter rules.

See also ASK PRICE; BID PRICE; MEMBER; SPECIALIST; UNITED STATES/AMERICAN STOCK EXCHANGE (AMEX); UNITED STATES/NEW YORK STOCK EXCHANGE (NYSE).

REGISTERED OPTIONS PRINCIPAL (ROP; United States)

A *Registered Options Principal (ROP)* is a registered representative who has completed a qualifying examination—known as the Series 4 exam—focusing on options.

A ROP will often supervise other registered representatives and their options work with investors. The ROP will check options tickets for accuracy and assume a certain amount of responsibility for a correct transaction being placed. It is the ROP's function to

ensure that the investor makes the desired options transaction and to help limit the firm's risk in relation to costly errors and misunderstandings.

See also OPTION; REGISTERED REPRESENTATIVE (RR); TICKET.

REGISTERED OPTIONS TRADER (United States/AMEX)

A *Registered Options Trader* is, effectively, an options specialist on the floor of the American Stock Exchange (AMEX). Like a share-trading specialist, it is the responsibility of the registered options trader to ensure a fair and orderly market in a specifically assigned group of options.

See also OPTION; TRADE; UNITED STATES/AMERICAN STOCK EXCHANGE (AMEX).

REGISTERED REPRESENTATIVE (RR; United States)

Registered Representative is a U.S. title for stockbrokers and other persons employed by a broker/dealer or other financial firm that is a member of the National Association of Securities Dealers (NASD) or Municipal Securities Rulemaking Board (MSRB). All registered representatives must have passed the Series 7 general securities examination.

People who make buy and sell recommendations, underwrite, and sell investment advice for a fee must be registered representatives under the requirements of the Securities and Exchange Commission and the New York Stock Exchange. A general state examination is also required.

Although the broker's exam at the state level is standardized to one test, individual license fees must be paid to each state in which the broker does business. Licensing keeps track of individual stock market professionals and can be revoked if the rules are not followed.

See also SECURITIES AND EXCHANGE COMMISSION (SEC); SERIES 7 REGISTERED; STOCKBROKER; UNDERWRITING.

REGISTERED SECONDARY DISTRIBUTION (United States)

Registered Secondary Distribution is the distribution of securities by an owner under registration with the Securities and Exchange Commission.

These distributions often originate through a control person or another holder of restricted securities. They might be done as part of a combined primary-secondary offering with a prospectus issued by the corporation, or as an offering from the owner making use of currently filed disclosure documents of the issuer. This is known as a shelf-registration.

See also AFFILIATED PERSON; ISSUE; PROSPECTUS; SECONDARY DISTRIBUTION.

REGISTERED SECURITY

A *Registered Security* is a security that has the investor's name recorded in the books of the issuer or the issuer's registrar. The registered investor receives any and all benefits attached to ownership. These benefits include voting rights, dividends, share splits, and, if they are attached, warrants.

The securities must be registered with a governmental agency, such as the Securities and Exchange Commission (SEC) in the United States.

The registration process was established by the Securities Exchange Act of 1933 and 1934. The SEC reviews issues of securities and, if approved, provides the registration, which allows issues to be publicly traded. The SEC neither approves nor disapproves of the quality of the investment.

The Registration Statement details financial and other operations of the company, its management, and the purpose of the offering. If the details sent to the SEC are inaccurate or incomplete, the issue will be delayed until the information is complete. A registration fee is charged by the SEC and paid by the issuer.

A bearer security is owned by the person who has it in his or her possession. Many countries are converting to the use of registered securities, as it is easier to keep track of the owner for paying dividends and taxation purposes.

See also BEARER CERTIFICATE/SECURITY/SHARE; DIVIDEND; SECURITIES AND EXCHANGE COMMISSION (SEC).

REGISTRAR

A *Registrar* is an agent who takes on the task of maintaining records of the legal ownership of securities.

The registrar keeps an up-to-date share register, which lists the names and addresses of shareholders and the number of shares they hold. He or she also monitors the quantity of shares in circulation to make certain it is the correct and authorized amount.

A bond registrar is responsible for certifying that a bond is a genuine debt obligation of the issuer.

In the United States, registrars work with transfer agents to keep current records of the owners of securities. In the United Kingdom, registrars often perform their duties in separately run subsidiaries of commercial banks.

See also ISSUE; REGISTERED SECURITY.

REGISTRATION
See REGISTERED SECURITY.

REGISTRATION STATEMENT
See REGISTERED SECURITY.

REGULAR-WAY SETTLEMENT

Regular-Way Settlement is a securities industry term for a transaction settled in the normal way, at the regular time. Settlement is achieved when a securities transaction has been completed, and is invariably marked by the delivery of securities or the payment of funds to a buyer.

Regular-way settlement for ordinary and preferred shares and municipal and corporate bonds is now Trade date + 3 days (T + 3) in the United States. Many options, government issues, and money market securities end with regular-way settlement. Settlement dates vary from country to country (T + 1, T + 3, and T + 4 are fairly common), but rarely occur more than two weeks after the date of the transaction.

An international investor who buys and sells securities in another country must be aware of the conventions for that country's regular-way settlement, as it will affect the date when funds must be available for use or can be repatriated.

See also MARGIN ACCOUNT; PRIMARY MARKET; WHEN ISSUED (WI).

REGULATION, TREND TOWARD

For most of the 20th century, capitalism around the world has demonstrated an increasing *Trend Toward Regulation*. This trend has been more pronounced in some countries, particularly the developed countries (although with some important differences among them), and it has emerged more during periods of depression and war. In some countries, such as the United States since the late 1970s, a countertrend of deregulation has become dominant, which has also been gaining ground in the 1990s in Japan and Western Europe. Regulation may be broadly defined as a diverse grouping of laws, policies, practices, and institutions by which governments seek to promote economic efficiency, equitability, and public health and safety.

Controversy over the justification, efficacy, and ramifications of government regulation is highly politicized. Advocates of laissez-faire capitalism argue that the capitalist economy works most efficiently when it is unfettered by regulation and can attend to the rational and equitable distribution of economic goods. If new needs arise, even at the level of society as a whole, the market is the best way to meet them. Government does not have as much information and is not well positioned as businesses are to carry out necessary modifications and to take advantage of opportunities to grow, reduce waste, and the like. These proponents of the virtues of the free market point to periods when countries' gross domestic products grew more rapidly and there was a trend away from regulation, or when the countries with the least regulation grew fastest. For example, during the period from 1981 to 1993, among all European Union countries, England and Ireland, which had the least regulated markets, showed the highest growth rates, whereas Greece, which had the most government regulation of the economy, grew at the slowest rate. One possible explanation is that countries with more regulatory baggage will not be able to compete in international trade.

Opponents of this view—many of whom are nonetheless advocates of capitalism—emphasize that while deregulated capitalism has produced rapid growth in some periods, at other times it has produced recession, breakdown, collapse, and depression. Further, it has always produced a distribution of wealth and income that was so skewed that, in addition to sacrificing the well-being of significant portions of the population, it also effectively removed them from among the productive ranks of society through unemployment, ill health, and so forth. It is also argued that the infatuation with the free market can lead to the corruption of public morality, the decay of social institutions, and the breakdown of international peace.

Of course, there are some nuances: many economists support the strengthening, or at least the maintenance, of regulation in some areas (for example, labor laws) while supporting deregulation in other areas (such as product quality). Regulation should not be seen as simply opposed to a competitive free market. On the contrary, one of the objectives of capitalist regulation is to promote competition by, for example, opposing the development of monopolies and creating a hospitable environment for the formation and growth of small businesses. Because a portion of the costs of complying with regulations is fixed, small companies carry a particularly heavy compliance burden. This has been mitigated to an extent by relaxing the application of regulatory requirements to such companies.

With regard to monopolies, some of them, such as in the railroad, oil, and telephone industries, were dismantled in the United States in the late 1800s and early 1900s. In Japan the major antimonopoly moves were made following World War II, with the breakup of the *zaibatsu*, conglomerates that were controlled by holding companies and had dominated Japanese industry. But in the United States in the 1990s, there remained numerous industries, from automobile manufacturing to retailing to publishing, in which a very small number of concerns dominated the market; and the trend was toward ever-greater concentration and centralization of capital. Their continued existence may be taken as an example of "capture"—in which government regulators end up supporting, rather than curbing, monopolies.

In other industries, such as the public utilities, the public interest is not served by redundancy, so the government's attitude is to permit the existence of monopolies but to monitor and regulate their activities. The means of regulation vary. In Great Britain, price regulation is practiced with regard to telephone, gas, electricity, and water providers. In such a system, price rises are pegged to a retail price index, and firms are offered the incentive of lowering their costs so as to increase profits. In the United States, a system of rate-of-return regulation is in effect, according to which an allowable profit rate is determined and prices are set at such a level as to yield it.

The biggest decade for regulation growth was the 1930s, when governments in all the major capitalist countries sought ways to prevent the recurrence, and buffer the effects of, the crash of 1929 and the Great Depression. For example, in the United States, several regulatory bodies were created, including the Securities and Exchange Commission and the National Association of Securities Dealers (stock markets), the Federal Trade Commission, the Federal Communications Commission, the National Labor Relations Board, and the Civil Aeronautics Board. Their effects varied. For example, with regard to financial markets, for several decades there was relative stability. By 1971 governments moved toward a system of flexible exchange rates. In the late 1970s all the world's principal countries except Japan had abolished the capital controls they had adopted at the end of World War II. They believed (wrongly) that financial instability would not result.

A major complication for many areas of regulation arises from technological advance and the greater mobility of capital. New technologies make obsolete many old regulations. There is, for example, no way to control the flow of capital across borders when it may be carried out at a computer. With regard to the stock market, following the October 1987 crash of the New York Stock Exchange, many regulators called for a ban on program trading, but in an atmosphere of computerization such a ban could scarcely be enforced. Governments that insist on more regulations may simply drive investors to some other country. The Eurodollar and Eurobond markets, in which U.S. dollars and bonds are traded, are a means of getting around regulations and taxes in the United States. The complicated derivatives of the Japanese stock market, whose trading the Japanese government sought to ban, may be traded on the Singapore stock exchange.

Stock market regulators, especially since the late 1980s, have sought to stop insider trading, in which investment house employees, or others with connections to them, use their advanced inside knowledge to secure better deals than are available to the public. The Amsterdam Stock Exchange ruled that insiders would no longer be allowed to trade two months before an annual earnings announcement. An unintended effect of this ban was a reduction in the Dutch market's liquidity and, according to one study, its ability to respond quickly to positive earnings news.

In terms of international competition, among the three most powerful capitalist countries—the United States, Japan, and Germany—the record of the early 1990s might be interpreted to mean that the economy that grew the fastest, that of the United States, did so because it had the least burden of regulation. According to this view, Japan and Germany—and Europe more generally—are held back by such things as uniform pay scales, strong unions, generous unemployment insurance, costly benefits, and inefficient regulations. The sectors in which deregulation is most seriously considered in America, Germany, France, Britain, and Japan are electricity, airlines, trucking, telecommunications, and retail distribution.

However, if one looks at gross domestic product per capita, and extends the time scale for comparison back to the early 1980s, then all three of the top countries have grown at approximately the same rate. Also, it has been pointed out that American productivity, in terms of output per worker hour, has not grown as rapidly as that of its leading competitors, and that the American economy has measured up only because the average number of hours per worker has increased. Perhaps it is best to conclude that the effects of regulation are multifaceted and that they interact in complex ways with other economic factors.

See also CAPITALISM; JAPANESE FINANCIAL MARKETS; MONOPOLY.

REGULATION A/B (United States)

Regulation A

An SEC provision for a simplified registration process for small issues of securities. It requires a shorter pro-spectus, and has less liability for officers and directors for false or misleading statements than for a full listing.

Regulation B

A Federal Reserve Board statement regarding the means and conditions by which the Federal Reserve banks make loans to members and other banks at the federal discount window.

See also FEDERAL DISCOUNT RATE/FED FUNDS; PROSPECTUS; REGISTERED SECURITY.

REGULATION G–X (United States)

Regulation G

A Federal Reserve Board rule that regulates lenders other than commercial banks, brokers, or dealers, who, in their ordinary course of business, extend credit to individuals to purchase securities. The rule also contains provisions for corporations that loan money by purchasing shares for employee stock option and stock purchase plans.

Regulation T

The Federal Reserve Board regulation that covers credit extension to customers by securities brokers, dealers, and members of the national securities exchanges. The regulation sets the initial margin requirement and strictly defines registered (eligible), unregistered (not eligible), and exempt securities.

Although the requirements can be changed, the initial equity in a margin account is a minimum of $2,000. Up to 50% of eligible marginable securities can qualify for a margin loan. For example, an investor buying 200 shares of XYZ Corporation at $50 per share will pay $10,000. The investor is able to borrow $5,000 and buy a further 100 shares at $50 per share. The short-term "Reg-T" is often used to describe the above situation.

Regulation T Call

If an investor makes a margin account purchase but doesn't have sufficient funds in his account to meet the minimum Regulation T requirements, the firm issues a Reg-T call. It is simply a request for additional funds.

The Federal Reserve requirement must be satisfied by regular-way settlement, currently Trade date + 3 days (T + 3).

Regulation U

A Federal Reserve requirement limiting the amount of credit that a bank is allowed to extend to a customer for the purchase or carry of corporate marginable securities.

Regulation X

The rule established by the Federal Reserve Board governing the amount and type of credit that can be accepted by a person buying, holding, or trading corporate marginable securities. It regulates the person receiving credit, rather than the individual or corporation granting the credit.

See also EMPLOYEE STOCK OWNERSHIP PLAN (ESOP); MARGIN; REGISTERED SECURITY; REGULAR-WAY SETTLEMENT.

REHYPOTHECATION/REHYPOTHECATE (United States)

Rehypothecation is the repledging of securities as collateral for a loan.

Hypothecation is synonymous with pledging. An investor generally agrees to allow the brokerage firm to repledge securities when the account agreement is signed.

The investor pledges (hypothecates) the securities to the brokerage firm as collateral against the margin loan. The broker then repledges, or rehypothecates, the securities to banks as collateral for broker loans as part of a General Loan and Collateral Agreement. Such broker loans are made to firms for their investors who have sold securities short.

See also COLLATERAL; MARGIN; SELLING SHORT.

RELATIONSHIP SHARES (Japan)

Relationship Shares refers to shares owned by business firms in which the firms have a working relationship.

Business firms in Japan will often own substantial equity positions in companies with which they have a working business relationship. These relationship shares are held as a permanent investment and are seldom traded publicly.

Holding the shares is believed to enhance the business relationship as well as show sincerity and respect. In some situations, the shares restrict the liquidity of trading and can act as an insurmountable barrier against any unwanted takeover threats.

See also EQUITY; LIQUIDITY; TAKEOVER/TAKEOVER BID.

REOPENING

Reopening refers to the reinitiation of trading after a temporary suspension.

When an order imbalance occurs on a stock exchange, it is not uncommon to halt trading to sort out the order imbalance or wait for the release of information that could have a significant effect on the price of the shares traded.

The temporary suspension of trading can also be caused by a price movement exceeding the maximum limit for the session. Some exchanges suspend trading for a specific period of time, such as 15 minutes, while others do not have a set time for such trading halts.

Once the reason for the halt in trading is dealt with, trading on the security is reopened and trading activity for the session is resumed.

See also AT THE CLOSE; AT THE OPEN; SESSION.

REORGANIZATION DEPARTMENT

In a brokerage firm, the *Reorganization Department* handles the exchange of securities when changes in capital structure have been made.

Events such as a security experiencing a reverse split or one company taking over another require an exchange of share certificates. Such changes are run through the Reorganization Department.

See also REVERSE SPLIT; SPLIT; TAKEOVER/TAKEOVER BID.

REPATRIATION

Repatriation refers to the return of funds to the investor in the country of origin.

Although each country has different rules regarding the transfer of funds into and out of the country, repatriation of funds for investors is usually easily accomplished. Some countries still have requirements regarding specific time periods during which funds must remain in the country, but these restrictions are expected to be changed as international investing becomes more common. The investor can learn the details of time requirements from a broker in the relevant country.

See also individual countries' stock exchange profiles.

RESEARCH AND DEVELOPMENT (R&D)

Research and Development (R&D) is a company's department for planning and improving products for the purpose of growth and increased earnings. It is listed as an expense item on the budgets of many companies. R&D costs include laboratory research, new product evaluation, and the testing of research findings.

There are several important issues to be addressed when accounting for R&D. At present, most companies charge R&D expenses to their profit and loss account in the year in which the expense is incurred.

However, many company accountants believe that the most accurate method of dealing with R&D costs is to amortize them over the life of the relevant product.

The development of new products enables a company to increase earnings and growth and also forms a broader revenue base. Single product companies can become highly vulnerable to economic cycles or industry sector changes. Having several products helps to sustain income through difficult times.

See also CYCLES; DIVERSIFICATION; FUNDAMENTAL ANALYSIS.

RESISTANCE LEVEL

The *Resistance Level* is the point at which investors believe the price of a stock or index has reached the highest possible level warranted at that time.

The first time a price trend reverses it is labeled as weak resistance. However, if the price level or index reverses several times, it is called strong resistance.

Technical analysts believe that if a price or index movement breaks through strong resistance the upward trend will continue and result in a breakout.

See also DOW THEORY; SUPPORT/SUPPORT LEVEL; TECHNICAL ANALYSIS.

RESTRICTED ACCOUNT (United States)

In the event that the equity in a margin account falls below the minimum currently required by Reg-T (50%), the account is referred to as a *Restricted Account*.

A restriction is not the same as a maintenance margin call, but rather is a technicality whereby the investor must deposit additional funds or marginable securities in order to make another transaction.

The investor can remove the restriction by putting additional funds or marginable securities into the account or by selling securities already held in the account. The restriction will also be removed if the prices of the securities in the portfolio increase enough to total the 50% equity requirement.

See also EQUITY; MARGIN; REGULATION G–X/REGULATION T.

RESTRICTED LIST (United States)

A *Restricted List* is a list of security issues that cannot be bought or sold by investors unless the transaction is clearly marked "unsolicited." The restriction list is comprised of issuers in the process of registering a new public offering with the Securities and Exchange Commission (SEC).

The SEC believes it would be inappropriate for brokers to solicit orders based on the potential impact of an upcoming issue that has not received the approval to be registered. The issue might be delayed, rejected, or have an impact on the current securities on the restricted list. By restricting the issues from solicitation, the SEC remains at arm's length and is not indirectly promoting a particular securities issue.

At the same time, the SEC does not want to restrict investment decisions of investors. Therefore, unsolicited buys and sells of securities on the restricted list remain unaffected. It is the stockbroker's responsibility to clearly mark any transaction as unsolicited.

See also INITIAL PUBLIC OFFERING (IPO); REGISTRATION; SECURITIES AND EXCHANGE COMMISSION (SEC).

RESTRICTIVE ENDORSEMENT

The *Restrictive Endorsement* of a securities certificate indicates who will receive the securities. The two sides of a securities certificate are equally important. The front is often beautifully engraved with designs and corporate logos, as well as information regarding the owner or owners, quantity, dates, and the CUSIP identification number. It is all information that identifies the owner, issuer, and quantity of securities.

The back side of a security contains a form with one purpose: to transfer those securities to someone else, either a person or a company, such as a brokerage firm, investment fund, or bank. It has some similarity in purpose to the reverse side of a check used for a person's checking account.

In order to transfer the securities when they are sold or deposited into an account, the certificate must be endorsed by the identical names appearing on the certificate's face. If this is not possible, other paperwork identifying the changes is required. The action is similar to writing "for deposit only" on the back of a check. It clearly identifies where the securities are to be deposited.

Restrictive endorsements can add a measure of safety when securities certificates are being mailed to a firm for deposit or sale.

See also CERTIFICATE; COMMITTEE ON UNIFORM SECURITIES IDENTIFICATION PROCEDURES (CUSIP); ENDORSE; GOOD DELIVERY.

RETAIL INVESTOR

Professional investors are people employed by companies to make investments for that firm. *Retail Investor* applies to all other investors, regardless of how active they are in their trading.

Many brokerage firms separate institutional investing and retail investing into two departments, each with a specific criteria. The reason for this is the different knowledge, expertise, and account maintenance necessary for each type of investor. The broker who handles institutional clients often will not have the current knowledge or expertise to meet the needs of individuals. Similarly, the broker handling retail investors might not be able to meet their needs adequately if his or her time is used in satisfying the different needs of institutional clients.

The decision to divide investors into the two categories is made by the individual brokerage firm, and is not required by the Securities and Exchange Commission.

See also BROKERAGE HOUSE; INSTITUTIONAL INVESTOR; REGISTERED REPRESENTATIVE (RR).

RETAINED EARNINGS

Also referred to as earned surplus, *Retained Earnings* are the earnings of a corporation that have not been paid out as dividends.

Retained earnings are affected by:
- Net income or loss for the current year
- All dividends, whether in the form of cash, property, or shares
- Adjustments or error corrections from earlier periods
- Appropriations of retained earnings whether legal, contractual, or discretionary

If the retained earnings balance is negative, it is referred to as a deficit. Deficits can be caused by accumulated prior net losses or dividends in excess of earnings.

Often labeled the Accumulated Retained Earnings Statement, a financial statement is included with the company's annual report and is effectively a retained earnings statement. It provides a record of dividend distributions made in the current year as well as a summary of previous years.

See also BALANCE SHEET; DIVIDEND; EARNINGS.

RETENTION REQUIREMENT (United States)
See RESTRICTED ACCOUNT.

RETURN
See RETURN ON INVESTMENT.

RETURN OF CAPITAL
Return of Capital refers to cash payments made to a company's investors that are not considered a distribution of dividends. These payments are regarded as the return of a portion of an investor's original investment and are therefore not taxable events. Return of capital might come from the sale of a capital asset or from the sales of securities in a portfolio (e.g., a unit trust).

Such distributions lower the cost basis of the investment, so an investor will have to adjust his or her calculations to account for a lower original purchase cost.

The returned funds are sent out or credited to an account, similar to a dividend payment, but are clearly designated as a return of capital.

Important to note: Any capital gains incurred when realized are still fully taxable.

See also ASSET; CAPITAL; DEPRECIATION.

RETURN ON EQUITY
Return on Equity is the post-tax income produced by a company over a 12-month period, expressed as a percentage of the company's equity capital.

Care must be taken when calculating the return on equity because there are several different ways of arriving at the figure. The most common form is:

$$\frac{\text{Net income for 12 months}}{(\text{Opening Equity Capital} + \text{Closing Equity Capital}) / 2} \times 100$$

Alternate versions of the formula do not use an average figure for the share capital, but instead use share capital at either the beginning or the end of the accounting period. There are also several different treatments for preferred share capital, preferred dividends, ordinary dividends, and taxes.

The ratio is employed by many fundamental analysts to show the effective use of money. Trends can be ascertained by comparing the return on equity for the current period to those rates experienced in prior periods. These trends can also be compared to those of other companies or the industry sector as a whole.

See also BUFFETT, WARREN; DIVIDEND; NET INCOME; NET WORTH; PREFERRED STOCK (PFD).

RETURN ON INVESTMENT
Return on Investment is the amount of money an investor receives from an investment.

For example: If an investor buys XYZ Corporation shares for a total of $10,000 and receives $11,000 back when the shares are sold, the return on investment is 10%. The initial investment of $10,000 is known as the principal. The gain of $1,000 is the return on investment.

Important to note: Calculations of return on investment should also account for any dividend or interest flows that arise as a result of holding the investment. These cash items should be added to any capital gain to provide a total return on investment. Different countries have different methods of taxation for dividends and capital gains, and an intelligent investor will adjust for local rules to find a post-tax return.

See also CAPITAL GAIN; DIVIDEND.

REUTERS

Paul Julius Reuter built the *Reuters* news agency with an entrepreneurial flair that continues to this day. From the start, German-born Reuter was determined to come up with solutions for clients. He delivered stock prices by carrier pigeon before telegraph cables were laid in Europe and became an innovator in the use of telegraphy to bring lightning-fast dispatches. He opened his office in London's growing financial district in 1851, serving subscribers throughout Europe in a company that was internationally focused from the very start.

Europe learned about the death of Abraham Lincoln from the Reuters news service, already established as a leading provider of stories to newspapers. By the 1870s, a global network of journalists was sending news from offices in the Far East, Asia, and Africa, as telecommunications technology spread to those regions.

War and political intrigue marked much of the first century, and Reuters' coverage of the great wars established its reputation as an accurate, up-to-date news source. To assure its independence and freedom from bias, the Reuter Trust was established. This ensures that Reuters will never fall into the hands of any interest group or faction.

Reuters' historic commitment to technology led the agency into computerized delivery of information. Its news retrieval system, the Stockmaster, launched in 1964, quickly became a success and was the precursor of modern digital information systems. Its main successor, the Reuter Monitor, expanded the Reuters franchise beyond merely carrying news to transmitting crucial information about foreign exchange transactions—making this product a centerpiece of the burgeoning global currency market.

Handling billions of dollars in transactions daily, the Monitor carried Reuters to a new level of financial success and allowed a huge expansion in its newsgathering capabilities. This growth also led to its flotation as a publicly traded company in 1984, furthering its development as the world's largest electronic publisher and provider of business information.

Customers in all parts of the world depend on Reuters to provide them with reliable and objective news and information. Reuters therefore has a special need to safeguard its independence and integrity and avoid any bias that may stem from control by any particular individuals or interests. Reuters' share structure includes the following two mechanisms specifically designed to prevent this:

- No shareholder may own 15% or more shares.
- There is a single founders share, in addition to the publicly traded ordinary shares. This may be used to out-vote all ordinary shares if other safeguards fail and there is an attempt to seize control of the company. "Control," for this purpose, means 30% of the shares.

Reuters is dedicated to preserving its independence, integrity, and freedom from bias in the gathering and dissemination of news and information. The Reuters Founders Share Company Limited, of which all Reuters trustees are directors, was established to safeguard those qualities.

The trustees have a duty to ensure, as far as they are able by the proper exercise of the powers vested in them, that The Reuter Trust Principles are observed.

These are:

- That Reuters shall at no time pass into the hands of any one interest, group, or faction.
- That the integrity, independence, and freedom from bias of Reuters shall at all times be fully preserved.
- That Reuters shall supply unbiased and reliable news services to newspaper, news agencies, broadcasters and other media subscribers and to businesses, governments, institutions, individuals, and others with whom Reuters has or may have contracts.
- That Reuters shall pay due regard to the many interests that it serves in addition to those of the media.
- That no effort shall be spared to expand, develop, and adapt the news and other services and products of Reuters so as to maintain its leading position in the international news and information business.

Reuters is currently organized into regional offices that provide sales, technical, and customer support to customers. These Front Line Business Units (FLBUs) are grouped into four areas: The United Kingdom and Ireland; Asia; the Americas; Continental Europe, the Middle East, and Africa.

The Front Line Business Units are as follows:
ASIA
Pacific (Australia, New Zealand)
East Asia
South East Asia
Far East (Japan and Korea)

Paul Julius Reuter. *(Courtesy of Reuters Limited)*

AMERICAS
North America, Western Region
North America, Eastern Region
Latin America

UK/IRELAND
UK/Ireland

CONTINENTAL EUROPE, MIDDLE EAST, AND
  AFRICA
Africa
Benelux
Central and Eastern Europe
East Mediterranean and North Africa
France
Germany
Gulf
Iberia
Italy
Nordic
Switzerland

Main Products

Information Products deliver news and prices to customer screens. They provide datafeeds to financial markets, and the software tools to analyze data. They cover currencies, stocks, bonds, futures, options, and other instruments. Triarch and TIBCO (formerly Teknekron) systems offer customers the means to manage their own information flows. Transaction Products enable traders to deal from their keyboards in such markets as foreign exchange, futures and options, and securities.

Media Products deliver news in all the dimensions of multimedia: text, television images, still pictures, sound, and graphics. Customers include broadcasters and newspapers around the world. Reuters also packages the news in electronic briefing products for corporate executives and insurance executives, and supplies news through online services including a number of Internet web sites.

REVALUATION

The opposite of "devaluation," *Revaluation* is an upward adjustment of a country's currency.

Rather than a response to fluctuations of a country's currency in the foreign exchange market, revaluation is the result of a conscious decision made by a government.

Revaluation makes imports more attractive to domestic buyers, while exports become relatively more expensive for buyers abroad.

Changes in the valuation of currency can directly affect the market prices of domestic shares, especially for companies that are dependent on foreign sales. The capital value of an investment made abroad, together with the values of any dividend or interest flows arising from the investment, will be affected by a currency revaluation.

See also CURRENCY; DEVALUATION; FLUCTUATION.

REVENUE ACT (United States)

The general term *Revenue Act* refers to any fiscal legislation concerned with the raising of public revenues and containing tax provisions. The Internal Revenue Code of 1939 unified current revenue acts and other laws relating to internal revenue, and codified them in an organized manner. The Internal Revenue Code of 1954 went even further by overhauling the tax laws, changing the arrangement and content of provisions of the 1939 code. It also contained new substantive provisions. Although modifications have been made, the following features of the 1954 code still pertain to internal revenue:

1. Depreciation

   The computation of depreciation was permitted under the 200% declining balance method at twice the straight line rate. In the straight line method, depreciable cost is divided by estimated years of useful life to determine the depreciation each year; in the declining balance method, twice the straight line rate per year is applied to the declining balance each year. The Treasury indicated that this conformed to "true" depreciation, because nearly two-thirds of the depreciable cost under this method is written off during the first half of the asset's life, as compared with only one-half under the straight line formula. The sum-of-the-digits method, in which the number of years of useful life is added up and the depreciation each year is in a decreasing progression, was also authorized for accelerated depreciation; in many aspects the sum-of-the-digits method is more liberal than the 200% declining balance method. Other consistent methods were also allowed, under the condition they not create deductions larger than the 200% declining balance method in the first two-thirds of the useful life of the asset.

2. Double Taxation of Dividends

   Each stockholder could exclude $50 received in the form of stock dividends and was allowed a credit against tax equal to 4% of the dividends in excess of the exclusion. The amount of the credit was limited to 2% of a stockholder's total taxable income in 1954, and 4% in the years that followed.

U.S. taxpayers are effectively taxed twice on dividends—first in the form of corporate tax and then with individual income taxes.

3. Research and Experimental Expenditures
This option allows taxpayers to deduct such expenses currently or to "capitalize" them and write them off over a period of not less than five years.

4. Carryback of Operating Losses
The period for carryback of losses was extended from one to two years, thereby providing a total span of eight years when used in combination with the five-year carryforward.

5. Tax on Unreasonable Accumulation of Surplus
The 1954 code required taxpayers to show that retained earnings were necessary to meet "reasonably anticipated" business requirements. As a concession to small business, $60,000 could be made without threat of penalty. When imposed, the tax was applied only to retained earnings found to be unreasonable.

6. Preferred Stock Bail-Outs
Proceeds of a sale or redemption of preferred stock, acquired through distributions by a corporation to common shareholders, was taxed as ordinary income and treated as nontaxable stock dividends in preferred stock later redeemed.

7. Net Operating Loss Carryovers
In order to reduce the trading of "tax-loss corporations," the code eliminated the carryover when more than 50% of the stock of the loss corporation was purchased by new owners within a two-year period and the loss corporation thereafter did not continue in the same business.

8. "Collapsible" Corporations and Partnerships
The code tightened provisions applicable to such corporations, formed and liquidated for the purpose of converting ordinary income tax liability into capital gains tax, and imposed restrictions on collapsible partnerships.

Other Tax Code Changes:
The following contains some of the major issues relating to alterations made to the Internal Revenue Code of 1954.

Tax Reform Act of 1969

Accomplished 30 December 1969, this was called ". . . one of the most sweeping and complex since the adoption of income tax in 1913."

The individual issues addressed were as follows:
1. Rate reductions for individuals
2. Low-income allowance
3. Single persons
4. Earned income rate limitation
5. Minimum tax on tax preference income
6. Income averaging
7. Charitable contributions
8. Alternative capital gains tax for individuals
9. Farm losses
10. Business moving expense and "hobby losses" not allowed

The following business issues were addressed:
1. Repeal of the 7% investment tax credit
2. Liberalized amortization
3. Restricted real estate depreciation
4. Tax-free corporate dividends
5. Allowances on natural resources
6. Restricted depreciation for regulated utilities
7. Taxability of stock dividends
8. Corporate securities issued in mergers
9. Multiple corporations
10. Financial corporations
11. Minimum corporate tax

Tax Reduction Act of 1975

An Act of Congress (P.L. 94-12), approved on 29 March 1975, created a $22.8 billion tax cut by amending the Internal Revenue Code of 1954 as follows:

1. Provide a 10% rebate of 1974 taxes up to a maximum $200.
2. Temporarily (meaning for 1975) increase the low-income allowance, increase the percentage standard deduction to 16% of adjusted gross income up to a maximum of $2,600, provide a $30 tax credit for each $750 personal exemption, and provide a 10% earned income credit for certain low-income taxpayers.
3. Provide an increase in the income limitation for the deduction of child care expenses from $18,000 to $35,000.
4. Authorize a tax credit of 5% of the purchase price of a new principal residence up to $2,000.
5. Extend the time in which a taxpayer must purchase a new principal residence in order to defer recognition of gain on the sale of a former residence from the prevailing 1 year to 18 months, and, if the taxpayer constructs a home, to 24 months.
6. Provide a $50 one-time payment to U.S. residents who receive a Social Security, supplementary security income, or railroad retirement benefit for the month of March 1975.

7. Authorize an increase in the investment tax credit (increase from 4% to 10% for utilities, and from 7% to 10% for all other businesses, on equipment acquired after 21 January 1975 and placed in service before 1 January 1977).

8. Provide an increase in the corporate surtax exemption from $25,000 to $50,000, with a corresponding reduction of the tax rate on the first $25,000 of corporate income from 22% to 20%.

Revenue Adjustment Act of 1975

Act (P.L. 94-164), approved 23 December 1975, continued the 1975 tax cut reductions at an $8.4 billion level, through 30 June 1976.

Tax Revision

(P.L. 94-331), approved 30 June 1976. Congress extended the tax cuts provided by the Tax Reduction Act of 1975 for two months, until 1 September 1976.

Tax Reduction and Simplification Act

(P.L. 95-30), approved 23 May 1977.

Revenue Act of 1978

(P.L. 95-600), approved 6 November 1978, addressed the following:

1. Liberalized personal income tax provisions by lowering the schedule of tax rates. The general tax credit (expiring in 1978) was replaced by a personal exemption of $1,000.

2. Provided for a five-step schedule for corporate taxes, maximum tax rate of 46%, and made the investment tax credit of 10% permanent.

3. Expanded the earned income tax credit for the working poor and reduced the effective rate on individual capital gains.

4. Established the intention of tax-writing committees of the Congress to report legislation providing "... significant tax reductions for individuals when certain goals for Federal expenditures are met and when justified in the light of prevailing and expected economic conditions over the next 4 years."

Reagan Administration's Tax Acts

1. Economic Recovery Tax Act of 1981 (ERTA)
   This was an act intended to be an integral part of the economic recovery program by providing incentives for work, saving, and investment. Reductions in individual income tax rates and other reductions in individual income taxes were approved. Beginning in 1985, annual inflation-related adjustments of the zero bracket amount, the personal exemption, and individual income tax brackets were provided, as were reductions on the increase in accelerated cost recovery of capital expenditures.

2. Tax Equity and Fiscal Responsibility Act of 1982 (TEFRA)
   This act to improve the fairness of the tax system, while preserving incentives for work, saving, and investment, was enacted in 1981. The act increased receipts by eliminating the unintended benefits and obsolete incentives, increased taxpayer compliance, and improved collection techniques.

After ERTA in 1981 and TEFRA in 1982, the next major tax legislation was the Deficit Reduction Act (DRA) of 1984. Congress passed the Tax Reform Act in 1986, making substantial changes in the tax law and changing the title to the Internal Revenue Code of 1986.

See also CAPITAL GAIN; CAPITAL LOSS; DEPRECIATION; DIVIDEND.

REVERSAL

A *Reversal* is a change of direction in a price or stock market index trend.

See also TECHNICAL ANALYSIS.

REVERSE CONVERSION

Reverse Conversion is a technique used by brokerage firms to earn interest on their client's investment portfolios.

Reverse conversion might proceed in the following way: the firm might sell short shares held in a customer's margin account and earn interest on the funds. The short position is hedged by the purchase of call options and the sale of put options, both of which have the same exercise price that is at or near the short sale price.

To unwind the position, the brokerage firm will sell the calls, buy back the puts, and buy back the stock sold short.

See also HEDGE; OPTION; SELLING SHORT.

REVERSE SPLIT

A *Reverse Split* reduces the number of shares a company has outstanding, without changing the market value of the company. Primarily undertaken for the purpose of raising the price per share to meet certain standards, reverse splits are commonly performed in quantities of 5 for one, 10 for one, or 25 for one.

For example: An investor has 100 shares of XYZ Corporation and the company announces a reverse split of 10 for 1. The investor will end up with ten of the new shares. If the prereverse split price was $1 per share, the post-reverse split price will be $10 per share.

Example: XYZ Corporation

Before a reverse split:

Quantity   100 shares

Price $1.00 per share

After a 10 for 1 reverse split:

Quantity   10 shares

Price $10.00 per share

All the financial data relevant to the company and its share price are adjusted to reflect the new share quantity.

Splits of any kind are considered neutral, except that the quantity of shares is changed. Reverse splits are also called "telescoping."

See also DIVIDEND; EX-DATE; SPLIT.

RICARDO, DAVID

David Ricardo was an English classical economist who developed economic thinking into a more logical, internally consistent system. Influenced by Adam Smith and encouraged by J.S. Mill, Ricardo's major contributions to economic theory were his theory of rent and theory of comparative cost.

Ricardo's early works were centered upon his experiences in the money and banking system, but it was his major work, *The Principles of Political Economy and Taxation* (1817), that dominated economics until Karl Marx. Ricardo's central concern was to determine the laws regulating distribution between the various classes within the economy and the relationship of these laws to the general circumstances of society.

Ricardo constructed a theoretical model that abstracted from the complexities of an actual economy to reveal the major influences within it. He was preoccupied with the importance of agriculture, and his model of the economy was reduced in particular to a corn-based example. He viewed production in agriculture as having a decisive bearing upon profit rates throughout the economy. With demand rising as a result of increasing population and a level of subsistence tending to rise over time, Ricardo argued that increasingly less fertile land had to be brought into production. The returns, in terms of corn, diminished to the point that it was no longer profitable to extend production to more land. Ricardo argued that costs and profits must be the same on all land, since, if profits were higher at one location than at another, capital would be attracted to the most profitable and would itself experience diminishing returns until profits

equilibrate. The equal level of surplus on all non-marginal land was rent.

The long-run expansion of population and the cultivation of less fertile land, Ricardo implied, would lead to the long-run decline in profits. Ricardo's theory of long-run growth was pessimistic, a view shared by other classical economists. Ricardo followed classical economic tradition in assuming that prices were determined principally by the quantity of labor used in production, but he diverged in his incorporation of capital costs. A production process dominated by direct labor inputs would be more vulnerable to an increase in money wage rates than a capital intensive process. If real wages rise, firms will substitute machinery for labor in a process known as the "Ricardo Effect."

Ricardo searched vainly for a measure of value in labor theory, and his idea of fixed capital embodying the labor input required to make it was later advanced by Marx. The short-run solution to the dilemma of diminishing returns lay in foreign trade and the import of cheap grain. This led Ricardo to argue against the Corn Laws in effect in 19th-century England and to develop his law of comparative costs. In a two-country, two-product model of international trade Ricardo demonstrated that by specialization in the product in which it experienced a relative cost advantage, a country could trade to the mutual benefit of both countries if the exchange rates were between the domestic relative cost ratios. The theory of comparative advantage provided the theoretical underpinning for the theory of international trade.

In the public debate between J.B. Say and Thomas Malthus, Ricardo refuted Malthus's claim of the possibility of a general glut, since he argued wages would fall and markets would clear. Ricardo was responsible for synthesizing much of earlier classical economics and providing it with a greater theoretical rigor. His analytical approach of theoretical model building has contributed substantially to economists' methodology, but shared the classical faith in unregulated markets determined by laws beyond the control of man.

See also CLASSICAL SCHOOL OF ECONOMICS; MALTHUS, THOMAS ROBERT; MARX, KARL; MILL, JOHN STUART; SAY, JEAN-BAPTISTE.

RIGHT OF ACCUMULATION

Right of Accumulation refers to a condition regarding open-end mutual funds that allows the investor to count the cash amount of previous purchases to receive lower prices on subsequent purchases at predetermined "break points."

If a mutual fund investor places $18,000 in a mutual fund that has a break point at $20,000, and later

David Ricardo, by T. Phillips. *(Mary Evans Picture Library)*

invests another $2,000 or more, the investor qualifies for a lower sales charge because of the right of accumulation.

Break points and right of accumulation are discussed in a mutual fund's prospectus.

See also MAXIMUM PRICE FLUCTUATION; MUTUAL FUND; SALES CHARGE.

RIGHTS OFFERING

A *Rights Offering* is an offering of common shares made to shareholders, entitling them to buy new shares at a price lower than that at which the shares will be offered to the public.

Rights offerings begin with a prospectus and security called "rights to present common shareholders." A shareholder can claim the discounted shares by presenting the rights and the additional funds to pay for them. Rights issues, a common way for a company to raise additional funds for expansion, offer new shares in a set proportion of a shareholder's existing holding. It is common to see phrases such as a "three for one" rights issue in the financial press.

Rights offerings are usually implemented by investment bankers under the auspices of a "standby commitment." The investment bank will normally agree to purchase shares that are not subscribed to by current shareholders.

If a shareholder does not wish to buy more shares of the company, the rights can be sold separately. Since rights issues tend to be priced at a level below the current market price of the shares, there is an intrinsic value in rights and they can be traded separately from the underlying shares.

See also INITIAL PUBLIC OFFERING (IPO); INVESTMENT BANKER; SHAREHOLDER.

RISK ARBITRAGE

Risk Arbitrage is a financial maneuver designed to take advantage of a risk situation.

The most common form of risk arbitrage is takeover arbitrage, in which a professional investor takes a stake in a company that is rumored to be a takeover target, while simultaneously taking a short position in the stock of the potential acquirer. The investor buys on the hope of a merger, in which case the market value of the target is expected to increase and the market value of the acquiring firm is expected to fall.

The risk involved with this strategy is that the merger will fail to materialize and there will be an adverse effect on prices.

See also INVESTOR; MERGER; SELLING SHORT.

RISKLESS TRANSACTION (United States and Others)

Although there are many transactions that are considered without risk (government securities, insured certificates of deposit, money market funds), *Riskless Transaction* also refers to a specific investment industry transaction.

When a brokerage firm receives an order from an investor to purchase over-the-counter securities in which the firm currently has no position, the firm can buy the securities for its own account, mark them up, and sell them to the customer at a riskless profit.

Although it is legal for an American brokerage firm to make such a transaction, the firm remains ethically bound by the National Securities Dealers Association 5% Rule. This rule stipulates that any additional mark-up to the investor must be no greater than 5% and must be disclosed to the investor.

See also FIVE PERCENT RULE; NATIONAL ASSOCIATION OF SECURITIES DEALERS (NASD); OVER THE COUNTER (OTC).

RISK/REWARD RATIO

A basic tenet of investing is that the greater the risk assumed by the investor, the greater the expected return on an investment. This is variously referred to as the *Risk/Reward Ratio*, the risk/return ratio, or the risk/return trade-off. The concept of return is relatively straightforward and readily quantified: It is the value added (or subtracted), the increase (or decrease), the profit (or loss) on the amount invested, usually expressed as a percentage of the original amount. The concept of risk, however, is multifaceted and much more complex, and is not easy to quantify.

Risk is usually defined as the chance, or probability, that the return on an investment will drop below the expected amount. The greater the probability and the more pronounced the potential drop, the greater the risk. Different investments fall into different risk categories. The following table indicates some possible risk categories and typical investments in those categories.

Risk Level	Approximate Expected Return	Type of Investment
Very high risk	20%	• New self-operated business
		• Futures or options trading
		• Stocks of new corporations
		• Oil/mineral exploration

Risk Level	Approximate Expected Return	Type of Investment
High risk	15%	• Undeveloped land • Real estate development • Junk bonds • Art
Moderate risk	12%	• Growth stocks • Medium-quality bonds • Residential real estate • Real estate second mortgages
Low risk	9%	• Treasury bonds (long term) • High-quality bonds
Very low risk	2%–6%	• Treasury bills • Money market funds • Insured savings accounts • Cash

In March 1995 the U.S. Securities and Exchange Commission attempted, without success, to find a simple comprehensive measure for indicating the risk for a mutual fund. Risk cannot be fully quantified with a single parameter, but there are some numerical gauges that academics and analysts have developed. The volatility, or the degree of ups and downs, inherent in the return on an investment is an indicator of the amount of risk. The standard deviation of a return on an investment is a measure of its volatility. The following table shows the average annual return on certain investments and their standard deviation for the 68-year period from 1926 to 1994.

Asset Class	Average Annual Return	Standard Deviation
Small-company stocks	12.22%	34.56%
Large-company stocks (S&P 500)	10.19%	20.35%
Long-term (20-year) corporate bonds	5.41%	8.41%
Long-term (20-year) government bonds	4.83%	8.75%
Intermediate-term (5-year) government bonds	5.09%	5.68%
Treasury bills (30-day)	3.69%	3.29%
U.S. inflation	3.12%	4.61%

Standard deviation is a statistical measure that indicates how tightly (or loosely) clustered the various data values are around the average. The smaller the standard deviation, the more tightly clustered the data. If data are normally distributed around the average, over two-thirds of the data values fall within one standard deviation above and below the average. Therefore, although small-company stocks had an average return of 12.22%, more than two-thirds of the returns were in the range –22.34% to 46.78% (12.22% ± 34.56%). More than two-thirds of the long-term corporate bonds, on the other hand, had returns in the range –3.00% to 13.82%. The narrower spread indicates less volatility and correspondingly lower risk. In general, the smaller the standard deviation of the return on an investment, the lower the risk.

Another numerical indicator of risk is the beta coefficient. This portfolio theory statistic is a measure of a security's volatility in relation to some index, such as the Standard and Poor's 500 for stocks or Lehman Brothers aggregate index for bonds. Betas are normally calculated on monthly returns over the preceding three years. A stock whose returns are statistically synchronous with those of the S&P 500 has a beta of 1.0. Stocks that are more volatile than the index stocks have betas greater than 1.0, while less volatile stocks have betas less than 1.0. The formula for computing the beta of a stock or portfolio j is

$$BETA_j = \frac{SD_j}{SD_i} CORR_{j,i}$$

where:

SD_j is the standard deviation of the returns for stock or portfolio j,

SD_i is the standard deviation of the returns for the index i (such as the S&P 500), and

$CORR_{j,i}$ is the correlation coefficient computed for the two sets of returns.

The correlation coefficient measures the tendency of j's returns to move with those of i, and is readily computed on a PC with statistical software.

Risk statistics, such as the standard deviation and beta coefficient, reflect past performance and do not necessarily predict future behavior. Changes in the management procedures for a portfolio can cause future volatility to vary substantially from past ups and downs. The period used to calculate a statistic may not be representative of future events because the risk factors may have changed.

There are several different risk factors; some are more significant for certain types of investments than for others. Common risk factors include the following:

Asset-class risk: Stocks, bonds, and cash are the three major asset classes. Allocating a disproportionate amount to one of these classes generally increases risk. An investor can manage asset-class risk by diversifying across all three of the asset classes.

Market risk: The stock market is influenced by investors' changing expectations for individual companies or for the economy as a whole. The bond market is affected by expectations about interest rates and inflation. Both markets respond to such emotional factors as hope and fear. As with asset-class risk, market risk can be managed with diversification. A second method for managing market risk is dollar cost averaging (DCA). This requires investing a fixed amount at regular intervals over a period of time, so the amount buys more shares when the value of the investment is declining and fewer shares when the value is increasing. DCA smoothes out the purchasing costs, yielding a middle-of-the-road average cost.

Interest-rate risk: When interest rates rise, bond prices fall. The stock market is also affected, but less directly, by investors shifting money into higher-yielding, interest-paying instruments.

Inflation risk: Inflation erodes fixed-income investments, especially those with longer terms. T-bills, CDs, and money market funds are highly susceptible. The following table shows the effect of inflation on three kinds of investments over the 70-year period from 1926 to 1996.

Asset Class	Annual Average Return	Annual Inflation	Real Return
Treasury bills	3.7%	3.1%	0.6%
Government bonds	5.1%	3.1%	2.0%
Stocks	10.7%	3.1%	7.6%

Currency risk: Fluctuating exchange rates can create a loss on foreign securities. For example, many who invested in Mexico before the peso crisis in late 1994 subsequently sold at substantial losses.

Country risk: Beyond exchange rates, this risk factor includes economic and political instability and is of concern to investors targeting developing markets.

Credit risk: Bonds are susceptible to the risk of default by the issuer. Lower-quality bonds have a greater credit risk and therefore offer a higher rate of return. Government bonds pay the lowest rates but have the highest credit rating and lowest risk of default.

Tax-rate risk: Changes in tax rates and how they are applied to various investments can have a significant impact on returns. For example, only a portion of long-term capital gains are taxed. An increase in the taxable portion could substantially reduce returns. Municipal bonds are tax exempt. If a flat rate income tax were approved and all investments became tax exempt, municipal bonds would lose value in relation to other investments.

See also BEAR MARKET; BETA; DIVERSIFICATION; DOWNSIDE RISK; INFLATION; PORTFOLIO THEORY.

ROAD SHOW

A *Road Show* is a series of presentations made to investment institutions that are designed to raise the profile of a company within the investment community. The presentations, which are normally prepared by the company's brokers, will stress the company's good features and detail its long-term plans. Road shows are becoming increasingly popular, especially for companies that seek to widen share ownership beyond their home countries.

ROCKEFELLER FAMILY

The *Rockefeller Family* has been one of the wealthiest and most powerful families in the United States for more than 125 years. The family fortunes were first established in oil refining during the career of John Davison Rockefeller (1839–1937) and further developed by his heirs, who were engaged in railroads, banking, mining, and other industries.

John D. Rockefeller was living in Cleveland in 1859 when he established a commission business that dealt in hay, grain, meats, and other products. Learning something of the potential of oil refining in the western Pennsylvania area, he had his first refinery built near Cleveland in 1863. Within two years it had become the largest refinery in the area. In the 1860s, John's brother William became the head of export operations in New York City.

In 1870 Rockefeller and some associates founded the Standard Oil Company (Ohio). Growing rapidly and buying out its competitors, Standard came to control nearly all the state's refineries by 1872. It then entered agreements with various railroads to receive discount rates on its oil shipments. It even worked out deals with some railroads whereby it would receive "drawbacks" or commissions whenever they transported oil for a competitor. Standard purchased pipelines and terminal facilities, continued to purchase other competing refineries, and endeavored to expand its markets throughout the country and abroad. By 1880 Standard Oil controlled the refining of up to 95% of all oil produced in the United States and had a virtual monopoly on its distribution and selling as

John D. Rockefeller, Sr., 1919. *(Spectrum Photo)*

well, including control of the pipelines and gathering system of the oil regions. By the mid-1880s three Standard refineries produced more than a quarter of the world's supply of kerosene. Rockefeller preferred to concentrate in these sectors of the oil industry and leave the production of oil to others.

Standard Oil became the first major U.S. trust, setting a pattern for other monopolies. Eventually the trust would govern 40 corporations. To Rockefeller, the combination of competing companies into one large trust was a mark of progress, of the elimination of some of the anarchy in the young oil industry. Excess production could be better controlled, and wild price fluctuations might be avoided.

For many others, however, Standard Oil's practices were considered outrageous and cutthroat. Some states passed antimonopoly laws. Eventually the U.S. Congress passed the Sherman Antitrust Act in 1890. Two years later the Ohio Supreme Court ruled that Standard Oil Trust violated the state's antimonopoly law. Maneuvering around this ruling, Rockefeller dissolved the trust and transferred its properties to companies in other states, while retaining the trust's basic structure of control. In 1899 these companies were united in the Standard Oil Company (New Jersey), a holding company that existed until 1911, when the U.S. Supreme Court declared it to be in violation of the Sherman Antitrust Act.

Rockefeller's only son, John D. Jr., was mainly engaged in philanthropy. He did, however, back the use of militiamen to attack miners that were striking against the Rockefeller-owned Colorado Fuel and Iron Company in Ludlow, Colorado in 1914. The militia burned down the miners' camp and gunned down its inhabitants, resulting in more than 40 deaths, including those of 11 children. At this point the elder Rockefeller's own fortune amounted to 2% of the total gross national product of the United States—and this did not include the huge wealth he had passed on to the rest of his family, which included banks, railways, and philanthropic foundations. Yet he remained a robber baron in the eyes of many; after the news of the deaths in Ludlow, he was so broadly reviled that he dared not emerge from his mansion to organize his wife's funeral for six weeks following her death.

Thereafter the Rockefellers gave a good deal more attention not only to philanthropy but to the management of public opinion. The senior Rockefeller's creation of tax-exempt foundations to handle donations was most timely, occurring as it did shortly before the passage of income tax laws in the United States and thus shielding much of the family fortune from taxation. Four of John D. Jr.'s five sons—John D. III, Lau-

rance, Winthrop, and David—spent at least significant portions of their careers on philanthropy, donating large sums of money to the arts, education, and medical research. Nelson was the most prominent in politics, a four-term governor of New York state and also the country's 41st vice president. Nelson Rockefeller worked early in his career as director of Creole Petroleum's operations in Venezuela and became expert at public relations while working during World War II as the Coordinator of Inter-American Affairs, from which office he disseminated news releases and cultivated relations with the media and government officials. John D. Jr. also had a daughter, Abby, who was not active in business or public life.

Standard Oil remained the core of the family fortune in the 20th century. After dissolution of the trust-like holding company in 1911, eight companies still had "Standard Oil" in their names. Companies that evolved from the trust included Mobil Oil, Amoco, Chevron, Exxon, Atlantic Richfield, and Pennzoil. However, the Rockefeller brothers, particularly Laurance and David, carried on and extended the family's activities in other businesses.

Laurance, a founder of Eastern Airlines in 1938, also helped finance the McDonnell Aircraft Corporation, one of the principal suppliers of aircraft for the U.S. Navy during World War II. After the war his investments were in such varied areas as resort hotels, nuclear equipment, and computers. He was also a member of the New York Stock Exchange.

The youngest of John Jr.'s sons, David, joined the staff of Chase National Bank in 1946 and continued to rise through its hierarchy, becoming chairman of the board and chief executive officer of what had become Chase Manhattan Bank in 1969. Under the leadership of David Rockefeller, a member of the Council on Foreign Relations and the Trilateral Commission, the bank became increasingly international. David was a strong supporter of the U.S. war in Vietnam and supported the governments in South Africa and Iran.

In 1947 the Rockefeller brothers founded the International Basic Economy Corporation (IBEC), whose purpose was to promote economic development in Latin America and other underdeveloped parts of the world. IBEC was most active in Brazil and Venezuela.

As Governor of New York in the 1960s, Nelson Rockefeller introduced a new way of funding some enormous public works projects. Because it was not politically possible to raise the money through taxes or long-term bonds, which had to be approved by voters at a referendum, Rockefeller devised special authorities that could issue bonds. He would then pledge the full moral authority of the state behind the bonds, which became known as "moral obligation" bonds. Large banks, especially Chase Manhattan, sold these to institutions and the public, and in this way Rockefeller raised more than $6 billion while avoiding the voting requirements of more conventional state bonds. Later, after Rockefeller left office, the value of these bonds declined, and many of their purchasers could never collect. The municipal bond market throughout the country was thereby undermined, contributing to New York City's fiscal crisis of the mid-1970s.

See also CHASE MANHATTAN CORPORATION; MONOPOLY; OIL; TRUST.

ROGERS, JIM

Jim Rogers is one of the most colorful members of the American investment community. A natural contrarian, Rogers has spent his life seeking out unexpected investment opportunities.

Born in the small town of Demopolis, Alabama, Rogers graduated from Yale in 1964. A summer job at the small brokerage of Dominick and Dominick awakened Rogers's interest in finance before a year's study at Oxford. He spent a further two years at Dominick and Dominick before joining the army. He met George Soros in 1970, and they formed their own investment company.

Starting with Soros as the trader and Rogers as the research expert they enjoyed massive success. In the ten years to 31 December 1980 their Quantum fund showed a gain of more than 3,300%, a stellar performance that guaranteed the wealth and reputation of both of the men.

Rogers has always employed a top-down approach to investing, putting his funds into countries and large sectors rather than picking individual stocks. His investment policy is to look for one of four different types of change that will affect a country or industry:

1. Disasters

    Rogers actively seeks stocks in industries that are in trouble. Super-cheap stocks in the automobile industry, bought when many companies were fighting against bankruptcy, produced spectacular gains when the industry consolidated and rid itself of wasteful practices and unrealistic pricing.

2. Over-Bought Stocks

    Rogers will sell short on those stocks that he feels have been over-bought by institutional investors. A scramble for ownership among these slow-moving behemoths of the investment world is often the first sign that a peak has been reached.

3. New Consumer Trends

    A fundamental shift in the buying patterns of consumers may lead to massive changes in share prices. The classic example, oft-quoted in business schools, is when Rogers and Soros noticed that women were spending less on makeup in the 1970s as the natural look became more popular. They shorted stock in a makeup company when it was at $130 and made money all the way down to $25 a year later.

4. Watch for Government Intervention

    Changes in government policy can also affect share prices. The provision of tax incentives, privatization, or the removal of subsidies will profoundly alter the nature of an industry.

Rogers's philosophy of life, as well as of investment, is well documented in his book, *Investment Biker: On the Road With Jim Rogers*, published in 1995. Together with his girlfriend, Tabitha Estabrook, Rogers fired up his trusty BMW and rode around the world. They covered 57,000 miles in their 18-month trip, visiting China, Russia, Africa, Australia, Latin America, and the United States. The couple's close shave with the Shining Path guerrillas in Peru and an attack by a knife-wielding fellow traveler in Zaire are among the highlights of the book.

As he records the sites and events of the journey, Rogers keeps his eye on possible investments, noting that the least well-known countries may contain some potential investment jewels if one is prepared to take a long-term view. Rogers's distrust of central planning and state control is one of the main tenets of the book. Countries such as Russia have lost the concept of responsibility because of excessive state intervention, while the Far East tiger economies show the benefits of entrepreneurship.

See also SOROS, GEORGE.

ROLL DOWN

The investment strategy of buying back a previously sold call option and simultaneously selling another call option with a lower strike price is known as a *Roll Down*. In order to take advantage of the greater time value in the premium, the call option sold has a later maturity date than the option bought back.

For example, the shares of XYZ Corporation dropped from 45 to 40 in a five-month period, and the 50 covered call originally sold at $2 is now 1/4. The four-month June calls are priced as follows:

XYZ June 40 call	2	($2)
XYZ June 45 call	1 1/2	($1.50)
XYZ June 50 call	1/4	($.25)

The investor could buy the XYZ 50 for 1/4 and sell the four-month June 45 call for 1 1/2, and be paid the additional premium income. The strategy would be used if the price of XYZ Corporation was expected to remain steady or rise only slightly.

If the share price is expected to drop further and stay down, the investor would sell the shares and close out the option position. The option position could also be allowed to expire, but if the shares are sold, it becomes uncovered. This increases the level of risk.

When investors use the strategy on a continual basis, it is referred to as a rolling covered write. These investors will roll down or up depending on the price movements.

See also CALL; OPTION; ROLL FORWARD; ROLL UP.

ROLL FORWARD

The closing out of a spread position and opening of another with a later expiration date is known as a *Roll Forward*. The strategy is used to gain additional premium income.

See also ROLL DOWN; ROLL UP.

ROLL UP

The closing out of a spread position and opening of another with a higher strike price for the purpose of gaining further premium income is referred to as a *Roll Up*.

See also ROLL DOWN.

ROLLOVER

Rollover is a description for the reinvestment of funds.

There are a number of ways in which funds might be reinvested. For example, the proceeds received from a bond that has reached maturity can be reinvested into a new bond issue that is similar to the original in all respects, except for the date of maturity. The funds from an Individual Retirement Account might be taken from one fund and then reinvested with another investment firm. A security can be sold and the proceeds used to buy a position in the same security for purposes of establishing a new cost basis.

When bank certificates of deposit mature, they may contain a rollover feature to reinvest the funds in a similar new CD.

See also COST BASIS; INDIVIDUAL RETIREMENT ACCOUNT (IRA); PROCEEDS.

ROTHSCHILD FAMILY

The *Rothschild Family* name is one of the most potent in investment. Their banking and stockbroking dynasty has lasted for nearly 200 years and has spread from the humblest of beginnings in Germany to the centers of modern finance. Even though the family's pre-eminent role in the financing of Europe has been taken over by the bulge bracket firm of Wall Street and the European-based global banks, the name of Rothschild is still synonymous with wealth, power, and banking.

The host of stories about the Rothschild bank's successes are the stuff of legend. Its close links with the British government were cemented when the bank provided the necessary financing to help the government buy the vital Suez Canal. The English poet Lord Byron famously asked which people held "the world in balance?" His rhetorical reply indicated that he believed the global economy, even in 1823, was controlled by just two families: "Jew Rothschild and his fellow, Christian Baring." The Rothschilds funded Wellington's armies in Spain and France. The family, showing a pioneering spirit that was the envy of their contemporaries, helped to develop oilfields in Russia and the first railway networks in Europe. Jokes about the incredible wealth amassed by the family are a staple of Jewish humor. The first Jewish Prime Minister of England, Benjamin Disraeli, included an unflattering portrait of a Rothschild-style banker in one of his novels. The Nazis used the strong public opinion against the Rothschilds as a means to attack the whole Jewish race, which was characterized by Hitler as a gang of money-grabbing usurers. More recently, a distrust of high finance has even led some conspiracy theorists to claim that the family is part of a global elite that manipulates flows of currency around the world.

The roots of the present-day banking dynasty can be traced back to Mayer Amschel Rothschild, a merchant who made a fortune from trading from his base in Frankfurt during the 18th century. He was brought up in the Judengass, a cramped, walled ghetto where the town's Jewish population was forced to live. The family name is taken from the German words for *red shield* (Rot Schild), a symbol that appeared on the house sign of Mayer Amschel Rothschild's descendants. Frankfurt was a strategically important city during the 18th and 19th centuries. It was placed at the intersection of five important land routes, a trade crossroad between England, Holland, Russia, Italy, and Northern Germany.

The terrible conditions that the Jewish people endured in Frankfurt were little improved since the

First Rothschild House, where Mayer Amschel (1743–1812) founded the dynasty in Frankfurt, Germany. *(Corbis)*

Middle Ages. They were kept behind thick stone walls and iron gates, locked in at night and forbidden to enter the rest of the city on Sundays and religious holidays. Only 500 families were allowed to live in the ghetto, so Jewish weddings were restricted to 12 each year. The German people were openly hostile to the Jews, making them doff their hats and bow on the order of *Jud mach Mores* (Jew, pay your duty).

Mayer's progress was hampered by German rules that, among many other restrictions, censored mail for Jewish traders. Mayer solved this problem by asking the sender to color code the envelopes: a blue envelope signified that the pound was strong but a red one told Mayer that sterling was in decline. He began his business in a modest manner, selling rare coins and medals to German collectors. In time, he became a broker to Wilhelm, the elector of Hesse-Cassel, an influential member of the German royalty, who accepted a select coterie of Jewish traders to act as his brokers. Mayer financed the elector's armies, which were growing rapidly in response to the threat posed by Napoleon. He proved his worth to Wilhelm in 1806 when the Napoleonic invasion of Prussia forced Wilhelm to escape from Frankfurt. Mayer Amschel hid

Wilhelm's assets from the invading French forces. The elector's fortune, hidden in 119 bulging wooden chests, was smuggled out by Mayer. The chests containing gold, silver, and coin were uncovered, but the resourceful Mayer bribed the French authorities to let those containing valuable bonds and property deeds stay in his possession. Both the elector and Mayer grew rich on the interest they received.

The prosperous father sent his five sons—Amschel, Salomon, Nathan, Carl, and James—abroad to work as merchants and bankers. The famous crest of the family, five arrows, represents the brothers who left the unsanitary conditions of the ghetto and the anti-Semitism of Frankfurt to set up businesses in London, Paris, Naples, and Vienna. Mayer Amschel sent one of his sons, Nathan, to England at the end of the 18th century.

Mayer's last great transaction before his death in 1812 was to buy civil rights for his fellow Jews from the Lutheran city fathers of Frankfurt. The negotiations ended with the Jews paying a one-off lump sum to the German authorities in exchange for further payments of the taxes that had been levied on the inhabitants of the ghetto for many hundreds of years.

Mayer Amschel Rothschild (1743–1812). *(Mary Evans Picture Library)*

His most gifted son, Nathan, established a flourishing textile export business in the newly industrialized England, but he made an even more substantial income from the Napoleonic wars. Nathan helped the British government finance the war and thereby provided the foundations for his family's fortunes in England. Speculating in gold, government-backed bonds, and foreign exchange was to prove far more lucrative than cotton. Nathan moved from Manchester, the center of the English cotton trade and a town with a large Jewish population, when the Napoleonic wars made trading difficult in continental Europe. He settled in London, marrying Hannah Cohen, the daughter of a well-known merchant, and left the Manchester business in the hands of three brothers-in-law, Reiss, Sichel, and Worms. His marriage provided him with an entree into the powerful Jewish families, such as the Montefiores and the Goldsmids, that lived and worked in the City of London.

As news of the family's financial acumen spread across Europe, the doors of politicians, company leaders, and fledgling tycoons opened for the Frankfurt Jews. Using the most advanced technology available at the time, the bank sent carrier pigeons and human couriers across Europe in order to fulfill its business obligations and to find new opportunities. A major coup came with a bond issue for the hapless Prussian government, which was paying an astronomical 24% interest rate on its heavy borrowings. Nathan worked with his family colleagues in France to win the contract for the bonds, which were eventually issued in London, Berlin, Frankfurt, Hamburg, and Amsterdam. Such extensive coverage was out of the reach of most firms at the time.

Nathan chose to specialize in bonds and gold rather than investing in the fashionable world of railways and the fast-expanding industrial sector. As early as 1815 he had written to a cousin in Frankfurt to assert that, "[My] chief business is in the banking line only." However, when the right opportunity arose, Nathan was always prepared to deviate from his set plan. In 1824 he formed a joint-stock company, the Alliance Insurance Company, which was set up as a rival to Lloyds. When a stake in the Almaden quicksilver mines in Spain began to lose money, the Rothschilds sent an agent to Mexico City to tap into newly discovered supplies.

The economic crisis of 1848 led to heavy losses for the bank. Despite worries that the family would go bankrupt because of failures in Austria, the family expanded its operations into the New World. The California Gold Rush of 1849 attracted a flock of bankers to California, but it was the Rothschilds who became the major importer of gold to the United Kingdom. Rivals such as Lazard Brothers were not able to match the Rothschilds' business acumen and financial muscle. Encouraged by their success in silver and gold, the family sent agents to Cuba and New Orleans to trade in tobacco, sugar, and coffee.

The Rothschilds issued bonds to finance the world's first state-owned railway in Belgium, together with other rail networks in Germany and France. Salomon Rothschild, based in Vienna, helped to fund the Austrian rail network. The brothers set up the prosperous oilfields of Baku (now known as Azerbaijan) in Russia and eventually sold their stake, at a substantial profit, to Royal Dutch-Shell. Expansion into copper (Rio Tinto), nickel (Société le Nickel), and diamonds (De Beers) soon followed. The speculative stakes taken in South African mining companies were to prove immensely profitable for the family.

The bank's spectacular successes in the last years of the Victorian Era were not without controversy. Lord Randolph Churchill, who was Secretary of State for India and later Chancellor of the Exchequer in Salisbury's Cabinets, was criticized for his close personal links with the family. Churchill's biographers have reported rumors that the politician told his friend "Natty" Rothschild cabinet secrets, and that he helped advance the bank's interests in India and Persia. When Churchill died, he owed the London office of Rothschilds £66,000.

World War I marked a major shift in the fortunes of all the family-owned merchant banks in Europe. The desire of presidents and politicians to be publicly associated with rich financiers was replaced by the wish to appease a predominantly suspicious electorate. At the same time, the United States was becoming the economic powerhouse of the world at the expense of Europe, which was undergoing a costly, traumatic reconstruction. Investment power was moving inexorably toward Wall Street. Furthermore, new supranational organizations (The League of Nations, The Bank for International Settlement) and powerful central banks were in the ascendancy, and the influence of the European family banks began to wane.

Rothschilds had grown comfortable in the last years of the 19th century and the first decade of the 20th century. Naturally conservative, the manners and methods of the bank seemed to be rooted in an antiquarian age. When Guy de Rothschild first entered the Paris office he was dismayed at how old-fashioned the firm was in comparison with its rivals. "The past clung to everything and everyone. The history of the House was as evident in visible relics as in the old stories that everyone loved to tell."

Nathan Mayer, 1st Baron Rothschild, 1907. *(Mary Evans Picture Library)*

There was also a distinct lack of natural bankers in the family ranks. Hunting and horse racing appeared to be more attractive than trading and making deals. One English Rothschild, Lionel, professed to be "a gardener by profession and a banker by hobby."

The rise of the Nazis in Germany caused the German family to flee to the United Kingdom and the United States. Although their possessions were confiscated and their property looted, the family members united against the anti-Semitism of the age. Those scions of the family who eschewed banking found success in the arts, politics, and, most notably, science.

The ultimate controlling company for the bank, Rothschilds Continuation Holdings AG, was originally set up by a fifth-generation Rothschild, Anthony Gustave de Rothschild, just after the outbreak of World War II. Anthony was concerned about the future survival of the firm, since the number of partners had fallen to two. Under partnership law, if either of them had died, the partnership would have to be dissolved.

The post-World War II years saw Anthony take control of N.M. Rothschild. A flood of new issues to fund reconstruction and redevelopment after the war brought significant profits to the family. New earnings opportunities were achieved in the global currency markets, which were rejuvenated after the prewar slump and the restrictions placed on trading during the war were lifted. The firm also extended its corporate finance department, opened further offices abroad, and placed a greater emphasis on investment management services.

In 1960 the family selected David Colville as the first nonfamily member to become a partner. The Rothschilds ignored Mayer Amschel Rothschild's exhortation that no person from outside the family should ever reach such a level. The acceptance that bankers should be chosen because of their business skills rather than just their breeding was a step that ensured the family's success in the difficult years that followed.

Edmund, a nephew of Anthony, became senior partner on his uncle's death in 1961. He replaced many of the firm's arcane practices with more up-to-date methods of working. For example, it had been enshrined in the bank's rules of conduct that nobody could knock on the door of a partner's room. Any important messenger or lowly clerk would have to loiter by the door until beckoned in by the partners.

In 1967 the family, in a very definite break with the past, decided to discontinue its involvement in bullion refining. However, the family, which had been in charge of the fixing of gold in London since 1919, persevered with its business on the international bullion market. The Rothschilds had been intimately linked with precious metals for many years, and in 1852 they were granted a lease for the Royal Mint refinery. For more than 100 years the Rothschilds were responsible for refining gold and silver before presenting ingots to the Bank of England and the Royal Mint for official acceptance.

N.M. Rothschild was the last merchant bank in the City of London to cling to the partnership structure. In 1970, to the general relief of partners who faced unlimited personal losses if there was a business failure, the bank adopted a corporate structure, and with it came the comfort of limited liability. When the Rothschild partnership became a public limited company, Edgar was named its chairman.

Sir Claus Moser, a German Jew who became a naturalized Englishman in 1947, was one of the bank's most interesting characters. As well as being vice-chairman of N.M. Rothschild for six years beginning in 1978, he was Professor of Social Statistics at the London School of Economics, Chairman of the Royal Opera House, and Warden of Wadham College in Oxford. He had escaped Nazi Germany with his immediate family in 1936.

The private squabbles of any family business become worthy of public attention if the combatants are as well known as the Rothschilds. In the 1970s two scions of the family, Evelyn and Jacob, fought bitterly over the future of the firm. Evelyn stayed at the family bank, rising to take on the chairman's mantle.

Jacob had worked at the U.S. bulge bracket firm, Morgan Stanley, in New York, where he learned just how quickly the financial world was changing. He established and ran a successful investment trust, Rothschild Investment Trust, for many years before eventually splitting from the bank. Forbidden by legal clauses to use the Rothschild name in the new venture, Jacob combined the trust with Great Northern to produce RITN. To complicate the matter still further, RITN paid $63 million in 1983 for a 50% stake in a U.S. investment bank called L.F. Rothschild, Unterberg, Towbin. Commentators were unable to prove a direct connection between L.F. Rothschild, who had founded his firm at the turn of the century, and his far more illustrious namesakes in Europe. RITN soon expanded still further, joining with the Charterhouse group, which owned industrial holdings and a medium-sized investment bank.

Evelyn, far richer than Jacob, was at heart a more traditional Rothschild. He also expanded his operations, albeit at a slightly more cautious pace. The bank used its excellent contacts with the British government to take a full part in the extensive program of privatizations proposed by Margaret Thatcher. Departments involved in capital raising, precious metals, and foreign exchange dealing were augmented. Business in the new markets of South America, the Far East, and Africa were developed. Evelyn proved his all-around talents when he acted as the chairman of *The Economist* magazine for many years: he was also chairman of United Racecourses.

The holding company was eventually moved to Switzerland in 1982. Many commentators saw the move as a defensive measure by Evelyn, who, it was assumed, feared that a socialist government would soon appear in the United Kingdom. The French side of the family had seen their business nationalized by French President François Mitterand, and Evelyn was certainly determined not to lose his valuable franchise in the same manner.

Baron Guy de Rothschild, a colorful member of the French side of the family, was a very public critic of the French nationalization program. His book *Contre Bonne Fortune* scorned Mitterand while painting an ostentatious picture of the wealth and power enjoyed by the upper-class banking elite. The book was a controversial best-seller in the newly Socialist France, but it did little to improve the public's perception of the family. Baron Guy continued his attack on the French president in an article in the magazine *Le Monde*, which bitterly denounced the treatment his family had received in France. He made an explicit comparison between the nationalizing Mitterand and the wartime Vichy government which, on the command of Pétain, had sequestered the bank's assets: "For Pétain I was a Jew, for Mitterand I am a pariah—for me it's enough. To rebuild on ruins two times in a lifetime is too much. Forced into retirement, I have decided to strike."

Sir Michael Richardson, the managing director of N.M. Rothschild, created a scandal of another kind in the 1980s when he tried to sell the famous Royal Masonic Hospital in Hammersmith, London, against the wishes of many freemasons. Richardson, who made no secret of his prominent position as a mason, eventually saw his sell-off plans end in defeat in the High Court.

In 1992 the family lost 150 million Swiss francs (£68 million) in one of the largest frauds then uncovered in Switzerland. Jurg Heer, a senior executive in charge of credit risk at the Zurich affiliate branch of the Rothschild bank, was indicted after loans made to the Coutinho Caro property group went into default. The Zurich bank was completely refinanced by the Rothschild family in London, Paris, and Zurich.

The suicide of Amschel Rothschild in 1996 cast a long shadow over the bank. The 41-year-old chairman of Rothschild Asset Managements, the fund management arm of the firm, was found hanging in a Paris hotel room. Amschel, the great-great-great-grandson of Nathan Rothschild, joined the bank in 1987 at the relatively advanced age of 32. He had enjoyed an unconventional early career for a Rothschild, working on a literary magazine and winning a succession of classic car races. He had often been described as uncomfortable with the glare of publicity that accompanies the super-rich, and he was known to prefer farming to banking. Amschel, whose personal fortune was estimated to be as high as £100 million, did not leave a suicide note but was known to have been very depressed following the death of his mother, Lady Teresa Rothschild.

Rothschilds faces something of an uncertain future in the rapidly changing world of banking. It lacks sufficient size to compete head-on with the major players in the global banking arena and has too little capital to make major inroads into the profitable areas of proprietary trading and derivatives. However, it is probably too unwieldy in size to be successful as a niche player. Other banks, which until recently were controlled by powerful families, now appear to be anachronisms in the fast-changing world of international finance; both Barings and Morgan Grenfell have lost their independence in recent years, albeit for markedly different reasons. There are also concerns about who will win the latest succession battle and lead the bank into the millennium. Baron David de Rothschild, who revived the fortunes of the family after the nationalization of the French bank, is currently favored to head the London bank. In 1996 he was made chairman of the new group investment banking committee that coordinated the bank's corporate finance interests in Europe, the Far East, Latin America, and the United States. Some commentators believe that the committee is the first step toward a more integrated bank, where the resources of all the different entities are combined for the common good of the family.

See also BARINGS COLLAPSE OF 1890; *ECONOMIST, THE.*

ROUND LOT

A *Round Lot* is a specified unit of shares for which a market maker will customarily pay a higher price than for odd lots.

In the United States the most common unit for share trading is 100 shares. However, there are also round lots of 10 shares, 500 shares, and in special circumstances in which the price is unusually high, a single share. Other countries have their own version of the round lot, sometimes called board lots or trading units, and their own policies regarding them.

The original purpose of the round lot was to maximize the speed of executing a transaction and minimize the chances of error. However, as computerized trading becomes more prevalent, the need for specified units of trading becomes less of an advantage.

While shares that are not in round lots can be bought and sold, they may incur an extra charge called the "odd lot differential."

See also BOARD LOT; EXECUTION; ODD LOT DIFFERENTIAL.

ROUND TRIP

A securities transaction that is completed, then followed by an opposite transaction within a relatively short period of time, is referred to as a *Round Trip*.

For example: If an investor buys 100 shares of XYZ Corporation and ten days later sells 100 shares of XYZ Corporation it would be referred to as a round trip.

The same would be true if the shares were sold short and repurchased. Some brokerage firms offer a discounted commission on a round trip transaction, usually if it is completed within a set period of time.

Frequent trading is considered a speculative activity. If frequent trading is encouraged by a stockbroker, it could be construed as churning, which is an illegal activity.

See also CHURNING; COMMISSION; SPECULATION.

THE ROYAL BANK OF CANADA

ROYAL BANK OF CANADA (RBC)

The *Royal Bank of Canada (RBC)* is the largest bank in Canada and the sixth largest in North America. As of mid-1997 it had assets of approximately $172 billion and employed 55,000 people. It has more than 100 branches and offices in 35 foreign countries. In Canada it operates 276 brokerage offices, 74 business banking offices, 26 private banking offices, 27 full service trust offices, and more than 1,300 retail bank branches. Its 10 million customers include 350,000 small businesses. RBC's domestic operations include deposit services, mutual funds, credit products, brokerage services, insurance products, investment banking, and wealth management custody and transfer. Its international services comprise corporate banking,

correspondent banking, investment banking, Treasury, private banking, equipment leasing, and mortgage insurance.

RBC was founded in 1864 in Halifax, Nova Scotia as the Merchants Bank, a name that it kept until 1901, when it assumed its present name. The bank thrived in the context of a surge in commercial activity in the area as a result of the U.S. Civil War. In 1868 it was incorporated.

Following several years of depression in the mid- and late 1870s, the Merchants Bank rebounded in the 1880s. In 1882 it opened its first branch outside Canada.

The gold rush in the early 1890s in southern British Columbia created favorable conditions for the bank to open two agencies there in the late 1890s. Then in 1899 two more branches were opened in New York and Havana, Cuba. With the consolidation of U.S. power in Cuba in the coming years, the bank opened several more branches there.

In 1907 RBC relocated from Halifax to Montreal. In the next five years it acquired the Union Bank of Halifax, the Traders of Bank of Canada, and the Bank of British Honduras. RBC continued to grow during World War I, buying the Quebec Bank in 1917, the Northern Crown Bank in 1918, and two other banks in British Guiana and Nassau. By the end of the war, RBC had 540 branches.

Continuing to expand, by 1925 the bank purchased the Bank of Central and South America and the Union Bank of Canada. RBC weathered the 1929 stock market crash and the subsequent Depression relatively well.

After World War II, RBC provided banking services to Canada's oil, gas, and minerals exploration industries. In 1951 it founded the Royal Bank of Canada Trust Company in New York. The only reversal of RBC's overseas expansion occurred after the revolution in Cuba, where it sold its assets to the Banco Nacional de Cuba in 1960.

In the early 1960s the bank improved its consumer-oriented financial services with a package of credit and insurance benefits and a credit card. In 1967 the revision of the Bank Act led to heightened competition among Canada's banks while removing or limiting the scope of various constraints on their activities. This opened the way for RBC to move in the direction of becoming a universal bank, combining bank, investment house, trust company, and insurance institution.

In the early 1970s RBC joined with five other banks to form Orion, a merchant banking organization based in London that was to provide financial services.

Orion became a wholly owned subsidiary of RBC in 1981, as RBC prepared for the possibility of international banking deregulation.

In the 1980s, RBC expanded the Royal Bank and Trust Company in New York. Overall, the bank reorganized into four groups, two of them responsible for Canadian retail and commercial business, and the other two for corporate and international banking. In 1987 the Canadian government relaxed the rules for ownership of brokerage firms by banks. RBC proceeded to acquire Dominion Securities, the largest investment house in Canada. Two years later, Dominion acquired Pemberton Securities, western Canada's largest investment dealer. By 1997 it had acquired three brokerage firms, a trust company, two insurance companies, and two institutional and pension custody portfolios.

In 1989 RBC opened subsidiaries in Paris and London. In 1990 it purchased International Trustco Inc. In 1993 it acquired the principal Canadian subsidiaries and some international units of Gentra Inc., including Royal Trust Company and Royal Trust Corporation of Canada. In 1996 RBC purchased the brokerage house Richardson Greenshields of Canada, which it intended to merge with RBC Dominion Securities to form the country's largest investment sales force of 1,600 brokers. It also set up a merchant banking subsidiary in Toronto to complement the operations of the Royal Bank Capital Corporation, the oldest venture capital firm in Canada.

In 1995 RBC became listed on the New York Stock Exchange. It planned more focused U.S. operations, dealing with fewer corporate clients and emphasizing trade finance, syndicated loans and standby lines of credit, foreign exchange, capital markets derivatives, and equity derivatives. Overall, RBC aimed to achieve international earnings that were 35% to 40% of its total earnings, and to become one of the top 20 global trade-finance banks by 2001.

See also BANK OF MONTREAL; CANADA.

RULE 390 (United States/New York Stock Exchange)

Rule 390 requires that execution of trades in securities listed on the New York Stock Exchange (NYSE) takes place only on the floor of the NYSE.

Important exceptions to this NYSE rule are transactions in Europe, prior to the opening of the NYSE, and transactions in Asia, after the NYSE closes.

See also EXECUTION; TRADING FLOOR; UNITED STATES/ NEW YORK STOCK EXCHANGE (NYSE).

RULE 405 (United States/New York Stock Exchange)

Rule 405, or the "Know Your Customer" rule, requires registered representatives and brokerage firms to know financial information about their customers, agents, and all securities transactions entered by customers or agents.

Additionally, the rule requires the broker to know a customer's investment objectives and to make suitable recommendations within the scope of those objectives.

The intent and language of the rule are written to prohibit a broker or firm to use "I didn't know" as an excuse for making an improper or unsuitable investment recommendation.

See also OBJECTIVE; PROFILE A CUSTOMER; REGISTERED REPRESENTATIVE (RR); SUITABILITY/SUITABILITY RULE; UNITED STATES/NEW YORK STOCK EXCHANGE (NYSE).

RULE OF 72

The *Rule of 72* is a simple mathematical formula for calculating the amount of time it will take a sum of money to double at a certain rate of compound interest.

$$\frac{72}{\substack{\% \text{ compound interest rate} \\ \text{(stated as a whole number)}}} = \text{The number of years to double}$$

For example, if the compound interest rate is currently 6%:

$$\frac{72}{6} \quad \text{The money will double in value in 12 years}$$

The Rule of 72 provides a quick way for an investor to calculate the potential of an investment, as compared to a compound interest rate.

See also FUNDAMENTAL ANALYSIS; INTEREST/INTEREST RATES; TECHNICAL ANALYSIS.

RULES (United States)

See SECURITIES AND EXCHANGE COMMISSION (SEC).

RULES OF FAIR PRACTICE (United States)

The *Rules of Fair Practice* are a set of rules established by the National Association of Securities Dealers (NASD) outlining norms of ethical conduct for its members and registered representatives. The rules address fairness of treatment, prices, proper disclosure of information, and avoidance of conflicts of interest with other members and investors.

The rules of fair practice make use of federal laws and regularly accepted industry practice to keep the market fair and orderly. Rule violations can lead to severe penalties, including censure, fines, suspensions, and banishment from the NASD. If laws are violated, criminal and civil penalties can also be applied.

See also NATIONAL ASSOCIATION OF SECURITIES DEALERS (NASD).

RUNNING AHEAD

Running Ahead is an action taken by disreputable brokers, involving the purchase of a security that is expected to rise before placing the orders of client investors. To prevent such actions occurring, many brokerage firms now issue restrictions on certain securities. A typical restriction states that a broker cannot make any transactions in the security for 48 hours.

Some restrictions limit any broker trades to "closing transactions only," meaning brokers can sell, but can't sell short. They will only be allowed to buy in order to close out a short position. They are prohibited from creating any new positions for their own accounts until the restriction expires.

See also CLOSING PURCHASE; CLOSING SALE; PIGGYBACKING; SELLING SHORT.

RUSSELL INDEXES

The widely followed, weighted *Russell Indexes* are published by the Russell Company of Tacoma, Washington, in the United States.

The following indexes are currently available:

Russell 3,000: Largest market capitalization of 3,000 U.S. companies' shares.

Russell 1,000: Largest market capitalization of 1,000 U.S. companies' shares (from the 3,000 list).

Russell 2,000: Remainder of 3,000 list, representing approximately 11% of the 3,000 capitalization.

Russell Top 200: The largest 200 blue chip companies from the Russell 1,000 list.

Russell 1,000 and 2,000 Value Indexes: Companies with less than average forecast growth. Companies in these two indexes have low price-to-book and price/earnings ratios, and dividend yields higher than the market average.

Russell 1,000 and 2,000 Growth Indexes: Companies with better than average growth histories, often displaying a higher price-to-book and price/earnings ratios.

See also DOW JONES AVERAGES; DOW THEORY; INDICATOR; TECHNICAL ANALYSIS.

RUSSIA

Russia (Rossiyskaya Federatsiya) is the world's largest country. It is bordered on the west by Finland, Estonia, Latvia, Lithuania, Belarus, and Ukranine, and on the south by Georgia, Azerbaijan, Kazakhstan, Mongolia, China, and North Korea.

Area: 6,592,800 square miles (17,075,400 square km)

Population: 147,168,000 (73.1% urban; 26.9% rural)

Form of Government: Federal multiparty republic, with a bicameral legislative body: Federation Council—178 members; State Duma—450 members. Head of state: President. Head of government: Prime Minister.

Official Language: Russian

Capital: Moscow

Largest Cities: Moscow, 8,570,200; St. Petersburg, 4,320,900; Nizhny Novgorod, 1,424,600; Novosibirsk, 1,418,200; Yekaterinburg, 1,347,000; Samara, 1,222,500; Omsk, 1,161,200; Chelyabinsk, 1,124,500; Kazan, 1,092,300; Ufa, 1,091,800; Perm, 1,086,100; Rostov-na-Donu, 1,023,200

Economy:

Currency: Ruble (R)

National Budget: Revenue—R 329.0 trillion; expenditures—R 410.8 trillion (current expenditure: 74.3%, of which economy: 23.3%; defense: 20.9%; education: 5.8%; health: 3.0%; interest on foreign debt: 2.4%; development expenditure: 25.7%)

Public Debt: US$130.8 billion

Gross National Product: US$349.1 billion

Principal Products: Agricultural produce; livestock; oils; metals; chemicals; industrial products

Foreign Trade (Imports): US$28.1 billion (machinery and transport equipment: 35.8%; food: 29.4%; chemicals: 10.6%; textiles: 7.4%; fuels and lubricants: 4.0%; ferrous and nonferrous metals: 3.7%; from Germany: 19.9%; United States: 7.3%; Finland: 5.8%; the Netherlands: 5.7%; Italy: 5.4%; Japan: 3.9%)

Foreign Trade (Exports): US$49.9 billion (fuels and lubricants: 44.0%; ferrous and nonferrous metals: 26.3%; chemicals: 7.7%; machinery and transport equipment: 5.0%; forestry products: 4.2%; food: 4.2%; to Germany: 10.6%; United Kingdom: 7.3%; United States: 6.9%; China: 5.7%; Italy: 5.5%; Japan: 4.3%)

Stock Exchanges: 70

Moscow Central Stock Exchange (MCSE)
9B, Bolshaya Maryinskaya Street
129626 Moscow
Russia
Phone: (7-095) 229 8882
Fax: (7-095) 202 0667

Internet Address: www.fe.msk.ru/infomarket

Trading Hours:
Monday–Friday, 11:00 to 5:00
Saturday, 10:00 to 3:00

Office Hours: Monday–Friday, 9:30 to 6:00

Listed Companies: 220

Market Capitalization: US$20 billion

Major Sectors: Oil, utilities, retail, food, and commodity based industries

History: The birth of the Moscow Stock Exchange followed the country's first privatization, that of Kamaz, a large manufacturer of heavy-duty trucks, in 1990. The first exchanges, organized by banks and trading companies, opened in the same year. Originally, these exchanges began by trading commodities, such as oil, grain, lumber, and currencies. Within a short time, brokerage firms developed and started trading securities and commodities.

In mid-1992, the Ministry of Finance passed a regulation requiring brokers and financial institutions to be licensed. They were also required to choose between dealing in securities or commodities for specialization.

Even though there are more than 70 officially registered stock exchanges and commodity exchanges, the vast majority of securities in Russia trade on the over-the-counter market.

Classes of Securities: Registered shares (common and preferred), bearer shares, vouchers (privatization checks)

Indices:

AK&M Cumulative Index (1 September 1993 base = 1)

AK&M Bank Index (1 September 1993 base = 1)

AK&M Industrial Index (1 September 1993 base = 1)

Moscow Times Index of 30 Companies (capitalization-weighted index)

Supervisory Organizations: Ministry of Finance

Depository: Depository Clearing Corporation (DCC)

Settlement Details:

Shares: Currently settlement can take from one day to several months. The equity market is primarily made up of paperless shares traded via a book-entry system that lacks centralization. Every domestic company with more than 1,500 shareholders is required to have a third party act as registrar to maintain the shareholder list. Even though ostensibly separate, the registrars remain under the influence of the company directors. This can expose investors to a certain amount of risk because of flaws in the system for the proper registration of ownership.

Russia lacks the communications infrastructure to allow a book-entry system to function well. The current system has been criticized for being risky and cumbersome. The licensed broker/dealer representing the buyer is required to present documents to the company registrar, who then authenticates that documentation and adds the investor's name to the list of shareholders. An extract is issued by the registrar and serves as proof of ownership for the buyer.

Since registrars are usually found in the city in which the company is located, brokers must travel all over the country to settle trades. The Depositary Clearing Corporation (DCC) has been set up to re-register shares. It is also expected that the DCC will act as a central transfer agent or depository for much of the Russian securities market.

Trading: Equity trading in Russia is largely decentralized, although it primarily takes place in Moscow. Broker/dealers buy shares from voucher and cash auctions, employees and managers of privatized companies, and regional brokerage firms and banks. Much of what they buy is quoted in US$ and sold to Western investors.

The risk of defaults on trades can be high and each broker/dealer needs to assess the risk of trading with counterparts. Prices are often not firm and only the buyer and seller know the price of execution on concluded transactions. Most transactions are executed over the counter.

Types of Shares:

Registered Shares
Both common and preferred shares can be issued in registered form. The shares come from privatized companies. Common registered shares fall into two categories: type A or type B.

Type A shares consist of common shares bought at a discount by government workers. Holders are restricted from selling their shares to certain people. Type B shares have been distributed by the government and held in trust by regional state property funds. Shares are sold by voucher cash auctions, and then the B shares are converted to common shares.

Bearer Shares

New companies commonly issue bearer shares to raise capital from Russian investors.

Vouchers (privatization checks)

150 million vouchers were issued by the Russian government in 1992. Each citizen had a right to receive a voucher that could be converted into shares of a privatized company. The vouchers were distributed through public auction.

Vouchers for the State Property Fund were the most actively traded in 1993, making them the most liquid security available. Trading in vouchers ceased on 30 July 1994, when they became invalid.

Listing Requirements: By law, companies are required to report statutory accounts to tax inspectors. The reports are then made available to the shareholders at annual meetings. Several issuing companies publish their financial statements in Russian newspapers. Although some of the large companies hire Western accountants to draw up financial reports in line with GAAP standards, these reports are often not available to the public.

A company with more than 5,000 shareholders must report and publish financial statements quarterly in a publication with a circulation of more than 50,000 readers.

Investor Taxation: There is 0.3% stamp tax on purchasing and transferring ownership of shares.

If shares are sold to a Russian legal entity, there is a 20% withholding on the gain that is technically based on the currency involved in the transaction.

Dividends have a 15% withholding tax on dividends (withheld at the source). Theoretically this is partly refundable (to a 10% tax) but there is no regular system to have the tax reduced.

Limitations: Ownership of more than 30% of a company's common shares requires a report to the Anti-Monopoly Committee.

Brokerage Firms:

Aktiv
Novaya Basmanaya No. 12
Pod 6 Floor 5
Moscow
Russia
Phone: (7-095) 265 9088, 925 8419
Fax: (7-095) 261 2153, 923 3658

Analaiz
Raspletina No. 3
Moscow
Russia
Phone: (7-095) 192 7931, 192 9766
Fax: (7-095) 192 9872

ANTON
Leningradsky Prospekt No. 24a
Moscow
Russia
Phone: (7-095) 212 7840, 212 7807
Fax: (7-095) 212 7127

Brunswick
Tzvetnoi Boulevard No. 25
Str. 3, Pod. 2, Fl. 3,
Moscow
Russia
Phone: (7-095) 929 9800
Fax: (7-095) 929 9799, 929 9802

Center Investment Securities
Vrubeya No. 5.
Moscow
Russia
Phone: (7-095) 564 8295
Fax: (7-095) 564 8299

CS First Boston
Belinskova No. 5
Moscow
Russia
Phone: (7-095) 564 6755, 654 8777
Fax: (7-095) 564 8798

Fineol
Malyi Tolmachevskyi 6/7
Office Suite 17
Moscow
Russia
Phone: (7-095) 233 3278
Fax: (7-095) 233 3647

Grant
Bolshaya Yakimanka No. 38a
Moscow
Russia
Phone: (7-095) 238 3278
Fax: (7-095) 238 9933

Nika
Trubnikovsdy Preulok 21

Stroenie 2
Moscow
Russia
Phone: (7-095) 956 6182
Fax: (7-095) 956 6181

Nikoil
Usievicha No. 22
Moscow
Russia
Phone: (7-095) 155 4220
Fax: (7-095) 152 6611

Olma
Maly Karetnyi No. 7, Stroenie 1
Moscow
Russia
Phone: (7-095) 209 2637
Fax: (7-095) 209 4062

Rating Invest
Pudovking No. 4
Moscow
Russia
Phone: (7-095) 143 0287
Fax: (7-095) 143 3845

Rinako Plus
Novaya Pl. 3/4, Pod. 4
Moscow
Russia
Phone: (7-095) 262 0916
Fax: (7-095) 928 5241

Russian Brokerage House
Olkhovskaya No. 22 Floor 3
Moscow
Russia
Phone: (7-095) 264 5645, 164 3801
Fax: (7-095) 264 5545

Trinfico
Vtoraya Baimanskaya 9/23
Korp. 18
Moscow
Russia
Phone: (7-095) 265 7912
Fax: (7-095) 254 7868

Trika-Dialog
Krasikova 32, Office 322
Moscow
Russia

Phone: (7-095) 129 0800, 332 4480
Fax: (7-095) 128 1144

Unitrust
Jitnaya no. 6
Moscow
Russia
Phone: (7-095) 236 5257
Fax: (7-095) 230 7116

Tserikh
Prospekt Mira No. 101
Moscow
Russia
Phone: (7-095) 287 8151
Fax: (7-095) 287 8506

Yalos Bank
Goglevksky Boulevard 12
Moscow
Russia
Phone: (7-095) 291 2965
Fax: (7-095) 290 4156

Moscow Partners
3rd Frunzinskaya No. 6
Moscow
Russia
Phone: (7-095) 245 9103, 245 9371
Fax: (7-095) 242 0428, 297 0299

Company Information:

The Best Performing Shares in the Country

Company Name	Share Price Change 1 January 1997 to 31 December 1997 (%)
Sberbank Of Russia	465
Avtovaz	431
Gaz Auto Plant	395
Nizhnevartoskneftegaz	279
Unified Energy Systems	249
Magnitogorsk Metal	208
Purneftegaz	205
Condpetroleum	200
Novolipetsk Ferrous Metal Factory	193
Severstal	179
Samaraneftegas	175
Komineft	173
Primorskoe Sea Shipping	154
Tomskneft	146
Surgutneftegaz	133
Orenburgneft	117

Company Name	Share Price Change 1 January 1997 to 31 December 1997 (%)
Lukoil Holding	104
Nizhny Tagil Ferrous Metal Factory	98
Aviastar	92
Lenenergo	92
Moscow Telephone	82
Nizhnovsvyazinform	80
Novorossiysk Shipping Company	76
Inkombank	71
Lukoil Permneft	58
Varyeganneftegaz	52
Megionneftegaz	52
Yuganskneftegaz	51
Neftekhimbank	48
Irkutskenergo	48
Rostelecom	45
Kamaz	43
Krasnoyarskenergo	41
Krasnoyarsk Aluminium Plant	36
Syktyvkarsky Forestry	31

The Largest Companies in the Country by Market Capitalization as of 31 December 1997

Company Name	Market Capitalization Local Currency (Millions)	Market Capitalization US Dollars (Millions)
Lukoil Holding	15,467	15,467
Unified Energy Systems	12,313	12,313
Mosenergo	3,249	3,249
Rostelecom	2,436	2,436
Sberbank of Russia	2,412	2,412
Moscow Telephone	1,305	1,305
Irkutskenergo	944	944
Bratsk Aluminium Factory	699	699
Purneftegaz	662	662
Novolipetsk Ferrous Metal Factory	659	659
Norilsk Nickel	600	600
Yuganskneftegaz	590	590
Lenenergo	555	555
St. Petersburg Telephone	526	526
Megionneftegaz	513	513
Gaz Auto Plant	488	488
Tomskneft	405	405

Company Name	Market Capitalization Local Currency (Millions)	Market Capitalization US Dollars (Millions)
Noyabrskneftegaz	405	405
Orenburgneft	386	386
Lukoil Permneft	372	372
Nizhnevartovsknefte gaz	311	311
Chernogorneft	306	306
Severstal	299	299
Avtovaz	277	277
Kamaz	228	228
Krasnoyarsk Aluminium Plant	212	212
Magnitogorsk Metal	206	206
Trade House Gum	181	181
Krasnoyarskenergo	180	180
Condpetroleum	165	165
Komineft	163	163
Kotlassk Pulp & Paper	150	150
Red October Krasny Octyabr	146	146
Novorossiysk Shipping Company	141	141
Nizhnovsvyazinform	105	105

Regional Exchanges:

Ekaterinburg Stock Exchange
Ul. Furmanova 109
620144 Ekaterinburg
Russia
Phone: (7-3432) 221 225, 208 581
Fax: (7-3432) 294 941

Moscow Inter-Bank Currency Exchange
Zubovxky Boulevard 4
119021 Moscow
Russia
Phone: (7-095) 201 5904
Fax: (7-095) 201 2723

Moscow International Stock Exchange
Slavyanskaya Pl 4, Building 2
103074 Moscow
Russia
Phone: (7-095) 923 2611
Fax: (7-095) 923 3339

St. Petersburg Stock Exchange
274 Ligovsky Pr.
196084 St. Petersburg

Russia
Phone: (7-812) 298 8931
Fax: (7-812) 296 1080
Internet Address: www.lse.spb.su/english

Siberian Stock Exchange
Ul. Frunze 5
630091 Novosibirsk
Russia
Phone: (7-812) 296 0591
Fax: (7-812) 296 0645

Vladivostock Stock Exchange
21, Zhertv Revolyutsi Str
690091 Vladivostock
Russia
Phone: (7-4232) 227 887
Fax: (7-4232) 228 009

Other Investment Information:
Ministry of External Economic Relations
Smolenskaya-Sennaya Square, 32-34
121200 Moscow

Russia
Phone: (7-095) 220 1350

Ministry of Ecology and Use of Natural Resources
Vadkovsky, 18-20
101474 Moscow
Russia
Phone: (7-095) 289 3065

State Bank of the Russian Federation
Zhitnaya, 4
Moscow
Russia
Phone: (7-095) 237 3065

Chamber of Commerce and Industry of the Russian
  Federation
Ilyinka, 6
103864 Moscow
Russia
Phone: (7-095) 923 4323
Fax: (7-095) 230 2455

S

SACRIFICATE (Italy)

To *Sacrificate* means to miss out on a price increase by selling a security too soon.

See also LEAVE ON THE TABLE.

SAFEKEEPING

Safekeeping refers to assets, documents, and other property held by an institution serving as a custodial agent. Safekeeping items cannot be commingled and must be kept separate from anything that might compromise their safety.

Investors can provide their own safekeeping with a rented safety deposit box.

See also BOOK-ENTRY; HYPOTHECATE; MARGIN.

SAITORI (Japan)

Saitori is the title given to a member of the Tokyo, Osaka, and Nagoya exchanges. Saitori receive buy and sell orders and notify the respective dealers when the trade is executed. They do not deal with the public.

See also BROKER/DEALER; JAPAN/TOKYO STOCK EXCHANGE (TSE); SPECIALIST.

SAKURA BANK LIMITED

Sakura Bank Limited was the world's eighth largest bank in early 1997, with assets of $441.1 billion and an international network of nearly 630 affiliates, subsidiaries, and branches in 32 countries. The Sakura Bank was the name adopted by the Mitsui Taiyo Kobe Bank Limited in 1992, two years after the merger of the Mitsui Bank Limited and the Taiyo Kobe Bank Limited.

The Mitsui Bank did not start its business as a bank. The company actually began trading in textiles and entered banking only after Takatoshi Hachirobei, one of the company's founders, decided that currency would soon replace the barter system. In 1863 Mitsui purchased a money exchange. Mitsui's dry-goods business, meanwhile, declined steadily, primarily due to insufficient management.

In the mid-1860s, Mitsui switched its allegiance to rebel Meiji forces from the failing Tokugawa government, which had repeatedly levied costly tax assessments against the company. After the restoration of the Meiji emperor, Mitsui lobbied for and won a highly favored status in government. By the early 1870s, Mitsui had become the unofficial state Treasury, holding large sums of money for the government.

Rizaemon Minomura, the Mitsui director credited with being the architect of the company's rise to power, strongly advocated moving the firm to Tokyo, the new center of government and commerce, and in 1876 the Mitsui Bank was incorporated as a separate entity.

The Mitsui Bank served as the exclusive finance agent for the Mitsui trading company, the Bussan, which had begun a new and highly profitable trade in cottons and textiles. Challenged with the increasing cost and dependence on its rival Mitsubishi Bank for shipping and warehousing services, the Mitsui Bussan created its own shipping company. This began a tremendous era of competition between the two companies; Mitsui eventually lost. The strain of the competition was great, and the Mitsui Bank emerged financially exhausted.

The Mitsui companies experienced unprecedented growth after Hikojiro Nakamigawa, a former president of the Sanyo Railway, joined Mitsui Bussan in 1891. Nakamigawa introduced the motto "People make Mitsui," a clever response to its rival's assertion that "Organization makes Mitsubishi."

Nakamigawa died in 1901, leaving the directorship to his rival and predecessor, Takashi Masuda. Masuda emerged from years of semiretirement, determined to shake Mitsui out of stagnation. He introduced foreign exchange services, secured special trading rights for Mitsui in China, and even proposed purchasing Manchuria in 1911.

Although it was a separate company, the Mitsui Bank was very broadly influenced by the Mitsui Bussan and its directors; Masuda in many ways retained authority over the bank's director, Shigeaki Ikeda. Ikeda distinguished himself at the bank by providing Masuda and his successor, Takuma Dan, with even-keeled leadership that ensured reliability.

In 1932, as a result of this group's rise to power, director Takuma Dan was assassinated. Masuda designated Ikeda, a more neutral figure, to run the Bussan, and Naojiro Kikumoto was named chairman of the bank.

Ikeda, effectively the leader of both the Bussan and the bank, was additionally named governor of the Bank of Japan in 1937, and in 1938 was named Minister of Finance and Minister of Trade and Industry. The Mitsui Bank, meanwhile, was renamed the Teikoku Bank in 1943, following its merger with the Dai-Ichi Bank. Teruo Akashi was made chairman of the new bank. When World War II ended in 1945, Ikeda was designated a "Class A war criminal" and purged from public life by the occupation authority.

Chairman Akashi was replaced by Junshiro Mandai in 1945. However, Mandai and six others resigned in 1946, shortly before the occupation authorities were to purge them as well. Kiichiro Satoh was then elected president of the bank.

The bank was permitted to establish correspondent agreements with American banks in 1950, which laid the groundwork for the reestablishment of Mitsui's international operation. Mitsui incorporated an IBM punch-card computing system that permitted the bank to centralize more of its operations at its head office. In 1954, following the relaxation of antimonopoly laws in 1949 and 1952, Teikoku reverted to its former name, Mitsui Bank.

Satoh was made chairman in 1959, and was succeeded as president by Masuo Yanagi, a career Mitsui employee, who in 1961 initiated an effort to control the bank's lending activities more efficiently.

The Mitsui Bank continued to bring itself closer to the public by marketing financial products specifically for private savers. In 1968 it merged with the Toto Bank, a small, consumer-oriented bank, whose 16 branches greatly strengthened Mitsui's presence in Tokyo.

Kyubei Tanaka, who succeeded Yanagi in 1965, was himself succeeded in 1968 by Goro Koyama. Koyama presided over the widespread computerization of Mitsui and ordered the improvement of communications between branches to accommodate people who lived in the suburbs but worked in the city.

Also in 1968, Mitsui participated with the Sanwa Bank in the creation of a national credit card company, the Japan Credit Bureau, and during the early 1970s the bank introduced automatic teller machines.

The decisions to remove the United States from the gold standard and the subsequent revaluation of the British pound had a devastating impact on the Japanese banking industry. The Mitsui Bank, which had grown heavily involved in international transactions, was forced to reorganize the following year.

Under President Joji Itakura and his successor Ken-ichi Kamiya, the Mitsui Bank became a much more business-oriented financial institution. One such venture included a 19-company collaboration on new software technologies. Kamiya was promoted to chairman in June 1988, and was succeeded as president by Ken-ichi Suematsu.

In the early 1980s the Mitsui Bank restructured to emphasize its business in the consumer and corporate fields and to develop groups of market specialists. The bank also introduced a cash management system (CMS) that linked its newly established continental headquarters in New York, London, and Tokyo.

The Taiyo Kobe Bank, the other part of the 1990 merger, was itself the product of a merger between the Bank of Kobe and the Taiyo Bank in 1973. It had been a very successful commercial or "city" bank that was not associated with any of Japan's major trading *keiretsu* (conglomerates). One of its predecessors, the Bank of Kobe, was established in 1936 through the amalgamation of seven banks in the Kobe-Osaka-Kyoto region of western Japan. It remained independent of control by the conglomerates during World War II. After the war, the Bank of Kobe was reorganized, and in 1945 it added trust operations, although it had to turn these over to Toyo Trust and Banking in 1960 in accordance with Japanese financial regulations. The bank got involved in international banking starting in the late 1950s, setting up operations in London, New York, Los Angeles, and Sydney.

The Taiyo Bank was also founded just before World War II, incorporating in 1940 as the Dai Nippon Mujin following the merger of four small mutual savings and loan companies. In 1951 it was rechartered as a mutual bank called Nippon Sogo Bank. Nippon Sogo did not establish itself as a major city bank, but in 1968 it got permission to conduct foreign exchange operations. It therefore changed its name to Taiyo Bank to create a new image.

When Bank of Kobe and Taiyo Bank merged in 1973, they formed the largest banking network in Japan, with more than 300 branches. Taiyo Kobe Bank opened a series of overseas offices in the mid-1970s. Through the 1980s it opened a foreign office an average of once every eight months.

Shortly after its formation through the merger of Mitsui Bank and Taiyo Kobe Bank in 1990, Sakura Bank had to deal with a $1.6 billion capital shortfall resulting from the sharp decline of the Nikkei Index in 1990, which pushed Sakura's capital-to-assets ratio below the 8% level recommended by the Bank for International Settlements. Sakura continued to develop, however. Much of its expansion during the following six years was in eastern and southern Asia.

See also BANK OF TOKYO-MITSUBISHI LTD.; DAI-ICHI KANGYO; MITSUBISHI TRUST & BANKING CORPORATION; SANWA BANK.

SALE DOCKET (United Kingdom)

Upon settlement, the stock exchange document attached to a security in order to identify the transaction is known as the *Sale Docket*.

See also CONFIRMATION.

SALES CHARGE

Sales Charge is a fee charged by a brokerage firm for investment products not ordinarily having any commission charges attached.

Mutual funds, unit investment trusts, limited partnerships, annuities, insurance products, and other special combination products have a sales charge added—either at the time of purchase (at which time the charge is referred to as a front end load), or in the event that the money invested is withdrawn within the first few years (at which time it is referred to as a back end load).

Sales charges are often reduced as the size of the investment is increased, so there will be a lower charge for a larger money purchase amount. These price breakpoints are fully described in the prospectuses of these funds.

Investment products with sales charges normally also have annual management fees attached. Management fees are customarily deducted from the earnings of the fund.

See also COMMISSION; MUTUAL FUND; UNIT INVESTMENT TRUST/UNIT TRUST.

SALES LITERATURE

Any graphically displayed or written materials used as an aid to sell a product or service is referred to as *Sales Literature*.

Sales literature is commonly used by brokers to promote investment products to their clients. It might also be used to sell shares, mutual funds, unit investment trusts, options, or other investment programs. The most complete details on an investment can usually be found in the prospectus.

Sales literature may appear in the form of colorful brochures, graphs, and charts showing progress, or in the form of a letter composed by a broker. Brokerage firms designate a compliance officer to approve any sales literature sent to prospective investors.

In the United States, the Securities and Exchange Commission has strict rules regarding the truth, accuracy, and use of any sales literature.

See also PROSPECTUS; SECURITIES AND EXCHANGE COMMISSION (SEC).

SALES LOAD

See SALES CHARGE.

SALES WRAPPER

A *Sales Wrapper* is any additional sales literature that accompanies a prospectus and features further details about the investment. A sales wrapper cannot contain any new information that does not appear in the prospectus and tends to place emphasis on the most beneficial attributes of the investment.

The language of prospectuses is often difficult for nonprofessional investors to follow. The sales wrapper emphasizes the main advantages and makes them easier to understand. Sales wrappers tend to be more sales oriented and are frequently used with new offerings.

See also INITIAL PUBLIC OFFERING (IPO); PROSPECTUS; SALES LITERATURE.

SALOMON INC.

The Salomon brothers, founders of *Salomon Inc.*, one of Wall Street's most powerful companies, were experts in money broking. The three siblings, Arthur, Herbert, and Percy, had learned their trade from their father, Ferdinand Salomon. They set up in a small office in New York City with an initial capital of $5,000 in 1910. Less than a century later, the market value of the business that began so humbly was valued in billions of dollars.

From their cramped premises on Broadway, close to the financial heartland of Wall Street, the brothers arranged loans for equity brokers and bought and sold bonds and bills for clients. Within a year of setting up their own business the Salomon brothers added a Wall Street broker, Morton Hutzler, to their firm, and thereby gained a valuable seat on the New York Stock Exchange (NYSE).

The brothers saw the big profits available to bond underwriters but had neither the capital nor the reputation to compete with the more established Wall Street firms. All this changed, however, with America's involvement in World War I. The U.S. government became desperate for money to finance the war effort and passed the Liberty Loan Act in 1917. Salomon took advantage of the increased demand for issues and undertook its first underwritings. The great industrial boom that followed the end of the war brought many profitable years for the firm, which grew across the United States. The New York office was expanded, and new businesses were opened up in Boston, Chicago, Cleveland, Minneapolis, and Philadelphia.

Salomon's partners had made a conscious effort to focus their attention on bonds, and as a consequence, they missed out on the huge profits to be gained from investing in the great bull run of the 1920s. However, the decision to stay out of equities was vindicated when the Wall Street Crash of 1929 wiped out many other firms and individuals. Arthur Salomon, the eldest and most forceful of the brothers, had astutely realized that the market was in danger of overheating and had discouraged investment in equities from as early as 1927.

The death of Arthur Salomon in 1928 created the first in a seemingly never ending series of power struggles that continued to afflict the firm for decades after. Herbert, the youngest of the three brothers, was sure that he would succeed Arthur at the expense of the slightly aloof Percy. Other partners, however, were unconvinced by Herbert's claim for leadership and believed that another partner, Ben Levy, should head up the firm.

The first task facing the partners after Arthur Salomon died was to ensure that the firm survived the Great Depression, which followed the Wall Street Crash. A bold stroke moved the relatively small firm of Salomon onto the main stage. The period from 1933 to 1935 saw the "capital strike" on Wall Street, when the major investment banks, angered at the regulatory regime that would be forced on them by Roosevelt's plans for a Securities and Exchange Commission, refused to issue any new securities. Salomon, which was not considered a major threat by any of the banks, brought the face-off between the government and the banks to an abrupt end when it underwrote an issue of bonds for a meat packing company called Swift and Company.

World War II was a difficult time for Salomon. Its unilateral breaking of the capital strike caused resentment among its Wall Street peers and led to the firm's unofficial exclusion from a number of syndicated deals. The continuing power struggle at the top of the firm diverted management from winning new business. Herbert Salomon had died in 1951 and Rudolf Smutny, who became senior partner in 1955, was an unpopular and ineffective leader. Under Smutny's management, the firm recorded an unexpected loss in 1956.

William Salomon, son of the original founder Percy Salomon, was elected as managing partner in 1963 and embarked on a huge expansion program. A successful issue of $218 million in AT&T bonds in 1962 had confirmed Salomon as a major player in underwriting. The firm now joined with Merrill Lynch, Blyth, and Lehman Brothers in an unofficial alliance against their more established rivals. This grouping, known as the "fearsome foursome," put together syndicates to bid for the new wave of bond issues. The Mergers and Acquisitions Department was strengthened, and the firm's first overseas offices were opened in London (1971) and Hong Kong (1972).

The firm bought seats on all of the major U.S. exchanges and developed a reputation for block trading. The new SEC regulations did away with fixed commissions and Salomon aggressively cut the rate it charged its clients for trading. Volumes soared but the firm actually took a loss in 1973. Two years later Salomon made healthy profits, boosted by its involvement in the refinancing of New York City, which had found itself on the verge of bankruptcy. The city issued Municipal Assistance Corporation (MAC) bonds through Salomon and Morgan Guaranty that paid for essential services and staff costs. Similar large-scale deals for the Government Employee Insurance Company (1976) and the Chrysler Corporation (1979) followed.

William Salomon was replaced by John Gutfreund in 1978. Gutfreund, who had once considered a career in teaching English after graduating from Oberlin College, had joined the firm in 1953. He was noted for his mixture of intelligence and aggression and became a partner in 1963 at the relatively young age of 34. Gutfreund led the firm during the 1980s, the decade that was to prove the best and the worst of times for Salomon. The firm developed a reputation for expertise in the oil industry, advising on the mega-mergers between Santa Fe and Southern Pacific and between Gulf and Standard. Salomon also provided financing and advisory services for Texaco's takeover of Getty Oil. The mania for junk bonds and the takeover boom guaranteed huge profits for the firm and, by 1985, Salomon underwrote nearly one-quarter of the debt issued in the country. It was also the largest dealer in debt securities issued by the U.S. government.

The firm developed a reputation for innovative financial products. Mortgage-backed securities, bundles of mortgages sold as a single package to institutional investors, were introduced in the late 1970s. The securities were normally guaranteed by the government but offered a higher yield than that available on bonds. By 1987 Salomon dominated the market for mortgage-backed securities, which was worth $600 billion per year.

In June 1986 Wall Street was shocked by the sudden departure of Lou Ranieri, head of the mortgage-backed securities desk. Ranieri, who rejoiced in the nickname of "Mr. Mortgage," had joined Salomon when still a teenager and had risen in classic Wall

Street style from a menial job in the post room to become one of the firm's biggest money earners. A close friendship had developed between Ranieri and Gutfreund over the two decades they had worked together at the firm, and outsiders were amazed when it emerged that Gutfreund had sacked him. Ranieri was ousted for his aggressive style and dislike of formal management structures, qualities that had characterized Salomon's best traders for many years.

The public perception of Gutfreund now altered. The urbane aficionado of English literature was now seen as a ruthless hatchet man who was incapable of compassion. This image was compounded by a notorious article in *New York Magazine* that portrayed Gutfreund as an extravagant socialite and his second wife, Susan, as a social-climbing spendaholic. As details of their $20 million refurbishment of their already luxurious apartment in Manhattan appeared in the press, Salomon's chairman became a symbol for excess.

Other, more serious, problems faced Gutfreund. The partners of the firm followed the lead given by many other Wall Street firms and incorporated their partnership as a limited liability company. The partners sold the partnership to Phibro, a large commodities trading company, for $550 million in 1981. A new company, called Phibro-Salomon, was established, and the former Salomon partners were rewarded with a mixture of hefty cash payments, equity stakes in Phibro-Salomon, and large salaries.

The new corporate structure was designed to protect partners from unlimited liability in the event of heavy losses. The downside, from the partners' point of view, was that the demands of external shareholders would now have to be considered on a constant basis. Limited liability also brought the problem of disgruntled senior management. Highly valuable staff members were now denied the financial rewards of a partnership and the firm realized that salaries and bonuses would have to increase to counter the threat of headhunting by other firms.

Gutfreund's attempts to appease those employees who had foregone the partnership prize created more problems. The top 100 executives at Salomon were given a stake in a phantom pool of money that would increase in line with the firm's share price. Loyalty to the firm was guaranteed by a rule that held that any person who left the firm in the following five years would lose his or her entitlement to the pool.

The bond-trading department continued to dominate the firm's profitability. The lion's share of revenues, which topped $5 billion in 1986, were earned on the bond desk, with a much smaller contribution received from the equities desk and the M&A department. As the share price rose, the pool grew to $100 million, and the bond traders began to agitate for a larger slice of the rewards.

The global stock market crash of 1987 brought Salomon's boom years to an abrupt end. Higher interest rates took the heat out of the market and the firm incurred big losses on the BP underwriting in the United Kingdom and on a junk bond offering for the Southland Corporation, a Texas-based retail chain. Bonuses were cut and 800 staff were made redundant after the firm reported a sixth consecutive fall in profits. A large block of shares in Salomon was offered to the market by Minorco, a holding company based in Bermuda. Bruce Wasserstein, head of the rival bank First Boston, contacted Ron Perelman, head of Revlon and a well-known corporate raider, and suggested a bid for the whole of Salomon. Gutfreund, worried about losing his job to Wasserstein and his firm to Perelman, spoke to Warren Buffett, the famous investor and fund manager. The two men were good friends and Gutfreund offered Buffett an attractive deal to buy the shareholding.

John Meriwether, a former academic who was head of the bond-arbitrage desk at Salomon, demanded increased compensation, as his department consistently outperformed the other divisions of the firm. Gutfreund, who was facing pressure from many different sides, came up with a solution that would ultimately lead to his downfall. In 1990 he allowed the arbitrageurs to secretly keep 15% of their own profits to pay for a confidential performance-related pay scheme. The payouts were spectacular, with one trader making an astonishing $23 million in one year.

Paul Mozer, one of the most successful traders in government bonds at Salomon during the 1980s, was angered when news of the secret deal reached his ears. He had moved from the bond arbitrage department to head the government bonds department, thereby foregoing the huge bonuses that Gutfreund was now offering. He pleaded with Gutfreund to extend the profit-sharing deal to all bond traders. Gutfreund agreed to Mozer's plea and Mozer was thereby given the opportunity to make immense personal profits.

Mozer then instigated a series of transactions that aroused the attentions of the regulatory authorities. In February 1991 Salomon made a fake bid for an auction of bonds using the name of a client. The bid was contrary to SEC rules, which prohibited any single firm from bidding for more than 35% of any government bond issue.

A series of improper transactions followed over the next few months, with Mozer buying 35% of each

Salomon Brothers Vice Chairman John Meriwether. *(AP/Wide World Photos)*

issue in Salomon's name and then buying extra bonds in the name of a client. In February, Mozer controlled 57% of the new issue. By May, Mozer, acting as a principal buyer and as an agent for two institutional clients, owned 85% of the bond issue. Salomon effectively controlled the market, and any other investor wanting to buy the bonds found that the supply was restricted. The imbalance between supply and demand caused the value of the bonds to increase. Salomon made huge profits and Mozer looked forward to a large slice of the pool.

Subsequent investigations proved that Gutfreund, Meriwether, and the firm's president, Thomas Strauss, had all known of Mozer's activities for many months. Gutfreund was widely criticized for attempting to cover up the irregular transactions. Mozer was forced to resign, and Gutfreund and Meriwether were soon to follow in what was a black period for the firm. Warren Buffett, who had held Salomon's shares since 1987, became the new temporary chairman. He instigated wide-sweeping reforms at the bank, forcing management to recognize the importance of creating shareholder wealth. The firm was forced to pay civil damages and Buffett, who once went on the record to say that "John Gutfreund runs an extremely good operation at Salomon," was left to rue his judgment.

Michael Lewis' famous book *Liar's Poker* presents an insider's view of the decade at Salomon. Lewis, a highly paid bond salesman who had started as a graduate trainee with the firm, accurately portrays the back-biting and internal disagreements that so disastrously afflicted Salomon during the 1980s.

The firm reported a massive loss of $831 million for 1994, the biggest in the group's history. A turbulent bond market had contributed to the loss, but investors were disgruntled to learn that $303 million had to be written off because of accounting errors in 1993. Such an adjustment did little to convince investors that the much-promised reforms of management practices and internal reporting had been successful.

Warren Buffett, through his Berkshire Hathaway fund, owned two types of Salomon shares. He was the biggest holder of ordinary shares, with some 6.3% of this class of shares. His fund also owned 560,000 preference shares that paid a 9% dividend annually. The preference shares were convertible to ordinary shares or could be redeemed for cash. In 1995 Buffett chose to redeem a tranche of preference shares for cash, indicating that his patience with the bank was at an end. In 1996, however, Buffett decided to convert the second tranche into ordinary shares, a gesture of confidence in Deryck Maughan, who took over management of the firm in 1991.

Maughan faced the same problems that bedeviled his predecessors. In 1994 he attempted to change the way traders were rewarded, aligning their salaries more closely to the performance of the firm as a whole. The move resulted in the loss of approximately 10% of Salomon's senior staff in a matter of months. Maughan's compensation scheme, which had been devised by Buffett, was soon dropped.

Salomon's profits continued to slide until late September 1997, when the firm was bought by Travelers Group Inc., a financial services firm. The deal was valued at approximately $9 billion. The merger with Travelers, along with its Smith Barney brokerage division, created Salomon Smith Barney Holdings, Inc. The new investment firm ranks number three in capital behind Morgan Stanley, Dean Witter Discover and Company and Merrill Lynch, with $22.3 billion in total assets.

See also GUTFREUND, JOHN; *LIAR'S POKER*; MOZER, PAUL; SMITH BARNEY SHEARSON.

SAME-DAY SUBSTITUTION

Same-Day Substitution is the designation given to two transactions—one a buy, the other a sell—identical in money amounts, and made during the same day. It might also refer to a purchase followed by a sale or a long sale and a short sale.

Such transactions by themselves do not change the amount of equity or debit in an account and do not generate a margin call.

The concept is that any lowering of risk (a long sale) combined with an increase in risk (a long purchase) is a same-day substitution if the money amounts remain the same.

See also MARGIN; REGULATION G–X/REGULATION T; SELLING SHORT.

SANTA CLAUS RALLY (United States)

A share price rally often seen on or around the Christmas holiday (December 25) is known as the *Santa Claus Rally*.

The Dow Jones Industrial Average has recently shown rallies during this period:

Year	Starting Level	Point Level Reached	Rally Points +
1990	2527.23	2633.66	106.43
1991	2902.73	3050.98	148.25
1992	3266.26	3294.36	28.1
1993	3687.58	3769.46	81.88
1994	3674.63	3833.43	158.8
1995	5048.84	5199.13	150.29
1996	6471.76	6547.79	76.03
1997	7808.95	8149.31	340.36

Santa Claus rallies are of limited use when forecasting the future level of a market and do not occur every year.

See also BULL MARKET; MARKET CORRECTION/MARKET CRASH; RALLY.

SANWA BANK

With a long history of being a "people's bank," *Sanwa Bank* became increasingly involved in investment and international banking in the last quarter of the 20th century. The sixth largest bank in the world, Sanwa had first-quarter assets of $447 billion in 1997. With its subsidiaries, the firm engages in a full line of retail and commercial banking services. Its global banking activities include aircraft, project, and trade finance; international merger and acquisition transactions; investment advisory and custodial services; securities underwriting; international private banking; and structured finance arrangements. It maintains a domestic network of more than 1,000 outlets and more than 200 offices in 30 foreign countries—the largest international branch network of any Japanese bank.

Sanwa Bank was the product of a three-bank merger in 1933. Among the banks that merged was a history dating back to the mid-17th century. In 1656 the Konoike family in Osaka began a business brewing sake. During the next 200 years they became involved in shipping and moneylending, and in 1877 they received a national banking charter.

Konoike Bank was a small city bank that refrained from foreign business even when the Japanese controlled Taiwan, Korea, and Manchuria. It proceeded in this way for several decades, but in the 1930s it began to suffer from competition from the *zaibatsu* (conglomerate) banks. Thus in 1933 Konoike Bank merged with Yamaguchi Bank and Sanjushi Bank. The resulting entity was named *sanwa*, meaning "three harmony." Unlike the larger Japanese banks that had connections with heavy industry, Sanwa was tied to the local textile industry.

Sanwa was the first Japanese bank to offer network banking, in which deposits, withdrawals, and general-purpose consumer loans could be made at any branch. In the 1930s it had the largest deposits of any Japanese commercial bank, even while it continued to avoid international involvements. But after Japan went to war with the United States in 1941, Sanwa absorbed, under the government's impetus, an affiliated trust company and several local banks. At the end of the war, however, it was ordered by the occupation authority to sell off these acquisitions.

After World War II, although the *zaibatsu* were officially broken up, there continued to be tight clusters of financial and industrial interests that worked closely together. Sanwa, which had never been a part of those groupings, continued to focus on individual banking and the financing of small businesses. However, finally entering international banking, in 1953 Sanwa opened its first overseas office, in San Francisco. It then opened offices in London (1957), New York (1963), and Hong Kong (1964).

Domestically, Sanwa began to do some work with larger corporate accounts. It made loans to companies in steel production, shipbuilding, automobile manufacturing, and petrochemicals. In this way it was able to become a part of Japan's first period of export-led growth (1955–65).

In the late 1950s Sanwa moved its center of activity to Tokyo, even though its official headquarters remained in Osaka. In 1959 Sanwa became the first Japanese bank to introduce computers. Focusing more attention on credit cards and leases, it founded the Japan Credit Bureau in 1961 and Orient Leasing in 1964.

In the 1970s Sanwa built up its international network. It 1973 it was listed on the Frankfurt Stock Exchange. In 1972 it established the Sanwa Bank of California, which later changed its name to Golden State Sanwa Bank and expanded to 106 branches. By the late 1980s Sanwa had established North American offices in New York, Chicago, Atlanta, Dallas, Boston, Los Angeles, Toronto, and Vancouver. U.S. operations accounted for 11% of Sanwa's net earnings in 1993–94. Also, beginning in the late 1980s Sanwa acquired a number of leasing companies and trust companies abroad.

Sanwa's most marked international gains were in Asia, especially in Hong Kong and China. In 1986 Sanwa became the first Japanese bank to establish a Chinese branch, and by 1994 it had 18 branches. It also had established a merchant banking joint venture in Shanghai, and commercial, merchant banking, and leasing operations in Jakarta, Bangkok, Singapore, Kuala Lumpur, and other Asian cities.

Sanwa emerged from the Japanese real estate and stock market collapse of the late 1980s in relatively good shape, although it did have to cut back on some of its operations in Europe and the United States. By 1994 only 2.7% of its loans were classified as bad, one of the lowest figures among major Japanese banks.

One of Sanwa's chief goals for the 1990s was to increase the percentage of its net income that came from fees (as opposed to interest on loans). This figure stood at 20% in the mid-1990s, and Sanwa's aim was to increase it to 50%.

See also JAPAN; JAPANESE BOOM AND BUST 1988–90; JAPANESE FINANCIAL MARKETS.

SAUDI ARABIA, KINGDOM OF

Saudi Arabia is bordered by Kuwait, Iraq, and Jordan in the north; Yemen and Oman in the south; United Arab Emirates and Quatar in the east; and the Red Sea in the west.

Population: 18,729,576

Form of Government: Monarchy. Chief of state: King and Prime Minister.

Official Language: Arabic

Capital: Riyadh

Largest City: Riyadh

Economy:

Currency: Saudi Riyal

Foreign Trade (Imports): $28.9 billion (commodities: machinery and equipment, chemicals, foodstuffs, motor vehicles, textiles; to United States: 21%; Japan: 14%; United Kingdom: 11%; Germany: 8%; Italy: 6%; France: 5%

Foreign Trade (Exports): $39.4 billion (commodities: petroleum and petroleum products 92%; from United States: 20%; Japan: 18%; Singapore: 5%; France: 5%; South Korea: 5%)

Gross National Product: $173.1 billion

Public Debt: $18.9 billion

National Budget: Revenues—$39 billion, expenditures—$50 billion

Principal Products: Oil and oil products; dates, wheat, barley, citrus fruit; livestock

Stock Exchanges: 1
Saudi Arabian Monetary Authority
Governor's Office
PO Box 2922
Riyadh, 11169
Saudi Arabia
Phone: (966-1) 1-466-2300
Fax: (966-1) 463-3223
Telex: 201736

Trading Hours: Saturday–Thursday, 10:00 to 12:00 and 4:00 to 6:30

Office Hours: Monday–Friday, 7:30 to 2:30

Exchange Holidays:
26–31 January   6–10 April
1 February

Investment Information:
Foreign Investment Capital Committee
PO Box 5729
Omar bin Al-Khatab Road
Riyadh 11127
Saudi Arabia
Phone: (966-1) 477-5302

Ministry of Industry and Electricity
PO Box 5729
Omar bin Al-Khatab Road
Riyadh 11127
Saudi Arabia
Phone: (966-1) 477-2722
Telex: 401154 INDEL SJ

Saudi Arabian Monetary Agency
PO Box 2992
Riyadh 11461
Saudi Arabia
Phone: (966-1) 477-4002
Telex: 401065 SAMA SJ

Council of Saudi Arabian Chambers of Commerce
PO Box 16683
Riyadh Chamber of Commerce and Industry Building
Riyadh 11474
Saudi Arabia
Phone: (966-1) 405-3200
Fax: (966-1) 402-747
Telex: 405808

SAY, JEAN-BAPTISTE

Jean-Baptiste Say was a French classical economist and industrialist who introduced the concept of the entrepreneur into economic theory and divided the factors of production into land, labor, and capital. Say was largely responsible for introducing Adam Smith's views to Europe and was a powerful advocate of the laissez-faire policy.

Say identified the role of the entrepreneur, who supplies productive agents and arranges them to create products to satisfy consumers. As a broker between producers and purchasers, the entrepreneur's profits are for his own services and capital risked.

Rejecting the English classical theory of value based on labor inputs, Say attempted to replace it with a subjective theory of markets developed in *Trait d'Economie Politique* (1803). Say's law of markets was based on the propositions that, first, products were given in exchange for products, and second, that goods constituted the demand for goods. Say restricted the role of money to that of a medium of exchange. His second proposition was interpreted to mean that the act of production generated income sufficient to buy back the product, or more simply, "supply creates its own demand."

According to Say's Law the possibilities of general overproduction or a deficiency in aggregate demand were ruled out. To Say, the persistence of gluts, or overproduction, could only exist as temporary phenomena. Say's Law of markets was accepted and clarified by David Ricardo and John Stuart Mill, but challenged by Thomas Malthus's observation of persistent gluts in post-Napoleonic England.

Say's Law was based on the implicit assumption that all income was spent. His orthodox classical economic approach denied the possibility of idle money balances, since rationally, such money could be lent out at interest. Partial overproduction was possible but could not develop into general overproduction. Say's doctrine maintained that if one seller was unable to sell all his or her product, others would enjoy extra demand and there would be a reallocation of productive resources. The labor theory of value was replaced, since the demand for a commodity determined the demand for a factor of production and the price of that factor.

Say was a forerunner of the neoclassical school of economics and equilibrium analysis. His influence upon economic thinking and economic policy for more than two centuries was severely criticized by Keynes. The experience of prolonged mass unemployment in the 1930s challenged the apparent impossibility of deficient aggregate demand in an economy. In his *General Theory of Employment, Interest and Money* (1936), Keynes attacked the neoclassical version of Say's Law, which assumed that the market system self-adjusted to a full-employment equilibrium. Money, Keynes argued, was held in idle balances as a store of value and the economy, therefore, would remain in equilibrium at below full-employment output.

See also CLASSICAL SCHOOL OF ECONOMICS; KEYNES, JOHN MAYNARD; MALTHUS, THOMAS ROBERT; MILL, JOHN STUART; NEOCLASSICAL SCHOOL OF ECONOMICS; RICARDO, DAVID; SMITH, ADAM.

SAY'S LAW
See SAY, JEAN-BAPTISTE.

SCALPER
A *Scalper* is a short-term speculator who buys shares and bonds to make small one-point or two-point profits before selling out and switching to another investment. Before the tightening up of regulations around the world, scalping was common, especially when shares were first issued by a company. New issues, which often had an element of undervaluation built into their price to make them more attractive, were firm favorites with several generations of scalpers.

See also PSYCHOLOGY OF SPECULATION.

SCARICARE (Italy)
See BEAR MARKET.

SCHEDULE 13D (United States)
Many countries have laws that govern the level of company ownership held by an institution, individual, or group of individuals acting in concert. In the United States, *Schedule 13D* is the form that the Securities and Exchange Commission (SEC) requires to be filed within ten business days of a shareholder reaching an ownership level of 5% or more of the equity shares of a company registered with the SEC.

The purpose of the form is to inform regulators and company management of the shareholder's intentions regarding the management and control of the target company.

See also MERGER; SECURITIES AND EXCHANGE COMMISSION (SEC); TAKEOVER/TAKEOVER BID; TARGET COMPANY.

SCHEDULE 13G (United States)
Similar to Schedule 13D, a *Schedule 13G* form is required to be filed within 45 days of the end of the calendar year in which an institution, individual, or group of persons acting in concert has acquired 5% or more of the equity shares of a company that is registered with the Securities and Exchange Commission (SEC).

The short form is used when the acquirer has acquired the shares through normal transactions and has no intention of changing or otherwise controlling the business activities and management of the company. The form is commonly used by broker/dealers, banks, and investment companies (mutual funds).

See also BROKER/DEALER; MUTUAL FUND; SCHEDULE 13D.

SCHLUSSKURS, SCHLUSSNOTIERUNG (Germany)
See CLOSING PRICE.

SCHNEIDER, JÜRGEN

Jürgen Schneider was the perpetrator of the biggest property crash in the history of postwar Germany. He fled Germany in April 1994, leaving behind debts of 5.2 billion deutschemarks (£2.3 billion). Schneider was accused of setting up a secret network of 200 offshore companies that siphoned money away from the German banks to prop up his construction empire. He used his existing properties as collateral in order to borrow more money from compliant banks.

Schneider, who was the son of a property developer, used money from his heiress wife, Claudia Schneider-Granzow, to buy his first properties. As their financial standing improved, the couple became regular features on the German social circuit.

Schneider's company, which was privately owned, had enjoyed many years of success in developing and restoring dozens of sites in Germany. From a slow start in 1981, the company grew to own 121 different properties in 14 German cities, including high-class hotels, prestigious retail sites, and luxury business accommodations.

By the end of the 1980s Schneider had moved into Leipzig and other East German cities as the post-reunification boom pushed up property prices. It was estimated that 1,000 of the 3,000 workers employed by the company were based in Leipzig. Expansion in the newly unified former East Germany, however, strained the company's finances. In April 1994 Schneider shocked his fellow board members by announcing his withdrawal from the company's affairs on the grounds of ill health.

The German police force were criticized by the German media for their inability to catch the Schneiders. More than 50 sightings of the Schneiders were made in places as far apart as the Isfahan mountains in Iran and a ranch in Tierra del Fuego, on the tip of Argentina. Other eagle-eyed Germans placed them in Hong Kong, Northern Ireland, and a hospital in Calcutta. Schneider was eventually arrested in his rented apartment in a suburb of Miami in South Florida, an area known for its high proportion of retired residents. He was charged with fraud and falsifying financial records, denied bail, and told to prepare himself for extradition.

When arrested, Schneider was pictured without his famous toupee, tanned, and looking healthier than expected and with a new mustache. He denied that he had fled Germany to avoid the repercussions from the collapse of his company despite the fact that he first registered in the United States under an assumed name. He likewise justified the transfer of 245 million deutschemarks from his business account to a bank in Switzerland as normal business practice. Unsurprisingly, Deutsche Bank was dismissive of Schneider's defense. A spokesman for the bank said at the time that, "Mr. Schneider's comments lie between the nonsensical and the outrageous. It is high time this U.S. comedy is brought to an end, and that he face a German court."

Schneider used popular mistrust about the big German banks as part of his public relations campaign following his arrest. He accused Deutsche Bank of an "arrogance of power," and claimed that its lending policy had put unbearable pressure on his company. He believed that Deutsche's eagerness to bankrupt him was inspired by personal animosity, rather than business sense, and he also thought that the bank had hastily rejected a proposal to rescue his company.

The chairman of Deutsche Bank, Hilmar Kopper, emerged with little credit from the collapse. When questioned about the size of the claims of small creditors relative to the total losses caused by the Schneiders, his reply—"peanuts"—was viewed as indiscreet and arrogant. Such an attitude added fuel to the fire of the debate about the power of the banks over German industry and the lack of interest in creating shareholder value. Problems at other industrial companies, Metallgesellschaft and KHD foremost among them, were not stymied by having representatives from the banks on their boards of directors.

Schneider, who worked closely with his wife to build up his property empire, had been granted loans by 50 banks in Germany. The small Konigsteiner Volksbank, based in a small village outside Frankfurt where the Schneiders lived in a castlelike, 100-room villa, was unable to bear the losses and was absorbed by the larger Frankfurter Volksbank. Four directors at Deutsche Centralbodenkredit, the Deutsche Bank subsidiary that had lent millions of deutschemarks to Schneider, were forced to resign. After an independent investigation, the bank cited "woefully inadequate" credit controls as a major contributing factor to the scandal.

See also DEUTSCHE BANK.

SCHULD (Germany)

See DEBT.

SCOPERTA (Italy)

See SELLING SHORT.

SCOPERTISA (Italy)

See BEAR MARKET.

SCOTTISH WIDOWS FUND AND LIFE ASSURANCE SOCIETY

The *Scottish Widows Fund and Life Assurance Society* was started in 1815 in Edinburgh, Scotland by a group of wealthy seamen and merchants. They pooled their money to create a fund to secure provisions for the Scottish widows, sisters, mothers, and other female survivors of soldiers who had died in the Napoleonic Wars. That aim was the substance of their charter. Until 1832 their business was confined to Scotland, but in that year they appointed agents to England, and in 1839 an office was opened in London.

In 1841 Scottish Widows became a formal company, the only private company ever created by an act of parliament. For more than 150 years it has continued to operate under its original charter. As a mutual company, it has no shareholders; its policy owners are its members and co-owners.

In 1997 Scottish Widows still maintained its head office in Edinburgh. It had 11 regional offices in the northern part of Great Britain, 10 sales branches in the southern region, and 8 direct sales branches throughout the United Kingdom. It had only one international office, which was in Princeton, New Jersey, in the United States.

Scottish Widows is an insurance holding company. Through its subsidiaries it has two business sectors: long-term insurance business and noninsurance business. The latter sector includes banking, estate agency, unit trust management, investment management, and building contracting. At the end of 1995 it had 4,103 employees and assets of $37.2 billion. The second largest life insurance firm in the country, it had nearly $41 billion invested in the stock market. Of its funds under management, roughly 30% were life insurance, 65% were pensions funds, and 5% were unit trusts (mutual funds) or other investment vehicles.

Scottish Widows' investments were diversified in many countries. For example, its $3.5 billion invested in Western Europe in 1995 was distributed as follows: France, 25.4%; the Netherlands, 17%; Germany, 15.6%; Finland, 10.7%; Switzerland, 8.2%; Spain, 7.9%; Sweden, 6.7%; and Italy, 5.8%. Scottish Widows was active in the emerging markets of Central and Eastern Europe as well, especially Poland. The managers of Scottish Widows' European fund place great importance on personally visiting companies before deciding whether to invest in their stock.

In the 1990s, Scottish Widows was able to expand its market share despite the decline of the pensions market, thanks to its development of new products and finding ways to connect them with customers. In 1993 Scottish Widows purchased a new computerized database system. As a result, focused direct mailings—to customers, potential customers, and independent financial advisers—became a much more useful part of its marketing strategy.

Also in 1993, Scottish Widows set up its first U.S. office. This office handled marketing and client services for U.S. clients, while headquarters in Edinburgh took care of investment management for these clients. The U.S. office targeted the U.S. pension funds of the 140 U.S.-based parent companies whose UK subsidiaries had some of their pension funds managed by Scottish Widows.

Scottish Widows Investment Management Limited, a subsidiary pension and trust investment company, did very well in the late 1980s and early 1990s by utilizing derivatives to allocate assets, expedite cash flow, and enhance prices, and by making astute options investments. It was able to get through the 1987 market crash in relatively good condition.

In 1995 Scottish Widows created a wholly owned subsidiary, Scottish Widows Bank. In 1996 Scottish Widows entered into a strategic alliance with the Royal Bank Group. Scottish Widows provided administration for and acquired a 20% interest in Royal Scottish Assurance, which is the life insurance subsidiary of the Royal Bank of Scotland. By mid-1997 this share had increased to 30%. In 1997 Scottish Widows created its first credit card, with its business administered by the Royal Bank.

Also in 1996 Scottish Widows transferred the administration of its investment portfolio to WM Company, a subsidiary of Bankers Trust. Scottish Widows would continue to manage its portfolio and allocate investments, but WM would be responsible for trade settlements, securities reconciliation, income collection, and tax recovery. The purpose of this move was to allow Scottish Widows to restructure and focus on its core businesses, namely, managing money, selling products (especially life assurance, pensions, and investment funds), and developing relationships with clients.

See also INSURANCE; MUTUAL FUND.

SCRIP

A *Scrip* is any paper representation of investment securities.

See also CERTIFICATE.

SCRIP DIVIDEND

See STOCK DIVIDEND.

SCRIP ISSUE (Europe)

The issue of shares to holders in proportion to their current holdings is referred to as the *Scrip Issue*. Made by transferring some reserves to the share capital account, the scrip issue brings the share capital in line with current business needs while reducing share prices according to the number of shares issued. The lower price makes the shares more marketable.

Important to note: A scrip issue—also referred to as a bonus issue or capitalization issue—does not lead to a transfer of any funds between the company and its shareholders.

See also ISSUE; REVERSE SPLIT; SPLIT.

SCRIPOPHILY

Scripophily is the collecting of old or unusual securities certificates.

Certificates are collected for their beauty or historical significance. They often look attractive and are framed and hung on the wall, much like other works of graphic art. Many of the collectible companies—typically old railroads, manufacturers, and utilities—no longer exist, but the certificates have appreciated in value as works of art.

New forms of scripophily will disappear as the world does away with paper certificates and keeps track of security ownership by computer book-entries. The Internet has many links to companies that offer certificates for sale as collectibles.

See also BOOK-ENTRY; CERTIFICATE; GOOD DELIVERY.

SÉANCE COMPLIMENTAIRE (France)

Séance Complimentaire refers to the late afternoon trading on the Paris Bourse, which occurs at the same time as trading on the New York Stock Exchange. Foreign securities are traded during this session. It is also known by the nickname petite bourse.

See also FRANCE; UNITED STATES/NEW YORK STOCK EXCHANGE (NYSE).

SEAQ (United Kingdom)

See UNITED KINGDOM/STOCK EXCHANGE AUTOMATED QUOTATION SYSTEM.

SEAT

A membership on the stock exchange or commodities exchange is commonly referred to as a *Seat*. Becoming a member on the stock exchange or commodities exchange is referred to as "having a seat on the exchange" with all the rights and privileges the membership position offers.

Some exchanges are limited to the number of seats allowed, but they can be bought and sold. Seats can be purchased as an investment and leased to someone else on some exchanges.

Membership Prices New York Stock Exchange (US$):

Year	High Price	Low Price
1990	430,000	250,000
1991	440,000	345,000
1992	600,000	410,000
1993	775,000	500,000
1994	830,000	760,000

See also MEMBER; SPECIALIST; TRADE.

SEATS (Australia)

See STOCK EXCHANGE AUTOMATED TRADING SYSTEM (SEATS).

SEC FEE (United States)

The *SEC Fee* is a minor fee charged on securities sold that are registered on U.S. stock exchanges.

The SEC Fee amounts to $.01 per $300 or fraction thereof of securities sold. Therefore, a person selling securities worth $300 would pay one cent (a penny) extra to the Securities and Exchange Commission.

Exceptions to the SEC fee are registered new issues of securities, listed options, private placements, exercises of rights, warrants, conversions of convertible securities, and a sale that comes as part of a tender offer or exchange.

See also COMMISSION; INITIAL PUBLIC OFFERING (IPO); SECURITIES AND EXCHANGE COMMISSION (SEC).

SECOND MARCHÉ (France)

Second Marché is the unlisted securities market of France.

Requirements for trading on the Second Marché are less stringent than on the exchanges. Ten percent of shares must be made available for trading and there is no minimum required capitalization. Also, a company is not required to have auditors approved by the Commission des Operations de Bourse (COB).

Shares may trade on the Second Marché permanently, but after a three-year history the auditors need COB approval, and the company must publish quarterly reports.

See also FRANCE; LISTED SECURITIES; OVER THE COUNTER (OTC).

SECOND MARKET

See OVER THE COUNTER (OTC).

SECOND SECTION (Japan)

Second Section refers to a second class of securities traded on the Tokyo, Osaka, and Nagoya exchanges. The Second Section was established in 1961 in order to provide a better market for over-the-counter securities. Listing involves fewer criteria than First Section securities. Some Japanese securities use the Second Section to begin trading.

See also FIRST SECTION; JAPAN/TOKYO STOCK EXCHANGE (TSE); OVER THE COUNTER (OTC).

SECONDARY DISTRIBUTION (United States)

Secondary Distribution refers to the sale of a block of securities to other investors. In the United States, if such sales are registered with the Securities and Exchange Commission (SEC), they are referred to as registered secondaries. If the sale of a block of securities is not registered with the SEC, they are referred to as spot secondaries.

Secondary distributions are customarily sold on a net price basis, with the sales charges paid by the seller. They are usually announced by the exchange.

See also NET PRICE; OVER THE COUNTER (OTC).

SECONDARY MARKET

The *Secondary Market* is the market in which securities are bought and sold publicly. The term refers to all trading, whether on a stock exchange or over-the-counter, that occurs after the initial public offering (primary market), when the shares begin to trade. A healthy secondary market guarantees liquidity and spreads risk.

See also LIMIT ORDER; OVER THE COUNTER (OTC); PRIMARY MARKET.

SECONDARY TREND

When a market index or average turns and moves in a direction opposite of what has been the primary trend for a period of days or weeks, it is referred to as a *Secondary Trend*.

The appearance of secondary trends can signal growing weakness or, if repeated, show the strongest areas of support.

The description is an important part of market technical analysis and originally comes from Dow Theory analysis.

See also DOW THEORY; SUPPORT/SUPPORT LEVEL; TECHNICAL ANALYSIS.

SECTOR

Sector refers to the grouping of companies on the basis of similarities between product or service lines.

Among the many sectors of quoted stocks are airlines, automobiles, banking, health, and technology. Sectors are frequently further subcategorized; for example, the technology sector can be divided into subsectors such as computers and telecommunication. The distinction between sectors and subsectors appears, at times, to be rather arbitrary.

Economic changes can have an effect on all of the companies of a specific sector. Therefore, it is common for analysts to compare the growth of a specific company to others in the same sector. If a company's growth is slower or faster than its industry average, a good analyst will investigate further to learn why the discrepancy exists. The difference could mean the existence of a problem or an undervalued growth situation.

See also DOW JONES AVERAGES; STANDARD AND POOR'S 500 INDEX (S&P 500).

SECURITIES ACT OF 1933 (United States)

The *Securities Act of 1933* was the first U.S. congressional law regulating the securities market. It was primarily concerned with guaranteeing the full disclosure of material information to shareholders and preventing fraud.

The law requires the registration of securities before any public sale and adequate disclosure of pertinent financial and other data in a prospectus that permits analysis by informed investors.

The law also contains antifraud provisions prohibiting false representation and disclosure. Enforcement of the Act was granted to the Securities and Exchange Commission by the Securities Exchange Act of 1934.

See also SECURITIES EXCHANGE ACT OF 1934.

SECURITIES ANALYST

See ANALYST.

SECURITIES AND EXCHANGE COMMISSION (SEC; United States)

The *Securities and Exchange Commission* is the United States Federal Government agency established by the Securities Exchange Act of 1934 that is empowered to monitor, regulate, and prosecute rule violations in the securities industry. All corporations with securities listed on a national exchange must file detailed registration statements with the SEC and are required to disclose financial information on a periodic basis. The SEC retains discretionary power over the form and detail of such disclosures. The SEC also requires periodic audits of these firms by independent accountants. A side aspect of this last requirement is that it places the auditor in a position of becoming legally liable to third parties (including investors) who might be harmed because of their information.

See also REGULATION A/B; SECURITIES ACT OF 1933; SECURITIES EXCHANGE ACT OF 1934.

The following are a number of the more important SEC rules:

SEC Rule 10a-1 States that short sales of securities registered on an exchange can only be executed on a price up tick or zero plus tick. An up tick is a price that is higher than the most immediate trade execution. A zero plus tick is a price the same as the immediate trade execution, if that price was an up tick.

SEC Rule 10b-2 Prohibits the solicitation of buy orders for an exchange listed security while that security is involved in a distribution

See also SECONDARY DISTRIBUTION.

SEC Rule 10b-4 Prohibits the short sale of securities that are involved in a tender offer.

See also TENDER OFFER.

SEC Rule 10b-6 Restricts any and all solicitation of buyers for a new issue of securities until the public offering is made. Underwriters are allowed to accept indications of interest but cannot make any sales of such securities.

SEC Rule 10b-7 Sets the regulations for an underwriter's attempt to stabilize the bid to implement the distribution of securities.

SEC Rule 10b-8 Prohibits price manipulation of a security involved in distribution through a rights offering.

SEC Rule 10b-10 Regulates the preparation as well as distribution of trade confirmations to investors. It defines the minimum required information and necessary disclosures to customers.

SEC Rule 10b-13 Prohibits investors who are involved in a tender offer from making additional purchases of the security so involved, until the same tender offer has expired.

See also TENDER OFFER.

SEC Rule 10b-16 Provides investors with complete information on borrowing (i.e., for margin accounts), including financial terms, conditions and arrange-ments; the securities industry's version of the Truth in Lending Law.

See also MARGIN.

SEC Rule 10b-18 Permits companies under certain conditions to repurchase their own shares in order to avoid price manipulation.

SEC Rule 11a Governs trades made by exchange members for their own accounts.

SEC Rule 13D Provides reporting and disclosure requirements for any person or group buying 5% or more of any one company's shares, when that company is registered with the SEC.

SEC Rule 13E Sets regulations for an issuer or affiliate when purchasing its own shares from the public market.

SEC Rule 14A Regulates the preparation and distribution of proxy information to shareholders. It defines the kind of information necessary, the supporting documents, and the format. It includes the requirement to submit the information to the SEC.

SEC Rule 15c2-1 Sets rules regulating the safekeeping of securities purchased in a margin account. It prohibits commingling of the investor's and the firm's securities and sets limits on hypothecation.

See also HYPOTHECATION; MARGIN.

SEC Rule 15c2-6 Attempts to reduce the fraud involved with many penny stocks. It establishes a suitability test, as well as a cooling off period for shares with a market price under $5, if the company has less than $2 million in tangible assets. Exchange listed and NASDAQ traded securities are exempt.

See also PENNY STOCK.

SEC Rule 15c3-1 Sets rules and a requirement formula used by broker/dealers to calculate "net capital." The basic rule states that investor-related indebtedness may not exceed net capital by more than 15 to 1.

SEC Rule 15c3-2 States that an investor must be notified of any credit balance left in an account with a broker/dealer and that the balance can be withdrawn at any time.

If the credit balance is left with the firm, the firm is allowed to make use of the funds in order to conduct day-to-day business. The investor still retains the right to withdraw the funds at any time.

SEC Rule 16a-1 Covers the reporting of beneficial ownership of equity ownership by all officers, directors, and principal shareholders (10% or more) of a registered company. Additional reports must be filed if the equity positions are increased or decreased.

SEC Rule 17a-3 and 17a-4 Governs the maintenance and record-keeping of broker/dealers. Record-keeping documents are defined; they must be prepared and preserved for regulatory inquiries.

SEC Rule 17a-8 Requires a report to the U.S. Treasury of any receipt of U.S. currency in excess of $10,000 and the import or export of U.S. currency in excess of $5,000 to a bank, securities, or other financial account in any foreign country in which a citizen or resident has an interest; a parallel rule to the Foreign Currency Transaction Reporting Act of 1970.

SEC Rule 17a-12 Sets the filing requirements for broker/dealers making a market in over-the-counter margin securities and receiving preferential credit terms for financing the positions.

SEC Rule 17a-17 Sets criteria for broker/dealers registering with the SEC as block positioners and who obtain preferential credit terms for the financing.

SEC Rule 17f-1 Requires broker/dealers, banks, and transfer agents to promptly report any knowledge of lost, stolen, counterfeit, or misplaced securities to a computer service maintained to keep track of such occurrences. The service National Crime Information Center (NCIC) acts as a central clearing service for those wishing to inquire about a missing security.

SEC Rule 17f-2 Requires the fingerprinting of virtually every employee, partner, or officer of a broker/dealer as a condition of affiliation with the firm. Subsequent fingerprints are sent to the U.S. Attorney General for identification and background checks.

SEC Rule 19b-3 Prohibits the fixing of commissions or floor broker rates by a national securities exchange.

SEC Rule 19c-4 Enforces the one share one vote rule.

SEC Rule 134 Defines the type of language that can be used by a dealer for the sale of a registered offering. It provides guidelines for information regarding the issuer and defines inappropriate materials for use in a prospectus.

SEC Rule 144 Permits a holder to sell unregistered securities to a public sale without a formal registration statement, under well-defined conditions.

SEC Rule 147 Sets terms and conditions for an intrastate offering without requiring SEC registration.

SEC Rule 156 Prohibits the use of false and misleading advertising when selling investment company securities.

SEC Rule 415 Enforces shelf registration requirements. Qualified issuers can register an offering to be sold during the following two year period.

SEC Rule 433 Sets rules under which a dealer can use a preliminary prospectus.

See also RED HERRING.

SECURITIES AND INVESTMENTS BOARD (SIB; United Kingdom)

The *Securities and Investments Board (SIB)* is the official organization in charge of implementing regulations set down in the Financial Services Act of 1986, as authorized by a delegation order of the Secretary of State for Trade and Industry. The board annually reports its activities to the secretary of state.

The SIB is responsible for authorizing various self-regulating organizations, recognized investment exchanges, recognized professional bodies, and recognized clearing houses. Its purpose is to ensure the protection of the investor through the self-regulating organizations and their conduct of business rules.

The SIB also maintains a compensation fund to protect investors from loss if an investment firm defaults.

See also SELF-REGULATING ORGANIZATION (SRO); UNITED KINGDOM.

SECURITIES ASSOCIATION, THE (TSA; United Kingdom)

A self-regulating organization authorized under the Financial Services Act of 1986, *The Securities Association (TSA)* regulates the actions of members engaged in the buying and selling of securities. It reports to the Securities and Investments Board.

See also SELF-REGULATING ORGANIZATION (SRO); UNITED KINGDOM.

SECURITIES DEALERS ASSOCIATION (Japan)

The *Securities Dealers Association* is the self-regulatory organization that sets entry standards and examinations for all securities dealers and sales representatives. It also sets rules on how much action can be taken by members to stabilize prices.

See also JAPAN; SELF-REGULATING ORGANIZATION (SRO).

SECURITIES EXCHANGE ACT OF 1934 (United States)

The *Securities Exchange Act of 1934* is the act that empowered the Securities and Exchange Commission (SEC) to enforce the Securities Act of 1933. The following are among the regulations covered by the act:

1. Registration of securities listed on stock exchanges and periodic disclosures by issuers of changes in financial status and condition
2. Regular disclosures of holdings and transactions by insiders, officers, directors, and shareholders owning 10% or more of the equity securities
3. Solicitation of proxies that enables shareholders to vote on proposals
4. Registration with the SEC of stock exchanges and broker/dealers, to ensure compliance with SEC rules through self-regulation
5. Surveillance by the SEC of trading practices on stock exchanges and the over-the-counter markets to minimize broker/dealer insolvencies
6. Regulation of margin requirements for securities purchased with credit
7. Subpoena power of the SEC for investigation of violations and other enforcement activities

See also SECURITIES ACT OF 1933; SECURITIES AND EXCHANGE COMMISSION (SEC).

SECURITIES INVESTORS PROTECTION CORPORATION (SIPC; United States)

Under the provisions of the Securities Protection Act of 1970, the *Securities Investors Protection Corporation (SIPC)* was established to provide protection to the customers of member firms in cases of insolvency.

In the event that a brokerage firm becomes insolvent, SIPC first attempts to find another firm with which to merge the insolvent one. If this fails, SIPC liquidates the insolvent firm and pays the investors on losses. The maximum amount of coverage per customer is $500,000 of which $100,000 in cash is covered.

SIPC is a non-profit organization.

See also HYPOTHECATION; INSOLVENCY; MARGIN.

SECURITIZATION

Securitization refers to the pooling together and repackaging of loans with similar risk profiles and maturities that can then be sold to investors. These packages, which can include residential mortgages, Eurobonds, and business loans, can be traded on stock exchanges.

SECURITY

In terms of finance, *Security* represents the collateral used to secure a loan. Real estate, equipment, or other assets might be used as loan collateral. If the borrower defaults on the loan, the lender may take possession of the collateral.

In terms of investing, a security is an instrument showing ownership in a business as signified by shares or shares of stock. A security can also be an instrument showing debt by a company or government entity. In this case the security is referred to as a bond. Securities can also be instruments that grant the right to buy or sell other securities, such as options, rights, and warrants. For purposes of regulation, derivatives of options, index options, and futures can also be classified as securities.

See also COMMON STOCK; OPTION; SUBSCRIPTION RIGHTS; SUBSCRIPTION WARRANT.

SECURITY PACIFIC CORPORATION (SPC)

See BANKAMERICA CORPORATION.

SEDOL

See STOCK EXCHANGE DAILY OFFICIAL LIST (SEDOL).

SEGREGATED SECURITIES (United States)

Segregated Securities refers to those securities that must be held in a separate place and not used by the broker/dealer to conduct the firm's business activities.

According to U.S. federal laws, securities that are fully paid and held in investor's cash accounts, those that are held in margin accounts, and those used as collateral on debit balances must be segregated.

The broker/dealer cannot commingle a customer's securities with any others except those of a bona fide customer. The firm is also prohibited from borrowing more against the aggregate value of customers' securities than the amount that is owed on the securities.

See also HYPOTHECATE; MARGIN; SECURITIES AND EXCHANGE COMMISSION (SEC)/SEC RULE 15C2-1; SECURITY.

SEGREGATION ACCOUNT 100 (United States)

A *Segregation Account 100* is maintained at the Depository Trust Corporation (DTC) and is used to keep shares of communications and maritime issues held by members for non-residents.

Because of certain limitations on foreign ownership, these issues are held in nominee name in a special segregated account at the DTC, where the amount of foreign ownership is easily identified.

See also DEPOSITORY TRUST CORPORATION (DTC); ISSUE; UNITED STATES.

SELF-REGULATING ORGANIZATION (SRO)

A *Self-Regulating Organization (SRO)* monitors adherence to all laws, rules, and regulations, and maintains the fair practice of securities trading.

Because of the need for those creating or enforcing regulations to understand the technical subtleties of the industry, securities trading remains largely self-regulated. Laws passed without an understanding of the securities industry could easily become too stifling for a free market or, conversely, such laws might not have sufficient strength to be effective. SROs are close enough to the action on the trading floor to recognize, stop, or prevent improper and fraudulent activities before they become a serious problem.

Although some top-level government restrictions and actions are necessary, an effective approach appears to be for governments to require the self-regulatory organizations to enforce compliance with a fair and orderly securities market.

See also COMPLIANCE; FAIR AND ORDERLY MARKET; NATIONAL ASSOCIATION OF SECURITIES DEALERS (NASD); SECURITIES AND EXCHANGE COMMISSION (SEC).

SELF-REGULATION

See SELF-REGULATING ORGANIZATION (SRO).

SELF-TENDER

A *Self-Tender* is one of a number of strategies used to ward off a takeover attempt.

Similar to a tender offer, a self-tender is made when the issuing corporation offers to buy back a certain number of its shares in exchange for cash or assets.

See also POISON PILL; SHARK REPELLENT; TENDER OFFER.

SELL

In the securities industry a *Sell* is an order to exchange securities (shares, bonds, options or other securities) for cash.

For example, an investor places a sell order for 200 shares of XYZ Corporation as a market order. The shares are sold for $50 per share and the investor receives $10,000, less commission and fees.

If an investor receives more money than was originally paid it is referred to as a capital gain and is taxable in many countries. If, however, the investor sells for a smaller amount of money than was originally paid, it is a capital loss and may be tax deductible.

See also CAPITAL GAIN; CAPITAL LOSS.

SELL AT BEST

Sell at Best is an instruction given by one broker/dealer to another broker/dealer when asking him or her to help sell parts of a large market order.

The instruction tells the broker/dealer to sell at the best available bid price.

See also LIMIT ORDER; MARKET ORDER; STOP LIMIT ORDER; STOP ORDER.

SELL ON THE CLOSE

Sell on the Close is an order designation that instructs to sell during the last period of trading at the end of the day. Many stock exchanges have set procedures with differing time considerations of between half an hour and half a minute for selling at the market close. Designating an order to sell on the close does not guarantee the closing price or even an execution. The market order always takes priority over all other orders.

The strategy of selling on the close may have been more successful when trading was slower than it is these days. An investor would observe that share prices were rising during the day and figured they would close on the highest level. An order would be placed to take advantage of the day's trend. Although a share price can still end at its high, with computerized trading an order can be entered as a market order up until the final bell.

See also CLOSING PRICE; LIMIT ORDER; MARKET ORDER; ON THE OPENING.

SELL ON THE OPEN

Sell on the Open is an instruction (given by the investor) to sell a specific amount of shares, but only in the event that the order is part of the initial transaction for the security involved on that market day. If the instruction cannot be followed, the order is canceled.

This differs from the rule that all market orders received before the open must be included in the initial transaction, as it is a specification entered by the investor.

See also LIMIT ORDER; MARKET ORDER; ON THE OPENING.

SELL OUT

Sell Out is the command given by a brokerage firm to sell securities positions belonging to an investor who owes money to the firm, or whose account is in arrears. The firm will sell enough securities to cover the amount overdue. A confirmation notice of the transaction is sent to the investor.

Sell out can also refer to securities sold at the market as the result of a trade made between broker/dealers in which a buy is made, but the buyer fails to pay. The buyer is responsible for any loss.

See also LIQUIDATION; MARGIN; SETTLE.

SELL STOP ORDER

An order placed through a stock exchange with instructions to sell a security when the market price trades at or through the stop price designated is known as a *Sell Stop Order*. Also called stop loss orders, their use is hotly debated as a defensive strategy.

Although some advise placing a stop order 10% away from the current market price, others suggest the strategy will doom a portfolio to a consistent 10% loss. Still others recommend placing stop orders at least two points ($2 in the United States) away from the current price, a strategy dating back more than 100 years.

There is little doubt that many investors place stop orders in the hope that the order will never be filled, as it will mean a loss. However, there are some investors who want the protection that a sell stop order offers from a severe price decline.

See also BUY STOP ORDER; LIMIT ORDER; MARKET ORDER.

SELLERS' MARKET

A strong market with prices rising is called a *Sellers' Market*. This is the time at which the demand for shares exceeds supply, thereby driving prices higher.

One of the oldest concepts in the stock market is to sell when others are buying and buy when others are selling. Charles Dow, one of the founders of *The Wall Street Journal* and the publication's first managing editor, believed that professional investors are aware of this, but often reverse the process. Many investors have trouble selling into a sellers' market, even though they are advised by professional share traders to "sell into strength."

See also DOW THEORY; SELL; TECHNICAL ANALYSIS.

SELLING CONCESSION

Selling Concession is the fee paid to the selling group of a new issue.

New issues are sold on a net basis, meaning there is no commission added to the price of the transaction. However, an amount is paid by the issuer to cover the costs of selling the new issue. This amount includes the selling concession and other related costs. These costs are paid out of the proceeds received for the new issue.

Some brokers follow the questionable tactic of promoting new issues as being available without a commission charge. Technically, this is true, but it is also misleading. The promotion implies a saving for the investor, but in fact the costs are similar to those of regular commissions charged by brokerage firms.

As always, the cost of any fees or commissions should not be the primary reason for selecting an investment. An appraisal of the quality of the investment should be the focus for the prudent investor.

See also COMMISSION; FEE; INITIAL PUBLIC OFFERING (IPO); SALES CHARGE; SELLING GROUP.

SELLING GROUP

The *Selling Groups* for an initial public offering are the broker/dealer groups affiliated with underwriters. They perform the function of obtaining "indications of interest" from investors and place the issue with investors. The selling group is not financially involved by owning part of the issue, but is allocated a certain amount of securities and receives the selling concession for the placements made.

See also COMMISSION; INITIAL PUBLIC OFFERING (IPO); SELLING CONCESSION.

SELLING SHORT

The act of selling a security that is not owned by the seller, or the selling and delivery of any security borrowed by or for the account of the seller is referred to as *Selling Short*. Short sales can take various forms, but all involve the selling of a security that the investor does not own.

An investor does not own a security unless it has been acquired either by purchase or as a gift. Nor does an investor own an underlying security—with the ownership of a right, warrant, option, or convertible security that can be exchanged—when that right, warrant, option, or convertible has not been exercised.

There are two basic classes of short sales:

1. A regular short sale, in which the investor sells an unowned security with the intention of buying it later. The later purchase repays the loan of the security borrowed to make the original sale.
2. A short sale against the box, in which the client owns the security, but does not wish to deliver

those shares. The client sells the security, but has the firm borrow other shares to complete the transaction. Shares left with a brokerage firm are called "box stock," hence the phrase "short against the box."

In light of the numerous market corrections in past years, it is easy to come up with reasons for selling short. Selling short is the classic way for an investor to profit in a declining stock market.

For example, Investor Johnson believes that the price of shares XYZ is about to drop. Johnson does not own those particular shares, but has a significant margin account with a brokerage firm. Investor Johnson might proceed in the following manner:

1. XYZ shares are currently trading at $50 a share on the New York Stock Exchange.
2. Johnson sells 100 shares short at the market for $50.25 per share.
3. News comes out that XYZ is having financial problems.
4. XYZ's price drops to $40 a share.
5. Johnson buys back to close out the short position at $40.25 per share, a $10 difference.
6. 100 shares at $10 equals $1,000 total profit.

The disadvantage to selling short is that the maximum gain is definite (the price cannot drop below $0) but the risk is virtually unlimited, since there is no maximum price for any share. If Johnson's XYZ shares didn't drop, but rather went to $60.25 a share, there could have been a $1,000 loss.

Another potential disadvantage to selling short lies in the need to have the brokerage firm borrow the securities for delivery. It is possible, especially with thinly traded issues, to have a situation in which the borrowed shares are called back. This means the brokerage firm must find other shares to borrow or close out the short position. If other shares are unavailable the position must be closed out whether profitable or not, possibly leaving the investor in a difficult position.

Short selling is a controversial investment technique and, until recently, has been very closely linked in the minds of the general public and stock market regulators with market manipulation. Wall Street's boom years before the Great Crash of 1929 were characterized by numerous "bear raids," in which short sellers would act together to bring down a company's share price. Common techniques included spreading false rumors about a company's profitability or tipping a company's direct competitors. Sometimes, the very knowledge that a group of investors on the inside

track were preparing to go short on a stock would be enough to drive the price down.

Defenders of short selling believe that their technique is an effective antidote to the natural upward trend of the stock market. Their skepticism acts as a brake on the unfounded optimism that rules the world's investors. They also point to other commercial practices in which prices are lowered to affect a sale: examples include farmers who sell their crops on the agricultural futures markets or manufacturers who pre-sell products. Short sellers also increase the liquidity of the markets by providing sellers who are willing to transact with buyers of the stock. The ability to sell short reflects the real nature of the market, giving a means for pessimists to benefit financially from their research.

Opponents of short selling point to its historical links with market manipulation and questionable practices. Short selling, they argue, tends to focus on one stock and does little to control the upward trend of the market as a whole. Short sellers may increase volatility by exaggerating the importance of bad news affecting a company.

Short Sale Rules (United States)

1. The order must be entered as a short sale and marked accordingly. Every "sell" order itself must be marked "long" or "short." (SEC Rule 10a-1(b))
2. "No person shall, for his own account or for the account of any other person, effect on a national securities exchange a short sale of any security (1) below the price at which the last sale thereof, regular way, was effected on such exchange, or (2) at such price unless such price is above the next preceding different price at which a sale of such security, regular way, was effected on such exchange." (SEC Rule 10a-1(a))
3. In determining the price at which a short sale may be effected after a security goes ex-dividend, ex-rights, or ex-any other distribution, all sale prices prior to the "ex" date may be reduced by the value of distribution.

Plus Tick and Zero Plus Tick Rules: A *tick* is a price movement. A plus tick is the next price higher than the previous transaction price. If shares trade three times—first at $20, second at $19 7/8, and third at $20—the third trade is an up tick.

If the most immediate transaction price is a plus tick and the next transaction price is identical, it is called a zero plus tick. If shares trade three times—

first at $19 7/8, second at $20, and third at $20—the third trade is a zero plus tick.

Plus tick and zero plus tick rules prevent short selling from further hammering down a declining share price.

Insider Rules on Selling Short (United States): A law known as the Securities Exchange Act of 1934 (Sec. 16c) forbids corporate insiders (i.e., directors, officers, and beneficial owners of more than 10% of any class of any equity nonexempt security) from both the ordinary speculative short sale and short sale against the box of shares in their corporation.

These insiders may not sell short the corporation's shares if they do not own any of the shares, or if the securities they do own are not delivered against the sale within 20 days thereafter or deposited in the mails within five days.

These regulations are designed to prevent investors from profiting on "inside information" not available to the general public.

NASDAQ Short Sale Rule The NASDAQ Short Sale Rule prohibits NASD members from selling a NASDAQ National Market stock at or below the inside best bid when that price is lower than the previous inside best bid in that stock.

See also LONG POSITION; MARGIN; SECURITIES AND EXCHANGE COMMISSION (SEC); SHORT AGAINST THE BOX.

SELLING THE SPREAD

Selling the Spread refers to the simultaneous buying and selling of two options of the same type. When this occurs, the option sold short trades at a higher premium than the option purchased, thereby creating a net credit from the option premiums.

Selling the spread can also involve the purchase of a call with a higher strike price and the sale of a call with a lower strike price. In this case, both options have the same expiration date.

See also CALL; CREDIT SPREAD; OPTION; PREMIUM; PUT.

SELLING TO CLOSE

When an investor purchases five calls on XYZ Corporation, then decides to sell the options for a profit on the premium, the order entered will be designated *Selling to Close*, meaning selling to close the option position.

This designation helps brokerage and exchange personnel understand the transaction and avoid an unintentional sale of uncovered options. The terminology limits risk, both for the brokerage firm and for the investor.

See also OPTION; PREMIUM; SELLING TO OPEN.

SELLING TO OPEN

When the sale to open a position occurs before any purchase has been made, the option writer (seller) is said to be *Selling to Open*. Options are sold in this manner in order to obtain income from the option premium. Such sales can be covered or uncovered.

An option is covered, for example, if an investor who owns 500 shares of XYZ Corporation sells 5 calls to open a position. The investor receives the premium as income and can deliver the shares if the option is called.

A position is naked or uncovered if an investor sells 5 calls on XYZ Corporation without owning the underlying shares. Premium income would still be received, but if the option is exercised the investor would have to buy the shares at the market price. Naked call options have unlimited risk, since there is no way to know how much the shares will cost.

Although selling a put might be uncovered, the amount of risk is known. If the put is exercised, the investor will have to buy the shares at the designated strike price.

See also CALL; OPTION; PUT.

SENIOR REGISTERED OPTION PRINCIPAL (SROP; United States)

Senior Registered Option Principal (SROP) is the title given to the officer or general partner in an investment firm who has the overall responsibility of monitoring investors' option transactions and accounts.

The same individual might also hold a separate title: Compliance Registered Option Principal (CROP). The duties of the CROP include monitoring activities in advertising, sales literature, account setup, and broker training. In larger firms, however, the two positions are covered by separate individuals.

See also COMPLIANCE; OPTION; PRINCIPAL; REGISTERED OPTIONS PRINCIPAL (ROP).

SEPON (United Kingdom)

See STOCK EXCHANGE POOL OF NOMINEES (SEPON).

SERBIA, REPUBLIC OF

Serbia and Montenegro form a joint independent state. Landlocked Serbia occupies the central part of the Balkan Peninsula, and Montenegro forms a bridge southwestward from southern Serbia to the Adriatic Sea.

Area: Serbia 21,609 square miles; Montenegro 5,333 square miles

Population: 11,101,833 (Serbia: 10,393,585; Montenegro: 708,248)

Form of Government: Republic. Legislative branch: Bicameral Federal Assembly: Chamber of Republics—40 members; Chamber of Citizens—138 members. Head of state and government: President. Head of government: Prime Minister.

Official Languages: Serbo-Croatian; Albanian

Capitals: Belgrade (Serbia); Podgorica (Montenegro)

Largest City: Belgrade

Economy:

Currency: Dinar

Gross National Product: US$10 billion

Public Debt: US$4.2 billion

Stock Markets: 3
Belgrade Stock Exchange (BSE)
Omladinskih Brigada 1
11070 Belgrade
Serbia
Phone: (38-1) 11 19 84 77
Fax: (38-1) 11 13 82 42

Trading Hours: Tuesday–Thursday, 10:00 to 11:30

Office Hours: Monday–Friday, 8:00 to 4:00

Exchange Holidays:

1, 2 January	1 May
27 April	7, 13 July

Listed Companies: 2 in 1994 (withdrawn 1996)
Most trading in short-term securities: 300 companies, 80 banks, and other financial institutions

Growth: *See* History.

History: The idea of a stock exchange appeared in Serbia as early as 1830, but only after the dinar was introduced as the official currency and the Act on Stock Exchanges was passed in 1886 did Serbian merchants found the Belgrade Stock Exchange in 1894. Shares, bonds, commodities, and foreign currency in compliance with world trading standards of the time were traded at this general and mixed stock exchange. Owing to its constant and successful operations, the stock exchange became a significant center of the country's economy. By its organization and the achieved level of development, it ranked with other similar stock exchanges and actively took part in the international economy. The securities traded at the Belgrade Stock Exchange were also listed at the exchanges in Paris, London, and Frankfurt. Its work was interrupted by World War II in April 1941, and in 1953 the stock exchange officially closed. After nearly 50 years, today's Belgrade Stock Exchange was reestablished in December 1989 as the Yugoslav Capital Market-Belgrade. The first trading took place on 28 February 1990. The stock exchange was founded by 32 major Yugoslav banks, and it was the first stock exchange in Yugoslavia that resumed its former activities. The present name, the Belgrade Stock Exchange, was restored to it on 28 May 1992. The Belgrade Stock Exchange is a corresponding member of the International Federation of the Stock Exchanges, and it maintains business contacts and closely cooperates with its domestic and foreign partners.

On 21 November 1994, the Belgrade Stock Exchange celebrated its hundredth anniversary.

When the Belgrade Stock Exchange was reestablished (under a different name) at the end of 1989, many parallel reforms were being carried out regarding the privatization process, accounting system, taxes, and financial infrastructure. Owing to the privatization process of big companies and the fast development of many new, small enterprises, it was expected that these reforms would facilitate rapid development of the stock exchange, not only on government or corporate debt securities but also on equities.

Political instability, the rapid decline of economic activities, and the escalation of inflation tendencies throughout 1992 and 1993 negatively affected the performance of all participants in the Serbian financial market. Economic sanctions imposed by the international community drastically affected the performance of the weakening economy, and the security market was constantly facing low liquidity and a relatively small trading volume.

In the past five years, due to the overall economic situation, the trading at the exchange was predominantly performed with short-term financial instruments, such as commercial paper of companies and banks. The main feature of the business operation of the stock exchange was an initial intensification of trade and increase in the number of transactions. There were 1,643 transactions in 1992, 9,153 in 1993. But there were only 4,725 transactions in 1994, and because of social conditions in the former Yugoslavia, there was no equity trading in 1995, 1996, and 1997.

In order to increase liquidity and trading efficiency, the Belgrade Stock Exchange introduced an automated trading system. The BSE is also taking measures toward establishing a central depository and a clearing house.

In spite of all the difficulties, one of the major objectives has been the establishment and promotion of a market-oriented economy with a stimulating stock exchange. In the last five years, financial market institutions headed by the Securities and Exchange Commission have made a significant effort to upgrade the regulations; reconcile the local standards and regulations with international practice; train personnel in administration, banking, and the economy; and recognize the significance of financial market operations.

It is realistic to expect that the forthcoming period will be more stimulating for the recovery of the Serbian economy and further development of the financial market. Reasons for optimism can be found in the gradual lifting of the economic sanctions and a successful start of the Program of Economic Recovery and Monetary Reconstruction that was introduced in January 1996. The first stage of the program was completed successfully and was characterized by the budget income and expenses balance, low inflation rate, and stability of the national currency. Within the distinctly market-oriented concept of the program, the development of the financial market plays one of the leading roles.

The implementation of the privatization programs, passing the new Act on Stock Exchanges and Broker and Dealer Organizations, and the improvement of existing legislation regulating organization and performance of companies are expected to give incentive to further develop the regulated financial market in Serbia. The rapid development of the stock exchange and of all the complementary institutions of the securities industry, such as the settlement and depository institutions, brokerage houses, and institutional investors, will allow the inflow of foreign capital and the participation of international financial institutions.

Classes of Securities: Money market instruments, common shares

Indices: None

Supervisory Organizations:
Ministry of Finance
Securities and Exchange Commission
Belgrade Stock Exchange

Depository: None

Settlement Details:

Shares: By arrangement

Trading: *See* History.

Listing Requirements: Decisions on admission of securities to exchange listing is accomplished by two Stock Exchange Commissions, which are appointed by the Stock Exchange Board of Directors. Short-term securities are approved for trading by the Short-Term Securities Commission, and the listing of shares, bonds, and other long-term securities is approved by the Stock Exchange Quotation Committee.

The quotation committee reviews the request for listing submitted by the issuer, together with the application form containing all information prescribed by the stock exchange rules, and also reviews all relevant facts relating to the issuers business. The application for listing must include the federal authority issuance approval for the specific issue.

Securities Lending: None

Brokerage Firms:
Jugobanka, Belgrade
Beobanka, Belgrade
Kreditna banka, Belgrade
Union banka, Belgrade
Panonska banka, Novi Sad
Vojvodanska banka, Novi Sad
Dinara, Belgrade
Agrobanka, Belgrade
JIK banka, Belgrade
MB PKB banka, Belgrade
Stocar banka, Cacak
EKI Broker, Belgrade
Beogradska banka, Belgrade
Karic banka, Belgrade
YUBMES, Belgrade
Novosadska banka, Novi Sad
AIK Banka Senta, Senta
Prva preduzetnicka banka, Belgrade
Investbanka, Belgrade
MB Dunav-Tisa-Dunav, Novi Sad
ASI banka, Belgrade
Continental banka, Novi Sad
Jorgic Broker, Belgrade
Mark Broker, Belgrade

Regional Exchange:
Montenegro Exchange
Podgorica

SÉRIE D' OPTIONS (France)
See OPTION SERIES.

SERIES 7 REGISTERED (United States)

Series 7 Registered is the designation given to a brokerage firm employee who has successfully completed the required Series 7 securities examination administered by the New York Stock Exchange and the National Association of Securities Dealers.

Usually, in order to obtain a ticket to take the six-hour examination (administered periodically in the United States), an individual must be sponsored by a NASD member. However, under limited circumstances the NASD can waive the Series 7 examination for persons with extensive experience in the securities industry.

See also NATIONAL ASSOCIATION OF SECURITIES DEALERS (NASD); REGISTERED REPRESENTATIVE (RR); UNITED STATES.

SETTLE

To *Settle* is to meet one's financial obligations.

With regard to securities, to settle is to complete a transaction between brokerage firms or between a brokerage firm and an investor. A trade is settled when the investor delivers money on a buy or securities on a sell.

See also BOOK-ENTRY; CERTIFICATE; TRADE.

SETTLEMENT

See SETTLE.

SETTLEMENT DATE (S/D)

The *Settlement Date (S/D)* is the day on which an investor or brokerage firm must deliver cash or securities to complete the transaction details.

Settlement dates vary from one exchange to another around the world. Some exchanges demand same-day settlement, while others extend a settlement option to several days. Three day settlement (T + 3) is becoming a popular settlement period in many countries, and in 1995 it became the regular-way settlement for the United States.

Details of the settlement of cash or securities, including the settlement date, are stated in the trade confirmation, sent out shortly after a transaction is executed. Although most exchanges can grant extensions from settlement, policies differ as to how they are handled by brokerage firms.

Brokerage firms also set their own policy with regard to having cash in an investor's account for buys or securities in the account for sells. Large transactions might require the cash or securities to be present in an account before the trade is entered.

See also BOOK-ENTRY; EXECUTION; GOOD DELIVERY; STREET NAME.

SEVERALLY AND JOINTLY

Severally and Jointly refers to a securities underwriting situation involving the purchase of an issue in which the members of the syndicate agree as one part of the group (severally) and for the whole group (jointly) to be responsible for buying the securities for resale.

SEVERALLY BUT NOT JOINTLY

Severally But Not Jointly refers to a securities underwriting situation involving the purchase of an issue in which the members of the syndicate agree to be responsible only for their portion of an underwriting.

See also INITIAL PUBLIC OFFERING (IPO); SYNDICATE, UNDERWRITING.

SHAPE (United Kingdom)

See SIZE.

SHARE

A *Share* is a unit of ownership of a company.

Ordinary shares, common shares, common stock, or stock all refer to units of ownership of a company. If the shares trade on a stock exchange or over-the-counter, it is a publicly traded company.

A shareholder receives all the benefits attached to the ownership of shares including voting rights, dividends, share splits, rights, and any warrants attached to the shares.

The number of shares authorized is the total amount of shares the company can issue as provided by the Articles of Incorporation. This number is in excess of the shares issued and outstanding, and usually appears on a company's balance sheet. The number of authorized shares can only be changed by an amendment to the corporate charter, which requires approval from shareholders. The number of authorized shares is often increased to accommodate the additional shares created by a share split.

See also REVERSE SPLIT; SPLIT; SUBSCRIPTION RIGHTS; SUBSCRIPTION WARRANT.

SHARE CAPITAL

Share Capital is the total amount of money shareholders have invested in a company.

See also ISSUED SHARE CAPITAL.

SHARE CERTIFICATE

See CERTIFICATE.

SHARE DIVIDEND

See DIVIDEND.

SHARE INDEX

See individual countries' stock exchange profiles.

SHARE SPLIT

See SPLIT.

SHAREHOLDER

A *Shareholder* is an investor who either owns shares of a company, is registered on the books as an owner, or owns shares in an investment company mutual fund.

A holder of ordinary shares is usually granted the following privileges of ownership:

1. A claim on a company's undivided assets in proportion to the shares held
2. Voting power (in proportion to the number of shares held) for the election of directors or other issues put to a vote
3. Dividends when earned and declared by the board of directors
4. A preemptive right to subscribe to additional share offerings before they are publicly offered, except if prohibited by the company's Articles of Incorporation or in special circumstances such as a merger

Shareholders of registered, publicly traded shares normally have a liability limited to the cost of buying the shares and assume no personal liability for actions taken by creditors or lawsuits brought against the company.

See also DIVIDEND; PREFERRED STOCK (PFD); SUB-SCRIPTION RIGHTS; SUBSCRIPTION WARRANT.

SHAREHOLDER OF RECORD

Shareholder of Record is the statement issued by a company announcing the board of directors' decision to pay a cash or share dividend. Such payments are made to shareholders of record as of a specified date. In order to be a shareholder of record, the investor must purchase the shares before the set ex-date.

Purchasing on or after the ex-date will not make an investor the shareholder of record and, as such, the investor will not qualify for such payments.

See also DIVIDEND; EX-DATE; SHAREHOLDER.

SHAREHOLDERS' EQUITY

Shareholders' Equity is represented by the net assets (the excess of assets over liabilities) of a corporation. It is the book value of any claim to a share in the assets after all debts are settled.

Shareholders' equity increases when shares are issued by the company. It also increases with the addition of funds from additional earnings. Equity is decreased when a company pays dividends, buys back shares, and experiences losses.

Fundamental analysis investors look at shareholders' equity as an important part of a company's value, and in particular, focus on how much of the equity is returned to the investor as a dividend.

See also BUFFETT, WARREN; DIVIDEND; FUNDAMENTAL ANALYSIS.

SHARK REPELLENT

Shark Repellent refers to dramatic steps taken by a corporation in order to prevent a takeover attempt.

While some companies welcome takeovers, others will take steps to prevent them from happening. These steps usually involve tactics that make the company a less attractive target or make a potential takeover too expensive. These tactics might include contingency plans for selling off any assets or subsidiaries that make the company attractive, or the issuing of convertible securities (which would add to the takeover expense).

See also MERGER; POISON PILL; TAKEOVER/TAKEOVER BID.

SHARP, ALBERT E.

Albert E. Sharp is a stockbroker based in Birmingham and is the largest broker in the United Kingdom outside of London. At the end of 1995 it also had offices in Bristol, London, and Manchester, and it managed approximately £2 billion in funds for private investors, pensions, and charities. Services provided by Albert E. Sharp for private client investors include discretionary management (including capital gains tax planning), personal equity plans, traded options, investment trust service, personal financial planning, and advice on ethical investment.

On 1 January 1996 Albert E. Sharp purchased Brown Shipley Stockbroking from the Guinness Peat Group for £7.4 million. This purchase made Albert E. Sharp the United Kingdom's largest independent stockbroking firm (having no outside shareholders). Brown Shipley Stockbroking had 14 offices throughout Great Britain, including in Chichester and Leicester, where Albert E. Sharp had not been represented.

Brown Shipley managed approximately £2 billion, mainly for private investors and primarily on an advisory basis. Its unit trust and asset management divisions had already been sold by Guinness Peat in 1994. Brown Shipley's pretax profits in 1994 were £532,000.

Brown Shipley has a long history. In 1800 Alexander Brown, an auctioneer from Northern Ireland who worked in the Belfast linen market, migrated to the United States. He went into business in Baltimore as an importer of Irish linens and an exporter of tobacco and cotton. His four sons became partners in the firm of Alexander Brown and Sons. Two of the sons established a firm in Liverpool, England, in 1810, known as William and James Brown and Company. This was an accepting house, or merchant bank, that financed trade by lending its name, and credit, to trade bills drawn by importers who were ordering from abroad. In recognition of the contributions of Joseph Shipley during the financial panic of 1837, the firm changed its name to Brown, Shipley and Company in 1839. Brown Shipley was a merchant bank that focused first on the textile trade and later financed all forms of trade and transportation, including the export of manufactured goods from such major centers as Birmingham, Manchester, and Sheffield.

For several decades Brown Shipley enjoyed the advantage of being based in Liverpool, the largest and the best port in Europe. It weathered the panic of 1857 with no major problems. But during the U.S. Civil War in the 1860s, cotton exports to the United Kingdom, which formed a major component of Brown Shipley's import business, were cut off. In 1866, just after the war ended, the establishment of intercontinental telegraph communications between the two countries provided a new means for merchants to place orders for cotton. Given this and other technological changes, as well as the increased concentration of finance in London and the fact that Brown Shipley's financial business had assumed more importance while its mercantile business had become smaller, Brown Shipley moved its headquarters to London, while retaining its Liverpool office.

Throughout the rest of the 19th century and for most of the 20th, Brown Shipley remained a relatively small, conservative institution that continued to excel at what it did best—merchant banking. Its strength rivaled that of major British houses such as Barings and Rothschilds. In 1914 Brown Shipley was a founding member of the United Kingdom's Accepting Houses Committee, the country's top merchant bank-

ers' club. It also provided the longest-serving governor of the Bank of England, Montagu Norman.

In the 1960s Brown Shipley's merchant bank business began to fall off as other forms of trade finance emerged. Believing it was necessary to diversify, Brown Shipley formed a holding company and got into other lending operations, including leasing and consumer credit. In 1979 the Bank of England began to accept the bills of many banks authorized under that year's Banking Act on terms similar to those granted the accepting houses. In the face of this increased competition, Brown Shipley diversified further. Its holding company bought four small stockbroking firms in the 1980s. By 1988 it held 32 businesses.

In the late 1980s and early 1990s Brown Shipley's leasing company extended some high-risk loans. In 1991 some of these loans went bad, and Brown Shipley suffered losses of £3.34 million. These were concentrated in its merchant banking and investment management and stockbroking activity. Only its insurance broking showed a consistent profit. Brown Shipley sold its bank to Kredietbank in 1992. The bank's management vowed to refocus on merchant banking, which had been its forté for so long. The Brown Shipley holding company, with its unit trust, asset management, and stockbroking businesses, was sold to Guinness Peat in 1993. Three years later the latter sold the stockbroker to Albert E. Sharp for a tidy profit.

See also UNITED KINGDOM.

SHELF REGISTRATION (United States)

Securities and Exchange Commission Rule 415 allows widely traded leading companies to file a single *Shelf Registration* (S-3) statement form with the SEC to cover entire new bond and/or share offerings for the following two-year period. This procedure expedites public offerings and avoids the customary waiting period. The securities are "kept on the shelf" until needed, then sold in the event that market conditions are favorable or a company needs to raise funds.

Shelf registrations and a prospectus are still required by the SEC in order to reflect any facts or events representing fundamental changes in the company.

See also INITIAL PUBLIC OFFERING (IPO); SECURITIES AND EXCHANGE COMMISSION (SEC)/ SEC RULE 415.

SHORT

See SELLING SHORT.

SHORT AGAINST THE BOX

Also called the perfect hedge, a *Short Against the Box* position is one in which an investor sells short shares that are owned. The short position can be closed by either delivering the same quantity of the shares that are owned or by buying back an equal number of shares.

Once such a position is taken, there is neither a gain nor a loss on the combined position. If the share price drops, the investor closes out the position and receives proceeds based on the short selling price. On the other hand, if the price rises and the investor closes out the position there is no additional gain, since the investor receives only the proceeds based on the short selling price. The scenario of no gain and no loss is why the short against the box is called the perfect hedge.

The strategy can be especially useful in a situation in which the investor is receiving shares but doesn't currently have the shares in hand, such as with a corporate share option. The investor must still meet all margin loan requirements and remains dependent upon the brokerage firm's ability to borrow shares to place against the short position. If the shares are held in the brokerage account, this will not be a problem, as they will be against the short position.

Example:

1. Investor owns 100 shares of XYZ, currently $50 a share, but bought at $40 a share.
2. 100 shares XYZ sell short at $50.25.
3. XYZ price drops to $40.25 a share.
4. Investor delivers 100 shares and closes the short position.
5. Investor earns $1,025 on the short sell.

Another use of the short against the box strategy is a situation in which an investor believes owned shares are experiencing a short-term price weakness, but will recover in a reasonable time. The investor sells short, watches the price drop, then buys the short position back for a profit. As the share price recovers, the investor retains the long position of shares.

See also HEDGE; HYPOTHECATION; MARGIN ACCOUNT.

SHORT COVERING

Buying back or delivering securities previously sold short is known as *Short Covering*.

See SELLING SHORT; SHORT AGAINST THE BOX.

SHORT HEDGE

A *Short Hedge* is a short sale against a long position, giving partial moderation to the risk.

To hedge is to moderate risk. If the risk is totally moderated it is a perfect hedge. A short hedge would

be to sell short calls to open a position where an equal number of the underlying shares to the option are held long in the account. The option position is called a covered call, and it is considered more conservative than owning the shares alone.

Example:

An investor owns 500 shares of XYZ Corporation and sells 5 calls to open an option position. The investor receives a premium of $2 for selling the calls.

$2 × 500 equals $1,000. The investor has hedged the long share position by $1,000.

Note that commissions and fees will have to be taken into account when evaluating the strategy.

See also PUT; SELLING SHORT; SHORT AGAINST THE BOX.

SHORT INTEREST

Short Interest is a figure representing the total number of shares that are currently being sold short in a specific security. Some market analysts use the short interest information as a measure of investor sentiment. Sentiment is negative as short interest increases.

U.S. stock exchanges gather and report the short interest numbers on selected securities around the 15th of every month, and most financial newspapers list the short interest reports.

See also SELLING SHORT; SHORT AGAINST THE BOX.

SHORT POSITION

See SELLING SHORT.

SHORT SALE

See SELLING SHORT.

SHORT SWING (United States)

Short Swing refers to short-term trades made by corporate insiders (officers, directors, and major shareholders) of the shares of their own company, in which a significant purchase is followed by a profitable sell. Because it was presumed that such persons were trading on inside information, short swing trades have been prohibited by the Securities and Exchange Commission.

See also INSIDER DEALING/INSIDER TRADING; SECURITIES AND EXCHANGE COMMISSION (SEC); SELLING SHORT.

SHORT-TERM

Short-Term is generally accepted to mean any period shorter than one year. However, share investing for the short-term might be as short as two days, or as long as three years. Some institutional investors consider bonds out two years as short-term investments.

Tax authorities around the world are often forced to provide a definition for short-term, as there can be different tax treatments for short-term and long-term investments.

Short-term securities investors are considered speculative, while long-term investors are considered conservative.

See also FUNDAMENTAL ANALYSIS; LONG-TERM; SPECULATION.

SHORT-TERM TRADING INDEX
See TRIN.

SIDE CAR RULE (United States)
The *Side Car Rule* is New York Stock Exchange Rule 80A, which moderates the use of the DOT system when the market experiences a sharp decline.

When the Standard & Poor's 500 Index drops more than 12 points—a fall that correlates to approximately a 96-point decline on the Dow Jones Industrial Average—programmed trades from institutional investors are routed to a special file, delayed, then executed after a five-minute period.

The move allows the transactions of individual investors to take priority over the computer programmed trades of institutions. In the slang of Wall Street, individual orders take "the express lane" for exchange execution.

See also DESIGNATED ORDER TURNAROUND (DOT); MARKET ORDER; PROGRAM TRADING; UNITED STATES.

SIGNIFICANT ORDER IMBALANCE
A *Significant Order Imbalance* causes a wide spread between bid and ask prices, and as a result, trading is occasionally halted in order to correct the problem.

An order imbalance can occur when an important announcement is pending. The reason for the halt or suspension is to clear up the order imbalance, arrive at a new market price, and allow the trading public access to the information contained in the announcement.

On the New York Stock Exchange, the parameters between the bid and ask are set at the lower of 10% or $3 for shares priced under $100, or the lower of 10% or $5 for shares above $100.

See also ASK PRICE; BID PRICE; LAST TRADE.

SILVER
Like gold, *Silver* is a precious metal that has functioned in the international stock market both as a com-

modity and as a form of money. Many countries use silver as one component of their coins and keep silver bullion in their national reserves.

Like that of the other precious metals, the price of silver tends to move independently of the rest of the stock market. Silver's price is much more volatile than the price of gold, and some analysts consider silver to be the better investment. Silver's large price swings mean that the same level of risk reduction in a portfolio can be accomplished with a smaller amount of silver as can be accomplished with a larger amount of gold. The volatility of silver's price also means that it is possible to make more money—or lose more money—in a shorter time period than would be possible with gold. Because of the volatility of silver prices, many analysts recommend that it be only one of several precious metals that are part of a portfolio, and that the total quantity of precious metals not exceed 10% of the portfolio's value.

An analysis of silver prices should not be based purely on fundamentals of supply and demand. Like other precious metals prices, silver prices also move in response to world events such as wars, political and economic crises, and inflation. This can make silver's future difficult to predict. Investors who are interested in silver can buy bullion or coins, stock in mining companies or mutual funds that specialize in precious metals, or futures contracts. Silver bullion and coins do not pay interest and dividends and may be expensive to store and insure. Investors should investigate the legitimacy of bullion and coin dealers, some of whom misrepresent risk and return or actually practice fraud. Mining company stock prices are often more volatile than the price of silver itself. Futures contracts are the riskiest, and the most potentially profitable, way to invest in silver.

Silver is widely used by industries because it resists oxidization and conducts heat and electricity better than any other metal. Silver is more ductile and malleable than any other metal except gold. In fact, silver is so soft that copper or steel must be added to it to make it hard enough to be made into coins or jewelry.

The photographic industry consumes more silver than any other industry. Photographic film is covered with silver bromide, a light sensitive chemical. Silver is also necessary for the production of photocopiers. In electronics, silver is used to make wires, electromechanical switching systems, and integrated circuits. Silver is important to the defense industry and is used to make jewelry, batteries, dental fillings, tableware, and an alloy for brazing and soldering. The demand for silver jewelry, however, falls when silver prices rise. Because silver has antibacterial qualities, doctors use silver wires, plates, and tubes during surgery. Silver salts are used in silver plating and silver mirrors and are also used to cauterize wounds and treat certain diseases of the skin and eyes.

Silver deposits exist in most countries. However, most ores that contain silver also contain lead, copper, and/or zinc. It is usually most efficient to mine these three metals and remove the silver as a by-product. Consequently, the primary supply of silver is influenced very little by changes in price. Few countries find it economical to mine silver. Mexico, the United States, and Peru produce most of the world's supply. Mexico and Peru are likely to continue to expand their silver production, since these nations need hard currency to pay their heavy foreign debts.

The amount of silver produced by mining is not enough to satisfy the international demand for it. In addition, government reserves of silver are more limited than reserves of gold, and central banks sell less silver than gold. As a result, some of the demand for silver must be met by other sources. Secondary sources of silver determine whether the international market is saturated or is experiencing a deficit. Industries produce scrap silver from melted silverware, used photographic solutions, and old electrical parts. The amount of scrap silver that is recovered in a given year varies greatly depending on the price of silver.

India is one of the most important sources of secondary supplies of silver. Traditionally, Indian families have hoarded silver jewelry, ornaments, coins, and ingots. These hoards, like gold hoards in Europe, provided a hedge against poverty and times of crisis. During times when silver prices are high or India's economy is floundering, families sell off large quantities of hoarded silver. However, in recent years India's government has taken steps to protect silver as a national treasure, limiting its export and making it illegal to smuggle bullion. Consequently, the Indian practice of unloading hoarded silver has decreased.

See also GOLD; PRECIOUS METALS.

SIMPLIFIED EMPLOYEE PENSION PLAN (SEP; United States)

The *Simplified Employee Pension Plan (SEP)* is a retirement plan for individuals that combines some of the features of an Individual Retirement Account (IRA) plan or a Keogh retirement plan without some of the lengthy paperwork.

An employer with fewer than 25 employees can establish an SEP. Elective contributions up to $7,000 per employee can be made to an SEP, with a maximum employer contribution of $30,000.

SEP plans can be deducted from income for taxes, but not for employment tax (FICA and FUTA). An individual can convert an SEP to an IRA when he or she leaves the company.

See also INDIVIDUAL RETIREMENT ACCOUNT (IRA); KEOGH PLAN; PENSION PLAN/FUND.

SINGAPORE, REPUBLIC OF

Singapore (Hsin-chia-p' o Kung-ho-kuo (Mandarin Chinese); Republik Singapura (Malay); Singapore Kudiyarasu (Tamil)) is an island city-state situated at the southern tip of the Malay Peninsula.

Area: 240 square miles (622 square km)

Population: 2,989,000 (100.0% urban)

Form of Government: Unitary multiparty republic, with one legislative house: Parliament—87 members. Chief of state: President. Head of government: Prime Minister.

Official Languages: Chinese, Malay, Tamil, English

Capital: Singapore

Economy:

Currency: Singapore dollar (S$)

National Budget: Revenue—S$23.3 billion; expenditures—S$14.1 billion (security: 34.7%; education: 22.5%; general services: 7.3%; health: 6.6%; communications: 6.2%; national development: 5.1%)

Public Debt: US$11.6 million

Gross National Product: US$55.4 billion

Principal Products: Fruits and vegetables; livestock; machinery and industrial products

Foreign Trade (Imports): S$156.4 billion (office machines: 9.7%; telecommunications apparatus: 7.2%; crude petroleum: 5.7%; electric power machinery: 3.9%; petroleum products: 3.1%; scientific instruments: 3.1%; musical instruments: 2.8%; from Japan: 22.0%; Malaysia: 16.4%; United States: 15.3%; Thailand: 4.8%; Taiwan: 3.8%; Saudi Arabia: 3.6%; Hong Kong: 3.4%)

Foreign Trade (Exports): S$147.3 billion (office machines: 23.3%; telecommunications apparatus: 10.4%; petroleum products: 7.7%; optical instruments: 2.2%; electrical circuit apparatus: 2.1%; clothing: 1.6%; industrial machinery: 1.5%; to Malaysia: 19.7%; United States: 18.8%; Hong Kong: 8.7%; Japan: 7.0%; Thailand: 5.6%; Taiwan: 4.0%; Germany: 3.5%; United Kingdom: 2.7%)

Stock Exchanges: 1

Stock Exchange of Singapore (SES)
20 Cecil Street #26-01/08
The Exchange
Singapore 049705
Phone: (65) 535-3788
Fax: (65) 535-6994

Internet Address: www.ses.com.sg/

Trading Hours: Monday–Friday, 9:00 to 12:30 and 2:00 to 5:00

Listed Companies: 294

Market Capitalization: US$282.6 billion

Major Sectors: Industrial and commercial, finance, property, hotels, mining

History: Share trading in Singapore can be traced to the late 19th century. The rubber boom of 1910 made share trading a major economic activity. Trading activity was also increased with the growth of the tin mining industry.

First incorporated on 24 May 1973, the Stock Exchange of Singapore Ltd. (SES) has its origins in the establishment of the Singapore Stockbrokers' Association in 1930.

The exchange has 33 member companies comprised of brokers, dealers, and dealers' representatives. Although supervision comes from regulations set by the elected Stock Exchange of Singapore Committee, it is regulated by the Securities Industry Act of 1986.

The exchange moved to new premises in July of 1988. With its new quarters came the addition of a new trading system. Instead of a big board for large companies and a separate section for smaller capitalization companies, all trading shares were linked by electronic TV monitor screen display. In March of 1988, full computerization began with the Central Limit Order Book (CLOB), a trading system with no trading floor. CLOB International is an over-the-counter market for international securities.

Classes of Securities: Ordinary shares, preference shares, debentures, bonds and loan stocks, warrants, covered warrants, equity options and other derivatives

Indices: Straits Times Industrial Index

Singapore. *(Spectrum Photo)*

Supervisory Organizations: Stock Exchange of Singapore

Depository: Central Depositary Pte Ltd. (CDP)

Settlement Details: Book-entry as of July 1994

Shares: Trade date + 7 days (T + 7)

Cash Market:
Trade date (T + 5:00 p.m.) seller
Trade date + 1 day buyer

Trading: The CLOB is a computerized trading system with workstations located in the brokerage firm's offices. The system enables orders to be entered and matched by CLOB, and confirmations to be sent automatically to brokers. Orders are held in the system according to price and time priority and are matched to the most favorable prices. Shares trade in board lots of 1,000.

SES also has a dealing and automated quotation system (SES-DAQ)—a second securities market in Singapore—designed for the trading of growing small and mid-sized companies.

At the end of 1994, the SES-DAQ traded 43 companies with a combined market capitalization of S$2.22 billion.

SES equity option trading began in early 1993 and, at present, calls and puts on the underlying shares of four companies are traded. CLOB International is Singapore's computer-operated over-the-counter market. It enables investors to trade in several international equities listed on foreign exchanges.

Institutional Delivery and Affirmation System (IDAS): An electronic, on-line communication system, IDAS facilitates settlement of institutional trades and allows for confirmation of a trade between the broker and the settlement agent of an institutional investor.

Listing Requirements: The Stock Exchange of Singapore receives and approves all applications for new listings. A new listing manual was published in 1993 to outline requirements for companies wishing to have their securities listed on the exchange.

Main Listing: Minimum paid-up capital for a main listing is S$15 million. SES approval is required on all substantial acquisitions.

Pretax profits must total at least S$7.5 million for the most recent three years, with a minimum pre-tax profit of S$1 million for each of those three years.

Foreign Requirements: Paid-up capital of a minimum S$30 million is required.

Cumulative pretax profits must total at least S$15 million for the most recent three years, with a minimum pretax profit of S$1 million for each of those years.

Information on the assets, earnings, and aggregate market value of the company must be provided.

Information must be provided regarding the degree of market interest in the company, its products, relative stability and industry position, as well as whether or not its industry is expanding.

Once SES approval has been granted, a prospectus must be issued to the public. A listed company must disclose any developments that might affect the price of its securities.

Investor Taxation:
Tax is not levied on dividends paid to non-residents.
27% dividend tax is levied against the company.
No capital gains tax is due on sales made by non-residents.
There is a clearing fee of 0.05% of value to a maximum $100.
There is a contract stamp duty of 0.05% of value of the contract.
There is a transfer stamp duty of 0.2% on the value, when shares are sent for registration. This is not charged on book-entry transactions.
A goods and services tax of 3% is levied on brokerage and clearing fees.

Limitations: There are no controls or limits on the repatriation of income, capital gains, or capital.

Brokerage Firms:
Alliance Securities (Pte)
156 Cecil Street #08-02
FEB Building
Singapore 0106
Phone: (65) 222-2811
Fax: (65) 225-0797
Telex: RS 22440

Baring Securities (Singapore) Pte Ltd
20 Raffles Place #24-00
Ocean Towers
Singapore 0104
Phone: (65) 535-3688
Fax: (65) 535-3233

BZW-Pacific Union Pte Ltd
50 Raffles Place #10-01
Shell Tower
Singapore 0104
Phone: (65) 225-7400
Fax: (65) 225-5698
Telex: RS 43451

Crédit Lyonnais Securities (Singapore) Pte Ltd
16 Collyer Quay #32-00
Hitachi Tower
Singapore 0104
Phone: (65) 534-3268
Fax: (65) 533-8922

DBS Securities Singapore Pte Ltd
22 Malacca Street
DBS Securities Building
Singapore 0104
Phone: (65) 533-9688
Fax: (65) 535-7785
Telex: RS 20438

GK Goh Stockbrokers Pte Ltd
50 Raffles Place #33-00
Shell Tower
Singapore 0104
Phone: (65) 225-1228
Fax: (65) 225-1522, 224-6906
Telex: RS 26624

J.M. Sassoon & Co (Pte) Ltd
1 Raffles Place #44-00
OUB Center
Singapore 0104
Phone: (65) 535-288, 535-2866
Fax: (65) 533-7956
Telex: RS 21288

Keppel Securities Pte Ltd
10 Hoe Chiang Road #08-01
Keppel Towers
Singapore 0208
Phone: (65) 221-5688
Fax: (65) 226-1543
Telex: RS 21185

Lee & Co (Stock & Share Brokers) Pte Ltd
10 Collyer Quay #27-05/07
Ocean Building
Singapore 0104
Phone: (65) 533-5288
Fax: (65) 532-5288
Telex: RS 29223

Lum Chang Securities Pte Ltd
16 Raffles Quay #28-01
Hong Leong Building
Singapore 0104
Phone: (65) 223-8282

Fax: (65) 225-6801
Telex: RS 24964

The Nikko Securities (Singapore) Pte Ltd
6 Battery Road #28-02
Singapore 0104
Phone: (65) 223-3800
Fax: (65) 225-2854

Nomura Securities Singapore Pte Ltd
6 Battery Road #39-04
Singapore 0104
Phone: (65) 420-1811
Fax: (65) 420-1888

ONG & Company Pte Limited
76 Shenton Way #06-00
Ong Building
Singapore 0207
Phone: (65) 223-9466
Fax: (65) 224-0253
Telex: RS 22071

Phillip Securities Pte Ltd.
95 South Bridge Road #11-17
Pidemco Centre
Singapore 0105
Phone: (65) 533-6001
Fax: (65) 535-3834
Telex: RS 20188

SBCI & Associates (Singapore) Pte Ltd
11 Collyer Quay #18-01
The Arcade
Singapore 0104
Phone: (65) 221-9991
Fax: (65) 225-9948
Telex: RS 20225

Summit Securities (S) Pte Ltd
20 Raffles Place #15-01/05
Ocean Towers
Singapore 0104
Phone: (65) 533-3388
Fax: (65) 532-6333, 532-6356
Telex: RS 20763

Tsang & Ong Stockbrokers (Pte) Ltd
80 Robinson Road #02-00
Singapore 0106
Phone: (65) 224-5877
Fax: (65) 224-6632
Telex: RS 28142

UOB Securities Pte Ltd
80 Raffles Place #18-00
UOB Plaza 1
Singapore 0104
Phone: (65) 535-6868
Fax: (65) 533-1747
Telex: RS 362237

Vickers Ballas & Co Pte Ltd
30 Raffles Place #07-00
Caltex House
Singapore 0104
Phone: (65) 535-8111
Fax: (65) 532-2331
Telex: RS 21425

Yamaichi Securities (Singapore) Pte Ltd
138 Robinson Road #19-03/08
Hong Leong Centre
Singapore 0106
Phone: (65) 226-1848
Fax: (65) 222-1049

SES Member Companies, London Offices:
Baring Securities (Singapore) Pte Ltd
Baring Securities Ltd
1 America Square
London EC3N 2LT
England
Phone: (44-171) 522-6000
Fax: (44-171) 702-0008

Crédit Lyonnais Securities
(Singapore) Pte Ltd
Crédit Lyonnais Securities Ltd
Broadwalk House
5 Appold Street, Broadgate
London EC2
England
Phone: (44-171) 696-9190
Fax: (44-171) 214-5401

Nomura Securities Singapore Pte Ltd
Nomura International Plc
Nomura House
1. St. Martin's le-Grand
London, EC1A 4NP
England
Phone: (44-171) 929-2366
Fax: (44-171) 626-0851

Vickers Ballas & Co Pte Ltd
Vickers Ballas (UK) Plc

5th Floor
78-80 Cornhill
London EC3
England
Phone: (44-171) 816-6700
Fax: (44-171) 816-6730

Company Information:

10 Most Active Companies

Name of Company	Shares Traded (add 000)
Amcol Holdings	748,878
RF-JAMA Warrant 96	705,320
Guthrie GTS	687,410
DBS Land	650,064
Hong Kong Land	595,769
Tuan Sing	468,064
DBS Land B Warrant 95	445,903
DBS Land A Warrant 95	410,396
IPC Corporation	383,171
Dairy Farm Holdings	346,628

10 Top Performers

Name of Company	Price Increase in US$	% Increase
Transmarco	3.79	71.1
Great Eastern Life Assurance	2.60	13.9
Fraser & Neave	2.04	19.2
L&M Group Investments	1.97	270.8
OCBC Foreign	1.90	18.0
Van Der Horst	1.9	59.5
Fraser & Neave Warrant 98	1.9	42.1
DBS Foreign	1.82	17.3
Bukit Sembawang Estates	1.76	8.7
Van Der Horst Warrant 98	1.76	70.5

10 Major Companies

Company	Market Capitalization (US$ Millions)
Singapore Telecom	33,673.00
Singapore Airlines	7,260.19
OCBC Bank	7,139.94
United Overseas Bank	5,896.62
City Developments	5,680.02
DBS Bank	4,937.41
Keppel Corporation	4,578.05
Singapore Press Holdings	3,327.70
Overseas Union Bank	3,154.01
DBS Land	3,086.50

Regional Exchanges: None.

Other Investment Information:

Economic Development Board
250 North Bridge Road #24-00
Raffles City Tower
Singapore 0617
Phone: (65) 336-2288
Fax: (65) 339-6077
Telex: RS 26233 SINEDB

Trade Development Board
1 Maritime Square #10-40 (Lobby D)
World Trade Centre
Telok Blangah Road
Singapore 0409
Phone: (65) 271-9388
Fax: (65) 278-2518
Telex: RS28617 TRADEV

Singapore International Chamber of Commerce
50 Raffles Place #03-02
Shell Tower
Singapore 0104
Phone: (65) 224-1255
Fax: (65) 224-2785

SIZE

Stated in round lots and appearing on every order form, *Size* refers to the amount or number of securities in an order.

For example, a quote for XYZ Corporation might appear as:

XYZ:	Bid	Ask	Size	Last
	49 1/4	50	100 × 150	50

This indicates that there are 100 lots (1,000 shares) available to buy at $49 1/4 and 150 lots (1,500 shares) available to sell at $50.

The size of a quote, like the price of a quote, is good for a moment only, and can change before any new order is entered and executed.

See also ASK PRICE; BID PRICE; LAST TRADE.

**The S·E·Bank Group
Skandinaviska Enskilda Banken**

SKANDINAVISKA ENSKILDA BANKEN (S-E-BANKEN)

Skandinaviska Enskilda Banken (S-E-Banken) is one of Sweden's Big Four banks. At the end of 1995 its assets stood at approximately $66 billion. It had approximately 275 branch offices in Sweden as well as branches, subsidiaries, and representative offices in 15 foreign countries. S-E-Banken is a member of the S-E Bank Group, the largest banking group in Scandinavia, which provides a full range of commercial and merchant banking services both domestically and internationally. S-E-Banken itself is the product of a 1971 merger of Stockholms Enskilda Bank and Skandinaviska Banken, each of which had a history dating back more than 100 years.

Stockholms Enskilda Bank, formed in 1856, played a part in Sweden's dynamic export economy of the mid-19th century. With its profits from this activity it funded the building of much of Sweden's industrial infrastructure. Later, when the export boom ended, Enskilda acquired several businesses but also incurred some large losses on bad loans.

The bank's history was largely unremarkable until the 1960s. With the rapid expansion of Swedish industry, there was increased demand for financial resources. However, ever more restrictive government regulations made it difficult for Swedish banks to rise to this challenge. As a result, and with an eye toward getting into international banking, Stockholms Enskilda Bank was interested in finding a merger partner.

Skandinaviska Banken, formed in 1864, from the beginning had been a commercial bank supplying investment capital to Swedish industry. One of its first transactions was to market an 8 million mark government-railway loan for Hamburg Banco, which put it on the road to eventually becoming one of the world's largest foreign exchange dealers.

Skandinaviska opened branches in Sweden's major cities, but it relied on its role as agent for Sweden's provincial banks to extend its influence throughout the provinces. Later, it used mergers to build up its branch network. In 1910 Skandinaviska merged with Sweden's second largest bank, Skanes Enskilda Bank, which had numerous provincial branches, and in 1949 with Göteborgs Handelsbank, which had 40 provincial branches.

At the beginning of 1972 Enskilda and Skandinaviska merged, forming S-E-Banken. The new bank soon got involved in the investment management business. In 1974 it became the full owner of Aktiv Placering A.B. in Stockholm, which managed individuals' portfolios, provided legal services for families, and advised clients on taxes and life insurance. This subsidiary grew both in Sweden and overseas, and by the 1990s it managed approximately 40 mutual funds.

In 1976 S-E-Banken made its first international acquisition, gaining an interest in Deutsch-Skandinavische Bank in Germany. It then formed Skandinaviska Enskilda Banken (Luxembourg) S.A. In 1979 it established a subsidiary in Singapore, called Skandinaviska Enskilda Banken (South East Asia) Limited.

In the late 1970s, the Swedish government began to gradually deregulate the banking industry. It dropped the requirement that Swedish banks purchase new issues of fixed-rate, long-term priority bonds each year to balance the national budget. In 1980 the Swedish government granted Swedish banks permission to issue certificates of deposit. In the next few years the government created Swedish Treasury bills, a commercial paper market, and market-rate state bonds. Together, these instruments did help stimulate the banking industry, although they did little to increase the national savings rate.

In 1982 Deutsch Skandinavische Bank, which S-E-Banken had founded six years earlier in Frankfurt, opened a branch in Hamburg. S-E-Banken Corporation was opened in New York as a means to get involved in American business. In London, S-E-Banken set up a subsidiary which offered full-service banking to Swedish and international clients.

S-E-Banken, along with Den norske Bank of Norway, Union Bank of Finland, and UNIBank of Denmark, formed Scandinavian Banking Partners. This grouping facilitated fast money transfers and cash management for clients in any of the participating banks' countries.

In 1985 the Swedish government removed controls on interest rates and lending volume. The next year, the big banks' profits nearly doubled.

Also in the mid-1980s S-E-Banken formed a new division to conduct investment banking in Sweden, and Enskilda Securities of London opened a subsidiary in Paris. Additional branches followed in London, Hong Kong, New York, and Singapore. A new subsidiary in Stockholm, Kortbetalning Servo A.B., developed new routines for redeeming credit and charge card bills. In 1995 S-E-Banken established branches in Oslo and Helsinki.

In the early 1990s Swedish banks lost large sums on nonperforming loans. For its part, in 1992 S-E-Banken lost nearly $4 billion. The government set up the Bank Support Authority to help the banks through the crisis. A few years later it was disbanded, as the banks had recovered to become among the best capitalized and most profitable in Europe.

In 1997 S-E-Banken merged with Trygg-Hansa, a Scandinavian insurance company. With SEK 300 billion in assets under management, the combined entity planned to become a leader in the Nordic market for asset management and a frontrunner in selling insurance products through branch banks.

See also SVENSKA HANDELSBANKEN.

SLATER, JIM

Jim Slater has enjoyed the highs and endured the lows in the City of London. During the early 1970s he ran a high-profile merchant bank worth many millions of pounds, only to see it crash in spectacular fashion. After many years, apparently in the wilderness, Slater returned as a stock picker and investment adviser of some note.

The son of a builder from the London suburb of Wembley, Slater left school at the age of 16 to become an accountant. He had a natural ability for math but found the exams difficult to pass. He joined the Army for two years to do compulsory National Service and, on leaving, finished his exams and qualified as an accountant. He joined a small industrial firm and soon found himself running the company with great success. He joined the UK car giant British Leyland and rose through the ranks to become deputy head of sales. While in Spain he caught a serious virus that prevented him from working for two years.

Slater used his forced layoff to learn about the stock market. He bought old copies of fusty investment magazines such as *Investors' Chronicle* and gave himself an instant education in high finance. Within two years Slater was making enough money from his share trading—which he initially treated as a hobby on a par with his beloved bird-watching and chess—to seriously consider it as a profession. He began to write a column on share tips for the City pages of the *Daily Telegraph*, which was then edited by Nigel Lawson.

Slater was named in the now defunct *London Evening News* as one of the most dynamic young businessmen in the United Kingdom. He met Peter Walker, who also appeared on the list, at a dining club. Slater persuaded Walker that his investment ideas would make them rich, and for a long time he was right. The firm they set up in 1964, Slater Walker Securities, was known for its astute stock selections, especially in the high-risk, high-return field of small companies. Slater Walker bought into property just as the UK residential and commercial property market exploded. The firm also developed a reputation for aggressive takeover bids and asset stripping.

Slater's investment philosophy was summed up in the phrase "small is beautiful." He believed that the growth potential for small companies was far greater than for mature corporates. A new innovation or a well-judged marketing campaign will have a great impact on the earnings of a small company, but a large company will need many such successes to achieve the same percentage gain in earnings. Furthermore, small companies tend to have a relatively limited distribution of shares. When earnings rise, and demand increases, the shortage of supply may push up the price still further. As Slater memorably once said when contrasting large companies against small companies: "Elephants can't gallop."

By 1972 Slater Walker was worth more than £200 million and had taken a preeminent role in the property boom. However, the rise in property prices came to an abrupt end in 1973. After a winter of strikes, political unrest, and the turmoil caused by the oil crisis, investors found themselves with plummeting property portfolios, and Slater Walker found itself overextended. The instability of many of the British banks who were also heavily exposed to property lending exacerbated Slater Walker's problems. The final straw was an extradition order from Singapore for Slater. He refused to go, and the firm had to be rescued by a bailout from the Bank of England.

After the closure of Slater Walker in 1975, Slater successfully fought the extradition order. Within two years a series of successful private property deals allowed him to fully pay off his creditors. Ever a versatile man, he wrote a series of best-selling children's books.

Slater has continued to publicize his investment ideas via newsletters and books. In the early 1990s he became a well-known proponent of the O'Higgins method of picking stocks. This technique, invented by U.S. fund manager Michael O'Higgins, starts by selecting the ten shares in an index with the highest dividend yield. From this group of ten, the five stocks with the lowest price are bought and kept in a portfolio. Slater marketed this technique as the basis for a Personal Equity Plan (PEP) in the United Kingdom and enjoyed success for a number of years in identifying falling stocks that were due to rebound in price.

The other investment method favored by Slater is slightly more complex. The price/earnings ratio for future earnings is compared to the growth rate of earnings per share that is forecast by analysts. This ratio produces the PEG, the price/earnings growth factor.

$$PEG = \frac{\text{Prospective price/earnings ratio}}{\text{Forecast growth rate of earnings per share}}$$

For example, ABC Limited trades on a prospective p/e ratio of 16. The percentage expected growth rate of earnings is 18% per annum.

$$PEG = \frac{16}{18} = 0.89$$

A PEG of less than 1 indicates that a stock is undervalued, while a high PEG indicates that a stock is fully valued.

See also HEMMINGTON SCOTT PUBLISHING; PRICE/EARNINGS RATIO.

SLD

SLD is an abbreviation for sold.

A report back to a brokerage firm might appear: SLD 100 shares XYZ at 49 1/8. When the execution is sent to the originating broker, that person informs the investor and all details relating to the transaction are sent out in a trade confirmation.

See also BUY; LIMIT ORDER; MARKET ORDER.

SLOVAK REPUBLIC (Slovakia)

Slovakia (Slovenska Republika) is a landlocked nation in central Europe. It is bordered by its former federal partner, the Czech Republic, to the west, Poland to the north, Ukraine to the east, Hungary to the south, and Austria to the southwest.

Area: 18,933 square miles (49,035 square km)

Population: 5,355,000 (56.8% urban; 43.2% rural)

Form of Government: Unitary multiparty republic, with one legislative house: National Council—150 members. Chief of state: President. Head of government: Prime Minister.

Official Language: Slovak

Capital: Bratislava

Largest Cities: Bratislava, 448,785; Kosice, 238,886; Presov, 90,963; Nitra, 86,679; Zilina, 85,686; Banska Bystrica, 84,575

Economy:

Currency: Koruna (Kcs)

National Budget: Revenue—Kcs 115.9 billion; expenditures—Kcs 124.8 billion (education, health, social welfare, and culture: 71.9%; defense: 3.5%)

Public Debt: US$2.1 billion

Gross National Product: US$10.2 billion

Principal Products: Cereals, sugar beets; livestock; chemicals; manufactured goods

Foreign Trade (Imports): Kcs 201.5 billion (machinery and transport equipment: 29.2%; petroleum and petroleum products: 21.1%; semimanufactured products: 15.0%; chemical products: 11.3%; manufactured products: 9.0%; from Czech Republic: 35.5%; former U.S.S.R.: 23.1%; Germany: 11.4%; Austria: 6.1%; Italy: 3.0%; Poland: 1.9%)

Foreign Trade (Exports): Kcs 167.7 billion (semimanufactured products: 38.8%; machinery and transport equipment: 19.4%; manufactured goods: 13.4%; chemical products: 12.0%; food, beverages, and tobacco: 5.5%; to Czech Republic: 42.4%; Germany: 15.2%; former U.S.S.R.: 8.3%; Austria: 5.0%; Hungary: 4.5%; Poland: 2.9%)

Stock Exchanges: 1

The Bratislava Stock Exchange
Vysoká 17
PO Box 151
814 99 Bratislava
Slovak Republic
Phone: (421-7) 503-6102
Fax: (421-7) 503-6121

Internet Address: www.bsse.sk

Trading Hours: Monday–Friday, 10:30 to 2:00

Exchange Holidays:

1, 6 January	1, 15 September
10, 13 April	24, 25 December
1 May	

Listed Companies: 45

Market Capitalization: US$2.0 million

Major Sectors: Steel, banking, pulp and paper, pharmaceuticals, engineering

History: The Bratislava Stock Exchange began trading in 1993 as part of the voucher privatization program instituted by the federal government. Shares of more than 500 companies and investment funds began to trade publicly. The market is split into the official Bratislava Stock Exchange and the over-the-counter RMS market.

In July 1995 the Ministry of Finance made amendments to the Securities Act and the Investment Companies Act to improve transparency in the market. Recent regulations have banned off-exchange trading.

Classes of Securities: Ordinary shares, fixed-income securities, a limited number of derivatives.

Indices: The SAX Index (September 1993, base = 100) was changed in May of 1995 to adjust for weighting and composition. The index was then based on 12 share issues.

Supervisory Organizations:
The Ministry of Finance
The Bratislava Stock Exchange

Depositories: Securities Centre (owned and supervised by the Ministry of Finance)

Settlement Details:

Shares: Trade date + three days (T + 3)

Trading: All shares are issued book-entry and are registered to the owner. Physical securities are held at a custodian bank.

Continuous trading is accomplished with a computerized system.

Listing Requirements:

Main Requirements:

	Main Market	Junior Market
Minimum share capital (SKK million)	500	500
Issue size of securities (nominal value, SKK million)	100	100
Minimum period an issuer must be in business	3 yrs.	1 yr.
Period covered by a company prospectus	3 yrs.	1 yr.
Frequency of submission for financial statements (per annum)	4	2

All issues, except government bonds, must first list on the junior market. Six months after the initial listing, and at the company's request, the committee will re-evaluate the listing and decide whether to reclassify the security to the Main Market or to delist the security.

Taxation: A 15% withholding tax is due on dividends and interest except when received from government securities. Double taxation agreements exist where the specified amount is withheld at the source.

There are no capital gains taxes for non-residents.

Limitations: Ownership at 5%, 10%, 20%, 30%, 50%, or more than 65% of any publicly traded issue requires a disclosure of ownership report under the regulations of the Securities Act.

A disclosure report from the Securities Registry is published. It includes the issuer's name, type of security, ISIN number, name of the shareholder, and the shareholder's previous and new positions.

Any acquisition of more than 30% of an issue triggers a public offer. The public offer may not be valid for less than 30 days nor more than 60 days. The purchase price of a public offer cannot be lower than the average price of the share during the most recent six months.

Brokerage Firms:

Creditanstalt Securities
Dubravska cesta 2
SK-81703 Bratislava
Slovak Republic
Phone: (421-7) 377-828
Fax: (421-7) 371-769

Company Information:

10 Most Active Companies

Name of Company	Trading Value (US$ millions)
Nafta	118.60
VSZ	87.32
Slovakofarma	64.25
JCaP	43.45
Skoplast	39.73
Slovnaft	38.09
Biotika	23.78
Hirochem	16.29
Chirana-Prema	16.25
Vegum	16.22

9 Largest Companies

Name of Company	Type of Business	Market Capitalization (US$)
Slovnaft	Oil and Gas	526,756
VSZ	Steel	328,094
Nafta	Energy	267,893
VUB	Banking	189,632
IRB	Banking	42,475
JCaP	Pulp and Paper	40,134
Biotika	Pharmaceuticals	40,134
Chemolak	Chemical	32,107
Plastika	Plastics	30,769

Regional Exchanges: None

SLOVENIA

Slovenia (Republika Slovenija) is a country in the far northwestern Balkans. It is bordered by Italy on the west, Austria on the north, Hungary on the northeast, and Croatia on the south and southeast.

Area: 7,821 square miles (20,256 square km)

Population: 1,971,000 (48.9% urban; 51.1% rural)

Form of Government: Multiparty republic, with two legislative houses: State Council—40 members; State Assembly—90 members. Head of state: President. Head of government: Prime Minister.

Official Langauge: Slovene

Capital: Ljubljana

Largest Cities: Ljubljana, 276,133; Maribor, 108,122; Celje, 41,279; Kranj, 37,318; Velenje, 27,665

Economy:

Currency: Tolar (SIT)

National Budget: Revenue—SIT 335.4 billion; expenditures—SIT 332.6 billion

Gross National Product: US$12.6 billion

Principal Products: Fruits and vegetables; livestock; machinery; manufactured goods; fuels

Foreign Trade (Imports): SIT 737.4 billion (machinery and transport equipment: 30.4%; basic manufactures: 12.1%; chemicals: 11.4%; mineral fuels: 10.7%; food: 7.7%; from Germany: 25.1%; Italy: 16.2%; Croatia: 9.1%; Austria: 8.5%; France: 8.0%)

Foreign Trade (Exports): SIT 688.8 billion (machinery and transport equipment: 27.5%; basic manufactures: 25.6%; chemicals: 9.1%; mineral fuels: 5.1%; food: 4.6%; to Germany: 29.5%; Italy: 12.4%; Croatia: 12.1%; France: 8.7%; Austria: 4.9%)

Stock Exchanges: 1
Ljubljana Stock Exchange (LSE)
Slovenska cesta 56
61 000 Ljubljana
Slovenia
Phone: (386-61) 171 0211
Fax: (386-61) 171 0213

Internet Address: www.ljse.si

Trading Hours:

Monday, Wednesday, Friday	9:30 to 1:00	BIS electronic system exchange
Tuesday, Thursday	10:00 to 12:00	

Office Hours: Monday–Friday 8:00 to 4:00

Exchange Holidays:

1, 2 January	25 June
13, 27 April	25, 26 December
1 May	

Listed Companies: 31

Market Capitalization: US$3.8 billion

Major Sectors: Banking, pharmaceutical, brokerage firms, consultants, publishing, construction, health resorts

History: In 1924 the Ljubljana Stock, Commodities and Foreign Exchange was established to trade government bonds and corporate debentures. It closed in 1941 due to World War II, and was abolished in 1953. The exchange reopened in 1989 as the Ljubljanska Borza.

Separated into two markets—Tier A and Tier B—the Ljubljanska Borza is a self-governing, self-regulating legal entity funded by membership fees and commissions charged on the volume of trading. There is also an OTC market trading about 20 different securities between brokerage firms.

As a result of the acceleration of Slovenia's privatization program (in part, due to the 1994 deadline for application), it is estimated that an additional 115 of the major Slovenian companies will become publicly traded by the end of 1995.

Exchange activities are monitored by the Securities and Exchange Commission (SEC) under authorization of the Investment Companies Act.

Classes of Securities: Ordinary shares, corporate bonds, government bonds, others as provided by law

Indices: Slovenian Stock Index (SBI)

Supervisory Organizations:
Securities and Exchange Commission
Ljubljana Stock Exchange

Depository: Slovenian Payment Institution/KDD Clearing Corporation

Settlement Details:

Shares: Trade date + 2 days (T + 2)

Trading: The majority of exchange trading is conducted using the open-outcry system. Occasionally, however, trading can be done through the BIS electronic system, originally designed for the Alberta Stock Exchange in Canada.

Listing Requirements: Listing on the LSE requires appropriate information to be contained within a prospectus. The prospectus must include details of the company's legal status, main activities, recent business results, and prospects. Continuing disclosure of audited annual financial statements and semiannual statements is required by law. Complete information pertaining to corporate actions, including shareholder's meetings, dividend and interest payments, new securities issues, the appointment and recall of directors, changes in substantial shareholder holdings (10%, 25%, 50%, and 75% of the voting rights), and other material changes is also required.

Investor Taxation: Dividends are taxed at 15% for foreign investors and at 25% for domestic investors.

While capital gains are taxed at 30% through corporate taxes, there is no capital gains tax for individuals or other investors.

Limitations: Listed securities can be traded by foreign or domestic investors. Repatriation is guaranteed by legislation. Repatriation of foreign and domestic securities is subject to approval of the Bank of Slovenia.

Brokerage Firms:
ABH
Slovenska 50
1000 Ljubljana
Slovenia
Phone: (386-61) 125 6145
Fax: (386-61) 125 7053

BPH
Tomsiceva1
1000 Ljubljana
Slovenia
Phone: (386-61) 125 6145
Fax: (386-61) 125 7053

Dadas
Kotnikova 5
1001 Ljubljana
Slovenia
Phone: (386-61) 132 8246
Fax: (386-61) 321 450

Mariborska
Vita Kraigherja 4/III
2000 Maribor
Slovenia
Phone: (386-61) 221 878
Fax: (386-61) 227 576

Nika BDP
Dunajska 20
1116 Ljubljana
Slovenia
Phone: (386-61) 133 155
Fax: (386-61) 133 1347

Nova LB
Subiceva 2
1000 Ljubljana
Slovenia
Phone: (386-61) 125 5333
Fax: (386-61) 222 518

Poteza BD
Miklosiceva 7a
1000 Ljubljana
Slovenia
Phone: (386-61) 133 2132
Fax: (386-61) 328 267

SKB Banka
Ajkovscina 4
1000 Ljubljana
Slovenia
Phone: (386-61) 133 2132
Fax: (386-61) 328 267

UBK Banka
Trzaska 116
1111 Ljubljana
Slovenia
Phone: (386-61) 123 1131
Fax: (386-61) 273 082

Company Information:

10 Most Active Companies

Name of Company	Trading Value (US$ millions)
Dadas	79.95
SKB Bank	75.10
Blag Trgovinski Centre	30.89
MK Zalozba	28.95
Nika	23.81
GPG	20.87
Probanka	20.35
Salus	14.30
Terme Eatez	10.04
Finmedia	9.41

10 Major Companies

Name of Company	Market Capitalization (US$ millions)
SKB Bank	119.07
Blag Trgovinski Centre	37.13
GPG	32.68
Salus	18.46
Nika	17.49
Dadas	16.64
Probanka	14.36
Hmezad Banka	13.16
MK Zalozba	12.94
Finmedia	11.01

Regional Exchanges: None

SMALL ORDER EXECUTION SYSTEM (SOES; United States)

The *Small Order Execution System (SOES)* is a trading system used by the NASD over-the-counter market. This system is designed for eligible issues with five market makers or more and applies to orders of 1,000 shares or less.

Trades are submitted for immediate execution, then routed to a clearing corporation for on-line comparison between the two members.

See also DESIGNATED ORDER TURNAROUND (DOT); NATIONAL ASSOCIATION OF SECURITIES DEALERS (NASD); OVER THE COUNTER (OTC).

SMITH, ADAM

Adam Smith was a Scottish classical economist educated at the University of Glasgow and Balliol College Oxford. As Professor of Logic, he wrote *The Theory of Moral Sentiments* (1759) before his appointment as tutor to the son of the Duke of Buccleugh. As tutor Smith traveled extensively in Europe and retired at an early age to concentrate on writing.

Influenced by his friend J. S. Mill and the work of Sir William Petty (1623–87), Smith published his seminal work after ten years of study. *An Inquiry into the Nature and Causes of the Wealth of Nations* (1776) is often interpreted as the foundation of English classical economics and its subsequent traditions.

Smith developed the focus on economic surplus, or the creation of wealth, from the Mercantile and Physiocrat schools, which viewed trade and agriculture respectively as the source of surplus. The five-volume *The Wealth of Nations* provided a comprehensive and integrated view of the economic process and the framework for much of classical analysis. Writing at the onset of the industrial revolution, Smith's major explanation for economic growth was the division of labor. Labor, he argued, was the fundamental measure of value, although actual prices were determined by the forces of supply and demand in the market. The division of labor referred primarily to the specialization of the labor force—the subdivision of tasks that was possible within the economy but limited by the extent of the market. Smith used the example of a pin manufacturer who, by organizing his labor into specialist tasks, could increase his output a hundredfold. Smith also applied the term *division of labor* to the proportion of the productive to unproductive labor in the economy.

The allocation of the labor force between various lines of employment played an important role for Smith in capital accumulation and the subsequent

Adam Smith, 1787, relief by James Tassie. *(Courtesy of National Portrait Gallery, London)*

"progress of improvement." In his historical context, Smith viewed productive employment as producing tangible objects that generated a surplus, which could be made available for future investment and the employment of labor. Capital provided a fund for wages to pay workers during production in advance of any income generated by output. The rate of return on capital invested was for Smith the rate of interest in the economy, the income accruing to the owner of capital.

Smith's underlying argument was that market economies generally serve the public interest well, guiding production and consumption like an "invisible hand." Individual self-interests interacting in the market led to the maximum social good. Smith believed the system to be harmonious, requiring the minimum of government interference. Free competition was the essential ingredient of the efficient economy, free enterprise for firms, and free trade for countries. To Smith, the basic goal of economic growth was beyond dispute, by its consequences for the accumulation of capital and the specialization of labor, and was not served by state regulation and control as in the mercantilist pattern. Economic growth and a competitive order were mutually reinforcing.

Smith's praise of the free market has led many to regard him as the father of the "libertarian movement," which advocates the absolute minimum of state intervention in the free market. Smith was, however, aware of the potential of monopoly power and his arguments can be interpreted as suggesting that problems may arise as a result of inequalities of income that develop.

In his discussion of public finance, Smith laid down four canons or principles of taxation: a tax should be proportionate to the ability to pay, certain in its impact in similar circumstances, convenient to pay, and economical to collect. Smith's work was the basis of much development and criticism by classical economists and later schools of thought. Little of the content of *The Wealth of Nations* was original to Smith, but in his ability to synthesize and communicate to a wider audience the impact and importance of Smith's work cannot be doubted.

See also CLASSICAL SCHOOL OF ECONOMICS; MILL, JOHN STUART; RICARDO, DAVID; SAY, JEAN-BAPTISTE.

SMITH BARNEY SHEARSON

Since the end of 1993, *Smith Barney Shearson* has been a wholly owned subsidiary of Travelers Group, Inc., and in 1997, with the purchase of Salomon Inc. by the Travelers Group, the company became part of Salomon Smith Barney Holdings, Inc. A leader in the U.S. securities industry, Smith Barney Shearson offers brokerage, investment banking, and asset management services to corporations, governments, and individuals throughout the world. The firm's core services include security sales, research, and trading for individuals and institutions; underwriting, advisory, and specialty financing for corporations and governmental entities; mutual fund services; futures; and asset management.

Smith Barney Shearson is the second largest brokerage company in the United States. With more than 10,000 retail brokers and more than 450 offices worldwide, the firm provides a wide range of investment products, including stocks, bonds, mutual funds, CDs, insurance, and annuities, as well as services such as retirement planning, asset allocation, overall money management, college funding, estate planning, trust services, and special services for affluent investors.

In mid-1997 Smith Barney Shearson had $156 billion in assets under its management. The company's 1996 net income was $889 million on total revenue of $6.3 billion. Its stock is traded on the New York and the Pacific stock exchanges.

The history of Smith Barney Shearson dates back to 19th-century Philadelphia and meanders through a complex series of mergers and acquisitions involving more than 40 companies that contributed to the formation of today's financial titan. In 1873 a young broker, Charles D. Barney, founded a firm in Philadelphia; in the same city in 1892, a young investment banker, Edward B. Smith, started his own company. The two firms operated independently for a number of decades, with each firm eventually purchasing a seat on the New York Stock Exchange and moving its base of operations to New York. The two companies merged in 1937, when the Smith firm ran into financial difficulty during a Wall Street slump. By that time, Charles D. Barney was no longer with the firm he started, having retired 30 years before. The merged company had 27 general partners, 4 limited partners, and a staff of 730.

The firm prospered as a private partnership until 1964, when it became a public corporation. In 1975 Smith Barney merged with another old-line investment firm, Harris, Upham and Company. Then in 1987 Primerica, a diversified financial services company, purchased Smith Barney, Harris Upham and Company.

Sanford Weill, who would gain control of Primerica in 1988, was Shearson's guiding force through much of its history. Weill started as a runner for Bear

Stearns, and after five years as a broker, joined three friends in 1960 in forming the investment firm of Carter, Berlind, Potoma and Weill. This fledgling enterprise would eventually become Shearson, which Weill left in the early 1980s, reacquired in the early 1990s, and made a part of Smith Barney Shearson.

In 1965, Carter, Berlind, Potoma and Weill became Carter, Berlind, Weill and Levitt, Inc. (CBWL), with Weill as its chairman, and two years later the firm made its first acquisition, taking over Berstein Macauley, an investment management firm. This first deal typifies Weill's mode of operations: a long-established, well-respected firm would run into difficulty, and Weill's company would take it over, merging it smoothly into their operations, usually cutting its back office staff but keeping its sales staff. Often the merged company specialized in an area of investment banking in which Weill's company was weak. In 1970 CBWL acquired Hayden Stone, an old-line brokerage that had expanded too rapidly, resulting in a serious backlog in its back office operations, and leading its investors to threaten legal action. The new firm was named CBWL-Hayden Stone. During the recession of the early 1970s, Wall Street suffered along with the economy in general. Many firms decided to merge as a means of survival. In 1973 CBWL-Hayden Stone acquired H.L. Hentz, another brokerage, and Saul Lerner and Company. Then in 1974 came the most ambitious takeover yet—Shearson Hammill and Company. Despite a strong retail sales force, Shearson Hammill ran into serious cash flow difficulties, so it decided to merge with the better capitalized though smaller CBWL-Hayden Stone.

The new company was called Shearson Hayden Stone, keeping the Shearson name prominent because it was known as a major underwriter, a status its partner firms lacked. The new firm made two major acquisitions in 1976—Faulkner, Dawkins and Sullivan, a regional brokerage with an excellent research division, and Lamson Brothers, a highly regarded commodities broker. By 1977 Shearson's holdings were consolidated, resulting in the seventh largest U.S. investment banking firm.

In 1979 Shearson acquired Loeb Rhodes, Hornblower and Company, one of Wall Street's oldest and most successful firms. Shearson Loeb Rhodes was now the second largest U.S. investment banking house. Then in 1981 Weill gambled on the takeover of Boston Company, a money-management firm, in violation of laws prohibiting a firm from engaging in both commercial and investment banking. The gamble was successful as Shearson was allowed to keep the Boston Company.

In 1982 Weill engineered the sale of Shearson Loeb Rhodes to American Express. He wanted access to American Express's capital to finance further expansion. However, after an initial period of success, the move proved to be Weill's undoing. American Express and Shearson turned out to be a good fit, and during the next 18 months Shearson took over four more firms. In 1983 Weill became president of American Express and oversaw the takeover of Lehman Brothers, the oldest continuous partnership on Wall Street. In 1985 Weill quit as president of American Express when he learned he would not succeed James Robinson as the CEO. It appeared to many that Weill's career was over, but he started rebuilding it almost immediately. In 1986 Weill engineered the spin-off from Control Data of a troubled firm called Commercial Credit in an initial public offering worth $850 million. Weill became the head of Commercial Credit and a year later bought Control Data's remaining interest in the firm.

Meanwhile, back at the "Weill-less" Shearson, its parent American Express took the firm public in 1987, retaining 61% of the firm. Two months after the stock market crash of 19 October 1987, Shearson purchased E.F. Hutton, which had been struggling for some time. The merger created Shearson Lehman Hutton, with a retail force second only to Merrill Lynch on Wall Street.

At Commercial Credit Weill was also making deals as he continued to rebuild his career. In 1988 he acquired Primerica, whose holdings included Smith Barney and the A.L. Williams Insurance Company. Later, he sold several of its divisions, such as Fingerhut. In 1992 Weill purchased 27% of the insurer Travelers. In 1993 Weill purchased the remainder of Travelers, and he came full circle by buying the Shearson brokerage operation from American Express. Thus, Weill and the fortunes of Shearson were once again linked. The new firm was called Smith Barney Shearson, and it was part of the Travelers Group.

In 1997 the Travelers Group purchased Salomon Inc., the parent company of Salomon Brothers, Inc. The brothers Arthur, Herbert, and Percy Salomon, who left their father's firm and started operations with a $5,000 investment, founded Salomon Brothers in 1910. Soon they merged with Morton Hutzler, an established firm with a seat on the New York Stock Exchange. For more than 85 years Salomon grew and prospered on Wall Street, and at the time it was purchased by the Travelers Group the firm had $25 billion in assets under its management. In 1996 Salomon Brothers had a net income of $617 million on total revenues of $4.4 billion.

The new firm was named Salomon Smith Barney Holdings, Inc. As with most Weill-engineered mergers, Salomon Brothers had strengths that Smith Barney Shearson was lacking. Smith Barney was a predominantly domestic firm concentrated in retail trading in stocks, while Salomon Brothers' strength was bond trading. Salomon also had a solid international presence, which Smith Barney sorely needed.

See also LEHMAN BROTHERS HOLDINGS INC.; SALOMON INC.

SMITH NEW COURT

See MERRILL LYNCH.

SOCIALLY RESPONSIBLE INVESTMENT (SRI)

Proponents of *Socially Responsible Investment (SRI)* believe that investment decisions should take into account broad social and environmental, as well as economic, criteria. According to the SRI viewpoint, investors should utilize a number of "screens," evaluating companies' records with regard to issues such as treatment of employees, opportunities for advancement within the company, discriminatory practices, business with repressive regimes, animal testing, pornography, consumer safety, and pollution. Investors should then weigh companies' overall score according to economic criteria in addition to these, with the economic emphasis on long-term gains rather than short-term profitability. The SRI philosophy holds that any economic system that does not contain this kind of ethical component is bound for self-destruction.

Such an investment philosophy is rather unusual from the traditional capitalist viewpoint, according to which investment decisions should be made solely on the basis of profitability. Critics of this traditional viewpoint have pointed out that many capitalist concerns carry on business and are able to realize high levels of profit because they do not have to assume many of the costs of their operations. For example, it has been argued that the petrochemicals industry is responsible for a great deal of environmental pollution, yet it is not the industry that has to bear the economic consequences, whether in the form of health care, resource destruction, or cleanup. It has been argued that if such costs were included in the ledgers of petrochemical companies, their profitability would be much lower, if not nil, with the result that investment dollars would tend to flow into the development of alternative kinds of products.

The SRI movement engages in economic and political action to change investing and business practices, and has grown rapidly since the 1970s. By 1996 the total value of social investment was estimated at approximately $1 trillion (roughly 10% of all investments), and the number of socially and environmentally screened funds had grown to more than 100.

Naturally, no investment—and certainly none under present-day conditions—can achieve a perfect score, meeting all the various social screens and also being viable economically. Therefore, SRI investors seek those companies that do the best overall, or the best in their industry. For example, the by-products of the pharmaceuticals industry include a great many carcinogens, but some firms, particularly multinational corporations such as Merck and Company and Johnson and Johnson, have done far better with pollution control, even exceeding what is required by government regulations.

During the 1980s, a major issue that galvanized the SRI movement was apartheid in South Africa. SRI investors refused to invest in funds whose activities were judged to be supporting the apartheid system. In most cases this came down to not investing in funds that carried out any economic activity in South Africa. In some cases, however, socially concerned investors did invest in companies doing business in South Africa, provided that those companies had good equal employment opportunity practices, their products and services did not have any direct connection with the maintenance of the apartheid system, and/or their community policies were directed toward the elimination of apartheid. The advocates of SRI feel that their stance played an important part in creating the conditions for the end of apartheid.

Another example involves opposition to animal testing. Under pressure from SRI advocates, companies such as the multinational corporation Procter and Gamble made serious attempts to reduce the number of animals used in product testing and to develop alternatives to animal testing.

Sometimes SRI investors have considered how an investment might have a secondary involvement with a social problem. For example, some fast-food companies have been criticized for purchasing beef from around the world, especially South America, where the clearing of ground for cattle ranching has involved destruction of the rain forest.

Evidence is mixed on how well socially responsible investments compare to other investments from a profitability standpoint. Some long-term studies have shown, for example, that the stocks of more socially responsible industrials and utilities have fared better than those of their less socially responsible counterparts. The weight of the evidence to date indicates that, taken as a whole, the more socially responsible companies have shown more growth than those that were less socially responsible. Proponents of SRI argue that this is to be expected and that as awareness spreads among consumers about the importance of social responsibility and to what extent different companies embody it, they will tend to purchase products from the companies that are doing better, thus boosting their sales and profits and, in all likelihood, increasing their advantage over the non-socially responsible companies.

The Social Investment Forum is a national membership association that promotes the concept and practice of SRI. It has five major areas of activity: networking and continuing education, research, direct member services and information, industry growth and client services, and industry advocacy.

See also ETHICAL INVESTMENT; QUALITATIVE ANALYSIS.

SOCIETA MADRE (Italy)
See COMPANY.

SOCIETA QUOTATA IN BORSA (Italy)
See COMPANY; LISTED SECURITIES.

SOCIÉTÉ (France)
See COMPANY.

SOCIÉTÉ DE CAPITAL (French)
See PUBLICLY HELD AND TRADED COMPANY.

SOCIÉTÉ D'INVESTISSEMENT À CAPITAL VARIABLE (SICAV; France)
See UNIT INVESTMENT TRUST/UNIT TRUST.

SOCIÉTÉ GÉNÉRALE
As of June 1997, *Société Générale* was the leading private sector bank in France and the 16th largest in the world. It had assets of $340 billion, 2,600 branches in France, 500 offices in more than 70 foreign countries, and 54,000 employees.

Société Générale's history began in 1864, when a group of French industrialists and bankers in Paris formed the Société pour Favoriser le Développement du Commerce et de l'Industrie en France S.A. Functioning as a deposit bank and an investment bank, it grew rapidly. In its first year it opened a branch in Bordeaux, and in the following two years it added additional branches in Orleans, Lyons, Tours, Toulouse, Lille, Marseilles, Nantes, Rennes, and other cities. In 1871 Société Générale opened its first foreign branch, in London. By 1875 there were 71 Société Générale branches.

The bank's growth slowed in the 1880s and 1890s, but got a stimulus after 1900 when the bank focused on deposits. By the start of World War I Société Générale had 114 branches covering nearly all the commercial and industrial towns in France, plus 560 ancillary offices.

Société Générale continued its overall pattern of slow, steady growth after the war. This was interrupted by the Great Depression, which hit France in 1930. But Société Générale survived, entering an agreement with Crédit Lyonnais to curtail expansion.

Following World War II, Société Générale, like France's other large deposit banks, was nationalized. Three more decades of steady growth ensued. During this period, Société Générale expanded overseas, and it had 35 branches in French colonies and foreign countries by 1955.

In the early 1960s, however, the French government imposed restrictions on lending as part of anti-inflationary efforts. As a result, many French banks got involved in the Eurodollar market, merchant banking, or overseas banking. Société Générale itself began dealing in Eurocurrencies during this period. By the end of the decade its international role had become strengthened, with its focus on commercial trading and foreign currency.

In 1975 Société Générale introduced Agrifan, a food products trading company, and two years later it formed trading companies for medical supplies and food industry equipment. The three trading companies were controlled by Sogexport, Société Générale's subsidiary. Playing an active role on the stock market, Société Générale handled nearly one-fourth of all new French security introductions and almost half of all new foreign ones in the mid-1970s.

In the late 1970s Société Générale began a period of rapid international growth. In 1978 it opened a branch in New York; in 1979, it opened branches in Latin America and Asia and formed a joint banking group with the National Bank of Egypt. In 1980 Société Générale acquired a controlling interest in the London stockbrokers Strauss Turnbull and Company and opened bank branches in Milan, Bucharest, Manila, Taipei, Athens, and Panama City.

In the early 1980s Société Générale began to move out of commercial banking and into corporate finance and investment banking. It developed its business with small- and medium-sized companies. After suffering international losses of $2.4 million in 1984, it refocused its international operations on wholesale and financial activities and specialized financing.

Société Générale was privatized in June 1987, the year after conservatives returned to power in France. In 1988 it acquired Touche Remnant Holdings Limited, a British asset management firm, and in 1989 it acquired Ingwerson and Company, a Dutch brokerage house. By 1997 Société Générale's asset management operation in Britain was managing assets of approximately $75 billion. In the mid-1990s Société Générale was the largest foreign bank in the Baltics. The bank also expanded into some of Europe's emerging markets. It was the first investment bank to set up a private equity fund for Romania. Its operations were growing in the former East Germany and Yugoslavia, Hungary, and the Czech Republic.

In general, in its international operations, Société Générale sought to maintain a balance between commercial and investment banking, and its earnings in these two areas were roughly equal. It ranked second in worldwide leasing among all banks in 1993.

In 1994 Société Générale opened commercial banking offices in Egypt, the Czech Republic, Pakistan, Slovenia, Malaysia, and Latvia. The following year it opened commercial branches in Ireland, Mexico, Brazil, China, India, Pakistan, and Thailand.

In 1994 Société Générale introduced a new derivative product called a Boost (Banking On Overall Stability). Boosts were aimed at long-term institutional investors who thought that volatility in a particular market would decline. They were listed on major stock exchanges in France, Germany, Italy, Spain, and other countries.

In 1995 Société Générale reorganized into three divisions: retail banking, resources and services, and international and finance.

See also FRANCE.

SOFT DOLLARS

Soft Dollars refers to any payment for services provided by a brokerage firm in the form of business, as opposed to cash. For example, a mutual fund may pay for the use of research facilities supplied by a brokerage firm by agreeing to do transactions for a specific dollar amount. Such a deal would guarantee the use of the research facilities at no charge if the fund generates commissions of, for instance, a minimum of $100,000 in a year.

Note: Despite the use of *dollars* as currency, such arrangements exist throughout the world.

See also COMMISSION; HARD DOLLAR COMMISSION.

SOFT MARKET

A *Soft Market* is a market in which relatively little selling pressure causes a decline and advances are weak and short in duration. Under these conditions, demand is not strong and supply is adequate for current transactions. Such markets can go through a time of accumulation, during which buyers slowly accumulate positions, or distribution, and sellers slowly sell positions.

If the volume strengthens on declines of market indexes it is often a sign of the presence of distribution. If, however, advances show the stronger volume, it can be a signal of accumulation and building strength.

See also DOW THEORY; FORMING A LINE; TECHNICAL ANALYSIS.

SOLD

Sold is the word used by a trader confirming the execution of an order.

For example, if a broker/dealer (OTC) or a specialist (stock exchange) bids 49 1/8 for 500 shares, a contra broker accepts the bid by saying "sold" and then delivers the 500 shares through the normal clearing procedure.

Sold appears on the written confirmation sent to the investor. It also shows on the account activity computer screen, and subsequently appears on periodic account statements.

Once securities are sold, they must be delivered by the selling investor on or before the settlement date.

See also ASK PRICE; BID PRICE; CONFIRMATION; LAST TRADE; SETTLE.

SOROS, GEORGE

George Soros is the best known, most influential, and, arguably, the most enigmatic fund manager in the world. He holds the best long-term investment record of any fund manager; $10,000 invested with Soros in 1969, when he began his investment partnership with Jim Rogers, would have been worth a staggering $13 million dollars in 1992.

George Soros was born in Hungary—the original family name was Dieu-de Shorosh—and his family was forced into hiding during the German occupation. Soros's father, a lawyer and editor of an Esperanto journal, forged official documents to hide his family's Jewish roots. The young Soros spent many months posing as the godson of a Christian government official to avoid the concentration camps.

After World War II Soros studied at the London School of Economics and worked in the arbitrage

George Soros speaks at a press conference, 14 March 1994. *(Reuters/Corbis-Bettmann)*

department of Singer and Friedlander. He moved to the United States and worked for a number of firms before running an offshore fund for Arnhold and Bleichroeder. In 1969 he set up the Quantum Fund and has since enjoyed many years of remarkable investment success.

Soros's books, articles, and lectures have explained his views of the market at considerable length. He has posited that the markets are inherently inefficient and that the efficient market hypothesis does not hold water. It is investors' perceptions that form market values, but because investors' perceptions are subjective they are inherently flawed. Changing perceptions cause the cycle of boom and bust that moves share prices, and the intelligent fund manager can use this pattern to make money.

Soros is best known as the man who "broke the Bank of England" by selling sterling to such an extent that the pound was forced to leave the European exchange rate mechanism. Soros's gamble on the exchange rate netted him an estimated $1 billion in one frenetic day of trading. The sterling strategy sealed Soros's reputation to such an extent that the market will now tend to follow any of his decisions; indeed the sheer size of Soros's highly leveraged fund is sufficiently large to move the markets.

Soros's hedge fund, which speculated in the market on behalf of several other funds and a group of wealthy individuals, was reviled for its part in the "Black Wednesday" collapse. In his defense, Soros stated that his trading technique was only successful because of the weaknesses inherent in the capitalist system. Many contrasts can be made between the trading styles of Soros and his contemporary Warren Buffett. Buffett is a patient, long-term investor, prepared to hang on to shares for years. Soros, on the other hand, is a short-term player, pouring in huge sums to back changes in the markets and pulling out as soon as a profit is made. And, while Buffett presents a home-spun, almost rural image, Soros is determined to be seen as an intellectual and internationalist.

Soros appears to some commentators as a frustrated academic who may have been happier, if not richer, if he had lived his life as a theoretical economist. His recent life has been characterized by a desire to be seen on the world stage, and his views on politics and capitalism have appeared in a book, *The Alchemy of Finance* (1994), and a number of heavyweight articles in the financial press. In 1994 Soros published *Soros on Soros*, which he described as "a summing up of my life's work." He has opened a number of foundations to promote open societies in eastern Europe and is eager to advise statesmen on how their economies should be run.

The Soros Foundation, headquartered in Hungary, provides aid worth approximately $300 million a year to 30 countries. For a man who has made a fortune through the application of strict capitalist policies, it is perhaps surprising to see such a left-wing inclination in his donations. Some commentators on the political right accuse Soros of trying to rewrite history by replacing communist dictatorships with left-wing democracies and of using his millions to produce socially engineered solutions in the former communist countries.

See also ROGERS, JIM.

SOUTH AFRICA, REPUBLIC OF

South Africa (Afrikaans Suid-Afrika, or Republic van Suid-Afrika) is the southernmost country on the African continent. It is bordered by Namibia on the northeast, Botswana and Zimbabwe on the north, Mozambique and Swaziland on the northeast.

Area: 473,290 square miles (1,225,815 square km)

Population: 41,465,000 (48.8% urban; 51.2% rural)

Form of Government: Multiparty republic, with two legislative houses: Senate—90 members; National Assembly—400 members. Head of state and government: President.

Official Languages: (11 official languages) Afrikaans, English, Ndebele, Pedi, Sotho, Swazi, Tsonga, Tswana, Venda, Xhosa, Zulu

Capitals: Pretoria (executive); Bloemfontein (judicial); Cape Town (legislative)

Largest Cities: Cape Town, 2,350,157; Johannesburg, 1,916,063; Durban, 1,137,378; Pretoria, 1,080,187; Port Elizabeth, 853,204

Economy:

Currency: Rand (R) (the financial rand was discontinued on 13 March 1995)

National Budget: Revenue—R 88.2 billion; expenditures—R 114.2 billion (education: 23.9%; interest on debt: 19.4%; economic services: 14.8%; health: 11.3%; defense: 9.3%)

Public Debt: US$2.3 billion

Gross National Product: US$119.0 billion

Principal Products: Fruits, vegetables, beef and poultry; gold and diamonds; metals

Foreign Trade (Imports): R 59.1 billion (machinery and apparatus: 29.1%; motor vehicles: 15.1%; chemicals and chemical products: 11.1%; food: 6.5%; from Germany: 16.3%; United States: 15.7%; United Kingdom: 11.3%; Japan: 9.9%; Italy: 3.8%; France: 3.4%)

Foreign Trade (Exports): R 79.5 billion (gold: 28.0%; gem diamonds: 12.8%; base metals and metal products: 12.5%; to Switzerland: 6.7%; United Kingdom: 6.6%; United States: 4.9%; Japan: 4.6%; Germany: 4.1%)

Stock Exchanges: 1

Johannesburg Stock Exchange (JSE)
PO Box 1174
17 Diagonal Street
Johannesburg, 2001
South Africa
Phone: (27-11) 377-2200
Fax: (27-11) 834-3937

Internet Address: www.jse.co.za/

Trading Hours: Monday–Friday, 9:30 to 1:00 and 2:00 to 4:00

Office Hours: Monday–Friday, 8:00 to 5:00

Exchange Holidays:

1 January	10 August
10, 13, 27 April	24 September
1 May	16, 25 December
16 June	

Listed Companies: 759

Total Market Capitalization:

At 31 December 1997

Local Currency (Millions)	US Dollars (Millions)
641,459	131,815

Major Sectors: Industrial holdings, mining houses, building and construction, insurance, diamonds

Share Price Performance:

(% Change)

1992	-9
1993	63
1994	44
1995	3
1996	7
1997	-2

History: Founded by Benjamin Woollan in November 1887, the Johannesburg Stock Exchange (JSE) was created to provide a marketplace for the shares of the many mining and financial companies that were established by 1886. Its first home was in Simmonds Street, between Market and Commissioner Streets. In 1889, the building was demolished to make way for a double story exchange on the same site. This survived until 1903, when the third exchange was built, this time on Hollard Street. It served for 54 years. In 1958 it was demolished and a new building was erected in its place. Trading took place there from November 1960 to December 1978, when the JSE moved to its new home in Diagonal Street.

During its first 50 years the JSE existed essentially as a mining-based market. With South Africa's postwar industrial development, its character changed dramatically, and there are now three times as many industrial companies listed as mining companies.

South Africa produces about 40% of the free world's gold. The JSE, by virtue of the number of mining companies it lists, has been from the beginning the most significant gold mining stock market in the world.

Chronology of Major Developments:

1881 Diamonds are discovered in Kimberly and the Kimberly Stock Exchange is established.

1886 Gold is discovered on the Witwatersrand.

1887 The JSE is founded by Benjamin Woollan and the first JSE building is established on Simmonds Street. Later it is rebuilt on Commissioner Street.

1890 The second JSE building is again established on Simmonds Street and, due to space constraints, trading activities expand into the street, which is chained off, hence the phrase to "trade between the chains."

1933 The Open Call Exchange is established in Johannesburg; it later becomes the Union Stock Exchange.

1958 The government closes the Union Stock Exchange and transfers listing to the JSE.

1963 The JSE is admitted as a member of the Federation of International Stock Exchanges.

1985 For the first time, an independent businessman is appointed as JSE executive president.

1993 The first African Stock Exchanges Conference is held in Nairobi in April. This leads to the formation of the African Stock Exchanges Association of which the JSE is an active member.

1994 The research sub-committee's report into the structure of the JSE is published in May. The second African Stock Exchange Conference is held in Johannesburg in October, during which the signing of a Memorandum of Understanding between the JSE and the Nairobi Stock Exchange takes place. A redevelopment sector is established on the Main Board. An international securities identification numbering (ISIN) system is introduced in compliance with international standards for equities and bonds.

Classes of Securities: Preference and ordinary shares, debentures, government or municipal bonds, Krugerrands, financial futures, options, and money market instruments

Indices:

JSE 80% Overall Index (January 1960 = 100)

JSE Actuaries All Share Index

JSE Actuaries Top Forty Company All Share Index

JSE Actuaries Top Ten Company Gold Index

JSE Actuaries Top Twenty-Five Company Industrial Index

Supervisory Organizations:

Registrar of Stock Exchanges

Financial Services Board

JSE Committee

Financial Services Board

Securities Regulation Panel

Depository: None currently, but a depository is to be developed with Electronic Script Registry.

Settlement Details: Settlement of shares with banks is normally concluded on the basis of scrip against the rand. Settlement takes about one week to complete and can take place in any currency by converting from U.S. dollars to the currency of choice.

In situations in which a broker operates a foreign client's account as a discretionary account, the broker arranges for endorsements or cancellations and settles cash through the client's financial account with an authorized dealer. In all instances the purchase and sale transaction must be supported by broker's notes.

Trading: Equity trading, which can be watched by the public from the observation gallery, takes place on the market floor between 9:30 and 4:00 every Monday through Friday. Trading is in the form of a two-way, open-outcry auction, in which brokers and their dealers call out the names of the shares for which they have orders to buy or sell. When a sale is concluded, the price must be recorded on the prices board in the market whenever it is different from the price of the previous sale. Prices find their levels according to supply and demand. In busy periods, up to 29,000,000 shares change hands each week. Dealing is between the broker and broker: there are no market makers or specialists.

Listing Requirements:

Main Board Listing: An applicant seeking a listing on the Main Board must satisfy the following criteria:

1. It must have subscribed capital of at least R 2 million (including reserves but excluding minority interests, revaluations of assets that are not supported by a valuation by an independent professional expert acceptable to the committee prepared within the last six months, and intangible assets).

2. It must have at least one million equity shares in issue.

3. It must have a satisfactory profit history for the preceding three financial years, the last of which reported an audited profit of at least R 1 million before taxation.

4. 10% of each class of equity shares must be held by the public.

5. The number of the public shareholders of listed securities must be at least:
   a. 300 for equity shares
   b. 25 for preference shares
   c. 10 for debentures

6. The minimum initial issue price of securities must not be less than 100 cents per security.

Venture Capital Market: The following are the guidelines and requirements relating to the granting of a listing on the Venture Capital Market (VCM).

Prior Approval:

Prior to submission of an application for the listing of a company on the VCM the following procedure will apply:

1. A memorandum giving a summary of the nature of the applicant, its method of operation, its business plans and its prospects must be submitted to the Listings Division through a sponsoring broker.

2. If this memorandum meets the approval of the Listings Division, it will be referred, together with such other documentation as may be deemed necessary, to the committee, which will consider a full application for a listing.

3. The committee will not list securities held by the entrepreneurs in the VCM company amounting to 75% of their shareholding(s) for a period of at least two years subsequent to a listing being granted for the balance of the securities.

Suitability:

A venture capital conglomerate must hold a portfolio of investments in ventures, each of which is characterized by the fact that the venture capital conglomerate:

1. Has an investment in each underlying venture that is substantially an equity one.

2. Is able to support each underlying venture project with added value by virtue of support services and proper financial disciplines.

3. Has conducted adequate research into the management strength and commercial viability of each of its underlying ventures.

4. Has drawn up a business plan for the coming three years in respect to each underlying venture, and of the combined portfolio, with forecast balance sheets, profit and loss accounts, and cash flows.

5. A single venture company must have drawn up an analysis of its prospects based on market segment growth, competitive analysis, and market share. From this it should present a three-year business plan with forecast balance sheets, profit and loss accounts, and cash flows.

Criteria:

An applicant seeking a listing on the VCM must satisfy the following criteria:

1. It must have a subscribed capital of at least R 500,000 (including reserves but excluding minority interests, revaluations of assets that are not supported by a valuation by an independent professional expert acceptable to the committee prepared within the last six months, and intangible assets).

2. It must have at least one million equity shares in issue.

3. A profit history is not necessary, but the applicant should, in its analysis of future earnings, indicate credible returns on capital that are above average on a time-weighted basis.

4. A minimum of 5% of each class of equity share must be held by the public.

5. The number of public shareholders shall be at least 75 for equity shares, 25 for preference shares, and 10 for debentures.

6. The minimum initial issue price of equity shares shall not be less than 50 cents per share.

7. The majority of the directors and managers should have successful records of achievement in their respective roles.

8. At the beginning of its prospectus or prelisting statement, there must be a warning, in bold, block letters, of the speculative nature of investment in such a company.

Development Stage Sector: The committee may allow the listing of substantial industrial companies that are in the development stage on the "Development Stage Sector" (DSS) of the Main Board. These companies must comply with all of the criteria for a Main Board listing, with the exception that they do not have to show a satisfactory profit history.

Procedure for listing on the DSS:

Prior to submitting application for listing on the DSS, the following procedure will apply:

1. A memorandum, giving a summary of the nature of the applicant, its operating plan, its business plan, prospects and particulars regarding the management's experience, must be submitted to the Listings Division through a sponsoring broker.

2. After consideration of the memorandum, the committee will decide whether it will consider a full application for listing on the DSS.

Criteria for DSS listing applicants:

1. The applicant should have a subscribed permanent capital of at least R 20 million (inclusive of reserves, but exclusive of minority interests, revaluations of assets not supported by a valuation by an independent professional expert acceptable to the committee prepared within the last six months, and intangible assets) prior to the offering of any securities to the public.

2. A profit history is not necessary, but the applicant should provide a forecast of future profits and losses for at least one year after completion of the development stage.

3. At the beginning of the prospectus or prelisting statement, there must be a warning, in bold letters, that the applicant is still in the development stage and that it does not have a profit history that meets the criteria for a Main Board listing.

Once listed, a company's share certificates must be endorsed to reflect that the securities are listed on the DSS. A company that has listed on the DSS and that has produced a satisfactory profit history for three consecutive financial years (the last of which was an audited pretax profit of at least R 1 million) may request, and the committee may require, the transfer of its listing to another sector of the Main Board.

Investor Taxation: Broadly speaking, there is no capital gains tax and from 1 October 1995 there has been no non-resident shareholders tax. Share dealings are tax-free within South Africa if they are held beyond a five-year safe-haven period. If sold prior to the five-year period, it is presumed that the transaction is in the nature of a trade and will be assessed for tax.

Limitations: There are no limitations on trading and foreign ownership of companies. There are no restrictions on investments made by persons or legal entities residing abroad, provided such investment is made in accordance with South African Exchange Control regulations. Realized investment amounts and income on investments owned by foreign investors are freely transferable to countries outside the Common Monetary Area of Southern Africa through the medium of the commercial rand.

Securities Lending: Restricted

Brokerage Firms:

J.D. Anderson & Co. Inc.
2nd Floor
JSE Annexe Building
1 Kerk Street
Johannesburg 2001
South Africa
Phone: (27-11) 836-2601/9
Fax: (27-11) 834-2772

Ryan Anderson & Co. Inc.
301 The Stock Exchange
17 Diagonal Street
Johannesburg 2001
South Africa
Phone: (27-11) 838-1058
Fax: (27-11) 838-2742

BP Bernstein
920 The Stock Exchange
17 Diagonal Street
Johannesburg 2001
South Africa
Phone: (27-11) 833-1560/6
Fax: (27-11) 836-0392

Cahn Price Shapiro, Inc.
236 The Stock Exchange
17 Diagonal Street
Johannesburg 2001
South Africa
Phone: (27-11) 833-1430/5
Fax: (27-11) 836-5911

De Witt Morgan & Co.
4th Floor
The Stock Exchange
17 Diagonal Street
Johannesburg 2001
South Africa
Phone: (27-11) 832-1266
Fax: (27-11) 836-6173

JM Folscher & Co. Inc.
5th Floor
The Stock Exchange
17 Diagonal Street
Johannesburg 2001
South Africa
Phone: (27-11) 833-2009
Fax: (27-11) 833-7792

Frankel Pollak Vinderine, Inc.
2nd Floor
The Stock Exchange
17 Diagonal Street
Johannesburg 2001
South Africa
Phone: (27-11) 833-5640
Fax: (27-11) 836-0402

Golding & Slabbert, Inc.
7th Floor
The Stock Exchange
17 Diagonal Street
Johannesburg 2001
South Africa
Phone: (27-11) 836-7151
Fax: (27-11) 836-4502

Ed Hern Rudolph, Inc.
640 The Stock Exchange
17 Diagonal Street
Johannesburg 2001
South Africa
Phone: (27-11) 836-5211
Fax: (27-11) 838-3488

Price, Potgeiter, Inc.
PO Box 61069
Marshalltown 2107
South Africa
Phone: (27-11) 833-1975
Fax: (27-11) 838-7928

Company Information:

The Best Performing Shares in the Country

Company Name	Share Price Change 1 January 1997 to 31 December 1997 (%)
Board Of Executors	492
African Life Asr.	192
Coronation Hdg.N Ord.	184
Orion Selections	181
Bidvest Group	170
Fedsure Hdg.	148
Metropolitan Life	106
Momentum Life Assurers	102
Rmb Holdings	99

Company Name	Share Price Change 1 January 1997 to 31 December 1997 (%)
Jd Group	99
Investec Group	93
Amal.Beverages Ind.	92
Dimension Data	92
First Nat.Bank Holdings	89
Pepkor	81
Nedcor	78
Shoprite	68
Anglo American Plat.	65
Metro Cash & Carry	55
Imperial Holdings	35

The Largest Companies in the Country by Market Capitalization as of 31 December 1997

Company Name	Market Capitalization Local Currency (Millions)	Market Capitalization US Dollars (Millions)
Anglo Am. Corp.of Sa.	46,036	9,460
Sa.Breweries	41,877	8,605
De Beers Cons.Mines	37,640	7,735
Liberty Life As.	32,939	6,769
Sasol	30,859	6,341
Billiton	26,725	5,492
Std.Bk.Inv.	25,905	5,323
Nedcor	24,805	5,097
First Nat.Bank Holdings	18,828	3,869
Rembrandt Group	18,531	3,808
Absa Gp.	17,720	3,641
Liberty Holdings	16,417	3,374
Orion Selections	15,424	3,170
Nbs Boland Gp.Ltd.	14,806	3,042
Anglo American Plat.	13,922	2,861
Investec Group	13,393	2,752
Bev.& Consumer Ind.Hdg.	12,604	2,590
Dimension Data	11,636	2,391
Momentum Life Assurers	10,499	2,158
Liblife Stgc.Investors	10,322	2,121
Imperial Holdings	10,309	2,119
Rmb Holdings	10,250	2,106
Tiger Oats	10,127	2,081
Anglo Amer.Inv.Tst.	10,025	2,060
Cg Smith	9,748	2,003
Anglo America Indl.	9,342	1,920
Bidvest Group	9,341	1,919
Metropolitan Life	9,276	1,906
Persetel Q Data	8,842	1,817
Rembrandt Behrend	8,640	1,775

Company Name	Market Capitalization Local Currency (Millions)	Market Capitalization US Dollars (Millions)
Barlow	8,613	1,770
Johnnies Industrial	8,077	1,660
Southern Life As.	8,043	1,653
Board Of Executors	7,832	1,609
Gold Fields Of Sa.	7,575	1,557
Fedsure Hdg.	7,518	1,545
Nampak	7,415	1,524
Samgro Inv.Hdg.	7,218	1,483
Cg Smith Foods	6,889	1,416
Driefontein Cons.	6,732	1,383
Anglo Amer.Coal	6,193	1,273
Tongaat-Hulett Group	6,042	1,242
Mutual & Federal In.	6,004	1,234
Pepkor	5,404	1,111
Woolworths Hdg.Ltd.	5,111	1,050
Premier Group	5,091	1,046
Liberty Investors	5,023	1,032
Safmarine & Rennies Hdg.	4,956	1,018
Edgars Stores	4,625	950
First Intl.Tst.	4,543	933
Nasionale Pers Bpk 'N'	4,473	919
Anglo Amer.Gold.Investg.	4,443	913
Engen	4,432	911
Coronation Hdg.N Ord.	4,378	900
Shoprite	4,270	877
Samancor	4,252	874
African Oxygen	4,023	827
African Life Asr.	4,011	824
Metro Cash & Carry	3,984	819
Sappi	3,900	801
Amal.Beverages Ind.	3,866	794
Plate Glass Ind. Inds.	3,865	794
Vaal Reefs Exp.&Mng.	3,829	787
Ingwe Coal	3,827	786
Wooltru 'N'	3,813	783
Iscor	3,688	758
Jci	3,377	694
Foschini	3,339	686
Mih Holdings	3,309	680
Jd Group	3,187	655

Regional Exchanges: None

Other Investment Information:

Department of Trade and Industry
Ministry of Finance, Trade and Industry

PO Box X84
240 Vermeulen Street
Pretoria
South Africa
Phone: (27-12) 26061
Telex: 320153

Ministry of Home Affairs and Environment Affairs
PO Box X152
Post Office Building
Pretoria
South Africa
Phone: (27-12) 2931911
Telex: 350013

Department of Immigration
Ministry of Justice
PO Box X276
Presidia Building
Pretoria
South Africa
Phone: (27-12) 3238581
Fax: (27-12) 211708

South African Reserve Bank
PO Box 427
Pretoria
South Africa
Phone: (27-12) 261611
Fax: (27-12) 3133197
Telex: 320455

SOUTH SEA BUBBLE

The foundation of Great Britain's trading empire, which spanned the globe until the 1950s, was the great industrial boom of the 18th century. It was a time of unprecedented national growth, when the rapid industrialization of the north of England combined with improvements in transportation to make Britain the world's dominant trading country. Britain's first real boom in demand for shares took place at this time: investors could choose to buy stock in the Bank of England, the successful and reputable East India Company, or the newly formed South Sea Company, which in the end became the source of a scheme known as the *South Sea Bubble*.

The South Sea Company was set up to establish a trading monopoly over half of the globe. The company announced plans to establish operations on the west coast of North America and Canada, as well as in the newly discovered countries of South America. The South Sea Company claimed that it would eventually enlarge its territories as far as the Far East. The company received a royal warrant in 1711, and King George I was named as its first governor. A prospectus was issued that highlighted the gold and silver resources of Latin America and the huge sums to be made from trading in the East. Rumors of beneficial agreements with Spain, at that time one of Britain's most dangerous trading competitors, began to circulate.

The South Sea Company enjoyed a successful share launch, boosted by holders of British government securities who had been forced to swap the debt instruments for shares in the new venture. Despite poor initial trading and a slide in the share price, the company was allowed to increase its share capital by £2 million when the government passed the South Sea Act in 1717. Three years later, the directors made an audacious attempt to pay off the UK's national debt—valued at £51 million at the time—by incorporating it into the company's share capital. The company promised to pay off the national debt within 25 years. Insiders at parliament, including the Chancellor John Aislabie, were rumored to be heavy buyers of South Sea stock. Despite the protestations of the Bank of England, the bill was passed in February 1720 and the shares jumped up to £300, providing huge paper profits to those who had bought into South Sea at the issue price of £100.

As new rumors of unimaginable wealth began to appear with increasing regularity, the shares marched forward on speculation and frenzy. A new issue of partly paid shares in April 1720 was oversubscribed, and the company even offered low interest rate loans to help investors buy the shares. A 10% dividend in 1720, paid despite the absence of any worthwhile profits from trading, only served to whip up investors' interest in the shares. Other businessmen, seeing the huge sums that flowed into South Sea, began to promote their own schemes, and a new breed of company, the "bubble company," was born.

Pressured by the South Sea directors, parliament passed the Bubble Act, which made it illegal for any company without a royal charter to issue shares. The act protected the South Sea Company by ensuring that cash subscriptions would continue to be sent in, propping up the company against any sudden withdrawal of funds. Many bubble companies were forced to close, leaving the investment-crazed public with nowhere to park their funds. South Sea, one of the few firms still open for business, benefited from the jump in demand for its shares, which reached £1,000 by June.

The collapse of South Sea was even swifter than its meteoric rise. Many investors did not believe that the shares would break the psychologically important £1,000 barrier, and sold to realize their gains. The legal maneuverings that had banned the other bubble companies created a climate of unease, which also adversely affected the South Sea Company. Panic gripped investors when they found no willing buyers for their shares, and within two days the price fell to £640. The South Sea Company tried to shore up its finances with a further flotation of shares, but investors, who were becoming skeptical about the company's fortunes, were slow to take up the offer. By mid-September the price slid to £400. Deliberately spread rumors of a bond issue and a huge dividend payout were counter-balanced by the scandal of directors secretly selling their shares in South Sea. Banks and deposit-holding goldsmiths shut their doors as investors scrambled to pull out of the stock. The Bank of England, which also suffered from a run on its own deposits, withdrew its support and the South Sea Company collapsed.

As the crash gathered pace, details of the behind-the-scenes corruption were covered up, or, to use the 18th-century word, *skreened*. The prime minister, Robert Walpole, worked tirelessly to prevent the public from knowing that phony projects had been created and that the king and his mistress had been heavily bribed.

Among those to suffer from the South Sea Bubble was Sir Isaac Newton, who allowed greed to get in the way of his financial judgment. The scientist and discoverer of gravity initially sold his shares in April 1720, doubling his money at a stroke. Caught up in the market mania, he bought more shares in the following weeks, only to see them become worthless in a matter of days. Newton lost more than £20,000, and could never mention the name of the South Sea Company without anger. The Canton of Berne, Switzerland, was more fortunate, selling shares at the peak, and making a £2 million profit on an initial investment of £200,000.

The mania created by the South Sea Company boom ended in riots in the City, the closure of many banks that had accepted the company's shares as security for loans, and the financial ruin of many investors. Instead of being enhanced by the South Sea Company's grandiose plans, Britain's standing in the inter-

The South Sea Bubble, 1720, engraving by J. Moore after William Hogarth. *(Mary Evans Picture Library)*

national trading community was ruined for many years.

See also MISSISSIPPI BUBBLE; PONZI SCHEME; TULIP-MANIA.

SPAIN, KINGDOM OF

Spain (Reino de Espana), one of Europe's largest countries, is located on the Iberian Peninsula at the southwestern corner of Europe. It is bordered on the northeast by France and on the west by Portugal.

Area: 194,898 square miles (504,783 square km)

Population: 39,188,000 (78.4% urban; 21.6% rural)

Form of Government: Constitutional monarchy, with two legislative houses: Senate—255 members; Congress of Deputies—350 members. Chief of state: King. Head of government: Prime Minister.

Official Language: Castilian Spanish

Capital: Madrid

Largest Cities: Madrid, 2,909,792; Barcelona, 1,623,542; Valencia, 752,909; Seville, 659,126; Zaragoza, 586,219

Economy:

Currency: Peseta (PTA)

National Budget: Revenue—PTA 13.2 trillion; expenditures—PTA 16.5 trillion (current transfers between public administrations: 53.2%; interest payments: 17.3%; wages: 16.0%)

Public Debt: PTA 34.4 trillion (US$257.0 billion)

Gross National Product: US$534.0 billion

Principal Products: Fruits and vegetables; livestock; wine; machinery

Foreign Trade (Imports): PTA 12.3 trillion (agricultural products: 11.6%; machinery: 11.0%; energy products: 9.4%, of which crude petroleum: 9.2%; transportation equipment: 8.1%; from France: 17.5%; Germany: 14.6%; Italy: 8.9%; United Kingdom: 7.8%; Japan: 3.6%)

Foreign Trade (Exports): PTA 9.8 trillion (transport equipment: 21.1%; agricultural products: 14.9%; machinery: 7.7%; to France: 20.1%; Germany: 14.2%; Italy: 9.2%; United Kingdom: 8.2%)

Stock Exchanges: 4
Madrid Stock Exchange (MSE; Bolsa de Madrid)
Plaza de Lealtad 1
28014 Madrid
Spain

Phone: (34-1) 589 2600
Fax: (34-1) 531 2290

Internet Address: www.bolsamadrid.es

Trading Hours: Monday–Friday, 11:00 to 5:00

Options and Futures: Monday–Friday, 10:45 to 5:15

Exchange Holidays:

1, 6 January	1 June
19 March	12 October
9, 10 April	25, 26 December
1 May	

Listed Companies: 388

Total Market Capitalization:

At 31 December 1997

Local Currency (Millions)	US Dollars (Millions)
33,688,960	221,034

Major Sectors: Banks and finance companies, utilities, food, construction, investment, communications, metal-working, oil-chemicals, other industries and services

Share Price Performance:

(% Change)
1992	-7
1993	61
1994	-5
1995	13
1996	39
1997	39

History:

1831 The MSE is founded by King Ferdinand VII.

1854 The Madrid Stock Exchange Daily Official List (Bulletin) begins.

1866 The Bank of Spain is established.

1868 The Spanish peseta is created following the Latin Monetary Union.

1893 The Madrid Stock Exchange is inaugurated by Queen Maria Cristina on 7 May. Trading begins on 8 May.

1898 Spain's loss of Cuba, Puerto Rico, and the Philippines results in 20% drop in share prices.

1900 The Madrid Stock Exchange booms due to funds from Cuba and the Philippines. Sixty-one companies trade on the Madrid Stock Exchange, up from 28 in 1874.

1914–18 (World War I) The Madrid Stock Exchange remains open and trading increases.

1929 NY stock crash has limited impact on the Madrid Stock Exchange.

1930 Negotiated stocks increase to 182.

1936 Political unrest and civil war cause the index to fall and the MSE to close in June.

1959 Stabilization plan leads to rapid growth of the Madrid Stock Exchange.

1973 Oil crisis has negative effect on trading.

1974 A new settlement system similar to "book-entry" system begins.

1975 The Madrid Stock Exchange is hit hard by political and economic factors, including the death of General Franco, the gradual transition to democracy, and a banking scandal.

1981 150th anniversary of the Madrid Stock Exchange.

1986 Spain joins the EEC, and the massive inflow of foreign investment triggers an economic boom. Membership of the European Monetary System (EMS) in 1988 makes Spain even more attractive for investment.

1988 Starting point of the reform:

• In July, the new Stock Market Act is published (Ley del Mercado de Valores).

• Toronto Computer Assisted Trading System (CATS) is selected for the continuous market.

1989 The continuous market for shares begins. It starts with seven blue chips and finishes the year with 51.

The following bodies are established:

• CNMV (Comision Nacional de Mercado de Valores), which is responsible for supervision, inspection, and registration. It reports to the Ministry of Finance.

• Sociedad de Bolsas, Interconnection Co. for the continuous market.

• Market members change from individual agents to Sociedades and Agencias (dealers and brokers).

• The governing body changes from Juntas Sindicales to Sociedad Rectora de la Bolsa de Valores.

1991 Creation of the electronic trading system for fixed-income securities, which starts in October with 31 bonds.

1992 SCL, the new clearing and settlement service and center for the new book-entry system, is formed.

1993 Bonds change from the trading floor to electronic market.

Classes of Securities: Shares, preference shares, fixed income, options, and futures

Indices:

IBEX 35 Index (the official index for the continuous market)

Madrid General Index (base = 100 31 December 1985)

MSE Total Index (base = 100 31 December 1985)

Calculation of the IBEX 35 Index:

The official index for the continuous market of the Spanish Stock Market is calculated, published, and distributed in real time by the Sociedad de Bolsa S.A.

IBEX 35 serves as underlying asset for trading, compensation, and settlement of futures and options contracts in stock options and futures market. It is weighted by capitalization and is composed of the 35 most liquid companies traded on the continuous market. The definition and supervision of the IBEX 35 is in the hands of a Committee of Experts made up of at least five independent representatives from the Spanish financial world. The index is revised on a semiannual basis. It is distributed by Sociedad de Bolsas through CATS terminals as well as the primary national and international networks.

The price per share for companies making up the index at any given time is based on the last transaction on the continuous market. For the calculation, the number of shares of each company making up the IBEX 35 Index is determined by the index manager at any given time.

Technical Adjustments: The IBEX 35 Index is not adjusted for either dividends or convertible bonds issues.

The number of shares is adjusted on the day the shares begin to trade without preferential subscription rights in the Stock Market Interconnection System. It is assumed that the increase is fully subscribed.

Calculation of the MSE General Index: Shares are selected on the basis of market capitalization, liquidity, and trading frequency at the end of each year. The Lasperyres formula, weighted by prices and year-end market capitalization, is used to calculate the General Index each year. The weighting of each share in its sector is calculated as the quotient of its market capitalization against total capitalization of these shares selected for the index.

Each sector's weighting in the General Index is calculated by dividing the MSE's total capitalization at year-end by the capitalization of each sector. In both cases foreign shares are excluded. No changes are made during the year. Daily corrections are made for factors that affect share prices but are not due to market forces, such as dividend payments and capital increases.

Supervisory Organizations:

Economy and Finance Ministry

Comision Nacional del Mercado de Valores (CNMV)
Sociedad de Bolsas (technical management of national computer system)
Madrid Stock Exchange

Depository: Clearing and Settlement Service, which acts as central registry for the book-entry system

Settlement Details:

Shares: Trade date + 5 days (T + 5)

Trading:

Continuous Market for Shares: Since its beginning in 1989, the Spanish continuous market has been managed by the Sociedad de Bolsas, in which each stock exchange (Madrid, Barcelona, Bilboa, and Valencia) has a 25% stake. Beginning 1995, there were 127 companies traded on this market, accounting for more than 96% of the total share trading volume of 1994.

The order-driven system gives an immediate disclosure of trading data and real time dissemination of information, with guaranteed transparency. It replaces the traditional open-outcry floor trading system and allows the four exchanges to drive orders through terminals connected to the central computer. Orders are executed on the basis of price and time of introduction. If a counterpart exists, the trade is matched, or if necessary it is held to be traded. Orders have a set period of time and are canceled automatically after one month.

Sub-Markets for Continuous Trading:

1. Principal Trading: This accounts for 99% of daily trading and is the submarket that sets the official prices. Positions can be adjusted between the hours of 10:30 and 11:00, and the market trades from 11:00 to 5:00.

2. Special Terms: The block trading market, in which minimum prices can be introduced and maintained. The market allows the counterpart to be chosen, provided the price is within the range of the best prices of the principal market. Orders can be introduced during the adjustment period, but cannot be executed until the market opens.

Listing Requirements:

1. Domestic Securities:
   Shares
   a. Minimum capital of PTA 200 million is required.
   b. In determining minimum capital, the part of the capital corresponding to shareholders who, directly or indirectly, have a stake of 25% or more will not be taken into account.
   c. Profits in the past two years or three non-consecutive years from a period of five years must have been sufficient to distribute a dividend of at least 6% of the paid-out capital, after paying taxes and making necessary allocations to reserves.
   d. There must be at least 100 shareholders, each with less than 25% of the capital.
   Second-Tier Market:
   a. Minimum capital of PTA 25 million is required.
   b. At least 20% of the capital to be circulated in the second-tier market must be entrusted to a market maker.

2. Foreign Shares:
   a. According to stock market law, foreign shares have the same freedom to list as domestic Spanish companies.
   b. Requirements must be fulfilled and approval given by the National Securities Market Commission.
   c. Requirements:
      1. The public offering in Spain of securities in circulation in the issuer's country of origin or the issue of securities on the Spanish market must entail at least PTA 200 million placed among at least 100 resident investors in Spain, none representing an individual holding equal to or more than 25% of the volume placed in the Spanish market. This must be previously verified by the National Securities Market Commission.
      2. The issuer must appoint a representative brokerage firm and deposit agents.
      3. Pricing must be in pesetas.
      4. Shares must be included in the book-entry system.
      5. A dealer or broker must mediate, acting on behalf of the buyer.
      6. Documentation must be legalized in the country of origin and be translated by a qualified translator.
      7. The amount paid for studies, procedures, and fees for the listing of a security is allowed a tax credit of 50%. The same applies to long-term investment in a stock.

Investor Taxation:

Withholding tax: Foreign and domestic investors suffer a 25% withholding tax on dividends, zero coupons, and bonds with private coupons, but public debt coupons, including Treasury bills, are exempt. This exemption does not apply to coupons of debt domiciled in tax paradises.

Direct taxes: There are double taxation treaties between Spain and many other countries. In almost all cases, the direct tax, except the small amount withheld and which is deductible in the country of origin, is the one applied where the investor resides. This situation applies to individuals, companies, and collective investment entities.

Countries with Double Taxation Agreements:

Austria
Belgium
Brazil
Bulgaria
Canada
China
Czech Republic
Denmark
Finland (exchange of notes)
France (additional agreement)
Germany
Hungary
Italy
Japan
Luxembourg
Morocco
Netherlands
Norway
Poland
Portugal
Rumania
Soviet Union (former)
Sweden
Switzerland
Tunisia
United Kingdom
United States

Countries with Double Taxation Treaties:

Andorra
Anguilla
Antigua and Barbuda
Aruba
Bahamas
Bahrain
Barbados
British Virgin Islands
Brunei
Cayman Islands
Cook Islands
Cyprus
Dominican Republic
Dutch Antilles
Falkland Islands
Fiji
Gibraltar
Granada
Guernsey and Jersey (channel islands)
Hong Kong
Isle of Man
Jamaica
Jordan
Lebanon
Liberia
Liechtenstein
Luxembourg
Maco
Malta
Mariana Island
Mauritius
Monaco
Montserrat
Nauru
Oman
Panama
Salomon Islands
San Marino
Seychelles
Singapore
St. Lucy
St. Vincent and the Grenadine Islands
Trinidad de Tobago
Turks and Caicos Islands
United Arab Emirates
Vanuatu
Virgin Islands

Limitations:

Treatment of Foreign Capital: There is freedom for foreign investment in Spain with the following exceptions:

a. Non-European Union investment in gambling, television, radio, air transport, and defense-related activities require the Cabinet's prior authorization.

b. Investments made by public authorities other than EU member states require the Cabinet's prior authorization, except for those that are liberalized under international agreements ratified by Spain.

c. Investments from non-EU countries that could harm the Spanish state's interests require the Cabinet's prior authorization when the amount is more than PTA 5,000 million. If the investment is less, the Economy Ministry may grant the authorization.

Registry: Although freedom of investment exists, the investments are monitored. Foreign investments in Spain and their settlements have to be declared to the Investment Registry at the Economy and Finance Ministry. The holders of the investment, the public notaries involved, and the broker/dealers or brokers acting in the subscription or transfer of securities, all have to make declarations.

Limits on Ownership: Prior administrative verification is required for direct investments when the foreign participation is more than 50% of the share capital of the Spanish company and the following conditions are in effect:

a. The investment is more than PTA 500 million.

b. The foreign participation in the capital plus reserves is more than PTA 500 million.

c. When any of the foreign investors is an individual or an entity resident in a country or territory is regarded as a tax paradise.

Repatriation of Capital and Transfer of Capital Gains: Foreign investment in accordance with the regulations will enjoy the right to transfer abroad the funds from the sale and legally obtained profits. Exchange controls have been liberalized, although certain limitations still exist.

Significant Holdings Information Rules: For information purposes, investors must inform the MSE and the National Securities Market Commission of purchases of shares in listed companies above a certain level. These packets are regarded as significant holdings when they amount to 5% of the capital or successive multiples of 5%. In accordance with article 53 of the Securities Market Law, owners of such holdings must inform the company concerned, the MSE, and the National Securities Market Commission.

Securities Lending: Securities lending is available.

Brokerage Firms:

AB Asesores Bursatiles Bolsa
Plaza de la Lealtad, 3-3^0
28014 Madrid
Spain
Phone: (34-1) 580 1100
Fax: (34-1) 531 2811

A.B.N. Amro
C/Serrano, 55-2^0
28006 Madrid
Spain

Phone: (34-1) 520 9150
Fax: (34-1) 520 9163

Banesto Bolsa
C/Mesena, 80
28033 Madrid
Spain
Phone: (34-1) 338 9030
Fax: (34-1) 338 9024

Beta Capital
C/Claudio Coello, 78 4^0
28001 Madrid
Spain
Phone: (34-1) 435 2741
Fax: (34-1) 435 7137

Central Hispano Bolsa
PZA, Canalejas, 11^0 E
28014 Madrid
Spain
Phone: (34-1) 558 1111
Fax: (34-1) 531 9778

Europea Popular Inversiones
C/Profesor Waksman, 5 1^{0}C
28036 Madrid
Spain
Phone: (34-1) 345 7755
Fax: (34-1) 345 7835

Gestemar Securities
C/Principe Vergara, 131 2^a
28002 Madrid
Spain
Phone: (34-1) 337 2250
Fax: (34-1) 337 2508

Indosuez Capital Securities Espana
C/Almagro, 34
28010 Madrid
Spain
Phone: (34-1) 319 6011
Fax: (34-1) 310 0364

J.P. Morgan
C/Jose Ortega y Gasset, 29
28006 Madrid
Spain
Phone: (34-1) 577 8507
Fax: (34-1) 577 8705

Company Name	Market Capitalization Local Currency (Millions)	Market Capitalization US Dollars (Millions)
Obrascon	123,960	813
Cortefiel	119,970	787
Elec.Reunidas	119,386	783
Bnc.Pastor	116,755	766
Electra De Viesgo	110,949	728
Cementos Portland	106,620	700
Bnc.Atlantico	105,927	695
Valderrivas	99,462	653
Carburos	98,241	645
Agf Union Fenix	96,442	633
Catalana Occidente	93,120	611
Prosegur	91,800	602
Uralita	91,162	598
Campofrio	91,155	598
Banco De Castilla	89,838	589
Viscofan	88,931	583
Bnc. Zaragozano	88,434	580
Asturiana	87,709	575
Bnc.De Valencia	87,281	573
Bp Oil Espana	81,916	537
Koipe	69,379	455
Aldeasa	69,216	454
Cofir Limited Data	66,830	438
Bnc.Herrero	65,407	429
Europistas	62,833	412
Bnc. Galicia	61,773	405
Corp.Banesto	61,432	403
Urbis Series 2	59,564	391
Azucarera Espana	58,895	386
Amper	57,421	377
Puleva Union	55,315	363
Agroman E Constrc.	54,212	356
Tubacex	54,210	356
Hisalba	53,835	353
Vidrala	50,040	328
Citroen Hispana	48,417	318
Finca.Y Minera	47,991	315
Bnc.Guipuzcoano	47,600	312
Abengoa	47,237	310
Empresa Nat. Celulosas	44,044	289
Energia Aragonesas	39,396	258
Uniland Cementera	39,096	257
Adolfo Dominguez	37,790	248
Bnc.De Vasconia	37,600	247
Azkoyen	34,357	225
Sarrio	34,274	225
Faes	31,066	204
Bnc.Cdt.Balear	30,835	202
Finanzauto	28,764	189

Company Name	Market Capitalization Local Currency (Millions)	Market Capitalization US Dollars (Millions)
Constrc.Lain	28,128	185
Prima	28,021	184
Bodegas Y Bebidas	26,187	172
Ercros	25,068	164
Tafisa	24,118	158
Bnc.De Vitoria	24,014	158
Iberpapel Gestion	23,904	157
Huarte	23,427	154
Miquel Y Costas	22,425	147
Dinamia Capital Privado S.C.R.	21,915	144
Baron De Ley	20,880	137
Midesa	20,528	135
Bnc.Alicante	20,183	132
Tudor	20,038	131
Duro Felguera	19,798	130
Caf	19,265	126
Algodonera	17,956	118
Filo	17,301	114
Unipapel	16,074	105
El Aguila	15,235	100
Banco Simeon	13,578	89
Zabalburu	12,799	84
Indo Intl.	11,687	77
Comp. Vinicola Del Nortede Espana	11,486	75
Grupo Anaya	11,284	74
Essa	11,190	73
Saltos Del Nansa	10,800	71

Regional Exchanges:

Barcelona Stock Exchange (BSE; Bolsa de Barcelona)

Paseo Isabel II,

08003 Barcelona

Spain

Phone: (34-3) 401 3555

Fax: (34-3) 401 3859

Internet Address: www.borsabcn.es

Trading Hours: 9:45 to 5:00

History: The roots of the Barcelona Stock Exchange can be traced to the Middle Ages when commodity exchanges grew out of the Commercial Revolution in Catalonia. The Ordinacions proclaimed by King James I in 1271 is the oldest and most complete text regulating the role of the mercantile mediator. The Casa Llotja de Mar, which today houses the Barcelona Exchange, was built in 1392.

The middle of the 19th century brought a period of industrial growth, the beginnings of the first Catalan corporations, and early trading in securities. The Barcelona market quickly became active with the role of mediators assumed by the Corredores Reales, stockbrokers who would later be known as Agentes de Cambio y Bolsa.

The Official Stock Exchange started in 1915, with its regulation and administration entrusted, until 29 July 1989, to the Colegio de Agentes de Cambio y Bolsa, the stockbrokers' association of Spain.

The Stock Market Act of 1988 placed the Barcelona Stock Exchange under the control of the Sociedad Rectora de la Bolsa de Valores de Barcelona, S.A., whose only shareholders are the stock exchange members—the companies, and agencies who operate in the stock exchange.

Indicators:

Barcelona Stock Exchange General Index (1 January 1986=100): A trade-weighted index, made up of the 65 most traded companies quoted on the Barcelona Stock Exchange.

The Annual Index (1 January 1994=100): A general index and nine sectorial indexes are computed daily in real time.

The Historical Index (1 January 1963=100): A general index and eight sectorial indexes are calculated daily. Returns Index FIBV (1 January 1985=1,000). A general index according to FIBV standards is calculated weekly. Spanish Stock Exchanges Index IBEX 35 (1 January 1990)

The IBEX 35: The official index for the continuous market of the Spanish Stock Exchanges. It is weighted by market value and is comprised of the 35 most traded companies on the continuous market of the four Spanish Stock Exchanges.

Classes of Securities: Public debt securities, fixed income, common shares, options, futures

Supervisory Organizations:

Economy and Finance Ministry
Comision Nacional del Mercado de Valores (CNMV)
Sociedad de Bolsas (technical management of national computer system)
Bolsa de Valores de Barcelona, S.A.

Depository: BSE Deposit Management Service (S.G.D.)

Settlement Details:

Shares:
Trade date + 5 days (T + 5) (expected to be changed to 3 days)
Physical and book-entry

Trading:

Interconnected Stock-Market System: Computer-assisted trading for stocks in the ISMS is transacted through the CATS system. The system gives equal access to all members of the Spanish Stock Exchanges in a single national market. More than 95% of the traded volume on Spanish Stock Markets is executed on this computerized system.

Floor Trading: Open-outcry trading in fixed income securities and shares is accomplished during the trading hours of 9:45 to 10:20 during the business day.

Stock Market System for Fixed Income and Public Debt: Electronic trading for fixed income and public debt securities is integrated in the stock market system.

Stock Market System Trading Hours:
9:00 to 2:00 (private fixed income)
9:00 to 1:00 (public debt)

Catalan Public Debt Market: Telephone trading, assisted by computer screens containing information regarding public debt issues by the Generalitat of Catalonia

Catalan Trading Hours: 9:00 to 2:00

Barcelona Stock Exchange Second Market for Small and Medium-Sized Corporations: This market was established to offer access to an organized stock market for those companies that, due to their size or other special characteristic, were not eligible for direct admission to the official market. All transactions are expected to be done on a cash basis, although credit-based operations are allowed with certain stocks.

Options and Futures Market: All Barcelona Stock Exchange members have access to the options and futures market. Products traded include options and futures on the IBEX 35 stock market index and options on shares in Telefonica, Endesa, Banco Bilbao Vizcaya, Repsol, and Iberdroia.

Market on Credit: Following the ministerial order made 25 March 1991, and in keeping with the rules established by the Barcelona Stock Exchange, once an investor has provided a cash guarantee of 50% of the total amount involved in the transaction, securities and stock exchange companies as well as other financial institutions may grant a credit in cash in the case of purchases, and a loan of share certificates in the case of sales, against payment of interest.

The credit may be granted for up to three and a half months. Trading on credit may only be done in blocks equal to a minimum of 500 stocks.

Investor Taxation:

Dividends and General Assembly Bonuses: 25% is retained at the source on the total amount. In addition to the amount retained, the taxpayer may deduct from his or her income tax quota 40% of the amount included in the taxable income (which includes the total amount of the dividends received multiplied by 1.4).

Interest: There is a 25% retention at the source on the total amount, which can be deducted from the income tax quota.

Capital Gains and Losses: With personal income tax, the capital gains and losses arising from the transfer of shares acquired more than two years in advance (except with investment companies) will be reduced by 11.11% for each year of permanent investment over two years, and will not be subject to tax after ten years.

The capital gains and losses produced are integrated and can be used to offset each other. If the balance is negative, the losses can be used to offset any capital gains produced during the following five years.

Capital gains resulting from onerous transmissions not exceeding PTA 500,000 in the course of the year are not subject to tax, unless they come from selling shares or unit trust participations.

Double Taxation: In the case of a double taxation treaty between Spain and the country of residence of the foreign investor, the tax system should abide by the rules established in the said treaty. The majority of treaties rule for a retention of 15% of dividends and 10% of interest payments. (See the section on Madrid above for details of taxation agreements and treaties.)

Limitations:

Rules for Foreign Investing: Foreign investment is regulated in Spain by Law 18/1992 and the Royal Decree 671/1992 on foreign investment in Spain. In addition to specific existing regulations of foreign investment in Spain, regulations on overseas economic transactions have to be taken into consideration. Full details of these regulations are contained in Royal Decree 1816/1991 and the Resolution of 7 January 1992.

A. Foreign investors are considered to be either individuals not resident in Spain or private legal entities that have their head offices overseas. The definition of foreign investment includes the creation of Spanish companies, taking participation stakes in Spanish companies, and the setting up of branches and establishments by non-residents.

B. Foreign investment in Spain is deregulated with the following exceptions:

• When investment planned by residents in non-community countries may have harmful consequences for the interests of the Spanish State

• Investments in gambling, television, radio, air transportation, and all activities directly related to national defense; the mining of minerals of strategic interest; and the operation of end services and carriers of telecommunications

• Foreign investment by governments and entities under the sovereignty of another country, unless they belong to EEC member states

• Investment made in Spain by private legal entities with their head office in non-EEC countries if subject to nationalization in their country of origin

C. Direct investment is considered to be:

• Participation in Spanish corporations when the investor can, by this act of participation or together with previously acquired shares, effectively influence the management or control the corporation

• The setting-up and extension of branches and establishments as well as the granting to these bodies of repayable loans

• The granting of loans with an average weighted life of over five years with the aim of establishing or maintaining long-lasting economic links

Direct investment does not require prior administrative verification except in cases where investment is in excess of PTA 500 million or comes from tax havens.

D. Portfolio investment is constituted by:

• The subscription and acquisition of Spanish company shares; the acquisition of securities such as subscription rights, debentures convertible into shares, or other similar securities which, by their nature, confer the right to become a shareholder, are comparable to the acquisition of shares

• The subscription and acquisition of negotiable securities representing debenture loans, issued by resident public or private individuals or legal entities, and financial instruments issued by residents

• Participation in Spanish collective investment funds. Portfolio investment is deregulated with no need for prior verification.

E. Foreign investment in Spain and its settlements must be declared to the Investment Registry of the Ministry of Economy and Finance, and the following are obliged to declare the investment and its clearing:

1. Principles of foreign investment
2. Public notaries who intervene in any of the transactions connected with the investment
3. The stock exchange companies or agencies or any other entity whose intervention is manda-

tory for the subscription or transfer of securities or who act as depositories for the securities acquired

Securities Lending: Securities lending is available.

Other Regional Exchanges:
Bilbao Stock Exchange (Bolsa de Bilbao)
Olabarri 1
48001 Bilbao (Vizcaya)
Spain
Phone: (34-4) 423 6818
Fax: (34-4) 424 4620
Internet Address: www.bolsabilbao.es

Valencia Stock Exchange (Bolsa de Valencia)
San Vincente 23
46002 Valencia
Spain
Phone: (34-6) 387 0100
Fax: (34-6) 387 0133

Other Investment Information:
National Securities Market Commission (CNMV)
Paseo de la Castellana, 19
28046 Madrid
Spain
Phone: (34-1) 585 1500

Derivatives Market
M.E.F.F. (Renta Fija)
Via Laietana, 58
08003 Barcelona
Spain
Phone: (34-3) 412 1128

M.E.F.F. (Renta Variable)
Pza. P. Ruiz Picasso, s/n Planta, 26
28020 Madrid
Spain
Phone: (34-1) 585 0800

Spanish Institute for Foreign Trade (ICEX)
Paseo de la Castellana, 14-16
28012 Madrid
Spain
Phone: (34-1) 431 1240
Fax: (34-1) 431 6128
Telex: 44838

General Directorate for External Investment
Ministry of Industry, Trade and Tourism
State Department of Trade
Paseo de la Castellana, 162
28046 Madrid
Spain

Phone: (34-1) 583 7400
Fax: (34-1) 458 1766
Telex: 42112

Banco de Espana (Bank of Spain)
Alcalá 50
28014 Madrid
Spain
Phone: (34-1) 446 9055
Fax: (34-1) 521 6356
Telex: 49461

SPECIAL CASH ACCOUNT

A brokerage account in which transactions are only settled on a cash basis is referred to as a *Special Cash Account*. There are no margin transactions and often no options transactions. Although often referred to as a cash account, the technical term is as listed above and such accounts can be designated to hold securities and cash or automatically have all cash and securities sent out.

Debits are not allowed in cash accounts, although the brokerage firm is not required to sell out or buy in if a debit is less than $500. Settlement in cash accounts is regular-way for such transactions. Current regular-way settlement in the United States is trade date plus three days (T + 3).

See also MARGIN ACCOUNT; REGULAR-WAY SETTLEMENT; SETTLE.

SPECIAL MEMORANDUM ACCOUNT (SMA; United States)

Formerly called the special miscellaneous account, the *Special Memorandum Account (SMA)* is an accounting record of those funds in an investor's account that are in excess of the margin requirement. It documents cash deposits, dividends paid into the account, interest received, and some of the proceeds from long sales of securities.

The SMA is a gauge as to how far an account is from a margin call, based on current status. Any cash the investor wishes to withdraw will be based on the "cash available" information in the margin account.

See also CASH ACCOUNT; MARGIN ACCOUNT; REGULATION G–X/REGULATION T.

SPECIAL OFFERING (United States/New York Stock Exchange)

A *Special Offering* is the process by which a member of the New York Stock Exchange (NYSE) can sell a large block of securities. A special offering is announced on the consolidated tape at a fixed price and is limited to NYSE members. All costs are paid by the seller.

Buyers of a special offering are member firms buying for either their own account or on behalf of investors. Special offerings need approval from the Securities and Exchange Commission.

See also BLOCK TRADE; MEMBER; SECONDARY DISTRIBUTION.

SPECIALIST (United States/New York Stock Exchange and Others)

A *Specialist* is a stock exchange member charged with maintaining a fair and orderly market in assigned securities.

Specialists and their specialist units (three or more specialists working together) perform many important functions, including the following:

- Quoting firm prices for bids and offer
- Executing orders for other stock exchange members
- Holding sufficient stock to guarantee liquidity
- Bringing together buyers and sellers in the market
- Buying, selling, and selling short for their own account

Buying, selling, or selling short is undertaken to moderate order imbalances. The specialist acts as a buyer when there are no buyers and as a seller when there are no sellers.

Specialists are not allowed to buy for their own accounts if they have an unexecuted order for the same security at the identical price in the specialist's book. Orders from off the exchange floor have priority.

The specialist is required to meet minimum capital requirements and must receive approval from the New York Stock Exchange. Persons performing functions similar to the specialist exist on many of the world's stock exchanges.

See also FAIR AND ORDERLY MARKET; LIMIT ORDER; SELLING SHORT; SPECIALIST'S BOOK.

SPECIALIST'S BOOK

A *Specialist's Book* is the record kept by Stock Exchange specialists of orders left with them. It might be a loose leaf notebook, a file of actual order tickets, or a computer list of orders waiting to be executed. As the orders are executed they are removed from the book and a notice of the order execution is sent to the place of origin.

See also EXECUTION; SPECIALIST; UNITED STATES/NEW YORK STOCK EXCHANGE (NYSE).

SPECJALISTA (Poland)

A *Specjalista* is a brokerage house appointed by an issuer of shares to establish the day's price for a given security and to act in such a way as to maximize turnover. This is best achieved by acting as a buyer when there are fewer buyers present and as seller if there are fewer sellers present.

A brokerage firm acting in this manner aggressively quotes prices with a relatively small spread between the bid and the offer in order to attract orders.

See also BROKERAGE HOUSE; MARKET MAKER; SPECIALIST.

SPECULATION

Speculation is an investment objective based on the strategy of obtaining a higher reward in return for the acceptance of greater risk.

The purchase of government Treasury securities is considered to offer a very high degree of safety, but if one buys and sells government securities, interest rate movements can cause considerable price changes. If an investor trades options or futures on government securities, the strategy becomes even more speculative.

Most speculative share prices are volatile, often showing wide swings between annual highs and lows. Speculative share price growth is usually based more on anticipation than on the actual earnings growth. These earnings can be volatile, often displaying losses in one year followed by increases of several hundred percent in the following years. Price/earnings ratios for such companies might seem high, but sometimes can be deceptively low when averaged over a period of time.

Some speculative situations are as follows:

- Market damage shares; those shares belonging to a company that has suffered a decline in price due to a severe market correction or bear market, but the fundamentals of the company itself have not been changed
- New companies, whose stocks have only traded for a short period, or who have been the subject of a recent initial public offering (IPO)
- New growth situations
- Turnarounds, in which a company has experienced business difficulties and expects to recover, or cyclical companies, such as those in the automotive and pulp industries. Sales, earnings, and stock prices tend to follow a cyclical pattern, and the strategy is to purchase stocks at the bottom of the cycle and to sell them as the cycle approaches its perceived peak. Other cyclically traded stocks include airlines, tire

companies, steel companies, chemical companies, and defense companies.

- Companies with high dividend yields

See also EARNINGS; GROWTH; OBJECTIVE; PSYCHOLOGY OF SPECULATION; RISK/REWARD RATIO; TOTAL RETURN.

SPECULATOR

A *Speculator* is an investor for whom speculation is a general investment objective.

See also SPECULATION.

SPECULAZIONE (Italy)

See SPECULATION.

SPEKULATION (Germany)

See SPECULATION.

SPIN OFF

A *Spin Off* is a share distribution made by a parent company to current shareholders of shares in a subsidiary. The action turns the subsidiary into an independent company, which has its own shares and listing on the market.

For example, if XYZ Corporation owns BBC Corporation, but wants to divest itself of BBC, it issues shares proportionately to the current shareholders of XYZ Corporation. BBC Corporation becomes a separate entity and trades independently of XYZ.

A spin off can also be performed as a leveraged buyout, in which management and venture capitalists seek to unlock the value hidden in the subsidiary.

See also ISSUE; LEVERAGED BUYOUT (LBO); SHAREHOLDER; SUBSIDIARY COMPANY.

SPLIT

A *Split* occurs when the number of outstanding shares is changed as a result of a vote approved by shareholders and authorized by the company's board of directors. There is no change in the market value of the company.

A split is also referred to as a split up or forward split when it increases the number of outstanding shares, and as a split down or reverse split when it decreases the number of outstanding shares. Shares are frequently split on a basis of 2 for 1, 3 for 1, or 4 for 1 when a company is increasing the number of shares. Reverse splits can frequently be seen as 1 for 10 or 1 for 5. If an investor owns 100 shares of XYZ Corporation with a current price of $50 and the company does a forward split of 2 for 1, the investor will own 200 shares with a current price of $25 per share.

A reverse achieves the opposite result. An investor owning 100 shares at $5 when a company does a 1 for 5 reverse split will own 20 shares worth $25 per share. All other financial figures are also adjusted to reflect the split. Other than the quantity and the price changing, the effect is neutral on a per share basis. The market value of the total shares also remains unchanged.

See also AUTHORIZED SHARES; CURRENT MARKET VALUE; MARKET PRICE; OUTSTANDING SHARES.

SPLIT DOWN

See SPLIT.

SPONSOR

A *Sponsor* is either the general partner for a limited partnership or the distributor (wholesaler, underwriter) of the shares of an investment company (mutual fund).

See also MUTUAL FUND; UNDERWRITING.

SPREAD

Spread is the difference between the bid and ask price of a security. For example, computer screens may display a quote for a share in XYZ Corporation as:

$49 3/4 – $50

The spread is 1/4 of a dollar (25 cents).

See also ASK PRICE; BID PRICE; CALL; COMBINATION; OPTION; PUT; STRADDLE.

SPREAD (Options)

Spread is an options strategy that combines a put and a call on the same underlying security. In this case the options will have different strike prices, different expiration dates, or a combination of both.

The following three variations are:

1. Spread with different strike prices
   - buy the November 50 XYZ Corporation calls
   - and sell the November 45 XYZ Corporation calls
2. Spread with different expiration dates
   - buy the April 50 XYZ Corporation calls
   - and sell the July 50 XYZ Corporation calls
3. Spread with different strike prices and different expiration dates
   - buy the August 60 XYZ Corporation puts
   - and sell the November 50 XYZ Corporation puts.

Investors wishing to transact a spread enter the order as a spread, rather than as two individual option orders.

See also CALL; OPTION; PUT; STRADDLE.

SQUEEZE

In the stock market, a *Squeeze* (often called a short squeeze) refers to a situation involving price increases while short interest is high. Investors who have sold short are squeezed by the higher prices and are often forced to close positions with a loss. If done intentionally, a short squeeze is illegal, because it is an example of price manipulation. However, if the upward market move is broad, affecting the shares of many companies, it can be difficult to determine whether manipulation is involved.

A profits squeeze affects businesses (invariably, those in highly competitive industries) which cannot pass on increased costs to their customers.

Credit squeezes and income squeezes are popular names for government controls on an economy which is perceived to be overheating.

See also INTEREST/INTEREST RATES; SELLING SHORT; SHORT INTEREST.

SRI LANKA, DEMOCRATIC REPUBLIC OF

Sri Lanka (Sri Lanka Prajathanthrika Samajavadi Janarajaya (Sinhala), Ilangai Jananayaka Socialisa Kudiarasu (Tamil)) is an island country in the Indian Ocean.

Area: 25,332 square miles (65,610 square km)

Population: 18,090,000 (22.0% urban; 78.0% rural)

Form of Government: Unitary multiparty republic, with one legislative house: Parliament—225 members. Head of state and government: President.

Official Languages: Sinhala; Tamil

Capitals: Colombo (administrative), and Sri Jayewardenepura Kotte (legislative)

Largest Cities: Colombo, 615,000; Dehiwala-Mount Lavinia, 196,000; Moratuwa, 170,000; Jaffna, 129,000; Sri Jayewardenepura Kotte, 109,000

Economy:

Currency: Sri Lankan Rupee (Rs)

National Budget: Revenue—Rs 98.5 billion; expenditures—Rs 134.7 billion (public debt service: 21.5%; transfer payments: 15.8%; defense: 11.4%; education: 10.4%; general public services: 8.1%; transport: 6.1%; health: 5.2%; agriculture: 5.1%)

Public Debt: US$5.9 billion

Gross National Product: US$10.6 billion

Principal Products: Rice; coconuts; sugarcane; cassava; tea; rubber; livestock; apparel; ceramics

Foreign Trade (Imports): Rs 181.5 billion (textile fibers: 24.5%; machinery and transport equipment: 23.0%; chemical products: 10.8%; vegetable products: 7.8%; mineral fuels: 7.7%; from Japan: 12.1%; India: 9.1%; Hong Kong: 8.3%; South Korea: 7.0%; Taiwan: 6.0%; Singapore: 5.5%)

Foreign Trade (Exports): Rs 137.3 billion (readymade apparel: 45.4%; tea: 15.9%; ceramic products: 12.3%; pearls: 8.0%; natural rubber: 4.8%; collectible art: 2.0%; to United States: 35.4%; Germany: 8.0%; United Kingdom: 7.2%; Belgium: 6.2%; Japan: 5.2%; the Netherlands: 3.8%; France: 3.0%)

Stock Exchanges: 1
Colombo Stock Exchange (CSE)
World Trade Center
Echelon Square
Colombo 1
Sri Lanka
Phone: (94-1) 44 6581
Fax: (94-1) 44 5279

Internet Address: www.lanka.net

Trading Hours: Monday–Friday, 9:00 to 12:30

Office Hours: Monday–Friday, 8:30 to 4:30

Exchange Holidays:

1 January	7, 9 July
4, 10 February	7 August
12 March	5 October
13, 14 April	3 November
1 May	25, 26 December
9 June	

Listed Companies: 239

Market Capitalization: US$2.9 billion

Major Sectors:
Banks, finance and insurance
Beverages, food and tobacco
Construction and engineering
Chemicals and pharmaceuticals
Footwear and textiles
Hotels and travels
Investment trusts
Land and property
Manufacturing
Motors
Stores and supplies
Services
Trading

History: First formed in 1896 to finance the Plantation Sector, the Sri Lanka exchange was known as the

Colombo Share Brokers' Association until 1984. Trading was enacted by a "call over" system.

The free market economic policies of 1978 and the emergence of the private sector as a dominant force in the economy caused a restructuring of the stock market. A trading floor that could meet increasing demand was launched on 2 July 1984.

Organized as a company limited by guarantee, the Colombo Share Market functions under the Colombo Stock Exchange. Policy is formed by a board of directors consisting of five brokers elected by members and four non-brokers who are appointed by the finance minister on the recommendation of the Securities and Exchange Commission of Sri Lanka. Among the appointments made by the board are the Rules and By-Laws Committee, the Disciplinary and Arbitration Committee, the Finance Committee, the Listings Committee, and the Research and Development Committee.

Membership is restricted to stockbrokers who are permitted to act as intermediaries or agents for buyers and sellers of securities. There are presently 15 member firms operating on the exchange floor.

Classes of Securities: Ordinary voting shares, preference shares

Indicators:

The All Shares Price Index (weighted and contains all quoted shares)

The Sensitive Price Index (January 1985 = 100) top 30 stocks weighted by market capitalization

Supervisory Organizations:

The Securities and Exchange Commission

The Ministry of Finance

The Federal Trade Commission

The Colombo Stock Exchange

Depository: Central Depository System (CDS)

Settlement Details:

Shares: A two tiered cycle; buyer to broker is on T + 5 and broker to seller and inter broker is T + 7.

Trading: Trading is controlled by four trading post managers and is achieved with the "open-outcry" system. Controls are imposed when prices move more than 10% in either direction.

Listing Requirements:

Ordinary Shares Listings of ordinary shares on the Colombo Stock Exchange must meet the following requirements:

1. The company must have paid up capital of at least Rs 5,000.000.

2. 25% of the ordinary share capital should be offered to the public and should be continuously held by the public.

3. Holdings of directors, their family members, and/or their nominees, parent, subsidiary or associate companies are not considered public holdings.

Other Securities

1. Ordinary shares are already quoted on the official list.

2. The value of such classes of security cannot exceed 50% of the issued ordinary capital of the company.

Investor Taxation:

1. There is no capital gains tax on the sale of shares.

2. There is no withholding tax on dividends. An imputation credit system of 50% is available, where shareholders are given credit for half the tax paid by the company. This is treated as an advance tax payment by shareholders.

3. Some companies approved by the board of investment may qualify for tax exemption on profits and dividends.

Limitations:

Ownership Limits: The vast majority of listed companies can have 100% foreign ownership. However, there are a number of exceptions:

• Banks falling under the purview of the Banking Act No. 30 of 1988 can have foreign ownership up to 49%

• BOI-approved companies that have an original agreed ration between national and non-national shareholdings

• Insurance companies incorporated in Sri Lanka

• Companies restricting non-national participation beyond a limit with a provision in the Articles of Association. A list is available from the stock exchange

• Companies in residential housing and mining must restrict non-national ownership to 40%

Procedure for Foreign Investment: Share investment and proceeds repatriation take place through a Share Investment External Rupee Account (SIERA) opened through commercial banks. Individuals, regional funds, and companies incorporated outside Sri Lanka are permitted to open a SIERA. Proceeds from investments repatriated after 5 June 1990 are not subject to exchange control regulations.

Regional Fund: A Regional Fund is floated abroad for purposes of investment in a specific region by persons or institutions who are not residents of Sri Lanka. The following requirements apply to regional funds:

1. Sufficient arrangements to transfer fund management technology to Sri Lanka
2. Experience in investments in world securities markets, particularly in Asia
3. Suitability of fund structure (within the fund itself), fund management, investment advice, custodianship, investment guidelines
4. Professionalism and experience of the fund manager

Country Funds: A Country Fund is floated abroad to make investments in a specific country for persons or institutions who are non-residents. The following requirements apply:

1. The developmental character of the fund, which includes investing in initial public offerings and unlisted shares
2. Sufficient arrangements to transfer fund management technology to Sri Lanka and a willingness to participate in the equity of a fund management company in Sri Lanka
3. Experience in investments in world securities markets, particularly in Asian regions
4. Suitability of fund structure (within the fund itself), fund management, investment advice, custodianship, investment guidelines, and arrangements for listing
5. Reasonableness of fee structure
6. Initial investment of US$25 to 30 million

Securities Lending: None

Brokerage Firms:
Colombo Brokers' Association
PO Box 101
59 Janadhipathi Mawatha
Colombo 1
Sri Lanka

Bartleet Mallory Stockbrokers (Pvt) Ltd.,
"Bartleet House" 65, Braybrook Place
Colombo 2
Sri Lanka
Phone: (94-1) 341772-9, 437227-8
Fax: (94-1) 434985

Forbes & Walker Stockbrokers (Pvt) Ltd.
"Seva Mandiraya" 46/38, Navam Mawatha
Colombo 2

Sri Lanka
Phone: (94-1) 446021-2, 446031, 446034
Fax: (94-1) 437149

John Keells Stockbrokers (Pvt) Ltd.
130, Glennie Street
Colombo 2
Sri Lanka
Phone: (94-1) 421101-15, 326003, 3268863

Allied Phillip Securities Ltd.
17-3/1, Standard Chartered Bank Building
Janadhipathi Mawatha
Colombo 1
Sri Lanka
Phone: (94-1) 433904, 433906, 433945

TA Securities Lanka (Pvt) Ltd.
81, Ward Place
Colombo 1
Sri Lanka
Phone: (94-1) 684363 (10 lines)
Fax: (94-1) 684368

Somerville Stock Brokers (Pvt) Ltd.
134, Vauxhall Street
Colombo 2
Sri Lanka
Phone: (94-1) 329201-5, 332827, 328144
Fax: (94-1) 430829

JB Securities (Pvt) Ltd.
150, St. Joseph Street
Colombo 14
Sri Lanka
Phone: (94-1) 449191-3, 447921, 447923

Lanka Securities (Pvt) Ltd.
189, Galle Road
Colombo 3
Sri Lanka
Phone: (94-1) 423800-6
Fax: (94-1) 337641

Asia Securities (Pvt) Ltd.
108, W.A.D. Ramanayake Mawatha
Colombo 2
Sri Lanka
Phone: (94-1) 423903-5, 336012-16

Commercial Stock Brokers (Pvt) Ltd.
61, Janadhipathi Mawatha
Colombo 1

Sri Lanka
Phone: (94-1) 332900-3
Fax: (94-1) 422835-36

De Silva & Abeywardena Stock Brokers (Pvt) Ltd.
1st Flr, State Bank of India Bldg.
Sir Baron Jayathilake Mawatha
Colombo 1
Sri Lanka
Phone: (94-1) 422826, 341573
Fax: (94-1) 422768

CDIC Sassoon Cumberbatch Stock Brokers (Pvt) Ltd.
65C, Dharmapala Mawatha
Colombo 7
Sri Lanka
Phone: (94-1) 439941-3, 445573, 445584
Fax: (94-1) 439945

CT Smith Stock Brokers (Pvt) Ltd.
1st Floor, Cargills Building
40, York Street
Colombo 1
Sri Lanka
Phone: (94-1) 433958, 433973, 433982
Fax: (94-1) 434038

HDF Securities (Pvt) Ltd.
27- 1/1, York Arcade Building
York Arcade Rd.
Colombo 1
Sri Lanka
Phone: (94-1) 331075-82
Fax: (94-1) 431848-9

NDBS Stock Brokers (Pvt) Ltd.
"Sayuru Sevana" 46/12, Navam Mawatha
Colombo 2
Sri Lanka
Phone: (94-1) 445601-3, 4455598, 445624
Fax: (94-1) 439251

Company Information:

The Best Performing Shares in the Country

Company Name	Share Price Change 1 January 1997 to 31 December 1997 (%)
Ceylon Tea	150
Ceylon Grain Elevators	134
Ceylon Brewery	88
Central Finance	73
Champs Development	68
Aitken Spence	56

Company Name	Share Price Change 1 January 1997 to 31 December 1997 (%)
Bairaha Farms	53
Ceylon Holiday Resorts	51
Ahungalla	50
Associated Electrical	49
Associated Motorways	48
Carsons Cumberbatch	47

The Largest Companies in the Country by Market Capitalization as of 31 December 1997

Company Name	Market Capitalization Local Currency (Millions)	Market Capitalization US Dollars (Millions)
Ceylon Tobacco	3,178	51
Asian Hotels Corp.	2,199	36
Ceylon Grain Elevators	1,965	32
Aitken Spence	1,812	29
Central Finance	1,236	20
Carsons Cumberbatch	1,070	17
Ceylon Tea	1,048	17
Brown & Co.	700	11

Regional Exchanges: None

Other Investment Information:

Greater Colombo Economic Commission
PO Box 1768
14 Sir Baron Jayatilleke Mawatha
Colombo 1
Sri Lanka
Phone: (94-1) 448880 or (94) 422447 or (94) 434403
Fax: (94-1) 447995
Telex: 21332 ECONCOM CE

Ministry of Trade and Commerce
21 Rakshana Mandlraya
Vauxhall Street
Colombo 2
Sri Lanka
Phone: (94-1) 421191
Telex: 21245

Central Bank of Sri Lanka
34-36 Janadhipathi Mawatha
PO Box 590
Colombo 1
Sri Lanka
Phone: (94-1) 421191
Fax: (94-1) 540353
Telex: 21176

Federal Chambers of Commerce and Industry
People's Bank Building
220 Deans Road
Colombo 1
Sri Lanka
Phone: (94-1) 699530

SRO

See SELF-REGULATING ORGANIZATION (SRO).

STABILIZATION (United States)

Supporting the price of a security to keep it from dropping below the bid is known as *Stabilization*.

Stabilization is illegal in the United States except as a means for supporting the price of a new registered offering. This form of stabilization is considered in the best interest of the public and is allowed under Securities and Exchange Commission Rule 10b-7. The price is pegged by the syndicate and the bids are identified as being stabilized.

Many investors are nervous about the market trading of new issues. Because of the uncertainty of acceptance, many will sell their purchases as soon as trading begins in the hope that the issue will be "hot" and experience a rapid increase in price. If the opening proves unexciting and the share price quickly drops, people will suffer losses and investors may lose faith. To give the company a fair chance for survival, syndicates are allowed to peg the price and give it support in the early trading. This action keeps confidence and helps to prevent the shares from being hammered down.

See also INITIAL PUBLIC OFFERING (IPO); SECURITIES AND EXCHANGE COMMISSION (SEC)/SEC RULE 10B-7; SYNDICATE.

STAMP DUTY (United Kingdom)

Stamp Duty is the name given to an extra fee, usually charged by a stock exchange, on the buying or selling of securities. The United Kingdom has Stamp Duty Reserve Tax (SDRT), which is imposed by the British government on equity security transactions. The SDRT is not charged if both the buyer and seller live outside the United Kingdom.

The purpose of the SDRT is to pay the cost of re-registration. Although many countries have some form of stamp duty, charged either to the seller or both participants to the trade, other countries have discontinued the practice.

See also individual countries' stock exchange profiles; COMMISSION; SALES CHARGE.

STANDARD & POOR'S (United States)

An investment information service owned by McGraw-Hill, Inc., *Standard & Poor's* provides a wide range of financial services, including bond ratings of corporate and municipal securities and the publication of several indices.

The most widely used indices are:

• Standard & Poor's Composite Index of 500 Stocks

• Standard & Poor's 400 Industrial Index

• Standard & Poor's 100 Index

The company also publishes a variety of statistical data, investment advisory reports, and other financial information. The most well-known titles include the following:

Bond Guide—A summary of information on corporate and municipal bond issues.

Earnings Forecaster—Earnings estimates for more than 1,600 companies.

New Issue Investor—Analysis of newly trading share issues.

Stock Guide—Financial data on listed and OTC common and preferred shares and mutual funds.

Analyst's Handbook—Data on the industry groups and companies of the 400 index.

Corporation Records—A collection of six volumes of information on more than 10,000 publicly traded companies.

Stock Reports—Analytical reports on both listed and OTC companies.

The Blue List—Information on municipal and corporate bonds.

Poor's Register—A national directory of companies and their officers.

Securities Dealers of North America—Information on brokers, dealers, and other financial organizations.

See also DOW JONES AVERAGES; STANDARD & POOR'S 500 INDEX (S&P 500).

STANDARD & POOR'S 500 INDEX (S&P 500; United States)

The *Standard & Poor's 500 Index (S&P 500)* is a list of stocks assembled as a broad market index for the U.S. stock market. The index is weighted to reflect the market value of the companies.

The price of each stock in the index is multiplied by the number of shares outstanding for that company, and that value for each of the S&P 500 issues is totaled. For the S&P 500 the total value of those stocks in the base period 1941–43 is given an index price of 10. The S&P 100 is calculated in a similar way with the index value of 100 set equal to the market value of the stocks on 2 January 1976. After the issues are totaled, the resulting value is divided by the base divisor to arrive at the index.

For the more technically inclined, the actual formula is:

$$\text{Index} = \frac{\Sigma P_1 Q_1}{\Sigma P_0 Q_0} \times \begin{array}{c} 100 \text{ (for S\&P 100)} \\ \text{(or)} \\ 10 \text{ (for S\&P 500)} \end{array}$$

where:

P_1 represents the current market price,

P_0 the market price in the base period,

Q_1 the number of shares outstanding, and

Q_0 the number of shares outstanding in the base period, subject to adjustment when necessary to offset changes in capitalization.

The majority of the stocks contained in the S&P 500 are those quoted on the New York Stock Exchange, but over-the-counter issues and a few American Exchange stocks are also included. Many institutional investors use the S&P 500 as a benchmark for evaluating their annual performance and for comparing the performance of different portfolios of stocks.

The Standard and Poor's 500 Index serves as a broad market indicator due to its diversification. However, the market weighted quality can cause the index to favor large capitalization companies, such as those listed in the Dow Jones Averages. Any comparison chart between the S&P 500 Index and the Dow Jones Industrial Average (DJIA) will demonstrate a definite tendency of each to track the other in major market moves.

Although the DJIA and the S&P 500 tend to mirror each other in directional movement, the larger 500 index tends to moderate the volatility. An institutional investor managing a large portfolio of stocks needs a larger index with which to compare performance results.

The S&P 500, like other market averages or indicators, is constantly changing. These changes often reflect changing economic conditions and a growth in relative importance of various industries. In addition, changes in the composition of the index are indicative of changes in the composition of the stock market.

The S&P 500 Index can provide useful information to the institutional and individual investor alike, both as a means for those who make use of it to monitor the considerable amount of money in motion and as an indicator of moves and trends in the stock market.

See also DOW JONES INDUSTRIAL AVERAGE (DJIA); INSTITUTIONAL INVESTOR.

STANDARD & POOR'S RATINGS

Standard & Poor's Ratings provides one of the three leading bond rating services available in the United States. Fitch and Moody's round out the triumvirate.

See also RATING.

Standard ⚡ Chartered

STANDARD CHARTERED PLC

Standard Chartered PLC is a holding company whose principal subsidiary is Standard Chartered Bank. The group engages in four main businesses: personal banking, corporate and institutional banking, investment banking, and Treasury operations. The personal banking division offers a range of products and services, including a variety of deposit and loan products, insurance, bank cards, and offshore banking products. The corporate and institutional division links the group's clients to its substantial international network. Investment banking activities include the Standard Chartered Equitor businesses, which provide custodial services in Asia to institutional and corporate clients, private banking and trust services to private clients, merchant banking, and stockbroking. The group's Treasury operations link 20 financial centers and provide to clients products such as foreign exchange, trade finance, and risk management.

Standard Chartered operates in more than 40 countries through a network of more than 600 offices. Although its headquarters are in London, Standard Chartered lacks a strong domestic network and depends largely on its vast overseas network, much of it in Third World countries. The group's business strategy is to grow its strong businesses in the Asia Pacific region (East and Southeast Asia), to enhance its historical position in the Middle East and South Asia, and to develop its African businesses in a focused way. At the end of 1995 the group had a market capitalization of US$10 billion. Standard Chartered stock is traded on the London Stock Exchange.

Standard Chartered is to a large extent a vestige of the British Empire. It emerged in 1969 when the Standard Bank, which did business throughout Africa, merged with the Chartered Bank, which operated branches throughout India, China, and Southeast Asia. Both banks had been in business for more than 100 years. Since both banks were products of the colonial era, with similar structures and experience, they made an excellent match. Also, the markets they served were geographically complementary. These factors made for a smooth transition.

Chronology of Significant Events

1850s To assist in the development of British colonial trade throughout Asia, the Chartered Bank of India, Australia, and China is incorporated in 1853 under a charter from Queen Victoria. The first overseas branches of the Chartered Bank open in Calcutta, Bombay, and Shanghai in 1858, followed by branches in Hong Kong and Singapore in 1859.

1862 The Standard Bank is incorporated in England under the name of the Standard Bank of British South Africa Limited.

1870–1900 The Chartered Bank opens branches in Indonesia (1863), the Philippines (1872), Malaysia (1875), Japan (1880), and Thailand (1894). The Standard Bank opens 15 branches in South Africa by 1864, absorbs 5 other banks by 1865, and opens a branch in Zimbabwe in 1892.

1901–14 Both the Chartered and the Standard open branches in Hamburg and New York during 1902–04. The Standard Bank opens branches in Malawi (1901), Zambia (1906), Kenya (1911), and Uganda (1912).

1957 The Chartered Bank acquires the Eastern Bank, a Middle Eastern bank with a branch network in India, Malaysia, Singapore, and the Persian Gulf area.

1960s The Standard Bank acquires the Bank of West Africa Limited, with more than 60 branches in Nigeria, nearly 30 in Ghana, and others in Sierra Leon and Gambia (1965). The Standard and the Chartered merge by incorporating as Standard and Chartered Banking Group Limited (1969).

1970s The group diversifies in 1973, acquiring Mocatta and Goldsmith, a trade broker in precious metals, and forming a partnership in a merchant bank. The group also acquires The Hodge Group, which later becomes Chartered Trust Limited (1973). In 1979 the group purchases the Union Bancorp of California.

1980s In the early and middle parts of the decade Standard and Chartered business fortunes reflect the bad economic times of many of the countries in which it operates. In 1985 the parent company of the group is renamed Standard Chartered PLC, and the bank becomes a clearing bank within the UK clearing system. The bank successfully rejects a takeover bid by Lloyds Bank. In 1988 the bank sells two of its assets in the United States—United Bank of Arizona and Union Banking Group. A new rights offering in 1988 also helps repair the bank's capital balance.

1990s The group decides to concentrate its assets on core banking activities, so it sells some peripheral assets such as Compass Credit Limited and Stan-Chart Business Credit. The group also sells a number of commercial and residential properties in Hong Kong, Singapore, and Malaysia. In 1992 Standard Chartered signs an agreement with First Interstate Group of California to combine some of First Interstate's international operations with its own. As part of this agreement, Standard Chartered absorbs 20 of First Interstate's offices, mainly in the Asia Pacific region and Latin America.

See also GREAT BRITAIN.

STANDARD INDUSTRIAL CLASSIFICATION (SIC)

The *Standard Industrial Classification (SIC)* is a numerical system for the uniform categorizing of a country's economic activities. The United Nations' Statistical Committee established the International Standard Industrial Classification (ISIC) in 1948 and revised it in 1958, 1968, and 1980. A number of other countries have set up their own SICs that follow the same principles and are compatible with the ISIC, while the European Community has established the Nomenclature des Activités établies dans les Communautés Européennes (NACE).

The SIC covers all economic activities, dividing them into major divisions, divisions, major groups, and groups. The major divisions are as follows:

- Agriculture, forestry, hunting, and fishing
- Mining and quarrying
- Manufacturing
- Electricity, gas, and water
- Construction
- Wholesale and retail trade, and catering and accommodation services
- Transport, storage, and communication
- Financing, insurance, real estate, and business services
- Community, social, and personal services
- Activities not adequately defined, unemployed persons, and persons not economically active

When it originally established the SIC, the United Nations recommended that member governments either adopt it as a national standard or rearrange their statistical data in accordance with it for the purpose of international compatibility.

The United States had its own SIC since the 1930s, which was used by federal, state, and local governments as well as businesses. In 1997 this SIC was replaced by a new North American Industrial Classification System (NAICS), which was devised jointly by the U.S. Census Bureau and U.S. Economic Classification Policy Committee, Statistics Canada, and the Instituto Nacional de Estadística of Mexico. The common industrial codes arrived at by the three countries were particularly important in the context of the North American Free Trade Agreement. The three planned to update the NAICS every five years.

NAICS has six-digit classification codes, as compared to the four-digit codes in the old SIC. This allows for a more finely grained categorization of economic activities. The first two digits, which are for the major economic sectors such as agriculture or manufacturing, are compatible with those of the ISIC. The third digit designates an economic subsector, such as crop production or apparel manufacturing. The fourth digit signifies an industry group, such as grain and oil seed farming or fiber, yarn, and thread mills. The fifth digit indicates the industry, such as wheat farming or broadwoven fabric mills. Each country may define additional digits for a more detailed description of industries, provided that the additional detail aggregates to a five-digit level of NAICS.

NAICS increased the number of industry categories from 1,005 to 1,160. It affected more than 3 million businesses and 55 million employees in the United States. A new feature of NAICS is its inclusion of emerging high-tech industries and service industries. The old SIC system focused on manufacturing and other traditional industries. As a result, unrelated services such as telemarketing, wig styling, and racetrack cleaning all had similar codes, leading to peculiar statistical aggregations. To take another example, the old SIC system had a four-digit code for eating places; there was therefore no distinction among beaneries, caterers, hamburger stands, restaurants, and tea rooms, a flaw that is corrected with NAICS.

To more accurately reflect the changes that have occurred in a modern economy, NAICS includes three new sectors in its industrial classification scheme. First, the information sector, which includes industries that create, distribute, or provide access to information, including satellite, cellular, and pager communications; on-line services; software and database publishing; motion pictures; video and sound recording; and radio, television, and cable broadcasting. Second, the health care and social assistance sector, comprising health maintenance organization medical centers, outpatient mental health care, and elderly continuing care. Third, the professional, scientific, and technical services sector, which includes legal, architectural, engineering, interior design, and advertising services.

Use of the new codes will facilitate the collection, analysis, and presentation of data by businesses, as well as the uniformity and comparability of statistical data for the government economic census. NAICS will be used in many different contexts. Attorneys will use it for filing required government documents, banks for evaluating loan applications, marketing agencies for assisting clients with targeted marketing, insurance companies for assessing employment risks, job services for assisting applicants seeking employment, city planning and zoning boards for monitoring compliance with zoning requirements, environmental protection agencies for monitoring emissions, power and utility companies for projecting usage needs, and publishers for soliciting advertisers based on classified readership.

See also ECONOMIC INDICATORS.

STATED PERCENTAGE ORDER

A *Stated Percentage Order* is an order to buy or sell a large quantity of listed shares, in which an instruction specifies a percentage of the total market volume in the security. The instruction keeps the order from creating an imbalance.

Many exchanges have established a variety of procedures designed to facilitate the purchase and sale of large quantities of shares. Every possible attempt is made to obtain a fair price for the block transaction, while maintaining price stability.

An investor wishing to sell a large block of shares is usually better off arranging a block trade rather than trying to sell the quantity a few thousand shares at a time. Selling in several transactions will continue to push the price lower and is likely to be much more expensive in terms of commissions.

See also BLOCK TRADE; MARKET PRICE; VOLUME.

STATED VALUE (United States)

The value assigned when shares are issued with no par value is referred to as the *Stated Value*. Such shares will appear on a balance sheet with the stated value and the total number of shares outstanding.

See also INITIAL PUBLIC OFFERING (IPO); PAR; SHARES.

STATEMENT

See ACCOUNT STATEMENT.

STATEMENT IN LIEU OF PROSPECTUS (United Kingdom)

A *Statement In Lieu of Prospectus* is the statement delivered to the Registrar of Companies by a company not needing to issue a full prospectus.

See also PROSPECTUS; RED HERRING.

STATUTORY DISQUALIFICATION (United States)

Statutory Disqualification is the inability to qualify as an associated person of a broker/dealer as a result of one of a number of offenses listed in the Securities and Exchange Act of 1934.

Both the New York Stock Exchange and the National Association of Securities Dealers have a similar prohibition to disqualify would-be members.

See also NATIONAL ASSOCIATION OF SECURITIES DEALERS (NASD); SECURITIES ACT OF 1933; SECURITIES AND EXCHANGE COMMISSION (SEC).

STATUTORY UNDERWRITER (United States)

If a stockbroker does not exhibit due diligence when selling shares owned by a control person, the broker and the firm could be penalized as a *Statutory Underwriter* in violation of the Securities and Exchange Act of 1933.

United States securities laws define an underwriter as any person or group purchasing securities from an issuer for purposes of reselling.

See also DUE DILIGENCE; SECURITIES ACT OF 1933; UNDERWRITING.

STATUTORY VOTING

Statutory Voting is the act of shareholders placing a single vote for or against each candidate proposed for the board of directors of a corporation. The votes cannot be summed together and cast for one candidate.

The purpose of voting in this manner is to make the board of directors elections dependent on more than 50% of share ownership. Most United States corporations have statutory voting procedures for electing their directors to the board.

See also DIRECTOR; VOTING SHARE.

STEENTH

A *Steenth* is verbal shorthand for 1/16 of a dollar for dollar denominated securities. As applied to bonds (which are quoted in points) it represents $62.50 per $1,000 face amount of bonds. So, for 10 bonds with a face amount of $1,000 per bond, a steenth would be $625.00.

Steenthing occurs when a floor broker undercuts another member with an order to buy a minimal amount, then when the order is executed claims parity for a larger amount with an order that had the time priority at the price. Steenthing usually happens in stock options contracts. Steenthing is considered unethical practice due to the exchange rules covering priority, parity, and precedence in verbal bids and offers.

See also ALL THE EIGHTS; OPTION; UNITED STATES/ NEW YORK STOCK EXCHANGE (NYSE).

STEINHARDT, MICHAEL

Michael Steinhardt (b. 1941) began his money managing career at the age of 13, when his father gave him 100 shares each of Penn Dixie Cement and Columbia Gas System for his bar mitzvah. Steinhardt began stopping at Merrill Lynch's Brooklyn office after school to check the price of stock, and used the shares his father gave him as capital to buy more stock. He didn't have much success in his first foray into the stock market. However, he was to become known as one of the best investors of the 20th century. By 1992 Steinhardt was the fifth highest paid money manager on New York's Wall Street. He started managing hedge funds in 1967, and one dollar invested with him then would have been worth more than $462 by 1995. The same dollar, if invested in an index fund such as Standard and Poor's 500, would have been worth only $17 by 1995.

Steinhardt has always been an overachiever. He graduated from high school at age 16 and zipped through the University of Pennsylvania's four-year Wharton School of Business program in three years. He worked for two years as a mutual funds research assistant at *Financial World* and then became a highly respected conglomerate analyst for Wall Street's Loeb Rhoades and Company. He became famous for recommending two companies whose stock doubled or tripled in a short period of time: Gulf and Western Industries and City Investing. In 1967, at age 26, Steinhardt started his own business, Steinhardt Fine and Berkowitz, with two equally young friends and $7.7 million in capital. Twenty years later, Steinhardt reflected on the youthful confidence that made him believe that he could "do a better job of managing money than people substantially my senior." He noted that for people growing up in the 1940s, 1950s, and 1960s, technological innovation was everywhere, and it was possible to estimate the long-term viability of companies. Times have changed—but then and now, Steinhardt could do a better job of managing money than most people.

Steinhardt's new business was managing hedge funds, private limited partnerships that are exempt from the Securities and Exchange Commission's mutual fund regulations if they stay within a maximum of 99 investors and have a minimum stake of $1 million. Steinhardt's basic philosophy, like that of many money managers, was to find companies whose stock is over- or undervalued. If the stock was overvalued, he sold it short—selling borrowed shares in the expectation that he could replace them later by buying them at a lower price, and keeping the difference as profit. Selling stock short is risky, and in 1987 Steinhardt noted that he had probably sold more stock short than anybody alive. While Steinhardt is adept at selling short—he followed his firm's assets minute by minute on six computers and seven phones, and often held stock for only a few hours before selling it—he did not attribute his success to this strategy. In fact, he went long in the market more often than short, buying undervalued stock and holding it until its value rose days or years later.

By going long and short in the market simultaneously, Steinhardt usually could make money in both bull and bear markets, if he went long and short on the right stocks. He usually did. In 1974 the S&P 500 dropped 41.4%, but Steinhardt's funds gained 34%. In 1981 he began buying five-year U.S. Treasury bonds (with borrowed money), sustaining paper losses at first but eventually gaining 97% at a time when the S&P 500 increased only 2.8%. Occasionally, however, Steinhardt lost big. In late 1992 he ventured into the international bond and currency markets, new arenas for him. At first he did well, but in the first quarter of 1994, he lost $1 billion—and that was just the beginning of a very bad year. Overall, his funds were down 27% in 1994. It was a new experience for a money manager whose funds generally outperformed the market by 24%.

Even after his 1994 losing streak, Steinhardt's funds were still worth approximately $2.5 billion, and in 1995 his funds rose 23%. However, in 1995, amid much skepticism, the 54-year-old Steinhardt decided to retire and pursue his dream of bringing secular Jewish values into mainstream American society. Wall Street pundits predicted he would be back, and he did return in 1996, managing an account containing $25 million of his own money. He increased the $25 million by 44% in 1996, and almost doubled his account in early 1997. Nevertheless, Steinhardt claimed he would not return to managing hedge funds.

See also HEDGE; SELLING SHORT.

STELLAGE (France)

Bourse transactions that are effectively put options are referred to as *Stellage*. The buyer of an option pays out a premium for the right to sell shares at a set price until a specific date.

See also MARCHÉ À OPTIONS; MARCHÉ À PRIMES.

STILLHALTER (Germany)

See OPTION WRITER.

STIMMBERECHTIGTE AKTIE (Germany)

See VOTING SHARE.

STOCK

Originating in the United States, *Stock* is the general term for equity shares. Stock can also refer to a company's current inventory of products.

Important to note: In the United Kingdom, *Stock* also refers to some debt securities.

See also COMMON STOCK; EQUITY.

STOCK AHEAD (United States)

Stock Ahead refers to an explanation offered by a stock exchange trading floor for a limit order not being filled, in spite of the fact that the price traded at, but not through, an investor's limit price.

This usually occurs when other orders at the same limit were entered earlier and, as a result, had time priority. As it was not possible to fill the investor's limit order, the message "stock ahead" is then sent back to the originating broker.

See also LIMIT ORDER; MARKET ORDER; STOP ORDER.

STOCK BUYBACK

See BUYBACK/STOCK BUYBACK.

STOCK CERTIFICATE

A *Stock Certificate* is the physical document that shows proportional ownership—identified by the number of shares owned—in a corporation. The face of the certificate indicates the number of shares, and displays the date, the CUSIP number (depending on the certificate's age), and the name of the owner of the stock. The reverse side of a stock certificate contains a form for selling or depositing the shares.

The Committee on Uniform Securities Identification Procedures (CUSIP) assigns a number to each individual company's stock, preferred stock, or bond issue. The nine-digit CUSIP number (appearing on certificates and often used with book-entries) allows quick identification of the security and enables the broker to rapidly access all important details regarding a specific issue. Such access can be important if a company's security is undergoing reorganization.

At the request of the U.S. Securities and Exchange Commission, the CUSIP International Numbering System (CINS) is being developed. This international system will help to unify settlement procedures.

Great care should be taken to retain stock certificates in a safe place. Although certificates can be replaced, the process is often time consuming. Lost, stolen, or destroyed certificates are just some of the reasons many stock exchanges are adopting paperless trading systems, in which all securities are bought, sold, and transferred electronically.

See also CERTIFICATE.

STOCK DIVIDEND

Stock Dividend refers to company shares that are distributed to current shareholders of record in proportion to their current holdings prior to the ex-date.

Stock dividends need the approval of the board of directors, but not the shareholders, unless the number of authorized shares is increased. The distributed shares can be additional shares of the company or can be shares in a company spin off.

If the shares are identical to those currently held by investors, the dividend is considered a stock split and is usually stated as 2 for 1, 3 for 1, or 5 for 1.

For example: If a shareholder owns 200 shares of XYZ Corporation and the company declares a 2 for 1 stock dividend, the shareholder will then own 400 shares. All financial data, including the share price, is adjusted to reflect the new number of shares. (Essentially, if the dividend is 2 for 1, all the price and data numbers are divided by 2). If the price of XYZ Corporation is $50 and a stock dividend of 2 for 1 is declared, the price will become $25.

Companies prefer distributing stock dividends. The distributions increase trading liquidity and lower the price per share, making shares available to a larger base of investors. Publicity surrounding stock dividends and splits is also positive and occurs at no cost to the company.

See also DIVIDEND; EX-DATE; SHAREHOLDERS' EQUITY.

STOCK EXCHANGE

A *Stock Exchange* is a place where securities are bought and sold for investors. Basic securities of shares (stocks), bonds (debentures), options, derivatives, and other securities are traded on exchanges throughout the world. Many exchanges are conducted on a trading floor, where members meet to perform securities transactions.

Although continuous auction is the usual means by which trading is accomplished, most exchanges have sophisticated computer systems that automatically match buy and sell orders for immediate execution. Some stock exchanges, such as Australia's ASX, are fully computerized and order driven. Every buyer has a seller, and price changes are determined by the transactions entered.

Amsterdam has the oldest stock exchange, organized in 1602. However, trading was conducted as early as 1586. At that time, securities—as designated by Amsterdam city authorities—were traded in St. Olof's Church. A large bell started and ended trading sessions from 11:00 A.M. to 12:00 noon and from 6:30 P.M. to 7:30 P.M. The ringing of a bell began and ended each trading session at St. Olof's; this tradition continues on today's Amsterdam Stock Exchange, as well as on the exchanges of other countries.

As with its 500-year-old predecessor, the New York Stock Exchange (NYSE) also begins and ends with the ringing of a bell. It is the largest stock exchange in the world. By the end of 1994, the NYSE traded more than 3,000 share issues from more than 2,500 different companies listed. As many as 73.4 billion shares were traded in 1994, making it a record year for trading volume on the NYSE. Additionally, record numbers of other securities were traded.

Stock exchanges continue to grow and increase in number. As of 1996, more than 100 countries had some form of stock exchange. Many have several regional exchanges that are centrally organized, all operating under the same procedures, rules, and regulations. Some exchanges such as Switzerland's Swiss Exchange (SWX) are consolidating into one main stock exchange with two regional arms. Other countries operate under the same industry regulations but have different listing requirements on each separate exchange.

As the popularity of computer enabled international trading continues to grow, the number of corporate issues will grow, as will the stock exchanges on which they trade.

See also individual countries' stock exchange profiles.

STOCK EXCHANGE AUTOMATED QUOTATION (SEAQ; United Kingdom)

The *Stock Exchange Automated Quotation (SEAQ)* is a securities dealing system that allows market makers

The New York Stock Exchange. *(Spectrum Photo)*

on the London Stock Exchange to report their quotes and volumes to system users.

See also UNITED KINGDOM/TRADING.

STOCK EXCHANGE AUTOMATED TRADING SYSTEM (SEATS; Australia)

The *Stock Exchange Automated Trading System (SEATS)* is a national network enabling stockbrokers to enter transactions through a computer. This system is responsible for transporting trading from the trading floor to the broker offices.

SEATS displays all information regarding the day's trading, including exactly how many buyers and sellers there are for a company's shares, thereby allowing brokers to easily obtain and assess market information and make a responsive decision. As a result, in many cases brokers can make bids or offers and confirm sales while the investor remains on the telephone.

All shares listed on the Australian Stock Exchange are traded by SEATS. As a result, six exchanges—including those of Adelaide, Brisbane, Hobart, Melbourne, Perth, and Sydney—have merged into one order-driven national stock exchange.

See also AUSTRALIA/HISTORY; BOOK-ENTRY; CLEARING HOUSE ELECTRONIC SUBREGISTER SYSTEM (CHESS); TRADING; UNITED KINGDOM/TRADING.

STOCK EXCHANGE DAILY OFFICIAL LIST (SEDOL; United Kingdom)

The *Stock Exchange Daily Official List (SEDOL)* is a publication of the UK Stock Exchanges that provides daily share trading information. This publication includes details of when shares were last quoted, whether or not a share is ex-dividend, daily trading prices, and closing price quotes.

SEDOL is the numbering system used to identify the securities traded on London's International Stock Exchange. It is similar to CUSIP, which is used in the United States.

The seven-digit numbers which make up each SEDOL code are used for both security identification and for purposes of trading, clearing, and settling transactions on the stock exchange.

See also CLEAR; COMMITTEE ON UNIFORM SECURITIES IDENTIFICATION PROCEDURES (CUSIP).

STOCK EXCHANGE INDICES

See individual countries' stock exchange profiles.

STOCK EXCHANGE OF SINGAPORE INDEX (SESI; Singapore)

The *Stock Exchange of Singapore Index (SESI)* is a comprehensive index for the Singapore exchange.

Six weighted indices cover the following sectors of the market:

1. Industrial and commercial
2. Finance
3. Hotels
4. Property
5. Mining
6. Plantations

Other indices include the Straits Times Industrial Index, Kuala Lumpur Stock Exchange Index, Business Times Index, Fraser's Singapore Industrial Index, Kay Hian Geometric Indexes, and Overseas Chinese Banking Corporation Index.

See also SINGAPORE/STOCK EXCHANGE OF SINGAPORE, LTD. (SES).

STOCK EXCHANGE POOL OF NOMINEES (SEPON; United Kingdom)

The *Stock Exchange Pool of Nominees (SEPON)* acts as a depository for settlement in the computerized Transfer Accounting, Lodgement for Investors and Stock Management (TALISMAN) equity settlement system on the International Stock Exchange in London.

See also TALISMAN BOUGHT TRANSFER (TBT); TALISMAN SOLD TRANSFER (TST); TRANSFER ACCOUNTING LODGEMENT FOR INVESTORS AND STOCK MANAGEMENT (TALISMAN); UNITED KINGDOM/DEPOSITORY.

STOCK INDEX FUTURES

Stock Index Futures settle in cash and combine the features of commodity futures trading with securities trading of share indices. They can be traded by themselves or used as a portfolio hedge against either a long or short position.

In the United States, stock index futures are traded on several indexes, including the following:

- New York Stock Exchange Composite Index
- Standard & Poor's 500 Index
- Value Line Composite Index

Option contracts settle in delivery of the underlying stock index futures contracts.

See also FUTURES CONTRACT; STOCK INDEX OPTION.

STOCK INDEX OPTION (United States and Others)

Stock Index Options are call and put options traded on the movement of a stock market index, such as the

Standard & Poor's 100 Index, whose options trade under the symbol OEX. Index options trade just like equity options, but they are settled for cash instead of shares.

An exercise notice can be tendered on any business day and results in the delivery of cash on the following business day. The cash delivered is equal to the difference between the closing value of the index on exercise date and the exercise price of the option. Exercise price intervals are 5 points on either side of the current index level. New strike prices are introduced when the index trades on or through an existing option exercise price.

S&P100 Index options have monthly expirations with a total of four months traded at the same time. As one month expires another is added. They are traded on the Chicago Board of Trade.

See also CALL; OPTION; PUT; STOCK INDEX FUTURES.

STOCK LIST

A *Stock List* is a general reference made to the complete listing of companies trading on a stock exchange. Listed companies must meet certain financial, size, and reporting requirements to trade on an exchange. Individual stock exchanges set their own requirements for a company to qualify. Even if a company meets the qualifications, final approval will not be automatically granted by the exchange.

Listings are normally managed by a listing committee that has the responsibility of monitoring compliance with exchange regulations. The committee approves or disapproves listings and has the authority to remove securities from the list.

Companies not qualified for listing on an exchange can often be traded using a Second List with less stringent requirements. They can also trade over the counter (OTC) on an unlisted market.

Listing details for many of the world's stock exchanges are summarized in this reference book. Full and current listing requirements should be obtained from the individual exchanges.

See also individual countries' stock exchange profiles/ listing requirements; OVER THE COUNTER (OTC).

STOCK MARKET

A *Stock Market* (or stock exchange) is the place where securities (such as shares, debt instruments, derivatives, and other financial instruments) are bought and sold for investors.

At present, more than 100 countries around the world make use of stock exchanges. As computeriza- tion increases—replacing floor trading with electronic trading systems that are more easily established and less costly to maintain—the number of stock exchanges is likely to increase. The world is moving toward a capital-driven economic system.

See also individual countries' stock exchange profiles; STOCK EXCHANGE.

STOCK MARKET EFFICIENCY THEORY

From an everyday, operational viewpoint, the *Stock Market Efficiency Theory* presents the following picture of the stock market: a large group of well-trained, fully informed analysts and brokers operate in the U.S. stock market, following all the major stocks. For example, if each broker concentrates on approximately two dozen stocks, then an average of approximately 1,000 brokers concentrate on each stock. As new information about a stock evolves, these 1,000 brokers all assimilate the information and take the appropriate action virtually simultaneously. The price of the stock adjusts accordingly and reflects the new information. Therefore at any given time the prices of the major stocks reflect all the information about them, and the price of every security always equals its value.

A key element of stock market efficiency theory is the efficient market hypothesis (EMH), which has been a tenet of modern financial analysis for decades. The EMH has been applied to such diverse financial markets as the U.S. stock market and the foreign exchange market, which consists of a network of brokers and banks based in London, New York, Tokyo, Toronto, and other financial centers. In the context of the EMH, *efficient* refers exclusively to the manner in which the market processes information. A market is defined as efficient if and only if prices in the market always reflect fully all the available information.

As the wording of the definition implies, the set of information is variable, and this leads to three forms of the EMH.

1. *Weak-form efficiency:* A market is weakly efficient if current prices fully reflect all historical market data. Included in historical market data are the complete histories of market prices, volumes traded, the amount of short positions outstanding, and other similar market data. If the market is weakly efficient, technical analysis cannot succeed because stock prices already reflect any information such analysis might yield. Technical analysts make predictions by analyzing historical market data.

2. *Semistrong-form efficiency:* A market has semistrong efficiency if current prices fully reflect all public information. Included in public information are all market data, all government publications, and all information disseminated by the media, including news reports and investigative reports issuing from newspapers, television, and radio. If the market is semistrong efficient, fundamental analysis cannot succeed. Fundamental analysts make predictions by analyzing public information and applying the straightforward model:

stock value = expected earnings × justified p/e ratio

The justified p/e ratio is the correct ratio of the price of a share of stock to its earnings. The p/e ratio reflects the stock's prospective growth in earnings and the level of risk associated with future earnings.

3. *Strong-form efficiency:* A market is strongly efficient if current prices fully reflect all information, whether publicly available or privately held. Included in private information is any information known to government officials or company insiders but not yet announced to the public. For example, a government official may know about a new regulation that will be imposed on an industry that may affect its profitability, or a few company employees may know about a new process or discovery that will greatly increase company revenues and profits. If the market is strongly efficient, even insider trading cannot succeed because stock prices already reflect any private information that an insider might have.

Many studies have been conducted to determine whether stock markets, as well as other capital markets, are efficient, and if so, in which form. Testing for weak-form efficiency consists of testing whether past data on stock prices can be used to predict future prices. Semistrong-form efficiency is tested by investigating the speed with which securities prices reflect new information. Testing for strong-form efficiency requires comparing the performance of insiders, such as officers of corporations or managers of large financial funds, to the performance of the market.

Most tests of market efficiency conclude that any well-developed capital market exhibits weak-form efficiency to a high degree and semistrong-form efficiency to a considerable degree, but clearly strong-form efficiency is absent. Two recent tests have been conducted on the Australian stock market and the Polish stock market. A study in 1993 concluded that the Australian stock market is efficient in the semistrong form and, therefore, in the weak form also, since the latter is a prerequisite for the former. But three earlier (1981–83) studies of the Australian stock market concluded that semistrong-form efficiency did not exist. The 1995 test of the Polish stock market also concluded that semistrong efficiency was absent.

However, the Polish market, which opened in 1990 after being closed for more than 50 years because of World War II and subsequent communist rule, is an emerging market, and poses special problems for researchers. For example, tests of weak-form efficiency could not be conducted because no significant historical data is available. As they emerge, the Polish market and other central European markets will provide researchers with fresh data for further tests of market efficiency.

There is a close relationship between the EMH and the capital asset pricing model (CAPM). The CAPM is a mathematical model used to analyze the risk and the required rates of return of stocks held in portfolios. Together the EMH and the CAPM are the basis for modern portfolio theory. Recent studies have discovered a large number of so-called market anomalies that should not exist in an efficient market for which the CAPM is valid. These anomalies cast doubt on the validity of the CAPM or the semistrong form of the EMH or both. The following are a few examples of these anomalies:

- *Monday effect:* Stocks tend to perform poorly on Mondays.
- *Price reversal effect:* If one stock in a group performs much differently on a day than other stocks in that group, its performance will usually catch up with the group by the next day.
- *Earnings surprise effect:* Stocks of companies whose reported earnings are better or worse than expected perform better or worse than the market.
- *Price/earnings effect:* Stocks with low p/e ratios tend to outperform the market.

Supporters of the EMH feel the CAPM is at fault for the observed anomalies and needs revision. However, adherents of the fractal market hypothesis and chaos theory fault both the EMH and the CAPM.

See also RANDOM WALK THEORY.

STOCK POWER

Also called a stock/bond power, a *Stock Power* is a completed form—virtually a duplicate of the form found on the reverse side of paper certificates—that grants to the bearer limited power of attorney. It must be signed, witnessed, and guaranteed by a member firm or commercial bank (a signature guarantee is not always required) before it is accepted by a transfer agent. The certificates identified on the stock power will be registered in the name of the new owner.

For security reasons, many investors prefer to mail certificates in one envelope and a stock power in another. Endorsing a certificate is somewhat similar to endorsing a bank check, although there is a further level of identification required for protection.

See also BOOK-ENTRY; CERTIFICATE; POWER OF ATTORNEY.

STOCK RECORD

A *Stock Record* is a transcript of the movements of all securities within a brokerage firm.

Keeping track of securities is an important but costly function for all brokerage firms and is undertaken as part of their due diligence for the accounts of their clients. The Stock Record Department is that part of a brokerage firm that monitors all movements of securities within the firm. As part of a brokerage firm's internal controls, the department identifies securities and owners by name. Daily audits on the securities are regularly performed, as well.

If a discrepancy is discovered, it is referred to as a *stock record break* and must be reconciled as soon as possible. If there is a position without a corresponding credit or a credit without a position, it is important to clear the matter up as quickly as possible due to the effect it may have on a firm's net capital requirements.

As the world stock exchanges move from paper securities to fully computerized book-entry, it is expected that record keeping will become easier to manage and less costly to both the brokerage firm and the investor.

See also BOOK-ENTRY; CERTIFICATE; SHARE.

STOCK TICKER

See TICKER/STOCK TICKER.

STOCK WATCHER (United States/New York Stock Exchange)

Stock Watcher is an NYSE computer system designed to locate situations that involve potential violations of insider trading regulations.

See also STOCKWATCH AUTOMATED TRACKING SYSTEM (SWAT).

STOCKBROKER

Stockbroker is both title and job description for one who works for a brokerage firm and assists investors when placing buy and sell orders for securities through a stock exchange or over-the-counter.

Other titles and terms for the position include:
- Account Executive
- Broker
- Customer's Man
- Financial Planner
- Intermediary
- Registered Representative

Generally, stockbrokers are licensed by professional organizations, government agencies, stock exchanges, or provincial authorities. Applicants are usually required to have an affiliation with a recognized brokerage firm. Licenses are granted only after successful completion of standardized examinations that cover both procedure and regulations. Novice brokers are expected to know these areas intimately when placing securities transactions. Error or failure to comply with regulations can result in the loss of a broker's license.

Setting up new accounts and generating income are the primary responsibilities for all brokers.

Broker compensation is based upon both a portion of commissions generated and the sales charges attached to various securities. For the compensation received, the broker is expected to place orders in a responsible and diligent manner, provide a variety of services to investors, and perform those duties specified by and for the brokerage firm.

See also COMMISSION; NATIONAL ASSOCIATION OF SECURITIES DEALERS (NASD); SALES CHARGE; SECURITIES AND EXCHANGE COMMISSION (SEC).

STOCKHOLDER

Stockholder refers to any person or group of persons owning shares of a company.

See also SHAREHOLDER.

STOCKHOLDER OF RECORD

Stockholder of Record is the person or group registered on a company's books as owner of the company's stock or preferred stock as of a specific date. The stockholder of record will often appear with the announcement of a dividend or a split approved by the board of directors.

The term *stockholder of record* is also used when announcing a vote to be put to the common stockholders. *Note*: Preferred stock is usually non-voting.

See also DIVIDEND; EX-DATE; SPLIT.

STOCKJOBBER (United Kingdom)
See MARKET MAKER.

STOCKWATCH AUTOMATED TRACKING SYSTEM (SWAT; United States)
The *Stockwatch Automated Tracking System (SWAT)* is an automated computer system designed to locate and identify any unusual trading activity in the over-the counter market.

Effectively, SWAT screens for potential violations of insider trading regulations. The system is programmed to set performance parameters in both price and volume. Any activity exceeding the parameters is investigated. Once suspicious trades are identified they can be examined more closely to see if insider trading might have been involved.

See also INSIDER; INSIDER DEALING/INSIDER TRADING; STOCK WATCHER; UNITED STATES/NEW YORK STOCK EXCHANGE (NYSE).

STOP LIMIT ORDER
A stop order sent to the exchange with a limit specifying a minimum acceptable price is called a *Stop Limit Order*.

Like a stop order, a stop limit order can be used to buy or sell. However, a regular stop order stipulates that the order be filled when the market price trades on or through the stop, at which time the stop order becomes a market order. With a stop limit order, when the market price trades on or through the stop, the stop order becomes a limit order. This prevents completion of the transaction unless the order can be executed at the limit price or better.

For example, if XYZ Corporation is trading at $50 per share, an investor might check the recent trading pattern and decide to place a sell stop at $43, with a limit of $42. If the price trades on or under the $43 level, the stop order triggers the limit order and the shares will be sold if the trade can be executed at $42 per share or higher.

As it is possible for a sharp decline to cause the price to fall through a sell stop and keep dropping, the disadvantage to putting a limit on a stop order is that the order cannot be executed until the share price recovers to the limit.

See also LIMIT ORDER; MARKET ORDER; STOCK AHEAD; STOP ORDER.

STOP ORDER
A *Stop Order* is an order placed through a stock exchange giving instructions to buy or sell a security when the market price trades at or through the designated stop price. Also called *stop loss orders*, the use of such orders is hotly debated as a defensive strategy.

Although some advise placing a stop order 10% away from the current market price, others believe that the strategy will doom a portfolio to a consistent 10% loss. Still others recommend placing stop orders at least two points ($2 in the United States) away from the current price, a strategy dating back more than 100 years.

There is little doubt that many investors place stop orders with the hope that the order is never filled, since it will mean a loss is realized. However, some investors want protection from a severe price decline.

Although some brokerage firms have tried stop orders for over-the-counter trading on an experimental limited basis, they are usually only available for exchange-traded securities.

See also BUY STOP ORDER; LIMIT ORDER; MARKET ORDER.

STOPPED STOCK
Stopped Stock is a price guarantee made by an exchange specialist or other member to a broker who has sent in an investor's order to buy or sell securities. It allows the stock exchange member to seek a better price without the concern of having the market move against the order.

For example: An investor places a market order with a broker to buy 100 shares with the current market price at $50. The broker wires the order to the stock exchange. If a specialist at the stock exchange believes he might fill the order at better than $50, he sends a message back to the broker saying "you are stopped at $50 for 100 shares of XYZ Corporation." If a better price can be obtained, the order is executed at the better price. If a better price is not available, the order is executed at the $50 price.

See also LIMIT ORDER; MARKET ORDER; STOP ORDER.

STRADDLE
A *Straddle* is an options strategy that involves the combination of a put and a call on the same underlying security.

The holder of a straddle is granted the right to require the maker to purchase and/or sell a security at an agreed price at some time in the future. The price agreed upon when purchasing the options is almost invariably the market price of the underlying share at the time the straddle is executed. The straddle is often employed when the market value of the security shows volatility. Profitability is dependent on the price moving and staying either above or below the agreed price by the date of expiration.

The following are several types of straddle:

Long Straddle: To buy an at-the-money call and put option on the same security

Short Straddle: To write (sell) an at-the-money call and put option on the same security

Strangle: When the options bought or sold are out of money

Long Straddle

Buy one November 70 call on XYZ Corporation at the money, for a premium of $3 1/2. Buy one November 70 put on XYZ Corporation at the money, for a premium of $1 1/2. Total cost = $500.

The risk is that the price remains between $65 and $75 until expiration. The maximum loss potential at expiration is the cost of the two options (i.e., $500). The reward if the price rises is unlimited. The position will become profitable above $75, before any commission costs are taken into account. If the price falls the maximum gain is $65 per share, taking out the $500 for premiums and commissions.

The long straddle can be a profitable strategy in a volatile stock market, where prices experience strong up and down movements.

Short Straddle

Write (sell) one November 70 call on XYZ Corporation at the money, for a premium of $3 1/2. Write (sell) one November 70 put on XYZ Corporation at the money, for a premium of $1 1/2. The total premium income is $500, less any commisions.

(Short) Strangle

The (short) strangle is essentially the same as the short straddle, except the strike prices are away from the money and would not necessarily be identical. Because of the strangle having different strike prices away from the market, the investor can add some cushion against loss potential.

It is important for the investor to be well aware of any risk when selling options. The maximum risk of every transaction should be fully understood.

See also CALL; OPTION; PUT; STRANGLE.

STRANGLE

A *Strangle* is similar to a straddle, with the exception that the options are away from the money instead of at the money. The two kinds of strangles are:

Long Strangle: Buy an out-of-the-money call and put option on the same underlying security.

Short Strangle: Sell an out-of-the-money call and put option on the same underlying security.

See also STRADDLE.

STREET, THE (United States)

The Street can specifically refer to the Wall Street financial district or it can refer to the industry of investing and finance in general. For example, one might hear from a colleague, "The word on the street is: XYZ Corporation is being taken over by ABC Corporation."

The daily financial publication *The Wall Street Journal* has a feature called "Heard on the Street," detailing small pieces of information about happenings in the world of investment and finance.

See also WALL STREET; *WALL STREET; WALL STREET JOURNAL, THE*.

STREET NAME

Street Name refers to a brokerage account containing investor-owned securities.

Brokerage firms require margined securities to be kept in street name, as the securities are collateral against the money borrowed. Since brokerage firms no longer store the actual paper, all certificates deposited with a brokerage firm in the United States are sent to the transfer agent for destruction, and the securities are placed in an account with the details on computer. Essentially, the securities are converted to book-entry.

When securities are kept at the brokerage firm in street name they can be borrowed against in a margin account, sold, or shipped out again in certificate form as long as certificates are still being used for investments.

See also BOOK-ENTRY; CERTIFICATE; GOOD DELIVERY.

STRIKE PRICE

In reference to options, *Strike Price* is the price paid or received if an option is exercised. For example, if an investor holds the March 30 calls on XYZ Corporation, the option can be exercised any time before expiration. The investor can purchase the shares for $30 per share, even if the price of XYZ may have risen to $50 per share.

If the investor owns the March 30 puts and exercises the option before expiration, the investor sells the shares at $30 per share no matter what the current price.

See also CLASS OF OPTIONS; OPTION.

SUBJECT

When referring to a price quotation, *Subject* means subject to change. In other words, the price quoted is not firm. This situation might occur when an investor or dealer is looking for a price estimate on a block trade.

The term *subject* can also be used when obtaining a price on a thinly traded security, meaning the firm quote will be given when an order is placed.

See also FIRM PRICE; LIMIT ORDER; MARKET ORDER; STOP ORDER.

SUBSCRIBED CAPITAL

Subscribed Capital is proceeds from shareholders that form the issued capital of a company after an initial public offering. It is the money received by the company for selling shares to the public.

See also INITIAL PUBLIC OFFERING (IPO); PRIVATE PLACEMENT; PUBLICLY HELD AND TRADED COMPANY.

SUBSCRIPTION PRIVILEGE

See PREEMPTIVE RIGHTS.

SUBSCRIPTION RIGHTS

Subscription Rights are granted to the holders of a company's stock. They allow the holders to buy a new issue of shares in that company at a price which is invariably below the prevailing market price. The owners will be able to buy a certain number of shares which is in proportion to their current holdings.

The beneficiaries of subscription rights are not obliged to take up the offer of new shares. In many stock exchanges it is now possible to buy and sell subscription rights without buying the underlying shares.

In recent years, the growth of shareholder awareness across Europe has resulted in an increased emphasis on subscription rights. In 1993 a group of German shareholders began legal proceedings against Deutsche Bank, which sought to raise capital from foreign investors without offering subscription rights to existing owners of the stock. The Swiss investment company BZ Vision took the Union Bank of Switzerland to court after the bank decided to issue shares to foreign institutional investors without offering them to existing Swiss shareholders.

See also SHARES; STOCK DIVIDEND; SUBSCRIPTION WARRANT.

SUBSCRIPTION WARRANT

Attached to a bond or a preferred stock, a *Subscription Warrant* gives the holder the right, but not the obligation, to subscribe to further shares and purchase those shares at a certain price for a designated time.

Although similar to rights, warrants are usually valid for a longer time period and allow for a subscription price higher than the current market price of the stock. Immediate conversion would be an unprofitable move for the investor.

Warrants do not carry voting rights and do not pay dividends.

See also SHARE; STOCK DIVIDEND; SUBSCRIPTION RIGHTS.

SUBSIDIARY COMPANY

A *Subsidiary Company* refers to any company operating as nearly a separate entity, but remains more than 50% owned and controlled by another company. For example, Pillsbury is a subsidiary of Grand Metropolitan PLC.

When a company owns several subsidiary companies, it is referred to as a parent company and defined as a conglomerate.

See also CONGLOMERATE.

SUITABILITY/SUITABILITY RULE

Self-Regulatory Organizations, such as the National Association of Securities Dealers in the United States, have set certain *Suitability* rules for brokers and brokerage firms when they make investment recommendations to investors.

The general concept is that any recommended investment should be appropriate based on the investor's investment objectives, financial capability, and the quality and quantity of other investments currently owned. An investor who has a portfolio of utility companies and is drawing a pension might not be the ideal investor for speculative new issues. It would be inappropriate for a broker to make such a recommendation, unless it is something the investor demands as an unsolicited order.

Many brokerage firms now require their stockbrokers to profile each customer's financial condition and investment objectives. The profiles must be updated as necessary and used by the broker for making appropriate investment recommendations.

See also NATIONAL ASSOCIATION OF SECURITIES DEALERS (NASD); OBJECTIVE; PROFILE A CUSTOMER; RULE 405.

SUMITOMO BANK LIMITED

In 1997 *Sumitomo Bank Limited* was one of the world's five largest banks, with assets of $485.6 billion and approximately 16,000 employees. In mid-1995 it had 363 offices in Japan as well as 73 offices in 33 foreign countries. It is one of the *keiretsu* (conglomerate) banks in Japan today and one of a group of Sumitomo enterprises that stretch over a broad range of industries.

The Sumitomo group originated in the early 17th century as a medicine and book shop near Kyoto. The Sumitomo family discovered a new method of copper smelting and built its early fortune in the copper trade. In the late 1800s Sumitomo bought some state enterprises as part of a modernization campaign. It established a banking division, the Sumitomo Bank, in 1895. In 1912 the bank was incorporated.

Sumitomo Bank expanded during World War I, opening branch offices in San Francisco, Shanghai, Bombay, New York, and London, and establishing an affiliate, the Sumitomo Bank of Hawaii. After the war, the bank followed the expansion of the Japanese empire, setting up operations in Korea, Taiwan, and China.

In 1925 Sumitomo Bank, which was prevented by regulations from doing trust banking itself, established the Sumitomo Trust Company. In 1950 Sumitomo Trust was authorized to deal in foreign exchange, and the following year it started trusteeships for investment trusts. Also during the 1950s, it introduced loan trusts and began pension trust management. Sumitomo Trust set up foreign offices in New York, London, and Los Angeles. By the late 1980s it was the second largest trust and banking company in Japan.

With the militarization of the Japanese economy in the 1930s, Sumitomo Bank played a role in financing the country's preparations for war. As a result of this military buildup, and World War II itself, the Sumitomo group became larger and more concentrated. In 1948, Sumitomo Bank was reorganized as the Bank of Osaka in accordance with the laws of the occupation authority. By 1952, however, a relaxation of these laws made it possible for Sumitomo Bank to resume its old name.

In the 1950s the bank grew rapidly and became able to finance larger industrial enterprises. Sumitomo Bank's financing of Toyo Kogyo (the manufacturer of Mazda trucks) at a critical stage in that company's development was particularly noteworthy, as was its restructuring of the ailing Ataka and Company, a major trading firm. These successes brought Sumitomo Bank more customers.

By the late 1970s the bank had greater deposits than any other Japanese bank. In 1979 it was divided into four divisions: business, sales, international, and planning and administration. In 1986, as part of a strategic plan to develop its operations in the Tokyo area, Sumitomo Bank merged with Heiwa Sogo Bank, which had approximately 100 branches.

In the 1980s Sumitomo put more emphasis on international expansion, purchasing the Swiss Banca de Gottardo in 1984 and becoming the leading Japanese bank in foreign markets. In 1986 Sumitomo announced its purchase of an interest in the New York–based investment bank Goldman Sachs. This purchase was viewed with alarm among American banks. While it was ruled legal by the U.S. Federal Reserve, it was decided that Sumitomo could not increase its interest, exercise management rights, or expand to other countries.

During the 1980s Sumitomo established branches in Seoul, Madrid, the Cayman Islands, Milan, Barcelona, Los Angeles, Frankfurt, and Paris. In 1990 Sumitomo created Sumitomo Bank Securities Inc. to enter the U.S. securities markets. It also created three other U.S. subsidiaries. Sumitomo Bank of California, chartered in 1952, had become the state's sixth largest bank by the mid-1990s, with 48 branch offices. In early 1996 Sumitomo purchased the commercial loan portfolio and 15 offices of Daiwa Bank Limited in the United States.

In 1990 Ichiro Isoda, who had been chairman of Sumitomo Bank for 17 years, was forced to resign in connection with a scandal in which a branch manager had been arrested for allegedly encouraging customers to make huge illegal loans to stock market speculators.

Like many Japanese banks, Sumitomo suffered serious losses on nonperforming loans in the 1990s, which by early 1995 had amounted to $15.8 billion. In early 1995 the bank announced it would write off $8 billion in bad loans and take a $3.2 billion loss for the previous fiscal year. This loss was the biggest by any Japanese company ever and the first by a major Japanese bank since World War II. On the Japanese stock market, however, this way of handling the problem was welcomed, since it was seen as a signal that major Japanese banks, which were holding an estimated $133 billion in bad loans, would begin to deal with the situation realistically. The share prices of these banks, including Sumitomo's, jumped by more than 15%.

SUMITOMO COPPER SCANDAL

The *Sumitomo Copper Scandal* that hit Sumitomo Corporation in 1996 created panic in the normally staid world of the London Metal Exchange (LME). The secretive realm of the metal traders was unexpectedly thrust into the limelight as details of illicit trading worth billions of dollars were released to the authorities.

Sumitomo's most senior trader was Yasuo Hamanaka, who was nicknamed "Mr. Five Percent" because his trading team was widely believed to control 5% of the world's copper trade. Sumitomo, which was the world's biggest copper trader, announced that it had discovered large unreported losses in its nonferrous metals division. These losses, caused by unauthorized trading, had built up over a decade of trading and were initially thought to be valued at $1.8 billion. This figure was soon revised upward to $2.6 billion.

Hamanaka had had many close brushes with the regulators in the United Kingdom but had always managed to stay one step ahead of the authorities. In 1991 Hamanaka was scrutinized by the Securities and Investments Board (SIB) after he was accused by the LME of attempting to validate false invoices for copper trades. In the following years the LME informed the SIB that Sumitomo's broker, Winchester Commodities, was trading huge quantities of copper on Sumitomo's behalf, even though it was not a full member of the LME.

The Serious Fraud Office (SFO) examined computer records at Winchester's headquarters. The firm had been set up by two brokers with many years of experience in the copper market. Charlie Vincent was known as "Copperfingers" because of the vast number of trades he conducted. His partner, Ashley Levett, is the owner of the prestigious Richmond Rugby Union Club. They were both paid bonuses of £10 million by Winchester in 1994 when Hamanaka put many trades through their brokerage. Both men had left the company and moved to Monte Carlo before Hamanaka's unauthorized trades became public and have vehemently denied any connection with the frauds.

Sumitomo first became aware of Hamanaka's illegal trading while taking part in an investigation of copper price movements at the insistence of the Securities and Investments Board in the United Kingdom and the Commodities Futures Trading Commission in the United States. As attention started to focus on his trades, Hamanaka confessed to concealing a number of unauthorized transactions by deliberately falsifying books and records.

In October 1996 Hamanaka was arrested by the Japanese police and was charged with the forging of documents. His home in Kawasaki, Japan, was raided and several boxes of papers pertaining to copper trading were removed.

The Sumitomo scandal cast a pall over the Japanese trading community. The financial probity of the country, which had been taken for granted for so long, had been hit by scandals at Daiwa and Nomura and was tainted by the involvement of the Yakuza in the collapse of the *jusen* banks. The sheer size of the Hamanaka scandal, and the apparent ease with which he carried it out, has forced financial regulators in Japan to improve their standards. And, perhaps even more significant, the series of scandals has rocked the confidence of the Japanese people in their business and political leaders. The mood of national disgrace, a powerful feeling in a country where the opinion of others is so vital, may be more important in the long term than any financial loss suffered by the banking and trading communities.

See also DAIWA BANK SCANDAL; NOMURA SECURITIES COMPANY LIMITED.

SUPER BOWL THEORY

The *Super Bowl Theory*, based on the end-of-season competition for American football, states that the stock market will rise if the game is won by a team from the former National Football League (NFL), but will fall back if a team from the former American Football League (AFL) takes the honors. The present National Football League is composed of teams from each former league. The game, which traditionally takes place in the second week of January, has been a statistically accurate portent of the direction of the stock market in the following 12 months. Since the first Super Bowl was played in 1967, the Super Bowl Theory has shown an 86% accuracy rate.

However, before basing any investment decisions on the strength of this superstition, a number of caveats should be considered. First, the theory is statistically biased: there are more teams from the old NFL than the old AFL, and the market rises in more years than it falls. Consequently, there are likely to be more years in which the NFL wins and the stock market rises. Second, there is, of course, no causal link between the two phenomena and anyone who says otherwise is almost certainly trying to sell some of their shares.

Buying stocks in the years in which the NFL triumphs is as valid a strategy as not buying stocks in a year that has three Friday the 13ths, traditionally the unluckiest day in the calendar. During the last 40 years, six years have had triple Friday the 13ths: three of these years saw recession and two experienced milder economic downturn. The last year with three Friday the 13ths was 1987, the year of the great Black Monday crash.

See also CHAOS THEORY; PENTAPHILIA.

SUPER DESIGNATED ORDER TURNAROUND (SUPER DOT; United States/New York Stock Exchange)

Super Designated Order Turnaround (SUPER DOT) is a system used by the NYSE to automatically process orders and trading reports. It can execute orders up to 30,099 shares if orders are received before the opening of the stock market.

As it is the world's largest stock exchange and executes trades for hundreds of millions of shares in each daily session, the NYSE rquires powerful computerized systems to complete most of its transactions. Due to the sophistication of the DOT systems and their ability to handle large volumes of transactions, some of the pressure on members involved in making the transactions is removed. Eventually all stock exchange trading will become computerized and people will handle only special trades or problem orders.

See also AUCTION MARKET.

SUPPLY-SIDERS

Supply-Siders refers to the school of economic thought that hypothesizes that a significant cut in government taxation and size will lead to the stimulation of a country's economy.

This theory is based on the belief that governments can grow to such a size that the cost of taxation will stifle the public's ability to purchase goods and services, and purports that supply-side economics would reverse the process by reducing the size of the government, public spending, and the accompanying level of taxation.

The theory further purports that such a move would put more money into the hands of the public, resulting in an increase in disposable income. Increased income in the hands of the general population would lead to an increase in the purchase of goods and services, thereby stimulating the economy.

See also KEYNES, JOHN MAYNARD; MACROECONOMICS.

SUPPORT/SUPPORT LEVEL

A technical analysis term originating as part of the Dow Theory, *Support* describes a market index level or security price level at which buyers are entering the market in greater numbers than sellers. The increased buying causes price or index declines to halt and reverse direction. Support is considered strong if the same turning point is repeated. Prices continue to rise until resistance—the level at which sellers are entering the market in greater numbers than buyers— is encountered. Heavy selling causes a price or index rise to halt and change direction.

The area between support and resistance establishes a current trading range for a security or market index. It is also believed by many that resistance becomes support when it is penetrated and the level reaches new highs.

See also DOW THEORY; MARKET PRICE; RESISTANCE LEVEL; TECHNICAL ANALYSIS.

SUSPENDED TRADING

Occasionally, *Suspended Trading* is the result of share price movement that exceeds the maximum percentage allowed.

On the New York Stock Exchange, trading will be suspended if the spread between the bid and ask for shares with a price under $100 reaches the lower end of 10%, or $3. For shares with a market price above $100, the parameters are the lower end of 10%, or $5.

An order imbalance can cause a temporary trading halt in a share pending an important announcement. The reason for the halt or suspension is to allow time to correct the order imbalance, arrive at a new market price, and allow the trading public access to the information contained in the announcement.

Allowing the information to be disseminated to the investing public is an essential part of creating a fair and orderly market.

See also ASK PRICE; BID PRICE; LAST TRADE.

SUSPENSION OF LISTING

Listed companies are required to meet certain ongoing requirements of size (based on market price), reporting, and marketability. If these requirements are not met, the stock exchange can request a *Suspension of Listing* a company's securities.

Suspensions might be temporary, or a company's securities can be delisted from trading on the stock exchange. Delisted securities can still be traded over the counter as long as a market for them exists.

See also CAPITALIZATION; LISTED SECURITIES; OVER THE COUNTER (OTC).

SVENSKA HANDELSBANKEN

With headquarters in Stockholm, *Svenska Handelsbanken* is Sweden's largest bank by asset value, which in 1997 was SKr 913 billion. As a universal bank, Svenska Handelsbanken offers a wide range of services to both individuals and corporate clients, including depository transactions, lending, property management, property mortgages, payment facilities, investment banking, factoring, leasing, and life insurance. The bank's explicit business strategy is to concentrate its operations in Sweden and the other Nordic countries (Denmark, Norway, and Finland). To that end, the bank has almost 500 branches in Sweden and several branches in each of the other Nordic countries. The bank does maintain international offices in world financial centers, such as London, Paris, and New York, but those are for the stated purpose of serving Nordic clients who do business abroad.

The bank is organized into eight regional units, each of which reports to the Central Head Office. Seven of the regional units cover different parts of Sweden, and the eighth covers the rest of the world, with its primary focus being the Nordic area. The regional units are highly autonomous with regard to market policy, lending, and administration. Each regional unit offers the bank's full range of services and is headed by an executive vice president. The Central Head Office in Stockholm consists of the Central Executive Office and three operating divisions—Handelsbanken Markets, the Central Treasury Department, and the Central Premises and Real Estate Department.

The bank is a securities underwriter, broker, and dealer, and it is a member of the Stockholm Stock Exchange, on which the bank's stock is also traded. Branches of the bank are members of other stock exchanges, namely, Copenhagen, Helsinki, Oslo, Frankfurt, and London. A subsidiary in Luxembourg is a member of the Luxembourg Stock Exchange.

Overall responsibility for the administration of the bank rests with the board of directors, which must number at least five according to the Swedish Banking Companies Act of 1987. The Articles of Association of the bank provide that the shareholders may elect not less than 8 nor more than 25 full members of the board at the annual general meeting. According to special legislation, the employees of the bank may appoint two additional members to the board. The board normally meets at least ten times a year; it meets additionally, if required, to consider major policy matters, large lending proposals, and other relevant business. The president is the chief executive officer of the bank, and is responsible for carrying out the policies of the board, for the current management of the bank's operations, and for coordinating the bank's regional units.

The branch managers report to the regional executive vice presidents, who report directly to the president, cutting out the layers of bureaucrats found in other banks. As a result, the bank is the most efficient bank in Sweden.

Chronology of Significant Events

1871 Stockholms Handelsbank, the predecessor of Svenska Handelsbanken, is founded by former directors of Stockholms Enskilda Bank, who left after an internal power struggle. The bank remains small and regional until the start of Sweden's industrial revolution in the 1890s.

1893–1913 The bank's loan volume increases nearly sevenfold from SKr 17 million to SKr 114 million, and the bank secures a substantial volume of underwriting and investment banking business.

1914–19 Stockholms Handelsbank acquires two banks in northern Sweden and one bank in southern Sweden, expands its branch network from 7 offices in Stockholm to 250 offices nationwide, and changes its name to Svenska Handelsbanken to reflect its national stature. In 1919 the bank's assets total SKr 1.6 billion and it is Sweden's largest bank.

1920s The bank is drawn into one of the largest financial frauds in history by Ivar Krueger, an engineer and match business owner who turned into a pyramid-scheme perpetrator.

1930s Sweden fares better than most of the world's depressed economies, and Svenska Handelsbanken fares better than most banks.

1940s The bank divests itself of much of its holdings in industrial enterprises and begins to reorient itself toward small- and medium-scale lending.

1950s The bank acquires Stockholms Inteckrings Garanti, a real estate lender, and begins to expand its branch network.

1960s Svenska Handelsbanken becomes the largest bank in all of Scandinavia and begins to establish overseas offices to serve Swedish companies doing business abroad.

1970s The bank loses its position as the largest bank in Scandinavia when Stockholms Enskilda Bank and Skandinaviska Bank merge. The bank establishes subsidiaries in Luxembourg and New York and otherwise expands its international presence.

1980s The bank establishes a merchant bank subsidiary in London—Svenska International—and establishes subsidiaries in Norway and Singapore.

1990s The bank acquires Stadshypotek, Sweden's leading mortgage lender; AS Aktoris, an Estonian corporate finance firm; and R.S. Platou Securities, a Norwegian company operating in the fields of securities research, corporate finance, and institutional equity trading.

See also SKANDINAVISKA ENSKILDA BANKEN; SWEDEN.

SWAP

Swap is the investment industry term for the act of selling one security to buy another similar security with an enhancement in yield, quality, or maturity.

The term can be used to describe any type of security, but is most often used for fixed income instruments.

Yield swaps can be motivated by a transaction that would bring in money faster, thus capitalizing on present values. Quality swaps could be motivated by a desire to lower the risk of a portfolio, particularly during a period of increased market volatility or an expected change in the movement of interest rates. Maturity swaps can be used to extend maturities for a longer term, alter the yield profile of a portfolio, or shorten maturities for an earlier availability of funds.

See also YIELD.

SWAPPING

See SWAP.

SWAZILAND, KINGDOM OF

Swaziland (Umbuso weSwatini (Swazi)) is a land-locked country in southern Africa. It is bordered by South Africa on the north, west and south, and by Mozambique on the east.

Area: 6,704 square miles (17,364 square km)

Population: 913,000 (34.3% urban; 65.7% rural)

Form of Government: Monarchy, with two legislative houses: Senate—30 members; House of Assembly—65 members. Head of state and government: King.

Official Languages: Swazi, English

Capitals: Mbabane (administration), Lobamba (royal and legislative)

Largest Cities: Manzini, 52,000; Mbabane, 38,290; Nhlangano, 4,107; Piggs Peak, 3,223; Siteki, 2.271

Economy:

Currency: Lilangeni (E)

National Budget: Revenue—E 1.2 billion; expenditures—E 1.5 billion (recurrent expenditure: 61.6%, of which education: 18.3%; general administration: 13.7%; economic services: 9.9%; health: 5.9%; justice and police: 5.6%; defense: 5.3%; public-debt payments: 1.8%)

Public Debt: US$217.8 million

Gross National Product: US$933.0 million

Principal Products: Sugarcane; grapefruit; seed cotton; lint cotton; corn and other vegetables; livestock; wood products; minerals

Foreign Trade (Imports): E 3.0 billion (machinery and transport equipment: 26.4%; foodstuffs: 14.8%; manufactured items: 10.6%; minerals, fuels, and lubricants: 10.2%; chemical products: 9.5%; from South Africa: 81.7%; United Kingdom: 2.5%; the Netherlands: 0.4%; Switzerland: 0.3%; France: 0.1%)

Foreign Trade (Exports): E 1.7 billion (sugar: 24.6%; canned fruits: 5.0%; wood and wood products: 4.1%; mineral products: 3.9%; to South Africa: 47.0%; United States: 3.6%; United Kingdom: 3.3%; Mozambique: 2.4%; South Korea: 2.2%; Zimbabwe 2.2%)

Stock Exchanges: 1
Swaziland Stockbrokers
Suite 205, 2nd Floor
Walker St.
PO Box 2818
Mbabane
Swaziland
Phone: (268) 46163
Fax: (268) 44132

Trading Hours: Monday–Friday, 10:00 to 12:00

Office Hours: Monday–Friday, 8:15 to 4:15

Exchange Holidays:
14, 17, 19, 25 April   6 September
25 May   25, 26 December
22 July

Listed Companies: 4

Market Capitalization: US$338 million

Indices: SSM Index (July 1990 = 100)

Other Investment Information:
Ministry of Commerce, Industry and Tourism
PO Box 45
Mbabane
Swaziland
Phone: (268) 43201
Telex: 2232

Swaziland Industrial Development Company
Tin and Walker Streets
PO Box 866
Mbabane
Swaziland
Phone: (268) 43391
Fax: (268) 45619
Telex: 2052

Swaziland Chamber of Commerce and Industry
PO Box 72
Mbabane
Swaziland

Phone: (268) 44408

Fax: (268) 44408

Telex: 2032

SWEDEN, KINGDOM OF

Sweden (Konungariket Sverige) is a nation of northern Europe. It is bordered by Norway on the west and northwest, and Finland on the northeast.

Area: 173,732 square miles (449,964 square km)

Population: 8,826,000 (83.1% urban; 16.9% rural)

Form of Government: Constitutional monarchy and parliamentary state, with one legislative house: Parliament—349 members. Chief of state: King. Head of government: Prime Minister.

Official Language: Swedish

Capital: Stockholm

Largest Cities: Stockholm, 703,627; Goteborg, 444,553; Malmo, 242,706; Uppsala, 181,191; Linkoping, 130,489

Economy:

Currency: Swedish Krona (SKr)

National Budget: Revenue—SKr 344.0 billion; expenditures—SKr 549.7 billion (health and social affairs: 23.0%; interest on national debt: 17.5%; education and culture: 9.9%; defense: 7.1%)

Public Debt: US$119.4 billion

Gross National Product: US$216.3 billion

Principal Products: Vegetables; livestock; machinery and transport equipment; electrical machinery; chemicals; iron and steel

Foreign Trade (Imports): SKr 399.1 billion (machinery and transport equipment: 37.9%, of which electrical machinery: 11.7%; transport equipment: 9.3%; chemicals: 11.3%; food: 7.5%; clothing: 4.9%; from Germany: 18.4%; United Kingdom: 9.7%; United States: 8.6%; Denmark: 6.8%; Finland: 6.3%; Norway: 6.1%)

Foreign Trade (Exports): SKr 471.6 billion (machinery and transport equipment: 45.1%, of which transport equipment: 15.2: electrical machinery: 12.0%; paper products: 9.5%; chemicals: 9.5%; wood and wood pulp: 6.3%; iron and steel products: 6.2%; to Germany: 13.3%; United Kingdom: 10.2%; Norway: 8.1%; United States: 8.0%; Denmark: 6.9%; Finland: 4.8%)

Stock Exchanges: 1

Stockholm Stock Exchange (SSE; Stockholm Fondbors)
Källargränd 2
S-111 82 Stockholm
Sweden
Phone: (46-8) 613 8800
Fax: (46-8) 246 8612

Internet Address: www.xsse.se

Trading Hours: Monday–Friday, 10:00 to 4:00

Exchange Holidays:

1, 5 January	30 October
4, 5, 8, 30 April	1 November
1, 16, 27 May	24, 25, 26, 31 December
21 June	

Listed Companies: 261 total
100 Official List
161 OTC and O-List

Total Market Capitalization:

At 31 December 1997

Local Currency (Millions)	US Dollars (Millions)
1,792,175	225,875

Major Sectors: Engineering industry, chemicals and pharmaceuticals, telecommunications, investment companies, forest industry

Share Price Performance:

(% Change)

1992	98
1993	88
1994	8
1995	10
1996	56
1997	21

History: Although trading of shares can be traced back to the year 1717, when a royal concession was granted to a salting company, 1776 marks the year that organized trading started on the Stockholm Stock Exchange. Trading was mostly in commodities until the enactment of securities legislation in 1862, and trading began on the Stockholm Stock Exchange in 1863. The Stockholm Stock Exchange began international trading in 1901.

Recent improvements have made the SSE more compatible with European Union directives. In 1992, the Act on Stock Exchanges and Clearing Operations changed the SSE to a limited company, with exchange members and listed companies as shareholders. The agencies that control banks and insurance companies have been merged into the Financial Supervisory Authority and are considered the competent authority for the purposes of European Union legislation.

Stockholm's stock exchange has been dominated by institutional investors (insurance companies, mutual funds, foundations, corporate investors) for many years—a situation caused, for the most part, by previous Exchange rules and regulations. Today, foreign interest in Swedish companies continues to grow. Due to the removal of many restrictive rules and regulations, foreign investors make up nearly 30% of share trading on the Stockholm Exchange and hold an estimated 27% of the total market capitalization.

Classes of Securities: Ordinary shares ("A" with full voting rights and "B" with reduced voting rights), preference shares, bonds, and derivatives

Indices:
SSE All Share Index (SX General) weighted by market value
Affarsvalden General Index
SX-OTC and SX-O for over-the-counter and unlisted securities

Supervisory Organizations: Financial Supervisory Authority

Depository: Swedish Central Securities Depository (VPC)

Settlement Details:

Shares: Book-entry, Trade date + 3 days (T + 3)

Trading: The Stockholm Stock Exchange uses an electronic trading system called the Stockholm Automated Exchange (SAX), now fully integrated for share trading. Fixed-income securities are traded on a parallel system called SOX. Call-over auction and after-market trading have been replaced by decentralized computer terminals. The computer system also matches orders for odd lot trading.

Round lots for shares are normally 50, 100, 500, 1,000, or 2,000, with size determined by the convention of trading and market value of approximately SKR 18,000 on the official list and SKR 9,000 on the parallel markets.

The main market is called the A-list. Two parallel markets also exist for equity shares. The small company market, OTC, created in the 1980s, and the O-list established in the late 1980s, bring unlisted securities under the rules and regulations of the official list.

The Swedish Options Market (OM Stockholm) acts as exchange and clearing house for derivatives. OM Stockholm offers futures and options on Swedish shares and the Swedish OMX equity index, as well as a standardized interest rate swap and interest rate options. It also operates a clearing service for the interbank trade in futures on national bonds, T-bills, and mortgage bonds, as well as market/clearing services for standardized stock loan contracts.

Listing Requirements: Issuers of securities are required by the Equity Market and Clearing Act to issue listing particulars in a prospectus, which is to be filed with the exchange with the company's application for registration. The required information must enable investors to make an informed appraisal of the business and financial position of the company and describe the rights attached to the securities.

A-List:
- Three years of audited records
- Meet the requirements for internal organization and disclosure of information
- Publish a Stock Exchange Listing Prospectus
- Minimum market value of SKr 300 million
- Distribution of 25% of the share capital, and a minimum of 10% of voting rights in the market distributed to at least 2,000 investors, each holding at least one round lot (trading unit). Investors holding 10% or more of share capital are not included in the distribution requirement.

Trading of shares cannot begin before the exchange approves the listing particulars and the information has been made public by the issuer. A prospectus approved by the EEA within the three months prior to application for trading in Sweden needs no further approval. Rules of the Financial Supervisory Board relating to the contents of listing particulars normally correspond to the requirements set by the EU Directive 89/390/EEC.

Documentation for listed companies is handled mainly through the Vardepapperscentralen (VPC), which has a computer system that maintains a list of shareholders of each company. It also registers voting rights and handles the distribution of shares and dividends.

OTC List:
- Minimum three years of audited records
- Meet requirements for organization and information disclosure
- Publish a listing prospectus
- Minimum market value of SKr 50 million
- Have distribution of at least 25% of share capital, and no less than 10% of voting rights, distributed to a minimum of 500 investors holding at least one round

Stockholm Stock Exchange. *(Courtesy of Stockholm Stock Exchange Limited)*

lot (trading unit) but not those exceeding 10% total equity

O-List

• Meet requirements for internal organization and disclosure of information

• Publish a prospectus

• Distribute a minimum of 10% of the share capital and no less than 10% of the voting rights in the market to a minimum of 300 investors, each holding a minimum of one round lot, but not exceeding 10% of the total equity

Registration of Shares: Swedish companies are required to deposit shares with the Swedish Central Securities Depository (VPC), in order to be listed on the Stockholm Stock Exchange. Foreign companies listed on the exchange can choose to deposit some of their shares with the VPC or through a depository arrangement with a Swedish bank to facilitate the dematerialized book-entry system for securities transactions. A foreign company may also choose to deposit shares with their own domestic Central Securities Depository (CSD) and execute all clearing and settlement in Sweden through Euroclear or Cedel.

Investor Taxation: Dividend withholding tax of 30% is levied on dividends if there is no tax treaty. Sweden has recently signed double taxation agreements with Belarus, Gambia, Germany, and Vietnam. Agreements will soon come into effect with Namibia, Russia, the United States, and Venezuela.

The VPC withholds appropriate relevant taxes on dividends.

Takeover and merger agreements between a Swedish company and another EU member are not subject to any form of taxation.

Limitations: All restrictions on foreign ownership of Swedish company shares were abolished in 1993. All foreign investors must register with the VPC in order to receive dividends. Such registration can be done through a broker or a bank.

Brokerage Firms:

Exchange Members:
Banque Indosuez Stockholm Filial
PO Box 7734
S-103 95 Stockholm
Sweden

Phone: (46-8) 454 5800
Fax: (46-8) 411 0686

Den Danske Bank A/S
Holmens Kanal 2-12
DK-1092 Copenhagen K
Denmark
Phone: (45-33) 44 00 00
Fax: (45-33) 44 09 40

Foreningsbanken
S-114 91
Stockholm
Sweden
Phone: (46-8) 782 3000
Fax: (46-8) 783 5555

Jysek Bank, A/S
Vertergade 8-16,
DK-8600 Silkeborg
Denmark
Phone: (45-8) 922 4536
Fax: (45-8) 922 2483

Morgan Grenfell & Co. Ltd (UK)
PO Box 5781
S-114 87 Stockholm
Sweden
Phone: (46-8) 463 5500
Fax: (46-8) 463 5550

Skandinaviska Enskilda Banken (Enskilda)
S-106 40 Stockholm
Sweden
Phone: (46-8) 763 8000
Fax: (46-8) 676 9019

Sveriges Riksbank
S-103 37 Stockholm
Sweden
Phone: (46-8) 787 0000
Fax: (46-8) 210 531

Trygg-Banken
PO Box 70270
S-107 22 Stockholm
Sweden
Phone: (46-8) 693 5000
Fax: (46-8) 693 5075

Unibank A/S
Torvegade 2
DK-1786 Copenhagen V

Denmark
Phone: (45-33) 33 33 33
Fax: (45-31) 54 53 75

Ostgota Enskilda Bank
PO Box 7523
S-103 92
Stockholm
Sweden
Phone: (46-8) 796 0400
Fax: (46-8) 796 0570

Stockbroker Firms

Aktiespararnas Investerings AB (Aktieinvest)
Norrtullsgatan 6, 4 tr
S-113 89 Stockholm
Sweden
Phone: (46-8) 457 1700
Fax: (46-8) 457 1875

Aragon Fondkommission
PO Box 7794
S-103 96 Stockholm
Sweden
Phone: (46-8) 457 1700
Fax: (46-8) 457 1875

Alfred Berg Transferator
PO Box 7643
S-103 94 Stockholm
Sweden
Phone: (46-8) 463 6400
Fax: (46-8) 678 0725

D. Carnegie
S-103 38 Stockholm
Sweden
Phone: (46-8) 676 8800
Fax: (46-8) 676 8895

FIBA Nordic Securities AS
PO Box 1351 Vika
N-0113 Oslo
Norway
Phone: (47-22) 83 88 70
Fax: (47-22) 83 09 50

Hagstromer & Qviberg Fondkommission
S-103 71 Stockholm
Sweden
Phone: (46-8) 696 1700
Fax: (46-8) 696 1701

Nordiska Fondkommission
PO Box 7362
S-103 90 Stockholm
Sweden
Phone: (46-8) 791 4800
Fax: (46-8) 678 6150

Erik Penser Fondkommission
PO Box 7405
S-103 91 Stockholm
Sweden
Phone: (46-8) 463 8000
Fax: (46-8) 611 2705

Servisen Fondkommission
PO Box 7405
S-103 91 Stockholm
Sweden
Phone: (46-8) 701 0900
Fax: (46-8) 611 8647

Timber Hill Europe AG
Gotthardstrasse 3
CH-6300 Zug
Switzerland
Phone: (41-42) 26 50 60
Fax: (41-42) 23 93 05

Company Information:

The Best Performing Shares in the Country

Company Name	Share Price Change 1 January 1997 to 31 December 1997 (%)
Kalmar Industries	1,972
Jm Bygg 'B'	268
Netcom Systems 'B'	132
Europolitan	103
Active Biotech 'B'	101
Foreningssparbanken 'A'	95
Skandia	94
Assa Abloy 'B'	86
Hennes & Mauritz 'B'	85
Atle	63
Skand.Ensk.Bkn.'A'	61
Trygg-Hansa 'B'	60
Sydkraft 'C'	55
Ericsson Lm Telfn 'A'	46
Sydkraft 'A'	45
Incentive 'B'	45
Incentive 'A'	44
Ericsson Lm Telfn. B	44
Atlas Copco 'A'	44
Industrivarden 'A'	43

Company Name	Share Price Change 1 January 1997 to 31 December 1997 (%)
Atlas Copco 'B'	42
Om Gruppen	41
Svenska Handbkn. 'A'	40
Electrolux 'B'	39
Volvo 'A'	39
Sas Sverige	34
Volvo 'B'	33
Scancem Series 'A'	30

The Largest Companies in the Country by Market Capitalization as of 31 December 1997

Company Name	Market Capitalization Local Currency (Millions)	Market Capitalization US Dollars (Millions)
Ericsson Lm Telfn. B	266,390	33,574
Astra 'A'	183,899	23,178
Hennes & Mauritz 'B'	72,410	9,126
Volvo 'B'	64,521	8,132
Foreningssparbanken 'A'	63,513	8,005
Abb 'A'	62,811	7,916
Svenska Handbkn. 'A'	59,470	7,495
Nordbanken Holding Ab	57,149	7,203
Skand.Ensk.Bkn.'A'	56,537	7,126
Investor 'B'	43,711	5,509
Sandvik 'A'	42,816	5,396
Astra 'B'	40,821	5,145
Electrolux 'B'	39,250	4,947
Skandia	38,332	4,831
Incentive 'A'	35,832	4,516
Skanska 'B'	34,097	4,297
Investor 'A'	30,156	3,801
Kalmar Industries	30,089	3,792
Volvo 'A'	29,384	3,703
Atlas Copco 'A'	29,033	3,659
Pharmacia & Upjohn Sdr	28,247	3,560
Stora Kopparberg 'A'	26,179	3,300
Ericsson Lm Telfn 'A'	25,798	3,251
Abb 'B'	25,218	3,178
Svenska Cellulosa Sca'b'	24,143	3,043
Sydkraft 'A'	23,889	3,011
Assidoman	23,793	2,999
Autoliv Sdb	18,667	2,353
Scania 'B'	17,900	2,256
Scania 'A'	17,750	2,237
Securitas 'B'	16,528	2,083

Company Name	Market Capitalization Local Currency (Millions)	Market Capitalization US Dollars (Millions)
Trygg-Hansa 'B'	16,472	2,076
Sandvik 'B'	15,719	1,981
Sydkraft 'C'	15,579	1,963
Netcom Systems 'B'	14,492	1,827
Atlas Copco 'B'	14,431	1,819
Aga 'A'	14,240	1,795
Assa Abloy 'B'	13,976	1,761
Industrivarden 'A'	13,895	1,751
Scancem Series 'A'	13,633	1,718
Modo 'B'	13,578	1,711
Jm Bygg 'B'	13,318	1,679
Incentive 'B'	13,092	1,650
Europolitan	12,382	1,561
Swedish Match	12,284	1,548
Ssab 'A'	12,151	1,531
Aga 'B'	11,907	1,501
Svenska Cellulosa Sca'a'	11,496	1,449
Skf 'B'	10,914	1,376
Trelleborg 'B'	10,534	1,328
Gullspangs Kraft 'B'	10,267	1,294
Perstorp 'B'	8,950	1,128
Wm Data Nordic 'B'	8,863	1,117
Graninge	8,816	1,111
Avesta Sheffield	8,295	1,045
Sas Sverige	8,108	1,022
Skf 'A'	7,832	987
Atle	6,846	863
Om Gruppen	6,809	858
Diligentia	6,647	838
Svedala Industri	6,290	793
Cardo	6,210	783
Active Biotech 'B'	6,196	781
Hoganas 'B'	6,038	761
Lundbergforetagen 'B'	6,018	758
Stora Koppg 'B'	5,881	741
Kinnevik Ind. 'B'	5,861	739
Bure Investment	5,700	718
Marieberg Tid.'A'	5,551	700
Custos 'A'	5,537	698

Regional Exchanges: None

Other Investment Information:
Ministry of Industry and Commerce
Invest in Sweden Office
Fredsgt. 8 103 33
Stockholm
Sweden

Phone: (46-8) 763-10-00
Fax: (46-8) 11-36-16
Telex: 14180

SWEETENER

Features added to the issue of a security to make it more attractive are referred to as *Sweeteners.* Such features include making bonds convertible, subscriptions rights, subscription warrants, and put features. These benefits are added when an issuer desires an active market for the securities in as short a time as possible.

See also CONVERTIBLE; SUBSCRIPTION RIGHTS; SUBSCRIPTION WARRANT.

SWISS BANK CORPORATION

The roots of the *Swiss Bank Corporation*, one of the "big three" banks in Switzerland, are found in the large number of small private banks that sprang up during the 1830s and 1840s. In 1854 six private banks based in and near Basel forged an alliance that gave them sufficient size to raise capital for public authorities and industry. The alliance, which was called the Bank-Verein, issued bonds and shares to the Swiss public.

The bitterly fought Franco-Prussian War provided an incentive to the growth of the Bank-Verein. A consortium of three non-Swiss banks, the Frankfurter, Berliner, and Wiener Bankverein, attempted to set up a bank in Basel to benefit from the flow of capital into Switzerland that was a result of the war in France. The Bank-Verein entered into an agreement with the three foreign banks to jointly set up a larger venture in Basel. A foundation protocol was signed in 1871 and on 15 April 1872 a new entity, the Basler Bankverein, opened for business.

The Basler Bankverein was chosen to be the Swiss issuing bank for French government loan notes in 1772. This promising start was soon reversed, however, by the onset of recession in Switzerland and the collapse of the Austrian Stock Exchange. A spate of bad loans and a fall in the value of equity holdings forced the Basler Bankverein to withhold its annual dividend payments.

As Swiss industry grew in the latter half of the 19th century, the patchwork of individual banks began to be replaced by larger groups that were better able to raise the large sums of capital that were demanded. The Basler Bankverein strengthened its operations by buying up the Zurcher Bankverein, the Basler Depositen-Bank, and the Schweizerische Unionbank. In 1897 the group changed its name to the Schweizerischer Bankverein (the Swiss Bank Corporation) and, in the following year, the first overseas office was opened in London. Banks in Geneva and Lausanne were also added to the network.

World War I halted the Swiss Bank Corporation's ambitious expansion plans. Although the bank was not as badly hit as some of its peers by the downturn in trade, the directors were forced to curtail their activities abroad for the duration of the war. Switzerland's neutrality, and the increasing stability of the Swiss franc, ensured that the country would be in a strong position to influence the global economy during the 1920s. The Swiss Bank Corporation was instrumental in setting up the Bank for International Settlements, which dealt with the payment of war reparations. The bank was also used by many foreign individuals and governments as a deposit-taking haven when hyperinflation threatened the value of their savings.

The repercussions of the Wall Street Crash in 1929 and the Great Depression that followed were felt across Europe. The Swiss Bank Corporation was called upon to shore up the Swiss banking sector and make substantial loans to the government. The devaluation of the Swiss franc in 1936 added to the woes of those involved in the sector. A New York office was opened in the month before the outbreak of World War II, but its impact was severely limited by the hostilities. Earnings dropped as international trade came to a halt, and the bank was forced to cut its dividend payments.

The bank issued the first postwar foreign bond in Switzerland in 1947. The wealth of the country increased dramatically after the war, and the Swiss franc became one of the most favored currencies for international trade. Between 1958 and 1964 the bank's assets doubled. The process of consolidation in the banking sector continued, and the Swiss Bank Corporation expanded its network of branches. Abroad, new offices were opened in San Francisco (1965), Chicago (1973), Houston (1976), and Miami (1987). The bank also developed a strong presence in Asia, with offices opening up in Tokyo (1966), Hong Kong (1964), and Singapore (1975).

The Swiss Bank Corporation has continually shown a commitment to the country's domestic industry. The watch-making industry had been a justifiably famous section of the Swiss economy for many years, but in the 1960s and 1970s competition from Japanese companies threatened some of Switzerland's best-known names. The Swiss Bank Corporation advanced large sums to enable the replacement of mechanical watches with their more advanced quartz competitors. In 1987 the board of the Swiss Bank Corporation announced that they were eager to take part in the "Big Bang" in the City of London with the acquisition of the securities broker Savory Milln.

Other events in the bank's history have been less pleasing. In 1985 the bank was ordered by the Supreme Court of Switzerland to release information to the British police forces concerning the alleged deposit of blackmail money from the Irish terrorist organization, the Irish Republican Army (IRA). In 1988, all three of the large Swiss banks were implicated in a substantial money laundering operation set up by Turkish drug criminals. In the following year the Swiss Bank Corporation was prohibited from taking part in a Canadian issue of Eurobonds because the Canadian government believed it had business links with pro-apartheid figures in South Africa.

In 1995 the Swiss Bank Corporation announced a major deal, the acquisition of the troubled UK merchant bank SG Warburg. Warburg had been negotiating with the U.S. bank Morgan Stanley for several months, but the talks were abruptly called off because of apparently insoluble disagreements over pricing and corporate culture. The chief executive of the Swiss Bank Corporation, George Blum, and the head of the bank's international operations, Marcel Ospel, visited Sir David Scholey, chairman of Warburg, and convinced him of the wisdom of the deal. A dozen senior executives drawn from both firms met in a hotel near London's Heathrow airport in April 1995 and thrashed out the details. The deal, which was announced in May 1995, guaranteed the Swiss Bank Corporation a valuable position in the European equity and bond markets. The new entity, SBC Warburg, has contributed a valuable stream of earnings to the Swiss holding company.

In May 1997 SBC bought the Wall Street company Dillon Read for $600 million and merged it with SG Warburg to produce a new investment banking entity, Warburg Dillon Read. Marcel Ospel, who became the chief executive of SBC in May 1996, hopes that Warburg Dillon Read will eventually have a worldwide staff of 20,000 and contribute profits of approximately Fr 3 bn (£1.2 bn) each year by the year 2002.

In February 1998 an extraordinary general meeting was convened in Basle to vote on SBC's merger with long-time rival UBS. Shareholders voted to accept the merger and end 125 years of independence at SBC. Many commentators, however, interpreted the merger as a takeover and viewed SBC as the dominant partner.

See also BANK FOR INTERNATIONAL SETTLEMENTS (BIS); WARBURG DYNASTY.

SWITCHING

Switching is a mutual fund feature that allows an investor to move investments from one fund to another.

Switching must occur within the same family of funds, but may be applied funds having differing investment objectives. Many funds have set limits as to the number of switches an investor can make within a specific time period. Generally, an additional fee is charged for making a switch.

Although some investors use funds for market timing, more often a change is made to increase or decrease risk exposure. An investor might begin with the popular approach of growth fund investing in early years, then switching to conservative growth, and eventually switching to more income-oriented funds.

Investing in three or more funds with different objectives and balancing the amounts invested in each fund according to varying investment climates can be another approach worth following for private investors.

See also MUTUAL FUND; OBJECTIVE; UNIT INVESTMENT TRUST/UNIT TRUST.

SWITZERLAND (SWISS CONFEDERATION)

Switzerland (Confederation Suisse (French); Schweizerische Eidgenossenschaft (German); Confederazione Svizzera (Italian)) is a landlocked country in central Europe. It is bordered by France on the west, Germany on the north, Austria and Liechtenstein on the east, and Italy on the south.

Area: 15,940 square miles (41,284 square km)

Population: 7,039,000 (67.9% urban; 32.1% rural)

Form of Government: Federal state, with two legislative houses: Council of States—46 members; National Council—200 members. Head of state and government: President.

Official Languages: French, German, Italian

Capitals: Berne (administrative); Lausanne (judicial)

Largest Cities: Zurich, 343,045; Basel, 176,220; Geneva, 171,744; Berne, 129,423; Lausanne, 117,153

Economy:

Currency: Swiss Franc (Fr)

National Budget: Revenue—Fr 36.3 billion; expenditures—Fr 42.4 billion (social services: 25.8%; transportation: 15.0%; defense: 14.0%)

National Debt: Fr 77.8 billion

Gross National Product: US$254.1 billion

Principal Products: Milk; fruits and vegetables; livestock; machinery; chemicals; metals and finished products

Foreign Trade (Imports): Fr 87.3 billion (machinery and electronics: 20.5%; chemical products: 13.5%; vehicles: 9.0%; textiles and clothing: 9.0%; from Germany: 34.4%; France: 11.4%; Italy: 10.5%; United States: 5.7%; the Netherlands: 4.9%)

Foreign Trade (Exports): Fr 90.2 billion (machinery and electronics: 27.3%; chemical products: 24.5%; watches: 8.3%; base metals and finished products: 8.1%; to Germany: 24.3%; France: 9.4%; United States: 8.7%; Italy: 7.7%; United Kingdom: 5.4%)

Stock Exchanges: 1
Swiss Exchange (SWX)
Selnaustrasse 32
CH-8021 Zurich
Switzerland
Phone: (41-1) 229 21 11
Fax: (41-1) 229 22 33

Internet Address: www.bourse.swx.ch

Trading Hours:

Monday through Friday	9:30 to 4:30	bonds
	10:00 to 4:30	equities
	10:15 to 4:30	derivatives
	4:30 to 10:00	off exchange activity
EBS Trading:	9:30 to 4:30	

The trading system is also available for entries and inquires from 4:30 P.M. to 10:00 P.M. and from 6:00 A.M. until trading resumes.

Office Hours: Monday through Friday, 8:30 to 5:30

Exchange Holidays:

1 January	1 June
9, 10, 13 April	24, 25 DecemberAugust
1 May	

Listed Companies: 427 total
216 domestic
211 foreign equities

Total Market Capitalization:

At 31 December 1997

Local Currency (Millions)	**US Dollars (Millions)**
813,826	557,968

Major Sectors: Pharmaceuticals, banks, insurance, machinery

Share Price Performance:

(% Change)

1992	20
1993	64
1994	-8
1995	23
1996	17
1997	58

History: Financial markets in Switzerland were born in 1849, when a stockbroker decided to publish a securities price list in Geneva. Officially founded in 1856, the Geneva Stock Exchange became the first organized financial market in the country. The first major technical development came in 1884 when a telephone was installed to link the Geneva and Zurich exchanges.

The structure of the markets remained virtually unchanged from 1938 to 1988. The early markets were structured under the federal political system of Switzerland. Seven regional exchanges, regulated by cantonal laws, were in operation until the late 1980s. Regional exchanges in Zurich, Geneva, and Basle evolved into the predominant trading exchanges.

Due to consolidation—made necessary by loss of market share and the desire to form a strong, centralized, and competitive securities market—most regional exchanges closed in the early 1990s. Bern remains the only exception, continuing to be a regional exchange trading a modest volume of regional company shares.

The Swiss exchange system underwent a profound change during the early 1990s. The seven existing stock exchanges, as well as the exchange for options and financial futures (SOFFEX), were combined into one organization known as the Swiss Exchange. Reporting requirements were introduced, meeting the need of exchange customers who desired the publication of the daily turnover of each stock. The exchanges of Berne, Lausanne, Neuchatel, and St. Gall stopped trading in 1991. In the same year, the listing autonomy of individual exchanges became concentrated in the Swiss Admissions Board.

The Swiss Electronic Exchange project (EBS-Elektronische Borse, Schweiz), began as a joint venture set up in 1992 by the exchanges of Basle, Geneva, and Zurich, together with SOFFEX. The Exchanges' Swiss Market Feed (SMF) began to supply prices and other data from the Swiss exchanges to information services around the world.

The Swiss Exchange was founded in 1993, with its board of directors given the authority for all major decisions concerning the future of the Swiss exchange system. The consolidation of exchanges began so that the Swiss Exchange operations could commence in 1995. A milestone was reached in 1993 when the Swiss securities clearing organization (SEGA) began operating the electronic SEGA communications system (SECOM), a complex EDP system ensuring Switzerland a top international position in clearing and settling technology. In 1994 Intersettle was formed as the settlement organization of the Swiss banks.

From those original seven stock exchanges, SOFFEX, and several umbrella organizations, one organization has emerged with one electronic system, one operating organization, and only one administration. The final step will be the technical integration of the SOFFEX system of trading and clearing into the electronic exchange system.

Classes of Securities: Bearer shares, registered shares, dividend-right certificates, participation certificates, bonds, straight bonds, convertible bonds, investment trust units, covered warrants, derivatives

Indices:

Swiss Market Index (SMI) (blue chip index with 21 securities)

SMIC

Swiss Performance Index (SPI) (all shares index with 338 securities)

SPIX

SPI Dienstielstungen/Services/Services

SPI Industrie/ Industrials/Industrie

Swiss Bid/Ask Index (SBAI)

Supervisory Organizations:

Federal Banking Commission

The General Assembly: Represents the top level of the exchange and elects the board of directors.

Board of Directors: Has 16 members and is in charge of Swiss Exchange supervision. The board enacts regulations, sets the budget, closes accounts, and admits and expels members. It is also in charge of selecting the general management and a six-member Executive Committee of the Board of Directors.

Supervisory Office: Subordinate to the Executive Committee of the Board of Directors. It is the Supervisory Office's charge to ensure the supervisory function of the Swiss Exchange and it is the main contact point for such issues as they arise.

Swiss Admissions Board: Made up of representation from the Swiss Exchange and the Swiss Trade and Industry Association (Vorort). The board has autonomy to decide listings of securities on the Swiss Exchange. It also determines reporting obligation for all the companies listed on the exchange.

Commission on Regulation: Another suborganization of the board of directors, which mostly deals with public takeover offers. The commission is temporary and will be discontinued after new federal exchange legislation is introduced to form a government body known as the Federal Takeover Commission.

General Management: Comprised of the four divisions of trading, listing, information technology, and planning/marketing/administration. The divisions are in charge of the technical and administrative organization of the exchange business.

Special Commissions: Similar to the Index Commission, it advises the board of directors and the management board on technical issues.

SOFFEX AG: A subsidiary of the Swiss Exchange. It is planned to integrate SOFFEX in the mid-term into the new electronic trading system of the Swiss Exchange. For legal purposes and peculiarities of an exchange trading derivatives, the clearing organization for SOFFEX derivatives will continue as an independent company. Organization integration is of interest to many investors and exchange members, as derivatives and their underlying securities are increasingly linked together in investment strategies.

Depository: Swiss Securities Clearing Corp. (SEGA)

Settlement Details:

Shares: Trade date + 3 days. Trading and settlement are linked electronically. Buyers and sellers are required to complete business with delivery and payment within three days of the date on which the transaction occurred.

Trading: Important Changes for Investors

Electronic Exchange: Although orders are still placed with banks, the banker now enters the order on the electronic exchange.

Longer Trading Hours: Trading begins at 9:30 A.M. and continues until 4:30 P.M. The system is also available for entries and inquiries from 4:30 P.M. to 10:00 P.M. and 6:00 A.M. until trading resumes.

Types of Orders: The new electronic exchange provides for some new types of orders, offering facilities for the direct entry of the following:

Fill or Kill: Orders require the entire order to be filled immediately or it lapses.

Stop Order: Becomes a market order as soon as the price given is reached.

Accept Order: Allows a trader to "clear off" all offers up to a specific limit in the order book without entering his order in the book.

Hidden Size Order: Allows a trader to enter an order in the order book in such a way that only part of it is visible to third parties at any given time.

New Round Lot Sizes (stocks, derivatives, investment funds, rights)

Price Range From:	Up To	Number of Shares
	incl. Fr 10.–	1,000
over Fr 10.–	incl. Fr 250.–	100
over Fr 250.–	incl. Fr 2,500.–	10
over Fr 2,500.–	incl. Fr 5,000.–	5
over Fr 5,000.–		1

New Price Increments (stocks, derivatives, investment funds, rights)

Price Range From:	To	Increment
	Fr 49.95–	Fr 0.05
Fr 50.–	Fr 249.75–	Fr 0.25
Fr 250.–	Fr 2,499.–	Fr 1.–
Fr 2,500.–		Fr 5.–

According to clearly defined rules, odd lots are combined into round lots and traded at the reference price. Special rules exist for orders of one or more round lots plus an odd lot.

In adherence with the principle of best execution, the following orders may, exceptionally, be traded off exchange without going through the matcher:

• Individual orders for stocks with a market value of Fr 200,000 and over

• Individual orders for options with a market value of Fr 100,000 and over

• Individual orders for bonds with a nominal value of Fr 100,000 and over

• Aggregate orders with a market or nominal value of Fr 1 million and over

During pre-opening, orders under these limits may only be traded outside of the matcher at the client's explicit request. In the trading statement, all transactions done via the matcher must be designated as exchange transactions, and all transactions not done via the matcher must be designated as off-exchange transactions.

In Switzerland, the contractual arrangement between members and clients ensures that orders must be executed at the best possible price, barring explicit instructions to the contrary. The exchange further obliges its members to execute orders above the exchange obligation limits outside of the matcher, but only if they can ensure best execution elsewhere. Members must therefore be able to verify if an off-exchange execution would produce the better price for the client.

All supervisory activities are subject to surveillance by a special independent unit of the Swiss Exchange. The federal banking commission is the government authority responsible for the Swiss Exchange.

Listing Requirements: The listing department examines criteria of capital base, market capitalization, marketability, and level of debt as part of the new Listing Rules for the Main Board issuer or guarantor.

Companies quoted on the market have to provide financial reporting according to Swiss Accounting Standards, and these reports must be of a standard equivalent to or higher than IAS, US-GAAP, or 4th and 7th EU Directives. Half-yearly interim reports and timely announcements of price-sensitive information through public news services are further requirements.

Investor Taxation:
35% withholding tax on dividends is funded back if a tax agreement exists between countries.
There is no capital gains tax.
Eurobond and Euro-stock issues, as well as bond trading between foreign investors, are tax free.
Funds can be freely repatriated.

Limitations: Listed companies may restrict the voting rights to a foreign investor holding registered shares. Dividend rights remain unaffected.

Brokerage Firms:
ABN Amro Bank (Schwetz)
Talstr. 41/Postfach 5239
8022 Zurich
Switzerland
Phone: (41-1) 631 41 11
Fax: (41-1) 631 53 80

Banque Bonhote & Cie. SA
1, Rue Pury CH 2001
Neuchatel
Switzerland

Phone: (41-38) 22 10 21
Fax: (41-38) 21 43 42

Banque Cantonale Vaudoise
Place Saint-Francois 14bis
1003 Lausanne
Switzerland
Phone: (41-21) 317 11 11
Fax: (41-21) 642 11 22
Telex: 454.304

Banque Nationale de Paris (Schweiz) AG
Zweigniederlassung Zurich
Seinaustrasse 30/31
8001 Zurich
Switzerland
Phone: (41-21) 317 11 11
Fax: (41-21) 642 11 22

Banca Unione di Credito
Bellariastrasse 82
8038 Zurich
Switzerland
Phone: (41-1) 211 00 24
Fax: (41-1) 221 36 10

BWO Bank fur Wertschriften und Optionen
Bahnhofstrasse 84
8023 Zurich
Switzerland
Phone: (41-1) 212 17 01
Fax: (41-1) 212 11 88

Cantrade Privatbank AG
Morgartenstr. 1/Postfach
8038 Zurich
Switzerland
Phone: (41-1) 295 22 53
Fax: (41-1) 295 25 73

Coop Bank
Aeschenplatz 3/Postfach
4002 Basel
Switzerland
Phone: (41-61) 286 24 13
Fax: (41-61) 272 84 14

Bank Ehinger & Cie AG
Rittergasse 12
4001 Basel
Switzerland
Phone: (41-61) 295 44 00
Fax: (41-61) 295 44 01

E. Gutzwiller & Cie AG, Banquiers
Aeschenvorstadt 14-16
4001 Basel
Switzerland
Phone: (41-61) 272 88 33
Fax: (41-61) 272 57 16

Bank Hoffman AG
Telstrasse 27
8022 Zurich
Switzerland
Phone: (41-1) 217 52 00
Fax: (41-1) 217 58 96

Bank J. Vontobel & Co. AG
Bahnhofstr. 3/ Postfach
8022 Zurich
Switzerland
Phone: (41-1) 283 72 87
Fax: (41-1) 283 58 30

MM. Lombard, Odier & Cie (MM.)
Rue de la Corraterie 11
1204 Geneva
Switzerland
Phone: (41-22) 709 21 11
Fax: (41-22) 709 29 11
Telex: 422.148 loc

Merrill Lynch Capital Markets AG
Stauffacherstrasse 5
8039 Zurich
Switzerland
Phone: (41-1) 297 75 91
Fax: (41-1) 291 33 41

Ruegg Bank AG
Talstrasse 66/Postfach
8039 Zurich
Switzerland
Phone: (41-1) 218 56 11
Fax: (41-1) 218 58 17

Rahn & Bodmer, Banquiers
Talstr. 15/Postfach
8022 Zurich
Switzerland
Phone: (41-1) 211 38 50
Fax: (41-1) 211 64 63

Banque Rothschild S.A.
Dpt. de Negoce
Rue de Hesse 18

1211 Geneva
Switzerland
Phone: (41-22) 818 91 11
Fax: (41-22) 818 91 21

Bank Sarasin & Cie.
Lowenstrasse 11
8022 Zurich
Switzerland
Phone: (41-1) 213 91 91
Fax: (41-1) 221 04 54

Union de Banques Suisses
Dpt. de Negoce
8, rue du Rhone
Case postale 2950
1211 Geneva
Switzerland
Phone: (41-1) 388 64 15
Fax: (41-1) 388 96 52

Société de Bourse Lémanique
6, rue de Rive/Case postale 797
1211 Geneva
Switzerland
Phone: (41-22) 312 04 55
Fax: (41-22) 312 07 60

Company Information:

The Best Performing Shares in the Country

Company Name	Share Price Change 1 January 1997 to 31 December 1997 (%)
Swiss Life B	2,013
Batigroup R	409
Clariant	287
Feldsch.-Hurlimann R	283
Kudelski P	264
Cft R	191
Infranor Br.	182
Cementia Hdg. P	163
Cft 'B'	156
Feldsch.-Hurlimann P	149
Credit Suisse R	132
Helvetia Patria R	127
Bt&T Telekommunikations	115
Basell Kb 'B'	104
Kaba	104
Bk Vision 'B'	101
Pirelli Intl. P	98
Schlatter R	97
Julius Baer 'B'	93

Company Name	Share Price Change 1 January 1997 to 31 December 1997 (%)	Company Name	Share Price Change 1 January 1997 to 31 December 1997 (%)
Zurich In. R	93	Novartis 'B'	55
Swissair Gsh.	93	Novartis R	55
Usego R	92	Moevenpick 'B'	54
Swiss Re R	91	Mikron R	54
Moevenpick R	90	Vp Bank Vaduz P	53
Baloise R	89	Sarna R	53
Enr Eastern Natural	89	Nestle R	52
Ares-Serono 'B'	89	Pharma Vision 'B'	51
Sulzer R	88	Roche Holding 'B'	49
Sairgroup R	85	Bcv 'B'	48
Saurer Ag.Arbon R	83	National-In. R	48
Golay Buchel P	80	Bucherer P	47
Union Bank Switz. 'B'	80	Galenica 'B'	46
Belimo Automation	80	Sbsi Hdg. 'B'	46
Union Bank Switz. R	79	Swisslog Hdg. R	46
Swiss Bank Co R	78	Sika 'B'	45
Tecan 'B'	75	Balair-Cta R	45
Moevenpick P	75	Hero R	44
Allgem. Fin. 'B'	74	Georg Fischer 'B'	44
Huber & Suhner R	73	Ems-Chemie 'B'	44
Crossair R	73	Siegfried R	43
Also Hdg. R	73	Llb 'B'	43
Jelmoli R	72	Sika R	43
Pirelli Intl. 'B'	72	Bank Sarasin R	43
Globus P	71	Villars R	42
Golay Buchel 'B'	71	Ciment Port. 'R'	42
Edipresse R	70	Georg Fischer R	41
Jelmoli 'B'	70	Graub Kb P	40
Prodega P	69	Stillhalter Vis.	40
Rieter Holding R	69	Roche Holding Gsh.	39
Zuerch.Ziegel 'B'	69	Hero 'B'	39
Kuoni Reisen R	68	Publigroup R	39
Fig R	68	Asklia R	39
Crossair Genuss	67	Big Star	38
Globus R	66	Bucher Hdg. 'B'	38
Eichhof 'B'	63	Ascom 'B'	38
Cos Computer 'B'	63	Simplon 'B'	38
Prodega R	63	Micronas 'R'	36
Eichhof R	62	Accu-Oerlikon 'B'	35
Gurit Heber 'B'	62	Sez Reg -A-	33
Edipresse 'B'	62	Alusuisse 'B'	33
Vp Bank Vaduz 'B'	61	Kuehne & Nagel	33
Tege Montreux	60	Baumgartner R	33
Vontobel 'B'	59	Calida 'B'	33
Wmh 'B'	59	Liecht.Glb.Tst.Pc.	32
Nationalbank R	58	Alusuisse R	31
Hottinger Zueri	57	Villars 'B'	30
Oz Holding 'B'	57	Ascom R	30
Cementia Hdg. 'B'	57	Zehnder 'B'	30
Oerlikon-Buehrle R	55	Kardex P	30

The Largest Companies in the Country by Market Capitalization as of 31 December 1997

Company Name	Market Capitalization Local Currency (Millions)	Market Capitalization US Dollars (Millions)
Novartis R	147,016	100,796
Roche Holding Gsh.	101,907	69,868
Nestle R	86,297	59,166
Credit Suisse R	60,093	41,201
Union Bank Switz. 'B'	44,836	30,740
Swiss Re R	39,942	27,385
Roche Holding 'B'	36,000	24,682
Swiss Bank Co R	35,106	24,069
Zurich In. R	32,644	22,381
Novartis 'B'	16,209	11,113
Abb Ag 'B'	14,845	10,178
Ciba Specialty Chems. R	12,023	8,243
Union Bank Switz. R	9,294	6,372
Swiss Life B	8,982	6,158
Clariant	8,872	6,083
Richemont B 'A'	8,300	5,690
Adecco 'B'	6,973	4,780
Ares-Serono 'B'	6,375	4,371
Holderbank 'B'	6,067	4,160
Alusuisse R	5,743	3,938
Pharma Vision 'B'	5,551	3,806
Baloise R	5,522	3,786
Elektrowatt 'B'	4,546	3,117
Sairgroup R	4,336	2,973
Stillhalter Vis.	4,070	2,790
Bk Vision 'B'	3,928	2,693
Ems-Chemie 'B'	3,457	2,370
Surveillance 'B'	3,455	2,369
Sulzer Medica	3,395	2,328
Sulzer R	3,365	2,307
Smh R	2,961	2,030
Smh 'B'	2,917	2,000
Alusuisse 'B'	2,820	1,933
Pargesa 'B'	2,638	1,809
Julius Baer 'B'	2,532	1,736
Holderbank R	2,404	1,648
Aare-Tessin R (Atel)	2,398	1,644
Pirelli Intl. 'B'	2,204	1,511
Oerlikon-Buehrle R	2,197	1,506
Llb 'B'	2,177	1,493
Helvetia Patria R	2,061	1,413
Abb Ag R	1,993	1,366
Surveillance R	1,712	1,174
Bcv 'B'	1,656	1,135
Kuoni Reisen R	1,643	1,126
Saurer Ag.Arbon R	1,617	1,108

Company Name	Market Capitalization Local Currency (Millions)	Market Capitalization US Dollars (Millions)
Motor-Columbus 'B'	1,383	948
Gotthard Bank 'B'	1,363	934
Rieter Holding R	1,351	926
National-In. R	1,255	860
Valora R	1,240	850
Schindler R	1,197	821
Neue Aarg Bank R	1,120	768
Sbsi Hdg. 'B'	1,101	755
Georg Fischer 'B'	1,000	686
Vontobel 'B'	975	669
Feldsch.-Hurlimann R	879	602
Gas Vision 'B'	878	602
Forbo R	875	600
Crossair R	861	590
Suedelektra 'B'	855	586
Bb Biotech	839	575
Phoenix Mecano 'B'	820	562
Schindler P	806	553
Publigroup R	790	541
Hilti P	784	538
Stratec Holdings B R	784	538
Sika 'B'	773	530
Bobst 'B'	753	516
Eg Laufenburg 'B'	752	516
Cementia Hdg. 'B'	752	516
Liecht.Glb.Tst.Pc.	738	506
Danzas R	723	496
Michelin Fin. 'B'	717	491
Tag Heuer	684	469
Cortaillod 'B'	673	461
Esec Holding	661	453
Pirelli Intl. P	661	453
Kw Laufenburg 'B'	655	449
Sig R	634	435
Hero 'B'	625	428
Vp Bank Vaduz 'B'	618	424
Intershop 'B'	595	408
Ascom 'B'	595	408
Generali (Schweiz) R	579	397
Jelmoli 'B'	573	393
Huber & Suhner R	570	391
Lindt&Sprungli R	564	387
Agie Charmilles R	562	385
Immuno 'B'	552	378
Zuerch.Ziegel 'B'	526	361
Disetronic 'B'	520	357
Berner Allgem. R	512	351
Oz Holding 'B'	508	348
Von Roll 'B'	506	347

Company Name	Market Capitalization Local Currency (Millions)	Market Capitalization US Dollars (Millions)	Company Name	Market Capitalization Local Currency (Millions)	Market Capitalization US Dollars (Millions)
Siegfried R	501	344	Lindt&Sprungli 'B'	219	150
Sig 'B'	491	336	Apg R	214	147
Selecta	490	336	Kudelski P	210	144
Valiant R	472	324	Castle Alternative Inv.R	209	143
Sez Reg -A-	470	323	Apg Genuss	201	138
Zuger Kantonal 'B'	468	321	Christ R	200	137
Sarna R	466	319	Usego R	200	137
Ciment Port. 'R'	458	314	Indholding. R	200	137
Bobst R	443	304	Canon (Schweiz) R	199	136
Hero R	419	287	Bell R	198	136
Cementia Hdg. P	414	284	Asklia R	198	135
Coop Bank	411	282	Bucherer P	195	134
Vp Bank Vaduz P	401	275	Schweizerhall R	192	132
Bb Medtech	401	275	Tege Montreux	188	129
Logitech R	397	272	Moevenpick R	185	127
Bt&T Telekommunikations	387	265	Arbonia Forsterb	181	124
			Intershop R	181	124
Jelmoli R	384	263	Netstal 'B'	181	124
Globus R	381	261	Basler Kb P Limited Data	180	124
Tecan 'B'	365	250			
Fig R	364	250	Hiestand R	179	123
Bank Sarasin R	363	249	Keramik	177	121
Gurit Heber 'B'	362	248	Also Hdg. R	176	120
Micronas 'R'	358	245	Vaudoise 'B'	175	120
C K W 'B'	343	235	Kuehne & Nagel	171	117
Sika R	331	227	Unigestion 'B'	170	117
Belimo Automation	325	223	Balair-Cta R	166	114
Lindt&Sprungli P	319	219	Gretag-Macbeth R	164	113
Bucher Hdg. 'B'	316	217	Zehnder 'B'	162	111
Galenica 'B'	315	216	Komax	161	111
Globus P	309	212	Georg Fischer R	159	109
Swisslog Hdg. R	296	203	Fuchs Petrolub 'B'	155	106
Fotolab 'B'	293	201	Ascom R	153	105
Kaba	286	196	Orior 'B'	148	101
Moevenpick 'B'	282	193	Bossard 'B'	147	101
Rothschild 'B'	275	189	Luzerner Kb P	143	98
Daetwyler 'B'	272	187	Altin 'B'	141	96
Phonak	271	186	Eichhof R	141	96
Creinvest 'B'	260	178	Unilabs 'B'	139	95
Sbsi Hdg. P	258	177	Sbsi Hdg. R	138	94
Zellweger 'B'	258	177	Jungfraubahn R	133	91
Moevenpick P	241	165	Nokia-Maillefer 'B'	133	91
Feldsch.-Hurlimann P	241	165	Sopracenerina R	132	91
Attisholz R	240	164	Prodega R	130	89
Interroll	238	163	Henniez R	126	86
Edipresse R	234	161	Enr Eastern Natural	116	80
Mikron R	232	159	Harwanne 'B'	115	79
Edipresse 'B'	231	158	Orell Fussli R Limited Data	110	75
Basell Kb 'B'	230	158			

Company Name	Market Capitalization Local Currency (Millions)	Market Capitalization US Dollars (Millions)
Graub Kb P	110	75
Kardex P	110	75
Porst 'B'	108	74
Batigroup R	107	73
Kardex B	99	68
Allgem. Fin. 'B'	96	66
India Investment	95	65
Nationalbank R	91	62
Zschokke R	90	62
Gonset 'B'	89	61
Lem 'B'	89	61
Ums Swissmetal 'B'	88	60
Spgp.B	84	58
New Venturetec B	83	57
Warteck R	80	55
Maag 'B'	78	53
Metallwaren P	74	51
Big Star	71	49
Baumgartner R	69	47
Vetropack 'B'	66	46
Sihl R	66	45
Prodega P	65	44
Winterthur In. R	62	43
Wmh 'B'	62	43
Swissair Gsh.	60	41
Walliser Kb. 'B'	60	41
Schlatter R	58	40
Eichhof 'B'	58	40
Calida 'B'	52	36
Loeb P	50	34
Cft 'B'	50	34
Quadrant B	49	34
Pelikan 'B'	46	32
Elma Electronic	45	31
Cos Computer 'B'	45	31
Sunstar 'B'	43	30
Simplon 'B'	42	29
Infranor Br.	41	28
Gavazzi(Carlo) 'B'	40	28
Swiss Steel R	40	27
Distefora 'B'	37	25
Scana Holding	36	25
Haldengut R	34	23
Warteck P	33	23
C.K.W. P	31	21
Crossair Genuss	30	21
Golay Buchel 'B'	30	20
Bq.Cant Jura 'B'	29	20
Hugli 'B'	28	19

Company Name	Market Capitalization Local Currency (Millions)	Market Capitalization US Dollars (Millions)
Cft R	28	19
Sihl 'B'	27	19
Intersport R	26	18
Calanda R	23	16
Hpi Hldg. R	20	14
Quadrant R	19	13
Buero Fuerrer 'B'	19	13
Hpi Hldg. 'B'	18	12
Haldengut 'B'	18	12
Zueblin Hdg. 'B'	17	12
Balair-Cta P	16	11
Calanda 'B'	16	11

Regional Exchanges: None

Other Exchanges:

Swiss Options and Financial Futures Exchange (SOFFEX)
Selnaustrasse
8021 Zurich
Switzerland
Phone: (41-1) 229 21 11
Fax: (41-1) 229 22 33
Internet: www.swx.ch

Other Investment Information:

Swiss National Bank
Bundesplatz
3033 Berne
Switzerland
Phone: (41-31) 210211
Fax: (41-31) 210207

Federal Banking Commission
Marktgasse 37
3001 Berne
Switzerland
Phone: (41-31) 331 69 11
Fax: (41-31) 322 69 26

SEGA (Swiss Securities Clearing Corp.)
Brandschenkestr. 47
8022 Zurich
Switzerland
Phone: (41-1) 288 45 70
Fax: (41-1) 288 48 92

SYMBOL (United States and Others)
See TRADING SYMBOL.

SYNDICAT (France)

See SYNDICATE.

SYNDICATE

A *Syndicate* is a group of investment bankers who purchase a new issue and resell the issue to the general public at a fixed price. Compensation comes from the difference between the issue price and the amount of money paid to the issuer, less any fees, expenses, and considerations paid to selling groups.

A syndicate might also be a group of investment bankers involved in bidding for a competitive issue, but are unsuccessful in the bid.

The broker/dealers acting as agents for the issuer, or as agents for the underwriters in the syndicate, are part of the selling group, but technically not a part of the syndicate.

See also AGENT; SELLING GROUP; UNDERWRITING.

SYNDICATE ACCOUNT LETTER

A *Syndicate Account Letter* is a document in the form of a letter sent by the syndicate manager to other members. The letter details conditions for the syndicate operations.

For issues of corporate offerings, the agreement is a formal document known as an "Agreement Among Underwriters."

A contractual agreement drawn up between investment banking participating members who form a syndicate, the Agreement Among Underwriters is also referred to as a syndicate contract or purchase group agreement. It differs from the Underwriting Agreement that is drawn up between the syndicate manager and the company issuing the securities.

An Agreement Among Underwriters:

• Appoints the originating investment banker as syndicate manager and agent

• Appoints additional managers, if necessary

• Defines the members' liability, which generally is limited to the amount of the participation, and agrees to pay each member's share on settlement date

• Authorizes the manager to form and allocate units to a selling group, and agrees to adhere to the rules of the selling group agreement

• Defines the lifetime of the syndicate, generally to 30 days past the termination of the selling group, or earlier if by mutual agreement

Syndicates are formed among investment bankers to bring out new issues and have the shares quickly sold into the public market in a way that is fair to investors as well as the company.

See also INVESTMENT BANKER; SELLING GROUP; UNDERWRITING.

SYNDICATE MANAGER (United States and Others)

The lead underwriter in a group is called the *Syndicate Manager*. Responsibilities include the organizational details (including contracts and agreements), formation of selling groups, allocation, confirmation of subject orders, closing financial accounting details, and reports of the underwriting activity.

A fee is paid to the manager of negotiated underwritings. Competitive underwritings can have more than one syndicate manager.

See also SYNDICATE; UNDERWRITING.

SYNDIKAT (Germany)

See SYNDICATE.

SYNERGY

Derived from the Greek for "working together," the word *Synergy* has taken on a modern meaning describing a situation in which the effect of the whole is greater than the sum of the individual components.

This concept can relate to corporate mergers, as the joining together of two organizations is expected to produce cost savings and increase the market share power. Diversification—in which a parent company spreads risk by acquiring a company—can be positive if it adds synergy to a company and makes it more efficient and productive. The disparaging term "diworsification" is sometimes used by financial analysts to describe a situation in which a company buys other smaller companies unrelated to their main business just for the sake of being involved with takeovers.

See also CONGLOMERATE; MERGER; TAKEOVER/TAKEOVER BID.

T

TAILGATING

When a broker buys securities for his personal account after performing the same transaction for a client, his actions are described as *Tailgating*.

Also known as trailing, tailgaiting is not strictly illegal. Many firms, however, prohibit their brokers from tailgating on ethical grounds. They see the activity as not being in the best interest of the customer or the brokerage firm.

Tailgaiting is considered an illegal act if the broker is trading on inside information.

See also INSIDER DEALING/INSIDER TRADING; STOCK-BROKER.

TAIWAN, REPUBLIC OF CHINA

Taiwan (Chung-hua Min-Kuo [Republic of China]) is an island situated 100 miles (160 km) off the southeast coast of Mainland China.

Area: 13,900 square miles (36,000 square km)

Population: 21,268,000 (74.7% urban; 25.3% rural)

Forms of Government: Multiparty republic with two legislative houses: National Assembly—402 members; Legislative Yuan—161 members. Chief of state: President. Head of government: Premier.

Official Language: Mandarin Chinese

Capital: Taipei

Largest Cities: Taipei, 2,652,685; Kao-hsiung, 1,416,160; T'ai-chung, 836,560; T'ai-nan, 702,704; Chi-lung, 365,312

Economy:

Currency: New Taiwan dollar (NT$)

National Budget: Revenue—NT$1.9 trillion; expenditures—NT$1.9 trillion (economic development: 29.3%; administration and defense: 24.8% education: 18.8%)

Public Debt: NT$553.5 billion

Gross National Product: US$244.7 billion

Principal Products: Sugarcane; rice; citrus fruits and other fruits and vegetables; livestock; machinery; plastics

Foreign Trade (Imports): NT$2.3 trillion (electronic machinery: 19.7%; nonelectrical machinery: 12.3%; chemicals: 10.5%; road motor vehicles: 7.1%; iron and steel: 6.7%; crude petroleum: 3.2%; from Japan:

29.0%; United States: 21.1%; Germany: 5.6%; Korea: 3.5%; Singapore: 2.8%; Malaysia: 2.7%)

Foreign Trade (Exports): NT$2.5 trillion (electrical machinery: 20.3%; nonelectrical machinery: 19.7%; plastic articles: 6.1%; synthetic fibers: 5.5%; transportation equipment: 5.2%; to United States: 26.2%; Hong Kong: 22.9%: Japan: 11.0%; Singapore: 3.6%; Germany: 3.5%)

Stock Exchanges: 1
Taiwan Stock Exchange (TSE)
7-10th Floor, City Building
85 Yen-Ping South Road
Taipei
Taiwan
Phone: (886-2) 311 4020
Fax: (886-2) 311 4004

Internet Address: www.tse.com.tw/

Trading Hours:
Monday–Friday, 9:00 to 12:00
Saturday, 9:00 to 11:00

Office Hours:
Monday–Friday, 9:00 to 12:00 and 2:00 to 5:00
Saturday, 9:00 to 12:00

Listed Companies: 404

Total Market Capitalization:

At 31 December 1997

Local Currency (Millions)	US Dollars (Millions)
5,852,647	179,161

Major Sectors: Banking and insurance, textiles, cement, steel, plastics

Share Price Performance:

(% Change)	
1992	–27
1993	100
1994	28
1995	–22
1996	38
1997	19

History: With the establishment of the Communist Party in 1949, new laws were created to provide each citizen of the new Republic of China with a decent standard of living. By 1952 social and political reform was being introduced in a number of ways, including Land Laws, which provided for the redistribution of land ownership. As a part of land reform, private land owned by a handful of wealthy landlords was cut into small pieces and redistributed among the peasant class.

Although the government's actions were drastic (and sometimes violent), they proved to be fair. All landowners received bonds and shares in four significant government-owned businessess as compensation for their losses. These landowners were the original investors in one of Asia's most successful "tiger economies," and the period of economic prosperity that followed led to the growth of a middle class eager to invest in a securities market. Eventually, a Securities and Exchange Commission with the authority to oversee securities trading and public offerings was created in Taiwan in 1960.

Today, the Taiwan Stock Exchange (TSE) is one of the most technologically advanced stock markets in Asia. The TSE has focused efforts on computerization and improving the quality of accounting, financial analysis, and clarifying legal procedures for issuing and trading securities. The SEC is in charge of appointing one-third of the TSE's directors.

Foreign institutional investors have been allowed to invest directly in Taiwan since 1991. Plans to begin the trading of futures and options on the TSE Index and the trading of government bonds are well advanced.

Classes of Securities: Common and preferred shares, government bonds, corporate bonds, money market securities, and debentures

Indices: The Taiwan Stock Exchange Index (TSE) (1966 = 100)

Supervisory Organizations: The Securities and Exchange Commission (SEC) regulates all securities markets.

Depository: The Taiwan Securities Central Depository (TSCD) serves as clearinghouse and depository.

Settlement Details:

Shares:

Trade date + 0 days (T + 0) sales by brokers and traders

Trade date + 1 days (T + 1) sales with stock delivery or cash payment

Trade date + 2 days (T + 2) book-entry through the TSCD

Physical or book-entry

Receive and delivery versus payment is allowed.

Turnaround same day trades are prohibited.

Trading: All shares trade through the TSE by way of the FAST computer system, which handles most of the transactions. Brokers and traders enter buy and sell orders, which are executed by computer according to exchange rules. FAST has the ability to:

- Collect orders from brokers
- Sort orders by price and time priority
- Execute orders
- Log the market price
- Send order confirmation reports to brokers
- Send trading reports to brokers
- Send market data to brokers and quote vendors

Margin transactions are now common after being introduced in 1974. Forty-six securities firms and ten banks are licensed to lend money or securities for transactions on the TSE.

Share prices are limited to a 7% fluctuation as compared to the closing price of the previous session. The Securities and Exchange Commission expects to relax the price fluctuation rule and eventually eliminate it altogether.

Standard board lots (round lots) are 1,000 shares.

Listing Requirements: Listing requirements are set by the Securities and Exchange Commission and the Taiwan Stock Exchange. Listed companies are required to submit annual, semiannual, and quarterly financial statements as well as monthly operating reports to the SEC.

Financial reports of listed companies must be audited by accounting firms consisting of a minimum of three certified public accountants, and must be signed by at least two certified public accountants. SEC standards for audit and budget systems must be followed.

A listed company has two days to report any event that might have a significant impact on the price of the shares. Any purchase or sale of assets exceeding 20% of a company's paid-up capital must be reported in two days.

Investor Taxation:

Dividends are subject to a 15% withholding tax.

No capital gains tax.

Share transfer tax of 0.3% of transaction value on the sell side.

Limitations:

Foreign investment 5% of a company's shares.

Total foreign investment of all investors in a single company is limited to 10%.

Total foreign investment quota is US$5 billion.

Ceiling per foreign institutional investor is $100 million.

Unlisted, open-end unit trusts are not bound by the ceiling.

Four areas are allotted for the placement of foreign investment funds.

They are:

1. Mutual funds established by the five Securities Investment Trust Enterprises (SITEs)

   a. SITE purchases the securities

   b. SITE issues "beneficial certificates" to a foreign depositary or to a special-purpose foreign investment company. These companies, in turn, issue depositary receipts or shares to investors that trade on overseas exchanges.

2. Qualified Foreign Institutional Investors (QFII), those organizations allowed to invest specified amounts of money in shares on the TSE.

   a. QFIIs can be major banks, insurance companies, fund managers, or foreign brokerage firms that meet the SEC requirements for total assets, net worth, years of experience, and value of securities holdings.

   b. QFIIs apply for an investment quota between US$5 million and US$20 million.

   c. The initial investment must be made within the six months following approval.

   d. Cash cannot be repatriated for a minimum of three months.

   e. Earnings can be repatriated once a year.

QFIIs can invest in listed shares, government and corporate bonds, beneficiary certificates, or money market instruments. QFIIs are prohibited from investing in convertible bonds. They can hold up to 5% of the shares of a listed company, but all QFIIs together are not allowed to hold more than 10% of the shares of any listed company. Additional restrictions may be applied. Margin trading is not allowed. As much as 10% of the available funds are allowed to be invested in time deposits of up to three months, but other cash must be kept in demand accounts.

A local custodian and a local agent are appointed to exercise shareholder's rights. A local broker must also be selected. Every transaction made by the QFII is supported by a submitted written order and settlement is confirmed by the custodian on the following trading day.

3. Global Depository Receipts (GDRs), issued by nine companies in Taiwan. Dividends received from GDRs are subject to a 25% withholding tax.

4. Euro-convertible bonds, available from 32 Taiwanese companies. Euro-convertible bonds are subject to 25% withholding tax.

Securities Lending: Prohibited

Brokerage Firms:

Core Pacific Securities Co.
Taipei
Taiwan
Phone: (886-2) 706 7777

Polaris Securities Co.
Taipei
Taiwan
Phone: (886-2) 776 6288

Cathay Investement & Trust Co.
Taipei
Taiwan
Phone: (886-2) 311 4881

China Securities
Taipei
Taiwan
Phone: (886-2) 521 5001

Jin Hsin Securities Co.
Taipei
Taiwan
Phone: (886-2) 314 1141-9

Taiwan Development & Trust
Taipei
Taiwan
Phone: (886-2) 394 4333

Taiwan Securities Investment Co.
Taipei
Taiwan
Phone: (886-2) 551 5161

The Overseas Trust Corporation
Taipei
Taiwan
Phone: (886-2) 713 9911

Well-Phone Securities Co.
Taipei
Taiwan
Phone: (886-2) 581 6111

Traders:

China Investment & Trust Co.
Taipei
Taiwan
Phone: (886-2) 731 5111

China Stock & Investment Co.
Taipei
Taiwan
Phone: (886-2) 713 3322

Oriental Investment Corporation
Taipei
Taiwan
Phone: (886-2) 311 5015

Company Information:

The Best Performing Shares in the Country

Company Name	Share Price Change 1 January 1997 to 31 December 1997 (%)
Taiyu Products	397
Asustek Computer	347
Pan-International	345
Yee Chen Construction	232
Aurora	218
Opto Tech	217
Compeq Manufacturing Co.	204
Ritek Incorporation	200
Ase	198
Taiwan Semiconductor	197
Hon Hai Prec. Ind. Co.	183
Wei Chuan Food	181
Ub Office Systems	172
Pou Chen	159
Taichung Machinery Works	154
Cis Technology	147
Union Leather & Printing	144
Lian Hwa Foods	141
Liton Electronic	135
China Chm. Pharm.	134
Master Home Frtr. Co.	131
Yang Iron	130
Fu I Indl. Co.	129
Kuo Feng	128
Taih Yung Enter.	128
Cmc Magnetics	127
Synnex Tech. Intl.	126
Shin Shin Sprmkt.	123
Taiwan Mask	123

Company Name	Share Price Change 1 January 1997 to 31 December 1997 (%)
Delta Elt. Indl. Co.	117
Silitek	116
United Micro Eltn.	113
Chinese Automobile	113
Phoenixtec Power	113
Tai Fang Foods	109
Chin-Poon Indl.	105
Compal Electronics	103
Yue Loong Motor	102
Chroma Ate	102
Kwong Fong Inds.Corp.	101
Holtek Microelectronics	99
Inventec	95
Pony Leather	94
Yageo Corporation	92
Tonlin Dept. Store	90
Systex Corp.	89
Siliconware Precn.	86
Delphan Construction	86
Nien Hsing Textile Co.	84
Taiwan Pineapple	83
Orient Semiconductor	81
Winbond Eltn.	81
Wei Chih Steel Indl.	79
Rectron	78
Kuoyang Construction	77
Chou Chin Indl. Co.	77
Lee Chi Ents. Co.	76
Formosa Oilseed Proc.	73
Pacific Elec.Wire & Cable	73
Falcon Cycle-Parts	73
Chung Hsin Elec. & Mch.	72
Chuntex Electronic	72
S&T Copper Inds.	70
Minchali Metal Ind. Co.	70
Continental Engr.	70
Top Con. & Dev.	69
Nan Kang Rub. Tyre Co.	68
Tay Feng Tire	68
Sun Splendor	66
Great Electronics	66
China Motor	66
Sdi Corporation	66
First Hotel	65
Tay-Shan Enterprise	63
Macronix Intl. Co.	63
Universal Scien. Indl.	63
Rexon Industrial	62
Everest Textile	60

Company Name	Share Price Change 1 January 1997 to 31 December 1997 (%)
China Development	60
Lite-On Tech.	59
China Wire & Cable Co.	58
Solomon Tech. Corp.	58
Hong Yi Fiber Ind. Co.	58
Sunko Ink	58
Min Hsing Cotton Mill	56
Mitac International	55
Mosel Vitelic	52
Kang Na Hsiung Enter. Co.	52
Eternal Chemical Co.	51
Taiwan Fluorescent	50
Kindom Construction	49
Standard Foods Taiwan	48
Kee-Tai Properties	48
Bes Engr. Corp.	47
Primax Electronics	47
Kinpo Electronics	46
Long Bon Con.	46
Ctci	45
Acer Peripherals	45
Wus Printed Circuit	45
Taian Electric	44
Taiwan Tea	44
China Container Terminal	44
Hung Sheng	43
Ensure Co.	42
U-Lead Industrial	41
Chung Fu Textile	40
Da-Cin Construction	40
First Intl. Computer	38
Far Eastern Textiles	37
Ruentex Industries	37
Yu Foong Spinning	36
Tong Lung Metal Industry	36
New Sun Metal Indl. Co.	34
Feng Tay Ents. Co.	34
Shihlin Paper	33
Hong Tai Elec. Ind. Co.	33
Ho Tung Chemical	33
Lan Fa Textile Co.	32
Taiwan Sogo Shinkong	32
Taiwan Secom	31
Der Pao Construction	31
Ace Union Foods	30
Taroko Textile	30
Picvue Electronics	30
Collins Co.	30

The Largest Companies in the Country by Market Capitalization as of 31 December 1997

Company Name	Market Capitalization Local Currency (Millions)	Market Capitalization US Dollars (Millions)
Cathay Life In. Co.	506,471	15,504
Taiwan Semiconductor	457,105	13,993
First Coml. Bank	246,303	7,540
United Micro Eltn.	243,160	7,444
China Development	242,830	7,433
Hua Nan Coml. Bank	236,844	7,250
Chang Hwa Coml. Bank	223,103	6,830
Shin Kong Life Insurance	188,004	5,755
China Steel	181,649	5,561
Nan Ya Plastics	175,638	5,377
Asustek Computer	166,991	5,112
Formosa Plastics	157,681	4,827
Wei Chuan Food	133,901	4,099
Utd. Wld. Chs. Coml. Bank	127,568	3,905
Intl. Coml. Bank of China	122,572	3,752
Ase	116,446	3,565
Chiao Tung Bank	104,805	3,208
Tatung	103,194	3,159
Acer	95,207	2,914
Formosa Chemical & Fiber	93,843	2,873
China Trust Business Bk.	92,594	2,834
President Ents.	86,176	2,638
Hon Hai Prec. Ind. Co.	84,447	2,585
Mosel Vitelic	78,835	2,413
Far Eastern Textiles	76,333	2,337
Inventec	75,267	2,304
Winbond Eltn.	74,714	2,287
Taipei Bank	74,200	2,271
Fubon Insurance	71,589	2,191
Yue Loong Motor	70,021	2,143
Taipei Bus. Bank	65,741	2,012
Macronix Intl. Co.	64,834	1,985
Taiwan Cement	63,855	1,955
Pacific Elec. Wire & Cable	63,145	1,933
Evergreen Mar. Corp.	59,366	1,817

Company Name	Market Capitalization Local Currency (Millions)	Market Capitalization US Dollars (Millions)	Company Name	Market Capitalization Local Currency (Millions)	Market Capitalization US Dollars (Millions)
Asia Cement	58,421	1,788	Cheng Shin Rub. Ind. Co.	28,399	869
China Air Lines	58,275	1,784	Ta Yih Indl.	28,035	858
Compeq Manufacturing Co.	57,820	1,770	Dah An Coml. Bank	26,563	813
Delta Elt. Indl. Co.	57,330	1,755	Pacific Construction	25,298	774
Cathay Con. Co.	56,522	1,730	China Life Insurance	25,038	766
Compal Electronics	55,213	1,690	Taiwan Secom	24,826	760
Fuh-Hwa Securities Fin.	54,000	1,653	Taichung Machinery Works	24,788	759
Taichung Bus. Bank	53,745	1,645	Tainan Spinning	24,395	747
China Motor	52,146	1,596	Shihlin Paper	24,078	737
Chinese Automobile	50,950	1,560	Goldsun Dev. & Con. Co.	23,977	734
Pou Chen	50,782	1,555	Intl. Bills Finance	23,786	728
Siliconware Precn.	50,373	1,542	Far Eastern Dept. Stores	23,611	723
Teco Elec.& Machinery	49,649	1,520	Cis Technology	23,443	718
Taiwan Tea	46,933	1,437	Umax Data Systems	23,069	706
Yageo Corporation	46,925	1,436	Synnex Tech. Intl.	22,950	703
The Medm. Bus. Bk. Hsin Chu	45,625	1,397	Ritek Incorporation	22,860	700
Taiwan Pineapple	44,969	1,377	Ever Fortune	22,683	694
Kuoyang Construction	43,050	1,318	Aurora	22,329	684
Hualon-Teijran	42,657	1,306	Clevo	22,125	677
Sanyang Ind.	42,345	1,296	Ton Yi Industrial	21,687	664
China Utd. Tst. Inv.	42,091	1,288	Taiwan Mask	21,638	662
Walsin Lihwa Wire	41,709	1,277	Universal Scien. Indl.	21,625	662
First Intl. Computer	41,581	1,273	Hotai Motor Co.	21,539	659
Taiwan Glass	40,500	1,240	The Medium Bk. of Tainan	21,407	655
Taiyu Products	39,453	1,208	China Bills Finance	21,375	654
Farmers Bank of China	38,610	1,182	Hung Fu Construction	20,833	638
China Petrochemical	36,403	1,114	The Chinese Bank	20,384	624
President Chain Store	35,762	1,095	Nan Kang Rub. Tyre Co.	20,344	623
Cmc Magnetics	34,976	1,071	Gvc Corporation	20,338	623
Chung Hsing Bills Fin.	34,843	1,067	Orient Semiconductor	20,298	621
Tuntex Distinct	34,500	1,056	Continental Engr.	20,085	615
Wan Hai Lines	34,344	1,051	Mitac International	19,909	609
Liton Electronic	32,105	983	Shihlin Elec. & Engr.	19,893	609
Yang Ming Marine Tran.	31,786	973	Lite-On Tech.	19,828	607
Formosa Taffeta Co.	31,708	971	Ta-Jung Transportation	19,730	604
Grand Commercial Bank	31,500	964	China Rebar Co.	19,551	599
Holtek Microelectronics	31,055	951	Shinkong Synthetic	19,378	593
			Ruentex Industries	19,263	590
			Yuen Foong Yu Paper	19,049	583
Acer Peripherals	29,024	888	Yung Tay Engr.	18,837	577

Company Name	Market Capitalization Local Currency (Millions)	Market Capitalization US Dollars (Millions)	Company Name	Market Capitalization Local Currency (Millions)	Market Capitalization US Dollars (Millions)
Hung Sheng	18,716	573	Taiwan Styrene Monomer	13,339	408
Usi Far East	18,444	565	The Medm. Bk. of Kaohsiung	13,239	405
Sampo	18,324	561	Fu-Sheng Ind.	13,119	402
Kuo Feng	17,693	542	The Medm. Bk. of Taitung	13,114	401
Eternal Chemical Co.	17,648	540	Tong Lung Metal Industry	13,107	401
Phoenixtec Power	17,585	538	Lien Hwa Industrial	12,899	395
Prince Housing Dev.	17,475	535	Formosan Rubber Gp.	12,865	394
Yee Chen Construction	17,233	528	U-Ming Marine	12,801	392
Silitek	16,822	515	Microtek Intl.	12,564	385
Mercuries & Associates	16,773	513	Taiwan Life Insurance	12,422	380
Kwong Fong Inds. Corp.	16,730	512	Opto Tech	12,400	380
Tay Feng Tire	16,618	509	Nien Hsing Textile Co.	12,305	377
Leofoo Development	16,525	506	Taiwan Sogo Shinkong	12,264	375
Twinhead Intl. Corp.	16,492	505	Wus Printed Circuit	12,238	375
Kindom Construction	16,448	504	Standard Foods Taiwan	12,171	373
Tung Ho Steel	16,185	495	Yieh Phui Enterprise	12,000	367
Pan-International	16,148	494	Feng Hsin Iron & Stl. Co.	11,997	367
China Manmade Fiber	15,879	486	Union Petrochemicals	11,987	367
Taiwan Synthetic Rub.	15,590	477	Feng Tay Ents.Co.	11,963	366
Master Home Frtr. Co.	15,281	468	Chungkuo Insurance	11,908	365
Sinkong Spinning	14,956	458	Delphan Construction	11,736	359
Chia Hsin Flour	14,922	457	Hung Ching Dev. & Con.	11,706	358
Uniglory Marine	14,830	454	Everest Textile	11,689	358
Oriental Un. Chemical	14,529	445	Primax Electronics	11,636	356
Chia Hsin Cement	14,515	444	Chung Hsin Elec. & Mch.	11,439	350
Chuntex Electronic	14,348	439	Taiwan Paper	11,334	347
Der Pao Construction	14,332	439	D-Link	11,332	347
Taiwan Sakura	14,278	437	Silicon Integrated Sys.	11,321	347
Pao Shiang Indl.	14,196	435	Tidehold	11,149	341
Grd. Pac. Petrochem.	14,181	434	Top Con. & Dev.	11,147	341
China Chm. Pharm.	14,142	433	Hua Engr. Wire Cable Co.	11,052	338
Taiwan Fluorescent	14,056	430	Lealea Enterprise Co.	10,955	335
Hsing Ta Cement Co.	14,024	429	Kuei Hung Indl. Co	10,833	332
Wei Chih Steel Indl.	13,972	428			
Kinpo Electronics	13,962	427			
Cheng Loong Co.	13,932	426			
Adi	13,773	422			
Hocheng Corp.	13,700	419			
Chia Hsin Livestock	13,585	416			
Ctci	13,411	411			

Company Name	Market Capitalization Local Currency (Millions)	Market Capitalization US Dollars (Millions)	Company Name	Market Capitalization Local Currency (Millions)	Market Capitalization US Dollars (Millions)
Kao Hsing Chang Iron	10,818	331	Chroma Ate	8,406	257
Chien Tai Cement Co.	10,785	330	Ta Ya Elec. Wire	8,388	257
Tera Electronic	10,570	324	Union Insurance	8,387	257
Fu I Indl. Co.	10,542	323	Da-Cin Construction	8,356	256
Far East Silo & Ship.	10,515	322	Chia Her Indl. Co.	8,349	256
Sheng Yu Steel	10,500	321	Megamedia Corp.	8,306	254
Sun Splendor	10,485	321	Tong Yang Industry	8,233	252
Bao-Chen Con.	10,390	318	Mag Technology	8,204	251
Taih Yung Enter.	10,335	316	Chin-Poon Indl.	8,090	248
Everlight Chm. Indl.	10,271	314	China Gen. Plastic	8,068	247
Mustek System	10,232	313	Lee Chi Ents. Co.	8,030	246
Chung Shing Textile Co.	10,231	313	Ub Office Systems	7,963	244
Hung Poo Con.	10,027	307	Sakura Development	7,941	243
Kenda Rubber Ind. Co.	10,010	306	Ho Tung Chemical	7,872	241
Ruentex Con. & Dev.	10,009	306	Eagle Food	7,820	239
Sin Yih Ceramics	10,002	306	Taiwan Indl. Dev.	7,805	239
Great Taipei Gas	9,939	304	Lucky Cement	7,746	237
Chief Construction	9,755	299	Central Insurance	7,680	235
Kee-Tai Properties	9,740	298	First Steamship Co.	7,624	233
Long Bon Con.	9,711	297	Microelectronics Tech.	7,612	233
Ambassador Hotel	9,588	293	Systex Corp.	7,520	230
Taian Electric	9,565	293	Chun Yuan Stl. Indl. Co.	7,478	229
Lee Chang Yung Chm. Ind.	9,527	292	Min Hsing Cotton Mill	7,455	228
Solomon Tech. Corp.	9,520	291	Gtm	7,427	227
Accton	9,506	291	Acer Sertek	7,410	227
Kolin	9,476	290	Giant Mnfg. Co.	7,400	227
Yung Shin Pharm.	9,475	290	Lan Fa Textile Co.	7,399	227
Picvue Electronics	9,402	288	Core Pacific Con.	7,327	224
Asia Polymer	9,381	287	Chang Ku Building	7,283	223
Tonlin Dept. Store	9,315	285	Hong Tai Elec. Ind. Co.	7,273	223
Chung Hwa Pulp	9,283	284	Universal Cement	7,260	222
Shin Yen Industrial	9,124	279	Sanyo Elec. (Taiwan)	7,190	220
Taiwan Polypropylene	8,884	272	Shin Shin Sprmkt.	7,177	220
Southeast Cement	8,819	270	Great Chin. Mtl. Ind. Co.	7,077	217
First Hotel	8,816	270	Hong Chung	7,070	216
Dong Ho Textile	8,649	265	China Synthetic Rub.	7,059	216
S&T Copper Inds.	8,644	265	Tah Shin Industrial	7,053	216
Yieh Loong	8,613	264	U-Lead Industrial	7,009	215
China Wire & Cable Co.	8,601	263	Kye Systems Corporation	6,979	214
Collins Co.	8,550	262	Crowell Development	6,867	210
Li Peng Enterprise	8,515	261	Wan Hwa Enterprise	6,811	209
New Sun Metal Indl. Co.	8,409	257	Dahin	6,803	208

Company Name	Market Capitalization Local Currency (Millions)	Market Capitalization US Dollars (Millions)	Company Name	Market Capitalization Local Currency (Millions)	Market Capitalization US Dollars (Millions)
Hung Chou Chems. Ind. Co.	6,723	206	Sdi Corporation	4,988	153
Yi Jinn Industrial	6,723	206	Formosa Oilseed Proc.	4,987	153
Zig Sheng Industrial	6,636	203	Taroko Textile	4,965	152
Minchali Metal Ind. Co.	6,592	202	Yieh-Hsing	4,957	152
Agv Products	6,401	196	Chun Hsin Plywood & Lum.	4,940	151
Yang Iron	6,395	196	Kang Na Hsiung Enter. Co.	4,896	150
Tay-Shan Enterprise	6,362	195	Wa Chu Wool Ind. Co. (Tw.)	4,895	150
China Electric Mnfg.	6,360	195	Taiwan Fire & Marine In.	4,893	150
Right Way Industrial	6,340	194	Pao-Ku	4,800	147
Tong-Hwa Synthetic	6,253	191	First Copper & Iron	4,650	142
Taita Chemical	6,210	190	Hong Yi Fiber Ind. Co.	4,643	142
Tai I Elec. Wire & Cab.	6,094	187	Fortune Electric	4,620	141
Lian Hwa Foods	6,065	186	Hong Ho Prec. Tex. Co	4,613	141
Ve Wong	6,034	185	Chun Yu Works & Co.	4,600	141
Tycoons Group Enterprise	5,937	182	United Ceramics	4,558	140
Tecom	5,913	181	Shin Yih Fiber	4,549	139
Great Wall Ents. Co.	5,839	179	San Fang Chemical	4,478	137
Falcon Cycle-Parts	5,720	175	Carnival Text. Indl.	4,373	134
Sincere Navigation	5,702	175	Wan Yu Paper	4,370	134
New Asia Const & Dev.	5,700	174	Hsinhsin Natural Gas	4,333	133
Sino Japan Feed	5,645	173	Tahchung Supr. Qlt. Iron	4,317	132
Lily Textile Co.	5,580	171	Hwang Dih Lon Tex. Co.	4,312	132
Namchow Chm. Indl. Co.	5,568	170	Sunko Ink	4,299	132
Shinung	5,541	170	Ability Enterprise	4,298	132
Tai Fang Foods	5,522	169	Evergreen Transport	4,285	131
China Container Terminal	5,518	169	China Glaze Co.	4,200	129
Ensure Co.	5,467	167	De Licacy Indl.	4,187	128
Chia I Indl. Co.	5,386	165	Chien Shiang Stainless	4,153	127
Asia Chemical Corp.	5,349	164	Charoen Pok Phand Ents.	4,151	127
Evertop Wire	5,320	163	Kpt Inds.	4,133	127
Great Electronics	5,298	162	Standard Chemical	4,088	125
Tyc Brother Indl.	5,191	159	Apex Science & Engr.	4,009	123
Long Chen Paper Co.	5,156	158	King-Wei Fiber Co.	3,969	121
Ornatube Enterprise	5,156	158	Tnc Industrial	3,891	119
Cathay Chemical Works	5,153	158	Lee Tah Farm Inds.	3,847	118
I-Hwa Industrial	5,112	156	Formosan Un. Chemicals	3,829	117
Rexon Industrial	5,106	156			
Feng An Metal Indl. Co.	5,094	156			
Behavior Tech. Cmp.	5,034	154			
Elitegroup Cmp. Sy.	4,991	153			

Company Name	Market Capitalization Local Currency (Millions)	Market Capitalization US Dollars (Millions)
Corner Corporation	3,694	113
Nantex Ind.	3,600	110
Ding Ing Enterprise	3,556	109
Southeast Soda	3,492	107
Pony Leather	3,477	106
Tah Tong Textile	3,451	106
Universal Textile	3,434	105
Jen Hsian Con.	3,368	103
Grape King	3,321	102
Nan Yang Dyeing Co.	3,306	101
Fwu Sow Products	3,296	101

Regional Exchanges: None

Other Investment Information:
Industrial Development and Investment Center
10th Floor
7 Roosevelt Road
Sec. 1
Taipei,
Taiwan
Phone: (886-2) 394-7213
Fax: (886-2) 392-6835
Telex: 10634 INVEST

Investment Commission
8th Floor
7 Roosevelt Road
Sec. 1
Taipei,
Taiwan
Phone: (886-2) 351-3151
Fax: (886-2) 396-3970

Ministry of Economic Affairs
15 Foo Chow Street
Taipei,
Taiwan
Phone: (886-2) 321-2200
Fax: (886-2) 391-9398
Telex: 19884

Council for Economic Planning and Development
9th Floor
87 Nanking E. Road
Sec. 2
Taipei,
Taiwan,

Phone: (886-2) 351-0271
Fax: (886-2) 331-5387

Board of Foreign Trade
Ministry of Economic Affairs
1 Hu Kou Street
Taipei,
Taiwan
Phone: (886-2) 351-0271
Fax: (886-2) 331-5387

Industrial Development Bureau
Ministry of Economic Affairs
41-2 Hsin Yi Road
Sec. 3
Taipei,
Taiwan
Phone: (886-2) 754-1255
Fax: (886-2) 7030160

TAKE
Take is a term used between brokers and dealers when one buys a position from another.

TAKE A BATH
Take a Bath means to incur a substantial loss on taking a position in a security.

TAKE A FLYER
Take a Flyer means to buy or sell securities based on rumor or a hunch, without fully analyzing the company, its sector, or the market as a whole.

TAKE A POSITION
To *Take a Position* is to establish a net inventory position, either long or short, in a security.

See also OFFER; POSITION; SPECULATION.

TAKEOVER/TAKEOVER BID
When an individual, a group of individuals, or a company attempts to take control of another company by acquiring majority interest in the outstanding shares of that company, it is referred to as *Takeover.* Takeovers can be friendly, with both sides cooperating, or they can be unfriendly, with opposition from the target company occasionally ending up in a court battle.

Sometimes a company being taken over is broken up and sold off in pieces, and other times it is kept as a division of the acquiring company. Buying companies often court the senior management of their target company by offering generous "golden parachutes," to make the transaction more attractive if they accept the offer. Some target companies will have contingency plans that will be implemented to ward off a serious takeover attempt. These tactics, commonly referred to as poison pills or shark repellent, are designed to make the takeover too expensive and time consuming to be attractive.

An unfriendly suitor might build a strong share position and offer the target company a choice between being taken over or buying back their shares at the current higher prices. This strategy is known as greenmail.

If a company does not wish to be taken over and resists the efforts of the suitor, the takeover attempt will be described as a hostile bid or a hostile takeover. Hostile bids often push up the share price of the target company, but if the company is successful in preventing the takeover, the price generally drops back to its prebid trading range. Payment for a takeover may be made with cash, securities, or a combination of both.

See also ACQUISITION; ASSET; MERGER; POISON PILL; SHARK REPELLENT.

TALISMAN BOUGHT TRANSFER (TBT; United Kingdom)

Talisman Bought Transfer (TBT) is a legal means by which shares are transferred from the Stock Exchange Pool of Nominees (SEPON) company into the name of the new owner.

See also STOCK EXCHANGE POOL OF NOMINEES (SEPON); TRANSFER ACCOUNTING LODGEMENT FOR INVESTORS AND STOCK MANAGEMENT (TALISMAN).

TALISMAN SOLD TRANSFER (TST; United Kingdom)

Talisman Sold Transfer (TST) is a legal means by which shares are transferred into the name of the Stock Exchange Pool of Nominees (SEPON) company from the share seller.

See also STOCK EXCHANGE POOL OF NOMINEES (SEPON); TRANSFER ACCOUNTING LODGEMENT FOR INVESTORS AND STOCK MANAGEMENT (TALISMAN).

TANGIBLE ASSETS

Tangible Assets are material assets (e.g., real estate, buildings, equipment, inventories, cash, and cash equivalents), as distinguished from intangible assets (e.g., goodwill, brand names, patents, and trademarks).

On a company's balance sheet, tangible assets normally appear as property, plant, and equipment used for the normal operation of business. The balance sheet also includes items that are held for use and not for investment, have a life expectancy of more than one year, and are tangible in nature.

See also ASSET; BALANCE SHEET; BOOK VALUE.

TAPE

Tape originally referred to the paper tape used in electronic tickers developed in the United States in the late 1800s as a faster means of disseminating stock market information.

Each investor had a ticker machine in his or her home or office by which he or she could receive price quotes from the stock exchange. Quotes came electronically in the form of a special code displayed as a series of holes on the ticker machine's paper tape. Although there was some time delay, the ticker was considerably faster than the previous method of periodic deliveries of trading reports by messenger.

As a result of technological advances and with the advent of television, tape later became a screen known as the "broad tape" or "composite tape," across which last trade transactions move. Fully electronic versions of this tape machine are still used, but mostly for decoration, as the quotes have to run slower than 900 characters per minute in order to be readable. Realtime quotations are now received by computers.

The term *tape* also has a broader meaning as a synonym for the market trend. It is best illustrated by the Wall Street maxim "Don't fight the tape," which means an investor should not invest in a direction contrary to the current market trend.

See also ASK PRICE; BID PRICE; QUOTATION; TICKER/ STOCK TICKER.

TARGET COMPANY

A *Target Company* is one that is viewed as attractive for either a merger or a takeover by another company.

In the United States takeovers are not usually announced to the public until the takeover company has acquired at least 5% of the outstanding shares of the target company. At the 5% level the takeover regulations are enforced and information must be filed with the Securities and Exchange Commission (SEC). Once filed with the SEC, the takeover bid becomes public information and the news media spreads the word.

Mutual funds investing in common shares often state in their prospectus that they will not buy more than 5% of the outstanding shares of any one company. This is done to avoid the 5% reporting requirements. Furthermore, it may not be in their best interest to buy more than 5% of a company if they want to remain as diversified as possible.

The public announcement of a takeover usually causes a sharp increase in the price of shares in the target company. The market price will quickly rise toward the takeover price and will frequently trade higher. If the market price continues to soar it may lead to an increase in the value of the takeover bid.

Some companies will take drastic measures to prevent being taken over. Measures colorfully described as the poison pill or shark repellent can make the cost of acquisition unacceptable to the company planning the takeover.

See also ACQUISITION; ASSET; GREENMAIL; MERGER; TAKEOVER/TAKEOVER BID.

TARGET LETTER (United States)

A *Target Letter* is sent by the U.S. Securities and Exchange Commission (SEC) to an individual, notifying the individual that he or she is under investigation by the SEC for violations of securities laws. The letter indicates that the findings could lead to an indictment on federal charges.

The recipient of a target letter from the SEC is advised to seek legal counsel in order to defend himself or herself against the allegations and to expedite the legal process. Fraud and insider trading violations are among frequent charges originated by the SEC and detailed in a target letter.

See also CHURNING; INSIDER DEALING/INSIDER TRADING; SECURITIES AND EXCHANGE COMMISSION (SEC).

TASSO D'INTERESSE (Italy)

See INTEREST/INTEREST RATES.

TAX SELLING

Tax Selling (also referred to as tax loss selling) is the selling of securities that are in a loss position near the end of a calendar year.

Market declines in December are often attributed to tax selling. Such losses are taken in order to reduce the tax liability on any gains taken during the year.

See also CAPITAL GAIN; CAPITAL LOSS; ORDINARY INCOME.

TAX SHELTER

A *Tax Shelter* is a legal method of avoiding the payment of personal and corporate taxation.

In the United States, popular tax shelters include Individual Retirement Accounts (IRAs), Keogh Plans, Salary Reduction Plans, Simplified Employee Pension Plans (SEPs), and Single Premium Life Insurance. Municipal bonds also retain their tax-exempt status. In the United Kingdom, TESSAs (Tax Exempt Savings Plan) and PEPs (Personal Equity Plan) are among the many investment products that provide a tax shelter.

See also INDIVIDUAL RETIREMENT ACCOUNT (IRA); KEOGH PLAN; SIMPLIFIED EMPLOYEE PENSION PLAN (SEP).

TAXABLE EVENT

A *Taxable Event* is any transaction that has tax consequences.

Tax may become due as the result of purchases, sales, dividends, or transactions in investments. The majority of countries in the world regard the payment of dividends and interest and capital gains on the sale of investments as taxable events.

See also individual countries' stock exchange profiles/ investor taxation.

TECHNICAL ANALYSIS

Technical Analysis is a method used primarily for forecasting short-term trends in stock market averages (e.g., Dow Jones Averages), trends in index levels (e.g., FT-SE 100 Index), trends in selective classes of securities, or movements of individual security prices.

Technical analysts compare recent trends with defined historical patterns and use the resulting information to determine current market strengths or weaknesses, as well as to predict the next turning point.

Charles Henry Dow, the founding father of Dow Jones & Company, is credited with creating technical analysis with the establishment of the Dow Jones Averages in 1884. Later work by William Hamilton, managing editor of *The Wall Street Journal*, and Robert Rhea clarified and reinforced the Dow Theory of stock market analysis.

In the 1920s, former *Forbes* editor Richard Shabacker showed how trend analysis could also be used with share price movements. John Magee and Robert D. Edwards further developed the idea of technical analysis with their book *Technical Analysis of Stock Trends*, first published in 1948. The book became the definitive work on pattern recognition analysis.

Patterns, appearing on a graphical representation of price trends, are essentially historic trends repeated often enough to provide some forecasting ability. Some important patterns are:

- Head and shoulders
- Tops
- Bottoms
- "W" formations
- Triangles

- Rectangles
- Rounded bottoms
- Drooping necklines

These patterns (also known as "reversal patterns") are recognized by the technical analyst as an indicator of investor sentiment or strategy. For example:

Head and shoulders is a reversal pattern and is created by a graph of prices forming an abstract drawing of a person. This abstraction (usually from the neck up) shows a right and left shoulder appearing on either side of a central head. The technical analysis of this pattern is as follows:

1. The right shoulder is formed by a slow extensive advance followed by a significant rally during which trading volume becomes heavy. The rally eventually reaches a high point, or top, at which volume declines and selling takes hold, sending prices lower.

2. The head is formed by a second rally, stronger and higher than the first, which also reaches a peak at which the volume weakens and the price declines to a level similar to the decline level of the first rally.

3. The left shoulder is formed by a third rally. Although it will not significantly increase volume, this rally usually results in a rise up to or near the top level of the right shoulder. It is then followed by a decline.

4. Eventually, prices drop through the neckline (a line drawn across the bottoms of the rallies). This final drop is referred to as the breakout or confirmation.

Head and shoulders patterns can invlove a multitude of minor variations; however, any head and shoulders patterns that do not include these basic characteristics are of doubtful use for forecasting.

In a technical analysis, each increase or decline in the degree of volume and each corresponding change is as necessary to the technical analyst as the pattern itself. As compared to previous rallies of the same shares, heavy volume is essential to the first shoulder—as is the weakening after the peak is achieved. In most cases the degree of volume for the head formation is close to, but less than, the degree of volume that forms the left shoulder; it too should involve heavy volume followed by volume weakness. The degree of volume on the third rally is usually less than that which occurred on the first two. The confirmation of the head and shoulders pattern occurs when the price has a breakout (breaks the neckline) and is considered a signal that the price will decline significantly further.

Dow Theory analysis examines the head and shoulders pattern from a slightly different view. The tops or peaks achieved in trend lines are also known as resistance; buyers are resisting the urge to buy more shares and begin to sell. The bottoms or valleys are known as support—the point at which selling stops and more buyers come to the market. If rising prices penetrate the resistance level, it is considered a positive signal. A new point of resistance is formed, with the previous point of resistance becoming the new level of support. When the price reaches the top, turns and breaks down through the former resistance level, it is now breaking through support. This is considered a signal of increasing weakness. This weakness is confirmed by declining volume. The price drops and is reconfirmed with lower volume on the ensuing rally. Again, the weakness displayed suggests a further significant decline.

The main advantage to technical analysis lies in its use for short-term forecasting. The technique is especially useful to futures and options traders. Although there are many facets to analyzing share prices and markets through technical analysis, all involve observation of share price or market indices movement and do not consider fundamental information about a company or its sector.

See also BUFFETT, WARREN; DOW THEORY; FUNDAMENTAL ANALYSIS.

TECHNOLOGY
See individual countries' stock exchange profiles; COMPUTER TRADING; DEALING ROOM TECHNOLOGY; NEURAL NETWORK; QUOTATION.

TEENIE (United States)
Teenie is a broker slang term for 1/16 of a dollar. Also called a *steenth*, the slang term will be used when discussing options below $3 or subscription rights. On some occasions, it might be used when discussing short-term municipals or other securities.

Brokers also use the term to describe their commission on a particular trade. "I only made a teenie on that trade," is a frequently heard lament on Wall Street.

See also COMMISSION; OPTION; STEENTH; SUBSCRIPTION RIGHTS.

TEGNINGSRET (Denmark)
Tegningsret refers to subscription and bonus rights. These rights enable shareholders to obtain a subscription and receive new shares when a company announces a capital increase. The amount of the

bonus is dependent on the number of shares held at the time of the capital increase. Rights begin trading three days prior to the subscription period (which lasts approximately 14 days) and are allowed to continue trading throughout.

The nominal value of subscription right or bonus right will not necessarily correspond to the nominal amount of shares to be subscribed for or received free of charge.

See also SUBSCRIPTION RIGHTS; SUBSCRIPTION WARRANT.

TEILRECHT (Germany)
See RIGHTS OFFERING.

TEL QUEL (Italy)
See EX-DIVIDEND (XD).

TELEFONVERKEHR (Germany)
The telephone market or over the counter market for securities in Germany is known as the *Telefonverkehr*. Both listed and unlisted securities can be traded in this manner by a dealer called a Freie Makler. Investors using this system include banks and other financial institutions.

See also BROKER/DEALER; FREIE MAKLER; LISTED SECURITIES; OVER THE COUNTER (OTC).

TELESCOPING (United States)
Telescoping is the slang term for a reverse share split.

See also REVERSE SPLIT.

TEMPLETON, SIR JOHN
For many years *Sir John Templeton* has been one of the world's most successful fund managers. He has built up a devoted group of followers who accept his judgment, which is often contrary to prevailing market opinion, and who have invested many billions of dollars with Templeton in the last four decades. A $10,000 investment with Templeton in 1954 would have grown into a fund worth $300 million by 1996.

Templeton has always eschewed the secular and country-based approach to investing in favor of picking individual stocks that are regarded as undervalued. Fundamental analysis and a long-term horizon are preferred to playing the markets. Templeton has often stressed that a trailblazing spirit is essential for long-term investment success. Many of Templeton's funds have deliberately been set up in Bermuda, far away from the direct influence and herd mentality engendered by Wall Street, the City of London, and Tokyo. Indeed, one of Templeton's favorite axioms is to con-sider opportunities that others have yet to identify: "Never follow the crowd. Superior performance is possible only if you invest differently from the crowd." The contrarian Templeton philosophy involves "investing at the time of maximum pessimism," resisting current investment fads to buy when prices are low, and selling as prices reach their peak.

During the late 1960s Templeton was one of the first Western investors to recognize the strength of the rebuilt Japanese economy. He identified that the economy in postwar Japan would reward long-term investors with far greater returns than those available in the traditional investment arenas. This ability to spot international opportunities ahead of the competition has been a vital factor in the success of Sir John's funds.

Templeton's most famous venture remains the London-listed fund management firm Templeton Galbraith and Hansberger (TGH), which was sold to the American-based Franklin Resources group in 1992. TGH was run by Templeton, John Galbraith, Tom Hansberger, and Templeton's son, John Templeton Jr. During the Franklin takeover, Hansberger criticized Templeton and his cofounder Galbraith for continuing to charge heavy front-end fees for their funds despite moves away from this practice throughout the industry. The fund has grown considerably since Franklin bought into the company. During the three years prior to 1995, funds under management increased from $20 billion to $50 billion.

Templeton published his ten golden rules for investment success in 1995. Like his contemporary, Warren Buffett, he reduced a complex investment philosophy into a number of deceptively simple rules. It would, however, be a mistake to ascribe Templeton's immense success solely to the following short list of simple, common sense commandments:

1. Avoid the popular and move away from the majority.
2. Always learn from your mistakes.
3. Buy stocks during times of pessimism.
4. Search for value in all securities that you consider.
5. Spread the risk of investing by diversification. Only fools put all their eggs in one basket.
6. Invest for real returns.
7. Keep an open mind and be prepared to entertain new ideas.
8. Buy when others are despondently selling and sell when others are buying.
9. Everything changes. Bull runs and bear markets are always temporary.

10. An investor who has all the answers does not even understand the questions.

A committed Christian, Sir John has displayed a marked philanthropic streak. He has endowed Templeton College in Oxford, one of the foremost schools of management in the United Kingdom. More controversially, Templeton has personally endowed a prize, the Templeton Prize for Progress in Religion, since 1972. The annual award, currently worth $1 million (£650,000) to the recipient, is awarded for innovative work in the religious sphere. The list of winners has included Mother Teresa of Calcutta, Alexander Solzhenitsyn, and the U.S. evangelist Billy Graham.

John Train's book *The Money Masters* (1980) contains a lengthy and informative interview with Templeton, with more details about his investment techniques.

See also BUFFETT, WARREN.

TENDER

There are three common meanings for *Tender* on the world's stock exchanges. Tender can refer to:
1. A method of auctioning a security to the highest bidders. A formal bid submitted to buy a security such as a U.S. Treasury bond or a U.K. government debt issue is called a tender.
2. The offering of money or goods to settle a debt or claim, such as the delivery of goods on a futures contract due date.
3. Any acceptable form of compensation for a transaction, product, or service. Legal tender includes cash, which is acceptable for all public and private bills, and securities.

See also CASH; FUTURES CONTRACT; TENDER OFFER.

TENDER OFFER (United States)

A *Tender Offer* is sometimes announced by a company planning a takeover. The goal of a tender offer is to obtain enough shares for the acquiring company to gain control of the target company. Tender offers are usually relied upon in the event that friendly takeover measures have not been successful.

A tender offer is made by a public announcement, usually appearing in the media, inviting shareholders to surrender their shares for a specific price. This publicized price is usually considerably higher than the current market price. The premium above the current market price is designed to provide an incentive for current shareholders to tender their shares.

Sections 13 D and E and sections 14 D, E, and F of the Securities Exchange Act of 1934 (enacted in 1968 and amended in 1970) require that the acquiring firm provide 30 days' notice to both the management of the target company and the SEC of their intention to effect the acquisition of the target company. These rules are affected by tender offers or open market purchases, and the beneficial owner of the securities and the name of the party supplying funds must be disclosed.

Such notices are implemented by the filing of Schedule 13D by persons or groups having made an acquisition of 5% or more of any class of a company's securities as well as tender offers that, in effect, will result in more than a 5% ownership. Schedule 14D can be used for reports filed on solicitations or recommendations in a tender offer made by someone other than the maker of the offer.

In addition to SEC regulations on takeovers, more than 30 states have laws designed to delay and prevent tender offers, allowing the company management time to establish a defense or seek better terms.

See also GOLDEN PARACHUTE; SCHEDULE 13D; TAKEOVER/TAKEOVER BID; TARGET COMPANY.

TENEUR DE MARCHÉ (France)

See MARKET MAKER.

TERMINE (FERMO; Italy)

See FORWARD CONTRACT.

TERZO MERCATO (Italy)

Terzo Mercato is a third, unregulated market for unlisted securities in Italy.

See also OVER THE COUNTER (OTC).

THAILAND, KINGDOM OF

Thailand (Prather, Prades, Sayam, Muang Thai) is a country situated in the west of the Indochinese Peninsula of Southeast Asia. It is bordered on the northwest by Myanmar (Burma), on the northeast by Laos, on the southeast by Cambodia, and on the south by Malaysia.

Area: 198,115 square miles (513,115 square km)

Population: 58,791,000 (17.6% urban; 82.4% rural)

Form of Government: Constitutional monarchy, with two legislative houses: Senate—270 members; House of Representatives—391 members. Chief of state: King. Head of government: Prime Minister (2).

Official Language: Thai

Capital: Bangkok

Largest Cities: Bangkok, 5,620,591; Nonthaburi, 264,201; Nakhon Ratchasima, 202,503; Chiang Mai, 161,541; Khon Kaen, 131,478

Economy:

Currency: Thai baht (B)

National Budget: Revenue—B 569.3 billion; expenditures—B 504.7 billion (economic services: 26.2%; education: 21.1%; defense: 17.2%; health: 8.1%; general public services: 5.7%; internal security: 5.5%; external debt service: 4.2%; social security: 4.0%)

Public Debt: US$14.6 billion

Gross National Product: US$120.2 billion

Principal Products: Sugarcane; rice; corn; rubber; bananas; livestock; clothing

Foreign Trade (Imports): B 1.2 trillion (nuclear reactors: 18.2%; electrical machinery: 16.8%; road vehicles: 7.9%; iron and steel: 7.6%; mineral fuels and lubricants: 7.4%; plastics: 3.3%; organic chemicals: 3.0%; from Japan: 30.2%; United States: 11.6%; Singapore: 6.4%; Germany: 5.4%; Taiwan: 5.1%; South Korea: 4.2%; Malaysia: 3.6%; China: 2.4%; United Kingdom: 2.3%)

Foreign Trade (Exports): B 951.4 billion (garments: 9.4%; precious jewelry: 4.4%; plastic articles: 4.1%; fresh prawns: 4.0%; rice: 3.5%; natural rubber: 3.1%; canned seafoods: 3.0%; footwear: 2.9%; integrated circuits: 2.8%; furniture: 2.1%; tapioca products: 2.1%; to United States: 21.3%; Japan: 16.8%; Singapore: 11.9%; Hong Kong: 5.2%; Germany: 3.9%; United Kingdom: 3.2%; the Netherlands: 3.1%; Malaysia: 2.8%; United Arab Emirates: 2.2%)

Stock Exchanges: 1

The Stock Exchange of Thailand (SET)
Sindhorn Building 2nd Floor
Wireless Road
Bangkok 10330
Thailand
Phone: (66-2) 254-0960-9
Fax: (66-2) 254-3040, 263-2734-6, 254-3032

Internet Address: www.set.or.th

Trading Hours: Monday–Friday, 10:00 to 12:00 and 2:30 to 4:30

Office Hours: Monday–Friday, 8:30 to 5:00

Exchange Holidays:

1, 2 January	12 July
11 February	14 August
6, 12–14 April	23 October
1, 5, 15 May	5, 11, 31 December

Listed Companies: 431

Total Market Capitalization:

At 31 December 1997

Local Currency (Millions)	US Dollars (Millions)
779,011	16,179

Major Sectors: Banking, property development, finance and securities, building and furnishing materials, transportation

Share Price Performance:

(% Change)

1991	52
1992	87
1993	116
1994	7
1995	1
1996	–27
1997	–53

History: In 1975, public unfamiliarity with stock trading led to sluggish daily turnover rates on the Stock Exchange of Thailand (SET), with values ranging from B 3.4 to 4 million (US$160,000 to US$190,000). In 1976 the SET Index lingered at 82.7 points, down from its opening day of 100 points. As the political climate in Thailand became more settled in the late 1970s, and high liquidity in the money market helped to create a decline in interest rates, the market began to grow. New funds came into the market, and in 1978 the daily average turnover value rose to B 232 million (US$11.4 million). The SET index rose to 257.7 points by the end of the year.

The first major growth came in the second half of 1986 as a booming Thai economy, lower interest rates, and new tax incentives encouraged more investment from both domestic and foreign investors. The daily average turnover value increased to B 101.2 million (US$19.2 million) in 1987. The SET Index continued its bullish streak, reaching a new high of 472.86 points on 16 October 1987, shortly before Black Monday. However, on 11 December 1987, the SET Index crashed by 244 points. This drop represented a loss of 48% of the value of the market. The market closed the year at 285 points.

The SET Index closed at 386.7 points in 1988, and rose to 879.2 by the end of 1989. At that time the average daily turnover value for the year was B 1.5 billion (US$59.4 million). With the Persian Gulf crisis and high interest rates, the SET Index fell from a high of 1,143.8 points to 612.9 points by the end of 1990.

The economic and political situation caused significant market fluctuations in 1991 and 1992.

Market transactions were inactive from February until the end of the third quarter of 1993. Investor confidence was undermined by a number of factors. A finance company listed on the SET was temporarily closed down, and there was a high-profile legal case launched against people accused of share manipulation. Political upheaval led to a cabinet reshuffle and disputes among coalition parties, and southern Thailand suffered from separatist terrorism.

Trading activities rebounded in the fourth quarter of 1993, and the SET Index closed the year at an all-time high of 1,683 points on 30 December. Daily average turnover had grown to B 9.0 billion (US$354.83 million).

A new historic high of 1,753.7 points was reached on 4 January 1994. However, increases in the Federal Funds Rate by the U.S. Federal Reserve designed to curb inflation in the United States, coupled with domestic political uncertainty, led to negative sentiment among investors, who slowed down their investment activities for the first half of 1994. The SET Index closed at 1,273.3 points in June 1994, achieving an average daily turnover of B 8.9 billion (US$353.13 million) during the first half of the year.

Classes of Securities: Common shares, preferred shares, unit trusts, warrants, debentures, government bonds, convertible bonds

Indices: The Stock Exchange of Thailand Index (30 April 1975 = 100). Weighted by market capitalization, the index compares the current market value of all listed and authorized ordinary shares with the market value on the base date. It is adjusted for new listings or delistings and includes all types of capitalization changes.

Supervisory Organizations:

The Ministry of Finance is in charge of the SET and securities industry.

The Securities and Exchange Commission is in charge of all financial organizations.

The SET Board of Directors controls policies and operations.

The Association of Members of the Securities Exchanges sets regulations for stock exchange member firms.

Depository: The Share Depository Centre (SDC) is a division of the Stock Exchange of Thailand.

Settlement Details:

Shares: Trade date + 3 days.
  Book-entry.
  Receive and delivery versus payment are allowed.
  Turnaround trades on the same day are allowed.

Trading: The Automated System for the Stock Exchange of Thailand (ASSET) replaced the floor trading system in April 1991. The ASSET made trading more orderly, equitable, liquid, and efficient. The two trading alternatives offered by the ASSET are:

1. Automatic Order Match (AOM):
   Brokerage members key in orders from their offices. The orders are sent through the SET's mainframe computer and are executed according to price and time priority. Each transaction is confirmed back to the member's office within seconds.
2. Put-Through (PT):
   Buying and selling brokers conduct negotiations privately and confirm the transaction through the SET computer.

The type of trading system partly depends on which board the shares are traded:

Type of Board	Trading System
Main Board	AOM
Special Board	AOM or PT
Big-Lot Board	PT
Foreign Board	AOM or PT

Since 8 February 1993, the SET has allowed four alternative orders for buying and selling shares:

- Non-limit Price Order
  1. Market Price Order (MPO)
  2. At-the-Open-Order (ATO)
- Conditioned Order
  3. Immediate-or-Cancel Order (IOC)
  4. Fill-or-Kill Order (FOK)

Board Lot

On the main board, a minimum transaction is one board lot or multiple thereof. The Stock Exchange of Thailand has set a standard trading board lot at 100 shares for all securities traded on the main board.

Trading is conducted on three separate boards:

1. The main board for regular trading
2. The special board for big lots, odd lots, and bonds
3. The foreign board for foreigners to trade on once an investor has reached the limit for the foreign ownership

Listing Reguirements:

Qualifications	Listed Company	Listed Company in a Provincial Zone	Infrastructure/Basic Industry (Newly Established Company)
1. Registered capital in form of ordinary shares	≥ B 60 million	≥ B 40 million	≥ B 60 million
2. Total market capitalization	≥ B 500 million	≥ B 200 million	≥ B 500 million
3. Cash payment for ordinary shares in 1	≥ 75% of the registered capital	same as a listed company	same as a listed company
4. Distribution of ordinary shares			
4.1 Number of small shareholders	≥ 600 shareholders	≥ 300 shareholders	≥ 600 shareholders
4.2 Total shares held by small shareholder in 4	≥ 30% of registered capital	≥ 20% of registered capital	≥ 30% of registered capital
5. Nature of business	Main business is beneficial to economy and society	same as listed company	1. Having an investment in a basic infrastructure project with a concession period ≥ 20 years or Operating in a large scale basic industry 2. Project cost ≥ B 10,000 million 3. Having the need to raise funds to commence the project 4. Having an investment in a project by the promoters ≥ 50% of the paid up capital for the whole project 5. Having a feasibility study
6. Business Operations 6.1 Operations	At least 3 years of operating track record under substantially the same management	1. same as listed company 2. Having the main operation and most of the labor in provincial zone (Samutprakarn, Samutsakorn, Nakornprathom, Nonthaburi, Prathumthani)	Having competent and experienced management in finance, production, and marketing
6.2 Past Financial Status	Company Profit • Year 1 ≥ B 5 million • Year 2 ≥ B 5 million • Last year before filing application ≥ B 25 million and total for past 3 years ≥ B 50 million or profit for the last 3 years ≥ B 80 million	Profit for the most recent year or for the past two years ≥ B 15 million	

Investor Taxation:

10% withholding tax on dividends

Capital gains tax for foreign institutional and corporate investors is 15%. Individual investors pay no capital gains.

Tax treaties can reduce the tax liability on capital gains.

Thailand Tax Treaties:

Australia	Hungary	Pakistan
Austria	India	The Philippines
Belgium	Indonesia	Poland
Canada	Italy	Singapore
China	Japan	Sri Lanka
Denmark	Korea	Sweden
Finland	Malaysia	United Kingdom & North Ireland
France	The Netherlands	Vietnam
Germany	Norway	

Stamp-Duty: Foreign and domestic transferors of share certificates, debenture certificates, and bond certificates must pay for stamps to be affixed on the certificates according to the value of the paid-up shares or the value of the transfer instruments, whichever is greater.

The stamp rate is one baht (4 cents) for every B 1,000 (US$40) or fraction thereof except for:

1. Transfers of listed securities with the SET as registrar
2. Transfer of government bonds, state enterprise bonds, and unit trusts

Limitations: Foreign ownership of an individual company is limited to 49%, but further limits can be imposed by individual companies.

Foreign investors are not entitled to dividends, rights offerings, or voting where "local shares" are involved.

Securities Lending: None

Brokerage Firms:

Dynamic Eastern Finance Thailand
459-471 Asoke-Dindaeng Road
Bangkok 10310
Thailand
Phone: (66-2) 245-5010-7

Nava Finance and Securities Public Co., Ltd.
422 Navathanakit Bldg., Phyathai Road
Bangkok
Thailand
Phone: (66-2) 215-0969-98

Krungthai Thanakit Public Co., Ltd.
15-16th Floor, Sermmit Tower
159 Sukhumvit 21 Road
Bangkok 10110
Thailand
Phone: (66-2) 261-7373-5

Union Securities Co., Ltd.
19th Floor, P.S. Tower
36/63-66 Sukhumvit 21 Road
Bangkok 10110
Thailand
Phone: (66-2) 261-1850

Capital Nomura Securities Public Co., Ltd.
Thai-Wah Tower
21/3 Sathorn Tai Road
Bangkok 10120
Thailand
Phone: (66-2) 285-0060, 285-0096

National Finance and Securities Public Co., Ltd.
7, 12, 14-16, 20th Floor, MBK Tower
444 Phyathai Road
Bangkok 10330
Thailand
Phone: (66-2) 217-9595, 217-9622, 217-8000

Kaitnakin Finance & Securities Public Co., Ltd.
12th Floor, World Trade Center Bldg.
4 Rajdamri Road
Bangkok 10330
Thailand
Phone: (66-2) 256-9898

Bara Development Finance & Securities Co., Ltd.
968 Rama IV Road
Bangkok 10330
Thailand
Phone: (66-2) 233-2534, 234-0463, 234-5021

Multi-Credit Corporation of Thailand Ltd.
17-18th Floor, Kian Gwan House 2
140/1 Wireless Road
Bangkok 10330
Thailand
Phone: (66-2) 252-9830-49, 256-0170-89

International Trust and Finance Public Co., Ltd.
ITF-Silom Palace Bldg.
160 Silom Road
Bangkok 10500

Thailand
Phone: (66-2) 236-0313, 231-6090-6110

The Ocean Securities & Finance Public Co., Ltd.
163 Surawong Road
Bangkok 10500
Thailand
Phone: (66-2) 234-9125-9, 234-7500-4

Union Asia Finance Public Co., Ltd.
Ruamsermkij Bldg.
132 Silom Road
Bangkok 10500
Thailand
Phone: (66-2) 236-7511, 237-2040-9

Ayudhya Investment and Trust Public Co., Ltd.
3rd Floor, Ploenchit Tower
898 Ploenchit Road
Bangkok 10330
Thailand
Phone: (66-2) 254-875-93, 264-0355-0383

CMIC Finance and Securities Public Co., Ltd.
9-10th Floor, B.B. Bldg.
54 Sukhumvit 21 Road
Bangkok 10110
Thailand
Phone: (66-2) 259-9000-24

Dhana Siam Finance and Securities Public Co., Ltd.
3rd Floor, Sintorn Tower
132 Wireless Road
Bangkok 10330
Thailand
Phone: (66-2) 250-0250-9, 254-3450-69

First Asia Securities Public Co., Ltd.
6-7th Floor, Bangkok of Asia Bldg.
191 Sathorn Tai Road
Bangkok 10120
Thailand
Phone: (66-2) 213-2680-6

Wall Street Finance and Securities Public Co., Ltd.
G, 1-2, 25 Wall Street Tower
33/18 Surawong Road
Bangkok 10500
Thailand
Phone: (66-2) 234-4141, 237-2301

Thanapol Finance and Securities Public Co., Ltd.
133 Sukhumvit 21 Road

Bangkok 10110
Thailand
Phone: (66-2) 258-0490-6

Thai Fuji Finance and Securities Co., Ltd.
7-10th Floor, Quality House Bldg.
38 Convent Road
Bangkok 10400
Thailand
Phone: (66-2) 237-8904-28, 237-8936-44

First Bangkok City Finance Co., Ltd.
22-24 Yukhon 2 Road
Bangkok 10400
Thailand
Phone: (66-2) 223-5856-9, 223-7174, 223-0331-3

Company Information:

The Best Performing Shares in the Country

Company Name	Share Price Change 1 January 1997 to 31 December 1997 (%)
Delta Electronics	376
Thai Union Frozen Prds.	191
New Imperial Hotel	73
Thai Airways Intl.	44
Hana Microelectronic	33

The Largest Companies in the Country by Market Capitalization as of 31 December 1997

Company Name	Market Capitalization Local Currency (Millions)	Market Capitalization US Dollars (Millions)
Ptt Exp. & Prdn.	127,100	2,640
Bangkok Bank	86,129	1,789
Thai Airways Intl.	74,900	1,556
Advanced Info. Service	54,288	1,128
Thai Farmers Bank	48,000	997
Bec World	38,400	798
Electricity Gnrt.	33,280	691
Siam Cement	28,800	598
Siam Commercial Bank	24,390	507
Delta Electronics	24,000	498
Bangkok Expressway	20,598	428
Telecom Asia	19,562	406
Shinawatra Computer	17,464	363
Advance Agro	17,289	359
Cogeneration	15,191	315

Company Name	Market Capitalization Local Currency (Millions)	Market Capitalization US Dollars (Millions)
Krung Thai Bank	14,499	301
Siam Makro	13,800	287
Grammy Entertainment	10,500	218
Bank of Ayudhya	10,000	208
Thai Petrochemical Inds.	8,970	186
Saha-Union	8,325	173
First Bangkok City Bank	8,197	170
Siam City Cement	7,998	166
National Petrochem.	7,905	164
Thai Plastic Chm.	7,613	158
Hana Microelectronic	6,938	144
Thai Military Bank	6,843	142
C P Feedmill	6,840	142
Banpu Public	6,811	141
Serm Suk	6,760	140
Phatra Thanakit	6,267	130
New Imperial Hotel	5,800	120
Tuntex	5,657	117
Bangkok Insurance Co.	5,400	112
Bank Of Asia	5,079	105
Preecha	5,040	105
Ayudhya Insurance	5,000	104
Siam Pulp Paper	4,884	101
Kr Precision	4,841	101

Regional Exchanges: None

Other Investment Information:

Office of the Board of Investment
555 Vipavadee Rangsit Road
Bankhen, Bangkok 10900
Thailand
Phone: (66-2) 270-1400, 270-1410, 270-1420
Fax: +(66-2) 271-0777
Telex: 72435 BINVEST TH
Cable Address: BINVEST

THEORY OF MARKETS

The *Theory of Markets* owes the development of its main outlines to economists such as Adam Smith, Léon Walras, and Alfred Marshall. As formulated up to approximately 1920 by the neoclassicist Marshall, the theory of markets refers to competitive markets in static equilibrium, with complete mobility of labor and capital (force plays no role) and perfect knowledge and (what was considered) rationality on the part of all participants. Since then it has been further developed to allow for monopolistic competition, monopoly, and oligopoly, as well as the introduction of more realistic assumptions about barriers to mobility, imperfect knowledge, the role of expectations about the future, and the like.

In the classical conception of the market, prices are a given for all participants and are brought into equilibrium by the overall relation of supply and demand. No buyer or seller is of sufficient size to alter the price of any commodity. If demand for some commodity exceeds supply, the price increases, thus increasing the profitability of its production. This causes capital and labor to produce more of the commodity until a point of balance is restored between capital and labor and the price falls back to its former equilibrium level. The opposite process occurs when there is an excess of supply over demand. In this conception, the result is the most efficient possible allocation of natural resources, capital, and labor.

The chief contributions of neoclassical economics include the market's greater mathematical formalization and its development of marginal theory, in which, for example, a consumer purchases a good up to the point at which the declining marginal utility of an additional unit of that good is equal to its price, or a capitalist produces a commodity up to the level at which the marginal cost of producing an additional unit is equal to the price.

Capitalism in the 20th century has been marked by many highly dynamic, indeed explosive, economic phenomena that have seldom conformed to the traditional microeconomic models. In all the developed countries, many of the most productive sectors are characterized by a degree of oligopoly bordering on monopoly. The role of the state produces further displacements of macroeconomic reality from neoclassical theory. Markets themselves have become much more complex and geographically extended. Finally, more recent studies of individual and group market behavior have led to further divergence from classical assumptions.

Stock Market Theories

Over the long haul, stock prices tend to vary in the same direction as, and in advance of, general economic indicators. In one study, the lag time between the two was approximately six months, making stock prices what economists call a "leading indicator." This lead time may result from investors' tendency to focus on the future.

Stock prices have demonstrated a general tendency to increase, especially since World War II. Aside from this long-term trend, stock prices also show extremely complex variation when one analyzes shorter time periods, whether days, weeks, or months, and technical analysts have come up with different ideas about how to better predict these variations.

Other theorists claim that there is no way to predict the stock market accurately—that price fluctuations arise from new information that becomes available in an essentially random way. Diverse influences on stock prices have increased greatly with the heightened globalization of the world economy, the closer interpenetration of economic and political forces, and the greater interlinking of securities markets themselves. Nevertheless, other studies do show that stocks tend to display "persistence," that is, a price move in one direction will usually be followed by another move in the same direction, thus producing a nonrandom trend.

Although the volatility of the stock market makes it especially difficult to predict its future, many analysts have devised methods to identify stock market trends. In the past, one approach put emphasis on the "stock cycle," which for many decades in the United States averaged approximately four years. However, in recent years there has been too much variation in the duration and amplitude of these cycles for them to have much predictive value.

The conventional theory for some time has held that the basic cause of stock market price changes is the anticipation of changes in corporate earnings, which affect dividends. The price of a stock reflects the present value of expected future earnings. Any condition that suggests a change in the earnings of a particular company, an industry, or the economy as a whole will affect stock prices, which will move in advance of actual changes in earnings and dividends. An alternative theory, known as the confidence theory of stock prices, focuses on the rise and fall of trader and investor confidence in the future of stock prices, earnings, and dividends. There are also structural theories, which study seasonal and other variation patterns. How these theories translate into investment strategies has been a matter of much conjecture and debate.

See also CLASSICAL SCHOOL OF ECONOMICS; NEO-CLASSICAL SCHOOL OF ECONOMICS.

THINLY TRADED

Thinly Traded is a designation given to securities or shares that do not have an active market.

Thinly traded shares often belong to smaller companies that have fallen in price after a period of trading difficulty or to new companies that have yet to establish a steady level of investor interest. In the United States, thinly traded share prices are quoted daily and appear only on pink sheets. A broker must call the market maker if an investor wants to make a trade. These shares might trade only a few times a day or go several days without having any trades.

Investing in thinly traded securities is considered a highly speculative strategy. Such investors are usually looking for a fast turnaround on their investment. As the shares are infrequently traded, it is common to find a wide spread between bid and offer prices.

See also ACTIVE MARKET; OBJECTIVE; PINK SHEETS; TRADE.

THIRD MARKET (United Kingdom)

Companies that had a trading record of one year and were sponsored by a member firm were traded on the *Third Market*, phased out in 1990, on the International Stock Exchange in London. Many of the more stringent requirements for formal trading were waived for companies that joined the Third Market.

See also UNITED KINGDOM.

THIRD WORLD DEBT

Third World Debt is a phenomenon that has largely come into being since 1965. According to World Bank statistics, in 1994 a total debt of approximately $923 billion was owed by some 51 countries in Africa, Asia, and Latin America. Among these, the leading debtors were Brazil, $94.5 billion; India, $87.9 billion; China, $84.6 billion; Mexico, $79.1 billion; Indonesia, $63.8 billion; and Argentina, $55.8 billion. There were many other countries, particularly in Africa, whose total debt, although smaller, presented a profound problem given the stagnation of their economies. In Latin America as well as in certain countries in Asia, particularly East Asia, there was more economic development, including industrialization, but current account deficits forced many of these countries to rely on debt financing to continue their development. In 1996 there were 32 states classified by the World Bank as severely indebted low-income countries; 25 of these were in Africa. Collectively, these countries owed $210 billion, or four times as much as they had in 1980, and the average ratio of debt to national income in these countries was more than 110%.

It was in Latin America, in the late 1970s and into the 1980s, that the most serious debt problems became concentrated. These problems were caused by a combination of factors: capital flight, in which money was withdrawn from the economies of the leading debtor countries and invested abroad; protectionist barriers in the United States and other developed countries; increased interest rates and fees imposed by foreign banks; and the oil price hikes that began in 1973. Beginning in 1983, when the amount of debt service paid by Latin America as a whole began to exceed new loans flowing into the continent, a number of countries faced liquidity crises. The associated decline in living standards in many Third World countries in the 1980s—one group of economists estimated that unemployment rose above 30% in some countries, real wages fell by one-third, and half the population suffered a drop in income—increased the pressure on governments to default on their loans.

The phenomenon of net capital outflows from the developing to the developed countries, which first occurred in Latin America, spread to Africa and then the Third World as a whole during the 1980s. Thus, from 1982 to 1990, while total resource flows to developing countries in the form of bilateral and multilateral aid, private grants, trade credits, direct private investment, and bank loans totaled $927 billion, the developing countries remitted $1,345 billion in debt service alone. Allowing for inflation, the net flow from the developing countries was the equivalent of six Marshall Plans for the wealthy countries. Despite their debt service payments, by 1990 the debtor countries faced a debt 61% higher than in 1982. Many had reached their borrowing limit and were seeking more capital inflows from foreign private equity investors. Some developing countries have established stock markets, and where these are striving, studies show that future growth in productivity and per capita GDP will follow.

Although signs of the forthcoming crisis appeared in the mid-1960s, private banks in the developed countries were eager to make loans to the Third World, since despite the risks these loans were extremely profitable in the short run. Many of the biggest banks made huge loans, far in excess of the capital that they held. But when the debtor countries were unable to make their payments in the early 1980s, these overexposed banks relied on the governments of the United States and other countries, the International Monetary Fund (IMF), and the Bank for International Settlements—acting as intermediary for the central banks of countries in the Organization for Economic Cooperation and Development—to bail them out. Numerous refinancing loans and restructuring requirements were imposed. In response, in 1987 Bra-

zil stopped paying interest on the commercial bank portion, or $69 billion, of its $108 billion total debt; several smaller debtors—Ecuador, Peru, and Bolivia—had previously suspended interest payments. In the Dominican Republic, Peru, Sudan, and elsewhere, governments' efforts to conform to IMF austerity measures led to political unrest.

In 1996 the World Bank, the IMF, and the United States proposed a plan to reduce the debt burden of the poorest countries. As part of this plan, the IMF would sell some of its gold stock and invest the proceeds to raise money to reduce the debt payments of some Third World borrowers. The World Bank and the IMF would also pressure donor countries to write off between 67% and 90% of their loans to these heavily indebted countries. The debtor countries would have to adopt a strict program of market reforms to be monitored by the World Bank and the IMF. Yet even under this proposal, it would be six years, for example, before some of the poorest countries in sub-Saharan Africa got any relief from their debt burdens.

See also INTERNATIONAL MONETARY FUND (IMF); ORGANIZATION FOR ECONOMIC COOPERATION AND DEVELOPMENT (OECD); PRE-EMERGING MARKETS; WORLD BANK.

THRIFTS

The term *Thrifts* originated in the United States and is now being used internationally to refer to financial institutions whose primary function, historically, was to provide an interest-bearing depository for personal savings. A distinguishing characteristic of thrifts is their structure as mutually owned institutions—they are owned by their clients, the lenders and borrowers. Thrift institutions include savings and loan associations, credit unions, and savings banks.

Savings and loan associations originated in the United Kingdom during the late 1700s as house-building cooperatives, called "building societies." A local group of workers' families banded together and made regular deposits to the society to finance the building of their homes. As savings grew, the funds were allocated, often by lottery, to member families for home building. When each family had a home, the building society broke up. Soon the societies started to borrow money from nonmembers to speed up the house-building process, and many became permanent organizations that provided mortgages and other financial services.

Building societies spread to other European countries and to the Americas. The first such institution in the United States was the Oxford Provident Building Association founded with 40 members in 1831 in

Frankford, Pennsylvania, now a part of Philadelphia. By 1890 these "building associations" had spread to all the states and territories, and they had broadened the scope of their financial activities.

Through much of their history savings and loan associations (and building societies) have been organized as mutuals, with each client having one vote in the company's management and sharing in company earnings in some way, such as receiving higher rates on savings, paying lower rates on loans, or getting a year-end bonus dividend. Today, the mutual structure is common on the European continent, where the financial services sector is dominated by mutually owned financial institutions, such as France's Crédit Agricole Mutuel, the Netherlands' Rabobank, and Germany's DB Bank. In recent years, however, outside Europe the trend has been away from mutuals in the financial services sector, with a large number of these institutions making public stock offerings. This is occurring in the United States, South Africa, Australia, and New Zealand, and to a lesser extent in the United Kingdom.

A credit union is a banking cooperative that operates strictly for the mutual benefit of its members. The members usually have some common bond, such as their place of employment, a labor union, a farm group, or an educational, a religious, or a social organization. The primary function of a credit union, besides being a depository for its members' savings, is to provide low cost credit to its members in the form of relatively short-term consumer loans, mainly for cars, household items, medical bills, and emergencies.

The credit union movement began in cooperative credit societies organized during the mid-1800s by Friedrich Wilhelm Raiffeisen in Germany and Luigi Luzzati in Italy. Alphonse Desjardins founded the first credit union in the Western Hemisphere in 1900 at Lévis, Quebec. He also helped start the first credit union in the United States in 1908 at Manchester, New Hampshire. Desjardins saw credit unions as a way to combat usury, whose harmful effects had been impressed on him in his work as a legislative reporter.

In 1921, Edward A. Filene, a Boston merchant, provided funding for the Credit Union National Extension Bureau, whose function was to aid the growth of credit unions in the United States. The work of this bureau was taken over in 1932 by the Credit Union National Association (CUNA), formed by the credit unions themselves. CUNA has progressively broadened its membership—in 1940 to include the Western Hemisphere, in 1954 to include Australia and Africa, and in 1958 to be a worldwide organization. In many developing countries, credit unions are the only source of credit for a large segment of the population, and they provide loans that serve as an impetus for the growth of farm production and small business.

Originally, savings banks differed from savings and loan associations mainly in their primary focus; the former were fixated on savings, the latter on loans. Savings banks often started as the result of philanthropic efforts of leading citizens to reduce poverty by encouraging saving among emerging wage-earner groups. The earliest municipal savings banks grew out of the municipal pawnshops in Italy during the 1700s. The first savings bank in the United Kingdom was the Savings and Friendly Society founded in 1810 by the pastor of a church in a poor area. In the United States the first savings banks were established for charitable purposes in the early 1800s as nonprofit institutions.

Nearly all savings banks were originally mutual savings banks, run by a board of trustees who elected their own successors. But since the 1980s many have issued stock offerings and become stock savings banks, run by a board of directors elected by the stockholders. As economies develop and become more complex, the thrifts tend to compete with the more diversified financial institutions. Relaxation of governmental regulations has made such competition possible.

See also BUILDING SOCIETIES; PAWNBROKING.

THROGMORTON STREET

Throgmorton Street is the location of the International Stock Exchange in London. The name is used in the same way as Wall Street in the United States or Beursplein 5 for the Amsterdam Stock Exchange.

See also NETHERLANDS; UNITED KINGDOM.

TICK

Tick is the minimum price movement for securities or a stock market index.

For example, if XYZ Corporation shows a last trade of $55 and the next trade is at $55 1/8, the price has moved up a tick. If a stock is trading at a price higher than the previous trade, it is referred to as an up tick. If it is trading at a price lower than the previous price, the term used in description is down tick.

Tick also functions as a short-term broad market indicator by providing investors with some idea of what is happening in the market at the present moment. For instance, if all of the current down ticks of individual stocks are added together and subtracted from the up ticks, the resulting cumulative tick is regarded as a broad market indicator because this calculation involves all of the stocks trading on the stock exchange.

The significance of the current tick is a matter of degree. On the New York Stock Exchange, any movement between the levels of –100 tick to +100 tick is considered to be neutral. Levels exceeding these limits can be instantly indicative of the market's current direction and give some idea as to the momentum of the trend. Since this is a broad market indicator of all the New York Stock Exchange stocks, it may disagree with the market averages at any given time. Sometimes, this may be an early warning of a turn in the market. At other times, the tick may quickly reverse and line up with the averages.

One situation in which the tick consistently disagrees with the market averages is when the market stages a sudden rally. The Dow Jones Industrials may be up 15 or 20 points, but the tick may be showing –150 or –200. The most probable reason for the phenomena is that as the market surges upward, limit sell orders are activated, causing sufficient selling to create the negative tick. If the market continues to advance upward, the tick eventually comes in line on the positive side.

The tick can also indicate the existence of program trading, in which computers are activating buys or sells of large blocks of stock. A level of 300 or more generally signifies the existence of this type of trading. A +400 tick can indicate programmed buying, whereas –350 could be the beginning of some programmed selling. Institutional traders will also carefully watch the tick; they do not want to miss out on an important rally or be left holding stock that is decreasing in value during a sharp decline.

In a panic sell situation the tick becomes meaningless, simply confirming what is already known—that everyone is selling. Although the meaning of the numbers of the tick is not absolute, the tick is always worth checking when placing a trade, as it gives an indication of the strength and momentum of the immediate market.

See also DOWNTICK; UPTICK; ZERO PLUS TICK.

TICKER/STOCK TICKER

The *Ticker* or *Stock Ticker* proved to be the invention with the greatest impact on the stock exchange in the late 19th century. Before its development, messenger boys (known as "pad shovers") ran from the trading floor to private homes and brokerage offices delivering reports of sales and purchases. The delay caused by delivery time made the stock ticker and its nearly instantaneous dissemination of information an important development for trading.

Ticker companies stationed "reporters" on the trading floor. These reporters recorded all stock transactions and sent the information to operating rooms nearby. The name of the stock, the price, and the number of shares traded were then typed on a keyboard. Electronic circuits transmitted the pulses created by the keyboard to a receiving device. Wheels inside this device either printed letters and numbers or perforated code symbols on paper tape. As a result of this technology, each person with a receiving device obtained fast, reliable information regarding the transaction of securities.

In 1890, members of the New York Stock Exchange established the New York Quotation Company and bought up all the ticker companies in a move intended to improve accuracy and the distribution of reliable information.

See also ASK PRICE; BID PRICE; BROAD TAPE; QUOTATION; TAPE.

TICKER SYMBOL

See TRADING SYMBOL.

TICKER TAPE

See QUOTATION; TAPE; TICKER/STOCK TICKER.

TICKET

A *Ticket* is the slip of paper on which an order is written and is the means by which an order is entered onto the securities market.

Tickets have been the method of entering trades from the stockbroker to the securities market ever since the orders were first written down on the first organized market in Amsterdam nearly 400 years ago. Although many firms now compose tickets on a computer screen, there are many who still use the handwritten order ticket. Such tickets contain all the details of the transaction, including instructions to buy or sell; designations (limit order, stop order, market order, day order, or good till canceled); investor's account identification; and whether the securities or cash should be held in the account or mailed out.

When an order ticket is written, it is first read back to the customer, then sent to the exchange for execution, unless it is kept on the books as an open order.

See also DAY ORDER; GOOD TILL CANCELED (GTC); LIMIT ORDER; OPEN ORDER; STOP ORDER.

TIESIOGINIAL SANDORAI (Lithuania)

Tiesioginial Sandorai refers to block trading transactions that are concluded when two parties agree on the quantity and price of the securities to be traded. They are not covered by the guarantee fund.

Although they can be the result of a corporate take-over attempt, block trades are usually conducted by institutional traders. Such trades are normally executed separately from regular trading on an exchange in order to moderate the price impact on a company's securities. The purpose of this is to help maintain a fair and orderly stock market.

Reports of block trades are used by some individual investors as a market indicator.

See also BLOCK TRADE; FAIR AND ORDERLY MARKET; LITHUANIA.

TIGHT MONEY

Tight Money refers to a period of time (marked by high interest rates) during which money is difficult to borrow, even with high-grade collateral.

Interest rates are raised by a government in an effort to slow down an overheating economy. Higher interest rates make money more difficult to borrow and, as a result, production is lowered and the economy slows.

If the interest rates rise high enough, it is possible to have an inverted yield curve, in which fixed-income securities with shorter maturities pay higher interest than those securities with longer maturities.

See also FEDERAL RESERVE SYSTEM; INTEREST/INTEREST RATES; INVERTED YIELD CURVE.

TIME BARGAIN (United Kingdom)

A *Time Bargain* is a stock exchange deal in which settlement is delayed to the next settlement period.

See also SETTLEMENT DATE (S/D).

TIME ORDER

The *Time Order* is the means by which orders to buy and sell securities are prioritized.

If two orders have the same limit price and can be executed at the limit, the order received first has the highest priority. The time order of "first in-first out" is important to the concept of maintaining a fair and orderly market.

The time at which an order is received is either notated on the computer system or stamped on a paper order ticket. In this way, an accurate chronology of orders received is kept.

See also FIRST IN FIRST OUT (FIFO); LIMIT ORDER; MARKET ORDER; STOP ORDER.

TIME VALUE

Time Value is the market value of an option's premium above its intrinsic value and is the price an option buyer pays to buy an option or an option writer receives for selling an option.

The premium, or price of an option, is made up of two parts: intrinsic value, which is based on the current price of the underlying security, and time value, which is based on the remaining time until expiration.

For example, shares in XYZ Corporation trade at $55. An investor wants to buy the November 50 calls, which have an option premium at $8. The $5 difference between the strike price and the current market price is the intrinsic value and the remaining $3 in the option premium is the time value.

Time value declines as the option approaches the expiration date.

See also CALL; INTRINSIC VALUE; OPTION; PUT; SELLING TO OPEN.

TIP

A *Tip* is any recommendation made by anyone to buy or sell a security for any reason. It might be made by the barber, a friend, a stockbroker, or by a financial newspaper. The tip might be good information or prove to be nothing more than an inaccurate rumor.

If a tip is made by someone with access to inside information—information that has not been released to the public—any trading based on this information is deemed illegal. No one is immune from the rules prohibiting trading on inside information. These rules apply to every buying and selling transaction, and do so in order for the market to remain fair and orderly.

See also FUNDAMENTAL ANALYSIS; INSIDER DEALING/ INSIDER TRADING; TECHNICAL ANALYSIS.

TITOLI (Italy)
See SECURITY.

TITOLI QUOTATA IN BORSA (Italy)
See LISTED SECURITIES.

TITOLO (A) PORTATORE (Italy)
See BEARER CERTIFICATE/SECURITY/SHARE.

TITRE (France)
Titre is a certificate or other document of securities ownership that often can be traded in lieu of the actual certificate.

See also CERTIFICATE.

TITRE SUPPORT (France)
See UNDERLYING SECURITY.

TITRES DE PLACEMENT (France)
See BLUE CHIP.

TITULOS AL PORTATOR (Colombia)
Titulos al Portator, or bearer securities, are certificates that are not registered on the books of an issuing company. Bearer securities are negotiable and payable to the holder. Ownership of bearer securities is transferred by simply handing over the appropriate bearer certificate.

In Colombia, mortgage documents can be issued as bearer securities.

The use of bearer securities differs from country to country. In many countries they are being eliminated as fully computerized trading is adopted by the exchange. When a system becomes computerized, all securities are kept in book-entry form, and certificates are "dematerialized."

See also BEARER CERTIFICATE/SECURITY/SHARE; COLOMBIA; TITULOS NOMINATIVOS.

TITULOS NOMINATIVOS (Colombia)
Titulos Nominativos are securities in certificate form that are recorded on the books of the issuing company. When endorsed on the back by the current registered owner, these securities can be transferred over to new ownership.

Registered securities are a necessity for fully computerized trading systems. Although the certificates are "dematerialized," the registration is necessary to keep track of the owners.

Shares, mortgages, and certificates of deposit can be issued in registered form in Colombia.

See also BEARER CERTIFICATE/SECURITY/SHARE; BOOK-ENTRY.

TOCCARE (DI) FONDO (Italy)
See BOTTOM.

TOCHTERGESELLSCHAFT (Germany)
See SUBSIDIARY COMPANY.

TOKAI BANK, LIMITED
The *Tokai Bank, Limited* is one of the top commercial banks in Japan. It is based in the Chukyo region of central Japan, a highly industrialized area. As of 31 March 1997, Tokai had assets of $285.4 billion and employed 11,625 workers. In addition to 285 branches, 9 subsidiaries, and 12 affiliates in Japan, Tokai Bank had 15 branches and agencies, 21 representative offices, 17 subsidiaries, and 8 affiliates in 42 cities spread over 27 countries overseas.

Tokai Bank was founded in 1941, approximately six months before Japan entered World War II. As part of a banking consolidation ordered by the military to increase efficiency, three small banks, the Aichi Bank, the Nagoya Bank, and the Ito Bank, merged. The oldest of the three, the Aichi Bank, had been founded in 1877. The three newly merged banks adopted the name *Tokai*, meaning "East Sea."

Tokai Bank did not have the opportunity to engage in any large wartime projects. As a result, after Japan was defeated and the country came under the power of the occupation authority, Tokai Bank was judged not to have contributed significantly to the Japanese war effort and was permitted to keep its management and its name. In 1947 it was awarded a foreign exchange license, and the following year it was permitted to increase its capitalization substantially.

During the 1950s Tokai aided the recovery in the Chukyo region, working to raise the large amounts of capital needed by some factories. During this period Tokai grew rapidly. In 1960 it issued checking accounts; in 1963 it began loan services; in 1965 it established the country's first on-line money order system; and in 1968 it opened a foreign trade information center. In addition, in 1962 Tokai's successful trust business had to be spun off as a separate firm, Chuo Trust and Banking Company, in accordance with Japan's financial regulations.

Tokai also worked to expand abroad. It opened its first overseas branch in London in 1963, upgraded an office to a branch in New York in 1965, and opened additional offices during the 1960s in Los Angeles, Amsterdam, Hong Kong, Zurich, Sydney, and Singapore. During this period, Tokai Bank's business was repeatedly stimulated by its close association with the Toyota Motor Company, also based in the Chukyo region.

Tokai continued its expansion in North America by establishing the subsidiary Tokai Bank of California in 1974. In the 1980s Tokai opened the Tokai Trust Company of New York, the Tokai Bank of Canada, a branch in Chicago, and offices in Atlanta, Dallas, Lexington (Kentucky), and other locations. In the 1990s Tokai seized the opportunity to work with non-Japanese clients in leveraged buyouts, corporate restructuring, and large-scale real estate development.

In 1988 Tokai reorganized itself and created a Treasury and capital market group as well as a corporate planning group. In 1989 it established a wholly owned subsidiary, Tokai Securities, Inc. in New York. Tokai Bank was listed on the exchanges in London, Paris, Geneva, Zurich, and Basel. In 1990 it created Tokai Morgan Grenfell International Funds Management Limited in Great Britain, as well as Tokai Bank (Deutschland) GmbH. That same year, Tokai Bank opened representative offices in Vienna, Brussels, San Francisco, Columbus, and Minneapolis. In 1991 Tokai Bank opened branches in Madrid and Paris, and in October of that year it merged with Sanwa Shinkin Bank.

In 1992 Tokai Bank acquired Japan International Bank Limited and established Tokai Bank Europe Limited. Also, Tokai Bank created Tokai Bank Europe Limited and Tokai Capital Markets Limited in the United Kingdom. In 1994 the bank established its Asia Department and China Department. The next year it opened branches in Taipei and Tianjin, and in 1997 it opened a branch in Shanghai.

In mid-1993 Tokai Bank had to write off $654 million in bad loans. All things considered, this was a relatively small figure compared to some of the bad loan write-offs that other major Japanese banks were forced to make in the early 1990s.

Domestically, Tokai Bank strove to provide the same full range of banking and financial services to its small and medium-size business clients that it would provide to large corporations. Tokai Bank's development of a multifaceted network, both domestically and overseas, was expected to allow it to meet the regulations for market risk management that were imposed by the Bank for International Settlements at the end of 1997.

See also JAPAN; JAPANESE FINANCIAL MARKETS.

TOMBSTONE

Tombstone refers to the advertisement (usually found in a financial newspaper) that announces a new offering or loan agreement, while listing the investment bankers and underwriting group. The name comes from the tombstone-like appearance of the advertisements and their presentation of information.

Tombstones might also appear in order to publicize a corporate merger, acquisition, a major business deal, or a significant real estate transaction. They may also be used to announce an investment banker's participation in a private placement.

See also INITIAL PUBLIC OFFERING (IPO).

TONTINE COFFEE HOUSE (United States)

The *Tontine Coffee House* was an early trading location for the New York Stock Exchange.

See also BUTTONWOOD AGREEMENT.

TOP

Top refers to the highest point reached by a share price or market index.

From the viewpoint of a technical analyst, the top is the strongest point of resistance, the point at which sellers enter the market to take profits. If enough buyers remain and outnumber the sellers, the resistance level will be penetrated and a breakout can occur. This will send the market or share price to new highs.

Once the former point of resistance is penetrated, it becomes the level of support. The logic behind the adoption of the new support level is that this price level has attracted buyers before and will again, if sellers drive the price back to that level.

See also BOTTOM; DOW THEORY; RESISTANCE LEVEL; SUPPORT/SUPPORT LEVEL; TECHNICAL ANALYSIS.

TORONTO-DOMINION BANK

The *Toronto-Dominion Bank* is one of the largest banks in Canada. As of 31 July 1997 it had assets of approximately $110 billion and had approximately 1,000 branches within the country as well as offices in more than a dozen other countries. The bank offers consumer and business services, including checking and savings accounts, credit cards, mortgage loans, student loans, trusts and wills and estate planning, and investment management services.

Toronto-Dominion Bank was formed in 1955 through a merger of the Bank of Toronto and the Dominion Bank. Each of these banks had originated during the mid-19th century when Canada's economy was beginning to take off.

The Bank of Toronto was originally chartered on 18 March 1855. It was founded by flour producers. While its initial customers were wheat farmers, millers, and merchants, the Bank of Toronto soon was serving the lumber industry and other agricultural interests. The bank survived a few years of slowdown when the demand for flour and timber in both the United States and England collapsed, but it emerged from this period in relatively good condition, since it had not been heavily invested in Canadian railroads.

Following the end of the U.S. Civil War, the U.S. market revived. In Canada, while grain production remained central, several new industries grew up, including leather tanning and liquor distillation. The volume of business in Ontario created the need for another bank, and the Dominion Bank was founded on 1 February 1871. The Dominion Bank emphasized commercial banking, investing in railroad expansion and construction.

During the rest of the 1800s, the Canadian economy grew through a series of booms and busts. Dairy farming, textiles, pulpwood, mining, and petroleum were among the new industries that sparked the country's growth.

During the 1930s both the Bank of Toronto and Dominion Bank closed branches, wrote off bad debts, and reduced assets. The Bank of Canada was founded in 1934 to issue currency, set interest rates, and formulate national monetary policy. During World War II, the Foreign Exchange Control Board (FECB) issued regulations. Both the Bank of Toronto and Dominion Bank worked with the Bank of Canada under the FECB's restrictions to raise C$12.5 billion to help finance the war effort.

The two banks were in good condition following the war. However, to be able to extend loans of the size demanded by Canadian industry during its next growth phase, each needed more operating capital. For this reason, they merged on 1 February 1955. It was the first amalgamation of chartered banks in Canada since 1908 and only the third in the country's history. The new Toronto-Dominion Bank had 450 branches and assets of $1.1 billion.

When it formed, Toronto-Dominion had offices in New York and London. During the 1970s, the bank expanded internationally. It established branches in such geographically diverse locations as Bangkok, Frankfurt, and Beirut.

In the 1980s Toronto-Dominion played an important role in handling Third World debt. Brazil, which owed the bank $836 million when it suspended payments on its entire foreign debt in 1987, was an important test case. Toronto-Dominion participated along with several other Canadian banks in a plan to extend an additional $6 billion loan to Brazil, which helped prevent banking crises in both Canada and the United States. Toronto-Dominion also sold off C$411 million in loans for 66 cents on the dollar, thus further reducing the risk from all Third World debt.

Throughout its history, Toronto-Dominion had emphasized the building of assets rather than the buying of the assets. It departed from this tradition in the 1990s with some important acquisitions.

In January 1993 Toronto-Dominion acquired the bulk of the assets and liabilities of Central Guaranty Trust Company, a failing financial institution. The $125 million purchase was the biggest such acquisition in Canada's history. This acquisition added $4.4 billion of residential mortgages, $900 million of personal loans, $2 billion of business loans, and $9.7 billion of personal deposits to Toronto-Dominion's portfolio.

In October 1996 Toronto-Dominion acquired Waterhouse Investor Services, a United States-based holding company of both Waterhouse National Bank and Waterhouse Securities. Waterhouse Securities, founded in 1979, served more than 700,000 individual investors through more than 100 branch offices in the United States. (Toronto-Dominion also owned Green Line Investor Services, Canada's largest discount broker.)

Also in 1996, the bank supported the creation of Canada's first aboriginal bank, First Nations Bank of Canada. Supported by 73 Saskatchewan aboriginal chiefs and the Saskatchewan Indian Equity Foundation, First Nations Bank aimed to be a full-service financial institution, fully owned by native people, within ten years.

In the mid-1990s, Toronto-Dominion decided to limit its high-yield and investment banking to four industries: communications, forest products, health care, and energy.

See also CANADA.

TOTAL CAPITALIZATION

Total Capitalization is an extension of market capitalization (the total value of a given company) and includes long-term debt and every form of equity.

See also MARKET CAPITALIZATION.

TOTAL RETURN

Total Return refers to any and all money generated from an investment.

Total return represents all dividends received and any capital gain realized as the result of holding the shares. The total return investor is usually looking for safety of principal, steady capital growth, and regular dividend payments that might fall somewhere between income-producing investments and growth shares.

Total return can be used as a general classification of an investor's objective. Companies favored by total return investors tend to be large, slightly conservative companies. Frequently, conglomerates such as General Electric are chosen.

See also CONGLOMERATE; DIVIDEND; EARNINGS; GROWTH; OBJECTIVE; SPECULATION.

TOTAL VOLUME

Total Volume can refer to the number of securities traded in a specific issue for a defined time period (usually one trading session).

As a market indicator, total volume refers to the number of all shares traded on a major stock exchange during one session or over some specific period of time.

Although total volume (as a broad market indicator) can reflect the activity of an entire stock market, the raw numbers can, at times, be deceptive. A more accurate picture can be obtained by a detailed examination of the up volume and the down volume for the trading session.

According to the Dow Theory, market advances on weakening volume are not expected to last. However, market advances on strong volume tend to hold their strength.

See also DOW THEORY; MARKET INDEX.

TOUCH, THE (United Kingdom)
See SPREAD.

TRADE

Trade is most often used as a synonym for a transaction or bargain, and refers to the placement of an order by an investor to buy or sell a security through an exchange or broker/dealer. Upon the execution of a trade, the seller transfers to the buyer any and all investment risk.

To make a trade is to conduct a business transaction in which properties, goods, or services are exchanged for compensation. Those active in such exchanges are referred to as traders. Often institutional investors or individuals who do a considerable amount of buying and selling securities, traders are responsible for implementing transactions on a stock exchange or on an over-the-counter-trading desk.

Trade can also refer to total levels of buying and selling between countries, such as in the phrase *balance of trade*.

See also EXECUTION; SECTOR.

TRADE DATE (T/D)
The date on which a transaction is executed is called the *Trade Date*.

The trade date is important for determining both the holding time period and whether or not an investor will receive a dividend payment or qualify for a split.

The trade date is noted on a confirmation notice sent to the investor immediately after a transaction has been executed. It is usually mailed on the day following execution. The trade date also appears on any monthly, quarterly, or semiannual statements sent out to investors from a brokerage firm.

See also CONFIRMATION; EX-DATE; EX-DIVIDEND (XD).

TRADER
See TRADE.

TRADING
Trading is the buying and selling of stocks with the hope of making a profit in the short term.

See also PROPRIETARY TRADING; TRADING FLOOR; SPECULATION.

TRADING AND SETTLEMENT
See SETTLE; TRADE.

TRADING AUTHORIZATION

Trading Authorization is a form—required by many brokerage firms—that grants limited power of attorney to someone other than the beneficial owner of the account and allows this individual to make purchases and sales of securities. Individuals, trusts, groups of investors pooling their funds, or investment clubs will make use of trading authorizations.

Individuals will sometimes allow a person who has significant investment experience or a registered investment adviser to manage the trading in their brokerage account. The trading authorization · form enables this.

See also INVESTMENT ADVISER; MUTUAL FUND; POWER OF ATTORNEY.

TRADING DESK

Over the counter securities are traded on a *Trading Desk*, which is located on the premises of a market maker.

Traders are located at computer terminals and make buy and sell transactions as orders are given to them. They can act as either principals, buying and selling for their firm's account or for securities in which they make a market, or as agents, arranging transactions for other securities through another market maker.

The capacity in which the firm acts normally appears on the confirmation mailed out to the investor.

The following two statements commonly appear on confirmations:

"We purchased for your account . . ." (agent)

or

"We sold to your account . . ." (principal)

The function of the trading desk is much like that of the specialist market maker on a stock exchange. Traders are subject to all government regulations and self-regulatory organization rules or recommendations.

See also OVER THE COUNTER (OTC); SELF-REGULATING ORGANIZATION (SRO); SPECIALIST.

TRADING DIVIDENDS
See DIVIDEND.

TRADING DOWN
Selling lower risk securities and buying securities with higher risk for the purpose of increasing gain potential is referred to as *Trading Down.*

This strategy can be accomplished with bonds by increasing yield and involves buying bonds with longer term maturities, or those that are higher risk.

With shares, trading down can be accomplished by purchasing stocks exhibiting higher volatility or those shares that trade at high p/e ratios.

Some mutual fund managers will trade down in order to increase the growth potential of their funds by increasing the risk. Such funds are normally widely diversified in order to moderate the increased risk.

See also DIVERSIFICATION; MUTUAL FUND; TRADING UP.

TRADING FLOOR
Trading Floor refers to the main area of a stock exchange where the daily trading sessions of listed securities occur. It is the place where traders, specialists, and other members gather to implement the trading of securities.

Some countries have replaced trading floors with computer systems to conduct the daily trading.

See also MEMBER; SPECIALIST; TRADE.

TRADING HALT
See SUSPENDED TRADING.

The floor of the New York Stock Exchange near closing time. *(UPI/Corbis-Bettmann)*

TRADING PATTERN

The *Trading Pattern* of the price of a company's shares is constructed by plotting each trade (using the prices at the close of each session) on a graph. Two lines are then drawn, one along the lowest levels and another along the highest levels. The trading pattern is thus defined. It is the movement of the share's price between the two lines.

Trading patterns are used by technical analysts to determine buy and sell signals. They are also observed by analysts looking for price growth and stability and can be used by investors considering entering a stop order.

See also BREAKOUT; STOP ORDER; TECHNICAL ANALYSIS.

TRADING POST

A *Trading Post* is an assigned location where specific securities are traded.

On any organized stock exchange all listed securities have an assigned location and an assigned specialist. The specialist acts as market maker in the assigned securities, and crowds of traders gather periodically to fill orders.

On the New York Stock Exchange, approximately 100 issues are traded at each one of 22 trading posts.

See also FLOOR BROKER; MARKET MAKER; SPECIALIST; TWO-DOLLAR BROKER.

TRADING RANGE

The *Trading Range* is the amount of movement between the level of support and the point of resistance of a stock market index, and is reflected in the trading pattern of the price of shares. Technical analysts use this information to help forecast short-term trading.

Fundamental analysts also make use of trading ranges as part of trend observation and to forecast future ranges. For example, if XYZ Corporation is trading at a range of $35 to $50 per share, it might be forecast to trade at $50 to $60 per share with a specified increase in earnings.

A general range for both shares and indexes is the Year High and Year Low. These figures contain both the growth and volatility for a 52-week period of time.

See also FUNDAMENTAL ANALYSIS; TECHNICAL ANALYSIS; YEAR HIGH/YEAR LOW (HI-LO).

TRADING SESSION

Trading Session refers to officially established days for trading as well as the time per day during which securities are allowed to be traded on a stock exchange.

Although some exchanges allow after-hours trading and permit orders to be placed before the exchange opens, trading session hours represent the time period during which actual stock exchange trading takes place. These hours and days differ from exchange to exchange. Some exchanges only trade a few days a week, and others only trade as announced.

The most common hours among the world's stock exchange are from 8:30 A.M. to 4:30 P.M. Monday through Friday.

See also individual countries' stock exchange profiles.

TRADING SYMBOL

A *Trading Symbol* is a short series of letters, numbers, or a combination of both used to identify a security for trading purposes. Markets around the world use some kind of trading symbol for the fast identification of a security. For example:

Trading Symbol	Company
IBM	International Business Machines
T	American Telephone & Telegraph
XON	Exxon
MMM	Minnesota Mining & Manufacturing (3-M)
GE	General Electric

A trading symbol is also entered on a ticket to buy or sell a quantity of shares and is also used to identify closing price quotations in daily publications. Standard & Poor's Stock Guide, published monthly, contains trading symbols for shares of U.S. companies, as well as recent financial information regarding company shares. Brokers usually keep a copy on their desk.

On NASDAQ in the United States, over the counter issues have similar symbols but normally begin with a base symbol of at least four letters. Additional letters are added to some symbols as qualifiers:

A—Class A

B—Class B

C—Issuer continuance and qualifications exceptions, used as a fifth character in a NASDAQ security symbol

D—New

E—Delinquent in required filings with the SEC

F—Foreign

G—First convertible bond

H—Second convertible bond, same company

I—Third convertible bond, same company

J—Voting

K—Nonvoting

L—Miscellaneous situations, such as depositary receipts, stubs, additional warrants, and units

M—Fourth preferred, same company

N—Third preferred, same company

O—Second preferred, same company

P—First preferred, same company

Q—Bankruptcy Proceedings

R—Rights

S—Shares of beneficial interest

T—With warrants or with rights

U—Units

V—When issued and when distributed

W—Warrants

Y—American Depositary Receipt (ADR)

Z—Miscellaneous situations such as depositary receipts, stubs, additional warrants, and units.

A more official identification for securities is the number that is assigned by the Committee on Uniform Securities Identification Procedures (CUSIP number).

See also COMMITTEE ON UNIFORM SECURITIES IDENTIFICATION PROCEDURES (CUSIP); STANDARD & POOR'S; TICKET.

TRADING UNIT
See ROUND LOT.

TRADING UP
Trading Up is a technique that involves selling off speculative securities and buying more conservative, investment-grade securities. Such trading is generally done to reduce risk exposure in a portfolio of securities.

Trading up is also undertaken by some investors when the market begins to appear unstable. This action is commonly known as a flight to quality.

When trading up occurs in a mutual fund, prior to the information being included in a report to shareholders, it is often referred to as "window dressing." Some mutual fund managers dress up their mutual funds to make them look less risky to shareholders in the semiannual report. While this practice might seem questionable to some, it is not considered illegal or unethical to the securities industry.

Value-oriented investors might tend to believe that trading up or a flight to quality are unnecessary moves if shares are selected on fundamentals of value. When the price of shares in a company selected on the basis of value drops because of market influences, funda-

mental analysts believe it is the time to buy more securities in that company.

See also BUFFETT, WARREN; MUTUAL FUND; RISK/REWARD RATIO.

TRANSACTION
See TRADE.

TRANSACTION CHARGES
See COMMISSION; SALES CHARGE.

TRANSACTION COSTS
Any and all costs incurred when buying or selling securities, other than the actual market value of the security, are *Transaction Costs*. Typical transaction costs include commissions, fees, mark-ups, markdowns, stamp tax, state tax, custodial fees, Securities and Exchange Commission tax, exchange fees, and any transfer or value-added taxes.

Transaction costs vary from country to country; however, differences are rarely large enough to materially affect the decision to trade in one country or another.

Although investors must pay attention to the costs involved in making transactions, the primary focus of analysis should be on the opportunities available when buying or selling the security.

See also COMMISSION; MARK DOWN; MARK UP.

TRANSACTIONS DE BLOC (France)
See BLOCK TRADE.

TRANSAK (United Kingdom)
TRANSAK is a network system that links members of the London International Financial Futures Exchange (LIFFE) to the clearing system and LIFFE matching system.

See also UNITED KINGDOM.

TRANSAKCJA PAKIETOWA (Poland)
Transakcja Pakietowa is a block trade, off-session transaction implemented by two brokerage houses that are members of the Warsaw Stock Exchange (WSE). The block transaction will be confirmed by the WSE.

Exchanges generally isolate block trades in order to avoid severe price changes in the regular market trading of a security. Price stability is now regarded as essential if a fair and orderly market is to be achieved by an exchange.

See also BLOCK TRADE; POLAND/TRADING.

TRANSFER

Transfer refers to the changing ownership of securities.

Whenever an investor buys securities, the name of the previous owner is removed from the registration list by the transfer agent (often a commercial bank or the company itself) and is replaced by the name of the new owner.

Sometimes, securities themselves must be sent to the transfer agent to be exchanged for new securities. Exchanges requiring the transfer of securities can occur during takeovers, mergers, or reverse splits. Investors holding securities are notified of the exchange and the new securities must be obtained before they can be traded. If the securities are held in a brokerage account, the firm will handle the details of the exchange.

See also REGISTRAR; REVERSE SPLIT.

TRANSFER ACCOUNTING, LODGEMENT FOR INVESTORS AND STOCK MANAGEMENT (TALISMAN; United Kingdom)

The *Transfer Accounting, Lodgement for Investors and Stock Management (TALISMAN)* is an equity settlement system for the UK Stock Exchange.

All shares of a company sold in a session by market makers are placed in a pool account that matches the shares to buyers. This pool account is operated by the Stock Exchange Pool of Nominees (SEPON).

The system communicates share details to the registrar in order to change the ownership documentation and send out certificates.

See also STOCK EXCHANGE POOL OF NOMINEES (SEPON); UNITED KINGDOM/SETTLEMENT DETAILS.

TRANSFER AGENT

See REGISTRAR.

TRANSFER AND AUTOMATED REGISTRATION OF UNCERTIFIED STOCK (TAURUS; United Kingdom)

Transfer and Automated Registration of Uncertified Stock (TAURUS) refers to the book-entry transfer system of the London Stock Exchange that was abandoned in 1993.

See also BOOK-ENTRY.

TRANSFER AND SHIP

Transfer and Ship describes the process of registering a security for a new owner.

When a investor buys a security position and wants the certificate mailed out, instructions to that effect can either be given when the order is placed, or the account can be set up to have the security certificate automatically shipped. Special instructions can also be given if the account owner wants to have a certificate shipped out in someone else's name, for example, making a gift of securities to a relative or friend.

Securities can only be sent out from an account if there are no outstanding debit balances against the securities. If a security is sent out from a margin account, the amount of cash or other securities remaining must provide sufficient equity. Some firms require the securities to be transferred to a cash account before being mailed out.

See also BOOK-ENTRY; REGISTRAR.

TRANSFER INITIATION FORM (TIF; United States)

As required by the New York Stock Exchange, a *Transfer Initiation Form (TIF)* must be used by brokerage firms to transfer all assets, including cash and securities, from one brokerage account to another.

The form contains a space for the investor's authorization signature and the list of securities in the account as well as an estimate of any cash balances.

A TIF form is filed with the receiving brokerage firm, which sends the request to the holding firm. The account will then be transferred in a few days, provided there is not a hold or other restriction on the account.

See also CASH ACCOUNT; MARGIN ACCOUNT.

TREASURY STOCK

Treasury Stock is capital stock of a corporation that has been fully paid by shareholders, legally issued, and then bought back by the corporation.

Such stock buybacks effectively reduce shareholder's equity but are not an asset to the company. Corporations cannot realize a gain or loss when buying or reissuing their own shares. Treasury stock does not have any voting power or preemptive rights and does not receive dividends. Furthermore, treasury stock does not receive assets in the event of a corporate liquidation.

The following are several reasons why a company might buy its own shares:

1. To supply employee stock purchase plans
2. To increase the earnings per share figure by reducing the number of shares outstanding
3. To thwart a takeover attempt by reducing the number of shares outstanding
4. To encourage the making of a market in the stock

TRILON FINANCIAL CORPORATION / 1061

5. To implement a leveraged buyout

When shares are reacquired and held for reissue, the capital of a company is reduced. This reduction is shown in financial reports as a deduction from shareholder's equity or a deduction from issued shares in the same class of security.

See also EARNINGS; LEVERAGED BUYOUT (LBO); SHAREHOLDERS' EQUITY; TAKEOVER/TAKEOVER BID.

TREND

Direction, as shown by closing prices of securities or levels of indices plotted on a line graph, is referred to as *Trend*.

See also TREND LINE.

TREND LINE

Trend Line is the line drawn on a plotted graph of market index or share closing prices.

If there is an up trend, a line connecting the peaks is drawn. If the trend is downward, the line can be drawn along the valleys. Trend lines add a visual dimension to market movements and assist the technical analyst in attempting to forecast reversals, which are directional changes in the trend of a market index or a company's share price.

The technical analyst looks for reversals as a place to buy, sell, or sell short.

See also DOW THEORY; FUNDAMENTAL ANALYSIS; TECHNICAL ANALYSIS.

TRIANGLE FORMATION

A *Triangle Formation* is a geometric pattern formation on a graph plotting a trend line.

See also TECHNICAL ANALYSIS.

TRIGGER

An event that causes a change is a called a *Trigger*.

A stop order is triggered and becomes a market order if the share price trades on or through the stop price. A limit order is executed when triggered by the share price, if the order can be filled at the price specified.

Takeover attempts often trigger poison pill or shark repellent tactics. These antitakeover strategies are intended to ward off any unwanted suitors by making the takeover attempt too time consuming and expensive.

See also LIMIT ORDER; POISON PILL; SHARK REPELLENT; STOP ORDER; TAKEOVER/TAKEOVER BID.

TRILON FINANCIAL CORPORATION

Trilon Financial Corporation is a diversified Canadian financial services group operating in three distinct financial spheres that accounted for the following percentages of 1995 revenues: life and general insurance (93%), investment banking and brokerage (6%), and commercial financing (1%). Trilon's insurance offerings include life, health, property, and casualty insurance products and related activities, as well as pension and annuity products. Its investment banking and brokerage services include capital markets, principal investment positions, asset management, and real estate brokerage operations. Commercial financing includes loans and investment activities.

Trilon, along with Hees International Bancorporation, Inc., form the financial services segment of Canada's largest corporate group, Edper Equities, the Toronto-based holding company of Peter and Edgar Bronfman, two of the heirs of the Seagram Company. Edper's holdings also include interests in some of Canada's largest companies in real estate, natural resources, and consumer products. Edper controls approximately 360 companies, including Labatts Breweries, Noranda Group (minerals and forest products), and the Toronto Bluejays baseball team. The acknowledged architect of the complex and controversial pyramid structure on which the Edper group is built is Jack Cockwell, a South African who moved to Canada in 1966. Cockwell's primary business principle is "maximum control at minimum cost." Pyramids, which are restricted and considered inefficient in the United Kingdom and the United States, employ multilevel holding companies. For example, a 50% stake in one holding company that holds a 50% stake in another holding company that holds a 50% stake in an operating company allows for control with only a 12.5% actual stake.

Trilon is 34% owned by Brascan, Limited, which since 1979 has been controlled by Edper. Originally Brascan was a natural resource recovery and power production company founded in 1899 by Brazilian and Canadian entrepreneurs. Since its founding by Brascan in 1982, Trilon has moved aggressively. In 1983 Trilon took over Brascan's minority stake in London Life Insurance Company, then increased its share to 98%. At the time, London Life was Canada's sixth largest insurance company with assets of C$5.5 billion. Shortly thereafter, Trilon acquired a 42% controlling interest in Royal Trust, Limited, the largest trust company in Canada, with assets of C$10.6 billion.

With the backing of Brascan's substantial capital base, Trilon grew to be Canada's sixth largest financial institution during its first six months of operation. In keeping with Jack Cockwell's preferred corporate structure, Trilon formed intermediate holding companies corresponding to its various service areas—Lonvest to manage insurance operations, Royal Trustco for trust operations, and a corporate division to manage Trilon's own investments and to provide brokerage services. The latter division became Trilon Bancorp, an independent subsidiary, in 1986. Each intermediate company expanded its operations.

In 1984 Royal Trustco merged its real estate operations with A.E. LePage, the third largest property broker in North America, with Royal Trustco owning 50.5% of the new company. In 1987 Royal Trustco introduced several innovative products in the guaranteed investment certificates market (GICs), including guaranteed market index investments, stock price adjusted rate certificates, and diversified guaranteed investment certificates. These instruments allowed investors to protect their principal while taking advantage of rises in the stock market.

In 1985 Lonvest acquired Fireman's Fund of Canada for C$143 million, and subsequently renamed the general insurer Wellington. In 1986 Lonvest acquired a 59% interest in the Holden Group for C$57 million. The Holden Group, based in the United States, provides specialty individual and group insurance plans for educational institutions and public employees. In 1987 Lonvest acquired a 60% stake in Optimum Financial Services Limited, which manages property and automobile insurance for members of professional and alumni associations in Quebec, Ontario, and Alberta. In 1995 Wellington Insurance Company was sold for C$205 million.

Trilon Bancorp also expanded actively. In 1985 it formed a leasing division by acquiring 50.6% of CVL Inc., an automobile leasing firm. The next year CVL changed its name to Triathlon Leasing. Triathlon expanded into computer leasing by acquiring City National Leasing in 1986 and Kompro Computer Leasing in 1987. Then Bancorp purchased Trustco's 50.5% share of Royal LePage and also formed Trilon Capital Markets and Trivest Insurance Network to conduct mercantile banking activities for small- and medium-size firms. In 1994 Triathlon was sold for C$225 million with the proceeds used to reduce bank debt.

In 1986 Trilon also began to expand internationally, acquiring Dow Financial Services Corporation, a Dow Chemicals subsidiary. It also established subsidiaries in Amsterdam and opened an office in Tokyo. In 1987–88 international expansion continued with offices opening in Geneva, Hong Kong, Luxembourg,

Austria, and Singapore. In 1987 Trilon entered into a joint venture with Taiwanese investors in China Canada Investment and Development Company.

In late 1997 Trilon was negotiating to sell some of its insurance and real estate services holdings and to purchase Hees International Bancorporation from its parent company Edper Equities.

See also HOLDING COMPANY; PYRAMIDING.

TRIN

Trin, also called the Short-Term Trading Index, measures buying and selling pressure by comparing the number of advancing and declining stocks to the advancing and declining volumes.

The formula for the trin looks like this:

$$\frac{\frac{\text{The number of issues advancing in price}}{\text{The number of issues declining in price}}}{\text{Total up volume / Total down volume}}$$

A trin of less than 1.0 indicates buying pressure while a trin of more than 1.0 indicates selling pressure. The numbers are not absolute. A trin level of .90 to 1.10 is considered neutral.

As an example, this might be the Trin at mid-morning on the New York Stock Exchange for a given trading day.

$$\frac{\dfrac{\text{Total issues of stock advancing (600)}}{\text{Total issues of stock declining (300)}} = 2}{\dfrac{\text{Total up volume (30,000)}}{\text{Total down volume (10,000)}} = 3}$$

$$2 \text{ divided by } 3 = .67$$

Because this number (.67) is less than 1.0, it indicates the existence of buying pressure.

The trin has a tendency to move by degrees. It may open at 1.50, then drop lower as buyers come on the scene. For example, the trin may at first drop to 1.35, then a few minutes later to 1.30, and within an hour show neutral at 1.0. There is often a tendency for an established trend to continue, in this case toward more buying pressure. There can be times when selling pressure returns and the trin will increase to 1.0, 1.3, 2.0, 3.0, or higher.

The trin tends to be most helpful in an uncertain market, when the investor doesn't know if the market will end the session with an overall advance or decline. In a strong up market or extremely weak market, the trin loses meaning and will only further confirm what is already known.

Understanding and observing the trin when placing a buy or sell transaction can provide some insight as to where the market is likely to be heading for the next few minutes or hours. This can help the investor decide whether or not to place an order and whether that order should be a limit order or a market order.

See also LIMIT ORDER; TICK; VOLUME.

TRINIDAD AND TOBAGO, REPUBLIC OF

The *Republic of Trinidad and Tobago* is an island republic of the West Indies. It is located just off the coast of Venezuela.

Area: 1,980 square miles (5,128 square km)

Population: 1,265,000 (71.3% urban; 28.7 rural)

Form of Government: Multiparty republic, with two legislative houses: Senate—31 members; House of Representatives—36 members. Chief of state: President. Head of government: Prime Minister.

Official Language: English

Capital: Port of Spain

Largest Cities: Chaguanas, 56,601; Port of Spain, 50,878; San Fernando, 30,092; Arima, 29,695; Port Fortin, 20,025; Scarborough, 4,000

Economy:

Currency: Trinidad and Tobago dollar (TT$)

National Budget: Revenue—TT$7.5 billion; expenditures—TT$7.5 billion (current expenditures: 93.7%; development expenditures: 6.3%)

Public Debt: US$1.7 billion

Gross National Product: US$4.8 billion

Principal Products: Sugarcane, coconuts, rice, oranges, and other fruit; livestock; petroleum

Foreign Trade (Imports): TT$7.5 billion (capital goods: 25.4%; nondurable consumer goods: 18.6%, of which food: 11.9%; mineral fuels and lubricants: 15.9%; chemical products [mostly medicines and plastics]: 11.0%; from United States: 38.9%; EC: 19.3%, of which United Kingdom: 8.1%; Venezuela: 16.8%; Canada: 4.9%; Japan: 3.8%)

Foreign Trade (Exports): TT$8.8 billion (refined petroleum: 33.3%; crude petroleum: 21.8%; anhydrous ammonia and urea: 8.9%; steel wire rods: 6.7%; food: 5.7%, of which raw sugar: 1.6%; to United States: 45.6%; Caricom: 20.2%, of which Barbados: 4.4%; Jamaica: 4.4%; Guyana: 3.6%; EC: 4.7%)

Stock Exchanges: 1
Trinidad and Tobago Stock Exchange (TTSE)
65 Independence Square
Port of Spain
Trinidad and Tobago

West Indies
Phone: (1-868) 625-5107-9
Fax: (1-868) 623-0089

Trading Hours: Tuesday, Wednesday, Thursday, 9:30 to close

Office Hours: Monday–Friday, 8:00 to 4:00

Exchange Holidays:

1 January	11, 19 June
27, 28 February	1, 31 August
30 March	24 September
10, 13 April	25, 26 December
30 May	

Listed Companies: 27

Market Capitalization: US$1.2 billion

Major Sectors: Banking, holding companies, tobacco, insurance, communications, publishing

History: An informal securities trading market existed for more than 20 years before the formal opening of the Trinidad and Tobago Stock Exchange (TTSE). In the early 1970s, the government localized the foreign-owned commercial banking and manufacturing sectors of the economy by encouraging companies to sell a majority of divested shares to resident investors.

The Capital Issues Committee was established to direct the primary market and the Call Exchange was empowered to monitor activities in the secondary market. Rules and regulations were set up to develop the capital market in an orderly fashion.

The TTSE began operations in October 1981 with 29 listed shares. It is managed by a nine-strong board of directors, which receives and approves all appropriate policy changes. The second-tier market, for companies whose securities are not fully transferable and cannot be granted a full listing, was approved in 1992. A bond market began operations in 1993.

Requirements for membership include standards regarding minimum capital requirements, independence, skill, and suitability. The Membership Committee works to ensure conformity with all rules governing the conduct of its membership, as well as ensuring compliance with the capital requirements. A fee of 2% of commissions is charged by the exchange.

Classes of Securities: Ordinary shares, bonds

Indices: TTSE Index (January 1983 = 100)

Supervisory Organizations:
Capital Issues Committee
Call Exchange

Trinidad and Tobago Stock Exchange

Depository: n.a.

Settlement Details:

Shares: Trade date + 5 days (T + 5) cash basis

Trading: A call-over procedure is used on the TTSE trading floor. Securities are traded in alphabetical order and the call-over is accomplished before trading ends.

Members can act either as agent or principal on transactions, but client orders always take precedence over broker trades.

Listing Requirements: Companies with a minimum capitalization of TT$1,000,000 who want a listing on the TTSE must submit an application to the exchange. At least 25% of the equity capital must be in the hands of the public, not counting persons associated with the company's directors or major shareholders. This requirement can be lowered in some circumstances.

Companies must enter a listing agreement with the TTSE that governs all disclosure and reporting regulations. Companies must also notify the exchange of any important changes and produce six-month reports. These reports must be published in the daily newspapers.

Investor Taxation: Dividend distributions to a parent company are taxed at 10% taxes. Dividends to any company other than a parent company are taxed at 15%.

Payments, other than interest on a debt, mortgage, or other security, are taxed at 20%. Any interest payment on any debt, mortgage, or other security will be taxed at 20%.

There is no tax on capital gains.

Limitations: Foreign investors can invest in or establish private companies without any restrictions on shareholdings.

Brokerage Firms:
Money Managers
2nd Floor, Union Club Building
65 Independence Square
Port of Spain
Trinidad, West Indies
Phone: (1-868) 623 1763
Fax: (1-868) 623 7815

Reliance Stockbrokers
Gordon Grant Building
10 St. Vincent Street
Port of Spain

Trinidad, West Indies
Phone: (1-868) 623 6945
Fax: (1-868) 623 8241

West Indies Stockbrokers
23A Chacon Street
Port of Spain
Trinidad, West Indies
Phone: (1-868) 623 4861
Fax: (1-868) 627 5002

Caribbean Stockbrokers
67 Independence Square
Port of Spain
Trinidad, West Indies
Phone: (1-868) 624 4415
Fax: (1-868) 624 4416

Company Information:

10 Most Active Companies

Name of Company	Trading Value (US$ millions)
Royal Bank T&T	34.61
Trinidad Cement	24.93
Republic Bank	21.02
Guardian Life of the Caribbean	14.26
Lever Brothers (WI)	12.00
Bank of Nova Scotia	6.26
Angostura Holdings	5.74
Neal & Massy Holdings	3.87
West Indian Tobacco Company	2.70
Ansa McAl Group	2.55

5 Major Companies

Name of Company	Market Capitalization (US$ millions)
Republic Bank	198.50
Trinidad Cement	166.61
Royal Bank T&T	158.00
Bank of Nova Scotia	111.91
CIBC (WI) Holdings	102.12

Other Investment Information:
The General Manager
Industrial Development Corporation
PO Box 949
Port of Spain
Trinidad, West Indies
Phone: (1-868) 623 7291, 623 7298
Fax: (1-868) 625 9124

Central Bank of Trinidad and Tobago
Eric Williams Plaza

PO Box 1250
Port of Spain
Trinidad, West Indies
Phone: (1-868) 625 4835
Fax: (1-868) 627 4696
Telex: 22532

TRIPLE WITCHING HOUR

The *Triple Witching Hour* is the day when equity options, index options, and futures on index options have their last trading day before expiration. It occurs on the third Friday of March, June, September, and December.

Positions will be unwound by investors as assets are realigned. Prices can become quite volatile as these changes occur, but many commentators believe that volatility has been moderated since circuit breaker measures were implemented in the late 1980s.

Extremely large sums of money are switched between options, index options, futures, and shares. These transactions will often be instigated by large institutional investors looking for arbitrage situations. Large-scale programmed trades, instigated by computers, may also increase the number of transactions.

See also INSTITUTIONAL INVESTOR; MUTUAL FUND; OPTION; PROGRAM TRADING.

TRITTBRETTFAHRER (Germany)

A German term for a speculator, *Trittbrettfahrer* literally translates as "traveler on the running board." A *trittbrettfahrer* will attempt to profit from short-term moves in the stock market.

See SPECULATION; TECHNICAL ANALYSIS.

TRUMP, DONALD

Donald Trump is an American real estate tycoon notorious for amassing what appeared to be billions of dollars of wealth but instead turned out to be millions of dollars worth of debt. Trump became a symbol of 1980s excess. By 1989 he had built, developed, or acquired the Grand Hyatt Hotel, Trump Tower, Trump Palace, Trump Plaza, Trump Parc, Trump Parc East, and the Plaza Hotel in Manhattan; and Trump Regency, Trump Plaza, Trump Castle, and the Trump Taj Mahal in Atlantic City, New Jersey. He owned a private jet, helicopter, and yacht as well as two large estates, one in Florida and one in Connecticut. In 1989, just before his downfall, Forbes included Trump on its list of the 400 richest Americans—but as it turned out, at least on paper, he may have actually been one of the 400 poorest. Trump was financing his real estate developments with an ever-increasing mound of debt in the form of bank loans and junk bonds.

One of Trump's first brushes with the stock market occurred when his competitor, Steve Wynn, made a hostile bid to take over the Hilton corporation. Wynn offered to pay $5 a share more than the market value for Hilton's stock. After Wynn made his tender offer, Trump bought Hilton's Atlantic City casino hotel for $320 million. To seal the deal, Trump borrowed a total of $350 million. Then he tried to decrease his own liability for the debt by selling $350 million worth of junk bonds of the casino hotel that he named Trump Castle. However, Bear Stearns, Trump's broker, was only able to get $300 million for the bonds. Some of the money was used as operating capital for the casino, and Trump remained personally responsible for $70 million of Trump Castle's debt. Trump Castle, of course, was indebted to its bondholders. Meanwhile, Holiday Inn, Trump's partner at Trump Plaza, expressed disappointment in that property's performance. Trump again turned to junk bonds, buying Holiday Inn's half interest in Trump Plaza with $250 million in bonds.

In 1987 Trump made his own takeover bid for Resorts International, a corporation that was $740 million in debt and owned an unfinished gaming hall called the Taj Mahal. He borrowed the entire purchase price for a controlling interest in Resorts stock, $96.2 million, from Citibank. Then Trump lost $100 million in the 1987 stock market crash—more than $75 million of it on his Resorts stock. Nevertheless, in March 1988 he offered to buy the rest of the Resorts stock, in order to make the company private. Resorts was still $650 million in debt, but Trump hoped to pay off that debt with another junk bond offering. However, T.V. talk show host Merv Griffin stepped in, and offered to pay $35 per share for Resorts stock, $13 per share more than Trump was offering. When Griffin's offer was made public, the market value of Resorts stock shot up. Ultimately, Griffin bought Trump out, giving him the opportunity to walk away with a $63 million profit. Trump, though, was determined to keep the Taj Mahal. He bought it from Resorts for $273 million, renamed it the "Trump Taj Mahal," and persuaded Merrill Lynch to sell $675 million in Taj Mahal junk bonds.

Trump's kingdom began to fall apart in 1990. *The Wall Street Journal* reported that Trump was responsible for more than $2 billion in bank and junk bond debts. Then *Forbes* reevaluated its 1989 estimate of how much Trump was worth, revising its figure from $1.3 billion to $500 million, based on an estimate of $3.7 billion in assets and $3.2 billion in debt. A few months later, an independent audit of Trump's finances revealed that if he liquidated all his debts, he would have a net worth of negative $295 million. And some estimates put him $900 million in debt. Fortunately for Trump, his debts were so high that his debtors, particularly the banks, were forced to work together to help him in order to prevent him from declaring bankruptcy. A group of Trump's bankers reached an agreement with him to deleverage, or divest himself of assets in return for having some of his debts written off. They put him on a spending allowance of $450,000 a month.

With the help of his banks, Trump made a comeback in the 1990s. The banks forced Trump to hire a financial officer to manage his money, and Trump hired Steve Bollenbach of Holiday Corporation. Trump has formed a public company to hold his casino assets, making it possible for him to raise money by selling stock, instead of personally guaranteeing bank loans. Trump recovered so quickly that by 1994, he managed to buy the top half of the Empire State Building. In 1997 the *Economist* reported that Trump's net worth, despite the fact that many of his assets remained heavily leveraged, was up to $2.5 billion.

See also JUNK BONDS.

TRUST (Internationally)

A *Trust* is defined as a fiduciary relationship in which one person acts as holder of legal title to property and is subject to an equitable obligation to keep or use the property for the benefit of another. The establishment of a trust involves three persons:

1. The trustor—the one creating the trust
2. The beneficiary
3. The trustee—the individual charged with the management and preservation of the property of the trust estate

Common types of trusts include:

1. Trusts in which income is periodically paid over to the trustor, such as a wife, child, parent, or friend, or to a charitable or other institution
2. Trusts in which income is accumulated for a minor until the age of majority is reached
3. Trusts in which the principal is paid to one beneficiary at a certain age, the income meanwhile being paid to either the same beneficiary or another person
4. Trusts in which the principal is paid to a beneficiary upon marriage as a marriage settlement

Various safeguards have been instigated to guarantee the integrity of trusts:

1. A trustee is required to keep accurate records of funds held, invested, and distributed, and trust funds must be kept entirely segregated from individual or corporate assets.
2. A trustee must comply with the wishes of the trustor in carrying out the terms of the trust.
3. A trustee cannot take advantage of his or her position to profit to the disadvantage of the beneficiaries unless the character of investments has been proscribed by the trustor; the trustee is bound to invest in classes of investments as permitted by state law.

Setting up a trust can be a complicated legal process and is often best accomplished by the appropriate legal counsel.

See also CASH ACCOUNT; MARGIN ACCOUNT.

TRUST (United States)

In the United States, *Trust* refers to a monopoly, or group of separate businesses acting as a monopoly, that controls the supply and demand factors of busi-

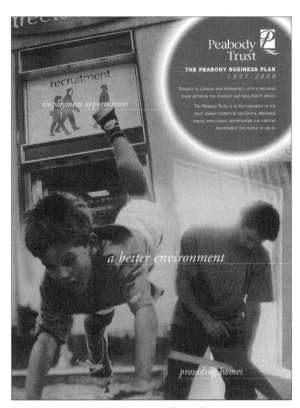

The cover of the Peabody Trust Business Plan, 1997–2000. *(Courtesy of Peabody Trust)*

ness activity. Such actions are usually illegal in the United States as well as in other countries.

See also MONOPOLY; ROCKEFELLER FAMILY.

TRUSTEE

A *Trustee* is a person who administrates a trust.

See also TRUST.

TULIPMANIA

Tulipmania is the first recorded instance of market mania. It paralyzed the economy of Holland and spread throughout Europe, leading to speculation and bankruptcy on a previously unimaginable scale.

The roots of the crisis lie in the humble tulip, a flower that was first imported into Northern Europe in the 16th century. A Swiss botanist, Conrad Gesner, introduced the bulbs to Austrian polite society, and the popularity of the flowers soon spread throughout the continent. Tulips became fashionable items among the aristocracy in England and Germany; aficionados in French court circles were increasingly prepared to bid against each other for the best examples.

Tulips became status symbols, displayed by merchants and courtiers as a sign of their wealth and good taste. In Holland, which was rich because of trading in the East Indies and the newly established colonies of Latin America, the fashion for tulips spread through all strata of society. Tulip brokers sprang up, buying and selling rare specimens that were imported from the tulip fields of Turkey. New methods of transportation and storage were introduced to save rare examples from perishing. Dutch growers began to experiment with cultivation methods, paying for guards to protect their valuable stocks from theft. The Dutch insurance industry began to issue expensive policies against tulips lost during transportation, stolen by collectors, or destroyed by bad weather.

The demand for tulips exploded, and tulip growers greedily pushed up prices. Suddenly the flowers became a vehicle for investment and were used as collateral for loans and mortgages. Banks had to construct tulip vaults and employed experts to value their inventory. At one stage there was even a call to replace the gold standard with a tulip standard, a move that would have invested a perishable flower with the same qualities as a precious metal. Bulbs became the major driver of the Dutch economy as people rushed to become part of the scramble to get rich. Speculation gripped all sections of Netherlands society. According to popular legend, some distinguished Dutch artists paid for tulip bulbs with certain paintings that are now recognized as Old Masters.

Markets were set up to trade tulips in the larger Dutch towns, and tulip brokers would scurry across the country, offering hot tips and searching out new trades. As prices spiraled, a futures market was set up. Contracts were struck for spring, summer, and autumn trading to complement the established winter market. An options market for tulips soon followed. Money flowed into Holland from abroad as speculators jumped on the bandwagon and inflation became endemic. Tulip riggers, the direct ancestors of today's stock exchange insider dealers, set up concert parties to control the market and began to spread rumors about crops. One story, about a tulip farmer whose stock was gobbled up by a hungry cow, ended in his bankruptcy and suicide. Other rumors to move the market included tales of a tulip-preserving machine, weather forecasts, and new plantings of rare hybrids.

The rapid end of Tulipmania came in 1637. The trend of rising prices suddenly hit a plateau, and investor confidence wavered. Prices tumbled on a wave of panic selling. Many people were bankrupt, unable to sell their bulbs for anything more than a pittance. The nation collapsed into an economic depression and also suffered a serious blow to its image as a financial innovator. The pattern of boom and bust that was to be repeated on many occasions over the next three and a half centuries had been set.

See also MARKET MANIA; MISSISSIPPI BUBBLE; SOUTH SEA BUBBLE.

TUNISIA, REPUBLIC OF

Tunisia (Al- Jumhuriyah at-Tunisyah) is a country of North Africa. It is bordered by Algeria to the west and southwest and Libya to the southeast.

Area: 59,664 square miles (154,530 square km)

Population: 8,896,000 (53.0% urban; 47.0% rural)

Form of Government: Multiparty republic, with one legislative house: Chamber of Deputies—163 members. Chief of state: President. Head of government: Prime Minister.

Official Language: Arabic

Capital: Tunis

Largest Cities: Tunis, 674,100; Safaqis, 230,900; Aryanah, 152,700; Ettadhamen, 149,200; Susah, 125,000

Economy:

Currency: Tunisian Dinar (D)

National Budget: Revenue—D 4.9 billion; expenditures—D 5.7 billion (finance: 17.9%; education: 12.4%; interior affairs: 5.8%; national economy: 4.9%; health: 4.9%)

Public Debt: US$7.6 billion

Gross National Product: US$15.3 billion

Principal Products: Olives; wheat; tomatoes, sugar beets, watermelons, and other fruits and vegetables; livestock; clothing; petroleum products; machinery

Foreign Trade (Imports): D 6.6 billion (textiles: 23.0%; machinery and electrical equipment: 20.0%; petroleum and petroleum products: 6.9%; transportation equipment: 6.5%; iron and steel products: 4.6%; plastics and plastic products: 3.2%; pharmaceutical products: 2.0%; from France: 27.4%; Italy: 15.4%; Germany: 12.2%; United States: 6.6%; Belgium: 4.3%; Spain: 3.6%; United Kingdom: 2.2%)

Foreign Trade (Exports): D 4.7 billion (clothing and accessories: 43.3%; petroleum and petroleum products: 9.4%; olive oil: 6.5%; machinery and electrical products: 6.5%; chemical products: 4.9%; to France: 27.2%; Italy: 19.6%; Germany: 15.5%; Belgium: 6.5%; Spain: 4.7%)

Stock Exchanges: 1
Tunis Stock Exchange (TSE)
rue Jean-Jacques Rousseau, Montplaisir
Tunis 1002
Tunisia
Phone: (216-1) 780 288
Fax: (216-1) 789 189
Telex: 14 931

Internet Information: mbendi.co.za/extu

Trading Hours: Monday–Friday, 10:00 to 11:30

Office Hours: Monday–Friday, 8:00 to 12:00 and 2:00 to 6:00

Exchange Holidays:

1 January	13 August
20, 21 March	7 November
6, 25 July	

Listed Companies: 304

Market Capitalization: US$3.9 billion

Major Sectors: Banking, industry, airlines

History: The Tunis Stock Exchange (TSE) was established in 1969. Until 1989 the exchange was only open for trading on Tuesdays and Fridays. Since then the exchange has become enlarged and modernized.

The Conseil de Marché Financier (Securities and Exchange Commission) was established in 1995 to oversee the activities of the stock exchange.

Classes of Securities: Ordinary shares, preference shares

Indices:
TSE Index (1990 = 100) all listed companies, except newly listed
Indice General BVM (30 September 1990 = 100)

Supervisory Organizations: Conseil de Marché Financier (Securities and Exchange Commission)

Settlement Details:

Shares: Settlement and transfer is implemented by STICODEVAM, a centralized clearing house.

Trading: The TSE is non-automated and uses a floor trading system, which makes use of charcoal and boards. Reuters and Telerate transmit quotations, although real-time quotations are not yet available. Share prices are only allowed to fluctuate by a maximum of 3% in a day's trading.

Listing Requirements: Companies seeking TSE listing must be public companies and meet minimum requirements for size, number of shareholders, and trading record. Full details are available from the TSE.

Taxation: Foreign investors are exempt from dividend and capital gains taxation.

Double taxation treaties exist with the following countries:

Austria
Belgium
Canada
Denmark
Egypt
France
Germany
Indonesia
Italy
Jordan
North African Countries
Norway
South Korea
Sweden
United Kingdom
United States

Limitations: Foreign investors are not allowed to hold more than 10% of the capital of listed companies or more than 30% of the capital of unlisted companies.

Securities Lending: None

Brokerage Firms:

International Maghreb Merchant Bank
Boulevard du 7 Novembre 1987
Immeuble Maghrebia Tour A 2035
Charguia II, Tunis
Tunisia
Phone: (216-1) 708 220
Fax: (216-1) 708 020

Company Information:

10 Most Active Companies

Name of Company	Trading Value (US$ millions)
Société Tunisienne de Banque	68.98
Banque International Arabe de Tunise	54.61
Banque de l'Habitat	46.49
TU	41.94
Union Bancaire pour le Commerce	37.19
Banque du Sud	34.54
Banque Nationale Agricole	32.54
BDET	30.42
Banque National de Développement	23.34
BTEI	18.17

10 Major Companies

Name of Company	Market Capitalization (US$ millions)
Société Tunisienne de Banque	432.52
Union Bancaire pour le Commerce et l'Industrie	351.40
Banque Nationale Agricole	294.62
Banque du Sud	276.34
Banque de l'Habitat	268.26
Banque Internationale Arabe de Tunise	241.61
Banque de Tunisie	255.58
Tunis Air	225.03
Amen Bank	194.84
Banque Nationale de Développement de Tunisia	166.65

Regional Exchanges: None

TURKEY, REPUBLIC OF

Turkey (Turkiye Cumhuriyeti) is a Middle Eastern country that lies primarily (95%) in southwest Asia. It is bordered by Iran, Armenia, and Georgia to the east; Iraq and Syria to the south; and Greece and Bulgaria to the west.

Area: 300,948 square miles (779,452 square km)

Population: 62,526,000 (65.6% urban; 34.4% rural)

Form of Government: Multiparty republic, with one legislative house: Turkish Grand National Assembly—450 members. Chief of state: President. Head of government: Prime Minister

Official Language: Turkish

Capital: Ankara

Largest Cities: Istanbul, 7,331,927; Ankara, 2,719,981; Izmir, 1,920,807; Adana, 1,010,363; Bursa, 949,810; Gaziantep, 683,557; Konya, 558,308

Economy:

Currency: Turkish Lira (TL)

National Budget: Revenue—TL 753.4 trillion; expenditures—TL 899.4 trillion (interest payments: 33.2%; personnel: 30.3%; investments: 8.5%)

Public Debt: US$52.6 billion

Gross National Product: US$126.3 billion

Principal Products: Wheat, sugar beets, barley, potatoes, grapes, apples, and other fruits and vegetables; livestock; iron and steel; machinery

Foreign Trade (Imports): US$23.3 billion (nonelectrical machinery: 16.0%; mineral fuels: 12.2%; iron and steel: 10.3%; road vehicles: 9.2%; electrical and electronic equipment: 7.7%; from Germany: 15.7%; United States: 10.4%; Italy: 8.6%; former U.S.S.R.: 7.9%; France: 6.3%; Saudi Arabia: 5.3%)

Foreign Trade (Exports): US$18.1 billion (textiles: 34.7%; iron and steel products: 13.1%; edible fruits: 6.1%; electrical and electronic machinery: 3.8%; to Germany: 21.7%; United States: 8.4%; former U.S.S.R.: 7.9%; Italy: 5.7%; United Kingdom: 4.9%; France: 4.7%)

Stock Exchanges: 1

The Istanbul Stock Exchange (ISE; Istanbul Menkul Kiymetler Borsasi)
Istinye 80860
Istanbul
Turkey
Phone: (90-212) 298 21 00
Fax: (90-212) 288 25 00

Internet Address: www.ise.org

Trading Hours:

Monday–Friday

Secondary:

National	Index & other major companies	10:00 to 12:00
		2:00 to 4:00
Regional	Unlisted/delisted companies	9:30 to 9:45
Wholesale	Block trades	9:00 to 9:15

Primary:

Initial Public Offering	Shares offered initially to the public	9:00 to 9:15
Rights Issues	Rights issues left unsubscribed in rights coupons market	9:00 to 9:15
Official Auction	Shares requested to be sold by courts/ tax authorities	9:00 to 9:15
Rights Coupons	Rights issues that are not desired to be subscribed	2:00 to 4:00
Mutual Funds	Mutual fund certificates	10:00 to 12:00
		2:00 to 4:00

Office Hours: Monday–Friday, 8:30 to 5:30

Exchange Holidays:

1, 28–30 January	19 May
6, 7–10, 23 April	28, 29 October

Listed Companies: 258

Total Market Capitalization:

At 31 December 1997

Local Currency (Millions)	US Dollars (Millions)
9,673,089,024	46,703

Major Sectors: Financial, automotive and parts, electrical and electronics, holding companies, foods

Share Price Performance:

(% Change)

1992	5
1993	534
1994	63
1995	41
1996	173
1997	278

History: As part of the 19th-century Ottoman trading empire, Turkey provided a central location for trade in Ottoman Treasury bonds and corporate stocks and bonds as well as foreign currencies. The first securities market, the Dersaadet Securities Exchange, began trading in 1866 following the Crimean War. Operating as a secondary market, it centralized trading and increased the efficiency with which the government could borrow funds. At the time, railroad bonds were the main securities traded. They were bought and sold by professional traders, banks, insurance companies, and other large corporations. Many Ottomans bought government bonds as a source of income.

The exchange of the 19th century disseminated information; in the later 1800s, Istanbul became connected to European markets by telegraph. Innovations such as joint-stock funding for urban amenities helped advance the Ottoman financial and economic development. The innovations also influenced new European techniques of financing. In its current form, the Istanbul Stock Exchange (ISE) dates from 1986.

The exchange relocated on 15 May 1995 to a new building in the business district of Istinye. In May 1995, an "Investor Counseling Center" was established to provide information on the exchange's operations, listed companies, and member firms. Short-selling procedures began on 3 April 1995.

Effective in 1995, the ISE restructured existing markets into new segments:

National Market (formerly the main market)	86 companies
Regional Markets	13 companies
Wholesale Market	Block Trades
New Companies Market	New

Classes of Securities: Common and preferred shares, corporate bonds, government bonds, and money market securities are available

Indices:

The ISE Composite Index (January 1986 = 100) float-capitalization weighted

The International Finance Corporation (IFC) Turkish Index, market capitalization weighted

The Istanbul Stock Exchange Index (IMKB), market capitalization weighted

It is also free-floated to reflect daily trading volume

The Morgan Stanley Capital International (MSCI)

Supervisory Organizations:

The Capital Markets Board regulates the securities industry.

The Istanbul Stock Exchange has surveillance authority.

An Executive Council serves as the governing body.

Depository: Takasbank

Settlement Details:

Shares:

Trade date + 2 days (T + 2)

After each session the exchange transmits trade results to the Settlement Company.

The Company faxes positions to the parties on T + 1 morning and members settle trades on T + 2.

The following are deadlines:

14:00—physical delivery of stocks

15:00—electronic transfer of stocks

14:30—cash deposits to the authorized bank

15:00—electronic fund transfers

Payments are cleared by same-day funds with delivery versus payment (DVP).

Turnaround trades on the same day can be done.

Trading: A lot (the standard unit of trading) is 1,000 shares. Odd lot orders and orders for "rights coupons" can also be executed on the ISE. Stock trading activities are carried out in two separate two-hour sessions, one in the morning and one in the afternoon.

Price determination follows the continuous auction method in which buyers and sellers enter bids and offers into the computer system via workstations at the ISE. The computer system enables members to execute several types of orders, including market orders, limit orders, limit value orders, fill or kill orders, and all or none orders. Members can also enter orders with differing validity periods of up to 15 business days. Unmatched orders without a specific validity period are canceled at the end of the trading session.

The ISE provides a daily trading report by each member and by individual stock at the end of the day, and a list of outstanding orders before each trading session. Trading information is broadcast to data vendors and one public nationwide television channel on a real-time basis.

Listing Requirements:

Listing: The free-zone status entitles the Istanbul Stock Exchange to apply procedures of admittance to this market. A listing committee scans issues prior to trading. In general, to obtain trading approval, the security shall be listed on at least one exchange in the country of origin or should meet the ISE normal listing criteria. When the ISE Executive Council approves trading, securities will be deposited with the Clearing and Custody Bank or with a bank or custody company in the country of origin that issues depository receipts and formally requests that these be circulated. The International Market Listing Committee along with experts from the exchange oversees the listing process.

Investor Protection: Securities issued on the International Market will be subject to the rules and regulations of the ISE concerning the public dissemination of information, documentation, and regular submission of information. A domestic intermediary may be assigned to take on joint responsibility for these obligations. The tax-free status of the International Market is assured by the free trade zone status granted on 1 April 1995.

Collateral: Intermediary institutions engaged in trading in the market are required to place a deposit in either U.S. dollars or government bonds with the Central Bank or a bank designated by the Executive Council. Alternatively, they can submit a letter of guarantee on sight drafted by an international bank and affirmed irrevocably.

Settlement: The Istanbul Stock Exchange may require the custody of the securities or certificates to be traded be regulated by the Clearing and Custody Bank or a bank designated by the Executive Council. The settlement period of T + 2 may be extended to facilitate access to investors.

To ensure full compliance with international settlement norms and procedures, the Clearing and Custody Bank will collaborate with international settlement companies such as Euroclear and Cedel with the aim of eventual full integration through the existing system.

Investor Taxation:

There is no withholding tax on dividends or government bond interest.

There is no capital gains tax.

Banking service fees have a 5% transaction tax.

There are no stamp or duty taxes.

Limitations:

There are no foreign ownership limits.

There are no foreign exchange restrictions.

Cash movements in and out of the country of more than $50,000 have to be reported to the Central Bank.

Approval from the federal government is required on a corporate takeover.

Permanent representation in Turkey is required for reporting activities. This can be achieved by appointing a local custodian bank that reports to the Capital Market Board and the tax authorities to benefit from tax exemption.

Decree 32 on the Protection of Value of Turkish Currency constitutes the legal base for cross-border transactions. The decree allows foreign investors to trade in Turkish securities without restrictions and to freely repatriate capital gains, dividends, and interests. Investments in securities must be made through authorized banks and brokerage houses, and proceeds must be repatriated through the banking system. The Turkish currency has been fully convertible since 1990. Under the same decree, residents are free to issue, buy, and sell securities abroad through brokerage houses, while non-residents may issue securities in Turkish capital markets subject to the provisions of the Capital Market Law.

The "Special Situations Communique" issued by the Capital Market Board in 1993, requires shareholders who control a minimum 10% of the paid-in capital to disclose any transactions that equal or exceed 1% of the paid-in capital of the company. In addition, foreign investors who wish to exercise their voting rights must register their shares with the General Directorate of Foreign Investment.

Securities Lending: Available for short-selling of the ISE 100 Composite securities

Brokerage Firms (Intermediary institutions providing custodian services for foreign investors):

The Chase Manhattan Bank
Yilduz posta C.
Dederman Ticaret Markazi
Istanbul
Turkey
Phone: (90-212) 275 12 90
Fax: (90-212) 275 42 94

Citibank N.A.
Boyukdere C. No. 100
80280 Istanbul
Turkey
Phone: (90-212) 288 77 00
Fax: (90-212) 288 77 58

Ottoman Bank (Bank Paribas)

Takasbank (central depository)

Other Brokerage Firms:
Acar Menkul Degerler A.S.
buyokdera c. 108/1 Oyak Ishani K: 6
Istanbul
Turkey
Phone: (90-212) 275 48 24
Fax: (90-212) 274 04 75

Aaks Menkul Degerler A.S.
Buyukdere C. Bentek is Markazi No: 47 K:
  4 Mecidiyekoy
Istanbul
Turkey
Phone: (90-212) 274 09 00
Fax: (90-212) 212 01 40

Alan Menkul Degerler A.S.
Halaskargazi C. No: 401 Kat:
  B4 80260 Ihiamur-Besiktas
Istanbul
Turkey
Phone: (90-212) 232 65 81
Fax: (90-212) 234 52 91

Ar Menkul Degerler A.S.
Kucuidanga C. 16-18 Biliar Is Merkazi K:3 Aksaray
Istanbul
Turkey
Phone: (90-212) 529 11 19
Fax: (90-212) 587 46 80

Arigil Menkul Degerler A.S.
Havyer S. 44/1-5 Cihangir Belyogiu
Istanbul
Turkey
Phone: (90-212) 418 47 20
Fax: (90-212) 346 45 05

Bahadir Menkul Degerler A.S.
Inebolu Sok. Set Apt. No: 79/1
  Setosto 80040 Kababas
Istanbul
Turkey
Phone: (90-212) 251 61 79
Fax: (90-212) 251 61 25

Basak Menkul Degerler A.S.
Abdi Ipekci Cad. Kizilkaya Apt. No: 59/7 Nisantasi
Istanbul
Turkey
Phone: (90-212) 230 05 54
Fax: (90-212) 234 42 62

Bayindir Menkul Degerler A.S.
Tahran Cd. No. 2/3 Kaavaldidere
Ankara
Turkey
Phone: (90-312) 467 41 00
Fax: (90-312) 426 17 30

Numerang Yatirim Menkul Degerler A.S.
Esid Buyukdere C. Yunus Emra S. Topcu Han No: 1
    D: 124 Levent
Istanbul
Turkey
Phone: (90-212) 280 91 00
Fax: (90-212) 268 43 00

Eczacibasi Menkul Degerler A.S.
19 Mayis Cd. Nova Baran Is Merkazi Sisli
Istanbul
Turkey
Phone: (90-212) 234 35 01
Fax: (90-212) 230 62 66

Ericiyes Menkul Degerler A.S.
Sogutiucesme cad. Kuyumcular Carsisi No: 9
    Kadikoy
Istanbul
Turkey
Phone: (90-212) 349 84 13
Fax: (90-212) 348 15 02

Garanti Menkul Kiymetler A.S.
Meta Cad. No. 38/3
Sarhan 80090 Takairn
Istanbul
Turkey
Phone: (90-212) 251 08 80
Fax: (90-212) 251 31 03

Sinai Yatirim ve Kredi Bankasi A.O.
Barbaros Bulven Akdogen S. 41/43 Besadas
Istanbul
Turkey
Phone: (90-212) 227 11 11
Fax: (90-212) 227 28 56

Tat Yatirim Bankasi A.S.
Kemeraita C. No.: 24/2 90030 Karakdy
Istanbul
Turkey
Phone: (90-212) 249 46 85
Fax: (90-212) 257 77 77

Tekfen Yatirim ve Finansman Bankasi A.S.
Ulus Mahelesi Tekfen Sitesi D. Blok 90600 Ebler
Istanbul
Turkey
Phone: (90-212) 287 00 00
Fax: (90-212) 257 77 77

T. Ihracat Kredi Bankasi A.S. (EXIMBANK A.S.)
Mili MQdfaa C. 20 Bakenlider
Ankara
Turkey
Phone: (90-312) 417 13 00
Fax: (90-312) 425 78 96

T. Merchang Bank A.S.
Cevdtpasa C. 288 80810 Bebek
Istanbul
Turkey
Phone: (90-212) 257 76 84
Fax: (90-212) 257 73 27

T. Kalkinma Bankasi A.S.
Buyukdere C. Resit Riza S. No. 3 Mecidiyelrdy
    80300
Istanbul
Turkey
Phone: (90-212) 212 00 20
Fax: (90-212) 211 97 02

T. Sinai Kalkinma Bankasi A.S.
Meclia-i Mebusan C. 137 Findildt
Istanbul
Turkey
Phone: (90-212) 251 27 92
Fax: (90-212) 243 29 75

Yatirim Bank A.S.
19 Mayrs Mah. Dr. Seviret Bay Sok. No. 5 Sisli
    80200
Istanbul
Turkey
Phone: (90-212) 225 70 90
Fax: (90-212) 231 95 99

Company Information:

The Best Performing Shares in the Country

Company Name	Share Price Change 1 January 1997 to 31 December 1997 (%)
Pimas Plastik	2,951
Milliyet Gazetcilik	1,286
Alternatifbank	1,083
Turkiye Is Bank 'C'	1,037
Enka Holding Yatirim	900
Teletas Telekomunikasyon	692
Nergis Holding	609
Aktas Elektrik	595
Yapi Kredi Bk.	582
Hurriyet Gazetecilik	550
Aksigorta	521

Company Name	Share Price Change 1 January 1997 to 31 December 1997 (%)
Dogan Holding	493
Carsi	482
Tupras	457
Demirbank	404
Kepez Elektrik	387
Petrol Ofisi	374
Vestel	367
Turkiye Garanti Bankasi	365
Cukurova Elektrik	338
Tofas Otomobil Fab.	315
Ford Otomotive Sanay	314
Koc Hdg.	309
Akbank	244
Cimsa Cimento	238
Alarko	222
Netas Telekomunik	206
Trakya Cam	197
Baticim	193
Akcansa	190
Ihlas Holding	174
Ardem	169
Arcelik	166
T Sise Cam	165
Petkim Petrokimya Hldg.	159
Migros Turk	148
Erciyas Biracilik	147
Eregli Demir Ve Celik	146
Aygaz	144
Bekoteknik	118
Sasa Elyas	116
Goodyear Lastikleri	90
Turkiye Kalkinma Bankasi	79
Aksa Akrilik Kimya	76
Ege Biracilik Ve Malt	61
Peg Profilo Elektrikli	52
Turk Hava Yollari	52

The Largest Companies in the Country by Market Capitalization as of 31 December 1997

Company Name	Market Capitalization Local Currency (Millions)	Market Capitalization US Dollars (Millions)
Turkiye Is Bank 'C'	1,898,773,760	9,168
Akbank	912,499,712	4,406
Koc Hdg.	777,239,040	3,753
Tupras	702,668,544	3,393
Sabanci Holding	637,499,648	3,078
Yapi Kredi Bk.	474,524,928	2,291
Turkiye Garanti Bankasi	409,999,872	1,980

Company Name	Market Capitalization Local Currency (Millions)	Market Capitalization US Dollars (Millions)
Turk Hava Yollari	364,999,680	1,762
Petrol Ofisi	346,499,840	1,673
Petkim Petrokimya Hldg.	337,499,648	1,630
Cukurova Elektrik	284,999,936	1,376
Ford Otomotive Sanay	240,206,112	1,160
Eregli Demir Ve Celik	202,751,984	979
Arcelik	197,437,296	953
Pimas Plastik	179,999,888	869
Migros Turk	177,187,360	855
T Sise Cam	170,799,984	825
Aktas Elektrik	164,999,984	797
Tofas Otomobil Fab.	148,049,984	715
Trakya Cam	127,559,904	616
Enka Holding Yatirim	125,999,984	608
Turkiye Kalkinma Bankasi	119,999,984	579
Akcansa	110,349,504	533
Demirbank	103,949,984	502
Aygaz	96,249,984	465
Netas Telekomunik	93,554,992	452
Erciyas Biracilik	86,999,984	420
Aksa Akrilik Kimya	86,545,376	418
Sasa Elyas	81,112,416	392
Uzel Makina	80,499,984	389
Ege Biracilik Ve Malt	79,810,880	385
Hurriyet Gazetecilik	77,013,280	372
Aksigorta	74,531,216	360
Vestel	67,999,984	328
Kepez Elektrik	67,199,984	324
Ihlas Holding	64,483,728	311
Teletas Telekomunikasyon	60,999,984	295
Anadolu Isuzu	56,470,672	273
Goodyear Lastikleri	49,673,520	240
Milliyet Gazetcilik	48,076,768	232
Cimsa Cimento	47,384,976	229
Dogan Holding	46,370,896	224
Alarko	44,329,680	214
Baticim	43,199,984	209
Ardem	41,279,984	199
Bekoteknik	40,162,464	194
Nergis Holding	38,999,984	188
Peg Profilo Elektrikli	36,996,736	179
Alternatifbank	33,047,968	160
Carsi	29,699,984	143

Regional Exchanges: None

Other Investment Information:

Broker and Bank Research
TEB Research
Meclis-i Mebusan Caddesi 35
Findikli
80040 Istanbul
Turkey
Phone: (90-212) 151 21 21

Global Securities
Halaskargazi Caddesi 368/11
Cifkurt Apt.
Sisli
80220 Istanbul
Turkey
Phone: (90-212) 132 30 40

Guis Securities
Yapi Kredi plaza
C/Blok Kat 9
Levent
80620 Istanbul
Turkey
Phone: (90-212) 180 50 00

Iktisat Bankasi
Buyukdere Caddesi
80504 Istanbul
Turkey
Phone: (90-212) 174 70 26

TURNAROUND

When a profitable company undergoes setbacks that result in extreme difficulty in selling its products and making a profit and then improves its business practices and once again becomes profitable, the company is said to have made a *Turnaround.*

Turnaround is also used to describe a type of speculative investing in which the investor looks for unprofitable companies that he or she believes will make a turnaround.

When a company experiences difficult times, the price of company shares tends to be low. As the turnaround begins and earnings improve, company share prices tend to rapidly accelerate. It is this price acceleration that the turnaround investor wants to find.

See also EARNINGS; OBJECTIVE; THEORY OF SPECULATION.

TURNER, TED

Broadcasting entrepreneur *Ted Turner* (Robert Edward Turner III), noted for being an innovator in television broadcasting, a champion yachtsman, and an owner of professional sports teams, rose to prominence as a U.S. business leader during the late 1900s. He was born in Cincinnati, Ohio, in 1938, but his family moved to Savannah, Georgia, when he was nine. Expelled from Brown University during his third year for flagrant dormitory rules infractions, he never completed his college education. However, he has since been awarded several honorary degrees.

Turner's father, the wealthy owner of a billboard-advertising company based in Atlanta, committed suicide in 1963 as the result of business pressures and depression. At the age of 25, Turner assumed control of the financially troubled enterprise, Turner Advertising, and restored it to a fiscally sound condition. During the late 1960s, Turner began purchasing struggling radio stations in the southeastern United States and transformed Turner Advertising into Turner Communications Company. He saw broadcasting as a natural extension of his billboard business. Each medium could be used to advertise the other.

Turner entered the television business in 1970 by acquiring Channel 17 WJRJ in Atlanta, an ailing independent UHF station owned by Rice Broadcasting, a public company. Turner took his company public by effecting a reverse merger with Rice, swapping 3.6 shares of Rice stock for one share of Turner Communications stock. He renamed the station WTCG, and the company became Turner Communications Group. The next year Turner bought a bankrupt television station in Charlotte, North Carolina. Soon WTCG began broadcasting Atlanta Braves major league baseball games and other sporting events. In two years Turner had brought his company to profitability.

1976 was a watershed year for Turner. At the beginning of the year he purchased the Atlanta Braves, and at the end of the year he pioneered the super station concept, transmitting WTCG's signal via satellite to cable systems across the country. The next year he acquired a controlling interest in the National Basketball Association's Atlanta Hawks. Throughout Turner's business career he has pursued an intense interest in yachting, and in 1977 he piloted his yacht *Courageous* to win the prestigious America's Cup races.

Cable News Network (CNN), the first live, 24-hour, all-news television network made its initial broadcast on 1 June 1980. A subsidiary of Turner Broadcasting System, CNN maintains news bureaus in major cities throughout the world and provides continuous live coverage of major news events as they are happening, transmitting via satellite around the globe. CNN received worldwide acclaim in 1991 for its coverage of the Persian Gulf War and events attending the breakup of the Soviet Union. A second Turner all-news service, Headline News, began operating in 1982. Then in 1985 Cable News Network International (CNNI) launched worldwide news service and is now distributed to 210 countries and territories.

In partnership with the former Soviet Union, in 1985 Turner originated the Goodwill Games, a quadrennial, international, multisport competition held in Olympic off years. The inaugural 1986 games were held in Moscow and were followed by the 1990 games in Seattle, Washington, and the 1994 games in St. Petersburg, Russia.

In 1986 Turner acquired MGM Entertainment, with its library of more than 3,300 feature films and the former Metro-Goldwyn-Mayer motion picture studios. Michael Milken, the junk bond specialist of Drexel Burnham Lambert, was engaged to raise the $1.6 billion required to close the deal. Reportedly Milken solicited the assistance of corporate raider Ivan Boesky, requesting that Boesky buy MGM stock to raise investor's confidence in the bond issues Milken was in the process of floating. Later, government prosecutors were not able to prove that Milken gave Boesky any insider information.

Turner raised a firestorm of protest from film buffs when he proceeded to colorize many of the black-and-white films in the MGM library. The large debt incurred in the MGM acquisition required Turner to immediately sell off many MGM assets. He also sold a 21% share of Turner Broadcasting System to Tele-Communications, Inc. (TCI), the largest cable company in the United States. With the MGM film library as the programming foundation, Turner launched Turner Network Television (TNT) in 1988.

In 1991 Turner acquired the entertainment assets of Hanna-Barbera Cartoons, including its 3,000-episode library and production facilities, and the next year he launched the Cartoon Network, the first 24-hour, all-animation television service. Then in 1993 Castle Rock Entertainment, a television and motion picture producer, joined the Turner empire. In 1994 Turner Broadcasting merged with New Line Cinema, an independent producer and distributor of motion pictures. In 1995 Turner initiated CNNfn, the financial network. Each weekday CNNfn broadcasts 12 hours of programming focusing on market news, personal finance, consumer issues, and world business developments.

In 1996 Turner sold Turner Broadcasting to Time Warner, Inc., for $6.2 billion, creating the world's largest media company, and he became a vice chairman of Time Warner. The deal was approved by the Federal Trade Commission only after TCI agreed to place its 21% of Turner Broadcasting, which would convert to a 9% Time Warner stake, in a special subsidiary and make it nonvoting stock.

In 1997, Turner's net worth increased from $2.2 billion to $3.2 billion, largely as a result of a 50% rise in the value of Time Warner stock. Turner, while traveling to New York to address a UN Association dinner, decided to donate the $1 billion profit to the United Nations in support of its worldwide programs. Turner set aside that amount in Time Warner stock to support ten gifts of $100 million each over the course of a decade. The gifts may or may not be made in stock, and their value may be less than $1 billion if Time Warner shares fall in value. The gift is earmarked for nonadministrative programs. At the time of the announcement Turner had not worked out any of the details. "I couldn't wait, because I had the whole United Nations there and all their supporters. I was kind of winging it."

TURNOVER

The word *Turnover* is used in several ways in the world's financial markets. They are as follows:

1. Turnover is used when describing the total number of buying and selling transactions in a market or for a single share.
2. In the United Kingdom, turnover normally refers to a company's annual sales volume. In this sense, turnover is a measure of a company's total revenues.
3. In industrial relations, turnover is the rate of employees changing companies or sectors. Some employment experts take the total number of employees and divide this number by the number of new employees to get a yearly percentage figure.
4. For accounting, turnover may refer to the number of times an asset is replaced in a measured period, normally a year.

See also ANNUAL REPORT; NET WORTH; VOLUME.

TWELVE B-1 (12B-1) Fund (United States)

The *Twelve B-1 (12B-1) Fund* refers to paragraph 12B-1 in the Investment Company Act of 1940. This important paragraph indicates that a mutual fund, registered with the Securities and Exchange Commission, may charge costs taken from income earned by the fund if the costs are to be used for advertising, certain general corporate purposes, and for distribution fees to reward securities salespersons. Because of this, the fees of 12B-1 mutual funds tend to be more expensive than the management fees of other funds.

12b-1 Funds generally have no front end load (sales charge). Instead, they have a deferred contingent sales charge in the first few years of redemption. Normally, each year an investor is in the fund means a lower sales charge if the shares are redeemed. After a minimum number of years, there is no sales charge for redemption of the shares.

See also BACK END LOAD; MUTUAL FUND; SALES CHARGE; UNIT INVESTMENT TRUST/UNIT TRUST.

TWENTY-DAY PERIOD (United States)

Also known as the cooling-off period, the *Twenty-Day Period* is the time period, after the filing of the Registration Statement and Preliminary Prospectus, for a new issue or secondary distribution. The twenty-day period is required by the Securities and Exchange Commission (SEC).

During this period the SEC may file a deficiency letter requesting more or corrected information on the issue. If the time period passes without further requests for information, the date of its passing becomes the effective date on which securities can be issued.

Any deficiencies can extend the twenty-day period as decided by the SEC.

See also INITIAL PUBLIC OFFERING (IPO); PRELIMINARY PROSPECTUS; SECONDARY DISTRIBUTION.

TWISTING

Twisting is a term used to describe overtrading to generate commissions.

See also CHURNING.

TWO-DOLLAR BROKER (United States)

Two-Dollar Broker is securities industry jargon for an exchange member who acts as a broker's broker and conducts transactions for member firms when their own brokers are too busy.

The term *two-dollar broker* came from an old traditional fee of two dollars per 100 shares transacted in such a manner. These fees are now negotiable.

See also MEMBER; SPECIALIST; TRADE.

TWO-SIDED MARKET

A *Two-Sided Market* is a securities market in which firm bid and ask prices are regularly presented. It is a market in which shares are constantly bought and sold and, therefore, both buyers and sellers are reasonably assured of gaining a firm price for their transaction.

See also ASK PRICE; BID PRICE; LAST TRADING DAY.

U

UNCERTIFIED SHAREHOLDING

See BOOK-ENTRY.

UNCOVERED OPTION

See NAKED OPTION/NAKED CALL.

UNCTAD

See UNITED NATIONS CONFERENCE ON TRADE AND DEVELOPMENT (UNCTAD).

UNDERLYING SECURITY

Underlying Security refers to those ordinary shares that could be purchased (with a call option) or sold (with a put option) if the option owner chooses to exercise his or her right before the expiration.

Equity options are sold and bought with ordinary shares as the underlying security. For example, an investor owns 5 April 50 calls on XYZ Corporation. The investor can exercise the call option at anytime prior to the April expiration and pay $50 per share for the 500 shares.

An underlying security also refers to the securities a corporation must deliver to the investor who either exercises a corporate stock option, subscribes to a rights offering, exercises a warrant, or converts a convertible security.

See also OPTION; SUBSCRIPTION RIGHTS; SUBSCRIPTION WARRANT.

UNDERVALUED

Undervalued is a fundamental analysis term used to describe a company's market price if it is perceived to be below its fair value. Undervalued companies are often the focus of fundamental analysis, especially if the price weakness is believed to be a temporary condition.

One sign of an undervalued company is an unusually low price/earnings ratio when compared to other companies in the same industry. If the p/e ratio is at 11x and similar companies trade at 18x, the company could be undervalued and, therefore, worth a closer look to explain the situation.

See also EARNINGS; FUNDAMENTAL ANALYSIS; PRICE/EARNINGS RATIO.

UNDERWRITER

See UNDERWRITING.

UNDERWRITING

Underwriting is an integral part of bringing securities to the public trading market. The following are the most commonly used underwriting terms:

Underwriter: Investment bankers buy a new issue of securities from an issuing corporation or government entity and resell the securities to the investing public. This is usually accomplished through a brokerage firm. The underwriter profits from the difference between the price they pay for the securities and the public offering price. This profit is known as the underwriting spread. The brokerage commission fee is also included in the underwriting spread, so the issue is sold to the public at a net price.

Underwriting Group (Purchase Group): Underwriters often work as a group with a new issue, especially when dealing with issues of a significant size. Working as a group spreads the risk and enhances a wide distribution of the issue. The underwriting group operates through an Agreement Among Underwriters (Syndicate Contract or Purchase Group Contract).

The Managing Underwriter: The underwriting group appoints a managing underwriter (lead underwriter, syndicate manager, manager) who also acts as originating investment banker and prepares all the necessary registration documentation for the regulatory authorities.

Underwriters' Agreement: This agreement is between an issuing organization and the managing underwriter as agent for the underwriting group. The agreement can also be referred to as the Purchase Agreement or Purchase Contract, as it contains the underwriter's commitment to purchase the issue of securities. It also details the public offering price, the underwriting spread (including discounts and commissions), as well as the net proceeds to the issuer and the settlement date.

See also COMMISSION; INITIAL PUBLIC OFFERING (IPO); PUBLIC OFFERING PRICE (POP); SPREAD; SYNDICATE; SYNDICATE MANAGER.

UNIFORM GIFT TO MINORS ACT (UGMA; United States)

The *Uniform Gift to Minors Act (UGMA)* establishes procedures for adults to make gifts of money and securities to minors. Normally a parent, relative, guardian, or independent trustee will open the account using an UGMA form standardized in all states. When the children become adults they will take charge of the property, unless other arrangements are made.

See also CASH ACCOUNT; CUSTODIAL ACCOUNT; MUTUAL FUND.

UNION BANK OF SWITZERLAND (UBS)

The *Union Bank of Switzerland (UBS)* formed in 1912 as the result of a merger between two Swiss banks, the Bank in Winterthur and the Toggenburger Bank, both of which had been founded during the 1860s. The Bank in Winterthur had operated predominantly as a commercial bank, and in 1906 it bought a seat on the Zurich Stock Exchange. It transacted more business abroad than many of its peers. The Toggenburger Bank, based in the east of Switzerland, was more focused on domestic savings and the granting of mortgages.

The mixture offered by the two banks—one mercantile, one retail—was complementary. The large number of small, private banks that stretched across Switzerland were gradually bought up by the "big three" banks, who were eager to reduce costs through economies of scale. By 1923 UBS had a branch in all of the major towns in Switzerland. The downturn in trade caused by World War I soon became a distant memory as the international economy boomed. The Great Depression, which began in 1931, provided a reminder of just how dependent banks are on the state of the economy. The size of the bank's balance sheet more than halved, and the equity capital had to be restructured. Further strictures came with World War II.

In 1945 the bank moved its headquarters from Winterthur and St. Gall to Zurich. Widely regarded as the center of the Swiss banking industry, and bolstered by an inflow of foreign capital, Zurich was now only behind New York and London in terms of importance. UBS's present headquarters, on the famous Banhofstrasse in central Zurich, are on the same site as the original office. A takeover of the Eidgenossiche Bank increased the bank's assets by more than 40%.

A merger in 1967 with Interhandel, a specialized financial company, ensured UBS's position as one of the "big three" banks in Switzerland. The Interhandel deal was followed by an extensive reorganization of the bank's management structure that reflected the increased need for the specialization that clients demanded. The bank was less eager than its competi-

tors to expand abroad, and it did not open a branch office in the United States until 1970.

In 1985 UBS bought London-based stockbrokers Phillips and Drew in one of the most significant deals of the "Big Bang" era. The process of integrating Phillips and Drew into a new merchant banking subsidiary, UBS Phillips and Drew, was not without problems. Heavy losses were incurred during the Black Monday crash of 1987, and the bank's dealing and settlements technology proved inadequate to deal with customer orders.

In 1994 the first rumblings of a row between the directors of UBS and the aggressive investor Martin Ebner threatened the cozy peace of the Swiss banking sector. Ebner, through his BK Vision investment fund, began a civil action in the courts as a protest against proposals to convert the bank's registered shares into bearer shares without offering adequate compensation to those investors who would lose voting power. BK Vision, which held more than four million of the registered shares, subsequently brought forth a criminal action alleging that in order to ensure a majority, UBS had bought its own shares before the vote on the proposal.

In 1997 UBS announced that it had incurred a loss on loans made in Indonesia, Thailand, and South Korea, three of the countries most badly hit by the financial crises that affected Asia during the year. The bank also lost money on equity derivatives: difficult market conditions led to losses of SFr 150 million while changes in UK tax law and a computer error were blamed for a further SFr 200 million deficit. Losses were also incurred on proprietary trading in Japanese convertible bonds. At the end of 1997 the board of UBS announced that it had accepted a merger deal with the Swiss Bank Corporation (SBC).

See also SWITZERLAND.

UNISSUED STOCK

Unissued Stock refers to ordinary shares that are authorized in the corporate charter but remain unissued. Unissued stock can be issued by a decision of the board of directors; however, any shares necessary for unexercised options, rights, warrants, or convertible securities must not be issued while they are still outstanding obligations.

Unissued shares do not pay dividends and are not voting shares in their unissued state. They do, however, appear on a company's balance sheet even though they are neither an asset nor a liability.

See also BOARD OF DIRECTORS; CONVERTIBLE; SUBSCRIPTION RIGHTS; SUBSCRIPTION WARRANT; TREASURY STOCK.

UNIT INVESTMENT TRUST/UNIT TRUST

Also known as bond funds, *Unit Investment Trusts* or *Unit Trusts* are portfolios of fixed-income securities such as corporate, municipal, and government bonds or mortgage backed securities. Units are purchased in blocks (usually of $1,000) and suffer a sales charge rather than a commission or fee. Investors in the units receive proportional income in the form of interest, which is usually paid monthly, and the principal is paid as securities in the trust mature.

The portfolio is fixed and unmanaged, meaning that securities might be substituted for similar securities with longer maturities, but are not actively traded. The trust format is closed-end, so new investors are not accepted once all of the units are sold. Brokerage firms maintain a secondary market for unit trusts so they can be bought and sold by the investor.

Although the terms *unit investment trust*, *unit trust*, or *trust* are at times used casually to describe any unmanaged but supervised fund of securities in a closed-end format, strictly speaking the label applies to debt securities.

See also COMMISSION; MUTUAL FUND; SALES CHARGE; WIDER SHARE OWNERSHIP.

UNIT OF TRADING

Virtually every stock exchange has a *Unit of Trading* for different securities, derivatives, and commodities traded. In the United States, probably the most common unit of trading is for ordinary shares to be traded in "round lots" of 100 shares.

The unit of trading concept serves to make exchanges more efficient and accurate, especially where the transactions are handled by more than one person. As the world of securities trading becomes totally computerized, the need for trading units may become obsolete, but for the present it is the norm.

Trading in shares can usually be done in odd lots, but this is often more expensive due to the extra handling necessary to receive an order execution.

See also BLOCK TRADE; ODD LOT; ROUND LOT.

UNITED KINGDOM OF GREAT BRITAIN AND NORTHERN IRELAND, THE

The *United Kingdom of Great Britain and Northern Ireland* is an island country off the northwestern coast of Europe.

Area: 94,251 square miles (244,110 square km)

Population: 58,586,000 (89.3% urban; 10.7% rural)

Form of Government: Constitutional monarchy, with two legislative houses: House of Lords—1,198 members; House of Commons—651 members. Chief of state: Sovereign. Head of government: Prime Minister.

Official Language: English

Capital: London

Largest Cities: Greater London, 6,933,000; Birmingham, 1,012,400; Leeds, 724,500; Glasgow, 681,500; Sheffield, 531,900; Bradford, 488,000; Liverpool, 477,000; Edinburgh, 441,600; Manchester, 432,000; Bristol, 397,600

Economy:

Currency: Pound Sterling (£)

National Budget: Revenue—£222.1 billion; expenditures—£260.8 billion (social security benefits: 32.0%; national health service: 13.0%; education and science: 12.0%; defense: 8.0%; debt interest: 7.0%)

National Debt: £223.9 billion

Gross National Product: US$1.0 trillion

Principal Products: Wheat, sugar beets, potatoes, barley, and other vegetables; livestock; machinery and transport equipment; electrical equipment; trucks and automobiles; chemicals; petroleum; clothing; iron and steel

Foreign Trade (Imports): £145.1 billion (machinery and transport equipment: 40.7%, of which electrical equipment: 18.0%; road vehicles: 10.9%; chemicals and chemical products: 9.8%, of which plastics: 2.5%; organic chemicals: 2.4%; food and live animals: 8.3%, of which vegetables and fruits: 2.3%; meat and meat preparations: 1.3%; petroleum and petroleum products: 3.1%; textile yarn and fabrics: 3.0%; paper and paperboard: 2.8%; nonferrous metals: 2.0%; iron and steel products: 2.0%; from Germany: 15.3%; United States: 12.2%; France: 10.6%; the Netherlands: 6.8%; Japan: 6.1%; Italy: 5.0%; Belgium-Luxembourg: 4.9%; Ireland: 3.9%; Switzerland: 3.3%; Norway: 2.6%)

Foreign Trade (Exports): £134.5 billion (machinery and transport equipment: 41.4%, of which electrical equipment: 18.6%; road vehicles: 7.0%; chemicals and chemical products: 14.0%, of which organic chemicals: 3.5%; petroleum and petroleum products: 6.4%; professional, scientific, and controlling instruments: 4.0%; iron and steel products: 2.7%; clothing and footwear: 2.4%; to Germany: 13.0%; United States: 12.5%; France: 10.0%; the Netherlands: 7.2%; Belgium-Luxembourg: 5.7%; Italy: 5.1%; Ireland: 4.9%; Spain: 3.7%; Sweden: 2.5%; Japan: 2.2%; Switzerland: 1.8%)

Stock Exchanges: 5

London STOCK EXCHANGE

London Stock Exchange (LSE; International Stock Exchange)

Old Broad and Threadneedle Streets

London EC2N 1HP

England

Phone: (44-171) 797 1000

Fax: (44-171) 334-8916

Internet Address: www.londonstockex.co.uk

Trading Hours: Monday–Friday, 8:30 to 4:30

Exchange Holidays:

1 January	31 August
10, 13 April	25, 28 December
4, 25 May	

Listed Companies: 2,683

Total Market Capitalization:

At 31 December 1997

Local Currency (Millions)	US Dollars (Millions)
1,169,412	1,924,149

Major Sectors: Health, household, oil, gas, banking, brewers, distillers, telephone networks

Share Price Performance:

(% Change)

1992	21
1993	31
1994	−8
1995	17
1996	12
1997	25

History: The London Stock Exchange originated in the coffee houses of the 17th century, where people met to invest or raise money. They bought and sold shares in joint-stock companies. As interest and volume grew, so did the number of brokers and stockjobbers. The brokers opened a subscription room on Threadneedle Street, and in 1773, voted to name the building the Stock Exchange. The demand for new capital grew with Britain's industrial revolution, and more than 20 other stock exchanges were formed in various parts of the country.

In 1965 these regional stock exchanges joined to form a Federation of Stock Exchanges, becoming a fully unified Stock Exchange in 1973. The unification included the Irish Stock Exchange in Dublin, which separated again in 1995 when it became independent.

In 1979 the abolition of foreign exchange controls made it easier for UK savings institutions to invest money overseas in non-UK securities. This exposed the exchange's member firms to foreign competition for the first time. When compared to major foreign brokers, the smaller London firms often lacked the necessary capital to trade in large volumes and therefore they had difficulty competing. In the early 1980s, the government challenged the exchange for having unfair rules that were restrictive to trade. A court case was averted when the exchange and the government reached an out-of-court agreement, with the exchange agreeing to major reforms.

Major trading changes occurred on the London Stock Exchange on 27 October 1986, when reforms referred to as the "Big Bang" took effect. The structure of the exchange was altered in the following ways:

• Ownership of member firms by an outside corporation became allowable, enabling the firms to build a larger base of capital.

• Separation of member firms into brokers and jobbers came to an end. All firms became broker/dealers, enabling them to act as agent or principal in exchange transactions. The firms were also allowed to register as market makers and commit to firm buying and selling prices at all times.

• Minimum commission scales were abolished and members competed with other firms on fees and commissions.

• Exchange voting rights transferred from individual members to member firms.

After the Big Bang, the exchange installed three new computer trading systems: The Stock Exchange Automated Quotations (SEAQ) for the United Kingdom equity market, SEAQ International for foreign securities, and the Stock Exchange Alternative Trading Service (SEATS) for less liquid securities.

Classes of Securities: Ordinary shares, preferred shares, sterling bonds, fixed interest stocks, UK government gilts, depositary receipts, Eurobonds, options

Indices:

The FT-SE 100 Share Index (Footsie), is made up of the 100 largest UK companies and serves as the

Bank of England. *(Spectrum Photo)*

basis for futures and traded options listed on the London International Financial Futures and Options Exchange (LIFFE)

The FT-SE Mid 250 is the real-time (recalculated each minute) benchmark for mid-size United Kingdom companies. It is made up of the next 250 largest companies (after the FT-SE 100) and has been calculated back to 31 December 1985. Futures and options for the FT-SE Mid 250 also trade on the exchange. The index is calculated both with and without investment trusts.

The FT-SE Small Cap index began in January 1993. It is calculated on 500 smaller companies at the end of each trading session.

The FT-SE Actuaries 350 is an index focusing on actively traded companies that are both large and medium-size. It is a combination of the FT-SE 100 and the FT-SE Mid 250 indices.

Supervisory Organizations:

The Treasury

Securities & Investments Board (SIB)

Competent Authority of the London Stock Exchange (parallel authority to the SIB)

Recognized Clearing Houses (RCHs)

Recognized Investment Exchanges (RIEs)

Self-Regulating Organizations (SROs)

Depository: Stock Exchange Pool of Nominees (SEPON) acts like a depository for settlement in the computerized Transfer Accounting, Lodgement for Investors and Stock Management (TALISMAN) settlement system.

Settlement Details:

Shares: Trade date + 5 days (T + 5) as of 26 June 1995. Rolling ten-day settlement was successfully introduced in July 1994, closing the 250 year old traditional method. The exchange's TALISMAN service is a computerized settlement system acting as a central clearing house for equity transactions. The process has a "presettlement" for the delivery of funds or securities that must be delivered to the broker before the settlement day. Details of each transaction are transmitted to the TALISMAN on the day before settlement.

Institutional clients or their custodians can participate in the exchange's Institutional Net Settlement (INS) service. An INSP client or custodian is able to deposit shares directly to the TALISMAN office and to make or receive a single net payment to or from the exchange to cover all trades settling on the settlement date.

Most foreign equity trades are settled in the originating country of the security. However, the exchange does settle trades for Australia, Ireland, and South Africa.

Trading: The exchange conducts markets for the trading of securities by:

- Providing a market structure
- Regulating the market operations
- Supervising activities of member firms
- Providing trade confirmation and settlement services

The UK equity market is a competing market maker system. During each session the 30 registered market makers are obliged to display their bid and offer prices and the maximum bargain size to which these prices relate. Prices are firm to other exchange member firms. Large bargain prices are negotiable.

The market makers compete for the best quote, earning their income by buying and selling securities at a profit. The competing quote system is supported by the Stock Exchange Automated Quotation (SEAQ) service.

SEAQ: bid and offer prices are digitally distributed through SEAQ. Registered market makers must maintain their prices during the mandatory quote period 8:30 A.M. to 4:30 P.M. every Monday through Friday.

SEAQ information, viewed through computer screens, includes:

- The price display service, showing the market makers quotes to the market
- The trade ticker that shows all trades valued at £1,000 or more reported to SEAQ (75% in real time)
- The SEAQ Automatic Execution Facility (SAEF), allowing broker/dealers to transact small private client orders automatically
- Market makers' bid and offer prices and sizes, which make up the yellow strip that identifies the best bid and offer price for every SEAQ security, and then identify up to three market makers with the best quote

When an SEAQ security cannot support competing quotes from market makers it is transferred to the exchange's SEATS service for less liquid securities.

SEATS: the Stock Exchange Alternative Trading Service (SEATS) for shares traded infrequently and that cannot support competing market makers.

SEATS shows:

- A SEAQ market maker quote, when applicable
- Current member firm orders
- Company information
- Past trading activity for each stock

- Name of the corporate broker

When more than one market maker registers in a security on SEATS, the security is transferred to the SEAQ system.

SEAQ International: The international equity market draws strength from the competing market maker system with quotes being displayed on SEAQ International. Companies quoted on SEAQ International benefit from exposure to an international market, and investors are provided with a visible, regulated trading facility.

The system is similar to SEAQ but is divided into 20 country sectors and one developing markets sector. The 52 market makers represent major international securities houses and quote continuous two-way prices in SEAQ International.

Share prices are quoted in the currency of each country, and transactions are settled through the local settlement system. International equity market trading can occur 24 hours a day, but quotations may only be input to SEAQ International between 7 A.M. and 8:30 P.M., UK time.

Listing Requirements: A company applying for listing on the exchange must provide a complete profile of the company including:

- Trading history
- Financial record
- Management and business prospects

The information is included in a document known as the company's listing particulars. The information provides investors with the data on which to make an informed decision and helps to market the shares. Companies can enter the trading market by one of the following methods:

- An introduction placing
- Intermediaries offer
- Offer for sale
- Offer for subscription

The company must appoint a sponsor to handle its application to the exchange. Sponsors can include banks, brokers, firms of solicitors, accountants, and other financial advisers.

To assist potential applicants to the official list, the exchange produces a guide called *Why Go Public? A Guide to Going Public*, and for overseas applicants, *Listing in London.*

When a company becomes listed, rules governing listed companies are set down in "The Listing Rules," which is informally also known as the "Yellow Book."

Depositary receipts: In August 1994 new rules were introduced that allow the listing for depositary receipts. These negotiable certificates, giving evidence of ownership of company shares, come primarily from developing economies that are raising capital from international investors. The receipts are marketed internationally mainly to financial institutions and institutional investors. They allow the international investor greater liquidity for trading, and simplify settlement, foreign exchange, and foreign ownership difficulties. The listing process comes under the aegis of the Capital Markets Group.

Options: A traditional options market exists on the London Exchange for virtually all UK listed securities with the exception of gilt-edged stock. Options trade mainly on equities but are also arranged on warrants to subscribe for ordinary shares, convertibles, and preference shares. Traditional options are also available on many foreign securities.

Investor Taxation:

Withholding Tax:

Taxpayer	Interest %	Dividends*
Resident corporations	25	Nil
Resident individuals	25	Nil
Nonresident corporations and individuals		
Non-treaty	25	Nil
Treaty	Nil–25	Nil–25

*A tax credit equivalent to the advance corporation tax paid by the corporation, is available to UK resident shareholders on dividends received. Double taxation treaties are being renegotiated to allow a tax credit (normally less a 15% withholding) to nonresident individuals and corporate portfolio investors. (In the case of Trinidad and Tobago and Zimbabwe, the 15% withholding tax is increased to 20%, and in the case of the Philippines, the increase is 25%.)

Limitations: There are no exchange controls on foreign investment in the UK nor on the repatriation of funds. Acquisitions of listed companies may be investigated by the EU or UK on the grounds of competition, especially in a regulated sector such as banking or insurance. Regulatory approval may be necessary.

Securities Lending: Available

Brokerage Firms:
Barclays de Zoete Wedd Securities
Ebbgate House
2 Swan Lane
London EC4R 3TS
England
Phone: (44-171) 623 2323
Fax: (44-171) 623 6075

Robert Fleming Securities
25 Copthall Avenue
London EC2R 7DR
England
Phone: (44-171) 636 5858
Fax: (44-171) 628 0683

Hoare Govett Securities
4 Broadgate
London EC2M 7LF
England
Phone: (44-171) 601 0101
Fax: (44-171) 374 1134

Kleinwort Benson Securities
20 Fenchurch Street
London EC3P 3DB
England
Phone: (44-171) 623 8000
Fax: (44-171) 929 2983

James Capel & Co.
James Capel House
6 Bevis Marks
London EC3A 7JQ
England
Phone: (44-171) 621 0011
Fax: (44-171) 621 1096

Merrill Lynch Europe
Ropemaker Place
25 Ropemaker Street
London EC2Y 9LY
England
Phone: (44-171) 628 1000
Fax: (44-171) 867 2867

County Natwest Securities
135 Bishopgate
London EC2M 3UR
England
Phone: (44-171) 375 5000
Fax: (44-171) 375 5050

Nomura International
Nomura House
1 St. Martins-Le-Grand
London EC1A 4NP
England
Phone: (44-171) 236 8811
Fax: (44-171) 236 7711

UBS Phillips & Drew
100 Liverpool Street
London EC2M 2RH
England
Phone: (44-171) 901 3333
Fax: (44-171) 901 2345

Smith New Court Securities
PO Box 293
20 Farringdon Road
London EC1M 3NH
England
Phone: (44-171) 772 1000
Fax: (44-171) 772 2905

SG Warburg Securities
1 Finsbury Avenue
London EC2M 2PA
England
Phone: (44-171) 606 1066
Fax: (44-171) 382 4800

Morgan Stanley International
25 Cabot Square
London E14 4QA
England
Phone: (44-171) 513 8000
Fax: (44-171) 513 8990

Brokerage Firms: (International)
Argentina
    Baring Securities (Argentina) SA
Australia
    Barclays
    Cazinove Australia PTY Limited
    County Natwest Securities Australia Ltd.
    James Capel & Co Limited
Brazil
    Baring Securities do Brasil Ltda.
Canada
    Deacon Barclays de Zoete Wedd Ltd.
    First Marathon (UK) Limited
    SG Warburg Securities
Colombia
    Baring Securities (Andean Pact) Ltda.
France
    Banque Paribas SA
    Baring Securities (France) SA
    Bzw Societe de Bourse SA
    Hoare Govett Securities Ltd.
    Natwest Sellier SA
Germany
    Barclays de Zoete Wedd Deutschland GMBH

James Capel & Co Limited
Natwest Securities GMBH
Hong Kong
  Barclays de Zoete Wedd Securities (Asia) Ltd.
  Baring Securities (Hong Kong) Ltd.
  Cazenove & Co (Overseas) Limited
  Marlin Partners Limited
India
  James Capel & Co Ltd.
  Marlin Partners Uk Ltd.
Indonesia
  PT Baring Securities Indonesia
Japan
  Barclays de Zoete Wedd Securities (Japan) Ltd.
  Baring Securities (Japan) Limited
  Cazenove & Co (Japan) Limited
  Citicorp Scrimgeour Vickers International Ltd.
  County Natwest Securities Japan Ltd.
Malaysia
  Barclays de Zoete Wedd Securities Ltd.
  Baring Securities (Singapore) Pte Ltd.
  Cazenove & Co (Overseas) Limited
  James Capel & Co Limited
  SG Warburg Securities (Malaysia)
Mexico
  Baring Research SA DE C V
Netherlands
  Barclays de Zoete Wedd Nederland Ltd.
Norway
  Fiba Nordic Securities AS
New Zealand
  Bzw New Zealand Ltd.
Philippines
  Baring Securities (Philippines) Inc.
Republic of Korea
  Barclays de Zoete Wedd Securities Ltd.
  Baring Securities Ltd.
  Citicorp Scrimgeour Vickers International Ltd.
  James Capel & Co Limited
  SG Warburg Securities
Singapore
  Baring Securities (Singapore) PTE Ltd.
  Bzw Pacific Union PTE Ltd.
  Cazenove & Co (Singapore) PTE Limited
South Africa
  Cazenove & Co
Spain
  Barclays Pizarro Y Recorder SA
Switzerland
  Baring Securities Ltd.
  Cazenove & Co
  Cazenove Financiere SA
  James Capel & Co Limited

Natwest Securities Limited
Townsley & Co
SG Warburg Securities
Taiwan
  Barclays de Zoete Wedd Asia International Ltd.
  Baring Securities (Taiwan) Ltd.
Thailand
  Barclays de Zoete Wedd Securities Ltd.
  Baring Research Ltd.
  Cazenove & Co (Overseas) Limited
  Warburg Phatra Securities
United States
  Barclays de Zoete Wedd Securities Ltd.
  Baring Securities Inc.
  Cazenove Incorporated
  Natwest Securities Corporation
  Washington Analysis Corporation

Company Information:

The Best Performing Shares in the Country

Company Name	Share Price Change 1 January 1997 to 31 December 1997 (%)
Signet Group	458
Jarvis	281
Amvescap	264
Skyepharma	246
Aggregate Industries	230
Nycomed Amersham	222
Verity Group	188
Taylor Nelson Agb	178
Benchmark Group	171
Diageo	154
Sun Life & Provincial Holdings	153
Micro Focus Gp.	152
St. James's Place Cap.	149
Capita Group	149
Shire Pharmaceuticals	144
Northern Leis.	139
Waste Recycling	133
Jardine Lloyd Thompson	131
Colt Telecom	119
Jjb Sports	118
Misys	115
Alliance Unichem	110
Jba Holdings	108
Grantchester Holdings	106
Cap.&Regl.Pr.	101
Admiral	98
Gerrard Group	97
Shaftesbury	95
Inde.Insurance Gp.	95

Company Name	Share Price Change 1 January 1997 to 31 December 1997 (%)	Company Name	Share Price Change 1 January 1997 to 31 December 1997 (%)
Brit.Borneo Ptl.	93	Asda Group	48
Holliday Chm.Hdg.	87	National Express	48
Ashtead Group	86	Close Brothers	48
Bank Of Scotland	86	Pizzaexpress	48
Lloyds Tsb Gp.	84	Lex Service	47
Cmg	82	Bespak	47
Vodafone Gp.	79	T & N	47
Fi Group	78	Unilever (Uk)	47
Mcalpine (Alfred)	75	Hays	47
Select Appt.Hdg.	75	Aea Technology	47
Cox In.Holdings	74	Boots	47
British Energy	73	Invesco Eng.& Intl.	46
Paragon Gp.Of Cos.	72	Unigate	46
Finelist Group	71	Whatman	45
Railtrack Gp.	69	Ryl.Bk.Of Sctl.	45
Tr European Growth	69	Vardon	45
Hiscox	66	Logica	45
Fortune Oil	64	Legal & General	45
Kwik-Fit Hdg.	64	Rugby Group	45
Parity	63	Investors Cap.Growth	45
Pillar Pr.	63	Man(E D & F)Gp.	44
Barclays	60	Wetherspoon (Jd)	44
Geest	60	Chelsfield	44
Abbot Group	60	Nat.Wstm.Bank	44
Airtours	59	Robert Wsm.Drs.	43
Headlam Group	59	Enterprise Inns	43
Courtaulds Text.	58	Bodycote Intl.	43
Sage Group (The)	58	Abbey National	43
Btg	57	Perkins Foods	43
British Land	57	Fleming Claverhouse	43
South West Water	56	British Assets	42
Provident Finl.	56	Morrison(Wm)Spmkts.	42
Alexon Group	56	Severn Trent	42
Scottish Power	55	Fleming American	41
Smithkline Bhm.	55	Anglian Water	41
Scot.Hydro-Elec.	54	Tesco	41
Britannic Asr.	54	Sema Group	41
Glaxo Wellcome	53	Orange	40
Hazlewood Foods	53	Goode Durrant	40
Meggitt	53	Eng.China Clays	40
Cattles	52	Senior Engr.	40
Firth Rixson	51	Powergen	40
Premier Oil	51	Partco	40
Daily Mail'a'	51	Devro	40
F&C Enterprise	51	Allied Colloids	39
Greggs	51	Greycoat	39
Prudential Corp.	51	Nthn.Ire.Elty.	39
Thames Water	50	Morrison Construction	39
Crt Group	49	General Accident	38
National Grid	49	Cobham	38

Company Name	Share Price Change 1 January 1997 to 31 December 1997 (%)
Allders	38
Peel Holdings	38
Yates Bros.Wine	38
Edinburgh Us Tracker Tst	37
Brit.Aerospace	37
Britax International	37
Chrysalis Group	36
Royal & Sun All.In.	36
Dewhirst Group	36
Sainsbury (J)	35
Kingfisher	35
First Choice Hols.	35
Triplex Lloyd	34
Corporate Svs.Gp	34
Hunting	34
Schroders Nv.	34
Wessex Water	34
Gt.Portland Est.	34
Fenner	33
Powell Duffryn	33
H & C Furnishings	33
Meyer Intl.	33
City Of London It	33
Land Securities	33
Reckitt & Colman	32
Williams	32
Hyder	32
Berkeley Group	32
Derwent Valley	32
House Of Fraser	31
Domestic&General Gp.	31
Mcbride	31
Watson & Philip	31
Berisford	31
Minerva	31
Shell Transport & Trdg.	31
Davis Ser.Gp.	30
Zeneca	30
Serco Group	30
Graham Group	30
Northern Foods	30

The Largest Companies in the Country by Market Capitalization as of 31 December 1997

Company Name	Market Capitalization Local Currency (Millions)	Market Capitalization US Dollars (Millions)
Brit.Petroleum	46,096	75,846
Shell Transport & Trdg.	43,754	71,992

Company Name	Market Capitalization Local Currency (Millions)	Market Capitalization US Dollars (Millions)
Lloyds Tsb Gp.	42,459	69,861
Smithkline Bhm.	34,441	56,669
British Telecom.	30,638	50,412
Hsbc Holdings (L)	27,012	44,445
Barclays	24,638	40,539
Diageo	22,464	36,962
Zeneca	20,259	33,334
Halifax	19,176	31,553
Nat.Wstm.Bank	17,518	28,824
Bat Inds.	17,207	28,313
Marks & Spencer	17,083	28,109
Unilever (Uk)	17,005	27,981
Abbey National	15,402	25,343
Prudential Corp.	14,232	23,418
Hsbc Holdings	13,633	22,431
Vodafone Gp.	13,495	22,204
Cable & Wireless	12,152	19,994
Reuters Holdings	11,258	18,525
General Elec.	11,030	18,149
Tesco	10,821	17,804
Bg	10,773	17,725
Sainsbury (J)	9,645	15,870
Royal & Sun All.In.	9,428	15,513
Bass	8,368	13,769
Granada Group	8,277	13,619
Rio Tinto (Reg)	8,022	13,199
Boots	7,994	13,153
Brit.Sky Bcast.	7,843	12,906
Gt.Unvl.Stores	7,714	12,693
Norwich Union	7,652	12,590
Rentokil Initial	7,574	12,462
Brit.Aerospace	7,547	12,418
Btr	7,432	12,228
National Power	7,284	11,985
Reed Intl.	6,954	11,442
Imp.Chm.Inds.	6,914	11,376
Bank Of Scotland	6,849	11,269
Ryl.Bk.Of Sctl.	6,686	11,002
Legal & General	6,682	10,994
Std.Chartered	6,448	10,610
Scottish Power	6,343	10,437
Cadbury Schweppes	6,184	10,175
Siebe	6,047	9,949
Commercial Union	5,824	9,583
British Airways	5,802	9,546
Kingfisher	5,741	9,446
Allied Domecq	5,455	8,976
Asda Group	5,360	8,820
Baa	5,222	8,592

Company Name	Market Capitalization Local Currency (Millions)	Market Capitalization US Dollars (Millions)	Company Name	Market Capitalization Local Currency (Millions)	Market Capitalization US Dollars (Millions)
General Accident	5,106	8,402	Next	2,588	4,258
Powergen	5,093	8,379	Blue Circle Inds.	2,585	4,254
Woolwich	5,088	8,372	British Steel	2,537	4,175
Land Securities	5,052	8,312	Compass Group	2,458	4,045
National Grid	4,962	8,165	Southern Elec.	2,420	3,981
Boc Group	4,875	8,021	Burmah Castrol	2,250	3,703
Railtrack Gp.	4,874	8,019	Tate & Lyle	2,250	3,702
Assd.Brit.Foods	4,767	7,844	Anglian Water	2,246	3,696
Alliance & Leicester	4,656	7,661	Gallaher Group	2,229	3,667
Scot.& Newcastle	4,607	7,581	Ti Group	2,221	3,654
Pearson	4,548	7,484	Rmc Group	2,201	3,622
Gkn	4,417	7,267	Nycomed Amersham	2,183	3,592
Whitbread	4,358	7,171	Britannic Asr.	2,138	3,517
Pen.&Orntl.Dfd.	4,252	6,996	Mepc	2,136	3,514
United Utilities	4,196	6,905	Provident Finl.	2,126	3,497
Emi Group	4,047	6,658	Misys	2,039	3,355
Centrica	3,970	6,533	Stagecoach Hdg.	2,013	3,312
Reckitt & Colman	3,887	6,395	Smith & Nephew	2,003	3,296
Safeway	3,752	6,173	Imperial Tobacco Gp.	2,000	3,291
Sun Life & Provincial Holdings	3,729	6,135	Burton Group	1,984	3,265
British Land	3,507	5,771	Wpp Group	1,984	3,265
Energy Group	3,500	5,759	Scot.Hydro-Elec.	1,969	3,240
Rolls-Royce	3,476	5,719	Electrocomp.	1,931	3,178
Thames Water	3,445	5,668	Daily Mail'a'	1,911	3,144
Tomkins	3,434	5,650	Emap	1,896	3,119
Utd.News & Media	3,423	5,633	Foreign & Colonial	1,847	3,039
Hays	3,419	5,625	Yorkshire Water	1,834	3,018
Billiton	3,335	5,488	United Assurance Group	1,823	2,999
Vendome Luxury U	3,326	5,473	Hanson	1,771	2,914
Severn Trent	3,315	5,455	Airtours	1,759	2,894
Orange	3,163	5,204	Bpb	1,739	2,862
Ladbroke Group	3,115	5,126	Securicor	1,719	2,828
Amvescap	3,079	5,066	Morrison (Wm) Spmkts.	1,716	2,824
Guardian Ryl.Ex.	3,026	4,980	Sema Group	1,700	2,797
Lucasvarity	3,025	4,977	Bba Group	1,698	2,793
3i Group	3,000	4,936	Argos	1,582	2,604
British Energy	2,961	4,872	Northern Foods	1,538	2,531
Enterprise Oil	2,883	4,743	Rexam	1,506	2,478
Schroders	2,883	4,743	Unigate	1,437	2,364
Carlton Comms.	2,853	4,694	Imi	1,419	2,335
Wolseley	2,753	4,530	Hyder	1,396	2,297
Lasmo	2,663	4,382	Liberty Intl.	1,358	2,235
Northern Rock	2,646	4,354	T & N	1,358	2,235
Rank Group	2,644	4,350	Hammerson	1,350	2,221
Williams	2,638	4,341	Slough Estates	1,349	2,220
Dixons Gp.	2,609	4,293	Cookson Group	1,346	2,214
Smiths Inds.	2,603	4,284			

Company Name	Market Capitalization Local Currency (Millions)	Market Capitalization US Dollars (Millions)	Company Name	Market Capitalization Local Currency (Millions)	Market Capitalization US Dollars (Millions)
Arjo Wiggins Apl.	1,344	2,211	Vickers	802	1,319
Pilkington	1,328	2,185	Schroders Nv.	800	1,316
Laporte	1,299	2,137	Perpetual	792	1,304
Greenalls Gp.	1,299	2,137	Cobham	781	1,286
Alliance Trust	1,274	2,096	Booker	779	1,282
Edinburgh Inv.Trust	1,241	2,043	Sedgwick Group	774	1,273
Witan Inv.Co.	1,232	2,027	Arriva	773	1,272
South West Water	1,215	1,999	Berkeley Group	772	1,270
Courtaulds	1,210	1,991	National Express	762	1,253
Premier Farnell	1,196	1,969	Racal Electronic	757	1,245
United Biscuits	1,188	1,954	Scottish Eastern	744	1,225
Scottish Mortgage	1,183	1,947	Nthn.Ire.Elty.	741	1,220
Johnson Matthey	1,176	1,935	Lonrho	738	1,214
Assd.Brit.Ports	1,155	1,901	Bowthorpe	735	1,209
Allied Colloids	1,155	1,900	Stakis	733	1,206
Smith (Wh) Group	1,108	1,823	Bicc	722	1,188
Fki	1,089	1,791	Charter	719	1,183
Wessex Water	1,086	1,788	Mfi Furniture	714	1,174
Bunzl	1,071	1,762	Taylor Woodrow	708	1,166
Tarmac	1,067	1,756	First Group	707	1,164
Nfc	1,058	1,741	Capita Group	706	1,161
Hillsdown Hdg.	1,055	1,736	St. James's Place Cap.	687	1,130
M&G Group (Hdg.)	1,053	1,732	British Biotech	686	1,128
Morgan Crucible	1,052	1,731	Anglo & Overseas	680	1,118
Avis Europe	1,007	1,658	Mercury Eur.Pvtn.	670	1,103
Elementis	1,004	1,652	Trinity Intl.Hdg.	670	1,103
Storehouse	1,001	1,647	Wetherspoon (Jd)	653	1,074
Brit.Borneo Ptl.	999	1,644	Man (E D & F) Gp.	652	1,073
Thistle Hotels	978	1,610	Telewest Comms.	649	1,068
Cmg	977	1,607	Coats Viyella	643	1,059
Caradon	932	1,533	Close Brothers	643	1,058
Ocean Group	927	1,525	Glynwed	642	1,057
Electra Inv.Tst.	920	1,514	Smith (David S)	635	1,045
Scottish Inv.	917	1,509	Somerfield	632	1,041
Alliance Unichem	910	1,497	Laird Group	631	1,038
Bodycote Intl.	909	1,496	Willis Corroon	628	1,033
Gt.Portland Est.	905	1,489	Kwik-Fit Hdg.	625	1,028
Sage Group (The)	897	1,476	Btg	624	1,027
De La Rue	889	1,463	Aggregate Industries	616	1,014
Rugby Group	881	1,450	Ldn.&Manc.Gp.	615	1,012
Mirror Gp.	873	1,437	Meyer Intl.	611	1,005
Inchcape	856	1,408	Brown (N) Group	610	1,003
Logica	847	1,393	Millennium & Copthorne Hotels	609	1,001
Cairn Energy	841	1,385	Caledonia Invs.	605	995
Flextech	828	1,362	Devro	602	990
Eng.China Clays	827	1,361	Btp	601	988
Chelsfield	823	1,354	Monument Oil&Gas	591	973
Dalgety	808	1,330			
Sears	802	1,319			

Company Name	Market Capitalization Local Currency (Millions)	Market Capitalization US Dollars (Millions)	Company Name	Market Capitalization Local Currency (Millions)	Market Capitalization US Dollars (Millions)
Jjb Sports	587	966	Tt Group	468	770
Thorn	583	959	Mayflower Corp.	466	767
Ashtead Group	575	946	Aea Technology	465	765
Medeva	575	946	House Of Fraser	463	762
Aegis Group	569	937	Senior Engr.	463	762
Croda Intl.	569	935	British Assets	458	753
London Intl.Gp.	561	924	Spirax-Sarco	456	751
Templeton Emrg.Mkt.	561	923	Jarvis	456	750
			Admiral	455	748
Colt Telecom	559	920	Beazer Group	454	747
Fleming Mercantile	557	917	Pillar Pr.	453	746
Scapa Group	557	916	Kwik Save Gp.	451	742
Eurotunnel Units	556	915	Hambros	450	741
Cattles	556	915	Greene King	450	741
Premier Oil	549	903	Albright & Wilson	450	740
Nycom.Amsh. (Nv)	546	899	Powell Duffryn	448	737
Weir Group	546	898	Mersey Docks	445	733
Powerscreen	546	898	Hewden-Stuart	445	732
Dfs Furniture Co.	540	888	Scottish Media	440	725
Monks Inv.Trust	540	888	Scottish American	428	705
Hepworth	538	886	Second Alliance	427	702
Barratt Developments	538	884	Davis Ser.Gp.	426	701
			Aggreko	424	698
Danka Bus.Sys.	534	878	Burford Hdg.	424	697
Newsquest	533	877	Halma	420	691
Lex Service	533	877	Galen Holdings	419	689
Serco Group	528	869	Investors Cap.Growth	413	680
Murray Intl.	528	868			
Inde.Insurance Gp.	528	868	Tbi	412	678
Travis Perkins	527	868	Inspec	411	676
British Vita	526	866	Johnston Press	411	676
St.Ives	522	859	Manchester Utd.	410	675
Wassall	521	858	Limit	410	675
Fairey Group	517	851	Bradford Pr.	405	666
Rit Capital Partners	512	842	Britax International	398	655
Crt Group	508	837	Pentland Group	398	654
Brixton Estate	505	831	Henderson Smaller Cos.	396	652
Kalon Group	504	829			
Signet Group	502	827	Delta	394	649
Peel Holdings	500	822	Highland Distl.	389	640
Pizzaexpress	497	817	Wimpey (George)	387	636
Select Appt.Hdg.	496	816	Murray Income	386	636
First Leisure	495	814	Bankers Inv.Trust	385	634
Mckechnie	490	805	Hazlewood Foods	383	630
Fleming Overseas	487	801	Fleming American	379	624
City Of London It	487	801	Govett Strategic	377	620
Wilson Bowden	486	800	Jba Holdings	376	619
Ldn.Clubs Intl.	477	784	Vaux Group	375	617
Christies Intl.	470	773	Ldn.Forfaiting	372	612

Company Name	Market Capitalization Local Currency (Millions)	Market Capitalization US Dollars (Millions)	Company Name	Market Capitalization Local Currency (Millions)	Market Capitalization US Dollars (Millions)
Micro Focus Gp.	370	609	Business Post Gp.	294	484
Securities Tst.Sctl.	370	609	Geest	294	484
Courtaulds Text.	369	608	Regent Inns	294	483
Edinburgh Us Tracker Tst	367	604	Benchmark Group	294	483
Capital Radio	366	603	Yule Catto	293	482
Merchants Trust	365	601	Waddington	290	477
Biocompatibles	364	600	Seton Hlthcr.	290	477
Carpetright	362	596	Stanley Leisure	290	477
Hardy Oil & Gas	358	588	Care First Group	288	473
Shire Pharmaceuticals	355	583	Shanks & Mcewan	287	472
Govett Oriental	352	580	Berisford	286	470
Corporate Svs.Gp	345	568	Dunedin Inc.Growth	283	465
Meggitt	343	564	Singer&Fried.Gp.	282	465
Jardine Lloyd Thompson	340	560	Finelist Group	282	465
Bellway	340	559	Temple Bar	282	464
Eurotherm	339	558	Fleming Japanese	282	464
Psion	338	557	Body Shop Intl.	281	463
Bryant Group	338	557	Dairy Crest	280	460
Persimmon	335	551	Transport Dev.	280	460
Atkins,Ws	334	550	Kleinwort Overseas	274	451
Savoy Hotel 'A'	329	541	Greycoat	272	447
Expro Intl.	326	536	Ellis & Everard	271	446
Schroder Uk Growth	326	536	Frogmore Estates	269	443
Redrow Gp.	325	535	Tibbett&Britten	269	443
Marley	323	531	Brammer	269	442
Low & Bonar	320	526	Tr European Growth	268	441
Dewhirst Group	319	525	Jarvis Hotels	267	439
Henderson	319	525	Ldn.Mer.Secs.	265	436
Wolv.&Dudley	318	523	Courts	263	433
Taylor Nelson Agb	315	518	F&C Pacific	263	433
More Group	313	516	Go-Ahead Group	263	433
Mcbride	312	513	Albert Fisher	263	432
Wilson(Connolly)	310	511	Salvesen(Chris.)	263	432
Vitec Group	309	509	Daejan Holdings	262	431
Fleming Cont.Europe	307	506	City Ctr.Rest.	262	431
Parity	306	504	Vosper Thncft.	262	430
General Cable	305	502	Throgmorton Trust	261	430
Fi Group	300	494	Gerrard Group	261	430
Sig	298	491	English & Scottish	260	427
Brake Brothers	297	489	Henderson Elec.&Gen.	259	426
Kleinwort Charter	296	487	Law Debenture	257	423
Dunedin Worldwide	295	486	Cox In.Holdings	255	420
Goode Durrant	295	485	Renishaw	254	419
Polypipe	295	485	Mercury World Mng.	254	417
Forth Ports	295	485	Ultra Electronics Hdg.	251	412
			Abbott Mead Vickers	250	411
			Baird (William)	245	404

Company Name	Market Capitalization Local Currency (Millions)	Market Capitalization US Dollars (Millions)	Company Name	Market Capitalization Local Currency (Millions)	Market Capitalization US Dollars (Millions)
Saatchi & Saatchi	244	402	British Empire Secs.	204	336
Marston Thompson	243	399	Scotia Holdings	204	335
Cordiant Comms.Gp.	242	398	Ascot Hdg.	203	333
Derwent Valley	241	397	Murray Smaller Mkts.	203	333
Holliday Chm.Hdg.	241	396	Minerva	202	333
Yates Bros.Wine	240	396	F&C Emerging Mkts.It.	199	328
Amec	240	395	Verity Group	199	327
Baring Tribune	240	395	Mansfield Brew.	198	325
Headlam Group	240	395	Skyepharma	197	323
Hiscox	240	395	H & C Furnishings	196	323
Ibstock	239	393	Moss Bros.Gp.	196	323
First Choice Hols.	238	391	Filtronic Comtek	195	321
Abbot Group	237	390	Evans Of Leeds	195	321
Chiroscience Gp.	237	389	Delphi Gp.	194	320
Rotork	237	389	South Stf.Water	194	319
Fleming Claverhouse	236	388	Cap.&Regl.Pr.	194	319
Graham Group	235	387	Britton Gp.	192	316
Shaftesbury	234	385	Boxmore Intl.	192	315
Greggs	233	383	Anglian Group	192	315
Wstm.Hlth.Care	233	383	Rjb Mining	191	314
Ionica	233	383	Grantchester Holdings	189	311
Iceland Group	230	379	Fenner	189	311
Bilton	230	378	Bemrose Corp.	188	310
Guinness Peat Gp.	229	378	Chrysalis Group	188	309
Celltech	227	374	F&C Smaller Cos.	187	308
F&C Eurotrust	225	371	Soco International	186	307
Dialog Corp.	225	370	Fortune Oil	186	307
Wates Cty.Ldn.	223	367	Gwr Group	186	305
Northern Leis.	222	365	Whatman	186	305
Watson & Philip	222	365	Firth Rixson	185	305
Henlys Group	220	363	Watmoughs Hdg.	185	304
Hogg Robinson	220	362	Tlg	183	302
Black (Peter)	220	362	Triplex Lloyd	182	299
Bovis Homes Group	219	360	Intm.Capital Group	181	298
Perpetual Inc.& Gw.	219	360	Robert Wsm.Drs.	181	298
Morrison Construction	218	359	Games Workshop	181	298
Partco	216	356	Scholl	181	297
Macfarlane Group	214	353	Victrex	181	297
Tr Property Inv.	213	350	Aberforth Smcos.	180	296
Westbury	213	350	Renold	179	294
Hunting	213	350	Vardon	178	293
Wickes	211	346	Bespak	177	291
Menzies (John)	210	346	Brit.Polythene	176	290
Heywood Williams	209	344	Benfield & Rea	176	290
Allders	208	343	F&C Enterprise	175	288
Brunner Inv.Tst.	207	341	Dennis Group	174	287
Bulmer (Hp)	206	339			
Field Group	204	336			

Company Name	Market Capitalization Local Currency (Millions)	Market Capitalization US Dollars (Millions)
Oxford Molecular	174	285
Paragon Gp.Of Cos.	172	283
Avon Rubber	171	281
Domestic&General Gp.	169	279
Ultraframe	168	277
Overseas Inv.	168	277
Eis Group	168	277
Thorntons	168	276
Staveley Inds.	167	275
Wembley Gp.	167	275
Candover Invs.	166	273
Tilbury Douglas	165	271
Mcalpine (Alfred)	163	269
Api Group	163	269
Enterprise Inns	163	269
Invesco Eng.& Intl.	162	267
Perkins Foods	162	267
Pendragon	162	266
Capital Corp.	161	265
Marshalls	161	264
Schroder Ventures	160	264
Allied Carpets	160	263
Fidelity Eur.Values	159	262
Wagon Ind.Hdg.	157	259
Mitie Group	157	258
Boosey & Hawkes	157	258
Alexon Group	156	257
Waste Recycling	156	256
Mowlem (John)	156	256

Regional Exchanges:

Midland and West
The Stock Exchange
Margaret Street
Birmingham B3 3JL
England
Phone: (44-121) 236 9181

North West
The Stock Exchange
76 King Street
Manchester M2 4NH
England
Phone: (44-171) 833 0931

North East
The Stock Exchange
Enterprise House

12 St. Paul's Street
Leeds LS1 2LQ
England
Phone: (44-113) 243 0738

Scotland
The Stock Exchange
Stock Exchange House
PO Box 141
7 Nelson Mandela Place
Glasgow G2 2BU
Scotland
Phone: (44-141) 221-7060

Other Investment Information:

Invest in Britain Bureau
Department of Trade and Industry
Kingsgate House
66-74 Victoria Street
London SW1E 6SW
England
Phone: (44-171) 215-8438, 215 8439
Fax: (44-171) 215 8451
Telex: 8811074

Department of the Environment
2 Marsham Street
London SW1E 3EB
England
Phone: (44-171) 276 3000
Fax: (44-171) 276 0818
Telex: 22221

Bank of England
Threadneedle Street
London EC2R 8AH
England
Phone: (44-171) 601 4444
Telex: 885001

UNITED NATIONS CONFERENCE ON TRADE AND DEVELOPMENT (UNCTAD)

The *United Nations Conference on Trade and Development (UNCTAD)* is the main organ of the UN General Assembly dealing with trade and development. Its principal task is to accelerate economic growth and development, especially in the developing countries. It has 188 member states and an annual operational budget of approximately $55 million.

UNCTAD was first convened in 1964 because of concerns about the gap in the standard of living between the developing and the developed countries.

Since 1964, full conferences have been held every three to four years.

According to calculations done in the 1960s by UNCTAD's director-general, R.D. Prebisch, taking into account the population growth of the developing countries, they needed to attain a growth rate of 5% per year to achieve real per capita growth. However, their exports were not sufficiently high to support such a growth rate. In addition, the trend in the terms of trade was going against them; that is, the prices of the primary products that the developing countries mainly exported had been declining relative to the prices of the industrial goods that they imported from the developed countries. As a result, rather than achieving real per capita economic growth, these countries were experiencing balance of payments deficits every year, which were worsening their economic conditions.

The solution, according to Prebisch, lay in a combination of measures to counteract the unfavorable terms of trade and to promote the developing countries' exports. In pursuit of these aims, international commodity agreements were designed to prevent the prices of primary products from falling, and compensatory finance arrangements were established. Further, Prebisch suggested that a differentiated policy be adopted, in which developing countries could discriminate against manufactured goods from the developed countries, whereas the developed countries should give preference to the developing countries' primary products.

In support of the same objectives, in 1965 a new chapter was added to the General Agreement on Tariffs and Trade (GATT) (which had mainly dealt with trade among the developed countries) calling for the reduction of tariffs and quotas on developing countries' exports. And in 1970, developed countries in the European Free Trade Association and the European Community, plus the United States, reached an agreement to give preferences in specified manufactured goods to the developing countries.

Despite these agreements and resolutions, the gap between the developed countries and the great majority of developing countries continued to widen. At the fourth UNCTAD in 1976, developing countries put forth a plan for debt rescheduling, technical aid, development of manufacturing industries, and the diversification of one-crop economies. Their principal opposition came from the wealthy countries. By the fifth UNCTAD in 1979, conditions in the poor countries had deteriorated further, and their collective external debt, whose servicing diverted needed funds from development, had climbed to $300 billion. In 1980 UNCTAD set guidelines for international action in debt rescheduling. But the 1980s saw an accelerated growth of this debt (which by 1996 had grown to approximately $1 trillion), expanded environmental destruction, and a deepening of poverty in many developing countries, especially in South Asia and Sub-Saharan Africa. According to 1996 UNCTAD reports, among developing countries China was the biggest recipient of foreign direct investment (FDI), with an inflow of $38 billion the previous year. However, Africa was expected to show the biggest percentage growth in incoming FDI in the 1990s.

These trends took hold despite a number of UNCTAD initiatives in the 1980s and 1990s, including:

• A set of principles and rules for controlling restrictive business practices (1980)

• A Common Fund for Commodities, intended to promote commodity agreements and support research and development (1989)

• The Agreement on the Global System of Trade Preferences among developing countries (1989)

• Conventions in maritime transport (1980–93)

• The Global Trade Point Network (1994)

• The Substantial New Programme of Action for the 1980s for the Least Developed Countries (1981)

• Action in favor of land-locked countries (1995)

UNCTAD continues to focus on the issues of globalization and development; international trade in goods and services and commodity issues; investment, enterprise development, and technology; and services infrastructure for development and trade efficiency. At present UNCTAD is implementing approximately 300 projects and, in addition, is promoting international technical cooperation with financial support from nonbudgetary sources.

The Trade and Development Board, which has 144 member states, is the executive body of UNCTAD. It meets annually to review the progress of the Programme of Action for the Least Developed Countries for the 1990s and of the United Nations New Agenda for the Development of Africa in the 1990s. The Board has established commissions on Trade in Goods and Services; on Investment, Technology, and Related Financial Issues; and on Enterprise, Business Facilitation, and Development. In addition, the UNCTAD secretariat is responsible for the Commission on Transnational Corporations and the Commission on Science and Technology for Development.

UNCTAD's publications include *Trade and Development Report* and *World Investment Report*, both of which are published annually.

See also COUNCIL FOR MUTUAL ECONOMIC ASSISTANCE (COMECON); EUROPEAN FREE TRADE ASSOCIATION (EFTA); GENERAL AGREEMENT ON TARIFFS AND TRADE (GATT); PRE-EMERGING MARKETS.

UNITED STATES OF AMERICA

The *United States of America* is a country of North America consisting of 48 contiguous states occupying the mid-latitudes of the continent, together with the state of Alaska at the northwest extreme of North America and the island state of Hawaii lying in the mid-Pacific Ocean. It is bordered by Canada to the north, and Mexico to the south.

Area: 3,679,192 square miles (9,529,063 square km)

Population: 263,057,000 (75.8% urban; 24.2% rural)

Form of Government: Federal republic, with two legislative houses: Senate—100 members; House of Representatives—435 members. Head of state and government: President.

Official Language: None

Capital: Washington, D.C.

Largest Cities: New York, 7,333,253; Los Angeles, 3,448,613; Chicago, 2,731,743; Houston, 1,702,086; Philadelphia, 1,524,249; San Diego, 1,151,977; Phoenix, 1,048,949; Dallas, 1,022,830; San Antonio, 998,905; Detroit, 992,038

Economy:

Currency: U.S. dollar (US$)

National Budget: Revenue—US$1.3 trillion; expenditures—US$1.5 trillion (social security and medicare: 32.0%; defense: 17.6%; interest on debt: 15.2%; income security: 14.5%; health: 7.5%; other: 13.2%)

National Debt: US$4.6 trillion

Gross National Product: US$6.7 trillion

Principal Products: Soybeans, hay, wheat; corn, grapes, oranges, and other fruits and vegetables; livestock; machinery and transport equipment; industrial products; chemicals; petroleum

Foreign Trade (Imports): US$683.8 billion (machinery and transport equipment: 46.4%, of which motor vehicles and parts: 15.6%; office and data-processing machines: 7.8%; petroleum and petroleum products: 7.4%; wearing apparel: 7.3%; chemicals and related products: 3.4%; food and live animals: 3.1%; from Canada: 19.4%; Japan: 17.9%; Mexico: 7.5%; China:

5.8%; Germany: 4.8%; Taiwan: 4.0%; United Kingdom: 3.8%; South Korea: 3.0%; France: 2.5%; Singapore: 2.3%; Italy: 2.2%; Malaysia: 2.1%; Thailand: 1.6%; Hong Kong: 1.5%; Brazil: 1.3%)

Foreign Trade (Exports): US$512.4 billion (machinery and transport equipment: 49.2%, of which motor vehicles and parts: 15.3%; electrical machinery: 10.3%; chemicals and related products: 10.2%; food and live animals: 6.4%; scientific and precision equipment: 4.3%; to Canada: 22.3%; Japan: 10.4%; Mexico: 9.9%; United Kingdom: 5.2%; Germany: 3.8%; South Korea: 3.5%; Taiwan: 3.3%; France: 2.6%; the Netherlands: 2.6%; Singapore: 2.5%; Hong Kong: 2.2%; Belgium: 2.1%)

Stock Exchanges:
New York Stock Exchange (NYSE)
11 Wall Street
New York, NY 10005
U.S.A.
Phone: (1-212) 656-3000
Fax: (1-212) 656-5557

Internet Address: www.nyse.com

Trading Hours:
Monday–Friday, 9:30 to 4:00
After-hours crossing sessions: 4:00 to 5:00 and 5:00 to 5:15

Exchange Holidays: (all U.S. stock exchanges have the same holidays)

1 January	4 July
16 February	7 September
10 April	26 November
25 May	25 December

Listed Companies: 2,575

Total Market Capitalization: US$8.6 trillion at 31 December 1997

Major Sectors: Automotive, consumer, petroleum, high tech/computer, insurance, banking, food, telecommunications

Share Price Performance:

(% Change)

1992	10
1993	11
1994	−1
1995	34
1996	21
1997	33

History: The birth of the United States of America's securities industry can be traced to the federal govern-

The floor of the New York Stock Exchange. *(Spectrum Photo)*

ment's issue of $80 million of bonds, known as "public stock," to pay for debts incurred during the Revolutionary War. A secondary market to buy and sell these securities quickly joined the previously established markets of commerce.

At this time, businesses began to raise capital for expansion by selling fractional shares of their companies. These securities were known as scrip, as they were initially bought by subscription, and were actively traded by the brokers of the day for their investing clients. In fact, there was enough business in government bonds, fire insurance companies, and banks to keep brokers busy in Boston, Philadelphia, and New York.

On 17 May 1792 a group of 24 stockbrokers and merchants met in New York to form an agreement that aimed to avoid dealing with the monopoly over securities sales held by auctioneers. The group pledged to avoid public auctions and agreed to collect minimum commissions on all sales of public stock. Further, they decided to give preference to each other in all securities dealings.

This compact, formed under a buttonwood tree near Wall Street, became known as the Buttonwood Agreement. The tree had been a meeting place for brokers for some time. In colder weather the brokers moved inside, usually to the comfortable quarters of the Tontine Coffee House.

Trade continued to grow and was aided by the establishment in 1818 of the regularly scheduled shipping service between New York and Liverpool, England. Growing trade opportunities drew new people to the city to find their fortunes. By 1817, when banks resumed specie payment, which had been suspended in 1814, several banks had become established in the city. Wall Street continued to be the site for the concentration of financial institutions. Among these banks were the Union Bank (founded in 1811), the Manhattan Bank (1700), the Bank of America (1812), the Bank of New York (1812), and the City Bank (1812).

In 1817 the securities business became large and strong enough to establish an organization of stockbrokers that agreed to meet regularly at set hours. The constitution drawn up and adopted on 8 March 1817 formed the New York Stock and Exchange Board (NYS&EB). The members rented a room at 40 Wall Street and began trading, following the procedures of Europe's London, Amsterdam, and Paris exchanges. For the next two decades trading consisted largely of an expansion of federal securities; state or private bond issues raising capital for the construction of bridges, roads, and canals; or municipal debt instru-

ments for water, sewer, and lighting systems. Also gaining in popularity were stocks of banks as well as fire and marine insurance companies. The successful sale of $8 million New York State bonds enabled the state to build the Erie Canal, which opened in October 1825. The famous 360-mile canal connected the Hudson River to the Great Lakes, thereby opening up commerce with the midwestern United States.

Business continued to grow and accelerate with additional finances from Europeans interested in the growth potential of the new country. General incorporation laws created favorable conditions for new securities and enabled several new companies to start up or expand. Daily share trading averaged 100 in 1827, but grew to 5,000 shares a day by 1834.

After a few moves, always close to Wall Street, in 1828 the NYS&EB rented space alongside the Post Office in the new Merchants Exchange on Wall Street's south side. A fire, consuming 17 blocks, forced the exchange to find temporary quarters in 1835. The exchange then endured the panic of 1837, started by the closing of the federally chartered Second Bank of the United States (1836). Several financial failures followed, many of them due to rash speculation in land and securities.

Economic recovery followed quickly in 1840, causing new growth in the economy and the securities market. In 1842 NYS&EB located new space for increased trading in a large hall on the second floor of the new Merchants Exchange at 55 Wall Street, where trading continued for the next decade. It was the decade of the telegraph's invention and the California gold discovery. It was also the time of the Mexican-American War.

Listing of stocks became more formalized in 1853, when the board began to require "full statements of the Capital-number of shares-resources and certified to" before a firm could began trading. New railroad stocks became the most popular traded securities in the 1850s and 1860s.

The first railroad security traded by the NYS&EB had been the Mohawk and Hudson Railroad, in 1830. By 1853 other listings included the Chesapeake and Ohio Steam Transportation and Mining Company, the Mohawk Valley Railroad, the Little Miami Railroad, the Marine Railroad, the Cleveland and Pittsburgh Railroad, the Galena and Chicago Union Railroad, the New York Central Railroad, the Central Railroad, and the Cleveland and Toledo Railroad.

Many stocks were of interest to the brokers of the 1850s, but when railroad stocks and bonds were being traded, the men in silk top hats came running. As a reporter of the Portland Transcript put it, ". . . there were scenes of excitement that baffle description." Crowds gathered around the central desk like a colony of buzzing bees.

Investment language took on the tone of speculation, as those who knew talked of "bears" and "bulls" on Wall Street. James Medbery, a stockbroker, wrote in his memoirs *Men and Mysteries of Wall Street,* published in 1870, "If you are long, you're a bull: if short, a bear." It is generally believed that both terms originated in London during the 18th century. There are several stories as to why the bull and bear financial symbols of buyers and sellers. Possibly the most popular is that the behavior of the animals describe what they symbolize. The bull is pushing ahead, often without caution, whereas the bear can be easily frightened and frequently turns vicious when cornered. How the terms originated is not as important as remembering the jargon. Bulls are buyers and bears are sellers. Bull markets are rising markets and bear markets occur when prices are falling.

The surging wave of investor interest during the Civil War led to the NYS&EB deciding to build their own premises. They changed the name to the New York Stock Exchange (NYSE) and with $625,000 built a four-story building, nearly 100 feet high, with an Italian marble front. A commemoration dinner celebrated the opening in December 1865.

As the Civil War ended, heavy industry came into full bloom. Stock issues provided gigantic sums of capital for growth and expansion. Competition accompanied the growth. New exchanges opened for trading petroleum, mining shares, cotton, corn, dry goods, produce, and gold. The NYSE received strong competition from an exchange that opened next door. The Open Board of Brokers began trading on the sidewalks of lower Manhattan, and in 1866 rented space next to the NYSE. Both did well and they eventually joined, along with members of the Government Bond Department, which had organized in 1867 to trade Civil War bonds. The combined entity kept the name New York Stock Exchange and drafted a constitution. With this merger the new organization gained trading control of $3 billion worth of securities in 1869. On 8 May of that year the Union Pacific and Central Pacific Railroads met at Promontory Point, Utah, to drive the last spike joining the east and west coast.

The roll-call method of trading gave over to continuous trading by 1873. The market started trading at 10:00 A.M. and continued through 3:00 P.M. The NYSE was open for business Monday through Friday, and from 10:00 A.M. to 12 noon on Saturdays. Brokers dealt in stocks of certain companies and would remain in one location marked with a sign on a pole on the trading floor. Other brokers could approach to buy or sell stock from a particular "trading post." The procedure marked an early form of the NYSE "specialist system."

With the speed of communication so essential to securities trading, it was inevitable that technological advances would have an effect. Securities trading was affected by the development of Samuel F.B. Morse's telegraph, operational in 1884, which made countrywide rapid communication a reality. Completion of the transatlantic cable in 1866 made international trading feasible.

The development with the greatest impact, however, was the stock ticker. Before its development, messenger boys, known as "pad shovers" delivered reports of sales and purchases, running from the trading floor to brokerage offices. The obvious delay caused by delivery time made the nearly instantaneous stock ticker an important development for trading. Ticker companies stationed "reporters" on the trading floor. They recorded transactions and sent the information to operating rooms nearby. The name of the stock, price, and number of shares traded were then typed on a keyboard. Electronic circuits transmitted the pulses created by the keyboard to a receiving device where wheels either printed letters and numbers or perforated code symbols on paper tape. The person with the receiving device had fast, reliable information regarding the securities transactions occurring. In 1890 members of the exchange established the New York Quotation Company and bought up all the ticker companies, a move intended to improve accuracy and the distribution of reliable information.

Several "bucket shops" sprang up during the later part of the 1800s. The term arose from the use of buckets to hold investor's orders. The shops didn't actually buy any shares on the exchange, but they did keep a running blackboard tally of various share prices. Speculative investors would place an "order" for a specified number of shares with an order to sell at a higher price. The quotes were often rigged and most investors lost money due to the large amount of fraud. The NYSE worked to prevent the shops from obtaining quotes on which to base their operations, but some of them survived even into the early 1900s.

On 29 October 1929 the stock market crash saw more than 16 million shares traded in a single session, a record that would stand for 39 years.

The 1930s began a period of scandal and regulatory reform for the exchange and the entire securities industry. Trading volume and public confidence reached new lows. The years that followed saw procedures and practices put into place that would provide both greater operating efficiencies and public safeguards utilizing the most modern equipment of the day.

In 1971, some 179 years after the Buttonwood Agreement, the NYSE was incorporated as a not-for-profit corporation. By 1982 the NYSE recorded its first 100-million-share day, a milestone that was surpassed one year later with a record 200 million shares traded in a single session.

On 17 May 1992, the NYSE marked its 200th Anniversary.

Operations: Today, as when it began more than 200 years ago, the NYSE still functions as an auction-style marketplace, where buyers and sellers meet. Brokers around the world route their orders to booths on the exchange's trading floor. From these booths, floor brokers take the orders to the various specialists' posts, where particular issues are traded. The trade will then be announced and specialists or floor brokers representing other brokerage firms will bid and counter-bid in historic auction fashion. Price information, including critical last-sale data, is displayed at the post, as well as on electronic displays in brokers' offices and financial institutions around the world. Each trade that occurs is entered by a post reporter and reflected in the display. Virtually retracing his steps, the floor broker returns to the firm's booth and sends information confirming that the trades were executed to the brokers who initially sent the buy or sell orders to the floor. The exchange has the capability of processing millions of such confirmations each day through the most technically advanced systems available.

Since 1973 the NYSE and the American Stock Exchange have consolidated computer facilities in the jointly owned Securities Industry Automation Corporation (SIAC).

Innovations: Historically, change comes slowly to markets where tradition is slow to bend. The New York Stock Exchange has long been regarded as an innovator, albeit sometimes reluctantly. By its very creation in 1792, the pact arranged by 24 merchants established a commission system and regular trading times, bringing structure to a frequently unruly process. The formal organization in 1817 reflected the growing maturity of the market and its participants. Brokers began communicating with other brokers and investors outside of New York by telegraph as early as 1844. By 1866 trans-Atlantic cable made communication between London and New York possible.

In 1871 the NYSE introduced a system of continuous trading that provided more liquid markets for stocks. That same year, the role of the specialist on the exchange was defined to position brokers to trade in particular stocks at a single location. The creation of the NYSE Clearing House in 1892 centralized the process of transferring securities from broker to broker. In 1920, with the establishment of Stock Clearing Corporation, the process was further streamlined and enhanced.

Utilizing advanced technology, the black box ticker, a central processing unit, replaced the existing ticker system in 1964. This move nearly doubled the speed at which trading information could be transmitted to brokers. Four years later, electronic transfer of securities became a reality. In 1973 the NYSE's Designated Order Turnaround (DOT) system became the first fully automated system to electronically route smaller orders.

The consolidated tape was introduced in 1975 to report trades in NYSE-listed stocks traded on all markets. The Intermarket Trading System (ITS) was launched in 1978 to provide an electronic link between competing exchanges so that brokers could monitor various markets for the best available prices. In 1979 the exchange moved to extend NYSE experience to the aggressive futures market with the organization of the New York Futures Exchange (NYFE). A link between the NYSE and the Chicago Mercantile Exchange was created in 1988 to coordinate trading procedures between the equities and futures markets.

In 1991 the NYSE inaugurated two trading sessions after the traditional 4:00 P.M. market close, paving the way for the possibility of 24-hour trading.

Classes of Securities: Ordinary shares, preferred shares, corporate bonds, government bonds, derivatives

Indices:
NYSE Composite Index
Dow Jones Industrial Average

Supervisory Organizations:
The Securities and Exchange Commission (SEC)
The New York Stock Exchange (NYSE)

Depository: The Depository Trust Company (DTC)
The DTC is industry owned with the NYSE being the primary owner.

Settlement Details:

Shares: Trade date + 3 days (T + 3) (all exchanges and OTC)

Trading: Trading is accomplished in a centralized continuous auction at a designated location (trading post) on the trading floor. Brokers represent investors with buy and sell orders. Approximately 90% of the transactions are automatically executed by an electronic computerized system.

SuperDot, the designated order turnaround system, links members directly to the NYSE trading floor. It directs market orders as well as limit orders to the appropriate post where the shares are traded or to the member firm's booth on the trading floor. Executions are promptly reported to the registered representatives and from them to the investor.

The largest category of members is the commission broker, employees of nearly 500 brokerage houses that handle trading on the stock exchange. They execute orders for their firm and for their investors at agreed commission rates. The houses deal for their own account and for the accounts of clients. Banks can only deal for customers.

Floor brokers execute orders for other exchange members when they have an overload or for those needing assistance with large orders. A commission is charged for the assistance.

Registered traders are individuals who buy and sell for their own accounts. They might also be trustees maintaining memberships for the convenience of dealing and saving costs.

Specialists are dealers who are assigned to specific groups of shares. They execute orders as specialists, and as dealers they buy and sell for their own accounts. Precedence is always given to public orders. Specialists are also charged with maintaining a fair and orderly market. They are required to buy when there are no buyers and sell when there are no sellers.

Off-Hours Trading On 13 June 1991 the NYSE created two crossing sessions that facilitate trading after the regular session closing time of 4:00 P.M. They are as follows:

Crossing Session I

Crossing Session I, with a 5:00 P.M. cross in individual stocks at the NYSE regular day's closing price, commences at 4:15 P.M. (EST) and enables members to enter one-sided, two-sided, or good-till-executed

(GTX) orders in specific company shares into the SuperDot system. Matched orders are filled at the day's NYSE closing price (determined during the exchange's 9:30 A.M. to 4:00 P.M. regular trading session) and appear on the consolidated tape. All orders are executed at 5:00 P.M.

In 1995 Crossing Session I averaged 248,000 shares per day.

Crossing Session II

Created to expedite portfolio crossing, Crossing Session II commences at 4:00 P.M. (EST). It is designed to facilitate the trading of baskets with a minimum of 15 NYSE securities and a value of $1 million or more. Members that have either performed a basket trade or have paired two customers' baskets submit aggregate information to the exchange for execution. At 5:15 P.M., the NYSE prints the aggregate information of all baskets executed in the current session to the consolidated tape. On the third day after trade date (T + 3), the individual component stocks executed as part of a basket trade are printed in combined form in the NYSE Daily Sales Report. The session ends at 5:15 P.M.

In 1995 Crossing Session II averaged 1.3 million shares per day.

Listing Requirements: An alternative set of listing standards is established for companies outside the United States. The standards meet the normal sales and earnings requirements for domestic NYSE listings. The NYSE considers the acceptability of a company's shares on an international basis.

Due to the existence of bearer shares in non-U.S. countries (as opposed to registered shares in the U.S. market), an individual company could have difficulty certifying the 5,000 round lot shareholder requirement. To compensate for this difficulty, the NYSE requires a member firm to attest to the liquidity and depth of the market for the company's shares. The standards apply where a broad, liquid market exists in the company's home market.

NYSE Alternative Listing Standards—Non-U.S. Companies (as of 20 May 1976)

Pre-tax Income	Net Tangible Assets	Aggregate Market Value Publicly Held Shares	Shares Not Concentrated (Publicly Held)	No. of Holders of Round Lots (100 Shares or More)
$100 million cumulative in latest 3 years with minimum of $25 million in any one of the 3 years	$100 million worldwide	$100 million worldwide	$2.5 million worldwide	5,000 worldwide

Investor Taxation: For non-resident investors, dividends on U.S. companies are subject to a withholding tax of 30%, although in most situations the rate can be

reduced to 15% for portfolio investments and between 5% and 10% for dividends paid by companies to non-residents who have substantial holdings.

Rents and royalties are also subject to U.S. withholding tax, but tax treaties often provide exemptions or reduced rates. Interest paid on deposits with banks and insurance companies is exempt from U.S. withholding tax. Usually, interest not qualified as portfolio interest is subject to withholding unless reduced or eliminated by a tax treaty.

Limitations: The United States doesn't impose exchange controls and, as a consequence, foreign investors are not restricted to the repatriation of capital, loans, and income to a home country. Dividends, interest, royalties, and service fees may also be repatriated freely.

The U.S. does have certain "earnings stripping" limitations that might restrict the ability of a U.S. corporation to claim interest deductions for interest paid to related foreign shareholders.

Restrictions on direct foreign investment do exist in sensitive areas of communication, aviation, mining on federal land, energy, banking, insurance, real estate, agricultural land, coastal shipping, and defense.

Securities Lending: Available

Brokerage Firms: (*See also* DISCOUNT BROKER.)
Bear Stearns & Co.
245 Park Avenue
New York, NY 10167
U.S.A.
Phone: (1-212) 272-2000

Sanford C. Bernstein & Co.
767 Fifth Avenue
New York, NY 10153
U.S.A.
Phone: (1-212) 486-5800

Alex Brown & Sons
135 E. Baltimore Street
Baltimore, MD 21202
U.S.A.
Phone: (1-410) 727-1700

Dean Witter Reynolds
Two World Trade Center
New York, NY 10047
U.S.A.
Phone: (1-212) 392-3200

Donaldson, Lufkin & Jenrette Securities Corp.
140 Broadway
New York, NY 10005
U.S.A.

Phone: (1-212) 504-3000

The First Boston Corporation
Park Avenue Plaza
55 E. 52nd Street
New York, NY 10055
U.S.A.
Phone: (1-212) 909-2000

Goldman, Sachs & Co.
85 Broad Street
New York, NY 10004
U.S.A.
Phone: (1-212) 902-1000

Hambrecht & Quist
One Bush Street
San Francisco, CA 94104
U.S.A.
Phone: (1-415) 576-3300

Kidder, Peabody & Co.
10 Hanover Square
New York, NY 10005
U.S.A.
Phone: (1-212) 968-2600

Lawrence (CJ)
1290 Avenue of the Americas
New York, NY 10019-6008
U.S.A.
Phone: (1-212) 468-5000

Smith Barney Shearson
388 Greenwich Street
New York, NY 10013
U.S.A.
Phone: (1-212) 566-4592

Merrill Lynch Capital Markets
World Financial Center
North Tower
250 Vesey Street
New York, NY 10281
U.S.A.
Phone: (1-212) 449-1000

Morgan Stanley & Co.
1251 Avenue of the Americas
New York, NY 10001-0190
U.S.A.
Phone: (1-212) 703-4000

Oppenheimer & Co.
One World Financial Center
New York, NY 10281
U.S.A.
Phone: (1-212) 667-7000

Paine Webber
1285 Avenue of the Americas
New York, NY 10019
U.S.A.
Phone: (1-212) 713-2000

Prudential Securities
1 Seaport Plaza
New York, NY 10038-3517
U.S.A.
Phone: (1-212) 214-1000

Robertson, Stephens & Co.
555 California Street
San Francisco, CA 94104-1501
U.S.A.
Phone: (1-415) 781-9700

Salomon Brothers
7 World Trade Center
New York, NY 10048-1100
U.S.A.
Phone: (1-212) 783-7000

Charles Schwab & Co.
241 California Street
San Francisco, CA 94111-4901
U.S.A.
Phone: (1-415) 398-1000

Wertheim Schroder & Co.
1 World Trade Center
New York, NY 10048-0001
U.S.A.
Phone: (1-212) 938-0404

Company Information:

The Best Performing Shares in the Country

Company Name	Share Price Change 1 January 1997 to 31 December 1997 (%)
Hsn	1,237
Patriot Amer.Hospitality	732
Suiza Foods	699
Tyco Intl.	644
Yahoo	562

Company Name	Share Price Change 1 January 1997 to 31 December 1997 (%)
Ballard Pwr Sys	463
Washington Mutual	425
Arterial Vascular Engr.	424
Chancellor Media 'A'	403
Allied Waste Inds.	332
Teleport Comms.Gp.A	298
Heftel Broadcasting-A	285
Us Airways	280
Assd.Bancorp	254
Best Buy	252
Foundation Health Sys.	244
Icn Pharmaceuticals New	229
National-Oilwell	222
Airborne Freight	213
America Online Del.	200
Us Bancorp Del.	199
Meyer(Fred)	195
Brooks Fiber Props.	195
Outdoor Systems	189
Comcast Special 'A'	187
Dell Computer	187
Sovereign Banc.	186
Quality Food Centres	185
Cendant	185
Jacor Comms.A	183
Clear Chl.Comms.	180
Fort James	180
Immunex New	178
Westamerica Bancorp.	168
Jp Foodservice	164
Compuware	161
Merc.Bancorp	159
Starwood Hotels& Resortstst.	157
North Fork Bancorp.	157
Worldcom Inc.Ga.	156
Barnes & Noble	153
Cvs	152
Firstplus Finl.Gp.	152
Caliber Sys.	152
Keane	150
Cbs.	150
Bell Atlantic	149
Universal Outdoor Hdg.	146
Vornado Realty Tst.	145
Catellus Dev.Corp.	143
Equitable Companies	141
Globalstar Telecom.	139
Safeskin	138
Provident Cos.Inco.	137
Nextel Comms.A	134

Company Name	Share Price Change 1 January 1997 to 31 December 1997 (%)	Company Name	Share Price Change 1 January 1997 to 31 December 1997 (%)
Platinum Tech.	133	Marshall & Iisly	99
Aes	133	Snyder Comms.	99
Veritas Software	133	Schwab (Charles)	99
Rexall Sundown	130	Legg Mason	98
Dime Bancorp	128	Peoples Bk.Bridgeport	98
Royal Crbn.Cruises	128	Ultramar Diamond Shamrock	98
Summit Bancorp	126	Frank.Res	97
Coca Cola Ents.	126	Sci Systems	96
Cke Restaurants	126	Southtrust	95
Berkshire Hathaway Cl.B	126	Owens Illinois New	95
Colonial Bancgroup	124	Mackenzie Finl.Corp.	95
Bb & T	122	Costco Companies	94
Mcdermott Intl.	122	Usa Waste Svs.	93
Quick And Reilly	121	Pier 1 Imports	92
Keystone Finl.	120	Firstenergy	92
Sofamor Danek Group	120	Nthn.Trust	92
Camco Intl.	119	Lehman Brothers Hdg.	92
Global Inds.	118	Itt Corp.New	92
Guidant Corp.	118	Lilly Eli	92
Belo A.H.	118	Deposit Guaranty	91
Family Dlr.Strs.	117	Nabors Inds.	90
Ccb Finl.	117	Fifth Third Bancorp.	90
Sbc Communications	114	First Security	90
Cincinnati Fin.	114	Schering-Plough	90
Duke Energy	114	Check Point Sftw.Tech Lt	90
Mckesson Corp.New	114	Equity Resd.Tst. Props.Shbi	90
Checkfree Holdings	113	Trustmark	89
Tenet Healthcare	113	Gen. Nutrition	88
Travelers Gp.	113	Spieker Properties	87
Compaq Computers	112	Dean Foods	87
Fremont Gen.	112	Bank Utd.'A'	87
Ocwen Finl.	112	Miller Herman	86
Donaldson Lufkin & Jenrette	111	Omnicom	86
Mercury General New	111	First Of Amer.Bank	85
Evi	110	Astoria Finl.Corp.	85
Federal Mogul	110	Mercantile Bank	85
Carnival Corp.A	108	Cnf Trsp.	85
Tcf Financial	108	Kohls	85
Southdown	107	Mcleod	85
Unisys	107	Nat.Commerce Bancorp.	85
1st.Coml.	106	Bergen Brunswig 'A'	85
Kansas Cty.Sthn.	106	Ahmanson (H.F.)	84
Charter One Finl.	106	Magna	83
Jabil Circuit	106	Hon Ind.	83
Unionbancal	103	Star Banc	83
Citrix Sys.	102	Cont.Airl.B	82
Union Planters	101	Thiokol	82
Proffitts	101	Amer.Bk.In.Group	82
Crestar Finl.	100	Liberty Properties Tst. Shbi	82
Mcdermott J Ray S A	99	Healthsouth	82

Company Name	Share Price Change 1 January 1997 to 31 December 1997 (%)	Company Name	Share Price Change 1 January 1997 to 31 December 1997 (%)
Norwest	82	Borders Gp.	72
Mack Cali Rlty	82	Cons.Stores	72
Gatx	81	Western National	72
Merrill Lynch	81	Sun	72
State Str.	81	First Va.Banks	71
Hntgtn.Bcsh.	80	Tosco	71
Kla Tencor	80	Solectron	71
Pfizer	80	Sw.Airlines	70
Halliburton	80	Applied Mats.	70
Progressive Corp.Ohio	80	1st.Ten.Nat.	70
I2 Technologies	79	Wal Mart Stores	70
Robert Half Intl.	79	Marsh & Mclennan	70
Maytag	79	Mgic Invt	69
Compass Bancshares	79	Peoplesoft	69
Edwards Ag	79	Maxim Integ.Products	69
Hbo	79	Publix Super Markets	69
Home Depot	79	Comerica	68
Paine Webber	79	Safety-Kleen	68
Dollar Gen.	78	Mellon Bank	68
Allmerica Finl.Corp.Com	78	Lci Intl.	67
Safeway	78	Puget Snd.Pwrlt.	67
City National	78	Uniphase	67
First Commerce (N.O.)	78	Centura Banks	67
Universal Health 'B'	78	Gap	67
Parker-Hannifin	78	Republic Inds.	67
Carramerica Realty	78	Delta Air Lines	66
Regions Finl.Corp.	78	Airtouch Communications	66
Wachovia Corp.	77	Torchmark Corp.	66
Valley Nat.Bk.	77	Warner Lambert	66
Emc Corp.Mass.	77	Gannett	66
Zions Bancorp.	76	Cooper Cameron	66
Stanley Works	76	Payless Shoesource	66
Conseco	75	Noble Drilling	65
Centex	75	Cmac Inv.	65
Lucent Technologies	74	Quantum	65
Health Man.As.A	74	Us Office Prds.	65
Banc One	73	Cox Communications 'A'	65
Dayton-Hudson	73	Bank Of New York	65
Tele Communications 'A'	73	Valassis Comms.	64
Old Kent Finl.	73	Nordstrom	64
Bear Stearns	73	Dollar Tree Stores	64
Barnett Banks	73	Century Tel.	64
Ny.Times 'A'	73	Biomet	63
Sunbeam	73	Vulcan Materials	63
Bristol Myers Squibb	72	Interpublic Gp.	63
Diamond Offshore Drilling	72	Schlumberger	63
Reliastar Finl.	72	Mcn Corp.	63
Watson Pharms.	72	Trimas	62
Golden St Bancorp	72	Gillette	62
1st.Amer.Tennessee	72	Minnesota Pwr. & Lt.	62

Company Name	Share Price Change 1 January 1997 to 31 December 1997 (%)	Company Name	Share Price Change 1 January 1997 to 31 December 1997 (%)
Exel	62	Nationsbank	54
Stewart Ents.'A'	61	Lafarge Corp.	54
Duke Realty Inv.	61	King World Production	54
A.C Nielson	61	Golden West Finl.	54
Amsouth Banc.	61	Synovus Finl.	53
Associates 1st.Cap.A	61	First Union	53
Northrop Grumman Corp.	61	United States Filter	53
Sungard Data Systems	61	Household Intl.	53
Colgate-Palm.	60	Us West Media Gp.	53
Wesco Financial	60	Commerce Bcsh.	52
Siebel Sys.	60	Financial Secs.Asr.Hdg. L	52
Bmc Software	60	Hibernia 'A'	52
Bed Bath & Beyond	60	Westpoint Stevens	52
Computer Assocs.Intl.	60	Liberty Finl.Cos.	52
Kroger	60	Comair Holdings	52
Mcgraw-Hill Co.	60	Illinois Tool Wks.	52
Telecom.New Liberty Media Gp.A	59	Time Warner	52
		Dial New	52
Staples	59	Provident Finl.Gp.	51
Tech Data	59	Timken	51
1st.Empire State	59	Medtronic	51
Finova Gp.	59	Transocean Offshore	51
Central Newspapers	58	Allstate Corp.	51
Amer.General	58	Tjx Cos.(New)	51
Sun Microsystems	58	Rite Aid	50
Clorox	58	Dana Corp.	50
Ny.State Elec. & Gas	58	Popular	50
Microsoft	58	Amer.Intl.Gp.	50
Martin Mrta.Mats.	58	Compusa	50
Tribune	58	Sara Lee Corp.	50
Countrywide Credit Inds.	57	Protect.Life	50
Pitney-Bowes	57	Ogden	50
Walgreen	57	R & B Falcon	49
Cadence Design Sys.	56	Starbucks	49
Bankers Tst.Ny.	56	Paychex	49
Fleetwood Ents.	56	Capital One Finl.Corp.	49
Block H R	56	Interstate Bakeries Del.	49
Wilmington Trust	56	Sealed Air	49
Neiman-Marcus	56	Old Republic Int.	49
Firstar	56	Houston Inds.	49
Reliance Group	56	Montana Power	49
Tandy	55	Ace	49
Health & Retirement Properties Trust	55	Teleflex	49
		Ual	48
Amer.Express	55	Baker Hughes	48
Fiserv	55	Trizec Hahn Sbvtg.U$	48
Comdisco	55	Oakwood Homes	48
Williams Cos.	55	Utilicorp Utd.	48
Firstmerit Corp.	55	Mbna Corp.	48
Paccar	55	Freddie Mac	48

Company Name	Share Price Change 1 January 1997 to 31 December 1997 (%)	Company Name	Share Price Change 1 January 1997 to 31 December 1997 (%)
Usg	48	Campbell Soup	42
Gen.Elec.	48	Bankamerica	41
Pittston Brinks Gp.	47	Dover	41
Kellogg	47	Hillenbrand	41
Fannie Mae	47	Nat.City	41
Price T.Rowe Assocs.	47	St.Paul	41
Weatherford Enterra	47	Heinz Hj	41
Ecolab	47	Quaker Oats	41
Sprint	47	Boston Edison	41
Sanmina	47	Xerox	41
Iomega	47	Cons.Edison.	41
Highwoods Props.	46	Lincare Holdings	40
Sybron	46	Deere & Co.	40
Amr (American Airlines)	46	Service Corp.Intl.	40
Aon Corp.	46	Valero En.New	40
Procter & Gamble	46	Black & Decker	40
P G & E	46	St.Joe Corp.	40
Panamerican Beverages'A'	46	Limited	40
Masco	45	Best Foods	39
Avery Dennison Corp.	45	Pnc Bank	39
Apollo Gp.A	45	Hartford Finl.Svs.Gp.	39
Texas Insts.	45	Crompton Knowles	39
Servicemaster	45	Electronic Arts	39
Lincoln Nat.	45	Ambac	39
Automatic Data Proc.	44	Grace Wr & Co. Del	39
Flowers Inds.	44	Health Care & Rtmt.Del.	39
Sonoco Prds.	44	Washington Pst.B	39
Fleet Finl.Gp	44	Bankboston	39
Mattel	44	Bellsouth	39
El Paso Nat.Gas New	44	Ensco Intl.	39
Bj Svs.	44	Fed.Express	39
K N Energy	43	Safeco	38
Everest Rein.Hdg.	43	Republic Ny.	38
Ford Motor	43	Ross Stores	38
Depuy	43	Inmc Mtg Hdg.	38
Sunamerica	43	Scripps Howard Cl.'A'	38
Lexmark Intl.Gp.A	43	Smith Intl.	38
Unum	43	Manor Care	38
Ashland	43	Genzyme	38
Shared Med.Sys.	42	Ingersoll-Rand	38
Tellabs	42	Chubb	38
Lear	42	Corestates Finl.	37
Crane	42	Long Isl.Ltg.	37
Cardinal Health	42	Suntrust Banks	37
Western Res.	42	Bay Networks	37
Disney (Walt)	42	Cintas	37
Usx-Marathon	42	Cisco Systems	37
First Chicago Nbd	42	Harris	37
At&T Corp.	42	Goodrich Bf	37
Us.West Communications	42	Nthn.States Pwr.	37

Company Name	Share Price Change 1 January 1997 to 31 December 1997 (%)	Company Name	Share Price Change 1 January 1997 to 31 December 1997 (%)
Jefferson Pilot	37	Ameritech	32
Forest Labs.	37	V F.	32
Keycorp	37	Teradyne	32
Cms Energy	37	Supervalu	32
Quintiles Transnational	37	Textron	32
Rowan Cos.	37	Helmerich Payne	32
Meredith	36	Csx	32
Mbia	36	Cambridge Tech.Ptns. Mass.	32
Leucadia Nat.	36	Secur Dyn.Tech.	32
Cummins Engine	36	Boeing	32
Adc Telecom.	36	Kennametal	32
Security Cap Pac Tst. Shbi	36	Sthn.New Engl.Telecom.	31
Winn-Dixie Strs.	36	Browning-Ferris	31
Millennium Chems.	36	Oge En.	31
Amer.Greeting 'A'	36	Ku Energy	31
Berkshire Hathaway	36	Rjr Nabisco Hdg.Corp.	31
Greenpoint Finl.Corp.	36	Thermo Insts.	31
Witco	36	Slm Hdg.	31
Aeroquip-Vickers	36	Wash.Wt.Pwr.	31
Allegiance	36	Conagra	31
Lowe's Cos.	36	Sterling Commerce	30
Danaher	35	Qualcomm	30
Newell	35	Cooper Inds.	30
Dsc Communications	35	Dun & Bradstreet	30
Linear Tech.	35	Meditrust Paired Ctf	30
Dresser Inds.	35	Sterling Software	30
Autodesk	35	Teco Energy	30
Dole Food	35	Symbol Techs.	30
Office Depot	35	Albertsons	30
Amer.Water Works	35	Intl.Bus.Mach.	30
Alleghany	35	Beneficial	30
Darden Restaurants	35	Lin Television Corp.	30
Dst Sys.Inc Del Com	34		
Pacificorp	34		
Quorum Health Gp.	34		
Penney (J.C.)	34		
Intuit	34		
Partnerre Hdg.	34		
Johnson & Johnson	34		
Sysco	34		
Cracker Barrel	33		
Tnsat.Hdg.	33		
Medpartners	33		
Office Max	33		
Clayton Homes	33		
Mapco	33		
Amer.Home Prds.	33		
Fina 'A'	33		
Midamericon En.Hdg.Co.	32		
Merck	32		

The Largest Companies in the Country by Market Capitalization as of 31 December 1997

Company Name	Market Capitalization US Dollars (Millions)
Gen.Elec.	240,136
Coca Cola	164,933
Microsoft	155,965
Exxon	150,883
Merck	127,015
Intel	114,718
Philip Morris	109,639
Procter & Gamble	107,267
Intl.Bus.Mach.	101,713
AT&T Corp.	99,587
Pfizer	96,428
Bristol Myers Squibb	94,084

Company Name	Market Capitalization US Dollars (Millions)	Company Name	Market Capitalization US Dollars (Millions)
Wal Mart Stores	88,573	Kimberly-Clark	27,433
Johnson & Johnson	88,515	Dell Computer	27,421
Lilly Eli	77,236	Worldcom Inc.Ga.	27,327
Amer.Intl.Gp.	76,287	Cendant	27,193
Bell Atlantic	70,674	Sara Lee Corp.	27,028
Du Pont E I De Nemours	67,922	Campbell Soup	26,531
Sbc Communications	67,140	Atlantic Rich.	25,700
Disney (Walt)	67,113	Monsanto	24,905
Hewlett-Packard	64,932	Emerson Electric	24,834
Travelers Gp.	61,637	Medtronic	24,605
Fannie Mae	60,543	Merrill Lynch	24,299
Citicorp	57,920	First Chicago Nbd	24,292
Mobil	56,625	Xerox	24,075
Cisco Systems	56,568	Tyco Intl.	24,008
Gillette	56,253	Mci Comms.	23,996
Bellsouth	55,840	Chrysler	23,311
Berkshire Hathaway	55,108	Dow Chemicals	23,016
Pepsico	54,994	Allied Signal	21,895
Ford Motor	54,834	Oracle Corp.	21,877
Lucent Technologies	51,345	Us.West Communications	21,824
Bankamerica	50,623	Bank Of New York	21,776
Chevron	50,570	Colgate-Palm.	21,742
Abbott Labs.	50,100	Electronic Data Systems	21,572
Gte	50,032	Anheuser-Busch	21,557
Amer.Home Prds.	49,699	Airtouch Communications	20,980
Boeing	48,918	Cbs .	20,938
Chase Manhattan	46,150	Kellogg	20,391
Schering-Plough	45,485	Sprint	20,141
Ameritech	44,054	Morgan (Jp)	20,052
Nationsbank	43,247	Duke Energy	19,927
Home Depot	42,980	Eastman Kodak	19,677
General Motors	42,967	Lockheed Martin Corp.	19,146
Compaq Computers	42,771	Fleet Finl.Gp	18,798
Amer.Express	41,482	Pharmacia Upjohn	18,584
Amoco	41,451	Heinz Hj	18,570
Schlumberger	40,067	Columbia/Hca Healthcare	18,562
Allstate Corp.	38,808	Caterpillar	18,056
Motorola	34,138	Automatic Data Proc.	17,952
Warner Lambert	33,816	Pnc Bank	17,871
Minnesota Mng.& Mnfg.	33,536	Southern	17,857
Mcdonalds	32,889	Sears Roebuck	17,738
Time Warner	32,321	Texas Insts.	17,562
First Union	32,180	Gannett	17,535
Banc One	31,879	Us West Media Gp.	17,510
Texaco	29,756	United Technologies	16,964
Wells Fargo	29,429	Safeway	16,774
Norwest	29,268	Gen.Re	16,628
Freddie Mac	29,125	Wachovia Corp.	16,561
Computer Assocs.Intl.	28,981	Carnival Corp.A	16,456
Us Bancorp Del.	27,478	Washington Mutual	16,421

Company Name	Market Capitalization US Dollars (Millions)	Company Name	Market Capitalization US Dollars (Millions)
Corestates Finl.	15,924	Gen.Mills	11,334
Conagra	15,634	Schwab (Charles)	11,138
Keycorp	15,556	Equitable Companies	11,048
Best Foods	15,534	Hartford Finl.Svs.Gp.	11,045
Walgreen	15,523	Cvs	11,032
Union Pacific	15,481	Bankers Tst.Ny.	11,015
Mellon Bank	15,434	Applied Mats.	10,983
Penney (J.C.)	15,075	Frank.Res	10,956
Suntrust Banks	15,050	Healthsouth	10,924
Illinois Tool Wks.	14,998	Mattel	10,829
Sun Microsystems	14,938	Fpl Group	10,767
Dayton-Hudson	14,753	Rockwell Intl.New	10,676
Deere & Co.	14,685	Aetna	10,486
Burlington Nthn.Santa Fe C	14,516	Edison Intl.	10,371
Amgen	14,246	Cox Communications 'A'	10,284
Baxter Intl.	14,125	Textron	10,270
Nat.City	14,049	Ppg Industries	10,175
Gap	14,022	Tenet Healthcare	10,111
Barnett Banks	13,863	Republic Inds.	10,009
Coca Cola Ents.	13,737	Goodyear Tire	9,950
Mbna Corp.	13,689	Occidental Ptl.	9,930
Household Intl.	13,657	Ralston Purina Ral-Pur Gp.	9,916
Bankboston	13,647	Texas Utilities	9,867
Emc Corp.Mass.	13,607	Aon Corp.	9,832
Halliburton	13,590	Weyerhaeuser	9,794
Amer.General	13,168	Amer.Elec.Pwr.	9,789
Tele Communications 'A'	13,093	Comcast Special 'A'	9,734
Intl.Paper	13,036	Usx-Marathon	9,734
Chubb	12,869	Air Prds.& Chems.	9,722
Phillips Ptl.	12,796	Itt Corp.New	9,678
Cigna	12,766	Cons.Edison .	9,636
P G & E	12,757	Tellabs	9,595
Pitney-Bowes	12,756	Hbo	9,592
Marsh & Mclennan	12,665	Unocal	9,568
Fifth Third Bancorp.	12,662	Costco Companies	9,563
First Data	12,520	Comerica	9,481
Waste Man.	12,513	Kroger	9,367
Enron Corp	12,426	United Healthcare	9,358
Loew's	12,204	State Str.	9,357
May Dept.Stores	12,184	America Online Del.	9,313
Rjr Nabisco Hdg.Corp.	12,141	Summit Bancorp	9,307
Aluminum Co.Of Am.	12,138	Service Corp.Intl.	9,256
Archer-Danls.-Midl.	12,091	Amp	9,241
3com	12,087	Guidant Corp.	9,221
Raytheon 'B'	11,935	Williams Cos.	9,109
Csx	11,783	Federated Dept.Strs.	9,035
Viacom 'B'	11,754	Toys R Us	8,928
Amr (American Airlines)	11,715	Boston Scientific	8,928
Albertsons	11,604	Marriott Intl.	8,838
Norfolk Southern	11,497	Delta Air Lines	8,807

Company Name	Market Capitalization US Dollars (Millions)	Company Name	Market Capitalization US Dollars (Millions)
Bb & T	8,770	Fed.Express	7,026
Honeywell	8,719	Slm Hdg.	7,021
Progressive Corp.Ohio	8,661	Hershey Foods	6,963
Peoplesoft	8,658	Limited	6,949
Corning	8,582	Aflac	6,941
Conseco	8,561	Hntgtn.Bcsh.	6,885
Usa Waste Svs.	8,502	Eaton	6,881
Sgs-Thomson Microels.	8,487	Safeco	6,881
Masco	8,404	Omnicom	6,866
Lowe's Cos.	8,341	St.Paul	6,864
Cardinal Health	8,215	Ust Inco.	6,807
Clorox	8,202	Newell	6,764
Aes	8,143	Tenneco New	6,725
Avon Products	8,102	First Of Amer.Bank	6,721
Pacificorp	8,100	Ingersoll-Rand	6,705
Dover	8,034	Diamond Offshore Drilling	6,704
Merc.Bancorp	8,013	Transamerica	6,692
Fort James	7,987	Bmc Software	6,673
Dominion Res.	7,956	Firstenergy	6,670
Lincoln Nat.	7,920	Thermo Electron	6,658
Burlington Res.	7,911	Unicom	6,657
Cna Financial	7,895	Trw	6,574
Houston Inds.	7,893	Coastal	6,546
Sysco	7,793	Southtrust	6,526
Clear Chl.Comms.	7,790	Winn-Dixie Strs.	6,505
Nthn.Trust	7,781	Cmp.Sciences	6,483
Cincinnati Fin.	7,727	Associates 1st.Cap.A	6,446
Northrop Grumman Corp.	7,680	Crown Cork Seal	6,434
Tribune	7,653	Panamst New	6,431
Sunamerica	7,641	Carolina Pwr.Lt.	6,371
Alltel	7,611	Nextel Comms.A	6,367
Equities Office Properties Trust	7,610	Fortune Brands	6,361
Mgic Invt	7,592	Ahmanson (H.F.)	6,320
Telecom.New Liberty Media Gp.A	7,558	Ny.Times 'A'	6,318
		Crestar Finl.	6,286
Unum	7,545	Interpublic Gp.	6,274
Hilton Hotels	7,447	Marshall & Iisly	6,271
Baker Hughes	7,386	Republic Ny.	6,238
Nike 'B'	7,380	Union Pacific Resources Group	6,155
Pub.Ser.Enter.Gp.	7,379	Qwest Comms.Intl.	6,148
Wrigley William	7,358	Firstar	6,144
Dresser Inds.	7,356	Ciena	6,069
Rite Aid	7,327	Genuine Parts	6,064
Mcgraw-Hill Co.	7,326	Becton Dickinson	6,059
Browning-Ferris	7,319	Cinergy Corp.	6,041
Quaker Oats	7,305	Parametric Tech.	6,034
Entergy Corp.Common Stk.	7,302	Lehman Brothers Hdg.	6,021
Cognizant	7,237	Grace Wr & Co. Del	5,972
Praxair	7,095	Mbia	5,971
Pion.Hi-Bred Intl.	7,052	Cooper Inds.	5,929

Company Name	Market Capitalization US Dollars (Millions)	Company Name	Market Capitalization US Dollars (Millions)
Union Carbide Am.	5,922	Dte Energy	5,033
Torchmark Corp.	5,907	Amerada Hess	5,031
Tosco	5,907	New Century Energies	5,015
Unionbancal	5,902	Mckesson Corp.New	5,006
Rohm & Haas	5,861	Dana Corp.	4,989
Cons.Natural Gas	5,776	Union Planters	4,978
Regions Finl.Corp.	5,744	Newmont Gold	4,976
Ctl.& Sw.	5,744	Star Banc	4,899
Synovus Finl.	5,728	Transocean Offshore	4,863
Us Airways	5,705	First Security	4,851
V F.	5,681	Dollar Gen.	4,839
Publix Super Markets	5,642	Hercules	4,836
Georgia Pacific	5,626	Grainger W W	4,825
Intl.Flav.& Frag.	5,623	Sherwin-Williams	4,797
Amer.Stores	5,620	Solectron	4,781
K Mart	5,599	Ensco Intl.	4,766
Compuware	5,591	Seagate Tech.	4,708
Bear Stearns	5,590	Block H R	4,705
Golden West Finl.	5,556	Eastman Chemicals	4,670
Tjx Cos.(New)	5,548	Nordstrom	4,668
Jefferson Pilot	5,518	Santa Fe Intl.	4,666
Adc Telecom.	5,513	Ascend Comms.	4,644
Paychex	5,498	Countrywide Credit Inds.	4,628
Digital Equp.	5,487	Staples	4,627
Micron Tech.	5,483	Newmont Mining	4,596
Gen.Dynamics	5,455	Morton Intl.	4,576
Ual	5,437	Paine Webber	4,576
Sw.Airlines	5,435	Case Corp.	4,539
Donnelley R R	5,434	Northwest Airlines 'A'	4,538
Bay Networks	5,422	Arco Chemicals	4,514
Peco Energy Co.	5,397	Allegheny Teledyne	4,509
Kohls	5,371	Maxim Integ.Products	4,485
Avery Dennison Corp.	5,357	Analog Devices	4,470
Servicemaster	5,355	Chancellor Media 'A'	4,450
Exel	5,349	Donaldson Lufkin & Jenrette	4,440
Tele Comms.Tci Vent.'A'	5,341	Reynolds Metals	4,435
Owens Illinois New	5,328	Union Electric	4,417
Equifax	5,322	Linear Tech.	4,413
Corn Prods Intl.	5,292	Beneficial	4,412
Dun & Bradstreet	5,267	Medpartners	4,404
Ace	5,261	Autozone	4,392
Provident Cos.Inco.	5,218	Knight-Ridder	4,391
Parker-Hannifin	5,121	Amsouth Banc.	4,371
Cadence Design Sys.	5,117	Champion Intl.	4,356
Gpu	5,088	Columbia Energy Gp.	4,356
Raytheon 'A'	5,072	Nthn.States Pwr.	4,337
Edperbrascan Corp.'A' Ltd Voting Share	5,063	Loral Space & Comms.	4,304
		Providian Finl.	4,299
Gateway 2000	5,046	Times Mirror 'A'	4,295
Balt.Gas & Elec.	5,039	1st.Ten.Nat.	4,279

Company Name	Market Capitalization US Dollars (Millions)	Company Name	Market Capitalization US Dollars (Millions)
Nat.Semiconductor	4,260	Price T.Rowe Assocs.	3,676
Cms Energy	4,249	Raychem	3,671
Washington Pst.B	4,249	Harris	3,662
Nucor	4,247	Starwood Hotels& Resortstst.	3,661
Global Marine	4,229	Phelps Dodge	3,658
Adaptec	4,219	Long Isl.Ltg.	3,656
Hasbro	4,219	Robert Half Intl.	3,638
Cincinnati Bell	4,216	Gartner Group 'A'	3,634
Stanley Works	4,212	Anadarko Ptl.	3,633
Thermo Insts.	4,188	Sunbeam	3,611
Harley-Davidson	4,150	Dime Bancorp	3,590
Health Man.As.A	4,127	Pinnacle West Cap.	3,590
Whirlpool	4,126	Stryker	3,581
Paccar	4,086	Willamette	3,579
Mirage Resorts	4,082	Ecolab	3,578
Western Atlas	4,034	Green Tree Finl.	3,566
Ashland	4,028	Capital One Finl.Corp.	3,557
Charter One Finl.	4,025	Maytag	3,544
Leggett&Platt	4,022	Hillenbrand	3,522
Noble Drilling	4,021	Circuit City Stores	3,510
Johnson Controls	4,016	Ceridian	3,499
Dow Jones	4,011	Diebold	3,492
Host Marriott	3,998	Vastar Res.	3,479
Sigma Aldrich	3,988	Qualcomm	3,462
Tandy	3,987	Old Republic Int.	3,451
Allegheny En.	3,979	Sterling Commerce	3,448
El Paso Nat.Gas New	3,977	Vulcan Materials	3,440
Pp&L Res.	3,971	Kansas Cty.Sthn.	3,417
Intel Wts.	3,958	Humana	3,400
Frontier Corp.	3,940	Royal Crbn.Cruises	3,382
New Holland N V	3,939	Tidewater	3,370
Sonat	3,923	Trizec Hahn Sbvtg.U$	3,365
Equity Resd.Tst. Props.Shbi	3,921	Teleport Comms.Gp.A	3,360
Cintas	3,814	Popular	3,350
Florida Progress	3,810	Sthn.New Engl.Telecom.	3,348
Office Depot	3,785	Autoliv	3,341
Gen.Motors 'H' Shs.	3,785	Talisman Energy	3,326
Dillard 'A'	3,774	Enron Oil & Gas	3,325
Ikon Office Sltn.	3,771	Sonoco Prds.	3,321
Edwards Ag	3,763	Storage Tech.	3,316
Rubbermaid	3,745	Starbucks	3,310
Union Camp	3,742	Simon Debartolo Gp.	3,284
Old Kent Finl.	3,728	Kla Tencor	3,268
Reliastar Finl.	3,718	Cooper Cameron	3,247
Itt Industries	3,716	Iomega	3,232
Imc Global	3,710	Ambac	3,225
Cons.Stores	3,708	Scana	3,213
Black & Decker	3,703	Westvaco	3,204
Danaher	3,690	Meyer(Fred)	3,203
Teco Energy	3,681	Total System Services	3,201

Company Name	Market Capitalization US Dollars (Millions)	Company Name	Market Capitalization US Dollars (Millions)
Wisconsin Energy	3,199	Travelers Pr.Clty.	2,864
Arrow Electronic	3,185	Manpower	2,860
Nabors Inds.	3,182	Ncr	2,859
Wendy's Intl.	3,180	Biomet	2,858
Lear	3,174	Pioneer Nat.Res.	2,855
Meditrust Paired Ctf	3,173	Watson Pharms.	2,849
Pennzoil	3,173	Genentech Spl.	2,849
Apache	3,171	Viacom 'A'	2,842
Estee Lauder Cl.A	3,160	Depuy	2,836
Solutia	3,160	Dsc Communications	2,831
Mcn Corp.	3,155	Compusa	2,829
Vornado Realty Tst.	3,151	R & B Falcon	2,822
Tcf Financial	3,146	United States Filter	2,813
Pacific Ents.	3,138	Western Res.	2,813
Fluor	3,133	Quintiles Transnational	2,811
Perkin Elmer	3,122	Mercantile Bank	2,810
Outdoor Systems	3,109	Deluxe	2,807
Nipsco Inds.	3,101	St.Jude Med.	2,802
Greenpoint Finl.Corp.	3,070	Lci Intl.	2,798
1st.Empire State	3,068	Liz Claiborne	2,795
Dpl	3,065	Ultramar Diamond Shamrock	2,793
Panamerican Beverages'a'	3,062	Finova Gp.	2,791
Enova	3,061	Bj Svs.	2,782
Potomac Elec.Pwr.	3,059	Lsi Logic	2,779
Sun	3,053	Gen. Nutrition	2,776
Bank East Asia	3,047	Mallinckrodt	2,772
Mercury General New	3,045	New England Elec.Sys.	2,767
Armstrong-World Ind.	3,032	St.Joe Corp.	2,766
Public Storage	3,026	Assd.Bancorp	2,765
Brunswick	3,022	Hubbel 'B'	2,761
Century Tel.	3,019	Newcourt Cr.Group	2,757
Kerr-Mcgee	3,018	Amer.Standard Co.	2,756
Adobe Sys.	3,011	Woolworth	2,749
Sundstrand	2,996	Dole Food	2,746
Allmerica Finl.Corp.Com	2,995	Interstate Bakeries Del.	2,740
Scty.Cap.Gp.'A'	2,993	Quantum	2,732
Chiron Corp	2,986	Dqe	2,728
Yahoo	2,985	Alza Corp.	2,717
Goodrich Bf	2,977	Networks Associates	2,710
Belo A.H.	2,967	Amer.Greeting 'A'	2,709
Temple Inland	2,959	Jd Edwards	2,705
Altera	2,952	Zions Bancorp.	2,704
Scripps Howard Cl.'A'	2,948	Oryx En.	2,696
Wellpoint Hlth.Net.New A	2,946	Biogen Nv.	2,694
Corrections Amer.	2,938	Usx-Us.Steel	2,692
1st.Amer.Tennessee	2,938	Avnet	2,684
Mead	2,936	Sungard Data Systems	2,679
Galileo Intl.	2,895	First Va.Banks	2,677
Compass Bancshares	2,884	Keane	2,675
Intl.Game Tech.	2,873	Lexmark Intl.Gp.A	2,675

Company Name	Market Capitalization US Dollars (Millions)	Company Name	Market Capitalization US Dollars (Millions)
Gt.Lakes Chm.	2,670	Unisys	2,439
Teradyne	2,670	Evi	2,438
Snap-On	2,656	Murphy Oil	2,432
Ngc	2,654	Security Cap.Indl.Tst. Shbi	2,432
Bed Bath & Beyond	2,651	Unitrin	2,426
Litton Inds.	2,647	Dean Foods	2,425
Whitman	2,646	Jacor Comms.A	2,421
Nextlevel Sys.	2,644	Cont.Airl.B	2,408
Rowan Cos.	2,642	Apollo Gp.A	2,403
Harcourt Gen.	2,639	Cons.Papers	2,397
Commerce Bcsh.	2,639	Ny.State Elec. & Gas	2,396
Nalco Chemical	2,635	Cabletron Sys.	2,370
Sealed Air	2,632	Amer.Finl.Gp.Ohio	2,368
First Commerce (N.O.)	2,625	Calenergy	2,364
Novell	2,622	Spieker Properties	2,361
Sci Systems	2,607	Allied Waste Inds.	2,356
Thomas & Betts	2,599	Pmi Group	2,347
Xilinx	2,594	Witco	2,345
Us Office Prds.	2,588	Borders Gp.	2,336
Pall	2,581	Bemis	2,335
Tri-Continental	2,581	Manor Care	2,335
Fiserv	2,575	Centocor	2,331
Mylan Laboratories	2,557	Deposit Guaranty	2,321
Puget Snd.Pwrlt.	2,553	Peoples Bk.Bridgeport	2,319
Mapco	2,537	Accustaff	2,316
Omnicare	2,522	Olin	2,312
Family Dlr.Strs.	2,517	Silicon Graphics	2,305
Supervalu	2,517	Weatherford Enterra	2,304
Wheelabrator Tech. $ 0.01	2,517	Echlin	2,285
Advd.Micro Devc.	2,516	Usg	2,283
Nabisco Hdg.A	2,512	Molex 'A'	2,282
Engelhard	2,510	Tyson Foods 'A'	2,271
Miller Herman	2,506	Barnes & Noble	2,265
Ryder System	2,506	North Fork Bancorp.	2,265
Payless Shoesource	2,506	Sybron	2,261
Hormel Foods	2,487	Biochem Pharma	2,260
Usf & G	2,486	Synopsys	2,256
Molex	2,485	Security Cap Pac Tst. Shbi	2,255
Fmc	2,477	Amer.Power Conv.	2,249
Comdisco	2,476	Hsn	2,249
Unifi	2,475	Us Industries	2,245
Cummins Engine	2,475	Mercantile Strs.	2,237
Smith Intl.	2,474	Ccb Finl.	2,231
Foundation Health Sys.	2,474	Electronic Arts	2,231
Tnsat.Hdg.	2,471	Us Surgical	2,219
Hibernia 'A'	2,467	At Home 'A'	2,217
Amer.Nat.In.	2,463	Brown-Forman 'B'	2,210
360 Comms.	2,459	Netscape Communications	2,210
Camco Intl.	2,454	Oge En.	2,208
Tel.& Data Sys.	2,451	Jones Apparel Group	2,207

Company Name	Market Capitalization US Dollars (Millions)	Company Name	Market Capitalization US Dollars (Millions)
Leucadia Nat.	2,203	Nicor	2,040
Partnerre Hdg.	2,197	Mack Cali Rlty	2,036
Allergan	2,190	Provident Finl.Gp.	2,035
Bausch & Lomb	2,189	Arterial Vascular Engr.	2,029
Rouse	2,188	Giant Food A.	2,014
1st.Coml.	2,186	Dura Pharms.	2,014
Polaroid	2,186	Tektronix	2,010
Stewart Ents.'A'	2,186	Noble Affiliates	2,006
Amer.Water Works	2,172	Readers Digest 'A'	1,999
Gulfstream Aeros.	2,168	Food Lion A.	1,993
Timken	2,165	Pac.Cen.Finl.	1,990
Icn Pharmaceuticals New	2,162	Forest Labs.	1,987
Genzyme	2,152	Health & Retirement Properties Trust	1,983
Nat.Service Inds.	2,145		
Immunex New	2,144	Erie Indty Co Cl 'A'	1,977
Brooks Fiber Props.	2,140	Warnaco Group	1,962
Wesco Financial	2,136	Patriot Amer.Hospitality	1,959
Clayton Homes	2,136	Intuit	1,954
Callaway Golf	2,134	Circus Circus Ents.	1,949
Catellus Dev.Corp.	2,130	Crompton Knowles	1,949
Bergen Brunswig 'A'	2,124	Quorum Health Gp.	1,944
Andrew	2,123	Ibp	1,939
King World Production	2,117	Mid Ocean Ltd.	1,939
Midamericon En.Hdg.Co.	2,117	Eci Telecom.	1,938
Intl.Home Foods	2,116	Gulf Indonesia Resources	1,932
Dial New	2,113	Illinova	1,931
Amb Pr.	2,110	Trinity Inds.	1,929
Lubrizol	2,108	Excel Comm.	1,921
Cytec Inds.	2,106	Food Lion'b'	1,920
Lyondell Ptl.	2,105	Lafarge Corp.	1,920
Advanced Fibre Comms.	2,105	Cooper Tire Rub.	1,920
Cambridge Tech.Ptns. Mass.	2,101	Amer.Bk.In.Group	1,908
Gen.Signal	2,099	Harrahs Entmt.	1,905
Wilmington Trust	2,098	Caliber Sys.	1,896
Dst Sys.Inc Del Com	2,096	Crane	1,893
Citrix Sys.	2,096	Golden St Bancorp	1,889
Mgm Grand	2,095	Cabot	1,884
Illinois Central Sr.A	2,092	Alumax	1,877
Keystone Finl.	2,091	Keyspan Energy	1,876
Utilicorp Utd.	2,087	Tech Data	1,873
Everest Rein.Hdg.	2,082	Ipalco Ents.	1,871
Lna.Pacific	2,081	Fina 'A'	1,870
Harsco	2,079	Centex	1,868
Georgia Pac.Com-Timber Gp.	2,076	Tele-Comms.Intl.Ser 'A'	1,865
Alleghany	2,066	Viad	1,864
Western National	2,065	Nat.Fuel Gas	1,861
Allegiance	2,056	Darden Restaurants	1,857
Cracker Barrel	2,053	Sovereign Banc.	1,853
Mcdermott Intl.	2,051	Atmel	1,850
Rexall Sundown	2,048	Cameco	1,849

Company Name	Market Capitalization US Dollars (Millions)	Company Name	Market Capitalization US Dollars (Millions)
Carramerica Realty	1,844	Helmerich Payne	1,706
Protect.Life	1,841	Tig Holdings	1,705
Agco	1,840	Vencor	1,704
Viking Office Prds.	1,839	Boise Cascade	1,701
Boston Edison	1,838	Tupperware	1,701
Hannaford Bros.	1,837	K N Energy	1,699
Questar	1,834	Utd. Asset Man.	1,697
Ucar Intl.	1,834	City National	1,690
Kansas Cty.Pwr.Lt.	1,830	Martin Mrta.Mats.	1,690
Duke Realty Inv.	1,826	Mcleod	1,685
Owens-Corning	1,824	Trustmark	1,685
Flowers Inds.	1,818	I2 Technologies	1,685
Freeport-Mcmoran Copper & Gold Cl.B	1,816	Liberty Finl.Cos.	1,678
Cnf Trsp.	1,814	Wallace Cmp.Ser.	1,672
Millennium Chems.	1,813	Apple Computers	1,671
Corporate Express	1,811	Valley Nat.Bk.	1,663
Hon Ind.	1,811	Quick And Reilly	1,663
Fremont Gen.	1,808	Pittston Brinks Gp.	1,655
Millicom Intl.Cellular S A	1,806	Shared Med.Sys.	1,651
Bowater (Us.)	1,801	Lg&E Energy Corp.	1,651
Snyder Comms.	1,798	Us.Cellular	1,650
Premark	1,798	Hertz 'A'	1,649
Mccormick & Co.Nv.	1,795	Dentsply Intl.	1,647
Health Care & Rtmt.Del.	1,789	Berkshire Hathaway Cl.B	1,645
Cadillac Fairview	1,783	Steris	1,643
Centura Banks	1,783	York Intl.	1,638
Bard C.R.	1,782	Jp Foodservice	1,635
Betzdearborn	1,781	Lancaster Colony	1,635
Platinum Tech.	1,778	Primedia	1,634
Gatx	1,774	Sofamor Danek Group	1,633
Union Texas Ptl.	1,771	1st.Health Gp.	1,629
Cke Restaurants	1,769	Federal Mogul	1,628
Office Max	1,768	Central Newspapers	1,626
Mcdermott J Ray S A	1,766	Avx	1,626
Valero En.New	1,764	Johns Manville	1,626
Firstmerit Corp.	1,762	Lincare Holdings	1,625
Ballard Pwr Sys	1,757	Lin Television Corp.	1,624
Proffitts	1,746	Reebok Intl.	1,622
Harnischfeger	1,743	Reliance Group	1,622
National-Oilwell	1,743	Dollar Tree Stores	1,619
Bce Mobl.Comm.	1,742	Comair Holdings	1,619
Phycor	1,741	Northeast Utilities	1,616
Suiza Foods	1,737	Best Buy	1,615
Highwoods Props.	1,737	Microchip Technology	1,614
Montana Power	1,735	Safety-Kleen	1,602
Ross Stores	1,733	Worthington Inds.	1,597
Fruit Of The Loom 'A'	1,730	Cornerstone Props.	1,596
Autodesk	1,726	Sterling Software	1,582
Nat.Commerce Bancorp.	1,722	Uici	1,580
Teleglobe	1,722	Promus Hotel New	1,578

Company Name	Market Capitalization US Dollars (Millions)	Company Name	Market Capitalization US Dollars (Millions)
Shaw Inds.	1,569	Reynd.& Reynd.	1,450
Jefferson Smurfit Corp. New	1,568	Wash.Fed.Com.	1,449
Veritas Software	1,563	Siebel Sys.	1,446
Gt.Amer.Communications Inactive 1/7/93	1,560	Universal	1,445
		Liberty Properties Tst. Shbi	1,443
Global Inds.	1,550	Amazon	1,438
Airborne Freight	1,546	Cyprus Amax Minerals	1,437
Mackenzie Finl.Corp.	1,537	Firstplus Finl.Gp.	1,435
Concord Efs	1,535	Beverly Enterprise	1,433
Oakwood Homes	1,531	Intl.Speciality Products	1,432
Brown-Forman 'A'	1,529	Kimco Realty	1,424
Fleetwood Ents.	1,527	Pacificare Hlth.Sys.'B'	1,423
Pier 1 Imports	1,527	Uniphase	1,423
Varian Assocs.	1,522	Trimas	1,421
Fore Systems	1,520	Idaho Power	1,415
Coltec Inds.	1,518	Ogden	1,415
Niagara Mohawk Pwr.	1,516	Secur Dyn.Tech.	1,415
Universal Health 'B'	1,516	Delmarva Pwr.&Lt.	1,412
Ocwen Finl.	1,516	Westpoint Stevens	1,409
Pep Boys-Manny	1,515	Quality Food Centres	1,405
Magna	1,514	Southdown	1,404
Checkfree Holdings	1,512	Inmc Mtg Hdg.	1,404
Ohio Casualty	1,511	Heftel Broadcasting-A	1,401
Neiman-Marcus	1,510	Plum Creek Timber Lp.	1,401
New Plan Realty Trust	1,509	A.C Nielson	1,399
Cipsco	1,508	Teleflex	1,397
Globalstar Telecom.	1,505	Western Digital	1,397
Financial Secs.Asr.Hdg. L	1,499	Valspar	1,396
Rpm	1,496	Mark Four Inds.	1,394
Lhs Group	1,495	Sanmina	1,391
Safeskin	1,493	Universal Outdoor Hdg.	1,389
La Quinta Inns	1,491	Bank Utd.'A'	1,388
Amf Bowling	1,491	Peoples Energy	1,384
Symbol Techs.	1,491	Legg Mason	1,382
Thiokol	1,487	Aeroquip-Vickers	1,382
Ku Energy	1,484	Outback Steakhouse	1,375
Millipore	1,480	Pentair	1,369
Salomon Bros.Fd.	1,477	Kennametal	1,367
Scherer R P	1,475	Credicorp Ltd.Com	1,361
Astoria Finl.Corp.	1,473	Wash.Wt.Pwr.	1,361
Jabil Circuit	1,472	Cmac Inv.	1,360
Blyth Industries	1,469	Check Point Sftw.Tech Lt	1,351
Meredith	1,467		
Valassis Comms.	1,465		
Colonial Bancgroup	1,464		
Westamerica Bancorp.	1,463		
Weis Markets	1,462		
Prec.Castparts	1,459		
Meritor Autv.	1,454		
Minnesota Pwr. & Lt.	1,453		
Fastenal	1,451		

Other Exchanges:

The NASDAQ (OTC) Stock Market

1735 K Street NW

Washington, DC 20006-1500

U.S.A.

Phone: (1-202) 728-8000

Fax: (1-202) 728-8882

Internet Address: www.nasdaq.com

Trading Hours:

	Monday–Friday	8:00 to 5:15 (Eastern Time)
The Nasdaq SmallCap Market	Monday–Friday	9:30 to 4:00
SelectNet (extended trading times)	Monday–Friday	8:00 to 9:30
		4:00 to 5:15

Exchange Holidays: See NYSE

Listed Companies: 6,208 domestic and foreign companies

Market Capitalization:
US$1.2 trillion 1995
US$1.5 trillion 1996
US$1.8 trillion 1997

Major Sectors: Pharmaceuticals; commercial banks/ holding companies; communications equipment; computer manufacturers; electronic components; life insurance; electric, gas, and sanitary services; printing and publishing; medical instruments and supplies; machinery; property and casualty insurance

Growth:
39.9% increase in the NASDAQ Composite Index 1995
23.0% increase in the NASDAQ Composite Index 1996
19.0% increase in the NASDAQ Composite Index 1997

History: The National Association of Securities Dealers Automated Quotations System (NASDAQ) uses computers and a telecommunications network to create an electronic trading system that allows participants to meet on the computer. Containing more companies than any other stock market in the world (over 6,000 domestic and foreign companies), NASDAQ'S share trading volume reached 101.2 billion shares in 1995, and dollar trading volume reached $2.4 trillion. In 1995 NASDAQ share volume exceeded that of all other U.S. stock markets.

A distinguishing feature of NASDAQ is its use of multiple market makers. On NASDAQ the typical stock has 11 market makers actively competing with one another for investor order flow.

Classes of Securities: Shares, small cap shares

Indices: NASDAQ Composite Index, 1995

Supervisory Organizations:
Securities and Exchange Commission (SEC)
National Association of Securities Dealers (NASD)
NASDAQ

Settlement:

Shares: Trade date + 3 days (T + 3) (All exchanges and OTC)

Trading: NASDAQ uses several market makers for the same securities, thereby providing a competitive market for those securities traded. More than 500 total market makers aggressively compete when buying and selling for their own accounts on the NASDAQ computerized system. At least two competing market makers are required for each listing, although it is common for each security to have as many as ten. Heavily traded issues might have as many as 40 or more market makers. In 1995 there were 266,616 computer terminals attached to the NASDAQ trading information service, with 55 countries included.

Listing Requirements: A listing agreement must be signed by a company desiring a NASDAQ listing. Companies must also meet quantitative and qualitative minimum standards.

Quantitative Standards:

Standard	Initial NASDAQ National Market Listing		Continued NASDAQ National Market
	Alternative[1]	Alternative[2]	Inclusion
Registration Under Section 12(g) of the Securities Exchange Act of 1934 or its equivalent	Yes	Yes	Yes
Net Tangible Assets[3]	$4,000,000	$12,000,000	$1,000,000
Net Income (last fiscal or two of the last three fiscal years)	$400,000	—	—
Pretax income (last fiscal or two of the last fiscal years)	$750,000	—	—
Public Float (Shares)[3]	500,000	1 million	200,000
Operating History	—	3 years	—

Standard	Initial NASDAQ National Market Listing		Continued NASDAQ National Market
	Alternative[1]	Alternative[2]	Inclusion
Market Value of Float	$3,000,000	$15,000,000	$1,000,000
Minimum bid per share	$5	$3	$1[4]
Shareholders		400[5]	
• if between 0.5 and 1 million shares publicly held	800	400	—
• if more than 1 million shares publicly held	400	400	—
• if more than 0.5 million shares publicly held and average daily volume more than 2,000 shares	400	400	—
Number of Market Makers	2	2	2

1. "Net Tangible Assets" refers to total assets (excluding goodwill) minus total liabilities.
2. Continued NASDAQ National Market inclusion requires net tangible assets of at least $2 million if the issuer has sustained losses from continuing operations and/or net losses in two of its three most recent fiscal years or $4 million if the issuer has sustained losses from the continuing operations and/or net losses in three of its four most recent fiscal years.
3. Public float is defined as shares that are not "held directly or indirectly by any officer or director of the issuer and by any person who is the beneficial owner of more than 10 percent of the total shares outstanding."
4. Market value of public float of $3 million and $4 million of net tangible assets.
5. Minimum of 300 shareholders with round lots.

NASDAQ requires a company qualifying for a listing to:
• Have at least two independent directors on its board
• Establish and maintain an audit committee comprised of a majority of independent directors
• Provide shareholders with quarterly and annual reports
• Examine related-party transactions for conflicts of interest
• Hold an annual meeting for shareholders and notify The NASDAQ Stock Market, Inc. of the meeting
• Specify in bylaws a quorum of not less than 33 1/3% of the outstanding shares of the company's common stock
• Solicit proxies and provide appropriate statements for all meetings of shareholders, as well as file the proxy solicitations with The NASDAQ Stock Market, Inc.
• Secure shareholder approval for certain transactions and increases in the amount of stock outstanding
• Refrain from taking certain actions on share issues that would disparately reduce or restrict the voting rights of existing shareholders
• Execute a NASDAQ National Market listing agreement
Foreign issuers may be exempted if compliance would be in contravention of law or business practices in the issuer's country of issue.

Investor Taxation: See New York Stock Exchange

Limitations: See New York Stock Exchange

Securities Lending: Available

Company Information:

10 Most Active Companies 1997

Name of Company	Share Trading Volume ('000)
Intel Corporation	3,887,851
Cisco Systems, Inc.	2,693,288
3Com Corporation	2,200,433
Microsoft Corporation	2,097,889
Oracle Systems Corp.	818,472
Ascend Communications, Inc.	1,945,994
Dell Computer Corporation	1,859,496
Applied Materials, Inc.	1,804,236
WorldCom Inc. Cl A	1,784,807
Sun Microsystems, Inc.	1,490,324

10 Major Companies 1997

Name of Company	Market Capitalization ($ US in millions)
Microsoft Corporation	156,004.75
Intel Corporation	114,830.37
Cisco Systems	56,441.80
Dell Computer Corporation	27,972.00
WorldCom, Inc.	27,441.59
Oracle Systems Corporation	21,877.36
Sun Microsystems, Inc.	14,938.41
Amgen	14,938.41

Name of Company	Market Capitalization ($ US in millions)
Tele-Communications Cl A	13,199.91
Fifth Third Bancorp	12,662.01

American Stock Exchange (AMEX)
86 Trinity Place
New York, NY 10006-1881
U.S.A.
Phone: (1-212) 306-1000
Fax: (1-212) 306-1152

Internet Address: www.amex.com

Trading Hours: 9:30–4:00

Exchange Holidays: (*See* New York Stock Exchange)

Listed Companies: 791

Market Capitalization:
US$137.3 billion 1995
US$135.1 billion 1996
US$162.2 billion 1997

Major Sectors: Energy, technology, mining, communications

Growth: AMEX Composite Index (XAX) up 101.33 points, 17% in 1997

History: Although the American Stock Exchange (AMEX) is second in size to NASDAQ, it remains the largest exchange in the United States for the trading of both equities and equity derivative securities. AMEX is an investment institution that commands international recognition, leading exchanges worldwide in trading floor technology, new product development, and services to its listed companies.

AMEX started as the "Curb Exchange" more than 100 years ago. The name originated from the hundreds of brokers and traders engaged in business on the streets of downtown New York City, near Trinity Place. After adopting their original charter in 1921, the brokers and traders moved indoors. Throughout its history, the American Stock Exchange has specialized in providing share trading for the more entrepreneurial companies. It has enabled many new companies to obtain capital in order to grow and prosper, thereby filling an important niche in the nation's economic development.

Companies listed on the AMEX choose a specialist unit made up of three or more specialists who trade the stock. The units operate from a trading post and act as auctioneers to provide a fair and orderly market for traded securities. Securities are traded by continuous auction, either through the specialist units or by computer, thereby providing fast and accurate order executions.

The AMEX is owned by its 661 regular members and 203 options principal members. Seats on the exchange allow members to trade on the exchange floor. Membership consists of many of the country's leading brokerage firms including Smith Barney, Bear Sterns, Merrill Lynch, and Paine Webber.

Classes of Securities: Common shares, preferred shares, corporate debt, government debt, options, and warrants on stock indices and equities

Indices: AMEX Composite Index (XAX)

On 2 January 1997 the American Stock Exchange introduced a new AMEX Composite Index with a new ticker symbol, XAX. The XAX is a market capitalization-weighted, price appreciation index, and replaces the AMEX Market Value Index (XAM) which, since its inception, had been calculated on a "total return basis" to include the reinvestment of dividends paid by AMEX companies. The new AMEX Composite Index is comparable to other major indices, which reflect only the price appreciation of their respective components.

In addition, AMEX has introduced five subindices that track the performance of companies in key AMEX market sectors: information technologies (ticker symbol XIT), financial (XFI), healthcare (XHL), natural resources (XNA), and industrials (XID). Sixteen industry and geographic subindices were discontinued on 31 December 1996.

Due to the changes in the way XAX is calculated, historical comparisons between old and new AMEX indices should not be made. In order to allow for year-to-date comparisons, historical data on XAX since 27 December 1995 has been provided to all major vendors.

Supervisory Organizations:
The Securities and Exchange Commission (SEC)
National Association of Securities Dealers (NASD)
American Stock Exchange (AMEX)

Settlement Details:

Shares: Trade date + 3 days (T + 3)

Trading: AMEX is an auction market where prices of securities are determined by public bids to buy and offers to sell. Procedures centralize order flow, which requires professionals to yield priority to public investors, thereby ensuring public buyers and sellers the best available prices. Surveillance systems provide the tools to keep high standards of public investor protection.

Listed companies choose specialist units made up of three or more individual specialists to trade their shares. Specialists function as auctioneers and provide a fair and orderly market, buying when there are no buyers and selling when there are no sellers. Stationed at a trading post on the trading floor, the specialist unit is responsible for overseeing all trading in its assigned stocks and options. Customer orders are sent to the specialist by computer or delivered in person by floor brokers. Most orders execute through the computer system without specialist intervention.

Listing Requirements: Approval for listing is granted at the discretion of the American Stock Exchange. The basic requirements for listing include:

- The nature of the business
- The market for the company's products
- The company's management reputation
- A historical record
- The company's growth pattern
- The financial integrity of the company
- The company's demonstrated earning power
- The company's future outlook

The numerical guidelines are important, but the AMEX has the flexibility to reject companies that do not meet the guidelines or accept companies that do not achieve all of the parameters.

Guideline/ Financial	Regular Requirement	Alternate Requirement
Pre-Tax Income	$750,000 latest fiscal year or 2 of most recent 3 years	n.a.
Market Value of Public Float	$3,000,000	$15,000,000
Minimum Price	$3	$3
Operating History	n.a.	3 Years
Stockholder's Equity	$4,000,000	$4,000,000

Guideline/ Distribution (For regular and alternative guidelines)	Regular Requirement		Alternate Requirement
	Alternative 1	Alternative 2	Alternative 3
Public Float	500,000	1,000,000	500,000
Stockholders	800	400	400
Average Daily Volume	n.a.	n.a.	2,000

AMEX acknowledges that some financially sound companies will be unable to fully comply with the listing guidelines. These companies may qualify for listing, provided they meet the numerical criteria out-lined above, have sufficient financial resources to conduct business for an extended period, and are otherwise considered suitable for AMEX listing.

Investor Taxation: See New York Stock Exchange

Limitations: See New York Stock Exchange

Securities Lending: Available

Company Information:

10 Most Active Companies 1997

Company Name	Trading Volume (millions)
Viacom Inc. (Cl. B)	223.1
Trans World Airlines, Inc.	222.8
Harken Energy Corporation	214.5
Echo Bay Mines Ltd.	188.7
JTS Corporation	177.0
Nabors Industries, Inc.	172.9
Hasbro, Inc.	159.1
Royal Oak Mines, Ltd.	14X.X
Grey Wolf Industries	132.9
IVAX Corporation	132.5

10 Major Companies

Name of Company	Market Capitalization (US$ millions)
B.A.T. Industries p.l.c.	29,122
Viacom, Inc.	14,597
Imperial Oil Ltd.	9,690
EdperBrascan Corporation	5,063
Hasbro, Inc.	4,219
Thermo Instrument Systems, Inc.	4,188
Nabors Industries, Inc.	3,189
Canadian Occidental Petroleum Ltd.	3,091
First Empire State Corporation	3,068
Keane, Inc.	2,675

Boston Stock Exchange (BSE)
One Boston Place
Boston, MA 02108
U.S.A.
Phone: (1-617) 723-9500
Fax: (1-617) 523-6603

Trading Hours: Monday–Friday, 9:30 to 4:00

Exchange Holidays: (*See* New York Stock Exchange)

Listed Companies:
160 exclusive listing
2,300, 95% of which are listed NYSE

Growth: See New York Stock Exchange

History: The third oldest stock exchange in the United States, the Boston Stock Exchange, Inc. (BSE) was established in 1834. Originally a market center for some of the country's largest companies, including banks, railroads, and insurance companies, the BSE played an important role in the nation's economy and in the financial prominence of New England.

Over the past decade, the BSE has been a rapidly growing participant in the National Market System through the Intermarket Trading System (ITS), a system that electronically links nine stock exchanges. The BSE is a self-regulatory organization run in accord with the rules and regulations of the Securities and Exchange Commission.

The exchange serves broker/dealer members, institutions, banks, pension funds, and their customers in the United States and abroad through the operation of a competitive marketplace for securities trading. The BSE operates as a central, continuous, open market where traders act as agents for buyers and sellers. The BSE trades more than 2,300 companies and the average daily trading volume is more than 6 million shares. The exchange trades more than 160 exclusively listed companies.

Trades are executed through the Boston Exchange Automated Communications and Order routing Network (BEACON), a fully integrated electronic trading and information system, and the Boston Exchange Automated surveillance Monitor (BEAM), the first real-time on-line surveillance system, which monitors all BSE trading activity while providing members with risk management information. The BSE Report Card provides measurement of execution quality and cost savings and is the most comprehensive customer report of any exchange to date. The Competing Specialist Initiative (CSI) is a program increasing competition for price improvement, adding both depth and liquidity for customers by allowing more than one specialist to compete for order flow. Another unique program offered by the BSE is Focus In/Out, designed to acquaint buy- and sell-side institutional traders and portfolio managers with the BSE services.

Supervisory Organizations:

The Securities and Exchange Commission (SEC)
The Boston Stock Exchange (BSE)

Depository: New England Securities Trust Company

Settlement Details:

Shares: Trade date + 3 days (T + 3)

Trading: The BEACON trading system was developed by and for the BSE. It is a real-time system designed to improve and expedite operations, while reducing cost and enhancing the quality of customer service.

As trading has moved toward screen-based systems, the BSE's BEACON system has led the way in fast, error-free trading, with its automated execution for trades of specified size. BEACON also offers the following refinements:

- Electronic limit order book
- On-line P&L inventory control
- Open order comparison
- On-line, real-time surveillance
- Interaction with ITS

BEACON also allows BSE members to enter orders and to cancel and change them without manual intervention or extra charge. Market orders are executed at or better than the national best bid or offer in less than 15 seconds, unless they are out of range and are stopped. This guarantees the best price to customers.

Market orders and marketable limit orders automatically cross with the electronic book and reports are simultaneously issued to the customer, the tape, and clearing. As markets move, messages alert the specialists, thus preventing reports on limit orders from being delayed. The system helps to give the investor the best price and fastest turnaround possible in the continuous auction market.

Listing Requirements:

Application Process:

1. Applicants send a non-refundable application fee accompanied by preliminary financial data and a recent annual report. Financial statements and balance sheets for the last two years, as well as the most recent opinion letter by an independent auditing firm, must also be included.

2. A preliminary review of the information (or prospectus, if the applicant is an initial public offering) along with the company's 10K and 10Q forms is performed by the exchange's listing department to determine the company's eligibility. Any company whose application does not meet the minimum standards will be rejected in writing at this stage in the process.

3. Applications fulfilling the preliminary requirements are forwarded to the BSE's vice president of listings for additional review. Those applicants meeting the listing requirements up to this point might be rejected due to any number of extraordinary circumstances, including the inappropriate use of proceeds, anticipated dilution of shareholder value, high percentage of

assets pledged, or problems with regulatory history. The vice president of listings prepares a written analysis that is presented to the exchange's Stock List committee for a vote.

4. The Stock List committee of eight members has broad experience in areas such as trading, investment banking, and finance. For approval, five of the committee members must vote in favor of the listing. Committee members consider both the corporate documents and the written analysis of the listings department in making their decisions. Considerations made by the Stock List committee include the viability of the security specialist interest and other factors not previously considered thus far in the review.

Basic Listing Requirements:

Category	Current Initial Requirements*	Maintenance Requirements
Assets	Total assets $3,000,000	$1,000,000
	[1]Tangible assets $2,000,000	
Earnings	$100,000 net income two of past three years or $2,000,000 net tangible assets	
Float	750,000 shares	150,000 shares
Market Value of Float	$1,500,000	$500,000
Beneficial Holders	[2]600	250
Minimum Bid Price	[3]$2	
Stockholders Equity	$1,000,000	$500,000

*As of 13 July 1994

1. Intangibles are "as defined" by the Exchange.
2. IPOs must meet requirements within 6 months of listing or face suspension and delisting after 30 days of such suspension.
3. IPOs must meet $2 per share requirement at time of listing. Non-IPOs must maintain $2 per share for 45 days prior to listing.

Investor Taxation: *See* New York Stock Exchange

Limitations: *See* New York Stock Exchange

Securities Lending: Available

Chicago Stock Exchange (CHX)
One Financial Place
440 South LaSalle Street
Chicago, IL 60605-1070

U.S.A.
Phone: (1-312) 663-2222, 2183
Fax: (1-312) 663-2396

Internet Addresses: www.chicagostockex.com

Trading Hours: Monday–Friday, 9:30 to 4:00

Exchange Holidays: See New York Stock Exchange

Listed Companies:
24 exclusively listed
3,278 total listed

Growth: *See* New York Stock Exchange

History: The original Chicago Stock Exchange (CHX) was formed in 1882. In 1949 this early organization merged with the St. Louis, Cleveland, and Minneapolis-St. Paul exchanges and became known as the Midwest Stock Exchange. The New Orleans Stock Exchange joined the Midwest in 1959. The name Chicago Stock Exchange came back into being on 8 July 1993.

The CHX responds to the needs of its member firms by providing fast, reliable, cost-effective trade executions in the National Market System. The CHX uses a computerized order execution system for trading called the Midwest Automated Execution System (MAX), which enables customer orders to be executed quickly at the best quoted price on any U.S. exchange without brokerage charges.

The CHX provides a facility for members to trade shares with each other and with members of other stock exchanges. As many as 2,630 New York Stock Exchange (NYSE) issues can be traded through the CHX, an amount equal to 94% of the total number of NYSE issues. Also traded are listed common shares, preferred shares, warrants, exclusive issues, and 100 of the most active OTC shares. Security issues are dually traded with the Pacific Exchange (PCX) as well as with the Boston Stock Exchange (BSE). The total number of issues traded on the CHX as of 24 February 1995 was 3,278.

Classes of Securities:
NYSE listed common shares, preferred shares, and warrants
AMEX listed common shares, preferred shares, and warrants
CHX exclusively listed equities
OTC equities
PCX dually listed issues
BSE dually listed issues

Indices: n.a.

Supervisory Organizations:
The Securities and Exchange Commission (SEC)
The Chicago Stock Exchange (CHX)

Depository: Midwest Securities Trust Company

Settlement Details:

Shares: Trade date + 3 days (T + 3)

Trading:

Floor Trading: After receiving an order to buy or sell, a brokerage firm sends the order to a floor broker on the CHX. The floor broker time-stamps the order ticket and checks the current price quote on the quote computer monitor, which continually updates price information from all regional and primary markets in the United States. The floor broker then approaches the specialist post where the company's shares are traded and asks the specialist to "quote the market" for the company. If the specialist on the CHX quotes the "best price available" and the order is a buy, the trade ticket is time stamped again and the contra broker's (selling broker's) trading acronym, or "give-up," is written on the ticket along with the agreed-upon price.

After the order is executed the ticket is placed in the tray on top of the specialist's post. A recorder (runner) retrieves the ticket from the specialist post and delivers it to one of the trade input operator stations located around the outside of the floor broker area.

To fill an order, the specialist may execute the order from an open order book or from the specialist book. The specialist book is an inventory of all open orders received from other floor brokers for a particular company's shares for which the specialist acts as agent. This includes limit orders. The specialist may also act as the seller (principal) on the contra side of the transaction and sell from inventory to fill the order.

Intermarket Trading System (ITS): If a price is better on another exchange and the CHX specialist is unable to better the price, the floor broker can send a commitment to a specialist on another exchange for execution via the Intermarket Trading System (ITS). ITS is an electronic link between all major U.S. exchanges. ITS input stations are placed around the outside of the floor broker area. An input operator types the information and sends the commitment to the designated exchange. If the order is executed, a confirmation message is received within two minutes. If the order is not executed, a cancellation notice is sent within two minutes.

MAX System: Floor brokers represent customers but are not always involved with customer trades. Often the transactions are automated. Orders for 2,099 shares or less, traded on the CHX, can be executed through the Midwest Automated Execution System (MAX). The specialist must accept and guarantee execution on all agency market orders of 100 shares up to and including 2,099 shares. MAX ensures fast, error-free executions at the best bid or offer price quoted in the National Market System

MAX directs the orders to the proper specialist and those within the parameters of execution criteria are filled in less than 15 seconds. A confirmation of the trade is sent to the Securities Industry Automation Corporation (SIAC), and the trade is displayed on the composite tape. Nearly 85% of the orders executed on the Chicago Stock Exchange are executed by the MAX system.

Chicago Match: A unique institutional trading system, the Chicago Match electronically matches users' orders through an allocation procedure. As an exchange-based system, it provides a facility for brokering trades, integrating the best of stock crossing systems with the advantages of the auction market. It is the only crossing system that combines the liquidity of the buy side, the sell side, and the exchange trading floor.

Chicago Match has several important features:

• It is designed to attract both passive and active trading styles.

• It allows buyer and seller to meet without disclosing their interests.

• It allows orders to be entered with premiums, providing a mechanism for handling buy and sell imbalances.

• It allows the use of disclosed orders with limits or premiums for price discovery.

• It makes match rates much higher than other systems.

• It provides a role for the broker to make markets and broker "near match" orders.

• It provides a facility for satisfying soft dollar and research commitments.

• Because it is an exchange-based system, it allows NYSE members participation as principal or agent.

Listing Requirements:

Minimum Listing Standards (foreign or domestic issuers):

Adequate Distribution	
Publicly held shares	250,000
Public shareholders	1,000 recommended
Minimum Bid	$5.00 recommended

Financial Strength

Net Tangible Assets*	$2,000,000
Net Income	Ability to earn $100,000
Working Capital	Adequate
Years in active business	Three

Corporate Governance

Management	Good character and integrity
Independent Directors	Two
Audit Committee	Independent Director Majority

Computed as total assets less intangible assets less total liabilities

Investor Taxation: *See* New York Stock Exchange

Limitations: *See* New York Stock Exchange

Securities Lending: Available

Brokerage Firms:
Advest, Inc.
29 South Main Street
West Hartford, CT 06107-2420
U.S.A.
Phone: (1-860) 521-7350

Andover Securities Corp.
401 South LaSalle Street
Chicago, Illinois 60606
U.S.A.
Phone: (1-312) 697-3300

Julius Baer Securities, Inc.
330 Madison Avenue
New York, NY 10017-5001
U.S.A.
(1-212) 297-3600

Robert W. Baird & Company Inc.
175 East Wisconsin Avenue
Milwaukee, WI 53202-4802
U.S.A.
Phone: (1-414) 567-9320

Baum (George K.) & Company, Inc.
120 West 12
Kansas City, MO 64116-4135
U.S.A.
Phone: (1-816) 421-3355

Bear Stearns & Company, Inc.
30 South Wacker Drive
Chicago, IL 60606-7410
U.S.A.
Phone: (1-312) 474-4600

Burke, Christensen & Lewis Securities, Inc.
30 South Wacker Drive
Chicago, IL 60606-7410
U.S.A.
Phone: (1-312) 474-4600

Credit Lyonnais Secs. (USA) Inc.
95 Wall Street
New York, NY 10005-4201
U.S.A.
Phone: (1-212) 428-6100

Dillon, Read & Company, Inc.
120 Wall Street
New York, NY 10005-3900
U.S.A.
Phone: (1-212) 701-2800

Donaldson, Lufkin & Jenrette Securities Corporation
140 Broadway
New York, NY 10005
U.S.A.
Phone: (1-212) 504-3000

CS First Boston Corporation
227 West Monroe
Chicago, Illinois 60606
U.S.A.
Phone: (1-312) 750-3000

Goldman, Sachs & Company
233 South Wacker Drive
Chicago, IL 60606-6391
U.S.A.
Phone: (1-312) 655-4600

Hambrecht & Quist, Inc.
One Bush Street
San Francisco, CA 94104
U.S.A.
Phone: (1-415) 576-3300

Merrill Lynch, Pierce, Fenner & Smith, Inc.
1 South Wacker Drive
Chicago, IL 60606-4676
U.S.A.
Phone: (1-312) 845-5500

The Pacific Exchange (PCX)
301 Pine Street
San Francisco, CA 94104
U.S.A.
Phone: (1-415) 393-4000

233 South Beaudry Avenue
Los Angeles, CA 90012
U.S.A.
Phone: (1-213) 977-4500

Internet Address: www.pacificex.com

Trading Hours:
Monday–Friday, 7:30 to 2:00 (Pacific Time)
50 minutes extra, extended session

Exchange Holidays: See New York Stock Exchange

Listed Companies: 1,770 (90% dually listed on other stock exchanges)

Growth: *See* New York Stock Exchange

History: The Pacific Exchange (PCX) dates back to 1882, when the San Francisco Stock and Bond Exchange formed during the California Gold Rush. The Los Angeles Oil Exchange was established during the Southern California oil boom in 1899. The San Francisco and Los Angeles exchanges operated as separate entities until 1956, when they joined to become the Pacific Coast Stock Exchange. In 1973 the exchange incorporated and became the Pacific Stock Exchange. Later the name was changed to the Pacific Exchange.

The exchange is a marketplace for publicly owned companies, security firms, broker/dealers, and individual and institutional investors. The PCX trades shares in more than 1,770 companies, options on more than 248 companies, LEAPS (extended term options), options on the Wilshire Small Cap Index., bonds, and several foreign index warrants.

The PCX is the only U.S. exchange with two separate trading floors, one in San Francisco and the other in Los Angeles, California. In the PCX auction market, the public customer's orders are filled before any dealer orders. The PCX also offers "Daylight Trading Time," which is an extension of the daily trading session, giving an additional fifty minutes after the New York Stock Exchange closes. More than 90% of transactions on the PCX are accomplished electronically through Pacific Computerized Order Access System (P/COAST), which is an integrated system that automatically executes market orders in only a few seconds.

Options trading on the PCX is through an open-outcry auction market. Open-outcry enables traders and brokers to transact option buys and sells face-to-face, and obtain the fairest price available. It is a market maker system that allows an easy shift of capital to meet trading demands.

Classes of Securities: Common shares, preferred shares, bonds and debentures, warrants, options

Supervisory Organizations:
Securities and Exchange Commission (SEC)
Pacific Exchange (PCX)

Depository: Pacific Depository

Settlement Details:

Shares: Trade date + 3 days (T + 3)

Trading: The Pacific Exchange operates as a continuous auction market where buyers or sellers of securities make bids to buy and asks to sell. The auction then ranks the bids and offers from highest to lowest. The highest outstanding bid and the lowest outstanding offer provide the quote. Of the many kinds of orders an investor can submit to the exchange, the most common is "at the market," which requests the order to be filled at the best available price.

Pricing is a matter of supply and demand. If the sellers predominate, the price of the security will decline. If buyers are eager, the price will rise. Public customer's orders must be filled before any dealer orders can be executed.

A vital component of the PCX auction market is the Intermarket Trading System (ITS), an electronic system that links all the U.S. stock exchanges. ITS helps to guarantee the best possible trade execution on all dually traded securities.

Orders are sent to the floor brokers of the Pacific Exchange by member brokerage firms on behalf of their retail and institutional investors. A member firm may have its own floor broker operation or may choose an independent broker. Independent floor brokers contract their services to various brokerage firms that do not have floor brokerage representation. The floor broker takes the order to the proper specialist.

Specialists are located at various trading posts on the trading floor. Every stock at the PCX is allocated to a specialist post. Specialists maintain a fair and orderly market in the daily trading of shares traded at their posts, matching and filling public orders. Specialists also act as "brokers' brokers" by helping with the filling of limit orders that are left with them by the floor brokers. When no public buyers or sellers are present in the market, the specialist acts as principal, buying or selling from the specialist's own account. The specialist can be in the position of "buyer or seller of last resort" when trading levels become extra active.

Listing Requirements: The Pacific Exchange has established a list of criteria to assist companies considering listing. Issues failing to meet the requirements are not considered for listing. Approval or rejection of any application is at the discretion of the exchange. Other criteria are also evaluated, including the nature of a company's business, the market for its product, the reputations of its management, and any other relevant factors. Meeting the basic criteria does not guarantee a listing on the Pacific Stock Exchange.

Step 1: Preliminary Review

To begin the listing process, the prospective issuer should submit the following:

For Initial Public Offering	For Secondary Offering
Current registration statement (with exhibits)	Most recent Form 10-K and subsequent 10-Qs
	Most recent proxy materials (NASDAQ and foreign-listed companies should also provide the last six months trading reports)
A legal opinion that the issuer complies with the PCX Rules of Corporate Governance	A legal opinion that the issuer complies with the PCX Rules of Corporate Governance
A $500 processing fee	A $500 processing fee

If the issue is approved, the processing fee is applied to the original listing fee.

Received materials are forwarded to a listings analyst for review. If the exchange listing criteria are met, the analyst schedules the issue for presentation to the Equity Listing Committee (ELC), which recommends approval or rejection to the exchange board of governors.

Step 2: Approval to List

The Pacific Stock Exchange's Senior Listing Representative contacts the company on approval by the ELC and remains the company's liaison throughout the listing.

1. The company submits materials for listing:

   a. Original listing application

   b. Listing agreement

   c. Resolutions authorizing listing by issuer's board of directors

   d. Opinion of counsel regarding legality of issue and issuer

   e. Statement of purpose

   f. Specimen stock certificate

   g. Agreement with registrar/transfer agent/warrant agent

   h. Remainder of listing fee

      (for initial public offerings)

   i. Any amendments to registration statement

2. Company files Exchange Act registration statement with the SEC:

   Securities must be registered with the Securities and Exchange Commission (SEC) under Section 12(b) of the Securities Exchange Act of 1934, before being admitted to trading on the exchange.

3. Company reserves a ticker symbol:

   The exchange can reserve a one-, two-, or three-character ticker symbol. Issuer requests for specific symbols should be made as early as possible.

When all the materials are received, the exchange's board of governors reviews those issues recommended by the ELC and votes on a final approval. The exchange then certifies that approval to the SEC.

In situations of simultaneous listing on the New York or American exchanges, some duplication of forms may occur. The PCX may accept some New York or AMEX exhibits instead of its own materials.

Step 3: Admission to Listing

When the board of governors grants approval, the issue will be allocated to a specialist. Issues that trade exclusively on the PCX are allocated to one specialist. Issues that also trade on the AMEX or NYSE are allocated to a specialist in both San Francisco and Los Angeles.

Preparations for issuers in the public offering stage:

1. At least four business days before the effective date of the offering, the issuer notifies the exchange of an anticipated pricing date and SEC approval of the registration statement.

2. When the registration is declared effective, the issuer sends three copies to the exchange and commences sale of offering.

The exchange distributes a press release announcing the trading of the security, its trading symbol, and the specialist firm handling its trading, four business days before the anticipated trading date. When the SEC grants effectiveness of the certification, the issue becomes a listed security.

Initial Quantitative Listing Requirements:

	Common Shares		Preferred[1]	Bonds & Debentures	Warrants[2]
	Basic	**Alternate**			
Net Tangible Assets	$2,000,000		$2,000,000	$2,000,000	
Net Worth		$8,000,000			
Pre-Tax Income					
After-Tax Income	$100,000[3]		$100,000	$100,000	
Public Float (Shares)	500,000	1,000,000	500,000		500,000
Market Value of Float	$1,500,000	$2,000,000	$1,000,000	$5,000,000	
Principal Amount			$5,000,000		
Bid Price	$3[4]	$1			
Public Beneficial Holders	500	500	250	200	250
Operating History	3 years		3 years		
Corporate Governance	Yes	Yes	Yes	Yes	

1. If the security is convertible into a class of equity security, the security must meet the applicable equity listing requirements.
2. The underlying security of the warrants must also qualify for listing on the exchange.
3. The issuer must meet the $100,000 net income requirement in the past fiscal year, two of the last three fiscal years, or have total net tangible assets of $2,500,000.
4. The closing bid price must have been held for the majority of business days for the most recent six-month period prior to the date of application by the user.

SCOR and Regulation A Shares:

Step 1: Obtain permit from every state where the offering will be sold.

Step 2. Sell the offering either directly or through a broker/dealer syndicate.

Step 3: Apply to the Pacific Exchange when the minimum listing criteria are met:

Minimum Company Requirements:

Total net tangible assets:	$500,000
Total net worth:	$750,000

Minimum Offering Requirements:

Offering price per share	$5
Publicly held shares (float)	150,000
Public beneficial holders	250

*Qualitative criteria must also be satisfied.

Qualitative Listing Requirements for All Issues:
1. Financial Condition
   a. Accounting practices
   b. Ability to service existing debt and other obligations
   c. Financing availability for current programs and expansion
   d. Development expenses in relation to equity and revenues
2. Nature and Scope of Operations:
   a. Demonstrated ability to develop new products or properties
   b. Potential or proven market for existing future products
   c. Plans for future development and resources expansion
3. Purpose of Offering Proceeds
   a. Product development
   b. Marketing and licensing
   c. Fund acquisitions of complementary businesses
   d. Repayment of debt
   e. Working capital
   f. Compensation to insiders
4. Composition of Assets
   a. Reserves
   b. Royalties
   c. Rights and patents
5. Management's Experience and Reputation
6. Governmental Policies on Products or Properties
7. Extent of Competition, Economic Conditions Within Industry
8. Bond/Debenture Credit Rating by S&P and Moody's

Foreign Issuers: Non-U.S. companies desiring to list on the Pacific Exchange must meet the regular requirements and file an Original Listing Application Foreign Issuer.

Investor Taxation: *See* New York Stock Exchange

Limitations: *See* New York Stock Exchange

Securities Lending: Available

Brokerage Firms:
Bear, Stearns & Co., Inc.
245 Park Avenue
New York, NY 10167
U.S.A.
Phone: (1-212) 272-2000

Blair (Williams) & Company
222 West Adams Street
Chicago, IL 60606
U.S.A.
Phone: (1-312) 236-1600

Deutsche Morgan Grenfell/C.J. Lawrence, Inc.
31 West 52nd Street
New York, NY 10019
U.S.A.
Phone: (1-212) 469-5000

Dillon, Read & Company, Inc.
120 Wall Street
New York, NY 10005-3900
U.S.A.
Phone: (1-212) 701-2800

Donaldson, Lufkin, & Jenrette Securities Corporation
140 Broadway
New York, NY 10005
U.S.A.
Phone: (1-212) 504-3000

Edwards (A.G.) & Sons, Inc.
One North Jefferson Avenue
St. Louis, MO 63103
U.S.A.
Phone: (1-314) 289-3000

Hambrecht & Quist L.L.C.
One Bush Street, 16th Floor
San Francisco, CA 94104
U.S.A.
Phone: (1-415) 576-3300

Kemper Securities, Inc.
77 West Wacker Drive
Chicago, IL 60601
U.S.A.
Phone: (1-312) 574-6600

Lehman Brothers, Inc.
American Express Tower, 20th floor
New York, NY 10285

U.S.A.
Phone: (1-212) 526-7000

Mabon Securities Corp.
One Liberty Plaza
165 Broadway
New York, NY 10038
U.S.A.
Phone: (1-212) 346-5400

Merrill Lynch, Pierce, Fenner & Smith, Inc.
World Financial Center
250 Vesey Street
North Tower, Building D
New York, NY 10281
U.S.A.
Phone: (1-212) 449-1000

Montgomery Securities
600 Montgomery Street, Suite 2100
San Francisco, CA 94111
U.S.A.
Phone: (1-415) 627-2000

Morgan (J.P.) Securities, Inc.
60 Wall Street
New York, NY 10005-2836
U.S.A.
Phone: (1-212) 483-2323

Morgan Stanley & Co., Inc.
1251 Avenue of the Americas
New York, NY 10001-0190
U.S.A.
Phone: (1-212) 703-4000

Nomura Securities International, Inc.
Two World Financial Center
Building B, 18th Floor
New York, NY 10281-1198
U.S.A.
Phone: (1-212) 667-9300

Paine Webber, Inc.
1285 Avenue of the Americas
New York, NY 10019
U.S.A.
Phone: (1-212) 713-2000

Smith Barney, Inc.
388 Greenwich Street
New York, NY 10013
U.S.A.
Phone: (1-212) 566-4592

Company Information: *See* New York Stock Exchange

Philadelphia Stock Exchange (PHLX)
1900 Market Street
Philadelphia, PA 19103-3584
U.S.A.
Phone: (1-215) 496-5000, (1-800) THE-PHLX
Fax: (1-215) 496-5653

Internet Address: www.phlx.com

Australia: (1-800) 12-7570
Hong Kong: (800) 6893
Japan: 0031-122868
Singapore: 800-1200542
Other Countires: 1(215) 496-1611

European Office:
Philadelphia Stock Exchange
12th Floor
Moor House
119 London Wall
London EC2Y 5ET
England
Phone: (44-171) 606-2348
Fax: (44-171) 606-3548

Trading Hours:

| Monday–Friday | 9:30 to 4:15 | (Eastern Standard Time) |
| | 6:00 P.M. to 2:30 P.M. | Currency Options |

Exchange Holidays: See New York Stock Exchange

Listed Companies:

2,700 share issues
  500 equity options
    12 sectors index options

Major Sectors: Airline, banking, forest products, gold-silver, phone, semiconductor, utility

History: The Philadelphia Stock Exchange (PHLX) is the oldest marketplace in America for securities. The PHLX continues to be a market leader in innovative products and services and currently trades more than 2,700 stocks, 500 equity options, 12 index options, and 10 currency options.

The roots of the exchange were formed through the efforts of a group of Philadelphia brokers who set up signal stations on high points across New Jersey. Signalmen stationed across the New Jersey countryside watched through telescopes as people flashed light signals transmitting news of stock prices and other important information from the center of New York. The information could be sent from New York to Philadelphia in approximately 10 minutes, negating the advantage of New York speculators. The system remained in use until the implementation of the telegraph in the 1840s.

The history of the PHLX can be traced back to 1754 when a group of some 200 local merchants and businessmen subscribed £348 to finance the opening of the London Coffee House. In a parallel to the spread of coffee houses in England and Continental Europe, Philadelphia's Coffee House soon became the focal point of the city's business and political life. The Coffee House was a meeting place for traders across the United States and became a center for protest against the restrictive tax practices imposed by the English on the fast-growing economies of the New World. The Coffee House was closed during the British occupation of Philadelphia and was replaced by the City Tavern, later renamed the Merchants Coffee House, as the exchange for the city.

The securities brokers who met at the Merchants Coffee House attempted to distinguish themselves from other merchants by establishing the Philadelphia Board of Brokers in 1790. The founding president, Matthew McConnell, was a military man who had served in the French and Indian War. In an age before the widespread trading of company shares, the exchange focused on the buying and selling of government paper. However, the first issues of shares in the First Bank of the United States and Schuylkill and Susquehanna Navigation Company were heavily oversubscribed by investors eager to profit from the booming U.S. economy. Similar capital-raising exercises for the Philadelphia and Lancaster Turnpike Company, owners of the first turnpike in the United States, were followed by new issues in the Pennsylvania Bank (1793), the Philadelphia Bank (1803), and the Farmers' and Mechanics' Bank (1807).

The earliest years of the 19th century saw rapid growth on the Philadelphia Stock Exchange. The War of 1812 led to a boom in both banking and insurance. The Second Bank of the United States was one of over 120 banks to receive a charter. Twenty-eight million dollars of the Second Bank's initial capital was raised via a public stock issue, with one investor buying some $3 million in equity for his own portfolio. Other merchants were now able to pay for insurance on their maritime cargo, so many new firms came to the fledgling insurance market to raise capital. The War of 1812 altered America's well-established trading links with Europe, with many entrepreneurs setting up manufacturing plants to replicate imported goods

The original stock exchange building of Philadelphia, Pennsylvania. *(Spectrum Photo)*

from England and France, which were no longer available.

The Philadelphia Stock Exchange was widely recognized as the premier capital market in the fledgling country. Brokers from New York, who had set up an informal exchange under the famous buttonwood tree on Wall Street, sent a young emissary, William Lamb, to Philadelphia to learn everything he could about the successful exchange. Lamb returned to New York with the basis of a constitution that was to provide the regulatory framework for stockbroking on Wall Street. The canal boom of the 1820s led to the building of the Erie Canal, which eventually made New York the most important exchange in the United States.

In 1837 the economy of the United States overheated, and the mania for borrowing led to defaults and a lack of investor confidence. The collapse of 1837 marked the end of Philadelphia's position as the financial center of the United States, and the railway boom, which followed the rush to build canals, was largely financed by the increasingly powerful Wall Street bankers. A boom in the building of streetcars for inner-city transportation was, however, largely centered on the streets of Philadelphia.

In 1870 PHLX set up a clearing house to facilitate the settlement and delivery of securities. Three years later the bankruptcy of Jay Cooke, the man behind the Northern Pacific Railroad and much of the financing of the Civil War, rocked the PHLX and led to a demand for tougher regulation of new issues and trading. However, the exchange has closed only on two occasions during its long history: first, in 1914 when the outbreak of World War I saw the market close for four months, and second, in 1933 when President Roosevelt declared a ten-day bank holiday.

With the ending of World War II, the PHLX sought partnership with other exchanges on the East Coast. PHLX merged with the Baltimore Stock Exchange in 1949 and, four years later, with the Washington Stock Exchange. The growing network of exchanges also signed up Pittsburgh, Boston, and Montreal as associate members.

New computer technology in the 1960s and 1970s led to more efficient trading and the introduction of new trading products. The introduction of exchange traded currency options in 1982 created a boom in currency trading that attracted clients from outside the United States to the exchange. Philadelphia responded to this global demand by introducing round-the-clock trading in 1990. The introduction of the United Currency Options Market in 1994 further increased customer demand for currency options.

Classes of Securities: Common shares, preferred shares, government and corporate bonds, derivatives

Supervisory Organizations:
Securities and Exchange Commission (SEC)
Philadelphia Stock Exchange (PHLX)

Depository: The Philadelphia Depository Trust Company

Settlement Details:

Shares: Trade date + 3 days (T + 3)

Trading: Trading of equities is accomplished through use of the specialist system either on computer or by open-outcry.

Original Listing Criteria for Common Stocks

Standard	Tier 1	Tier 1 (Alt)	Tier 2	Tier 2 (Alt)
Shares Outstanding	none	none	none	none
Public Float	**	**	750,000	750,000
Aggregate Market Value	$3,000,000	$15,000,000	$2,250,000	$2,250,000
Net Tangible Assets	$4,000,000	$12,000,000	$1,500,000	$2,000,000
Net Income	$750,000 latest year or $400,000 in 2 of 3 most recent years	none	$100,000 in 3 of last 4 years	none
Share Price	$5.00	$3.00	$3.00	$3.00
Shareholders	**	**	500	500
Audit Committee	no	no	yes*	yes*

*A majority of the members comprising the audit committee must be independent directors.
**The public distribution original listing standard covers public float and share holders of record in the chart below.

Public Float	Shareholders
If >1,000,000	400
If >500,000, but <1,000,000	800
If >500,000 & average	400
6 month daily volume of 2,000 shares	

Investor Taxation: *See* New York Stock Exchange

Limitations: *See* New York Stock Exchange

Securities Lending: Available

Arizona Stock Exchange (AZX)

AZX, Inc., formerly Wunsch Auction Systems, Inc., operates the Arizona Stock Exchange, an equity trading system now conducting daily auctions in over 8,000 equities. In November 1991 the Arizona Corporation Commission voted approval for the exchange's move to Phoenix. In December 1991 Arizona's Commerce and Economic Development Commission voted to fund the plan. Trading commenced on 30 March 1992.

AZX has offices in the following cities:
Phoenix
2800 N. Central Avenue
Suite 1230
Phoenix, AZ 85004
U.S.A.
Phone: (1-602) 222-5858
Internet Address: www.azx.com

New York
20 Exchange Place
31st Floor
New York, NY 10005
U.S.A.
Phone: (1-212) 514-8890

San Francisco
2215 Chestnut St.
San Francisco, CA 94123
U.S.A.
Phone: (1-415) 776-4100

Introduction: The Arizona Stock Exchange, operated by AZX, Inc., is the only open-screen call market for equity trading. The single price auction is designed to allow anonymous participants to trade at the truest market prices with the lowest possible transaction costs.

The Arizona Stock Exchange conducts one daily auction ending at 5 P.M. Eastern time. Prior to 5 P.M., participants enter limit orders into the system. Orders can be displayed in the Open Book or concealed in the Reserve or Balanced Book. Orders placed in the Open Book can be viewed by all participants, creating an advertisement to trade, which attracts counterparties. NYSE, AMEX, and NASDAQ NMS stocks are eligible for trading.

During the auction, the central computer in Phoenix continuously calculates and displays the single price that matches the most shares based on the participant's limit prices. Once the single price of the trade is calculated, participation is determined by time priority. After the auction, matched order instructions are transmitted to and executed by ITG, Inc. The trade date is the next business day, and settlement occurs between three and five days after the trade date. Other than next-day trade date, AZX trades are cleared and settled like ITG POSIT trades.

Accessing the System: AZX provides software free of charge to enter the auction. The software installs on any existing personal computer with a modem.

Participants can also access the auction via:
- ITG's Trading Desk
- ITG's QuantEX order routing system
- Proprietary methods tailored to the participant's needs

Order Placement: Participants have four books into which to place their orders.

Open Book: Orders entered in the Open Book are displayed to other participants in the system.

Early Open Book orders receive three primary benefits:
- Lower commissions
- Higher fill ratios
- Priority over Reserve and Balanced Book orders

Reserve Book: Participants who do not wish to advertise sensitive order flow can place their orders in the Reserve Book. These orders will remain in the Reserve Book until a match occurs, in which case the exact number of shares filling in the Reserve Book gets "flushed out" into the Open Book. Orders can also be flushed out of the Reserve Book into the Open Book at any time during the auction.

Balanced Book: Participants who have strict constraints (net dollar buy/sell, minimum share size, etc.) can use the Balance Book. Orders placed in the Balanced Book become eligible to match with other Open, Reserve, or Balanced Book orders only at the end of the auction. This guarantees that constraints are honored and that orders are not seen unless filled.

Match Book: Participants who wish to do internal crosses between accounts can use the Match Book. Users select the price and trade date, either same day or next day.

Commissions: AZX only charges for matched trades. Reserved and Balanced Book orders are charged 1 cent per share. Commissions for orders entered directly into the Open Book range from 1/3 of a cent up to 1 cent per share, depending on the time of order entry. The earlier the order placement in the Open Book, the lower the commission. Match Book commissions are 1/2 cent per share.

Over 8,000 stocks are eligible to trade on the Arizona Stock Exchange. These stocks include listed as well as over the counter National Market issues. Non-National Market issues on the "small cap" list, however, are not eligible for trading.

The SEC requires all customers with direct access to be institutions, such as mutual funds, pension funds, bank trust departments, broker/dealers, and insurance companies. Individuals are not allowed to trade on the AZX.

National Association of Securities Dealers Automated Quotation System (NASDAQ)
National Association of Securities Dealers
1735 K Street, NW
Washington, DC 20006-1506
Phone: (301) 590-6500

Internet Address: www.nasdaq.com

The Maloney Act of 1934 provided a framework for the self-regulation of over-the-counter securities in the United States. The NASDAQ system was set up in 1971 to provide a computer-based system for the execution of orders and the dissemination of information with regard to over-the-counter issues. In recent years, NASDAQ has been the fastest growing stock exchange in the United States and has developed a reputation for dealing in fast-growth companies, especially in the high technology sectors.

NASDAQ provides three primary services to its subscribers:
1. The NASDAQ Quotation System
2. The Small Order Execution System (SOES)
3. The Trade Acceptance and Reconciliation Service

NASDAQ Quotation System: The NASDAQ Quotation System gathers, verifies, and distributes quotation information to system subscribers. Level 1 service provides the best bid and ask prices in all securities to salespeople and dealers in the OTC market. It also broadcasts last-sale price and volume data on more than 3,000 issues of the NASDAQ National Market System.

Level 2 service is provided through NASDAQ-owned computer terminals. It is available to both member and non-member subscribers and is a composite display with current quotes submitted by the market makers in each issue. The quotes provide the best available bid and ask prices (referred to as "the inside market"), indexes, volume, and market summary information.

Small Order Execution System (SOES): SOES is a Tandem-based system that enables all securities orders of up to 1,000 shares for the 3,000 NASDAQ National Market System issues and all securities orders of up to 500 shares for nearly 3,000 other NASDAQ issues to be automatically executed by computer.

Trade Acceptance and Reconciliation Service (TARS): Also a Tandem-based system, the TARS assists the back offices of member firms to resolve uncompared and advisory OTC transactions processed through participating clearing organizations.

NASDAQ is also linked electronically to London's International Stock Exchange.

Other Investment Information:
Securities and Exchange Commission
Judiciary Plaza
450 Fifth Street NW
Washington, DC 20549
U.S.A.
Phone: (1-202) 272-2800

International Trade Administration
Department of Commerce
14th Street and Constitution Avenue, NW
Washington, DC 20230
U.S.A.
Phone: (1-202) 482-2000

US Chamber of Commerce
1615 H Street, NW
Washington, DC 20062
U.S.A.
Phone: (1-202) 566-8195

United States International Trade Commission
500 E Street SW
Washington, DC 20436
U.S.A.
Phone: (1-202) 252 1822

UNLISTED SECURITIES MARKET (USM; United Kingdom)

Set up in 1980, the *Unlisted Securities Market* (USM) facilitated trading in those shares that were not listed on the main market of the London Stock Exchange.

The USM has now been superseded by the Alternative Investment Market (AIM).

See also ALTERNATIVE INVESTMENT MARKET (AIM); LISTED SECURITIES; OVER THE COUNTER (OTC); STOCK MARKET.

UNREALIZED PROFITS/LOSSES

Sometimes referred to as paper gains or paper losses, *Unrealized Profits/Losses* are those trades that have not been finalized with a closing transaction. For example, a person buys XYZ Corporation at $40 per share. If the share later trades at $50, the investor will have an unrealized gain of $10 per share. It will become a realized gain only if the investor sells at $50 per share.

If another investor sold short XYZ Corp. at $40 per share and the price is now $50, the investor has an unrealized loss of $10 per share. This will become a realized loss if the investor buys back the shares at the $50 level.

See also CAPITAL GAIN; CAPITAL LOSS; DIVIDEND; SELLING SHORT.

UNSOLICITED CALL

See COLD CALL.

UNWIND A TRADE

To *Unwind a Trade* is to reverse a securities position with an offsetting transaction. Unwinding will mean buying a security if it has been sold short or selling a security if one was purchased.

Unwinding is also used to describe transactions made to correct an error. If a broker enters a sell order instead of a buy order, it will be necessary to buy the shares back to close out the short position and place the originally intended buy order.

See also BUYING TO CLOSE; ERROR; SELLING SHORT.

UPTICK

When a securities trade is executed at a price higher than the most recent transaction it is called an *Uptick*. If XYZ Corporation trades at $50 and that trade is followed by another at $50 1/8, it is called an uptick. If it trades at $50, then at $50 1/8 and again at $50 1/8 it is known as a zero plus tick. The terms are important to selling short on an exchange. Exchange short sells can only be done on upticks or zero plus ticks.

If a security price trades at a lower price than the most recent transaction, it is called a downtick.

See also DOWNTICK; LAST TRADE; SELLING SHORT; TICK; ZERO PLUS TICK.

URUGUAY, REPUBLIC OF

Uruguay (Republica Oriental del Uruguay) is South America's second smallest country. It is bordered on the north and northeast by Brazil, on the south by the estuary of the Rio de la Plata, and on the west by Argentina.

Area: 68,037 square miles (176,215 square km)

Population: 3,186,000 (89.6% urban; 10.4% rural)

Form of Government: Republic, with two legislative houses: Senate—31 members; Chamber of Representatives—99 members. Head of state and government: President.

Official Language: Spanish

Capital: Montevideo

Largest Cities: Montevideo, 1,311,976; Salto, 80,823; Paysandu, 76,191; Las Piedras, 58,288; Rivera, 57,316

Economy:

Currency: Uruguayan Peso ($)

National Budget: Revenue—$15.3 billion; expenditures—$17.0 billion (social security and welfare: 60.0%; general public services: 14.1%; capital investments: 8.7%; interest on Public Debt: 6.1%; subsidies: 4.0%)

Public Debt: US$4.6 billion

Gross National Product: US$12.3 billion

Principal Products: Rice, sugar cane, wheat, barley, and other vegetables; livestock; rubber; textiles

Foreign Trade (Imports): US$2.8 billion (machinery and appliances: 21.1%; transport equipment: 15.5%; chemical products: 11.5%; mineral products: 10.2%; synthetic plastics, resins, and rubber: 6.0%; textile products: 6.0%; base metals and products: 5.3%; from Brazil: 25.6%; Argentina: 23.5%; United States: 9.4%; Italy: 4.9%; Spain: 4.4%; Germany: 3.6%)

Foreign Trade (Exports): US$1.9 billion (live animals and live-animal products: 25.6%; textiles and textile products: 20.5%; vegetable products: 13.0%; hides and skins: 11.1%; synthetic plastics, resins, and rubber: 3.3%; processed foods: 3.0%; to Brazil: 25.7%; Argentina: 20.0%; United States: 6.8%; Germany: 6.3%; United Kingdom: 3.8%; Italy: 3.2%)

Stock Exchanges: 1
Montevideo Stock Exchange (MSE; Bolsa de Valores de Montevideo; BVM)
Misiones 1400
Montevideo 11000

Uruguay
Phone: (598-2) 442 951
Fax: (598-2) 442 961

Internet Address: www.bvm.com

Trading Hours: Monday–Friday, 2:00 to 3:00

Office Hours: Monday–Friday, 9:00 to 5:00

Exchange Holidays:

1–6 January	18 July
14, 15 February	25 August
31 March	5 September
19 April	12 October
1, 18 May	2 November
19 June	25 December

Listed Companies: 20

Market Capitalization: US$1.3 billion

Major Sectors: Money market instruments

History: In 1994 more than 80% of trading on the Montevideo Stock Exchange (MSE) was in U.S. dollar-denominated state bonds and bills. Only 3% of trading was in shares.

The MSE is considering cross-listing with other stock exchanges within the Federation of Ibero-American Stock Exchanges. It is also in the process of converting to an electronic trading system. The exchange is also part of the Mercosur agreement that will provide a common market between Brazil, Argentina, Uruguay, and Paraguay.

Classes of Securities: Ordinary shares, U.S. dollar-denominated state bonds and bills, participations (derivatives)

Indices: None

Supervisory Organizations: Uruguay government

Trading:

1. Main market trades mostly money market instruments and relatively few share issues.
2. A parallel market, the Electronic Stock Market of Uruguay (ESMU), was established in 1994.

Listing Requirements: Contact the Montevideo Stock Exchange for full information.

Investor Taxation: There are no personal income tax or interest rate taxes.

Limitations:

1. There are no ownership restrictions on foreign investors.

2. Capital movement is unrestricted for investment by foreigners, with the exception of the broadcasting industry.
3. Repatriation conditions are set in a system contract signed by the foreign investor and government:
    a. Capital cannot be repatriated in the three years following the investment.
    b. Earnings not transferred abroad within two years shall be considered capitalized as of the date of their generation.
    c. Remittances abroad shall be charged first against earnings and subsequently against capital.

The system guarantees such transfers of capital and earnings, even in the event of any modification of the current system of free remittance of capital. The system is not commonly used, because of the general freedom to invest, withdraw, and remit capital and earnings.

Company Information:

9 Most Active Companies

Name of Company	Trading Value (US$ millions)
Montevideo Refrescos	76.1
Alcan	14.2
Fabrica Nacional de Papel	9.2
CINOCA	7.6
Malteria Oriental	6.7
Fabrica Nac. de Cerveza	5.8
Frigorifico Modelo	5.2
Cristalerias del Uruguay	4.8
FUNSA	0.9

Other Investment Information:

Committee for Investment Development
Executive Government Office
Edeficio Libertad
Avda Luis Alberto de Herrera 3050
Montevideo
Uruguay
Phone: (598-2) 808 110
Telex: UY-DICOPRE 22280

Ministry of Economy and Finance
Colonia 1089
Montevideo
Uruguay
Phone: (598-2) 919 102
Telex: 6269

Ministry of Industry and Energy
Rincon 747
Montevideo
Uruguay
Phone: (598-2) 902 600
Telex: 22072

Central Bank of Uruguay
Avda Juan P. Fabini
Montevideo
Urguay
Phone: (598-2) 917 117
Telex: 6659

U.S. AND EUROPEAN STOCK EXCHANGE REGULATIONS

U.S. and European Stock Exchange Regulations have been created to simplify dual compliance. The regulations of the European Association of Securities Dealers Automated Quotation System (EASDAQ) are based upon the rules and requirements of the National Association of Securities Dealers Automated Quotation System (NASDAQ) and the information disclosure requirements of the Securities and Exchange Commission (SEC). This allows a company admitted to NASDAQ to gain a dual trading facility on EASDAQ with few additional obligations with which to comply. A company admitted to EASDAQ will find that the steps necessary to fully comply with NASDAQ and SEC rules have been greatly reduced.

Dual trading of a company's shares on EASDAQ and NASDAQ will mean the initial public offering, secondary offerings, and the trading in the company's stock will be directly accessible to intermediaries and investors across Europe and the United States, and the bouts of daily trading in their securities will be almost doubled. EASDAQ is able to offer a dual trading facil-

ity for those companies listed on NASDAQ. This provides companies with the opportunity to have their shares traded across Europe and the United States. Dual trading offers two primary advantages: first, the hours of trading in a dual listed company's shares will be extended; second, the company will gain access to, and profile with, a wider range of investors.

A prospectus issued by an EASDAQ company is required to be approved by the relevant competent authority, which could be the Belgian Banking and Finance Commision (CBF) or the relevant body in the company's home state. Once approved, the prospectus can be issued throughout Europe. This means the issue and trading of EASDAQ securities can take place across Europe and the United States in a practical and cost-effective way. There is also the possibility of providing EASDAQ admission and trading facilities to companies from non-European Union countries.

A competent authority is defined by the European Union's Investment Services Directive. Each European Union country has been required to nominate a financial regulator to be its competent authority. The role of the competent authority is to supervise the content of prospectuses for the public issue of securities. The approval of a prospectus by a competent authority allows the prospectus to be used throughout the rest of the European Union.

See also EUROPEAN ASSOCIATION OF SECURITIES DEALERS AUTOMATED QUOTATION (EASDAQ); NATIONAL ASSOCIATION OF SECURITIES DEALERS AUTOMATED QUOTATION SYSTEM (NASDAQ); SECURITIES AND EXCHANGE COMMISSION (SEC).

UTILE (Italy)

See PROFIT.

V

VALEUR ADMISE À LA BOURSE (France)
See LISTED SECURITIES.

VALEUR AU PORTER (France)
See BEARER CERTIFICATE/SECURITY/SHARE.

VALEURS NON COTÉES (France)
See LISTED SECURITIES.

VALEUR SOUS JACENTE (France)
See UNDERLYING SECURITY.

VALORA DE MAERCATO (Italy)
See CURRENT MARKET VALUE; MARKET PRICE.

VALORE (Italy)
See COMMON STOCK.

VALORE (AL) PORTATORE (Italy)
See BEARER CERTIFICATE/SECURITY/SHARE.

VALUATION
See MARKET CAPITALIZATION.

VALUE LINE INVESTMENT SURVEY
Value Line Publications
220 E. 42nd Street
New York, NY 10017
Phone: (1-212) 907-1500

Value Line Investment Survey is a subscription investment advisory and information service that provides company and industry historical data, analysis, and specific price objective forecasts to investors. By making use of a computer model based on earnings momentum, Value Line analysts rank company shares by "timeliness" and "safety."

Risk ratings are assigned to each company's shares, identifying the price volatility of each issue in relation to the market average. Industry groups are also ranked for timeliness and safety.

The ranking system is as follows:

Rank	Safety
1	Highest
2	Above average
3	Average
4	Below average
5	Lowest

Value Line reports provide detailed company financial information stretching back over several years, including such items as annual earnings, revenues, average p/e ratio, and dividends. Current debt, insider buying and selling, percentage of shares held by institutions, and analysts' comments regarding changes in a company are also included.

Publications by Value Line include:
Value Line Investment Survey
Value Line Convertibles
Value Line Mutual Fund Survey
Value Line Options
Value Line OTC Special Situations

See also FITCH INVESTOR'S SERVICE INC.; MOODY'S INVESTOR'S SERVICES; RATING; STANDARD & POOR'S RATINGS.

VANDERBILT FAMILY
The *Vanderbilt Family* fortune was established by "Commodore" Cornelius Vanderbilt (1794–1877), who, at the time of his death, left behind the first American estate worth more than $100 million. At the time, a skilled worker earned approximately $600 a year, and the budget of the federal government of the United States was less than $350 million. The Commodore made his first fortune in sail and steamboat lines, buying his first boat with $100 that he borrowed from his mother. He specialized in breaking monopolies by running cheap ships at lower rates and forcing his competition to buy him out if they wanted to stay in business. In 1853, *Town and Country* reported that he was "the largest owner of steamboat property in the world," and that he was "worth 10 cents a minute."

The Commodore made his first foray into the stock market during the 1849 California gold rush. He formed a transit company that could carry passengers and goods from New York to San Francisco via Nicaragua, bypassing the longer Panama route. At first the Commodore schemed to build a canal in Nicaragua. He sold stock in his transit company to many private investors, making them think that he might also get financing from Barings in London. Vanderbilt promised Nicaraguan politicians $10,000 for approving the contract to build the canal, along with $200,000 in stock and 20% of the canal's profits for 20 years. The value of the stock shot up, but when Vanderbilt announced that Barings would not finance the canal, shares dropped again, and he bought them at par. Then he began transporting passengers across a combined steamboat and overland route, building Accessory Transit into a thriving company. When the gold

Cornelius Vanderbilt. *(Spectrum Photo)*

rush began to pan out after four years, the Commodore sold his shares at a huge profit, and bragged that he now had a fortune worth more than $11 million, "invested better than any other eleven millions in the United States."

The Commodore's steamboat fortune was indeed well invested. In the 1840s and 1850s, he began buying securities. In keeping with his lifelong interest in transportation, he bought stock in several railroads. Although he managed railroad operations skillfully, the Commodore made his greatest profits not from the railroads' revenues but from manipulating his shares of railroad stock. He began buying shares of the New York and Harlem line in the late 1850s, when its prices were low. By 1857 he had a major interest of 1,001 shares. In 1863 the New York City Common Council announced that it was granting the New York and Harlem line a franchise for a street railway from the Battery to Union Square. In response to this news, the Commodore began buying stock in the line again, pushing the price from $9 to $50 per share. Many corrupt New York City councilmen began selling New York and Harlem stock short, because they planned to cancel the franchise and force the price to fall. Unfazed, the Commodore kept buying, and the stock price rose to $170 per share. The short-sellers had to pay a price that was several times what they had expected to pay—and they had to pay it to the Commodore and his partners, who by now owned most New York and Harlem stock.

Next, the Commodore took over a major interest in the New York and Hudson line, in response to another short-selling scheme by corrupt officials. This time the short-sellers were Daniel Drew, one of the Commodore's partners, and several corrupt members of the New York State Legislature, which set rail routes and rates. The legislators planned to pass a bill merging the New York and Hudson with the New York and Harlem, increasing stock prices, and then defeat the bill, causing the stock to plunge. The Commodore bought all the New York and Hudson shares that were then on the market and 27,000 more that Drew issued illegally. Drew and the legislators proved unable to meet their calls and deliver the stock they had sold short. Finally, the Commodore sold them the stock at $285 per share, after he was informed that if the price went any higher, every broker on Wall Street would go out of business. In the end, the Commodore was left with 18,000,000 New York and Hudson shares out of a total of 28,500,000—enough to make him president of the line. He issued more stock, improved service on the line, and managed to pay stockholders a dividend of 8% annually.

The Commodore used actual coercion to gain control of the New York Central line, which he hoped to merge with the New York and Hudson. During a brutally cold winter, he announced that the New York and Hudson line would not carry passengers all the way to their connection with the Central, instead dropping them off a mile away and leaving them to struggle through the snow with their baggage. Vanderbilt was investigated by the legislature, but he got the Central, and promptly inflated its stock by issuing 80% more. Then he merged it with the New York and Hudson, and inflated the joint company's stock still more. Revenues from the lines increased steadily as New York City grew, and the Commodore became ever more wealthy. To consolidate his railroad monopoly, however, Vanderbilt needed the Erie Railroad. To attain it, he fought an expensive legal battle with Daniel Drew, who had become his partner again and then double-crossed him by issuing new Erie Railroad stock every time the Commodore thought he had already bought it all. The Erie Railroad War, as it became known, may have been the only battle the Commodore ever lost—it cost him between $1–$2 million, and in the end, he sold his Erie stock and gave up control of the line to Jim Fisk and Jay Gould.

The Commodore made money on the railroads he still controlled by watering the stock and then making the water good by cutting costs and improving services. At the time of his death in 1877, he left a personal fortune worth more than $100 million. Not wanting to split the wealth among his numerous children, Vanderbilt left most of it to his oldest son, William Henry. With the assistance of financier J.P. Morgan, William Henry sold approximately 200,000 New York Central shares for $35 million. He still held enough stock to control the railroad, but he took the money he made from the sale and invested in U.S. government and state and local securities, which were mostly tax-free. In the meantime, he expanded the New York Central and acquired other railroads. Between his management of the rail lines and his government security investments, William Henry managed to double the family fortune by the time of his death in 1885. At the same time, his son Cornelius, an able railroad manager, was trebling the $5 million bequest his grandfather had left him.

At William Henry's death, his fortune was divided among various family members. Control of most of the New York Central stock passed to J.P. Morgan by 1903. The Vanderbilt family fortune was large enough that the Vanderbilts remained famous as one of America's richest families for much of the 20th century. However, few Vanderbilts today are millionaires, and none is on the *Forbes* list of the 400 richest people in America. Today, the most famous Vanderbilt is probably Gloria Vanderbilt, who built a career as a designer in the 1970s and 1980s.

See also SELLING SHORT; WATERED STOCK.

VARIABLE ANNUITY

A *Variable Annuity* is a life insurance company product similar to a mutual fund. A purchaser pays a premium to the company, either on a one-off basis or over a number of periods. Income from an annuity is first available when a person "annuitizes" and can be paid immediately or on a regular basis over a number of months. Income generated by a variable annuity depends on the success of the securities in the "separate account." A fixed annuity pays out a constant rate. The backing behind any annuity is provided by the insurance company involved.

See also MUTUAL FUND; PREMIUM; UNIT INVESTMENT TRUST/UNIT TRUST.

VEDETTES (France)
See BLUE CHIP.

VEGA

The opposite of Delta, *Vega* is an analyst's description of the volatility of an equity issue and is the measurement of the relationship between a market price and option premium in the market.

See also EQUITY; OPTION; PREMIUM.

VEKEHRSWERT (Germany)
See CURRENT MARKET VALUE; MARKET PRICE.

VENDEUR D'UNE POSITION (France)
See OPTION WRITER.

VENDITA (IN) DANNO (Italy)
See SELL OUT.

VENEZUELA, REPUBLIC OF

Venezuela (Republica de Venezuela) is a country at the northern extremity of South America. It is bordered on the east by Guyana, on the south by Brazil, and on the west by Colombia.

Area: 352,144 square miles (912,050 square km)

Population: 21,844,000 (84.6% urban; 15.4% rural)

Form of Government: Federal multiparty republic, with two legislative houses: Senate—53 members;

Chamber of Deputies—199 members. Head of state and government: President.

Official Language: Spanish

Capital: Caracas

Largest Cities: Caracas, 1,822,465; Maracaibo, 1,249,670; Valencia, 903,621; Barquisimeto, 625,450; Ciudad Gualyana, 453,047

Economy:

Currency: Venezuelan Bolivar (B)

National Budget: Revenue—B 961.5 billion; expenditures—B 1.2 trillion (subsidies: 29.8%; goods and services: 28.9%; capital transfers: 17.6%; interest payments: 16.6%)

Public Debt: US$26.9 billion

Gross National Product: US$58.9 billion

Principal Products: Sugarcane, bananas, corn, rice, coffee, livestock; petroleum; metal manufactures

Foreign Trade (Imports): B 997.5 billion (machinery: 32.8%; transport equipment: 17.9%; chemicals: 12.0%; basic metal manufactures: 6.6%; textile products: 3.8%; cereals and preparations: 3.6%; precision and photographic equipment: 2.7%; from United States: 46.2%; Japan: 7.6%; Germany: 5.6%; Italy: 4.7%; Colombia: 4.2%; Brazil: 3.5%; Canada: 3.2%; France: 2.9%)

Foreign Trade (Exports): B 1.3 trillion (crude petroleum and petroleum products: 77.5%; basic metal manufactures: 8.2%; to United States: 56.4%; Netherlands Antilles: 9.0%; Colombia: 6.1%; Brazil: 2.5%; Germany: 2.3%; the Netherlands: 2.2%; Mexico: 1.5%; Japan: 1.5%)

Stock Exchanges: 2

Caracas Stock Exchange (CSE; Bolsa de Valores de Caracas)
Calle Sorocaima, Edificio Atrium
Piso 1, El Rosal, Caracas 1060
Venezuela
Phone: (58-2) 905-55-11/905-55-60
Fax: (58-2) 905-58-14

Internet Addresses: www.caracasstock.com

Trading Hours:
Monday–Friday, 9:45 to 11:45
Pre-opening, 9:00 to 9:45
Pre-closing, 11:45 to 12:15

Office Hours: Monday–Friday, 8:30 to 12:30 and 1:30 to 5:00

Exchange Holidays:

1, 5 January	12 October
19 March	11, 25 December
24 July	

Listed Companies: 159

Total Market Capitalization:

At 31 December 1997

Local Currency (Millions)	**US Dollars (Millions)**
4,165,690	8,261

Major Sectors: Banking, financial services, utilities, textiles

Share Price Performance:

(% Change)

1992	–35
1993	62
1994	69
1995	69
1996	296
1997	20

History: The Caracas Stock Exchange originated in the mid-19th century. The Commercial Code of 1873 contained a legal framework for an exchange, and in 1917 a law was passed to regulate operations. However, the Bolsa de Comercio de Caracas was not founded until 1947. Trading began with 18 share issues and six government bonds.

The name changed to Bolsa de Valores de Caracas in 1974, and the exchange became an active member of the IberoAmerican Federation of Stock Exchanges (FIABV).

Fifty-five members, primarily brokerage firms, are a part of the stock exchange. Management is by a board of directors and an internal administration for operations. The exchange is supervised by the National Securities Commission (CNV).

Class of Securities: Common shares and Treasury bills

Indices:

Caracas Stock Exchange Price Index (CSE Index) (1971 base = 100)

Indice de Capitalization de la BVC (December 1993 = 1,000)

Supervisory Organizations:

Comision Nacional de Valores (CNV) (National Securities Commission)

The Superintendency of Foreign Investment (SIEX)

Superintendency of Banks of the Central Bank

Depository: None

Settlement Details:

Shares:

Trade date to trade date +1 day (T to T + 1)

Regular: Trade date + 5 days (T + 5)

Forward: Trade date + 6 to 60 days (T + 6 to 60)

Trading: The Automated System for Stock Transactions (SATB) executes transactions. It replaced the traditional floor trading system in late 1992. Brokers enter orders from their offices rather than on the exchange floor.

Listing Requirements: A company seeking a listing must have minimum paid-up capital of B 20 million. If the company is not registered at the CNV, the public offering must be for at least 20% of its subscribed capital.

Listed companies are required to submit quarterly financial statements within a 30-day period following the end of the quarter. Audited annual statements must be submitted within 30 days of the shareholder's general meeting.

Other relevant market information, such as dividend announcements, rights issues, and any changes in accounting procedures, must also be reported. Companies must also report shareholdings of 5% and more.

Investor Taxation:

Non-resident income tax is 34%.

Capital gains tax is 1% of all security sells.

Dividends are tax exempt.

Limitations: Foreign Investment Law Decree #727 allows foreign participation in stock markets. The law does not require prior approval for foreign investors. Venezuela allows the free repatriation of investment proceeds and has eased many other restrictions for foreign investors. Foreign investment in shares of some industries (e.g., oil and gas) is prohibited, and share ownership in banks or other financial institutions in Venezuela is limited to 19.9%.

Securities Lending: Available, but seldom used

Brokerage Firms:

Alcantara V. Rafael, Cavelba S.A.

Edf. Sudameris, piso 9 Ofc. 902,

Av. Urdaneta

Caracas

Venezuela

Phone: (58-2) 562-13-33

Bancaracas Casa de Bolsa C.A.
Edif. Ibarras, Piso 7, Esq Ibarras,
Av. Urdaneta
Caracas
Venezuela
Phone: (58-2) 561-63-21

Bancor Mercado de Capitales C.A.
Torre Europa, Nivel oficinas,
Av. Fco de Miranda
Caracas
Venezuela
Phone: (58-2) 951-00-18

Banguaria Mercado de Capitales C.A.
Torre K.L.M., Piso 12, Av. Romulo
Gallegos. Sta Eduvigis
Caracas
Venezuela
Phone: (58-2) 283-55-45

C.A. Sofimara Mercado De Capitales
Casa de Bolsa "Sofimerca"
Edif. Grupo Financiero Bancomara
Av. Bolivia
Caracas
Venezuela
Phone: (58-2) 781-78-77

Capitales Noroco-Casa De Corretaje, C.A.
Torre Banhorien, PH-A Av Casanova
c/Las Acacias
Caracas
Venezuela
Phone: (58-2) 781-55-33

Coronado, Fernando
Edif. Citibank, Mezzanina,
Camelitas a Altagracia
Caracas
Venezuela
Phone: (58-2) 82-58-22

Escotet Valores C.A.
Torre Orinoco, P.H, Cruce Calle Orinoco
c/Veracruz, Las Mercedes
Caracas
Venezuela
Phone: (58-2) 920-13-1

Financorp Valores C.A.
C.C.C.T., Sector Yarey, Mezz. 2, Of.

M-2, Chuao
Caracas
Venezuela
Phone: (58-2) 959-08-56

Flores R., Victor Julio
Edif. Karam, Piso 4, Ofc. 421,
Pelota a Ibarras, Av. Urdaneta
Caracas
Venezuela
Phone: (58-2) 563-03-9

Company Information:

The Best Performing Shares in the Country

Company Name	Share Price Change 1 January 1997 to 31 December 1997 (%)
Cantv	53
Electricidad De Caracas	45
Corimon	32
Banco Provincial	32

The Largest Companies in the Country by Market Capitalization as of 31 December 1997

Company Name	Market Capitalization Local Currency (Millions)	Market Capitalization US Dollars (Millions)
Electricidad De Caracas	1,176,668	2,333
Cantv	1,022,862	2,028
Banco Provincial	488,702	969
Sivensa	351,322	697
Vencemos '1'	288,628	572
Mavesa	190,650	378
Vencemos '2'	155,356	308
Manpa	128,464	255
Banco Venz.De Credito 'A&B'	90,331	179
Banco Mercantil 'A'	84,000	167
Ceramica Carabobo 'A'	27,494	55
Mantex	26,161	52
Ceramica Carabobo 'B'	21,413	42
Envases Venezolanos	21,168	42
Hl Boulton & Co.	18,306	36
Dominguez & Cia. Caracas	17,325	34
Sudamtex 'B'	16,261	32
Sudamtex 'A'	13,448	27
Corimon	11,828	23
Venepal 'A'	6,193	12

Regional Exchanges:
Maracaibo Stock Exchange (MSE; Bolsa de Valores de Maracaibo)
Edif. Banco Central de Venezuela
Calle 96, Esq Con Avda. 5
Maracaibo
Venezuela
Phone: (58-61) 22-69-77
Fax: (58-61) 22-76-63

Other Investment Information:

Investment Banks:
Financorp
CCCT, Sector Yarey, Mezz. 2.
Chuao
Venezuela
Phone: (58-2) 959-00-02

Finantrust-Capitales Noroco
Torre Banhorien, PH-A,
Av. Casanova con Las Acacias
Caracas
Venezuela
Phone: (58-2) 781-74-44

M. M. Fintec
Av. Andrés Bello, Urb. Mariperez,
Edificio Las Fundaciones, Piso 4.
Caracas
Venezuela
Phone: (58-2) 573-69-22

Merinvest
Av. Andrés Bello, Urb. Mariperez,
Edf. Fondo Comun, Piso 13.
Caracas
Venezuela
Phone: (58-2) 574-97-11

Oberto, Sosa y Asociados
Av. Francisco de Miranda,
Urb. Los Palos Grandes,
Edif. Mene Grande, Mohedano,
Piso 2
Caracas
Venezuela
Phone: (58-2) 285-50-80

Venezuelan Asset Management
Av. Los Chaguaramos, Urb. La Castellana,
Centro Grencial Mohedano

Oficina 3-D
Caracas
Venezuela
Phone: (58-2) 761-07-10

General Information
Economic Planning Advisory Board
Ministry of Development
Edif. Sur
Centro Simon Bolivar
Caracas
Venezuela
Phone: (58-2) 41-93-41
Telex: 22753

National Securities Commission
Avenida Urdaneta, de Santa Capilla a Carmelitas,
Edificio Banco Central de Venezuela
Caracas
Venezuela
Phone: (58-2) 81-93-83

Superintendency of Foreign Investment
Esquina Bolsa a Mercaderes
Edif. La Perla
El Silencio
Caracas
Venezuela
Phone: (58-2) 483-66-66

Ministry of Development
Edif. Sur
Centro Simon Bolivar
Caracas
Venezuela
Phone: (58-2) 41-93-41
Telex: 22753

Superintendency of Foreign Investment
Esquina Bolsa a Mercaderes
Edif. La Perla
El Silencio
Caracas
Venezuela
Phone: (58-2) 483-66-66

VENTE À DECOUVERT (France)
See SELLING SHORT.

VENTURE CAPITAL
Venture Capital is money supplied by persons or organizations to fund new or growing businesses.

Because of the inherent risk in starting a new business, venture capitalists require a large return on their investment, often in the form of a significant equity stake. In most situations, venture capitalists will take equity positions by receiving ownership shares in the company. Their gain comes when the company performs an initial public offering and its shares begin to trade on the market. Investors can also be repaid by receiving a percentage of profits, a royalty on sales, or preferred shares.

Typical sources for venture capital include high networth individuals, bank subsidiaries, Small Business Investment Companies (SBICs), pooled venture capital funds, and venture capital limited partnerships. In the United States, the Small Business Administration promotes venture capital programs by licensing and financing SBICs.

Although they are more expensive than other sources of capital, entrepreneurs will seek venture capital if they are unable to obtain enough financing through more conventional means. Finding a venture capital partner who has knowledge of the business or sector in which a company operates will often bring significant intangible benefits in addition to the supply of capital.

See also CAPITAL; LISTED SECURITIES; MARKET CAPITALIZATION; OVER THE COUNTER (OTC).

VERKAUFEN (France)
See SELL.

VERTICAL SPREAD
To buy an option at one strike price and sell an option of the same class at the next higher or lower strike price is known as a *Vertical Spread*. Both options have the same expiration dates.

Essentially there are four types of vertical spreads:
Vertical bull call spreads
Vertical bull put spreads
Vertical bear call spreads
Vertical bear put spreads

Vertical Bull Spread: With the price of XYZ Corporation at $63 per share, write (sell) a January 70 call at $3 (premium) and buy an XYZ Corporation January 60 call at $6 (premium). The net difference is a cost of $300 (maximum risk) without including commissions in the calculations.

The maximum return is limited to $700. The maximum profit is attained when the market share price of XYZ Corporation rises to $70 per share and stays above that level until expiration.

Vertical Bear Spread: A bear spread is a vertical spread with the simultaneous purchase of one option and the sale of a second option, both having the same underlying shares and expiration date, but differing strike prices. The term "vertical" comes from the same expiration date for both options. A bear spread position can be taken with either puts or calls.

A vertical bear spread is a strategy to achieve profitability from the price decline of the underlying security.

For example, if an investor believes the price of XYZ Corporation will drop from its current $55 level, a bear spread could be a way to take advantage of the decline. If the shares are owned, the investor could sell the stock or sell a covered call on the shares. If the shares are not owned, the investor could sell naked (uncovered) calls on the shares, but the action carries the high risk. The price of XYZ Corporation could rise and the investor would be forced to pay a high price to deliver the shares when they are called.

Option quotes on XYZ Corporation show:
XYZ October 60s at $2
XYZ October 50s at $8

The investor sells one XYZ 50 call at $8 and simultaneously buys one XYZ 60 at $2, thus netting the difference of $6, for a total dollar amount of $600 ($6 x 100 shares).

Risk: If the price rises and the XYZ 50 call (short call) is exercised, the investor can exercise the 60 call to cover. The loss would amount to $400, not including commissions.

If the price rises to $65 and the 50 call is assigned to the investor:

• Exercise the XYZ 60 and deliver the shares (below $60 the investor could buy at market)

• Investor pays $60 per share and sells at $50 per share, equals a difference of $1,000

• $1,000 minus the $600 received in option premiums equals a loss of $400 (not including commissions)

Reward: If the investor's assessment is correct and the price of XYZ Corporation drops, both options will expire worthless and the investor profits the $600 difference in premiums paid and received.

$800 received for the 50s – $200 paid for the 60s = $600 profit (less commissions)

See also CALENDAR SPREAD; OPTION; SPREAD.

VERTRILUNGSBRIEF (Germany)
See ALLOTMENT LETTER.

VERTYBINIAI POPIERIAI (Lithuania)

Vertybiniai Popieriai is the term for securities traded on the National Stock Exchange of Lithuania. This class includes ordinary shares, ordinary bearer shares, preference named shares, and Lithuanian Government Securities (LGS).

National Stock Exchange of Lithuania activity growth:

	1994 Turnover (US$ millions)	1995 Turnover	Change %
PC shares	11.844	30.309	156
IC shares	0.537	1.815	238
Bank shares	3.988	4.969	25
Total	16.368	37.093	127

(PC is Public Corporation, IC is Investment Company)

See also BEARER CERTIFICATE/SECURITY/SHARE; LITHUANIA; SECURITY.

VERTYBINIY POPIERIY JYVKIA (Lithuania)

Vertybiniy Popieriy Jyvkia is an event such as the payment of dividends and interest, a change in a share's nominal value, or a change in the authorized capital, which alters the characteristics of an issuer's securities.

These changes can have an impact on the trading price of a company's issued securities, and, therefore, investors must be notified of their occurrence.

Exchanges have specific reporting rules on such events. Companies failing to report information can be subject to delisting from the exchange.

See also DELISTING; LISTING; LITHUANIA.

VERTYBINIY POPIERIY KOTIRAVIMAS (Lithuania)

Vertybiniy Popieriy Kotiravimas is a price quotation for securities.

See also LITHUANIA; QUOTE.

VERWALTUNGSRAT (Germany)

See BOARD OF DIRECTORS.

VOLATILE

When the price of a share or a market moves in a highly active way, displaying rapid advances and sudden declines, it is described as being *Volatile*.

Individual share price volatility can be influenced by factors relating to the company's industry or specific influences on the business activity of the company. Earnings reports, litigation, financing difficulties, labor relations, exporting, or pending acquisi-

tions can all be factors that contribute to the volatility of a share's market price.

Stock markets have a tendency to be theme driven. Sometimes the theme is a change in interest rates, the strength of the currency or the balance of trade, inflation, or a combination of these factors. All of these factors can influence investor activities in the stock market.

Low liquidity for a specific share or market index can be a major influence on volatility.

High volatility stocks show far greater price fluctuations than those with low volatility. Market timing becomes very important when buying or selling volatile issues.

See also BETA; INTEREST/INTEREST RATES.

VOLATILITY

See VOLATILE.

VOLUME

Volume refers to a total number of securities traded, and is usually quoted on a daily basis. It can refer to the total volume of shares or bonds traded for a specific company, or to the total volume of shares or bonds traded on a major stock exchange.

Some analysts see volume as an indicator of strength. If the stock market index advances on weak volume, the advance is thought unlikely to continue and is expected to turn and drop. It signals the presence of a small number of buyers at this price level. If the market index turns and begins to decline and the volume becomes strong, it is considered a sign of great weakness with the selling expected to continue. Declines are always caused by a greater presence of sellers than buyers.

Although heavy volume on advances is a sign of strength, there are times when market direction suddenly changes, especially when it approaches new highs or pushes through resistance levels. Volume is one of the key indicators closely watched by technical analysts.

See also RESISTANCE LEVEL; SUPPORT/SUPPORT LEVEL; TECHNICAL ANALYSIS.

VORLAUFIGE DOVODENDE (Germany)

See INTERIM DIVIDEND.

VORSTAND (Germany)

See BOARD OF DIRECTORS.

VORZZUGSAKTIE (Germany)

See PREFERRED STOCK (PFD).

VOTING SHARE

A *Voting Share* is any share of a company that grants voting and proxy rights to the shareholder. Normally the ratio is one vote per share, but there may be exceptions in the shares allowed for cumulative voting.

With cumulative voting, the number of shares owned by a shareholder is multiplied by the number of directors being elected. The shareholder can cast all the votes for one director or spread them equally, up to the total number of votes calculated.

If a shareholder owns 500 shares and there are 3 directors being elected, the shareholder has 1,500 votes for cumulative voting. The 1,500 votes can be cast for one, divided equally, or mixed in any way the shareholder desires.

See also BOARD OF DIRECTORS; PROXY.

W FORMATION
See TECHNICAL ANALYSIS.

WACHSTUMSWERTE (Germany)
See GROWTH.

WALK-AWAY MERGER (United States)
Walk-Away Merger describes a situation in which a target company walks away from a merger agreement because the acquiring company's share prices have fallen below a predetermined level.

In the United States, mergers generally require regulatory approval, which often takes a long time to be granted. Meanwhile, the acquiring company may experience a price decline in the shares that were intended to fund the acquisition, and the target company can decide to cancel the agreement.

See also ACQUISITION; MERGER; TAKEOVER/TAKEOVER BID.

WALL STREET
Wall Street refers to both the street name and the general location in New York City of the largest financial district in the United States. This area contains the New York Stock Exchange, American Stock Exchange, a large number of brokerage firms, and a variety of other financially related firms.

Wall Street is also a synonym for the general concept of capital finance in the United States, where hundreds of billions of dollars are exchanged every year. It is often referred to as "the Street."

See also THROGMORTON STREET; UNITED STATES.

WALL STREET
If one film sums up the heady days of the stock market boom of the 1980s, it is Oliver Stone's *Wall Street* (1987). Michael Douglas won an Academy Award for Best Leading Actor for his role in *Wall Street* as the avaricious corporate raider Gordon Gekko.

Looking up Wall Street in New York City. *(Spectrum Photo)*

The plot line is a fairly simple tale of how a young broker, Bud Fox (Charlie Sheen), is corrupted by his stock market hero, the ruthless Gekko. Fox works for a second-tier brokerage, spending long hours cold-calling clients from a computerized printout and studying share movement charts in his bedroom at night. By contrast, Gekko lives the life of a tycoon, complete with subservient wife, glamorous mistress, huge estate, and expensive *objets d'art*. He makes money through stock market scalping and insider trading.

The naive Fox's attempts to meet Gekko are futile until his 40th visit to Gekko's impressive office. A box of Havana cigars is deemed sufficient tribute, and he is granted a brief audience with the tycoon. Fox is immediately seduced by the sense of power that Gekko radiates as he shouts buy and sell orders at his underlings and checks his personal wealth on a vast bank of dealing screens. When Fox passes a valuable piece of inside information to Gekko, his fate is as good as sealed.

Gekko persuades Fox to spy on a competitor and obtain more insider information. Fox's rewards come in the shape of a promotion, an expensive Manhattan apartment, and Gekko's cast-off mistress. Fox takes on many of Gekko's personality traits, becoming aggressive with clients and jettisoning old friends who he fears will hold back his meteoric rise. Gekko's philosophical gems, such as "lunch is for wimps" and "every battle is won before it is fought" guide Fox on his relentless march toward success.

In contrast to the naked greed espoused by Gekko is Fox's father, a humble worker at BlueStar Airlines. His homespun ethics and distrust of those who make money trading the assets of others are, unfortunately, ignored by his headstrong son. In a pivotal moment in the movie, Gekko whips the BlueStar's shareholders into a frenzy with a speech that champions the belief that "greed is good." Any vestige of morality has been subsumed by a collective avarice.

Gekko, the ultimate predator, has plans to buy Blue-Star only to break it up and resell the stripped down assets to the highest bidder. Almost too late, the young wheeler-dealer Fox realizes that he has put the livelihoods of his father and his father's colleagues at risk.

Martin (left) and Charlie Sheen in *Wall Street* (1988). *(AP/Wide World Photos)*

Only a last-ditch effort by Fox, the airline unions, and one of Gekko's rivals can halt the break-up.

Wall Street accurately catches the flavor of the real Wall Street during the bull run of the 1980s. Now the film appears dated, but it is still intriguing as an example of the decade's get-rich-quickly mentality.

See also BECK, JEFF.

WALL STREET JOURNAL, THE

The Wall Street Journal is the most respected financial newspaper in the United States, and has a larger readership than any other daily newspaper in the country. It is published Monday through Friday. The structure of the paper has changed very little in more than 100 years since it was founded. It includes tables reporting the stock market activity of the previous day; analyses of business topics; and editorials and readers' letters. The *Journal* prints the prices of active stocks and bonds, government Treasury bills, mutual funds, puts and calls from the options exchanges, government agency securities, foreign currencies, and commodities futures. Since the 1960s, the *Journal*'s front page has also carried one or two feature articles on subjects other than business and economic news.

Charles Dow of Dow Jones and Company founded *The Wall Street Journal* in 1889. At the time, few reliable sources of information about the stock market existed. Speculators could manipulate the stock market by spreading rumors that would cause the price of a particular stock to rise or fall. Charles Dow and his partners, Edward Davis Jones and Charles Milford Bergstresser, were determined to provide accurate, reliable, up-to-date information about the stock market. They warned their reporters against accepting bribes, and refused to accept outside financial assistance for the paper. At first they delivered bulletins, called "flimsies," to Wall Street financial houses several times a day. They also published the Dow Jones averages, which were the average closing prices of certain stocks, railroads, and industrials that Dow considered to be reflective of market trends. The flimsies and a news bulletin called *Customers' Afternoon News Letter* established the reputation of Dow Jones and Company for covering the markets accurately and honestly. The *Afternoon News Letter* grew into *The Wall Street Journal*, which takes its name from the street that even before the American Civil War was recognized as the financial capital of the United States.

Today *The Wall Street Journal* is respected around the world, and millions of investors read it every day. In the 1990s, the *Journal* began producing an electronic, interactive edition on the World Wide Web. This edition contains everything that is in the print *Journal*, but it is updated all day long, seven days a week, and includes real time stock prices. Readers of the electronic edition can choose to have breaking news e-mailed to them throughout the day. In addition, the electronic edition contains links to other financial web pages, a searchable archive, and bulletin boards on financial and economic subjects. It also includes the *Personal Journal*, a version of the electronic edition that can be customized for each user. The *Personal Journal* provides news that is of particular interest to an individual user, and includes a portfolio that an individual can use to track the progress of particular stocks or mutual funds.

Journal readers who want to do extremely in-depth research can link to another Dow Jones electronic tool: the Publications Library. The Publications Library is a full-text archive that contains articles from major business publishers, including *The Wall Street Journal*, and major U.S. and international newspapers and newswires.

Unlike most World Wide Web media sites, the *Wall Street Journal* charges a subscription fee. When its fees were first introduced in 1996, the readership of the electronic *Journal* dropped from 600,000 to 60,000. But by 1997 its readership was back up to 115,000. However, the interactive edition of *The Wall Street Journal* does not rely solely on subscription revenues. It offers advertising that can be precisely targeted to a certain type of reader. For example, some ads appear only when readers access the *Journal* from a particular location, such as America Online or Netcom. Other ads appear only to readers with a certain level of income or education. Still other ads appear only to readers of a certain age. Most readers of the *Journal*'s electronic edition have advanced degrees, make more than $115,000, and do not read the print version of the *Journal*.

The Wall Street Journal's foray into electronic publishing is setting the standard for other business publishers. In 1997, for the first time, electronic publishing accounted for half of the business publishing industry. By the year 2001, revenues for on-line business publishers are expected to reach $37.9 billion.

See also DOW JONES INDUSTRIAL AVERAGE (DJIA).

WALLPAPER (United States and Others)

Wallpaper is a colorful expression used by some U.S. stockbrokers to describe a worthless or nearly worthless security. The implication is that since the security

The *Wall Street Journal*s presses. (AP/Wide World Photos)

has no monetary value, it could be hung on a wall for decoration.

See also BOOK-ENTRY; CERTIFICATE; SCRIPOPHILY.

WANDELOBLIGATION (Germany)
See CONVERTIBLE; SECURITY.

WAR AND STOCK MARKETS
Historically, the relationship between *War and Stock Markets* has been a complex one. Certainly many wars have been fought principally for economic reasons, yet it would probably be impossible to prove that any particular war was fought for the purpose of stimulating stock markets. It would be more accurate to say that changes in stock markets have reflected underlying economic forces that have, in particular political conditions, given rise to war. War has often had such economic effects as a major increase in debt associated with military spending, while at the same time stimulating technical innovation, organization, and productivity, all of which has had an impact on stocks. Thus the relationship under consideration concerns how war has affected the stock market—in periods of preparation for or threat of war, during the actual fighting, and in the aftermath of war. Some examples will illustrate the varying effects of wars on stock markets.

An initial boost to U.S. markets resulted from the sale of Revolutionary War bonds in 1790. The new government funded all of these bonds, those of both the Continental Congress and the 13 colonies. A wave of speculation swept the country.

During the U.S. Civil War, there was a great deal of speculation in securities, gold, and commodities. Four stock exchanges operated in New York during the war.

Following the destruction of the U.S. battleship *Maine* off the coast of Cuba in 1898, the Dow Jones Industrial Average fell 16% in less than six weeks. But by two months later, with the United States at war with Spain, the market had recovered. And by September 1899, with the war turned in the United States' favor, the Dow had increased by 83% over its low of 18 months earlier.

On 31 July 1914, shortly after the outbreak of World War I, the London Stock Exchange shut down. In response, stocks fell approximately 20 points on the New York Stock Exchange. Leading bankers and exchange officials met and decided to shut down the New York Stock Exchange in an attempt to avert a decline in the market values of gold and U.S. securities. However, the anticipated bust in these markets did not occur, and before long, clandestine trading began. The market reopened after four months. It turned out that the prices of gold and U.S. securities had actually risen. Trading was at first restricted, but as war orders poured in from Europe, speculation took off, particularly in some favored industries known as "war brides."

It should be noted that during World War I, Britain took measures to promote economic expansion among its allies by promising to buy at a fixed price as much wheat, wool, and other primary commodities as its suppliers could produce. This helped these countries reduce their foreign debts during the war, but a steep price decline for their exports after the war made it harder for these primary product exporters to service their debts.

In the United States during World War II, the U.S. stock market at first rose slightly with Germany's invasion of Poland on 1 September 1939. Obviously, Germany was not an ally of the United States, but there were those investors who were pleased to see German troops marching eastward (toward the Soviet Union) rather than westward. The market rose sharply when England and France declared war on Germany two days later. The market continued to rise for several months, but then slumped following Germany's attack on Belgium and the Netherlands in May 1940. Within two weeks, as it was apparent that these countries as well as France would fall to the Nazis, the market had fallen 21%. For two more years it continued to fall, eventually dipping 36% before it began to recover with some U.S. victories in the Pacific. As the tide of the war in Europe began to change following the Soviets' victory at Stalingrad, the U.S. market continued to rise steadily. By May 1946 it was 56% higher than four years earlier.

Sometimes political settlements and redivisions that have resulted from a war have determined the fate of particular stock markets. Following World War II, the Berlin Stock Exchange became far less important, whereas the exchanges in Frankfurt and Düsseldorf assumed more prominence. In Japan the securities markets were transformed after the war and reorganized according to the U.S. model. Much stock formerly held by large *zaibatsu* (family-owned companies) or jointly held by corporations and the government was distributed, increasing public stock ownership and stimulating growth on the nine Japanese exchanges. In a number of developing countries, stock markets grew after World War II as part of efforts to encourage foreign investment.

The onset of the Korean War in 1950 brought an immediate, sharp price decline in the U.S. market that lasted for two months. A pronounced recovery and a bull market then emerged and lasted until early 1953, when a mild recession began.

A near-war can also have a major effect on the stock market. During the Cuban missile crisis in October 1962, the Dow Jones Industrial Average fell sharply. Later, following the resolution of the crisis, the Dow began a rally that lasted more than three years.

With the outbreak of the Six Day War in 1967, when U.S. ally Israel fought against Egypt and Syria, the Dow fell more than 50 points. However, with Israel's victory, it recovered and gained more than 100 points.

A period during the Vietnam War illustrates how domestic political changes associated with a war can affect the stock market. The Dow fell following the Tet offensive in January 1968. But with President Lyndon Johnson's announcement at the end of March that he would not run in that year's presidential election, the market began to recover. Key investors, who saw the war as costly and unwinnable, hoped that Johnson's successor would move to get out of the war quickly. One month after the elections the market had climbed 20% above its post-Tet low. However, when it became apparent that the United States would not extract itself from the war soon, the market fell again.

In August 1990, the Dow reacted very negatively to Iraq's invasion of Kuwait. But once the United States declared war on Iraq, and even more once the United States had won, the Dow soared.

Taking all these historical examples into account, it can be said that the usual pattern in war crises has been as follows: The stock market falls, sometimes very sharply, in the period leading up to war or immediately following war's outbreak. But the market recovers, often climbing far above its prewar highs, especially if the war ends favorably. Industries that have particular technical, logistical, or supply tie-ins to the war effort tend to do better, and the stimulus they experience during the war can often spur ongoing growth. The stability of currencies can vary greatly, usually depending on whether a country is victorious.

The effects of a war on the stock market are one thing; the effects on the overall economy are another. Even among countries that are allied with the victors, the burdens of war debt are often long-lasting and crippling. The negative effects on a country's economy can, of course, be all the greater, depending on the degree of destruction to its plant and equipment and its infrastructure.

WAR CHEST

A *War Chest* is the assemblage of funds for the financing or defending of takeover attempts.

Fending off and attempting takeovers can be expensive in terms of legal fees and other costs, especially if the target company is desperate to avoid being absorbed by another company. One strategy for a target company is to build cash reserves in a war chest and develop contingency plans to make the company less attractive to an acquirer.

See also ACQUISITION; POISON PILL; TAKEOVER/TAKEOVER BID.

WARBURG DYNASTY

The firm S.G. Warburg, built on the image of Siegmund G. Warburg, lost its independence in 1995 after 50 years of immense success. The origins of the *Warburg Dynasty* have been traced back to Simon von Cassel, a trader who set up business in the German town of Warburg in the 16th century. In the 18th century the von Cassel family moved to Hamburg, via Danish Altona, and a new surname, von Warburg, was adopted. Jews living in Germany at this time were prohibited from having surnames and, therefore, many adopted the name of the town or the city in which they were based.

The sojourn in Danish Altona marked the beginning of the Warburg fortune. Altona was an independent principality and a neighbor of Hamburg. Its rulers were from Denmark, a country whose attitude toward Jews was far more accepting than Germany's. The country placed no restrictions on the number of Jews that could live within its borders and allowed Jewish settlers to set up their own schools and courts. Jacob Samuel von Warburg, who was the first member of the clan to move to Altona, established himself as a leader of the Jewish community in the principality. One of Jacob Samuel's grandsons first established a money-lending and merchant trading business in 1774. Over the coming years more family members joined the firm, which was sold in 1907 to the related partnership of M.M. Warburg.

M.M. Warburg and Company was established by Marcus Gombrich Warburg, who arrived in Hamburg in 1773. With his sons, Moses and Gerson, Marcus Warburg set up a moneychanging business that benefited from Hamburg's strategic position as a European trading crossroads. The growth of the firm was not, however, without incident. In 1804 Gerson Warburg was taken hostage by the Napoleonic army that was besieging the city. Reports at the time suggest that Moses was reluctant to pay the ransom demanded by the French forces and that he had to be coerced to hand over the money for Gerson's release.

The French army occupied Hamburg until 1814. As soon as they left, M.M. Warburg and Company began to search out new business. The firm corresponded with N.M. Rothschild and Sons in London and the two firms dealt together in silver and bills of exchange. Beginning in 1849, Jews were entitled to full citizenship in Hamburg, and the firm was finally allowed to use the designation "banker" in its title. It grew cautiously, employing 11 members of staff by 1869 and rarely straying from its primary areas of business. Expansion came in the shape of a loan taken out by the French government to pay reparations after the Franco-Prussian war of 1870–71. M.M. Warburg and Company took a full participation in the loan, which was issued by the Rothschilds.

During the latter years of the 19th century the Hamburg scion of the Warburg family went from strength to strength. Sara Warburg (d. 1884) held much of the power in the firm after her husband, Abraham Samuel, passed away in 1856. A series of marriages, and the friendship between Sara Warburg and chief minister Bismarck, guaranteed the success of the family firm into the next century. When Siegmund Warburg was born in 1902, his family was well established in the banking business. The background of the firm's successes between the wars was in constant upheaval as the Weimar Republic faltered and was replaced by a growing surge of nationalism and anti-Semitism. Hamburg, rich from international trade and finance, was the seat of the powerful banking families. Siegmund's older cousin, Max Warburg, was the city's most influential private banker.

The young Siegmund gained firsthand experience in banking at a national level from his involvement in the financing of reparations that had been imposed on the German government at the end of World War I. In 1930 Siegmund became a partner in the family firm. He came to London after extended sojourns in New York and Boston, where he learned about the U.S. banking business. In 1934, at the age of 32, Warburg set up a new venture, the New Trading Company. His copartner, Henry Grunfeld, was to work with him for the next 50 years. Warburg chose to renounce his German nationality but had to wait the mandatory five years before he was granted British nationality. The rise of the Nazis made a return to Germany an impossibility. The New Trading Company spent most of the war years arranging finance for the Allied war effort. Warburg used his knowledge of German politics and his vast array of contacts for the benefit of UK intelligence services.

In 1946 the New Trading Company was renamed S.G. Warburg and Company. With share capital and reserves of £233,108 and 30 eager staff members, the bank faced the postwar years with optimism. The bank's progress was steady rather than spectacular, but Warburg took care to encourage young talent to stay with the firm. An all-important presence in the United States was achieved through an agreement with the New York investment bank Kuhn, Loeb and Company. Siegmund Warburg was made a partner at Kuhn, Loeb in 1953 and remained a partner until the end of the association between the two firms in 1964.

In 1953 the corporate structure of S.G. Warburg was altered and the firm became a fully-owned subsidiary of the stock exchange-listed company Mercury Securities. The Mercury holding company also had interests in insurance, marketing, and metal trading. The firm bought the long-established London bank, Seligman Brothers, which had considerable expertise in the credit business. Seligman Brothers was an acceptance house that was authorized to have discount facilities at the Bank of England. The takeover led to Warburg's membership in the Accepting Houses Committee, and deposits increased dramatically over the following years.

Siegmund Warburg carefully developed a strategy that would protect his company from the short-term volatility that characterizes the merchant banking business. Besides the addition of marketing, insurance, and metal broking to the fast-growing Warburg portfolio, during the next two decades the company claimed a large stake in the French bank Paribas, bought a shipping line in Norway, and bought two well-known British advertising agencies, Masius Wynn Williams and D'Arcy MacManus.

In 1958 S.G. Warburg and Company took a central role in one of the defining moments of British corporate history. The first large-scale hostile takeover of a UK company occurred when American companies Reynolds Metals and Tube Investments joined to make a bid for British Aluminium, which manufactured one-third of all the aluminum products in the United Kingdom and owned refineries in Scotland and Canada. Reynolds Metals was eager to expand and followed the advice of its investment bankers, Kuhn, Loeb, to make the takeover more acceptable in the United Kingdom by cooperating with a UK company, Tube Investments, to make the bid.

Warburg, with support from Wagg and Schroders, advised Reynolds and Tube Investments in the bidding battle against the Aluminum Corporation of America. The bank bought British Aluminium shares in the open market for both companies, employing nominee companies to obscure the true owners of the shares. The struggle for British Aluminium—which was dubbed the "Great Aluminium War" by the British press—developed Warburg's reputation for expertise in mergers and acquisitions. Lazard Frères and Hambros, who advised British Aluminium, were distraught when the previously agreed-upon bid from the Aluminum Corporation of America was rejected in favor of the plan inspired by Warburg. A series of inconclusive meetings between all parties to the deal came to an abrupt end on New Year's Eve in 1958. With neither party having secured a majority of shares, the banks that supported the Aluminum Corporation of America made an offer for British Aluminium. Reynolds and Tube Investments responded by buying all the available shares, and the consortium soon owned 80% of the shares. Warburg's success was greeted with animosity by some sections of the City and the bank's relationship with several of its peers suffered for a number of years.

In 1966, Siegmund Warburg was knighted for his services to the banking world. His strategy of nurturing talent in-house appeared to be paying off. In contrast to many of its competitors, half of the Warburg board was under 45 years of age and—almost unheard of in the City of London—four of the directors were still in their 30s. Moreover, Warburg also encouraged non-British nationals on the board as a way of bolstering foreign business. Warburg established a strong presence in the nascent Eurobond market. In 1963 the bank issued the first Eurodollar bond issue on behalf of Autostrada, the Italian highway authority. Warburg also floated the first dollar-denominated loan in London for one of the new breed of pan-European organizations, the European Coal and Steel Community. In 1969 Warburg was lead manager for the first issue of an innovative financial instrument, the floating rate note.

On New Year's Day 1970, Siegmund Warburg relinquished the chairman's seat of Mercury Securities and was replaced by Henry Grunfeld. Warburg moved to Blonay, a small village in Switzerland, where he built a large home. Any thoughts of retirement, however, were banished as he supervised banking activities in London from his base in Switzerland. Henry Grunfeld retired as chairman in 1974 and was replaced by Lord Roll.

In 1973 Warburg struck an associate deal with the French bank Banque de Paris et des Pay-Bas, commonly known as Paribas. This agreement led to a $25 million joint investment in the U.S. regional bank A.G. Becker, which was one of the leading players in the market for U.S. Treasury bills, responsible for 3% of transactions on the New York Stock Exchange.

Siegmund Warburg worked indefatigably to develop his firm's business abroad. He paid particular attention to the Far East and was one of the few bankers to realize the immense potential of postwar Japan. In 1978 the Emperor of Japan together with the prime minister of the country presented Siegmund Warburg with the Order of the Sacred Treasure (Second Class) in recognition for his contribution to the Japanese economic revival. The company also worked closely with Lazard Frères in Paris and Kuhn, Loeb in New York to provide funding for the governments of Third World countries such as Indonesia, Gabon, and Nigeria. Warburg's growth was hampered by the boycott of Jewish-owned banks by the oil-producing countries during the mid-1970s. It slipped in the league table of debt-issuing banks in Europe, tumbling from the top three to the position of also-rans.

The Becker investment proved to be problematic, leading to a certain amount of friction between Warburg and Paribas. At the end of 1980 Becker entered into a loss-making slump, and several directors chose to resign. Two hundred fifty staff members, representing some 10% of the bank's workforce, were made redundant in 1982, and clients began to close accounts.

Siegmund Warburg fell increasingly ill and was unable to exert his customary influence over the bank that carried his name. He devoted an increasing amount of time to reading and worked on a pet project, an anthology of aphorisms collected from books and colleagues. His wife, Lady Warburg, organized a lavish party at Claridge's hotel in London to celebrate his 80th birthday, but two days before, on 28 September 1982, Siegmund suffered a stroke. After being transported to London by air ambulance, he died on 18 October. An obituary in the *Financial Times* summed up the immense influence Siegmund Warburg had exerted over the British banking business: "Sir Siegmund Warburg was perhaps the most influential financier in the City of London. . . . He brought about radical changes in the practice of corporate finance and was instrumental in reshaping the role played by merchant bankers."

Warburg displayed an aggressive attitude to the opportunities afforded by the Big Bang in the City of London. The investment in Becker was sold off and the new chairman, David Scholey, began an assault on the major American investment banks that were expanding their operations in the United Kingdom. A new holding company, S.G. Warburg Group PLC, was set up in 1987 to combine Warburg's banking interests with three important acquisitions. Akroyd and Smithers, a stock jobbing firm founded in 1875, offered proven expertise in government and corporate bonds and equities. The cost, £41 million for a 29.5% stake, was partly paid in paper issued by Mercury. Rowe and Pitman was a major player in the provision of corporate finance services and was responsible for nearly one-fifth of London's trade in foreign equities. Mullens and Company, which could trace its roots back to the 18th century, was a government broker and official adviser to the Bank of England. London's regulatory authorities eventually allowed banks to wholly own their broking subsidiaries, and a fully merged group soon evolved. The fund management division of the firm, Mercury Asset Management (MAM), was listed as a separate entity on the stock exchange even though Warburg kept 75% of the shares.

In 1994 Warburg achieved record results, and many within the firm believed that it would soon challenge the North American powerhouses. David Scholey, who was now Sir David Scholey, and the firm's chief executive, Lord Cairns, realized that the bond-trading division needed to be strengthened, and they publicly announced plans to recruit more traders. This ambitious expansion plan was, however, doomed to failure. Less than a month before the board of directors agreed to the proposal, the chairman of the U.S. Federal Reserve, Alan Greenspan, had announced a tightening of the country's monetary policy. On the day the agreement was reached, the markets for British and European bonds fell sharply.

Scholey was much praised for his ability to meld the disparate Big Bang acquisitions into a unified entity but was frustrated by slow progress in bonds. Other banks, especially Salomon Brothers, made spectacular profits from betting the firm's own capital on proprietary bond trading. Large fees were available for arranging and underwriting new issues.

The cost of the new traders, who were among the highest paid individuals in finance, was not matched by increased profitability in the bond division. The fall in the market led to sustained trading losses. The volume of client orders declined. Other ventures, such as the Chicago-based derivatives firm KC-CO, which had been bought in 1993, drained resources from the firm. The U.S. market for European equities also cooled down as the markets stagnated. Staff began to blame management for being old-fashioned, bureaucratic, and ineffectual. Cultural problems emerged as the rather stuffy, private school spirit of Rowe and Pitman clashed with the meritocracy at Warburg.

By September 1994 it became clear that the expansion into bonds had been ill-timed and poorly executed. Warburg's profitable run was coming to an abrupt end. Salvation appeared to come in the form of Morgan Stanley's president, John Mack, who lunched with Lord Cairns in September. Mack, who was largely responsible for building up Morgan Stanley's extremely successful bond operation, explained how both firms could save money by sharing the cost of new technology in emerging markets. Eventually the discussion led to the benefits that would accrue if the firms were to merge.

Morgan Stanley was a much larger firm than Warburg, so any deal would in reality have the characteristics of a takeover rather than a merger. A member of Wall Street's "bulge bracket" elite, Morgan Stanley had well-established equity and bond operations on Wall Street. In London the firm employed some 2,000 people in its futuristic offices at Canary Wharf. The directors of Morgan Stanley knew that a merger would give them control over MAM, the fund managers of which Warburg owned 75%. MAM would be a perfect acquisition for Morgan Stanley, which lacked presence in international fund management, and would propel Morgan Stanley to the top of the investment banking league.

The financial woes at Warburg continued and the firm issued a profit warning ahead of its half-year results. Senior representatives from both firms met at a series of confidential meetings to thrash out the details of a deal. It soon became apparent that the 25% of MAM that was owned by minority shareholders would be a problematic stumbling block. Duplication among the two workforces would lead to costly, morale-sapping redundancies. The talks even floundered around the appropriate name for the merged entity. On 8 December the news of the planned merger leaked out to the City of London and shares in Warburg soared.

The directors of both firms hurriedly admitted to the merger talks, but it soon became clear that there were insurmountable problems. The MAM minority shareholders demanded a hefty premium for their shares, while staff became worried about losing their highly-paid positions. The Morgan Stanley operating committee met in New York and reluctantly decided to call off the merger. The directors and staff at Warburg were angered by the perfunctory way in which Morgan Stanley announced the ending of their interest, and were incensed when a senior manager went on record with his remark that MAM, and not Warburg, had been the primary reason for the planned deal.

Executives at MAM now realized that the asset management business was far more attractive to predators than Warburg's core business of investment banking. The doubts about Warburg's future that surfaced during the bid talks with Morgan Stanley had a detrimental effect on MAM. Some commentators stated that Warburg had advertised its weaknesses during the bid talks and that a takeover was inevitable.

Things went from bad to worse. On 9 January 1995 Warburg announced that it was pulling out of the majority of the Eurobond markets and that its continental European government bond business was to shut down. The two co-heads of Warburg's equity capital markets operation, Maurice Thompson and Michael Cohrs, announced on 5 February that they were leaving to join Deutsche Morgan Grenfell. Within a week Cairns resigned, citing the loss of faith his staff showed in him as a contributory factor.

Scholey took over as chief executive. The unwieldy management structure was slimmed down and, although Scholey remained at heart committed to independence, he investigated other options. The collapse of Barings in February was a salutary experience for all those who believed in the primacy of the British merchant banks in the international arena. As details emerged of how one solitary trader had destroyed a 200-year-old bank, Scholey increasingly realized that only well-capitalized banks would be able to compete in the volatile markets. The firm faced two stark options; either rein in the expansion plans to concentrate on core businesses or seek a partner with extensive cash reserves.

Approaches were received from a number of big banks. Smith Barney, the second tier U.S. investment bank, suggested a strategic alliance, while National Westminster Bank, a UK retail bank, considered a full acquisition. In March, George Blum, the chief executive of Swiss Bank Corporation (SBC), visited Scholey in London. With Marcel Ospel, SBC's head of corporate finance, they concluded that expansion in the United States would be costly and difficult. Europe, however, was different, and an influx of capital from SBC to Warburg was mooted. Importantly, SBC already owned a large fund management company in the United States, Brinson Partners, and was therefore not overly concerned by the minority shareholders at MAM. A bid was agreed upon, and SBC Warburg was formed.

The takeover of Warburg was symptomatic of the increasing power held by the large American and European firms in the City of London. British firms, in the age of global capitalism, were shown to be too small and financially stretched to compete with the powerhouses from abroad. The Big Bang, designed to strengthen London's position as a financial center, actually resulted in an influx of foreign firms.

Other scions of the Warburg family remain active in the banking world. Siegmund's second cousin, Eric Warburg, fled from Nazi Germany in the year before World War II broke out and set up a bank called E.M. Warburg in New York. He later sold half of the bank to Lionel Pincus and the firm was renamed E.M. Warburg Pincus and Company Inc. in 1970. Siegmund, who apparently detested Eric, had always regarded the use of the Warburg name by his cousin to be something of an irritant. One of Max Warburg's descendants, also called Max, has taken control of the private bankers Max Warburg and Company, which is still based in Hamburg.

See also COMPAGNIE FINANCIÈRE DE PARIBAS; KUHN LOEB & CO.; LAZARD FRÈRES; MERCURY ASSET MANAGEMENT LTD.; ROTHSCHILD FAMILY; SWISS BANK CORPORATION.

WAREHOUSING
See PARKING.

WARRANT
See SUBSCRIPTION WARRANT.

WASH SALE RULE (United States)
A wash sale is the simultaneous purchase and sale of the same security, and as defined by the Securities and Exchange Commission (SEC), is illegal. The *Wash Sale Rule* states that if an investor attempts to repurchase an identical (or substantially identical) security within 30 days of the time it was sold for a capital loss, the disposal cannot be considered a loss for tax purposes. If the investor purchases the same security after the 30-day period, the capital loss remains. The rule also applies to closing out a loss in a short-sale position and reselling within the 30 days.

The rule does not apply to business firms, such as securities dealers, trading securities as part of the normal course of their business.

See also BUY; CAPITAL GAIN; CAPITAL LOSS; SECURITIES AND EXCHANGE COMMISSION (SEC).

WASSERSTEIN, BRUCE
Bruce Wasserstein (b. 1948) earned a reputation during the 1980s, the decade of "merger mania," as a brilliant, extremely aggressive strategist in the mergers and acquisitions arena. Born in Brooklyn, Wasserstein is the son of a ribbon manufacturer who also earned a substantial fortune in real estate. He entered the University of Michigan at the age of 16, graduating at 19 with a degree in political science. By the age of 23, he received two degrees from Harvard University—a doctorate in law and a Master of Business Administration (MBA). He attended Cambridge for a year on a

fellowship and received a graduate degree in economics.

In 1973 Wasserstein began working as an associate in the prestigious New York law firm of Cravath, Swaine and Moore. A few years later he was assigned to assist one of the law firm's clients, First Boston Corporation, an investment banking firm in New York. First Boston was advising Combustion Engineering in its acquisition of Gray Tool. During these dealings Wasserstein greatly impressed Joseph Perella, First Boston's manager of mergers and acquisitions (M&A), with his ability to grasp all the details of the deal and to completely control a meeting. A few months later, Perella hired Wasserstein as a member of First Boston's M&A department. Thus began a 15-year association, during which the pair would become one of the most successful M&A teams on Wall Street.

At Perella's request, Wasserstein was made co-director of the M&A department. Soon Wasserstein was outshining his mentor, and by 1987 his annual earnings, mainly from bonuses on transactions, were $6 million compared to Perella's $5 million. M&A transactions at First Boston went from four per year in the late 1970s to 200 in 1987. Wasserstein became adept at structuring M&A deals and was a masterful tactician of deal-making.

The first major deal that made First Boston's M&A team widely known was DuPont's purchase of Conoco in 1981. Both Mobil Oil and Seagram's opposed the acquisition. Wasserstein's structure of the $7.6 billion deal was so complex that the participants at First Boston called it the "Big Rube," alluding to the fanciful, convoluted contraptions that Rube Goldberg drew in his cartoons. The key element of this structure was a two-part tender offer that enabled the buyout to be accomplished quickly by attracting the majority of the stockholders to the early all-cash part of the offer. Latecomers received so-called rump or stub securities, also known as junk bonds, representing the remaining equity in the company that may or may not have been worth its estimated value. The two-part tender offer had never before been used on a deal of such magnitude.

Soon Michael Milken of Drexel Burnham Lambert began using junk bonds as a takeover device. Wasserstein's response was a new application of the bridge loan, making a temporary loan of First Boston's own capital so that a client could close a hostile buyout quickly. The client could then arrange for long-term financing by securing a bank loan or issuing junk bonds. This strategy facilitated the issuance of junk bonds because First Boston's commitment of a large

sum in the bridge loan had already demonstrated its faith in the deal.

Other deals that Wasserstein structured while at First Boston included the acquisition of ABC by Capital Cities, the purchase of Pet Foods by IC Industries, and the takeover of Allied Stores and later Federated Department Stores by Campeau Corporation, a Canadian retailer. Wasserstein used a bridge loan for Campeau's purchase of Allied. With the loan and other funds, Campeau was able to purchase 50% of Allied stock from the aftermarket specialist Boyd Jefferies, who trades after the major East Coast markets have closed. This deal was destined to come back and haunt Wasserstein.

By 1988 the majority of First Boston's business was in M&A, and Wasserstein was the unquestioned star of the M&A department. Wasserstein made overtures to the top management, proposing that he be made chief executive officer and change the direction of the firm. He wanted to cut back on other departments, particularly trading. His suggestions were for the most part rejected, so both Wasserstein and Perella left First Boston to start their own company, Wasserstein, Perella and Company, which soon became known on Wall Street as "Wasserella." The principals of the new firm saw great opportunity in Europe and Asia, so they shopped for a foreign partner. Within a few months the giant Japanese securities brokerage Nomura bought a 20% share of the company for $100 million.

Early activity at Wasserella was frenetic. They advised Philip Morris in its $13.2 billion purchase of Kraft, and at the same time participated with four other investment firms in unsuccessfully defending Pillsbury against a hostile raid by Grand Metropolitan PLC of Britain. When Kohlberg Kravis Roberts acquired RJR Nabisco, they paid Wasserella a $25 million retainer, mainly to keep Wasserstein from helping the opposition. Wasserstein advised and assisted in the following transactions: the purchase by WPP, the British advertising giant, of the Olgilvy Group, a U.S. advertising agency; the formation of the world's second largest pharmaceutical company through the merger of Britain's Beecham and the U.S. company Smith Kline Beckman; the takeover of Northwest Airlines' parent NWA by the investor Alfred A. Checchi; and the purchase of Warner Communications by Time, Inc., despite strong opposition from Paramount.

Throughout his career Wasserstein has not been without setbacks and detractors. While he was still at First Boston, his competitors began calling him "Bid-'em-up Bruce," a reference to what they felt was a fiscally reckless style in structuring takeover bids. In 1990 the Campeau Corporation placed both Allied Stores and Federated Department Stores in Chapter 11 bankruptcy, covering a combined debt of $7.5 billion—the largest mercantile failure in U.S. history. Robert Campeau and many in the financial community placed the blame on Wasserstein. However, Wasserstein responded that Robert Campeau could have saved his companies by doing any one of the following in a timely manner: float a new junk-bond issue; mortgage his properties; or sell some assets. He also pointed out that he had not been Campeau's adviser for 18 months.

In 1991, Interco Inc., a former Wasserella client, initiated an $89.5 million malpractice suit against the firm, charging that in 1988 Wasserstein gave poor advice. Interco, a conglomerate based in St. Louis, had been facing a hostile takeover. On Wasserstein's advice the firm went heavily into debt to pay a large dividend, assuring stockholder loyalty. Most of the debt was to be retired by selling one of Interco's holdings, the Ethan Allen furniture chain, which according to Wasserstein's calculations would yield $500 million. The sale actually brought $357 million, and unable to pay its debts, Interco was forced into bankruptcy. The suit was later settled for $18.25 million.

Wasserstein's longtime associate, Joseph Perella, left the firm in 1993, reportedly unhappy with Wasserstein's domineering style and some of his recent business decisions, such as the firm's $350 million investment in Isosceles, the holding company for Gateway, a struggling British supermarket chain. The latter investment is part of Wasserella's merchant banking operations, which were started with a $1 billion fund. Besides the Isosceles investment, the merchant banking fund invested $155 million in Maybelline, the cosmetic manufacturer. Under Wasserella's guidance Maybelline accomplished an impressive turnaround, and in 1996 was sold to France's L'Oreal. Wasserstein engineered the sale, which involved a bidding war between L'Oreal and the German firm Joh, and earned his firm a $200 million profit.

When the M&A business dropped off in the early 1990s, Wasserstein's firm also suffered a slowdown, and ironically, Wasserstein found it necessary to place more emphasis on areas of investment banking, such as trading, which he had earlier urged First Boston to de-emphasize. In the mid-1990s the M&A business was again on the ascendancy, and Wasserstein began to hire additional specialists from other firms. In 1997 Wasserstein, Perella and Company raised $250 million for a corporate buyout fund from such investors as BankAmerica, SunAmerica, and BankBoston. The firm's strategy was to focus on medium-size companies, leaving larger corporations to larger investment firms with bigger war chests.

See also NOMURA SECURITIES COMPANY LIMITED; PERELLA, JOSEPH R.

WATERED STOCK

Watered Stock is stock that has a par value greater than the net tangible assets that it represents.

Analysts may find examples of "watering" in the balance sheets of some companies. Typical signs would include aggressive revaluations of fixed assets and a heavy premium placed on intangible assets, such as patents, brand names, and purchased goodwill.

Watered stock occurs in a number of ways. The company may give away stock to stockholders in the form of a bonus issue or may give away stock to promoters and advisers in exchange for their services. Stock may be issued at a price lower than the par value stated. Operating deficits, especially if occurring over a number of years, will impair the value of net tangible assets. In some cases, a company may fraudulently issue stock against an asset that is either non-existent or overvalued.

See also CONVERTIBLE; OPTION; SECURITY; SUBSCRIPTION WARRANT.

WELLS FARGO & COMPANY

WELLS FARGO AND COMPANY

Wells Fargo and Company is the eighth largest bank holding company in the United States. As of 31 March 1997, the company had assets of $101.9 billion, employed approximately 34,500 people, and operated 1,984 branches in ten western states. Wells Fargo and Company stock is traded on the New York, Pacific, London, and Frankfurt stock exchanges. Approximately 91 million shares of common stock are outstanding. At $240 a share, the stock was the fourth most expensive traded on the New York Stock Exchange.

Wells Fargo is a leader in employing computer technology to modernize its business. The bank first provided on-line banking in 1989 and Internet accessibility in 1995.

Chronology of Significant Events

1852 Wells Fargo and Company opens its first office in July, located in San Francisco. The company, a joint-stock association with initial capitalization of $300,000, is formed to provide express and banking services to California. Principals in the company's formation are Henry Wells and William G. Fargo. Wells is also the president of American Express Company and Fargo is its vice president. The company offers diverse and mutually supportive services: general forwarding and commissions; buying and selling gold dust, bullion, and specie; and freight services between New York and California. The American Express Company serves as its eastern representative.

1855 Wells Fargo expands rapidly until 1866, becoming the West's all-purpose business, communications, and transportation agent. The company develops its own stagecoach business, helps start and then takes over the Overland Mail Company, and participates in the Pony Express.

1871–1900 The number of Wells Fargo banking and express offices grows from 436 to 3,500 at the turn of the century. During this period, Wells Fargo also establishes the first transcontinental express line and expands its express services to Japan, Australia, Hong Kong, South America, Mexico, and Europe.

1905 Wells Fargo separates its banking and express operations. Wells Fargo Bank merges with the Nevada National Bank to form Wells Fargo Nevada National Bank. Wells Fargo and Company Express has already moved to New York City in 1904. Wells Fargo continues some overseas express operations until 1924 when American Express acquires controlling interest and gradually absorbs the remaining Wells Fargo express business. During the years under American Express, Wells Fargo develops security services, such as armored cars, guard services, and alarm systems. These operations along with the right to the Wells Fargo name will be sold to Baker Industries, Inc. in 1967, and will continue as its subsidiary Wells Fargo Armored Service Corporation.

1923 The Wells Fargo Nevada National Bank merges with the Union Trust Company to form the Wells Fargo Bank and Union Trust Company.

1960 The bank merges with American Trust Company to form Wells Fargo Bank American Trust Company. In 1962 the name is shortened to Wells Fargo Bank. Following the merger, Wells Fargo's involvement in international banking greatly accelerates. The company opens a representative office in Tokyo, then branch offices in Seoul, Hong Kong, and Nassau, and additional representative offices in Mexico City, São Paulo, Caracas, Buenos Aires, and Singapore.

1967 Wells Fargo, together with three other California banks, introduces a Master Charge card (now MasterCard).

1968 Wells Fargo changes from a state to a federal banking charter.

1969 Wells Fargo forms a holding company and purchases the rights to its own name from the American Express Corporation.

1975 According to *Institutional Investor*, between 1975 and 1980 Wells Fargo acquires more new domestic accounts from the 350 largest pension funds than any other money manager. However, in response to a variety of costly international operations setbacks, the bank slows its overseas expansion and concentrates on developing its own branches rather than tying itself to the fortunes of other banks.

1980 Wells Fargo's performance sharply declines during the early part of this decade. The bank retrenches its overseas operations and concentrates on the California market while attacking costs by closing 100 branches and cutting 3,000 jobs.

1986 Wells Fargo purchases the Crocker National Corporation from Britain's Midland Bank. The acquisition doubles the strength of Wells Fargo's primary market, making it the tenth largest U.S. bank.

1989 The company expands into full-service brokerage and launches a joint venture with the Japanese company Nikko Securities. The bank also begins to pursue a new international banking strategy—cooperative agreements with overseas banks. Wells Fargo reaches a cooperative agreement with the Hong Kong and Shanghai Banking Corporation, Limited (HSBC) whereby each bank agrees to serve the overseas banking needs of the other bank's clients in their respective geographic areas.

1995 Wells Fargo enters into another international cooperative agreement with the Banco Nacional de Mexico (Banamex) and strengthens its association with HSBC by establishing the jointly owned Wells Fargo HSBC Trade Bank in California.

1996 Wells Fargo purchases First Interstate Bancorp (FIB) for $11.6 billion in the largest bank merger in U.S. history, making Wells Fargo the eighth largest U.S. bank with $108 billion in assets. At the time of the merger Wells Fargo has 983 offices throughout California. FIB is one of the largest U.S. bank holding companies, with 55 banks that operates 1,140 offices in 13 states; 406 of its offices are in California. FIB offers a variety of financial services, including discount securities, broking, venture capital, and mortgage banking.

FIB had been incorporated in 1957 as Firstamerica Bancorporation, although its history could be traced back to the founding of the Bank of Italy in San Francisco in 1904. It had been one of 13 banks that originated the Cirrus automated teller machine network in 1982. Actively acquiring a number of other banks, FIB made an attempt to take over the Bank of America in 1986–87 but was rebuffed.

In October 1995 Wells Fargo made the first of a series of offers to buy FIB. For several months FIB resisted these offers, largely because it anticipated the closing of all or nearly all its California offices. Wells Fargo's bids assumed the form of a hostile takeover, the first such attempt against a major U.S. bank in nine years. Opposition was widespread in Los Angeles, with even the mayor speaking out against the takeover. By March 1996, however, FIB had to accept Wells Fargo's offer, which was better for its stockholders than any it had been offered by other banks. As a condition of approving the merger, the Justice Department and the state of California required Wells Fargo to divest itself of 61 of its own offices as an antitrust measure. As part of the consolidation of the two banks, Wells Fargo closed approximately 85% of FIB's branches in California, resulting in an anticipated annual savings of $800 million. By May 1996, partly as a result of the successful acquisition of FIB, the value of Wells Fargo's stock had increased 55% in 12 months.

See also HONGKONG AND SHANGHAI BANKING CORPORATION LIMITED.

WERTSCHRIFTENTRUST (Germany)
See UNIT INVESTMENT TRUST/UNIT TRUST.

WERTZUWACHSTEUER (Germany)
Wertzuwachsteuer is value added tax.

WestLB

WESTDEUTSCHE LANDESBANK GIROZENTRALE (WESTLB)
Westdeutsche Landesbank Girozentrale (WestLB) is the central bank for North Rhine-Westphalia, Germany's most populous region. A major force in the German economy and the clearing bank for more than 150 savings institutions in the region, WestLB is also an increasingly important international bank. WestLB

had assets in early 1997 of $302.8 billion and employed 26,349 people. It had affiliates, branches, and representative offices in 35 countries. Its strength derives in part from the fact that it is jointly owned by the state government, regional banks, and local authorities.

In 1832 the president of Westphalia used reparations received from the Swedish government following the Napoleonic Wars to create the first assistance bank in Prussia, the Westphalian Provinzialbank-Hülfskasse. Frederick William IV, the king of Prussia, was impressed by this bank and decided to establish a similar bank in the Rhineland in 1847. Seven years later, the Provinzial-Hülfskasse of the Rhineland was created. Both of these banks greatly expanded their services by the end of the 19th century and played a major role in the industrial growth of the Rhine-Westphalia region. They became known as the Landesbank für Westfalen Girozentrale, Münster and the Rheinische Girozentrale und Provinzialbank, Düsseldorf.

These two banks survived the world wars and the intervening depression. After World War II, both banks expanded their services to include clearing transactions for savings banks. They anticipated merging with each other beginning in the 1950s, but for political reasons the merger could not be carried out until 1 January 1969, when they became the Westdeutsche Landesbank Girozentrale. In doing so, they achieved the size necessary to constitute a significant rival to Germany's Big Three banks—Deutsche Bank, Dresdner Bank, and Commerzbank.

During its early years WestLB offered a diverse range of services, including tailor-made long-term loans. Its commercial loan operations expanded to include larger firms. Internationally, WestLB joined the Chase Manhattan Bank and two other banks in 1970 in starting Orion Bank Limited, a global merchant bank. By 1976 WestLB had become Germany's third largest lending institution.

During the 1970s the bank was involved in an extended scandal. Its founding chairman, Ludwig Poullain, was charged with bribery, fraud, and malfeasance in relation to various loans ranging from roughly $500,000 to $1 million. He was found not guilty in 1981.

In the early 1980s WestLB experienced some difficulties, and had to stop paying dividends for six years. With profits down, WestLB sold its stakes in two industrial companies to raise funds. In the mid-1980s WestLB raised more than DM 1 billion in new capital from its shareholders; the biggest contributor was the North Rhine-Westphalia government, which raised its stake in the bank to 43%. WestLB bulked up its loan loss reserves during the 1980s in anticipation of possible defaults by Third World debtors.

In 1984 WestLB and four other German banks created a new venture capital company. In 1985–86 WestLB increased its international business, purchasing a 58% share of Gerreshiemer Glas AG from Owens-Illinois Inc. and taking part in an arrangement to sell securities on the Tokyo stock exchange. In 1987 WestLB led a banking syndicate that bought a 25% share in the Deutsche Babcock AG engineering group from the Iranian government.

In 1987 WestLB underwent a reorganization designed to strengthen its investment banking operations. Some private banks expressed concern that WestLB had unfair competitive advantages because of its support from the state. In addition to functioning as clearing house for the savings banks in North Rhine-Westphalia and Brandenburg, providing them with trade finance and foreign exchange services, WestLB served as a development bank for the region, supporting new businesses and providing housing finance. And increasingly, it was able to draw on resources from its foreign operations.

In 1988 WestLB was one of several major German banks that made large loans to the Soviet Union. After the collapse of the Soviet Union and its bloc, WestLB was active in extending its operations into Eastern Europe, with offices in Moscow, Belgrade, Prague, Budapest, and Warsaw.

In 1991 the bank opened a branch in Singapore, its third Asian branch following Tokyo and Hong Kong. In 1992 WestLB planned a major push into the U.S. securities market. Two years later the bank set up a U.S. public finance department to market municipal and related derivative products.

In the mid-1990s WestLB mapped out "Project Omega," a major plan to develop a leading European investment bank headquartered in London that would deal in bond markets of leading currencies other than deutsche marks; build derivatives trade; boost primary market origination; provide research, sales, and trading in equity markets outside Germany; and eventually expand asset management business and investment banking in America and Asia. In 1996 West Merchant Bank, WestLB's London investment bank, made a pre-tax return of 31% on capital. WestLB continued its expansion in the City of London, and by 1997 West Merchant had increased its staff to 1,000, more than double what it was in 1995.

See also GERMANY.

WESTPAC BANKING CORPORATION

Westpac Banking Corporation, at one time Australia's largest banking and financial services group in terms of assets, now vies for the second spot with ANZ Banking Group. Westpac is Australia's oldest bank, founded in 1817 and incorporated in 1850 as the Bank of New South Wales. When the bank merged in 1982 with the Commercial Bank of Australia Limited, which was founded in the state of Victoria, it changed its name to Westpac Banking Corporation to signify the area it has historically served—the western Pacific.

Westpac provides a wide variety of financial services, offering general banking services to retail, commercial, and institutional customers and providing investment management and insurance as well. The company operates more than 1,100 branches, approximately 850 teller machines, and approximately 3,000 electronic funds transfer-at-point-of-sale terminals. It also maintains a nationwide telephone banking service. For institutional and international clients, Westpac provides leveraged leasing, working-capital loans, trade financing, project finance loans, foreign currency loans, and interest rate and currency products.

Chronology of Significant Events

1817 Bank of New South Wales is founded in Sydney.

1850 The bank is incorporated by an act of the New South Wales Parliament, and is allowed to establish branches. The first branch opens in the Moreton Bay area of the emerging colony of Queensland.

1853 The Bank of New South Wales opens a branch in London.

1864 The Bank of New South Wales has 46 offices and agencies.

1866 The Commercial Bank of Australia (CBA) opens in Melbourne.

1876 CBA has 34 offices and agencies.

1886 The Bank of New South Wales has expanded its operations to more than 140 sites, including locations in Adelaide (1877) and Perth (1883).

1891 Profiting from the boom of the 1880s, CBA takes over three other banks and increases its branches and agencies to more than 100.

1893 All Australian banks face a depression caused by a severe drop in wool prices and the bursting of the land boom in the colony of Victoria. Over half of the banks close, but the Bank of New South

Wales and CBA both survive, and are able to resume expansion with the start of the new century.

1900–10 CBA expands into Tasmania and New Zealand. The "Wales," as the Bank of New South Wales came to be called, expands into Fiji, Papua New Guinea, and Samurai Island.

1911–19 The Wales helps Australia finance the war effort, and its general manager is knighted for his service.

1920s Australian banks experience the worldwide economic boom that culminates in the bank crash of 1929.

1930s By the middle of the decade the Australian economy is recovering from the Great Depression.

1940s Bank growth is stifled by the war effort. After the war, Australia's banks become embroiled in the government's attempt to nationalize all private banks and place them under the control of Australia's central bank. The banks challenge the constitutionality of the move and win.

1950s Throughout the decade, Australia's economy is improving. In the second half of the decade, the government-owned Commonwealth Bank relinquishes its monopoly of savings accounts, and the Wales enters the field of savings. Complying with government regulations, the Wales channels a certain percentage of its savings deposits to housing construction loans. The Wales purchases 40% of Australian Guarantee Corporation (AGC), the country's largest finance company, which is active in consumer and business loans, investment and merchant banking, and insurance.

1960s Australia's banks have the difficult job of switching the country from the imperial pound system of currency to a decimal system of Australian dollars and cents.

1970s Both the Wales and CBA diversify their services and their geographic areas of operation. Both banks open more overseas offices. The Wales increases its interest in AGC to 54%, while CBA operates a finance company, General Credit Limited, as a wholly owned subsidiary. The Wales acquires significant holdings in three merchant banking firms, and CBA follows suit with substantial shares in two merchant banks.

1980s Australia deregulates its financial markets. Spurred by increasing competition at home and abroad, the Wales and CBA merge, forming Westpac (1982). The merger is the largest in Australian history. Technological innovation and diversification are Westpac's main goals for the decade. By 1988 Westpac claims to have the most advanced computerized banking system in the world. The bank increases its operations in the Eurocurrency markets, and opens new offices in New Jersey, Los Angeles, Seoul, Kuala Lumpur, and Taipei. Westpac acquires the remaining shares in AGC, making it a wholly owned subsidiary. Bank assets more than double between 1982 and 1986.

1990s Early in the decade Westpac sustains losses of more than A$2 billion, due largely to increased provisions for problem loans and charges for bad debts. The bank begins pulling out of less profitable markets and overseas regions (1992). The following year the bank returns to profitability but slips out of first place when the National Australia Bank and the Bank of New Zealand merge. By mid-decade the bank is again pursuing new holdings, acquiring Challenge Bank in western Australia (1995) and Trust Bank New Zealand (1996), which together increase the bank's assets by 14.8%. In 1996 Westpac reports a 32.2% increase in profits over the previous year to more than A$1.5 billion. In 1997 the bank merges with the Bank of Melbourne.

See also AUSTRALIA AND NEW ZEALAND BANKING GROUP LIMITED (ANZ); NEW ZEALAND.

WHARTON SCHOOL

The *Wharton School* at the University of Pennsylvania is the first, and by some accounts the best, school to offer a business education in an academic environment. Joseph Wharton, an entrepreneur from Philadelphia, founded the school in 1881 by giving the University of Pennsylvania $100,000 (which today would be closer to $1.4 million) to start the school. Wharton was the first exclusively business school, and went on to set other milestones in business education, including publishing the first business textbooks and creating the first Master of Business Administration (MBA) program in international management. In 1996 *Business Week* rated Wharton's MBA program number one in the United States, while *U.S. News and World Report* rated Wharton's undergraduate program number one among business schools. The same year, a group of international corporate recruiters surveyed by London's *Times* ranked Wharton as the best business school in the world.

The key to Wharton's success may be its willingness to change with the times. In recent years, students at Wharton have been required to take courses on the global business environment and to become proficient in a foreign language. Wharton has several student and faculty exchange programs with universities in Europe, Asia, Latin America, and Australia. It also offers MBA students the opportunity to work together with students from universities in other countries to design marketing strategies for companies that want to enter international markets. Almost 30% of Wharton's MBA students and 11% of its undergraduates come from countries outside the United States. Perhaps because of their exposure to a global curriculum, 24% of Wharton MBA alumni accept positions in countries other than the United States, and 57% accept jobs that include international responsibilities.

Wharton has changed its curriculum not only in response to international changes, but also in response to criticism from the domestic business community. In the early 1990s, the U.S. Graduate Management Admission Council noted that business schools were teaching their students to build "abstract models," rather than teaching them to work within "the messy, concrete reality of international business." In response, Wharton overhauled its already prestigious MBA program. It replaced the traditional two-term academic year with a series of six-week courses, and changed its curriculum to focus on leadership skills and a multidisciplinary approach. In addition to completing their academic coursework, students in the MBA program must now make themselves available as consultants to the rest of the university and to local businesses. Faculty members are evaluated on their teaching and leadership, rather than their research.

The efficacy of Wharton's graduate and undergraduate programs may best be demonstrated by the job offers received by its graduates: Wharton undergraduates receive an average of three job offers upon graduation, and make an average starting salary of $37,000, while 98% of its MBAs receive job offers at graduation and make an average of $95,000 in the first year after they graduate.

Chronology of Significant Events

1881–1910 Wharton publishes the first textbooks for business students.

1921 Wharton becomes the first business school to have its own research center.

1953 Wharton starts the first executive education program.

1970 Wharton creates the first health care management MBA program.

1973 Wharton begins the first center for entrepreneurship.

1976 Wharton institutes the first and only dual-degree program in management and technology. Students graduate with a Bachelor of Science (BS) in economics from Wharton and a BS in Engineering or a Bachelor of Applied Science from the University of Pennsylvania's School of Engineering.

1983 Wharton establishes the first MBA in international management. Students graduate with an MBA from Wharton and a Master of Arts (MA) in international studies from the University of Pennsylvania's School of Arts and Sciences.

1994 Wharton establishes a unique international studies degree for undergraduates, emphasizing business, language, and liberal arts. Students graduate with a BS in economics from Wharton and a Bachelor of Arts (BA) from the University of Pennsylvania School of Arts and Sciences. They are required to become fluent in a foreign language and study abroad for one semester in a part of the world where their target language is spoken.

1997 Wharton institutes a joint-degree program in nursing and health care management. Students graduate with two BAs, one in nursing and one in economics. The school establishes a sub-matriculation program with the University of Pennsylvania Law School. After six years, students graduate with a BS in economics from Wharton and a Juris Doctor (JD) from the Law School.

See also HARVARD BUSINESS SCHOOL; KEIO BUSINESS SCHOOL; MASTER OF BUSINESS ADMINISTRATION (MBA).

WHEN DISTRIBUTED (WD)

When Distributed (WD) refers to conditional transactions of shares previously issued but closely held.

See also BLOCK TRADE; INITIAL PUBLIC OFFERING (IPO); WHEN ISSUED (WI).

WHEN ISSUED (WI)

Short for when, as, and if issued, *When Issued (WI)* refers to conditional transactions on a security that is authorized, but has not yet been issued. New issues of shares, bonds, split shares, and Treasury securities are examples of items that trade on a when issued basis. The designation "WI" appears in stock listings in newspapers to illustrate the when issued status of a security.

See also INITIAL PUBLIC OFFERING (IPO); SPLIT; WHEN DISTRIBUTED (WD).

WHIPSAW

Named for the large wood cutting saw worked by two operators, *Whipsaw* refers to a market cutting in both directions. For example, a person buys 100 shares of XYZ Corporation at $50 and sells when the market price falls to $40. If the investor sold just before the price moved up to $51, the person would have been whipsawed.

Technical analysts will also use the term *whipsaw* to describe a market giving unreliable signals in the chart trends.

See also DOW THEORY; FUNDAMENTAL ANALYSIS; TECHNICAL ANALYSIS.

WHITE COLLAR CRIME

White Collar Crime is a catch-all term that includes many different financial crimes. The crimes embraced by the term include stock market manipulation, insider trading, fraud, theft, and concealment.

White collar crime is very much regarded as a problem of the modern age, where success in business counts more than ethics and the pressure on executives to perform is increasing on a daily basis. People who bend the rules in the commercial world tend to be highly regarded by their peers until they get caught. The company takeover and property booms of the 1980s inspired the "greed is good" culture and provided many opportunities for insider dealing.

Because of the complexity of some white collar crimes, some jury members have acquitted defendants rather than convict them of crimes they do not understand. It is estimated that £500 billion ($750 billion) of hot money is laundered through the world's financial markets each year. The laundering process requires the complicity of bankers, lawyers, accountants an other professional financial experts who profit financially from their tangential involvement with crime.

Some judges have been accused of favoritism toward offenders who share their social status and cultural background. Many of the white collar crime cases that come to trial in the United Kingdom and the United States have resulted in lower-than-expected court sentences for the guilty. As a consequence, the public's faith in the legal system and the motivation of the prosecutors have suffered. Different countries have different attitudes toward white collar crime. In Malaysia, for example, the list of punishments for white collar crime is far more extensive than in Europe. Those found guilty of market manipulation, short selling, insider trading, and giving misleading information to investors may be sentenced to be whipped by the authorities.

See also BANK OF CREDIT AND COMMERCE INTERNATIONAL (BCCI) COLLAPSE; BARLOW CLOWES; LEESON, NICK; MONEY LAUNDERING.

WHITE KNIGHT

A *White Knight* is a company that rescues another company from bankruptcy or from a hostile takeover.

In the case of a bankruptcy reorganization, the white knight provides the funding needed for the rescued firm to pay creditors and continue operations. In exchange, the white knight acquires controlling interest in the other firm. In the arena of corporate takeovers, the management and directors of a company being raided may perceive the so-called suitor as being undesirable because it will exercise control that is in some way unfavorable to existing management and the shareholders. On the other hand, the management and directors may support takeover by a white knight because they envision pending benefits to themselves and the shareholders.

See also CORPORATE RESCUE; FRIENDLY TAKEOVER; HOSTILE BID; HOSTILE TAKEOVER; RAIDER.

WIDER SHARE OWNERSHIP

Wider Share Ownership refers to a decrease in the concentration of stock ownership, such as happens when a greater number of individuals own the same number of shares, or a given number of shares are distributed more equally among a given number of stockholders. Policy makers and planners often see it as a desirable objective, although there are disagreements as to how to evaluate it when it is indirect (through institutional investors) or is not deep (many people owning few shares), as well as numerous questions related to its overall economic and political effects. Wider share ownership has been promoted as a means of increasing liquidity and perhaps reducing volatility in stock markets, providing more equity to new and small businesses, and strengthening free-market ideology.

One other issue concerns the relationship between stock ownership and the control of a corporation. Here it must be emphasized that even where there is broader individual ownership of shares in some companies, an effectively controlling interest may be retained by those who own a small majority of shares, such as 5% or 10%. There is, however, some evidence that broader share ownership, usually exercised through institutional investors, has affected the direction of some corporations and limited their management's independence.

In the United Kingdom, there was a significant increase in the number of people owning shares of stock in the late 20th century. In 1979, 3 million adults, or 7% of the adult population, owned shares, whereas 15 years later, there were 10 million adult shareowners, constituting 22% of the adult population. Further, the percentage of stockholders who owned shares in more than one company had reached

49% in 1993, while those who owned shares in four to ten companies amounted to 17% of all shareholders.

These developments toward wider share ownership were stimulated by two new instruments: venture capital trusts (VCTs) and collective investment schemes. In addition, broad policy initiatives that increased the number of stockholders in Britain included a program of privatizing state-owned companies; employee share schemes, in which employees receive tax relief on money used to buy shares; and Personal Equity Plans (PEPs), which offer tax relief on investment in British and European Union companies.

VCTs were introduced in April 1995. The government's main objectives in doing so were threefold: to foster better conditions for the establishment of new businesses and for the growth of small businesses; to create jobs in growth industries; and to help meet the shortage of equity and other long-term financing needs that such businesses often face. The VCTs are companies quoted on the stock exchange that invest in a range of unquoted companies, thus spreading investors' risk.

In the mid-1990s the British government planned to develop a new type of collective investment scheme, known as open-ended investment companies. These are similar to unit trusts, but they have a corporate structure, and investors buy shares in a company.

In the privatization program, which was given particular impetus during the Thatcher administration, both building societies and brokers were very active in purchasing shares during the public offerings. The methods of privatization included trade sales, private placements, public flotations, and employee or management buyouts.

Employee share schemes were promoted by the British government and many British employers as a means of giving employees a direct stake in the ownership and prosperity of the companies for which they worked. In turn, it was felt that this would stimulate the workers' productivity, an especially important consideration to capitalism in the increasingly competitive global marketplace of the 1990s.

PEPs were introduced in Britain in 1987. By April 1994 approximately £16 billion had been invested in more than 4.5 million plans. Adults could invest up to £6,000 in a general PEP and up to £3,000 in a single company PEP in one tax year. Once the government allowed a broader range of instruments to come under the PEP category, including corporate bonds, preference shares, and convertibles, total investments in PEPs increased further.

In Britain the organization ProShare worked to advance wider share ownership. In November 1993 it launched a new series of investment clubs that built on Britain's 30 years of investment club experience and its 1,000 existing clubs. In 1995 the London Stock Exchange opened a new public equity market, the Alternative Investment Market (AIM). This market was designed to assist the special funding needs of small, young, or developing companies that wanted to have their shares more widely traded. It is a low-cost but high-risk market.

Overall in Britain, wider share ownership was seen by the government and many businesses as beneficial. Studies showed that it contributed to the liquidity and efficiency of capital markets: individual shareholders performed 70% of transactions even though they owned only 20% of the market. Companies, particularly new and small companies, enjoyed an increase in equity funding. And, it was believed, a broader spectrum of individuals—provided they prospered on the market—would identify with the companies they invested in and with the status quo more generally.

Others, however, criticized the idea that a very broad individual share ownership was viable or even desirable. They pointed out that while British share ownership was wide, it was not deep. Most people did not have the necessary knowledge or the ready cash to build diversified portfolios on their own, but were better off relying on indirect investments.

Indeed, while the number of Britons who invested directly in the shares of particular companies had increased, their share of the total market value had declined. More of the share was held by those investing in unit trusts, pension funds, and insurance companies, which were often considered less risky. Whereas individuals directly owned 50% of British equities in the early 1960s, that figure fell gradually but steadily for the next 30 years, by which time they owned only 20% (by value) of British shares, whereas more than half the market was owned by unit trusts, pension funds, and insurance companies. By comparison, in the mid-1990s individuals still owned one-third of the value on the Paris stock exchange.

In other European countries, similar efforts were made to stimulate wider share ownership. In Italy in the early 1990s the government began a privatization program that included the banking system, which it considered bureaucratic and stifling of competition. In Sweden the government put numerous state-owned enterprises up for sale. During the 1980s the government had floated minority shareholdings in various state enterprises, principally to institutional investors, to raise investment capital, while seeking to preserve a majority of state ownership. By contrast, in the 1990s the Swedish government had abandoned the principle of majority state ownership, except perhaps for utilities, and was aiming for broader individual ownership.

In Asian countries such as Thailand, India, Singapore, and Malaysia, there were efforts to promote broader public investment in mutual funds. This was seen as the best way to raise funds for business while also limiting volatility in the markets.

In the United States, there was an overall movement following World War II from direct individual to institutional (such as mutual fund) ownership of shares. Direct ownership by individuals fell from 90% of all shares in the early 1950s to just under 50% in the early 1990s.

It was not clear how these changes had affected the pace of new business formation, which had increased during that period. Institutional investors might focus on a smaller number of companies, yet they could also have a greater effect than individuals on the companies in which they selected to invest.

As for stock market volatility, some research showed that the increased concentration of ownership in the hands of fewer institutional investors would lead to large price movements and thus increased volatility. Much of the increased institutional ownership was in the form of corporate or government-sponsored pensions, Keogh plans, and individual retirement accounts. The transition from mainly defined-benefit plans to mainly defined-contribution plans in the private pension sector had the effect of transferring risk from the sponsoring companies to the individuals.

See also BUILDING SOCIETIES; MUTUAL FUNDS; PRIVATIZATION; UNIT INVESTMENT TRUST/UNIT TRUST.

WIDOW-AND-ORPHAN STOCKS

Widow-and-Orphan Stocks is a description given to the shares of a conservative company. The implication is that investment in these shares is safe enough for widows and orphans (people who can't afford to lose money). Traditional companies for the widow-and-orphan share description include utilities that tend to offer a high degree of safety and yield a good dividend.

See also BUFFETT, WARREN; FUNDAMENTAL ANALYSIS.

WIGGIN, ALBERT

Albert Wiggin (1868–1951) headed Chase National Bank in the early 20th century, at a time when it expanded to become the largest bank in the world (Chase later merged with the Manhattan Company to become the Chase Manhattan Corporation). Wiggin

also advised the U.S. government regarding national and international banking crises, including the problem of collecting German war reparations after World War I. But shortly after he retired from Chase, Wiggin was investigated by a Senate committee and found to have speculated in the stock market with bank funds, and to have benefitted from his inside knowledge of the bank in several personal stock deals.

Wiggin was born in Medfield, Massachusetts, on 21 February 1868. After graduating from high school in Boston, he became a clerk for the Commonwealth Bank of Boston and later served as a bank examiner. Then he moved to New York City, where he worked as an officer at several banks, participating in numerous bank mergers. Consequently, it was with an extensive banking background that Wiggin was hired as a vice-president of Chase National Bank in 1905. At age 36 he was Chase's youngest vice president ever. In 1907 Wiggin became a member of an emergency committee formed to hold the country's banking situation together during an economic panic. In 1911 he became president of Chase and in 1917, chairman of its board of directors.

Wiggin expanded Chase from a relatively small bank into one of the largest in the world. He expanded Chase's services, especially its trust services, and was thus able to expand the bank's list of corporate accounts. In 1917 Wiggin created Chase Securities Corporation as an affiliate of the bank. The establishment of Chase Securities made Chase one of the first U.S. banks to have its own security underwriting affiliate (however, Chase Securities was dismantled after passage of the Glass-Steagall Act of 1933, which made it illegal for commercial banks to underwrite securities). At the time, the country was in the midst of World War I, and the security affiliate made it possible for Chase to distribute, and add to its own portfolio, U.S. war bonds.

International developments after World War I produced many opportunities for banks to lend money to companies and industries, and Chase's assets tripled during this period, reaching $535 million by 1920. During the 1920s and early 1930s, Wiggin engineered a series of mergers for Chase, which absorbed seven of New York City's major banks. One of these was Equitable Trust Company, owned by John D. Rockefeller and, at the time, the eighth largest bank in the world. Equitable Trust's assets totaled more than $1 billion at the time of its acquisition. Under Wiggin's direction, Chase also merged with the Metropolitan Bank and the Mechanics National Bank, and purchased its first foreign branches. The series of mergers made Chase the largest bank in the world, and Wiggin became its chairman. When Wiggin became president of Chase in 1911, the bank's resources had totaled only $250 million, but by 1933, its resources were up to $2.75 billion.

Wiggin first came under public scrutiny in 1931 when the World Bank invited him to head a committee of experts in London to study the possibility of converting Germany's short-term credits into long-term credits. Germany had been borrowing money abroad in order to pay its reparations for World War I. Wiggin was lambasted by the American press when the committee recommended that the United States reduce Germany's war debts, since Germany's credit was too poor for banks to provide it with long-term loans.

The criticism of Wiggin's 1931 committee report, however, was nothing compared to the opprobrium Wiggin suffered when he was investigated by the Senate in 1933. Wiggin had recently been forced to resign from Chase, partly because he was speculating in the stock market with bank funds. The Senate investigation revealed that additionally Wiggin had made $4 million before, during, and after the 1929 stock market crash by short-selling shares in the bank. Wiggin apparently based his decisions about when to sell Chase stock short on inside information. In a transaction completed in 1929, he sold 59,522 shares of Chase stock and made a profit of $4.5 million for his family corporation. In another transaction, completed in 1931, he sold 42,506 shares at a profit of more than $4 million. He was also criticized for raising his own salary as bank president (from 1929 to 1932 he earned approximately $1,500,000) at the same time that he was cutting the salaries of the average bank worker, and when Chase Bank was losing money. Wiggin's speculation was to cost him more than $3 million in lawsuit settlements in the years to come. He died in 1951 at the age of 83.

See also CHASE MANHATTAN CORPORATION; SELLING SHORT.

WIGGLE ROOM

The placing of a stop order far enough away from the current market price to avoid making it a tempting target for the specialist allows for *Wiggle Room*. This is especially important with sell stop orders. Some investors follow the 10% strategy, where sell stops are placed 10% below the purchase price. Others believe this strategy guarantees a consistent 10% loss.

A logical approach with stop orders is to:

1. Avoid using them except in situations in which the investor is unable to watch the market.

2. Place sell stop orders based on the observation of a recent price chart.

If an investor believes a price will show weakness in the near future and the investor doesn't want to ride out the decline, it is better to sell the shares before the price starts to weaken.

See also LIMIT ORDER; MARKET ORDER.

WILL

A *Will* is a legal document granting assets to individuals or organizations at the request of the person originating the document. The assets are appropriately transferred after the death of the person drawing up the will. Assets granted in a will are often subject to estate taxes imposed by the country of the decedent's residence.

When ordinary shares and other securities are granted with a will, the inheritor will have a cost basis for capital gains tax selected from the decedent's date of death.

See also ASSET; ESTATE.

WILSHIRE 5,000

Wilshire 5,000 is a stock market index published by Wilshire Associates of Santa Monica, California. It is a market value-weighted index and includes more than 6,500 U.S. company ordinary shares traded on the New York Stock Exchange (NYSE), American Stock Exchange (AMEX), and the over the counter National Association of Securities Dealers Automated Quotation System (OTC NASDAQ). The calculation is based from 31 December 1980.

The Wilshire 5,000 is widely followed as a broad market indicator for share prices. Some mutual funds attempt to mirror the index.

See also DOW JONES INDUSTRIAL AVERAGE (DJIA); INDICATOR; STANDARD & POOR'S 500 INDEX (S&P 500).

WINTERFLOOD SECURITIES

Winterflood Securities is a London-based stockbroker that specializes in small company stocks. The chairman of the company, Brian Winterflood, is a well-known commentator on small company stocks.

Many of the companies bought and sold by Winterflood originally appeared on the Unlisted Security Market (USM) in the United Kingdom. Companies joining the USM were subject to less strict regulations and reporting restrictions than their larger counterparts on the main markets. The USM has since been superseded by the Alternative Investment Market

(AIM), the preferred exchange for companies with a market capitalization of less than £50 million.

Brian Winterflood set up his firm in 1986. Winterflood was bought out by the merchant bank Close Brothers in 1993. In 1995 Winterflood was elected to the main board of Close Brothers.

See also ALTERNATIVE INVESTMENT MARKET (AIM).

WITHHOLDING TAX

Withholding Tax is the amount due when interest or dividends are paid or a capital gain is achieved.

Individual countries set their own rules regarding withholding tax on investments. Some countries maintain the same rules for residents and non-residents, while others have different sets of rules. Rules on withholding can be affected by the existence of a tax treaty between two countries.

See also individual countries' stock exchange profiles.

WITHHOLDING TAX AT THE SOURCE

Countries often withhold tax on share dividends by taxing the corporation paying the dividend. Taxes paid before the dividends are paid out to the shareholders is referred to as *Withholding Tax at the Source.* Many countries have tax treaties in effect that allow the investor to recover all or part of the withheld taxes on dividends.

See also CAPITAL GAIN; COMMON STOCK; DIVIDEND.

WOMEN IN THE STOCK MARKET

The first *Women in the Stock Market* in the United States earned $500,000 in their first year of business—1870. The women were Victoria Woodhull and her sister Tennessee Claflin. They opened a brokerage house (financed by Cornelius Vanderbilt) half a century before women achieved suffrage, partly because Woodhull believed that the power of money was more important than the right to vote. However, like many brokerage houses, Woodhull, Claflin and Company went out of business in the Panic of 1873. After Woodhull and Claflin got out of the business, women in the U.S. stock market were relatively invisible for almost 100 years. Although women, like men, have been managing money ever since money was invented, U.S. brokerage houses refused to allow women to represent them. The situation began to change in 1967 when Muriel Siebert became the first woman to buy her own seat on the New York Stock Exchange.

Even so, women achieved entrance to the stock market in the United States sooner than they achieved

it in most other countries. Women were not allowed to become members of Lloyds of London until 1970. The first woman to trade on the floor of Canada's Toronto Stock Exchange started in 1973. In Japan, the best job a Harvard-educated woman can expect at a brokerage house is running routine statistics and making tea—until age 25, when she would be expected to leave and get married. In some countries, such as Saudi Arabia, women have no chance to become stockbrokers because they are forbidden by law from working in fields where they might come into contact with men. On the other hand, at least half the traders in Singapore are women, and the first woman to own a seat on the Manila stock exchange in the Philippines did so in the early 20th century. While the number of women investors, business owners, and stockbrokers varies widely from country to country, in most of the world the trend is toward women becoming more involved in the stock market, rather than less.

Brokerage houses are not becoming interested in women because they have an altruistic desire to give women a fair chance. On the contrary, they are paying attention to women because women are becoming ever more prosperous. Worldwide, women still earn 30% to 40% less than men for the same work (in the United States, they earn 25% less), but their wages are increasing much faster than men's. In some cases, this wage disparity helped women to get jobs at brokerage firms that took advantage of the opportunity to get equally well-trained workers for lower salaries. Even though women earn less, their combined incomes add up: 56% of adult women in the United States work, and they earn more than $1 trillion every year. Women constitute 40% of the segment of the U.S. population made up of people holding assets in excess of $500,000. Women make up almost half of the U.S. workforce, own 30% of U.S. businesses, invest in the stock market equally as often as men do, and invest just as high a percentage of their portfolios in equities as men do. Women also make up more than 60% of the membership of the National Association of Investors, an organization for individual investors in the United States. In Canada, a recent survey showed that two out of three decisions to invest in mutual funds are made by women, and that women are responsible for investment decisions in one out of three households.

Women Investors

Statistics like these provide brokerages with every reason to actively court women investors. Many firms, including Merrill Lynch, Smith Barney Shearson, and

Prudential Securities, run ad campaigns targeting women. Women and men have similar investment needs, but women usually need to make their money earn more to compensate for the fact that they earn less, have smaller pensions and fewer retirement benefits, and live longer than men. Many brokers are finding that women often approach investing differently than men do. Women tend to be more risk averse and want more information than men do. They prefer brokers who are willing to take the time to answer questions, and they are less likely to jump at the chance to buy a stock based on a hot tip, preferring to research and consider investment decisions carefully.

Despite their risk averseness, or perhaps because of it, women investors frequently do very well in the stock market. In 1995 the National Association of Investors Corporation (NAIC) reported that women-only investment clubs had outperformed men's clubs for 9 of the previous 13 years. In 1996 the NAIC reported that women-only investment clubs earned an average annual return on their investments of 21.3%, while men-only clubs earned 15%. Of course, investment clubs of any kind tend to outperform the stock market, perhaps partly because their members tend to hold their stocks over the long term. Although the NAIC was reporting on investment clubs in the United States, women are forming investment clubs all over the world. For example, every year women in the Zurich Investment Club (a subgroup of Switzerland's Zurich International Women's Association) start a portfolio containing international shares worth 500,000 Swiss francs.

Women Business Owners

In the United States, women are the fastest-growing group of entrepreneurs. In 1996, while only eight of the 2,577 companies traded on the New York Stock Exchange and 10 of the 788 companies listed on the American Stock Exchange were owned by women, 69 of the National Association of Securities Dealers Automated Quotation System's (NASDAQ) 5,074 listed companies were women-owned. NASDAQ caters to small companies run by entrepreneurs. Many of these businesses are extremely successful. NASDAQ tracked their progress from September 1994 through December 1995, and discovered that they were up 31%—a respectable performance, compared with Standard and Poor's 500 (up 33.1%) and the NASDAQ composite (up 37.7%).

The trend toward women entering the workplace as entrepreneurs is not limited to the United States, however. Many Asian women are flourishing entrepreneurs. For example, in 1991, Charlene Wang Chien sold 10% of the stock in her computer business on the Taiwan Stock Exchange. Chien's company, First International Computer, was worth approximately $180 million.

Women Who Work in the Stock Market

People who work in the stock market usually go into one of three areas: sales and trading, investment banking, or research and marketing. Traditionally, sales and trading was a male preserve, while women occupied a research and marketing ghetto. However, research and marketing have become more important than they used to be, as brokering becomes a more information-dependent business and competition for clients increases. Women are also making inroads into sales, trading, and investment banking. In 1984, Columbia Business School reported that 26% of its graduates going into investment banking jobs were women—up from 3.8% in 1974.

Fairness has little to do with why brokerage firms are hiring more women—for these companies, making more money is the bottom line, although U.S. companies that have gone public do have to submit to public scrutiny of their employment practices. Businesspeople and investors are ever more amenable to working with women, since many work with, went to school with, or *are* women. In circles where women are still rare, being female can give a broker an edge over her male peers, because she stands out compared to them and may have better listening skills. Moreover, women who succeed in the male-dominated world of the stock market are generally extremely competent—they may have to work much harder than men in order to be promoted to the same positions. As a result, some women brokers now have legendary reputations. Wall Street's Elaine Garzarelli became famous for predicting the 1987 stock market crash in an interview with CNN a week before it happened. At the time, few people listened to her, but now Garzarelli, who has since predicted several important market swings, is known as the Guru of Wall Street.

See also GARZARELLI, ELAINE.

WORKING CAPITAL

Working Capital is the sum of the current assets of a company. These may include cash, accounts receivable, inventory, and other assets.

Working capital is the funding with which a company does business. It finances the cash conversion cycle in which the company takes time to convert its product or service to cash.

Sources of working capital within the company are retained earnings, operating efficiencies, and cash flow allocation from depreciation or deferred taxation. External sources can include banks and trade credit.

See also ASSET; CURRENT LIABILITIES; CURRENT RATIO; NET CURRENT ASSETS.

WORKING CONTROL

Working Control describes the ability of a shareholder or group of shareholders to effectively control a corporation, even though their combined holdings are at minority level. Such control is possible where the shareholdings are widely dispersed. Working control enables such shareholders to influence the company's decisions and strategies.

See also AFFILIATED PERSON; BOARD OF DIRECTORS; TAKEOVER/TAKEOVER BID.

WORKOUT/WORKOUT MARKET

Workout is a designation given to an order whose details are not yet available. A *Workout Market* provides an investor with an estimated price for selling a block of securities, as the details are being estimated and must be worked out when an actual trade is placed.

In a constantly trading market, it is virtually impossible to give a firm price to any securities until the investor is ready and willing to make a transaction. Limit orders exist to guarantee a price, but do not guarantee an order execution.

Block transactions require special handling and negotiation to be executed. The aim is to provide the investor with an acceptable order execution, with minimal impact on the current market price. It is part of keeping the market fair and orderly.

See also BLOCK TRADE; FAIR AND ORDERLY MARKET; LIMIT ORDER; MARKET PRICE.

WORLD BANK

The *World Bank* is made up of five organizations:
1. International Bank for Reconstruction and Development (IBRD)
2. International Development Association (IDA)
3. International Finance Corporation (IFC)
4. Multilateral Investment Guarantee Agency (MIGA)
5. International Center for Settlement of Investment Disputes (ICSID)
1. IBRD was founded in 1944 and is the World Bank's primary lending organization. IBRD lends money to developing countries that have relatively high per capita incomes. Money is used to pay for development projects such as the construction of highways, schools, and hospitals. Funds are also available to help governments improve management of their countries' economies.

Interest rates change every six months. Sources of funds are the world's financial markets. IBRD sells bonds and other debt securities to pension funds, insurance companies, corporations, other banks, and individuals on a worldwide basis.

IBRD is owned by 177 member countries, each with voting power based on the country's shareholding, which is based on the country's economic strength.

In the past five years, the IBRD approved an annual average of US$15.6 billion in loans for a variety of development projects.
2. The IDA began in 1960 to provide assistance on concessional terms to the poorest developing countries that did not qualify for loans from IBRD. IDA loans (called credits) are provided to countries with average annual per capita income of less than $800. IDA credits are interest-free, although there is a small service charge. Terms are 35 to 40 years, with an additional 10-year grace period.

IDA raises money from contributions by governments, IBRD profits, and repayment of IDA credits. IDA consists of 155 member countries, all of which are also members of IBRD.

In the past five years, IDA funded an annual average of US$6.4 billion in credits for development projects.
3. The IFC started in 1956 with the aim of strengthening the private sector in developing countries. IFC lends directly to the private sector, while the IBRD and IDA lend to governments. IFC provides long-term loans, equity investments, guarantees, stand-by financing, risk management, and quasi-equity instruments, such as subordinated loans, preferred stock, and income notes.

The interest rate on IFC loans and financing varies between countries and projects. Loans have maturities of 3 to 13 years; some have grace periods of 8 years. Eighty percent of funds are borrowed in the international financial markets through public bond issues or private placements, and the remaining 20% are borrowed from the IBRD.

The IFC is owned by 161 member countries. Every year, IFC approves approximately US$4 billion in financing, which includes syndications and underwriting for private-sector projects in developing countries.
4. MIGA came into being in 1988 to help developing countries attract foreign investment. MIGA

provides investors with investment guarantees against "non-commercial risk," such as expropriation and war. It also provides governments with advice on improving the climate for foreign investment. MIGA may insure up to 90% of an investment, with a current limit of US$50 million per project. 119 countries are members of MIGA.

5. ICSID originated in 1966 to promote increased flows of international investment by providing facilities for the conciliation and arbitration of disputes between governments and foreign investors. ICSID also provides advice, performs research, and publishes in the area of foreign investment law. ICSID has a membership of 109 countries. The organization hears 7–10 cases per year and publishes a multi-volume collection of investment laws and treaties and a semi-annual law journal.

See also INTERNATIONAL MONETARY FUND (IMF).

WRAP ACCOUNT (United States)

Sometimes referred to as a managed account or an asset management account, a *Wrap Account* is set up with a brokerage firm by large net worth individuals. Minimums vary from firm to firm, but $250,000 is common. The firm and the investor establish investment objectives and a plan to achieve them. The firm hires a money manager who is compensated from the investor's assets. The money manager executes trades through the brokerage firm.

An annual fee is charged for this service, often on a basis of "assets under management." Periodic reports are made to the investor regarding the achievement of objectives.

See also CASH ACCOUNT; INVESTMENT ADVISER; MARGIN ACCOUNT.

WRITER

See OPTION WRITER.

X-Y

XD (United Kingdom)

See EX-DIVIDEND (XD).

XR (United Kingdom)

See EX-RIGHTS (XR).

YAKUZA

The *Yakuza* is a criminal organization that has had influence over many companies in Japan. It is currently believed to have some 165,000 members.

The history of the Yakuza is shrouded in myth. Some people believe that its origins lie in the *machi-yokko*, an informal grouping of shopkeepers, farmers, and laborers that banded together in the early 17th century to fight the threat posed to villages and towns by criminal gangs. This was an age when gangs of rebel samurai warriors, carrying distinctive long swords, roamed through Japan. An extended period of peace during the Tokugawa epoch had caused many samurai to lose both their jobs and their masters. Forced into crime by a lack of work, these *ronin* (leaderless warriors) terrorized feudal Japan.

The *machi-yokko* became popular heroes, eulogized in songs and paintings. As word spread of their brave resistance against the better-trained *ronin*, new recruits joined and individual *machi-yokko* gangs established links with each other across Japan. A new breed of gang began to appear, less interested in doing good works for the community as a whole but eager to make money from gambling and protection. The level of organization increased, groups developed operating structures, and the members started to call themselves Yakuza.

The Yakuza split into "families," each led by an *oyabun*, or father, who guided the family and demanded loyalty from his *kobun*, or children. New members were required to take part in an initiation ceremony in which the exchange of sake cups symbolized acceptance into the Yakuza family. The amount of sake in the cups denoted a new member's status in the family and his relationship with the father. The ceremony was usually enacted in a Shinto temple.

A number of different groups existed at this time. The *Tekiya* were traveling merchants who made a living from peddling poor quality products and miracle cures. They banded together to protect themselves from extortion and to warn each other of any unwanted attention from local authorities. The oyabun of the Tekiya made a living from renting stalls at fairs, demanding protection money and selling goods. The feudal authorities accepted the Tekiya and gave their oyabun the right to carry two swords, a traditional mark of respectability that their behavior did not merit.

The *Bakuto* were a gang of professional gamblers who contributed many of the customs and traditions of the modern Yakuza. Indeed the word *Yakuza* is believed to have come from a losing hand in the Japanese card game *hanafuda*, which was popular with the gambling-obsessed Bakuto. In the game, a losing hand of 20 consists of the cards eight-nine-three: the term used to describe this hand, pronounced "ya-ku-za" in Japanese, was widely used to indicate that something was worthless. The punishment of finger cutting is also a Bakuto invention, designed to reduce a warrior's ability to hold his sword with power. The cutting of the first joint of the little finger, *yubitsume*, was required if an underling had transgressed against the oyabun and could be followed by the loss of other fingers before expulsion from the family. The Bakuto also popularized tattoos among the Yakuza, enduring many hours of pain to display their loyalty to their father and family. Tattoos, which were originally a way of branding criminals by the authorities, became a badge of honor within the Yakuza gangs.

The Meiji Restoration (1867) began the transformation of Japan from a feudal to an industrial society. The Yakuza benefited from the increase in trade, recruiting new members and setting up protection rackets in the docks and on construction sites. The birth of a new political system offered further opportunities, and Yakuza members tried to infiltrate the parliament, seeking patronage and immunity from prosecution in exchange for protection and bribes. Right wingers in the Japanese government who wanted to hold on to certain aspects of the feudal system were implicated in the reign of terror that followed. Evidence suggests that the Yakuza were employed by the ultranationalists to take part in attacks on politicians, industrialists, and the forces of law.

World War II radically altered the role of the Yakuza. Many members were either conscripted or interred, and faced an uncertain future once peace was achieved. The American occupation force launched an investigation into the Yakuza but mistakenly concluded that it was a spent force. The reality was that many gang members had used the postwar black market to make a fortune from rationed goods. A new strand was added to the diverse history of the group: the *gurentai* (gangsters) were far more aggressive than their predecessors and were ready to use violence to protect their black market activities.

Automatic machine guns replaced ceremonial swords and the gurentai began to dress like American gangsters, using the Chicago crime boss, Al Capone, as their role model. The 1950s and 1960s saw a great boom in the number of members eager to swear allegiance to their Yakuza oyabun. Violent turf wars broke out between the 5,000 gangs (believed to contain a total of 184,000 members) as the families struggled for supremacy.

The man to unite the disparate elements into a single Yakuza was the ultranationalist Yoshio Kodama, who had been a spy for the Japanese government in East Asia before World War II. He developed strong links with military leaders and high-ranking politicians, including the prime minister, and acted as the go-between between the Yakuza and the government for many years. A fervent anti-Communist, he perceived the Yakuza as a bulwark against the spread of communism from China and did everything in his power to put an end to the inter-group struggles. He forged alliances between strong factions and mediated between the oyabuns to achieve a truce.

The Yakuza began to branch out, making vast amounts from trade in amphetamines and other narcotics. The traditional areas of organized crime—money lending, pornography, prostitution, illegal gambling, and result rigging—were soon making billions of yen for the crime bosses.

A lucrative new type of crime was, however, added to the Yakuza's repertoire. The *sokaiya* is a professional racketeer who demands money from public companies. The name comes from the Japanese phrase for shareholders' meeting—*kabunishi sokai*—and their power derives from the traditional Japanese fear of a public loss of face. Their favored technique is to disrupt annual shareholders' meetings by aggressive behavior and physical threats to directors and shareholders. The performance is repeated until the company pays a fee to the sokaiya. Many of the sokaiya have become experts in the company they are attacking and may use insider information when trading the company's shares.

The Japanese government tightened the laws against sokaiyas in 1982 and made it illegal for corporates to pay off gangsters. In 1991 more than 2,000 Japanese companies united to conspire against the sokaiya threat. They held their annual general meetings at the same time and on the same day, making it impossible for the Yakuza to disrupt every meeting.

Many companies are also forced to pay large subscription fees to poor quality business magazines run by the Yakuza. The spiraling cost of development land in Japan, especially in the Tokyo region, led to another new type of Yakuza criminal, the *jiageya*, or land turner. Their specialty was forcing individuals from small properties or strips of land in prime development areas and then charging a fortune to property speculators for the same premises.

In March 1992 the Japanese government passed the Act for Prevention of Unlawful Activities by Boryokudan Members. *Boryokudan* are groups that contain criminal elements and have used violence to achieve their aims. The Yakuza have tried to circumvent these laws by setting up front companies. At the same time, certain Yakuza members have attempted to change the public profile of their organization by stressing its samurai traditions and its Robin Hood-style interest in helping. So far, their public relations efforts have met with little success.

The close links between the Yakuza and Japanese banking were highlighted by the *jusen* crisis of 1996. Seven jusen companies, set up to provide housing loans, collapsed under total bad debts of 13.2 trillion yen. Conservative estimates suggest that at least half of this money had been lent to Yakuza-fronted companies and is now impossible to recover. Criminal investigators have found that since the 1970s Yakuza criminals have diversified away from street-level crime into high finance. The heady profits made from jiageya business encouraged the Yakuza to enter the real estate business on a full-time basis. Loans from banks, eager to profit from the property boom and frightened by the reputation of the Yakuza, were easily obtained. When the property market collapsed, several jusen were forced to close.

The National Police Agency's criminal investigation bureau in Japan estimated that approximately 10% of the banks' loans were directly related to gangsters, with another 30% to 40% probably linked to organized crime.

The Yakuza, who had attained a greater level of financial sophistication because of their involvement in financial institutions, began to take an increasing part in the noncriminal Japanese economy. The distinction between informal and formal economies became blurred. The Yakuza defaulted on loans and collaterized the same property assets for different obligations. As the market soured, the Yakuza bought into debt-ridden companies in order to profit from their bankruptcy. Bank officials who were accustomed to the traditional customs of Japanese business showed an understandable reluctance to discuss these non-performing loans with Yakuza representatives.

Stockbroking, long a useful method to launder money, has been infiltrated by the Yakuza in Japan since the early 1970s. With the help of other Asian gangs, the Yakuza established brokerages in Indonesia, Malaysia, and Singapore. Their business soon spread to Australia, New Zealand, Hong Kong and, it is rumored, as far as the City of London and Wall Street. The Yakuza use their brokerages to invest "hot" money from criminal activities, which reappears, after several transactions, in the legitimate form of dividends and capital gains.

Via sokaiya activities, the Yakuza infiltrated many Japanese brokers and bankers, both in mainland Japan and in the offices abroad. In 1991 the chairman and president of Nomura Securities resigned after the bank was accused of lending money to the Yakuza and helping to manipulate share prices to make huge profits on the stock exchange. In 1997 one-third of the board of Nomura Securities was forced to resign after the president of the bank admitted paying ¥38 million ($300,000) to a sokaiya who threatened to disrupt the broker's annual meeting. Many customers moved their account from Nomura and the firm lost its position as the leading broker on the Tokyo Stock Exchange.

Several other large companies have also been revealed as sokaiya payers. The processed food group Ajinomoto and the large retailer Takashimaya were among the list of companies that have been tainted by the scandal. The eagerness of businessmen to pay off the sokaiya is understandable: when a manager at Fuji Film refused to pay the bribe, he was killed by gangsters wielding traditional Samurai swords. The future of the Yakuza, despite the efforts of the Japanese government, appears to be secure. It is even possible to buy a directory, the *Tantosha Hikkei*, which advertises the services of nearly 700 sokaiya.

See also MONEY LAUNDERING; WHITE COLLAR CRIME.

YAMAICHI SECURITIES COMPANY, LIMITED

Along with Nomura Securities, Daiwa Securities, and Nikko Securities, *Yamaichi Securities Company, Limited* is the smallest of the so-called big four Japanese securities brokerages. Yamaichi engages in a wide range of securities activities in Japan and abroad. The company's principal services include executing securities transactions for both Japanese and foreign investors; underwriting public offerings; providing advisory services for mergers and acquisitions; managing funds; performing transactions related to marketable securities; subscribing stocks; privately placing securities; researching securities and economic conditions; providing investment counseling; acting as paying agent; leasing security deposit boxes; and overseeing investment trusts.

Yamaichi's headquarters are in Tokyo, and as of late 1996, the company had 118 domestic branches, 35 overseas offices, and 11 affiliates, with representation in locations such as the United States, United Kingdom, Germany, Hong Kong, France, Singapore, Malaysia, Canada, the Netherlands, Switzerland, Bahrain, Italy, and Australia. The firm and its affiliates hold seats on the world's major stock exchanges, including the New York, American, Boston, Pacific, Chicago, Montreal, Toronto, London, Amsterdam, Frankfurt, Hong Kong, Singapore, Jakarta, Philippine, and Tokyo exchanges, as well as on several futures exchanges, including the London International Financial Futures Exchange (LIFFE) and the Singapore International Monetary Exchange (SIMEX).

Yamaichi was incorporated as a public company in 1943, and its stock is traded on the Tokyo, Osaka, Nagoya, and Paris exchanges. In 1996 Yamaichi had a net income of US$163 million on total revenue of US$2.6 billion. Overseas revenues accounted for 29.9% of the total.

Chronology of Significant Events

1897 The Koike Shoten, the predecessor firm, is licensed as a broker on the Tokyo Stock Exchange, at a time when securities trading is very primitive and Japanese industrialization is struggling to gain momentum. (*Shoten* means "store" or "shop.")

1917 The company changes its name to Yamaichi.

1920s and 1930s Yamaichi grows steadily, even though stock trading remains poorly developed, with very few joint-stock companies, no government regulation of exchanges, and many corrupt brokers. The *zaibatsu* (family-controlled industrial groups) dominate the economy.

1940s Yamaichi incorporates as a public company in 1943, but Japanese successes in World War II have already peaked. Prices drop sharply, and trading is sporadic until the end of the war. After the war, as part of the breakup of the zaibatsu, the occupation forces close the securities exchanges and reorganize the principal securities companies. The exchanges reopen in 1949, and Yamaichi leads the management of the first Japanese convertible bond issue for the Tosa Electric Railway Company.

1950s The Japanese markets, in a downward trend since their reopening, begin to pick up when spurred by the production demands of the Korean War. By mid-decade the Japanese economy is well on the way to full recovery. In 1959 the Yamaichi Investment Trust Management Company is set up to manage the new and very popular investment trusts.

1960s At the start of the decade the Japanese economy is growing 10% per year. In an attempt to tighten the money supply in 1963, the government incites a recession in 1964–65. Yamaichi, which has borrowed heavily to finance rampant expansion, nearly goes bankrupt, but it survives with the help of its major creditors and the government. By 1967 the company has recovered. At the end of the decade, the government relaxes somewhat the barriers to foreign investment.

1970s Yamaichi begins to assert itself in foreign markets, setting up offices in France and Germany and opening banks in the Netherlands and Switzerland. Japan's strong export industries make the country capital-rich, and Japanese investors look for opportunities in Europe and the United States. Yamaichi is aggressive in serving their needs.

1980s By 1980 Yamaichi is firmly established in many foreign markets, particularly London and New York. At mid-decade the company is very active in mergers and acquisitions. Since hostile takeovers are still virtually nonexistent in Japan, Yamaichi's role is that of corporate matchmaker. The New York stock market crash of 1987 forces Yamaichi to cut back its New York operations. Nevertheless, by the end of the decade 20% of Yamaichi's profits are from overseas.

1990s At the start of the decade, a scandal hits Yamaichi and the rest of the big four brokerages. They are subjected to restrictions and penalized for illegally compensating special clients for losses and for using insider information to benefit these clients. The Japanese Ministry of Finance requires the firms to erect "Chinese Walls" to better control the flow of information. The Japanese markets stagnate and, in the face of increased competition, Yamaichi's profits plunge an estimated 92%. Some of its affiliates struggle, and one of them goes bankrupt, the first Japanese brokerage house to do so in 17 years. Near the end of the decade another scandal hits the big four. They are investigated for paying off a racketeer—Ryuichi Koike, a so-called sokaiya racketeer, one who seeks payoffs for not disrupting annual meetings and for not harassing corporate executives. Yamaichi's president, chairman, and board of directors resign. Amid these mounting difficulties, some observers feel that Yamaichi will have trouble surviving upcoming deregulation of Japanese financial markets.

See also CHINESE WALLS; NIKKO SECURITIES COMPANY LIMITED; NOMURA SECURITIES COMPANY LIMITED.

YASUDA TRUST AND BANKING COMPANY, LIMITED

The *Yasuda Trust and Banking Company, Limited* is one of the Japanese institutions licensed for both banking and trust management. The regulations under which it operates are more stringent than for other banks, requiring that it maintain higher reserves. Its activities include commercial banking, asset and pension fund management, real estate brokerage and development, stock transfer agency services, financing, money market operations, trustee services, and the trading and underwriting of securities. Its assets were $68.7 billion on 31 March 1997.

Yasuda was once one of Japan's most powerful *zaibatsu* (conglomerates), with origins in the mid-19th century. Its wealth was mainly built on financial services, including banking (the Yasuda Bank was established in the 1860s), insurance, and lending. Soon after trust banking laws were passed in 1923, Yasuda entered the trust business. Two years later, several financiers, led by Yasuda, founded the Kyosai ("mutual aid") Trust Company. Yasuda expanded its interest in the trust bank and, in 1926, changed its name from Kyosai to Yasuda.

Unlike other *zaibatsu*, Yasuda concentrated on finance. The institutions in its group included Yasuda Bank, the Yasuda Fire and Marine Insurance Company, Yasuda Mutual Life Insurance, and the Yasuda Trust Company. In the 1930s there was much competition and little regulation in the provision of financial services in Japan. Nevertheless, Yasuda was one of the *zaibatsu* that prevailed.

Most of the *zaibatsu* were drawn into Japan's war effort in the 1940s, given their essential role in promoting the country's economic efficiency and growth. Yasuda itself took over some accounts from other institutions and was deeply involved in financing the war.

After the war, the American occupation authority dissolved the *zaibatsu* into thousands of smaller companies with new names. Yasuda Bank, which stood at the center of the Yasuda group, became the Fuji Bank, which went on to become one of the world's largest banks. In 1948, under new trust laws, Yasuda Trust was reincorporated as Chuo Trust and Banking. When these laws were relaxed in 1952, and with the new Loan Trust Law, Chuo changed its name back to Yasuda Trust and Banking.

With its trust and long- and short-term finance products, Yasuda developed ties with Japan's largest industrial companies. The various companies of the former Yasuda group reestablished cross-ownership of stock and formed the new Fuyo industrial group.

Yasuda Trust and Banking built a reputation for conservative trust and asset management. As a principal manager for Japan's largest and fastest growing companies' funds, Yasuda benefited from the rapid expansion of Japan's heavy industry between 1955 and 1970. Yasuda itself grew extremely quickly.

The combination of the end of the Bretton Woods system of currency valuation in 1971, which undercut the market for Japanese exports, and the OPEC oil embargo of 1973 wreaked havoc on some Japanese financial institutions. Yasuda, however, experienced only a slowing of its growth rate, since its investments were sufficiently diversified. This diversification policy also helped Yasuda survive the second oil crisis in 1979.

After 1970 Yasuda looked increasingly to enter foreign financial markets. As part of this it expanded its overseas operations. By the mid-1990s cities where it had branches or agencies included Hong Kong, London, Los Angeles, New York, and Singapore. By 1995, it had 58 branches and 28 offices, agencies, and representative offices in 15 foreign countries.

In the 1990s Yasuda was affected by the bad-loan problems that ran through the entire Japanese banking industry. The collapse of the real estate and stock markets in 1990 threw many banks into chaos. Yasuda emerged from the crash in a weakened condition, having undergone substantial asset shrinkage, so that even by 1997 its assets were approximately 20% lower than they had been prior to the crash. The difficulties experienced by Yasuda and other Japanese banks in the mid-1990s rebounded on the stock market, making it harder for the market to recover. In 1992, 1995, and 1997 declines in bank stocks precipitated sharp drops in the overall market. The decline of 1997 resulted from Moody's downgrading of the credit ratings of four medium-size Japanese banks, including Yasuda.

In early 1997 Western bank analysts estimated the total bad debt held by Japanese financial institutions at $656 billion, with perhaps another $135.6 billion held by their affiliates. The continued critical condition of the financial sector caused the government to postpone its "Big Bang" deregulation of the stock market, intended to give it the same degree of flexibility enjoyed by the markets in London and New York. Finally in 1997 the government unleashed the deregulation, one feature of which was lifting a ban on financial holding companies.

See also FUJI BANK; JAPANESE BOOM AND BUST 1988–90.

YEAR HIGH/YEAR LOW (HI-LO)

Usually listed together, *Year High/Year Low (Hi-Lo)* figures show the upper and lower price limits for a share, bond, or market index over the past 52 weeks. A brokerage report might list the year high of XYZ Company at $52 and the low at $35 to illustrate the peak and trough prices for the security over the last year. Analysts will use the range of prices, in conjunction with technical analysis or in comparison to earnings, in order to forecast future price potential.

See also EARNINGS; INDEX NUMBERS; TRADING RANGE.

YIELD

Yield is the amount of money an investor receives on a security or a property in proportion to the amount of the investment.

Usually stated as a percentage, yield is calculated on an annual amount, or on a total amount. For example, if an investor buys a security for $1,000 and receives $100 in return, the yield is 10%. If that investor receives 10% for five years, the yield is 10% annual interest.

Where bonds are concerned, calculations of yield can become more complicated. The simplest to understand is current yield—the annual interest amount divided by the current market price of the bond. Also known as interest yield, running yield, earnings yield, and flat yield, current yield is useful for making comparisons between bonds at a fixed point in time.

Of more interest to investors is the yield to maturity. Also known as the yield to redemption, yield to maturity accounts for both the annual interest payments and any capital gain or loss realized from holding the bond. The yield to maturity is more informative than the current yield because it accounts for the initial purchase price, the interest payments, the value of the bond at maturity, and the time remaining until the bond matures.

See also CAPITAL GAIN; DIVIDEND; INTEREST/INTEREST RATES.

YIELD CURVE

A *Yield Curve* is a graph that plots the respective yields of a group of securities, identical in all respects except for their maturity dates, against the time remaining until maturity. The line, invariably a smooth curve, highlights differences between short-term yields and long-term yields.

Yield curves appear in three major shapes. Most common is an upward slope, which reflects lower yields on short-term maturities than those on long-term maturities. A downward sloping curve, also known as an inverted yield curve, suggests higher demand for short-term loans and expectations of future interest rate cuts. A flat line denotes a narrowing of yield spreads among the different maturities.

See also CAPITAL GAIN; INVERTED YIELD CURVE; YIELD.

YIELD TO MATURITY

See YIELD.

YUGOSLAVIA, REPUBLIC OF

See SERBIA AND CROATIA.

YUPPIE

The term *Yuppie* first came into use in the United States in approximately 1980. It is slang for a young urban professional; it deliberately invited comparison to such terms as *hippie* and *yippie* from the 1960s and early 1970s, and the contrast in meaning highlighted the changes in social and political climate that had occurred in the intervening years.

The yuppie social category was based partly on age, partly on class, and partly on residency. But beyond the data about occupations and income, the yuppies were identified by their lifestyle and their values. The term yuppie, most heavily employed in the major media between 1983 and 1988, came to connote single-minded devotion to wealth, success, and extravagance. The yuppies were a particular substratum of the upper middle class who probably comprised no more than 5% of the "baby boom" generation (those born between 1945 and 1960). If yuppies were defined as those baby boomers who earned more than $40,000 a year in a professional or managerial occupation, and lived in urban areas, there were probably no more than 1.5 million of them at most.

There was also a yuppie style of consumption. Yuppies were identified with a certain set of tastes. In consumer goods, these were typified by the Rolex watch; such cars as Porsches, Saabs, Volvos, and BMWs; high-priced, high-status foods epitomized by "nou-velle cuisine," mineral water, and sushi; residency in exclusive apartments or condominiums; and lavish vacations. In these consumption patterns, the yuppies exemplified many of the same characteristics of "conspicuous consumption" that Thorstein Veblen had identified 60 years earlier, although (as noted below) the yuppies were by no means part of the leisure class.

Politically, the yuppies tended to support the Republican Party, given their success in the business world, their relatively high incomes, and the fact that most of them had at best the vaguest memories of the social struggles of a generation earlier. However, they usually differed with the Republican positions on some issues, such as abortion and women's rights.

There was also a yuppie attitude toward work. Unlike many of their middle-class professional predecessors, the yuppies did not pursue social service careers such as medicine, social work, or education. When they did graduate work it tended to be in law or business, but many yuppies went directly into the world of work after receiving a bachelor's degree. The premise here was that with many jobs available in banks, corporations, law firms, consulting agencies, and brokerages that offered excellent starting salaries, there was no point in prolonging one's education and accumulating debts when one could be off and running in the business world. Further, the market for PhDs had been glutted. The financial/speculative boom that occurred in the United States up until the fall of 1987 provided the context in which the yuppie strategy could succeed.

In addition, during this period, the distribution of income became increasingly unequal. According to the Census Bureau, the income gap between the richest and poorest families was wider in the mid-1980s than at any time since the bureau began to keep statistics in 1946. This gap grew even greater in the following years with the further spread of what economists Robert Frank and Philip Cook have called "winner-take-all markets." These developments reinforced the tendency, perhaps most marked among the yuppies, to see the world in terms of winners and losers.

The yuppies were no group of 20-somethings born to join the idle rich and thus be assured of an affluent lifestyle regardless of their own efforts. The yuppies were quintessentially upwardly mobile. They engaged in long hours of work. This arose not only from the character of their jobs and the drive to "get ahead"; the fact of engagement in work became a moral imperative. Not to be frenetically busy, even on the weekends, was seen as a defect, a sign that one was not engaged wholeheartedly in the business of living. The yuppies took up residency in the "fast lane." They worked hard; they exercised hard (strenuous jogging and aerobic workouts); and they relaxed in a serious, calculated way, whether in a restaurant or on vacation.

The media attention given to the yuppies and the yuppie lifestyle increased their influence far beyond the level suggested by the yuppies' proportion of the population.

However, after the stock market crash of October 1987, in which some 40,000 people on Wall Street lost their jobs, many yuppies had to relocate to find new employment. By the 1990s the term *yuppie* largely fell out of use, although it was occasionally revived, such as in studies seeking to determine what had become of the yuppies as they grew older, or in projections about the future of certain businesses, such as those conducted on the Internet.

ZEICHNUNG (Germany)

Zeichnung is a subscription for a new issue.

See also INITIAL PUBLIC OFFERING (IPO).

ZEITGESCHAAFTE (Germany)

Zeitgeschaafte refers to trades on the forward market.

ZERO PLUS TICK

Zero Plus Tick is the instance in which a stock trades twice, both times higher than the previous price.

For example: If XYZ Corporation trades at $50. . . 50 1/8. . . 50 1/8, the first price over fifty is a plus tick and the second is a zero plus tick. If a price trades lower than the previous price it is a zero minus tick and a short sale cannot be executed at the price. If the price of XYZ Corporation goes back to $50, a short sale cannot be executed at that price. Either the price would have to go lower and uptick, or it would have to trade again at $50 1/8 for a market short sell to be executed.

A zero plus tick is important for traders on American exchanges because short sales can only be made on a plus tick or a zero plus tick. The rule helps to prevent the hammering of a share's price by the short sellers.

See also MARGIN; SELLING SHORT; TICK; UPTICK.

ZERTIFIKAT (Germany)

See CERTIFICATE.

ZIMBABWE, REPUBLIC OF

The *Republic of Zimbabwe*, formerly Southern Rhodesia, Rhodesia, or Zimbabwe Rhodesia, is a landlocked country of southern Africa. It is bordered on the north by Zambia, on the northeast and east by Mozambique, on the south by South Africa, and on the southwest and west by Botswana. It also touches Namibia with its far western corner.

Area: 150,873 square miles (390,759 square km)

Population: 11,261,000 (26.4% urban; 73.6% rural)

Form of Government: Multiparty republic, with one legislative house: House of Assembly—150 members. Head of state and government: President.

Official Language: English

Capital: Harare

Largest Cities: Harare, 1,184,169; Bulawayo, 620,936; Chitungwiza, 274,035; Mutare, 131,808; Gweru, 124,735

Economy:

Currency: Zimbabwean Dollar(Z$)

National Budget: Revenue—Z$13.3 billion; expenditures—Z$14.7 billion (recurrent expenditures: 78.7%; of which goods and services: 48.7%; transfer payments: 29.9%)

Public Debt: US$3.0 billion

Gross National Product: US$5.8 billion

Principal Products: Sugarcane, corn, wheat; tobacco leaves, soybeans; livestock; gold

Foreign Trade (Imports): Z$11.8 billion (machinery and transport equipment: 35.1%, of which transport equipment: 7.9%; fuels: 14.7%, of which petroleum products: 14.6%; chemicals: 13.9%; manufactured goods: 13.5%, of which textiles: 2.0%; paper and paperboard: 1.5%; from South Africa: 27.0%; United Kingdom: 10.1%; United States: 8.9%; Japan: 6.0%; Germany: 4.9%; the Netherlands: 2.6%; France: 2.5%; Switzerland: 1.9%; Italy: 1.5%)

Foreign Trade (Exports): Z$10.2 billion (domestic exports: 84.3%, of which tobacco: 24.3%; gold sales: 15.1%; ferroalloys: 6.4%; asbestos: 3.6%; nickel metal: 3.4%; cut flowers: 1.7%; cotton: 1.5%; corn: 1.2%; to South Africa: 12.0%; United Kingdom: 9.3%; Germany: 5.0%; Botswana: 4.7%; Zambia: 4.3%; Mozambique: 3.4%; Italy: 3.1%; the Netherlands: 3.0%; Switzerland: 2.8%; Malawi: 2.7%)

Stock Exchanges: 1
Zimbabwe Stock Exchange (ZSE)
8th Floor, Southampton House
Union Avenue/1st Street
PO Box UA 234
Harare
Zimbabwe
Phone: (263-4) 736861/791045
Fax: (263-4) 791045

Internet Address: www.meiklesafrica.com

Trading Hours: Monday–Friday, 9:00 to 12:00

Office Hours: Monday–Friday, 8:00 to 4:30

Exchange Holidays:

1 January	11 August
10, 13 April	25, 26 December
1, 25 May	

Listed Companies: 71

Market Capitalization: US$6,700 millions

Major Sectors: Banking, industrial, food, mining, metals

History: The Zimbabwe Stock Exchange is a small but active stock exchange in Africa. It was established in 1896 and has been open to foreign investment since 1993. Small by world standards, within the context of Africa it is second only to the much older established stock market in Johannesburg. It currently has 12 members and more than 60 listed securities. There are two indices, the Zimbabwe Industrial Index and the Zimbabwe Mining Index.

During 1996, the Zimbabwe Stock Exchange market capitalization surged 165%, from Z$19.9 billion to Z$52.8 billion (roughly US$4.87 billion), making it one of the star emerging market performers. This was due in some part to the listing of Ashanti Goldfields following its takeover of Cluff Resources.

The Zimbabwe Stock Exchange operates according to the Stock Exchange Act (Chapter 198). Companies may not allow more than 40% of their ownership (traded after 1993) to be foreign, and no single overseas shareholder can possess more than 10% of any company's shares. Those bringing in funds through a registered commercial bank may now repatriate their income and sales proceeds free of charge, but taxes of 15% on dividends and 10% on capital gains are levied on individuals. The Reserve Bank has placed fresh controls on dual-listed shares: those importing foreign bought scrip now need permission to sell locally, while locally acquired dual listed scrip remains unsaleable outside Zimbabwe.

Trading days and times are Monday to Friday, 9:00–12:00. There is a basic Z$20 charge per transaction and per registration. Brokerage fees are 2% on transactions less than Z$50,000 to 1% on transactions of more than Z$100,000. There is a 20% tax on dividends levied semiannually and a 30% capital gains tax, although this rate varies with the length of investment.

The value of quoted shares rose 92% in U.S. dollar terms (more than 12% in local currency terms) in 1996, but growth slackened in 1997 due to a 10% fall in the Zimbabwe dollar and an inflation rate above 20% during the same period. The reduction in interest rates by the end of 1996 to 19% and the end of the drought were factors stimulating growth in 1996. With more than 40% of company performances linked to farm output, the industrial index soared from 3972 to 8786 between January and December in 1996.

There have been four new issues in 1997 raising market capitalization 28.8%, from $5.2 billion to $6.7 billion. Sixty-seven companies are listed. The dual listing of Ashanti's 10 million shares contributed to the increase, along with those of Meikles (Northchart), Randalls, National Merchant Bank, Consolidated Farming Investments (the former farmers' co-operative) and Interfresh. A major challenge is to move to a central share register and scrip depository, with the aim of eventually getting the market on screen.

Classes of Securities: Ordinary shares and other securities

Indices: ZSE Industrial Index (1967 = 100)

Supervisory Organizations:
Ministry of Finance
Zimbabwe Stock Exchange

Settlement Details:

Shares: Trade date + seven days (T + 7)

Trading: Trading is implemented by a call-over system.

Listing Requirements: Available from Zimbabwe Stock Exchange

Investor Taxation: Withholding tax dividend payments are 15% at the source for residents and non-residents.

A deduction of 10% for annual inflation is allowed. Capital gains of less than Z$1,000 are not liable for taxation.

Limitations: Ownership of a Zimbabwe company is limited to 5% per individual investor and 25% (excluding multinational investors) collectively for all foreign investors.

Securities Lending: None

Brokerage Firms:
Corporate Securities
6th Floor, Livingstone House
Samora Machel Avenue
PO Box 7245
Harare
Zimbabwe
Phone: (263-4) 702005
Fax: (263-4) 702006

Edwards & Company
Club Chambers
Cnr. Baker Avenue/Third Street

PO Box 1475
Harare
Zimbabwe
Phone: (263-4) 727907
Fax: (263-4) 707932

Remo Investment Brokers
3rd Floor, Royal Mutual House
45 Baker Avenue
Harare
Zimbabwe
Phone: (263-4) 702398

Sagit Stockbrokers
20th Floor, Karigamombe Centra
53 Samora Machel Avenue
Harare
Zimbabwe
Phone: (263-4) 738811

Quincor Stockbrokers
2nd Floor, Kurima House
Baker Avenue
PO Box HG865
Highlands
Harare
Zimbabwe
Phone: (263-4) 725411

Company Information:

10 Most Active Companies

Name of Company	Trading Value (US$ in millions)
Delta	64.15
Bindura Nickel	9.23
TA Holdings	6.62
Wankie Colliery	4.88
Portland Holdings	4.84
Colcom Holdings	4.15
Zimbabwe Sun	3.65
Hippo Valley Estates	3.05
National Foods	2.43
Barclays Bank of Zimbabwe	2.26

10 Major Companies

Name of Company	Market Capitalization (US$ in millions)
Delta	436.38
Bindura Nickel	170.58
Barclays Bank of Zimbabwe	134.49
Zimbabwe Sun	125.22
Hippo Valley Estates	116.38
Tobacco Sales	84.37
Portland Holdings	75.98
Rio Tinto Zimbabwe	66.93
National Foods	62.73
Plate Glass Industries	60.96

Regional Exchanges: None

Other Investment Information:

Investment Center
Ministry of Finance, Economic Planning and
  Development
Munhumutapa Building
Samora Marchel Avenue
Causeway
Harare
Zimbabwe
Phone: (263-4) 794571
Telex: 22141

Ministry of the Environment and Tourism
Karigamombe Center
Causeway
Harare
Zimbabwe
Phone: (263-4) 794455

Reserve Bank of Zimbabwe
76 Samora Marchel Avenue
PO Box 1283
Harare
Zimbabwe
Phone: (263-4) 790731
Telex: 26075

ZIRKA AUFTRAG (Germany)
See LIMIT ORDER.

ZULASSUNGSSTELLE (Germany)
Zulassungsstelle are the listings or admissions committees of the German stock exchanges. The Listings Committee licenses securities before they are admitted to the official listing, and scrutinizes all relevant information to ensure that documentation is in order and full disclosure has been made to the public.

See also GERMANY/LISTING REQUIREMENTS.

ZUSAMMENSCHLUSS (Germany)

See MERGER; TAKEOVER/TAKEOVER BID.

ZUTEILUNGSSCHEIN (Germany)

See ALLOTMENT LETTER.

ZWISCHENBILANZ (Germany)

See INTERIM STATEMENT.

ZWISCHENHANDLER (Germany)

See AGENT.

APPENDICES

EMERGING STOCK MARKETS

The study of "emerging markets" has become popular only in recent years, as the world moves toward a global economy and as businesses in these markets become increasingly productive. Investors obviously have a purpose in such study: to select those market areas that provide strong opportunities for growth as their economies and stock markets develop and mature.

Emerging market countries are those countries experiencing or showing the potential for high economic growth, but frequently having substantial political, economic, and market-related risks. Although many stock exchanges are actively working to create fair and orderly markets, often they can do little to eliminate such problems as insider trading, inadequate disclosure of corporate cross holdings, or the influence of economic and political factors that affect share prices as well as the entire market. These problems can also occasionally occur in developed markets; however, developed markets generally have established monitoring mechanisms and will take strong punitive actions when they detect and prosecute violators. Such mechanisms, along with self-regulating organizations, act as a deterrent and help to keep the markets fair and orderly. For many years the attitude of many smaller countries appeared to be that their securities markets were economically insignificant, that such regulation was unimportant compared to their more pressing economic concerns. Some of these markets traded shares owned by wealthy families who used trading as a way of raising short-term capital. The markets had a very static aspect, showing little or no growth. In recent years stock exchanges in smaller countries have come to recognize the importance of establishing measures under the general category of "investor protection" as a way to build the confidence of savers and investors with an interest in the securities markets.

In 1970 there were 32 developing countries with securities or stock markets, but only a handful were active. A mere six were backed by legislation, and only two, Argentina and the Philippines, were under the control of a securities commission. By 1992 the number had grown to more than 50 developing countries with securities markets, 21 of which had securities commissions. In the same time period, the world equity market capitalization grew from US$50 billion to more than US$600 billion with the number of listed companies growing 100% (5,000 to 10,000). The growing world interest in trading equities is obvious, but this growth does not necessarily represent a maturing of the full regulatory, informational, and trading development of such markets.

Emerging markets can experience a short, speculative increase, frequently followed by a severe decline, or they can experience sustained growth as they take their places in the global economy. Prudent investors look for conditions and events that will encourage and nurture economic growth. These factors are likely to encourage economic growth:

Government deregulation of key industries (transportation, oil)
Privatization of important industries (airline, telecommunications, banking)
Introduction of fiscal prudence policies
Removal of price subsidies
Reduction and elimination of trade barriers
Introduction of tighter fiscal and monetary policies
Enhanced and encouraged international competitiveness
Stabilization of monetary exchange rates
Manageable inflation, with measures taken to contain it
Increased resources becoming available to the private sector
Decreasing foreign debt
Reliable investment alternatives
Expanding consumer base
Skilled, competitive labor force

Many of the world's stock markets are now taking steps to pass securities legislation, establish regulatory commissions and self-regulatory organizations, as well as build designated investor protection funds to encourage investment within the country or from the international investment community. The establishment, implementation, and active compliance of these organizations and funds is essential to any stock market's growth and development. It is compliance with rules, which make the market both fair and orderly, that will allow the market to have "transparency."

Compliance allows the institutional and individual investor a fair opportunity to profit from a successful business. The potential for profit is still the primary reason for investing in shares.

Taxation favorable to investors is developing as countries' stock markets grow. Favorable tax environments encourage investors to buy and trade securities, thereby lowering the businesses of various countries' dependence on debt. Many countries have created tax benefits for equity investors, and some have eliminated capital gains taxes entirely. Taxes are being further modified, through tax treaties or gains elimination, to attract international investors. Additional encouragement is coming from privatization programs, which provide for share ownership of what were previously government-owned companies.

Statistical and analytical socio-economic information on international emerging markets is becoming readily available. Books, available through bookstores or at public libraries, as well as on the Internet provide an abundance of information (search words: emerging markets). Internet information on emerging markets is normally provided by investment firms (i.e., brokerage firms, mutual funds, investment advisers), specializing in international investing. There are also several organizations supportive of international investing who can provide database information.

The International Finance Corporation (IFC), a member of the World Bank Group, is owned by more than 162 member countries. IFC has served as financial and technical support for businesses and developing member countries for the past 40 years. Since 1975, the IFC has maintained a performance statistical database on emerging stock markets. In their annual *Emerging Stock Markets Factbook*, IFC defines "emerging markets" as ". . . those which are in a developing economy, with the implications that all have the potential for development." IFC now provides quarterly and monthly analysis of emerging markets in the form of hard copy booklets, computer diskettes, or other data delivery systems. The "Emerging Markets Data Base (EMDB)" looks at local index performance, and provides indexes created by IFC, including:

IFC Global (IFCG) Indexes
Market Weights in the IFCG Composite Index
Comparative Valuations of the IFCG Indexes
IFCG Price Index Performance Summary
IFCG Price Indexes
Percent Change in IFCG Price Indexes
IFCG Total Return Index Performance Summary
IFCG Total Return Indexes
Percent Change in IFCG Total Return Indexes

IFC Investable (IFCI) Indexes
Market Weights in the IFCI Composite Index
Comparative Valuations of the IFCI Indexes
IFCI Price Index Performance Summary
IFCI Price Index
Percent Change in IFCI Price Indexes
IFCI Total Return Index Performance Summary
IFCI Total Return Indexes
Percent Change in IFCI Price Indexes

IFC Global (IFCG) Industry Indexes
Industry Weights in the IFCG Composite Index
Sector Distribution of the IFCG Composite Index by Market
IFCG Industry Price Indexes Performance Summary
IFCG Industry Price Indexes
Percent Change in IFCG Industry Price Indexes
IFCG Industry Total Return Indexes Performance Summary
IFCG Industry Total Return Indexes
Percent Change in IFCG Industry Total Return Indexes

IFC Investable (IFCI) Industry Indexes
Industry Weights in the IFCI Composite Index
Sector Distribution of the IFCI Composite Index by Market
IFCI Industry Price Indexes Performance Summary
IFCI Industry Price Indexes
Percent Change in IFCI Industry Price Indexes
IFCI Industry Total Return Indexes Performance Summary
IFCI Industry Total Return Indexes
Percent Change in IFCI Industry Total Return Indexes

Additionally, these publications comment on subjects of market performance and economic, as well as political, events.

As this *International Encyclopedia of the Stock Market* attests, it is not longer necessary to convince many economically developing countries of the value of an active equities market that follows the legislative and structural examples of more mature markets. It is also not necessary to convince the 95 countries listed here of the significance of international investing to their future economic success and growth. As the information for the *Encyclopedia* was being gathered from the various securities exchanges, it quickly became clear that countries are establishing meaningful legislation, building organizations for compliance, and setting in place structures for the implementation of securities trading. Transaction-clearing organizations and depositories are either established and functional, or are scheduled to be so in the near future. The numbers of traded companies are increasing, with strict requirements in place for their listings. Parallel markets are functional or being set in place for the trading of smaller growth companies. Trading floors are disappearing in favor of computerized book-entry (no certificate) systems for handling transactions and settlements. Information on performance of markets, individual share issues, and economic developments is now becoming more readily available. These developments and changes will encourage domestic and international investing in securities.

Historically, countries that have enabled companies to obtain money from foreign capital markets have flourished from the added leverage. Japan, Hong Kong, Singapore, Thailand, Malaysia, Chile, and Mexico have all benefited from an international market. During the 1980s more than a hundred emerging market funds were established, and they raised more than US$4 billion in new capital equity for investments in developing countries. In the 1990s the number is considerably higher.

All markets are subject to political, economic, and social influences; they are all part of investment risk. Even the United States stock market is sharply influenced by, for example, changes in interest rates, which can have more to do with politics than economics. Emerging markets involve another risk, however: the speculation that accompanies perceived high growth in anticipation of higher share prices is a prime motivation for institutional and individual investors alike. Such anticipation can create a price bubble in an individual company's share price or in a popular emerging market. Just as share prices of companies involved with the Internet during the mid-1990s advanced greatly beyond actual earnings levels, so can a general increase occur in the prices of companies in a popular market. Eventually, speculative profits are taken, and gains can be lost as quickly as they occur. Likewise, as quickly as privatizations are now taking place, changes in government can reverse the process. The main advantages at this time are high-speed communication, the strong need for economic expansion, and a growing trend toward democracy. Another important stabilizing factor could be the element of competition between the exchanges for the funds of the international investor. Many former political and economic systems have been dramatically unsuccessful. Real growth can only come from a country's entrance and development in the world economy. Market cycles and speculative anticipation eventually give way to steady growth investing.

The future of emerging markets depends on the ability of countries to establish a sound regulatory, organizational, and informational framework with fair and orderly trading for all investors. Obviously, the framework needs the backing of economic growth and development in a political atmosphere that encourages investing. Active international trading will likely require the direct involvement of all interested countries to set world standards of uniformity.

Investors can approach emerging market international investing through foreign banks or brokerage firms; they can make use of companies providing investment advisory services, buy shares of international open and closed-end funds traded locally, or invest in a variety of depository (depositary) receipts/depository shares that may be traded in the investor's country of residence. Price changes normally reflect the price fluctuation on the main market plus currency changes. Shares trade and pay dividends in terms of local currency. The receipts also have the advantage of not requiring any custodial or safekeeping charges and trade for regular domestic commission rates.

Sector analysis is frequently used to identify the strongest areas of economic development within a country or group of countries. Sectors in emerging market countries vary dramatically according to underlying factors influencing growth. India, with more than 200 million people in its middle class, could have strong growth in consumer-related sectors, whereas a country like Pakistan, which is placing emphasis on electrification and infrastructure improvements, would likely show the greatest growth in those areas.

Sector analysis can be obtained from many stock exchanges, but is also available from many subscription sources, including the Internet. Investing in emerging markets can be profitable. The prudent investor can research where to find them and how to take advantage of special growth situations.

Although the emerging markets investment theme has been popular in recent years, it should not eliminate investors' interest in developed markets. One need only look at the tremendous growth of the New York Stock Exchange or the NASDAQ (over the counter) markets to see incredible growth in the past couple of years, as well as excellent performance for the past five years and even ten years. These excellent profits come from some of the most developed markets in the world. Every market has opportunities—just as every market has risks. Whether a market is emerging, submerging, or developed should be a matter of concern for any investor, part of his or her investment philosophy and strategy.

Prudent investing involves a screening process. The screen attempts to sift out favorable and unfavorable factors of growth potential. Investment selections with the highest number of favorable and lowest number of unfavorable factors are often the selections that become most profitable.

WORLD CURRENCY

Issuing Country	1 Unit Main Currency	Abbr.*	Equals	Sub-Currency
Afghanistan	afghani	(AF)	100	puls
Albania	lek	(L)	100	quintars
Algeria	Algerian dinar	(DA)	100	centimes
American Samoa	US dollar	(US$)	100	cents
Andorra	French franc	(F)	100	centimes
Angola	new kwanza	(NKz)	100	lwei
Anguilla	EC dollar	(EC$)	100	cents
Antigua & Barbuda	EC dollar	(EC$)	100	cents
Argentina	nuevo peso argentino	(ARS)	100	centavos
Armenia	dram	(AMD)	100	luma
Aruba	Aruban florin	(Af)	100	cents
Australia	Australian dollar	($A)	100	cents
Austria	Austrian shilling	(S)	100	groschen
Bahamas	Bahamain dollar	(B$)	100	cents
Bahrain	Bahraini dinar	(BD)	1,000	fils
Bangladesh	taka	(Tk)	100	poiska
Barbados	Barbadian dollar	(Bds$)	100	cents
Belarus	Belarusian ruble	(BYB)	100	kopeks
Belgium	Belgian franc	(BF)	100	centimes
Belize	Belizean dollar	($)	100	cents
Benin	CFA franc	(CFA)	100	centimes
Bermuda	Bermudian dollar	($)	100	cents
Bhutan	ngultrum (Indian currency is also legal tender)	(Nu)	100	chetrum
Bolivia	boliviano	($)	100	centavos
Botswana	pula	(P)	100	thebe
Brazil	cruzerio real	(CR$)	100	centavos
British Virgin Islands	U.S. dollar	(US$)	100	cents
Brunei	Bruneain dollar	(B$)	100	cents
Bulgaria	lev	(Lv)	100	stotinki
Burkina	CFA franc	(CFAF)	100	centimes
Burma	kyat	(K)	100	pyas
Burundi	Burundi franc	(FBu)	100	centimes
Cambodia	new riel	(CR)	100	sen
Cameroon	CFA franc	(CFAF)	100	centimes
Canada	Canadian dollar	(Can$)	100	cents
Cape Verde	Cape Verdian escudo	(CVEsc)	100	centavos
Cayman Islands	Caymanian dollar	(CI$)	100	cents
Central African Republic	CFA franc	(CFAF)	100	centimes
Chad	CFA franc	(CFAF)	100	centimes
Chile	Chilean peso	(CH$)	100	centavos
China	yuan	(¥)	10	jiao
Christmas Island	Australian dollar	($A)	100	cents
Cocos (Keeling) Islands	Australian dollar	($A)	100	cents
Colombia	Colombian peso	(Col$)	100	centavos
Comoros	Comoran franc	(CF)	100	centimes
Congo	CFA franc	(CFAF)	100	centimes
Cook Islands	New Zealand dollar	(NZ$)	100	cents
Costa Rica	Costa Rican colón	(C)	100	centimos

Issuing Country	1 Unit Main Currency	Abbr.*	Equals	Sub-Currency
Côte d'Ivoire	CFA franc	(CFAF)	100	centimes
Croatia	Croation kuna	(HRK)	100	paras
Cuba	Cuban peso	(Cu$)	100	centavos
Cyprus	Cypriot pound	(£C)	100	cents
Czech Republic	koruna	(Kcs)	100	haleru
Denmark	Danish krone	(DKr)	100	cere
Djibouti	Djibouti franc	(F)	100	centimes
Dominica	EC dollar	(EC$)	100	cents
Dominican Republic	Dominican peso	(RD$)	100	centavos
Ecuador	sucre	(S/)	100	centavos
Egypt	Egyptian pound	(£E)	100	piasters
El Salvador	Salvadoran colón	(¢)	100	centavos
Equatorial Guinea	CFA franc	(CFAF)	100	centimes
Eritrea	birr (Ethiopian currency used)	(Br)	100	cents
Estonia	Estonian kroon	(EEK)	100	cents
Ethiopia	birr	(Br)	100	cents
Faulkland Islands	Faulkland pound	(£F)	100	pence
Faroe Islands	Danish krone	(DKr)	100	oere
Fiji	Fijian dollar	(F$)	100	cents
Finland	markka (or Finmark)	(Fmk)	100	pennia
France	French franc	(F)	100	centimes
French Guiana	French franc	(F)	100	centimes
French Polynesia	CFP franc	(CFPF)	100	centimes
Gabon	CFA franc	(CFAF)	100	centimes
Gambia	dalasi	(D)	100	butut
Gaza Strip	new Israeli shekel	(IS)	100	new agorot
Germany	deutsche mark	(DM)	100	pfennige
Ghana	new cedi	(¢)	100	pesewas
Gibraltar	Gibraltar pound	(£G)	100	pence
Greece	drachma	(Dr)	100	lepta
Greenland	Danish krone	(DKr)	100	oere
Grenada	EC dollar	(EC$)	100	cents
Guadeloupe	French franc	(F)	100	centimes
Guam	U.S. dollar	(US$)	100	cents
Guatemala	quetzal	(Q)	100	centavos
Guernsey	Guernsey pound	(£G)	100	pence
Guinea	Guinean franc	(GF)	100	centimes
Guinea-Bissau	Guinea-Bissau peso	(PG)	100	centavos
Guyana	Guyanese dollar	(G$)	100	cents
Haiti	gourde	(G)	100	centimes
Holy See (Vatican City)	Vatican lira	(VLit)	100	centesimi
Honduras	lempira	(L)	100	centavos
Hong Kong	Hong Kong dollar	(HK$)	100	cents
Hungary	forint	(Ft)	100	filler
Iceland	Icelandic krona	(Kr)	100	aurar
India	Indian rupee	(Re)	100	paise
Indonesia	Indonesian rupiah	(Rp)	100	sen
Iran	Iranian rial	(RI)	100	tomans
Iraq	Iraqi dinar	(ID)	100	fils
Ireland	Irish pound	(£)	100	pence
Israel	new Israeli shekel	(IS)	100	agorot

Issuing Country	1 Unit Main Currency	Abbr.*	Equals	Sub-Currency
Italy	Italian lira	(Lit)	100	centesimi
Jamaica	Jamaican dollar	(J$)	100	cents
Japan	yen	(JPY)	100	sen
Jersey	Jersey pound	(£J)	100	pence
Jordan	Jordanian dinar	(JD)	100	fils
Kenya	Kenyan shilling	(KSh)	100	cents
Kiribati	Australian dollar	($A)	100	cents
Korea, North	North Korean won	(Wn)	100	chon
Korea, South	South Korean won	(Wn)	100	chon
Kuwait	Kuwaiti dinar	(KD)	100	fils
Laos	new kip	(K)	100	at
Latvia	lat	(LVL)	100	cents
Lebanon	Lebanese pound	(L)	100	piasters
Lesotho	loti	(L)	100	lisente
Liberia	Liberian dollar	(L$)	100	cents
Libya	Libian dinar	(LD)	1,000	dirhams
Liechtenstein	Swiss franc, franken, or franco	(Fr)	100	centimes, rappen, centesimi
Luxembourg	Luxembourg franc	(Flux)	100	centimes
Macau	pataca	(P)	100	avos
Macedonia (former Yugloslav Rep. of)	denar	(MKD)	100	fils
Madagascar	Malagasy franc	(FMG)	100	centimes
Malawi	Malawian kwacha	(K)	100	tambaia
Malaysia	ringgit	(M$)	100	sen
Maldives	rufiyaa	(Rf)	100	laari
Mali	CFA franc	(CFAF)	100	centimes
Malta	Maltese lira	(Lm)	100	cents
Man, Isle of	pound	(£M)	100	pence
Marshall Islands	U.S. dollar	(US$)	100	cnts
Martinique	French franc	(F)	100	centimes
Mauritania	ouguiya	(UM)	5	khoums
Mauritius	Mauritian rupee	(Re)	100	cents
Mayotte	French franc	(F)	100	centimes
Mexico	New Mexican peso	($)	100	centavos
Micronesia, Fed. States of	U.S. Dollar	(US$)	100	cents
Monaco	French franc	(F)	100	centimes
Mongolia	tugrik	(Tug)	100	mongos
Montserrat	EC dollar	(EC$)	100	cents
Morocco	Moroccan dirham	(DH)	100	centimes
Mozambique	metical	(Mt)	100	centavos
Namibia	South African rand	(R)	100	cents
	Namibian dollar	(N$)	100	cents
Nauru	Australian dollar	($A)	100	cents
Nepal	Nepalese rupee	(Re)	100	paisa
Netherlands	Netherlands guilder, gulden, or florin	(G)	100	cents
Netherlands Antilles	Netherlands Antilles guilder, gulden, or florin	(G)	100	cents
New Caledonia	CFP franc	(CFPF)	100	centimes
New Zealand	New Zealand dollar	(NZ$)	100	cents

Issuing Country	1 Unit Main Currency	Abbr.*	Equals	Sub-Currency
Nicaragua	gold cordoba	(C$)	100	centavos
Niger	CFA franc	(CFAF)	100	centimes
Nigeria	naira	(N)	100	kobo
Niue	New Zealand dollar	(NZ$)	100	cents
Norfolk Island	Australian dollar	($A)	100	cents
Northern Mariana Islands	U.S. dollar	(US$)	100	cents
Norway	Norwegian krone	(NKr)	100	oare
Oman	Omani rial	(RO)	1,000	baiza
Pacific Islands, Trust Territory of the	U.S. dollar	(US$)	100	cents
Pakistan	Pakistani rupee	(Re)	100	paisa
Panama	balboa	(B)	100	centesimos
Papua New Guinea	kina	(K)	100	toea
Paraguay	guarani	(G)	100	centimos
Peru	nuevo sol	(S)	100	centimos
Philippines	Philippine peso	(P)	100	centavos
Pitcairn Islands	New Zealand dollar	(NZ$)	100	cents
Poland	zloty	(Zl)	100	groszy
Portugal	Portuguese escudo	(Esc)	100	centavos
Qatar	Qatari riyal	(QR)	100	dirhams
Reunion	French franc	(F)	100	centimes
Romania	leu	(L)	100	bani
Russia	ruble	(R)	100	kopeks
Rwanda	Rwandan franc	(RF)	100	centimes
St. Helena	St. Helenian pound	(£S)	100	pence
St. Kitts and Nevis	EC dollar	(EC$)	100	cents
St. Lucia	EC dollar	(EC$)	100	cents
St. Pierre and Miquelon	French franc	(F)	100	centimes
St. Vincent and the Grenadines	EC dollar	(EC$)	100	cents
San Marino	Italian lire	(Lit)	100	centesimi
Sao Tome and Principe	dobra	(Db)	100	centimos
Saudi Arabia	Saudi riyal	(SR)	100	halalah
Senegal	CFA franc	(CFAF)	100	centimes
Serbia and Montenegro	Yugoslav New Dinar	(YD)	100	paras
Seychelles	rupee	(SR)	100	cents
Sierra Leone	leone	(Le)	100	cents
Singapore	Singapore dollar	(S$)	100	cents
Slovakia	koruna	(Sk)	100	halierov
Slovenia	tolar	(SlT)	100	stotins
Solomon Islands	Solomon Island dollar	(Si$)	100	cents
Somalia	Somali shilling	(SoSh)	100	cents
South Africa	rand	(R)	100	cents
Spain	peseta	(PTA)	100	centimos
Sri Lanka	Sri Lankan rupee	(Re)	100	cents
Sudan	Sudanese pound	(£Sd)	100	piastres
Suriname	Surinamese guilder. gulden, or florin	(G)	100	cents
Svalbard	Norwegian krone	(Nkr)	100	oere
Swaziland	lilangeni	(E)	100	cents
Sweden	Swedish krona	(SKr)	100	oere

Issuing Country	1 Unit Main Currency	Abbr.*	Equals	Sub-Currency
Switzerland	Swiss franc, franken, or franco	(Fr)	100	centimes, rappen, or centesimi
Syria	Syrian pound	(£S)	100	piastres
Taiwan	New Taiwan dollar	(NT$)	100	cents
Tajikistan	ruble	(R)	100	kopeks
Tanzania	Tanzanian shilling	(TSh)	100	cents
Thailand	baht	(B)	100	satang
Togo	CFA franc	(CFAF)	100	centimes
Tokelau	New Zealand dollar	(NZ$)	100	cents
Tonga	pa'anga	(T$)	100	sentini
Trinidad and Tobago	Trin and Tobago dollar	(TT$)	100	cents
Tunisia	Tunisian dinar	(D)	1,000	millimes
Turkey	Turkish lira	(TL)	100	kurus
Tuvalu	Tuvaluan dollar or	($T)	100	100 cents
	Australian dollar	($A)		
Uganda	Ugandan shilling	(USh)	100	cents
United Arab Emirates	Emirian dirham	(DH)	100	fils
United Kingdom	British pound	(£)	100	pence
United States	U.S. dollar	(US$)	100	cents
Uruguay	Urguayan peso	($)	100	centesimos
Vanuatu	vatu	(VT)	100	centimes
Venezuela	bolivar	(B)	100	centimos
Vietnam	new dong	(D)	100	xu
Virgin Islands	U.S. dollar	(US$)	100	cents
Wallis & Futuna	CFP franc	(CFPF)	100	centimes
West Bank	new Israel shekel	(NS)	100	new agorot
	Jordanian dinar	(JD)	1,000	fils
Western Sahara	Moroccan dirham	(DH)	100	centimes
Western Samoa	tala	($)	100	sene
Zambia	Zambian kwacha	(K)	100	ngwee
Zimbabwe	Zimbabwean dollar	(Z$)	100	cen

*Many differences in currency abbreviations exist throughout the world.

OTHER INVESTMENT INFORMATION:
FINANCE, TRADE AND BANKING ORGANIZATIONS

Investment information can be obtained through these sources. Also contact the nearest embassy or consular office to obtain further business, investment, or trading information from a specific country.

Albania, Republic of
Ministry of Trade and Foreign Economic
    Cooperation
Government Offices
Tirana, Albania
Phone: (355) (42) 23791
Telex: 2164
Fax: (355) (42) 23791

Albanian State Bank
Sheshi Skenderbeu 1
Tirana, Albania
Phone: (355) (42) 22435
Telex: 2153

Chamber of Commerce of Albania
Konferenca e Prezes 6
Tirana, Albania
Phone: (355) (42) 27997
Telex: 2179

Algeria, Democratic and Popular Republic of
Ministry of Industry
rue Ahmad Bey
Immeuble le Colisée
Algiers, Algeria
Phone: (213) 601114
Telex: 52707

Central Bank of Algeria
28 ave Franklin Roosevelt
Algiers, Algeria
Phone: (213) 594200
Fax: (213) 603777
Telex: 66499

Chamber of Commerce and Industry of Algeria
1 rue de Languedoc
Algiers, Algeria
Phone: (213) 632525
Fax: (213) 637533
Telex: 66505

Angola, People's Republic of
Foreign Investment Office
Ministry of Planning
Largo do Palacio
Luanda, Angola
Phone: (244) (2) 339052
Telex: 3082

Ministry of Finance
Avda 4 de Fevereiro 25
Luanda, Angola
Phone: (244) (2) 344628
3363

Banco Nacional de Angola
Avda 4 de Fevereiro 151
Luanda, Angola
Phone: (244) (2) 339141
Fax: (244) (2) 393179
Telex: 3005

Anguilla
Ministry of Home Affairs, Tourism, Agriculture and
    Fisheries
The Secretariat
The Valley, Anguilla
Phone: (809) 497-2518
Fax: (809) 497-3389
Telex: 9313

Ministry of Finance and Economic Development
The Secretariat
The Valley, Anguilla
Phone: (809) 497-2451

Anguilla Chamber of Commerce
PO Box 321
The Valley, Anguilla
Phone: (809) 497-2701, (809) 497-2712
Telex: 9327

Antigua and Barbuda
Ministry of Economic Development and Tourism
Administration Building
Queen Elizabeth Highway
St. John's, Antigua, W.I.
Phone: (809) 462-0092
Telex: AK 2122
Cable: EXTERNAL ANTIGUA

Antigua and Barbuda Development Bank
27 St. Mary's Street
PO Box 1279
St. John's, Antigua, W.I.
Phone: (809) 462-0838

Argentina (The Argentine Republic)
Ministry of the Economy
Hipolito Yrigoyen 250
1310 Buenos Aires, Argentina
Phone: (54) (1) 34-6411
Telex: 21952

Central Bank of Argentina
Reconquista 266
1003 Buenos Aires, Argentina
Phone: (54) (1) 39-48411
Fax: (54) (1) 33-46489
Telex: 1137

Chamber of Commerce of Argentina
Avda Leandro N. Alem 36
1003 Buenos Aires, Argentina
Phone: (54) (1) 33-18051
Telex: 18542

Aruba
Aruba Foreign Investment Agency
85 Caya G.f. Betico Croes
Oranjestad, Aruba
Phone: (297) (8) 26070
Fax: (297) (8) 22743

Department of Economic Affairs, Commerce and
  Industry
L.G. Smith Boulevard 15
Oranjestad, Aruba
Phone: (297) (8) 21181
Fax: (297) (8) 34494

Centrale Bank van Aruba
Havenstraat 2
Oranjestad, Aruba
Phone: (297) (8) 33088
Fax: (297-(8) 32251
Telex: 5045

Aruba Chamber of Commerce and Industry
PO Box 140
Zoutmansraat 201
Oranjestad, Aruba
Phone: (297) (8) 21566 or (297) (8) 23500
Fax: (297) (8) 33962

Australia
Department of Foreign Affairs and Trade
Bag 8
Queen Victoria Terrace
Canberra, ACT 2600
Phone: (61) (6) 261-9111
Telex: 62007

Department of Industry, Technology and Commerce
51 Allara Street
Canberra, ACT 2601
Phone: (61) (6) 276-1000
Fax: (61) (6) 276-1111
Telex: 6654

Department of the Treasury
Parkes Place
Parkes, ACT 2600
Phone: (61) (6) 263-1111
Fax: (61) (6) 276-2614
Telex: 62010

International Chamber of Commerce
PO Box E118
Queen Victoria Terrace
Canberra, ACT 2600
Phone: (61) (6) 295-1961
Fax: (61) (6) 295-1076

Australian Chamber of Commerce
PO Box E139
Queen Victoria Terrace
Canberra, ACT 2600
Phone: (61) (6) 285-3523
Fax: (61) (6) 285-3590

Austria, Republic of
ICD Austria
Federal Agency for Industrial Cooperation and Devel-
  opment
Openring 3
1010 Vienna, Austria
Phone: (43) (1) 588580
Fax: (43) (1) 568659

Ministry of Economic Affairs
Section IV
Stubenring 1
1010 Vienna, Austria
Phone: (43) (1) 711000
Fax: (43) (1) 7139311
Telex: 111780

Ministry for the Environment
Radetzkystrasse 2
1031 Vienna, Austria
Phone: (43) (1) 711580
Fax: (43) (1) 7115842
Telex: 3221371

Ministry of Finance
Himmelpfortgasse 9
1010 Vienna, Austria
Phone: (43) (1) 514330
Fax: (43) (1) 5127869
Telex: 111688

Austrian National Bank
Otto Wagner Platz
1090 Vienna, Austria
Phone: (43) (1) 404200
Fax: (43) (1) 404209400
Telex: 114669

Austrian Chamber of Commerce
Wiedner Haupstrasse 63
1040 Vienna, Austria
Phone: (43) (1) 501050
Fax: (43) (1) 50206255
Telex: 11187

Bahamas, Commonwealth of
Ministry of Finance and Planning
Rawson Square
PO Box N-3017
Nassau, the Bahamas
Phone: (242) 322-4151
Telex: 20255

National Economic Council
c/o Secretary to the Cabinet
PO Box N-1747
Nassau, the Bahamas
Phone: (242) 322-2805 or (242) 322-2808
Fax: (242) 32-88294

Foreign Investment Board
c/o Secretary to the Cabinet
PO Box N-1747
Nassau, the Bahamas
Phone: (242) 322-2805 or (242) 322-2808
Fax: (242) 32-88294

The Central Bank of the Bahamas
Frederick Street
PO Box N-4868

Nassau, the Bahamas
Phone: (242) 322-2193
Fax: (242) 322-4321
Telex: 20115

Bahamas Chamber of Commerce
Shirley Street
PO Box N-665
Nassau, the Bahamas
Phone: (242) 322-2145
Fax: (242) 322-4649

The Registrar General's Department
Registry of Companies
PO Box N-532
Nassau, the Bahamas
Phone: (242) 322-3316 or (242) 322-3317
Fax: (242) 322-5553

Bahrain
Bahrain Marketing and Promotions Office
PO Box 11299
Manama, Bahrain
Phone: (973) 533886
Fax: (973) 531117

Bahrain Chamber of Commerce and Industry
PO Box 248
Manama, Bahrain
Phone: (973) 233913
Fax: (973) 241294
Telex: 8691

Bahrain Monetary Agency
PO Box 27
Manama, Bahrain
Phone: (973) 241241
Fax: (973)533342 or (973) 534170

Ministry of Development and Industry
PO Box 245
Manama, Bahrain
(973) 291511
Fax: (973) 290302

Bangladesh, The People's Republic of
Board of Investment
Bangladesh Secretariat
Storey Building
Dhaka, Bangladesh
Phone: (880) (2) 235111

Ministry of Industry
Shilpa Bhapan
91 Motiheel
Dhaka, Bangladesh
Phone: (880) (2) 236020
Telex: 7289

Ministry of Finance and Planning
Bangladesh Secretariat
Storey Building
Dhaka, Bangladesh
Phone: (880) (2) 236511
Telex: 65886

Ministry of the Environment, Forests, Fisheries and
   Livestock
Bangladesh Secretariat
Bhaban 4
Storey Building
Dhaka, Bangladesh
Phone: (880) (2) 236022

Bangladesh Bank
PO Box 325
Motiheel
Dhaka, Bangladesh
Phone: (880) (2) 235000
Fax: (880) (2) 412347
Telex: 65657

Federation of Bangladesh Chambers of Commerce
   and Industry
PO Box 2079
Federation Bhaban
60 Motiheel
Dhaka, Bangladesh
Phone: (880) (2) 250566
Telex: 624733

Barbados

Barbados Industrial Development Corporation
Pelican House
Princess Alice Highway
Bridgetown, Barbados
Phone: (809) 472-5350
Fax: (809) 431-7802
Telex: 2295

Ministry of Trade, Industry and Commerce
Reef Road
Fontabello
PO Box 1016
Bridgetown, Barbados

Phone: (809) 436-6870
Fax: (809) 427-9559
Telex: 2251

Barbados Chamber of Industry and Commerce
PO Box 189
Nemwil House
Lower Collymore Road
St. Michael, Barbados
Phone: (809) 426-0747
Fax: (809) 429-2907

Belarus, Republic of

State Committee on Foreign Economic Relations
vul. Lenina, 14
Minsk 220600, Belarus
Phone: (7) (172) 241756
Fax: (7) (172) 273924
Telex: 2252125 GKVS SU

State Committee on Ecology
Vul. Kollekfornaya, 10
Minsk 220084, Belarus
Phone: (7) (172) 206620
Fax: (7) (172) 205583

Ministry of Trade
Vul. Kirova 8, b/d. 1
Minsk 220050, Belarus
Phone: (7) (172) 270897

National Bank of the Republic of Belarus
Lenina 20
Minsk 220010, Belarus
Phone: (7) (172) 270946

Belgium, Kingdom of

Department of Economic Expansion and Foreign
   Investments
Ministry of Economic Affairs
rue de l'Industrie 10
1040 Brussels, Belgium
Phone: (32) (2) 513-9640
Fax: (32) (2) 514-0389
Telex: 61932

Banque Nationale de Bélgique
5 boulevard de Bérliment
1000 Brussels, Belgium
Phone: (32) (2) 221-2111
Fax: (32) (2) 221-3101

Belize

Ministry of Economic Development
PO Box 174
Belmopan, Belize
Phone: (501) 22322
Telex: 102

Central Bank of Belize
Treasury Lane
PO Box 852
Belize City, Belize
Phone: (501) 77216
Fax: (501) 77106
Telex: 225

Benin, Republic of

Investment Control Commission
Ministry of Planning and Economic Reorganization
PO Box 342
Cotonou, Benin
Phone: (229) 300541
Telex: 5252

Chamber of Commerce, Agriculture and Industry
PO Box 31
Ave du Général de Gaulle
Cotonou, Benin
Phone: (229) 313299

Bermuda

Office of Chief Immigration Officer
Ministry of Labour and Home Affairs
PO Box HM 364
Government Administration Building
30 Parliment Street
Hamilton, Bermuda
Phone: (441) 295-5151
Fax: (441) 295-4115

Ministry of the Environment
Government Administration Building
30 Parliment Street
Hamilton, Bermuda
Phone: (441) 295-5151
Fax: (441) 292-2348

Bermuda Monetary Authority
48 Church Street
Hamilton, Bermuda
Phone: (441) 295-5278
Fax: (441) 292-7471
Telex: 3567

Bermuda Chamber of Commerce
8 Front Street
Hamilton, Bermuda
Phone: (441) 295-4201
Fax: (441) 292-5779

Bolivia, Republic of

Ministry of Industry, Trade and Tourism
Avda Camacho y Bueno
Casilla 1372
La Paz, Bolivia
Phone: (591) 373050, (591) 372056, (591) 372045
Fax: (591) 35881
Telex: 3259 DICOMEX BV

The Central Bank of Bolivia
Ayacucho Mercado
Casilla 3118
La Paz, Bolivia
Phone: (591) 374151
Fax: (591) 35319
Telex: 3228

The National Chamber of Commerce
Avda Mariscal Santa Cruz
Casilla 7
Phone: (591) 354255
Fax: (591) 391004
Telex: 2305

Botswana, Republic of

Ministry of Commerce and Industry
Private Bag 4
Gaborone, Botswana
Phone: (267) 353024
Fax: (267) 356027
Telex: 2543

Botswana Development Corporation
Madirelo House
Mmanaka Road
Gaborone, Botswana
Phone: (267) 351811
Fax: (267) 373539
Telex: 2251

Bank of Botswana
PO Box 712
Gaborone, Botswana
Phone: (267) 351911
Fax: (267) 372984
Telex: 2448

Brazil, The Federated Republic of
Secretariat of the Environment
Esplanada dos Ministérios
Bloco B5 andar
70053 - Brasília, DF
Brazil
Phone: (55) (61) 223-0129
Fax: (55) (61) 226-1644

Brunei, Sultanate of
Economic Development Board
Ministry of Finance
Bandar Seri Begawan
Brunei Darussalem
Phone: (673) (2) 241991
Fax: (673) (2) 226132
Telex: EPUMOFBU 2676

Brunei Darussalem State Chamber of Commerce
PO Box 2246
Bandar Seri Begawan 1922
Brunei Darussalem
Phone: (673) (2) 228533
Fax: (673) (2) 228389
Telex: 2203

Bulgaria, Republic of
Bulgarian National Bank
Sofuska Komuna Street 2
1000 Sofia, Bulgaria
Phone: (359) (2) 85-51-40
Fax: (359) (2) 88-05-58
Telex: 24091

Bulgarian Chamber of Commerce and Industry
Boulevard A. Stamboliiski 11A
1040 Sofia, Bulgaria
Phone: (359) (2) 87-26-31
Fax: (359) (2) 87-32-09
Telex: 22374

Ministry of Industry, Trade and Services
Slavyanska Street 8
1000 Sofia, Bulgaria
Phone: (359) (2) 87-07-41

Ministry of the Environment
ul. William Gladstone 67
1000 Sofia, Bulgaria
Phone: (359) (2) 87-61-51
Fax: (359) (2) 52-16-34
Telex: 22145

Burkina Faso
Ministry of Economic Promotion
PO Box 7008
Ouagadougou
Burkina Faso
Phone: (226) 306361 or (226) 306370
Telex: 9855221 BF

Ministry of the Environment and Tourism
PO Box 7044
Ouagadougou
Burkina Faso
Phone: (226) 306015
Fax: (226) 310122
Telex: 5205

Cameroon, Republic of
Ministry of Industrial and Commercial Development
Yaoundé, Cameroon
Phone: (237) 23-40-40
Fax: (237) 22-27-04
Telex: 8638

Banque des Etats de l'Afrique Centrale
Blvd du 20 Mai
PO Box 1917
Yaoundé, Cameroon
Phone: (237) 23-24-74
Telex: 8275

Canada
Investment Development Division
Investment Canada
240 Sparks Street
PO Box 2800
Station D
Ottawa, Canada K1P 6A5
Phone: (613) 995-0465
Fax: (613) 996-2515

Environment Canada
Les Térrasses de la Chaudière
10 Wellington Street
Ottawa, Canada K1A 0G2
Phone: (613) 997-2800
Fax: (613) 953-6789
Telex: 053-3608

Bank of Canada
234 Wellington Street
Ottawa, Canada K1A 0G9
Phone: (613) 782-8111
Telex: 053-4241

Cape Verde, Republic of
Ministry of Finance and Planning
107 Avda Amílcar Cabral
Praia, Sao Tiago, Cape Verde
Phone: (238) 614329
Telex: 6058

Banco de Cabo Verde (Bank of Cape Verde)
117 Avda Amílcar Cabral
Praia, Sao Tiago, Cape Verde
Phone: (238) 614193
Telex: 99350

Channel Islands, The
Economic Adviser's Office
Cyril Le Marquand House
The Parade
St. Helier, Isle of Jersey
Phone: (44) (534) 25424

Chamber of Commerce
19 Royal Street
St. Helier, Isle of Jersey
Phone: (44) (534) 24536
Fax: (44) (534) 34942

Commercial Relations Office
States Office
North Esplanade
St. Peter Port, Isle of Guernsey
Phone: (44) (481) 727688

Guernsey Chamber of Commerce
States Arcade
Market Street
St. Peter Port, Isle of Guernsey
Phone: (44) (481) 727483
Telex: 419445

Chile, Republic of
Ministry of Economics
Teatinos 120
Santiago, Chile
Phone: (56) (2) 772-5522
Telex: 240558

Executive Secretariat
Foreign Investment Committee
Teatinos 120
Santiago, Chile
Phone: (56) (2) 698-4254
Fax: (56) (2) 698-9476

China, The People's Republic of
Ministry of Foreign Economic Relations and Trade
2 Dongchangan Jie
Beijing 10073, China
Phone: (86) (1) 553-0311
Telex: 22168

China Council for the Promotion of International
   Trade
1 Fu Xing Men Wai Jie
Beijing 100860, China
Phone: (86) (1) 801-3344
Fax: (86) (1) 801-1370
Telex: 22315

People's Bank of China
Cheng Qui
Beijing 100860, China
Phone: (86) (1) 841-3128
Telex: 22017

Colombia
National Planning Department
Calle 26 No. 13-19 Piso 18
Bogotá, Colombia
Phone: (57) (1) 342-7277
Fax: (57) (1) 281-3348
Telex: 45634 DNP B O

Banco Republica (Bank of the Republic)
Calle 16 No. 6-66 Piso 16
Bogotá, Colombia
Phone: (57) (1) 243-7937
Fax: (57) (1) 282-2162

Chamber of Commerce and Industry of Colombia
Calle 71 No. 9-92
Bogotá, Colombia
Phone: (57) (1) 235-9880

Comoros, The Federal Republic of
National Office of Commerce
PO Box 421
Moroni, The Comoros
Phone: (269) 2413
Telex: 233

Ministry of Finance, Economy, Budget and Planning
PO Box 324
Moroni, The Comoros
Phone: (269) 2767
Telex: 219

Ministry of Production, Industry, Rural Development
    and Environment
PO Box 41
Moroni, The Comoros
Phone: (269) 2292
Telex: 240

Banque Centrale des Comoros
PO Box 405
Moroni, The Comoros
Phone: (269) 731002
Telex: 213

The Congo, Republic of
National Investment Commission
Ministry of Finance, Economy and the Budget
PO Box 2031
Brazzaville, The Congo
Phone: (242) 834324
Telex: 5210

Costa Rica, Republic of
Center for Export and Investment Promotion
Apdo 5418
San José, Costa Rica
Phone: (506) 217166
Fax: (506) 200636
Telex: 2385

Ministry of Economy, Industry and Trade
Apdo 10216
San José, Costa Rica
Phone: (506) 221016
Fax: (506) 222305
Telex: 2415

Banco Central de Costa Rica
Apdo 10058
San José, Costa Rica
Phone: (506) 223322
Fax: (506) 234658
Telex: 2163

Côte d'Ivoire, Republic of
Ministry of Industry and Trade
PO Box 140
Abidjan, Côte d'Ivoire
Phone: (225) 210568

Ministry of the Environment, Construction, and Town
    Planning, Posts and Telecommunications
PO Box184
Avenue Jean Paul II

Abidjan, Côte d'Ivoire
Phone: (225) 291367
Telex: 22108

Banque Centrale de Etats de l'Afrique de l'Quest
PO Box 1769
Ave Terrasson de Fougères
Abidjan, Côte d'Ivoire
Phone: (225) 210466
Fax: (225) 222852
Telex: 23474

Cuba, Republic of
State Committee for Economic Cooperation
Calle 1a, Number 201, Vedado
Havana, Cuba
Phone: (53) 3-6661
Telex: 511297

Banco Nacional de Cuba
Lamarilla, Apda 736
Havana 1, Cuba
Phone: (53) 62-8001
Telex: 511822

Cyprus
Central Bank of Cyprus
International Division
PO Box 5529
36 Metochiou Street
Nicosia, Cyprus
Phone: (357) (2) 445281
Fax: (357) (2) 472012
Telex: 2424

Ministry of Commerce and Industry
6 Andreas Araouzos Street
Nicosia, Cyprus
Phone: (357) (2) 302422
Fax: (357) (2) 366120
Telex: 2283

Cyprus Chamber of Commerce and Industry
PO Box 1455
36 Grivas Dhingenis Avenue
Nicosia, Cyprus
(357) (2) 449500
Telex: 2077
Fax: (357) (2) 449048

Czech Republic
Agency for Foreign Investment and Development
Ministry of the Economy

Mabr. kpt. Jarose 1000
170 32 Prague 7, Czech Republic
Phone: (420) (2) 389-1111
Fax: (420) (2) 712-2263
Telex: 121044

Ministry of the Environment
Slezska' 9
120 29 Prague 2, Czech Republic
Phone: (420) (2) 215-1111
Fax: (420) (2) 215-1111

Czech State Bank
Na Prikope 28
110 03 Prague 1, Czech Republic
Phone: (420) (2) 235-2112
Fax: (420) (2) 235-4141
Telex: 121555

Czech Chamber of Commerce and Industry
Argentinska' 38
170 05 Prague 7, Czech Republic
Phone: (420) (2) 872-4111
Fax: (420) (2) 875-3940

Denmark, Kingdom of
Ministry of Foreign Affairs
Investment Secretariat
2 Asiatisk Pads
1448 Copenhagen, Denmark
Phone: (45) (1) 33-920000
Fax: (45) (1) 31-540533

Ministry of Industry
Information Office for Foreign Investment
Slotsholmsgade 12
1216 Copenhagen, Denmark
Phone: (45) (1) 33-923350
Fax: (45) (1) 33-123778

Ministry of the Environment
Slotsholmsgade 12
1216 Copenhagen, Denmark
Phone: (45) (1) 33-923388
Fax: (45) (1) 33-328030
Telex: 42230

Djibouti, Republic of
Investment Approval Committee
Council of Ministers
Office of the Prime Minister
PO Box 2086
Djibouti

Phone: (253) 351494
Fax: (253) 355049
Telex: 5871

Ministry of Industry and Industrial Development
PO Box 175
Djibouti
Phone: (253) 350340
Telex: 5871

Banque Nationale de Djibouti
PO Box 2118
Djibouti
Phone: (253) 352751
Fax: (253) 356288
Telex: 5838

Chamber of Commerce and Industry
PO Box 84
Djibouti
Phone: (253) 351070
Telex: 5957

Dominica, Republic of
Dominica National Development Corporation
PO Box 293
Valley Road
Roseau, Dominica
Phone: (767) (44) 82045 or (767) (44) 82046 or (767)
(44) 82760

Dominica Export-Import Agency (DEXIA)
PO Box 173
Charles Avenue
Roseau, Dominica
Phone: (767) (44) 82494 or (767) (44) 83496

Dominica Association of Industry and Commerce
PO Box 85
15 King George V Street
Roseau, Dominica
Phone: (767) (44) 82874

Agricultural, Industrial and Development Bank
PO Box 215
64 Hillsborough Street
Roseau, Dominica
Phone: (767) (44) 82853
Fax: (767) (44) 84903

Ministry of Health
Government Building
Kennedy Avenue

Roseau, Dominica
Phone: (767) (44) 82401

Dominican Republic, The
Directorate of Foreign Investment
Secretariat of State for Industry and Commerce
Government Offices
Avda Mexico
Santo Domingo, Dominican Republic
Phone: (809) 685-5171

Directorate of Industrial Development
Secretariat of State for Industry and Commerce
Government Offices
Avda Mexico
Santo Domingo, Dominican Republic
Phone: (809) 685-5171

Tourist Development Directory
Secretariat of State for Tourism
PO Box 497
Avda George Washington
Santo Domingo, Dominican Republic
Phone: (809) 682-8181
Telex: 346-0303

Agro-Industrial Development Board
Secretariat of State for Agriculture
Centro de los Heroes Costanza
Santo Domingo, Dominican Republic
Phone: (809) 533-7171
Telex: 346-0393

Banco Central de la Repùblica Dominicana
PO Box 1347
Calle Pedro Henriquez Urena
Santo Domingo, Dominican Republic
Phone: (809) 689-7121
Fax: (809) 686-7488
Telex: 346-0052

Dominican Center for Export Promotion
PO Box 199-2
Plaza de la Independencia
Santo Domingo, Dominican Republic
Phone: (809) 530-5505
Fax: (809) 530-8208
Telex: 346-0351

Ecuador
Ministry of Industries, Commerce, Integration and
  Fisheries (MICIP)
Roca 582 y Juan Léon Mera

Quito, Ecuador
Phone: (593) (2) 527-988
Telex: 2166

National Chamber of Commerce of Ecuador
Avda Olmedo 414
Cassila y Boyaca
Guayaquil, Ecuador
Phone: (593) (4) 323130
Fax: (593) (4) 323478
Telex: 3466

Egypt, Arab Republic of
Ministry of Economy
8 Sharia Adly
Cairo, Egypt
Phone: (20) (2) 907334

Ministry of Foreign Trade
Lazoghil Square
Cairo, Egypt
Phone: (20) (2) 25424

General Authority for Investment
8 Sharia Adly
Cairo, Egypt
Phone: (20) (2) 3906804
Telex: 92235

Federation of Chambers of Commerce
4 el-Falaki Square
Phone: (20) (2) 3551164
Telex: 92645

El Salvador, Republic of
Ministry of Economy
Investment Department
Paseo General Escalòn 4122
PO Box 19
San Salvador, El Salvador
Phone: (503) 243000
Fax: (503) 981965

Salvadoran Foundation for Economic and Social
  Development
Edificio FUSADES
Boulevard Santa Elena
Urbanización Santa Elena
Antiguo Cuscatlàn
La Libertad, El Salvador
Phone: (503) 783366
Fax: (503) 783356 or (503) 783369

Banco Central de Reserva de El Salvador
Calle Ruben Dario y Norte
San Salvador, El Salvador
Phone: (503) 225022
Fax: (503) 713581

Estonia, Republic of
Eesti Bank (Bank of Estonia)
Kentmanni 13
Tallinn, Estonia 200100
Phone: (372) (2) 445-331
Fax: (372) (2) 443-393
Telex: 173146

Ministry of the Environment
Toompuiestee
Tallinn, Estonia 200110
Phone: (372) (2) 452-507
Fax: (372) (2) 453-310
Telex: 173238

Chamber of Commerce and Industry
Toom Kooli 17
Tallinn, Estonia 200106
Phone: (372) (2) 444-929
Fax: (372) (2) 443-656
Telex: 173254

Ethiopia, People's Democratic Republic of
Ministry of Foreign Trade
PO Box 2559
Addis Ababa, Ethiopia
Phone: (251) (1) 151066
Telex: 21320

Ministry of Agriculture, Environmental Protection
  and Development
PO Box 1223
Addis Ababa, Ethiopia
Phone: (251) (1) 448040
Fax: (251) (1) 513042

National Bank of Ethiopia
PO Box 5550
Addis Ababa, Ethiopia
Phone: (251) (1) 447430
Telex: 21020

Chamber of Commerce of Ethiopia
PO Box 517
Addis Ababa, Ethiopia
Phone: (251) (1) 518240
Telex: 21213

Fiji, Republic of
Fiji Trade and Investment Board
Civic House
Town Hall Road
PO Box 2303
Government Building
Suva, Fiji
Phone: (679) 315988
Fax: (679) 301783
Telex: 2355

Reserve Bank of Fiji
PO Box 1220
Suva, Fiji
Phone: (679) 313611
Fax: (679) 301688
Telex: 2164

Fiji Trade and Investment Board
Civic House
Town Hall Road
PO Box 2303
Government Building
Suva, Fiji
Phone: (679) 315988
Fax: (679) 301783
Telex: 2355

Finland, Republic of
Commission for Foreign Investment
Ministry of Trade and Industry
Aleksanterinkatu 10
0017 Helsinki 17, Finland
Phone: (358) (0) 1601
Fax: (358) (0) 1603666
Telex: 124645

Ministry of the Environment
PO Box 339
00121 Helsinki 17, Finland
Phone: (358) (0) 19911
Fax: (358) (0) 1991499
Telex: 123717

Bank of Finland
PO Box 160
00101 Helsinki 17, Finland
Phone: (358) (0) 1831
Fax: (358) (0) 174872
Telex: 121224

France (The French Republic)
Delegation à l'Aménagement du Territoire et à
  l'Action Regionale (DATAR)
1 Avenue Charles Floquet
75005 Paris, France
Phone: (33) (1) 40651234
Fax: (33) (1) 43069901

Banque de France (Bank of France)
39 rue Croix des Petits Champs
Phone: (33) (1) 42924292
Fax: (33) (1) 42962300
Telex: 220932

Gabonese Republic, The
Ministry of Commerce, Industry and Scientific
  Research
PO Box 3906
Libreville, Gabon
Phone: (241) 763055
Telex: 5347

Ministry of Finance, the Budget and State Sharehold-
  ings
PO Box 2245
Libreville, Gabon
Phone: (241) 762270
Telex: 5238

Ministry of Tourism, the Environment and National
  Parks
PO Box 403
Libreville, Gabon
Phone: (241) 762695

Centre Gabonais de Commerce Exteriéur
PO Box 3906
Libreville, Gabon
Phone: (241) 761167
Telex: 5347

Chamber of Commerce, Agriculture, Industry and
  Mines
PO Box 2234
Libreville, Gabon
Phone: (241) 722064
Telex: 5554

The Gambia, Republic of
National Investment Board
71 Hagan Street
Banjul, The Gambia

Phone: (220) 28168
Fax: (220) 29220
Telex: 2230 NIG GV

Ministry of Economic Planning and Industrial Devel-
  opment
Central Bank Building
Banjul, The Gambia
Phone: (220) 28229
Telex: 2293

Ministry of Information and Tourism
The Quadrangle
Banjul, The Gambia
Phone: (220) 28496
Telex: 2204

The Central Bank of The Gambia
1-2 Buckle Street
Banjul, The Gambia
Phone: (220) 28103
Fax: (220) 26969
Telex: 2218

Germany, The Federal Republic of
Ministry of Foreign Affairs
Adenauerallee 00-103
Bonn, Germany
Phone: (49) (228) 170
Fax: (49) (228) 340
Telex: 886591

Ministry of the Environment, Natural Conservation
  and Nuclear Safety
Kennedyallee 5
Bonn, Germany
Phone: (49) (228) 8305
Telex: 885790

Deutsche Bundesbank
Wilhelm-Epstein Strasse 14
Frankfurt, Germany
Phone: (49) (69) 560-1581
Fax: (49) (69) 560 1071
Telex: 414431

Ghana, Republic of
Ghana Investment Centre
Central Ministerial Area
PO Box M-193
Accra, Ghana
Phone: (233) 665125

Fax: (233) 663801
Telex: 2229

Secretariat for Finance and Economic Planning
PO Box M-40
Accra, Ghana
Phone: (233) 665421
Telex: 2132

Secretariat for Information
PO Box M-41
Accra, Ghana
Phone: (233) 228011
Telex: 2201

Ghana Chamber of Commerce
PO Box 2325
Accra, Ghana
Phone: (233) 662427
Fax: (233) 662210

Greece
Ministry of National Economy
Department of Private Investment
Syntagma Square
101 80 Athens, Greece
Phone: (30) (1) 3230911, (30) (1) 3242711, (30) (1)
   3330801
Fax: (30) (1) 3234393
Telex: 221086

Hellenic Industrial Development Bank S.A.
87 Syngrou Avenue, 3rd Floor
117 45 Athens, Greece
Phone: (30) (1) 3237981
Fax: (30) (1) 3621023

Grenada
Grenada International Development Corporation
Frequente Industrial Park
St. George's, Grenada
Phone: (809) 444-1035 or (809) 444-1040
Fax: (809) 444-4828

Ministry of Trade
Export Development Office
Lagoon Road
St. George's, Grenada
Phone: (809) 440-2101

Granada Chamber of Commerce and Industry
PO Box 129

Decaul Building, Mt. Gay
St. George's, Grenada
Phone: (809) 440-2937 or (809) 440-4485
Fax: (809) 440-6627

Eastern Caribbean Central Bank
Grenada Office
Camerhogne House
Church Street
St. George's, Grenada
Phone: (809) 440-3016

Guatemala, Republic of
Bank of Guatemala
7a Avenida 22-01, Zona 1
Apartado Post 365
Guatemala City, Guatemala, C.A.
Phone: (502) (2) 534053
Fax: (502) (2) 534035

Guatemalan Chamber of Commerce
10a Calle 3-80, Zona 1
Guatemala City, Guatemala, C.A.
Phone: (502) (2) 82681

Guatemalan Chamber of Industry
Ruta 6, 9-21, Zona 4
Guatemala City, Guatemala, C.A.
Phone: (502) (2) 317069, (502) (2) 325380, (502)
   (2)316768

Industrial Policy Division
Ministry of Economy
6a Avenida 1-71, Zona 1
Guatemala City, Guatemala, C.A.
Phone: (502) (2) 81161, (502) (2)84247

Guinea-Bissau
Ministry of Planning and Economic Cooperation
Government Office
Avdo de Brasil
Bissau, Guinea-Bissau
Phone: (245) 213431

Banco Central da Guiné-Bissau (Central Bank of
   Guinea-Bissau)
Bissau, Guinea-Bissau
Phone: (245) 212434
Fax: (245) 201305
Telex: 241

Guinea, Republic of
National Investments Commission
Ministry of Planning and Finance
PO Box 707
Conakry, Guinea
Phone: 441637
Fax: 442148
Telex: 22311

Ministry of Natural Resources, Energy and the
   Environment
PO Box 295
Conakry, Guinea
Phone: 445001
Telex: 22350

Banque Central de la République de Guinèe
PO Box 692
12 Boulevard du Commerce
Conakry, Guinea
Phone: 441725
Telex: 22225

Chamber of Commerce of Guinea
PO Box 545
Conakry, Guinea
Phone: 444495
Telex: 609

Guyana, Cooperative Republic of
Ministry of Trade, Tourism and Industry
Main and Urquhari Streets
Georgetown, Guyana
Phone: (592) (2) 68695
Telex: 2288

Export Promotion Council
10 Fort Street
Kinston, Georgetown, Guyana
Phone: (592) (2) 56561
Fax: (592) (2)56313

Bank of Guyana
PO Box 1003
Church Street
Georgetown, Guyana
Phone: (592) (2) 63250
Fax: (592) (2) 72965
Telex: 2267

Georgetown Chamber of Commerce
PO Box 10110

156 Waterloo Street
Georgetown, Guyana
Phone: (592) (2) 56451

Honduras, Republic of
Ministry of Economy and Commerce
Edif. Salame
5a Avda
4a Calle
Tegucigalpa, Honduras
Phone: (504) 22351
Telex: 1396

Ministry of Foreign Affairs
Edif. Atala
Avda La Paz
Tegucigalpa, Honduras
Phone: (504) 314209
Telex: 1129

Ministry of Natural Resources
Boulevard Miraflores
Tegucigalpa, Honduras
Phone: (504) 323141

Banco Central de Honduras
7a Avda
1a Calle
Apdo 58-C
Tegucigalpa, Honduras
Phone: (504) 222270
Telex: 1121

Hong Kong
Inward Investment Office
Hong Kong Industry Development Department
14th Floor, Ocean Centre
5 Canton Road
Kowloon, Hong Kong
Phone: (852) (3) 737-2434
Fax: (852) (3) 730-4633
Telex: 50151 INDHK HX

Industrial Promotion Unit
Hong Kong Economic and Trade Office
7th Floor
Nishi-Azabu Mitsui Building
Minato 4-17-30
Nishi-Azabu
Tokyo, Japan
Phone: (81) (3) 3498-8806
Fax: (81) (3) 3498-8815

Industrial Promotion Unit
Hong Kong Economic and Trade Office
680 Fifth Avenue
22nd Floor
New York, NY USA 10019
Phone: (1) (212) 265-8888, (1) (212) 752-3650
Fax: (1) (212) 974-3209

Industrial Promotion Unit
Hong Kong Economic and Trade Office
180 Sutter Street
Fourth Floor
San Francisco, CA USA 94104
Phone: (1) (415) 956-4560
Fax: (1) (415) 421-0646
Telex: 216708 HKIND SFO

Industrial Promotion Unit
Hong Kong Economic and Trade Office
1233 20th Street N.W.
Washington, D.C. USA 20036
Phone: (1) (202) 331-8947
Fax: (1) (202) 331-8958
Telex: 023440484 HKWSH UI

Industrial Promotion Unit
Hong Kong Economic and Trade Office
6 Grafton Street
London W1X 3LB, England
Phone: (44) (171) 499-9821
Fax: (44) (171) 495-5033
Telex: 05128404 HKGOVT G

Industrial Promotion Unit
Hong Kong Economic and Trade Office
Avenue Louise, 228
1050 Brussels, Belgium
Phone: (32) (2) 648-39-66
Fax: (32) (2) 640-66-55
Telex: 04661750 HONREP B

Industrial Promotion Unit
Hong Kong Economic and Trade Office
37-39 rue de Vermont
1211 Geneva 20, Switzerland
Phone: (41) (22) 734-90-40
Fax: (41) (22) 733-99-04
Telex: 04528880 HKGV CH

Hong Kong Trade Development Council
38th Floor
Convention Plaza
1 Harbour Road

Hong Kong
Phone: (852) (5) 833-4333
Fax: (852) (5) 824-0249
Telex: 73595 CONHK HX

Hong Kong Chamber of Commerce
22nd Floor
95 Queensway
Hong Kong
Phone: (852) (5) 529-9229
Fax: (852) (5) 527-9843
Telex: 83535 TRIND HX

Chinese General Chamber of Commerce
Hong Kong
Phone: (852) (5) 525-6385
Fax: (852) (5) 845-2610
Telex: 89854 CGCC HX

Hungary, Republic of
Office for Investment Promotion
Ministry of International Economic Relations
Honvèd u. 13-15
1880 Budapest, Hungary
Phone: (36) (1) 1530000
Fax: (36) (1) 1532794

Hungarian Chamber of Commerce
Kossuth L. tèr. 6-8
1054 Budapest, Hungary
Phone: (36) (1) 1533333
Fax: (36) (1) 1531285

Ministry of Environmental Protection and Urban
  Development
Fò. u. 44-50
1011 Budapest, Hungary
Phone: (36) (1) 1154840
Fax: (36) (1) 1362198

National Bank of Hungary
Szabadsàg tèr. 8-9
1850 Budapest, Hungary
Phone: (36) (1) 1532600
Fax: (36) (1) 1324179

Iceland
Investment Information:
Ministry of Commerce
Arnarhvàli
150 Reykjavìk, Iceland
Phone: (354) (1) 621700
Fax: (354) (1) 621702

Central Bank of Iceland
Kalkifnsvegur 1
150 Reykjavìk, Iceland
Phone: (354) (1) 699600
Fax: (354) (1) 621802
Telex: 2020

Federation of Icelandic Industries
PO Box 1407
121 Reykjavìk, Iceland
Phone: (354) (1) 27577
Fax: (354) (1) 25380

India, Republic of
Foreign Investment Promotion Board
Office of the Prime Minister
South Block
New Delhi, India 110 011
Phone: (91) (11) 3012312

The Joint Secretary
Secretariat of Industrial Approval (SIA)
Department of Industrial Development
Ministry of Industry
Udyog Bhawan
New Delhi, India 110 011
Phone: (91) (11) 3011815
Fax: (91) (11) 3011770
Telex: 031-6565

Ministry of the Environment and Forests
Paryavaran Bhavan
CGO Complex II
Lodi Road
New Delhi, India 110 003
Phone: (91) (11) 3607210

Reserve Bank of India
New Central Office Building
Shaheed Bhagat Singh Road
Bombay, India 400 023
Phone: (91) (22) 2861602, (91) (22) 2860604
Fax: (91) (22) 2864667
Telex: 011-82318

Indonesia, Republic of
National Development Planning Agency
Jalan Taman Suropati 2
Jakarta, Indonesia 10310
Phone: (62) (21) 334811
Fax: (62) (21) 3105374
Telex: 61333

Indonesian Chamber of Commerce and Industry
Chandra Building, 3rd Floor
Thamrin 20
Jakarta, Indonesia 10350
Phone: (62) (21) 324000
Fax: (62) (21) 3106098
Telex: 61262

Ireland
Industrial Development Authority of Ireland
Wilton Park House
Wilton Place
Dublin 2, Ireland
Phone: (353) (1) 686633
Fax: (353) (1) 603703

The Chamber of Commerce of Ireland
7 Clare Street
Dublin 2, Ireland
Phone: (353) (1) 612888
Fax: (353) (1) 766043
Telex: 90716

Isle of Man
National Economic Council
Hill Street
Douglas, Isle of Man
Phone: (624) 626262

Department of Industry
30 Bucks Road
Douglas, Isle of Man
Phone: (624) 626262

Chamber of Commerce
17 Drinkwater Street
Douglas, Isle of Man
Phone: (624) 674941
Fax: (624) 663367

Israel, State of
Ministry of Trade and Industry
PO Box 229
30 Agron Street
Jerusalem, Israel 91490
Phone: (972) (2) 210111
Fax: (972) (2) 245110

Ministry of the Environment
PO Box 6158
2 Kaplan Street
Jerusalem, Israel 91061
Phone: (972) (2) 701411

Fax: (972) (2) 358038

Israel Investment Center
PO Box 29930 Agron Street
Jerusalem, Israel 91490
Phone: (972) (2) 210111
Fax: (972) (2) 245110

Israel Investment Authority
PO Box 883
3 Kaplan Street
Jerusalem, Israel 91008
Phone: (972) (2) 522194
Fax: (972) (2) 537207

Bank of Israel
PO Box 780
Bank of Israel Building
Tel Aviv, Israel 61013
Phone: (972) (3) 695245
Fax: (972) (3) 263195
Telex: 341217

Italy (The Italian Republic)

Institute for Assistance in the Development of Southern Italy
Viale Pilsudski, 124
00197 Rome, Italy
Phone: (39) (6) 4817636
Fax: (39) (6) 4817639
Telex: 332125 IASMM I

Ministry of the Environment
Piazza Venezia 11
00187 Rome, Italy
Phone: (39) (6) 6759320
Fax: (39) (6) 6759320

Banca d'Italia
Via Nazionale 91
00184 Rome, Italy
Phone: (39) (6) 47921
Fax: (39) (6) 4747820
Telex: 630045

Jamaica

Jamaica Promotions Limited
35 Trafalgar Road
Kingston 10
Jamaica, West Indies
Phone: (809) 929-9450
Fax: (809) 924-9650

Ministry of Finance, Development and Planning
30 National Heroes Circle
Kingston 4
Jamaica, West Indies
Phone: (809) 922-8600
Telex: 2447

Ministry of Mining, Production and Commerce
4 Winchester Road
Kingston 10
Jamaica, West Indies
Phone: (809) 926-9170

Bank of Jamaica
Nethersole Place
PO Box 621
Kingston, Jamaica
Phone: (809) 922-0750
Fax: (809) 922-0828
Telex: 2165

Jamaica Chamber of Commerce
7-8 East Parade
PO Box 172
Kingston, Jamaica
Phone: (809) 922-0150
Fax: (809) 924-9056

Japan

Ministry of International Trade and Industry
1-3 Kasumigaseki, Chiyoda-ku
Tokyo, Japan
Phone: (81) (3) 35011511
Telex: 22916

Environment Agency
1-22 Kasumigaseki, Chiyoda-ku
Tokyo, Japan
Phone: (81) (3) 35813351
Fax: (81) (3) 35014634
Telex: 33855

Nippon Ginko (Bank of Tokyo)
1-1 Hongoku-cho, 1-chome, Nihonbashi, Chuo-ku
Tokyo, Japan
Phone: (81) (3) 3279111
Fax: (81) (3) 32450358
Telex: 22763

Chamber of Commerce and Industry of Japan
2-2, 3-chome, Marunouchi, Chiyoda-ku
Tokyo, Japan
Phone: (81) (3) 32837851

Jordan, Hashemite Kingdom of
Ministry of Trade and Industry
PO Box 2019
Amman, Jordan
Phone: (962) 663191
Telex: 21163

Central Bank of Jordan
PO Box 37
King Hussein Street
Amman, Jordan
Phone: (962) 630301
Fax: (962) 638889
Telex: 21250

Kenya, Republic of
Ministry of Commerce
PO Box 47024
Cooperative House
Haile Selassie Avenue
Nairobi, Kenya
Phone: (254) (2) 728370
Telex: 33042

Ministry of the Environment
PO Box 30126
Kencom House
Nairobi, Kenya
Phone: (254) (2) 29261

Central Bank of Kenya
PO Box 60000
Haile Selassie Avenue
Nairobi, Kenya
Phone: (254) (2) 226431
Telex: 22324

Kenya Chamber of Commerce
PO Box 47024
Ufanisi House
Haile Selassie Avenue
Nairobi, Kenya
Phone: (254) (2) 334413

Korea, Republic of
Foreign Investment Advice Office
Bureau of Economic Cooperation
Ministry of Finance
1 Chungang-dong, Kwachon City
Kyonggi Province, Korea
Phone: (82) (2) 778-0521
Fax: (82) (2) 503-9324
Telex: 23243

Ministry of the Environment
7-16 Sincheon-dong, Songpa-ku
Seoul, Korea
Phone: (82) (2) 421-0247
Fax: (82) (2) 421-0280

Ministry of Justice
1 Chungang-dong, Kwachon City
Kyonggi Province, Korea
Phone: (82) (2) 503-7012
Fax: (82) (2) 504-3337
Telex: 24757

Bank of Korea
110 Namdaiemun-no, Chung-ku
Seoul, Korea
Phone: (82) (2) 759-4114
Fax: (82) (2) 752-7389
Telex: 24711

Chamber of Commerce and Industry of Korea
45 Namdaemun-no, Chung-ku
Seoul, Korea
Phone: (82) (2) 757-0757
Fax: (82) (2) 757-9475
Telex: 25728

Kuwait, State of
Ministry of Finance
PO Box 9
Ministries Complex
Kuwait City, Kuwait
Phone: (965) 2468200
Fax: (965) 2404025
Telex: 22101

Central Bank of Kuwait
PO Box 526
Ahmad al-Jaber Street
Kuwait City, Kuwait
Phone: (965) 2449200
Fax: (965) 2464887
Telex: 22101

Kuwait Chamber of Commerce
PO Box 775
Chamber Building
Ali as-Salem Street
Kuwait City, Kuwait
Phone: (965) 2433854
Fax: (965) 2433858
Telex: 22198

Laos, People's Democratic Republic of
Foreign Investment Management Committee
Ministry of Foreign Economic Relations
Government Offices
Vientiane, Laos
Phone: (856) (22) 2330

Banque de la RDP Lao
PO Box 19
Rue Yonnet
Vientiane, Laos
Phone: (856) (22) 2000
Telex: 4304

Lao National Chamber of Commerce and Industry
PO Box 1163
Vientiane, Laos
Phone: (856) (22) 3171

Latvia, Republic of
Division of Foreign Relations
Ministry of Finance
1 Smilsu Street
Riga 226-989, Latvia
Phone: (371) 211752
Fax: (371) 227220

Lebanon, Republic of
Central Bank of Lebanon
PO Box 11-5544
Beirut, Lebanon
Phone: (961) (1) 865303
Telex: 20744

Lesotho, Kingdom of
Lesotho National Development Corporation
Private Bag A96
Maseru 100, Lesotho
Phone: (266) 312012
Fax: (266) 310038
Telex: 4341 LO

Ministry of Trade and Industry
PO Box 747
Maseru 100, Lesotho
Phone: (266) 322802
Fax: (266) 3101121
Telex: 43840

Central Bank of Lesotho
PO Box 1184
Maseru 100 Lesotho
Phone: (266) 324281

Fax: (266) 310051
Telex: 4367

Liberia, Republic of
Investment Commission
PO Box 9043
Executive Mansion Building
Monrovia, Liberia
Phone: (231) 22163

National Bank of Liberia
PO Box 2048
Broad Street
Monrovia, Liberia
Phone: (231) 222497

Ministry of Commerce and Industry
PO Box 9041
Monrovia, Liberia
Phone: (231) 22141
Telex: 44331

Liechtenstein, Principality of
Liechtenstein Bank
Stadtle 44
Post Box 384
9490 Vaduz, Liechtenstein
Phone: (41) (75) 68811
Fax: (41) (75) 68358
Telex: 889400

Department of Environmental Protection
9490 Vaduz, Liechtenstein
Phone: (41) (75) 66111

Liechtenstein Chamber of Commerce and Industry
Josef-Rheinberger Str. 11
Post Box 232
9490 Vaduz, Liechtenstein
Phone: (41) (75) 22744
Fax: (41) (75) 84503

Lithuania, Republic of
Commercial Trade Department
Ministry of International Economic Relations
Gedimino Pr. 30/1
2695 Vilnius, Lithuania
Phone: (370) 226411, (370) 226917, (370) 226808
Fax: (370) 625432

Ministry of Economics
Gedimino Pr. 38/2
2326 Vilnius, Lithuania

Phone: (370) 622416
Fax: (370) 625604

Ministry of Trade
Gedimino Pr. 27
2326 Vilnius, Lithuania
Phone: (370) 621625
Fax: (370) 224601

Bank of Lithuania
Gedimino Pr. 6
2320 Vilnius, Lithuania
Phone: (370) 622079
Fax: (370) 221501
Telex: 261246

Chamber of Commerce and Industry of Lithuania
Algirdo 31
2326 Vilnius, Lithuania
Phone: (370) 661450
Fax: (370) 661550
Telex: 261114

Luxembourg, Grand Duchy of
Board of Economic Development
19-21 Boulevard Royal
2910 Luxembourg
Phone: (352) 4794-231

Ministry of the Economy
19-21 Boulevard Royal
2910 Luxembourg
Phone: (352) 4794-231
Fax: (352) 460448
Telex: 3405

Ministry of the Environment
5 Rue de Prague
2918 Luxembourg
Phone: (352) 478870
Fax: (352) 400410
Telex: 2536

Ministry of Labor
26 Rue Zithe
Luxembourg
Phone: (352) 499211
Fax: (352) 499212
Telex: 2958

Chamber of Commerce of Luxembourg
7 Rue Alcide de Gasperi
2981 Luxembourg

Phone: (352) 435853
Fax: (352) 438326
Telex: 60174

Madagascar, Democratic Republic of
Ministry of Finance
PO Box 268
Antaninarenina
101 Antananarivo, Madagascar
Phone: (261) (2) 21632
Telex: 22489

Central Bank of the Republic of Madagascar
PO Box 550
101 Antananarivo, Madagascar
Phone: (261) (2) 21751
Fax: (261) (2) 34552

Chamber of Commerce of Madagascar
PO Box 166
101 Antananarivo, Madagascar
Phone: (261) (2) 21567

Malawi, Republic of
Malawi Investment Promotion Agency
Plaza House
Private Bag 302
Capital City
Lilongwe 3, Malawi
Phone: (265) 780 800
Fax: (265) 781 781
Telex: 44944

Reserve Bank of Malawi
PO Box 30063
Capital City
Lilongwe 3, Malawi
Phone: (265) 732 488
Fax: (265) 731 145
Telex: 44788

Associated Chambers of Commerce and Industry
Chichiri Trade Fair Grounds
PO Box 258
Blantyre, Malawi
Phone: (265) 671 988
Fax: (265) 671 147
Telex: 43992

Malaysia, Federation of
Malaysian Industrial Development Authority (MIDA)
3rd-6th Floor
Wisma Damansara, Jalan Semantan

PO Box 10618
Kuala Lumpur, Malaysia
Phone: (60) (3) 2543633
Telex: MIDA MA 30752
Cable: FIDAMAL

Chamber of Commerce and Industry of Malaysia
Bangunan Angkass Raya, 13th Floor
Jalan Ampang
Kuala Lumpur, Malaysia
Phone: (60) (3) 433090

Maldives, Republic of
Ministry of Trade and Industries
Ghaazee Building
Ameer Ahmed Magu
Male, Republic of Maldives
Phone: 323668
Fax: 323756
Telex: 77076 TRADIND MF

Ministry of Planning and the Environment
Ghaazee Building
Ameer Ahmed Magu
Male, Republic of Maldives
Phone: 322965
Fax: 327351
Telex: 66110

Maldives Monetary Authority
Majeedhee Building
Marine Drive
Male, Republic of Maldives
Phone: 322290
Fax: 323862
Telex: 66055

Ministry of Finance
Ghaazee Building
Ameer Ahmed Magu
Male, Republic of Maldives
Phone: 324345
Fax: 324432

Malta, Republic of
Malta Development Corporation
PO Box 571
House of Catalunya
Marsamxewtto Road
Valletta, Malta
Phone: (356) 221431 or (356) 222691
Fax: (356) 606407
Telex: 1275

Central Bank of Malta
Castille Place
Valletta, Malta
Phone: (356) 247480
Fax: (356) 243051
Telex: 1262

Ministry of the Environment
Floriana
Valletta, Malta
Phone: (356) 222378
Fax: (356) 231293
Telex: 1861

Mauritania, Islamic Republic of
National Committee of Investment
PO Box 223
Government Offices
Nouakchott, Mauritania
Phone: 52935

Ministry of Fisheries and Marine Economy
PO Box 137
Nouakchott, Mauritania
Phone: 52476
Telex: 595

Ministry of Industries and Mines
PO Box 183
Nauakchott, Mauritania
Phone: 51318

Ministry of Rural Development and the Environment
PO Box 366
Nouakchott, Mauritania
Phone: 52020

Banque Central de Mauritanie
PO Box 623
Avenue de l'Independence
Nouakchott, Mauritania
Phone: 52206
Telex: 532

Mauritius, Republic of
Mauritius Export Development and Investment
 Agency
PAI Building, 2nd Floor
Port Louis, Mauritius
Phone: (230) 208-7750
Fax: (230) 208-5965

Mauritius Offshore Business Activities Authority
Government House
Port Louis, Mauritius
Phone: (230) 201-2557 or (230) 201-1840 or (230)
   201-1146
Fax: (230) 208-8622
Telex: 4249 EXTERN IW

Ministry of the Environment and Quality of Life
Barracks Street
Port Louis, Mauritius
Phone: (230) 208-2831
Fax: (230) 208-6579

Bank of Mauritius
Sir William Newton Street
Port Louis, Mauritius
Phone: (230) 208-4164
Fax: (230) 208-9204

Mauritius Chamber of Commerce and Industry
Royal Road
Port Louis, Mauritius
Phone: (230) 208-3301
Fax: (230) 208-0076

Mexico
National Commission on Foreign Investment
Office of the President
Los Pinos
Mexico City, Mexico
Phone: (52) (5) 5153353
Telex: 1760010

Secretariat of State for Commerce and Industrial
  Development
Alfonso Reyes 30
Mexico City, Mexico
Phone: (52) (5) 2861823
Telex: 1775718

Secretary of State for Foreign Affairs
Ricardo Flores Magon 1
Tiateloco 06995
Mexico City, Mexico
Phone: (52) (5) 2775470
Telex: 1763478

Bank of Mexico
Avda 5 de Mayo 2
Mexico City, Mexico
Phone: (52) (2) 7090044
Fax: (52) (2) 6251557
Telex: 1772669

Mongolia, People's Republic of
Ministry of Trade and Industry
Ulan Bator 11, Mongolia
Phone: 706143
Telex: 221

Mongolbank
Ulan Bator 6, Mongolia
Phone: 22847
Telex: 241

Mongolian Chamber of Commerce and Industry
Ulan Bator 11, Mongolia
Phone: 24620
Telex: 79336

Montserrat
Ministry of Trade
PO Box 272
Plymouth, Montserrat
Phone: (664) 491-2546 or (664) 491-2075
Fax: (664) 491-2367

Economic Development Unit
Government of Montserrat
PO Box 292
Plymouth, Montserrat
Phone: (664) 491-2066
Fax: (664) 491-4632

Montserrat Chamber of Commerce
PO Box 384
Marine Drive
Plymouth, Montserrat
Phone: (664) 491-3640
Fax: (664) 491-4660

Morocco, Kingdom of
Office of Industrial Development (ODI)
10 Rue Ghandi
PO Box 211
Rabat, Morocco
Phone: (21) (77) 708460
Fax: (21) (77) 707695
Telex: 36053

Moroccan Center for Export Promotion (CMPE)
23 Boulevard Giradot
Casablanca, Morocco
Phone: (21) 302210
Fax: (21) 301793
Telex: 27847

La Fédération des Chambres du Commerce et
  d'Industries du Maroc
56 Avenue de France
Rabat, Morocco
Phone: (21) (77) 765230
Telex: 31884

Mozambique, Republic of
Office for Foreign Investment Promotion
PO Box 4635
Maputo, Mozambique
Phone: (258) (1) 422456
Telex: 6876

Ministry of Trade
Praca 25 de Junho
Maputo, Mozambique
Phone: (258) (1) 426091
Telex: 6374

Banco de Mozambique
Avda 25 de Setembro 1695
Maputo, Mozambique
Phone: (258) (1) 428151
Fax: (258) (1) 429718
Telex: 6244

Chamber of Commerce of Mozambique
Rua Mateus Sansao Mutema 452
Maputo, Mozambique
Phone: (258) (1) 491970

Myanmar, Union of
Ministry of Trade
228-240 Strand Road
Yangon, Myanmar
Phone: (95) (1) 87034
Fax: (95) (1) 89578
Telex: 21338

Foreign Investment Commission
228-240 Strand Road
Yangon, Myanmar
Phone: (95) (1) 07034

Myanmar Economic Bank
PO Box 35
564 Merchant Street
Yangon, Myanmar
Phone: (95) (1) 81819 or (95) (1) 85257
Cable: BANKINDUST

Namibia, Republic of
The Investment Centre
Ministry of Trade and Industry
Private Bag 13340
Windhoek, Namibia
Phone: (264) 289911
Fax: (264) 220148

Namibia National Chamber of Commerce and
  Industry
PO Box 9355
Windhoek, Namibia
Phone: (264) 228809
Fax: (264) 228009

Nepal, Kingdom of
Foreign Investment Promotion Division
Ministry of Industry
Kathmandu, Nepal
Phone: (977) (1) 2-16692 or 2-15026 or 2-15030

Federation of Nepalese Chambers of Commerce and
  Industry
PO Box 269
Kathmandu, Nepal
Phone: (977) (1) 2-12096

Nepal Chamber of Commerce
PO Box 198
Kathmandu, Nepal
Phone: (977) (1) 2-21318
Fax: (977) (1) 226567
Telex: 2349

Netherlands, Kingdom of the
Netherlands Foreign Investment Agency
Ministry of Development Corporation
PO Box 20061
Bezuidenhoutseweg 67
2500 EB The Hague, Netherlands
Phone: (31) (70) 3486486
Telex: 31326

Ministry of Housing, Physical Planning and the
  Environment
Van Alkemadelaan 85
2597 AC The Hague, Netherlands
Phone: (31) (70) 3264201
Telex: 34429

Ministry of Social Affairs and Employment
PO Box 90801
Anna Van Hannoverstraat 4

2509 LV The Hague, Netherlands
Phone: (31) (70) 3334444
Fax: (31) (70) 3334023
Telex: 331250

De Netherlands Bank NV
PO Box 98
Westeinde 1
1000 AB Amsterdam, Netherlands
Phone: (31) (20) 5249111
Telex: 11355

Netherlands Antilles
Department of Trade, Industry and Employment
De Rouvilleweg 7
Willemstad
Curacao, Netherlands Antilles
Phone: (599) (9) 626400
Fax: (599) (9) 627590

Bank of the Netherlands Antilles
Breedesraat 1
Willemstad
Curacao, Netherlands Antilles
Phone: (599) (9) 613600
Fax: (599) (9) 615004

Curacao Chamber of Commerce and Industry
PO Box 10
Willemstad
Curacao, Netherlands Antilles
Phone: (599) (9) 613918

Foreign Investment Agency Curacao
ITC Building, Piscadera Bay
Curacao, Netherlands Antilles
Phone: (599) (9) 636603
Fax: (599) (9) 636481
Telex: 1456

New Zealand, Dominion of
Overseas Investment Commission
PO Box 2498
Wellington, New Zealand
Phone: (64) (4) 4722029
Fax: (64) (4) 4723262

Ministry of Commerce
PO Box 1473
32 Bowen Street
Wellington, New Zealand
Phone: (64) (4) 4720030
Fax: (64) (4) 473638

Ministry of the Environment
PO Box 10362
Wellington, New Zealand
Phone: (64) (4) 4734090
Fax: (64) (4) 4710195

Immigration Service
Business Immigration Section
PO Box 4130
120 The Terrace
Wellington, New Zealand
Phone: (64) (4) 4739100
Fax: (64) (4) 4712118

Reserve Bank of New Zealand
PO Box 2498
2 The Terrace
Wellington, New Zealand
Phone: (64) (4) 4722029
Fax: (64) (4) 4738554
Telex: NZ3368

Niger, Republic of
Investment Commission
Ministry of the Economy, Finance and Planning
PO Box 235
Niamey, Niger
Phone: (227) 723467
Telex: 5214

Chamber of Commerce and Industry of Niger
PO Box 209
Niamey, Niger
Phone: (227) 732210
Telex: 5242

Nigeria, Federal Republic of
Industrial Development Coordinating Committee
Ministry of Industry and Technology
Garki, Abuja
Federal Capital Territory
Nigeria

Investment Information and Promotion Centre
Federal Ministry of Industry and Technology
Garki, Abuja
Federal Capital Territory
Nigeria

Nigerian Association of Chambers of Commerce, Industries and Agriculture
Commerce House
Idowu Taylor Street

Victoria Island
Lagos, Nigeria
Phone: (234) (1) 964737
Telex: 21368

Norway, Kingdom of
Ministry of Industry
Ploensgt 8
PO Box 8014
Department 0030
Oslo 1, Norway
Phone: (47) (2) 34-90-90
Fax: (47) (2) 34-95-25
Telex: 21428

Ministry of the Environment
Myntgt 2
PO Box 8013
Oslo 1, Norway
Phone: (47) (2) 34-90-90
Fax: (47) (2) 34-95-60

Norges Bank (Bank of Norway)
Bankplassen 2
PO Box 1179
Sentrum 0107
Oslo 1, Norway
Phone:(47) (2) 31-60-00
Fax:(47) (2) 41-31-05
Telex: 71369

Oman, The Sultanate of
Committee on the Investment of Foreign Capital
Ministry of Commerce and Industry
PO Box 550
Muscat, Oman
Phone: (968) 79950
Fax: (968) 794238
Telex: 3665 WIZARA ON

Ministry of Environment and Water Resources
PO Box 323
Muscat, Oman
Phone: (968) 696444
Fax: (968) 602320
Telex: 54404 A/B MININVOY ON

Ministry of Finance and Economy
PO Box 506
Muscat, Oman
Phone: (968) 738201
Telex: 5333 MALIYA ON

Ministry of Social Affairs and Labor
PO Box 560
Muscat, Oman
Phone: (968) 602444
Telex: 5002 MOSAL ON

Central Bank of Oman
PO Box 4161
Ruwi, Oman
Phone: (968) 702222
Fax: (968) 707913
Telex: 3070 MARKAZI ON

Oman Development Bank
PO Box 309
Muscat, Oman
Phone: (968) 738021
Telex: 5179 OBEDE ON

Oman Chamber of Commerce and Industry
PO Box 4400
Ruwi, Oman
Phone: (968) 70764
Telex: 33889 AL-GURFA MB

Pakistan, Islamic Republic of
Investment Promotion Bureau
Kandawala Building
M.A. Jinnah Road
Karachi, Pakistan
Phone: (92) (21) 714289
Fax: (92) (21) 713572
Telex: 3137 SUPLS PK

Ministry of Industries
Block-A, Pak Secretariat
Islamabad, Pakistan
Phone: (92) (51) 820235
Fax: (92) (51) 825130
Telex: MIND PK 5774

Federation of Pakistan Chambers of Commerce and
  Industry
Federation House, Clifton
Karachi, Pakistan
Phone: (92) (21) 532179
Fax: (92 (21) 570277
Telex: 25370 FPCC&J

Panama, Republic of
Panama Trade Development Institute
Banco Exterior Building
PO Box 6-1897

El Dorado, Panama
Phone: (507) 25-7244
Fax: (507) 25-2193
Telex: 3499 Invest PG

Chamber of Commerce, Industry and Agriculture of
  Panama
Avda Samuel Lewis
Panama City, Panama
Phone: (507) 64-8498
Telex: 2434

Papua New Guinea, Independent State of
Investment Promotion Authority
PO Box 5053
Boroko, Papua New Guinea
Phone: (675) 258777
Telex: 93128

Tourism Development Corporation
PO Box 7144
Boroko, Papua New Guinea
Phone: (675) 272521
Fax: (675) 259119

Bank of Papua New Guinea
Douglas Street
PO Box 121
Port Moresby, Papua New Guinea
Phone: (675) 212999
Fax: (675) 211617
Telex: 22128

Paraguay, Republic of
Investment Council Office
Ministry of Industry and Commerce
Avda Espana 323
Ascunción, Paraguay
Phone: (595) (21) 204693
Fax: (595) (21) 210570
Telex: 259

Central Bank of Paraguay
Avda Pablo VI
Ascunción, Paraguay
Phone: (595) (21) 608019 or (595) (21) 608020
Fax: (595) (21) 608150
Telex: 134

Chamber of Commerce of Paraguay
Estrella 540
Ascunción, Paraguay
Phone: (595) (21) 47312

Peru, Republic of
National Commission on Foreign Investment and
  Technology (CONITE)
Ministry of Industry, Commerce, Tourism, and
  Integration
Calle 1 Oeste
Corpac, San Isidro
Lima, Peru
Phone: (51) (14) 407120
Telex: 21094

Confederation of Chambers of Commerce of Peru
Avda Gregorio Escobedo 398
Lima, Peru
Phone: (51) (14) 633434

Philippines, Republic of
Department of Trade and Industry
385 Sen. Gil J. Puyat Avenue
1200 Makatu, Metro Manila, Philippines
Phone: (63) (2) 868-403 or (63) (2) 867-895 or (63)
  (2) 875-602
Fax: (63) (2) 632-851166
Telex: 45555 BOI/PM OR 122661 BOI PH

Philippine Chamber of Commerce
ODC International Plaza Building
219 Salcedo Street
Makatu, Metro Manila 2801
Phone: (63) (2) 8176981
Telex: 62042

Poland, Republic of
Ministry of Privatization
ul. Krucza 36
00-525 Warsaw, Poland
Phone: (48) (22) 628-0281
Fax: (48) (22) 625-1114

Ministry of Industry and Trade
ul. Wspo'lna 4
00-921 Warsaw, Poland
Phone: (48) (22) 210-351
Fax: (48) (22) 212-550

Ministry of Environmental Protection, Natural
  Resources and Forestry
ul. Wawelska 52/54
00-922 Warsaw, Poland
Phone: (48) (22) 250-001 or (48) (22) 254-001
Fax: (48) (22) 253-335 or (48) (22) 253-972

National Bank of Poland
ul. Swietokrzyska 11/12
00-950 Warsaw, Poland
Phone: (48) (22) 200-321
Fax: (48) (22) 269-95

Polish Chamber of Commerce
Promotion Center
ul. Trebacka 4
00-074 Warsaw, Poland
Phone: (48) (22) 260-221 or (48) (22) 267-376
Fax: (48) (22) 2274-673 or (48) (22) 6355-137

Portugal, Republic of
Portugese Foreign Trade Institute
Avenue 5 de Outubro 101
Lisbon, Portugal
Phone: (351) (1) 7930103
Fax: (351) (1) 7935028
Telex: 16498

Ministry of Trade and Tourism
Avenue de República 79
Lisbon, Portugal
Phone: (351) (1) 730412
Telex: 13455

Bank of Portugal
Rua do Comercio 148
Lisbon, Portugal
Phone: (351) (1) 3462931
Fax: (351) (1) 3467341
Telex: 16554

Qatar, State of
Ministry of Economy and Trade
PO Box 1968
Doha, Qatar
Phone: (974) 434888
Telex: 4488

Ministry of the Interior
PO Box 3883
Doha, Qatar
Phone: (974) 330000
Fax: (974) 324430
Telex: 4238

Industrial Development Technical Center
PO Box 2599
Doha, Qatar
Phone: (974) 832121
Telex: 4323

Qatar Chamber of Commerce
PO Box 402
Doha, Qatar
Phone: (974) 425131
Fax: (974) 324338
Telex: 4078

Romania
Romanian Development Agency
7 Boulevard Magheru
Bucharest, Romania
Phone: (40) (0) 15686 or (40) (0) 154698
Fax:(40) (0) 120371
Telex: 11027

Ministry of the Environment
12 Boulevard Libertatii
Bucharest, Romania
Phone: (40) (0) 316104
Fax: (40) (0) 316486
Telex: 11457

National Bank of Romania
25 Lipscani Street
Bucharest, Romania
Phone: (40) (0) 155528
Fax: (40) (0) 154910
Telex: 1136 BN BUCR

Russia
Ministry of External Economic Relations
Smolenskaya-Sennaya Square, 32-34
121200 Moscow, Russia
Phone: (7) (095) 2201350

Ministry of Ecology and Use of Natural Resources
Vadkovsky, 18-20
101474 Moscow, Russia
Phone: (7) (095) 2893065

State Bank of the Russian Federation
Zhitnaya, 4
Moscow, Russia
Phone: (7) (095) 2373065

Chamber of Commerce and Industry of the Russian
 Federation
Ilyinka, 6
103864 Moscow, Russia
Phone: (7) (095) 9234323
Fax: (7) (095) 2302455

Saint Christopher and Nevis, Federation of
Investment Promotion Agency
PO Box 600
Bay Road, St. Christopher
Phone: (869) 465-4106
Telex: 6852 IPA KC

Ministry of Trade and Industry
PO Box 186
Government House
Church Street
Basseterre, St. Christopher
Phone: (869) 465-2302

Ministry of Finance
Government House
Church Street
Basseterre, St. Christopher
Phone: (869) 465-2612

Ministry of Agriculture, Lands, Housing and Development
Government House
Church Street
Basseterre, St. Christopher
Phone: (869) 465-2521

Eastern Caribbean Central Bank
PO Box 89
Basseterre, St. Christopher
Phone: (869) 465-2536
Fax: (869) 465-1051
Telex: 6828

St. Kitts-Nevis National Bank Ltd.
PO Box 343
Basseterre, St. Christopher
Phone: (869) 465-2205
Telex: 6826

Saint Lucia
National Development Corporation
PO Box 495
27 Brazil Street
Castries, St. Lucia, West Indies
Phone: (758) 452-3614 or (758) 452-3615
Telex: 341-6387 NDC SLU LC

Ministry of Finance, Statistics, Development and Negotiations
Old Government Buildings
Laborie Street
Castries, St. Lucia, West Indies

Phone: (758) 452-5315
Fax: (758) 453-1648
Telex: 6223

Ministry of Health, Housing and Labor
Chausée Road
Castries, St. Lucia, West Indies
Phone: (758) 452-2827

Ministry of Trade, Industry and Tourism
NIS Building
John Comption Highway
Castries, St. Lucia, West Indies
Phone: (758) 452-2429

Eastern Caribbean Central Bank
PO Box 89
Basseterre, St. Christopher
Phone: (758) 465-2537
Fax: (758) 465-1051
Telex: 6825

St. Lucia Chamber of Commerce, Industry and Agriculture
PO Box 482
Monplaisir Building
Brazil Street
Castries, St. Lucia, West Indies
Phone: (758) 452-3165
Fax: (758) 452-6907

Saint Vincent and the Grenadines
The Development Corporation
PO Box 841
Kingstown, St. Vincent
Phone: (809) 457-1358
Fax: (809) 457-2838

St. Vincent and the Grenadines Chamber of Commerce and Industry
PO Box 134
Kingstown, St. Vincent
Phone: (809) 457-1464
Fax: (809) 457-2944

Ministry of Health and Envrionment
Government Offices
Kingstown, St. Vincent
Phone: (809) 457-6111

Saudi Arabia, Kingdom of
Foreign Investment Capital Committee
PO Box 5729

Omar bin Al-Khatab Road
Riyadh, Saudi Arabia 11127
Phone: (966) (1) 4775302

Ministry of Industry and Electricity
PO Box 5729
Omar bin Al-Khatab Road
Riyadh, Saudi Arabia 11127
Phone: (966) (1) 4772722
Telex: 401154 INDEL SJ

Saudi Arabian Monetary Agency
PO Box 2992
Riyadh, Saudi Arabia 11461
Phone: (966) (1) 4774002
Telex: 401065 SAMA SJ

Council of Saudi Arabian Chambers of Commerce
PO Box 16683
Riyadh Chamber of Commerce and Industry Building
Riyadh, Saudi Arabia 11474
Phone: (966) (1) 4053200
Fax: (966) (1) 402747
Telex: 405808

Senegal, Republic of
Investment Committee
Office of the President
PO Box 168
Avenue Roume
Dakar, Senegal
Phone: (221) 231088
Telex: 258

Ministry of the Economy, Finance and Planning
PO Box 462
Rue Charles Laisné
Dakar, Senegal
Phone: (221) 22650
Telex: 61203

Ministry of Tourism and Environmental Protection
PO Box 4049
Avenue André Peytavin
Dakar, Senegal
Phone: (221) 225376

Central Bank of West Africa
PO Box 3108
Avenue Abdoulaye Fadiga
Dakar, Senegal
Phone: (221) 231615

Fax: (221) 239354
Telex: 21815

Seychelles, Republic of
Seychelles Industrial Development Corporation
PO Box 537
Victoria, Seychelles
Phone: 24911
Fax: 25121
Telex: 2415

Ministry of Finance
PO Box 313
State House
Victoria, Seychelles
Phone: 25252
Fax: 25265
Telex: 2363

Office of the President
State House
Victoria, Seychelles
Phone: 24391

Ministry of Administration and Manpower
PO Box 50
National House
Victoria, Seychelles
Phone: 24041
Fax: 24936
Telex: 2333

Central Bank of Seychelles
PO Box 791
Independence Avenue
Victoria, Seychelles
Phone: 25200
Fax: 24958
Telex: 2301

Chamber of Commerce and Industry
PO Box 443
Premier Building
Victoria, Seychelles
Phone: 23812

Seychelles Marketing Road
PO Box 516
Oceangate House
Victoria, Seychelles
Phone: 76618

Sierra Leone, Republic of
Industrial Development Department
Ministry of Trade and Industry
Ministry Buildings
George Street
Freetown, Sierra Leone
Phone: 25211
Telex: 3218

Bank of Sierra Leone
PO Box 30
Siaka Stevens Street
Freetown, Sierra Leone
Phone: 26501

Sierra Leone Chamber of Commerce
PO Box 502
Lanina Sankoh Street
Freetown, Sierra Leone
Phone: 26305

Singapore, Republic of
Economic Development Board
250 North Bridge Road #24-00
Raffles City Tower
Singapore 0617
Phone: (65) 3362288
Fax: (65) 3396077
Telex: RS 26233 SINEDB
Cable: INDUSPROMO

Trade Development Board
1 Maritime Square #10-4- (Lobby-D)
World Trade Center
Telok Blangah Road
Singapore 0409
Phone: (65) 2719388
Fax: (65) 2782518
Telex: RS 28617 TRADEV
RS 28170 TRADEV
Cable: SINTRADEV

Singapore International Chamber of Commerce
50 Raffles Place #03-02
Shell Tower
Singapore 0104
Phone: (65) 2241255
Fax: (65) 2242785
Telex: RS 25235 INTCHAM

Solomon Islands
Foreign Investment Advisory Committee
PO Box 26

Honiara, Solomon Islands
Phone: 23700
Telex: 66337

Ministry of Commerce and Primary Industries
PO Box G26
Honiara, Solomon Islands
Phone: 21140
Telex: 66311

Central Bank of Solomon Islands
PO Box 634
Honiara, Solomon Islands
Phone: 21791
Fax: 23513
Telex: 66320

South Africa, Republic of
Department of Trade and Industry
Ministry of Finance, Trade and Industry
PO Box X84
240 Vermeulen Street
Pretoria, South Africa
Phone: (27) (12) 26061
Telex: 320153

Ministry of Home Affairs and Environment Affairs
PO Box X152
Post Office Building
Pretoria, South Africa
Phone: (27) (12) 2931911
Telex: 350013

Department of Immigration
Ministry of Justice
PO Box X276
Presidia Building
Pretoria, South Africa
Phone: (27) (12) 3238581
Fax: (27) (12) 211708

South African Reserve Bank
PO Box 427
Pretoria, South Africa
Phone: (27) (12) 261611
Fax: (27) (12) 3133197
Telex: 320455

Spain, Kingdom of
Spanish Institute for Foreign Trade (ICEX)
Paseo de la Castellana, 14-16
28012 Madrid Spain
Phone: (34) (1) 4311240

Fax: (34) (1) 4316128
Telex: 44838

General Directorate for External Investment
Ministry of Industry, Trade and Tourism
State Department of Trade
Paseo de la Castellana, 162
28046 Madrid, Spain
Phone: (34) (1) 5837400
Fax: (34) (1) 4581766
Telex: 42112

Banco de Espana (Bank of Spain)
Alcalá 50
28014 Madrid, Spain
Phone: (34) (1) 4469055
Fax: (34) (1) 5216356
Telex: 49461

Sri Lanka, Democratic Socialist Republic of
Greater Colombo Economic Commission
PO Box 1768
14 Sir Baron Jayatilleke Mawatha
Colombo 1, Sri Lanka
Phone: (94) (1) 448880 or (94) (1) 422447 or (94) (1)
  434403
Fax: (94) (1) 447995
Telex: 21332 ECONCOM CE

Ministry of Trade and Commerce
21 Rakshana Mandlraya
Vauxhall Street
Colombo 2, Sri Lanka
Phone: (94) (1) 421191
Telex: 21245

Central Bank of Sri Lanka
34-36 Janadhipathi Mawatha
PO Box 590
Colombo 1, Sri Lanka
Phone: (94) (1) 421191
Fax: (94) (1) 540353
Telex: 21176

Federal Chambers of Commerce and Industry
People's Bank Building
220 Deans Road
Colombo 1, Sri Lanka
Phone: (94) (1) 699530

Sudan, Republic of
The Investment Public Corporation
21 Al Amarat

PO Box 701
Khartoum, Sudan
Phone: 42425
Telex: 24078

Swaziland, Kingdom of
Ministry of Commerce, Industry and Tourism
PO Box 45
Mbabane, Swaziland
Phone: (268) 43201
Telex: 2232

Swaziland Industrial Development Company
Tin and Walker Streets
PO Box 866
Mbabane, Swaziland
Phone: (268) 43391
Fax: (268) 45619
Telex: 2052

Swaziland Chamber of Commerce and Industry
PO Box 72
Mbabane, Swaziland
Phone: (268) 44408
Fax: (268) 44408
Telex: 2032

Sweden, Kingdom of
Ministry of Industry and Commerce
Invest in Sweden Office
Fredsgt. 8 103 33
Stockholm, Sweden
Phone: (46) (8) 763-10-00
Fax: (46) (8) 11-36-16
Telex: 14180

Switzerland (The Swiss Confederation)
Federal Office for Industry and Labor
Department of Industry
Mattenhofstrasse 5
Berne, Switzerland
Phone: (41) (31) 612871
Fax: (41) (31) 612768

Swiss National Bank
Bundesplatz
3033 Berne, Switzerland
Phone: (41) (31) 210211
Fax: (41) (31) 210207

Syrian Arab Republic
Higher Council for Investment
Office of the Prime Minister

Government Offices
Damascus, Syria
Phone: (963) (11) 113513
Telex: 227981

Central Bank of Syria
29 Ayar Square
Damascus, Syria
Phone: (963) (11) 224800
Telex: 269007

Taiwan/Republic of China
Industrial Development and Investment Center
10th Floor
7 Roosevelt Road
Sec. 1
Taipei, Taiwan, Republic of China
Phone: (866) (2) 394-7213
Fax: (866) (2) 392-6835
Telex: 10634 INVEST

Investment Commission
8th Floor
7 Roosevelt Road
Sec. 1
Taipei, Taiwan, Republic of China
Phone: (866) (2) 351-3151
Fax: (866) (2) 396-3970

Ministry of Economic Affairs
15 Foo Chow Street
Taipei, Taiwan, Republic of China
Phone: (866) (2) 321-2200
Fax: (866) (2) 391-9398
Telex: 19884

Council for Economic Planning and Development
9th Floor
87 Nanking E. Road
Sec. 2
Taipei, Taiwan, Republic of China
Phone: (866) (2) 351-0271
Fax: (866) (2) 331-5387

Board of Foreign Trade
Ministry of Economic Affairs
1 Hu Kou Street
Taipei, Taiwan, Republic of China
Phone: (866) (2) 351-0271
Fax: (866) (2) 331-5387

Industrial Development Bureau
Ministry of Economic Affairs

41-2 Hsin Yi Road
Sec. 3
Taipei, Taiwan, Republic of China
Phone: (866) (2) 754-1255
Fax: (866) (2) 7030160

Tanzania, United Republic of
Ministry of Industry and Trade
PO Box 9503
Dar es Salaam, Tanzania
Phone: (255) (51) 27251

Bank of Tanzania
PO Box 2939
Dar es Salaam, Tanzania
Phone: (255) (51) 21291
Telex: 41024

Dar es Salaam Chamber of Commerce
PO Box 41
Dar es Salaam, Tanzania
Phone: (255) (51) 36303
Fax: (255) (51) 36303
Telex: 41408

Thailand, Kingdom of
Office of the Board of Investment
555 Vipavadee Rangsit Road
Bankhen
Bangkok 10900
Thailand
Phone: (66) (2) 270-1400 or (66) (2) 270-1410 or (66) (2) 270-1420
Fax: (66) (2) 271-0777
Telex: 72435 BINVEST TH
Cable Address: BINVEST

Togo, Republic of
EPZ Promotion Board
P.B. 3250
Lome, Togo
Phone: (228) 21-13-74
Fax: (228) 21-52-31
Telex: (986) 5012

Ministry of Industry and State Enterprise
P.B. 2748
Lome, Togo
Phone: (228) 21-07-44
Telex: 5396

Ministry of Planning and Mines
Ave de la Marina

Lome, Togo
Phone: (228) 21-27-01
Telex: 5380

Trinidad and Tobago, Republic of
The General Manager
Industrial Development Corporation
PO Box 949
Port of Spain, Trinidad
Phone: (868) 623-7291 or (868) 623-7298
Fax: (868) 625-9124

Central Bank of Trinidad and Tobago
Eric Williams Plaza
PO Box 1250
Port of Spain, Trinidad
Phone: (868) 625-4835
Fax: (868) 627-4696
Telex: 22532

Tunisia, Republic of
Agency for Promotion of Industry
63 Rue du Syrie
1002 Tunis-Belvédère, Tunisia
Phone: (216) (1) 288091
Fax: (216) (1) 782482
Telex: 12280

Ministry of National Economy
Avenue Kheireddine Pacha
1002 Tunis, Tunisia
Phone: (216) (1) 780366
Telex: 14341

Chamber of Commerce and Industry
Rue de Entrepreneurs
Tunis, Tunisia
Phone: (216) (1) 242872
Fax: (216) (1) 354714
Telex: 14718

Turkey, Republic of
Foreign Investment Directorate
State Planning Organization
Ministry of Economy and Commerce
Sanayi ve Ticaret Bakanhgh
Ankara, Turkey
Phone: (90) (312) 229-2834
Telex: 44598

Union of Chambers of Commerce and Industry of
  Turkey
149 Ataturk Boulevard

Ankara, Turkey
Phone: (90) (312) 117-7700
Telex: 42343

Uganda, Republic of
Uganda Investment Authority
PO Box 7418
Crest House, Nkruman Road
Kampala, Uganda
Phone: (256) (41) 234105
Fax: (256) (41) 242903

Ministry of Commerce, Industry and Cooperatives
PO Box 7103
Kampala, Uganda
Phone: (256) (41) 759785
Telex: 61183

Ministry of Water, Energy, Minerals and Environment
  Protection
PO Box 7270
Kampala, Uganda
Phone: (256) (41) 234995
Telex: 61098

Bank of Uganda
PO Box 7120
Kampala, Uganda
Phone: (256) (41) 258441
Fax: (256) (41) 242903
Telex: 61059

Ukraine, Republic of
Ministry of External Economic Relations and Trade
vul. Pushkinska 4
Kiev, Ukraine
Phone: (380) (044) 2122951
Fax: (380) (044) 2125271

Ministry for the Protection of the Environment
vul. Kirova 7
Kiev, Ukraine
Phone: (380) (044) 2262205

National Bank of Ukraine
Zhovtnevoji Revolyutsiji 9
Kiev, Ukraine
Phone: (380) (044) 2934264
Fax: (380) (044) 2931698

Chamber of Commerce and Industry
vul. Bolshaya Zhitomarskaya 33
Kiev, Ukraine

Phone: (380) (044) 2122911
Fax: (380) (044) 2123353
Telex: 131379

United Arab Emirates, The
Ministry of Economy and Commerce
PO Box 901
Abu Dhabi, United Arab Emirates
Phone: (971) (2) 215455
Fax: (971) (2) 215339
Telex: 22897

Ministry of Finance and Industry
PO Box 433
Abu Dhabi, United Arab Emirates
Phone: (971) (2) 726000
Fax: (971) (2) 773301
Telex: 22937

Ministry of Petroleum and Mineral Resources
PO Box 59
Abu Dhabi, United Arab Emirates
Phone: (971) (2) 651810
Fax: (971) (2) 663414
Telex: 22544

Central Bank of the United Arab Emirates
PO Box 854
Abu Dhabi, United Arab Emirates
Phone: (971) (2) 368200
Fax: (971) (2) 668483
Telex: 22330

Federation of UAE Chambers of Commerce and
  Industry
PO Box 3014
Abu Dhabi, United Arab Emirates
Phone: (971) (2) 214144
Fax: (971) (2) 339210
Telex: 23883

**United Kingdom of Great Britain and Northern
Ireland, The**
Invest in Britain Bureau
Department of Trade and Industry
Kingsgate House
66-74 Victoria Street
London SW1E 6SW, England
Phone: (44) (171) 215-8438 or (44) (171) 215-8439
Fax: (44) (171) 215-8451
Telex: 8811074

Department of the Environment
2 Marsham Street
London SW1 3EB, England
Phone: (44) (171) 276-3000
Fax: (44) (171) 276-0818
Telex: 22221

Office of Northern Ireland
Whitehall
London SW1A 2AZ, England
Phone: (44) (171) 210-3000

Department of Employment
Overseas Labour Section
Caxton House
Tothill Street
London SW1H 9NF, England
Phone: (44) (171) 273-5336 or (44) (171) 273-5337
Telex: 915564

Bank of England
Threadneedle Street
London EC2R 8AH, England
Phone: (44) (171) 601-4444
Telex: 885001

United States of America
International Trade Administration
Department of Commerce
14th Street and Constitution Avenue, NW
Washington, D.C. USA 20230
Phone: (1) (202) 482-2000

Environmental Protection Agency
401 M Street, SW
Washington, D.C. USA 20460
Phone: (1) (202) 260-2090

US Chamber of Commerce
1615 H Street, NW
Washington, D.C. USA 20062
Phone: (1) (202) 566-8195

Uruguay, Republic of
Committee for Investment Development
Executive Government Office
Edificio Libertad
Avda Luis Alberto de Herrera 3050
Montevideo, Uruguay
Phone: (598) (2) 808110
Telex: UY-DICOPRE 22280

Ministry of Economy and Finance
Colonia 1089
Montevideo, Uruguay
Phone: (598) (2) 919102
Telex: 6269

Ministry of Industry and Energy
Rincon 747
Montevideo, Uruguay
Phone: (598) (2) 9026000
Telex: 22072

Central Bank of Uruguay
Avda Juan P. Fabini
Montevideo, Uruguay
Phone: (598) (2) 917117
Telex: 6659

Venezuela, Republic of
Economic Planning Advisory Board
Ministry of Development
Edif Sur
Centro Simon Bolivar
Caracas, Venezuela
Phone: (58) (2) 41-9341
Telex: 22753

Ministry of Development
Edif Sur
Centro Simon Bolivar
Caracas, Venezuela
Phone:(58) (2) 41-9341
Telex: 22753

Superintendency of Foreign Investment
Esquina Bolsa a Mercaderes
Edif. La Perla
El Silencio
Caracas, Venezuela
Phone: (58) (2) 483-6666

Vietnam, Socialist Republic of
State Committee for Cooperation and Investment
56 Quoc To Giam
Ho Chi Minh City, Vietnam
Phone: (84) (8) 53666

Chamber of Commerce and Industry of Vietnam
33 Ba Trieu
Hanoi, Vietnam
Phone: (84) (41) 52961
Fax: (84) (41) 56446
Telex: 411257

Western Samoa, Independent State of
Department of Economic Development
PO Box 862
Apia, Western Samoa
Phone: (685) 24071

Central Bank of Samoa
Private Bag
Apia, Western Samoa
Phone: (685) 24100
Fax: (685) 20293
Telex: 200

Development Bank of Western Samoa
PO Box 1232
Apia, Western Samoa
Phone: (685) 22861
Telex: 212

Yemen, Republic of
General Authority for Investment
Office of the Prime Minister
Government Offices
San a', Yemen
Phone: (967) (1) 247-6900

Central Bank of Yemen
PO Box 59
Ali Abd al-Mughni Street
San 'a, Yemen
Phone: (967) (1) 274371
Fax: (967) (1) 274131
Telex: 2280

Federation of Chambers of Commerce of Yemen
PO Box 16992
San 'a, Yemen
Phone: (967) (1) 224262

Zambia, Republic of
Investment Board
Office of the Prime Minister
PO Box 30208
Lusaka, Zambia
Phone: (260) (1) 218282
Telex: 42240

Ministry of the Environment and Natural Resources
PO Box 30055
Lusaka, Zambia
Phone: (260) (1) 214988

Bank of Zambia
PO Box 30080
Lusaka, Zambia
Phone: (260) (1) 216529
Telex: 41560

Confederation of Industries and Chambers of Commerce
PO Box 30844
Lusaka, Zambia
Phone: (260) (1) 252369
Fax: (260) (1)252483
Telex: 40124

Zimbabwe, Republic of
Investment Center
Ministry of Finance, Economic Planning and Development
Munhumutapa Building

Samora Marchel Avenue
Causeway
Harare, Zimbabwe
Phone: (263) (4) 794571
Telex: 22141

Ministry of the Environment and Tourism
Karigamombe Center
Causeway
Harare, Zimbabwe
Phone: (263) (4) 794455

Reserve Bank of Zimbabwe
76 Samora Marchel Avenue
PO Box 1283
Harare, Zimbabwe
Phone: (263) (4) 790731
Telex: 26075

ANNOTATED BIBLIOGRAPHY

African Equities: A Guide to Markets and Companies, by Christopher Hartland-Peel. London: Euromoney Publications, 1996.

An exceptionally well-researched book, *African Equities* offers an in-depth look at the stock markets and listed companies of nine African countries. South Africa is not included, as it is extensively covered by other sources. The countries covered by this book are:

Part 1: South and East Africa
          Botswana, Kenya, Namibia, Zambia,
          Zimbabwe
Part 2: West Africa
          Côte d'Ivoire, Ghana, Nigeria
Part 3: North Africa
          Morocco

Author Christopher Hartland-Peel has developed a reputation for the study of emerging markets. Based in Nairobi during the early 1990s, he worked on privatization and financial market development and realized the need for quality research on sub-Saharan stock markets. Mr. Hartland-Peel also formerly worked for International Finance Corporation in Washington, D.C. and also worked with the Asian Development Bank.

Although the book contains basic profile information on the various stock exchanges and their performance records, its main strength is in its detailed developmental information and fundamental analysis of the various listed companies. Comparative graphs and statistical growth tables are included.

Barron's Finance & Investment Handbook, 4th Edition, by John Downes and Jordan Elliot Goodman. Hauppauge, New York: Barron's, 1995.

A handbook of personal investment data and other information with the primary features being a description of several types of investments and an extensive glossary of investment terminology. The book is divided into five parts and has an appendix.

Part 1: How to Invest Your Money: 30 Key Personal
          Investment Opportunities
Part 2: How to Read an Annual Report
Part 3: How to Read the Financial Pages
Part 4: Dictionary of Finance and Investment
          (glossary)
Part 5: Finance and Investment Ready Reference
          (information sources)
Appendix Selected Further Reading
          Currencies of the World
          Abbreviations and Acronyms

The Warren Buffett Way: Investment Strategies of the World's Greatest Investor, by Robert G. Hagstrom, Jr. New York: Wiley, 1995.

A popular book describing one of the world's most successful investor's strategies: this book explains what Warren Buffett has done to become the wealthiest stock buyer in the United States. The key to Mr. Buffett's strategy is to determine the intrinsic value of a business and pay a fair price for the shares. His strategy also employs a "buy and hold" philosophy, rather than buying and selling shares for short-term profits. The idea is to invest in the growth of a business, not the inconsistencies of stock market psychology.

"Buying a Business" is the title of Chapter 4, and it describes four primary tenets:

Business Tenets:
1. Is the business simple and understandable?
2. Does the business have a consistent operating history?
3. Does the business have favorable long-term prospects?

Management Tenets:
1. Rationality
2. Candor
3. The institutional imperative

Financial Tenets:
1. Return on equity
2. Owner earnings
3. Profit margins
4. The one-dollar premise

Market Tenets:
1. Determine the value
2. Buy at attractive prices

The soundness of Warren Buffett's strategy and the evidence of his abilities is shown by his personal success; he has achieved a net worth estimated at $8.3 billion in 1993 and more than twice that amount in 1996.

The Business Week Guide to Global Investments Using Electronic Tools, by Robert Schwabach. New York: Osborne McGraw-Hill, 1994.

Although this book is somewhat dated in terms of data, software capabilities, and available information, the basic concept of giving the investor a thumbnail global view of investing is timeless. Since this book was published, Internet providers have improved as well as multiplied, and Internet stock market data has grown considerably in quantity and quality.

The book is in four parts.

Part 1:   Same Planet, New World

"Around the World in 80 Markets" gives Internet-available information on some of the world's markets.

"On-Ramps for the Information Highway" discusses primary Internet and other data providers. This area has experienced considerable growth since the book was published.

"The Tools of the Trade: What You Need to Turn on and Tune in." Again, many changes have occurred in computer hardware and software.

Part 2:

"A Closed-End View of an Open World" discusses closed-end investment funds for various areas.

Part 3:

"The Information Highway: Roadside Attractions" looks at details of services provided by various Internet connections including: CompuServe, Prodigy, America On-Line, Dow Jones News, GEnie and Delphi.

Part 4:

"Gentlemen Choose Your Weapons," describes various software programs designed specifically for market analysis. Tools that can access a large database for purposes of graph construction are examined—for example, Telescan, Metastock, The Technician, Windows on Wall Street. Demo version disks of the analytical tools are included with the book.

The book gives the investor a basic background on the use of computer databases for world stock market analysis.

Crises Investing for the Rest of the '90s, by Douglas Casey. Secaucus, New Jersey: Carol Publishing (Birch Lane Press), 1995.

Part 1 of this book, "What's Going On and Why?", analyzes economic periods of boom and bust, the destruction of the dollar, federal debt, taxes, and the Great Depression. Part 2, "What You Can Do About It", looks at a variety of investment selections and hedging opportunities including: low-risk portfolios, venture capital, low-priced stocks, mutual funds, Wall Street ethics, gold, energy, commercial properties, and others. Part 3, "What's Going To Happen Next?", examines a variety of future potential crises opportu-

nities including the former Soviet Union, a "new class" society, and the destruction of the rain forests.

The Dow Jones Guide to the World Stock Market, by the editors of Dow Jones in association with Morningstar. Englewood Cliffs, New Jersey: Prentice Hall, 1996.

The book contains data from 1994–95, relating to 2,500 companies listed on 20 stock exchanges around the world. The exchanges of Australia, Belgium, Canada, Denmark, Finland, France, Germany, Hong Kong, Italy, Japan, Malaysia, the Netherlands, New Zealand, Norway, Singapore, Spain, Sweden, Switzerland, the United Kingdom, and the United States are covered.

The work focuses on a general description of a country's economy and stock exchange, stock market performance, and statistics relating to the fundamentals of individual companies. Data on Sales, Net Income, Book Value, Price/Earnings Ratio, Price/Book Ratio, Yield %, Price, 52 Week High and Low Prices, Market Capitalization and a general description of the companies are presented.

Emerging Stock Markets: A Complete Investment Guide to New Markets Around the World, by Margaret M. Price. New York: McGraw-Hill, 1994.

As International Editor for *Pensions and Investments,* a periodical published in New York, Margaret Price was able to gather information from several international sources. Her strategy in describing countries is to take a "top down" macroeconomic view to partly explain market activities. The book presents information on 25 emerging markets around the world, including Argentina, Brazil, Chile, Colombia, Mexico, Venezuela, Hungary, Poland, Portugal, Greece, Turkey, South Korea, Taiwan, Indonesia, Malaysia, the Philippines, Thailand, India, Pakistan, the People's Republic of China, and the Commonwealth of Independent States. Some of the African markets and Papua New Guinea are also included.

The first three chapters describe:

• The selection process for emerging markets

• How to invest (direct, ADRs, mutual funds)

• A look at the best performing money managers

Although each country described has unique qualities, a basic format is used to describe the market as an opportunity with risk and reward potential, such as the format for Hungary:

• Government and politics

• History

- The Economy
    - Up from communism
    - Dealing with debt
    - Privatization
- The Markets
    - The stock exchange
    - Foreign investors
    - Investments to consider

The book ends with a discussion of NAFTA in the following areas:

- Sectors
- Services
- Regulations

This well-researched book makes use of information from the International Finance Corporation (a division of the World Bank), the Bank of New York, Baring America Asset Management Co. Inc., and SEI Corporation. It presents emerging market data, other research, and conclusions that are complete, concise, and useful to the international investor.

Emerging Stock Markets Factbook. Washington, D.C.: International Finance Corporation, annual editions.

The annual *Factbook* contains stock market analysis of current emerging markets in comparison to the world's developed markets. Areas examined are:

1. Introduction to Emerging Markets
2. World Stock Markets
3. IFC Global Indexes
4. IFC Investable Indexes
5. IFC Index Market Profiles
6. Other Equity Market Profiles

Appendix information is included:

Appendix 1:
   Sources and Notes
   Stock Market Reference List
   Macroeconomics Data Notes
   Currency Notes
   Standard Industrial Classification (SIC) Codes
   Glossary
   Abbreviations

Appendix 2:
   Investor Information
   Withholding Taxes for Emerging Markets
   Investment Regulations Summary for Entering and
      Exiting Emerging Markets
   Information Disclosure Summary for Emerging
      Markets

Appendix 3:
   Emerging Stock Market Directory

Addresses and Fax Numbers
Operating Information for Emerging Stock Market
   Exchanges
Summary of Major Changes to Coverage in (most
   recent year)
EMDB Publications and Products
News Service Access to Indexes

Encyclopedia of Banking and Finance, 10th edition, by Charles J. Woelfel. Chicago and London: Fitzroy Dearborn, 1994.

Dr. Charles J. Woelfel is Professor Emeritus of Accounting at the University of North Carolina, Greensboro. He was also editor of the 9th edition of this encyclopedia.

The encyclopedia contains nearly 4,200 entries, definitions and descriptions relating to banking and finance. The terms cover Abandonment (the relinquishment of title, possession, or claim) to Z-Tranche (the final class of securities in collateralized mortgage obligations called "CMOs"). Some entries are a few short paragraphs; others are several pages in length. The relevant material was updated through 1993. Although it is heavy on terms relative to banking, it also contains numerous investment and stock market-related entries.

This tenth edition marks 70 years since the original publication in 1924.

Getting Started In Futures, second edition, by Todd Lofton. New York: Wiley, 1993.

This introduction is intended to provide someone who knows nothing about futures a basic understanding of what they are and how they can be used. The author, Todd Lofton, is a former member of the Chicago Board Options Exchange (CBOE), a past president of Investor Publications, a publisher/editor for *Futures* magazine (then called *Commodities*) and is known as a popular speaker and writer on the subject of futures.

The clearly written book provides non-jargon examples of futures trading. The author's early description of futures sets the tone for the work: He describes a grower making an agreement to sell corn to a cattleman at a mutually agreeable price, the corn to be delivered in the future. Although this would be a "forward contract," a futures contract does basically the same thing but is standardized by the marketplace for reliability and consistency.

The 16 chapters describe basic terms and concepts, today's futures market, speculation, hedging, procedures, a description of the trading place, analysis (fundamental and technical) of financial futures, money management, futures options, rules and regulations, and contracts. Appendices A, B, and C describe chart patterns, "point-and-figure" charts, and moving averages. Appendix D goes into more depth with Stochastics and Relative Strength.

The investor who reads this book has the opportunity to gain a considerable amount of knowledge relating to the basics of trading futures.

The Global Investor: Opportunities, Risks and Realities for Institutional Investors in the World's Markets, by Gavin R. Dobson. Chicago: Probus Publishing, 1994.

Gavin Dobson's book is a look at the concerns and advantages of international investing. The book is in four parts:

Part 1:   Historical Background

Looks at state-sponsored international investing, infrastructure investing, private international investing, corporate investment, and international portfolio management. It then moves to the construction and history of three investment funds: The Scottish American Investment Company (SAINTS), The Alliance Trust, and The Edinburgh Investment Trust.

Part II: The Case for International Investing

The section first gives some background, then looks at developed markets as compared to emerging markets and draws conclusions such as: "The trend of faster economic growth by smaller countries is inexorable. As they grow, their stock markets will expand, and the pool of capitalization will correspondingly increase for foreign investment. For example, Colombia today has nearly twice the market capitalization that Norway had in 1980, yet is regarded as a greater risk today than Norway was then." Index performance, risk diversification, particular opportunities, and the weight of money are also analyzed.

Part III: The Practice of International Investment Management

Part three gives a brief background, then looks at a "top-down" approach to international investing with economically-related factors, stock market-related factors, country rankings, and the weighting decision. Portfolio construction using futures and stock selection using a variety of methods is discussed.

Part IV: Some Administrative Considerations
   Administrative concerns of:
   • Global custody
   • Corporate governance and social screening
   • International performance measurement

   • Investment vehicles
   • Technology and sources of information
   The book concludes with a modest glossary and the following appendices:

A: Withholding tax rates
B: The Cadbury Code of Best Practice
C: Environmental Declaration
D: Representative indices in world markets
E: Some key data providers

The Global Trade and Investment Handbook: A Country-by-Country Reference to Business Practices, Regulations and Laws, by Jack A. Gottschalk. Chicago: Probus Publishing, 1993.

This book contains investment information gathered from 155 countries, organized alphabetically by country name. The focus is not on stock markets, but rather on direct foreign investment and trade opportunities with descriptions of the political environment, foreign investment policy, the formation and types of permitted business organizations, environmental protection, rights and obligations of foreign investors, labor, accounting requirements, currency controls, taxation, legal system, customs and duties, protection of intellectual property, immigration and residence, and sources of foreign investment assistance.

International Investing with ADRs: Your Passport to Profits Worldwide, by Eric J. Fry. Chicago: International Publishing, 1994.

This book has a basic eight-chapter structure, with an appendix containing the international country and city telephone dialing codes. Chapters 1 through 3 contain information about American Depository Receipts (ADRs), a description of what they are, the differences between sponsored and unsponsored ADRs, Rule 144a, pricing characteristics, how to approach ADR investing, and where to find information.

The remaining five chapters contain lists of ADRs for various countries divided regionally around the world:
   European ADRs
   Asia and Pacific Basin ADRs
   Latin American ADRs
   Mediterranean and African ADRs
   144a ADRs
A brief description of each country's stock exchange appears at the beginning of each country, along with a graphic depiction of a popular index. The format for describing the ADRs is as follows:
   Exchange (where traded, e.g., NYSE)

Ticker Symbol (trading symbol)

Shares per ADR (the number of shares represented by one ADR share)

ADR Type (sponsored or unsponsored)

Depositary(ies)

Business Activities

Address (of the company)

Telephone

Fax

The objective of this book is to provide an initial screen, where the investor can select possible targets for further study, then contact the company or the stock exchange for detailed information.

Investment Biker: Around The World with Jim Rogers, by Jim Rogers. New York: Random House, 1994.

When stockbroker Jim Rogers talks about investment opportunities in many countries around the world, he has first-hand research on which to rely. He's been there. This fascinating and enjoyable book is about a 1990 motorcycle trip made around the world by Jim Rogers along with his friend and companion Tabitha.

Starting in Ireland, they traveled through Europe, Turkey, China, back along a northern Asia route through Russia and back to Ireland. Then they went south through Algiers, Tamanraset, Bangui, Harare, all the way to Capetown. They flew to Perth, Australia—traveled to Hobart—then went to New Zealand. After flying to Cape Horn in South America, they drove to New York, then to Anchorage and south. The worldwide trip ended in Palo Alto, California. It lasted 22 months with them traveling more than 65,000 miles.

Although the story of Jim Rogers' journey is interesting by itself, he also provides a traveler's view of the economic and political structures of many countries, as well as each country's infrastructure. These insights can help to complete a picture of investment opportunities in the world. The author has no hesitation to make investment recommendations such as: "Stick with nations where hard-nosed bureaucrats push fiscal reforms, maintain sound currencies, advocate free trade, and stay out of areas best left to the private sector."

The LGT Guide To World Equity Markets, by LGT Asset Management. London: Euromoney Books, annual editions.

This annual Guide is a collection of market overview essays, stock market profiles, and appendices.

The 1996 version had essays with the following headings and tables:

Introduction:

- Lichtenstein Global Trust
- Top Performing Markets 1985–1995
- The Importance of Global Investing
- The Challenge of Global Investing
- The LGT Asset Management Advantage
- LGT Asset Management Regional Investment Offices

International Equity Indices

- Evolution of World Equity Market Capitalization
- Considerations in Index Construction
- Weighting Methodology
- How Investors Use Indices
- Choosing the Right Index
- Summary

The Impact of Monetary Policies on World Markets

- United States of America
- Japan
- United Kingdom
- Germany
- France

Global Privatization and the Investor

- Notional Privatization in Central Europe and Russia
- 1994–95, Privatization Issues to Market Capitalization (%) for Selected Countries
- 1994–95, Privatization Issues by Region
- Economic Distortions
- Market Liberalization

Regulations

- Support or Restriction for the Markets
- Deregulation: The Common Standards Approach
- Daiwa Banned From the United States
- Thailand: Financing the Speculator
- Japan: Indemnifying the Investor
- France: Rescuing Credit Lyonnais

Stock exchange profiles are organized by:

- Global Markets
- Latin America and the Caribbean
- Asia
- Africa and the Middle East
- Central and Eastern Europe

Although there are differences between the profiles, most exchange profiles follow this basic format:

Introduction

Economic and Political Overview

Market Performance:
- In previous year
- Summary information
- Year-end share price index, price/earnings ratios and yields
- Market indices and their constituents

The Stock Market
- Brief history and structure
- Opening hours, names, and addresses
- Number of listed companies and market value of listed shares
- Equity raised

Market Size
- Number of listings and market value
- Largest quoted companies
- The 20 largest listed companies
- Equity turnover
- The 20 most actively traded shares

Types of Shares

Other Markets

Investors

Country Funds

Operations
- Trading system
- List of principal brokers
- Settlement and transfer
- Commission and other costs

Taxation and Regulations Affecting Foreign Investors
- Withholding tax
- Gains on disposal of shares
- Exchange control and cash transaction reporting
- Foreign acquisition and takeover acts

Reporting Requirements

Shareholder Protection Codes
- Significant shareholding
- Insider trading
- Compensation fund
- Research
- Prospective changes

Listed Stock Options: The Hands-On Study Guide for Investors and Traders, by Carl F. Luft and Richard K. Sheiner. Chicago: Probus Publishing, revised edition, 1994.

Listed Stock Options explains the basics of using stock options in a conservative manner to reduce risk and stabilize return. Early on, the book discusses option basics, the operations of the options market, and the properties of call and put options. Later chapters discuss the complexities of various option strategies. Worksheets included in the book enable the investor to become familiar with various phases of option strategies.

The book has eight chapters; Chapter 8 deals with the long-term options, called "Long-Term Equity Anticipation Securities," or LEAPS.

Appendix A contains a complete bibliography, and Appendix B gives a glossary of option terminology.

Chapters 5–7 include a problem-solving session at the end of the chapter to give the reader experience in dealing with option situations and strategies. Answers to the problems are given in Appendix C.

The NASDAQ Stock Market Fact Book. Gaithersburg, Maryland: National Association of Securities Dealers (NASD), annual editions.

Many stock exchanges publish an annual information piece known as a "Factbook." Each exchange follows its own format, but the general concept is similar for all. The books contain historical performance data for the stock exchange. The Factbook published by NASDAQ has the following contents:

Overview
Market Data
Market Makers
Index Data
National Market Data
Foreign and ADRs
Historical Data
National Market Stocks
Small Cap Market Stocks
Standard Industrialization Codes

Copies of the current directory can be obtained by calling the NASD Media Source at (1-301) 590-5678. Factbooks from other stock exchanges can be obtained by contacting their respective information services.

Standard and Poor's 500 Guide, by Standard & Poor's. New York: McGraw-Hill, Inc., 1997.

The book contains the Standard and Poor's analysis for all 500 companies included in the Standard and Poor's 500 Index. Financial analysis appears by company name in alphabetical order, with additional helpful information appearing at the front of the book:

- What Is the S&P 500?
- The Six Questions...Answered (a discussion of frequently asked questions)

- What You'll Find in This Book (a discussion of the analysis format used for each company)
  - How to Use This Book to Select Investments
  - Companies with Five Consecutive Years of Earnings Increases
    - Rapid Growth Stocks
    - Stocks with A+ Rankings
    - Fast Rising Dividends
    - Higher Dividends for Ten Years

The book is a wealth of information for investors specifically interested in Standard & Poor's 500 stocks.

Technical Analysis of Stock Trends, 7th edition, by Robert D. Edwards and John Magee. Chicago: John Magee, and New York: Amacom, 1997.

The first edition of this important work was published in 1948, and since that time has sold more than 800,000 copies. John Magee, a pioneer in technical analysis of stock trends, together with Robert D. Edwards, expanded the analysis ideas of Charles Henry Dow (founding father of *The Wall Street Journal)* and later *WSJ* editor William Hamilton. The work of Dow and Hamilton focused primarily on the Dow Industrial and Dow Railroad Averages trends.

Later, in the 1920s, Richard Schabacker (former editor of *Forbes*) showed how signals from trends could also be observed when tracking share prices.

The work of Magee emphasizes three main principles:

1. Stock prices move in trends
2. Volume goes with the trend
3. A trend, once established, tends to continue in force

A significant portion of this book is dedicated to pattern recognition: the trends form a pattern that can often be taken as the signal of change.

Patterns such as:

- Head and shoulders
- Tops and bottoms
- "W" shaped patterns
- Triangles
- Rectangles

They are patterns well known to practitioners of technical analysis.

The book explains basic concepts of technical analysis, discusses the Dow Theory (including its weaknesses), spends five chapters on reversal patterns, covers consolidation, gaps, support and resistance, and finishes Part 1 with significant coverage of trendlines and channels. Part 2 applies the lessons to practical situations and discusses selection, chart building, recognizing bottoms and tops, trendlines, implications, and the use of capital.

Appendix A discusses Tekniplat Charting, and Appendix B provides more chart examples. A glossary completes the historic work.

The World's Emerging Stock Markets: Structure, Regulations, and Opportunities, by Keith K.H. Park and Antoine W. Van Agtmael. Chicago: Probus Publishing, 1993.

A study of emerging markets, this book uses a modified essay approach, with local experts providing the information on their respective economies and stock exchanges. For example, Malaysia was composed by Nick Seaward, Research Director for Baring Securities in Kuala Lumpur. The advantage to the approach is in the insight provided by a person dealing with economic and market subtleties on a daily basis.

The work is divided into six sections with individual chapters as main headings for each essay.

Section: I   Introduction
Ch. 1   Enhanced Efficiency of Global Portfolio
            Diversification through Emerging
            Market Investing
Ch. 2   Investing in Emerging Markets
Ch. 3   Two Decades of Change in Emerging
            Markets
Ch. 4.   Portfolio Management in Emerging
            Markets: Country Allocation and
            Stock Research
Section: II   Asia
Section: III   Latin America
Section IV   Europe
Section V   Middle East
Section VI   Investment Strategies and Related
                Issues

The sections are followed by appendices A through H providing data and other factual information on regions and exchanges.

INDEX

Last Resort 635; Market Correction/Market Crash 676; Market Mania 677; Master of Business Administration (MBA) 682; Merrill Lynch 693; Mozer, Paul 726; PaineWebber 801; Regulation, Trend Toward 883; Super Bowl Theory 1005; Thailand, Kingdom of, History 1041; Trump, Donald 1065; Union Bank of Switzerland 1080; Women in the Stock Market 1172; Yamaichi Securities Company, Limited 1179; Yuppie 1182

Black Tuesday

Bank Brussels Lambert (BBL) 94; Bank of Montreal 102; Bank of Nova Scotia 104; BankBoston 93; Bankers Trust Company 110; Banque Nationale de Paris (BNP) 114; Bear Stearns 132; Black Monday 147; Caveat Emptor/Caveat Subscriptor 219; Deutschmark Crisis of the 1930s 334; Dresdner Bank AG 354; Durant, William 358; Federal National Mortgage Association 392; First Chicago NBD Corporation 407; *Fortune* 415; Générale Bank 445; Goldman, Sachs and Company 464; Graham, Benjamin 469; History of Commercial Banking in the United States 491; Household International Inc. 504; Istituto per la Ricostruzione Industriale 552; Japanese Boom and Bust, 1988–90 583; Kennedy, Joseph 596; Keynes, John Maynard 599; Kidder, Peabody & Company 603; Lloyds Bank PLC 645; Merrill Lynch 693; Morgan, J.P., and Company, Inc. 717; PaineWebber 801; Penn Square Failure 813; Prudential Securities 867; Regulation, Trend Toward 883; Salomon Inc. 919; Selling Short 935; Société Générale 961; Swiss Bank Corporation 1014; Union Bank of Switzerland 1080; United States/New York Stock Exchange 1097; Westpac Banking Corporation 1165; Wiggin, Albert 1170

Black-Scholes Options Pricing Model

Futures Trading 436

Block

Block Trade 152; Direct Placement 337; Distributing Syndicate 342; Exchange Distribution 386; Long-Term Credit Bank of Japan, Ltd. (LTCB) 652; Marketable Parcel 679; Position Offer/Bid 855; Secondary Distribution 930; Special Offering 982; Stated Percentage Order 992; Unit Investment Trust/Unit Trust 1081; Workout/Workout Market 1174

Block Positioner

SEC Rule 17a-17 932

Block Trade

Agency Facilitation Trader (AFT) 12; All or Any Part (AOAP) 15; Amsterdam Interprofessional Market (AIM) 33; Bank Hapoalim 97; Bear Stearns 132; Blockwatch 152; Lynch, Peter 656; Raccattore 877; Salomon Inc. 919; Tiesioginial Sandorai 1051; Transakcja Pakietowa 1059

Blue Chip

Aunt Millie 52; Basket Trading 129; Belgian Dentist 134; Flight to Quality 412

Board Lot

Odd Lot 781; Round Lot 908

Board of Directors

Accountant 4; Annual Meeting 38; Argentina, History/Buenos Aires Exchange 42; Audit 50; Australia, History 52; Ballot 78; Baltic Exchange 78; Banco Ambrosiano Scandal 80; Banco Central Hispano (BCH) 83; Bank for International Settlement (BIS) 96; Bank of New York 104; BankBoston 93; Bankers Trust Company 110; Barclays Bank 119; Board Room 153; Chairman of the Board 220; Chicago Mercantile Exchange (CME) 232; Common Stock 264; Costa Rica, Republic of, History 279; Declaration of Dividend 318; Dividend 344; Final Dividend 397; Friendly Takeover 434; Holding Company 495; Investment Company 541; Lloyd's Register of Shipping 650; Lloyds Bank PLC 645; Long-Term Credit Bank of Japan, Ltd. (LTCB) 652; Majority Control 659; Martillo System 680; Pac-Man Defense 801; Perelman, Ronald 816; Perot, H. Ross 818; Peterson, Peter G. 824; President 860; Principal Shareholder 862; Proxy Statement 867; Schneider, Jürgen 927; Shareholder of Record 941; Split 984; Sri Lanka, Democratic Republic of, History 985; Statutory Voting 993; Stock Dividend 995; Stockholder of Record 1000; Svenska Handelsbanken 1006; Trinidad and Tobago, Republic of, History 1063; Unissued Stock 1080

Boesky, Ivan

Den of Thieves 321; Drexel Burnham Lambert 355; Goldman, Sachs and Company 464; Guinness Trial 481; Kohlberg Kravis Roberts (KKR) 606; Milken, Michael 705; Morgan Grenfell Group PLC 720; Pickens, T. Boone 833; Turner, Ted 1075

Bolivia, Republic of

Banco Bilbao Vizcaya (BBV) 82; Mercosur 691; Third World Debt 1048

Brokerage House

Buffett, Warren

Building Societies

Bulgaria, Republic of

Bull

Bull Market

Business Cycle

Busted Trade
Error 374

Buttonwood Tree
United States/New York Stock Exchange 1097

Buy
Agency 12; Agency Trades 12; All or None (AON) 15; Alternative Order 32; Analyst 33; Apport 41; At Discretion 49; At Risk 49; At the Close 49; At the Market 50; At the Open 50; Auction Market 50; Backwardation 74; Bank Hapoalim 97; Barca 118; Book 160; Book-Entry Transfer (BET) 160; Broker 177; Call Option 191; Called Away 191; Cash Transaction 217; CAVAL 218; Chicago Mercantile Exchange (CME) 232; Clear 250; Close 252; Close a Position 252; Commission 263; Contrarion 276; Cross 295; Daisy Chain 312; Dealer 314; Debt 317; Delinquency 320; Desk 332; Discretionary Account 342; Dow Theory 351; Each Way 361; En Cours 373; Exchange Distribution 386; Execution 388; Exercise Price 388; Fill or Kill (FOK) 397; Floor Broker 412; Floor Trader 412; Free Riding 433; Futures Contract 436; Gain 439; Gap 443; Gilt Edged Market Maker (GEMM) 457; Giver 457; Good Delivery 467; Good Till Cancelled (GTC) 468; Goodwill 468; Horizontal Spread 503; Illiquid Investment 516; Immediate or Cancel (IOC) 516; In the Money 517; Index Option 518; Insider Dealing/Insider Trading 533; Interest Rate Futures 537; Investment Adviser 540; Investment Club 541; Investment Income 543; Issue Price 552; Kerkorian, Kirk 599; Kursmakler 616; Last Trading Day 626; Lay Off 628; Legal Transfer 633; Letter of Credit 636; Letter of Intent 637; Lynch, Peter 656; Making a Market 660; Managed Fund 670; Marché des Reports 673; Margin Account 674; Market Bottom 676; Market Maker 677; Market on Close 678; Market Top 679; Marketable Limit Order 679; Matched Orders 683; Maximum Price Fluctuation 687; Minneapolis Grain Exchange (MGE) 710; N/A 731; Net Balance System 746; Net Worth 747; Neural Network 753; New York Mercantile Exchange (NYMEX) 757; Nikko Securities Company Limited 766; Normal Investment Practice 774; Odd Lot Theory 781; Oferta 783; Offer 782; On Balance Volume 789; On the Opening 789; Ongoing Buyer/Ongoing Seller 789; Open Market Operations 790; Open Order 790; Opening Purchase 791; Option 792; Option Contract 792; Option Spread 793; Option Spreading 793; Or Better (OB) 794; Order Imbalance 795; Pac-Man Defense 801; Participate But Do Not Initiate (PNI) 809; Pawn-broking 810; Physical Access Member 833; Playing the Market 836; Portfolio Theory 845; Position Offer/Bid 855; Primary Dealer 861; Principal Shareholder 862; Profit 864; Profit Margin 864; Psychology of Speculation 868; Purchasing Power 870; Qualitative Analysis 873; Quotation 874; Raccattore 877; Rally 878; Registered Competitive Market Maker (RCMM) 882; Registered Representative (RR) 882; Regular-Way Settlement 883; Regulation G–X/Regulation G 885; Reverse Conversion 893; Risk Arbitrage 896; Rollover 902; Saitori 917; Same-Day Substitution 923; SEC Rule 10b-18 931; SEC Rule 10b-2 931; SEC Rule 13e 931; Secondary Market 930; Security 933; Sell Out 934; Sellers' Market 935; Selling Short 935; Selling the Spread 937; Settle 940; Specialist 983; Speculation 983; Stamp Duty 989; Stated Percentage Order 992; Stellage 994; Stock Exchange 995; Stockbroker 1000; Stop Limit Order 1001; Stopped Stock 1001; Support/Support Level 1006; Swap 1007; Syndicate 1025; Tip 1052; Trade 1056; Transaction Costs 1059; Trin 1062; Two-Sided Market 1077; Underlying Security 1079; Unwind a Trade 1137; Vertical Spread 1148; Wash Sale Rule 1160

Buy Stop Order
Buy 186; Do Not Reduce (DNR) 345

Buyback/Stock Buyback
Closing Purchase 252; Roll Down 901; Self-Tender 934; Short Covering 943; Treasury Stock 1060

Buying to Close
Unwind a Trade 1137

Cabinet Security
Cabinet Option Trade 189

CAC 40 Index
Indicators 527

Calendar Spread
Horizontal Spread 503

Call
Assign 48; Break Even Point 174; Called Away 191; Call 190; Chicago Board of Options Exchange (CBOE) 225; Debit Spread 317; Exercise Price 388; Forced Conversion 415; Futures Trading 436; Hedge 490; Junk Bonds 592; Naked Option/Naked Call 734; OEX 781; Option Contract 792; Option Writer 793; Portfolio Theory 845; Spread (Options) 984; Straddle 1001; Vertical Spread 1148

Commodity Futures Trading Commission (CFTC)

Common Stock

Company

Oversight and Surveillance System (MOSS) 678; Master of Business Administration (MBA) 682; Maxwell, Robert 687; Mercury Asset Management Ltd. 692; Merger 693; Minority Interest 711; Minority Shareholder 711; Mitsubishi Trust & Banking Corporation 714; Money Laundering 715; Morgan, J.P., and Company, Inc. 717; Multinational Company (MNC) 728; Multiple Listing 728; Nadir, Asil 731; Net Current Assets 746; Net Sales 747; Nikko Securities Company Limited 766; Nippon Credit Bank (NCB) 767; Nippon Shinpan Company, Ltd. 768; No-Par Value 773; No-Review Offering 773; Nomura Securities Company, Limited 770; Office of Fair Trading (OFT) 783; Offre Publique d'Acaht, Offre Publique d'Échange 783; Orphan Stock 798; Overvalued 799; Pac-Man Defense 801; Paid In Capital/Paid Up Capital 801; Panty Raid 807; Pension Reversion 814; Perella, Joseph R. 815; Perelman, Ronald 816; Performance Fund 818; Plan Company 836; Player 836; Pool 843; Pooling of Interests 843; Portfolio 845; Praeference Aktie 856; President 860; Principal Shareholder 862; Profit and Loss 864; Profit Margin 864; Profit Sharing Plan 864; Proxy 867; Qualitative Analysis 873; Quantitative Analysis 873; Quiet Period 874; Quotation Spread 875; Raccattore 877; Real Estate Investment Trust (REIT) 880; Regulation, Trend Toward 883; Research and Development (R&D) 886; Resistance Level 887; Retained Earnings 888; Return of Capital 888; Return on Equity 888; Road Show 898; Scripophily 929; SEC Rule 10b-18 931; Sector 930; Shareholder 941; Shareholder of Record 941; Short Swing 943; Split 984; Statement in Lieu of Prospectus 993; Stock Dividend 995; Stock List 998; Stockholder 1000; Subscribed Capital 1003; Subsidiary Company 1003; Suspension of Listing 1006; Synergy 1025; Takeover/Takeover Bid 1036; Target Company 1037; Tegningsret 1039; Tender Offer 1041; Transfer Accounting, Lodgement for Investors and Stock Management (TALISMAN) 1060; Turnaround 1075; Undervalued 1079; Unissued Stock 1080; Value Line Investment Survey 1141; Volume 1149; Voting Share 1150; Walk-Away Merger 1151; Widow-and-Orphan Stocks 1170; Wilshire 5,000 1171; Working Capital 1173

Compliance

Back Office 74; Broker/Dealer (BD) Form 177; Compliance Registered Options Principal (CROP) 268

Compliance Officer

Sales Literature 919

Compliance Registered Options Principal (CROP)

Senior Registered Option Principal (SROP) 937

Computer Trading

Arbitrage 42; Bank of Montreal 102; Canada, History/ Vancouver Exchange 192; Checking 225; Chicago Mercantile Exchange (CME) 232; Chile, Republic of, History 235; China, Republic of/Shanghai Stock Exchange 240; Circuit Breakers 247; Committee on Uniform Securities Identification Procedures (CUSIP) 263; Crowd 295; Dealing Room Technology 315; Delayed Tape 320; European Association of Securities Dealers Auto Quotation (EASDAQ) 378; Execution 388; Institutional Networks Corporation (Instinet) 534; Intermarket Trading System (ITS) 537; Japan, History 564; Luxembourg, Grand Duchy of, History 653; Maximum Price Fluctuation 687; Oferta 783; Over the Counter (OTC) 799; Pacific Computerized Order Access System (P/ COAST) 801; Philippines, Republic of, History 826; Program Trading 865; Property as Investment 865; Quotation 874; Stock Exchange 995; Stock Exchange Automated Trading System (SEATS) 997; Stock Exchange Pool of Nominees (SEPON) 997; Stock Market 998; Stock Record 1000; Stockwatch Automated Tracking System (SWAT) 1001; Tape 1037; Titulos al Portator 1053; Titulos Nominativos 1053; Unit of Trading 1081; United Kingdom/London Stock Exchange 1081; United States/ NASDAQ 1119; United States/Pacific Stock Exchange (PSE) 1127; United States/Philadelphia Stock Exchange 1132; Uruguay, Republic of, History 1137

Concert Party

Acting in Concert 8; Racketeer Influenced and Corrupt Organizations Act 877

Confirmation

Book-Entry 160; BOT 161; Contract Note 275; Dow Theory 351; Exercise Notice 388; SEC Rule 10b-10 931; Size 950; SLD 952; Trade Date (T/D) 1056; Trading Desk 1056

Conglomerate

Ahmanson, H.F. & Company 13; Dai-Ichi Kangyo Bank Ltd. 311; Defensive Shares 318; Drexel Burnham Lambert 355; Fuji Bank 434; Japanese Financial Markets 585; Kohlberg Kravis Roberts (KKR) 606; Ling, James 639; Mitsubishi Trust & Banking Corporation 714; Nadir, Asil 731; NatWest Group 740; Perelman, Ronald 816; Subsidiary Company 1003

Witter, Discover & Company 724; Morgan, J.P., and Company, Inc. 717; NationsBank 739; Nikko Securities Company Limited 766; Other Income 798; PaineWebber 801; Passed Dividend 810; Portfolio Manager 845; Quarterly Report 873; Raider 878; Retained Earnings 888; Revenue Act 891; Risk/Reward Ratio 896; Self-Tender 934; Statutory Voting 993; Treasury Stock 1060; Turkey, Republic of, History 1069; Wider Share Ownership 1168; Working Control 1174

Cost of Goods Sold
First In First Out (FIFO) 408

Côte d'Ivoire, Republic of
Pre-Emerging Markets 857

Coutts & Company
NatWest Group 740

Credit
Account Statement 4; Accrual Basis 7; Ancient Egypt, Banking in 34; Banco do Brasil (BB) 84; Bank of the United States (II) 107; BankAmerica Corporation 92; BankBoston 93; *Bonfire of the Vanities, The* 159; Cash 216; Cash Flow 217; Commercial Paper 260; Credit Analyst 289; Credit Rating 289; Credit Risk 289; Credit Spread 290; Deutsche Bank 332; Difference 337; Discount Market 341; Dun & Bradstreet (D&B) 358; Economic Indicators 363; First Chicago NBD Corporation 407; Fisher, Irving 409; Fitch Investor's Service Inc. 410; Japanese Financial Markets 585; Margin Account 674; Margin Call 674; Middle Ages, Banking in the 703; Monetary Policy 715; Nippon Shinpan Company, Ltd. 768; Profit and Loss 864; Rating 879; Revenue Act 891; Royal Bank of Canada 909; Schneider, Jürgen 927; SEC Rule 15c3-2 931; Sharp, Albert E. 941

Crédit Agricole
Building Societies 180; Lazard Frères 628; Thrifts 1049

Credit Rating
Debt Service 318; Debtor 318; Default 318

Credit Suisse
Maxwell, Robert 687

Cumulative Preferred Stock/Cumulative Preference Shares
Accumulated Dividend 7; Adjustable Rate Preferred Stock 10; Dividend 344; Dividend in Arrears 344

Curb
United States/American Stock Exchange 1122

Currency
Banco do Brasil (BB) 84; Bank of England, History of 100; Bank of Montreal 102; Bank of Tokyo-Mitsubishi, Ltd. (BMT) 108; Banking Act of 1979 112; Bretton Woods Agreement 175; Cash 216; Currency Futures 296; Depreciation 330; Derivative Instrument 331; Devaluation 335; Earnings 361; Emerging Growth Markets 372; Eurobond 376; Eurocurrency 377; European Currency Snake 381; European Monetary System (EMS) 385; European Options Exchange (EOE) 386; Exchange Rate 387; Fuji Bank 434; Gold 461; Gold Standard 462; Gresham, Sir Thomas 476; International Monetary Fund (IMF) 538; Junk Bonds 592; Latin Union 626; Money Supply 716; Pegging 813; Pound 856; Revaluation 891; SEC Rule 17a-8 932; United States/Philadelphia Stock Exchange 1132

Currency Futures
Financial Futures 397

Current Assets
Accounts Receivable 6; Acid Test Ratio 7; Current Liabilities 296; Current Ratio 297; Floating Capital 412; Net Current Assets 746; Quick Asset Ratio 873; Quick Assets 873; Working Capital 1173

Current Liabilities
Current Ratio 297; Net Current Assets 746; Quick Asset Ratio 873; Quick Assets 873

Current Market Value
Abandon 1; Acquisition 7; Agreement among Underwriters 13; All or Any Part (AOAP) 15; Any and All Bid 40; Appreciation 41; Bank of the United States (II) 107; Breakup Value 175; Call Option 191; Cash Flow 217; Cost Basis 278; Earnings 361; Equity 373; Equity Method of Accounting 373; Eurobond 376; Gold 461; Haircut 489; Issued Share Capital 552; Kohlberg Kravis Roberts (KKR) 606; Mark to the Market 675; Market Capitalization 676; Market Stabilization 679; Marketable Limit Order 679; Minneapolis Grain Exchange (MGE) 710; Naked Option/Naked Call 734; Narrowing a Spread 737; Nil Paid 767; Non-Qualifying Stock Option 773; Option Writer 793; Price/Earnings Ratio 860; Put Premium 870; Quote 875; Rally 878; Random Walk Theory 878; Reverse Split 893; Risk Arbitrage 896; Sell Stop Order 935; Standard & Poor's 500 Index 989; Stop Order 1001; Stopped Stock 1001; Sub-

Individual Retirement Account (IRA)

About-Amount Trade 2; Account 3; Margin Account 674; Phantom Income 826; Rollover 902; Simplified Employee Pension Plan (SEP) 945; Tax Shelter 1038

Indonesia, Republic of

Bank Brussels Lambert (BBL) 94; Junk Bonds 592; Pre-Emerging Markets 857; Standard Chartered PLC 990; Third World Debt 1048; Warburg Dynasty 1156; Yakuza 1177

Industrial Bank of Japan Ltd. (IBJ)

Long-Term Credit Bank of Japan, Ltd. (LTCB) 652; Nikko Securities Company Limited 766; Nippon Credit Bank (NCB) 767

Industrial Stocks

Dow Jones Industrial Average (DJIA) 349

Inflation

Banco do Brasil (BB) 84; Bank Hapoalim 97; Chicago School of Economics 234; Consumer Goods 272; Consumer Price Index (CPI) 273; Cost-of-Living Adjustment (COLA) 279; Credit 286; Credit Risk 289; Deflation 319; Dow Theory 351; European Currency Snake 381; Fiscal Policy 409; Fisher, Irving 409; Gold 461; Islamic Banking 547; Kleinwort Benson 604; Lazard Frères 628; Macroeconomics 659; Market Mania 677; Mexican Collapse of 1994 695; Mexican Debt Crisis of 1982 697; Money Supply 716; Morgan Grenfell Group PLC 720; Multinational Company (MNC) 728; Nadir, Asil 731; National Debt 738; PaineWebber 801; Phillips, Alban 832; Portfolio Theory 845; Precious Metals 856; Risk/Reward Ratio 896; Silver 944; Volatile 1149

Initial Margin

Adjusted Debit Balance (ADB) 10

Initial Public Offering (IPO)

All or None (AON) 15; Allotment 17; Application Form 41; Apportion 41; Bear Stearns 132; Blanket Certification Form (NASD Form Fr-1) 151; Bought Deal 164; Concession 269; Direct Placement 337; Donaldson, Lufkin & Jenrette 346; Due Diligence Meeting 357; Each Way 361; Effective Date 367; Émission/Emissione 372; European Association of Securities Dealers Auto Quotation (EASDAQ) 378; Fast Market (B) 392; Firm Commitment 407; Firm Order 407; Free Riding 433; Hot Issue 504; Impact Day 517; Issue 552; Junk Bonds 592; Kidder, Pea-

body & Company 603; Ling, James 639; Market Mania 677; Market Stabilization 679; Mozer, Paul 726; Net 745; Net Price 746; Nil Paid 767; Normal Investment Practice 774; Offer for Sale 782; Offering Date 783; Paid In Capital/Paid Up Capital 801; Pegging 813; Piggyback Registration 835; Plain Vanilla 835; Preliminary Agreement 859; Preliminary Prospectus 859; Presumptive Underwriter 860; Primary Distribution 861; Primary Market 862; Private Placement 863; Property as Investment 865; Pure Play 870; Quiet Period 874; Red Herring 881; Registered Company 881; Regulations; Rollover 902; Rothschild Family 902; Scalper 926; SEC Fee 929; SEC Rule 10b-6 931; Secondary Market 930; Selling Concession 935; Selling Group 935; Skandinaviska Enskilda Banken 950; Smith Barney Shearson 958; Speculation 983; Subscribed Capital 1003; Suitability/Suitability Rule 1003; Syndicate 1025; Twenty-Day Period 1077; Underwriting 1079; When Issued (WI) 1167; Zeichnung 1185

Insider

Tip 1052; Yakuza 1177; Yamaichi Securities Company, Limited 1179

Insider Dealing/Insider Trading

Board of Directors 153; Companies Act of 1980 266; Dealing in Advance 314; Dow Theory 351; Drexel Burnham Lambert 355; Emerging Growth Markets 372; Financial Services Act (FSA) 398; *Fortune* 415; Goldman, Sachs and Company 464; Harvard Business School 489; Investor Protection 543; Kennedy, Joseph 596; Kidder, Peabody & Company 603; Milken, Michael 705; Morgan Grenfell Group PLC 720; Nadir, Asil 731; Regulation, Trend Toward 883; Stock Market Efficiency Theory 998; Stock Watcher 1000; Tailgating 1027; Target Letter 1038; Tulipmania 1067; Turner, Ted 1075; Value Line Investment Survey 1141; *Wall Street* 1151; White Collar Crime 1168; Wiggin, Albert 1170

Insolvency

Acquisition 7; Bank of New England Corporation (BNEC) 103; BankBoston 93; Borrowing Power 161; Capital Adequacy 213; Corporate Rescue 277; Hammer 489; Lender of Last Resort 635; Nadir, Asil 731

Institutional Investor

Accompagnateur 3; Air Pocket 14; Clearing House Electronic Subregister System (CHESS) 252; Computer Trading 267; Cyclical Stocks 298; Delivery Versus Payment (DVP) 320; Direct Account Holder

Iran, Islamic Republic of

Ireland, Republic of

Israel, State of

Issue

Issue Price

Issued and Outstanding

Issuer

Kohlberg Kravis Roberts (KKR)
Barbarians at the Gate 118; Junk Bonds 592; Wasserstein, Bruce 1160

Korea, Republic of (South)
Bank of Tokyo-Mitsubishi, Ltd. (BMT) 108; Kennedy, Joseph 596; Khashoggi, Adnan 602; Nippon Credit Bank (NCB) 767; Pre-Emerging Markets 857

Kursmakler
Freie Makler 433

Kuwait, State of
Banco Central Hispano (BCH) 83; War and Stock Markets 1155

Laggard
Leader 629

Last Trade
Real Estate Investment Trust (REIT) 880

Last Trading Day (Futures)
Triple Witching Hour 1065

Late Tape
Delayed Tape 320

Latvia, Republic of
Bank for International Settlement (BIS) 96; Société Générale 961

Lazard Frères
Peterson, Peter G. 824; Rothschild Family 902; Warburg Dynasty 1156

Leader
Japanese Financial Markets 585

Leeson, Nick
Barings Collapse of 1995 123; Jett, Joseph 587; White Collar Crime 1168

Legal List
Prudent Man Rule 867

Lehman Brothers Holdings, Inc.
Catastrophe Bonds 217; Garzarelli, Elaine 443; Glucksman, Lewis L. 460; Junk Bonds 592; Maxwell, Robert 687; Peterson, Peter G. 824; Risk/Reward Ratio 896; Salomon Inc. 919; Warburg Dynasty 1156; Wasserstein, Bruce 1160

Lender of Last Resort
Bank of England, History of 100

Letter of Credit
Ancient Greece, Banking in 34; Commercial Paper 260; Kidder, Peabody & Company 603

Leverage
Capital Structure 215; Capitalization Ratio 216; Common Stock Ratio 264; Debt-to-Equity Ratio 318; European Bank for Reconstruction and Development (EBRD) 379; Exposure 390; Kidder, Peabody & Company 603; Lehman Brothers Holdings, Inc. 633; Margin 674; Nomura Securities Company, Limited 770; Perelman, Ronald 816; Player 836; Position Limit 855; Pyramiding 871

Leveraged Buyout (LBO)
Barbarians at the Gate 118; Drexel Burnham Lambert 355; Harvard Business School 489; Japanese Boom and Bust, 1988–90 583; Junk Bonds 592; Kohlberg Kravis Roberts (KKR) 606; Lehman Brothers Holdings, Inc. 633; Management Buy-Out (MBO) 670; Spin Off 984; Tokai Bank, Limited 1053; Treasury Stock 1060

Liability
Accounts Payable 6; Acid Test Ratio 7; Balance of Payments 77; Balance Sheet 77; Cash Ratio 217; Close a Position 252; Closing Purchase 252; Closing Sale 253; Compliance Officer 267; Corporation 278; Current Liabilities 296; Debt Restructuring 317; Debt-to-Equity Ratio 318; Deficit 319; Equity 373; Financial Planning 397; Fully Paid and Non-Assessable Shares 435; Gift Tax 457; Insolvency 533; Limited Company 639; Minority Interest 711; Mozer, Paul 726; Net 745; Net Worth 747; Non-Qualifying Stock Option 773; Open Order 790; Perelman, Ronald 816; Pooling of Interests 843; Publicly Held and Traded Company 870; Regulation A/B 885; Shareholder's Equity 941; Tax Selling 1038; Unissued Stock 1080

Liar's Poker
Mozer, Paul 726; Salomon Inc. 919

Limit Order
An Hand Lassen 33; At the Market 50; Away from the Market 72; Bid Price 144; Cabinet Security 189; Cancel 212; Daily Trading Limit 312; Day Order 313; Designated Order Turnaround (DOT) 332; Do Not Reduce (DNR) 345; Execution 388; Firm Order 407; In Prezzo 517; Limit Order System

Security Pacific Corporation (SPC)

Self-Regulating Organization (SRO)

Sell

Share Capital

Share Index

Shareholder

United States of America

Unlisted Securities Market (USM)

Unrealized Profits/Losses

Uptick

Uruguay, Republic of

Value Line Investment Survey

Vanderbilt Family

Venezuela, Republic of

Venture Capital

Vertical Spread

Volatile